THE ENGLISH AND SCOTTISH
POPULAR BALLADS

THE
ENGLISH AND SCOTTISH
POPULAR BALLADS

EDITED BY
FRANCIS JAMES CHILD

This Dover edition, first published in 1965, is an
unabridged and unaltered republication of the
work originally produced in Boston, Massachusetts

Copyright in 1882 as:

Vol. I—Parts I, 1882, and II, 1884.
Vol. II—Part III, Part IV, V, 1885.
Vol. III—Part IV, 1886; Part VI, 1889.
Vol. IV—Part VII, 1890; VIII, 1892.
Vol. V—Part IX, 1894; Part X, 1898.

This edition also contains as an appendix to
Part X an essay on Walter Scott's title entitled
"Professor Child and the Ballad" reprinted in
part from Vol. XXX No. 6 of the Harvard issue of
Studies and Notes in Philology, published by the
Department of English at Harvard University.

IN FIVE VOLUMES
VOLUME II

Library of Congress Catalog Card Number: A65-?????

Manufactured in the United States of America

Dover Publications, Inc.
180 Varick Street
New York, N.Y. 10014

NEW YORK
DOVER PUBLICATIONS, INC.

This Dover edition, first published in 1965, is an unabridged and unaltered republication of the work originally published by Houghton, Mifflin and Company, as follows:

Vol. I—Part I, 1882; Part II, 1884
Vol. II—Part III, 1885; Part IV, 1886
Vol. III—Part V, 1888; Part VI, 1889
Vol. IV—Part VII, 1890; Part VIII, 1892
Vol. V—Part IX, 1894; Part X, 1898.

This edition also contains as an appendix to Part X an essay by Walter Morris Hart entitled "Professor Child and the Ballad," reprinted *in toto* from Vol. XXI, No. 4, 1906 [New Series Vol. XIV, No. 4] of the *Publications of the Modern Language Association of America*.

Library of Congress Catalog Card Number: 65-24347

Manufactured in the United States of America

Dover Publications, Inc.
180 Varick Street
New York, N.Y. 10014

ADVERTISEMENT TO PART IV

NUMBERS 83–113

UPON concluding this Fourth Part, I have to express warm thanks to Mr JAMES BARCLAY MURDOCH for a punctilious recollation of MOTHERWELL'S manuscript, and to Mr MALCOLM COLQUHOUN THOMSON for again granting the use of the volume. Miss MARY FRASER TYTLER, to remove a doubt about a few readings, has generously taken the trouble to make a fac-simile copy of ALEXANDER FRASER TYTLER'S BROWN manuscript. Mr MACMATH, whose accuracy is not surpassed by photographic reproduction, has done me favors of a like kind, and of many kinds. Rev. Professor SKEAT, with all his engagements, has been prompt to render his peculiarly valuable help at the libraries of Cambridge; and Mr F. H. STODDARD, late of Oxford, now of the University of California, has allowed me to call upon him freely for copies and collations at the Bodleian Library. The notes which Dr REINHOLD KÖHLER, Professor FELIX LIEBRICHT, Professor C. R. LANMAN, and Mr GEORGE LYMAN KITTREDGE have contributed, in the way of Additions and Corrections, will speak for themselves. Miss ISABEL FLORENCE HAPGOOD, translator of the Epic Songs of Russia, has given me much assistance in Slavic popular poetry, and Lieutenant-Colonel W. F. PRIDEAUX, of Calcutta, Mr FRANK KIDSON, of Leeds, and Mr P. Z. ROUND, of London, have made obliging communications as to English ballads.

F. J. C.

NOVEMBER, 1886.

CONTENTS OF VOLUME II

THE CHERRY–TREE CAROL

A. a. 'Joseph was an old man,' Sandys, Christmas Carols, p. 123. **b.** Sandys, Christmastide, p. 241.

B. a. 'The Cherry-Tree Carol,' Husk, Songs of the Nativity, p. 59. **b.** Hone's Ancient Mysteries, p. 90. **c.** 'The Cherry-Tree Carol,' Sylvester, A Garland of Christmas Carols, p. 45. **d.** 'The Cherry-Tree,'

Birmingham chap-book, of about 1843, in B. Harris Cowper's Apocryphal Gospels, p. xxxviii.

C. 'The Cherry-Tree Carol,' Bramley and Stainer, Christmas Carols, p. 60.

D. Notes and Queries, Fourth Series, XII, 461.

THE proper story of this highly popular carol is derived from the Pseudo-Matthew's gospel, chapter xx; Tischendorf, Evangelia Apocrypha, p. 82; Thilo, Codex Apocryphus Novi Testamenti, Historia de Nativitate Mariæ et de Infantia Salvatoris, p. 395. What succeeds, after **A** 9, **B** 8, **C** 7, **D** 6, is probably founded on the angel's words to the shepherds in Luke ii, and on Jesus's predictions in the authentic gospels. This latter portion is sometimes printed as an independent carol, under the title of ' Joseph and the Angel.' *

On the third day of the flight into Egypt, Mary, feeling the heat to be oppressive, tells Joseph that she will rest for a while under a palm-tree. Joseph helps her to light from her beast, and Mary, looking up from under the tree, and seeing it full of fruit, asks for some. Joseph somewhat testily expresses his surprise that she should think of such a thing, considering the height of the tree: he is much more concerned to get a supply of water. Then Jesus, sitting on his mother's lap, bids the palm to bow down and refresh his mother with its fruit. The palm instantly bends its top to Mary's feet.

The truly popular carol would be sure to adapt the fruit to its own soil. In English the tree is always a cherry. We have the story also in the fifteenth of the Coventry Mysteries, ed. Halliwell, p. 146 (not omitting Joseph's quip in **A** 5, etc.), with the addition of a little more miracle: for it is not the season for cherries, and Mary's wish is anticipated by the tree's blooming before she has uttered it. In Catalan and Provençal the tree is an apple. On the way from Bethlehem to Nazareth, Mary and Joseph come upon a gardener who is climbing an apple-tree, and Mary asks for an apple. He politely gives her leave to pluck for herself. Joseph, who this time has not been disobliging, tries, but the branches go up; Mary tries, and the branches come to her: † Milá, Romancerillo, p. 3, No 4. Also p. 63, No 55, where again Joseph is *molt felló*, very crusty; further, Briz, III, 228; Arbaud, Chants populaires de la Provence, 'Lou premier Miracle,' I, 23, and 'La Fuito en Egypto,' II, 237 f. In other legendary ballads, not so entirely popular, the palm-tree is preserved: Meinert, p. 262; Böhme, p. 628, No 523 = Weinhold, Weihnachtspiele, p. 385; Lexer, Kärntisches Wörterbuch, p. 310; Feifalik, Die Kindheit Jesu, pp 101, 106 = Pailler, Weihnachtlieder aus Oberösterreich, No 314, p 338 f; Pailler, p. 332, No 310; Hoffmann, Horæ Belgicæ, Part Ten, p. 59; Alberdingk Thijm, I, 212. In Schmitz, Sitten und Sagen des Eifler Volkes, I, 116, and Pailler, as above, No 311, we have a fig-tree.

---

* A copy of the Cherry-Tree carol in The Guardian, Dec. 27, 1871, is partly compiled " from several ancient sources," and partly composed by the contributor: see Notes and Queries, Fourth Series, X, 73.

† Cf. the very naive **D** 5 : 'Mary shall have cherries, and Joseph shall have none.'

Some of these are very imperfect, or have even lost chief points in the story.

There are many narratives of the childhood of Jesus, based on the apocryphal gospels, in which this legend must needs be found: as,

Cursor Mundi, ed. Morris, II, 668 f, v. 11,657 ff; Horstmann, Altenglische Legenden, 1875, p. 6, 1878, pp 102, 112; Stephens, Fornsvenskt Legendarium, p. 71; Pitré, Canti popolari siciliani, II, 333.*

A

a. Sandys, Christmas Carols, p. 123, West of England.
b. Sandys, Christmastide, p. 241.

1 JOSEPH was an old man,
        and an old man was he,
    When he wedded Mary,
        in the land of Galilee.

2 Joseph and Mary walked
        through an orchard good,
    Where was cherries and berries,
        so red as any blood.

3 Joseph and Mary walked
        through an orchard green,
    Where was berries and cherries,
        as thick as might be seen.

4 O then bespoke Mary,
        so meek and so mild:
    ' Pluck me one cherry, Joseph,
        for I am with child.'

5 O then bespoke Joseph,
        with words most unkind:
    ' Let him pluck thee a cherry
        that brought thee with child.'

6 O then bespoke the babe,
        within his mother's womb:

' Bow down then the tallest tree,
        for my mother to have some.'

7 Then bowed down the highest tree
        unto his mother's hand;
    Then she cried, See, Joseph,
        I have cherries at command.

8 O then bespake Joseph:
    ' I have done Mary wrong;
    But cheer up, my dearest,
        and be not cast down.'

9 Then Mary plucked a cherry,
        as red as the blood,
    Then Mary went home
        with her heavy load.

10 Then Mary took her babe,
        and sat him on her knee,
    Saying, My dear son, tell me
        what this world will be.

11 ' O I shall be as dead, mother,
        as the stones in the wall;
    O the stones in the streets, mother,
        shall mourn for me all.

12 ' Upon Easter-day, mother,
        my uprising shall be;
    O the sun and the moon, mother,
        shall both rise with me.'

B

a. Husk, Songs of the Nativity, p. 59, from a Worcester broadside of the last century. b. Hone's Ancient Mysteries, p. 90, from various copies. c. Sylvester, A Garland of Christmas Carols, p. 45. d. Birmingham chap-book, of about 1843, in B. Harris Cowper's Apocryphal Gospels, p. xxxviii.

* Liber de Infantia Mariæ et Christi Salvatoris, O. Schade, 1869, p. 38 f, follows almost word for word the Pseudo-Matthew. In note 234 the editor points out passages

1 JOSEPH was an old man,
        and an old man was he,
    And he married Mary,
        the Queen of Galilee.

2 When Joseph was married,
        and Mary home had brought,

where the story occurs in Hróthsvítha, and other mediæval poetry. See, also, Schade, Narrationes de vita et conversatione beatæ Mariæ Virginis, 1870, pp 16, 24.

Mary proved with child,
and Joseph knew it not.

3 Joseph and Mary walked
through a garden gay,
Where the cherries they grew
upon every tree.

4 O then bespoke Mary,
with words both meek and mild :
' O gather me cherries, Joseph,
they run so in my mind.'

5 And then replied Joseph,
with words so unkind :
' Let him gather thee cherries
that got thee with child.'

6 O then bespoke our Saviour,
all in his mother's womb :
' Bow down, good cherry-tree,
to my mother's hand.'

7 The uppermost sprig
bowed down to Mary's knee :
' Thus you may see, Joseph,
these cherries are for me.'

8 ' O eat your cherries, Mary,
O eat your cherries now ;
O eat your cherries, Mary,
that grow upon the bough.'

9 As Joseph was a walking,
he heard an angel sing :
' This night shall be born
our heavenly king.

10 ' He neither shall be born
in housen nor in hall,
Nor in the place of Paradise,
but in an ox's stall.

11 ' He neither shall be clothed
in purple nor in pall,
But all in fair linen,
as were babies all.

12 ' He neither shall be rocked
in silver nor in gold,
But in a wooden cradle,
that rocks on the mould.

13 ' He neither shall be christened
in white wine nor red,
But with fair spring water,
with which we were christened.'

14 Then Mary took her young son,
and set him on her knee :
' I pray thee now, dear child,
tell how this world shall be.'

15 ' O I shall be as dead, mother,
as the stones in the wall ;
O the stones in the street, mother,
shall mourn for me all.

16 ' And upon a Wednesday
my vow I will make,
And upon Good Friday
my death I will take.

17 ' Upon Easter-day, mother,
my rising shall be ;
O the sun and the moon
shall uprise with me.

18 ' The people shall rejoice,
and the birds they shall sing,
To see the uprising
of the heavenly king.'

----◆----

C

Bramley and Stainer, Christmas Carols, p. 60.

1 JOSEPH was an old man,
an old man was he,
He married sweet Mary,
the Queen of Galilee.

2 As they went a walking
in the garden so gay,
Maid Mary spied cherries,
hanging over yon tree.

3 Mary said to Joseph,
with her sweet lips so mild,

'Pluck those cherries, Joseph,
  for to give to my child.'

4 O then replied Joseph,
  with words so unkind,
'I will pluck no cherries
  for to give to thy child.'

5 Mary said to cherry-tree,
  'Bow down to my knee,
That I may pluck cherries,
  by one, two, and three.'

6 The uppermost sprig then
  bowed down to her knee:
'Thus you may see, Joseph,
  these cherries are for me.'

7 'O eat your cherries, Mary,
  O eat your cherries now,
O eat your cherries, Mary,
  that grow upon the bough.'

8 As Joseph was a walking
  he heard angels sing,
'This night there shall be born
  our heavenly king.

9 'He neither shall be born
  in house nor in hall,

Nor in the place of Paradise,
  but in an ox-stall.

10 'He shall not be clothed
  in purple nor pall,
But all in fair linen,
  as wear babies all.

11 'He shall not be rocked
  in silver nor gold,
But in a wooden cradle,
  that rocks on the mould.

12 'He neither shall be christened
  in milk nor in wine,
But in pure spring-well water,
  fresh sprung from Bethine.'

13 Mary took her baby,
  she dressed him so sweet;
She laid him in a manger,
  all there for to sleep.

14 As she stood over him
  she heard angels sing,
'Oh bless our dear Saviour,
  our heavenly king.'

———•———

D

Notes and Queries, Fourth Series, XII, 461; taken from the mouth of a wandering gypsy girl in Berkshire.

1 O JOSEPH was an old man,
  and an old man was he,
And he married Mary,
  from the land of Galilee.

2 Oft after he married her,
  how warm he were abroad,

. .   . .

.   .   .   .

3 Then Mary and Joseph
  walkd down to the gardens cool;
Then Mary spied a cherry,
  as red as any blood.

4 'Brother Joseph, pluck the cherry,
  for I am with child:'
'Let him pluck the cherry, Mary,
  as is father to the child.'

5 Then our blessed Saviour spoke,
  from his mother's womb:
'Mary shall have cherries,
  and Joseph shall have none.'

6 From the high bough the cherry-tree
  bowd down to Mary's knee;
Then Mary pluckt the cherry,
  by one, two, and three.

7 They went a little further,
  and heard a great din:
'God bless our sweet Saviour,
  our heaven's love in.'

8 Our Saviour was not rocked
in silver or in gold,
But in a wooden cradle,
like other babes all.

9 Our Saviour was not christend
in white wine or red,
But in some spring water,
like other babes all.

———◆———

A. b. 2. When Joseph and Mary
walked in the garden good,
There was cherries and berries,
as red as the blood.

3 *is wanting.*
4⁸. some cherries.   5². so unkind.
5⁸. the cherries.
6¹, ². bespoke Jesus in.
6⁴. that my mother may.
7¹, ². tallest tree, it bent to Mary's.
After 8 :

Then Joseph and Mary
did to Bethlehem go,
And with travels were weary,
walking to and fro.

They sought for a lodging,
but the inns were filld all,
They, alas ! could not have it,
but in an ox's stall.

But before the next morning
our Saviour was born,
In the month of December,
Christmas Day in the morn.

9–12 *are wanting.*
B. b. 2². and his cousin Mary got.
2⁴. by whom Joseph knew not.
3¹. As Joseph.   3². the garden.
4⁸. Gather me some.
4⁵, ⁶. Gather me some cherries,
for I am with child.
5¹. O then bespoke.   5². with words most.

6. O then bespoke Jesus,
all in his mother's womb :
Go to the tree, Mary,
and it shall bow down.

7. Go to the tree, Mary,
and it shall bow to thee,
And the highest branch of all
shall bow down to Mary's knee.

And she shall gather cherries,
by one, by two, by three :
Now you may see, Joseph,
those cherries were for me.

13⁸. with the spring.

15. This world shall be like
the stones in the street,
For the sun and the moon
shall bow down at thy feet.

(my feet *in a Warwickshire broadside:
Sylvester.*)

17. And upon the third day
my uprising shall be,
And the sun and the moon
shall rise up with me.

18 *is wanting.*
*For 9–13 we have, as a separate carol, in
Chappell's Christmas Carols, edited by Dr
E. F. Rimbault, p. 22, the following
verses, traditional in Somersetshire :* *

1 As Joseph was a walking
he heard an angel sing :
' This night shall be the birth-time
of Christ, the heavnly king.

2 ' He neither shall be born
in housen nor in hall,
Nor in the place of Paradise,
but in an ox's stall.

3 ' He neither shall be clothed
in purple nor in pall,
But in the fair white linen
that usen babies all.

4 ' He neither shall be rocked
in silver nor in gold,

* The same in Christmas and Christmas Carols [by J. F.
Russell], p. 26, with an additional modern-sounding stanza.

But in a wooden manger,
    that resteth on the mould.'

5 As Joseph was a walking
    there did an angel sing,
And Mary's child at midnight
    was born to be our king.

6 Then be ye glad, good people,
    this night of all the year,
And light ye up your candles,
    for his star it shineth clear.

c. 1^3. When he.   2 *is omitted.*
  After 3 :

    Joseph and Mary walked
      through an orchard good,
    Where were cherries and berries,
      as red as any blood.

5 *is omitted.*

6, 7. Go to the tree, Mary,
      and it shall bow to thee,
    And the highest branch of all
      shall bow down to Mary's knee.

Go to the tree, Mary,
    and it shall bow to thee,
And you shall gather cherries,
    by one, by two, and three.

Then bowed down the highest tree
    unto his mother's hand :
See, Mary cried, see, Joseph,
    I have cherries at command.

17^2. my uprising. 17^3. moon, mother.
17^4. shall both rise.
18 *is wanting, and is suspiciously modern.*
d. 1^1. When Joseph. 1^2. and *wanting.*
  $2^{1,\,2}$. When Joseph he had
    his cousin Mary got.
  2^4. by whom Joseph knew not.
  3^1. As Joseph. 3^2. the garden gay.

$3^{3,\,4}$. Where cherries were growing
    upon every spray.
$4^{3,\,4}$. Gather me some cherries,
    for I am with child.

5. Gather me some cherries,
    they run so in my mind.
Then bespoke Joseph,
    with wordes so unkind,

I will not gather cherries.
    Then said Mary, You shall see,
By what will happen,
    these cherries were for me.

6^1. Then bespoke Jesus.
$6^{3,\,4}$. Go to the tree, Mary,
    and it shall bow down.

7. And the highest branch
    shall bow to Mary's knee,
And she shall gather cherries,
    by one, two, and three.

8 *wanting.*   10 *wanting.*
11^3. But in fine.
$13^{1,\,2}$. He never did require
    white wine and bread.
13^3. But cold spring.   13 *precedes* 12.
$14^{3,\,4}$. Come tell me, dear child, how.

15. This world shall be
    like the stones in the street,
For the sun and the moon
    shall bow down at my feet.

The rest is wanting.
D. 3^2. to the garden school.

The first stanza is said to have this variation in Worcestershire :

    Joseph was a hoary man,
      and a hoary man was he.

Notes and Queries, Fourth Series, III, 75.

55

THE CARNAL AND THE CRANE

'The Carnal and the Crane.' a. Sandys, Christmas Carols, p. 152, Christmastide, p. 246, from a broadside. b. Husk, Songs of the Nativity, p. 97, apparently from a Worcester broadside. c. Birmingham chap-book, of about 1843, in B. Harris Cowper's Apocryphal Gospels, p. xli.

MR HUSK, who had access to a remarkably good collection of carols, afterwards unfortunately dispersed, had met with no copy of 'The Carnal and the Crane' of earlier date than the middle of the last century. Internal evidence points us much further back. The carol had obviously been transmitted from mouth to mouth before it was fixed in its present incoherent and corrupted form by print.*

The well-informed Crane instructs his catechumen, the Crow, in several matters pertaining to the birth and earliest days of Jesus: the Immaculate Conception; the Nativity; the conference of Herod with the Wise Men, including the miracle of the roasted cock; the Flight into Egypt, with the Adoration of the Beasts and the Instantaneous Harvest; the Massacre of the Innocents. Of the apocryphal incidents, the miracle of the cock, sts 10, 11, has been spoken of under No 22. The adoration of the beasts, sts 15, 16, is derived from the Historia de Nativitate Mariæ, etc. (Pseudo-Matthæi Evangelium), c. 19, Thilo, p. 394, Tischendorf, p. 81, and is of course frequent in legendaries of the infancy of the Saviour,† but is not remarkable enough to be popular in carols. The miraculous harvest, by which the Holy Family evade Herod's pursuit, is, on the contrary, a favorite subject with popular poetry, as also, like the bowing of the palm-tree, with pictorial art. I do not know where and when this pretty and clever legend was invented. In the Greek Gospel of Thomas, ch. 12, Jesus sows one grain of wheat, in the Latin Gospel of Thomas, ch. 10, and ch. 34 of the Pseudo-Matthew, a very little, and reaps an immense crop at harvest time; Tischendorf, pp 143 f, 165 f, 97: but this passage would hardly even suggest the miracle in question.‡ In a Swedish carol, 'Staffans-Visan,' reprinted from a recent broadside, in Dansk Kirketidende, 1861, cols 35, 36, by Professor George Stephens, and afterwards by Grundtvig, Danmarks Folkeviser, III, 882, the legend of the Cock and that of the Sower are combined, as here. The legend of the Sower is followed by that of the Palm-tree, and others, in La Fuito en Egypto, Arbaud, Chants p. de la Provence, II, 235. Another Provençal version of the Sower is given by Briz, IV, 70; a Catalan at pp 65 and 68, 'Lo rey Herodes;' ten Catalan versions by Milá, 'Herodes,' Romancerillo, pp 6–9, No 10. To these add: 'La Fuite en Égypte,' Poésies p. de la France, MS., I, fol. 226, 'Le roi Hérode,' VI, 192; 'De Vlucht naar Egypten,' Lootens et Feys, p. 32, No 20, Hoffmann von Fallersleben, Horæ Belgicæ, Part Ten, p. 22, No 4; 'Die Flucht Maria's,' Haupt und Schmaler, Volkslieder der Wenden, I, 275, No 283; Bezsonof, Kalyeki Perekhozhie, II, 116, No 319. The legend of the Sower occurs also in Le Geu des Trois Roys,

---

* Carnal, *cornicula, corneille*, might be thought to have been long obsolete from the word not occurring in ordinary dictionaries, if in any: but it is hazardous to build conclusions on the omissions of dictionaries.

† As, Horstmann, Altenglische Legenden, 1875, p. 4, 1878, pp 101, 112; Cursor Mundi, 11,629 ff, Morris, II, 660; Fornsvenskt Legendarium, p. 71; Feifalik, Kindheit Jesu,

p. 103; Schade, Liber de Infantia, etc., p. 38, and note 226; etc.

‡ In Cursor Mundi, v. 12,323 ff, II, 707, the sowing is according to the Apocrypha. In Luzel's Breton Ballads, I, $\frac{80}{81}$, the Virgin, to keep a poor widow from killing one of her children to feed two others, makes corn sown at Christmas in early morning ripen before day.

Jubinal, Mystères inédits du 15ᵉ Siècle, II, 117–131.

It is ordinarily Mary, and not Jesus, who operates the miracle; in the French mystery it is perhaps Joseph.* In the Provençal and Catalan ballads the Virgin commonly hides behind a sheaf or a stack, and does not pass on.†

———

1 As I passd by a river side,
   And there as I did reign,
In argument I chanced to hear
   A Carnal and a Crane.

2 The Carnal said unto the Crane,
   If all the world should turn,
Before we had the Father,
   But now we have the Son!

3 'From whence does the Son come,
   From where and from what place?'
He said, In a manger,
   Between an ox and ass.

4 'I pray thee,' said the Carnal,
   'Tell me before thou go,
Was not the mother of Jesus
   Conceivd by the Holy Ghost?'

5 She was the purest virgin,
   And the cleanest from sin;
She was the handmaid of our Lord
   And mother of our king.

6 'Where is the golden cradle
   That Christ was rocked in?
Where are the silken sheets
   That Jesus was wrapt in?'

7 A manger was the cradle
   That Christ was rocked in:
The provender the asses left
   So sweetly he slept on.

8 There was a star in the east land,
   So bright it did appear,
Into King Herod's chamber,
   And where King Herod were.

9 The Wise Men soon espied it,
   And told the king on high
A princely babe was born that night
   No king could eer destroy.

10 'If this be true,' King Herod said,
   'As thou tellest unto me,
This roasted cock that lies in the dish
   Shall crow full fences three.'

11 The cock soon freshly featherd was,
   By the work of God's own hand,
And then three fences crowed he,
   In the dish where he did stand.

12 'Rise up, rise up, you merry men all,
   See that you ready be;
All children under two years old
   Now slain they all shall be.'

13 Then Jesus, ah, and Joseph,
   And Mary, that was so pure,
They travelld into Egypt,
   As you shall find it sure.

14 And when they came to Egypt's land,
   Amongst those fierce wild beasts,
Mary, she being weary,
   Must needs sit down to rest.

* Joseph stops a moment to speak to the sower, asks the direct road to Egypt, and begs that if any inquiry is made he will say that nobody has passed that way. The sower is not punctilious, and answers, Je le feray très volontiers, que je voy bien qu'estez prodoms. The Swede is scrupulous. When the Virgin says, If anybody asks after us, say that you have seen nobody, he replies, I have promised my God never to tell a lie, "thinking she was only a lady." In the Wendish ballad the Virgin's demand is simply, If the Jews pass, conceal me not, reveal me not.

† In one Provençal version, Arbaud, II, 245 f, Joseph and Mary ask a man at work in the fields to save them from Herod, and he tells them to hide under mint. The mint depresses its leaves so as to afford no concealment. For this the mint is cursed; though it flower, it shall not seed. The good man then tells them to hide under sage; the sage stretches itself out to cover them. The mint betrays the Virgin in many of the Catalan ballads: She is under the stack! The salvia answers in Milá, C, 'ment la menta y mentirá.' In D parsley is the good plant: the mint is cursed with barrenness as before. In Milá, J, the partridge (one symbol of the devil) sings: Catxacatatxá! Sota la garbera la Mare de Deu está! for which its head is cursed, never to be eaten. So Briz, IV, 69.

15 'Come sit thee down,' says Jesus,
    'Come sit thee down by me,
And thou shalt see how these wild beasts
    Do come and worship me.'

16 First came the lovely lion,
    Which Jesus's grace did bring,
And of the wild beasts in the field
    The lion shall be king.

17 We 'll choose our virtuous princes
    Of birth and high degree,
In every sundry nation,
    Whereer we come and see.

18 Then Jesus, ah, and Joseph,
    And Mary, that was unknown,
They travelled by a husbandman,
    Just while his seed was sown.

19 'God speed thee, man,' said Jesus,
    'Go fetch thy ox and wain,
And carry home thy corn again
    Which thou this day hast sown.'

20 The husbandman fell on his knees,
    Even upon his face:
'Long time hast thou been looked for,
    But now thou art come at last.

21 'And I myself do now believe
    Thy name is Jesus called;
Redeemer of mankind thou art,
    Though undeserving all.'

22 'The truth, man, thou hast spoken,
    Of it thou mayst be sure,
For I must lose my precious blood
    For thee and thousands more.

23 'If any one should come this way,
    And enquire for me alone,
Tell them that Jesus passed by
    As thou thy seed did sow.'

24 After that there came King Herod,
    With his train so furiously,
Enquiring of the husbandman
    Whether Jesus passed by.

25 'Why, the truth it must be spoke,
    And the truth it must be known;
For Jesus passed by this way
    When my seed was sown.

26 'But now I have it reapen,
    And some laid on my wain,
Ready to fetch and carry
    Into my barn again.'

27 'Turn back,' says the captain,
    'Your labor and mine 's in vain;
It 's full three quarters of a year
    Since he his seed has sown.'

28 So Herod was deceived,
    By the work of God's own hand,
And further he proceeded
    Into the Holy Land.

29 There 's thousands of children young
    Which for his sake did die;
Do not forbid those little ones,
    And do not them deny.

30 The truth now I have spoken,
    And the truth now I have shown;
Even the Blessed Virgin
    She 's now brought forth a son.

———◆———

8¹. West land. 16². spring; *perhaps a preposition has been dropped.*
1². did rein. 2². Sure all the world will turn.
3¹. Whence does the Son come from.
3³. Out of the land of Egypt. 4². goest.
5². all sin. 5³. of the. 7⁴. slept in.
8¹. East land. 9⁴. No prince should.
10². tellest me. 12⁴. Now slaughtered shall be.
13¹. aye and. 13³. Egypt land. 13⁴. find most.

14¹. Egypt. 14². Among some.
14³. Mary grown quite.
15³. see that these. 15⁴. Will come.
16². did bring. 16⁴. be king.
17³. every nation of the world.
18¹. aye and. 18³. passed by.
18⁴. As he his seed had. 19⁴. hath sown.
20³, ⁴. And made a lowly reverence
    To Jesus Christ His grace.

21. Long time thou hast been looked for,
    But now thou art come at last;
    And I myself do now believe
    Thy name is Jesus called.

22³. must shed.   23⁴. seed had sown.
24². train most.   25¹. spoken.
25⁴. As I my seed had sown.   26¹. And now.
26³. The other you see is fit to carry.
26⁴. barns.
27¹. said the Captain of the guard.
29¹. There were.
29². Who for.   29³. these little.

30³. Thus the.   30⁴. Brought forth our Lord the
    Son.
c. 1-7. *not given.*

8. There was a star in the west land,
   Which shed a cheerful ray
   Into King Herod's chamber,
   And where King Herod lay.

12⁴. Now shall destroyed be.
21, 22. *not given.*
25⁴. When I my seed had sown.
29, 30. *not given.*

56

DIVES AND LAZARUS

A. 'Dives and Lazarus.' **a.** Sylvester's Christmas Carols, p. 50. **b.** Husk, Songs of the Nativity, p. 94.

B. 'Diverus and Lazarus,' F. S. L., in Notes and Queries, Fourth Series, III, 76.

A BALLET " of the Ryche man and poor Lazarus " was licensed to Master John Wallye and Mistress Toye, 19 July, 1557 – 9 July, 1558. W. Pekerynge pays his license for printing " of a ballett, Dyves and Lazarus," 22 July, 1570 – 22 July, 1571. Arber, Registers of the Company of Stationers, I, 76, 436. A fiddler in Fletcher's Monsieur Thomas, printed 1639, says he can sing The merry ballad of Diverus and Lazarus: Act 3, Scene 3, Dyce, VII, 364. The name Diverus is preserved in C, and F. S. L., who contributed this copy to Notes and Queries, had heard only Diverus, never Dives. Dr Rimbault, Notes and Queries, as above, p. 157, had never met with Diverus. Hone cites two stanzas, a 10, b 11, nearly, in his Ancient Mysteries, p. 95, and Sandys the last three stanzas, nearly as in a, in Notes and Queries, p. 157, as above.

A copy in Bramley and Stainer's Christmas Carols, p. 85, seems to have been made up from Sylvester's and another copy. The few variations are probably arbitrary.

The subject could not escape the popular muse : e. g., Socard, Noëls et Cantiques imprimés à Troyes, Histoire de Lazare et du Mauvais Riche, p. 118 ff ; ' El mal rico,' Milá, Romancerillo, p. 16, No 16, A–F; 'Lazarus,' Des Dülkener Fiedlers Liederbuch, p. 53, No 63 ; ' Lazar a bohatec,' Sušil, Moravské Národní Písně, p. 19, No 18, Wenzig, Bibliothek Slavischer Poesien, p. 114 ; Bezsonof, Kalyeki Perekhozhie, I, 43–47, Nos 19–27.

There is a very beautiful ballad, in which the Madonna takes the place of Lazarus, in Roadside Songs of Tuscany, Francesca Alexander and John Ruskin, ' La Madonna e il Riccone,' p. 82.

A

a. Sylvester, A Garland of Christmas Carols, p. 50, from an old Birmingham broadside. b. Husk, Songs of the Nativity, p. 94, from a Worcestershire broadside of the last century.

1 As it fell out upon a day,
  Rich Dives he made a feast,
And he invited all his friends,
  And gentry of the best.

2 Then Lazarus laid him down and down,
  And down at Dives' door :
' Some meat, some drink, brother Dives,
  Bestow upon the poor.'

3 ' Thou art none of my brother, Lazarus,
  That lies begging at my door;
No meat nor drink will I give thee,
  Nor bestow upon the poor.'

4 Then Lazarus laid him down and down,
  And down at Dives's wall :
' Some meat, some drink, brother Dives,
  Or with hunger starve I shall.'

5 ' Thou art none of my brother, Lazarus,
  That lies begging at my wall ;
No meat nor drink will I give thee,
  But with hunger starve you shall.'

6 Then Lazarus laid him down and down,
  And down at Dives's gate :
' Some meat, some drink, brother Dives,
  For Jesus Christ his sake.'

7 ' Thou art none of my brother, Lazarus,
  That lies begging at my gate ;
No meat nor drink will I give thee,
  For Jesus Christ his sake.'

8 Then Dives sent out his merry men,
  To whip poor Lazarus away ;

They had no power to strike a stroke,
  But flung their whips away.

9 Then Dives sent out his hungry dogs,
  To bite him as he lay ;
They had no power to bite at all,
  But licked his sores away.

10 As it fell out upon a day,
  Poor Lazarus sickened and died ;
Then came two angels out of heaven
  His soul therein to guide.

11 ' Rise up, rise up, brother Lazarus,
  And go along with me ;
For you 've a place prepared in heaven,
  To sit on an angel's knee.'

12 As it fell out upon a day,
  Rich Dives sickened and died ;
Then came two serpents out of hell,
  His soul therein to guide.

13 ' Rise up, rise up, brother Dives,
  And go with us to see
A dismal place, prepared in hell,
  From which thou canst not flee.'

14 Then Dives looked up with his eyes,
  And saw poor Lazarus blest :
' Give me one drop of water, brother Lazarus,
  To quench my flaming thirst.

15 ' Oh had I as many years to abide
  As there are blades of grass,
Then there would be an end, but now
  Hell's pains will ne'er be past.

16 ' Oh was I now but alive again,
  The space of one half hour !
Oh that I had my peace secure !
  Then the devil should have no power.'

B

From memory, as sung by carol-singers at Christmas, in Worcestershire, at Hagley and Hartlebury, 1829–39 : F. S. L., in Notes and Queries, Fourth Series, III, 76.

1 As it fell out upon one day,
  Rich Diverus he made a feast,
And he invited all his friends,
  And gentry of the best.

2 And it fell out upon one day,
  Poor Lazarus he was so poor,
He came and laid him down and down,
  Evn down at Diverus' door.

3 So Lazarus laid him down and down
    Even down at Diverus' door :
  ' Some meat, some drink, brother Diverus,
    Do bestow upon the poor.'

4 ' Thou art none of mine, brother Lazarus,
    Lying begging at my door :
  No meat, no drink will I give thee,
    Nor bestow upon the poor.'

5 Then Lazarus laid him down and down,
    Even down at Diverus' wall :
  ' Some meat, some drink, brother Diverus,
    Or surely starve I shall.

6 ' Thou art none of mine, brother Lazarus,
    Lying begging at my wall ;
  No meat, no drink will I give thee,
    And therefore starve thou shall.'

7 Then Lazarus laid him down and down,
    Even down at Diverus' gate :
  ' Some meat, some drink, brother Diverus,
    For Jesus Christ his sake.'

8 ' Thou art none of mine, brother Lazarus,
    Lying begging at my gate ;
  No meat, no drink will I give thee,
    For Jesus Christ his sake.

9 Then Diverus sent out his merry men all,
    To whip poor Lazarus away ;
  They had not power to whip one whip,
    But threw their whips away.

10 Then Diverus sent out his hungry dogs,
    To bite poor Lazarus away ;
   They had not power to bite one bite,
    But licked his sores away.

11 And it fell out upon one day,
    Poor Lazarus he sickened and died ;
   There came two angels out of heaven,
    His soul thereto to guide.

12 ' Rise up, rise up, brother Lazarus,
    And come along with me ;
   There is a place prepared in heaven,
    For to sit upon an angel's knee.'

13 And it fell out upon one day
    Rich Diverus he sickened and died ;
   There came two serpents out of hell,
    His soul thereto to guide.

14 ' Rise up, rise up, brother Diverus,
    And come along with me ;
   There is a place prepared in hell,
    For to sit upon a serpent's knee.'

———◆———

A. a. 14–16. *There are only these trifling variations in the stanzas cited by Sandys :*
    16^2. of an. 16^3. I 'd made my peace.
  b. 1^3. his guests.
      7^3. I 'll give to thee.
      8^3. But they. 8^4. And flung.
      9^3. But they. 9^4. So licked.
      10^3. came an angel. 10^4. there for.
      11^2. come along.
      11^3. For there 's a place in heaven provided.
      12^3. There came a serpent.
      12^4. there for.

$13^{2\cdot4}$. And come along with me,
    For there 's a place in hell provided
    To sit on a serpent's knee.
  14^1. lifting his eyes to heaven.
  14^2. And seeing.
  $15^{3,\,4}$. Then there would be an ending day,
    But in hell I must ever last.
  $16^{3\,4}$. I would make my will and then secure
    That the.
B. 13, 14 *differ but slightly in Hone :*
    13^1. As it. 13^2. Rich Dives. 13^4. therein.
    14^1. Dives. 14^3. For you 've a place provided. 14^4. To sit.

57

BROWN ROBYN'S CONFESSION

Buchan's Ballads of the North of Scotland, I, 110.   Motherwell's MS., p. 580.

———◆———

THE only known version of 'Brown Robyn's Confession' is the one printed in Ballads of the North of Scotland, the copy in Motherwell's MS. having been derived from Buchan.

The ballad, as we have it in English, celebrates a miracle of the Virgin, and is our only example of that extensive class of legends, unless we choose to include 'The Jew's Daughter,' and to take Robin Hood's view of the restoration of his loan, in the fourth Fit of the Little Gest.   Of rescues on the sea, by which Mary " vere maris stella indiciis evidentissimis comprobatur," we have two in most of the collections of the Virgin's miracles, e. g., Vincent of Beauvais, l. VII, cc 88, 89, Gautier de Coincy, ed. Poquet, pp 515, 605. The deliverance, however, *is* for honor done to Mary, and *not* for a fair confession.

A fine ballad, very common in Sweden, and preserved by tradition also in Denmark and Norway, has the same story with a tragical termination for the hero, saving a single instance, in which there is also a supernatural interference in his behalf.

Swedish. 'Herr Peders Sjöresa.'   **A**, Afzelius, II, 31, No 36, new ed. No 30, from oral traditions, compared with a printed copy of the date 1787.   **B**, Atterbom's Poetisk Kalender, 1816, p. 52, apparently from Gyllenmärs' Visbok, after which it is given by Bergström, Afzelius, II, 158.   **C**, Arwidsson, II, 5, No 67, one of three closely resembling copies.   **D**, 'Herr Peder,' Wigström, Folkdiktning, I, 43,

No 21.   **E**, Fagerlund, p. 194, No 4.   **F, G,** Aminson, IV, 20, 22.

Norwegian.   'Unge herr Peder på sjöen,' Landstad, p. 617, No 82.

Danish.   **A**, manuscript of the fifteenth century, in a copy communicated by Professor Grundtvig.   **B**, 'Jon Rimaardssøns Skriftemaal,' Vedel, 1591, It Hundrede udvaalde Danske Viser, p. 3, No 2 (Bergström); Danske Viser, II, 220, No 92.   **C**, 'Lodkastningen,' Kristensen, I, 16, No 6.   **D**, 'Sejladsen,' the same, p. 322, No 119.

Swedish **C-E,** the Norwegian version, Danish **C, D,** are all from recent oral tradition.

With a partial exception of Danish **A, B,**[*] the story of these ballads is this.   Sir Peter asks his foster-mother what death he shall die. You are not to die in your bed, she says, and not in fight, but beware of the waves.   Peter cares not for the waves, and builds a splendid ship, the hulk and masts of whalebone (elm, Swedish **D**; walnut, Norwegian, Danish **D**), the flags of gold (oars, Danish **A**).   Let us drink to-day, while we have ale, says Peter; to-morrow we will sail where gain shall guide. The skipper and helmsman push off, forgetful of God the Father, God's Son, and the Holy Ghost.   They sail a year or two on the boiling sea, and when they come where water is deepest the masts begin to go, Swedish **A**; the ship stops, Swedish **C, D, F,** Norwegian, Danish **A, C, D;**[†] will not mind her helm, Danish **B.**   They cast lots to see who is the

———

[*] Danish **B** begins very like 'Sir Patrick Spens.'   A skeely skipper Haagen eyes the sky and tells his master that any one who sails to-day will never come back alive, etc.

[†] In Danish **A** the ship is stopped by a sea-troll that lay on the bottom.   The helmsman crying out, Why does not the ship sail? the troll replies, You have a sinful man among you; throw him over.   It certainly looks officious of a heathen

troll to be arresting sinners.   See also 'Germand Gladensvend,' Grundtvig, No 33, and the corresponding 'Sætrölls kvæði,' Íslenzk fornkvæði, No 5.

Hysmine is selected by lot and thrown over, in a storm, " according to sailor's custom," in the Greek romance of Hysmine and Hysminias, VII, 12, 15.

Serpents (någas) stop a ship in mid ocean and demand that

sinner; the skipper and captain do this while Peter is in his cabin sleeping,* in Swedish D, Norwegian, Danish C, D. The lot falls on Peter. He makes his shrift, since there is no priest, before the mast (which, with the yard, forms a cross), Swedish A, B, Norwegian, Danish B, C; before an oar, on which Our Lord stands written, Danish A. "Churches have I plundered, and convents have I burned, and stained the honor of many a noble maid. I have roamed the woods and done both robbery and murder, and many an honest peasant's son buried alive in the earth:" Swedish A. He then says his last words, Danish C, D, and nearly all.

> 'If any of you should get back to land,
>   And my foster-mother ask for me,
> Tell her I'm serving in the king's court,
>   And living right merrily.

> 'If any of you should get back to land,
>   And my true-love ask for me,
> Bid her to marry another man,
>   For I am under the sea.' †

In Swedish C, D, Danish C, they throw Peter over, on the larboard in the first, and the ship resumes her course; in Swedish D, F, he wraps a cloak round him and jumps in himself; in Swedish A the ship goes down.

In Danish B Jon Rimaardssøn binds three bags about him, saying, He shall never die poor that will bury my body.‡ It was a sad sight to see when he made a cross on the blue wave, and so took the wild path that lay to the sea's deep bottom. Sir Peter, in Danish A, made this cross and was ready to take this path; but when he reached the water the wild sea turned to green earth.

> Sir Peter took horse, the ship held her course,
>   So glad they coasted the strand;
> And very glad was his true-love too
>   That he had come to land.§

No explanation is offered of this marvel. In the light of the Scottish ballad, we should suppose that Sir Peter's deliverance in Danish A was all for the fair confession he made upon the sea.‖

Saxo relates that, in the earlier part of Thorkill's marvellous voyage, the crews of his three ships, when reduced almost to starving, coming upon an island well stocked with herds, would not heed the warning of their commander, that if they took more than sufficed to mitigate their immediate sufferings they might be estopped from proceeding by the local divinities, but loaded the vessels with carcasses. During the night which followed,

---

a certain holy man whose instructions they desire shall be delivered to them; when the holy man has thrown himself in, the vessel is free to move: Burnouf, Introduction à l'Histoire du Buddhisme indien, p. 316 f. (Rambaud, La Russie Épique, pp 175 f, 178 f.)

* A resemblance to Jonah, but a circumstance not unlikely to be found in any such story. In Danish C, Kristensen, I, 16, after the skipper and steersman have informed Peter that he is to be thrown overboard, they suggest the confession which he elsewhere makes unprompted. So Joshua to Achan, Joshua vii, 19, and Saul to Jonathan, 1 Samuel xiv, 43, in a similar emergency.

† These touching verses, which are of a kind found elsewhere in ballads (see 'The Twa Brothers,' I, 436 f), are preceded by a vow in Swedish A, and the same vow ends Swedish E:

> 'And if God would but help me,
>   That I might come to some land,
> So surely would I build a church
>   All on the snow-white sand.

> 'And if I might but come to some town,
>   And God would so much stead,
> So surely would I build a church,
>   And roof it over with lead.'

Slavic examples of these affecting messages are found in Roger, No 141, p. 80 = Konopka, No 14, p. 114; Woicicki, Pieśni, I, 76, II, 328, W. z Oleska, p. 507, No 27; Zegota Pauli, P. l. polskiego, p. 97, No 9, Lipiński, p. 90, No 47; Kolberg, No 16, pp 196–205, c, d, l, m, p, s, x; Kozłowski, p. 43, No 8; Sakarof, Pyesni, IV, 8. See also 'Mary Hamilton,' further on.

‡ Lord Howard throws Sir Andrew Barton's body over the hatchbord into the sea,

> And about his middle three hundred crowns;
>   'Wherever thou land, this will bury thee!'

§   Herre Peder han red, og skibet det skred,
>   De fulgte så glade hit strand;
> Så glad da var hans fæstemø
>   At han var kommen til land.

‖ The importance of confession for the soul's welfare is recognized by Jon Rimaardssøn.

> 'Now would I render thanks for his grace
>   To bountiful Christ in heaven,
> For in great peril my soul had been
>   Had I gone hence unshriven.'

he ships were beset by a crowd of monsters,
he biggest of whom advanced into the water,
rmed with a huge club, and called out to the
eafarers that they would not be allowed to
ail off till they had expiated the offence they
iad committed by delivering up one man for
ach ship. Thorkill, for the general safety,
urrendered three men, selected by lot, after
vhich they had a good wind and sailed on.
Book VIII; p. 161, ed. 1644.

King Half on his way home from a warlike
xpedition encountered so violent a storm that
iis ship was nigh to foundering. A resolution
vas taken that lots should be cast to determine who should jump overboard. But no
lots were needed, says the saga (implying, by
the way, that a vicarious atonement was sufficient), for the men vied with one another
who should go overboard for his comrade.
Fornaldar Sögur, Rafn, II, 37 f.*

A very pretty Little-Russian *duma*, or ballad,
also shows the efficacy of confession in such a
crisis: 'The Storm on the Black Sea,' Mak-
simovitch, Songs of Ukraine, p. 14, Moscow,
1834, p. 48, Kief, 1849; translated by Boden-
stedt, Die poetische Ukraine, p. 118. The
Cossack flotilla has been divided by a storm
on the Black Sea, and two portions of it have
gone to wreck. In the third sails the hetman.
He walks his deck in sombre composure, and
says to the sailors, Some offence has been
done, and this makes the sea so wild: confess
then your sins to God, to the Black Sea, and
to me your hetman; the guilty man shall die,
and the fleet of the Cossacks not perish. The
Cossacks stand silent, for no one knows who
is guilty, when lo, Alexis, son of the priest
of Piriatin, steps forth and says, Let me be
the sacrifice; bind a cloth round my eyes, a
stone about my neck, and throw me in; so
shall the fleet of the Cossacks not perish.
The men are astounded: how can a heavy sin
be resting on Alexis, who reads them the
sacred books, whose example has kept them

from wickedness! Alexis left home, he says,
without asking his father's and mother's blessing, and with an angry threat against his
brother; he wrenched the last crust of bread
from his neighbors; he rode along the street
wantonly spurning the breasts of women and
the foreheads of children; he passed churches
without uncovering, without crossing himself:
and now he must die for his sins. As he
makes this shrift the storm begins to abate;
to the amazement of the Cossacks, the fleet is
saved, and not one man drowned.

The rich merchant Sadko, the very entertaining hero of several Russian popular epics,
is nowhere more entertaining than when, during one of his voyages, his ship comes to a stop
in the sea. He thinks he has run upon a rock
or sand-bank, and tries to push off, but the
vessel is immovable. Twelve years we have
been sailing, says Sadko, and never paid trib-
ute to the king of the sea. A box of gold is
thrown in as a peace-offering, but floats like a
duck. It is clear that the sea-king wants no
toll; he requires a man. Every man is ordered to make a lot from pine-wood and write
his name on it. These lots are thrown into
the sea. Every one of them swims like a
duck but Sadko's, and his goes down like a
stone. That is not the proper wood for a lot,
says Sadko: make lots of fir-wood. Fir lots
are tried: Sadko's goes down like a stone, the
rest swim like ducks. Fir is not right, either;
alder, oak, are tried with the same result. We
are quite wrong, says Sadko; we must take
cypress, for cypress was the wood of the cross.
They try cypress, and still Sadko's lot sinks,
while all the others float. I am the man, says
Sadko. He orders his men to get for him an
oblation of silver, gold, and pearls, and with
this, taking an image of St Nicholas in one
hand and his gusli in the other, commits himself to the sea, and goes down like a stone.
But not to drown. It was quite worth his
while for the rare adventures that followed.†

* Cited by Dr Prior, Ancient Danish Ballads, II, 227, as
also Saxo.
† Rybnikof, Pĕsni, III, 241–48, No 41, reprinted in Kiryeevski, V, 34–41. Other versions in Rybnikof, I, 363–80,
Nos 61–64, III, 248 f, No 42; Hilferding, Onezhskiya By-

liny, No 70, coll 384–99, No 146, coll 738–40, No 174, coll
877–80; Kirsha Danilof, ed. Kalaidovitch, 1878, No 26, pp
182–87, Kiryeevski, V, 47–55, and No 44, pp 234–39, Kiryeevski, V, 41–47. (I owe this note to Dr Theodor Vetter.)
There is much variety in the details, as might be expected.

The casting of lots to find out the guilty man who causes trouble to a ship occurs in William Guiseman, Kinloch's Ancient Scottish Ballads, p. 156, Kinloch MSS, V, 43, a copy, improved by tradition, of the " lament " in ' William Grismond's Downfal,' a broadside of 1650, which is transcribed among the Percy papers, from Ballard's collection.

Captain Glen is thrown overboard without a lot, on the accusation of the boatswain, and with the happiest effect; broadside in the Roxburghe collection, Logan's Pedlar's Pack p. 47, Kinloch MSS, V, 278.

Translated by Gerhard, p. 66, Knortz, L. u R. Altenglands, p. 155, No 40. Swedish A by the Howitts, Literature and Romance of Northern Europe, I, 276; Danish B by Prior, II 227.

---

1 IT fell upon a Wodensday
    Brown Robyn's men went to sea,
    But they saw neither moon nor sun,
    Nor starlight wi their ee.

2 ' We 'll cast kevels us amang,
    See wha the unhappy man may be ; '
    The kevel fell on Brown Robyn,
    The master-man was he.

3 ' It is nae wonder,' said Brown Robyn,
    ' Altho I dinna thrive,
    For wi my mither I had twa bairns,
    And wi my sister five.

4 ' But tie me to a plank o wude,
    And throw me in the sea ;
    And if I sink, ye may bid me sink,
    But if I swim, just lat me bee.'

5 They 've tyed him to a plank o wude,
    And thrown him in the sea ;

He didna sink, tho they bade him sink ;
    He swimd, and they bade lat him bee.

6 He hadna been into the sea
    An hour but barely three,
    Till by it came Our Blessed Lady,
    Her dear young son her wi.

7 ' Will ye gang to your men again,
    Or will ye gang wi me ?
    Will ye gang to the high heavens,
    Wi my dear son and me ? '

8 ' I winna gang to my men again,
    For they would be feared at mee ;
    But I woud gang to the high heavens,
    Wi thy dear son and thee.'

9 ' It 's for nae honour ye did to me, Brown Robyn,
    It 's for nae guid ye did to mee ;
    But a' is for your fair confession
    You 've made upon the sea.'

4⁴. if I sink.

In Kirsha Danilof, No 44, Sadko's lot is a feather, the others of cork. He whose lot floats is a righteous soul ; he whose lot sinks is to be thrown overboard. All the lots swim like ducks but Sadko's. Now make lots out of twigs, says Sadko, and he whose lot sinks is a righteous soul. Sadko's lot is some forty pounds of metal, and his the only one that floats.

58

SIR PATRICK SPENS

A. a. 'Sir Patrick Spence,' Percy's Reliques, 1765, I, 71. **b.** 'Sir Andrew Wood,' Herd's Scots Songs, 1769, p. 243. 11 stanzas.

B. 'Sir Patrick Spence,' Herd's MSS, II, 27, I, 49. 16 stanzas.

C. 'Sir Patrick Spens,' Motherwell's MS., p. 493. 20 stanzas.

D. 'Sir Andro Wood,' Motherwell's MS., p. 496. 8 stanzas.

E. 'Young Patrick,' Motherwell's MS., p. 348. 16 stanzas.

F. 'Skipper Patrick,' Motherwell's MS., p. 153. 14 stanzas.

G. 'Sir Patrick Spence,' Jamieson's Popular Ballads, I, 157. 17 stanzas.

H. 'Sir Patrick Spens,' Scott's Minstrelsy, III, 64, ed. 1803. 29 stanzas.

I. 'Sir Patrick Spens,' Buchan's Ballads of the North of Scotland, I, 1; Motherwell's MS., p. 550. 29 stanzas.

J. 'Sir Patrick Spens,' Harris MS., fol. 4. 24 stanzas.

K. 'Sir Patrick Spens,' communicated by Mr Murison. 14 stanzas.

L. 'Sir Patrick,' Motherwell's Note-Book, p. 6, Motherwell's MS., p. 156. 5 stanzas.

M. Buchan's Gleanings, p. 196. 4 stanzas.

N. 'Earl Patricke Spensse,' Dr J. Robertson's Adversaria, p. 67. 4 stanzas.

O. 'Sir Patrick Spens,' Gibb MS., p. 63. 3 stanzas.

P. 'Earl Patrick Graham,' Kinloch MSS, I, 281. 4 stanzas.

Q. Finlay's Scottish Ballads, I, xiv. 2 stanzas.

R. 'Sir Patrick Spence,' communicated by Mr Macmath. 1 stanza.

STANZAS of **E** and of **L**, a little altered, are given by Motherwell in his Introduction, pp xlv, xlvi. The ballad in the Border Minstrelsy, **H**, was made up from two versions, the better of which was **G**, and five stanzas, 16–20, recited by Mr Hamilton, sheriff of Lanarkshire. Mr Hamilton is said to have got his fragment "from an old nurse, a retainer of the Gilkerscleugh family," when himself a boy, about the middle of the last century.* The copy in Finlay's Scottish Ballads, I, 49, is Scott's, with the last stanza exchanged for the last of **A**, and one or two trifling changes. The imperfect copies **K**, stanzas 6–10, **M** 1, 3, show admixture with the more modern ballad of 'Young Allan.' **L** 1, with variations, is found in 'Fair Annie of Lochroyan,' Herd, 1776, I, 150, and may not belong here. But ballad-ships are wont to be of equal splendor with Cleopatra's galley : see, for a first-rate, the Scandinavian 'Sir Peter's Voyage,' cited in the preface to 'Brown Robyn's Confession.' †

This admired and most admirable ballad is

---

* Scott's Minstrelsy, ed. 1833, I, 295 ; Notes and Queries, Second Series, X, 237.

† Christie, I, 7, makes up a copy from Scott and Buchan, "with some alterations from the way the editor has heard" the ballad "sung." I have not felt called upon always to register Christie's cursory variations, but the fourth stanza may be given as he prints it :

> The first word that Sir Patrick read
> A licht licht laugh gae he ;
> But ere he read it to an end
> The saut tear blint his ee.

'Sir Patrick Spens,' Aberdeen, printed by John Duffus, 1866, is composed from several versions, as Scott's, Buchan's, Aytoun's.

one of many which were first made known to
the world through Percy's Reliques. Percy's
version remains, poetically, the best. It may
be a fragment, but the imagination easily
supplies all that may be wanting; and if more
of the story, or the whole, be told in H, the
half is better than the whole.

The short and simple story in A-F is that
the king wants a good sailor to take command
of a ship or ships ready for sea. Sir Patrick
Spens * is recommended, and the king sends
him a commission. This good sailor is much
elated by receiving a letter from the king,
but the contents prove very unwelcome.† He
would hang the man that praised his seaman-
ship, if he knew him, B; though it had been
the queen herself, she might have let it be, F;
had he been a better man, he might ha tauld a
lee, D. The objection, as we learn from A 5,
C 5, is the bad time of year. Percy cites a law
of James III, forbidding ships to be freighted
out of the realm with staple goods between the
feast of Simon and Jude and Candlemas, October 28–February 2. There is neither choice
nor thought, but prompt obedience to orders.
The ship must sail the morn, and this without
regard to the fearful portent of the new moon
having been seen *late* yestreen with the auld
moon in her arm. They are only a few
leagues out when a furious storm sets in. The
captain calls for a boy to take the steer in
hand while he goes to the topmast to spy land,
B; or, more sensibly, sends up the boy, and
sticks to the rudder, C, E. The report is not
encouraging, or is not waited for, for the sea
has everything its own way, and now the

nobles, who were loath to wet their shoes, are
overhead in water, and now fifty fathoms
under. It would be hard to point out in ballad poetry, or other, happier and more refined
touches than the two stanzas in A which por-
tray the bootless waiting of the ladies for the
return of the seafarers.‡

In G-J we meet with additional circumstances. The destination of the ship is Norway. The object of the voyage is not told
in G; in H it is to bring home the king of
Norway's daughter; in J to bring home the
Scottish king's daughter; in I to take out the
Scottish king's daughter to Norway, where
she is to be queen. The Scots make the passage in two days, or three, G, H, I. After a
time the Norwegians begin to complain of the
expense caused by their guests, G, H; or reproach the Scots with staying too long, to their
own king's cost, I. Sir Patrick tells them
that he brought money enough to pay for
himself and his men, and says that nothing
shall induce him to stay another day in the
country. It is now that we have the omen of
the new moon with the old moon in her arm,
in G, H. In I this comes before the voyage
to Norway,§ and in G the stanza expressing
apprehension of a storm, without the reason,
occurs twice,‖ before the voyage out as well
as before the return voyage. In J, as in A-
F, the ship is lost on the voyage out. In G,
therefore, and I as well, two different accounts
may have been blended.

Whether there is an historical basis for the
shipwreck of Scottish nobles which this ballad sings, and, if so, where it is to be found,

---

* Sir Patrick Spens, or Spence, **A, B, C, G, H, J, M**;
Young Patrick, **E**; Skipper Patrick, **F**; Young Patrick
Spens, **I, K**; Sir Patrick, **L**; Earl Patrick Spens, **N**; Sir
Andrew Wood, **A** b, **D**; Earl Patrick Graham, **P**.

† It is so with the Conde Dirlos, when he receives a letter
from the emperor:

> De las cartas placer hubo,
> de las palabras pesar;
> que lo que las cartas dicen
> á él parece muy mal.
>   (Wolf y Hofmann, Primavera, II, 129.)

‡ There is a falling off in **C, E**, with the wives sewing
their silken seams and rocking the cradle, and in **B**, waiting
with their babies in their hands, till in **M** the ladies, still so
called, are reduced to fishers' wives, "wi their gown-tails
owre their crown!"

§ The reading in **I** 9, "To Noroway, wi our king's daughter," has been treated as if important. This version, says
Buchan, was taken down from the recitation of "' a wight of
Homer's craft,' who, as a wandering minstrel, blind from
his infancy, has been travelling in the North as a mendicant for these last fifty years. He learned it in his youth
from a very old person." The mendicant was, no doubt,
James Rankin, "the blind beggar whom I kept travelling
through Scotland, collecting ballads for me, at a heavy expense" (frontispiece to Buchan's MSS, vol. i.). A large
part of Buchan's ballads have the mint-mark of this minstrel
beggar and beggarly minstrel, who collected for pay. No
confidence can be placed in any of his readings: his personal
inspiration was too decided to make him a safe reporter.

‖ For consistency's sake, it has here been dropped from
the place where it first occurs, after stanza 4.

are questions that have been considerably discussed. A strict accordance with history should not be expected, and indeed would be almost a ground of suspicion.* Ballad singers and their hearers would be as indifferent to the facts as the readers of ballads are now ; it is only editors who feel bound to look closely into such matters. Motherwell has suggested a sufficiently plausible foundation. Margaret, daughter of Alexander III, was married, in 1281, to Eric, King of Norway. She was conducted to her husband, " brought home," in August of that year, by many knights and nobles. Many of these were drowned on the return voyage,† as Sir Patrick Spens is in **G**, **H**, **I**.

Margaret, Eric's queen, died in 1283, leaving a newly born daughter ; and Alexander III, having been killed by being thrown from his horse, in 1286, the crown fell to the granddaughter. A match was proposed between the infant Margaret, called the Maid of Norway, and the eldest son of Edward I of England. A deputation, not so splendid as the train which accompanied the little maid's mother to Norway, was sent, in 1290, to bring the Princess Margaret over, but she died on the way before reaching Scotland. The Scalacronica speaks of only a single envoy, Master Weland, a Scottish clerk. If " the chronicle will not lie," the Maid of Norway and the Scottish clerk perished, we must suppose in a storm, on the coasts of Boghan ‡ (Buchan?). This is not quite enough to make the ballad out of, and there is still less material in the marriage of James III with the daughter of the king of Norway in 1469, and no shipwreck chronicled at all.

No such name as Patrick Spens is historically connected with any of these occurrences. Spens has even been said not to be an early Scottish name. Aytoun, however, points to a notable exploit by one Spens as early as 1336, and Mr Macmath has shown me that the name occurred in five charters of David II, therefore between 1329 and 1370. We might allege that Spens, though called Sir Patrick in later days, was in reality only a skeely skipper,§ and that historians do not trouble themselves much about skippers. But this would be avoiding the proper issue. The actual name of the hero of a ballad affords hardly a presumption as to who was originally the hero. This ballad may be historical, or it may not. It might be substantially historical though the command of the ship were invariably given to Sir Andrew Wood, a distinguished admiral, who was born a couple of centuries after the supposed event ; and it might be substantially historical though we could prove that Patrick Spens was only a shipmaster, of purely local fame, who was lost off Aberdour a couple of hundred years ago. For one, I do not feel compelled to regard the ballad as historical.

A mermaid appears to the navigators in **J**, **L**, **P**, **Q**, and informs them, **J**, that they will never see dry land, or are not far from land, **L**, **P**, **Q**, which, coming from a mermaid, they are good seamen enough to know means the same thing. The appearance of a mermaid to seamen is a signal for despair in a brief little ballad, of no great antiquity to all seeming, given further on under the title of ' The Mermaid.' If nothing worse, mermaids at least bode rough weather, and sailors do not like to see them : Faye, Norske Folke-Sagn, ed. 1844, p. 55 (Prior). They have a reputation for treachery : there is in a Danish ballad, Grundtvig, II, 91, No 42, **B** 14, one who has betrayed seven ships.

The place where the ship went down was half owre to Aberdour, **A**, **C**, **F** ? ; ower by Aberdour, **I**, **J**, **N** ; forty miles off Aberdeen, **G**, **H** (**H** may only repeat **G**) ; nore-east, nore-

---

* Or a pure accident. Wyntoun says that Margaret sailed the 12th of August. Motherwell found, "from a laborious calculation," that the 12th of August, 1282 (a misprint, I suppose, for 1281), was a Monday, the sailing day in **G** 5. The account in **H** is probably taken from **G**.

† Fordun, ed. Skene, I, 307.

‡ Scalacronica, ed. Stevenson, p. 110. Fordun mentions Michael of Wemyss and Michael Scot as the envoys, I, 311.

§ He was not even that, according to **G** 4, which has the silly reading,

> For I was never a good seaman,
> Nor ever intend to be.

So in a mixed ballad which will be put with ' Young Allan.'

west frae Aberdeen, **D**; between Leith and Aberdeen, **K**. **B** and **E** transfer the scene to St Johnston (Perth), and **P** to the Clyde, down below Dumbarton Castle. We may fairly say, somewhere off the coast of Aberdeenshire, for the southern Aberdour, in the Firth of Forth, cannot be meant.

The island of Papa Stronsay is said to be about half way between Aberdour in Buchan and the coast of Norway, half owre to Aberdour; and on this island there is a tumulus, which Mr Maidment informs us is known now, and *has always been* known, as the grave of Sir Patrick Spens. Nothing more has been transmitted, we are assured, but only the name as that of a man buried there: Maidment, Scotish Ballads and Songs, Historical and Traditionary, I, 31 f. "The Scottish ballads were not early current in Orkney, a Scandinavian country," says Aytoun, "so it is very unlikely that the poem could have originated the name." With regard to this Orcadian

grave of Patrick Spens, it may first be remarked that Barry, who, in 1808, speaks of the Earl's Knowe in Papa Stronsay, says not a word of the tradition now affirmed to be of indefinite long-standing (neither does Tudor in 1883). The ballad has been in print for a hundred and twenty years. There are Scots in the island now, and perhaps there "always" have been; at any rate, a generation or two is time enough for a story to strike root and establish itself as tradition.*

A a is translated by Herder, Volkslieder, I, 89, Bodmer, I, 56, Döring, p. 157, Rosa Warrens, Schottische Volkslieder, No 16, 1; **G**, by Loève-Veimars, p. 340; **H**, by Grundtvig, Engelske og skotske Folkeviser, No 2, Schubart, p. 203, Wolff, Halle der Völker, I, 60, Fiedler, Geschichte der schottischen Liederdichtung, I, 13; **I**, by Gerhard, p. 1. Aytoun's ballad, by Rosa Warrens, Schottische Volkslieder, No 16, 2.

A

a. Percy's Reliques, 1765, I, 71: "given from two MS. copies, transmitted from Scotland." b. Herd's Scots Songs, 1769, p. 243.

1 THE king sits in Dumferling toune,
  Drinking the blude-reid wine:
' O whar will I get guid sailor,
  To sail this schip of mine ?'

2 Up and spak an eldern knicht,
  Sat at the kings richt kne :
' Sir Patrick Spence is the best sailor
  That sails upon the se.'

3 The king has written a braid letter,
  And signd it wi his hand,
And sent it to Sir Patrick Spence,
  Was walking on the sand.

4 The first line that Sir Patrick red,
  A loud lauch lauched he ;

The next line that Sir Patrick red,
  The teir blinded his ee.

5 ' O wha is this has don this deid,
  This ill deid don to me,
To send me out this time o' the yeir,
  To sail upon the se !

6 ' Mak hast, mak haste, my mirry men all,
  Our guid schip sails the morne :'
' O say na sae, my master deir,
  For I feir a deadlie storme.

7 ' Late late yestreen I saw the new moone,
  Wi the auld moone in hir arme,
And I feir, I feir, my deir master,
  That we will cum to harme.'

8 O our Scots nobles wer richt laith
  To weet their cork-heild schoone ;
Bot lang owre a' the play wer playd,
  Thair hats they swam aboone.

---

* I have not felt called upon to say anything of the attempt of the late Mr Robert Chambers·to prove ' Sir Patrick Spens a piece of literary work of the last century, by arguments which would make Lady Wardlaw author not only of most of the romantic Scottish ballads, but also of a good part of the ballads of Europe. The flimsy plea of Mr Chambers has been effectually disposed of by Mr Norval Clyne, The Romantic Scottish Ballads and the Lady Wardlaw Heresy, Aberdeen, 1859, and by Mr James Hutton Watkins, Early Scottish Ballads, Glasgow, 1867.

9 O lang, lang may their ladies sit,
  Wi thair fans into their hand,
Or eir they se Sir Patrick Spence
  Cum sailing to the land.

10 O lang, lang may the ladies stand,
  Wi thair gold kems in their hair,

Waiting for thair ain deir lords,
  For they 'll se thame na mair.

11 Haf owre, haf owre to Aberdour,
  It 's fiftie fadom deip,
And thair lies guid Sir Patrick Spence,
  Wi the Scots lords at his feit.

———•———

B

Herd's MSS., II, 27, I, 49.

1 THE king he sits in Dumferling,
  Drinking the blude reid wine : O
' O where will I get a gude sailor,
  That 'l sail the ships o mine ? ' O

2 Up then started a yallow-haird man,
  Just be the kings right knee :
' Sir Patrick Spence is the best sailor
  That ever saild the see.'

3 Then the king he wrote a lang letter,
  And sealld it with his hand,
And sent it to Sir Patrick Spence,
  That was lyand at Leith Sands.

4 When Patrick lookd the letter on,
  He gae loud laughters three ;
But afore he wan to the end of it
  The teir blindit his ee.

5 ' O wha is this has tald the king,
  Has tald the king o me ?
Gif I but wist the man it war,
  Hanged should he be.

6 ' Come eat and drink, my merry men all,
  For our ships maun sail the morn ;
Bla 'd wind, bla 'd weet, bla 'd sna or sleet,
  Our ships maun sail the morn.'

7 ' Alake and alas now, good master,
  For I fear a deidly storm ;
For I saw the new moon late yestreen,
  And the auld moon in her arms.'

8 They had not saild upon the sea
  A league but merely three,
When ugly, ugly were the jaws
  That rowd unto their knee.

9 They had not saild upon the sea
  A league but merely nine,
When wind and weit and snaw and sleit
  Came blawing them behind.

10 ' Then where will I get a pretty boy
  Will take my steer in hand,
Till I go up to my tap-mast,
  And see gif I see dry land ? '

11 ' Here am I, a pretty boy
  That 'l take your steir in hand,
Till you go up to your tap-mast,
  And see an you see the land.'

12 Laith, laith were our Scottish lords
  To weit their coal-black shoon ;
But yet ere a' the play was playd,
  They wat their hats aboon.

13 Laith, laith war our Scottish lords
  To weit their coal-black hair ;
But yet ere a' the play was playd,
  They wat it every hair.

14 The water at St Johnston's wall
  Was fifty fathom deep,
And there ly a' our Scottish lords,
  Sir Patrick at their feet.

15 Lang, lang may our ladies wait
  Wi the tear blinding their ee,
Afore they see Sir Patrick's ships
  Come sailing oer the sea.

16 Lang, lang may our ladies wait,
  Wi their babies in their hands,
Afore they see Sir Patrick Spence
  Come sailing to Leith Sands.

C

Motherwell's MS., p. 493, "from the recitation of —— Buchanan, alias Mrs Notman, 9 September, 1826."

1 THE king sat in Dunfermline toun,
    Drinking the blude red wine :
' Where will I get a bold sailor,
    To sail this ship o mine ? '

2 Out then spak an auld auld knicht,
    Was nigh the king akin :
' Sir Patrick Spens is the best sailor
    That ever sailed the main.'

3 The king's wrote a large letter,
    Sealed it with his own hand,
And sent it to Sir Patrick Spens,
    Was walking on dry land.

4 The first three lines he looked on,
    The tears did blind his ee ;
The neist three lines he looked on
    Not one word could he see.

5 ' Wha is this,' Sir Patrick says,
    ' That's tauld the king o me,
To set me out·this time o the year
    To sail upon the sea !

6 ' Yestreen I saw the new new mune,
    And the auld mune in her arm ;
And that is the sign since we were born
    Even of a deadly storm.

7 ' Drink about, my merry boys,
    For we maun sail the morn ;
Be it wind, or be it weet,
    Or be it deadly storm.'

8 We hadna sailed a league, a league,
    A league but only ane,
Till cauld and watry grew the wind,
    And stormy grew the main.

9 We hadna sailed a league, a league,
    A league but only twa,
Till cauld and watry grew the wind,
    Come hailing owre them a'.

10 We hadna sailed a league, a league,
    A league but only three,

Till cold and watry grew the wind,
    And grumly grew the sea.

11 ' Wha will come,' the captain says,
    ' And take my helm in hand ?
Or wha 'll gae up to my topmast,
    And look for some dry land ?

12 ' Mount up, mount up, my pretty boy,
    See what you can spy ;
Mount up, mount up, my pretty boy,
    See if any land we 're nigh.'

13 ' We 're fifty miles from shore to shore,
    And fifty banks of sand ;
And we have all that for to sail
    Or we come to dry land.'

14 ' Come down, come down, my pretty boy,
    I think you tarry lang ;
For the saut sea 's in at our coat-neck
    And out at our left arm.

15 ' Come down, come down, my pretty boy,
    I fear we here maun die ;
For thro and thro my goodly ship
    I see the green-waved sea.'

16 Our Scotch lords were all afraid
    To weet their cork-heeled shoon ;
But lang or a' the play was played,
    Their hats they swam abune.

17 The first step that the captain stept,
    It took him to the knee,
And the next step that the captain stepped
    They were a' drownd in the sea.

18 Half owre, half owre to Aberdour
    It's fifty fadoms deep,
And there lay good Sir Patrick Spens,
    And the Scotch lords at his feet.

19 Lang may our Scotch lords' ladies sit,
    And sew their silken seam,
Before they see their good Scotch lords
    Come sailing owre the main.

20 Lang lang may Sir Patrick's lady
    Sit rocking her auld son,
Before she sees Sir Patrick Spens
    Come sailing owre the main.

D

Motherwell's MS., p. 496, communicated by Kirkpatrick Sharpe.

1 THE king sits in Dumferling town,
  Drinking the blood red wine : O
' Where will I get a good skipper,
  To sail seven ships o mine ? ' O
Where will, etc.

2 O up then spake a bra young man,
  And a bra young man was he :
' Sir Andrew Wood is the best skipper
  That ever saild the sea.'

3 The king has written a bra letter,
  And seald it wi his hand,
And ordered Sir Andrew Wood
  To come at his command.

4 ' O wha is this, or wha is that,
  Has tauld the king o me ?
For had he been a better man,
  He might ha tauld a lee.'

* * * * *

5 As I came in by the Inch, Inch, Inch,
  I heard an auld man weep :
' Sir Andrew Wood and a' his men
  Are drowned in the deep ! '

6 O lang lang may yon ladies stand,
  Their fans into their hands,
Before they see Sir Andrew Wood
  Come sailing to dry land.

7 O laith laith were our Scottish lords
  To weit their cork-heeld shoon ;
But ere that a' the play was plaid,
  They wat their heads aboon.

8 Nore-east, nore-west frae Aberdeen
  Is fifty fathom deep,
And there lies good Sir Andrew Wood,
  And a' the Scottish fleet.

----◆----

E

Motherwell's MS., p. 348.

1 THE king sits in Dumfermline toun,
  Sae merrilie drinking wine ; O
Says, Whare will I get a fine skipper,
  Wud sail these ships of mine ? O

2 Out and spak an auld rich knicht,
  And an ill death may he die !
Says, Young Patrick is the best skipper
  That ever set sail on sea.

3 The king did write a lang letter,
  Sealed it with his own hand,
And he sent it to Young Patrick,
  To come at his command.

4 When Young Patrick read the letter lang,
  The tear blindit his ee ;
Says Wha is this, or wha is that,
  That 's tauld the king of me ?
Altho he had been better than what he is,
  He micht hae askt leave of me.

5 ' But busk, O busk, my merry men a',
  O busk and mak you braw,
For blaw the wind what airt it will,
  Our ship she must awa.

6 ' Drink, O drink, my merrie men all,
  Drink o the beer and wine,
For gin Wednesday by twal o'clock
  We 'll a' be in our lang hame.'

7 Out and spak a pretty little boy :
  ' I fear a deadlie storm ;
For I saw the new mune late yestreen,
  And the old ane in her arm,
And readilie, maister,' said he,
  ' That 's the sign of a deadly storm.'

8 Aye they sat, and aye they drank,
  They drank of the beer and wine,
And gin Wednesday gin ten o'clock,
  Their hair was wat abune.

9 ' Whare wuld I get a pretty little boy,
  That wants to win hose and shoon,

Wuld up to the top of my mainmast go,
  See if he could spy land ? '

10 ' O here am I, a pretty little boy,
  Wants to win hose and shoon ;
I 'll up to the top of your mainmast go,
  Though I should neer come doun.'

11 ' Come doun, come doun, my pretty little boy,
  I think thou tarries lang ;
For the jawe is coming in at my coat-neck,
  Going out at my richt hand.'

12 But there cum a shouir out o the Norewest,
  Of dreidfu hail and rain,
It made Young Patrick and his men
  A' flat wi the sea faem.

13 O is na it a great pitye
  To see feather-beds on the main ?

But it is a greater pitye, I think,
  To see men doing the same.

14 There 's a brig at the back o Sanct John's
    toun,
  It 's fifty fadom deep,
And there lies a' our brau Scots lords,
  Young Patrick's at their feet.

15 Young Patrick's lady sits at hame,
  She 's sewing her silken seam ;
And aye when she looks to the salt sea waves,
  ' I fear he 'll neer return.'

16 Young Patrick's lady sits at hame
  Rocking her oldest son ;
And aye when she looks to the salt sea waves,
  ' I 'm feared he 'll neer come hame.'

F

Motherwell's MS., p. 153, from the recitation of Mrs
Thomson.

1 THE king he sits on Dunfermline hill,
  Drinking baith beer and wine ; O
Says, Whare shall I get a good skipper,
  That will sail the salt sea fine ? O

2 But out then speaks an Irish knight,
  Sat by the king's right knee :
' Skipper Patrick is the best skipper
  That ever my eyes did see.'

3 The king has written a lang letter,
  And sealed it wi his hand,
And sent it to Skipper Patrick,
  As he walked alang the sand.

4 ' O wha is this, or wha is that,
  That 's tauld the king of me ?
For tho it had been the queen hersell,
  She might hae let it be.

5 ' But busk you, O busk, my merry men all,
  Sae merrily busk and boune,
For blaw the wind where eer it will,
  Our gude ship sails the morn.'

6 ' O no, O no, our dear master,
  It will be a deidly storm ;
For yestreen I saw the new new mune,
  Wi the auld mune in her arm ;
It 's a token, maister, or ye were born,
  It will be a deadly storm.'

7 ' But busk, O busk, my merrie men all,
  Our gude ship sails the morn,
For blow the wind whereer it will,
  Our gude ship sails the morn.'

8 They had na sailed a day, a day,
  A day but scarsely five,
Till Skipper Patrick's bonny ship
  Began to crack and rive.

9 It 's bonny was the feather beds
  That swimmed alang the main,
But bonnier was our braw Scots lords,
  They neer returned again.

10 Our Scots lords they are all laith
  To weet their coal black shoon;
But I trow or a' the play was played,
  They wat their hair abune.

11 Our ladies may stand upon the sand,
　　Kembing down their yellow hair,
　　But they will neer see Skipper Patrick's ship
　　Come sailing in nae mair.

12 Our ladies may stand upon the sand
　　Wi gloves upon their hand,
　　But they will never see Skipper Patrick's ship
　　Come sailing into the land.

13 O vour and o vour to bonnie Aberdour
　　It 's fifty fadoms deep ;
　　There you will find young Patrick lye,
　　Wi his Scots lords at his head.

14 Row owre, row owre to Aberdour,
　　It 's fifty fadom deep ;
　　And there lies Earl Patrick Spens,
　　His men all at his feet.

───────

G

Jamieson's Popular Ballads, I, 157, communicated by Scott.

1 THE king sits in Dunfermlin town,
　　Sae merrily drinkin the wine :
　　' Whare will I get a mariner,
　　Will sail this ship o mine ? '

2 Then up bespak a bonny boy,
　　Sat just at the king's knee :
　　' Sir Patrick Spence is the best seaman,
　　That eer set foot on sea.'

3 The king has written a braid letter,
　　Seald it wi his ain hand ;
　　He has sent word to Sir Patrick,
　　To come at his command.

4 ' O wha is this, or wha is that,
　　Has tald the king o me ?
　　For I was never a good seaman,
　　Nor ever intend to be.'

5 They mounted sail on Munénday morn,
　　Wi a' the haste they may,
　　And they hae landed in Norraway,
　　Upon the Wednesday.

6 They hadna been a month, a month
　　In Norraway but three,
　　Till lads o Norraway began to say,
　　Ye spend a' our white monie.

7 ' Ye spend a' our good kingis goud,
　　But and our queenis fee : '
　　' Ye lie, ye lie, ye liars loud,
　　Sae weel 's I hear you lie.

8 ' For I brought as much white money
　　As will gain my men and me ;
　　I brought half a fou o good red goud
　　Out oer the sea with me.

9 ' Be 't wind or weet, be 't snaw or sleet,
　　Our ships maun sail the morn : '
　　' O ever alack ! my master dear,
　　I fear a deadly storm.

10 ' I saw the new moon late yestreen,
　　Wi the auld moon in her arm ;
　　And if we gang to sea, master,
　　I fear we 'll suffer harm.'

11 They hadna sailed a league on sea,
　　A league but barely ane,
　　Till anchors brak, and tap-masts lap ;
　　There came a deadly storm.

12 ' Whare will I get a bonny boy
　　Will tak thir sails in hand,
　　That will gang up to the tap-mast,
　　See an he ken dry land ? '

13 Laith, laith were our good Scots lords
　　To weet their leathern shoon ;
　　But or the morn at fair day-light,
　　Their hats were wat aboon.

14 Mony was the feather bed,
　　That flotterd on the faem,
　　And mony was the good Scots lord
　　Gaed awa that neer cam hame,
　　And mony was the fatherless bairn
　　That lay at hame greetin.

15 It's forty miles to Aberdeen,
    And fifty fathoms deep;
  And there lyes a' our good Scots lords,
    Wi Sir Patrick at their feet.

16 The ladies crackt their fingers white,
    The maidens tore their hair,

A' for the sake o their true loves,
  For them they neer saw mair.

17 Lang, lang may our ladies stand,
    Wi their fans in their hand,
  Ere they see Sir Patrick and his men
    Come sailing to the land.

H

Minstrelsy of the Scottish Border, III, 64, ed. 1803; I, 299, ed. 1833; "taken from two MS. copies, collated with several verses recited by the editor's friend, Robert Hamilton, Esq., Advocate."

1 THE king sits in Dumfermline town,
    Drinking the blude-red wine: O
  'O whare will I get a skeely skipper,
    To sail this new ship of mine?' O

2 O up and spake an eldern knight,
    Sat at the king's right knee:
  'Sir Patrick Spens is the best sailor
    That ever saild the sea.'

3 Our king has written a braid letter,
    And seald it with his hand,
  And sent it to Sir Patrick Spens,
    Was walking on the strand.

4 'To Noroway, to Noroway,
    To Noroway oer the faem;
  The king's daughter of Noroway,
    'T is thou maun bring her hame.'

5 The first word that Sir Patrick read,
    Sae loud, loud laughed he;
  The neist word that Sir Patrick read,
    The tear blinded his ee.

6 'O wha is this has done this deed,
    And tauld the king o me,
  To send us out at this time of the year
    To sail upon the sea?

7 'Be it wind, be it weet, be it hail, be it sleet,
    Our ship must sail the faem;
  The king's daughter of Noroway,
    'T is we must fetch her hame.'

8 They hoysed their sails on Monenday morn,
    Wi a' the speed they may;
  They hae landed in Noroway,
    Upon a Wodensday.

9 They hadna been a week, a week
    In Noroway but twae,
  When that the lords o Noroway
    Began aloud to say:

10 'Ye Scottishmen spend a' our king's goud,
    And a' our queenis fee!'
  'Ye lie, ye lie, ye liars loud,
    Fu loud I hear ye lie!

11 'For I brought as much white monie
    As gane my men and me,
  And I brought a half-fou o gude red goud
    Out oer the sea wi me.

12 'Make ready, make ready, my merrymen a',
    Our gude ship sails the morn:'
  'Now, ever alake! my master dear,
    I fear a deadly storm!

13 'I saw the new moo late yestreen,
    Wi the auld moon in her arm;
  And if we gang to sea, master,
    I fear we 'll come to harm.'

14 They hadna sailed a league, a league,
    A league but barely three,
  When the lift grew dark, and the wind blew loud
    And gurly grew the sea.

15 The ankers brak, and the topmasts lap,
    It was sic a deadly storm,
  And the waves came oer the broken ship,
    Till a' her sides were torn.

16 'O where will I get a gude sailor,
    To take my helm in hand,
  Till I get up to the tall topmast,
    To see if I can spy land?'

17 'O here am I, a sailor gude,
    To take the helm in hand,
  Till you go up to the tall topmast;
    But I fear you 'll neer spy land.'

18 He hadna gane a step, a step,
     A step but barely ane,
   When a bout flew out of our goodly ship,
     And the salt sea it came in.

19 'Gae fetch a web o the silken claith,
     Another o the twine,
   And wap them into our ship's side,
     And letna the sea come in.'

20 They fetched a web o the silken claith,
     Another o the twine,
   And they wapped them roun that gude ship's side,
     But still the sea came in.

21 O laith, laith were our gude Scots lords
     To weet their cork-heeld shoon;
   But lang or a' the play was playd,
     They wat their hats aboon.

22 And mony was the feather-bed
     That flattered on the faem,

And mony was the gude lord's son
  That never mair cam hame.

23 The ladyes wrang their fingers white,
     The maidens tore their hair,
   A' for the sake of their true loves,
     For them they 'll see na mair.

24 O lang, lang may the ladyes sit,
     Wi their fans into their hand,
   Before they see Sir Patrick Spens
     Come sailing to the strand.

25 And lang, lang may the maidens sit,
     Wi their goud kaims in their hair,
   A' waiting for their ain dear loves,
     For them they 'll see na mair.

26 O forty miles off Aberdeen
     'T is fifty fathoms deep,
   And there lies gude Sir Patrick Spens,
     Wi the Scots lords at his feet.

I

Buchan's Ballads of the North of Scotland, I, 1; Motherwell's MS., p. 550.

1 THE king sits in Dunfermline town,
     A-drinking at the wine;
   Says, Where will I get a good skipper,
     Will sail the saut seas fine?

2 Out it speaks an eldren knight
     Amang the companie:
   'Young Patrick Spens is the best skipper
     That ever saild the sea.'

3 The king he wrote a braid letter,
     And seald it wi his ring;
   Says, Ye 'll gie that to Patrick Spens,
     See if ye can him find.

4 He sent this not wi an auld man,
     Nor yet a simple boy,
   But the best o nobles in his train
     This letter did convoy.

5 When Patrick lookd the letter upon
     A light laugh then gae he;
   But ere he read it till an end,
     The tear blinded his ee.

6 'Ye 'll eat and drink, my merry men a',
     An see ye be weell thorn;

For blaw it weet, or blaw it wind,
  My guid ship sails the morn.'

7 Then out it speaks a guid auld man,
     A guid death mat he dee!
   'Whatever ye do, my guid master,
     Tak God your guide to bee.

8 'For late yestreen I saw the new moon,
     The auld moon in her arm :'
   'Ohon, alas!' says Patrick Spens,
     'That bodes a deadly storm.

9 'But I maun sail the seas the morn,
     And likewise sae maun you ;
   To Noroway, wi our king's daughter,
     A chosen queen she 's now.

10 'But I wonder who has been sae base
     As tauld the king o mee;
   Even tho he ware my ae brither,
     An ill death mat he dee !'

11 Now Patrick he riggd out his ship,
     And sailed ower the faem,
   But mony a dreary thought had hee,
     While hee was on the main.

12 They hadna saild upon the sea
     A day but barely three,

Till they came in sight o Noroway,
  It 's there where they must bee.

13 They hadna stayed into that place
  A month but and a day,
Till he causd the flip in mugs gae roun,
  And wine in cans sae gay.

14 The pipe and harp sae sweetly playd,
  The trumpets loudly soun ;
In every hall where in they stayd,
  Wi their mirth did reboun.

15 Then out it speaks an auld skipper,
  An inbearing dog was hee:
' Ye 've stayd ower lang in Noroway,
  Spending your king's monie.'

16 Then out it speaks Sir Patrick Spens:
  ' O how can a' this bee ?
I hae a bow o guid red gowd
  Into my ship wi mee.

17 ' But betide me well, betide me wae,
  This day I'se leave the shore,
And never spend my king's monie
  Mong Noroway dogs no more.'

18 Young Patrick hee is on the sea,
  And even on the faem,
Wi five-an-fifty Scots lords' sons,
  That langd to bee at hame.

19 They hadna saild upon the sea
  A day but barely three,
Till loud and boistrous grew the wind,
  And stormy grew the sea.

20 ' O where will I get a little wee boy
  Will tak my helm in hand,
Till I gae up to my tapmast,
  And see for some dry land ? '

21 He hadna gane to his tapmast
  A step but barely three,

Ere thro and thro the bonny ship's side
  He saw the green haw sea.

22 ' There are five-an-fifty feather beds
  Well packed in ae room ;
And ye 'll get as muckle guid canvas
  As wrap the ship a' roun.

23 ' Ye 'll pict her well, and spare her not,
  And mak her hale and soun : '
But ere he had the word well spoke
  The bonny ship was down.

24 O laith, laith were our guid lords' sons
  To weet their milk-white hands ;
But lang ere a' the play was ower,
  They wat their gowden bands.

25 O laith, laith were our Scots lords' sons
  To weet their coal-black shoon ;
But lang ere a' the play was ower,
  They wat their hats aboon.

26 It 's even ower by Aberdour
  It 's fifty fathoms deep,
And yonder lies Sir Patrick Spens,
  And a 's men at his feet.

27 It 's even ower by Aberdour,
  There 's mony a craig and fin,
And yonder lies Sir Patrick Spens,
  Wi mony a guid lord's son.

28 Lang, lang will the ladyes look,
  Into their morning weed,
Before they see young Patrick Spens
  Come sailing ower the fleed.

29 Lang, lang will the ladyes look,
  Wi their fans in their hand,
Before they see him Patrick Spens
  Come sailing to dry land.

J

Miss Harris's MS., fol. 4, from the singing of her mother.

1 HIE sits oor king in Dumfermline,
  Sits birlin at the wine ;
Says, Whare will I get a bonnie boy
  That will sail the saut seas fine ?
That will hie owre to Norraway,
  To bring my dear dochter hame ?

2 Up it spak a bonnie boy,
  Sat by the king's ain knie :
' Sir Patrick Spens is as gude a skipper
  As ever sailed the sea.'

3 The king has wrote a broad letter,
  And signed it wi his hand,
And sent it to Sir Patrick Spens,
  To read it gif he can.

4 The firsten line he luikit on,
    A licht lauchter gae he ;
But ere he read it to the end,
    The tear blindit his ee.

5 ' O wha is this, or wha is that,
    Has tauld oor king o me ?
I wad hae gien him twice as muckle thank
    To latten that abee !

6 ' But eat an drink, my merrie young men,
    Eat, an be weel forn ;
For blaw it wind, or blaw it weet,
    Oor gude ship sails the morn.'

7 Up it spak his youngest son,
    Sat by Sir Patrick's knie :
' I beg you bide at hame, father,
    An I pray be ruled by me.

8 ' For I saw the new mune late yestreen,
    Wi the auld mune in her arms ;
An ever an alake, my father dear,
    It 's a token o diedly storms.'

9 ' It 's eat an drink, my merrie young men,
    Eat, an be weel forn ;
For blaw it wind, or blaw it weet,
    Oor gude ship sails the morn.'

10 They hadna sailed a league, a league,
    A league but only three,
When the whirlin wind an the ugly jaws
    Cam drivin to their knie.

11 They hadna sailed a league, a league,
    A league but only five,
When the whirlin wind an the ugly jaws
    Their gude ship began to rive.

12 They hadna sailed a league, a league,
    A league but only nine,
When the whirlin wind an the ugly jaws
    Cam drivin to their chin.

13 ' O whaur will I get a bonnie boy
    Will tak the steer in hand,
Till I mount up to oor tapmast,
    To luik oot for dry land ? '

14 ' O here am I, a bonnie boy,
    Will tak the steer in hand,
Till you mount up to oor tapmast,
    To luik oot for dry land.'

15 He 's gaen up to the tapmast,
    To the tapmast sae hie ;
He luikit around on every side,
    But dry land he couldna see.

16 He luikit on his youngest son,
    An the tear blindit his ee ;
Says, I wish you had been in your mother's
      bowr,
    But there you 'll never be.

17 ' Pray for yoursels, my merrie young men,
    Pray for yoursels an me,
For the first landen that we will land
    Will be in the boddam o the sea.'

18 Then up it raise the mermaiden,
    Wi the comb an glass in her hand :
' Here 's a health to you, my merrie young
      men,
    For you never will see dry land.'

19 O laith, laith waur oor gude Scots lords
    To weet their cork-heeled shoon ;
But lang, lang ere the play was played,
    Their yellow locks soomed aboun.

20 There was Saturday, an Sabbath day,
    An Monnonday at morn,
That feather-beds an silken sheets
    Cam floatin to Kinghorn.

21 It 's och, och owre to Aberdour,
    It 's fifty faddoms deep ;
An there lie a' oor gude Scots lords,
    Wi Sir Patrick Spens at their feet.

22 O lang, lang will his lady sit,
    Wi the fan into her hand,
Until she see her ain dear lord
    Come sailin to dry land.

23 O lang, lang will his lady sit,
    Wi the tear into her ee,
Afore she see her ain dear lord
    Come hieing to Dundee.

24 O lang, lang will his lady sit,
    Wi the black shoon on her feet,
Afore she see Sir Patrick Spens
    Come drivin up the street.

K

Communicated by Mr Murison, as taken down from recitation in Old Deer by Mrs Murison.

*   *   *   *   *

1 IT 's when he read the letter ower
   A licht lauch then leuch he;
But lang ere he wan the end o it
   The saut tear filled his ee.

2 'O woe be to the man,' he says,
   'That 's tauld the king o me;
Altho he be my ain brither,
   Some ill death mat he dee!

3 .   .   .   .   .   .

   'For be it weet, or be it win,
   My bonnie ship sails the morn.'

*   *   *   *   *

4 'For late the streen I saw the new meen,
   Bit an the auld ane tee.
An it fears me sair, my good maister,
   For a tempest in the sea.'

5 .   .   .   .   .

   Till up it rase the win an storm,
   An a tempest i the sea.

6 .   .   .   .   .   .

   It 's throch an throu the comely cog
   There comes the green raw sea.

*   *   *   *   *

7 'Call upo your men, maister,
   An dinna call on me,
For ye drank them weel ere ye tuke the gate,
   But O nane gae ye me.

8 'Ye beat my back, an beat my sides,
   When I socht hose an sheen;
So call upo your men, maister,
   As they lie drunk wi wine.'

9 'Come doon, come doon, my bonnie boy,
   An tak my helm in han;
Gin ever we live to gae to lan,
   I 'll wed ye wi my daughter Ann.'

10 'Ye used me ill, my guid maister,
   When we was on the lan,
But nevertheless, my gude maister,
   I 'll tak your helm in han.'

11 O laith, laith was oor bonny boys
   To weet their cork-heeled shoes;
But lang ere a' the play was played,
   They wat their yallow broos.

12 O laith, laith was oor bonnie boys
   To weet their cork-heeled sheen;
But lang ere a' the play was played,
   They wat their hair abeen.

13 'O lang, lang will my lady leuk,
   Wi the lantern in her han,
Afore she see my bonnie ship
   Come sailin to dry lan.'

14 Atween Leith an Aberdeen
   Lies mony a craig an sea,
An there it lies young Patrick Spens,
   An mony bonnie boys him wi.

L

Motherwell's Note-Book, p. 6, Motherwell's MS., p. 156, from Mrs Gentles, Paisley, February 1825.

1 OUR ship it was a gudely ship,
   Its topmast was of gold,
And at every tack of needlework
   There hung a silver bell.

2 Up started the mermaid by our ship,
   Wi the glass and the comb in her hand:
'Reek about, reek about, my merrie men,
   Ye are not far from land.'

3 'You lie, you lie, you pretty mermaid,
   Sae loud as I hear you lie;
For since I have seen your face this nicht,
   The land I will never see.'

4 We hadna sailed a league but ane,
  A league but barely three,
Till all we and our goodly ship
  Was all drowned in the sea.

———————

M

Buchan's Gleaning , p. 196, " from a very intelligent old
man."

1 THERE shall no man go to my ship
  Till I say mass and dine,
And take my leave of my lady ;
  Go to my bonny ship syne.

2 When he was up at the top-mast head
  Around could naething see,

5 Lang lang may our ladies stand,
  Wi their seams into their hand,
Looking for Sir Patrick's ship,
  That will never come to land.

But terrible storm in the air aboon,
  And below the roaring sea.

3 ' Come down, come down, my good master,
  You see not what I see ;
For thro an thro your bonny ship's side
  I see the green salt sea.'

4 Lang lang will the ladies look,
  Wi their gown-tails owre their crown,
Before they see Sir Patrick Spens
  Sailing to Dunferline town.

———————

N

Noted down from a female servant, by Joseph Robertson,
July 15, 1829, Adversaria, p. 67.

1 OWER and ower by Aberdour
  There 's mony a cloudy stone,
And there is mony a gude lord's son
  I fear will never come home.

2 Lang, lang will his lady look,
  Wi her baby in her arms,

But she 'll never see Earl Patrick Spens
  Com walkin up the stran.

3 ' I have a table in my room,
  It cost me guineas nine ;
I wad sink it in the sea
  For ae sight o dry lan.

4 ' There 's a coat o green velvet on my back,
  I got it for my fee ;
But tho I wad gie ten thousan punds,
  Dry land I will never see.'

———————

O

Gibb MS., p. 63.

1 BONNY were the feather beds
  Cam sailin ower the faem,
But bonnier was the sixteen lords
  Gaed out and neer cam hame.

2 Lang, lang may the nourice sit,
  Wi the bonny babe on her knee,

Ere ever she see her good lord come,
  To pay to her her fee.

3 An lang, lang will the lady sit,
  Wi the gowd fan in her hand,
Ere ever she see her ain gude lord
  Come skipping to dry land.

P

Kinloch MSS, I, 281.

1 Fu laith, fu laith was our braw Scots lords
  To weet their coal black shoon ;
  But ere the battle a' was foucht,
  Their hats war weet aboun.

2 Out and starts the mermaiden,
  Wi a fan into her hand :

Q

Finlay's Scottish Ballads, I, xiv, from a recited copy.

1 THEN up an cam a mermaid,
  Wi a siller cup in her han :
'Sail on, sail on, my gude Scotch lords,
  For ye sune will see dry lan.'

R

Communicated by Mr Macmath, from Mr William Tra-
quair, S. S. C., Edinburgh ; obtained originally in Perthshire.

' T WAS late, late on a Saturday night,
  And early on a Sunday morn,

'Keep up your hearts, my merry men a',
  For ye 're near the dry land.'

3 Out and spak Earl Patrick Graham,
  Wi the saut tear in his ee :
'Now sin we 've seen the mermaiden,
  Dry land we 'll never see.'

4 Down below Dunbarton castle,
  Full fifty fathoms deep,
There lies a' our braw Scots men,
  Earl Patrick at their feet.

---

2 'Awa, awa, ye wild woman,
  An let your fleechin be ;
For sen your face we 've seen the day,
  Dry lan we 'll never see.'

That robes of silk and feather beds
  Came floating to Kean-Gorn.

A. a. 1³. quhar. 5¹. quha.
   5³. zeir. 11¹. have owre, have owr.
   b. *In this copy* Sir Andrew Wood *replaces* Sir
     Patrick Spens *throughout.*
   8⁴. They wat thair heads aboone.
   At the end of version B *Herd says :* The
     foundation of the preceding song seems to
     have been the same story with that under
     the title of 'Sir Andrew Wood' in the
     former volume [of 1769]. In the Relicks
     of Antient Poetry is a copy somewhat dif-
     ferent from either. *We cannot suppose,
     after this, that Herd took his copy from
     Percy and altered it, and yet, excepting
     the variations noted above, and* haff *for*
     have *in* 11¹, *the copies are the same to a
     letter. If Herd's copy was one of the
     two used by Percy, what was the other ?
     Was there, after all, but one copy again,
     as in the case of 'King Estmere' ?*
B. O *is added, in singing, to every second and
   fourth verse. Also in* D, E, F, H.

C. 14². I thing.
F. 14. *In a smaller hand, and detached from the
   preceding, as if added later.*
G. *After 4 occurs this stanza, almost verbally repeated in 9, and improperly anticipating
   matters, according to the arrangement of
   the story in this version :*

    Be 't wind, be 't weet, be 't snaw, be 't
      sleet,
    Our ships maun sail the morn :
    Ever alack ! my master dear,
    For I fear a deadly storm.

H. 24⁴. perhaps driven.
K. 'Spendin the queen's meat an her fee' *was said
   by the reciter to belong to the ballad, though
   the connection was not remembered.*
   13². *Var. :* An langer will she stan.
L. 1 *is* 5 *and* 5 *is* 1 *in the MS.*

59

SIR ALDINGAR

A. 'Sir Aldingar,' Percy MS., p. 68; Hales and Furnivall, I, 166.

B. 'Sir Hugh le Blond,' Minstrelsy of the Scottish Border, III, 51, 1803.

C. 'Sir Hugh le Blond,' Dr Joseph Robertson's Note-Book, January 1, 1830, p. 6.

THIS ballad, one of the most important of all that the Percy manuscript has saved from oblivion, was first given to the world in the Reliques of Ancient English Poetry, II, 48, ed. 1765, II, 49, ed. 1767, with conjectural emendations by the editor, and the insertion of some stanzas to complete the story. A second version, very much humbled in diction, and otherwise corrupted, but of indubitable antiquity, as Scott remarks, was published in the Minstrelsy of the Scottish Border in 1803, as communicated by Mr Williamson Burnet, of Monboddo, from the recitation of an old woman. The story which this version relates was then, we are informed, universally current in the Mearns, and was supposed to be authenticated by the sword of the hero, preserved nearly down to that time by his reputed descendants.

Tales of the same general description — of a noble lady accused to her husband of infidelity, believed by him to be guilty, and in process of time demonstrated to have been faultless, to his entire conviction — are, 'as might be expected, extremely often to be met with in ballad, romance, chronicle, or saga; nor is the number small of those which have the special traits that the accusation is made by a trusted officer of the husband, who has attempted to seduce the lady, and has failed, and that the wife is cleared by a judgment of God. Our ballad belongs with a very distinct Scandinavian variety of these last, but has adopted one characteristic trait from another source.

The English version, as written down about the middle of the seventeenth century, narrates that Sir Aldingar, steward of King Henry, repulsed by the queen whom he has sought to make his paramour, cannot rest till he has revenge. He takes a lazar that happens to come to the king's gates, and lays him in the queen's bed, promising that in two hours the blind and lame shall be whole and sound ; he then goes to fetch the king. The king, convinced by his eyes, says he will hang the lazar and burn his wife, and immediately proceeds to tell the queen his discovery. The queen sees the hand of Aldingar in this, and also the meaning of a dream she has had: how a vulture, or griffin, had carried her crown away, and would have taken her to his nest * had it not been for a merlin, a little hawk, that came flying from the east and struck the big bird down. She claims the right to maintain her innocence by battle, and the king gives her forty days to provide herself with a champion, which failing she shall be burnt. No man in all the south country will undertake her cause, but a messenger who rides into the east meets what seems to be a child, who interrogates him, and, getting a slow answer, bids the queen by him to remember her dream and be of good cheer, for when bale is highest boot shall be nighest. The days of grace being out, and no champion found, the queen is put into a tun to burn, and looks only for death. At this moment a child is seen riding from the east, who, when he comes to the fire, or-

---

* Such dreams are not unusual in this connection : the empress has a like one in Octavian, Weber, Metrical Romances, III, 165, v. 195 ff; the emperor in The Erl of Tolous, Lüdtke, st. 68 ; the duke in the German Hirlanda.

ders the brands to be withdrawn and Aldingar to be produced. Aldingar, a very large man, would not have minded fifty such. The child claims the first stroke, and if Aldingar can give a second he need not spare him. Aldingar's legs are cut off at the knee with this stroke. Aldingar asks for a priest to shrive him, confesses everything, and begs the queen's forgiveness. The child enjoins King Harry to take back his wife and love her, for she is true as stone; the lazar under the gallows becomes a sound man at the same instant, and is made steward in Aldingar's place.

The Scottish ballad repeats the main part of this story, dropping all that is miraculous save the simple judgment of God. Rodingham, who represents Aldingar, does not cajole the leper with the promise of being restored to health, but intoxicates him with sweet liquors, and lays him asleep in the queen's bed. The king wishes to believe the queen guiltless, and proposes that she shall find a champion. The champion is an ordinary knight; the leper is neither better nor worse for the part he is made to play; and the knight is rewarded with a gift of lands. That the Scottish ballad is the original of the English is a singularly unhappy idea of Sir Walter Scott's, and it is hard to conceive what suggested such a notion, unless it were the allegation that the sword with which Sir Hugh defended the queen's honor was until a late day producible by his posterity, whereas no one pretends to have the other. But Sir Walter could not seriously have credited this tradition, for he himself observes that there is no instance in history in which the honor of a queen of Scotland was committed to the chance of a duel.

Cousin to the English ballad is the Scandinavian 'Ravengaard og Memering,' Grundtvig, No 13, I, 177–213, 426 f, II, 640–45, III, 779–82, IV, 722–31. There are eleven versions in all, besides a Norwegian copy, extant at the end of the last century, of which now only the story is at our command. Eight of the eleven texts are Danish, A–C, G–L. A is from a manuscript of the middle of the sixteenth century, and so a hundred years older than 'Sir Aldingar.' The other Danish copies are from recent tradition,* and so are Färöe D, E. An Icelandic version, F, is from a seventeenth-century manuscript.

The old Danish ballad affords the following story. Gunild [Gunder] lives at Spire, and many nobles from all quarters of the compass sue for her hand, which Henry, Duke of Brunswick and Schleswig, obtains. Henry, going to the wars, commits to Ravengaard the protection of his land, and especially of his wife. But no sooner is the duke fairly away than Ravengaard goes to "the queen," and demands of her the sword Adelring, which she has in keeping. This being refused, Ravengaard threatens that he will tell false tales of her, but the lady is not intimidated. The duke comes home, and asks Ravengaard how things are. The country remains as it was, but Gunild has been acting ill. The duke will not believe anything wrong of Gunild; but Ravengaard affirms that he has seen the archbishop with her with his own eyes. Henry, after repeating this charge to Gunild, beats her severely, and nobody dares come to the rescue, or to speak for her, save two ladies of the court, who maintain that Ravengaard has lied. Then let her find a man who will fight with him, says the duke. Bare-headed and bare-foot Gunild goes to the hall where the knights are drinking. They all rise; but when she asks, Is there anybody here who will fight for a woman? there is no response except from Memering. He had served her father fifteen years; never had he seen her so wretched, bare-shouldered, bare-foot. Ravengaard had had more of her father's bounty than anybody, and he has been the first to betray her. Memering had always been last when gifts were giving; but he will go into the lists for her if he can have the sword Adelring, and this Gunild promises him. A ring

* All these Scandinavian versions were printed for the first time by Grundtvig, save two out of eleven copies of K: these two in Kristensen, I, 124, No 49, 'Mimering,' and II, 306, No 87, 'Fru Gunder i Spire.' F was subsequently printed in Íslenzk Fornkvæði, No 12, I, 78, 'Gunnhildar kvæði.' Grundtvig devoted particular attention to this ballad, and has elucidated the history of the subject in a masterly way.

is marked on the ground for the fight. Raven-gaard requires Memering to swear that he knows not of the sword Adelring. Memering (who has thrust the blade into the earth) swears that he does not know of more than the hilt being above ground, and exacts in turn that Ravengaard shall swear that he has no knowledge of the sword Sudevind [Saade-ring], to which Ravengaard makes oath with-out qualification. With the first blow Raven-gaard cuts Memering's sword in two. This shows, says the duke, what deeds you have been doing. Memering strikes, and cuts Ra-vengaard's sword in two. Ravengaard asks his adversary to wait a moment till he can tie his shoe, stoops, and picks up the sword Sude-vind ; for which perjury, says Memering, thy foul soul is lost. Ravengaard now cuts a sec-ond sword of Memering's in two. Memering asks for time to tie his shoe, stoops down, and produces the sword Adelring ; for which per-jury, says Ravengaard, thy foul soul is lost. But Memering had been careful to swear with circumstance : he had sworn that he knew of nothing but the hilt being above ground. With one stroke he cuts Sudevind in two, and with a second Ravengaard's neck. And now Gun-ild may say to the duke, You see Ravengaard lied. Henry begs forgiveness. Memering, who has a broken head and leg, demands noth-ing more than bread the rest of his days, but Gunild says she will herself be his leech, and he shall have both bread to eat and scarlet to wear.

The trick of reserving a peculiarly formi-dable sword is a commonplace in northern sagas,* and we are not obliged to suppose that it belonged to the ballad from the beginning. No trace of it is found in the other Scandi-navian versions.

The Danish versions from recent oral tradi-tion, B, C, G-L, relate that Henry, going off on an expedition, commits Gunild to the care of Ravnlil, who forthwith demands that she shall do his will, otherwise he will tell a great lie about her. She trusts in the triumph of hon-esty, and defies him. Henry comes back, and inquires of Ravnlil about his wife, and Ravnlil tells his great lie : Gunild spares neither monk nor priest ; he has seen the archbishop with her, C. Henry seizes Gunild by the hair, throws her to the ground and beats her ; thus shall she be served till she find a kemp that will fight for her. Gunild goes to the kemp-house, and asks if there is any man that will fight for a woman. None who will fight for a whore, H, K. Memering jumps over the table, B, G, I, and offers to be her champion. At the first shock in the lists Memering's horse is brought to his knees ; in the second encounter Memering takes off Ravnlil's head. Henry offers tons of gold to redeem Gunild. Shame befall him that sells her, says Memering, and rides off with Gunild, leaving Henry wringing his hands.

K, like A, represents that Gunild was wooed from all quarters before she was won by Henry. Memering, who sits lowest at the board, says to Gunild, as in A 20–23, that he had served her father eleven years, and never seen her with bare feet. In C Memering finds Gunild weeping, and, learning the reason, asks the loan of her father's horse, receives horse and armor of proof, goes where the kemps are drinking, and challenges the slanderer. The burly villain says he will take him in his left hand and chuck him out of the country, crush all his limbs with his little finger. After the fight, Memering presents Gunild with "the head that has belied her," and she carries it to Henry, who asks in wonder, Who in all my land has hewn down a man so big ? Me-mering, the least of men, she says. Henry offers him his Sudselille, his Strudselille, his

---

* See Flóamannasaga, Vigfússon and Möbius, Fornsögur, p. 134 f, where the whole sword is hid in the sand ; Svarf-dælasaga, Íslendínga Sögur, 1830, II, 132–134 ; Gunnlaugs saga ormstúngu, Ísl. Sög., 1847, II, 225 f ; Þiðriks saga, Un-ger, p. 206, c. 222 ; Sturlaugs saga starfsama, c. 10, Rafn, Fornaldar Sögur, III, 608 f ; and cf. ' Orm Ungersvend og Bermer Rise,' Danmarks gamle Folkeviser, No 11 : Grundt-vig and Bugge. Besides the oath customary in judicial com-bats, that the parties believe in the justice of their cause, the old Frisian and Lombard laws require champions to swear that they will fight fairly and honestly, and that they have no charm concealed about them, " ne forte carminibus, vel machinis diabolicis, vel magicis artibus insidientur : " Grundt-vig, I, 194 note *. Jove seems to be expected to laugh at a qualified perjury in some of the above cases.

Spire, but will have Gunild for his own. Memering bids him keep his gifts; he will not resign Gunild, whom he has won. The diminutive size of Memering is noted also in B, H, I, K, and the hugeness of Ravnlil in B, G, I. In H Memering knocks off his opponent's hat in the first bout, and the head follows in the second. Now we will ride off, says Memering to Gunild; but Gunild will not budge till she has had vengeance on Henry.

The Norwegian story has lost the beginning, but agrees well with the Danish so far as it goes. Gunild goes into the kemps' hall, and asks if any man dare fight for a woman against huge Ronnegaar. All are silent but Mimmer, smallest of Christian men, who offers himself. Gunild holds him cheap for his low stature, and says he had better stay at home and keep his sheep; but he, not rebuffed, mounts his horse, seeks out Ronnegaar, and, after a three days' fight, vanquishes him and cuts off his head, which he ties to his saddle-bow and brings back in triumph.

The Icelandic ballad is in accord with the Danish until we come to the judicium dei, and then an ordeal by hot iron takes the place of the combat. So with the two Färöe copies, which, however, mix both forms, and inconsistently bring in Memering, with nothing for him to do. King Diderik replaces Henry in all three, but Spire remains the place of the action. When the returning king asks after Gunild, he is told that the archbishop has been seen lying with her, or the bishop's brother, and others besides. He seizes her by the hair and drags her from her bed, F, beats her for two days, E, F, and a third, and no one dares interfere. At last two of his children beg him to stop, D, E; ask what their mother has done, F. She has been untrue. Then let her carry iron and walk on steel. Nine times she carries iron and ten times she walks on steel, F. The conclusion is very much injured in all these copies. In the Ice-

landic, F, "all her iron bands fall off;" her accuser goes to infernal punishment, and she to heaven. In D, E, after the children have asked for the ordeal by fire, Gunild goes to the strand, or along the street, and meets Mimmering, smallest of Christian men, E, who says he has served her father eight years, and never saw her in such wretched plight. She then goes to another land, D; Mimmering takes her from heathen land (which at least makes him of some use), E; when she enters a church her iron bands burst. She is making gifts of a Yule day, and gives her traducer a red ring, meaning a rope round his neck.

The names of the four actors in the Scandinavian versions are: Henry, as in English, in all the Danish copies,[*] replaced by King Diderik in Färöe D, E, Icelandic F; Gunild, or Gunder, Gunni, Gunde, in all copies, including the Norwegian; Memering, Mimmering, in all but the Norwegian and Danish H, which have the slight modifications Mimmer, Nimmering, these last, as also Färöe D, E, adding the suffix Tand. There is considerable variety, always with some likeness, in the fourth name: Raffuengaard, Danish A; Röngård, H; Ronnegaar, the Norwegian; Ravnlil, B, G, K, L, Ravnhild, I; Rundkrud Hagensgaard, C; Roysningur, Färöe D, E; Rögnvaldr, Icelandic F. Ravengaard, Röngård, Ronnegaar, with the Anglo-Latin Rodingar, presently to be mentioned, are evidently the forerunners of the English Aldingar (Sir Raldingar) and Rodingham.[†] The English Eleanor is probably a later substitution for Gunild, become unfamiliar. Eleanor may have been meant or understood for Henry Second's queen (less likely for Henry Third's, though she went into a monastery), but considering how freely the name is dealt with in English ballads, the question is hardly worth raising, and assuredly it never was raised except by editors.[‡]

Memering is of diminutive size in B-E,

[*] Hans Hendrik in H; clearly, as Grundtvig says, a modern misunderstanding of Han Hendrik.

[†] The name Raadengaard occurs in Grundtvig, No 7, A, G, H, No 12, C; Ravengaard also in No 7, D, No 12, A; Raanegaard, Ronegaard, in No 12, B.

[‡] Percy says that it had been suggested to him that the author of 'Sir Aldingar' "had in his eye the story of Gunhilda, *who was sometimes called Eleanor*, and was married to the Emperor (here called King) Henry." I have not found that Gunhilda was ever called Eleanor.

H-K, the smallest of Christian men in E, and also in the Norwegian copy.* The large size of his antagonist is noted in B, C, G, I, and the Norwegian copy. His representative in English A seems no more in a man's likeness than a child of four years old. Aldingar would not have recked had there been half a hundred such; and Aldingar is as big as a fooder, " a tun of man," like Falstaff, though not so unwieldy.

Gunhild, daughter of Cnut the Great and Emma, was married in 1036 to King Henry, afterwards the Emperor Henry III, and died of the plague at Ravenna two years later, never having had any trouble with her husband. William of Malmesbury, who died only a little more than a hundred years after Gunhild, 1142 or 1143, writes of her as follows: She was a girl of extraordinary beauty, and had been sighed for in vain by many suitors before her hand was bestowed upon Henry. She was attended to the ship which was to take her to her husband by a procession so splendid that it was still in William's day the theme of popular song. After many years of married life she was denounced for adultery, and offered as her champion against her accuser (who was a man of gigantic bulk), others refusing, a mere boy that she had brought with her from England, who by miracle hamstrung her defamer. Gunhild then could not be induced by threats or blandishments to live longer with her husband, but took the veil, and passed the remainder of a long life in the service of God.†

It will be recognized that we have in this narrative many points of the English and Danish ballad: the beauty of the queen, English A 2; her numerous suitors, Danish A, K; the youth or under size of the queen's champion, who had previously been in the service of her family, and the huge dimensions of the other party; the triumph of weakness and innocence, and Gunhild's separating herself from Henry, Danish B, C, G-L. Nor can we well doubt that William of Malmesbury was citing a ballad, for the queen's wonderful deliverance in so desperate an extremity would be even more likely to be celebrated in popular song than her magnificent wedding, and a ballad is known to have been made upon a similar and equally fabulous adventure which is alleged in chronicle to have occurred to Gunhild's mother.

Malmesbury does not mention the names of the combatants, though he may very well have known them. These names are supplied by a French metrical life of Edward the Confessor, " translatée du Latin," of which the manuscript must have been written before 1272, and may, perhaps, be dated as early as 1245. In this poem we are told that Gunhild, having been calumniated to her husband, the Emperor Henry, was obliged by the custom of the empire to purge herself by battle, and with difficulty could find a champion, because her accuser was of gigantic size. But a dwarf, whom she had brought up, by name Mimecan,‡ undertook to fight for her, hamstrung the giant at the first blow, and at the second cut off his feet, " as the history says." The lady, thus acquitted, declined to have the emperor for her lord. The other name is given in verses describing a picture of the combat, one of many illustrations which adorn the manuscript: How the dwarf Mimecan, to redeem the honor of his mistress, fights with the huge old Rodegan, and cuts off his feet; where Rodegan is, perhaps, an adaptation of Rodingar, for rhyme's sake; § but we have Rodyngham in English B.

In The Chronica Majora of Matthew Paris, I, 515, ed. Luard, manuscript of the beginning of the fourteenth century, the passage in Malmesbury is repeated, with additions from other sources. The name of Gunhild's cham-

---

* Little Mimmering Tand is found in several ballads. He is one of King Diderik's kemps in Grundtvig, No 7, A, and appears again in his No 16, C. Mimering is the smallest of men in Grundtvig, No 14.

† De Gestis Regum Anglorum, l. ii, c. 12.

‡ Danish and Norwegian Mimecan, Mimmering, Memer-

ing, English mimicking, mimocking, and probably minnikin, Scottish memerkyn, mynmerkin, all denote a man or object of small size, and point to Icelandic minni = minor, minnkan, a minishing, etc. ; as Bugge remarks.

§ Lives of Edward the Confessor, edited by Henry Richards Luard, p. 39 f, vv 506–531, p. 3, VII.

pion is given as Mimecan, and the dwarf is further said to have cut off the giant's head, as in the Norwegian version of the ballad and Danish C, and to have presented it to his mistress, as in Danish C. Brompton's Chronicle, of the second half of the fourteenth century, reiterates the story of the duel, giving the names of both combatants, Mimecan (misprinted or misread Municon) and Roddyngar.*

It is highly probable that this story became connected with Gunhild, wife of Henry III, in consequence of her bearing the name Cunigund after her marriage, owing to which circumstance she might become confused with the consort of the Emperor St Henry II, St Cunigund, in whose legendary history there is a passage essentially similar. St Cunigund's married life extended from 1002 to 1024. After Henry's death she retired to a nunnery, and she died " in the service of God," 1033, which corresponds with what Malmesbury says of Gunhild. Notwithstanding the mutual asceticism of the imperial pair, reports obtained, instigated by the devil, that Cunigund had doubly broken her vows, nor did these fail to make an impression on her husband's mind. To justify herself, Cunigund offered to walk barefoot over red-hot ploughshares, or, according to another account, to carry red-hot iron in her hands, and she went through the test without injury.† This form of ordeal is of the nature of what is suggested in the Färöe and the Icelandic ballad, and executed in the latter, where Gunild both walks over hot steel and carries hot iron in her hands.

Emma, Gunhild's mother, had the misfortune to be subjected to the same aspersions as her daughter and the Empress Cunigund, and was favored with the like glorious vindication. Accused of having a bishop for her lover, she asked to be submitted to the ordeal of hot iron, and walked over nine glowing ploughshares, in the church of St Swithin, Winchester, not only without injury, but even without the consciousness of what she had done.‡ We are expressly informed that a ballad on the subject was sung by a minstrel in the hall of the prior of St Swithin on the occasion of a visit of the Bishop of Winchester in 1338, in conjunction with another about the giant Colbrand.§

Earlier instances of a miraculous exoneration, under similar circumstances, are those of Richarda, or Richardis, wife of the Emperor Charles III, 887, and of Gundeberg, wife of the Lombard king Arioald, c. 630.

Richarda, accused of adultery with a bishop, protests, like Cunigund, not only her innocence of crime, but her intact virginity after a marriage of ten or twelve years, and offers herself to the judgment of God, either by duel or hot ploughshares; or actually proves her integrity by some form of ordeal, divino [aquino] judicio, or by passing through fire in

---

* Twysden, Historiæ Anglicanæ Scriptores Decem, col. 933. In MS. A of the Abbreviationes of Ralph de Diceto, ed. Stubbs, I, 174, this note is inserted in the margin (at Gunnildam imperatori Romano cum ineffabilibus divitiis maritavit): Quam Rodingarus Alemannicus impetivit de adulterio, sed Mimekinus eam defendit et Rodingarum interfecit. The Abbreviationes were written before 1200, but the date of the insertion is of course uncertain.

† The second account in Alberti Krantzii Saxonia, lib. IV, c. 32, p. 97, ed. 1621: Grundtvig. Cunigund having publicly protested that she had never known man (not even her husband), Henry, who wished the secret kept, according to one account struck her lightly in the face, according to another squeezed her mouth together so roughly as to draw blood. Grundtvig sees in this story a correspondence with the severe beating that Henry is said, in some of the ballads, to have inflicted on Gunild.

‡ The trial is described with every detail in the Annals of Winchester, which may be of Henry II's time: Luard,

Annales Monastici, II, 20–25. See, also, Brompton's Chronicle, Hist. Angl. Scriptores X, col. 941 f ; Eulogium Historiarum, ed. Haydon, II, 184, c. 184; Rudbourn, in Wharton's Anglia Sacra, I, 233–35 ; etc.

§ Et cantabat joculator quidam, nomine Herebertus, canticum Colbrandi, necnon gestum Emme regine a judicio ignis liberate, in aula prioris: Registrum prioratus S. Swithini Wintoniensis, cited by Warton, History of English Poetry, I, 81, ed. 1840. While the ordeal was in process, we are told, the spectators were weeping "intolerably" and crying with one voice, St Swithin, help her! now or never! Deus vim patitur. Regina sine clamore faciebat orationem: Deus, qui liberasti Susannam, tu me liberare digneris! It may be the same or another ballad on the deliverance of Queen Emma which Langland refers to at the end of the Prologue to Piers Plowman, as sung by lazy dykers and delvers, "that drive forth the long day with Dieu vous saue, Dame Emme."

a waxed shift, or donning a wax shift, which is set on fire at her hands and feet. Disculpated thus, she goes, like Cunigund, into a monastery for the rest of her days.*

Gundeberg happening to praise a certain nobleman's figure, he solicited her in shameless style, and was most contemptuously rejected. Upon this he tells the king that Gundeberg means to poison her husband and take another man, and the queen is put under confinement. Remonstrance is made by the king of the Franks, to which race Gundberg belongs, and Arioald consents to allow her to clear herself by a champion. One Pitto (otherwise Carellus) fights with the accuser and kills him.† If Pitto, as Bugge has suggested, and as seems more than plausible, be Little (old Italian pitetto, etc.), then the root of the Scandinavian-English story is found in the early part of the seventh century. The name Carellus may also be a significant diminutive.

Henry, in the Scandinavian ballad, accepts the testimony of the man in whose charge he had left Gunild, without asking for proof. Circumstantial evidence is offered in the English ballad; the false steward shows the king a leper lying in the queen's bed. Aldingar induces the leper to conform to his orders by promising that he shall be a sound man in two hours. Rodyngham gives the leper a drink, and lays him in the bed asleep. The queen, to the advantage of good taste, but to the detriment of the proof, is not there in either case.

We have here a link with the story of Oliva, or Sibilla, in the Charlemagne cycle of fictions. We may begin with the second section of the Karlamagnus saga, because we know that it was translated from an English copy brought home by a Norseman resident in Scotland in 1287.

Olif is here sister to Charles, and married to King Hugo. Going to the chase, Hugo leaves his wife in the care of his steward, Milon, who had long had a passion for her, and takes advantage of this occasion to declare it. The queen threatens to have him hanged. Milon goes home, puts a potion in a mazer, returns to the queen, and, pretending that what he had said was only a jest and meant to try her virtue, asks her, in token of reconciliation, to drink the cup with him. He feigns to begin; the queen follows in earnest, and falls into a dead sleep. He lays her in her bed, administers the same drink to a black beggar, and, when it has had its effect, lays him by the queen, putting the arms of each about the other's neck. When the king comes back he wonders that his wife does not come to meet him, and asks where she is. The steward answers, as in A 8, that the queen has taken a new love, and conducts the king to his chamber. Hugo cuts off the black man's head. Every drop of his blood turns to a burning candle, which makes the king think that he has killed a holy man. But the steward says, Not so; rather she is a witch, that can make stones float and feathers sink, and urges the king, now that his sword is out, to take off the queen's head, too. The king refuses. Olif wakes, and is astounded at what her eyes behold. What means this black man in her bed! God wot, says Milon, he has long been your leman. The queen demands an ordeal, according to the law of the land; and successively proposes that she shall be put naked into a copper over a hot fire, or be thrown from a high tower on sword and spear points, or be taken in a boat out of sight of land and thrown into the water. The king is each time disposed to let her have her way, but is always dissuaded by Milon, who tells him that no such trial would signify anything with a witch of her powers. Hereupon a knight leaps up and knocks Milon down for a liar, and offers to fight him on these terms: Milon to be fully armed and on his best horse,

---

* Regino, † 915, in Pertz, I, 597; Hermannus Contractus, † 1054, and Compendium ex codice Bernoldi, Migne, Patrologia, CXLIII, col. 201; Massmann, Kaiserchronik, twelfth century, II, 415–22; Jac. von Königshofen's Chronicle, end of fourteenth century, ed. Schilter, p. 105, cited by Grimm, Rechtsalterthümer, p. 912, Grundtvig, I, 190.

In the Kaiserchronik the emperor gives his wife a blow with his fist.

† Fredegarius, Chronicon, c. 51, in Du Chesne, I, 755; Aimoinus, c. 1000, Historia Francorum, lib. IV, c. 10, in Du Chesne, III, 103. Paulus Diaconus, lib. IV, c. 47, has wrongly made Gundeberg wife of Rodoald, putting the event at 652.

and the challenger to have no armor, a mule for a steed, and a wooden wand for a weapon. Milon is immediately thrown, but the king is still induced to think this to be more of his wife's magic, calls his best men to council, and bids them determine what death she shall die. There is no further resemblance to our ballad. Karlamagnus Saga, Af Fru Olif ok Landres, Unger, p. 51.

A Färöe ballad, 'Óluvu kvæði,' Hammers-haimb, in Antiquarisk Tidsskrift, 1846–48, p. 281, repeats this story with variations, and as we are informed by Grundtvig, I, 201, so do Icelandic rimes, ' Landres rímur,' as yet un-printed. In the Färöe ballad, after Óluva's champion (who had come with her from home, like Memering) has unhorsed her accuser, she passes the ordeal of water and fire trium-phantly, and still another.

In the Spanish prose romance of Oliva (printed in 1498) and the French chanson de geste of Doon l'Alemanz (fifteenth-century manuscript), the heroine, who is now Pepin's sister, becomes the victim of slander, not in consequence of her having rebuffed an over-weening lover, but because the father or uncle of the arch-traitor Ganelon had been thwarted in his plan to match his daughter or sister with the nobleman upon whom Pepin has be-stowed Oliva. It is an ordinary young lad who is put into the lady's bed, and no loath-some leper or beggar. The injured woman asks for the ordeal of fire or of water, and, in the Spanish romance, when these are refused her, to be thrown from a tower. After much difficulty this right is conceded in the latter, and, like Richardis,* she walks through a blazing fire, in simple shift, without singeing hair or thread. But all this helps her not. F. Wolf, Ueber die neuesten Leistungen der Franzosen, u. s. w., p. 98 ff ; C. Sachs Bei-träge, u. s. w., p. 2 ff.

According to other forms of the same story, it is Sibilla, wife of Charles the Great, that is temporarily repudiated by her husband, owing to a false suspicion of unfaithfulness, seem-ingly justified by an ugly dwarf being found in bed with her. A French romance, which narrated this story, is described in the Chron-icle of Alberich, a monk of the cloister of Trois Fontaines, in the diocese of Liége, writ-ing in the first half of the thirteenth cen-tury.† A fragment of the latter half of such a romance, and of the same age, is preserved. A complete tale is extant in a variety of forms : Hystoria de la reyna Sebílla, in Spanish prose, French by origin, of which a full analysis is given by Ferdinand Wolf, Ueber die neuesten Leistungen, u. s. w., p. 124 ff, from a printed copy dated 1532 ; ‡ a Dutch volksbuch, also from the French, printed not far from the same time, of which an ample account is also given by Wolf in Denkschriften der kaiser-lichen Akademie der Wissenschaften, Phil. Hist. Classe, VIII, 180 ff ; Macaire, a French romance in verse, of the thirteenth or four-teenth century, Mussafia, Altfranzösische Ge-dichte aus venezianischen Handschriften, II, Guessard, Les Anciens Poëtes de la France ; a German metrical tale of uncertain date, ' Diu Künigin von Frankrich und der unge-triuwe Marschalk,' found in many manu-scripts, von der Hagen, Gesammtabenteuer, I, 169, Meyer und Mooyer, Altdeutsche Dich-tungen, p. 52 ; a meisterlied, ' Die Kunigin von Frankreich, dy der marschalk gegen dem Kunig versagen wart,' u. s. w., printed in the fifteenth century, and lately in Wolff's Halle der Völker, II, 255.§ The king and queen are nameless in the last two, and the queen bears the name of Blançiflor in ' Macaire.' In the two German versions the false marshal repeats the part of the false steward in the English and Norse story ; having failed with the queen, he

* In Königshofen's Chronicle.
† Edited by Leibnitz in Accessiones Historicæ, tom. II, Pars I, p. 105 f. The passage relating to this romance is cited from Leibnitz by Wolf, Ueber die neuesten Leis-tungen, u. s. w., p. 156 f, and from a manuscript by Gues-sard, Macaire, p. xii f. All that is said of the dwarf is : de quodam nano turpissimo, cujus occasione dicta regina fuit expulsa.
‡ This tale apparently exists also in a manuscript of the

end of the fourteenth century : Gayangos in Rivadeneyra' Biblioteca, Libros de Caballerias, p. lxxxiii, ' Sebilla.' Cited by Wolf.
§ See, for the last, and generally for the related litera ture, von Tettau, Ueber einige bis jetzt unbekannte Erfur ter Drucke aus dem 15. Jahrhundert, pp 8–65. Hans Sach has dramatized the story of the false marshal, VIII, 54, ed Keller.

lays a sleeping dwarf in her bed. The dwarf is principal in the Spanish and Dutch story, and after a discomfiture in which he loses some of his teeth at the vigorous hand of the queen, creeps into her bed while she is asleep. He does the same in the Venetian-French romance, thinking to get vengeance for rough handling from his mistress when acting as Pandarus for Macaire, of whose spite against the queen for rebuking his inordinate passion he is all the while the tool.

Sibilla appears again as Sisibe, daughter of a Spanish king, married to Sigmundr, father of Sigurðr Fáfnisbani. The king, summoned to arms, entrusts her to two of his nobles, one of whom, Hartvin, proposes that she shall accept him as a husband, and is threatened with the gallows. The two represent to the king, on his return, that the queen has had a handsome thrall for her partner during his absence. Hartvin advises that she be relegated to a desolate forest and have her tongue cut out, to which Sigmundr assents. þiðriks Saga, Unger, p. 159 ff, cc 156–59; Hyltén-Cavallius, p. 115, cc 149–51.

The first part of the English romance of Sir Triamour, or a little more than 600 verses, is derived from some French form of Sibilla. A king going on a crusade to the holy land commits his queen to the care of his steward; the steward sues the queen to accept him as a paramour, and is threatened with hanging; the steward pretends that he has only been proving her, but when the king comes home tells him that he has seen a man lying with the queen, and has slain the traitor; the king is minded to burn his wife, but is advised by the steward rather to banish her; three days are allowed the queen to quit the country, and if found after that she is to die in the fire. Percy Society, vol. XVI, ed. Halliwell; Percy MS., ed. Hales and Furnivall, II, 78; Utterson, Select Pieces of Early Popular Poetry, I, 5.

In like manner, Genoveva's husband is persuaded by the false Golo, who has been charged with the care of her and has abused his trust, that his wife has admitted a cook to her favor; and Octavian's mother, in the English romance, excites her son's resentment against his innocent queen by inducing a scullion, "lothly of face," to get into the empress's bed: Weber, III, 163, v. 153 ff.*

Another series of tales, that has likeness in parts with the story of Gunhild and of Sibilla, is represented in English by the pleasing romance of The Erl of Tolous,† dating from about 1400.

We read in this lay of Britain, as it is called in the last stanza, that Barnard, Earl of Toulouse, has become enamored of the Empress of Germany, with whose lord he is at strife, and has excited a certain interest in the mind of the lady. The emperor selects two knights to guard his wife; these conceive a violent passion for her, and declare it, one after the other, after having obtained from her a promise of secrecy. She tells the first that he is a traitor and deserves to be hanged, and the second that he should be hanged had she not hight to hold counsel. These knights, who have been in collusion from the first, think themselves unsafe, notwithstanding the empress's promise, and conspire to be her ruin. They induce a young gentleman, for a jest, to strip himself all but bare, and hide behind a curtain in her chamber while she is sleeping; then summon "lords of bed" to help take a traitor who is with their lady in her bower, find the young man where they had put him, and bear him through the body. The lady is cast into prison. Her husband, who is far off, has a dream of two wild bears tearing his wife to pieces, and returns home with all haste. The knights tell their story. A council is called the next day, and it is decided that the empress must die (be burned). An old knight calls attention to the circumstance that the young man's tongue is stopped, and that none ever found a fault in the lady before; he advises that proclamation be made for a champion, to which the king, who loves his wife

---

* For Genoveva see Seuffert, Die Legende von der Pfalzgräfin Genovefa, Würzburg, 1877.

† Ritson, A. E. Metrical Romanceës, III, 93; newly and

admirably edited, Berlin, 1881, by Gustav Lüdtke, with a thorough investigation of the related literature, the more material part of which is furnished in appendixes.

tenderly, gladly assents. The Earl of Toulouse hears of the lady's peril, and resolves to go to Germany and fight for her. This, as being on hostile terms with the emperor, he must do in disguise. By the help of an abbot, who is the empress's uncle, he obtains admission to the lady in a monk's dress, hears her shrift, and assures himself of her innocence; and then, monk as he seems, offers to do battle with the accusers. One is run through, the other yields as recreant and confesses the plot, and both are burned. The monk is revealed by the abbot, under a pledge that he shall receive no injury, to be Sir Barnard of Toulouse. The emperor treats his late foe graciously, and rewards him, even to the extent of dying in three years, when the earl is chosen his successor and weds the empress.

Of this story the following are repetitions, with variations: (1) Miracle de la Marquise de Gaudine, MS. of about 1400, Paris et Robert, Miracles de Notre Dame, II, 121 ff; (2) the German Volksbuch, Eine schöne und liebliche History vom edlen und theuren Ritter Galmien, printed 1539 or earlier, upon which Hans Sachs founded his play Der Ritter Galmi mit der Hertzogin auss Britanien, Keller, VIII, 261; (3) the Danish poem Den kydske Dronning, by Jeppe Jensen, 1483, Brandt, Romantisk Digtning, II, 89 ff; (4) a tale of Bandello, Second Part, No 44, Amore di Don Giovanni di Mendozza e della Duchessa di Savoia, printed 1554; (5) the French prose-romance L'Histoire de Palanus, Comte de Lyon, ed. A. de Terrebasse, 1833, put before 1539. In (1) a dwarf is made to conceal himself in the lady's chamber; in (2) a scullion to boast that he is the object of her passion; in (3) a servitor is the instrument of treachery; in (4) a young gentleman; in (5) this machinery is dropped, and a slanderous letter does the mischief. In none of these is the lady a German empress; in (5) she is an English queen; in (2) of British birth. In all there is a reciprocal predilection on the part of the lady and her champion.

Spanish and Provençal chroniclers and a Spanish ballad relate a story substantially according with what we find in The Earl of Toulouse, the injured heroine being an empress of Germany, and her champion a count, in all cases but one Count Ramon of Barcelona.

In the Spanish ballad ' Romance de cómo el conde don Ramon de Barcelona libró á la emperatriz de Alemaña que la tenian para quemar,' Duran, Romancero, II, 210, No 1228, Wolf y Hofmann, Primavera, II, 102, from the Silva de Romances of 1550, two knights, with no motive given but their own wickedness, tell the emperor that they have seen the empress toying with her chamberlain. The empress is imprisoned, and casts about for two knights to defend her life against the accusers. In all the chivalry of the court there is none that will venture against appellants so redoubtable, and she is to be burned in three days. The Count of Barcelona hears the distressing intelligence, and sets out to the rescue. No one being admitted to the lady except her confessor, the count makes known to the holy father that he has come for the defence, and begs, if possible, that he may first have a word with her majesty. He has an interview, in the guise of a monk, and is properly welcomed by the empress, who expresses her confidence that he will succeed in establishing her innocence, but will not permit him even to kiss hands. Asking only to take his adversaries one at a time, the count speedily disposes of the first, when the other surrenders. The emperor, delighted with the result, wishes to show due honor to the champion, who, however, is not to be found, having returned to his estates immediately after the fight; nor is the empress at liberty to tell who he is until the third day. He is then revealed to be the flower of chivalry, the lord of Catalonia. The empress, with the approval of her husband, goes to Barcelona, attended by a magnificent train and under conduct of two cardinals, to express her gratitude in person, and is very splendidly received and entertained.

The oldest of the chroniclers, the Catalan Bernart Desclot, writing about 1300, ascribes the misfortune of the empress to a harmless partiality for a young nobleman, which was misrepresented to the emperor by two of his councillors, out of envy and spite.* The empress is allowed a year and a day to find a champion, in default of which she is to be burned. None of the knights to whom she has shown kindness dare offer themselves in her cause, on account of the high favor in which her accusers, who engage to make good their charge by battle, stand with their master. But a minstrel attached to the court takes it in hand to find her a defender, goes to Barcelona, and so interests the count in the case that he sets out immediately for Germany. Carbonell, c. 1500, Beuter, c. 1530, and Pujades, † 1635, all of whom rely in part on popular tradition, make the count to be Ramon Berengar III, and Beuter says that, according to the Catalans, the empress was Matilda, daughter of Henry I of England, who was married to the emperor Henry V in 1114.†

Provençal chronicles, Cæsar de Nostradamus's Histoire et chronique de Provence, 1614, and La Royalle Couronne des Roys d'Arles, 1641, return to the baffled steward or maître d'hôtel and his revenge. The empress is Matilda in Nostradamus, as in Beuter, and the steward simply accuses her of adultery, and offers to sustain the charge by battle. No one dares to defend the lady, because the accuser is un fort rude et dangereux champion. The steward is hanged after his defeat. In La Royalle Couronne des Roys d'Arles the emperor is said to be Henry III and the empress Matilde, fille de Camet, qui avoit esté roy de Dannemarc et estoit roy d'Angleterre, The emperor Henry V was as king of Arles Henry III. Camet, whether miswritten or not, can mean only Canut, and there is an obvious confusion between Gunild, daughter of Cnut, wife of Henry III of Germany, and Matilda, daughter of Henry I of England, wife of Henry III of Arles and V of Germany.‡ This may be an historical blunder, pure and simple, or may have been occasioned by a knowledge of the tradition concerning Gunild.

There is little or nothing in all these tales that can be historically authenticated, and much that is in plain contradiction with history.§ Putting history out of the question, there is no footing firmer than air for him who would essay to trace the order of the development. Even if we exaggerate the poverty of

---

* This recalls Morant in Karl Meinet, Keller, 219 ff, and in La gran conquista de ultramar, Wolf, Denkschriften der kais. Akad., as before, VIII, 280. Olive, in the German volksbuch Hirlanda, seems to be patterned after Morant. Hirlanda is charged with an intrigue with Olive by a graceless nobleman, and is to be burned unless vindicated by battle. Everybody is afraid of the impeacher's strength and skill in fight, but he is vanquished by a mere boy (divinely assisted) and confesses his villainy. The boy is Hirlanda's long-lost son. This is a stale paraphrase of an old story.

† Diago in his history of the counts of Barcelona contends for Ramon Berengar IV and the wife of Alfonso VII, who was crowned Emperor of Spain in 1135: Wolf, Lüdtke.

‡ For these chronicles and for Palanus, see F. Wolf in Jahrbücher für wissenschaftliche Kritik, 1835, 945–56, and Lüdtke, 78 ff. In the Arles chronicle, as also in Desclot, Carbonell, Beuter, etc., the empress gives the count a ring when he visits her in prison, and the same is done earlier in The Erl of Tolous; see Lüdtke, pp 80, 171, 181, 185, 191, 201, and vv 392, 1076 of the English romance. It may be noted, without the intention of suggesting any particular inference, that Arthur's queen in Le lai du Corn, v. 325 ff, to clear herself from the suspicion of loving amiss, professes herself ready to be thrown into a fire of thorns, and, should a hair of her head or any of her dress be burned, then to be dragged at a horse's heels. She owns that she *had* given a ring to a young donzel, who had killed a giant that had slandered Gawain, and then wished modestly to withdraw.

§ Lüdtke has endeavored, by a very carefully conducted comparison, to show the probability of an historical foundation for The Erl of Tolous in the relations of Bernard I, Count of Barcelona, with the Empress Judith, second wife of Louis le Débonnaire. By the influence of this beautiful and clever woman, Bernard, son of the William of Orange of romance, and later in his life Count or Duke of Toulouse, as his father had been, was made imperial chamberlain or prime minister, with the object of forwarding the aspirations which the empress entertained for her son Karl. Hugo, Count of Tours, and Matfrid, Count of Orleans, partisans of Lothair, stand for the empress's two lovers and enemies. Judith was accused of adultery with Bernard, and shut up in a monastery. At an assembly of the estates of the empire in 831, she declared herself prepared to refute the charge against her, and no accuser appearing, did so, when required, by an oath, after which she was restored to her rights as wife and empress. Bernard, though already incidentally purged by the empress's oath, some months subsequently asked the privilege of a duel with anybody that was disposed to inculpate him, and, no such person offering, in turn cleared himself by an oath. See Lüdtke, p. 98 ff, p. 209 ff. Hildegard, Louis's mother, according to tradition, labored under the same imputation as Judith, his wife; a parallel to the case of Gunild and her mother Emma. The story of Hildegard (Grimms, Deutsche Sagen, II, 102) has some resemblance to that of Repsima, Les Mille et un Jours, p. 265, Paris, 1840, and Jonathan Scott's Arabian Nights, VI, 396, 'Adventures of the Cauzee,' etc.

human invention so far as to assume that there must have been a single source for stories so numerous and so diversified in the details, a simple exposition of the subject-matter, with subordinate connections, seems all that it is safe, at present, to attempt.*

A is translated, according to Percy's Reliques, by Bothe, p. 175, and by Knortz, Lieder u. Romanzen Altenglands, No 68; B by Gerhard, p. 71. The old Danish ballad, Grundtvig's A, by Dr Prior, I, 151.

A

Percy MS., p. 68; Hales and Furnivall, I, 166.

1 OUR king he kept a ffalse steward,
   Men called him Sir Aldingar,

  .   .   .   .   .

    .   .   .   .

2 He wold haue layen by our comely queene,
   Her deere worshipp to haue betraide ;
   Our queene shee was a good woman,
   And euer more said him nay.

3 Aldingar was offended in his mind,
   With her hee was neuer content,
   But he sought what meanes he cold find out,
   In a fyer to haue her brent.

4 There came a lame lazer to the kings gates,
   A lazar was blind and lame ;
   He tooke the lazar vpon his backe,
   Vpon the queenes bed he did him lay.

5 He said, Lye still, lazar, wheras thou lyest ;
   Looke thou goe not away ;
   Ile make thee a whole man and a sound
   In two howres of a day.

6 And then went forth Sir Aldingar,
   Our queene for to betray,
   And then he mett with our comlye king,
   Saies, God you saue and see !

7 'If I had space, as I haue grace,
   A message I wold say to thee :'
   'Say on, say on, Sir Aldingar,
   Say thou on and vnto me.'

8 'I can let you now see one of [the] greiuos-
    [est] sights
   That euer Christen king did see ;

Our queene hath chosen a new, new loue,
   She will haue none of thee.

9 'If shee had chosen a right good knight,
   The lesse had beene her shame ;
   But she hath chosen a lazar man,
   Which is both blinde and lame.'

10 'If this be true, thou Aldingar,
   That thou dost tell to me,
   Then will I make thee a rich knight
   Both of gold and fee.

11 'But if it be false, Sir Aldingar,
   That thou doest tell to me,
   Then looke for noe other death
   But to be hangd on a tree.
   Goe with me,' saide our comly king,
   'This lazar for to see.'

12 When the king he came into the queenes
    chamber,
   Standing her bed befor,
   'There is a lodly lome,' says Harry King,
   'For our dame Queene Elinor !

13 'If thou were a man, as thou art none,
   Here thou sholdest be slaine ;
   But a paire of new gallowes shall be built,
   Thoust hang on them soe hye.

14 'And [a] fayre fyer there shalbe bett,
   And brent our queene shalbee :'
   Fforth then walked our comlye king,
   And mett with our comly queene.

15 Saies, God you saue, our queene, Madam,
   And Christ you saue and see !
   Heere you [haue] chosen a new, new loue,
   And you will haue none of mee.

16 'If you had chosen a right good knight,
   The lesse had beene your shame ;

---

* Grundtvig, admitting that the time has not come for anything more, sketches an hypothesis of the evolution and transmission of the story, " as a mere experiment," I, 203 f.

But you haue chosen a lazar man,
That is both blind and lame.'

17 ' Euer alacke ! ' said our comly queene,
' Sir Aldingar is false to mee;
But euer alacke ! ' said our comly queene,
' Euer alas, and woe is mee !

18 ' I had thought sweuens had neuer been true ;
I haue prooued them true at the last;
I dreamed in my sweauen on Thursday at
eueninge,
In my bed wheras I lay,

19 ' I dreamed a grype and a grimlie beast
Had carryed my crowne away,
My gorgett and my kirtle of golde,
And all my faire heade-geere.

20 ' How he wold haue worryed me with his
tush,
And borne me into his nest,
Saving there came a little hawk,
Flying out of the east.

21 ' Saving there came a little hawke,
Which men call a merlion ;
Vntill the ground he stroke him downe,
That dead he did fall downe.

22 ' Giffe I were a man, as I am none,
A battell I would proue ;
I wold fight with that false traitor ;
Att him I cast my gloue !

23 ' Seing I am able noe battell to make,
You must grant me, my leege, a knight,
To fight with that traitor, Sir Aldingar,
To maintaine me in my right.'

24 ' I'le giue thee forty dayes,' said our king,
' To seeke thee a man therin ;
If thou find not a man in forty dayes,
In a hott fyer thou shall brenn.'

25 Our queene sent forth a messenger ;
He rode fast into the south ;
He rode the countryes through and through,
Soe ffar vnto Portsmouth.

26 .   .   .   .   .
.   .   .   .   .

He cold find never a man in the south country
That wold fight with the knight soe keene.

27 The second messenger the queen forth sent
Rode far into the east ;
But, blessed be God made sunn and moone !
He sped then all of the best.

28 As he rode then by one riuer side,
There he mett with a little child ;
He seemed noe more in a mans likenesse
Then a child of four yeeres old.

29 He askt the queenes messenger how far he rode;
Loth he was him to tell ;
The little one was offended att him,
Bid him adew, farwell.

30 Said, Turne thou againe, thou messenger,
Greete our queene well from me ;
When bale is att hyest, boote is att next ;
Helpe enough there may bee.

31 ' Bid our queene remember what she did dreame
In her bedd wheras shee lay ;
Shee dreamed the grype and the grimly beast
Had carryed her crowne away ;

32 ' Her gorgett and her kirtle of gold,
Alsoe her faire head-geere ;
He wold haue werryed her with his tushe,
And borne her into his nest.

33 ' Saving there came a little hawke,
Men call him a merlyon ;
Vntill the ground he did strike him downe,
That dead he did ffall downe.

34 ' Bidd the queene be merry att her hart,
Euermore light and glad ;
When bale is att hyest, boote is at next,
Helpe enoughe there shalbe.'

35 Then the queenes messenger rode backe,
A gladed man then was hee ;
When he came before our queene,
A gladd woman then was shee.

36 Shee gaue the messenger twenty pound,
O lord, in gold and ffee ;
Saies, Spend and spare not while this doth last,
Then feitch thou more of me.

37 Our queene was put in a tunne to burne,
   She thought no thing but death ;
   Thé were ware of the little one
   Came ryding forth of the east.

38 With a mu . . . . .
   A louelie child was hee ;
   When he came to that fier,
   He light the queene full nigh.

39 Said, Draw away these brands of fire
   Lie burning before our queene,
   And feitch me hither Sir Aldingar,
   That is a knight soe keene.

40 When Aldingar see that little one,
   Ffull litle of him hee thought ;
   If there had beene halfe a hundred such,
   Of them he wold not haue wrought.

41 Hee sayd, Come hither, Sir Aldingar ;
   Thou seemust as bigge as a ffooder ;
   I trust to God, ere I haue done with thee,
   God will send to vs [an] auger.

42 Saies, The first stroke that 's giuen, Sir Aldin-
      gar,
   I will giue vnto thee,
   And if the second giue thou may,
   Looke then thou spare not mee.

43 The litle one pulld forth a well good sword,
   I-wis itt was all of guilt ;
   It cast light there over that feild,
   It shone soe all of guilt.

44 He stroke the first stroke att Aldingar,
   He stroke away his leggs by his knee ;

·   ·   ·   ·   ·   ·

·   ·   ·   ·   ·

45 Sayes, Stand vp, stand vp, thou false traitor,
   And fight vpon thy feete ;

For and thou thriue as thou begins,
   Of a height wee shalbe meete.

46 'A preist, a preist,' sayes Aldingar,
   'Me for to houzle and shriue !
   A preist, a preist,' sayes Aldingar,
   'While I am a man liuing a-liue !

47 'I wold haue laine by our comlie queene ;
   To it shee wold neuer consent ;
   I thought to haue betrayd her to our king,
   In a fyer to haue had her brent.

48 'There came a lame lazar to the kings gates,
   A lazar both blind and lame ;
   I tooke the lazar vpon my backe,
   In the Queenes bed I did him lay.

49 'I bad him, Lie still, lazar, where he lay,
   Looke he went not away ;
   I wold make him a whole man and a sound
   In two houres of a day.

50 ·   ·   ·   ·   ·

·   ·   ·   ·   ·

   'Euer alacke !' sayes Sir Aldingar,
   'Falsing neuer doth well ;

51 'Forgiue, forgiue me, queene, Madam !
   For Christs loue forgiue me !'
   'God forgaue his death, Aldingar,
   And freely I forgiue thee.'

52 'Now take thy wife, thou King Harry,
   And loue her as thou shold ;
   Thy wiffe shee is as true to thee
   As stone that lies on the castle wall.'

53 The lazar vnder the gallow tree
   Was a pretty man and small ;
   The lazar vnder the gallow tree
   Was made steward in King Henerys hall.

———◆———

B

Minstrelsy of the Scottish Border, III, 51, 1803. Communicated to Scott by K. Williamson Burnet, of Monboddo,
as written down from the recitation of an old woman, long
in the service of the Arbuthnot family.

1 THE birds sang sweet as ony bell,
   The world had not their make ;

The queen she 's gone to her chamber,
   With Rodingham to talk.

2 'I love you well, my queen, my dame,
   Bove land and rents so clear,
   And for the love of you, my queen,
   Would thole pain most severe.'

3 'If well you love me, Rodingham,
   I'm sure so do I thee;
I love you well as any man,
   Save the king's fair bodye.'

4 'I love you well, my queen, my dame,
   'T is truth that I do tell;
And for to lye a night with you,
   The salt seas I would sail.'

5 'Away, away, O Rodingham!
   You are both stark and stoor;
Would you defile the king's own bed,
   And make his queen a whore?

6 'To-morrow you'd be taken sure,
   And like a traitor slain,
And I'd be burned at a stake,
   Altho I be the queen.'

7 He then steppd out at her room-door,
   All in an angry mood,
Untill he met a leper-man,
   Just by the hard way-side.

8 He intoxicate the leper-man,
   With liquors very sweet,
And gave him more and more to drink,
   Until he fell asleep.

9 He took him in his arms two,
   And carried him along,
Till he came to the queen's own bed,
   And there he laid him down.

10 He then steppd out of the queen's bower,
   As swift as any roe,
Till he came to the very place
   Where the king himself did go.

11 The king said unto Rodingham,
   What news have you to me?
He said, Your queen's a false woman,
   As I did plainly see.

12 He hastend to the queen's chamber,
   So costly and so fine,
Until he came to the queen's own bed,
   Where the leper-man was lain.

13 He looked on the leper-man,
   Who lay on his queen's bed;
He lifted up the snaw-white sheets,
   And thus he to him said.

14 'Plooky, plooky are your cheeks,
   And plooky is your chin,
And plooky are your armis twa,
   My bonny queen's layne in.

15 'Since she has lain into your arms,
   She shall not lye in mine;
Since she has kissd your ugsome mouth,
   She never shall kiss mine.'

16 In anger he went to the queen,
   Who fell upon her knee;
He said, You false, unchaste woman,
   What's this you've done to me?

17 The queen then turnd herself about,
   The tear blinded her ee:
'There's not a knight in a' your court
   Dare give that name to me.'

18 He said, 'T is true that I do say;
   For I a proof did make;
You shall be taken from my bower,
   And burned at a stake.

19 'Perhaps I'll take my word again,
   And may repent the same,
If that you'll get a Christian man
   To fight that Rodingham.'

20 'Alass! alass!' then cried our queen,
   'Alas, and woe to me!
There's not a man in all Scotland
   Will fight with him for me.'

21 She breathed unto her messengers,
   Sent them south, east, and west;
They could find none to fight with him,
   Nor enter the contest.

22 She breathed on her messengers,
   She sent them to the north;
And there they found Sir Hugh le Blond,
   To fight him he came forth.

23 When unto him they did unfold
   The circumstance all right,
He bade them go and tell the queen
   That for her he would fight.

24 The day came on that was to do
   That dreadful tragedy;
Sir Hugh le Blond was not come up,
   To fight for our lady.

25 'Put on the fire,' the monster said,
'It is twelve on the bell ; '
' 'T is scarcely ten, now,' said the king,
'I heard the clock mysell.'

26 Before the hour the queen is brought,
The burning to proceed ;
In a black velvet chair she 's set,
A token for the dead.

27 She saw the flames ascending high,
The tears blinded her ee :
'Where is the worthy knight,' she said,
'Who is to fight for me ?'

28 Then up and spak the king himsell :
'My dearest, have no doubt,
For yonder comes the man himsel,
As bold as eer set out.'

29 They then advanced to fight the duel,
With swords of temperd steel ;
Till down the blood of Rodingham
Came running to his heel.

30 Sir Hugh took out a lusty sword,
'T was of the metal clear,
And he has pierced Rodingham
Till 's heart-blood did appear.

31 'Confess your treachery, now,' he said,
'This day before you die ;'
'I do confess my treachery,
I shall no longer lye.

32 'I like to wicked Haman am,
This day I shall be slain :'
The queen was brought to her chamber,
A good woman again.

33 The queen then said unto the king,
Arbattle 's near the sea ;
Give it unto the northern knight,
That this day fought for me.

34 Then said the king, Come here, Sir Knight,
And drink a glass of wine,
And, if Arbattle 's not enough,
To it we 'll Fordoun join.

C

Dr Joseph Robertson's Note-Book, January 1, 1830, p. 6.

1 THEY 'VE putten her into prison strang,
A twalmon lang and mair,
Until the mice and wild rattens
Did tear her yallow hair.

*   *   *   *   *

2 'One shake o your han,' said Rodingham,
'One shak o your han gie me :'
'I cam na here for shaking hans,
But to fight maist desperatelie.'

3 'It 's nae ten strucken on the clock,
Nor eleven on the bell :'
'We 'll doe ill deeds anew ere night,
Tho it were strucken twall.'

A. 2². *Perhaps we should read* to betray.
4². was lind. 5⁴. in 2.
13³. be bul: t *torn off, and one stroke of the* u
dotted. Furnivall.
17⁴. Sᴿ *before* Euer *crossed out. Furnivall.*
19¹. dreamed the grype.
24¹, ³. 40. 28⁴. 4.
30³, 34³. next *should, perhaps, be* nyest.

32¹. kirt e. 32⁴. her nest.
36¹. 20ᴵᴵ.
38¹. *The rest of the line is cut away.*
40³. 100. 45³. thriue : *one stroke of the* u *is
left out. Furnivall.*
49⁴. 2. 52¹. thou K.
52³. is a.
B. 28⁴. as ere.

60

KING ESTMERE

a. Percy's Reliques, edition of 1794, I, 64. **b.** Reliques, edition of 1765, I, 58.

'KING ESTMERE' occurred at page 249 of Percy's folio manuscript, but the three leaves on which it was written were "unfortunately torn out" by Percy to send to the press, and the genuine form of the ballad thereby put beyond recovery. In the second and later editions of the Reliques the editor professes to give the ballad from two copies ("containing very great variations," 1794), one of them being that of the folio. But here and elsewhere Percy employs a singular periphrasis, as he has explained to us in the preface to the Reliques, and means only that he has amended his original more or less. Notwithstanding the seemingly explicit language, there is no second copy at all.*

We are told by Percy, in a note to stanza 63, that though liberties have been taken with that portion of the ballad which follows, yet wherever the fourth edition differs from the preceding ones it has been brought nearer to the folio.† Some notes of readings of the folio are also furnished in the fourth edition (and are here restored), which were not given in the others. While we cannot but be vexed that so distinguished a ballad, not injured

much, so far as we can see, by time, should not come down to us as it came to Percy, our loss must not be exaggerated. The changes made by the editor, numerous enough, no doubt, cannot be very material until we approach the end. Stanzas 63–66 are entirely suspicious, and it may even be questioned whether the manuscript contained a word that is in them.

The name of Bremor, son of the king of Spain, and "a heathen hound" (if this be not Percy's interpolation), taken with certain resemblances in the story, very naturally suggested to Professor Sophus Bugge (Grundtvig, IV, 704) a connection between this ballad and 'Young Orm and Bermer-Giant,' 'Orm Ungersvend og Bermer-Rise.'‡ The giant, who is described as a rabid berserker, presents himself at the Danish court (Grundtvig, A), and demands that the king shall give him his daughter and half his land, or find a man who will fight in the ring with him. The king refuses daughter and land, and says he will find a champion. He offers the chance of winning so fair a may to his men, and no one dares say a word except Young Orm, who sits low-

---

* "The editor . . . must plead guilty to the charge of concealing his own share in the amendments under some such general title as a Modern Copy, or the like:" Reliques, 1794, I, xvii. See, further, 'The Rising in the North' and 'Northumberland betrayed by Douglas,' in the same volume, pp 288, 297.

† We have *paynim* four times in the first edition, and only twice in the fourth. *And ever I feare that paynim king*, b 21³, gives place to *I cannot blame him if he doe. Laught loud laughters three*, b 58⁴, was not (as who needs to be told ?) the reading of the folio; but was *lough a loud laughter* the reading of the folio ?

The statement that 'King Estmere' was "unfortunately torn out in sending the . . . piece to the press" is far from intelligible. Since readings were given from the manuscript in the fourth edition for the first time, one would suppose that the original was still in the editor's hands when that

edition was prepared. But the three leaves from the manuscript would have been much less convenient to send to the press than the copy already three times printed in the Reliques; and Percy himself pleads in excuse for his taking out leaves from the manuscript, to save the trouble of transcribing, that he was very young, and "had not then learnt to reverence it." The readings from the manuscript, which first appear in the fourth edition, may possibly be from notes; one would hope that Percy would not trust his memory after the lapse of thirty years. Hales and Furnivall, I, lxxiv, II, 200; also II, 600 ff, where the texts of the first and of the fourth edition are printed in parallel columns.

‡ Grundtvig, No 11, A-F, I, 159–69, IV, 715, and Kristensen, I, 246, No 93; Swedish, A, Arwidsson, II, 445, B-E, Grundtvig, IV, 720–22; Norwegian, Landstad, No 8; Icelandic, 'Ormars rímur,' in an abstract, Grundtvig, III, 775–77.

est at the board : he will be the man. But first Orm provides himself with an irresistible sword, which is buried in his father's tomb, and is yielded by the dead man only upon the condition that his son shall take the revenge due for his death. With this sword Orm, like the child in ' Sir Aldingar,' cuts the giant through at the knees, being, he says, not tall enough to strike higher. He then goes to Iceland, and fights three days with the men who had slain his father, but without prevailing. A mermaid, from the sea-bottom, cries out to him that his sword is under a spell, and that he must whirl it three times round his head and then stick the point in the ground. This done, he has no difficulty in despatching his foes. He returns to the Danish court, and marries the princess.

The likeness between the English ballad and the Danish (which represents well enough the other Norse poems) is that a youthful champion wins a king's daughter by killing a truculent competitor, who has nearly the same name in both (Bremor, Bermer).

Further consideration led Bugge to maintain that the proper subject of ' King Estmere ' is rather the story of Hjalmar, Odd and Anganty, and that the English ballad is better represented by the tragic Färöe ballad of ' Arngrim's Sons ' than by ' Orm and Bermer-Giant,' which last he regards as a free reconstruction of an earlier and fuller form of ' Arngrim's Sons ' than has come down to us. The points in which the story of Hjalmar, Odd and Anganty * is like ' King Estmere,' in contrast with the Orm ballad, are that the hero does not fight single-handed with the giant, but has the help of . Odd (Adler) ; that the king's daughter chooses her husband for herself; that the bride is not won by a sword taken from a father's grave. The argument is, however, much too intricate and too long to be repeated here, even had the subtle and

accomplished advocate shown full confidence in the conclusion.

But this confidence he does not feel, for, as he conceives, King Estmere again exhibits resemblances to ' Ogier le Danois,' the basis of the Danish ballad ' Holger Danske og Burmand,' Grundtvig, No 30.† The name Adler, says Bugge, is about as near to Ogier, Oddgeir, as to Oddr. Adler's brother, Estmere, might be the chivalrous paynim Karaheus, despite the unlike name, and King Adland's daughter the amiral's daughter Gloriande, the beloved of Karaheus. Brunamons of Majorca, to whom the amiral offers his daughter after the defection of Karaheus, may be Bremer of Spain. Ogier, like Adler (in Percy's edition), kills the hateful interloper, and Karaheus, like Estmere, gets the lady, but without taking part in the fight. If this hypothesis is not quite so satisfactory as the other, we may combine both. The English ballad may have been derived from some form of ' Arngrim's Sons,' but have been modified under the influence of ' Ogier le Danois.' ‡

A brief statement of these speculations may suffice in view of their inconclusiveness, which is the greater by reason of our not knowing to what extent Percy interfered with his manuscript.

The names Adler and Estmere appear again in a short romance in the Percy manuscript, Hales and Furnivall, II, 296. The story is that of Hugdietrich in the Heldenbuch : von der Hagen, I, 169, ed. 1855, Amelung and Jänicke, I, 167 ; given by Weber in Illustrations of Northern Antiquities, p. 63. Adler is a king, and, like Estmere in the ballad, is exacting in the matter of a wife. In the Heldenbuch it is not the young man who is so difficult to suit, but his guardian. Estmere (v. 11, where there is corruption or defect) appears to be Adler's messenger to King Ardine, the father of a lady who answers all require-

---

* Derived from the Färöe ballad, 'Arngríms synir,' Hammershaimb, Færöiske Kvæder, p. 15, No 3 ; Hervarar saga, Örvar-Odds saga, Fornaldar Sögur, I, 411, II, 161, 504 ; etc. The pertinent chapters of the Hervarar saga are translated by Prior, I, 194, and ' Child Orm and the Berm Giant,' in the same volume, p. 132; the ballad also in the

London Magazine, 1821, IV, 415, and by George Borrow, in Targum, or Metrical Translations from Thirty Languages and Dialects, St Petersburg, 1835, p. 59 (Grundtvig).

† I, 384 ; translated by Prior, I, 297.

‡ Grundtvig's Gamle Folkeviser, IV, 704–712.

ments, and who, as it turns out, likes Adler, but is not to be had on easy terms.*

' King Estmere ' begins very much like the Danish ballad, ' Den farlige Jomfru,' Grundtvig, No 184, and especially like version D.

1 Ther stod drick paa felde,
  der druck kiemper snile.

2 Der druck innde her Ion Runnd,
  och ryder och her Rosenns-wannd.

3 ' Høre du, her Ion Rund, kiere stolbroder mynn,
  vilttu icki gifftis ennd ? '

4 ' Ieg ved icki denn yomffru y dette rige
  der yeg lader were minn lige.'

For knights and others to ride into hall, and up to the high board, is quite according to use. Every one will remember the passage in Chaucer's Squire's Tale, vv 30 ff. So again in Sir Perceval, Thornton Romances, p. 19, xxxi; Sir Degrevant, the same, p. 227, lxxvi; Libius Disconius, Percy MS., Hales and Furnivall, II, 486, v. 1951 (Skeat); Madden's Syr Gawayne, p. 8 ff, p. 111, v. 332; Perceval le Gallois, ed. Potvin, II, 125, vv 12,640–50; Messire Gauvain, p. 27, p. 146 ; Mabinogion, I, 70, 303 f, II, 257 ; Stowe's Survey of London (vol. II, book VI, p. 48, ed. 1720, following Walsingham), cited by Percy in his Essay on the Ancient Minstrels, Reliques, I, xli, lxxxvii, ed. 1794 ; Warton's History of English Poetry, II, 172, note d, ed. 1840.

The champion of England formerly rode into Westminster Hall in the coronation ceremony, but this part of the spectacle was omitted from the two last coronations.

King Estmere stables his steed at the hall board. Here again the minstrel is within the bounds of custom. " On voyait au moyen âge, dans la salle des chefs gallois, d'énormes crampons de fer, fixés au pavé de distance en distance, qui servaient aux chevaliers pour attacher leurs chevaux, car ils y entraient souvent avec eux ; quelques-uns les conduisaient même jusque dans leur chambre à coucher : " Villemarqué, Les Romans de la Table Ronde, etc., 1860, p. 416 (cited by Liebrecht).

For bribing to secrecy with an arm-ring, stanza 47, see, also, Grundtvig, No 82, A 14, 15, B 20, 21 ; No 95, D 16, 17, Kristensen, I, No 96, 16 ; Grundtvig, No 233, A 18, B 12, D 13 ; No 274, A 21.

Translated by Grundtvig, Engelske og skotske Folkeviser, p. 1 ; by Bodmer, I, 27 ; Herder, I, 195 ; Knortz, L. u. R. Alt-Englands, No 14.

---

1 HEARKEN to me, gentlemen,
    Come and you shall heare ;
  Ile tell you of two of the boldest brether
    That ever borne were.

2 The tone of them was Adler Younge,
    The tother was Kyng Estmere ;
  The were as bolde men in their deeds
    As any were, farr and neare.

3 As they were drinking ale and wine
    Within his brother's hall,
  ' When will ye marry a wyfe, brother,
    A wyfe to glad us all ? '

4 Then bespake him Kyng Estmere,
    And answered him hartilye :
  ' I know not that ladye in any land,
    That 's able to marrye with mee.'

* Esmer, or something similar, is, as Grundtvig remarks, I, 236, a name of rather frequent occurrence. King Esmer is one of King Diderik's champions; Grundtvig, I, 78. Esmère is a name in Le dit de Flourence de Romme, Jubinal, Nouveau Recueil de Contes, etc., I, 93 ; Esmerés, or Essmer, in the Knight of the Swan, Reiffenberg and Borgnet, Le Chevalier au Cygne, III, 533, Grimm, Deutsche Sagen, II, 302. It may be added, though the fact certainly appears to be of but slight moment, that there is a King Easter, with a King Wester, in the ballad of ' Fause Foodrage,' and these are called in one version (Motherwell's Minstrelsy, p. lix) the Eastmure King and the Westmure King. The fifteenth tale enumerated in The Complaint of Scotland is How the King of Estmure land married the King's daughter of Westmure land.

5 'Kyng Adland hath a daughter, brother,
　　Men call her bright and sheene ;
　If I were kyng here in your stead,
　　That ladye shold be my queene.'

6 Saies, Reade me, reade me, deare brother,
　　Throughout merry England,
　Where we might find a messenger
　　Betwixt us towe to sende.

7 Saies, You shal ryde yourselfe, brother,
　　Ile beare you companye ;
　Many a man throughe fals messengers is de-
　　　ceived,
　　And I feare lest soe shold wee.

8 Thus the renisht them to ryde,
　　Of twoe good renisht steeds,
　And when the came to King Adlands halle,
　　Of redd gold shone their weeds.

9 And when the came to Kyng Adlands hall,
　　Before the goodlye gate,
　There they found good Kyng Adland
　　Rearing himselfe theratt.

10 'Now Christ thee save, good Kyng Adland ;
　　Now Christ you save and see : '
　Sayd, You be welcome, King Estmere,
　　Right hartilye to mee.

11 'You have a daughter,' said Adler Younge,
　　'Men call her bright and sheene ;
　My brother wold marrye her to his wiffe,
　　Of Englande to be queene.'

12 'Yesterday was att my deere daughter
　　The king his sonne of Spayn,
　And then she nicked him of naye,
　　And I doubt sheele do you the same.'

13 'The kyng of Spayne is a foule paynim,
　　And 'leeveth on Mahound,
　And pitye it were that fayre ladye
　　Shold marrye a heathen hound.'

14 'But grant to me,' sayes Kyng Estmere,
　　'For my love I you praye,
　That I may see your daughter deere
　　Before I goe hence awaye.'

15 'Although itt is seven yeers and more
　　Since my daughter was in halle,

She shall come once downe for your sake,
　　To glad my guestës alle.'

16 Downe then came that mayden fayre,
　　With ladyes laced in pall,
　And halfe a hundred of bold knightes,
　　To bring her [from] bowre to hall,
　And as many gentle squiers,
　　To tend upon them all.

17 The talents of golde were on her head sette
　　Hanged low downe to her knee,
　And everye ring on her small finger
　　Shone of the chrystall free.

18 Saies, God you save, my deere madam,
　　Saies, God you save and see :
　Said, You be welcome, Kyng Estmere,
　　Right welcome unto mee.

19 'And, if you love me, as you saye,
　　Soe well and hartilee,
　All that ever you are comen about
　　Soone sped now itt shal bee.'

20 Then bespake her father deare :
　　My daughter, I saye naye ;
　Remember well the kyng of Spayne,
　　What he sayd yesterdaye.

21 'He wold pull downe my halles and castles,
　　And reave me of my lyfe ;
　I cannot blame him if he doe,
　　If I reave him of his wyfe.

22 'Your castles and your towres, father,
　　Are stronglye built aboute,
　And therefore of the king his sonne of Spaine
　　Wee neede not stande in doubt.

23 'Plight me your troth, nowe, Kyng Estmere,
　　By heaven and your righte hand,
　That you will marrye me to your wyfe,
　　And make me queene of your land.'

24 Then Kyng Estmere he plight his troth,
　　By heaven and his righte hand,
　That he wolde marrye her to his wyfe,
　　And make her queene of his land.

25 And he tooke leave of that ladye fayre,
　　To goe to his owne countree,

To fetche him dukes and lordes and knightes,
 That marryed the might bee.

26 They had not ridden scant a myle,
 A myle forthe of the towne,
But in did come the kyng of Spayne,
 With kempës many one.

27 But in did come the kyng of Spayne,
 With manye a bold barone,
Tone day to marrye Kyng Adlands daughter,
 Tother daye to carrye her home.

28 Shee sent one after Kyng Estmere,
 In all the spede might bee,
That he must either turne againe and fighte,
 Or goe home and loose his ladye.

29 One whyle then the page he went,
 Another while he ranne ;
Till he had oretaken King Estmere,
 I-wis he never blanne.

30 'Tydings, tydings, Kyng Estmere !'
 'What tydinges nowe, my boye ?'
'O tydinges I can tell to you,
 That will you sore annoye.

31 'You had not ridden scant a mile,
 A mile out of the towne,
But in did come the kyng of Spayne,
 With kempës many a one.

32 'But in did come the kyng of Spayne,
 With manye a bold barone,
Tone daye to marrye King Adlands daughter,
 Tother daye to carry her home.

33 'My ladye fayre she greetes you well,
 And ever-more well by mee ;
You must either turne againe and fighte,
 Or goe home and loose your ladye.'

34 Saies, Reade me, reade me, deere brother,
 My reade shall ryse at thee,
Whether it is better to turne and fighte,
 Or goe home and loose my ladye.

35 'Now hearken to me,' sayes Adler Yonge,
 'And your reade must rise at me ;
I quicklye will devise a waye
 To sette thy ladye free.

36 'My mother was a westerne woman,
 And learned in gramarye,
And when I learned at the schole,
 Something shee taught itt mee.

37 'There growes an hearbe within this field,
 And iff it were but knowne,
His color, which is whyte and redd,
 It will make blacke and browne.

38 'His color, which is browne and blacke,
 Itt will make redd and whyte ;
That sworde is not in all Englande
 Upon his coate will byte.

39 'And you shal be a harper, brother,
 Out of the north countrye,
And Ile be your boy, soe faine of fighte,
 And beare your harpe by your knee.

40 'And you shal be the best harper
 That ever tooke harpe in hand,
And I wil be the best singer
 That ever sung in this lande.

41 'Itt shal be written in our forheads,
 All and in grammarye,
That we towe are the boldest men
 That are in all Christentye.'

42 And thus they renisht them to ryde,
 Of tow good renisht steedes,
And when they came to King Adlands hall,
 Of redd gold shone their weedes.

43 And whan the came to Kyng Adlands hall
 Untill the fayre hall-yate,
There they found a proud porter,
 Rearing himselfe thereatt.

44 Sayes, Christ thee save, thou proud porter,
 Sayes, Christ thee save and see :
'Nowe you be welcome,' sayd the porter,
 'Of what land soever ye bee.'

45 'Wee beene harpers,' sayd Adler Younge,
 'Come out of the northe countrye ;
Wee beene come hither untill this place
 This proud weddinge for to see.'

46 Sayd, And your color were white and redd,
 As it is blacke and browne,

I wold saye King Estmere and his brother
    Were comen untill this towne.

47 Then they pulled out a ryng of gold,
    Layd itt on the porters arme :
  ' And ever we will thee, proud porter,
    Thow wilt saye us no harme.'

48 Sore he looked on Kyng Estmere,
    And sore he handled the ryng,
  Then opened to them the fayre hall-yates,
    He lett for no kind of thyng.

49 Kyng Estmere he stabled his steede
    Soe fayre att the hall-bord ;
  The froth that came from his brydle bitte
    Light in Kyng Bremors beard.

50 Saies, Stable thy steed, thou proud harper,
    Saies, Stable him in the stalle ;
  It doth not beseeme a proud harper
    To stable his steed in a kyngs halle.

51 ' My ladde he is so lither,' he said,
    ' He will doe nought that 's meete ;
  And is there any man in this hall
    Were able him to beate ? '

52 ' Thou speakst proud words,' sayes the king of
    Spaine,
  ' Thou harper, here to mee ;
  There is a man within this halle
    Will beate thy ladd and thee.'

53 ' O let that man come downe,' he said,
    ' A sight of him wold I see ;
  And when hee hath beaten well my ladd,
    Then he shall beate of mee.'

54 Downe then came the kemperye man,
    And looked him in the eare ;
  For all the gold that was under heaven,
    He durst not neigh him neare.

55 ' And how nowe, kempe,' said the kyng of
    Spaine,
  ' And how, what aileth thee ? '
  He saies, It is writt in his forhead,
    All and in gramarye,
  That for all the gold that is under heaven,
    I dare not neigh him nye.

56 Then Kyng Estmere pulld forth his harpe,
    And plaid a pretty thinge ;

The ladye upstart from the borde,
    And wold have gone from the king.

57 ' Stay thy harpe, thou proud harper,
    For Gods love I pray thee ;
  For and thou playes as thou beginns,
    Thou 'lt till my bryde from mee.'

58 He stroake upon his harpe againe,
    And playd a pretty thinge ;
  The ladye lough a loud laughter,
    As shee sate by the king.

59 Saies, Sell me thy harpe, thou proud harper,
    And thy stringës all ;
  For as many gold nobles thou shalt have
    As heere bee ringes in the hall.'

60 ' What wold ye doe with my harpe,' he sayd,
    ' If I did sell itt yee ? '
  ' To playe my wiffe and me a fitt,
    When abed together wee bee.'

61 ' Now sell me,' quoth hee, ' thy bryde soe
    gay,
    As shee sitts by thy knee ;
  And as many gold nobles I will give
    As leaves been on a tree.'

62 ' And what wold ye doe with my bryde soe
    gay,
    Iff I did sell her thee ?
  More seemelye it is for her fayre bodye
    To lye by mee then thee.'

63 Hee played agayne both loud and shrille,
    And Adler he did syng,
  ' O ladye, this is thy owne true love,
    Noe harper, but a kyng.

64 ' O ladye, this is thy owne true love,
    As playnlye thou mayest see,
  And Ile rid thee of that foule paynim
    Who partes thy love and thee.'

65 The ladye looked, the ladye blushte,
    And blushte and lookt agayne,
  While Adler he hath drawne his brande,
    And hath the sowdan slayne.

66 Up then rose the kemperye men,
    And loud they gan to crye :
  ' Ah ! traytors, yee have slayne our kyng,
    And therefore yee shall dye.'

67 Kyng Estmere threwe the harpe asyde,
   And swith he drew his brand,
And Estmere he and Adler Yonge
   Right stiffe in stour can stand.

68 And aye their swordes soe sore can byte,
   Throughe help of gramarye,

That soone they have slayne the kempery men,
   Or forst them forth to flee.

69 Kyng Estmere tooke that fayre ladye,
   And marryed her to his wiffe,
And brought her home to merry England,
   With her to leade his life.

———————

a. *Readings of the manuscript, cited in Percy's notes, have been restored.*

1[4]. *Percy prints* y-were.

13[2]. *misprinted* 'leeve thon.

34[2]. shall ryde ; *so* b. *Compare* 35[2], *where* rise *is said to be the reading of the MS.*

42[2]. On tow good renish. *Compare* 8[2].

59[3], thou shalt have, 60[1], he sayd, *are acknowledged changes, or additions, of Percy's.*

63. " Some liberties have been taken in the following stanzas ; but wherever this edition differs from the preceding, it hath been brought nearer to the folio MS." *Percy's note.*

68[1]. can fyte.

b. 5[4]. *Omits* my.

6[4]. Betweene us two.

8[3]. they came. 9[2]. yate.

10[2]. thee save. 10[4]. unto.

12[4]. And *wanting :* I feare. 15[1]. yeare.

15[2]. Syth. 15[3]. downe once. 16[5]. eke as.

16[6]. To waite. 17[2]. Hunge.

18[1, 2]. Christ you save. 18[3]. Sayes.

19[4]. may bee.

21[3]. And ever I feare that paynim kyng.

22[3]. of that foule paynim.

26[4]. many a. 27[2], 32[2]. grimme barone.

28[1]. Then shee sent after.

28[3]. returne and. 33[1]. That ladye.

34[3]. Which waye we best may turne.

34[4]. To save this fayre.

37[1]. groweth. 42[2]. On towe good renish ; *so* **a.**

46[3]. Ild saye. 49[1]. he light off.

49[2]. Up att the fayre hall. 49[4]. Light on.

50[1]. Stable thou. 50[2]. Goe stable.

50[4]. To stable him.

51[3]. And aye that I cold but find the man.

52[1]. sayd the Paynim kyng.

52[4]. That will. 55[3]. written.

56. Kyng Estmere then pulled forth his harpe,
    And playd thereon so sweete ;
Upstarte the ladye from the kynge,
    As hee sate at the meate.

57. ' Nowe stay thy harpe, thou proud harper,
    Now stay thy harpe, I say ;
For an thou playest as thou beginnest,
    Thou 'lt till my bride awaye.'

58. He strucke upon his harpe agayne,
    And playd both fayre and free ;
The ladye was so pleasde theratt
    She laught loud laughters three.

59. ' Nowe sell me thy harpe,' sayd the kyng of
    Spayne,
    ' Thy harpe and stryngs eche one,
And as many gold nobles thou shalt have
    As there be stryngs thereon.'

60[1]. And what.

61. ' Now sell me,' syr kyng, ' thy bryde soe gay,
    As shee sitts laced in pall,
And as many gold nobles I will give
    As there be rings in the hall.'

62[2]. her yee.

65[4]. hath Sir Bremor slayne. 68[1]. can byte.

61

SIR CAWLINE

Percy MS., p. 368; Hales and Furnivall, III, 3.

THE copy of this ballad in the Percy manuscript, the only one known to exist, shows very great carelessness on the part of the transcriber, or of some predecessor. It begins with these two stanzas, which manifestly belong to an historical ballad, and have only a verbal connection with what follows:

Jesus, lord mickle of might,
*Th*at dyed ffor us on the roode,
To maintaine vs in all our right *
*Th*at loues true English blood.

Ffor by a k*night* I say my song,
Was bold and ffull hardye;
S*i*r Robert Briuse wold fforth to ffight,
In-to Ireland ouer the sea.

There is a large omission after the 125th verse (the 28th stanza as here printed), though the writing is continuous. There are also several difficult or unintelligible passages, even more than are usually met with in this manuscript.

As published in the Reliques of Ancient English Poetry, I, 35, ed. 1765, I, 41, ed. 1794, 'Sir Cawline' is extended to nearly twice the amount of what is found in the manuscript, and a tragical turn is forced upon the story.

I have said that the copy of 'Sir Cawline' in the Percy manuscript is the only one known. There are nevertheless two Scottish ballads, one hitherto unpublished and one printed by Buchan, which narrate Sir Colvin's winning the king's daughter by vanquishing the elritch knight. These, I conceive, however, to be simple rifacimenti of the ballad in Percy's Reliques. They will be given in an appendix.

'Sir Cawline' may possibly be formed upon a romance in stanzas † which itself was composed from earlier ballads. There are two adventures in the ballad, one with an elritch knight, and a second with a five-headed giant who is at the same time a hend soldan, and there seem to be traces of another in the now unintelligible twenty-ninth stanza. The first adventure, though not of the same commonplace description as the second, is still by no means unique. We are immediately reminded of the beautiful romance of Eger, Grime and Gray-Steel: how Gray-Steel kept a forbidden country beyond seven days of wilderness, and how Grime slew the up to that time unmatched Gray-Steel with the sword Erkyin [Egeking], brought from beyond the Greekës sea, and cut off his hand, with fingers thrice a common man's size, and on every finger a gay gold ring.‡ Gray-Steel, to be sure, is pictured rather as a giant than an elf, but still gives the impression of something out of the ordinary, as having perhaps lost an elritch character in the course of tradition. The elritch knight in our ballad haunts the moors, far from any good town, like Grendel, who held the moors and fens, but there is only a hint of that supernatural terror which attends the awful "march-stepper" in Beówulf. Gervase of Tilbury has a story of an ancient entrenchment in the bishopric of Ely, where anybody could have a passage at arms with an unearthly warrior, by moonlight only, by simply calling out, "Come,

---

* So maintaine vs all in our right ?
† To this suggestion the actual form of stanzas 8, 11 lends a faint plausibility.

‡ Percy MS., Hales and Furnivall, I, 367, 372 f, 389, 391. For the name of the sword see Liebrecht, Zur Volkskunde, p. 500.

knight, and meet knight." * Scott has introduced a spectral combat of this sort into his
Marmion, Canto III, xxiii-xxv, and in a note
(4) cites a similar encounter from Heywood's
Hierarchy of Blessed Angels. He adds that a
forest in the North Highlands is believed to
be haunted by a martial spirit called Lham-
dearg, or Bloody Hand, who insists on all
whom he meets doing battle with him. Villemarqué has a tale like that of Gervasius, Les
Romans de la Table Ronde, etc., 1860, p. 392 f
(Liebrecht). These combatants and combats
are rather shadowy compared with Grendel,
Gray-Steel, our Elritch King, and an encounter
with them.

'Liden Grimmer og Hjelmer Kamp,' a ballad of the 'Orm Ungersvend' class, Grundtvig, No 26 (I, 352, from manuscripts of the
16th and the 17th century, IV, 762, from recent tradition), has the same remote and general resemblance to 'Sir Cawline' that 'Orm
Ungersvend' has to 'King Estmere,' the points
of agreement permitting the supposition of a
far-off connection, or of no connection at all.†
In Danish A, Grimmer, a young man who
never went to a dance except with a drawn
sword in his hand or sat down to table out of
his corselet, sails to the heathen-king's land
and asks him for his daughter. The king
tells him that he will not get the fair maid
unless he fights with Hjelmer Kamp and wins.
The king's daughter, who is as favorably in-
clined to Grimmer as King Adland's daughter
is to Estmere (and King Ardine's daughter to
Adler), though in neither case has there been
a previous meeting, tells him that no man ever
came back from a fight with Hjelmer, and
that Grimmer is far from understanding her
father, who really wishes his death. Grim-

mer is not at all daunted, and so the lady
gives him a sword with which he is sure to
prevail. Thus equipped he makes sail for
Hjelmer Kamp, who receives him with con-
temptuous remarks upon his size, but is presently cut to bits. Stopping only long enough
to make boot of Hjelmer's gold, Grimmer
returns to the heathen-king's court, and receives the princess in marriage. The resemblance of the Danish ballad is to be found
in Cawline's second adventure, that with the
giant, where the elritch sword represents the
invincible weapon bestowed by the princess.
In Danish B a coat of mail goes with the
sword, "som icke skal suerd paa bide." This
coat is like Estmere's after Adler has brought
his magic to bear, and Cawline's fight with the
giant, Estmere's with Bremor, and Hjelmer's
with the kemp have all an obvious simili-
tude.

Two verbal peculiarities in this ballad will
not fail to be remarked: a superfluous *and*,
7⁴, without and a good leedginge, 8³, and take
you doe and the baken bread, 27¹, and hee
tooke then vp and that eldryge sword, 39¹,
but take you doo and your lands broad, and
again 26¹ (?) ; *for* used, apparently, in the
sense of *but* (as in "for and a shrouding
sheet"), 11³, ffor if you wold comfort me
with a kisse, 13³, ffor some deeds of armes
ffaine wold I doe, 22⁵, ffor they tooke and two
good swords ; in this last we have the superfluous *and* again. These were, perhaps, only
tricks of some ballad-singer, eking out his
measure with half-articulated syllables.‡

Percy's ballad is translated by Bodmer, I,
134, and by Bothe, p. 25 ; Buchan's by Gerhard, p. 32.

---

* Cited by Scott, Minstrelsy, II, 273, ed. 1833; Otia Im-
perialia, ed. Liebrecht, LIX, p. 26.

† Grundtvig's **A, B** are translated by Dr Prior, I, 276.
The story is found also in Icelandic rímur of the 15th century printed in Björner's Kämpedater, 1737. Björner was
acquainted with an old Swedish ballad on the subject, but

this ballad has not been found. The story of these rímur is
given by Mallet, Histoire de Dannemarc, II, 312, ed. 1787,
and in Percy's translation, Northern Antiquities, II, 248.

‡ So, as to *and*, the German 'Ulinger,' Mittler, p. 68, sts
21, 22, 23 ; den ersten schrey *vnd* den sie thet, etc.

*   *   *   *   *

1 AND in *that* land dwells a king
   W*hi*ch does beare the bell ouer all,
   And w*i*th him there dwelled a curteous k*night*,
   S*i*r Cawline men him call.

2 And he hath a ladye to his daughter,
   Of ffashyon shee hath noe peere;
   K*night*s and lordes they woed her both,
   Trusted to haue beene her feere.

3 S*i*r Cawline loues her best of onë,
   But nothing durst hee say
   To discreeue his councell to noe man,
   But deerlye loued this may.

4 Till itt beffell vpon a day,
   Great dill to him was dight;
   The maydens loue remoued his mind,
   To care-bed went the knight.

5 And one while he spread his armes him ffroe,
   And cryed soe pittyouslye:
   'Ffor the maydens loue *that* I haue most minde
   This day may comfort mee,
   Or else ere noone I shalbe dead!'
   Thus can S*i*r Cawline say.

6 When our p*a*rish masse *that* itt was done,
   And our king was bowne to dine,
   He sayes, Where is S*i*r Cawline,
   That was wont to serue me w*i*th ale and wine?

7 But then answered a curteous k*night*,
   Ffast his hands wringinge:
   'S*i*r Cawline's sicke, and like to be dead
   W*i*thout and a good leedginge.'

8 'Ffeitch yee downe my daughter deere,
   Shee is a leeche ffull ffine;
   I, and take you doe and the baken bread,
   And drinke he on the wine soe red,
   And looke no daynti is ffor him to deare,
   For ffull loth I wold him tine.'

9 This ladye is gone to his chamber,
   Her maydens ffollowing nye;
   'O well,' shee sayth, 'how doth my lord?'
   'O sicke!' againe saith hee.

10 'I, but rise vp wightlye, man, for shame!
   Neuer lye here soe cowardlye!
   Itt is told in my ffathers hall,
   Ffor my loue you will dye.'

11 'Itt is ffor yo*u*r loue, ffayre ladye,
   That all this dill I drye;
   Ffor if you wold comfort me w*i*th a kisse,
   Then were I brought ffrom bale to blisse,
   Noe longer here wold I lye.'

12 'Alas! soe well you know, S*i*r k*night*,'
   .   .   .   .   .
   .   .   .   .   .

13 .   .   .   .   .   .
   I cannott bee yo*u*r peere:
   'Ffor some deeds of armes ffaine wold I doe,
   To be yo*u*r bacheeleere.'

14 'Vpon Eldrige Hill there growes a thorne,
   Vpon the mores brodinge;
   And wold you, s*i*r knight, wake there all night
   To day of the other morninge?

15 'Ffor the eldrige k*i*ng, *that* is mickle of might,
   Will examine you beforne;
   And there was neuer man *that* bare his liffe away
   Since the day *that* I was borne.'

16 'But I will ffor yo*u*r sake, ffaire ladye,
   Walke on the bents [soe] browne,
   And Ile either bring you a readye token,
   Or Ile neuer come to you againe.'

17 But this ladye is gone to her chamber,
   Her maydens ffollowing bright,
   And S*i*r Cawlin's gone to the mores soe broad,
   Ffor to wake there all night.

18 Vnto midnight [that] the moone did rise,
   He walked vp and downe,
   And a lightsome bugle then heard he blow.
   Ouer the bents soe browne;
   Saies hee, And if cryance come vntill my hart,
   I am ffarr ffrom any good towne.

19 And he spyed, ene a litle him by,
   A ffuryous king and a ffell,
   And a ladye bright his brydle led,
   That seemlye itt was to see.

20 And soe fast hee called vpon Sir Cawline,
   Oh man, I redd the fflye !
Ffor if cryance come vntill thy hart,
   I am a-feard least thou mun dye.

21 He sayes, [No] cryance comes to my hart,
   Nor ifaith I ffeare not thee ;
Ffor because thou minged not Christ before,
   Thee lesse me dreadeth thee.

22 But Sir Cawline he shooke a speare ;
   The king was bold, and abode ;
And the timber these two children bore
   Soe soone in sunder slode ;
Ffor they tooke and two good swords,
   And they layden on good loade.

23 But the elridge king was mickle of might,
   And stiffly to the ground did stand ;
But Sir Cawline, with an aukeward stroke,
   He brought ffrom him his hand,
I, and fflying ouer his head soe hye,
   [It] ffell downe of that lay land.

24 And his lady stood a litle thereby,
   Ffast ringing her hands :
' For the maydens loue *that* you haue most
   minde,
Smyte you my lord no more.

25 ' And hees neuer come vpon Eldrige [Hill],
   Him to sport, gamon, or play,
And to meete noe man of middle-earth
   And *tha*t liues on Christs his lay.'

26 But he then vp and *that* eldryge king,
   Sett him in his sadle againe,
And *that* eldryge king and his ladye
   To their castle are they gone.

27 And hee tooke then vp and *that* eldryge sword,
   As hard as any fflynt,
And soe he did those ringes fiue,
   Harder then ffyer, and brent.

28 Ffirst he presented to the kings daughter
   The hand, and then the sword,

   .   .   .   .   .

    .   .   .   .

   *   *   *   *   *

29 ' But a serre buffett you haue him giuen,
   The king and the crowne,' shee sayd :
' I, but four and *thirty* stripes
   Comen beside the rood.'

30 And a gyant that was both stiffe [and] strong,
   He lope now them amonge,
And vpon his squier fiue heads he bare,
   Vnmackley made was hee.

31 And he dranke then on the kings wine,
   And hee put the cup in his sleeue,
And all thé trembled and were wan,
   Ffor feare he shold them greeffe.

32 ' Ile tell thee mine arrand, king,' he sayes,
   ' Mine errand what I doe heere ;
Ffor I will bren thy temples hye,
   Or Ile haue thy daughter deere ;
I, or else vpon yond more soe brood
   Thou shalt ffind mee a ppeare.'

33 The king he turned him round about,
   Lord, in his heart he was woe !
Says, Is there noe knight of the Round Table
   This matter will vndergoe ?

34 ' I, and hee shall haue my broad lands,
   And keepe them well his liue ;
I, and soe hee shall my daughter deere,
   To be his weded wiffe.'

35 And then stood vp Sir Cawline,
   His owne errand ffor to say :
' Ifaith, I wold to God, Sir,' sayd Sir Cawline,
   ' *That* soldan I will assay.

36 ' Goe ffeitch me downe my eldrige sword,
   Ffor I woone itt att ffray : '
' But away, away ! ' sayd the hend soldan,
   ' Thou tarryest mee here all day ! '

37 But the hend soldan and Sir Cawline
   Thé ffought a sum*m*ers day ;
Now has hee slaine *that* hend soldan,
   And brought his fiue heads away.

38 And the king has betaken him his broade lands,
   And all his venison ;

   .   .   .   .   .

    .   .   .   .

39 ' But take you doo and *your* lands [soe] broad,
     And brooke them well *your* liffe ;
   Ffor you *promised* mee *your* daughter deere,
     To be my weded wiffe.'

40 ' Now by my ffaith,' then sayes our k*ing,*
     ' Ffor *that* wee will not striffe,
   Ffor thou shalt haue my daughter dere,
     To be thy weded wiffe.'

41 The other morninge S*ir* Cawline rose
     By the dawning of the day,
   And vntill a garden did he goe
     His mattins ffor to say ;
   And *that* bespyed a ffalse steward,
     A shames death *that* he might dye !

42 And he lett a lyon out of a bande,
     S*ir* Cawline ffor to teare ;
   And he had noe wepon him vpon,
     Nor noe wepon did weare.

43 But hee tooke then his mantle of greene,
     Into the lyons mouth itt thrust ;
   He held the lyon soe sore to the wall
     Till the lyons hart did burst.

44 And the watchmen cryed vpon the walls
     And sayd, ' S*ir* Cawline 's slaine !
   And w*ith* a beast is not ffull litle,
     A lyon of mickle mayne : '
   Then the k*ing*s daughter shee ffell downe,
     ' For peerlesse is my payne ! '

45 ' O peace, my lady ! ' sayes S*ir* Cawline,
     ' I haue bought thy loue ffull deere ;
   O peace, my lady ! ' sayes S*ir* Cawline,
     ' Peace, lady, ffor I am heere ! '

46 Then he did marry this k*ing*s daughter,
     W*ith* gold and siluer bright,
   And fiftene sonnes this ladye beere
     To S*ir* Cawline the knight.

The first two stanzas of the MS. have been omitted, as belonging to another ballad.

1². ouer all does beare the bell.
1⁴. men call him S*ir* Cawline.
2⁴. her peere.
3⁴. this mayd.
5⁵. *Only half the second* n *of* noone *in the MS. Furnivall.*
7². wringinge his hands.
8⁴. and eene on : *MS.* edne ? *Furnivall. I feel no confidence in the emendation.*
8⁵. no daytinesse.   8⁶. teene.

10². lye soe cowardlye here.
11⁵. *MS.* now ?   *Furnivall.*
12¹, 13², ³, ⁴ *make a stanza in the MS.*
18¹. they Moone.   22³, ⁵.   2.   23⁴. him ffrom.
23⁶. *There may be a bold ellipsis of* It.
24³. for they . . . most meed : *cf.* 5³.
25¹. heest.   27³.   5.
28². they hand . . . they sword.
29¹. serrett buffett.   29³. 34.   30³. 5.
32⁵. in or.   32⁶. mee appeare.   37⁴. 5.
39¹. you too.   46³. 15.

APPENDIX

THE first of the following pieces is described as having been learned by Mrs Harris, in Perthshire, about 1790, transmitted by recitation to her daughter, and written down from recollection in 1859. No account is given of the derivation of the other. Both make the princess marry Sir Colvin after his victory on the elritch hill, rejecting Percy's pathetic conclusion. Neither retains much of the phraseology of Percy's manuscript, and neither shows those traces of Percy's phraseology which would demonstrate its parentage. The first, though the style is stale enough, has not the decidedly stall-copy stamp of the other. It undoubtedly has passed through a succession of mouths (as is shown by the change of leech to match in 3²), but we may doubt whether the other was ever sung or said. 8⁴, in the Harris version,

     Sin the first nicht that I was born,

is close to the Percy manuscript, 17⁴,

     Since the day that I was borne,

where Percy's Reliques has,

But he did him scath and scorne.

In the old manuscript, when Sir Cawline cuts off the elritch knight's hand, the hand flies over the knight's head and falls down on that lay land; in Buchan, 25, 26, the hand also flies into the sky and lights on the ground ; but Percy says merely that the knight fell on that lay land.   So that there is one case in each of agreement with the Percy manuscript where the Reliques depart from it.   It may also be urged that Buchan, $22^{1, 2}$,

> To trouble any Christian one
> Lives in the righteous law,

is nearer to what we find in the manuscript, st. 25,

> And to meete noe man of middle-earth
> And that liues (= 'lieves) on Christs his lay,

than Percy's,

> That thou wilt believe on Christ his laye,
> And thereto plight thy hand ;

> And that thou never on Eldridge come.

Were there anything characteristic or otherwise remarkable in the passages where there is agreement with the Percy manuscript and divergence from the Reliques, even one case of such agreement could not be lightly set aside.*   But such agreements as these are not significant enough to offset the general character of the Scottish ballads, which is not that of a traditional waif, but of a fabrication of recent times.   It is most likely that the Harris ballad was put together by some one who was imperfectly acquainted with the copy in the Reliques. Whether Buchan's ballad was formed upon some copy of the Harris version it is not worth the while to ask.

SIR COLIN

Harris MS., fol. 5b.

1 THE king luikit owre his castle wa,
   To his nobles ane an a';
Says, Whare it is him Sir Colin,
   I dinna see him amang you a'?

2 Up it spak an eldern knicht,
   Aye an even up spak he:
' Sir Colin 's sick for your dochter Janet,
   He 's very sick, an like to dee.'

3 ' Win up, win up, my dochter Janet,
   I wat ye are a match most fine;
Tak the baken bread an wine sae ried,
   An to Sir Colin ye maun gieng.'

4 Up she rase, that fair Janet,
   An I wat weel she was na sweer,
An up they rase, her merrie maries,
   An they said a' they wad gae wi her.

5 ' No, no,' said fair Janet,
   ' No, no such thing can be;
For a thrang to gae to a sick man's bour,
   I think it wald be great folie.

6 ' How is my knicht, all last nicht? '
   ' Very sick an like to dee;
But if I had a kiss o your sweet lips,
   I wald lie nae langer here.'

7 She leant her doon on his bed-side,
   I wat she gae him kisses three ;
But wi sighen said that fair Janet,
   ' As for your bride, I daurna be.

8 ' Unless you watch the Orlange hill,
   An at that hill there grows a thorn;
There neer cam a liven man frae it,
   Sin the first nicht that I was born.'

9 ' Oh I will watch the Orlange hill,
   Though I waur thinkin to be slain ;
But I will gie you some love tokens,
   In case we never meet again.'

10 He gae her rings to her fingers,
   Sae did he ribbons to her hair ;
He gae her a broach to her briest-bane,
   For fear that they sud neer meet mair.

11 She put her hand in her pocket,
   An she took out a lang, lang wand;
' As lang 's ony man this wand sall keep,
   There sall not a drap o his blude be drawn.'

12 Whan een was come, an een-bells rung,
   An a' man boun for bed,
There beheld him Sir Colin,
   Fast to the Orlange hill he rade.

13 The wind blew trees oot at the rutes,
   Sae did it auld castles doon;
'T was eneuch to fricht ony Christian knicht,
   To be sae far frae ony toon.

---

* The Percy manuscript was inspected by many persons near the time of the first publication of the Reliques, and again while the fourth edition was going through the press, but it is not for a moment to be suggested or supposed that anything in the Scottish ' Sir Colvin ' is to be accounted for in that way.

14 He rade up, sae did he doon,
   He rade even through the loan,
   Till he spied a knicht, wi a ladie bricht,
     Wi a bent bow intil his han.

15 She cried afar, ere she cam naur,
   I warn ye, kind sir, I rede ye flee;
   That for the love you bear to me,
     I warn ye, kind sir, that ye flee.

16 They faucht up, sae did they doon,
   They faucht even through the loan,
   Till he cut aff the king's richt han,
     Was set aboot wi chains a' goud.

17 'Haud your hand now, Sir Colin,
   I wat you 've dung my love richt sair;
   Noo for the love ye bear to me,
     See that ye ding my love nae mair.'

18 He wooed, he wooed that fair Janet,
   He wooed her and he brocht her hame ;
   He wooed, he wooed that fair Janet,
     An ca'd her Dear-Coft till her name.

KING MALCOLM AND SIR COLVIN

Buchan's Ballads of the North of Scotland, II, 6 ; Motherwell's MS., p. 581.

1 THERE ance livd a king in fair Scotland,
   King Malcolm called by name,
   Whom ancient history gives record
     For valour, worth, and fame.

2 And it fell ance upon a day,
   The king sat down to dine,
   And then he missd a favourite knight,
     Whose name was Sir Colvin.

3 But out it speaks another knight,
   Ane o Sir Colvin's kin :
   ' He 's lyin in bed, right sick in love,
     All for your daughter Jean.'

4 'O wae 's me,' said the royal king,
   ' I 'm sorry for the same;
   She maun take bread and wine sae red,
     Give it to Sir Colvin.'

5 Then gently did she bear the bread,
   Her page did carry the wine,
   And set a table at his bed:
     ' Sir Colvin, rise and dine.'

6 ' O well love I the wine, lady,
   Come frae your lovely hand,

But better love I your fair body,
     Than all fair Scotland's strand.'

7 ' O hold your tongue now, Sir Colvin,
   Let all your folly be ;
   My love must be by honour won,
     Or nane shall enjoy me.

8 ' But on the head o Elrick's hill,
   Near by yon sharp hawthorn,
   Where never a man with life eer came,
     Sin our sweet Christ was born ;

9 ' O ye 'll gang there and walk a' night,
   And boldly blaw your horn;
   With honour that ye do return,
     Ye 'll marry me the morn.'

10 Then up it raise him Sir Colvin,
   And dressd in armour keen,
   And he is on to Elrick's hill,
     Without light of the meen.

11 At midnight mark the meen upstarts;
   The knight walkd up and down,
   While loudest cracks o thunder roard
     Out ower the bent sae brown.

12 Then by the twinkling of an ee
   He spied an armed knight,
   A fair lady bearing his brand,
     Wi torches burning bright.

13 Then he cried high, as he came nigh,
   ' Coward thief, I bid you flee !
   There is not ane comes to this hill,
     But must engage wi me.

14 ' Ye 'll best take road before I come,
   And best take foot and flee;
   Here is a sword, baith sharp and broad
     Will quarter you in three.'

15 Sir Colvin said, I 'm not afraid
   Of any here I see;
   You hae not taen your God before;
     Less dread hae I o thee.

16 Sir Colvin then he drew his sword,
   His foe he drew his brand,
   And they fought there on Elrick's hill
     Till they were bluidy men.

17 The first an stroke the knight he strake,
   Gae Colvin a slight wound ;
   The next an stroke Lord Colvin strake,
     Brought 's foe unto the ground.

18 ' I yield, I yield,' the knight he said,
  ' I fairly yield to thee;
Nae ane came eer to Elrick-hill
  Eer gaind such victorie.

19 ' I and my forbears here did haunt
  Three hundred years and more ;
I 'm safe to swear a solemn oath
  We were never beat before.'

20 ' An asking,' said the lady gay,
  ' An asking ye 'll grant me ; '
' Ask on, ask on,' said Sir Colvin,
  ' What may your asking be ? '

21 ' Ye 'll gie me hame my wounded knight,
  Let me fare on my way;
And I 'se neer be seen on Elrick's hill,
  By night, nor yet by day;
And to this place we 'll come nae mair,
  Coud we win safe away.

22 ' To trouble any Christian one,
  Lives in the righteous law,
We 'll come nae mair unto this place,
  Coud we win safe awa.'

23 ' O yese get hame your wounded knight,
  Ye shall not gang alane ;

But I maun hae a wad o him,
  Before that we twa twine.'

24 Sir Colvin being a book-learnd man,
  Sae gude in fencing tee,
He 's drawn a stroke behind his hand,
  And followed in speedilie.

25 Sae fierce a stroke Sir Colvin 's drawn,
  And followed in speedilie,
The knight's brand and sword hand
  In the air he gard them flee.

26 It flew sae high into the sky,
  And lighted on the ground;
The rings that were on these fingers
  Were worth five hundred pound.

27 Up he has taen that bluidy hand,
  Set it before the king,
And the morn it was Wednesday,
  When he married his daughter Jean.

Motherwell, who cites a manuscript of Buchan, prints the first three stanzas and the last with some variations : Introduction, p. lxvi, note **. The ballad is not in Buchan's two manuscript volumes.

62

FAIR ANNIE

A. 'Lord Thomas and Fair Annie,' Minstrelsy of the Scottish Border, II, 102, 1802; 31 stanzas.

B. 'Burd Helen,' Jamieson's Popular Ballads, II, 376; 26 stanzas.

C. 'Fair Annie,' Motherwell's MS., p. 351; 33 stanzas.

D. Herd, The Ancient and Modern Scots Songs, 1769, p. 307; 8 stanzas.

E. ' Lady Jane,' Jamieson-Brown MS., fol. 20, Jamieson's Popular Ballads, II, 371 ; 20 stanzas.

F. ' Fair Annie,' Motherwell's MS., p. 385, Motherwell's Minstrelsy, p. 327 ; 32 stanzas.

G. Communicated by Miss Reburn ; 5 stanzas.

H. Communicated by Dr Thomas Davidson; 2 stanzas.

I. 'Fair Annie,' Kinloch MSS, I, 155 ; 45 stanzas.

J. ' The Fause Lord,' Buchan's MSS, I, 66; 65 stanzas.

THE fragment D, printed in 1769, antedates the committing to writing of any of the other versions. E was taken down as early as 1783.

A and B are from the beginning of this century. A was obtained " chiefly from the recitation of an old woman," but we are not

informed who supplied the rest. Herd's fragment, **D**, furnished stanzas 2–6, 12, 17, 19. A
doubt may be hazarded whether stanzas 8–10
came from the old woman. **I** is a combination
of three recited versions, and **J**, perhaps a transcript of a stall-copy, is, like many of Buchan's
ballads, extended to twice the length of genuine versions by tedious, sometimes nauseous,
amplification and interpolation.

'Lady Jane,' Jamieson's Popular Ballads,
II, 73, is a combination of **B** and **E**, with a
good many bad verses of Jamieson's own. A
version in Motherwell's MS., p. 477, "from
the recitation of an old maid-servant of Mr
Alexander, of Southbar," was, as would be inferred from a memorandum at the end of the
transcript, derived from a printed book, and is
in fact an imperfect recollection of this compounded ballad of Jamieson's.

Grundtvig has attempted a reconstitution
of the ballad from versions **A, B, D, E, F,**
Danmarks gamle Folkeviser, V, 42.

Annie [Helen, **B**, Ellen, **G**, Jane, **E**] was
stolen from home in her childhood, **A** 15,
B 23, **C** 31, **E** 9, **F** 25, **I** 38, **J** 50, 51, by a
knight from over sea, to whom she has borne
seven sons, out of wedlock. Her consort bids
her prepare to welcome a bride, with whom
he shall get gowd and gear; with her he got
none. But she must look like a maid, comb
down her yellow locks, braid her hair.* Annie meekly assents, for love, she says, in **C** 12;
in **I** 4, **J** 15, the welcoming goes against her
heart; in **F** 9 she is told that she is to do it;
in **H** 2 she says the welcome will have to come
from him. Annie receives the bride and her
train and serves the tables, suppressing her
tears and drinking water to keep her cheek
from paling. She passes for servant or housekeeper, and in **I** 23, **J** 25, uses the word 'master,' not to anger the bride; in **C** 17 she calls
her lord brother, and the knight calls her sister in **C** 18 and (inconsistently) in **J** 38.

What 'n a lady's that? asks the bride, **E** 9,
J 37, and what means all these bonny boys
that follow at her heel? **J** 37.

When the married pair have gone to their
bed-chamber, Annie, in a room near by, bewails her sad lot in song; to the harp or her
virginals, **E, F, J, I**. The bride hears the
lament: it is that of a woman who will go
mad ere day, **B** 20, **C** 26, **J** 44, 48. The
bride goes to Fair Annie's chamber, **A, C**?
to see what gars her greet, inquires her parentage, and discovers that they are sisters; or
learns this fact from the song itself, **B, E**;
or recognizes her sister's voice, **F, I, J**. King
Henry was their father, **B, F, I**; King Easter,
C; † the Earl of Wemyss, of Richmond, **A,
E**. Queen Easter was their mother, **F**; Queen
Catherine, Elinor [Orvis], **B, I**. The bride,
who had come with many well-loaded ships,
gives all or most of them to her sister, **A, B,
C, F, I**, and goes virgin home, **A, B, F, I, J**;
expecting, as **B, J** add, to encounter derision
for going away wife and coming back maid.

In **C** 27 the bride suspects that the woman
who wails so madly is a leman, and urges her
husband to get up and pack her down the
stairs, though the woods were ne'er so wild.
He refuses. A similar scene is elsewhere put
earlier, during the bridal entertainment, **I** 29,
30, **J** 40: see also **G** 2, 3, which are partly explained by these passages, and partly by **J** 36.

There are other variations in the story, and
some additional particulars in one or another
version: none of these, however, seem to belong to the original ballad. The bride, as
soon as she sees Annie, is struck with the resemblance to her lost sister, **A** 14, **E** 9, **J** 29.
The bridegroom repents, and rejects the woman he has married, **E** 19, **F** 30, **J** 49. The
bridegroom confiscates without ceremony, as
tocher for Annie, six of the seven ships which
the bride had brought with her, **E, J**.‡
The name Lord Thomas in **A** was prob

---

* **F** 2 reads, "Bind up your hair, and tie it in your neck,"
which is deceptive. It was an imperative custom, as is well
known, that the married woman should bind up her hair or
wear it under a cap, while a maid wore it loose or in a braid;
a yard long, like Chaucer's Emily, if she had as much. See
D3, **E**3, **I**5, and Prior's Danish Ballads, II, 180 f.

† And John Armstrang her eldest brother, **C** 30: so the

Scottish king was right when he weened Johnie was a king
as well as he.

‡ "The tradition which commonly accompanies this tale,"
says Jamieson, Popular Ballads, II, 83, "says that he was
aware of his bride's being the sister of his mistress, and that he
had courted her, not with a view of retaining her as his wife,
but of securing from her father a portion for Lady Jane, whom

ably suggested by 'Lord Thomas and Fair Annet.'

A Danish ballad of Fair Annie has been known to the English for fourscore years through Jamieson's translation. The Scandinavian versions are the following.

Danish. 'Skjön Anna,' Grundtvig, No 258, V, 13, eight versions : A, 39 four-line stanzas, B, 34 sts, C, 45 sts, from manuscripts of the sixteenth century; D, 48 sts, E, 41 sts, G, 32 sts, from seventeenth-century manuscripts; F, 41 sts, from broadsides or stall-copies, the earliest dated 1648, from Peder Syv, 1695, and from copies lately taken down which were derived from printed texts; H, 43 sts, a version recently obtained from tradition in Norway. Of these, A, B, C, G are independent texts; D, E, F are derived from some copy of C, or from a version closely akin to C; H is essentially the broadside copy F, but has one stanza of its own. F, Syv, No 17, Danske Viser, IV, 59, No 177, the form through which the Danish ballad has been made known by English translations, is unfortunately an impure and sophisticated text.

Swedish. A, 'Skön Anna,' 19 sts, Arwidsson, I, 291, No 42 ; B, Afzelius, I, 24, No 5, 32 sts ; C, Wigström, Folkdiktning, I, 57, No 28, 37 sts. C follows in the main Danish F, but with a variation in st. 31 which is of much importance if traditional. A translation of Danish F has long circulated in Sweden as a broadside : see, besides Grundtvig, Bergström's Afzelius, II, 30.

The Scandinavian story will, for more brevity, be collected principally from Danish A, B, C, and some variations of the other copies be added.

Fair Annie [Anneck, Annecke, A], a king's daughter, is stolen in her early years, and sold to a man of rank, who is in fact heir to a crown. They have seven sons in eight [seven] years, and he then becomes king. Fair Annie begs the queen-mother to intercede with her son now to make her a lawful wife and legiti-

mate his children. The mother loves Annie, and heartily desires that he may. The son refuses ; she has great virtues, but he does not know Annie's friends [her forbears, lineage, Danish F, Swedish C]. He makes suit for a king's daughter in a distant land. Annie's heart all but breaks when the bride comes. The young king asks the bride what gift she will give his *amie*, A. I will give her my old shoes, she says, B, D, F. She must give something else if she would get his good will. Then she will give Annie seven mills that lie far over the Rhine and grind nought but cinnamon, B, D, F. Annie is now asked what gift she will make the bride. I will give her *you*, whom I can so ill spare, answers Annie. No, that is not enough ; she must give another gift to win the bride's good will. I will give her the seven sons I have borne, says Annie. Neither is that enough ; she must give the bride her gold brooch. This Annie will not surrender, for it was his morning-gift. Annie now asks her lord to let her go into the bride-house [hall] and see the bride. He refuses emphatically, but his kind mother says, Yes; she will even go with Annie, though it should cost her her life. Annie goes to the bride-house, preceded by her seven sons, who wear her father's color. She pours wine for the bride, with many tears, A, C. The bride asks who this fair woman is that weeps so sore. And who are these that wear her father's color ? * It is the king's sister's daughter, from a foreign land, C-F, H ; his sister, Danish A, Swedish A, B. "It is not your sister's daughter," says the bride; "that I plainly see. I fear it is your leman," C 34, D, E. The king now avows the truth. It is Fair Annie, my leman, Danish A 33, Swedish A 16 (which adds, "Her father I never knew"); she was stolen from a foreign land in her young days, and has been with me seven years, Danish B 31 ; she was sold to me from a foreign land ; these are her seven sons, they will be bastards now, and that is the cause of her grief, C 35, 36, D, E ; these are my seven sons, Fair

---

he intended to marry : " a canny project adopted into the degenerate and interpolated **J** (st. 53), but rather too sharp practice for an old ballad.

* The boys are all dressed in scarlet red in Danish **E** 24, **F** 27, **H** 21 ; so in English **E** 6, but in **J** 23 in black.

Annie is their mother, Swedish B 27. I had a sister, says the bride; she was stolen from my father's land; Fair Annie was her name, this must be she,* she shall keep her husband. The king sends the new-come bride home with due ceremony, and keeps Fair Annie for his heart's delight, C 37–44, D, E.

In Danish G 7, the king gives as a reason for not espousing Fair Annie that she has no fortune, ingen rente, which is the objection to her in English A 1, C 2, etc. The oldest [youngest] son of Fair Annie attends his mother's sister to her father's land in Swedish C, Danish F, K, as in English J 54. The king promises his brother to Annie's sister in Danish A 39 (compare also Swedish B 33). In English I 26, J 30, the bride thinks *her* brother would be a good match for Annie.

Swedish C, though in itself of little authority, has an advantage over the Danish copies and Swedish B in making Annie refuse to part with the gold brooch, not because it was a morning-gift, but because she had had it ever since she was a child and was kidnapped from her father's court; and again in making this brooch the means of her recognition as sister by the bride.

The Scandinavian ballad is regarded by Grundtvig as transmitted from Low German. The rhymes are frequently not after the Danish manner (see Grundtvig, V, 46, 7), and the heroine's name has a Low German look.

Dutch and German versions, all ill enough preserved, are:

Dutch. A. 'Schön Adelheid,' 22 four-line stanzas, Hoffmann, Niederländische Volkslieder, 2d ed., 1856, p. 46, No 11, 'Mooi Aeltje en Koning Alewijn,' Willems, p. 177, No 70; from Den Italiaenschen Quacksalver, Amsterdam, 1708. B. 'Madel,' 15 stanzas, Snellaert, Oude en nieuwe Liedjes, p. 70, No 65, 2d ed., 1864.

German. A. Longard, Altrheinländische Mährlein und Liedlein, 1843, p. 23, No 12; Wilhelm von Zuccalmaglio, Deutsche Volkslieder, 1840, p. 74, No 32, = Mittler, No 333: 21 four-line stanzas. B. Montanus (Vincenz von Zuccalmaglio), Die deutschen Volksfeste, 1854, p. 46, 17 stanzas, apparently rewritten.

According to Dutch A Aaltje, Ethel, Adeline, a king's daughter, is stolen, and sold for a great sum to King Alewijn. She asks the king's mother, who is quite disposed to have her for a daughter, when her son will marry her, and the mother asks her son how long Maid Aaltje is to live under disgrace. The king objects that Aaltje is a *vondeling*, a waif-woman (English C 2, I 2); Heaven only knows her friends and kin. He adds that he was over the Rhine yesterday, and that Aaltje will break her heart with sorrow. The young woman asks the mother's permission to go to the bride's house, and is told to go in good style, her seven sons before her and fourteen ladies-in-waiting behind. The king meets Aaltje half-way, and says, If you are going to the bride's house, what gift do you mean to make the bride? The bride will have enough, she replies; I will give her my old stockings and shoes. She must give something better to gain her friendship. Then Aaltje will give her " seven sons of yours and mine " to serve her. She will have your seven sons, says the king, but you must give her your brooch.† No, that you will not get, says Aaltje. There were two at my father's court; my sister and I each had one. Are you then of royal birth? says the king. Had you told me that, I would have married *you*. When Aaltje appears at the bride's house, they offer her to drink, and many a tear she drops in the cup. Who is this woman that weeps so piteously? asks the bride. These are some of our nieces and nephews, who have come from foreign parts

---

* And the young bride throws down a half gold-ring,
    Fair Annie she throws down the other,
  And a pair of loving sisters were they,
    And the rings they ran together.
                          Swedish B 32.

† Vorige span, sts 14, 15, for which Hoffmann reads voorge-span, meaning a fore-span. A span of horses is as absurd here as possible, but is adopted in the German version, and

made to point a gibe at the king. It would seem that the Dutch *voorspan*, brooch or clasp, German spange (see Hexham's Dictionary, 1658), must have been for some time obsolete. In Richthofen's Altfriesisches Wörterbuch we find simply *span, spon:* " verstanden ist darunter ein goldener Schmuck den die friesischen Weiber *vor* der Brust trugen." Stanza 15 is interpreted accordingly.

to bring you presents, is the king's answer. Nieces and nephews! says the bride; it is Maid Aaltje, my youngest sister. She takes the crown from her head: Take it, Aaltje, and keep your husband. Saddle my horse. I came in honor, I must go back in shame. (Cf. English B 26, I 45.)

B. Madel (M'Adel), the oldest of a king's two daughters, is stolen by a king's son to be his leman, and taken to a far country. They have seven sons, and he forsakes her and betroths himself to her sister. He asks his mother what present she will make his bride; she has seven mills which she will give her. Madel, asked in like manner, replies, My old stockings and shoes. Madel asks the queen-mother if she may go to the bridal, for the king is to marry, and is answered as in A. When she comes to the bride-loft they pour wine for her, and she drops tears in the cup. The bride asks who this is, and the king replies, One of my nieces from a far country, who came to do me honor, but only puts me to shame. You are not telling me the truth, says the bride. The king owns that it is Madel, his leman, with her seven sons. The bride recognizes a brooch* stiff with gold and silk. "There are but two such in all Flanders; I and my sister each had one." She tears the crown from her own head and puts it on her sister, saying, King, marry her in my place. The brooch is distinctly made the means of identification, which it by all likelihood was originally in all the Scandinavian ballads, though only Swedish C has retained (or restored) this feature.

The German ballad resembles Dutch A closely. The queen-mother gives Adelheid permission to go to the wedding, and her seven sons must walk before her. At the feast the king offers her to drink; she cannot drink for the grief he has caused her. The bride sees her weeping, and orders food and drink to be offered her (cf. English J 36), but

she cannot touch them. The king pretends that she is one of his nieces who has lived with him seven years [is fatigued by her journey, B]. The bride exclaims, I see the fore-span (by your fore-span, A), you are driving a pair! In A she asks the fair woman's name and country. Her country is over the Rhine, and thence she had been stolen. "Then you must be my sister," declares the bride somewhat hastily, gives up her seat and the crown, puts her ring on Adelheid's finger, and bids the news be sent to father and mother.

The lyric beauty of the Scottish version of this ballad, especially conspicuous in A, C, E, has been appreciatingly remarked by Grundtvig.

But Fair Annie's fortunes have not only been charmingly sung, as here; they have also been exquisitely *told* in a favorite lay of Marie de France, 'Le Lai del Freisne.' This tale, of Breton origin, is three hundred years older than any manuscript of the ballad. Comparison will, however, quickly show that it is not the source either of the English or of the Low German and Scandinavian ballad. The tale and the ballads have a common source, which lies further back, and too far for us to find.

The story of the lay is this.† There were two knights in Brittany, living on contiguous estates, and both married. The lady of one of the two gave birth to two boys, and the father sent information of the event to his neighbor and friend. His friend's wife was a scoffing, envious woman, "judging always for the worse," and said,

> I marvel much, thou messenger,
> Who was thy lordës counsellor,
> That did advise him not to spare
> This shame to publish everywhere,
> That his wife hath *two* children bore:
> Well may each man know therefore
> Two men have been with her in bower,‡
> Which is to both but small honour.

---

* "Voorgespan" again.

† Roquefort, Poésies de Marie de France, I, 138. There is a highly felicitous old English translation, unfortunately somewhat defective: Weber, Metrical Romances, I, 357, Ellis's Specimens, III, 282, what is missing being supplied in each case from the French.

‡ For this idea see Grimm's Rechtsalterthümer, p. 456 of the 2d ed., and Deutsche Sagen, 515, 534, 571; the English romance of Octavian, Weber, III, 162, vv 127–132, the French, in Conybeare's abridgment, p. 3, reprint of the Aungervyle Society, p. 23; the volksbuch Kaiser Octavianus, Simrock, II, 244; the Spanish ballad 'Espinelo,' Du-

In the course of the same year the woman that had made this hateful insinuation was brought to bed of twin girls. To save her reputation she was ready even to put one of them to death, but a favorite damsel in her house suggested a better way out of her perplexity, and that was to leave one of the children at the door of a convent. The child, wrapped in a rich pall that had been brought from Constantinople, with a jewelled ring bound to its arm to show that it was well born, was taken away in the night to a considerable distance, and was laid between the branches of a great ash-tree in front of a nunnery. In the morning it was discovered by the porter, who told his adventure to the abbess; and the abbess, having inspected the foundling, resolved to bring it up under the style of her niece. The girl, who received the name La Freisne from the tree in which she had been found, turned out a marvel of beauty and of all good qualities. A gentleman of the vicinity fell in love with her, and made large gifts to the monastery to constitute himself a lay-brother, and so have access to her without exciting suspicion. He obtained her love, and in the end induced her to fly with him to his château. This she did with sufficient deliberation to take with her the robe and ring which were the tokens of her birth; for the abbess had told her how she had been found in the ash, and had committed these objects to her care. She lived a good while with the knight as his mistress, and made herself loved by everybody; but his retainers had repeatedly remonstrated with him for not providing himself with a lawful successor, and at last forced him to marry the daughter and heiress of a gentleman near by. On the day of the nuptials La Freisne let no sign of grief or anger escape her, but devoted herself to the bride so amiably as even to win over the mother, who had accompanied her daughter, and had at first felt much uneasiness at the presence of a possible rival. Finding the marriage bed not decked with sufficient elegance, La Freisne took from a trunk the precious pall from Constantinople, and threw it on for a coverlet. When the bride's mother was about to put her daughter to bed, this robe was of course the first object that met her eyes. Her heart quaked. She sent for the chamberlain, and asked where the cloth came from. The chamberlain explained that "the damsel" had put it on to improve the appearance of the bed. The damsel was summoned, and told what she knew: the abbess who brought her up had given her the robe, and with it a ring, and charged her to take good care of them. A sight of the ring was asked; the lady cried, You are my daughter, and fainted. When she recovered she sent for her husband and confessed everything. The husband was only too happy to find that the damsel tant pruz è sage è bele was his daughter. The story was repeated to La Freisne, and then to the knight and to the archbishop who had performed the marriage ceremony. The marriage was dissolved the next day, and La Freisne formally espoused by the knight, who received with her half her father's heritage. The sister went home and made a rich marriage.

The common ground-work of the ballads and the lay is, that a man who has formed an irregular union with a woman whose family he does not know undertakes matrimony with another person, who is discovered on the day of the nuptials to be sister to his leman. A jewel in the possession of the latter, by itself or together with another token, reveals and proves the kinship in the lay and in the Scandinavian-German ballad, but there is no trace of such an instrumentality in the Scottish.

Single features, or even several features, of the story of Fair Annie or of La Freisne occur in many other ballads and tales, but there is no occasion to go into these resemblances here.

---

ran, I, 177, No 323, and again a 16th century ballad of Timoneda, II, 392, No 1346. This last may be the foundation of a broadside in the Pepys collection, I, 40, No 18: "The Lamenting Lady, who, for wrongs done by her to a poor woman for having two children at one burthen, was by the hand of God most strangely punished by sending her as many children at one birth as there are days in the year." But we have the same miracle in Grimm's Deutsche Sagen, No 578. Further, Grundtvig, V, 386, 'Grevens Datter af Vendel,' No 258, **E** 1; Li Reali di Francia, l. II, c. 42, p 180 of the edition of Venice, 1821. (Grundtvig.)

A Norse ballad has almost every point in 'Fair Annie' but the sisterly relation of leman and bride: see 'Slegfred og Brud,' Grundtvig, No 255, and 'Thomas o Yonderdale,' an apocryphal ballad of Buchan's, further on. Bare mention may be made of the beautiful Spanish romance 'Las dos Hermanas,' found also in Portuguese, in which the queen of a Moor or Turk discovers her sister in a slave who has been presented to her, or captured at her request.*

Translated after **A** by Schubart, p. 115; mainly after **E**, with stanzas from **A** and **C**, by Grundtvig, Engelske og skotske Folkeviser, No 28; after **E** by Wolff, Hausschatz, p. 209, Halle der Völker, I, 3; after **D** by Gerhard, p. 77; by Knortz, L. u. R. Alt-Englands, No 3, after Allingham.

Danish **F** by Jamieson, Popular Ballads, II, 103; by Prior, III, 300, No 148. Dutch **A** by Prior, III, 484.

———•———

A

Minstrelsy of the Scottish Border, II, 102, 1802, chiefly from the recitation of an old woman residing near Kirkhill, in West Lothian.

1 'It's narrow, narrow, make your bed,
　　And learn to lie your lane;
　For I'm ga'n oer the sea, Fair Annie,
　　A braw bride to bring hame.
　Wi her I will get gowd and gear;
　　Wi you I neer got nane.

2 'But wha will bake my bridal bread,
　　Or brew my bridal ale?
　And wha will welcome my brisk bride,
　　That I bring oer the dale?'

3 'It's I will bake your bridal bread,
　　And brew your bridal ale,
　And I will welcome your brisk bride,
　　That you bring oer the dale.'

4 'But she that welcomes my brisk bride
　　Maun gang like maiden fair;
　She maun lace on her robe sae jimp,
　　And braid her yellow hair.'

5 'But how can I gang maiden-like,
　　When maiden I am nane?
　Have I not born seven sons to thee,
　　And am with child again?'

6 She's taen her young son in her arms,
　　Another in her hand,
　And she's up to the highest tower,
　　To see him come to land.

7 'Come up, come up, my eldest son,
　　And look oer yon sea-strand,
　And see your father's new-come bride,
　　Before she come to land.'

8 'Come down, come down, my mother dear,
　　Come frae the castle wa!
　I fear, if langer ye stand there,
　　Ye'll let yoursell down fa.'

9 And she gaed down, and farther down,
　　Her love's ship for to see,
　And the topmast and the mainmast
　　Shone like the silver free.

10 And she's gane down, and farther down,
　　The bride's ship to behold,
　And the topmast and the mainmast
　　They shone just like the gold.

11 She's taen her seven sons in her hand,
　　I wot she didna fail;
　She met Lord Thomas and his bride,
　　As they came oer the dale.

* 'Las dos Hermanas,' Catalan, Castilian, Asturian. Milá, Observaciones, p. 117, No 19, = Briz, II, 159; p. 124, No 24, = Primavera, II, 38, No 130; Briz, II, 161. Milá, Romancerillo, p. 214, No 242, **A-E**, p. 216, No 242. Amador de los Rios, Historia de la Lit. Esp., VII, 455 f. Portuguese. 'Rainha e Captiva,' Almeida-Garrett, II, 193, No 11, 2d ed.; 'Romance de Branca-Flor,' Braga, Romanceiro Geral, p. 103, No 38; Romanceiro da Madeira, p. 211; Roméro e Braga, Cantos populares do Brazil, I, 41 ff, Nos 22, 23, II, 203. In some of these the queen identifies the captive by overhearing, while she lies in bed, words said or sung by her sister. In Chodzko, Chants de l'Ukraine, p. 88, No 17, the captive sister is replaced by a (Polish) mother in slavery among the Turks.

12 'You're welcome to your house, Lord Thomas,
        You're welcome to your land ;
    You're welcome with your fair ladye,
        That you lead by the hand.

13 'You're welcome to your ha's, ladye,
        Your welcome to your bowers ;
    You're welcome to your hame, ladye,
        For a' that's here is yours.'

14 'I thank thee, Annie ; I thank thee, Annie,
        Sae dearly as I thank thee ;
    You're the likest to my sister Annie,
        That ever I did see.

15 'There came a knight out oer the sea,
        And steald my sister away ;
    The shame scoup in his company,
        And land whereer he gae !'

16 She hang ae napkin at the door,
        Another in the ha,
    And a' to wipe the trickling tears,
        Sae fast as they did fa.

17 And aye she served the lang tables,
        With white bread and with wine,
    And aye she drank the wan water,
        To had her colour fine.

18 And aye she served the lang tables,
        With white bread and with brown ;
    And ay she turned her round about,
        Sae fast the tears fell down.

19 And he's taen down the silk napkin,
        Hung on a silver pin,
    And aye he wipes the tear trickling
        A' down her cheek and chin.

20 And aye he turn'd him round about,
        And smiled amang his men ;
    Says, Like ye best the old ladye,
        Or her that's new come hame ?

21 When bells were rung, and mass was sung,
        And a' men bound to bed,
    Lord Thomas and his new-come bride
        To their chamber they were gaed.

22 Annie made her bed a little forbye,
        To hear what they might say ;

'And ever alas !' Fair Annie cried,
    'That I should see this day !

23 'Gin my seven sons were seven young rats,
        Running on the castle wa,
    And I were a grey cat mysell,
        I soon would worry them a'.

24 'Gin my seven sons were seven young hares,
        Running oer yon lilly lee,
    And I were a grew hound mysell,
        Soon worried they a' should be.'

25 And wae and sad Fair Annie sat,
        And drearie was her sang,
    And ever, as she sobbd and grat,
        'Wae to the man that did the wrang !'

26 'My gown is on,' said the new-come bride,
        'My shoes are on my feet,
    And I will to Fair Annie's chamber,
        And see what gars her greet.

27 'What ails ye, what ails ye, Fair Annie,
        That ye make sic a moan ?
    Has your wine barrels cast the girds,
        Or is your white bread gone ?

28 'O wha was 't was your father, Annie,
        Or wha was 't was your mother ?
    And had ye ony sister, Annie,
        Or had ye ony brother ?'

29 'The Earl of Wemyss was my father,
        The Countess of Wemyss my mother ;
    And a' the folk about the house
        To me were sister and brother.'

30 'If the Earl of Wemyss was your father,
        I wot sae was he mine ;
    And it shall not be for lack o gowd
        That ye your love sall tyne.

31 'For I have seven ships o mine ain,
        A' loaded to the brim,
    And I will gie them a' to thee,
        Wi four to thine eldest son :
    But thanks to a' the powers in heaven
        That I gae maiden hame !'

B

Jamieson's Popular Ballads, II, 376, from the recitation of Mrs Arrot, of Aberbrothick.

1 THERE livd a lord on yon sea-side,
    And he thought on a wile,
How he would go over the saut sea
    A lady to beguile.

2 'O learn to mak your bed, Helen,
    And learn to ly your lane,
For I'm gaun over the saut seas
    A bright bride to bring hame.'

3 'How can I mak my bed,' she says,
    'Unless I mak it wide,
Whan I have seven o your sons
    To lie down by my side?

4 'And the first o your seven sons,
    He rides a milk-white steed;
The second o your seven sons
    He wears a milk-white weed.

5 'The third ane o your seven sons,
    He draws baith ale and wine;
The fourth ane o your seven sons,
    He serves you when you dine.

6 'The fifth ane o your seven sons,
    He can baith read and write;
And the sixth ane o your seven sons,
    He is a' your heart's delight.

7 'And the youngest o your seven sons,
    He sleeps on my breast-bane;
Whan him and I ly down at night,
    For him rest get I nane.'

8 'O wha will bake my bridal bread,
    And brew my bridal ale?
And wha will welcome my gae lady,
    That I bring oer the dale?

9 'And sin ye've taen the turn in hand,
    See that ye do it right,
And ilka chimly o the house,
    That they be dearly dight.'

10 O a' the day she washd and wrang,
    And a' the night she buik,
And she's awa to her chamber,
    To gie her young son suck.

11 'Come here, come here, my eldest son,
    And see what ye may see;
For yonder comes your father dear,
    Your mother-in-law side be.'

12 She's taen a cake o the best bread,
    A bottle o the best wine,
And a' the keys upon her arm,
    And to the yates she's gaen.

13 'Ye are welcome hame, gay lady,' she said,
    'And ay ye are welcome hame;
And sae is a' the gentlewomen
    That's wi you ridden and gane.

14 'You are welcome hame, gay lord' she said,
    'And ay ye are welcome hame;
And sae is a' the gentlemen
    That's wi you ridden and gane.'

15 She saird them up, she saird them down,
    She saird them till and frae;
But when she went behind their backs,
    The tear did blind her ee.

16 Whan day was gane, and night was come,
    And a' man boun to bed,
The bridegroom and the bonny bride
    In their chamber was laid.

17 Burd Helen and her seven sons
    Lay in a bower near by;
    .   .   .   .   .
      .   .   .   .   .

18 'If my seven sons were seven grey ratts,
    To rin frae wa to wa,
And I mysel a good grey cat,
    I would bite their back a-twa.

19 'If my seven sons were seven grey hares,
    And them to rin a race,
And I mysel a good greyhound,
    I would gie them a chace.'

20 Up and spak the bonny bride,
    In chamber where she lay:
'There is a lady in this bower,
    She will gae mad or day.'

21 'Lye still, lye still, my bonny bride,
    Lye still and tak a sleep;
It's but ane o my wine puncheons;
    Nae langer wad it keep.'

22 'King Henry was my father dear,
    Queen Catherine was my mother,
Lady Anne she was my sister dear,
    And Frederick was my brother.

23 'And whan I was six years of age,
    They ca'd me Mary Mild;
I was stown frae my father's yate,
    Whan I was but a child.'

24 Then up and spak the bonny bride,
    By her lord as she lay :

'Lye down, lye down, my dear sister,
    There's nae ill done for me.

25 'O seven ships conveyd me here,
    And seven came oer the main ;
And four o them shall stay wi you,
    And three convey me hame.

26 'But when I gae hame to my father's house,
    They will laugh me to scorn,
To come awa a wedded wife,
    Gae hame a maid the morn.'

C

Motherwell's manuscript, p. 351, from the recitation of Janet Holmes, an old woman in Kilbarchan, who derived the ballad from her mother ; July 18, 1825.

1 'LEARN to mak your bed, honey,
    And learn to lye your lane,
For I'm gaun owre the salt seas,
    A fair lady to bring hame.

2 'And with her I'll get gold and gear,
    With thee I neer got nane ;
I took you as a waaf woman,
    I leave you as the same.'

3 'What aileth thee at me, my lord,
    What aileth thee at me,
When seven bonnie sons I have born,
    All of your fair bodie ?

4 'The eldest of your seven sons,
    He can both read and write ;
The second of your sons, my lord,
    Can do it more perfyte.

5 'The third one of your sons, my lord,
    He waters your milk-white steed ;
The fourth one of your sons, my lord,
    With red gold shines his weed.

6 'The fifth one of your sons, my lord,
    He serves you when you dine ;
The sixth one now you do behold,
    How he walks out and in.

7 'The seventh one of your sons, my lord,
    Sucks hard at my breast-bane ;

When a' the house they are at rest,
    For him I can get nane.

8 'And if you leave me thus forlorn,
    A wainless wife I'll be,
For anybody's gold or gear
    That is beyond the sea.'

9 'O wha will bake my bridal bread,
    Or wha will brew my ale ?
Or wha will cook my kitchen neat,
    Or give my men their meal ?'

10 'For love I'll bake your bridal bread,
    To brew your ale I'm fain,
To cook your kitchen, as I have done,
    Till you return again.'

11 'O wha will bake my bridal bread,
    Or wha will brew my ale ?
Or wha will welcome my braw bride,
    That I bring owre the dale ?'

12 'For love I'll bake your bridal bread,
    For love I'll brew your ale,
And I will welcome your braw bride
    That you bring owre the dale.'

13 Her mind she keeped, but sair she weepd
    The time that he was gane

.   .   .   .   .   .

14 'Go up, go up, my eldest son,
    Go to the upmost ha,
And see if you see your father coming,
    With your mother-to-be-in-law.'

15 'Put on, put on, O mother dear,
  Put on your gouns so braw,
  For yonder is my father coming,
  With my mother-to-be-in-law.'

16 She's taen the wheat-bread in one hand,
  The red wines, which plenty were,
  And she's gane to the outmost gate,
  And bid them welcome there.

17 'You're welcome here, my brother dear,
  Ye're welcome, brother John;
  Ye're welcome a' my brethern dear,
  That has this journey gone.'

18 'I thank you, sister Annie,' he says,
  'And I thank you heartilie,
  And as you've welcomed home myself,
  You'll welcome my fair ladye.'

19 'If I had roses to my feet,
  And ribbons to my gown,
  And as leal a maid as your braw bride,
  I would speak without a frown.'

20 He's given her roses to her feet,
  And ribbons to her gown,
  And she has welcomed his braw bride,
  But weel that was her own!

21 'I thank you, sister Annie,' she says,
  'I thank you heartilie,
  And if I be seven years about this place,
  Rewarded you shall be.'

22 She served them up, she served them down,
  And she served all their cries,
  And aye as she came down the stair
  The tears fell from her eyes.

23 When mass was sung, and all bells rung,
  And all men boune for bed,
  The good lord and his fair lady
  Were in their chamber laid.

24 But poor Annie and her seven sons
  Was in a room hard by,
  And as she lay she sighed and wept,
  And thus began to cry:

25 'O were my sons transformed to cats,
  To speel this castle wa,
  And I mysell a red blood-hound
  That I might worry them a'!'

26 The bride she overhearing all,
  And sair she rued her fate:
  'Awauk, awauk, my lord,' she said,
  'Awauk, for well you may;
  For there's a woman in this gate
  That will go mad ere day.

27 'I fear she is a leman of thine,
  And a leman meek and mild;
  Get up and pack her down the stairs,
  Tho the woods were neer sae wild.'

28 'O yes, she is a leman of mine,
  And a leman meek and kind,
  And I will not pack her down the stairs,
  For a' the gear that's thine.'

29 'O wha's your father, Ann?' she says,
  'Or wha's your mother dear?
  Or wha's your sister, Ann?' she says,
  'Or brother? let me hear.'

30 'King Easter he's my father dear,
  The Queen my mother was;
  John Armstrang, in the west-airt lands,
  My eldest brother is.'

31 'Then I'm your sister, Ann,' she says,
  'And I'm a full sister to thee;
  You were stolen awa when very young,
  By the same lord's treacherie.

32 'I've seven ships upon the sea,
  All loaded to the brim,
  And five of them I'll give to thee,
  And twa shall carry me hame.

33 'My mother shall mak my tocher up,
  When I tell her how you thrive;
  For we never knew where you was gone,
  Or if you was alive.'

D

Herd, The Ancient and Modern Scots Songs, 1769, p. 307.

1 ' Wha will bake my bridal bread,
    And brew my bridal ale ?
  And wha will welcome my brisk bride,
    That I bring oer the dale ? '

2 ' I will bake your bridal bread,
    And brew your bridal ale,
  And I will welcome your brisk bride,
    That you bring oer the dale.'

3 ' But she that welcomes my brisk bride
    Maun gang like maiden fair ;
  She maun lace on her robe sae jimp,
    And braid her yellow hair.'

4 ' But how can I gang maiden-like,
    When maiden I am nane ?
  Have I not born seven sons to thee,
    And am with child agen ? '

5 She 's taen her young son in her arms,
    Another in her hand,
  And she 's up to the highest tower,
    To see him come to land.

6 ' You 're welcome to your house, master,
    You 're welcome to your land ;
  You 're welcome with your fair lady,
    That you lead by the hand.'

*   *   *   *   *

7 And ay she servd the lang tables,
    With white bread and with wine,
  And ay she drank the wan water,
    To had her colour fine.

8 Now he 's taen down a silk napkin,
    Hung on the silver pin,
  And ay he wipes the tears trickling
    Adown her cheek and chin.

E

Jamieson-Brown MS., fol. 20 ; Jamieson's Popular Ballads, II, 371.

1 ' O wha will bake my bridal bread,
    And brew my bridal ale ?
  Wha will welcome my bright bride,
    That I bring oer the dale ? '

2 ' O I will bake your bridal bread,
    An brew your bridal ale ;
  An I will welcome your bright bride,
    That you bring oer the dale.

3 ' O she that welcomes my bright bride
    Maun gang like maiden fair ;
  She maun lace her in her green cloathin,
    An braid her yallow hair.'

4 ' O how can I gang maiden like,
    Whan maiden I am nane ?
  Whan I ha born you seven sons,
    An am wi bairn again ? '

5 The lady stood in her bowr door
    An lookit oer the lan,

An there she saw her ain good lord,
    Leadin his bride by the han.

6 She 's dressd her sons i the scarlet red,
    Hersel i the dainty green,
  An tho her cheek lookd pale and wan,
    She well might ha been a queen.

7 She calld upon her eldest son :
    ' Look yonder what you see ;
  For yonder comes your father dear,
    Your step-mother him wi.

8 ' O you 'r welcome hame, my ain good lord,
    To your ha's but an your bowrs ;
  You 'r welcome hame, my ain good lord,
    To your castles an your towrs :
  Sae is your bright bride you beside,
    She 's fairer nor the flowers.'

9 ' O whatn a lady 's that ? ' she says,
    ' That welcoms you an me ?
  If I 'm lang lady about this place,
    Some good I will her dee.
  She looks sae like my sister Jane,
    Was stoln i the bowr frae me.'

10 O she has servd the lang tables,
    Wi the white bread an the wine ;
But ay she drank the wan water,
    To keep her colour fine.

11 , An she gid by the first table,
    An leugh amo them a' ;
But ere she reachd the second table,
    She let the tears down fa.

12 She 's taen a napkin lang an white,
    An hung 't upon a pin ;
It was to dry her watry eyes,
    As she went out and in.

13 Whan bells were rung, an mass was sung,
    An a' man boun to bed,
The bride but an the bonny bridegroom
    In ae chamber was laid.

14 She 's taen her harp intill her han,
    To harp this twa asleep ;
An ay as she harped an she sang,
    Full sorely did she weep.

15 · O seven fu fair sons I have born
    To the good lord o this place,
An I wish that they were seven hares,
    To run the castle race,

An I mysel a good gray houn,
    An I woud gi them chase.

16 ' O seven fu fair sons I have born
    To the good lord o this ha ;
I wish that they were seven rottons,
    To rin the castle wa,
An I mysell a good gray cat,
    I wot I woud worry them a'

17 ' The earle o Richmond was my father,
    An the lady was my mother,
An a' the bairns bisides mysel
    Was a sister an a brother.'

18 ' Sing on, sing on, ye gay lady,
    I wot ye hae sung in time;
Gin the earle o Richmond was your father,
    I wot sae was he mine.'

19 ' Rise up, rise up, my bierly bride ;
    I think my bed 's but caul ;
I woudna hear my lady lament
    For your tocher ten times taul.

20 ' O seven ships did bring you here,
    An an sal tak you hame ;
The leve I 'll keep to your sister Jane,
    For tocher she gat nane.'

F

Motherwell's MS., p. 385 ; Motherwell's Minstrelsy, p. 327. From the recitation of Mrs Rule, Paisley, August 16, 1825.

1 ' LEARN to mak your bed, Annie,
    And learn to lie your lane,
For I maun owre the salt seas gang,
    A brisk bride to bring hame.

2 ' Bind up, bind up your yellow hair,
    And tye it in your neck,
And see you look as maiden-like
    As the first day that we met.'

3 ' O how can I look maiden-like,
    When a maid I 'll never be ;
When seven brave sons I 've born to thee,
    And the eighth is in my bodie ?

4 ' The eldest of your sons, my lord,
    Wi red gold shines his weed ;
The second of your sons, my lord,
    Rides on a milk-white steed.

5 ' And the third of your sons, my lord,
    He draws your beer and wine,
And the fourth of your sons, my lord,
    Can serve you when you dine.

6 ' And the fift of your sons, my lord,
    He can both read and write,
And the sixth of your sons, my lord,
    Can do it maist perfyte.

7 ' And the sevent of your sons, my lord,
    Sits on the nurse's knee ;
And how can I look maiden-like,
    When a maid I 'll never be ?

8 ' But wha will bake your wedding bread,
          And brew your bridal ale ?
    Or wha will welcome your brisk bride,
          That you bring owre the dale ? '

9 ' I 'll put cooks in my kitchen,
          And stewards in my hall,
    And I 'll have bakers for my bread,
          And brewers for my ale ;
    But you 're to welcome my brisk bride,
          That I bring owre the dale.'

10 He set his fut into his ship,
          And his cock-boat on the main ;
    He swore it would be year and day
          Or he returned again.

11 When year and day was past and gane,
          Fair Annie she thocht lang,
    And she is up to her bower-head,
          To behold both sea and land.

12 ' Come up, come up, my eldest son,
          And see now what you see ;
    O yonder comes your father dear,
          And your stepmother-to-be.'

13 ' Cast off your gown of black, mother,
          Put on your gown of brown,
    And I 'll put off my mourning weeds,
          And we 'll welcome him home.'

14 She 's taken wine into her hand,
          And she has taken bread,
    And she is down to the water-side
          To welcome them indeed.

15 ' You 're welcome, my lord, you 're welcome,
              my lord,
          You 're welcome home to me ;
    So is every lord and gentleman
          That is in your companie.

16 ' You 're welcome, my lady, you 're welcome,
              my lady,
          You 're welcome home to me ;
    So is every lady and gentleman
          That 's in your companye.'

17 ' I thank you, my girl, I thank you, my girl,
          I thank you heartilie ;
    If I live seven years about this house,
          Rewarded you shall be.'

18 She served them up, she served them down,
          With the wheat bread and the wine ;
    But aye she drank the cold water,
          To keep her colour fine.

19 She servd them up, she servd them down,
          With the wheat bread and the beer ;
    But aye she drank the cauld water,
          To keep her colour clear.

20 When bells were rung and mass was sung,
          And all were boune for rest,
    Fair Annie laid her sons in bed,
          And a sorrowful woman she was.

21 ' Will I go to the salt, salt seas,
          And see the fishes swim ?
    Or will I go to the gay green-wood,
          And hear the small birds sing ? '

22 Out and spoke an aged man,
          That stood behind the door :
    ' Ye will not go to the salt, salt seas,
          To see the fishes swim ;
    Nor will ye go to the gay green-wood,
          To hear the small birds sing.

23 ' But ye 'll tak a harp, into your hand,
          Go to their chamber door,
    And aye ye 'll harp, and aye ye 'll murn,
          With the salt tears falling oer.'

24 She 's tane a harp into her hand,
          Went to their chamber door,
    And aye she harpd, and aye she murnd,
          With the salt tears falling oer.

25 Out and spak the brisk young bride,
          In bride-bed where she lay :
    ' I think I hear my sister Annie,
          And I wish weel it may ;
    For a Scotish lord staw her awa,
          And an ill death may he die !

26 ' Wha was your father, my girl,' she says,
          ' Or wha was your mother ?
    Or had you ever a sister dear,
          Or had you ever a brother ? '

27 ' King Henry was my father dear,
          Queen Easter was my mother,
    Prince Henry was my brother dear,
          And Fanny Flower my sister.'

28 'If King Henry was your father dear,
    And Queen Easter was your mother,
And Prince Henry was your brother dear,
    Then surely I 'm your sister.

29 'Come to your bed, my sister dear,
    It neer was wrangd for me,
But an ae kiss of his merry mouth,
    As we cam owre the sea.'

30 'Awa, awa, ye forenoon bride,
    Awa, awa frae me!
I wudna hear my Annie greet,
    For a' the gold I got wi thee.'

31 'There was five ships of gay red gold
    Came owre the seas with me;
It 's twa o them will take me hame,
    And three I 'll leave wi thee.

32 'Seven ships o white money
    Came owre the seas wi me;
Five o them I 'll leave wi thee,
    And twa 'll tak me hame,
And my mother will mak my portion up,
    When I return again.'

G

Communicated by Miss Margaret Reburn, as current in County Meath, Ireland, 1860–70.

1 SHE served them up, she served them down,
    She served them up with wine,
But still she drank the clear spring water,
    To keep her color fine.

2 'I must get up, she must sit down,
    She must sit in my place,
Or else be torn by wild horses
    And thrown over the gates.'

3 'You wont get up, she wont sit down,
    She wont sit in your place,
Nor yet be torn by wild horses,
    Nor thrown over the gates.'

4 She called up her seven sons,
    By one, by two, by three:
'I wish you were all seven gray-hounds,
    This night to worry me.'

5 'What ails you, fair Ellen? what ails you, fair?
    Or why do you sigh and moan?'
'The hoops are off my wine hogsheads,
    And my wine is overflown.'

H

From Dr Thomas Davidson. Aberdeenshire.

1 'BUT wha will bake my bridal bread,
    An brew my bridal ale,
And wha will welcome my bride hame,
    Is mair than I can tell.'

2 'It 's I will bake your bridal bread,
    And brew your bridal ale,
But wha will welcome your bride hame,
    It 'll need tae be yersel.'

3 An she 's hung up a silken towel
    Upon a golden pin,
. . . tae wipe her een,
    As she gaed but and ben.

I

Kinloch MSS, I, 155, May, 1827. "Composed of three recited versions obtained in the west of Scotland."

1 'LEARN to mak your bed, Annie,
    And learn to lie your lane;

For I am gaing oure the saut seas,
    A brisk bride to bring hame.

2 'Wi her I will get gowd and gear;
    Wi thee I neer gat nane;
I got thee as a waif woman,
    I 'll leave thee as the same.

3 ' O wha will bake my bridal bread,
    Or brew my bridal ale ?
Or wha welcome my brisk bride,
    That I 'll bring oure the dale ? '

4 ' O I will bake your bridal bread,
    And brew your bridal ale;
But I downa welcam your brisk bride
    That ye 'll bring frae the dale.'

5 ' She that welcomes my brisk bride,
    She maun look maiden-like;
She maun kaim doun her yellow locks,
    And lay them in her neck.'

6 ' O how can I look maiden-like,
    Whan maiden I am nane ?
For seven sons I hae born to thee,
    And the eighth lies in my wame.

7 ' But what aileth thee at me, my lord,
    What aileth thee at me,
Whan seven braw sons I 've born to thee,
    Out of my fair bodie ?

8 ' The first ane of your sons, my lord,
    Can baith read and write;
And the second of your sons, my lord,
    Can do it maist perfyte.

9 ' The third ane o your sons, my lord,
    Can water your grey steed ;
And the fourth ane o your sons, my lord,
    Can bake your bridal bread.

10 ' The fifth ane o your sons, my lord,
    Can serve ye whan ye dine;
And the sixth ane o your sons, my lord,
    Can brew your bridal wine.

11 ' The seventh ane o your sons, my lord,
    Lies close at my breist-bane ;
Whan a' the lave are fast asleep,
    It 's rest I can get nane.'

12 He set his foot into the stirrup,
    His hand upon the mane ;
Says, It will be year and day, ladie,
    Ere ye see me again.

13 Whan he had ae foot on the sea,
    The ither on dry lan,
' It will be year and day, ladie,
    Till I come back again.'

14 Whan year and day war past and gane,
    Fair Annie she thought lang;
And she went up to her hie tower,
    Wi a silk seam in her hand.

15 She lookit east, she lookit west,
    And south, below the sun,
And there she spied her ain gude lord,
    Coming sailing to the lan.

16 She called up her seven braw sons,
    By ane, twa, and by three:
' See, yonder comes your father,
    And your mother-for-to-be.'

17 And she called up her servants a':
    ' O come, behold and see !
O yonder comes your master dear,
    And a new mistress brings he.

18 ' Gae doun, gae doun, my eldest son,
    Into the outmost ha,
And if ye welcome ane o them,
    Be sure to welcome a'.'

19 Some ran east, and some ran west,
    And some ran to the sea;
There was na ane in a' his house
    To welcome his new ladie.

20 But Annie 's to her coffer gane,
    Tane out a silver kaim,
And she 's kaimd doun her yellow hair,
    As she a maid had been.

21 And Annie has kaimd her lang yellow locks,
    And laid them in her neck ;
And she 's awa to the saut, saut sea,
    To welcome his lady aff deck.

22 She durst na ca him her ain gude lord,
    For angering o the bride;
But she did ca him master dear,
    And I wat he was richt glad.

23 ' You 're welcome, you 're welcome, master,' she
    said,
    ' To your halls bot an your bouers ;
And sae are a' thir merry young men
    That come alang with you.

24 ' You 're welcome, you 're welcome, fair ladie,
    To your halls but an your bouers;
And sae are a' thir gay ladies;
    For a' that 's here is yours.'

25 ' I thank ye, I thank ye, fair maiden,
    I thank ye kindlie ;
If I be lang about this house,
    Rewarded ye sall be.

26 ' I have a brither o mine ain;
    He 's newly come from sea ;

I think it wad be a richt gude match
  To marry him and thee.'

27 'I thank ye, I thank ye, fair ladie;
  Gie your brither to whom like ye ;
But there 's never ane in this warld
  My wedding day sall see:
But one word o my master dear
  In private wad I be.'

*   *   *   *   *

28 The first dish that fair Annie set doun,
  She lookit baith pale and wan ;
The neist dish that fair Annie set doun,
  She was scarce able to stan.

29 'O is this your mistress, good lord,' she says,
  ' Although she looks modest and mild ?
Then we will hunt her frae our house
  Wi dogs and hawks sae wild.'

30 'She 's na my mistress, dear lady,' he says,
  ' Altho she looks modest and mild;
Nor will we hunt her frae our house
  Wi dogs and hawks sae wild.'

31 Whan bells war rung, and mass was sung,
  And a' men boun for bed,
The bonnie bride and the bridegroom
  In bride's bed they were laid.

32 Whan dinner was past, and supper was by,
  And a' were boun for bed,
Fair Annie and her seven sons
  In a puir bye-chamber war laid.

33 Fair Annie took out her virginals,
  And sadly did she play ;

.   .   .   .

.   .   .   .

34 'O gin my sons were yon grey rats,
  That climb the castle-wa,
And I mysel a bloody grey cat,
  I 'd rise and worry them a'.'

35 Then out and spak the bonny bride,
  In bride's bed whare she lay :
' I think this is like my sister Anne,
  That doth sae sadly play.'

36 'Lie still, lie still, my gay ladie,
  Lie still and sleep a wee;
It 's nathing but an auld servant,
  That waileth sae for me.'

37 'O gin my seven sons were seven young hares,
  That rin round the castle wa,
And I mysel a bluidy grewhund,
  I wad rise and worry them a'.'

38 The new bride waukenit in the nicht,
  And blew upon her horn:
' I think I hear my sister's voice,
  That was stown frae us a bairn.'

39 'Sleep on, sleep on, dear lady,' he says,
  ' It 's yon maiden in her dream,

.   .   .   .   .

40 'O wha was eer thy father, fair maid,
  Or wha was eer thy mither ?
Or wha was eer thy ae sister,
  Or wha was eer thy brither ? '

41 'King Henry was my father,' she said,
  ' Queen Elinore was my mither ;
Fair Marion was my ae sister,
  Earl Robert was my brither.'

42 'Sin King Henry was your father, fair maid,
  And Queen Elinore your mither,
O I am een your ae sister,
  And ye are just the ither.

43 'Come to your bed, fair Annie,' she said,
  ' Come to your bed full sune;
I may weel say, I daur weel say,
  There is na evil dune.

44 'Seven ships of gold did bring me here,
  But ane shall tak me hame;
Six I will leave to my sister Anne,
  To bring up her children young.

45 'But whan I gang to my father's ha,
  And tirl on the pin,
The meanest in a' my father's house
  Will ca me a forsaken ane.'

———◆———

J

Buchan's MSS, I, 66.

1 'LEARN, O learn, Fair Annie,' he said,
  ' O learn to lie your lane ;

For I am going ower the sea,
  To woo and to bring hame

2 ' A brighter and a fairer dame
  Than ever ye hae been ;

For I am going ower the sea,
    To chuse and bring her hame.'

3 ' What aileth thee, my ain gude lord,
    What aileth thee at me ?
For seven braw sons hae I born
    Unto your fair bodie.

4 ' The eldest o your sons, my lord,
    Is heir o a' your land;
The second o your braw young sons
    He rises at your right hand.

5 ' The third o your braw young sons
    He serves you when you dine;
The fourth o your braw sons, my lord,
    He brings to you the wine.

6 ' The fifth o your braw young sons
    Right well can use the pen ;
The sixth o your braw young sons,
    He 's travelling but and ben.

7 ' The seventh o your braw young sons,
    He lies on my breast-bane,
The fairest flower amo them a',
    That lay my sides between.'

8 ' But I am going ower the sea,
    To woo and to bring hame
A lady wi some gowd and gear;
    Wi you I never got nane.'

9 ' Ye staw me awa in twall years auld,
    Ye sought nae gowd wi me;
Ye put me to the schools o Ayr
    For fully years three.

10 ' But wha 'll be cook in your kitchen,
    And butler in your ha ?
And wha will govern your merry young men,
    When ye are far awa?'

11 ' O ye 'll be cook in my kitchen,
    And butler in my ha,
And ye 'll wait on my merry young men,
    And serve them ane and a'.'

12 ' But wha will bake your bridal bread,
    And wha will brew your ale ?
And wha will welcome that lady
    That ye bring ower the dale?

13 ' O ye will bake my bridal bread,
    And ye will brew my ale,
And ye will welcome that lady
    That I bring ower the dale.

14 ' Ye 'll bake bread, and ye 'll brew ale,
    For three score knights and ten ;

That day month I gang awa,
    The same day I 'll come again.'

15 ' O I will bake your bridal bread,
    And I will brew your ale ;
But oh, to welcome another woman
    My heart will nae be hale.'

16 ' Ye will put roses in your hair,
    And ribbons in your sheen,
And ye will look fair maiden like,
    Though maiden ye be nane.'

17 ' O I 'll put roses in my hair,
    And ribbons in my sheen,
And may be look as maiden-like
    As the bride ye bring hame.'

18 Two of his sons he sent before,
    And two rade by his side,
And three he left at hame wi her,
    She was the brightest bride.

19 As she was gazing her around,
    To view the rural plain,
And there she saw the bridal folk,
    Merrily coming hame.

20 ' Come here, come here, my boys a',
    Ye see not what I see ;
For here I see your fair father,
    And a step-mother to thee.

21 ' O shall I call him honey, Sandy,
    Husband, or my gude lord ?
Or shall I call him my gude master,
    Let well or woe betide ? '

22 ' Ye winna call him honey, mother,
    For angering o the bride;
But ye 'll call him your gude master,
    Let well or woe betide.'

23 She buskd her bonny boys in black,
    Herself in simple green,
A kaim o gowd upon her hair,
    As maiden she had been.

24 She 's taen the white bread in her lap,
    The wine glass in her hand,
And she 's gane out upo the green,
    To welcome the bride hame.

25 She woudna ca him her ain gude lord,
    For angering o the bride:
' Ye 're welcome hame, my gude master,
    Your lands lie braid and wide.'

26 ' O fair mat fa you, Fair Annie,
    Sae well 's ye 've welcomd me ;

Ye might hae welcomd my new bride ;
  Some gift to you she 'll gie.'

27 ' Ye 're welcome hame, ye new-come bride,
  To your ha's and your bowers ;
Ye 're welcome hame, my lady gay,
  Ye 're whiter than the flowers.'

28 ' O wha is this,' the bride did say,
  ' Sae well that welcomes me?
If I 'm lang lady o this place
  Some gift to her I 'll gie.

29 ' She 's likest to my dear sister
  That eer my eyes did see;
A landit lord staw her awa,
  An ill death mat he die !

30 ' I hae a brother here this day,
  Fairer ye neer did see ;
And I woud think nae ill a match
  Unto this fair ladie.'

31 ' Ye 'll wed your brother on a stock,
  Sae do ye on a stane;
I 'll wed me to the kingdom of heaven,
  For I 'll neer wed a man.'

32 She servd the footmen o the beer,
  The nobles o the wine;
But nane did cross her pale, pale lips,
  For changing o her min.

33 When she came in unto the room
  She leuch amo them a',
But when she turnd her back about
  She loot the saut tears fa.

34 She hanged up a silken cloath
  Upon a siller pin;
It was to dry her twa blue eyes,
  As she went out and in.

35 Her heart wi sorrow sair was filld,
  Her breast wi milk ran out;
She aft went to a quiet chamber,
  And let her young son suck.

36 ' There is a woman in this house
  This day has served me;
But I 'll rise up, let her sit down,
  She 's ate, that I may see.

37 ' O wha is this,' the bride coud say,
  ' That serves this day sae well?
And what means a' this bonny boys,
  That follow at her heel ? '

38 ' This is my sister, Fair Annie,
  That serves this day sae well,
And these are a' her bauld brothers,
  That follow at her heel.'

39 Then out it speaks the new-come bride,
  Was full o jealousie:
' I fear there 's something new, my lord,
  Ye mean to hide frae me.

40 ' But if she be your light leman
  Has me sae sair beguild,
She shall gae out at my window,
  And range the woods sae wild.'

41 When day was dane, and night drew on,
  And a' man bound for bed,
The bridegroom and the new-come bride
  In ae chamber were laid.

42 The lady being left alone,
  Nursing her fair young son,
She has taen up her gude lord's harp,
  She harped and she sung.

43 ' Seven braw sons hae I born
  To the lord o this place;
I wish they were seven hares
  To run the castle race,
And I mysel a gude greyhound,
  To gie them a' a chace.'

44 ' Lie near, lie near, my ain gude lord,
  Lie near and speak wi me ;
There is a woman in the house,
  She will be wild ere day.'

45 ' Lie still, lie still, my new-come bride,
  Lie still and take your rest ;
The pale 's out o my wine-puncheon,
  And lang it winna rest.'

46 She held the harp still in her hand,
  To harp them baith asleep,
And aye she harped and she sang,
  And saut tears she did weep.

47 ' Seven braw sons hae I born
  To the gude lord o this ha;
I wish that they were seven brown rats,
  To climb the castle wa,
And I mysel a gude grey cat,
  To take them ane and a'.'

48 ' Lie near, lie near, my ain gude lord,
  Lie near and speak wi me;
There is a woman in this house,
  She will be wild ere day.'

49 ' Lie yond, lie yond, my new-come bride,
        My sheets are wonderous cauld;
    I woudna hear my love's lament
        For your gowd ten thousand fauld.'

50 ' O wae be to you, ye fause lord,
        Some ill death mat ye die!
    For that 's the voice o my sister Ann,
        Was stown frae yont the sea.'

51 ' Fair mat fa ye, ye buirdly bride,
        A gude death mat ye die!
    For that 's the voice o your sister Ann,
        Was stown frae yont the sea;
    I came seeking Annie's tocher,
        I was not seeking thee.'

52 ' Seven gude ships I hae brought here,
        In seven I 'se gae hame;
    And a' the gowd that I brought here,
        It 's a' gang back again.'

53 ' Seven ships they brought you here,
        But ye 'll gang hame in ane;
    Ye 'll leave the rest to tocher Ann,
        For wi her I got nane.'

54 ' Seven ships they brought me here,
        But I 'll gang hame in ane;
    I 'll get my sister's eldest son
        To hae me maiden hame.

55 ' My father wants not gowd nor gear,
        He will get me a man;
    And happy, happy will he be
        To hear o his daughter Ann.

56 ' I hae my sheen upon my feet,
        My gloves upon my hand,
    And ye 'll come to your bed, Annie,
        For I 've dane you nae wrang.'

————◆————

C. ' Fair Annie ' I took this day from the recitation
      of Janet Holmes, an old woman in Kilbar-
      chan. It was, as she described it, a "lang
      rane " of her mother's. July 18, 1825.
      Motherwell.
    1¹. honey *is probably a corruption of* Annie.
    5⁴. his wig.
    19³. I *must be understood,* I *as leal, but does not
        require to be inserted.*
    20⁴. *Possibly not correct.* To all *would, no
        doubt, be an easy reading, but the abrupt
        exclamation is more like nature.*
    29¹. Oh.
E. 11². laugh.   14³. harpd.   20¹. you hame.
F. 12³. Oh.   22³. Ye wilt.
I. 28¹. sat.   45². tirls.
    41 ff. *In one of the Kinloch versions thus:*

        ' King Henry is my father,' she says,
            ' Queen Orvis is my mither,
        And a' the bairns about the house
            Are just my sister and brither.'

        ' O if ye be ane o thae, Fair Anne,
            Sure I 'm ane o' the same,
        And come to your gude lord, Anne,
            And be ye blythe again.

        ' For he never wed me for his love,
            But for my tocher fee,

And I am as free o him this day
    As the bairn on the nurse's knee.'

J. 36². hae served.
    *The following more obvious and entire
    ly superfluous interpolations have been
    omitted from the text.*
    After 9 :

        But ye were feard the Duke of York
            Should come and bide wi me,
        As he showed kindness and respect,
            Which greatly grieved thee.

    After 18 :

        But it fell ance upon a day,
            'T was aye day by it lane,
        Fair Annie was washing her fingers,
            Above a marble stane.

    After 28 :

        O he that staw my ae sister
            Did leave my bower full bare ;
        I wish a sharp sword at his breast,
            Cauld iron be his share !

        He looked ower his right shoulder,
            A light laugh then gie he ;

Said, Hear na ye my new-come bride,
  Sae sair as she brands me ?

The bride she patted wi her lips,
  She winked wi her ee,
Yet never thought by the words he
    spake
  'T was her sister, Annie.

After 35 :

When they had eaten and well drunken,
  And all had fared fine,
The knight he called his butlers all,
  For to serve out the wine.

After 38 :

Then out it speaks an English lord,
  A smart young lord was he :
' O if she be a maiden fair,
  Wi her I 'se wedded be.'

The bridegroom gae a laugh at that
  Amang his merry young men ;
Says, There 's a hynd chiel in the house
  Runs far nearer her mind.

After 53 :

O if this be my sister dear,
  It 's welcome news to me ;
I woud hae gien her thrice as much
  Her lovely face to see.

63

CHILD WATERS

A. ' Childe Waters,' Percy MS., p. 274 ; Hales and Furnival, II, 269.

B. a. ' Burd Ellen,' Jamieson's Brown MS., fol. 22. **b.** ' Lord John and Bird Ellen,' A. Fraser Tytler's Brown MS., No 9.

C. ' Lady Margaret,' Kinloch's annotated copy of his Ancient Scottish Ballads, p. 180.

D. Kinloch MSS, VII, 325.

E. 'Fair Margaret,' Harris MS., No 8, p. 12 b.

F. Jamieson's Popular Ballads, I, 114, from Mrs Arrot of Arberbrothick.

G. ' Cruel William,' Buchan's MSS, II, 129.

H. ' Burd Alone,' Motherwell's MS., p. 277.

I. Communicated by Dr Davidson, derived from Old Deer, Aberdeenshire.

J. ' Burd Helen,' Buchan's Ballads of the North of Scotland, II, 30.

A WAS printed in Percy's Reliques, III, 58, ed. 1765, with comparatively few changes. B a was published by Jamieson, from Mrs Brown's manuscript, in his Popular Ballads, I, 113, with some slight variation from the text, many acknowledged interpolations, and the addition of three sentimental stanzas to make Burd Ellen die just as her enduring all things is to be rewarded. In this tragic close, Jamieson was anticipated by Mrs Hampden Pye, in her ' Earl Walter,' 1771, Evans's Old Ballads, II, 208, 1777. C is given as it appears in Kinloch's annotated copy of his Ancient Scottish Ballads, where ten stanzas are inserted to enlarge and complete the copy published in 1827. This enlarged copy was communicated to Chambers, and seven of the supplementary stanzas were introduced into his compilation, The Scottish Ballads, p. 193. These supplementary stanzas, some of them certainly, and we may suppose all, belonged to a copy of which only the concluding portion, here given as D, is elsewhere preserved.

The variations in the several versions of this charming ballad, which has perhaps no superior in English, and if not in English perhaps nowhere,* are not material, and the story may therefore be given as it runs in A, the oldest copy. Fair Ellen comes to Child Waters, and tells him that her gown, which was too wide, is now too narrow. He bids her be content and take two shires of land; she would rather have one kiss from his mouth than Cheshire and Lancashire both. He must ride far into the North the next day; she asks to be his foot-page. This she may be if she will shorten her gown and clip her locks, so as not to be known for a woman. He rides hard all day, and she keeps up with him barefoot. They come to a broad piece of salt water; he lets her get through as she can, but Our Lady bears up her chin. Then he points out a splendid hall, where are four and twenty ladies, and the fairest is his love and wife. God give both good! is all she says. Arrived there, Ellen takes his horse to the stable. At bed-time he sends her to the town, to bring him the fairest lady that can be found, to sleep in his arms, and to bring this lady in *her* arms, for filing of her feet. Ellen lies at the foot of the bed, for want of other place, and before dawn is roused by Child Waters to feed his horse. The pains of travail come on her in the stable; Child Waters' mother hears her moans, and bids him get up. He stands at the stable-door and listens. Ellen sings:

> Lullaby, dear child, dear!
> I would thy father were a king,
> Thy mother laid on a bier!

This moves even his sturdy heart; he tells Ellen to be of good cheer, for the bridal and the churching shall both be on one day.

* Caution is imperative where so much ground is covered, and no man should be confident that he can do absolute justice to poetry in a tongue that he was not born to; but foreign poetry is as likely to be rated too high as to be undervalued. I will give Grundtvig's impression, at least as competent a judge of popular ballads as ever spoke: "Den

In B, C, E, G, I, J the man relents so far as, when they are in the water, to ask her to ride. She will not, C, E, I; he takes her on at a stone which stands in the middle of the stream, B, G, J. The stream is Clyde in B, C, E, G, J; the Tay in I. In C, E, F, H he tells her after they have passed the water, that it is three and thirty miles to his house; a (poetically) superfluous and meddling parrot says it is but three. In C, G he tells her that she will have a serving-man for a husband, and in H that he has already wife and bairns.

One stroke in A, the sending of Ellen to fetch a woman from the town, is wanting in the other versions, decidedly to their advantage. This exaggeration of insult, submitting to which only degrades the woman, is paralleled, though not quite reached, by the paramour in the forest in the otherwise exquisitely refined tale of The Nut-Brown Maid. As for the ballad, the disagreeable passage may be an insertion of some unlucky singer, and the perfect truth to nature and remarkably high taste of The Nut-Brown Maid, in every other particular, would almost drive us to assume an interpolation in this case too.

E 1, 2, 16, F 2, 3 show contact with the ballad of 'Lizzie Lindsay;' the passing of the water, particularly in E 8–12, with 'The Knight and Shepherd's Daughter;' and again, H 21.

An exceedingly popular Scandinavian ballad is manifestly of the same source, though the story is told in a very different way, the cruel trials to which the woman's love is put being entirely lacking: Danish, 'Jomfru og Stalddreng,' Grundtvig, V, 171, No 267, A-A. Swedish, A, 'Liten Kerstin Stalldräng,' Afzelius, II, 15, No 33; B, 'Stolts Botelid Stalldräng,' Afzelius, II, 20, No 34; C-E, 'Liten Kerstin Stalldräng,' Arwidsson, II, 179, No 109, Hofberg's Nerikes gamla Minnen, p. 254, Öberg in Aminson, I, 28; F-I, from Cavallius and Stephens's manuscript collection, Grundt-

Rigdom paa stemningsfuld Lyrik, som i det hele taget hjemler den engelsk-skotske Folkevise den højeste pœtiske Rang mellem alle sine Søskende, kommer ogsaa her til Syne, fordelt paa alle Opskrifter." Danmarks gamle Folkeviser, V, 187.

vig, V, 217 f; J, 'Liten Kerstin och Dane-
Peter,' Wigström, Folkdiktning, I, 66, No
32. Norwegian, A, 'Liti Kersti som stall-
dreng,' Landstad, p. 605, No 78; B-E, Grundtvig, V, 218–20; F, Landstad, p. 605, note.
(Several of these are only a verse or two.)
Danish A-F are from manuscripts of the sixteenth or seventeenth century; G was printed
at the end of the seventeenth; the other copies
are from recent tradition, but nevertheless
point to a higher antiquity than those which
were taken down earlier.   There is naturally
much variation in details among so many
copies, and it will be sufficient to indicate the
general character of the story.   A young
woman, who may be called Kirstin, clips her
hair and puts on man's clothes, seeks service
at court, and is taken as stable-boy, at the
instance of a man (often the king's son, or of
other high rank) who may be called Peter,
with whom she, in some copies, seems to have
had a previous connection.   Peter, as an ac-
commodation, lets the stable-boy sleep with
him.   In the course of time Kirstin cannot do
duty any more, cannot buckle on spurs, is ill
and requires woman's assistance, which the
queen renders.   She gives birth to twins in
the stable (among the horses' legs, as in English, B 30, F 30).   A merry wedding follows.*
   Another Scandinavian ballad has a limited
resemblance to 'Child Waters:' Danish, 'Den
trofaste Jomfru,' Grundtvig, IV, 494, No 249,
A-I; 'Den fredløse,' Kristensen, II, 191, No
57 (A-C), J-L.   Swedish, A, 'De Sju Gull-
bergen,' Afzelius, III, 71, No 79; B, C, from

Cavallius and Stephens's collection, Grundtvig, IV, 507 f.   Norwegian, A, 'Herre Per
og stolt Margit,' Landstad, p. 590, No 74;
B, Herr' Nikelus, Landstad, p. 594, No 75.
The ballad begins like Danish 'Ribold og
Guldborg' and 'Kvindemorderen.' A knight
carries off a maid, making her fine promises,
among which gold castles commonly figure.
He takes her over a very wide piece of water,
an arm of the sea, on his horse in most versions; in Danish B, K they swim it.   When
they come to land, she asks Where are the
promised castles? Danish C, D, J, K, L, Norwegian A, B.   He tells her that he is a pen-
niless outlaw (wanting in Swedish A, C); she
offers the gold she has brought with her to
buy him his peace (wanting in Swedish A, C,
Norwegian B).   He tells her he has another
love; she is willing to be their servant (wanting in Danish A, B, C, I, Norwegian B).
Here he ceases his trial of her; he is a royal,
or very opulent, person, she is to have a troop
of servants, the castles are not in the air, and
all ends happily.

   Percy's edition of A is translated (freely)
by Bürger, 'Graf Walter,' and Bürger's version is revised, to bring it slightly nearer the
original, by Bothe, Volkslieder, p. 199.   Percy
is translated by Bodmer, I, 41.   I is translated by Gerhard, p. 117, and Aytoun's compilation, I, 239, by Knortz, Schottische Balladen, p. 11.   The Danish ballad is translated
by Prior, III, 25, after Danske Viser, IV, 116,
Syv, Fourth Part, No 31, Grundtvig's G c.

A

Percy MS., p. 274; Hales and Furnivall, II, 269.

1 CHILDE Watters in his stable stoode,
      And stroaket his milke-white steede;
   To him came a ffaire young ladye
      As ere did weare womans wee[de].

* Except in Swedish A, where, apparently by a mixture
of two stories, the issue is tragic.

2 Saies, Christ you saue, good Chyld Waters!
      Sayes, Christ you saue and see!
   My girdle of gold, which was too longe,
      Is now to short ffor mee.

3 'And all is with one chyld of yours,
      I ffeele sturre att my side;
   My gowne of greene, it is to strayght;
      Before it was to wide.'

4 ' If the child be mine, Faire Ellen,' he sayd,
   ' Be mine, as you tell mee,
   Take you Cheshire and Lancashire both,
   Take them your owne to bee.

5 ' If the child be mine, Ffaire Ellen,' he said,
   ' Be mine, as you doe sweare,
   Take you Cheshire and Lancashire both,
   And make that child your heyre.'

6 Shee saies, I had rather haue one kisse,
   Child Waters, of thy mouth,
   Then I wold haue Cheshire and Lancashire
     both,
   That lyes by north and south.

7 ' And I had rather haue a twinkling,
   Child Waters, of your eye,
   Then I wold haue Cheshire and Lancashire
     both,
   To take them mine oune to bee.'

8 ' To-morrow, Ellen, I must forth ryde
   Soe ffarr into the north countrye ;
   The ffairest lady that I can ffind,
   Ellen, must goe with mee.'
   ' And euer I pray you, Child Watters,
   Your ffootpage let me bee ! '

9 ' If you will my ffootpage be, Ellen,
   As you doe tell itt mee,
   Then you must cutt your gownne of greene
   An inche aboue your knee.

10 ' Soe must you doe your yellow lockes,
   Another inch aboue your eye ;
   You must tell noe man what is my name ;
   My ffootpage then you shall bee.'

11 All this long day Child Waters rode,
   Shee ran bare ffoote by his side ;
   Yett was he neuer soe curteous a knight
   To say, Ellen, will you ryde ?

12 But all this day Child Waters rode,
   Shee ran barffoote thorow the broome ;
   Yett he was neuer soe curteous a knight
   As to say, Put on your shoone.

13 ' Ride softlye,' shee said, ' Child Watters ;
   Why doe you ryde soe ffast ?
   The child which is no mans but yours
   My bodye itt will burst.'

14 He sayes, Sees thou yonder water, Ellen,
   That fflowes from banke to brim ?
   ' I trust to god, Child Waters,' shee said,
   ' You will neuer see mee swime.'

15 But when shee came to the waters side,
   Shee sayled to the chinne :
   ' Except the lord of heauen be my speed,
   Now must I learne to swime.'

16 The salt waters bare vp Ellens clothes,
   Our Ladye bare vpp he[r] chinne,
   And Child Waters was a woe man, good Lord,
   To ssee Faire Ellen swime.

17 And when shee ouer the water was,
   Shee then came to his knee :
   He said, Come hither, Ffaire Ellen,
   Loe yonder what I see !

18 ' Seest thou not yonder hall, Ellen ?
   Of redd gold shine the yates ;
   There 's four and twenty ffayre ladyes,
   The ffairest is my wordlye make.

19 ' Seest thou not yonder hall, Ellen ?
   Of redd gold shineth the tower ;
   There is four and twenty ffaire ladyes,
   The fairest is my paramoure.'

20 ' I doe see the hall now, Child Waters,
   That of redd gold shineth the yates ;
   God giue good then of your selfe,
   And of your wordlye make !

21 ' I doe see the hall now, Child Waters,
   That of redd gold shineth the tower ;
   God giue good then of your selfe,
   And of your paramoure ! '

22 There were four and twenty ladyes,
   Were playing att the ball,
   And Ellen, was the ffairest ladye,
   Must bring his steed to the stall.

23 There were four and twenty faire ladyes
   Was playing att the chesse ;
   And Ellen, shee was the ffairest ladye,
   Must bring his horsse to grasse.

24 And then bespake Child Waters sister,
   And these were the words said shee :

You haue the prettyest ffootpage, brother,
   That euer I saw with mine eye ;

25 ' But *that* his belly it is soe bigg,
   His girdle goes wonderous hye ;
   And eu*er* I pray you, Child Waters,
   Let him goe into the chamber with mee.'

26 ' It is more meete for a little ffootpage,
   That has run through mosse and mire,
   To take his supper vpon his knee
   And sitt downe by the kitchin fyer,
   Then to goe into the chamber with any ladye
   That weares soe [rich] attyre.'

27 But when thé had supped euery one,
   To bedd they took the way ;
   He sayd, Come hither, my little footpage,
   Harken what I doe say.

28 And goe thee downe into yonder towne,
   And low into the street ;
   The ffairest ladye *that* thou can find,
   Hyer her in mine armes to sleepe,
   And take her vp in thine armes two,
   For filinge of her ffeete.

29 Ellen is gone into the towne,
   And low into the streete ;
   The fairest ladye *that* shee cold find
   Shee hyred in his armes to sleepe,
   And tooke her in her armes two,
   For filing of her ffeete.

30 ' I pray you now, good Child Waters,
   That I may creepe in att yo*ur* bedds feete ;
   For there is noe place about this house
   Where I may say a sleepe.'

31 This [night] and itt droue on affterward
   Till itt was neere the day :

He sayd, Rise vp, my litle ffoote-page,
   And giue my steed corne and hay ;
   And soe doe thou the good blacke oates,
   That he may carry me the better away.

32 And vp then rose Ffaire Ellen,
   And gaue his steed corne and hay,
   And soe shee did and the good blacke oates,
   That he might carry him the better away.

33 Shee layned her backe to the manger side,
   And greiuouslye did groane ;
   And *that* beheard his mother deere,
   And heard her make her moane.

34 Shee sayd, Rise vp, thou Child Waters,
   I thinke thou art a cursed man ;
   For yonder is a ghost in thy stable,
   That greiuouslye doth groane,
   Or else some woman laboures of child,
   Shee is soe woe begone.

35 But vp then rose Child Waters,
   And did on his shirt of silke ;
   Then he put on his other clothes
   On his body as white as milke.

36 And when he came to the stable-dore,
   Full still *that* hee did stand,
   That hee might heare now Faire Ellen,
   How shee made her monand.

37 Shee said, Lullabye, my owne deere child !
   Lullabye, deere child, deere !
   I wold thy father were a king,
   Thy mother layd on a beere !

38 ' Peace now,' he said, ' good Faire Ellen,
   And be of good cheere, I thee pray,
   And the bridall and the churching both,
   They shall bee vpon one day.'

B

a. Jamieson's Brown MS., fol. 22, taken down from Mrs Brown's recitation before 1783. **b.** A. Fraser Tytler's Brown MS., No 9, as recited by Mrs Brown in 1800.

1 ' I WARN ye all, ye gay ladies,
   That wear scarlet an brown,
   That ye dinna leave your father's house,
   To follow young men frae town.'

2 ' O here am I, a lady gay,
   That wears scarlet an brown,
   Yet I will leave my father's house,
   An follow Lord John frae the town.'

3 Lord John stood in his stable-door,
   Said he was bound to ride ;
   Burd Ellen stood in her bowr-door,
   Said she 'd rin by his side.

4 He 's pitten on his cork-heeld shoone,
  An fast awa rade he ;
  She 's clade hersel in page array,
  An after him ran she.

5 Till they came till a wan water,
  An folks do ca it Clyde ;
  Then he 's lookit oer his left shoulder,
  Says, Lady, can ye wide ?

6 ' O I learnt it i my father house,
  An I learnt it for my weal,
  Wenneer I came to a wan water,
  To swim like ony eel.'

7 But the firstin stap the lady stappit,
  The water came til her knee ;
  ' Ohon, alas ! ' said the lady,
  ' This water 's oer deep for me.'

8 The nextin stap the lady stappit,
  The water came till her middle ;
  An sighin says that gay lady,
  I 've wat my gouden girdle

9 The nextin stap the lady stappit,
  The water came till her pap ;
  An the bairn that was in her twa sides
  For caul begane to quake.

10 ' Lye still, lye still, my ain dear babe,
   Ye work your mither wae ;
   Your father rides on high horse-back,
   Cares little for us twae.'

11 O about the midst o Clyden water
   There was a yeard-fast stane ;
   He lightly turnd his horse about,
   An took her on him behin.

12 ' O tell me this now, good Lord John,
   An a word ye dinna lee,
   How far it is to your lodgin,
   Whare we this night maun be ? '

13 ' O see you nae yon castle, Ellen,
   That shines sae fair to see ?
   There is a lady in it, Ellen,
   Will sunder you an me.

14 ' There is a lady in that castle
   Will sunder you and I : '
   ' Betide me well, betide me wae,
   I sal go there an try.'

15 ' O my dogs sal eat the good white bread,
   An ye sal eat the bran ;
   Then will ye sigh, an say, alas !
   That ever I was a man ! '

16 ' O I sal eat the good white bread,
   An your dogs sal eat the bran ;
   An I hope to live an bless the day,
   That ever ye was a man.'

17 ' O my horse sal eat the good white meal,
   An ye sal eat the corn ;
   Then will ye curse the heavy hour
   That ever your love was born.'

18 ' O I sal eat the good white meal,
   An your horse sal eat the corn ;
   An I ay sall bless the happy hour
   That ever my love was born.'

19 O four an twenty gay ladies
   Welcomd Lord John to the ha,
   But a fairer lady then them a'
   Led his horse to the stable sta.

20 An four an twenty gay ladies
   Welcomd Lord John to the green,
   But a fairer lady than them a'
   At the manger stood alane.

21 Whan bells were rung, an mass was sung,
   Ar a' men boun to meat,
   Burd Ellen at a bye-table
   Amo the foot-men was set.

22 ' O eat an drink, my bonny boy,
   The white bread an the beer : '
   ' The never a bit can I eat or drink,
   My heart 's sae full of fear.'

23 ' O eat an drink, my bonny boy,
   The white bread an the wine : '
   ' O I canna eat nor drink, master,
   My heart 's sae full of pine.'

24 But out it spake Lord John's mother,
   An a wise woman was she :
   ' Whare met ye wi that bonny boy,
   That looks sae sad on thee ?

25 ' Sometimes his cheek is rosy red,
   An sometimes deadly wan ;
   He 's liker a woman big wi bairn,
   Than a young lord's serving man.'

26 'O it makes me laugh, my mother dear,
　　Sic words to hear frae thee ;
　He is a squire's ae dearest son,
　　That for love has followd me.

27 'Rise up, rise up, my bonny boy,
　　Gi my horse corn an hay : '
　'O that I will, my master dear,
　　As quickly as I may.'

28 She's taen the hay under her arm,
　　The corn intill her han,
　An she's gane to the great stable,
　　As fast as eer she can.

29 'O room ye roun, my bonny broun steeds,
　　O room ye near the wa;
　For the pain that strikes me thro my sides
　　Full soon will gar me fa.'

30 She's leand her back against the wa ;
　　Strong travail seizd her on ;
　An even amo the great horse feet
　　Burd Ellen brought forth her son.

31 Lord John'[s] mither intill her bowr
　　Was sitting all alone,
　Whan, i the silence o the night,
　　She heard fair Ellen's moan.

32 'Won up, won up, my son,' she says,
　　'Go se how a' does fare ;
　For I think I hear a woman's groans,
　　An a bairn greeting sair.'

33 O hastily he gat him up,
　　Stayd neither for hose nor shoone,
　An he's doen him to the stable-door,
　　Wi the clear light o the moon.

34 He strack the door hard wi his foot,
　　An sae has he wi his knee,
　An iron locks an iron bars
　　Into the floor flung he :
　'Be not afraid, Burd Ellen,' he says,
　　'Ther's nane come in but me.'

35 Up he has taen his bonny young son,
　　An gard wash him wi the milk;
　An up has he taen his fair lady,
　　Gard row her in the silk.

36 'Cheer up your heart, Burd Ellen,' he says,
　　'Look nae mair sad nor wae ;
　For your marriage an your kirkin too
　　Sal baith be in ae day.'

C

Kinloch's annotated copy of his Ancient Scottish Ballads,
Kinloch MSS, IV, 180.

1 'THE corn is turning ripe, Lord John,
　　The nuts are growing fu,
　And ye are bound for your ain countrie,
　　Fain wad I go wi you.'

2 'Wi me, Margret, wi me, Margret,
　　What wad ye do wi me?
　I 've mair need o a pretty little boy,
　　To wait upon my steed.'

3 'It's I will be your pretty little boy,
　　To wait upon your steed ;
　And ilka town that we come to,
　　A pack of hounds I 'll lead.'

4 'My hounds will eat o the bread o wheat,
　　And ye of the bread of bran ;
　And then you will sit and sigh,
　　That eer ye loed a man.'

5 The first water that they cam to,
　　I think they call it Clyde,
　He saftly unto her did say,
　　Lady Margret, will ye ride ?

6 The first step that she steppit in,
　　She steppit to the knee ;
　Says, Wae be to ye, waefu water,
　　For through ye I maun be.

7 The second step that she steppit in,
　　She steppit to the middle,
　And sighd, and said, Lady Margaret,
　　'I 've staind my gowden girdle.'

8 The third step that she steppit in,
　　She steppit to the neck;
　The pretty babe within her sides,
　　The cauld it garrd it squake.

9 'Lie still my babe, lie still my babe,
　　Lie still as lang's ye may,
　For your father rides on horseback high,
　　Cares little for us twae.'

10 It's whan she cam to the other side,
　　She sat doun on a stane;
　Says, Them that made me, help me now,
　　For I am far frae hame.

11 'How far is it frae your mither's bouer,
　　Gude Lord John tell to me?'
　'It's therty miles, Lady Margaret,
　　It's therty miles and three:
　And yese be wed to ane o her serving men,
　　For yese get na mair o me.'

12 Then up bespak the wylie parrot,
　　As it sat on the tree,
　'Ye lee, ye lee, Lord John,' it said,
　　'Sae loud as I hear ye lee.

13 'Ye say it's therty miles frae your mither's
　　bouer,
　　Whan it's but barely three;
　And she'll neer be wed to a serving man,
　　For she'll be your ain ladie.'

14 ['O dinna ye see yon bonnie castle,
　　Lies on yon sunny lea?
　And yese get ane o my mither's men,
　　For yese get na mair o me.']

15 ['Well see I yon bonnie castle,
　　Lies on yon sunny lea,
　But Ise neer hae nane o your mither's men,
　　Tho I never gat mair o thee.']

16 [Whan he cam to the porter's yett
　　He tirled at the pin,
　And wha sae ready as the bauld porter
　　To open and lat him in.]

17 Monie a lord and fair ladie
　　Met Lord John in the closs,
　But the bonniest face amang them a'
　　Was hauding Lord John's horse.

18 [Monie a lord and lady bricht
　　Met Lord John on the green,
　But the bonniest boy amang them a'
　　Was standing by, him leen.]

19 Monie a lord and gay ladie
　　Sat dining in the ha,
　But the bonniest face that was there
　　Was waiting on them a'.

20 O up bespak Lord John's sister,
　　A sweet young maid was she:
　'My brither has brought a bonnie young page,
　　His like I neer did see;
　But the red flits fast frae his cheek,
　　And the tear stands in his ee.'

21 But up bespak Lord John's mither,
　　She spak wi meikle scorn:
　'He's liker a woman gret wi bairn,
　　Than onie waiting-man.'

22 'It's ye'll rise up, my bonnie boy,
　　And gie my steed the hay:'
　'O that I will, my dear master,
　　As fast as I can gae.'

23 She took the hay aneath her arm,
　　The corn intil her hand,
　But atween the stable-door and the staw,
　　Lady Margret made a stand.

24 [Whan bells were rung, and mass was sung,
　　And a' men boun for bed,
　Lord John, mither, and sister gay
　　In ae bour they were laid.]

25 [Lord John had na weel gat aff his claise,
　　Nor was he weel laid doun,
　Till his mither heard a bairn greet,
　　And a woman's heavy moan.]

26 ['Win up, win up, Lord John,' she said,
　　'Seek neither hose nor shoon;
　For I've heard a bairn loud greet,
　　And a woman's heavy moan.']

27 [Lord John raise, put on his claise,
　　Sought neither hose nor shoon,
　Atween the ha and the stable-door
　　He made na a step but ane.]

28 'O open the door, Lady Margaret,
    O open and let me in;
I want to see if my steed be fed,
    Or my grey-hounds fit to rin.'

29 'I 'll na open the door, Lord John,' she said,
    'I 'll na open it to thee,
Till ye grant to me my ae request,
    And a puir ane it 's to me.

30 'Ye 'll gie to me a bed in an outhouse,
    For my young son and me,
And the meanest servant in a' the place,
    To wait on him and me.'

31 [He 's tane the door wi his fit,
    And he keppd it wi his knee,
He made the door o double deals
    In splinders soon to flee.]

32 ['An askin, an askin, grant me, Lord John,
    An askin ye 'll grant me;
The meanest maid about the place
    To bring a glass o water to me.']

33 'I grant, I grant, Lady Margret,' he said,
    'A' that, and mair frae me,
The very best bed in a' the place
    To your young son and thee,
And my mither, and my sister dear,
    To wait on him and thee.

34 'And a' thae lands, and a' thae rents,
    They sall be his and thine;
Our wedding and our kirking day,
    They sall be all in ane.'

35 And he has tane Lady Margaret,
    · And rowd her in the silk,
And he has tane his ain young son,
    And washd him in the milk.

D

Kinloch MSS, VII, 325.

*   *   *   *   *

24 Lord John rose, put on his clothes,
    Sought neither stockens nor shoon,
An between the ha and the stable
    He made not a step but one.

25 'O open, open, to me, Burd Ellen,
    O open an let me in : '
'O yes, O yes, will I, Lord John,
    But not till I can win;
O yes, will I, Lord John,' she says,
    'But I 'm lyin wi your young son.'

26 He 's taen the door wi his foot,
    An he kepped it wi his knee;
He made the door of double deals
    In splinders soon to flee.

27 'An askin ye 'll grant me, Lord John,
    An askin ye 'll grant me;
May the meanest maid about the place
    Bring a glass o water to me ? '

28 'O hold your tongue, Burd Ellen,' he said,
    'Lat a' your askins be;
For the best maid about the house
    Shall bring a glass o wine to thee.

29 'An the best bed about it a',
    For my young son an thee;
My mother and my ae sister
    Sal bear you company.

30 'Your marriage an your kirkin day
    They sal be both in ane,
An a' these ha's an bowers, Burd Ellen,
    They sal be yours an mine.'

E

Harris MS., No 8, fol. 12 b : originally from Jannie Scott,
an old nurse in Perthshire, about 1790.

1 'I BEG you bide at hame, Margaret,
    An sew your silken seam;

If ye waur in the wide Hielands,
    Ye wald be owre far frae hame.'

2 'I winna bide at hame,' she said,
    'Nor sew my silken seam;

For if I waur in the wide Hielands,
    I wald no be owre far frae hame.'

3 'My steed sall drink the blude-red wine,
    An you the water wan ;
  I 'll mak you sigh, an say, alace,
    That ever I loed a man ! '

4 'Though your steed does drink the blude-red
        wine,
    An me the water wan,
  Yet will I sing, an merry be,
    That ever I loed a man.'

5 ' My hounds shall eat the bread o wheat,
    An you the bread o bran ;
  I 'll mak you sigh, an say, alace,
    That ever you loed Lord John ! '

6 ' Though your hounds do eat the bread o wheat,
    An me the bread o bran,
  Yet will I sing, an merrie be,
    That ever I loed Lord John.'

7 He turned aboot his high horse head,
    An awa he was boun to ride ;
  She kilted up her green clieden,
    An after him she gaed.

8 Whan they cam to that water
    Whilk a' man ca the Clyde,
  He turned aboot his high horse head,
    Said, Ladie, will you ride ?

9 ' I learnt it in my mother's bour,
    I wish I had learnt it weel,
  That I could swim this wan water
    As weel as fish or eel.'

10 Whan at the middle o that water,
    She sat doon on a stone ;
  He turned aboot his high horse head,
    Says, Ladie, will ye loup on ?

11 ' I learnt in my mother's bour,
    I wish I had learnt it better,
  That I culd swim this wan water
    As weel as eel or otter.'

12 He has taen the narrow ford,
    An she has taen the wide ;
  Lang, lang ere he was at the middle,
    She was sittin at the ither side.

13 .   .   .   .   .
      .   .   .   .   .
  Wi sighen said that Fair Margaret,
    Alace, I 'm far frae hame !

14 ' Hoo many miles is 't to your castle ?
    Noo Lord John, tell to me ; '
  ' Hoo many miles is 't to my castle ?
    It 's thirty miles an three : '
  Wi sighen said that Fair Margaret,
    It 'll never be gane by me !

15 But up it spak the wily bird,
    As it sat on the tree,
  ' Rin on, rin on noo, Fair Margaret,
    It scarcely miles is three.'

16 Whan they cam to the wide Hielands,
    An lichted on the green,
  Every an spak Erse to anither,
    But Margaret she spak nane.

17 Whan they waur at table set,
    An birlin at the best,
  Margaret set at a bye-table,
    An fain she wald hain rest.

18 ' Oh mither, mither, mak my bed
    Wi clean blankets an sheets,
  An lay my futeboy at my feet,
    The sounder I may sleep.'

19 She has made Lord John his bed,
    Wi clean blankets an sheets,
  An laid his futeboy at his feet,
    But neer a wink culd he sleep.

20 ' Win up, win up noo, Fair Margaret,
    An see that my steed has meat ;
  See that his corn is in his travisse,
    Nor lyin amang his feet.'

21 Slowly, slowly rase she up,
    An slowly put she on,
  An slowly gaed she doon the stair,
    Aye makin a heavy moan.

        *   *   *   *   *

22 ' An asken, an asken, gude Lord John,
    I pray you grant it me ;
  For the warst bed in a' your hoose,
    To your young son an me.'

23 'Your asken is but sma, Margaret,
  Sune grantet it shall be ;
For the best bed in a' my hoose
  Is owre little for thee.'

24 'An asken, an asken, gude Lord John,
  I pray you grant it me ;
For the warst ale in a' your hoose,
  That ye wald gie to me.'

25 'Your asken is but sma, Margaret,
  Sune grantet it sall be ;
For the best wine in a' my hoose
  Is owre little for thee.

26 'But cheer up your heart noo, Fair Margaret,
  For, be it as it may,
Your kirken an your fair weddin
  Sall baith be on one day.'

F

Jamieson's Popular Ballads, I, 114, from Mrs Arrot of
Arberbrothick.

1 LORD THOMAS stands in his stable-door,
  Seeing his steeds kaimd down ;
Lady Ellen sits at her bower-door,
  Sewing her silver seam.

2 'O will ye stay at hame, Ellen,
  And sew your silver seam ?
Or will ye to the rank highlands ?
  For my lands lay far frae hame.'

3 'I winna stay at hame, Lord Thomas,
  And sew my silver seam ;
But I 'll gae to the rank highlands,
  Tho your lands lay far frae hame.'

* * * * *

4 'An asking, an asking, Lord Thomas,
  I pray thee grant it me ;
How many miles into your fair tower,
  And house where you would be ?'

5 'Your asking fair, Lady Ellen,' he says,
  'Shall now be granted thee ;
For to my castle where it stands
  Is thirty miles and three :'
'O wae is me,' says Lady Ellen,
  'It will never be run by me.'

6 But up and spak the wily pyot,
  That sat upon the tree :

'Sae loud, sae loud, ye fause, fause knight,
  Sae loud as I hear you lie !

7 'For to your dwelling-house,' it says,
  'Of miles it 's scantly three :'
'O weel is me,' says Lady Ellen ;
  'It shall be run by me.'

* * * * *

8 'O mither, mither, mak my bed,
  And mak it braid and wide,
And lay my little page at my feet,
  Whatever may betide.'

* * * * *

9 'An asking, an asking, Lord Thomas,
  I pray thee grant it me ;
O grant me a cup of cold water,
  Between my young son and me.'

10 'What you do ask, Lady Ellen,
  Shall soon be granted thee ;
The best bread and the best wine,
  Between my young son and thee.'

11 'I ask again, my good Lord Thomas,
  I ask again of thee ;
The poorest cot-house in your land,
  Between my young son and me.'

12 'Your asking now, dear Lady Ellen,
  I quickly grant to thee ;
The best bower about my tower,
  Between my young son and thee.'

G

Buchan's MSS, II, 129.

1 THE knight he stands in stable-door,
   Says he, I will go ride ;
  The lady 's kilted her gay cloathing,
   And ran low by his side.

2 He has ridden, and she has run,
   Till they came to yon water wan ;
  He has ridden, and she has run,
   Like to his waiting man.

3 He has ridden, and she has run,
   Till they came on to Clyde ;
  The knight he rode on high horseback,
   But the lady she bot wide.

4 The first step that the lady stepped,
   She stept into the knee ;
  The bairn that was between her sides
   There he gied spartles three.

5 'Lie still, lie still, my bonny boy,
   Ye work your mother woe ;
  Your father rides on high horseback,
   Cares little for us two.'

6 The nextand step that lady stepped.
   She stept into the pap ;
  The bairn that was between her sides
   There spartled and he lap.

7 'Ly still, ly still, my bonny boy,
   You work your mother's woe ;
  Your father rides on high horseback,
   Cares little for us two.'

8 In the middle of that water
   There stands a yird-fast stone ;
  He turnd his horse head back again,
   Said, Lady, loup ye on.

9 She hadna ridden a mile, a mile,
   O never a mile but ane,
  Till she grew sick, and so weary
   She couldna ride nor gang.

10 'Ride on, ride on, my gay lady,
   You see not what I see ;
  For yonder is my father's castle,
   A little beyond the lee,
  And ye 'll get ane of my father's men,
   But, lady, neer lippen on me.'

11 There were four and twenty bonny ladies
   Led Willie frae bower to ha,
  But the bonniest lady among them a'
   Led his steed to the sta.

12 When they were at the table set,
   And sitting at their dine,
  Out it spake his mother dear,
   And she spake aye in time.

13 'Sometimes your boy 's red, Willie,
   And other times he 's wan ;
  He looks like a woman wi bairn,
   But no ways like a man.'

14 'Win up, win up, my bonny boy,
   Go look your master's steed ;
  See that his meat be at his head,
   And not among his feet.'

15 O healy, healy raise she up,
   And healy gaed she down,
  And healy opend the stable-door,
   And as healy gaed she in,
  And even among that big horse feet
   She bear her dear young son.

16 As Willie's mother was walking alone,
   Between the bower and ha,
  She thought she heard a bairn's greet
   And lady's moan in the sta.

17 'Gude make ye safe, my ae son Willie,
   Gude keep ye safe frae harm ;
  Ye might hae chosen a lighter foot-boy
   Than a women in travilling.'

18 He hit the table wi his foot,
   He kept it wi his knee,
  Till silver cups and silver spoons
   Into the floor did flee.

19 There were fifteen steps into that stair,
   I wat he made them a' but three ;
  He 's to the stable gane in haste,
   And a' to see his gay lady.

20 'I am not come o sic low kin,
   Nor yet sic low degree,
  That you needed to banish me frae your sight,
   That ye left nae woman wi me.'

21 'I wish I 'd drunken the wan water
   When I did drink the wine,

Or when I left my lady gay,
  And her at sic a time.

22 'But up ye 'll take my dear young son,
  And wash him wi the milk,

And up ye 'll take my lady gay
  And row her in the silk ;
For her kirking and her fair wedding
  Shall baith stand in ae day.'

H

Motherwell's MS., p. 277, from Marjory Johnston, servant
to W. Parker, manufacturer, Paisley.

*   *   *   *   *

1 'TURN back, turn back, O Burd Alone,
  For the water 's both broad and long : '
First she went into the shoulders,
  And sine unto the chin.

2 'How far is it to your hall, Lord John?
  How far is it? I pray of thee : '
'The nearest way unto my hall
  Is thirty miles and three.

3 'Turn back, turn back, O Burd Alone,
  Ye 'll sink before ye win owre : '
'I am too big with bairn,' she says,
  'To sink or I win owre.'

4 'Turn back, turn back, O Burd Alone,
  Turn back, I pray of thee ;
For I 've got a wife and seven bairns,
  I like far better than thee.'

5 And then spak a wild parrot,
  Sat high upon the tree :
'Gang on, gang on, O Burd Alone,
  [He likes nane better nor thee.]

6 'For Lord John has neither wife nor bairns,
  He likes better than thee,
And the nearest way to Lord John's hall
  Is only short miles three.'

7 When she was come to Lord John's hall,
  Lords, knights and ladies braw
Was there to welcome them hame ;
  But the bravest in the ha,
She waited at Lord John's back,
  Serving the tables a'.

8 When she was laid into her bed,
  Amang the servants a' ilk ane,
The mother heard a babie greet,
  And a lady make a heavy maen.

9 'Rise up, rise up, Lord John,' she said,
  'Bind on thy hose and shoon ;
Thow might hae got some other lady
  Than a lady big wi bairn.'

10 Lord John awa to the hay-loft,
  Where his lady lay ;
'O rise, O rise, my love,' he says,
  'O rise and let me in ;
It 's I have got no loves without,
  But I 've got one within.'

11 'I ask three favours of you, Lord John,
  I ask three favours of thee ;
I ask a bottle of your sma, sma beer,
  For your old son and me.'

12 'O rise, O rise, my love,' he says,
  'O rise and let me in ;
My wine and gin is at your command,
  And that of my old son.'

13 'The next favour I ask of you, Lord John,
  The next favour I ask of thee,
Is the meanest room in all your house,
  For your young son and me.

14 'The next favour I ask of you, Lord John,
  The next favour I ask of thee,
Is the meanest maid in a' your house,
  To wait on your yong son and me.'

15 'O rise, O rise, my love,' he says,
  'O rise and let me in ;
For thy bridal and thy banquet day
  Shall both be held in ane.'

I

Communicated by Dr Thomas Davidson, as learned from his aunt at Old Deer, about 185

1 LORD JOHN stands in his stable-door,
　　Just on his way to ride ;
　Lady Ellen stands in her bower-door,
　　Says, Bide, Lord John, abide !

　　*　　*　　*　　*　　*　　.

2 He did ride, and she did run,
　　A lief-lang simmer's day,
　Until they came till a wan water,
　　That a' man did ca Tay.

3 The first step that she steppit in,
　　She steppit tae the cweet ;
　An sichan said that gay lady,
　　I fear this water's deep !

4 The next step that she steppit in,
　　She steppit tae the knee ;
　An sichan said that gay lady,
　　This water's deep for me !

5 Lord John hield down his high horse head,
　　Said, Lady, will ye ride ?
　' O no ! O no ! kind sir,' she said,
　　' I 'll rather choose tae wide.'

6 The next step that she steppit in,
　　She steppit tae the chin ;
　An sichan said that gay lady,
　　I 'll wide nae farrer in.

7 The firsten town that they cam till,
　　She got a leash o huns tae lead,
　.　　.　　.　　.　　.

　　*　　*　　*　　*　　*

8 When bells were rung, and mass was sung,
　　An a' was ready tae dine,
　.　　.　　.　　.　　.

9 When bells were rung, and mass was sung,
　　An a' were bound for bed,
　.　　.　　.　　.　　.

J

Buchan's Ballads of the North of Scotland, II, 30.

1 THE knight stands in his stable-door,
　　Says he, I will gae ride ;
　A lady stands in her bower-door,
　　Says, I 'll ride by your side.

2 ' Ye shall not follow me, Burd Helen,
　　Except ye do this deed;
　That is, to saddle to me my horse,
　　And bridle to me my steed,
　And every town that ye come to,
　　A liesh o hounds to lead.'

3 ' I will saddle to you your horse,
　　Sae will I bridle your steed ;
　And every town that we come to,
　　A liesh o hounds I 'll lead.'

4 Take warning a', ye maidens fair,
　　That wear scarlet and brown ;

In virtue leave your lammas beds,
　　To follow knights frae town.

5 ' My dogs shall eat the white bread, Helen,
　　And you the dust and bran ;
　And you will sigh, and say, alas !
　　That eer our loves began.'

6 ' Your dogs may eat the gude white bread,
　　And I the dust and bran ;
　Yet will I sing, and say, well 's me,
　　That eer our loves began.'

7 ' My horse shall drink the gude red wine,
　　And you the water wan ;
　And then you 'll sigh, and say, alas !
　　That eer our loves began.'

8 ' Your horse may drink the gude red wine,
　　And I the water wan ;
　But yet I 'll sing, and say, well 's me,
　　That eer our loves began.'

9 Then Willie lap on his white steed,
    And straight awa did ride ;
Burd Helen, drest in men's array,
    She walked by his side.

10 But he was neer sae lack a knight
    As ance woud bid her ride,
And she was neer sae mean a may
    As ance woud bid him bide.

11 Sweet Willie rade, Burd Helen ran,
    A livelang summer's tide,
Until she came to wan water,
    For a' men ca's it Clyde.

12 The first an step that she wade in,
    She wadit to the knee ;
'Ohon, alas !' said that fair maid,
    'This water's nae for me !'

13 The next an step that she wade in,
    She wadit to the pap ;
The babe within her sides twa,
    Cauld water gart it quack.

14 'Lie still, lie still, my bonny bairn,
    For a' this winna dee ;
Your father rides on high horseback,
    Minds neither you nor me.'

15 In the midst of Clyde's water,
    There stands a yird-fast stone ;
There he leant him ower his saddle-bow,
    And set that lady on,
And brought her to the other side,
    Then set her down again.

16 'O see ye not yon goodly towers,
    And gowd towers stand sae hie ?
There is a lady in yonder bower
    Will sinder you and me.'

17 'I wish nae ill to your lady,
    She neer wishd nane to me ;
But I wish the maid maist o your love
    That drees far mair for thee.

18 'I wish nae ill to your lady,
    She neer comes in my thought ;
But I wish the maid maist o your love
    That dearest hae you bought.'

19 Four an twenty gay ladies
    Led Willie thro bower and ha ;
But the fairest lady amo them a'
    Led his horse to the sta.

20 Four an twenty gay ladies
    Were a' at dinner set ;
Burd Helen sat at a by-table,
    A bit she coudna eat.

21 Out it spake her Dow Isbel,
    A skilly dame was she :
'O whare got ye this fine foot-page
    Ye've brought alang wi thee ?

22 'Sometimes his colour waxes red,
    Sometimes it waxes wan ;
He is liker a woman big wi bairn
    Nor be a waiting man.'

23 'Win up, win up, my boy,' he says,
    'At my bidding to be,
And gang and supper my gude steed,
    See he be litterd tee.'

24 Then she is into stable gane,
    Shut tee the door wi a pin,
And even amang Willie's horse feet
    Brought hame her bonny young son.

25 When day was gane, and night was come,
    And a' man bound for bed,
Sweet Willie and Dow Isbel
    In ae chamber were laid.

26 They hadna been well lien down,
    Nor yet well faen asleep,
Till up it wakens Sweet Willie,
    And stood at Dow Isbel's feet.

27 'I dreamd a dreary dream this night,
    I wish it may be for guid ;
Some rogue hae broke my stable-door,
    And stown awa my steed.

28 'Win up, win up now, Dow Isbel,
    At my bidding to be,
And ye'll gae to my stable-door,
    See that be true or lie.'

29 When she gaed to the stable-door,
　　She heard a grievous groan ;
　　She thought she heard a bairn greet,
　　　But and a woman's moan.

30 'When I was in my bigly bower,
　　I wore but what I would ;
　　This night I 'm lighter 'mang Willie's horse feet,
　　　I fear I 'll die for cold.

31 'When I was in my bigly bower,
　　I wore gold to my tae ;
　　This night I 'm lighter mang Willie's horse feet,
　　　And fear I 'll die or day.

32 'When I was in my bigly bower,
　　I wore scarlet and green ;
　　This night I 'm lighter mang Willie's horse feet,
　　　And fear I 'll die my lane.'

33 Dow Isbel now came tripping hame,
　　As fast as gang coud she ;
　　'I thought your page was not a man,
　　　Ye brought alang wi thee.

34 'As I gaed to your stable, Willie,
　　I heard a grievous groan ;
　　I thought I heard a bairn greet,
　　　But and a woman's moan.

35 'She said, when in her bigly bower,
　　She wore but what she would ;
　　But this night is lighter mang your horse feet,
　　　And fears she 'll die for cold.

36 'She said, when in her bigly bower,
　　She wore gold to her tae ;
　　But this night is lighter mang your horse feet,
　　　And fears she 'll die or day.

37 'Win up, win up, now Sweet Willie,
　　At my bidding to be,
　　And speak some comfort to the maid,
　　　That 's dreed sae much for thee.'

38 He is to the stable door gane,
　　As fast as gang coud he ;
　　'O open, O open, Burd Helen,' he says,
　　　'Ye 'll open the door to me.'

39 'That was never my mother's custom,
　　And hope it 's never be mine,

A knight into her companie,
　　When she drees a' her pine.'

40 'O open the door, Burd Helen,' he says,
　　'O open the door to me ;
　　For as my sword hangs by my gair,
　　　I 'll gar it gang in three.'

41 'How can I open, how shall I open,
　　How can I open to thee,
　　When lying amang your great steed's feet,
　　　Your young son on my knee ? '

42 He hit the door then wi his foot,
　　Sae did he wi his knee,
　　Till doors o deal, and locks o steel,
　　　In splinders gart he flee.

43 'An asking, asking, Sweet Willie,
　　An asking ye 'll grant me ;
　　The warst in bower in a' your towers,
　　　For thy young son and me.'

44 'Your asking 's nae sae great, Burd Helen,
　　But granted it shall be ;
　　The best in bower in a' my towers,
　　　For my young son and thee.'

45 'An asking, asking, sweet Willie,
　　An asking ye 'll grant me ;
　　The warst an woman about your bowers,
　　　To wait on him and me.'

46 'The best an woman about my bowers,
　　To wait on him and thee,
　　And that 's my sister Dow Isbel,
　　　And a gude woman is she.

47 'Ye will take up my little young son,
　　And wash him wi the milk ;
　　And ye 'll take up my gay lady,
　　　And row her in the silk.

48 'Be favourable to my lady,
　　Be favourable, if ye may ;
　　Her kirking and her fair wedding
　　　Shall baith stand on ae day.

49 'There is not here a woman living
　　But her shall be my bride,
　　And all is for the fair speeches
　　　I got frae her at Clyde.'

A. And *throughout for* &.

18³, 19³, 22¹, 23¹. four and twenty, *MS. has* 24.

26⁶. [rich]. *Percy.*

27². they way.

28¹. goe thy.   28³. ffarest.

28⁵, 29⁵. armes 2.

31¹. this and itt droue now. *The emendation,
   made without confidence, assumes, as
   does that to* 31¹, *and to be used as in* 'Sir
   Cawline.'

32³. did on.

B. a. 21². An a' man.

b. 1¹. I forbid you.

1³. To leave your father's families.

1⁴. And follow . . . frae the.

2¹. I am a gay ladie.   2². wear.

2³. father's castle.   3¹,³. stands.

3². Says I am boon to ride.

3⁴. Says I 'll run by your side.

4¹. He has mounted on his berry brown steed.

4³. She 's clad her in a page's weed.

4⁴. And ay as fast.   5². An folks.

5³. He 's lookd oer.

5⁴. Says Ellen will you ride.

6¹. O I learnd it when I was a bairn.

7¹, 8¹, 9¹. that ladie.

7². It was aboon her knee.

7³. Says Bird Ellen.

8². It was up till.

8³. Ohon alas says Bird Ellen.

9¹. The thirden step.   9². touched her pap.

9³. The bairn between her sides twa.

9⁴. begood to.

10². You gie your mother pain.

10⁴. And cares little for us twain.

11¹. O *wanting.* Clyde's.   11². There stands.

11³. He has turnd about his berry brown steed.

11⁴. And taen her up him behind.

12⁴. Where this night you mean to be.

13¹. Do not ye see.   13². so far and hie.

13³. ladie there, he says.

14. Altho there be a ladie there,
      Should sunder you and me,
    Betide my life, betide my death,
      I will go thither and see.

15², 16². brown.   15³. Then you will.

15⁴. That ever you lovd a man.

16¹. O 't is I shall.

16³, ⁴. But I neer shall live to cry alas,
      That ever I lovd a man.

17¹, ². My horse shall eat the baken meat,
      And you shall eat the corn.

17³. You then will.

18¹. O I shall eat the baken meat.

18³. And I still shall bless.

20⁴. her lane.

21². a' were.

22 = a 23.   ³. O I can neither eat nor drink.

23 = a 22.   ³. O I can neither eat nor drink.

24³, ⁴. My son, where gat ye that foot-page
      You have brought hame to me ?

25¹. cheeks look.   25². pale and wan.

25³. He looks mair like a ladie wi bairn.

26. He has looked oer his left shoulder,
      And a loud laugh laughed he ;
    Says, He 's a squire's ae dear son,
      I got in the north countrie.

27¹. Win up, win up.   27³. And so.

27⁴. As fast as ever I may.

28²⁻⁴. And the corn in her right hand,
      And she 's hied her to the stable-door,
      As fast as she could gang.

29². Stand nearer to.   29³. between my sides.

30¹, ². She has leand to the manger side
      And gien a grieveous groan.

30⁴. brought home a son.

31 = a 31, 32.
    Then out it spake Lord John's mother,
      As she stood on the stair,
    ' I think I hear a woman groan,
      And a bairn greeting sair.'

32 = a 33.   ¹. O quickly, quickly raise he up.
      ³. But hied him to the stable-door.

33, *wanting in* a.

    'Now open the door, Bird Ellen,' he says,
      ' O open and let me in,
    Or baith the door and the door cheeks
      Into the floor I 'll fling.'

34. He is struck the door wi his right foot
      And pushed it wi his knee,
    Till iron bolts and iron bars
      In flinders he has gard flee :
    ' Be not afraid, Bird Ellen,' he says,
      ' For there 's nane win in but me.'

35, *wanting in* a.

> The never a word spake that ladie,
> As on the floor she lay,
> But hushd her young son in her arms
> And turnd his face away.

36 = a 35.

> 'Now up ye take my bonny young son
> And wash him wi the milk,
> And up ye take my fair ladie,
> And row her i the silk.'

a 36 *is wanting in* b.

37. 'And smile on me now, Bird Ellen,
>   And cast awa your care,
>   For I 'll make you ladie of a' my lands,
>   And your son shall be my heir.'

38. 'Blessd be the day,' sayd Bird Ellen,
>   'That I followd you frae the town,
>   For I 'd rather far be your foot-page
>   Than the queen that wears the crown.'

C. *The stanzas bracketed are those which Kinloch interpolated in his later copy.*
27, 31, 32, *were derived from* D.
22[1]. *In his later copy Kinloch has made the change*, Win up, win up, my bonnie boy.

E. 20[4]. Or lyin : *see* G 14.

G. 22[6]. Aye.

H. 5[4]. *This line is included in* ( ) *in the MS., and was probably supplied by Motherwell.*

I. 3[3], 4[3], 6[3]. sichan : *MS.* "sich an, perhaps sich-in."

J. 4[3] *seems to be a corruption of* I forbid you leave your families, *or something of the kind : cf.* B a 1[1, 3].
10[1]. *The knight seems to be* lack (*wanting*) *rather in* not bidding, *or* letting, *her ride ; his lack is nothing but his leave ; but as the idea may conceivably be that it would be unknightly to ride with a lady behind — all ballads to the contrary — no emendation has been attempted.*
21[3]. five foot page.

64

FAIR JANET

A. 'Fair Janet,' Sharpe's Ballad Book, p. 1.

B. 'Fair Janet and Sweet William,' Motherwell's MS., p. 357.

C. 'Willie and Annet,' Herd's Scots Songs, 1769, p. 303.

D. 'Lord William,' Motherwell's MS., p. 271.

E. 'Willie and Janet,' Kinloch MSS, V, 283, II, 41.

F. 'Sweet Willie and Fair Maisry,' Buchan's Ballads of the North of Scotland, I, 97 ; Motherwell's MS., p. 606.

G. 'Sweet Willie,' Finlay's Scottish Ballads, II, 61.

G, AS printed by Finlay, was made up from various fragments. Of his twenty-seven stanzas fourteen were taken from C, and these are now omitted. A 13, D 5, G 4, 5, C 19, are found also in some copies of 'Fair Annie of Lochroyan ;' C 19 also in 'Sweet Willie and Fair Annie.' The very inappropriate question in F 4, "O will ye gang to the cards, Meggie," occurs in Jamieson's 'Clerk Saunders,' I, 84, st. 5. The inquiry in G 1, "Will you *burn* for Sweet Willie ?" may probably have been suggested by the ballad of 'Lady Maisry.' We have the oath by the thorn, G 13, in 'Glasgerion.' For the conclusion of A, E, see No 7, I, 96 ff.

Fair Janet, A, B, E [Annet, Maisry], loving Sweet Willie, and on the point of becoming a mother by him, is destined by her father to marry a French lord, A; a Southland lord, B, E, G. She implores Willie to fly with her over sea, B, C; to good green wood, F. They set sail, but her condition obliges her to return, B; her time comes before they can get away, C. She bears a child.* To avoid discovery, the babe is taken to Willie's mother, who very readily assumes charge of it. Scarcely has the child been born, when Janet's father comes with orders to busk the bride, A, B, C (?), E, F. She begs to be tenderly handled, as not being in good plight. They attire her gayly, and she selects Willie to lead her horse, or ride before her on her horse, to church, A, B, E. Her cheek is pale, her color goes and comes; it is suspected, and even suggested, that she has borne a bairn, or is near to doing so, A 22, C 14, D 10, E 11, F 25. She seeks to clear herself by an ambiguous oath, E 12, G 26, 27; Willie does this for her, G 11. After dinner, or supper, A, B, dancing is in order. Janet makes excuses to her brothers, her father, the bridegroom's man, and declines very decidedly the bridegroom's own invitation, with marked asperity in A, B. But with Willie she will dance though her heart should break in three. She takes three turns, and falls down dead. Willie gives the key of his coffer to his man, and bids him tell his mother that his horse has slain him. He would not survive Janet in any pure and full form of the story, and does not in A, C, E.

'Sweet William,' Motherwell's Minstrelsy, p. 307, borrows some stanzas at the beginning from 'Fair Janet.'

There are points of resemblance between 'Fair Janet' and a ballad very popular in Scandinavia and in Germany, which demand notice, though they may not warrant the assumption of community of origin.

The Scandinavian ballad is: Danish, 'Kong Valdemar og hans Søster,' Grundtvig, No 126, III, 63 ff, 911 f, A-I; G from a sixteenth-century manuscript, A-F from seventeenth-century manuscripts or print, the two last from recent tradition. Icelandic, 'Soffíu kvæði,' Íslenzk Fornkvæði, No 52, II, 152, A-F, all of which, according to Grundtvig, must be put, at latest, in the seventeenth century, though some are first met with in the eighteenth. Färoë, a single copy, almost Danish, from the beginning of this century, printed by Grundtvig, III, 67 f. Norwegian, three copies from recent tradition, Grundtvig, III, 69, 913 f. Swedish, all from this century, 'Liten Kerstin och Fru Sofia,' Arwidsson, No 53, I, 335–51, A-E; F, G, in Cavallius and Stephens' collection, Grundtvig, III, 70; H, 'Liten Kerstin och drottning Sofia,' Wigström, Folkdiktning, I, 79.†

The German ballad is: A. 'Graf Hans von Holstein und seine Schwester Annchristine,' Müllenhoff, p. 492, No 48. B. 'Der grobe Bruder,' Wunderhorn, II, 272, 1808, Birlinger und Crecelius, II, 24. C. 'Der grausame Bruder,' Parisius, p. 38, No 12, A. D. 'Das Lied vom Pfalzgrafen,' Düntzer und Herder, Briefe Goethe's an Herder, I, 154. E. 'Der grausame Bruder,' Erk, Liederhort, p. 153, No 45. F. 'Christinchen,' Pröhle, p. 4, No 2. G. Wunderhorn, Birlinger und Crecelius, II, 247, No 4. H. Parisius, No 12, C. I. Reifferscheid, p. 107. J. 'Der böse Bruder,' Zuccalmaglio, p. 185, No 89. K. 'Der Pfalzgraf vom Rhein,' Wunderhorn, I, 259, 1806, Birlinger und Crecelius, II, 24. L. 'Der grausame Bruder,' Hoffmann und Richter, Schlesische Volkslieder, p. 49, No 27. M. Parisius, No 12, B. A version in broadside style, Erlach, II, 585, Doenniges, p. 217; compounded copies,

---

* She bids Willie leave her bower while she is in travail, C 7; in default of bower-woman, Willie offers to bandage his eyes and do a woman's part, E 3, after which a stanza is doubtless lost, in which man's aid would be rejected: cf. No 15, I, 182. F has a strange passage, 6–10 (belonging, perhaps, to 'Leesome Brand'), in which the lady, after asking that she may have the attendance of three women, selects the top of a tree for her labor, and informs Willie that he will have to drie every pain that she herself has, which experience duly follows.

† Danish E is translated by Prior, II, 99.

Simrock, No 16, Scherer, Jungbrunnen, No 35, A.

According to the Scandinavian story, a king is informed by his queen, her inexorable enemy, that Kirstin, his sister, has just borne a child. The king sends for Kirstin, who is at some distance, to come to him immediately. She is obliged to make the journey on horseback. Upon her arrival the king puts her to a variety of tests, among these a long dance. Kirstin comes off so well that her brother says the queen has belied her. The queen then bares Kirstin's breast and makes milk flow from it. The king hereupon sends for heavy whips, and flogs his sister to the point of death. In the Icelandic and Färöe versions Kirstin dies of the dance, in her brother's arms. In the Swedish versions and in Danish I the king is Kirstin's father, not her brother. The Norwegian versions and Swedish F, H have a false conclusion: Kirstin survives, and is united to her lover. In Danish A the king had, before he learned the state of things, promised his sister to the son of the King of England, and in Danish F, H, I, Swedish F, and the Färöe ballad, Kirstin's lover is an English prince, who, in Danish H, comes to claim his mistress, and, finding her dead, kills the king. In Swedish A Kirstin dances with four, dances with five, dances with all the men of the court, and in Swedish C, H she tires out successively all the courtiers, the king, and the queen.

A, far the best preserved of the German versions, makes a hunter ask a count for his sister Annchristine. Being refused, as an unequal match, he tells the count that his sister, for all her nobility, has borne a child. The count maintains Annchristine to be a maid. The hunter says, Send for her, and see. The young lady is required to come on horseback. When her brother sees her approaching, with her long hair flowing, his confidence is strengthened. The hunter says, Make her dance. She dances seven hours, and her brother finds reason to continue of the same mind as before. The hunter says, Let us tighten her lacing, and, when that is done, milk springs from her breasts. Her brother gives her the choice between whipping and the sword. She chooses the former. He beats her till liver and lungs spring from her body. She then calls on him to stop; Prince Frederick of England is his brother-in-law. The count is much troubled, and promises everything if she will live. But Annchristine dies, and presently Prince Frederick appears. He has heard of what the count has done, cuts him to bits, and gives him to the crows.

In the other German versions the informant is generally of low rank, and sometimes professes to be father of the child. In B, C, G, H, K he is a kitchey-boy, a personage who plays no insignificant part in romantic story. The coming on horseback is wanting. The long dance is found in B-F. The father of the child is always the English King, who runs the brother through with his sword, B, D, E, G, K, L, or otherwise gives him his due.

The slight resemblance and the great difference of the Scottish story are apparent. Fair Janet has to go a certain distance on horseback, at a time when she is peculiarly ill fitted to do so, like the hapless Kirstin of the Scandinavian ballads and the German A, and she dies from dancing in her weak condition, as the lady does in the Icelandic and Färöe ballad. But both the ride and the dance are incidental to her forced marriage, and neither the ride nor the dance is employed as a test, as the dance always is in the other ballad, and as the ride is expressly devised to be in German A 6. The Scottish Janet is not constrained to dance, nor does she dance down all the men in the room. She declines every invitation except Willie's, and this, in some cases, she (very naturally and touchingly) encourages or incites; and her vital powers give way after three turns. All the unspeakably ferocious features of the Norse and German ballads are wanting, and the bound which divides the pathetic from the horrible is never passed.

A Breton ballad, 'Ar C'homt Gwillou,' 'Prinses ar Gwillou,' 'Le Comte Guillou,' 'La Princesse Le Guillou,' Luzel, II, 6–15, in three versions, has the probation by dancing. A count or prince, returning to his mistress after a considerable absence, happens to hear a shepherdess singing a song, of which he himself is unfortunately the subject. The lady has had a child. Fearing to encounter her injured lover, she tries to pass off a younger sister for herself, but, as may be imagined, this desperate artifice does not succeed. She is told what is said of her, and hopes she may melt like butter if ever she had daughter or son. The count calls out, Play up, musicians, that we may see how this damsel will step out. The young woman pleads that she is suffering from fever, and cannot dance just now, but the count strikes her on the breast so that milk spurts on her gown, **A**. He kills her.*

There is also a Magyar ballad, in which a jealous or offended lover makes his mistress dance till her boots are full of blood, as Kjersti's are in Norwegian **A**, **B**: 'Darvas Kis Clement,' Aigner, p. 110.

One or two correspondences with the Scandinavian-German ballad will require to be noted under 'Lady Maisry,' which immediately follows.

A is translated by Knortz, Schottische Balladen, No 7; **F** by Gerhard, p. 97; a combination of **A**, **C** and others by Grundtvig, No 39.

———————

A

Sharpe's Ballad Book, p. 1, as sung by an old woman in Perthshire.

1 ' YE maun gang to your father, Janet,
    Ye maun gang to him soon ;
Ye maun gang to your father, Janet,
    In case that his days are dune.'

2 Janet 's awa to her father,
    As fast as she could hie :
' O what 's your will wi me, father?
    O what 's your will wi me ? '

3 ' My will wi you, Fair Janet,' he said,
    ' It is both bed and board ;
Some say that ye loe Sweet Willie,
    But ye maun wed a French lord.'

4 ' A French lord maun I wed, father ?
    A French lord maun I wed ?
Then, by my sooth,' quo Fair Janet,
    ' He 's neer enter my bed.'

5 Janet 's awa to her chamber,
    As fast as she could go ;
Wha 's the first ane that tapped there,
    But Sweet Willie her jo ?

6 ' O we maun part this love, Willie,
    That has been lang between ;

There 's a French lord coming oer the sea,
    To wed me wi a ring ;
There 's a French lord coming oer the sea,
    To wed and tak me hame.'

7 ' If we maun part this love, Janet,
    It causeth mickle woe ;
If we maun part this love, Janet,
    It makes me into mourning go.'

8 ' But ye maun gang to your three sisters,
    Meg, Marion, and Jean ;
Tell them to come to Fair Janet,
    In case that her days are dune.'

9 Willie 's awa to his three sisters,
    Meg, Marion, and Jean :
' O haste, and gang to Fair Janet,
    I fear that her days are dune.'

10 Some drew to them their silken hose,
    Some drew to them their shoon,
Some drew to them their silk manteils,
    Their coverings to put on,
And they 're awa to Fair Janet,
    By the hie light o the moon.

*   *   *   *   *

11 ' O I have born this babe, Willie,
    Wi mickle toil and pain ;

---

* La Fidanzata Infedele, Nigra, Rivista Contemporanea, XXXI, 21, and ' L'adultera,' Ferraro, Canti p. monferrini, p. 5, are the same ballad as the Breton, but the dance is not proposed in these.

Take hame, take hame, your babe, Willie,
  For nurse I dare be nane.'

12 He 's tane his young son in his arms,
    And kisst him cheek and chin,
  And he 's awa to his mother's bower,
    By the hie light o the moon.

13 'O open, open, mother,' he says,
    'O open, and let me in;
  The rain rains on my yellow hair,
    And the dew drops oer my chin,
  And I hae my young son in my arms,
    I fear that his days are dune.'

14 With her fingers lang and sma
    She lifted up the pin,
  And with her arms lang and sma
    Received the baby in.

15 'Gae back, gae back now, Sweet Willie,
    And comfort your fair lady ;
  For where ye had but ae nourice,
    Your young son shall hae three.'

16 Willie he was scarce awa,
    And the lady put to bed,
  Whan in and came her father dear :
    'Make haste, and busk the bride.'

17 'There 's a sair pain in my head, father,
    There 's a sair pain in my side ;
  And ill, O ill, am I, father,
    This day for to be a bride.'

18 'O ye maun busk this bonny bride,
    And put a gay mantle on ;
  For she shall wed this auld French lord,
    Gin she should die the morn.'

19 Some put on the gay green robes,
    And some put on the brown ;
  But Janet put on the scarlet robes,
    To shine foremost throw the town.

20 And some they mounted the black steed,
    And some mounted the brown ;
  But Janet mounted the milk-white steed,
    To ride foremost throw the town.

21 'O wha will guide your horse, Janet ?
    O wha will guide him best ? '

'O wha but Willie, my true-love ?
  He kens I loe him best.'

22 And when they cam to Marie's kirk,
    To tye the haly ban,
  Fair Janet's cheek looked pale and wan,
    And her colour gaed an cam.

23 When dinner it was past and done,
    And dancing to begin,
  'O we 'll go take the bride's maidens,
    And we 'll go fill the ring.'

24 O ben than cam the auld French lord,
    Saying, Bride, will ye dance with me ?
  'Awa, awa, ye auld French lord,
    Your face I downa see.'

25 O ben than cam now Sweet Willie,
    He cam with ane advance :
  'O I 'll go tak the bride's maidens,
    And we 'll go tak a dance.'

26 'I 've seen ither days wi you, Willie,
    And so has mony mae,
  Ye would hae danced wi me mysel,
    Let a' my maidens gae.'

27 O ben than cam now Sweet Willie,
    Saying, Bride, will ye dance wi me ?
  'Aye, by my sooth, and that I will,
    Gin my back should break in three.'

28 She had nae turned her throw the dance,
    Throw the dance but thrice,
  Whan she fell doun at Willie's feet,
    And up did never rise.

29 Willie 's taen the key of his coffer,
    And gien it to his man :
  'Gae hame, and tell my mother dear
    My horse he has me slain ;
  Bid her be kind to my young son,
    For father he has nane.'

30 The tane was buried in Marie's kirk,
    And the tither in Marie's quire ;
  Out of the tane there grew a birk,
    And the tither a bonny brier.

B

Motherwell's MS., p. 357, from the recitation of Agnes yle, Kilbarchan.

1 'IF you do love me weel, Willie,
   Ye 'll shew to me truelie ;
   Ye 'll build to me a bonnie ship,
   And set her on the sea.'

2 He did love her very weel,
   He shewed to her trulie ;
   He builded her a bonnie ship,
   And set her on the sea.

3 They had not sailed one league, one league,
   One league but only three,
   Till sharp, sharp showers fair Janet took,
   She grew sick and like to die.

4 'If you do love me weel, Willie,
   Ye 'll shew to me trulye ;
   Ye 'll tak me to my mother's bower,
   Whare I was wont to be.'

5 He did love her very weel,
   He shewed to her trulye ;
   He took her to her mother's bower,
   Whare she was wont to be.

6 'It 's ye 'll stand up at my richt side,
   You will on tiptaes stand,
   Until you hear your auld son weep,
   But an your Janet mourn.

7 'Come take your auld son in your arms,
   He is both large and lang ;
   Come take your auld son in your arms,
   And for a nourice gang.'

8 He is to his mother's bowers,
   An hour or it struck nine :
   'I have a babe into my arms,
   He 'll die for nouricing.'

9 'Goe home, go home, my son,' she says,
   'And mak thy Jenny blythe ;
   If ae nurse winna sere her son,
   It 's I 'll provide him five.'

10 Fair Janet was nae weel lichter,
    Nor weel doun on her side,
    Till ben and cam her father dear,
    Saying, Wha will busk our bride ?

11 Ben and cam her brethren dear,
    Saying, Wha will busk our bride ?
    And wha will saddle our bride's horse ?
    Whom ahint will she ride ?

12 'Hold your tongue, my brethren dear,
    And let your folly be,
    For I 'm sae fair and full of hair
    Sma busking will serve me.

13 'Hold your tongue, my brethren dear,
    And let your folly be,
    For I will ride behint William,
    He will best wait on me.

14 'Willie, lay the saddle saft,
    And lead the bridle soun,
    And when we come to Mary's Kirk,
    Ye 'll set me hooly down.'

15 Supper scarslie was owre,
    Nor musick weel fa'n to,
    Till ben and cam the bride's brethren,
    Saying, Bride, ye 'll dance wi me :
    'Awa, awa, my brethren dear,
    For dancing 's no for me.'

16 Ben and came her ain bridegroom,
    Saying, Bride, ye 'll dance wi me ;
    She says, Awa, awa, ye southland dog,
    Your face I downa see.

17 Ben and cam then Sweet Willie,
    Saying, Bride, ye 'll dance wi me :
    'Oh I will dance the floor once owre,
    Tho my heart should break in three.'

18 'Oh no, oh no,' said Sweet William,
    'Let no such things eer be;
    But I will cut my glove in two,
    And I 'll dance for thee and me.'

19 She hadna danced the floor once owre,
    I 'm sure she hadna thrice,
    Till she fell in a deadly swound,
    And from it neer did rise.

20 Out and spak her ain bridegroom,
    And an angry man was he :
    'This day she has gien me the gecks,
    Yet she must bear the scorn ;
    There 's not a bell in merry Linkum
    Shall ring for her the morn.'

21 Out and spoke then Sweet William,
   And a sorry man was he :
' Altho she has gien you the gecks,
   She will not bear the scorn ;
There 's not a bell in merry Linkum
   But shall ring for her the morn.'

22 There was not a bell in merry Linkum
   But they tinkled and they rang,
And a' the birds that flew above,
   They changed their notes and sang.

—————•—————

C

Herd's Scots Songs, 1769, p. 303 : I, 162, ed. 1776.

1 Livd ance twa luvers in yon dale,
   And they luvd ither weel ;
Frae evning late to morning aire
   Of luving luvd their fill.

2 ' Now, Willie, gif you luve me weel,
   As sae it seems to me,
Gar build, gar build a bonny schip,
   Gar build it speedilie.

3 ' And we will sail the sea sae green,
   Unto some far countrie,
Or we 'll sail to some bonie isle,
   Stands lanely midst the sea.'

4 But lang or ere the schip was built,
   Or deckd, or rigged out,
Came sick a pain in Annet's back
   That down she coud na lout.

5 ' Now, Willie, gif ye luve me weel,
   As sae it seems to me,
O haste, haste, bring me to my bowr,
   And my bowr-maidens three.'

6 He 's taen her in his arms twa,
   And kissd her, cheik and chin ;
He 's brocht her to her ain sweet bowr,
   But nae bowr-maid was in.

7 ' Now leave my bower, Willie,' she said,
   ' Now leave me to my lane ;
Was nevir man in a lady's bower
   When she was travelling.'

8 He 's stepped three steps down the stair,
   Upon the marble stane ;
Sae loud 's he heard his young son's greet,
   But and his lady's mane !

9 ' Now come, now come, Willie,' she said,
   ' Tak your young son frae me,

And hie him to your mother's bower,
   With speed and privacie.'

10 He 's taen his young son in his arms,
   He 's kissd him, cheik and chin ;
He 's hied him to his mother's bower,
   By th' ae light of the moon.

11 And with him came the bold barone,
   And he spake up wi pride :
' Gar seek, gar seek the bower-maidens,
   Gar busk, gar busk the bryde.'

12 ' My maidens, easy with my back,
   And easy with my side ;
O set my saddle saft, Willie,
   I am a tender bryde.'

13 When she came to the burrow-town,
   They gied her a broch and ring,
And when she came to . . . ,
   They had a fair wedding.

14 O up then spake the norland lord,
   And blinkit wi his ee :
' I trow this lady 's born a bairn,'
   Then laucht loud lauchters three.

15 And up then spake the brisk bridegroom,
   And he spake up wi pryde :
' Gin I should pawn my wedding-gloves,
   I will dance wi the bryde.'

16 ' Now had your tongue, my lord,' she said,
   ' Wi dancing let me be ;
I am sae thin in flesh and blude,
   Sma dancing will serve me.'

17 But she 's taen Willie be the hand,
   The tear blinded her ee :
' But I wad dance wi my true-luve,
   But bursts my heart in three.'

18 She 's taen her bracelet frae her arm,
   Her garter frae her knee :

'Gie that, gie that to my young son,
He 'll neer his mother see.'

*　　*　　*　　*　　*

19 'Gar deal, gar deal the bread, mother,
Gar deal, gar deal the wyne;
This day hath seen my true-love's death,
This nicht shall witness myne.'

———•———

D

Motherwell's MS., p. 271, "from Margery Johnston, who had it of her grand-aunt, a very old woman."

*　　*　　*　　*　　*

1 'It never was my mother's fashion,
As little will 't be mine,
For to hae gay lords within my room
When ladies are travailing.'

2 Lord William was scarsely down the stair,
A step but only ane,
Till he heard his auld son gie a cry,
And his lady a heavy maen.

3 'Turn back, turn back, Lord William,' she says,
'Take thy auld son in thy coat-neuk,
And see and reach thy mother's bowers
Twa hours before day comes.'

4 He 's awa wi his auld son in his coat-neuk,
As fast as he can run,
And there he 's reached his mother's bowers,
Twa hours before day came.

5 'O rise, O rise, my mother dear,
O rise and let me in,
For I 've my auld son in my coat-neuk,
And he shivers at the chin.'

6 'Ye 're welcome hame to me, Lord William,
And so is thy auld son;
It 's where ye had but ae nourice,
Thy auld son he 'll hae four.'

7 His lady was scarsely in her bed,
Nor well faln owre asleep,
When four and twenty knights and lords
Came for the bride at last.

8 They dressed her up, they dressed her down,
They dressed her wondrous fine,
And just before her ain bedside
She lost her colour clean.

9 'Be hooly wi my head, maidens,
Be hooly wi my hair,
For it was washen late last night,
And now it 's very sair.'

10 Out then spoke a southern lord,
And oh but he spak bauld:
'She is the likest that bore a child
That eer my eyes did see.'

11 Up then spak her auld, auld father,
And oh he spoke in time:
'She neer bore a child since her birth
Except it was yestreen.'

12 Out then spoke a northern lord:
'It 's bride, will ye dance wi me?'
'Oh no, oh no, you northland lord,
It 's dancing 's no for me.'

13 Out then spoke a southland lord:
'It 's bride, will ye dance wi me?'
'Oh no, oh no, you southland lord,
I would as lief chuse to die.'

14 Out then spoke her ain bridegroom:
'O bride, will ye dance wi me?'
'Oh no, oh no, my ain bridegroom,
It 's dancing 's no for me.'

15 Out then spoke her ain Willy,
And oh he spoke fu fine:
'O bride, O bride, will ye dance wi me,'

.　　.　　.　　.　　.

16 'Oh yes, oh yes, Willie,' she said,
'It 's I will dance with thee;
Oh yes, I 'll dance, dear Willie,' she said,
'Tho my back it gaes in three.'

17 She leaned her head on Willie's breast,
And her back unto the wa:
'O there 's the key of my coffer,
And pay weel the nouriss fee,
And aye when ye look on your auld son,
Ye may aye think on me.'

E

Kinloch MSS, V, 283, II, 41, from Mary Barr, Clydesdale.

1 WILLIE and Fair Janet
　　Sat a' day on yon hill ;
　And Janet she took sair pains,
　　And O but she grew ill.

2 ' Fetch a woman to me, Willie,
　　O fetch a woman to me,
　For without the help of woman, Willie,
　　Surely I will dee.'

3 ' O tie a napkin on my face,
　　That naething I may see,
　And what can a woman do, Janet,
　　But I will do for thee ? '

　　*　　*　　*　　*　　*

4 She was na scarcely brought to bed,
　　Nor yet laid on her side,
　Till in and cam her father there,
　　Crying, Fy, gae busk the bride.

5 ' A wearyed bride am I, father,
　　A wearyed bride am I ;
　Must I gae wed that southlan lord,
　　And let Sweet Willie abe ? '

　　*　　*　　*　　*　　*

6 ' Now chuse, now chuse now, Fair Janet,
　　What shall your cleeding be ;
　Now chuse, now chuse now, Fair Janet,
　　And I will gie it to thee.

7 ' Whether will you hae it of the berry brown,
　　Or of the holland green ;
　Or will you hae it of the crimson red,
　　Most lovely to be seen ? '

8 ' I will not hae 't of the berry brown,
　　Nor yet o the holly green ;
　But I will hae 't of the crimson red,
　　Most lovely to be seen.'

9 ' Now chuse, now chuse now, Fair Janet,
　　What man you 'll ride behind : '
　' O wha sae fitting as Sweet Willie ?
　　He 'll fit my saddle fine.'

10 O they rode on, and they rode on,
　　Till they cam to Merrytown green ;
　But Sweet Willie and Fair Janet
　　Cam aye hoolie ahin.

11 O whan they cam to Merrytown,
　　And lighted on the green,
　Monie a bluidy aith was sworn
　　That our bride was wi bairn.

12 Out and spake the bonny bride,
　　And she swore by her fingers ten :
　' If eer I was wi bairn in my life,
　　I was lighter sin yestreen.'

13 Up and raise he the bridegroom,
　　Says, Bride, will ye dance wi me ?
　' Dance on, dance on, bridegroom,' she says,
　　' For I 'll dance nane wi thee.'

14 Up and raise her father then,
　　Says, Bride, will ye dance wi me ?
　' Dance on, my father,' she replied,
　　' I pray thee let me be.'

15 Then up and raise he Sweet Willie,
　　And he had meikle pride :
　' I 'll lay my gloves in the bride's han,
　　And I 'll dance for the bride.'

16 ' O no, O no, O Sweet Willie,
　　O no, that shall na be ;
　For I will dance wi thee, Willie,
　　Tho my back should fa in three.'

17 She had na run a reel, a reel,
　　A reel but barely three,
　Till pale and wan grew Fair Janet,
　　And her head took Willie's knee.

18 Out and spake then the bridegroom,
　　And he spake wi great scorn :
　' There 's not a bell in Merrytown kirk
　　Shall ring for her the morn.'

19 Out and spak he Sweet Willie,
　　And his heart was almost gane :
　' 'T is a the bells in Merrytown kirk
　　Shall ring for her the morn.'

20 Willie was buried in Mary's kirk,
　　etc., etc., etc.

F

Buchan's Ballads of the North of Scotland, I, 97 ; Motherwell's MS., p. 606.

1 HEY, love Willie, and how, love Willie,
   And Willie my love shall be;
   They 're thinking to sinder our lang love, Willie;
   It 's mair than man can dee.

2 'Ye 'll mount me quickly on a steed,
   A milk-white steed or gray,
   And carry me on to gude greenwood,
   Before that it be day.'

3 He mounted her upon a steed,
   He chose a steed o gray;
   He had her on to gude greenwood,
   Before that it was day.

4 'O will ye gang to the cards, Meggie?
   Or will ye gang wi me?
   Or will ye hae a bower-woman,
   To stay ere it be day?'

5 'I winna gang to the cards,' she said,
   'Nor will I gae wi thee,
   Nor will I hae a bower-woman,
   To spoil my modestie.

6 'Ye 'll gie me a lady at my back,
   An a lady me beforn,
   An a midwife at my twa sides,
   Till your young son be born.

7 'Ye 'll do me up, and further up,
   To the top o yon greenwood tree;
   For every pain myself shall hae,
   The same pain ye maun drie.'

8 The first pain that did strike Sweet Willie,
   It was into the side;
   Then sighing sair said Sweet Willie,
   These pains are ill to bide !

9 The nextan pain that strake Sweet Willie,
   It was into the back;
   Then sighing sair said Sweet Willie,
   These pains are women's wreck !

10 The nextan pain that strake Sweet Willie,
   It was into the head;
   Then sighing sair said Sweet Willie,
   I fear my lady 's dead !

11 Then he 's gane on, and further on,
   At the foot o yon greenwood tree;
   There he got his lady lighter,
   Wi his young son on her knee.

12 Then he 's taen up his little young son,
   And kissd him, cheek and chin,
   And he is on to his mother,
   As fast as he could gang.

13 'Ye will take in my son, mother,
   Gie him to nurses nine;
   Three to wauk, and three to sleep,
   And three to gang between.'

14 Then he has left his mother's house,
   And frae her he has gane,
   And he is back to his lady,
   And safely brought her hame.

15 Then in it came her father dear,
   Was belted in a brand:
   'It 's nae time for brides to lye in bed,
   When the bridegroom 's send 's in town.

16 'There are four-and-twenty noble lords
   A' lighted on the green;
   The fairest knight amang them a',
   He must be your bridegroom.'

17 'O wha will shoe my foot, my foot?
   And wha will glove my hand?
   And wha will prin my sma middle,
   Wi the short prin and the lang?'

18 Now out it speaks him Sweet Willie,
   Who knew her troubles best:
   'It is my duty for to serve,
   As I 'm come here as guest.

19 'Now I will shoe your foot, Maisry,
   And I will glove your hand,
   And I will prin your sma middle,
   Wi the sma prin and the lang.'

20 'Wha will saddle my steed,' she says,
   'And gar my bridle ring?
   And wha will hae me to gude church-door,
   This day I 'm ill abound?'

21 'I will saddle your steed, Maisry,
   And gar your bridle ring,
   And I 'll hae you to gude church-door,
   And safely set you down.'

22 'O healy, healy take me up,
      And healy set me down,
   And set my back until a wa,
      My foot to yird-fast stane.'

23 He healy took her frae her horse,
      And healy set her down,
   And set her back until a wa,
      Her foot to yird-fast stane.

24 When they had eaten and well drunken,
      And a' had thornd fine,
   The bride's father he took the cup,
      For to serve out the wine.

25 Out it speaks the bridegroom's brother,
      An ill death mat he die !
   'I fear our bride she's born a bairn,
      Or else has it a dee.'

26 She's taen out a Bible braid,
      And deeply has she sworn ;
   'If I hae born a bairn,' she says,
      'Sin yesterday at morn,

27 'Or if I 've born a bairn,' she says,
      'Sin yesterday at noon,
   There 's nae a lady amang you a'
      That woud been here sae soon.'

28 Then out it spake the bridegroom's man,
      Mischance come ower his heel !
   'Win up, win up, now bride,' he says,
      'And dance a shamefu reel.'

29 Then out it speaks the bride hersell,
      And a sorry heart had she :
   'Is there nae ane amang you a'
      Will dance this dance for me ?'

30 Then out it speaks him Sweet Willie,
      And he spake aye thro pride :
   'O draw my boots for me, bridegroom,
      Or I dance for your bride.'

31 Then out it spake the bride hersell :
      O na, this maunna be ;
   For I will dance this dance mysell,
      Tho my back shoud gang in three.

32 She hadna well gane thro the reel,
      Nor yet well on the green,
   Till she fell down at Willie's feet
      As cauld as ony stane.

33 He's taen her in his arms twa,
      And haed her up the stair ;
   Then up it came her jolly bridegroom,
      Says, What 's your business there ?

34 Then Willie lifted up his foot,
      And dang him down the stair,
   And brake three ribs o the bridegroom's side,
      And a word he spake nae mair.

35 Nae meen was made for that lady,
      When she was lying dead ;
   But a' was for him Sweet Willie,
      On the fields for he ran mad.

——•——

G

Finlay's Scottish Ballads, II, 61.

1 'WILL you marry the southland lord,
      A queen of fair England to be ?
   Or will you burn for Sweet Willie,
      The morn upon yon lea ?'

2 'I will marry the southland lord,
      Father, sen it is your will ;
   But I 'd rather it were my burial-day,
      For my grave I 'm going till.

3 'O go, O go now, my bower-wife,
      O go now hastilie,

O go now to Sweet Willie's bower,
      And bid him cum speak to me.'

   *   *   *   *   *

4 And he is to his mother's bower,
      As fast as he could rin :
   'Open, open, my mother dear,
      Open, and let me in.

5 'For the rain rains on my yellow hair,
      The dew stands on my chin,
   And I have something in my lap,
      And I wad fain be in.'

6 'O go, O go now, Sweet Willie,
    And make your lady blithe,
For wherever you had ae nourice,
    Your young son shall hae five.'

7 Out spak Annet's mother dear,
    An she spak a word o' pride ;
Says, Whare is a' our bride's maidens,
    They 're no busking the bride ?

8 'O haud your tongue, my mother dear,
    Your speaking let it be,
For I 'm sae fair and full o flesh
    Little busking will serve me.'

9 Out an spak the bride's maidens,
    They spak a word o pride ;
Says, Whare is a' the fine cleiding ?
    It 's we maun busk the bride.

10 'Deal hooly wi my head, maidens,
    Deal hooly wi my hair ;

For it was washen late yestreen,
    And it is wonder sair.'

*   *   *   *   *

11 And Willie swore a great, great oath,
    And he swore by the thorn,
That she was as free o a child that night
    As the night that she was born.

12 'Ye hae gien me the gowk, Annet,
    But I 'll gie you the scorn ;
For there 's no a bell in a' the town
    Shall ring for you the morn.'

13 Out and spak then Sweet Willie :
    Sae loud 's I hear you lie !
There 's no a bell in a' the town
    But shall ring for Annet and me.

*   *   *   *   *

E. *The copy in Kinloch MSS, II, 41, has been
revised by Mr Kinloch. His more important changes are as follows :*
    1^1. Sweet Willie. 1^3. took in labor-pains.
    2^1. Gae fetch. 2^3. For but.
    2^4. It 's surely.
    3^3. And what a woman can do, Janet.
    3^4. That I. 4^4. Says, Fy.
    $6^{1,\,3}$. now chuse thee, Fair Janet.
    7^2, 8^2. hollin.
    10^2, 11^1, 18^3, 19^3. Marytoun.
    10^4. Cam riding. 12^1. Then out.
    14^4. ye let me abee.
    18^1. the bridegroom then.
    19^1. But out. 19^2. His heart.

20. Fair Janet was buried in Mary's kirk,
    Sweet Willie in Mary's quier,
And out o the tane there sprang a rose,
    Out o the tither a brier.

21. And aye they grew, and aye they threw,
    Till thae twa they did meet,
That ilka ane might plainly see
    They war twa lovers sweet.

G. 1^3. *Var.* mourn for. 11, *in Finlay, follows* 13.
Fourteen stanzas, taken from C, *have been
omitted.*

65

LADY MAISRY

A. 'Lady Maisry,' Jamieson - Brown MS., fol. 24; Jamieson's Popular Ballads, I, 73.

B. Motherwell's MS., p. 422, communicated by Charles Kirkpatrick Sharpe.

C. 'Janet,' Motherwell's MS., p. 472.

D. 'Lady Margery,' Campbell MSS, II, 70.

E. 'Lady Marjory,' Motherwell's MS., p. 1; Motherwell's Minstrelsy, p. 234.

F. The Scots [Edinburgh] Magazine, 1822, LXXXIX, 734.

G. Notes and Queries, Second Series, IX, 193.

H. 'Young Prince James,' Buchan's Ballads of the North of Scotland, I, 103.

I. a. 'Bonnie Susie Cleland,' Motherwell's MS., p 235, Motherwell's Minstrelsy, p. 221. **b.** 'Susie Cleland,' Motherwell's MS., p. 179. **c.** 'Susie Cleland,' Motherwell's MS., p. 181.

A WAS No 12 in William Tytler's Brown manuscript, and stanzas 1, 21, 22, of that copy are cited by Anderson in his letter to Percy, Nichols's Illustrations, VII, 177. Jamieson, who made a few changes in printing from his manuscript, attributes, by an oversight, the ballad to Mrs Arrot: compare Popular Ballads, I, pp 66 and 59. His copy is repeated by Motherwell, p. 71. **C**, of which no account is given by Motherwell, is hardly more than a variety of **B**. There is a copy in the Abbotsford manuscript, "Scottish Songs," which is more considerably tampered with, in the way of change, omission, and insertion.*

All the versions are in accord as to the material points of the story. Lady Maisry rejects the suit of all the lords in the north country, **A**; she has given her love to an English lord. Her lover's seat is Strawberry Castle, **D**, **E**, **F**; Adam's Tower, **H**; he lives at London, **G**. Maisry has been at Strawberry Castle for a time, and has there learned some unco lair, **D**, **E**.† It is discovered that Maisry

goes with bairn. Her brother, **A**, **H**, father **I**, informed to this effect, requires her to renounce her English lord, but she refuses; her father offers her the choice of marrying an auld man or burning, **D**. In the other versions the family set about preparations for burning her without attempting any arrangement. Maisry, warned of her approaching fate, calls for a boy to carry word to England, and a light-footed and heartily devoted young messenger takes her errand. The English lord asks if his biggins are broken, his towers won, or is his lady lighter, and is told that his lady is to be burnt for him that very day. Horses are instantly saddled: a black, a brown, are foundered, a milk-white [a dapple-gray], fair fall the mare that foaled that foal! holds out, **B**, **C**, **E**, **F**. In **D** fifteen stout steeds are burst, yet the little foot-page runs aye before, crying, Mend your pace an you may! Maisry, in the flames, hears her lover's horn, hears his bridle ring, **A**, **E**, **F**, **H**. "Beet on!" she cries; "I value you not one straw. Mend up

---

* The genuineness of **H**, Buchan's version, may be doubted both on general and on particular grounds, and both because of its departures from the common story and because of its repeating some peculiarities of the Jamieson-Brown copy, **A**. If **H** was compiled, as I think it was, largely from **A**, the person that did the work may have seen the manuscript, which is not at all improbable; for the *English blude* of **H** 13 is found in the MS., **A** 16, and not in

the copy printed by Jamieson, and so with the *thistle* of **H** 15, **A** 17. Buchan, or Buchan's foreman, is entitled to copyright for the invention, in **H** 17, of Maisry's carrying peats in her petticoat, "her ainsell for to burn;" also for English James, that little prince, 10³, Adam's high tower, 20³, thro Linkum and thro Lin, 37⁴.

† Like the Clerk of Oxenford's two sons, and Sweet William, Motherwell, Minstrelsy, p. 307.

the fire, brother; I see him coming that will soon mend it up to thee." * In A, H she cries out, when her lover appears, that if her hands had been free she would have cast out his young son. He leaps into the fire for a last kiss; her body falls apart, B-G. He threatens an awful retaliation: he will burn father and mother, and the chief of all her kin (who, no doubt, had been concerned in this auto da fé). Vengeance glutted, he will throw himself into the flames, A, F; he will take the pilgrim's cloak and staff, C. The foot-page shall be heir of his land, C; he will remember the bonny boy that ran the errand, E.†

Maisry, Margery, is the heroine's name in A, D-H, J; Janet in B, C; Susie Cleland in I. The hero has a name only in A, Lord William, and in H, Prince James.

'Lady Maisry' has a limited, and perhaps quite accidental, resemblance to the Scandinavian-German ballad spoken of in the preface to 'Fair Janet.' The lapse of the heroine is visited with a fearful death at the hand of brother or father, and the lover who was partner to her trespass appears on the scene immediately after, and takes his revenge. A kitchey-boy is informant in A, as in some versions of the German story.

The regular penalty for incontinence in an unmarried woman, if we are to trust the authority of romances, is burning. This, accord-ing to the well-known passage in Ariosto, Orlando Furioso, IV, 58, 59, was l'aspra legge di Scozia, empia e severa, though it might be as difficult to point out a law to that effect in any European code as a corresponding patria potestas.‡ Some ballad cases are: Scandinavian (Danish, Swedish, Norwegian, Icelandic), 'Ildpröven' and 'Møen paa Baalet,' Grundtvig, Nos 108, 109, II, 577–590, III, 904 f, Eva Wigström, Folkdiktning, I, 30, No 13; Spanish and Portuguese, 'De la infanta y don Galvan,' Wolf and Hofmann, Primavera, No 159, II, 92; 'Conde Claros de Montalvan,' Primavera, No 191, II, 374; 'La infanta seducida,' Milá, Romancerillo Catalan, No 258, A–M, pp 249–54; 'L'infanta,' Briz, IV, 39; 'Dom Carlos de Montealbar,' etc., Braga, Romanceiro, p. 79 ff, Nos 31, 32, 33, Cantos pop. do Archipelago Açoriano, p. 246, No 25, Almeida-Garrett, II, 203; 'Dona Ausenda,' Almeida-Garrett, II, 177, 'Dona Aldonça,' Estacio da Veiga, p. 75; Hardung, Romanceiro Portuguez, I, 180–204. To these add the prose Merlin, ed. Wheatley, I, 16; L'Histoire plaisante du noble Siperis de Vinevaulx, etc., cited by Liebrecht, Dunlop, p. 467, note 117.§

A is translated, after Jamieson, I, 73, by Grundtvig, Engelske og skotske Folkeviser, p. 38; I, a, the same, p. 322.

---

* There is no word of quailing except in G, and in G she blesses her lover most touchingly, with almost her last words.

> She turned her head on her left shoulder,
> Saw her girdle hang on the free:
> 'O God bless them that gave me that!
> They 'll never give more to me.'

† According to Buchan, H 39, Maisry's true-love ran brain; so again in Buchan's version of Fair Janet, see F 35. This is Maisry's end in several versions of 'Auld Ingram,' and in all, I suppose, a modern substitute for the immediate death of older ballads.

‡ A champion may be offered even in Ariosto's Scotland.

§ In 'The Infanta and Don Galvan,' the lady, like Fair Janet, calls to Don Galvan to come and take her new-born child and carry it to his mother to nurse. The father superintends in person the preparation of the pile in 'Dona Au-senda.' In the romances of Conde Claros, the infanta, when she learns that she is to be burnt, asks for some one "que haya comido mi pan," to carry a letter to Don Claros, and a page does the errand, just as in the Scottish ballad: Primavera, II, 374, etc. Often a bird, hawk, dove, takes the message, as in 'Sweet William,' Motherwell's Minstrelsy, p. 307. Don Claros asks the infanta of her father in marriage, and is refused (because she is promised). He then informs the emperor that the infanta is with child. It is a *hunter* who informs the father of the love of his daughter and the count in one of the romances, Primavera, II, 362. Compare the German ballad, in 'Fair Janet,' p. 102. When the lover gets his letter, in Briz, IV, 43, he reminds us of Sir Patrick Spens:

> Quan D. Cárlos reb la carta, molt content y alegre estava:
> Al desclohent de la carta, llágrimas de sanch llansava.

A

Jamieson-Brown MS., fol. 24.

1 THE young lords o the north country
   Have all a wooing gone,
   To win the love of Lady Maisry,
   But o them she woud hae none.

2 O they hae courted Lady Maisry
   Wi a' kin kind of things ;
   An they hae sought her Lady Maisry
   Wi brotches an wi' rings.

3 An they ha sought her Lady Maisry
   Frae father and frae mother ;
   An they ha sought her Lady Maisry
   Frae sister an frae brother.

4 An they ha followd her Lady Maisry
   Thro chamber an thro ha ;
   But a' that they coud say to her,
   Her answer still was Na.

5 'O had your tongues, young men,' she says,
   'An think nae mair o me ;
   For I 've gien my love to an English lord,
   An think nae mair o me.'

6 Her father's kitchy-boy heard that,
   An ill death may he dee !
   An he is on to her brother,
   As fast as gang coud he.

7 'O is my father an my mother well,
   But an my brothers three ?
   Gin my sister Lady Maisry be well,
   There 's naething can ail me.'

8 'Your father and your mother is well,
   But an your brothers three ;
   Your sister Lady Maisry 's well,
   So big wi bairn gangs she.'

9 'Gin this be true you tell to me,
   My mailison light on thee !
   But gin it be a lie you tell,
   You sal be hangit hie.'

10 He 's done him to his sister's bowr,
   Wi meikle doole an care ;
   An there he saw her Lady Maisry,
   Kembing her yallow hair.

11 'O wha is aught that bairn,' he says,
   'That ye sae big are wi ?
   And gin ye winna own the truth,
   This moment ye sall dee.'

12 She turnd her right an roun about,
   An the kem fell frae her han ;
   A trembling seizd her fair body,
   An her rosy cheek grew wan.

13 'O pardon me, my brother dear,
   An the truth I 'll tell to thee ;
   My bairn it is to Lord William,
   An he is betrothd to me.'

14 'O coud na ye gotten dukes, or lords,
   Intill your ain country,
   That ye draw up wi an English dog,
   To bring this shame on me ?

15 'But ye maun gi up the English lord,
   Whan youre young babe is born ;
   For, gin you keep by him an hour langer,
   Your life sall be forlorn.'

16 'I will gi up this English blood,
   Till my young babe be born ;
   But the never a day nor hour langer,
   Tho my life should be forlorn.'

17 'O whare is a' my merry young men,
   Whom I gi meat and fee,
   To pu the thistle and the thorn,
   To burn this wile whore wi ? '

18 'O whare will I get a bonny boy,
   To help me in my need,
   To rin wi hast to Lord William,
   And bid him come wi speed ? '

19 O out it spake a bonny boy,
   Stood by her brother's side :
   'O I would rin your errand, lady,
   Oer a' the world wide.

20 'Aft have I run your errands, lady,
   Whan blawn baith win and weet ;
   But now I 'll rin your errand, lady,
   Wi sat tears on my cheek.'

21 O whan he came to broken briggs,
   He bent his bow and swam,

An whan he came to the green grass growin,
    He slackd his shoone and ran.

22 O whan he came to Lord William's gates,
    He baed na to chap or ca,
But set his bent bow till his breast,
    An lightly lap the wa ;
An, or the porter was at the gate,
    The boy was i the ha.

23 'O is my biggins broken, boy ?
    Or is my towers won ?
Or is my lady lighter yet,
    Of a dear daughter or son ? '

24 'Your biggin is na broken, sir,
    Nor is your towers won ;
But the fairest lady in a' the lan
    For you this day maun burn.'

25 'O saddle me the black, the black,
    Or saddle me the brown ;
O saddle me the swiftest steed
    That ever rade frae a town.'

26 Or he was near a mile awa,
    She heard his wild horse sneeze :

'Mend up the fire, my false brother,
    It's na come to my knees.'

27 O whan he lighted at the gate,
    She heard his bridle ring :
'Mend up the fire, my false brother,
    It's far yet frae my chin.

28 'Mend up the fire to me, brother,
    Mend up the fire to me ;
For I see him comin hard an fast
    Will soon men 't up to thee.

29 'O gin my hands had been loose, Willy,
    Sae hard as they are boun,
I would have turnd me frae the gleed,
    And castin out your young son.'

30 'O I 'll gar burn for you, Maisry,
    Your father an your mother ;
An I 'll gar burn for you, Maisry,
    Your sister an your brother.

31 'An I 'll gar burn for you, Maisry,
    The chief of a' your kin ;
An the last bonfire that I come to,
    Mysel I will cast in.'

B

Motherwell's MS., p. 422, communicated by Charles Kirkpatrick Sharpe.

1 In came her sister,
    Stepping on the floor ;
Says, It 's telling me, my sister Janet,
    That you 're become a whore.

2 'A whore, sister, a whore, sister ?
    That 's what I 'll never be ;
I 'm no so great a whore, sister,
    As liars does on me lee.'

3 In came her brother,
    Stepping on the floor ;
Says, It 's telling me, my sister Janet,
    That you 're become a whore.'

4 'A whore, brother, a whore, brother ?
    A whore I 'll never be ;
I 'm no so bad a woman, brother,
    As liars does on me lee.'

5 In came her mother,
    Stepping on the floor :
'They are telling me, my daughter,
    That you 're so soon become a whore.'

6 'A whore, mother, a whore, mother ?
    A whore I 'll never be ;
I 'm only with child to an English lord,
    Who promised to marry me.'

7 In came her father,
    Stepping on the floor ;
Says, They tell me, my daughter Janet,
    That you are become a whore.'

8 'A whore, father, a whore, father ?
    A whore I 'll never be ;
I 'm but with child to an English lord,
    Who promisd to marry me.'

9 Then in it came an old woman,
    The lady's nurse was she,

And ere she could get out a word
    The tear blinded her ee.

10 'Your father 's to the fire, Janet,
    Your brother 's to the whin ;
  All for to kindle a bold bonfire,
    To burn your body in.'

11 'Where will I get a boy,' she said,
    'Will gain gold for his fee,
  That would run unto fair England
    For my good lord to me ? '

12 'O I have here a boy,' she said,
    'Will gain gold to his fee,
  For he will run to fair England
    For thy good lord to thee.'

13 Now when he found a bridge broken,
    He bent his bow and swam,
  And when he got where grass did grow,
    He slacked it and ran.

14 And when he came to that lord's gate,
    Stopt not to knock or call,
  But set his bent bow to his breast
    And lightly leapt the wall ;
  And ere the porter could open the gate,
    The boy was in the hall,

15 In presence of that noble lord,
    And fell down on his knee:
  'What is it, my boy,' he cried,
    'Have you brought unto me ?

16 'Is my building broke into ?
    Or is my towers won ?
  Or is my true-love delivered
    Of daughter or of son ? '

17 'Your building is not broke,' he cried,
    'Nor is your towers won,
  Nor is your true-love delivered
    Of daughter nor of son ;
  But if you do not come in haste,
    Be sure she will be gone.

18 'Her father is gone to the fire,
    Her brother to the whin,

To kindle up a bold bonfire,
    To burn her body in.'

19 'Go saddle to me the black,' he cried,
    'And do it very soon ;
  Get unto me the swiftest horse
    That ever rade from the town.'

20 The first horse that he rade upon,
    For he was raven black,
  He bore him far, and very far,
    But failed in a slack.

21 The next horse that he rode upon,
    He was a bonny brown ;
  He bore him far, and very far,
    But did at last fall down.

22 The next horse that he rode upon,
    He as the milk was white ;
  Fair fall the mare that foaled that foal
    Took him to Janet's sight !

23 And boots and spurs, all as he was,
    Into the fire he lap,
  Got one kiss of her comely mouth,
    While her body gave a crack.

24 'O who has been so bold,' he says,
    'This bonfire to set on ?
  Or who has been so bold,' he says,
    'Her body for to burn ? '

25 'O here are we,' her brother said,
    'This bonfire who set on ;
  And we have been so bold,' he said,
    'Her body for to burn.'

26 'O I 'll cause burn for you, Janet,
    Your father and your mother ;
  And I 'll cause die for you, Janet,
    Your sister and your brother.

27 'And I 'll cause mony back be bare,
    And mony shed be thin,
  And mony wife be made a widow,
    And mony ane want their son.'

C

Motherwell's MS., p. 472.

1 BEN came to her father dear,
   Stepping upon the floor;
Says, It 's told me, my daughter Janet,
   That you 're now become a whore.

2 'A whore, father, a whore, father?
   That 's what I 'll never be,
Tho I am with bairn to an English lord,
   That first did marry me.'

3 Soon after spoke her bower-woman,
   And sorely did she cry:
'Oh woe is me, my lady fair,
   That ever I saw this day!

4 'For your father 's to the fire, Janet,
   Your brother 's to the whin,
Even to kindle a bold bonefire,
   To burn your body in.'

5 'Where will I get a bonnie boy,
   Will win gold to his fee,
That will run on to fair England
   For my good lord to me?'

6 'Oh here am I, your waiting-boy,
   Would win gold to my fee,
And will carry any message for you,
   By land or yet by sea.'

7 And when he fand the bridges broke,
   He bent his bow and swam,
But when he fand the grass growing,
   He slacked it and ran.

8 And when he came to that lord's gate,
   Stopt not to knock nor call,
But set his bent bow to his breast,
   And lightly lap the wall.

9 And ere the porter was at the gate
   The boy was in the hall,
And in that noble lord's presence
   He on his knee did fall.

10 'O is my biggins broken?' he said,
   'Or is my towers won?
Or is my lady lighter yet,
   Of daughter or of son?'

11 'Your biggins are not broken,' he said,
   'Nor is your towers won,
Nor is your lady lighter yet,
   Of daughter or of son;
But if you stay a little time
   Her life it will be gone.

12 'For her father 's gone to the fire,
   Her brother to the whin,
Even to kindle a bold bonefire,
   To burn her body in.'

13 'Go saddle for me in haste,' he cried,
   'A brace of horses soon;
Go saddle for me the swiftest steeds
   That ever rode to a town.'

14 The first steed that he rade on,
   For he was as jet black,
He rode him far, and very far,
   But he fell down in a slack.

15 The next steed that he rode on,
   He was a berry brown;
He bore him far, and very far,
   But at the last fell down.

16 The next steed that he rode on,
   He was as milk so white;
Fair fall the mare that foaled the foal
   Took him to Janet's lyke!

17 But boots and spurs, all as he was,
   Into the fire he lap,
Took ae kiss of her comely mouth,
   While her body gave a crack.

18 'O who has been so bold,' he said,
   'This bonfire to set on?
Or who has been so bold,' he cried,
   'My true-love for to burn?'

19 Her father cried, I 've been so bold
   This bonefire to put on;
Her brother cried, We 've been so bold
   Her body for to burn.

20 'Oh I shall hang for you, Janet,
   Your father and your brother;
And I shall burn for you, Janet,
   Your sister and your mother.

21 'Oh I shall make many bed empty,
    And many shed be thin,
    And many a wife to be a widow,
    And many one want their son.

22 'Then I shall take a cloak of cloth,
    A staff made of the wand,
    And the boy who did your errand run
    Shall be heir of my land.'

———◆———

D

Campbell MSS, II, 70.

1 LADY MARGERY was her mother's ain daughter,
    And her father's only heir,
    And she's away to Strawberry Castle,
    To learn some unco lair.

2 She hadna been in Strawberry Castle
    A year but only three,
    Till she has proved as big with child,
    As big as woman could be.

3 Word has to her father gone,
    As he pat on his shoon,
    That Lady Margery goes wi child,
    Unto some English loon.

4 Word has to her mother gane,
    As she pat on her gown,
    That Lady Margery goes wi child,
    Unto some English loon.

5 The father he likes her ill,
    The mother she likes her waur,
    But her father he wished her in a fire strang,
    To burn for ever mair.

*   *   *   *   *

6 'Will ye hae this auld man, Lady Margery,
    To be yeer warldly make?
    Or will ye burn in fire strang,
    For your true lover's sake?'

7 'I wunna hae that old, old man
    To be my worldly make,
    But I will burn in fire strang,
    For my true lover's sake.'

8 'O who will put of the pot?
    O who will put of the pan?
    And who will build a bale-fire,
    To burn her body in.'

9 The brother took of the pot,
    The sister took of the pan,
    And her mother builded a bold bale-fire,
    To burn her body in.

10 'O where will I get a bony boy
    That will run my errand soon?
    That will run to Strawberry Castle,
    And tell my love to come soon?'

11 But then started up a little boy,
    Near to that lady's kin:
    'Often have I gane your errands, madam,
    But now it is time to rin.'

12 O when he came to Strawberry Castle,
    He tirled at the pin;
    There was nane sae ready as that lord himsell
    To let the young body in.

13 'O is my towers broken?
    Or is my castle wone?
    Or is my lady Margery lighter
    Of a daughter or a son?'

14 'Your towers are not broken,
    Nor is your castle wone;
    But the fairest lady of a' the land
    For thee this day does burn.'

15 'Go saddle for me the black, black horse,
    Go saddle to me the brown;
    Go saddle to me as swift a steed
    As ever man rade on.'

16 They saddled to him the black horse,
    They saddled to him the brown;
    They've saddled to him as swift a steed
    As ever man rade on.

17 He put his foot into the stirrup,
    He bounded for to ride;
    The silver buttons lap of his breast,
    And his nose began to bleed.

18 He bursted fifteen gude stout steeds,
 And four o them were dappled gray,
And the little foot-page ran aye before,
 Crying, Mend it, an ye may !

19 When he came to the bale-fire,
 He lighted wi a glent,
Wi black boots and clean spurs,
 And through the fire he went.

20 He laid ae arm about her neck,
 And the other beneath her chin ;
He thought to get a kiss o her,
 But her middle it gade in twain.

21 ' But who has been so false,' he said,
 ' And who has been sae cruel,

To carry the timber from my ain wood
 To burn my dearest jewel ?

22 ' But I 'll burn for ye, Lady Margery,
 Yeer father and yeer mother ;
And I 'll burn for ye, Lady Margery,
 Yeer sister and yeer brother.

23 ' I 'll do for ye, Lady Margery,
 What never was done for nane ;
I 'll make many lady lemanless,
 And many a clothing thin.

24 ' And I 'll burn for yeer sake, Lady Margery,
 The town that yeer burnt in,
And [make] many a baby fatherless,
 That 's naething o the blame.'

———

E

Motherwell's MS., p. 1, from the recitation of Mrs Thomson, Kilbarchan, February 25, 1825 ; Motherwell's Minstrelsy, p. 234.

1 LADY MARJORY was her mother's only daugh-
 ter,
 Her father's only heir, O
And she is awa to Strawberry Castle,
 To get some unco lair. O

2 She had na been in Strawberry Castle
 A twelve month and a day,
Till Lady Marjory she gaes wi child,
 As big as she can gae.

3 Word is to her father gone,
 Before he got on his shoon,
That Lady Marjory she gaes wi child,
 And it is to an Irish groom.

4 But word is to her mother gane,
 Before that she gat on her gown,
That Lady Marjorie she goes wi child,
 To a lord of high renown.

5 ' O wha will put on the pot ? ' they said,
 ' Or wha will put on the pan ?
Or wha will put on a bauld, bauld fire,
 To burn Lady Marjorie in ? '

6 Her father he put on the pot,
 Her sister put on the pan,

And her brother he put on a bauld, bauld fire,
 To burn Lady Marjorie in ;
And her mother she sat in a golden chair,
 To see her daughter burn.

7 ' But where will I get a pretty little boy,
 That will win hose and shoon,
That will go quickly to Strawberry Castle
 And bid my lord come doun ? '

8 ' O here am I a pretty boy,
 That 'll win hose and shoon,
That will rin quickly to Strawberry Castle,
 And bid thy lord come doun.'

9 O when he came to broken brigs,
 He bent his bow and swam,
And when he came to good dry land,
 He let down his foot and ran.

10 When he came to Strawberry Castle,
 He tirled at the pin ;
None was so ready as the gay lord himsell
 To open and let him in.

11 ' O is there any of my towers burnt ?
 Or any of my castles broken ?
Or is Lady Marjorie brought to bed,
 Of a daughter or a son ? '

12 ' O there is nane of thy towers burnt,
 Nor nane of thy castles broken,

But Lady Marjorie is condemned to die,
 To be burnt in a fire of oaken.'

13 'O gar saddle to me the black,' he said,
 'Gar saddle to me the brown;
Gar saddle to me the swiftest steed
 That eer carried a man from town.'

14 He left the black into the slap,
 The brown into the brae,
But fair fa that bonny apple-gray
 That carried this gay lord away!

15 He took a little horn out of his pocket,
 And he blew 't both loud and shrill,
And the little life that was in her,
 She hearkend to it full weel.

16 'Beet on, beet on, my brother dear,
 I value you not one straw,
For yonder comes my own true-love,
 I hear his horn blaw.

17 'Beet on, beet on, my father dear,
 I value you not a pin,

For yonder comes my own true-love,
 I hear his bridle ring.'

18 But when he came into the place,
 He lap unto the wa;
He thought to get a kiss o her bonny lips,
 But her body fell in twa.

19 'Oh vow, oh vow, oh vow,' he said,
 'Oh vow but ye 've been cruel!
Ye 've taken the timber out of my own wood
 And burnt my ain dear jewel.

20 'Now for thy sake, Lady Marjorie,
 I 'll burn both father and mother;
And for thy sake, Lady Marjorie,
 I 'll burn both sister and brother.

21 'And for thy sake, Lady Marjorie,
 I 'll burn both kith and kin;
But I will remember the pretty little boy
 That did thy errand rin.'

—◆—

F

The Scots [Edinburgh] Magazine, 1822, LXXXIX, 734, communicated by W. W.

1 FAIR MARJORY 's gaen into the school,
 Between six and seven,
An she 's come back richt big wi bairn,
 Between twelve and eleven.

2 It 's out then sprung her mither dear,
 Stood stately on the flure:
'Ye 're welcum back, young Marjory,
 But ye 're sune becum a hure.'

3 'I 'm not a hure, mither,' she said,
 'Nor ever intend to be;
But I 'm wi child to a gentleman,
 An he swears he 'll marry me.'

4 [It 's out then sprung her father dear,
 Stood stately on the flure:
'Ye 're welcum back, young Marjory,
 But ye 're sune becum a hure.'

5 'I 'm not a hure, father,' she said,
 'Nor ever intend to be;

But I 'm wi child to a gentleman,
 An he swears he will marry me.'

6 It 's out then sprung her brother dear,
 Stood stately on the flure:
'Ye 're welcum back, young Marjory,
 But ye 're sune becum a hure.'

7 'I 'm not a hure, brother,' she said,
 'Nor ever intend to be;
But I 'm wi child to a gentleman,
 An he swears he will marry me.'

8 It 's out then sprung her sister dear,
 Stood stately on the flure:
'Ye 're welcum back, young Marjory,
 But ye 're sune becum a hure.'

9 'I 'm not a hure, sister,' she said,
 'Nor ever intend to be;]
Ye 're but a young woman, sister,
 An ye shuld speak sparinlie.'

10 Her father 's to the grene-wude gaen,
 Her brither 's to the brume;

An her mither sits in her gowden chair,
　To see her dochter burn.

　　*　　　*　　　*　　　*　　　*

11 .　.　.　.　.　.
　.　.　.　.　.　.

The sister she culd do naething,
　And she sat down to greet.

12 'Oh whare will I get a bonny boy,
　That wull win hose an shoon,
That wull rin to Strawberry Castle for me,
　And bid my true-love come?'

13 It 's out than spak a bonny boy,
　That stude richt at her knee :
'It 's I wull rin your errand, ladie,
　Wi the saut tear i my ee.'

14 It 's whan he cam to broken brigg,
　He bent his bow an swam,
An whan he cam whare green grass grew,
　Set doon his feet an ran.

15 An whan he cam to Strawberry Castle,
　He thirled at the pin,
An aye sae ready as the porter was
　To rise and let him in.

　　*　　　*　　　*　　　*　　　*

16 'Gae saddle to me the black,' he says,
　'Gae saddle to me the broun ;
Gae saddle to me the swiftest steed
　That eer set fute on grun.'

17 It 's first he burst the bonny black,
　An syne the bonny broun,
But the dapple-gray rade still away,
　Till he cam to the toun.

18 An aye he rade, an aye he rade,
　An aye away he flew,
Till the siller buttons flew off his coat ;
　He took out his horn an blew.

19 An aye he blew, an aye he blew,
　He blew baith loud an shrill,
An the little life that Marjory had,
　She heard his horn blaw weel.

20 'Beik on, beik on, cruel mither,' she said,
　'For I value you not a straw ;
For if ever I heard my love in my life,
　He 's comin here awa.'

　　*　　　*　　　*　　　*　　　*

21 When he cam unto the flames
　He jamp in, butes and a' ;
He thocht to hae kissd her red rosy lips,
　But her body broke in twa.

　　*　　　*　　　*　　　*　　　*

22 I 'll burn for thy sake, Marjory,
　The toun that thou lies in ;
An I 'll mak the baby fatherless,
　For I 'll throw mysel therein.

G

Notes and Queries, Second Series, IX, 193 ; communicated
by A. J., Edinburgh, as learned by himself and an elder sister
from an old washerwoman of East Dereham, Norfolk, in the
early part of this century.

　　*　　　*　　　*　　　*　　　*

1 'MY father was the first good man
　Who tied me to a stake ;
My mother was the first good woman
　Who did the fire make.

2 'My brother was the next good man
　Who did the fire fetch ;

My sister was the next good woman
　Who lighted it with a match.

3 'They blew the fire, they kindled the fire,
　Till it did reach my knee :
"O mother, mother, quench the fire !
　The smoke will smother me."

4 'O had I but my little foot-page,
　My errand he would run ;
He would run unto gay London,
　And bid my lord come home.'

5 Then there stood by her sister's child,
　Her own dear sister's son :

'O many an errand I've run for thee,
And but this one I'll run.'

6 He ran, where the bridge was broken down
He bent his bow and swam;
He swam till he came to the good green turf,
He up on his feet and ran.

7 He ran till he came at his uncle's hall;
His uncle sat at his meat:
'Good mete, good mete, good uncle, I pray,
O if you knew what I'd got to say,
How little would you eat!'

8 'O is my castle broken down,
Or is my tower won?
Or is my gay lady brought o bed,
Of a daughter or a son?'

9 'Your castle is not broken down,
Your tower it is not won;
Your gay lady is not brought to bed,
Of a daughter or a son.

10 'But she has sent you a gay gold ring,
With a posy round the rim,

To know, if you have any love for her,
You'll come to her burning.'

11 He called down his merry men all,
By one, by two, by three;
He mounted on his milk-white steed,
To go to Margery.

12 They blew the fire, they kindled the fire,
Till it did reach her head:
'O mother, mother, quench the fire!
For I am nearly dead.'

13 She turned her head on her left shoulder,
Saw her girdle hang on the tree:
'O God bless them that gave me that!
They'll never give more to me.'

14 She turned her head on her right shoulder,
Saw her lord come riding home:
'O quench the fire, my dear mother!
For I am nearly gone.'

15 He mounted off his milk-white steed,
And into the fire he ran,
Thinking to save his gay ladye,
But he had staid too long.

———•———

H

Buchan's Ballads of the North of Scotland, I, 103.

1 THERE stands a stane in wan water,
It's lang ere it grew green;
Lady Maisry sits in her bower door,
Sewing at her silken seam.

2 Word's gane to her mother's kitchen,
And to her father's ha,
That Lady Maisry is big wi bairn —
And her true-love's far awa.

3 When her brother got word of this,
Then fiercely looked he:
'Betide me life, betide me death,
At Maisry's bower I'se be.

4 'Gae saddle to me the black, the black,
Gae saddle to me the brown;
Gae saddle to me the swiftest steed,
To hae me to the town.'

5 When he came to Maisry's bower,
He turnd him round about,
And at a little shott-window,
He saw her peeping out.

6 'Gude morrow, gude morrow, Lady Maisry,
God make you safe and free!'
'Gude morrow, gude morrow, my brother dear,
What are your wills wi me?'

7 'What's come o a' your green claithing,
Was ance for you too side?
And what's become o your lang stays,
Was ance for you too wide?'

8 'O he that made my claithing short,
I hope he'll make them side;
And he that made my stays narrow,
I hope he'll make them wide.'

9 'O is it to a lord o might,
Or baron o high degree?

Or is it to any o your father's boys,
    Rides in the chase him wi?'

10 'It's no to any Scottish lord,
    Nor baron o high degree;
But English James, that little prince,
    That has beguiled me.'

11 'O was there not a Scots baron
    That could hae fitted thee,
That thus you've lovd an Englishman,
    And has affronted me?'

12 She turnd her right and round about,
    The tear blinded her ee:
'What is the wrang I've done, brother,
    Ye look sae fierce at me?'

13 'Will ye forsake that English blude,
    When your young babe is born?'
'I'll nae do that, my brother dear,
    Tho I shoud be forlorn.'

14 'I'se cause a man put up the fire,
    Anither ca in the stake,
And on the head o yon high hill
    I'll burn you for his sake.

15 'O where are all my wall-wight men,
    That I pay meat and fee,
For to hew down baith thistle and thorn,
    To burn that lady wi?'

16 Then he has taen her, Lady Maisry,
    And fast he has her bound;
And he causd the fiercest o his men
    Drag her frae town to town.

17 Then he has causd ane of his men
    Hew down baith thistle and thorn;
She carried the peats in her petticoat-lap,
    Her ainsell for to burn.

18 Then ane pat up this big bauld fire,
    Anither ca'd in the stake;
It was to burn her Lady Maisry,
    All for her true-love's sake.

19 But it fell ance upon a day,
    Prince James he thought full lang;
He minded on the lady gay
    He left in fair Scotland.

20 'O where will I get a little wee boy,
    Will win gowd to his fee,
That will rin on to Adam's high tower,
    Bring tidings back to me?'

21 'O here am I, a little wee boy,
    Will win gowd to my fee,
That will rin on to Adam's high tower,
    Bring tidings back to thee.'

22 Then he is on to Adam's high tower,
    As fast as gang coud he,
And he but only wan in time
    The fatal sight to see.

23 He sat his bent bow to his breast,
    And ran right speedilie,
And he is back to his master,
    As fast as gang coud he.

24 'What news, what news, my little wee boy?
    What news hae ye to me?'
'Bad news, bad news, my master dear,
    Bad news, as ye will see.'

25 'Are ony o my biggins brunt, my boy?
    Or ony o my towers won?
Or is my lady lighter yet,
    O dear daughter or son?'

26 'There's nane o your biggins brunt, master,
    Nor nane o your towers won,
Nor is your lady lighter yet,
    O dear daughter nor son.

27 'There's an has been [put up] a big bauld fire,
    Anither ca'd in the stake,
And on the head o yon high hill,
    They're to burn her for your sake.'

28 'Gae saddle to me the black, the black,
    Gae saddle to me the brown;
Gae saddle to me the swiftest steed,
    To hae me to the town.'

29 Ere he was three miles near the town,
    She heard his horse-foot patt:
'Mend up the fire, my fause brother,
    It scarce comes to my pap.'

30 Ere he was twa miles near the town,
    She heard his bridle ring:

'Mend up the fire, my fause brother,
    It scarce comes to my chin.

31 'But look about, my fause brother,
    Ye see not what I see ;
I see them coming here, or lang
    Will mend the fire for thee.'

32 Then up it comes him little Prince James,
    And fiercely looked he :
'I 'se make my love's words very true
    She said concerning me.

33 'O wha has been sae bauld,' he said,
    'As put this bonfire on ?
And wha has been sae bauld,' he said,
    'As put that lady in ? '

34 Then out it spake her brother then,
    He spoke right furiouslie ;
Says, I 'm the man that put her in :
    Wha dare hinder me ?

35 'If my hands had been loose,' she said,
    'As they are fastly bound,

I woud hae looted me to the ground,
    Gien you up your bonny young son.'

36 'I will burn, for my love's sake,
    Her father and her mother ;
And I will burn, for my love's sake,
    Her sister and her brother.

37 'And I will burn, for my love's sake,
    The whole o a' her kin ;
And I will burn, for my love's sake,
    Thro Linkum and thro Lin.

38 'And mony a bed will I make toom,
    And bower will I make thin ;
And mony a babe shall thole the fire,
    For I may enter in.'

39 Great meen was made for Lady Maisry,
    On that hill whare she was slain ;
But mair was for her ain true-love,
    On the fields for he ran brain.

———◆———

I

a. Motherwell's MS., p. 235 ; Motherwell's Minstrelsy,
p. 221. b. Motherwell's MS., p. 179, from Mrs Thomson,
of Kilbarchan. c. Motherwell's MS., p. 181, from Mrs
McLean, of Glasgow.

1 THERE lived a lady in Scotland,
    Hey my love and ho my joy
There lived a lady in Scotland,
    Who dearly loved me
There lived a lady in Scotland,
An she 's fa'n in love wi an Englishman.
    And bonnie Susie Cleland is to be burnt in
        Dundee

2 The father unto the daughter came,
    Who dearly loved me
Saying, Will you forsake that Englishman ?

3 'If you will not that Englishman forsake,
    Who dearly loved me
O I will burn you at a stake.'

4 'I will not that Englishman forsake,
    Who dearly loved me
Tho you should burn me at a stake.

5 'O where will I get a pretty little boy,
    Who dearly loves me
Who will carry tidings to my joy ? '

6 'Here am I, a pretty little boy,
    Who dearly loves thee
Who will carry tidings to thy joy.'

7 'Give to him this right-hand glove,
    Who dearly loves me
Tell him to get another love.
    For, etc.

8 'Give to him this little penknife,
    Who dearly loves me
Tell him to get another wife.
    For, etc.

9 ' Give to him this gay gold ring ;
　Who dearly loves me
Tell him I 'm going to my burning.'
　An, etc.

10 The brother did the stake make,
　Who dearly loved me
The father did the fire set.
　An bonnie Susie Cleland was burnt in Dun-
　　dee.

A. 11¹. she says.
　16¹. blood *I was disposed to change to* lord :
　　but see H 13¹.
　21³⁴. *As cited by Anderson from William
　　Tytler's MS.*,

　　. . . . to green grass growing
　　He took off his sheen.

B. 22⁴. Janet's exite : *in* C 16⁴ Janet's lyke.
D. *Stanzas 8, 9, 21, are the three last of the MS.*
　8¹⁻². *I should read* put on, *were it not for*
　　9¹⁻².
　23³. lady lamentless.
E. 3³. If *for* that *in the margin, without explana-
　　tion.*
　15–17. *The order in the MS. is* 16, 17, 15.
　*Motherwell, as often elsewhere, makes slight
　　changes in printing, as :* 11², broken *to*
　　won, *though not changed in* 12² ; 15³ [17³],
　And *to* And wi, *unnecessarily, see* F 19³.
F. 2–9. " Her father, brother, and sister succes-
　　sively address her in the same polite style,
　　and receive the same answer ; except that to
　　the latter, instead of the information con-
　　tained in the last two lines, she addresses a
　　piece of advice." *The phrase* stood stately
　　in 2², *most appropriate for the mother, was
　　probably varied for father, brother, and
　　sister.*
　15–16. " He delivers his message in the ap-
　　proved ballad style, and the lover speaks."
　20. " The few verses following contain her tes-
　　tamentary bequests to her relatives above
　　mentioned ; but the person from whom I got
　　the ballad could not repeat them."
G. 6². He bend.
I. a. 1. *Given in the Appendix to Motherwell's
　　Minstrelsy, p. xix, XIV, with this
　　slight difference in the burden :* And
　　she dearly loved me.
　3–9. at Dundee *in the burden.*
　8². Penknife *for* wife, *in my copy of the MS.*
　10. *In the Minstrelsy, from* b :

　　Her father he ca'd up the stake,
　　Her brother he the fire did make.

b. 1. There lived a lady in Scotland
　　O my love and O my joy
　　Who dearly loved an Englishman.
　　　And bonnie Susie Cleland is to be burnt
　　　　at Dundee

　2. The father to the daughter came :
　　' Will you forsake your Englishman ? '
　　For, etc.

　3 *is wanting.*

　4. ' My Englishman I 'll neer forsake,
　　Altho you burn me at your stake.
　　For, etc.

　5. ' O where will I get a pretty little boy,
　　That will bring tidings to my joy ? '
　　For, etc.

　6. ' O here am I, a pretty little boy,
　　And I 'll carry tidings to thy joy.'
　　For, etc.

　7. ' O take to him this right-hand glove,
　　Tell him to seek another love.'
　　For, etc.

　8 *is wanting.*

　9. ' O bring to him this gay gold ring,
　　And bid him come to my burning.'
　　For, etc.

　10. Her father he ca'd up the stake,
　　Her brother he the fire did make.
　　　And bonnie Susie Cleland is burnt at
　　　　Dundee

c. 1–4 *are wanting.*

5. 'Where will I get a bonny boy,
      Oh my love and oh my joy
   Where will I get a bonny boy,
      That dearly loves me
   Where will I get a bonny boy,
      Will carry tidings to my joy?'
         Bonnie Susie Cleland was burned at
            Dundee

6. 'Here am I, a little boy,
      That dearly loves thee
   Will carry tidings to thy joy.'

7. 'Carry my love this glove,
      Who dearly loves me
   Bid him seek another love.

8. 'Carry my love this knife,
      That dearly loves me
   Bid him seek another wife.

9. 'Carry my love this ring,
      That dearly loves me
   Bid him come to my burning.'

10 *is wanting.*

66

LORD INGRAM AND CHIEL WYET

A. a. 'Lord Ingram and Chiel Wyet,' Motherwell's Minstrelsy, p. 173. **b.** 'Child Vyet,' Maidment's North Countrie Garland, p. 24.

B. 'Lord Ingram and Gil Viett,' Skene MS., p. 16.

C. 'Auld Ingram,' Herd's MSS, I, 169, II, 84; 'Lord Wa'yates and Auld Ingram,' Jamieson's Popular Ballads, II, 265.

D. 'Lord Ingram and Childe Viat,' Kinloch MSS, V, 323.

E. 'Lord Ingram and Childe Vyet,' Buchan's Ballads of the North of Scotland, I, 234.

C WAS furnished Jamieson from Herd's MSS by Scott, and underwent a few slight changes in publication. Jamieson inquired through the Scots Magazine, October, 1803, p. 699, for the conclusion, which is wanting, but unsuccessfully.

The only variation of much moment in the five versions of this tragedy is that, in C, the bridegroom and the lover are not brothers, but uncle and nephew. Some inconsistencies have been created in the course of tradition. The bride's insisting on having twenty men before her and twenty on each side, ere she will go to kirk, not to mention the extrava- gance of twenty milk-white doves above her head, C 22,* is incompatible with her aversion to the "weary wedding," and with her lan- guage about the bridegroom's gifts in C 4, 5, D 4–6, E 8–10. There is much confusion at the end. After the death of the two rivals the lady, in E, imposes on herself the penance of begging her bread as a pilgrim for the rest of her days. This penance we find also in the two last stanzas of A, and a trace of it in B 20, D 10. Another, and probably later, repre- sentation is that she went mad, A 30, B 19, D 9. The two are blended in A, B, D; un- less we are to suppose that Maisry's adopting

---

* This stanza, which comes in here with flagrant impro- priety, is a commonplace, or movable passage. It occurs, as a feature in the ceremony of a brilliant wedding, in 'Fair Mary of Wallington,' E 6, 7, and in some copies of 'Lord Thomas and Fair Annet:' see that ballad, note to **A.**

a beggar's life was a consequence of her madness, which is not according to the simplicity of old ballads. That something was due the unfortunate Lord Ingram, especially if he was disposed to relinquish his wife to his brother, B 17, the modern sense of justice will admit; but that Maisry's remorse on account of the handsome wedding Ingram had given her should exceed her grief for Chiel Wyet, A 32, B 20, D 10, E 43, 44, is as little natural as romantic, and is only to be explained as an exhibition of imbecility, whether on her part or on the part of some reciter who gave that turn to the story. B confounds confusion by killing Maisry on the top of all.

The sword laid in bed between man and woman, B 14, E 30, as a sign or pledge of continence, does not occur often in popular ballads. We have it in 'Südeli,' Uhland, I, 275, No 121, st. 11, and in two of the Swedish forms of Grundtvig's 'Brud i Vaande,' Danmarks gamle Folkeviser, V, 345, No. 277, D, sts 26, 27, and Arwidsson, II, 248, No 132, sts 21, 22, 'Fru Margaretha.' In popular tales: Grimms, K. u. H. märchen, No 60; Asbjørnsen og Moe, Norske Folkeeventyr, No 3; Il Pentamerone, I, 9; Hahn's Griechische Märchen, I, 171, No 122. In Norse poetry and saga: Völsunga saga, 27, Rafn, Fornaldar Sögur, I, 187; Sæmund's Edda, Sigurðarkviða, III, 65, Lüning, p. 401, Bugge (68), p. 259; Snorri's Edda, Hafniæ, 1848, I, 362, Skáldskaparmál, 41; Saxo Grammaticus, Book 9, p. 162 of the Frankfort edition of 1576; Gaungu-Hrólfs saga, 24, Fornaldar Sögur, III, 303. Further, in Orendel und Bríde, ed. Ettmüller, p. 46, XII, 49, 50; Wolfdietrich, von der Hagen's Heldenbuch, I, 236, st. 592; Tristan, ed. Michel, I, 88, v. 1768 ff, Scott's Sir Tristrem, III. 20; Amis and Amiloun, Weber's Metrical Romances, II, 417, v. 1163 ff;

Aladdin in the Arabian Nights, J. Scott, IV 345.*

Lord Wayets, in C 17, kicks up the table and sends the silver cup into the fire. Young Beichan takes the table with his foot and makes the cups and cans to flee, B 18, D 23, F 28, J 5, N 42, or makes the table flee, H 42; so the knight in 'Child Waters,' G 18, the baron in 'Child Maurice,' E, F, and the mother in 'Fair Mary of Wallington,' A, B. Kinmont Willie, st. 9, takes the table with his hand and gars the red wine spring on hie. The table, being of boards laid on trestles, would be easy to ding over or make flee. Being also narrow, it might be jumped over, and those in whose way it might be seem to have preferred to clear it in that fashion, at least out of Britain. So the Danish Lord Lovel on hearing of his love's death, spilling the mead or wine, Kristensen, II, No 20, A 6, B 10, C 3, D 4; Sir Peter in Afzelius, No 9, I, 50, Grundtvig, No 210, IV, 220, etc. The king in the Icelandic Ribbalds kvæði, to be sure, kicks the table away and spills the mead and wine, Íslenzk Fornkvæði, No 16, B 8, C 2, so that Lord Wayets, Young Beichan, and others may have taken their cue from that island. But against this we may put Hervarar saga, c. 3, Fornaldar Sögur, I, 516; Olafs saga hins Helga, c. 50, Keyser and Unger, p. 36; Grundtvig, Danmarks Folkeviser, No 11, A 23, No 13, B 18, G 15, I 16; etc. In 'Magnus Algotsøn,' Grundtvig, No 181, D 18, the bride jumps over the table and goes off with her old love; in Sušil's Bohemian ballads, No 135, p. 131, the bride jumps over four tables and on to a fifth to get at her first betrothed; in the Novella della Figlia del Re di Dacia, ed. Wesselofsky, p. 38, the duke jumps over the table to get to his wife; in a German ballad in Schröer's Ausflug nach Gottschee, p. 210 f,

---

* These citations, which might easily be extended, are many of them repeated from Grimm's Rechtsalterthümer, pp. 168–70 of the second edition. Sir Walter Scott has pointed out that on the occasion of the marriage of Maria of Burgundy with the Archduke Maximilian, in 1477, the marriage being by proxy, Ludwig, Pfalzgraf of Vendelz, the bridegroom's representative, was formally bedded with the bride, a naked sword being laid between them. Scott also refers to a play called The Jovial Crew, acted in 1641, in

which one of the characters, to enrage another, proposes to be his proxy, marry his love for him, and lay a naked cudgel betwixt them : Sir Tristrem, p. 439, ed. 1833. In an Italian ballad the sword is reduced to a straw : Wolf, Volkslieder aus Venetien, No 95, Bolza, No 56, Ferraro, C. p. monferrini, No 76. In the Spanish and Portuguese romances of 'Gerineldo,' the sultan or king, having found the page asleep with the infanta, lays his sword between the two and retires : Duran, Nos 320, 321; Hardung, I, 101.

the bridegroom, who has lost the bride, jumps over the table to get out of the room as soon as possible; a French gentleman takes a vault over the table before him, Gautier, Les Épopées Françaises, I, 508, ed. 1865, and a lady in a ludicrous anecdote told in the Zimmerische Chronik, ed. Barack, 1881, II, 132 f. But Torello's wife, on the other hand, Decameron, X, 9, throws down the table which bars her way to her lord, and so does the steward in 'Sir Orfeo,' v. 576, ed. Zielke.*

Ebbe Skammelsøn, being obliged to absent himself from his plighted maid for a considerable time, loses her through the artifices of his brother [and mother], who pretends first that Ebbe is unfaithful, and then that he is dead. Ebbe is warned by a dream that his brother is about to wed his mistress, goes home in great haste, and arrives on the wedding-day. He kills the bride, and then his brother, who, at the last moment, offers to cede the bride to him, as Lord Ingram, in B 17, says he meant to do. Ebbe after this begs his bread, or goes on a pilgrimage weighted with iron on his hands and loins; wherein his part resembles Maisry's. Danske Viser, III, 75, No 120, translated by Prior, II, 380; Arwidsson, No 33, I, 216, 224, 412; Atterbom's Poetisk Kalender, 1816, p. 55.

It may be worth noting that Maisry's wedding, according to B 20, was "in good kirkdoor," like the five of The Wife of Bath.

Translated by Knortz, Lieder und Romanzen Alt-Englands, p. 166, No 44, after Allingham, p. 306.

A

a. Motherwell's Minstrelsy, p. 173, communicated by Charles Kirkpatrick Sharpe. b. Maidment's North Countrie Garland, p. 24, from tradition in Aberdeenshire.

1 LORD INGRAM and Chiel Wyet
    Was baith born in one bower;
    Laid baith their hearts on one lady,
    The less was their honour.

2 Chiel Wyet and Lord Ingram
    Was baith born in one hall;
    Laid baith their hearts on one lady,
    The worse did them befall.

3 Lord Ingram wood her Lady Maisery
    From father and from mother;
    Lord Ingram wood her Lady Maisery
    From sister and from brother.

4 Lord Ingram wood her Lady Maisery
    With leave of a' her kin;
    And every one gave full consent,
    But she said no to him.

5 Lord Ingram wood her Lady Maisery
    Into her father's ha;
    Chiel Wyet wood her Lady Maisery
    Amang the sheets so sma.

6 Now it fell out upon a day,
    She was dressing her head,
    That ben did come her father dear,
    Wearing the gold so red.

7 He said, Get up now, Lady Maisery,
    Put on your wedding gown;
    For Lord Ingram he will be here,
    Your wedding must be done.

* Some of the Norse examples were derived from notes of Grundtvig, three others from Liebrecht. Grundtvig cites an ordinance of Frederic II of Denmark, dated 1586, to this effect: Whereas a custom has come in of having a dance during a wedding-repast, which dance those that sit behind the tables are asked to as well as others, and therefore are obliged to step on the tables, on which the victuals are still standing, and whereas this, indecorous of itself, might even prove dangerous to women-folk, and others, who should attempt to jump over the tables, now therefore dancing during meal-time is forbidden until dishes and tables shall have been cleared away: IV, 754. The table-jumping above is mostly done under great excitement, and at weddings, in order that the right parties may come together; but nimble young men in England seem to have taken this short way to their places habitually in old times. Liebrecht cites this curious passage from the Jests of Scogin, Hazlitt's Shakespeare Jest-Books, II, 105: "Scogin did mark the fashions of the court, and among all other things he did mark how men did leap over the table in the king's hall to sit down at dinner and supper, which is not used now." The first edition of Scogin's Jests is of 1565.

8 'I'd rather be Chiel Wyet's wife,
  The white fish for to sell,
Before I were Lord Ingram's wife,
  To wear the silk so well.

9 'I'd rather be Chiel Wyet's wife,
  With him to beg my bread,
Before I were Lord Ingram's wife,
  To wear the gold so red.

10 'Where will I get a bonny boy,
  Will win gold to his fee,
And will run unto Chiel Wyet's,
  With this letter from me?'

11 'O here I am, the boy,' says one,
  'Will win gold to my fee,
And carry away any letter
  To Chiel Wyet from thee.'

12 And when he found the bridges broke,
  He bent his bow and swam;
And when he found the grass growing,
  He hastened and he ran.

13 And when he came to Chiel Wyet's castle,
  He did not knock nor call,
But set his bent bow to his breast,
  And lightly leaped the wall;
And ere the porter opend the gate,
  The boy was in the hall.

14 The first line he looked on,
  A grieved man was he;
The next line he looked on,
  A tear blinded his ee:
Says, I wonder what ails my one brother
  He'll not let my love be!.

15 'But I'll send to my brother's bridal —
  The bacon shall be mine —
Full four and twenty buck and roe,
  And ten tun of the wine;
And bid my love be blythe and glad,
  And I will follow syne.'

16 There was not a groom about that castle
  But got a gown of green,
And all was blythe, and all was glad,
  But Lady Maisery she was neen.

17 There was no cook about that kitchen
  But got a gown of gray,

And all was blythe, and all was glad,
  But Lady Maisery was wae.

18 Between Mary Kirk and that castle
  Was all spread ower with garl,
To keep Lady Maisery and her maidens
  From tramping on the marl.

19 From Mary Kirk to that castle
  Was spread a cloth of gold,
To keep Lady Maisery and her maidens
  From treading on the mold.

20 When mass was sung, and bells was rung,
  And all men bound for bed,
Then Lord Ingram and Lady Maisery
  In one bed they were laid.

21 When they were laid into their bed —
  It was baith soft and warm —
He laid his hand over her side,
  Says, I think you are with bairn.

22 'I told you once, so did I twice,
  When ye came me to woo,
That Chiel Wyet, your only brother,
  One night lay in my bower.

23 'I told you twice, I told you thrice,
  Ere ye came me to wed,
That Chiel Wyet, your one brother,
  One night lay in my bed.'

24 'O will you father your bairn on me,
  And on no other man?
And I'll give him to his dowry
  Full fifty ploughs of land.'

25 'I will not father my bairn on you,
  Nor on no wrongeous man,
Though ye would give him to his dowry
  Five thousand ploughs of land.'

26 Then up did start him Chiel Wyet,
  Shed by his yellow hair,
And gave Lord Ingram to the heart
  A deep wound and a sair.

27 Then up did start him Lord Ingram,
  Shed by his yellow hair,
And gave Chiel Wyet to the heart
  A deep wound and a sair.

28 There was no pity for that two lords,
        Where they were lying slain ;
    But all was for her Lady Maisery,
        In that bower she gaed brain.

29 There was no pity for that two lords,
        When they were lying dead ;
    But all was for her Lady Maisery,
        In that bower she went mad.

30 Said, Get to me a cloak of cloth,
        A staff of good hard tree ;
    If I have been an evil woman,
        I shall beg till I dee.

31 'For a bit I 'll beg for Chiel Wyet,
        For Lord Ingram I 'll beg three ;
    All for the good and honorable marriage
        At Mary Kirk he gave me.'

——◆——

B

Skene MS., p. 16 ; taken down in the North of Scotland,
1802–1803.

1 LORD INGRAM and Gil Viett
        Were baith born in ae ha ;
    They laid their love on ae lady,
        An fate they coud na fa.

2 Lord Ingram and Gil Viett
        Were baith laid in ae wame ;
    They laid their love on ae lady,
        The greater was their shame.

3 Lord Ingram wood her Lady Masery
        Frae father and frae mither ;
    Gill Viett wood her Lady Masery
        Frae sister and frae brither.

4 Lord Ingram courted her Lady Masery
        Among the company a' ;
    Gill Viett he wood her Lady Masery
        Among the sheets so sma.

5 'Get up, my daughter dear,
        Put on your bridal gown ;
    This day 's your bridal day
        Wi Lord Ingram.'

6 'How can I get up,
        An put on my bridal gown,
    Or how marry the ae brither,
        An the tither's babe in my womb ? '

*   *   *   *   *

7 'O laugh you at mysell, brither,
        Or at my companie?
    Or laugh ye at my bonnie bride,
        She wad na laugh at thee ? '

8 'I laugh na at yoursel, brither,
        Nor at your companie ;
    Nor laugh I at your buirlie bride,
        She wad na laugh at me.

9 'But there 's a brotch on a breast-bane,
        A garlan on ane's hair ;
    Gin ye kend what war under that,
        Ye wad neer love woman mair.

10 'There is a brotch on a breast-bane,
        An roses on ane's sheen ;
    Gin ye kend what war under that,
        Your love wad soon be deen.'

11 Whan bells were rung, and mass was sung,
        And a' man boun to bed,
    Lord Ingram and Lady Masery
        In ae chamer were laid.

12 He put his hand out oure his bonnie bride,
        The babe between her sides did quake :
    .   .   .   .   .   .
        .   .   .   .   .

13 'O father your babe on me, Lady Masery,
        O father your babe on me.'
    .   .   .   .   .   .
        .   .   .   .   .

14 'I may father my babe on a stock,
        Sae may I on a stane,
    But my babe shall never hae
        A father but its ain.'

15 He took out a brand,
        And laid it atween them twa ;
    .   .   .   .   .   .
        .   .   .   .   .

16 Gill Viett took out a long brand,
　　And stroakd it oer a stro,
　An thro and thro Lord Ingram's bodie
　　He made it come and go.

17 ' Wae mat worth ye, Gill Viett,
　　An ill died mat ye die !
　For I had the cup in my hand
　　To hae drunken her oer to thee.'

18 ' [For] ae mile [I wad gae] for Gil Viett,
　　For Lord Ingram I wad hae gaen three ;
　An a' for that in good kirk-door
　　Fair wedding he gave me.'

19 Gil Viett took a long brand,
　　An stroakd it on a stro,
　An through and thro his own bodie
　　He made it come and go.

20 There was nae mean made for that godd lords,
　　In bowr whar they lay slain,
　But a' was for that lady,
　　In bowr whar she gaed brain.

21 There was nae mean made for that lady,
　　In bowr whar she lay dead,
　But a' was for the bonnie babe
　　That lay blabbering in her bleed.

———◆———

C

Herd's MSS, I, 169, II, 84.　Jamieson's Popular Ballads,
II, 265.

1 LADY MAISDRY was a lady fair,
　　She maid her mither's bed ;
　Auld Ingram was an aged knight,
　　And hee sought her to wed.

2 ' 'Tis I forbid ye, Auld Ingram,
　　For to seek me to spouse ;
　For Lord Wayets, your sister's son,
　　Has been into my bowrs.

3 ' 'T is I forbid ye, Auld Ingram,
　　For to seek me to wed ;
　For Lord Wayets, your sister's son,
　　Has been into my bed.'

4 'T is he has bought to this lady
　　The robes of the brown ;
　' And ever alas,' says this lady,
　　' The robs will pit mee down ! '

5 And he has bought to this lady
　　The robs of the red ;
　' And ever alas,' says this lady,
　　' The robs will be my dead ! '

6 And he has bought to this lady
　　The chrystal and the lammer,
　Sae has hee bought to her mither
　　The curches of the cammer.

7 Every ane o her se'n brethren
　　They had a hawk in hand,

And every lady i the place
　They got a goud garland.

8 Every cuk in that kitchen
　　They gat a noble claith ;
　A' was blyth at Auld Ingram's cuming,
　　But Lady Maisdrey was wraith.

9 ' Whare will I get a bonny boy,
　　Wad fain wun hos and shoon,
　That wud rin on to my Wayets,
　　And quickly cume again ? '

10 ' Here am I, a bonny boy,
　　Wad fain wun hoes and shoon,
　Wha wull rin on to your Wayets,
　　And quickly cume again.'

11 ' Ye 'l bid him, and ye 'l pray him baith,
　　Gif ony prayer can dee,
　To Mary Kirk to cume the morn,
　　My weary wadding to see.'

12 Lord Wayets lay our his castle wa,
　　Beheld baith dale and down,
　And he beheld a bonny boy
　　Cume rinnen to the town.

13 ' What news, what news, ye bonny boy ?
　　What news ye hae to mee ?
　.　　.　　.　　.　　.
　　.　　.　　.　　.

14 ' O is my ladie's fauldis brunt ?
　　Or is her towrs wun ?

Or is my Maisdrey lighter yet
  A dear dochter or sun?'

15 'Your ladie's faulds they are not brunt,
  Nor yet are her towrs wun,
Neither is Maisdrey lighter yet
  A dear dochter or sun.

16 'But she bids ye and she prays ye baith,
  Gif ony prayer can dee,
To Mary Kirk to cume the morn,
  Her weary wadding to see.'

17 He dung the boord up wi his fit,
  Sae did he wi his tae;
The silver cup that sat upon 't
  I the fire he gard it flee:
'O what na a lord in a' Scotland
  Dare marry my Maisdrey?'

18 'O 't is but a feeble thought
  To tell the tane and not the tither;
O 't is but a feeble thought
  To tell 't is your mither's brither.'

19 ''T is I wull send to that wadding,
  And I wul follow syne,
The fitches o the fallow deer
  An the gammons o the swine,
An the nine hides o the noble cow;
  'T was slain in season time.

20 ''T is I wul send to that wadding
  Ten ton of the red wyne;
Much more I'll send to that wadding,
  An I wul follow syne.'

21 When he came in unto the ha,
  Lady Maisdrey she did ween,
And twenty times he kist her mou
  Before Auld Ingram's een.

22 Nor to the kirk she wud ne gae,
  Nor til 't she wudn ride,
Till four and twunty men she gat her before,
  An twunty on ilka side,
An four and twunty milk-white dows
  To flee aboon her head.

23 A loud laughter gae Lord Wayets
  Mang the mids o his men:
'Marry the lady wham they weel,
  A maiden she is nane.'

24 'O laugh ye at my men, Wayets?
  Or di ye laugh at me?
Or laugh ye at the beerly bride,
  That's gane to marry me?'

25 'I laugh na at your men, uncle,
  Nor yet dive I at thee,
Bit I laugh at my lands sae braid,
  Sae weel's I do them see.'

26 Whan ene was cume, and ene-bells rung,
  An a' man gane to bed,
The bride bit and the silly bridegroom
  In chambers they were laid.

27 Was na it a fell thing for to see,
  Twa heads lye on a coad,
Lady Maisdrey like the moten goud,
  Auld Ingram like a toad?

28 He turnd his face unto the stock,
  And sound he fell asleep;
She turnd her fair face unto the wa,
  An sa't tears she did weep.

29 It fell about the mark midnight,
  Auld Ingram began to turn him;
He pat his hands on 's lady's sides,
  An waly, sair was she murnin.

30 'What aileth thee, my lady dear?
  Ever alas and wae 's me,
There is a baube betwixt thy sides!
  O sae sair 's it grieves me.'

31 'Didn I tell ye that, Auld Ingram,
  Or ye saught me to wed,
That Lord Wayets, your sister's son,
  Had been into my bed?'

32 'O father that bairn on me, Maisdrey,
  O father it on me,
An ye sall hae a rigland shire
  Your mornin's gift to bee.'

33 'O sarbit,' says the Lady Maisdrey,
  'That ever the like me befa,
To father my bairn on Auld Ingram,
  Lord Wayets in my father's ha!

34 'O sarbit,' says the Lady Maisdrey,
  'That ever the like me betide,
To father my bairn on Auld Ingram,
  An Lord Wayets beside!'

D

Kinloch MSS, V, 323, in the handwriting of John Hill Burton.

1 LORD INGRAM and Childe Viat
Were both bred in one ha ;
They laid their luves on one ladye,
And frae her they could na fa.

2 Lord Ingram courted Ladye Maisery,
He courted her frae ha to bower ;
And even sae did Childe Viat,
Amang the summer flowers.

3 Lord Ingram courted Ladye Maisery,
He courted her frae bower to ha ;
And even sae did Childe Viat,
Among the sheets sae sma.

4 Sir Ingram bought her Ladye Maisery
The steed that paid him well ;
She wads he were ayont the sea,
Gin she had her true love.

5 Lord Ingram bought her Lady Maisery
The knives hafted wi steel ;
She wads they were in his heart's bluid,
Gin Childe Viat was weel.

6 Lord Ingram bought her Lady Maisery
The golden knobbed gloves ;

She wads they were ayone the sea,
Gin she had her true love.

*   *   *   *   *

7 ' There 's two swords in one scabbard,
They cost me many a pound ;
Take you the best, leave me the worst,
We 's fight till they be done.'

8 The firsten stroke Lord Ingram gae,
He wounded Childe Viat nigh ;
The nexten stroke Childe Viat gae,
Lord Ingram's head did flie ;
And fifty feet oer a burken buss
Lord Ingram's head did flee.

9 There was no mane made for these two lords,
In bower where they lay slain ;
But all was for this fair ladie,
In bower where she gaed brain.

*   *   *   *   *

10 ' For one word I would gie for Childe Viat,
For Lord Ingram I would gie three ;
And it 's a' for the brave wedding
That he did to me gie.'

E

Buchan's Ballads of the North of Scotland, I, 234.

1 LORD INGRAM and Childe Vyet
Were baith born in ae bower ;
They fell in love wi ae lady,
Their honour was but poor.

2 Lord Ingram and Childe Vyet
Were baith bred in ae ha ;
They laid their love on Lady Maisry,
The waur did them befa.

3 Lord Ingram gained Lady Maisry
Frae father and frae mother ;
Lord Ingram gained Lady Maisry
Frae sister and frae brother.

4 Lord Ingram gained Lady Maisry
Frae a' her kith and kin ;
Lord Ingram courted Lady Maisry
But she said nay to him.

5 Lord Ingram courted Lady Maisry
In the garden amo the flowers ;
Childe Vyet courted Lady Maisry
Amo her ha's and bowers.

6 Lord Ingram sent to Lady Maisry
A steed paced fu well ;
She wishes he were ower the sea,
If Childe Vyet were well.

7 Lord Ingram courted Lady Maisry
Frae her relations a' ;

Childe Vyet courted Lady Maisry
   Amo the sheets sae sma.

8 Lord Ingram bought to Lady Maisry
   The siller knapped gloves ;
She wishd his hands might swell in them,
   Had she her ain true love.

9 Lord Ingram bought to Lady Maisry
   The brands garnishd wi steel ;
She wishd the same might pierce his heart,
   Gin Childe Vyet were weell.

10 Childe Vyet bought to Lady Maisry
   The fancy ribbons sma ;
She had mair delight in her sma fancy
   Than o Lord Ingram, gowd and a'.

11 Lord Ingram 's gane to her father,
   And thus he did complain :
'O am I doomd to die for love,
   And nae be loved again ?

12 'I hae sent to your daughter
   The steed paced fu well ;
She wishes I were ower the sea,
   Gin Childe Vyet were well.

13 'I hae bought to your daughter
   The siller knapped gloves ;
She wishd my hands might swell in them,
   Had she her ain true love.

14 'I hae bought to your daughter
   The brands garnishd wi steel ;
She wishd the same might pierce my heart,
   Gin Childe Vyet were weell.

15 'Childe Vyet bought to your daughter
   The fancy ribbons sma ;
She 's mair delight in her sma fancy
   Nor o me, gowd and a'.'

16 Her father turnd him round about,
   A solemn oath sware he,
Saying, She shall be the bride this night,
   And you bridegroom shall be.

17 'O had your tongue, my father dear,
   Let a' your passion be ;
The reason that I love this man,
   It is unknown to thee.'

18 Sweetly played the merry organs,
   Intill her mother's bower ;
But still and dum stood Lady Maisry,
   And let the tears down pour.

19 Sweetly played the harp sae fine,
   Intill her fathers ha ;
But still and dum stood Lady Maisry,
   And let tears down fa.

20 Tween Marykirk and her mother's bower,
   Was a' clad ower wi gowd,
For keeping o her snaw-white feet
   Frae treading o the mould.

21 Lord Ingram gaed in at ae church-door,
   Childe Vyet at another,
And lightly leugh him Childe Vyet
   At Lord Ingram, his brother.

22 'O laugh ye at my men, brother ?
   Or do ye laugh at me ?
Or laugh ye at young Lady Maisry,
   This night my bride 's to be ? '

23 'I laugh na at your men, brother,
   Nor do I laugh at thee ;
But I laugh at the knightless sport
   That I saw wi my ee.

24 'It is a ring on ae finger,
   A broach on ae breast-bane ;
And if ye kent what 's under that,
   Your love woud soon be dane.'

25 Lord Ingram and his merry young men
   Out ower the plains are gane,
And pensively walkd him Childe Vyet,
   Him single self alane.

26 When they had eaten and well drunken,
   And a' men bound for bed,
Lord Ingram and Lady Maisry
   In ae chamber were laid.

27 He laid his hand upon her breast,
   And thus pronounced he :
'There is a bairn within your sides,
   Wha may the father be ?

28 'Wha ever be your bairn's father,
   Ye will father it on me ;

The fairest castle o Snowdown
 Your morning gift shall be.'

29 ' Wha ever be my bairn's father,
 I 'll neer father it on thee ;
For better love I my bairn's father
 Nor ever I 'll love thee.'

30 Then he 's taen out a trusty brand,
 Laid it between them tway ;
Says, Lye ye there, ye ill woman,
 A maid for me till day.

31 Next morning her father came,
 Well belted wi a brand ;
Then up it starts him Lord Ingram,
 He was an angry man.

32 ' If your daughter had been a gude woman,
 As I thought she had been,
Cauld iron shoud hae never lien
 The lang night us between.'

33 ' Ohon, alas ! my daughter dear,
 What 's this I hear o thee ?
I thought ye was a gude woman
 As in the north countrie.'

34 ' O had your tongue, my father dear,
 Let a' your sorrows be ;
I never liked Lord Ingram,
 Ye ken ye forced me.'

35 Then in it came him Childe Vyet,
 Well belted wi a brand ;
Then up it raise him Lord Ingram,
 He was an angry man.

36 ' Win up, win up, now Lord Ingram,
 Rise up immediately,
That you and I the quarrel try,
 Who gains the victory.

37 ' I hae twa brands in ae scabbard,
 That cost me mony pound ;
Take ye the best, gie me the warst,
 And I 'll fight where I stand.'

38 Then up it starts him Childe Vyet,
 Shook back his yellow hair ;
The first an stroke Childe Vyet drew,
 He wounded Ingram sair.

39 Then up it starts him Lord Ingram,
 Shed back his coal-black hair ;
The first an stroke Lord Ingram drew,
 Childe Vyet needed nae mair.

40 Nae meen was made for these twa knights,
 Whan they were lying dead,
But a' for her Lady Maisry,
 That gaes in mournfu weed.

41 Says, ' If I hae been an ill woman,
 Alas and wae is me !
And if I 've been an ill woman,
 A gude woman I 'll be !

42 ' Ye 'll take frae me my silk attire,
 Bring me a palmer's weed,
And thro the world, for their sakes,
 I 'll gang and beg my bread.

43 ' If I gang a step for Childe Vyet,
 For Lord Ingram I 'll gang three ;
All for the honour that he paid
 At Marykirk to me.

44 ' I 'll gang a step for Childe Vyet,
 For Lord Ingram I 'll gang three ;
It was into my mother's bower
 Childe Vyet wronged me.'

———————•———————

A. a. 1^4. their bonheur. 8^2. to kill.
  11^1. boy *wanting* : see b.
  11^2. And will. 19^1. and that.
  26^1. did stand.
 b. 1^1. Childe Vyet, *and always.*
  1^3, 2^3. Had . . . loves. 1^4. honour.
  3^1, 3^3, 4^1, 5^1, 5^3. the Lady.

7^1. He said *wanting.*
7^3. he *wanting*. 8^2. to sell. 9^3. I 'd be.
10^3. Will run. 11^1. I am the boy, says one.
11^2. Will win. 13^1. to Vyet's.
14^1. line that Childe Vyet read.
14^3. line that he.
$14^{5, 6}$, $15^{1, 2}$, *as* 15.

What ails my one brother, he says,
    He 'll not let my love be ?
But I 'll send to my brother's bridal,
    The woman shall be free.

15³. Take four and twenty bucks and ewes.
16⁴. was wi wean.   17¹. about the.
18². with gold.   18³, 19³. keep the lady.
18⁴. the mould.
20¹. bells were.   21¹. upon their.
21⁴. Says he, You are with bairn.
22². came as my wooer.   22³. your one.
23¹. so did I.   26¹. start him.
28¹, 29¹. for the.
28³, 29³. All was for Lady.
30¹. O get to me.   31. For ae.
31³. All for the honourable marriage that.
B. 1³. Their laid.   2². womb.

12, 13 *make one stanza in the MS.*
15, 16 *are written together in three long lines.*
18 *did not belong where it stands, cf.* A 31, E
    43, 44, *but as the text now runs, cannot*
    well change place.
C. *Herd's copies differ little except in spelling.*
    6⁴. cannell (*cinnamon*). *I have thought it best to*
    risk cammer, *for* camerik, cambric, *though*
    I have not found the word in English :
    Danish kammer-dug.
10³. *second copy omits* on.   11². due (?).
13, 14 *are written in one stanza.*
19⁵. *second copy* hidies.
25¹. men, Wayets : uncle *in second copy.*
26–28 *precede* 23–25.
D. 4². that paid : *cf.* E 6². 10 *follows* 6 *in MS.*
E. 31², 35². belted and a brand.

67

GLASGERION

A. ' Glasgerion,' Percy MS., p. 94; Hales and Furnivall, I, 248.

B. ' Glenkindie,' Jamieson's Popular Ballads, I, 93.

C. Kinloch MSS, III, 139.

' GLASGERION ' was first printed in Percy's Reliques, III, 43, 1765, and was not thought by the editor to require much correction. Certainly the English ballad is one which it would be hard to mend. Scottish B is mainly of good derivation (a poor old woman in Aberdeenshire), and has some good stanzas, but Jamieson unfortunately undertook to improve a copy in which the story was complete, but " the diction much humbled," by combining with it a fragment of another version. Dr John Hill Burton seems, in turn, to have compounded a portion of the ballad as printed by Jamieson with a fragment from tradition (C): Kinloch MSS, III, 147.

Cunningham, Songs of Scotland, II, 32, has fused Percy's and Jamieson's copies, as Motherwell remarks, " in a flux of his own which has disfigured and quite changed the features of each."

The grete Glascurion is joined in Chaucer's House of Fame, III, 13–18, with the harpers Orpheus, Orion (Arion), and Chiron, and with Orpheus again by Gavin Douglas, copying Chaucer, in his Palice of Honour, I, 21, vv 15, 16, ed. Small.

Y Bardd Glas Keraint, in English Keraint the Blue Bard (Blue Bard being an appellation of a chief bard, who wore an official robe of blue), is recorded, as Mr Edward Williams informs us, to have been an eminent poet of distinguished birth, son of Owain, Prince of Glamorgan. The English name Glasgerion, Mr Williams further remarks, differs not half o much from Glasgeraint as most Welsh names, as written by Englishmen, do from their true orthography. There is, therefore, at least no absurdity in the suggestion that the Glascurion of Chaucer and the Glasgerion of the ballad may represent the Welsh Glas Keraint.*

A peasant lad, tailor's lad, who had over-heard the troth-plight of a knight and lady, anticipates the lover in 'Den fule Bonde-dreng,' Kristensen, II, 25–27; 'Torpardrän-gen,' Hazelius, Ur de Nordiska Folkens Lif, p. 138; 'Die Betrogene,' Norrenberg, Des Dülkener Fiedlers Liederbuch, p. 79. The ad-venture is jocosely treated in the first two, and does not amount to a tragedy in the other. A groom forestalls Agilulf, King of the Lom-bards, in the Decameron, III, 2, again with-out a bloody conclusion.

The marvellous power of the harp in B 2, C 1 is precisely paralleled in the Scandinavian 'Harpans Kraft,' Arwidsson, No 149, II, 311–17; Afzelius, No 91, III, 144–47; Grundtvig, No 40, II, 65–68; Landstad, No 51, p. 475; Íslenzk Fornkvæði, No 3, p. 18 f. In these the fish is harped out of the water, the young from folk and from fee, the bairn from its mother's womb, the water from the brook, the wind from the wood, the horns from the hart's head, the bark from the tree, the dead out of the mould, etc., etc. These effects are of the same nature as those produced by the harp of Orpheus, and it is to be observed that in the ballad of 'Harpans Kraft' the harper is a bridegroom seeking (successfully) to recover his bride, who has been carried down to the depths of the water by a merman. We have had something like these effects in the 'Twa Brothers,' No 49, B 10, I, 439, where Lady Margaret harps the small birds off the briers and her true love out of the grave.† There is a fisherman in the Gesta Romanorum who has a harp so sweet that all the fish in the water come to his hand: Oesterley, No 85,

p. 413, Madden, No 35, p. 116, No 8, p. 293. Equally potent is pipe, flute, or song in many ballads of various nations; the fish come up from below, the stars are stopped, the brook rises, the pines vail their top, the deer stops in its leap, etc., the musician being some-times an elf, sometimes an inspired mortal: 'Hr. Tönne af Alsö,' Grundtvig, No 34, II, 15, 19, Afzelius, No 7, I, 33, 128; 'Elvehöj,' Grundtvig, No 46, II, 107–109, Afzelius, No 95, III, 170, Arwidsson, No 147, II, 301; Ku-drun, ed. Bartsch, sts 379, 381, 388; the Rou-manian 'Şalga,' 'Mihu Copilul,' 'Vidra,' Stan-ley, p. 29, Alecsandri, pp 58, 66, 98 f, the same, Ballades et Chants populaires, pp 118, 168, Murray, pp 44, 53 f, 83; 'El Poder del Canto,' Milá, Romancerillo, No 207, p. 165, Nigra, Rivista Contemporanea, XX, 78; 'Conde Arnaldos,' Wolf and Hofmann, No 153, II, 80. For the soporific effect of such music, as shown in B 5, C 2, there are par-allels in ' Albred Lykke, 'who sings a ballad which sets everybody asleep but the young bride who had been stolen from him, Kris-tensen, I, 281, No 105, sts 11, 12, II, 259 f, No 76, sts 13, 14; 'Den fortryllende Sang,' Grundtvig, No 243, IV, 470, Danish A 12, 473, Swedish G 25, 26; 'El Rey marinero,' Milá, No 201, p. 151, Briz, I, 117, IV, 15, V, 75; Campbell's West Highland Tales, I, 291 f.

The oath by oak, ash, and thorn, A 18, is a relic or trait of high antiquity. We have an oath by the thorn in 'Fair Janet,' G 13, 'Young Hunting,' K 26; by corn, grass sae green and corn, in 'Young Hunting,' A 16, D 19, G 7. It is to be supposed that the tree, thorn, corn, was touched while swearing, a sod taken up in the hand. See Grimm's Rechts-alterthümer, 2d ed., p. 896 f, p. 117 f.

For drying the sword on the sleeve, A 22, see ' Little Musgrave and Lady Bernard.'

Translated by Bodmer, I, 73, after Percy; by Knortz, Lieder und Romanzen Alt-Eng-lands, No 59, after Allingham, p. 358

---

* See The Cambrian Journal, September, 1858, pp 192–94, communicated to me by the kind courtesy of Rev. Pro-fessor D. Silvan Evans. As to Glasgerion's being a king's son, ballad titles count for little.

† In C 18, p. 440,

> She *wept* the sma brids frae the tree,
> She *wept* the starns adoun frae the lift,
> She *wept* the fish out o the sea.

A

Percy MS., p. 94; Hales and Furnivall, I, 248.

1 GLASGERION was a kings owne sonne,
   And a harper he was good ;
He harped in the kings chamber,
   Where cuppe and candle stoode,
And soe did hee in the queens chamber,
   Till ladies waxed wood.

2 And then bespake the kings daughter,
   And these words thus sayd shee :

  .   .   .   .

    .   .   .   .

3 Saide, Strike on, strike on, Glasgerrion,
   Of thy striking doe not blinne ;
There 's neuer a stroke comes ouer thin harpe
   But it glads my hart within.

4 ' Faire might you fall, lady ! ' quoth hee ;
   ' Who taught you now to speake ?
I haue loued you, lady, seuen yeere ;
   My hart I durst neere breake.'

5 ' But come to my bower, my Glasgerryon,
   When all men are att rest ;
As I am a ladie true of my promise,
   Thou shalt bee a welcome guest.'

6 But hom then came Glasgerryon,
   A glad man, Lord, was hee :
' And come thou hither, Iacke, my boy,
   Come hither vnto mee.

7 ' For the kings daughter of Normandye,
   Her loue is granted mee,
And beffore the cocke haue crowen,
   Att her chamber must I bee.'

8 ' But come you hither master,' quoth hee,
   ' Lay your head downe on this stone ;
For I will waken you, master deere,
   Afore it be time to gone.'

9 But vpp then rose that lither ladd,
   And did on hose and shoone ;
A coller he cast vpon his necke,
   Hee seemed a gentleman.

10 And when he came to that ladies chamber,
   He thrild vpon a pinn ;

The lady was true of her promise,
   Rose vp and lett him in.

11 He did not take the lady gay
   To boulster nor to bedd,
But downe vpon her chamber-flore
   Full soone he hath her layd.

12 He did not kisse that lady gay
   When he came nor when he youd ;
And sore mistrusted that lady gay
   He was of some churlës blood.

13 But home then came that lither ladd,
   And did of his hose and shoone,
And cast that coller from about his necke ;
   He was but a churlës sonne :
' Awaken,' quoth hee, ' my master deere,
   I hold it time to be gone.

14 ' For I haue sadled your horsse, master,
   Well bridled I haue your steed ;
Haue not I serued a good breakfast,
   When time comes I haue need.'

15 But vp then rose good Glasgerryon,
   And did on both hose and shoone,
And cast a coller about his necke ;
   He was a kingës sonne.

16 And when he came to that ladies chamber,
   He thrild vpon a pinn ;
The lady was more then true of promise,
   Rose vp and let him in.

17 Saies, Whether haue you left with me
   Your braclett or your gloue ?
Or are you returned backe againe
   To know more of my loue ? '

18 Glasgerryon swore a full great othe,
   By oake and ashe and thorne,
' Lady, I was neuer in your chamber
   Sith the time that I was borne.'

19 ' O then it was your litle foote-page
   Falsly hath beguiled me :'
And then shee pulld forth a litle pen-kniffe,
   That hanged by her knee,
Says, There shall neuer noe churlës blood
   Spring within my body.

20 But home then went Glasgerryon,
    A woe man, good [Lord], was hee;
  Sayes, Come hither, thou Iacke, my boy,
    Come thou hither to me.

21 Ffor if I had killed a man to-night,
    Iacke, I wold tell it thee;
  But if I haue not killed a man to-night,
    Iacke, thou hast killed three!

22 And he puld out his bright browne sword,
    And dryed it on his sleeue,
  And he smote off that lither ladds head,
    And asked noe man noe leaue.

23 He sett the swords poynt till his brest,
    The pumill till a stone;
  Thorrow *that* falsenese of *that* lither ladd
    These three liues werne all gone.

B

Jamieson's Popular Ballads, I, 93, taken from the recitation of an old woman by Professor Scott, of Aberdeen, and "somewhat improved" by a fragment communicated by the Rev. William Gray, of Lincoln.

1 GLENKINDIE was ance a harper gude,
    He harped to the king;
  And Glenkindie was ance the best harper
    That ever harpd on a string.

2 He'd harpit a fish out o saut water,
    Or water out o a stane,
  Or milk out o a maiden's breast,
    That bairn had never nane.

3 He's taen his harp intil his hand,
    He harpit and he sang,
  And ay as he harpit to the king,
    To haud him unthought lang.

4 'I'll gie you a robe, Glenkindie,
    A robe o the royal pa,
  Gin ye will harp i the winter's night
    Afore my nobles a'.'

    *   *   *   *   *

5 He's taen his harp intill his hand,
    He's harpit them a' asleep,
  Except it was the young countess,
    That love did waukin keep.

6 And first he has harpit a grave tune,
    And syne he has harpit a gay,
  And mony a sich atween hands
    I wat the lady gae.

7 Says, Whan day is dawen, and cocks hae
    crawen,
  And wappit their wings sae wide,

  It's ye may come to my bower-door,
    And streek you by my side.

8 But look that ye tell na Gib, your man,
    For naething that ye dee;
  For, an ye tell him Gib, your man,
    He'll beguile baith you and me.

9 He's taen his harp intill his hand,
    He harpit and he sang,
  And he is hame to Gib, his man,
    As fast as he could gang.

10 'O mith I tell you, Gib, my man,
    Gin I a man had slain?'
  'O that ye micht, my gude master,
    Altho ye had slain ten.'

11 'Then tak ye tent now, Gib, my man,
    My bidden for to dee;
  And but an ye wauken me in time,
    Ye sall be hangit hie.

12 'Whan day has dawen, and cocks hae crawen,
    And wappit their wings sae wide,
  I'm bidden gang till yon lady's bower,
    And streek me by her side.'

13 'Gae hame to your bed, my good master;
    Ye've waukit, I fear, oer lang;
  For I'll wauken you in as good time
    As ony cock i the land.'

14 He's taen his harp intill his hand,
    He harpit and he sang,
  Until he harpit his master asleep,
    Syne fast awa did gang.

15 And he is till that lady's bower,
    As fast as he could rin;

When he cam till that lady's bower,
  He chappit at the chin.

16 'O wha is this,' says that lady,
  'That opens nae and comes in?'
  'It's I, Glenkindie, your ain true-love,
  O open and lat me in!'

17 She kent he was nae gentle knicht
  That she had latten in,
For neither when he gaed nor cam,
  Kist he her cheek or chin.

18 He neither kist her when he cam,
  Nor clappit her when he gaed,
And in and at her bower window,
  The moon shone like the gleed.

19 'O ragged is your hose, Glenkindie,
  And riven is your sheen,
And reaveld is your yellow hair,
  That I saw late yestreen.'

20 'The stockings they are Gib, my man's,
  They came first to my hand,
And this is Gib, my man's shoon,
  At my bed-feet they stand;
I've reavelld a' my yellow hair
  Coming against the wind.'

21 He's taen the harp intill his hand,
  He harpit and he sang,
Until he cam to his master,
  As fast as he could gang.

22 'Won up, won up, my good master,
  I fear ye sleep oer lang;
There's nae a cock in a' the land
  But has wappit his wings and crawn.'

23 Glenkindie's tane his harp in hand,
  He harpit and he sang,
And he has reachd the lady's bower
  Afore that eer he blan.

24 When he cam to the lady's bower,
  He chappit at the chin :
  'O wha is that at my bower-door,
  That opens na and comes in?'
  'It's I, Glenkindie, your ain true-love,
  And in I canna win.'

*   *   *   *   *

25 'Forbid it, forbid it,' says that lady,
  'That ever sic shame betide,
That I should first be a wild loon's lass,
  And than a young knight's bride.'

26 He's taen his harp intill his hand,
  He harpit and he sang,
And he is hame to Gib, his man,
  As fast as he could gang.

27 'Come forth, come forth, now, Gib, my man,
  Till I pay you your fee ;
Come forth, come forth, now, Gib, my man,
  Weel payit sall ye be.'

28 And he has taen him Gib, his man,
  And he has hangd him hie,
And he's hangit him oer his ain yate,
  As high as high could be.

29 There was nae pity for that lady,
  For she lay cald and dead,
But a' was for him, Glenkindie,
  In bower he must go mad.

———◆———

C

Kinloch's MSS, III, 139, in the handwriting of John Hill Burton.

1 GLENKINNIE was as good a harper
  As ever harpet tone ;
He harpet fish out o the sea-flood,
  And water out of a dry loan,
And milk out o the maiden's breast
  That bairn had never neen.

2 He harpit i the king's palace,
  He harpit them a' asleep,
Unless it were Burd Bell alone,
  And she stud on her feet.

3 'Ye will do ye home, Glenkinnie,
  And ye will take a sleep,
And ye will come to my bower-door
  Before the cock's crowing.'

4 He 's taen out his milk-white steed,
    And fast away rode he,
Till he came to his ain castle,
    Where gold glanced never so hie.

5 ' Might I tell ye, Jeck, my man,
    Gin I had slain a man ? '
' Deed might [ye], my good master,
    Altho ye had slain ten.'

6 ' I 've faun in love wi a gay ladie,
    She 's daughter to the Queen,
And I maun be at her bower-door
    Before the cock's crowing.'

7 He 's taen out his master's steed,
    And fast awa rode he,
Until he cam to Burd Bell's door,
    Where gold glanced never so hie.

8 When he came to Burd Bell's door,
    He tirled at the pin,

And up she rose, away she goes,
    To let Glenkinnie in.

9 .   .   .   .   .

   .   .   .   .   .

    That I combed out yestreen.

*   *   *   *   *

10 She looked out at a shot-window,
    Atween her and the meen :
' There is twa lovers beguiled the night,
    And I fear I am ane.

11 ' Ye shall na hae to say, Glenkindie,
    When you sit at the wine,
That once you loved a queen's daughter,
    And she was your footman's quean.'

*   *   *   *   *

A. 1⁴. cappe . . . yoode.
    1⁵, ⁶, 2¹, ² *make a stanza in the MS.*
    3⁸. this harpe.   4¹. him fall?   4⁸. 7 yeere.
    6¹. whom then.
    7⁸, ⁴. & at her chamber must I bee
        beffore the cocke haue crowen.
    10². pinn : *one stroke of the n is left out, as
        frequently, in the MS.   Furnivall.*
    11². nor noe.   14⁴. times.   16⁴. him im.
    17¹. you you.   17⁸. you are.   21⁴. killed 3.
    22⁸. head : *there is a tag to the* d *as if for* s.
        Furnivall.
    23⁴. these 3.
B. 1⁸, ⁴, 2 *are cited by Jamieson in the Scots
    Magazine, October,* 1803, *p.* 698, *as the
    beginning of a fragment* [*Gray's*], *with
    only this variation* :

    Glenkindie was ance the best harper.

    *He has, therefore, combined the two ver-
    sions here.*
    Stanza 4, *as published, is the first of*
    " another copy [*Scott's*], in which the
    story is complete, but, it having been
    written from the recitation of a poor old
    woman in Aberdeenshire, the diction
    has been much humbled.   It begins* :

' I 'll gie you a robe, Glenkindy,
    A robe o the royal pa,
Gin ye will harp i the winter's night
    Afore my nobles a'.'

(Robe *is misprinted* rolu).
After 4 *follows this stanza, which, with
but a word or two of difference, is the
first of* ' Brown Robin,' *where, no doubt,
it belongs, but not here* :

    And the king but and his nobles a'
        Sat birling at the wine,
    And he wad hae but his ae dochter
        To wait on them at dine.

10 *may not be in the right place, and
    should, perhaps, be put just before Gib
    gets his deserts.   Some such stanza
    would come in well between* 20 *and* 21
    of A.
After 25 *follows* 29, *manifestly with no
    right.   If this commonplace is retained,
    it must come at the end.*
After 29 (27 *in Jamieson*) *follow these
    three stanzas, the first a superfluous
    and very improbable repetition ; the
    second altered by Jamieson,* " *to intro-*

duce a little variety, and prevent the
monotonous tiresomeness of repetition,"
*the last as little in traditional style as
the second.*

> He 'd harpit a fish out o saut water,
>   The water out o a stane,
> The milk out o a maiden's breast
>   That bairn had never nane.
>
> He 's taen his harp intill his hand,
>   Sae sweetly as it rang,
> And wae and weary was to hear
>   Glenkindie's dowie sang.
>
> But cald and dead was that lady,
>   Nor heeds for a' his maen ;
> An he wad harpit till domis day,
>   She 'll never speak again.

C. *8 follows 2 in the MS.*

*A fragment in Kinloch MSS, III, 147, six-
teen stanzas, in the writing of John Hill
Burton, is thus made up :* B 1, 2, C 2, B 6,
7, C 4, 5, B 11, C 6, B 14, C 7, 8, B 17,
18, B 19$^{1-3}$ *and* C 9^4, B 20 ; *with the following variations, probably arbitrary.*
Variations from

> B 1^1. a gude harper.
> 1^3. he was the.   1$^{4.}$ on string.
> 2^1. o the sea-flood.   2^2. o the.
> 2^3. And milk.
> C 2^3. Except it was.   B 7^4. streek down.
> C 4^3. Untill.   C 5^1. Now might.
> C 5^2. a man had slain = B 10^2.
> C 5^3. Indeed ye micht.
> B 11^1. Jock my man.   11^3. And but ye.
> C 7^1. And he 's.   C 8^1. bower-door.
> C 8^3. and away.

68

YOUNG HUNTING

A. 'Young Hunting.' **a.** Herd's MSS, I, 182. **b.** The
same, II, 67.

B. 'Young Redin,' Kinloch MSS, VII, 7, Kinloch's
Ancient Scottish Ballads, p. 1.

C. 'Young Riedan,' Harris MS., fol. 8.

D. Motherwell's MS., p. 377.

E. 'Lord William,' Scott's Minstrelsy, III, 265, 1803.

F. 'Earl Richard.' **a.** Motherwell's MS., p. 61, Motherwell's Minstrelsy, p. 218. **b.** Motherwell's Minstrelsy,
Appendix, p. xvii, one stanza.

G. Herd's MSS, I, 34 ; Herd's Scottish Songs, 1776, I,
148.

H. 'Clyde's Water,' Dr Joseph Robertson's Journal of
Excursions, No 1, 1829.

I. 'Lord John,' Motherwell's MS., p. 189.

J. 'Earl Richard,' Scott's Minstrelsy, II, 42, 1802, and
III, 184, 1833.

K. 'Young Hunting,' Buchan's Ballads of the North of
Scotland, I, 118.

J, Scott's version, and naturally the best
known, is described by the editor as made up
from the best verses of Herd's copies, A, G,
with some trivial alterations adopted from tradition. This account is far from being exact,
for there are many lines in the edition of 1802
which are not found in Herd's copies, and in
the edition of 1833 four additional stanzas, 11,
12, 13, 28. Such portions of Scott's version
as are not found in Herd are here distinguished by a larger type. K is perhaps a stall
copy, and certainly, where it is not taken from

other versions, is to a considerable degree a modern manufacture by a very silly pen.*

The copy in Pinkerton's Tragic Ballads, p. 34, is only the first five stanzas of **G**, a little altered.

A Scandinavian ballad begins somewhat like 'Young Hunting,' but ends like ' Elveskud' or 'Clerk Colvil.' A young man who has made up his mind to marry is warned by his mother against the wiles of a former mistress. He rides to his old love's house and is welcomed to beer and wine. He tells her that he is on the way to his bride. She wants a word with him, or a kiss, and as he leans over to her on his horse, stabs him to the heart. He rides home bleeding, pretends that he has hurt himself by running against a tree, asks that his bed may be made and a priest sent for, and dies. **Danish**, ' Frillens Hævn,' Grundtvig, IV, 203 f, No 208, **A-D**, **A** from a manuscript of the 17th century. **Swedish**, **A**, ' Herr Magnus,' Afzelius, No 13, I, 67, an imperfect copy; **B**, from Cavallius and Stephens' manuscript collection, **C-H**, fragments in the same collection, Grundtvig, IV, 203 ; **I**, ' Herr Samsing,' Eva Wigström, in Hazelius, Ur de nordiska Folkens Lif, p. 124. **Norwegian**, ' Herre Per og Gjöðalin,' a mixed form, Landstad, p. 564, No 68, and the first stanza in Lindeman, No 132, No 178.

The place where the dead body of the knight lies at the bottom of the river is discovered by candles burning bright, **A** 22 f, **C** 19 f, **H** 8, **K** 31, 35. Sir Walter Scott supposed these candles to mean " the corpselights . . . which are sometimes seen to illuminate the spot where a dead body is concealed." He had been informed that the body of a man drowned in the Ettrick had been discovered by means of these candles. Though the language in the ballad is not quite explicit, owing perhaps to the fact that the method of detection practised was more familiar formerly than now, the meaning is as likely to be that a candle, floated on the water, would burn brighter when it came to the spot where the body lay. A candle (a consecrated one in Catholic countries) stuck in a loaf of bread, or supported by cork, is still believed to be efficient for indicating the place of a drowned body ; in England, Henderson, Notes on the Folk Lore of the Northern Counties, ed. 1879, p. 60 ; in Bohemia, Wuttke, Deutscher Volksaberglaube der Gegenwart, ed. 1869, p. 239, No 371; in Brittany, Blätter für literarische Unterhaltung, 1837, p. 892 ; in Portugal, Vasconcellos, Tradições Populares, p. 80, No 178.†

That the body of a murdered man will emit blood upon being touched, or even approached, by the murderer is a belief of ancient standing, and evidence of this character was formerly admitted in judicial investigations. See especially Grimm, Rechtsalterthümer, 1854, p. 930 f, Bahrgericht, who cites from literature the Nibelungenlied (1043–45, Bartsch) Hartmann's Iwein, 1355–64, Shakespeare's Richard III, I, 2, besides instances of legal or historical description ; to which may be added others furnished by Sir W. Scott, Minstrelsy III, 190–93, ed. 1833, and Kinloch, Ancient Scottish Ballads, pp 10–12. See further Schmidt, Die Märchen des Straparola, pp 229, 346 ff, Holinshed's Chronicle of Scotland, p. 235, ed. 1808, Matthew Paris, Chronica Majora, ed. Luard, II, 344 f, Brand's Antiquities, ed. Ellis, II, 542–44.‡

There is a sort of *judicium ignis* in **A** 26–28, **B** 23 f, **C** 24, **K** 37 f : the fire which does not burn the innocent bower-woman consumes her guilty mistress.

For the oath by corn, **A** 16, **D** 21, grass

---

* For utter ineptness 7–9 even go beyond the ordinary Buchan mark.

† Other expedients are, a loaf of bread weighted with quicksilver, or without candle or quicksilver, or a chip of wood; Henderson, as above, p. 59, Gregor, Notes on the Folk Lore of the North East of Scotland, p. 208, Choice Notes from Notes and Queries, pp 40–43, and Liebrecht, Volkskunde, p. 344 f, who cites nearly all these places. J. S. C. observes in Notes and Queries : As there are in all run-

ning streams deep pools formed by eddies, in which drowned bodies would be likely to be caught and retained, any light substance thrown into the current would consequently be drawn to that part of the surface over the centre of the eddy hole.

‡ Also (not seen by me) Danske Samlingar, II, 274–76, 1867, Norsk Magazin, I, 401, 1860, cited by somebody (probably Grundtvig) whom I have neglected to note.

and corn, G 7, thorn, K 26, see 'Glasgerion.'

E is translated by Schubart, p. 173 ; F by Wolff, Halle der Völker, I, 24, Hausschatz,

p. 204 ; J by Schubart, p. 86, Gerhard, p. 134 ; Aytoun's copy by Rosa Warrens, Schottische Volkslieder, p. 46 ; Allingham's copy by Knortz, Lieder und Romanzen Alt-Englands, p. 42.

———•———

A

a. Herd's MSS, I, 182 ; b. the same, II, 67.

1 O LADY, rock never your young son young
    One hour longer for me,
For I have a sweetheart in Garlick's Wells
    I love thrice better than thee.

2 'The very sols of my love's feet
    Is whiter then thy face :'
'But nevertheless na, Young Hunting,
    Ye 'l stay wi me all night.'

3 She has birld in him Young Hunting
    The good ale and the beer,
Till he was as fou drunken
    As any wild-wood steer.

4 She has birld in him Young Hunting
    The good ale and the wine,
Till he was as fou drunken
    As any wild-wood swine.

5 Up she has tain him Young Hunting,
    And she has had him to her bed,
.   .   .   .   .   .
    .   .   .   .   .   .

6 And she has minded her on a little penknife,
    That hangs low down by her gare,
And she has gin him Young Hunting
    A deep wound and a sare.

7 Out an spake the bonny bird,
    That flew abon her head :
'Lady, keep well thy green clothing
    Fra that good lord's blood.'

8 'O better I 'll keep my green clothing
    Fra that good lord's blood
Nor thou can keep thy flattering toung,
    That flatters in thy head.

9 'Light down, light down, my bonny bird,
    Light down upon my hand,
.   .   .   .
    .   .   .   .

10 'O siller, O siller shall be thy hire,
    An goud shall be thy fee,
An every month into the year
    Thy cage shall changed be.'

11 'I winna light down, I shanna light down,
    I winna light on thy hand ;
For soon, soon wad ye do to me
    As ye done to Young Hunting.'

12 She has booted an spird him Young Hunting
    As he had been gan to ride,
A hunting-horn about his neck,
    An the sharp sourd by his side.

13 And she has had him to yon wan water,
    For a' man cɔlls it Clyde,
.   .   .   .
    .   .   .   .

14 The deepest pot intill it all
    She has puten Young Hunting in ;
A green truff upon his breast,
    To hold that good lord down.

15 It fell once upon a day
    The king was going to ride,
And he sent for him Young Hunting,
    To ride on his right side.

16 She has turnd her right and round about,
    She sware now by the corn,
'I saw na thy son, Young Hunting,
    Sen yesterday at morn.'

17 She has turnd her right and round about,
    She swear now by the moon,

'I saw na thy son, Young Hunting,
  Sen yesterday at noon.

18 'It fears me sair in Clyde Water
    That he is drownd therein : '
  O thay ha sent for the king's duckers,
    To duck for Young Hunting.

19 They ducked in at the tae water-bank,
    Thay ducked out at the tither :
  'We 'll duck no more for Young Hunting,
    All tho he wear our brother.'

20 Out an spake the bonny bird,
    That flew abon their heads,

  .   .   .   .   .   .

  .   .   .   .   .   .

21 'O he 's na drownd in Clyde Water,
    He is slain and put therein ;
  The lady that lives in yon castil
    Slew him and put him in.

22 'Leave aff your ducking on the day,
    And duck upon the night ;
  Whear ever that sakeless knight lys slain,
    The candels will shine bright.'

23 Thay left off their ducking o the day,
    And ducked upon the night,

And where that sakeless knight lay slain,
    The candles shone full bright.

24 The deepest pot intill it a'
    Thay got Young Hunting in ;
  A green turff upon his brest,
    To hold that good lord down.

25 O thay ha sent aff men to the wood
    To hew down baith thorn an fern,
  That they might get a great bonefire
    To burn that lady in.
  'Put na the wyte on me,' she says,
    'It was her May Catheren.'

26 Whan thay had tane her May Catheren,
    In the bonefire set her in ;
  It wad na take upon her cheeks,
    Nor take upon her chin,
  Nor yet upon her yellow hair,
    To healle the deadly sin.

27 Out they hae tain her May Catheren,
    And they hay put that lady in ;
  O it took upon her cheek, her cheek,
    An it took upon her chin,
  An it took on her fair body,
    She burnt like hoky-gren.

———◆———

B

Kinloch MSS, VII, p. 7, Kinloch's Ancient Scottish Ballads, p. 1 ; "from the recitation of Miss E. Beattie, of Edinburgh, a native of Mearns-shire, who sings it to a plaintive and melancholy, though somewhat monotonous, air of one measure."

1 YOUNG REDIN 's til the huntin gane,
    Wi therty lords and three ;
  And he has til his true-love gane,
    As fast as he could hie.

2 'Ye 're welcome here, my Young Redin,
    For coal and candle-licht ;
  And sae are ye, my Young Redin,
    To bide wi me the nicht.'

3 'I thank ye for your licht, ladie,
    Sae do I for your coal ;

But there 's thrice as fair a ladie as thee
    Meets me at Brandie's Well.'

4 Whan they war at their supper set,
    And merrily drinking wine,
  This ladie has tane a sair sickness,
    And til her bed has gane.

5 Young Redin he has followed her,
    And a dowie man was he ;
  He fund his true-love in her bouer,
    And the tear was in her ee.

6 Whan he was in her arms laid,
    And gieing her kisses sweet,
  Then out she 's tane a little penknife,
    And woundid him sae deep.

7 'O lang, lang is the winter nicht,
   And slawly daws the day;
   There is a slain knicht in my bouer,
   And I wish he war away.'

8 Then up bespak her bouer-woman,
   And she spak ae wi spite:
   'An there be a slain knicht in your bouer,
   It 's yoursell that has the wyte.'

9 'O heal this deed on me, Meggy,
   O heal this deed on me;
   The silks that war shapen for me gen Pasche,
   They sall be sewed for thee.'

10 'O I hae heald on my mistress
   A twalmonth and a day,
   And I hae heald on my mistress
   Mair than I can say.'

*   *   *   *   *

11 They 've booted him, and they 've spurred him,
   As he was wont to ride,
   A huntin-horn round his neck,
   And a sharp sword by his side;
   In the deepest place o Clyde's Water,
   It 's there they 've made his bed.

12 Sine up bespak the wylie parrot,
   As he sat on the tree:
   'And hae ye killd him Young Redin,
   Wha neer had love but thee?'

13 'Come doun, come doun, ye wylie parrot,
   Come doun into my hand;
   Your cage sall be o the beaten gowd,
   Whan now it 's but the wand.'

14 'I winna come doun, I canna come doun,
   I winna come doun to thee;
   For as ye 've dune to Young Redin,
   Ye 'll do the like to me;
   Ye 'll thraw my head aff my hause-bane,
   And throw me in the sea.'

15 O there cam seekin Young Redin
   Mony a lord and knicht,
   And there cam seekin Young Redin
   Mony a ladie bricht.

16 And they 've til his true-love gane,
   Thinking he was wi her;

   .   .   .   .   .   .

   .   .   .   .   .   .

17 'I hae na seen him Young Redin
   Sin yesterday at noon;
   He turnd his stately steed about,
   And hied him throw the toun.

18 'But ye 'll seek Clyde's Water up and doun,
   Ye 'll seek it out and in;
   I hae na seen him Young Redin
   Sin yesterday at noon.'

19 Then up bespak Young Redin's mither,
   And a dowie woman was scho:
   'There 's na a place in Clyde's Water
   But my son wad gae throw.'

20 They 've sought Clyde's Water up and doun,
   They 've sought it out and in,
   And the deepest place in Clyde's Water
   They 've fund Young Redin in.

21 O white, white war his wounds washen,
   As white as a linen clout;
   But as the traitor she cam near,
   His wounds they gushit out.

22 'It 's surely been my bouer-woman,
   O ill may her betide!
   I neer wad slain him Young Redin,
   And thrown him in the Clyde.'

23 Then they 've made a big bane-fire,
   The bouer-woman to brin;
   It tuke not on her cheek, her cheek,
   It tuke not on her chin,
   But it tuke on the cruel hands
   That pat Young Redin in.

24 Then they 've tane out the bouer-woman,
   And pat the ladie in;
   It tuke na on her cheek, her cheek,
   It tuke na on her chin,
   But it tuke on the fause, fause arms
   That Young Redin lay in.

C

Harris MS., fol. 8, from Mrs Harris, Perthshire.

1 THE ladie stude in her bour-door,
   In her bour-door as she stude,
   She thocht she heard a bridle ring,
   That did her bodie gude.

2 She thocht it had been her father dear,
   Come ridin owre the sand;
   But it was her true-love Riedan,
   Come hiean to her hand.

3 'You 're welcome, you 're welcome, Young
       Riedan,' she said,
   'To coal an cannel-licht;
   You 're welcome, you 're welcome, Young
       Riedan,
   To sleep in my bour this nicht.'

4 'I thank you for your coal, madame,
   An for your cannel tae;
   There 's a fairer maid at Clyde's Water,
   I love better than you.'

5 'A fairer maid than me, Riedan?
   A fairer maid than me?
   A fairer maid than ten o me
   You shurely neer did see.'

6 He leant him owre his saddle-bow,
   To gie her a kiss sae sweet;
   She keppit him on a little penknife,
   An gae him a wound sae deep.

7 'Oh hide! oh hide! my bourswoman,
   Oh hide this deed on me!
   An the silks that waur shappit for me at Yule
   At Pasch sall be sewed for thee.'

8 They saidled Young Riedan, they bridled
       Young Riedan,
   The way he was wont to ride;
   Wi a huntin-horn aboot his neck,
   An a sharp sword by his side.

9 An they are on to Clyde's Water,
   An they rade it up an doon,
   An the deepest linn in a' Clyde's Water
   They flang him Young Riedan [in].

10 'Lie you there, you Young Riedan,
   Your bed it is fu wan;

The [maid] you hae at Clyde's Water,
   For you she will think lang.'

11 Up it spak the wily bird,
   As it sat on the tree:
   'Oh wae betide you, ill woman,
   An an ill death may you dee!
   For he had neer anither love,
   Anither love but thee.'

12 'Come doon, come doon, my pretty parrot,
   An pickle wheat aff my glue;
   An your cage sall be o the beaten goud,
   Whan it 's of the willow tree.'

13 'I winna come doon, I sanna come doon,
   To siccan a traitor as thee:
   For as you did to Young Riedan,
   Sae wald you do to mee.'

14 Come doon, come doon, my pretty parrot,
   An pickle wheat aff my hand;
   An your cage sall be o the beaten goud,
   Whan it 's o the willow wand.'

15 'I winna come doon, I sanna come doon,
   To siccan a traitor as thee;
   You wald thraw my head aff my hase-bane,
   An fling it in the sea.'

16 It fell upon a Lammas-tide
   The king's court cam ridin bye:
   'Oh whare is it him Young Riedan?
   It 's fain I wald him see.'

17 'Oh I hae no seen Young Riedan
   Sin three lang weeks the morn;
   It bodes me sair, and dries me mair,
   Clyde's Water 's him forlorn.'

18 Up it spak the wily bird,
   As it sat on the tree;

   .   .   .   .

   .   .   .

19 'Leave aff, leave aff your day-seekin,
   An ye maun seek by nicht;
   Aboon the place Young Riedan lies,
   The cannels burn bricht.'

20 They gae up their day-seekin,
   An they did seek by nicht;

An owre the place Young Riedan lay,
    The cannels burnt bricht.

21 The firsten grip his mother got
    Was o his yellow hair;
An was na that a dowie grip,
    To get her ae son there!

22 The nexten grip his mother got
    Was o his milk-white hand;
An wasna that a dowie grip,
    To bring sae far to land!

23 White, white waur his wounds washen,
    As white as ony lawn;

But sune 's the traitor stude afore,
    Then oot the red blude sprang.

*   *   *   *   *

24 Fire wadna tak on her bourswoman,
    Niether on cheek nor chin;
But it took fast on thae twa hands
    That flang young Riedan in.

25 'Come oot, come oot, my bourswoman,
    Come oot, lat me win in;
For as I did the deed mysell,
    Sae man I drie the pine.'

D

Motherwell's MS., p. 377; from Agnes Lyle, Kilbarchan.

1 EARL RICHARD has a hunting gone,
    As fast as he can ride;
He 's a hunting-horn about his neck,
    And a broadsword by his side.

2 'Licht down, licht down, Earl Richard,' she
    says,
'O licht down and come in,
And thou 'll get cheer and charcoal clear,
    And torches for to burn.'

3 'I winna licht, I canna licht,
    I winna licht at all;
A fairer lady then ten of thee
    Meets me at Richard's Wall.'

4 He louted owre his saddle-bow,
    And for to kiss her sweet,
But little thocht o that penknife
    Wherewith she wound him deep.

5 'Why wounds thou me so deep, lady?
    Why stabs thou me so sore?
There 's not a lord like Earl Richard
    Could love false woman more.'

6 She called upon her waiting-maid,
    Long before it was day:
'I have a dead man in my bower,
    I wish he were away.'

7 'Keep ye your bower, my lily-flower,
    Keep it free of all men's blood;'
'Oh I will keep it een as weel
    As you or any maid.

8 'But siller will be thy wage,' she says,
    'And gold will be thy fee,
And I mysell will gang alang
    And bear thee companye.'

9 They booted him, and spurred him,
    As he was wont to ride,
And they 're awa to Lorn's Water,
    To Lorn's Water so wide.

10 They turned down his yellow hair,
    Turnd up his milk-white feet:
'Lye thou there, Earl Richard,' she said,
    'Till the blood seep from thy bane;
That fairer maid than ten of me
    Will look lang or thou come hame.'

11 As they were coming hame again,
    Upon the road so hie,
There they spy'd a small pyet,
    Was sitting on a tree.

12 'Where has thou been, fair lady?' it says,
    'Whare has thou been so soon?
Or what did thou wi Earl Richard,
    Was late wi thee yestreen?'

13 'Come down, come down, my wee pyet;
    An thou 'll come to my knee,

I have a cage of beaten gold,
    And I 'll bestow 't on thee.'

14 ' Keep thou thy cage of beaten gold,
    And I will keep my tree ;
For as thou did wi Earl Richard,
    So wad thou do wi me ;
Thou wad thraw the wee head aff my bouk,
    And drown me in the sea.'

15 ' Come down, come down, my wee pyet ;
    An thou 'll come to my hand,
I have a cage of beaten gold,
    And thou 's be put therein.'

16 ' Keep thou thy cage o beaten gold,
    And I will keep my tree ;
For as thou did wi Earl Richard,
    So would thou do wi me.'

17 ' Oh an I had my bow bendit,
    And set unto my knee,
I wad shoot this wee pyet
    Sits gabbing on the tree.'

18 ' Before thou get thy bow bendit,
    And set unto thy knee,

I 'll be at Earl Richard's father,
    Telling ill tales on thee.'

19 As they were coming hame again,
    Upon the road so bricht,
There they saw Earl Richard's father,
    Coming marching in their sicht.

20 ' Whare has thou been, fair lady ? ' he says,
    ' Whare has thou been back sae sune ?
O what did thou wi my auld son,
    Was late wi thee yestreen ? '

21 She did swear by stars o licht,
    And grass-green growing corn,
That she had not seen Earl Richard's face
    Since Saturday at morn ;
' But in Lorn's Water, indeed,' she says,
    ' I fear his days are done.'

22 ' There was not a ford in Lorn's Water
    But he could ride it weel ;
And what did thou wi my auld son,
    That went with thee afield ? '

*   *   *   *   *

E

Scott's Minstrelsy, III, 265, 1803, communicated by James Hogg, from the recitation of his mother (Motherwell).

1 LORD WILLIAM was the bravest knight
    That dwalt in fair Scotland,
And, though renowned in France and Spain,
    Fell by a ladie's hand.

2 As she was walking maid alone,
    Down by yon shady wood,
She heard a smit o bridle reins,
    She wishd might be for good.

3 ' Come to my arms, my dear Willie,
    You 're welcome hame to me ;
To best o chear and charcoal red,
    And candle burnin free.'

4 ' I winna light, I darena light,
    Nor come to your arms at a' ;
A fairer maid than ten o you
    I 'll meet at Castle-law.'

5 ' A fairer maid than me, Willie ?
    A fairer maid than me ?
A fairer maid than ten o me
    Your eyes did never see.'

6 He louted owr his saddle-lap
    To kiss her ere they part,
And wi a little keen bodkin,
    She pierced him to the heart.

7 ' Ride on, ride on, Lord William now,
    As fast as ye can dree ;
Your bonny lass at Castle-law
    Will weary you to see.'

8 Out up then spake a bonny bird,
    Sat high upon a tree :
' How could you kill that noble lord ?
    He came to marry thee.'

9 ' Come down, come down, my bonny bird,
    And eat bread aff my hand ;

Your cage shall be of wiry goud,
　　Whar now it 's but the wand.'

10 ' Keep ye your cage o goud, lady,
　　And I will keep my tree ;
　　As ye hae done to Lord William,
　　Sae wad ye do to me.'

11 She set her foot on her door-step,
　　A bonny marble stane,
　　And carried him to her chamber,
　　Oer him to make her mane.

12 And she has kept that good lord's corpse
　　Three quarters of a year,
　　Until that word began to spread ;
　　Then she began to fear.

13 Then she cryed on her waiting-maid,
　　Ay reády at her ca :
　　' There is a knight into my bower,
　　'T is time he were awa.'

14 The ane has taen him by the head,
　　The ither by the feet,
　　And thrown him in the wan water,
　　That ran baith wide and deep.

15 ' Look back, look back, now, lady fair,
　　On him that loed ye weel ;
　　A better man than that blue corpse
　　Neer drew a sword of steel.'

F

a. Motherwell's MS., p. 61, from the recitation of Miss Stevenson of Glasgow, January 22, 1825 ; Motherwell's Minstrelsy, p. 218. b. Motherwell's Minstrelsy, Appendix, p. xvii, VIII, one stanza.

1 EARL RICHARD is a hunting gone,
　　As fast as he can ride,
　　His hunting-horn hung about his neck,
　　And a small sword by his side.

2 When he came to my lady's gate
　　He tirled at the pin,
　　And wha was sae ready as the lady hersell
　　To open and let him in.

3 ' O light, O light, Earl Richard,' she says,
　　' O light and stay a' night ;
　　You shall have cheer wi charcoal clear,
　　And candles burning bright.'

4 ' I will not light, I cannot light,
　　I cannot light at all ;
　　A fairer lady than ten of thee
　　Is waiting at Richard's Wall.'

5 He stooped from his milk-white steed,
　　To kiss her rosy cheek ;
　　She had a pen-knife in her hand,
　　And wounded him so deep.

6 ' O lie ye there, Earl Richard,' she says,
　　' O lie ye there till morn ;

　　A fairer lady than ten of me
　　Will think lang of your coming home.'

7 She called her servants ane by ane,
　　She called them twa by twa :
　　' I have got a dead man in my bower,
　　I wish he were awa.'

8 The one has taen [him] by the hand,
　　And the other by the feet,
　　And they 've thrown him in a deep draw-well,
　　Full fifty fathom deep.

9 Then up bespake a little bird,
　　That sat upon a tree :
　　' Gae hame, gae hame, ye false lady,
　　And pay your maids their fee.'

10 ' Come down, come down, my pretty bird,
　　That sits upon the tree ;
　　I have a cage of beaten gold,
　　I 'll gie it unto thee.'

11 ' Gae hame, gae hame, ye fause lady,
　　And pay your maids their fee ;
　　As ye have done to Earl Richard,
　　Sae wud ye do to me.'

12 ' If I had an arrow in my hand,
　　And a bow bent on a string,
　　I 'd shoot a dart at thy proud heart,
　　Amang the leaves sae green.'

G

Herd's MSS, I, 34 ; Herd's Scottish Songs, 1776, I, 148.

1 SHE has calld to her her bower-maidens,
   She has calld them one by one :
'There is a dead man in my bower,
   I wish that he was gone.'

2 They have booted him, and spurred him,
   As he was wont to ride,
A hunting-horn around his waist,
   A sharp sword by his side.

3 Then up and spake a bonie bird,
   That sat upon the tree :
'What hae ye done wi Earl Richard ?
   Ye was his gay lady.'

4 'Cum down, cum down, my bonie bird,
   Cum sit upon my hand ;
And ye sall hae a cage o the gowd,
   Where ye hae but the wand.'

5 'Awa, awa, ye ill woman,
   Nae ill woman for me ;
What ye hae done to Earl Richard,
   Sae wad ye do to mee.'

* * * * *

6 'O there's a bird intill your bowir
   That sings sae sad and sweet ;
O there's a bird intill your bour
   Kept me frae my nicht's sleep.'

* * * * *

7 And she sware by the grass sae greene,
   Sae did she by the corn,
That she had not seen Earl Richard
   Sen yesterday at morn.

* * * * *

H

Dr Joseph Robertson's "Journal of Excursions," No 1, 1829.

* * * * *

1 'HAIL well, hail well, my little foot-page,
   Hail well this deed on me,
And ever I live my life to brook,
   I'se pay thee well thy fee.'

2 'It's we'l beet him, and we'l spur him,
   As gin he had been gain to ride,
Put a huntin-horn about his neck,
   And a small sword by his side.

3 'And we'll carry him to Clyde's Water,
   And there we'll fling him in,
That we may have it to be said
   In Clyde's Water he drownd.'

4 O they bet him, and they spurrd him,
   As gin he had been gain to ride,
Pat a huntin-horn about his neck,
   But the sword on his wrang side.

5 And they hae carried him to Clyde's Water,
   And there they flang him in,

That they might have it to be said
   In Clyde's Water he drowned.

* * * * *

6 'It's we'll sen for the king's doukers,
   And douk it up and doun ;
It's we'll sen for the king's doukers,
   And douk it out and in.'

7 Out it spak a little wee birdie,
   As it sat on yon burn-brae :

. . . . .
. . . . .

8 'Ye may lay by your day doukers,
   And turn you to the night,
And where the innocent blood lies slain,
   The candles will burn fou bricht.'

* * * * *

9 O they hae brunt that gay ladie,
   And blawn her in the air,
And nothing o that bower-man would burn
   But the hands that buskd him rare.

I

Motherwell MS., p. 189.

*   *   *   *   *

1 'Come down, come down, thou bonnie bird,
    Sit low upon my hand,
And thy cage shall be o the beaten gowd,
    And not of hazel wand.'

2 'O woe, O woe be to thee, lady,
    And an ill death may thou die!
For the way thou guided good Lord John,
    Soon, soon would thou guide me.'

3 'Go bend to me my bow,' she said,
    'And set it to my ee,
And I will gar that bonnie bird
    Come quickly down to me.'

4 'Before thou bend thy bow, lady,
    And set it to thy ee,
O I will be at yon far forest,
    Telling ill tales on thee.'

*   *   *   *   *

J

Scott's Minstrelsy, II, 42, 1802, and III, 184, 1833, from
Herd's copies (A, G), and from tradition.

1 ' O lady, rock never your young son young
    One hour langer for me;
For I have a sweetheart in Garlioch Wells
    I love far better than thee.

2 ' The very sole o that ladye's foot
    Than thy face is far mair white:'
' But, nevertheless, now, Erl Richard,
    Ye will bide in my bower a' night?'

3 She birled him wi the ale and wine,
    As they sat down to sup:
A living man he laid him down,
    But I wot he neer rose up.

4 Then up and spake the popinjay,
    That flew aboun her head:
'Lady, keep weel your green cleiding
    Frae gude Erl Richard's bleid.'

5 ' O better I 'll keep my green cleiding
    Frae gude Erl Richard's bleid,
Than thou canst keep thy clattering toung,
    That trattles in thy head.'

6 She has calld upon her bower-maidens,
    She has calld them ane by ane:
' There lies a deid man in my bowr,
    I wish that he were gane.'

7 They hae booted him, and spurred him,
    As he was wont to ride,

A hunting-horn tied round his waist,
    A sharp sword by his side;
And they hae had him to the wan water,
    For a' men call it Clyde.

8 Then up and spake the popinjay,
    That sat upon the tree:
' What hae ye done wi Erl Richard?
    Ye were his gaye ladye.'

9 ' Come down, come down, my bonny bird,
    And sit upon my hand;
And thou sall hae a cage o gowd,
    Where thou hast but the wand.'

10 'Awa, awa, ye ill woman,
    Nae cage o gowd for me;
As ye hae dune to Erl Richard,
    Sae wad ye do to me.'

11 She hadna crossd a rigg o land,
    A rigg but barely ane,
When she met wi his auld father,
    Came riding all alane.

12 ' Where hae ye been, now, ladye fair,
    Where hae ye been sae late?
We hae been seeking Erl Richard,
    But him we canna get.'

13 ' Erl Richard kens a' the fords in Clyde,
    He 'll ride them ane by ane;
And though the night was neer sae mirk,
    Erl Richard will be hame.'

14 O it fell anes upon a day
  The king was boun to ride,
And he has mist him Erl Richard,
  Should hae ridden on his right side.

15 The ladye turnd her round about,
  Wi mickle mournfu din :
'It fears me sair o Clyde water,
  That he is drownd therein.'

16 'Gar douk, gar douk,' the king he cried,
  'Gar douk for gold and fee ;
O wha will douk for Erl Richard's sake,
  Or wha will douk for me ?'

17 They douked in at ae weil-heid,
  And out aye at the other :
'We can douk nae mair for Erl Richard,
  Altho he were our brother.'

18 It fell that in that ladye's castle
  The king was boun to bed,
And up and spake the popinjay,
  That flew abune his head.

19 'Leave aff your douking on the day,
  And douk upon the night ;
And wherever that sackless knight lies slain,
  The candles will burn bright.'

20 'O there's a bird within this bower,
  That sings baith sad and sweet ;
O there's a bird within your bower
  Keeps me frae my night's sleep.'

21 They left the douking on the day,
  And douked upon the night,
And where that sackless knight lay slain,
  The candles burned bright.

22 The deepest pot in a' the linn
  They fand Erl Richard in ;

A green turf tyed across his breast,
  To keep that gude lord down.

23 Then up and spake the king himsell,
  When he saw the deadly wound,
'O wha has slain my right-hand man,
  That held my hawk and hound ?'

24 Then up and spake the popinjay,
  Says, What needs a' this din ?
It was his light lemman took his life,
  And hided him in the linn.

25 She swore her by the grass sae grene,
  Sae did she by the corn,
She had na seen him Erl Richard
  Since Moninday at morn.

26 'Put na the wyte on me,' she said,
  'It was my may, Catherine :'
Then they hae cut baith fern and thorn,
  To burn that maiden in.

27 It wadna take upon her cheik,
  Nor yet upon her chin,
Nor yet upon her yellow hair,
  To cleanse the deadly sin.

28 The maiden touchd the clay-cauld corpse,
  A drap it never bled ;
The ladye laid her hand on him,
  And soon the ground was red.

29 Out they hae ta'en her May Catherine,
  And put her mistress in ;
The flame tuik fast upon her cheik,
  Tuik fast upon her chin,
Tuik fast upon her fair bodye,
  She burnd like hollins grene.

K

Buchan's Ballads of the North of Scotland, I, 118.

1 LADY MAISRY forth from her bower came,
  And stood on her tower-head ;
She thought she heard a bridle ring,
  The sound did her heart guid.

2 She thought it was her first true-love,
  Whom she loved ance in time ;

But it was her new love, Hunting,
  Come frae the hunting o the hyn.

3 'Gude morrow, gude morrow, Lady Maisry,
  God make you safe and free ;
I'm come to take my last farewell,
  And pay my last visit to thee.'

4 'O stay, O stay then, Young Hunting,
  O stay with me this night ;

Ye shall hae cheer, an charcoal clear,
    And candles burning bright.'

5 ' Have no more cheer, you lady fair,
    An hour langer for me ;
I have a lady in Garmouth town
    I love better than thee.'

6 ' O if your love be changed, my love,
    Since better canno be,
Nevertheless, for auld lang syne,
    Ye 'll stay this night wi me.

7 ' Silver, silver shall be your wage,
    And gowd shall be your fee,
And nine times nine into the year
    Your weed shall changed be.

8 ' Will ye gae to the cards or dice,
    Or to a tavern fine ?
Or will ye gae to a table forebye,
    And birl baith beer and wine ? '

9 ' I winna gang to the cards nor dice,
    Nor to a tavern fine ;
But I will gang to a table forebye,
    And birl baith beer and wine.'

10 Then she has drawn for Young Hunting
    The beer but and the wine,
Till she got him as deadly drunk
    As ony unhallowed swine.

11 Then she 's taen out a trusty brand,
    That hang below her gare,
Then she 's wounded him Young Hunting,
    A deep wound and a sair.

12 Then out it speaks her comrade,
    Being in the companie :
' Alas ! this deed that ye hae done
    Will ruin baith you and me.'

13 ' Heal well, heal well, you Lady Katharine,
    Heal well this deed on me,
The robes that were shapen for my bodie,
    They shall be sewed for thee.'

14 ' Tho I woud heal it never sae well,
    And never sae well,' said she,
' There is a God above us baith
    That can baith hear and see.'

15 They booted him, and spurred him,
    As he 'd been gaun to ride,
A hunting-horn about his neck,
    A sharp sword by his side.

16 And they rode on, and farther on,
    All the lang summer's tide,

Until they came to wan water,
    Where a' man ca's it Clyde.

17 And the deepest pot in Clyde's water,
    And there they flang him in,
And put a turf on his breast-bane,
    To had Young Hunting down.

18 O out it speaks a little wee bird,
    As she sat on the brier :
' Gae hame, gae hame, ye Lady Maisry,
    And pay your maiden's hire.'

19 ' O I will pay my maiden's hire,
    And hire I 'll gie to thee ;
If ye 'll conceal this fatal deed,
    Ye 's hae gowd for your fee.'

20 Then out it speaks a bonny bird,
    That flew aboon their head :
' Keep well, keep well your green claithing
    Frae ae drap o his bluid.'

21 ' O I 'll keep well my green claithing
    Frae ae drop o his bluid,
Better than I 'll do your flattering tongue,
    That flutters in your head.

22 ' Come down, come down, my bonny bird,
    Light down upon my hand ;
For ae gowd feather that 's in your wing,
    I woud gie a' my land.'

23 ' How shall I come down, how can I come down,
    How shall I come down to thee ?
The things ye said to Young Hunting,
    The same ye 're saying to me.'

24 But it fell out on that same day
    The king was going to ride,
And he calld for him Young Hunting,
    For to ride by his side.

25 Then out it speaks the little young son,
    Sat on the nurse's knee :
' It fears me sair,' said that young babe,
    ' He 's in bower wi yon ladie.'

26 Then they hae calld her Lady Katharine,
    And she sware by the thorn
That she saw not him Young Hunting
    Sin yesterday at morn.

27 Then they hae calld her Lady Maisry,
    And she sware by the moon
That she saw not him Young Hunting
    Sin yesterday at noon.

28 ' He was playing him at the Clyde's Water,
    Perhaps he has fa'en in : '

The king he calld his divers all,
  To dive for his young son.

29 They div'd in thro the wan burn-bank,
  Sae did they outthro the other :
' We 'll dive nae mair,' said these young men,
  ' Suppose he were our brother.'

30 Then out it spake a little bird,
  That flew aboon their head :
' Dive on, dive on, ye divers all,
  For there he lies indeed.

31 ' But ye 'll leave aff your day diving,
  And ye 'll dive in the night;
The pot where Young Hunting lies in,
  The candles they 'll burn bright.

32 ' There are twa ladies in yon bower,
  And even in yon ha,
And they hae killd him Young Hunting,
  And casten him awa.

33 ' They booted him, and spurred him,
  As he 'd been gaun to ride,
A hunting-horn tied round his neck,
  A sharp sword by his side

34 ' The deepest pot o Clyde's Water,
  There they flang him in,
Laid a turf on his breast-bane,
  To had Young Hunting down.'

35 Now they left aff their day diving,
  And they dived on the night ;
The pot that Young Hunting lay in,
  The candles were burning bright.

36 The king he calld his hewers all,
  To hew down wood and thorn,
For to put up a strong bale-fire,
  These ladies for to burn.

37 And they hae taen her Lady Katharine,
  And they hae pitten her in ;
But it wadna light upon her cheek,
  Nor woud it on her chin,
But sang the points o her yellow hair,
  For healing the deadly sin.

38 Then they hae taen her Lady Maisry,
  And they hae put her in:
First it lighted on her cheek,
  And syne upon her chin,
And sang the points o her yellow hair,
  And she burnt like keckle-pin.

A. a. 1¹. than he. 2¹. lover's. 3⁸. drucken.
  7⁸. the green. 10¹. higher. 10⁸. On every.
  12². Or he.
  20¹, ² *and* 21 *in one stanza.*
  21¹. Clyd's. (?) 23⁸. lackless.
  25⁵, ⁶ *and* 26 *in one stanza.*
  b. *is a revised copy, in which most of the above*
    readings are corrected, with other changes.
    1¹. *second* young *omitted.*
    3⁸. love drucken. 4⁸. love drunken.
    6¹. her of. 13¹. wan *omitted.*
    14¹, 24¹. pit. 15². gan. 18¹, 21¹. Clyde's.
    19¹. tae *omitted.* 27¹, ². hae *omitted.*
    27⁶. hoky gren *wanting.*

B. 6, 7. *These stanzas, with the trivial variation*
  in 6⁸ *of* she 's taen out, *are given by Cham-*
  bers, Scottish Ballads, p. 259, note, from
  his recollection of a recited fragment.

D. " The catastrophe wanting, but the lady's
  treachery was discovered, and she was
  burned." *Motherwell's MS.*
  9⁴. so deep. 20¹. hast.

E. " Although much of the language seems somewhat modernized, this must be attributed to
  its currency, being much liked, and very
  much sung, in this neighborhood. I can
  trace it back several generations, but cannot
  hear of its ever having been in print. I
  have never heard it with any considerable
  variation, save that one reciter called the
  dwelling of the feigned sweetheart Castle-
  swa." *Hogg.*

G. " To a wild melancholy tune." *Herd.*
  Quhat, ze, *etc., are printed* what, ye, *as*
  usual.

H. 7¹, ² *and* 8 *one stanza.*

69

CLERK SAUNDERS

A. 'Clerk Sanders,' Herd's MSS, I, 177, II, 49.

B. 'Clerk Saunders,' Herd's MSS, I, 163, II, 46.

C. 'Clerk Saunders,' Kinloch's Scottish Ballads, p. 233.

D. 'Lord Saunders,' Motherwell's MS., p. 196.

E. 'The Seven Bluidy Brithers,' Motherwell's MS., p. 199.

F. 'Clerk Saunders,' Jamieson's Popular Ballads, I, 83.

G. 'Clerk Sandy,' Buchan's Ballads of the North of Scotland, I, 160.

'CLERK SAUNDERS' was first given to the world in the Minstrelsy of the Scottish Border, II, 33, 1802, and was there said to be "taken from Mr Herd's MS., with several corrections from a shorter and more imperfect copy in the same volume, and one or two conjectural emendations in the arrangement of the stanzas." Sir Walter arranged his ballad with much good taste, but this account of his dealing with Herd's copies is very far from precisely accurate. A, the longer of these, does not end, as here printed, with Margret's refusal to be comforted, a rather unsufficing conclusion it must be owned. The story is continued by annexing the ballad of 'Sweet William's Ghost,' the lack of which in B makes Scott call that version imperfect. This sequel, found also in F, is omitted here, and will be given in the proper place.* Jamieson's, F, as well as Scott's, is a made-up copy, "the stanzas where the seven brothers are introduced" having been "enlarged from two fragments, which, although very defective in themselves, furnished lines which, when incorporated with the text, seemed to improve it." About one half of G is taken from Herd's MSS, with trivial alterations. The ghostly vis-

itation at the end blends 'Proud Lady Margaret' with 'Sweet William's Ghost,' and this conclusion, not being worth transferring, has been allowed to stand.† The dream in E 13 may be derived from 'Fair Margaret and Sweet William.'

The austerities vowed in D 13–15, E 17–20, found also in A 20–22, G 23–25, make a very satisfactory termination to the tragedy, and supply a want that may be felt in B, and in A as it stands here. The like are found in 'The Clerk's Twa Sons o Owsenford,' 'Bonny Bee Ho'm,' 'Lord Livingston,' 'The Weary Coble o Cargill,' and 'The Lowlands of Holland.' Also in the French ballad of 'La Biche Blanche,' where a brother, having unwittingly been the death of his sister, who was maid by day but hind by night, vows himself to a seven years' penance :

J'en suis au désespoir, j'en ferai pénitence ;
Serai pendant sept ans sans mettr' chemise blanche,
Et coucherai sept ans sous une épine blanche.

or,

Et j'aurai sous l'épin', pour toit, rien qu'une branche.

---

* But it is, of course, not impossible that there may have been such a conclusion to 'Clerk Saunders.' It may be mentioned, though not as an argument, that there was a ballad in Boccaccio's time (of which he cites the first two lines), on the story of G. iv, N. 5, of the Decamerone ; a tale in which three brothers kill their sister's lover, and bury the body in a solitary place, and his ghost appears and informs the sister of what had happened.

† Buchan 1, 2 = **B** 1, 2 ; 3–9 = **A** 3–9 ; 11 = **A** 10 ; 12 = **B** 11 ; 15 is made from **A** 12 ; 16 = **B** 16 ; 17 = **A** 15 ; 23–25 = **A** 21, 22, 20 ; 26–29 are made from **A** 24–26, 23. The fatuity of 13^2, 14^2 is such as is found nowhere out of Buchan.

The stanza given in the Appendix to Motherwell's Minstrelsy, xix, XVI, is Scott's 13.

Vaugeois, Histoire des Antiquités de la Ville de l'Aigle, p. 585, repeated in Bosquet, La Normandie Romanesque, p. 83, Beaurepaire, Poésie p. en Normandie, p. 78; Haupt, Französische Volkslieder, p. 20, Souvestre, in Revue des Deux Mondes, 1849, Avril, p. 106, and Les Derniers Paysans, p. 36, ed. 1871.

The king, in 'Kong Valdemar og hans Søster,' Grundtvig, No 126, A, B, C, will live in a dark house where he shall never see fire nor light, nor shall the sun ever shine on him, till he has expiated his monstrous cruelty to his sister.

So the marquis, in the Romance del Marques de Mántua, swears, till he has avenged the death of Valdovinos,

> de nunca peinar mis canas,
> ni las mis barbas cortar,
> de no vestir otras ropas,
> ni renovar mi calzar, etc.

Wolf and Hofmann, Primavera, No 165, II, 192.

F, Jamieson's version, connects 'Clerk Saunders' with a Scandinavian ballad,* which seems to be preserved in abbreviated and sometimes perverted forms, also by other races. Full forms of this Northern ballad are:

Icelandic, 'Ólöfar kvæði,' eight versions, A-H, Íslenzk Fornkvæði, No 34, I, 332.

Färöe, 'Faðir og dottir,' communicated by Hammershaimb to the Antiquarisk Tidsskrift, 1849–51, p. 88.

Norwegian, 'Far aa dótter,' Bugge, Gamle Norske Folkeviser, p. 115, A (with two fragments, B, C).

A father [king, Icelandic A-H] asks his daughter if she is ready to marry. She has no such thought.† [She swore by God, by man, that she had never had the thought, had no private connection, was as clear as a nun; but nobody knew what was in her mind: Färöe.]

Who, then, he asks, is the fair knight that rode to your bower? No fair knight, but one of her knaves. Whose was that horse I saw at your door? It was no horse, but a hind from the fell. Who was that fair knight you kissed at the spring? It was no knight, but her maid that she kissed. Does her maid wear a sword at her side? It was no sword, but a bunch of keys. Does her maid wear spurs? It was no spurs, but gold on her shoes. Has her maid short hair? Her plaits were coiled on her head. Does she wear short clothes, like men? Maids hold up their coats when there is a dew. What babe was crying in her chamber? It was no babe, but her dog. What was that cradle standing by her bed? It was no cradle, but her little silk-loom.

In the Färöe ballad the father then rides to the wood, meets a knight, cuts him in two, hangs his foot, hand, and head to his saddle, and returns. Do you know this foot? he asks. It has often found the way to her chamber. Do you know this hand? Many a night it has lain on her arm. Do you know this head? Many a kiss have the lips had. In the other versions these bloody tokens are produced on the spot, with a more startling effect. The daughter wishes a fire in her father's house, him in it, and herself looking on. Instantly a blaze bursts forth, the king is burnt up, and all that belongs to him. The daughter sets the fire herself in the Färöe and the Norwegian ballad. She dies of grief in Icelandic C, takes to the wood in E, F,‡ goes into a cloister in D, G (cf. English C).

A briefer form of this same story is 'Den grymma Brodern,' Afzelius, No 86, III, 107. In this a brother takes the place of the father. After several questions he asks his sister if she knows the man's hand that hangs at his saddle. She bursts out into an exclamation of

---

* We may suppose that all the three versions, two of them fragmentary, which Jamieson combined, contained the passage which furnishes the link: but it would be much more satisfactory if Jamieson had given us all three as he received them.

† Icelandic A-C have an introductory incident not found in E-H. There is a trace of this in D, and it occurs also in two other ballads, I, K, of the same series, which lack the feature that A-H and English F have in common. A king

finds a young child that has been left on or in the cleft of a rock, takes it with him, and rides to his daughter's bower. He asks his daughter who the fair swain is that he has found, and how it comes to have her eyes. She feigns ignorance and indifference: many a man is like another. Then come the questions found in the other versions.

‡ "Goes brain," perhaps, as the editors suggest, like Lady Maisry in 'Lord Ingram,' and others in Scottish ballads.

grief. ' Thore och hans Syster,' Arwidsson, No 55, I, 358,* has lost its proper conclusion, for we have not come to the conclusion when the brother says that his sister's false inventions will never give out till the sea wants water, a comment which we also find in the Färöe ballad (where, however, it is misplaced). This is the case, also, with ' Det hurtige Svar,' Danske Viser, No 204, IV, 228 * and 362, but in the Danish ballad a perversion towards the comic has begun, the end being:

> ' Brother, would you question more,
> I have answers still in store.'

> ' When women lack a quick reply,
> The German Ocean shall be dry.'

In a **Spanish** and **Portuguese** romance a woman has received a lover in the absence of her husband. The husband returns before he is expected, and puts questions similar to those in the ballads already spoken of : whose horse, lance, sword, is this ? whose spurs, whose arms are these ? and is answered after the same fashion. There is considerable variety in the conclusion ; the husband kills his wife, kills the paramour, kills both, both he and his rival lose their lives, the wife dies of fright, or is even pardoned. Spanish : ' De Blanca-Niña,' Wolf and Hofmann, Primavera, No 136, II,

52 ; ' Romance del Conde Lombardo,' the same, No 136 a, II, 53 ; ' La adúltera castigada,' Milá, Romancerillo, No 254, A-M, pp 241–45 ; ' Lo retorn soptat,' Briz, IV, 183 ; Fernan Caballero, La Gaviota, p. 82, ed. Leipzig, 1868.†

In an Illyrian ballad, husband, wife, and a young Clerk are the parties. Three watches are set to give notice of the husband's return, one in the field, one in the house-court, one before the chamber. They give due warning, but the woman, like Lady Barnard, in ' Little Musgrave,' will not heed. After some questions and evasions the husband strikes off her head : ' Nevérnost,' Vraz, Narodne Pésni Ilirske, p. 72 ; ' Bestrafte Untreue,' A. Grün, Volkslieder aus Krain, p. 41.

Nothing could be easier than to give these questions, prevarications, and comments a humorous turn, and this is done in a large number of ballads : see ' Our good man came hame at een.'

The two ballads which immediately follow have connections with ' Clerk Saunders.'

Scott's copy is translated by Schubart, p. 79 ; Wolff, Halle der Völker, I, 45, Hausschatz, p. 202 ; Knortz, Lieder und Romanzen Alt-Englands, No 13. F, in Afzelius, III, 110.

A

Herd's MSS, a, I, 177 ; b, II, 419.

1 CLARK SANDERS and May Margret
  Walkt ower yon graveld green,
  And sad and heavy was the love,
  I wat, it fell this twa between.

2 ' A bed, a bed,' Clark Sanders said,
  ' A bed, a bed for you and I ;'
  ' Fye no, fye no,' the lady said,
  ' Until the day we married be.

3 ' For in it will come my seven brothers,
  And a' their torches burning bright ;
  They 'll say, We hae but ae sister,
  And here her lying wi a knight.'

4 ' Ye 'l take the sourde fray my scabbord,
  And lowly, lowly lift the gin,
  And you may say, your oth to save,
  You never let Clark Sanders in.

5 ' Yele take a napken in your hand,
  And ye 'l ty up baith your een,

---

* These are translated by Jamieson, Illustrations of Northern Antiquities, p. 424, Prior, II, 378 ; W. and M. Howitt, Literature and Romance of Northern Europe, I, 261.

† Fernan Caballero had another Andalusian version besides this.

An ye may say, your oth to save,
  That ye saw na Sandy sen late yestreen.

6 'Yele take me in your armes twa,
  Yele carrey me ben into your bed,
And ye may say, your oth to save,
  In your bower-floor I never tread.'

7 She has taen the sourde fray his scabbord,
  And lowly, lowly lifted the gin;
She was to swear, her oth to save,
  She never let Clerk Sanders in.

8 She has tain a napkin in her hand,
  And she ty'd up baith her eeen;
She was to swear, her oth to save,
  She saw na him sene late yestreen.

9 She has taen him in her armes twa,
  And carried him ben into her bed;
She was to swear, her oth to save,
  He never in her bower-floor tread.

10 In and came her seven brothers,
  And all their torches burning bright;
Says thay, We hae but ae sister,
  And see there her lying wi a knight.

11 Out and speaks the first of them,
  'A wat they hay been lovers dear;'
Out and speaks the next of them,
  'They hay been in love this many a year.'

12 Out an speaks the third of them,
  'It wear great sin this twa to twain;'
Out an speaks the fourth of them,
  'It wear a sin to kill a sleeping man.'

13 Out an speaks the fifth of them,
  'A wat they 'll near be twaind by me;'
Out an speaks the sixt of them,
  'We 'l tak our leave an gae our way.'

14 Out an speaks the seventh of them,
  'Altho there wear no a man but me,
. . . . .
  I bear the brand, I 'le gar him die.'

15 Out he has taen a bright long brand,
  And he has striped it throw the straw,
And throw and throw Clarke Sanders' body
  A wat he has gard cold iron gae.

16 Sanders he started, an Margret she lapt,
  Intill his arms whare she lay,
And well and wellsom was the night,
  A wat it was between these twa.

17 And they lay still, and sleeped sound,
  Untill the day began to daw;
And kindly till him she did say
  'It's time, trew-love, ye wear awa.'

18 They lay still, and sleeped sound,
  Untill the sun began to shine;
She lookt between her and the wa,
  And dull and heavy was his eeen.

19 She thought it had been a loathsome sweat,
  A wat it had fallen this twa between;
But it was the blood of his fair body,
  A wat his life days wair na lang.

20 'O Sanders, I 'le do for your sake
  What other ladys would na thoule;
When seven years is come and gone,
  There's near a shoe go on my sole.

21 'O Sanders, I 'le do for your sake
  What other ladies would think mare;
When seven years is come an gone,
  Ther's nere a comb go in my hair.

22 'O Sanders, I 'le do for your sake
  What other ladies would think lack;
When seven years is come an gone,
  I 'le wear nought but dowy black.'

23 The bells gaed clinking throw the towne,
  To carry the dead corps to the clay,
An sighing says her May Margret,
  'A wat I bide a doulfou day.'

24 In an come her father dear,
  Stout steping on the floor;
. . . . .
. . . . .

25 'Hold your toung, my doughter dear,
  Let all your mourning a bee;
I 'le carry the dead corps to the clay,
  An I 'le come back an comfort thee.'

26 'Comfort well your seven sons,
  For comforted will I never bee;
For it was neither lord nor loune
  That was in bower last night wi mee.'

B

Herd's MSS, **a**, I, 163; **b**, II, 46.

1 CLERK SAUNDERS and a gay lady
  Was walking in yonder green,
  And heavy, heavy was the love
  That fell this twa lovers between.

2 'A bed, a bed,' Clerk Saunders said,
  'And ay a bed for you and me;'
  'Never a ane,' said the gay lady,
  'Till ance we twa married be.

3 'There would come a' my seven brethern,
  And a' their torches burning bright,
  And say, We hae but ae sister,
  And behad, she's lying wi you the night.'

4 'You'll take a napkain in your hand,
  And then you will tie up your een;
  Then you may swear, and safe your aith,
  You sawna Sandy sin yestreen.

5 'You'll take me up upo your back,
  And then you'll carry me to your bed;
  Then you may swear, and save your aith,
  Your board [-floor] Sandy never tred.'

6 She's taen him upo her back,
  And she's carried him unto her bed,
  That she might swear, and safe her aith,
  Her board-floor Sandy never tread.

7 She's taen a napkin in her hand,
  And lo she did tie up her een,
  That she might swear, and safe her aith,
  She sawna Sandy syne yestreen.

8 They were na weel into the room,
  Nor yet laid weel into the bed,

   .   .   .   .   .
    .   .   .   .   .

9 When in came a' her seven brethern,
  And a' their torches burning bright;
  Says they, We hae but ae sister,
  And behold, she's lying wi you this night.

10 'I,' bespake the first o them,
   A wat an ill death mat he die!
   'I bear a brand into my hand
   Shall quickly gar Clerk Saunders die.'

11 'I,' bespake the second of them,
   A wat a good death mat he die!
   'We will gae back, let him alane,
   His father has nae mair but he.'

12 'I,' bespake the third o them,
   A wat an ill death mat he die!
   'I bear the brand into my hand
   Shall quickly help to gar him die.'

13 'I,' bespake the fourth o them,
   A wat a good death mat he die!
   'I bear the brand into my hand
   Shall never help to gar him die.'

14 'I,' bespake the fifth o them,
   A wat an ill death mat he die!
   'Altho his father hae nae mair,
   I'll quickly help to gar him die.'

15 'I,' bespake the sixth o them,
   A wat a good death mat he die!
   'He's a worthy earl's son,
   I'll never help to gar him die.'

16 'I,' bespake the seventh of them,
   A wat an ill death mat he die!
   'I bear the brand into my hand
   Shall quickly gar Clerk Saunders die.'

17 They baith lay still, and sleeped sound,
   Untill the sun began to sheen;
   She drew the curtains a wee bit,
   And dull and drowsie was his een.

18 'This night,' said she, 'the sleepiest man
   That ever my twa eyes did see
   Hay lyen by me, and sweat the sheets;
   A wite they're a great shame to see.'

19 She rowd the claiths a' to the foot,
   And then she spied his deadly wounds:
   'O wae be to my seven brethern,
   A wat an ill death mat they die!

20 'I'm sure it was neither rogue nor loun
   I had into my bed wi me;
   'T was Clerk Saunders, that good earl's son,
   That pledgd his faith to marry me.'

C

Kinloch's Scottish Ballads, p. 233, a North Country version.

1 It was a sad and a rainy nicht
    As ever raind frae toun to toun ;
Clerk Saunders and his lady gay
    They were in the fields sae broun.

2 ‘ A bed, a bed,’ Clerk Saunders cried,
    ‘ A bed, a bed, let me lie doun ;
For I am sae weet and sae wearie
    That I canna gae nor ride frae toun.’

3 ‘ A bed, a bed,’ his lady cried,
    ‘ A bed, a bed, ye ’ll neer get nane ;

.   .   .   .   .

.   .   .   .   .

4 ‘ For I hae seven bauld brethren,
    Bauld are they, and very rude ;
And if they find ye in bouer wi me,
    They winna care to spill your blude.’

5 ‘ Ye ’ll tak a lang claith in your hand,
    Ye ’ll haud it up afore your een,
That ye may swear, and save your aith,
    That ye saw na Sandy sin yestreen.

6 ‘ And ye ’ll tak me in your arms twa,
    Ye ’ll carry me into your bed,
That ye may swear, and save your aith,
    That in your bour-floor I never gaed.’

7 She ’s taen a lang claith in her hand,
    She ’s hauden ’t up afore her een,
That she might swear, and save her aith,
    That she saw na Sandy sin yestreen.

8 She has taen him in her arms twa,
    And carried him into her bed,
That she might swear, and save her aith,
    That on her bour-floor he never gaed.

9 Then in there cam her firsten brother,
    Bauldly he cam steppin in :
‘ Come here, come here, see what I see !
We hae only but ae sister alive,
    And a knave is in bour her wi.’

10 Then in and cam her second brother,
    Says, Twa lovers are ill to twin ;

And in and cam her thirden brother,
    ‘ O brother dear, I say the same.’

11 Then in and cam her fourthen brother,
    ‘ It ’s a sin to kill a sleepin man ; ’
And in and cam her fiften brother,
    ‘ O brother dear, I say the same.’

12 Then in and cam her sixthen brother,
    ‘ I wat he ’s neer be steerd by me ; ’
But in and cam her seventhen brother,
    ‘ I bear the hand that sall gar him dee.’

13 Then out he drew a nut-brown sword,
    I wat he stript it to the stroe,
And thro and thro Clerk Saunders’ body
    I wat he garrd cauld iron go.

14 Then they lay there in ither’s arms
    Until the day began to daw ;
Then kindly to him she did say,
    ‘ It ’s time, my dear, ye were awa.

15 ‘ Ye are the sleepiest young man,’ she said,
    ‘ That ever my twa een did see ;
Ye ’ve lain a’ nicht into my arms,
    I ’m sure it is a shame to be.’

16 She turnd the blankets to the foot,
    And turnd the sheets unto the wa,
And there she saw his bluidy wound,

.   .   .   .   .

17 ‘ O wae be to my seventhen brother,
    I wat an ill death mot he dee !
He ’s killd Clerk Saunders, an earl’s son,
    I wat he ’s killd him unto me.’

18 Then in and cam her father dear,
    Cannie cam he steppin in ;
Says, Haud your tongue, my dochter dear,
    What need you mak sic heavy meane ?

19 ‘ We ’ll carry Clerk Saunders to his grave,
    And syne come back and comfort thee : ’
‘ O comfort weel your seven sons, father,
    For man sall never comfort me ;
Ye ’ll marrie me wi the Queen o Heaven,
    For man sall never enjoy me.’

D

Motherwell's MS., p. 196, from the recitation of Mrs Thomson.

*   *   *   *   *

1 'O I HAVE seven bold brethren,
   And they are all valiant men,
If they knew a man that would tread my
      bower
   His life should not go along wi him.'

2 'Then take me up into your arms,
   And lay me low down on your bed,
That ye may swear, and keep your oath clear,
   That your bower-room I did na tread.

3 'Tie a handkerchief round your face,
   And you must tye it wondrous keen,
That you may swear, and keep your oath clear,
   Ye saw na me since late yestreen.'

4 But they were scarsley gone to bed,
   Nor scarse fa'n owre asleep,
Till up and started her seven brethren,
   Just at Lord Saunders' feet.

5 Out bespoke the first brither,
   'Oh but love be wondrous keen!'
Out bespoke the second brither,
   'It's ill done to kill a sleeping man.'

6 Out bespoke the third brither,
   'We had better gae and let him be;'
Out bespoke the fourth brither,
   'He'll no be killd this night for me:'

7 Out bespoke the fifth brother,
   'This night Lord Saunders he shall die;
Tho there were not a man in all Scotland,
   This night Lord Saunders he shall die.'

8 He took out a rousty rapier,
   And he drew it three times thro the strae;
Between Lord Saunders' short rib and his side
   He gard the rusty rapier gae.

9 'Awake, awake, Lord Saunders,' she said,
   'Awake, awake, for sin and shame!
For the day is light, and the sun shines bricht,
   And I am afraid we will be taen.

10 'Awake, awake, Lord Saunders,' she said,
   'Awake, awake, for sin and shame!
For the sheets they are asweat,' she said,
   'And I am afraid we will be taen.

11 'I dreamed a dreary dream last night,
   I wish it may be for our good,
That I was cutting my yellow hair,
   And dipping it in the wells o blood.'

12 Aye she waukened at this dead man,
   Aye she put on him to and fro;
Oh aye she waukend at this dead man,
   But of his death she did not know.

*   *   *   *   *

13 'It's I will do for my love's sake
   What many ladies would think lang;
Seven years shall come and go
   Before a glove go on my hand.

14 'And I will do for my love's sake
   What many ladies would not do;
Seven years shall come and go
   Before I wear stocking or shoe.

15 'Ther'll neer a shirt go on my back,
   There'll neer a kame go in my hair,
There'll never coal nor candle-light
   Shine in my bower nae mair.'

———◆———

E

Motherwell MS., p. 199, from Widow Smith, George Street, Paisley.

1 AN ensign and a lady gay,
   As they were walking on a green,
The ensign said to the lady gay,
   Will you tak me to your bower at een?

2 'I have seven bluidy brithers,
   Och and to you they have nae good will;
And if they catch you in my bower,
   They'll value not your bluid to spill.'

3 'O you may take me on your back,
   And carry me to your chamber-bed,

That I may swear, and avow richt clear,
That your flowery bower I did never tread.

4 'O take a napkin from your pocket,
And with it blindfold my een,
That I may swear, and avow richt clear,
That your flowery bower I have never seen.'

5 O she 's taen him upon her back,
And carried him to her chamber-bed,
That he might swear, and avow it clear,
That her flowery [bower] he did never
tread.

6 O she 's taen a napkin from her pocket,
And with it blinded baith his een,
That he might swear, and avow it clear,
That her flowery bower he had never seen.

7 They were not well into their bed,
Nor were they scarsely fallen asleep,
Till in there came her seven bluidy brithers,
And placed themselves at the ensign's feet.

8 Said the first one to the second,
'Och it is long since this love began;'
Said the second unto the third,
'It 's a sin to kill a sleeping man.'

9 Said the third one to the fourth,
'I will go to yon tavern hie;'
Said [the] fourth one to the fifth,
'O if you will go, so will I.'

10 Said the fifth to the sixth,
'Och it 's long since this love began;'
Said the sixth to the seventh,
'It 's a sin to kill a sleeping man.'

11 Out then spoke the seventh bluidy brither,
Aye and an angry man was he:
'Altho there was no more men alive,
The ensign's butcher I will be.'

12 He 's taen out his rusty broad-sword,
And ran it three times along his throat,

And thro and thro the ensign's body
The tempered steel it went thro and thro.

13 'O I have dreamed a dream,' she said,
'And such an dreams cannot be good;
I dreamed my bower was full of swine,
And the ensign's clothes all dipped in blood.

14 'I have dreamed another dream,
And such an dreams are never good;
That I was combing down my yellow hair,
And dipping it in the ensign's blood.'

15 'O hold your tongue, my sister dear,
And of your weeping let a be;
For I will get you a better match
Than eer the ensign, what was he?'

16 'So woe be to you, my seven bluidy brithers,
Aye and an ill death may you die!
For you durst not fight him in battle-field,
But you killed him sleeping in bed wi me.

17 'I 'll do more for my love's sake
That other lovers would not incline;
Seven years shall come and go
Before I wash this face of mine.

18 'I will do for my love's sake
What other lovers would not repair;
Seven years shall come and go
Before I comb down my yellow hair.

19 'I 'll do more for my love's sake,
What other lovers will not do;
Seven years shall come and go
Before I cast off stocking and shoe.

20 'I will do for my love's sake
What other lovers they will be slack;
Seven years shall come and go
Before I cast off my robes of black.

21 'Go make to me a high, high tower,
Be sure you make it stout and strong,
And on the top put an honour's gate,
That my love's ghost may go out and in.'

F

Jamieson's Popular Ballads, I, 83, communicated by Mrs Arrot, of Aberbrothick, but enlarged from two fragments.

1 CLERK SAUNDERS was an earl's son,
 He livd upon sea-sand ;
May Margaret was a king's daughter,
 She livd in upper land.

2 Clerk Saunders was an earl's son,
 Weel learned at the scheel ;
May Margaret was a king's daughter,
 They baith loed ither weel.

3 He 's throw the dark, and throw the mark,
 And throw the leaves o green,
Till he came to May Margaret's door,
 And tirled at the pin.

4 'O sleep ye, wake ye, May Margaret,
 Or are ye the bower within ? '
 O wha is that at my bower-door,
 Sae weel my name does ken ? '
' It 's I, Clerk Saunders, your true-love,
 You 'll open and lat me in.

5 'O will ye to the cards, Margaret,
 Or to the table to dine ?
Or to the bed, that 's weel down spread,
 And sleep when we get time ? '

6 'I 'll no go to the cards,' she says,
 ' Nor to the table to dine ;
But I 'll go to a bed, that 's weel down spread,
 And sleep when we get time.'

7 They were not weel lyen down,
 And no weel fa'en asleep,
When up and stood May Margaret's brethren,
 Just up at their bed-feet.

8 'O tell us, tell us, May Margaret,
 And dinna to us len,
O wha is aught yon noble steed,
 That stands your stable in ? '

9 'The steed is mine, and it may be thine,
 To ride whan ye ride in hie ;
. . . . .

. . . . .

10 'But awa, awa, my bald brethren,
 Awa, and mak nae din ;

For I am as sick a lady the nicht
 As eèr lay a bower within.'

11 'O tell us, tell us, May Margaret,
 And dinna to us len,
O wha is aught yon noble hawk,
 That stands your kitchen in ? '

12 'The hawk is mine, and it may be thine,
 To hawk whan ye hawk in hie ;
. . . . .

. . . . .

13 'But awa, awa, my bald brethren,
 Awa, and mak nae din ;
For I 'm ane o the sickest ladies this nicht
 That eer lay a bower within.'

14 'O tell us, tell us, May Margaret,
 And dinna to us len,
O wha is that, May Margaret,
 You and the wa between ? '

15 'O it is my bower-maiden,' she says,
 ' As sick as sick can be ;
O it is my bower-maiden,' she says,
 ' And she 's thrice as sick as me.'

16 'We hae been east, and we 've been west,
 And low beneath the moon ;
But a' the bower-women eer we saw
 Hadna goud buckles in their shoon.'

17 Then up and spak her eldest brither,
 Ay in ill time spak he :
' It is Clerk Saunders, your true-love,
 And never mat I the
But for this scorn that he has done
 This moment he sall die.'

18 But up and spak her youngest brother,
 Ay in good time spak he :
' O but they are a gudelie pair !
 True lovers an ye be,
The sword that hangs at my sword-belt
 Sall never sinder ye.'

19 Syne up and spak her nexten brother,
 And the tear stood in his ee :
'You 've loed her lang, and loed her weel,
 And pity it wad be
The sword that hangs at my sword-belt
 Shoud ever sinder ye.'

20 But up and spak her fifthen brother :
  ' Sleep on your sleep for me ;
  But we baith sall never sleep again,
  For the tane o us sall die.'

21 And up and spak her thirden brother,
  Ay in ill time spak he :
  ' Curse on his love and comeliness !
  Dishonourd as ye be,
  The sword that hangs at my sword-belt
  Sall quickly sinder ye.'

22 The eldest brother has drawn his sword,
  The second has drawn anither,
  Between Clerk Saunders' hause and collar-
    bane
  The cald iron met thegither.

23 ' O wae be to you, my fause brethren,
  And an ill death mat ye die !
  Ye mith slain Clerk Saunders in open field,
  And no in bed wi me.'

G

Buchan's Ballads of the North of Scotland, I, 160.

1 CLERK SANDY and a lady gay
  Where walking in the garden green,
  And great and heavy was the love
  That hae befa'en these twa between.

2 ' A bed, a bed,' said Clerk Sandy,
  ' A bed, my love, for you and me ; '
  ' O never a foot,' said the lady gay,
  ' Till ance that we twa married be.

3 ' My seven brithers will come in,
  And a' their torches burning bright ;
  They 'll say, We hae but ae sister,
  And here she 's lying wi a knight.'

4 ' Ye 'll take my brand I bear in hand,
  And wi the same ye 'll lift the gin ;
  Then ye may swear, and save your oath,
  That ye neer let Clerk Sandy in.

5 ' Ye 'll take that kurchie on your head,
  And wi the same tie up your een ;
  And ye will swear, and save your oath,
  Ye saw not Sandy sin yestreen.

6 ' Ye 'll lift me in your arms twa,
  And carry me unto your bed ;
  Then ye may swear, and save your oath,
  Clerk Sandy in your bower neer tread.'

7 She 's taen the brand he bare in hand,
  And wi the same lifted the gin ;
  It was to swear, and save her oath,
  She never loot Clerk Sandy in.

8 She 's taen the kurchie frae her head,
  And wi the same tied up her een ;
  It was to swear, and save her oath,
  She saw not Sandy sin yestreen.

9 She 's taen him in her arms twa,
  And she 's carried him to her bed ;
  It was to swear, and save her oath,
  Clerk Sandie in her bower neer tread.

10 They hadna kissd, nor love clapped,
  Like other lovers when they meet,
  Till in a quarter's space and less
  These two lovers fell sound asleep.

11 Then in it came her seven brothers,
  And a' their torches burning bright ;
  They said, We hae but ae sister,
  And here she 's lying wi a knight.

12 O out it speaks the first o them,
  ' We will awa and lat them be ; '
  Then out it speaks the second o them,
  ' His father has nae mair but he.'

13 Out it speaks the third o them,
  For he was standing on the birk :
  ' Nae sweeter coud twa lovers lye,
  Tho they 'd been married in a kirk.'

14 Then out it speaks the fourth o them,
  Mair fair and lovely is his buke :
  ' Our sister dear we cannot blame,
  Altho in him she pleasure took.'

15 Then out it speaks the fifth o them,
  ' It were a sin to do them ill ; '
  Then out it spake the sixth o them,
  ' It 's hard a sleeping man to kill.'

16 But out it speaks the seventh o them,
  I wish an ill death mat he dee !
  ' I wear the sharp brand by my side
  That soon shall gar Clerk Sandy die.'

17 Then he's taen out his trusty brand,
　　And he has stroakd it ower a strae;
　　And thro and thro Clerk Sandy's middle
　　I wat he's gart it come and gae.

18 The lady slept by her love's side
　　Until the dawning o the day,
　　But what was dune she naething knew,
　　For when she wak'd these words did say:

19 'Awake, awake, now Clerk Sandy,
　　Awake, and turn you unto me;
　　Ye're nae sae keen's ye were at night,
　　When you and I met on the lee.'

20 O then she calld her chamber-maid
　　To bring her coal and candle seen:
　　'I fear Clerk Sandy's dead eneuch,
　　I had a living man yestreen.'

21 They hae lifted his body up,
　　They hae searched it round and round,
　　And even anent his bonny heart
　　Discovered the deadly wound.

22 She wrung her hands, and tore her hair,
　　And wrung her hands most bitterlie:
　　'This is my fause brothers, I fear,
　　This night hae used this crueltie.

23 'But I will do for my love's sake
　　Woud nae be done by ladies rare;
　　For seven years shall hae an end
　　Or eer a kame gang in my hair.

24 'O I will do for my love's sake
　　What other ladies woud think lack;
　　For seven years shall hae an end
　　Or eer I wear but dowie black.

25 'And I will do for my love's sake
　　What other ladies woudna thole;
　　Seven years shall hae an end
　　Or eer a shoe gang on my sole.'

26 In it came her father dear,
　　And he was belted in a brand;
　　Sae softly as he trad the floor,
　　And in her bower did stately stand.

27 Says, Hold your tongue, my daughter dear,
　　And ye 'll lat a' your mourning be;
　　I 'll wed you to a higher match
　　Or eer his father's son coud be.

28 'Wed well, wed well your seven sons;
　　I wish ill wedded they may be,
　　Sin they hae killd him Clerk Sandy!
　　For wedded shall I never be.'

29 His corpse was laid in the cauld clay,
　　The bells went tinkling thro the town;
　　'Alas! alas!' said the lady gay,
　　'That eer I heard that waefu soun!'

30 When she had sitten intill her bower
　　A twalmonth lang and weary day,
　　Even below her bower-window
　　She heard a ghaist to knock an cry.

31 She says, Ye're thief or bauld robber,
　　Or biggin come to burn or brake;
　　Or are you ony masterfu man,
　　That is come seeking ony make?

32 'I am not thief nor bauld robber,
　　Nor bigging come to burn nor brake;
　　Nor am I ony masterfu man,
　　That is come seeking ony make;
　　But I'm Clerk Sandy, your first love,
　　And wants wi you again to speak.

33 'Gin ye're Clerk Sandy, my first love,
　　And wants wi me to speak again,
　　Tell me some o' the love tokens
　　That you and I had last between.'

34 'O mind not ye, ye gay lady,
　　Sin last I was in bower wi thee,
　　That in it came your seven brethren,
　　The youngest gart me sairly dree?'
　　Then sighd and said the gay lady,
　　'Sae true a tale as ye tell me.'

35 Sae painfully she clam the wa,
　　She clam the wa up after him;
　　'T was not for want of stockings nor sheen,
　　But hadna time to put them on;
　　And in the midst o gude greenwood,
　　'T was there she lost the sight o him.

36 The lady sat, and mourning there,
　　Until she coudna weep nae mair;
　　At length the cloks and wanton flies
　　They biggit in her yellow hair.

37 'O had your peace, my dearest dear,
　　For I am come to mak you wise;
　　Or this night nine nights come and gang,
　　We baith shall be in Paradise.'

A b, B b, Herd II, *seem to be revisions, and to possess no authority.*

A. a. 3¹. For an.

4². gin *has been altered to* pin, *according to a marginal suggestion, and* pin *stands at* 7² *in my copy.*

6¹. taw. (?)

14⁴. *Perhaps we should read* brand 'll.

15². throi. (?) 18³. and awa. 23³. his. (?)

After 18⁴ *is written, but struck out:*

O Sandie, ye are the sleepiest man
That ever I saw wi mine eeen.

And above the first verse of 19, *also struck out:*

Ye hae spoyled my sheets wi sweat, she said.

14³, ⁴ *stand thus in the second copy:*

I 'se bear the brand into my hand
Shall quickly gar Clark Sanders die.

20 *is wanting.*

Stanzas 27–41 *are transferred to* 'Sweet William's Ghost.'

B. a *is written in long lines, two to a stanza.*

D. 2⁴. my bower-room ye.

E. 12. "Recited as here written, but it was not thought to be right."

15². And if. 17³. shall I come.

F. *After* 20 *Jamieson introduced these two stanzas of his own,* "the idea of the rose being suggested by the gentleman who recited, but who could not recollect the language in which it was expressed:"

But up and spak her midmaist brother,
And an angry laugh leugh he:
'The thorn that dabs, I 'll cut it down,
Though fair the rose may be.

'The flower that smelld sae sweet yestreen
Has lost its bloom wi thee;
And though I 'm wae it should be sae,
Clerk Saunders, ye maun die.'

After 23 *follow ten stanzas, which are transferred to* 'Sweet William's Ghost.'

G. 32⁶. you to speak again.

70

WILLIE AND LADY MAISRY

A. 'Willie, the Widow's Son,' Motherwell's MS., p. 498; 'Sweet Willie and Lady Margerie,' Motherwell's Minstrelsy, p. 370.

B. 'Willie and Lady Maisry,' Buchan's Ballads of the North of Scotland, I. 155.

'WILLIE AND LADY MAISRY' has much in common with 'Clerk Saunders.' The chief point of difference is that of Willie's killing Maisry's brother and the guard, B 22–24.

Here the ballad has probably been affected by another, now represented in English only by a very corrupt version, 'The Bent sae Brown,' which immediately follows.

A

Motherwell's MS., p. 498; Motherwell's Minstrelsy, p. 370. From the recitation of Mrs Notman, then far advanced in years, with whose grandmother it was a favorite: September 9, 1826.

1 WILLIE was a widow's son,
And he wore a milk-white weed, O
And weel could Willie read and write,
Far better ride on steed. O

2 Lady Margerie was the first lady
   That drank to him the wine,
And aye as the healths gade round and round,
   'Laddy, your love is mine.'

3 Lady Margerie was the first ladye
   That drank to him the beer,
And aye as the healths gade round and round,
   'Laddy, you 're welcome here.'

4 'You must come into my bower
   When the evening bells do ring,
And you must come into my bower
   When the evening mass doth sing.'

5 He 's taen four and twenty braid arrows,
   And laced them in a whang,
And he 's awa to Lady Margerie's bower,
   As fast as he can gang.

6 He set ae foot on the wall,
   And the other on a stane,
And he 's killed a' the king's life-guards,
   And he 's killed them every man.

7 'Oh open, open, Lady Margerie,
   Open and let me in;
The weet weets a' my yellow hair,
   And the dew draps on my chin.'

8 With her feet as white as sleet
   She strode her bower within,
And with her fingers long and small
   She 's looten Sweet Willie in.

9 She 's louten down unto her foot
   To loose Sweet Willie's shoon;
The buckles were sa stiff they wudna lowse,
   The blood had frozen in.

10 'O Willie, Willie, I fear that thou
   Has bred me dule and sorrow;
The deed that thou has dune this nicht
   Will kythe upon the morrow.'

11 In then came her father dear,
   And a broad sword by his gare,
And he 's gien Willie, the widow's son,
   A deep wound and a sair.

12 'Lye yont, lye yont, Willie,' she says,
   'Your sweat weets a' my side;
Lye yont, lie yont, Willie,' she says,
   'For your sweat I downa bide.'

13 She turned her back unto the wa,
   Her face unto the room,
And there she saw her auld father,
   Walking up and down.

14 'Woe be to you, father,' she said,
   'And an ill deed may you die!
For ye 've killd Willie, the widow's son
   And he would have married me.'

15 She turned her back unto the room,
   Her face unto the wa,
And with a deep and heavy sich
   Her heart it brak in twa.

———•———

B

Buchan's Ballads of the North of Scotland, I, 155.

1 SWEET WILLIE was a widow's son,
   And milk-white was his weed;
It sets him weel to bridle a horse,
   And better to saddle a steed, my dear,
   And better to saddle a steed.

2 But he is on to Maisry's bower-door,
   And tirled at the pin:
'Ye sleep ye, wake ye, Lady Maisry,
   Ye 'll open, let me come in.'

3 'O who is this at my bower-door,
   Sae well that knows my name?'

'It is your ain true-love, Willie,
   If ye love me, lat me in.'

4 Then huly, huly raise she up,
   For fear o making din,
Then in her arms lang and bent,
   She caught sweet Willie in.

5 She leand her low down to her toe,
   To loose her true-love's sheen,
But cauld, cauld were the draps o bleed
   Fell fae his trusty brand.

6 'What frightfu sight is that, my love?
   A frightfu sight to see!

What bluid is this on your sharp brand?
  O may ye not tell me?'

7 'As I came thro the woods this night,
  The wolf maist worried me;
O shoud I slain the wolf, Maisry?
  Or shoud the wolf slain me?'

8 They hadna kissd, nor love clapped,
  As lovers when they meet,
Till up it starts her auld father,
  Out o his drowsy sleep.

9 'O what's become o my house-cock,
  Sae crouse at ane did craw?
I wonder as much at my bold watch,
  That's nae shooting ower the wa.

10 'My gude house-cock, my only son,
  Heir ower my land sae free,
If ony ruffian hae him slain,
  High hanged shall he be.'

11 Then he's on to Maisry's bower-door,
  And tirled at the pin:
'Ye sleep ye, wake ye, daughter Maisry,
  Ye'll open, lat me come in.'

12 Between the curtains and the wa
  She rowd her true-love then,
And huly went she to the door,
  And let her father in.

13 'What's become o your maries, Maisry,
  Your bower it looks sae teem?
What's become o your green claithing,
  Your beds they are sae thin?'

14 'Gude forgie you, father,' she said,
  'I wish ye be't for sin;
Sae aft as ye hae dreaded me,
  But never found me wrang.'

15 He turnd him right and round about,
  As he'd been gaun awa;
But sae nimbly as he slippet in
  Behind a screen sae sma.

16 Maisry, thinking a' dangers past,
  She to her love did say,
'Come, love, and take your silent rest;
  My auld father's away.'

17 Then baith lockd in each other's arms,
  They fell full fast asleep,
When up it starts her auld father,
  And stood at their bed-feet.

18 'I think I hae the villain now
  That my dear son did slay;
But I shall be revengd on him
  Before I see the day.'

19 Then he's drawn out a trusty brand,
  And stroakd it oer a stray,
And thro and thro Sweet Willie's middle
  He's gart cauld iron gae.

20 Then up it wakend Lady Maisry,
  Out o her drowsy sleep,
And when she saw her true-love slain,
  She straight began to weep.

21 'O gude forgie you now, father,' she said,
  'I wish ye be't for sin;
For I never lovd a love but ane,
  In my arms ye've him slain.'

22 'This night he's slain my gude bold watch,
  Thirty stout men and twa;
Likewise he's slain your ae brother,
  To me was worth them a'.

23 'If he has slain my ae brither,
  Himsell had a' the blame,
For mony a day he plots contriv'd,
  To hae Sweet Willie slain.

24 'And tho he's slain your gude bold watch,
  He might hae been forgien;
They came on him in armour bright,
  When he was but alane.'

25 Nae meen was made for this young knight,
  In bower where he lay slain,
But a' was for sweet Maisry bright,
  In fields where she ran brain.

2⁴, 3⁴. Lady *in MS.*, Laddy *in Minstrelsy.*
9¹. his foot *in Minstrelsy:* cf. B 5¹.
10⁸. hast *in both.*

Several slight changes are made by Motherwell in printing.

71

THE BENT SAE BROWN

Buchan's Ballads of the North of Scotland, I, 30.

———◆———

'THE BENT SAE BROWN' combines the story of 'Clerk Saunders' with that of another ballad, not found in an independent form in English, but sufficiently common in Danish and Swedish; whence the non-tragical conclusion, for the killing of a certain number of brothers is not regarded as a very serious matter by the heroine, whether in English or Norse. The introduction and conclusion, and some incidental decorations, of the Scottish ballad will not be found in the Norse, but are an outcome of the invention and the piecing and shaping of that humble but enterprising rhapsodist who has left his trail over so large a part of Buchan's volumes.*

Stanzas 21–34 contain the substance of the Norse ballad referred to, which has been printed in the following versions, and exists in others not yet given to the world, Danish, Norwegian, and Icelandic.

Swedish. A. 'Unger Sven,' Arwidsson, I, 295, No 43. B. 'Ung Hillerström,' Afzelius, II, 180, No 55.

Danish. A. An unpublished version, found in two manuscripts of the 17th century, communicated to me by Grundtvig. B. 'Jomfruen i Skoven,' "Tragica, No 15," Danske Viser, III, 99, No 123.† C. 'Kjærligheds Styrke,' Kristensen, I, 109, No 43. D, E, F. 'Jomfruens Brødre,' Kristensen, II, 276, No 80 A, B, C. G. Madsen, Folkeminder fra Hanved Sogn, p. 88, No 5.

A youth has passed the night with his love, either in her bower or in a wood. When they are about to part in the morning, she begs him to be on his guard against her seven brothers, on his way through the wood and over the heath. He makes light of the danger, and in the wood meets the seven brothers. They demand how he comes to be there, and he feigns to have been out with his hawk and hound, to have been coursing hares. No, they say, you were with our sister last night, and asked no read of us. He makes no denial; but her will was as good as his. They ask whether he will fly or fight. He has no thought of flight, kills all seven, and goes back to his love. She will not forsake him for killing her brothers; nor would she, Danish A, C, F, had he killed her father too.‡

---

* Several of Buchan's ballads, says Sir Walter Scott, Minstrelsy, I, 87, ed. 1833, " are translated from the Norse, and Mr Buchan is probably unacquainted with the originals." Scott seems to have meant only that the ballads in question had a Norse origin, not that they were deliberately translated within what we may call historical times. In this particular instance the resemblances with the Norse are remarkably close, but the very homeliness of the Scottish ballad precludes any suspicion beyond tampering with tradition. The silliness and fulsome vulgarity of Buchan's versions often enough make one wince or sicken, and many of them came through bad mouths or hands: we have even positive proof in one instance of imposture, though not of Buchan's being a conscious party to the imposture. But such correspondences with foreign ballads as we witness in the present case are evidence of a genuine traditional foundation.

Stanzas 25, 26 are remarkably like F 3, 5 of 'Earl Brand,' the Percy copy, and may have served in some Scottish version of the 'Douglas Tragedy.'

Stanzas 36–41 are borrowed from the 'Knight and Shepherd's Daughter.' Folly could not go further than in making the mother clip her locks and kilt her clothes, as in 36 : unless it be in making a boat of a coat and a topmast of a cane, as in 3, 4.

† Translated by Prior, III, 234.

‡ In Danish B the maid has grace enough to weep for her brothers seven : " and almost more for the knight." But this last line is probably taken up from another ballad. In 'Herr Helmer,' a ballad which has some of the traits of 'Ribold,' Afzelius, No 54, II, 178, 226, Arwidsson, No 21, I, 155, Eva Wigström, Folkdiktning, I, 25, and the same, Skånska Visor, p.1, Helmer kills six of his love's seven brothers, and is treacherously slain by the seventh, whom he has spared. The seventh brother cuts off Helmer's head and takes it to his sister. A Danish version of 'Herr Helmer,' Danske Viser, No 209, IV, 251, ends differently : the seventh brother offers his sister to Helmer as ransom for his life.

1 ' THERE are sixteen lang miles, I 'm sure,
    Between my love and me ;
  There are eight o them in gude dry land,
    And other eight by sea.

2 ' Betide me life, betide me death,
    My love I 'll gang and see ;
  Altho her friends they do me hate,
    Her love is great for me.

3 ' Of my coat I 'll make a boat,
    And o my sark a sail,
  And o my cane a gude tapmast,
    Dry land till I come till.'

4 Then o his coat he 's made a boat,
    And o his sark a sail ;
  And o his cane a gude tapmast,
    Dry land till he came till.

5 He is on to Annie's bower-door,
    And tirled at the pin :
  ' O sleep ye, wake ye, my love, Annie,
    Ye 'll rise, lat me come in.'

6 ' O who is this at my bower-door,
    Sae well that kens my name ? '
  ' It is your true-love, Sweet Willie,
    For you I 've crossd the faem.'

7 ' I am deeply sworn, Willie,
    By father and by mother ;
  At kirk or market where we meet,
    We darna own each other.

8 ' And I am deeply sworn, Willie,
    By my bauld brothers three ;
  At kirk or market where we meet.
    I darna speak to thee.'

9 ' Ye take your red fan in your hand,
    Your white fan ower your een,
  And ye may swear, and save your oath,
    Ye sawna me come in.

10 ' Ye take me in your arms twa,
    And carry me to your bed ;
  And ye may swear, and save your oath,
    Your bower I never tread.'

11 She 's taen her red fan in her hand,
    The white fan ower her een ;
  It was to swear, and save her oath,
    She sawna him come in.

12 She 's taen him in her arms twa,
    And carried him to her bed ;
  It was to swear, and save her oath,
    Her bower he never tread.

13 They hadna kissd, nor love clapped,
    As lovers do when they meet,
  Till up it waukens her mother,
    Out o her drowsy sleep.

14 ' Win up, win up, my three bauld sons,
    Win up and make ye boun ;
  Your sister's lover 's in her bower,
    And he 's but new come in.'

15 Then up it raise her three bauld sons,
    And girt to them their brand,
  And they are to their sister's bower,
    As fast as they coud gang.

16 When they came to their sister's bower,
    They sought it up and down ;
  But there was neither man nor boy
    In her bower to be foun.

17 Then out it speaks the first o them :
    ' We 'll gang and lat her be ;
  For there is neither man nor boy
    Intill her companie.'

18 Then out it speaks the second son :
    ' Our travel 's a' in vain ;
  But mother dear, nor father dear,
    Shall break our rest again.'

19 Then out it speaks the third o them,
    An ill death mat he die !
  ' We 'll lurk amang the bent sae brown,
    That Willie we may see.'

20 He stood behind his love's curtains,
    His goud rings showd him light ;
  And by this ye may a' weell guess
    He was a renowned knight.

21 He 's done him to his love's stable,
    Took out his berry-brown steed ;
  His love stood in her bower-door,
    Her heart was like to bleed.

22 ' O mourn ye for my coming, love ?
    Or for my short staying ?
  Or mourn ye for our safe sindring,
    Case we never meet again ? '

23 'I mourn nae for your here coming,
       Nor for your staying lang;
   Nor mourn I for our safe sindring,
       I hope we 'll meet again.

24 'I wish ye may won safe away,
       And safely frae the town;
   For ken you not my brothers three
       Are mang the bent sae brown?'

25 'If I were on my berry-brown steed,
       And three miles frae the town,
   I woudna fear your three bauld brothers,
       Amang the bent sae brown.'

26 He leint him ower his saddle-bow,
       And kissd her lips sae sweet;
   The tears that fell between these twa,
       They wat his great steed's feet.

27 But he wasna on his berry-brown steed,
       Nor twa miles frae the town,
   Till up it starts these three fierce men,
       Amang the bent sae brown.

28 Then up they came like three fierce men,
       Wi mony shout and cry:
   'Bide still, bide still, ye cowardly youth,
       What makes your haste away?

29 'For I must know before you go,
       Tell me, and make nae lie;
   If ye 've been in my sister's bower,
       My hands shall gar ye die.'

30 'Tho I 've been in your sister's bower,
       I have nae fear o thee;
   I 'll stand my ground, and fiercely fight,
       Aud shall gain victorie.'

31 'Now I entreat you for to stay,
       Unto us gie a wad;
   If ye our words do not obey,
       I 'se gar your body bleed.'

32 'I have nae wad, says Sweet Willie,
       Unless it be my brand,
   And that shall guard my fair body,
       Till I win frae your hand.'

33 Then two o them stept in behind,
       All in a furious meed;
   The third o them came him before,
       And seizd his berry-brown steed.

34 O then he drew his trusty brand,
       That hang down by his gare,
   And he has slain these three fierce men,
       And left them sprawling there.

35 Then word has gane to her mother,
       In bed where she slept soun,
   That Willie had killd her three bauld sons,
       Amang the bent sae brown.

36 Then she has cut the locks that hung
       Sae low down by her ee,
   Sae has she kiltit her green claithing
       A little aboon her knee.

37 And she has on to the king's court,
       As fast as gang coud she;
   When Fair Annie got word o that,
       Was there as soon as she.

38 Her mother, when before the king,
       Fell low down on her knee;
   'Win up, win up, my dame,' he said,
       'What is your will wi me?'

39 'My wills they are not sma, my liege,
       The truth I 'll tell to thee;
   There is ane o your courtly knights
       Last night hae robbed me.'

40 'And has he broke your bigly bowers?
       Or has he stole your fee?
   There is nae knight into my court
       Last night has been frae me;

41 'Unless 't was Willie o Lauderdale,
       Forbid that it be he!'
   'And by my sooth,' says the auld woman,
       'That very man is he.

42 'For he has broke my bigly bowers,
       And he has stole my fee,
   And made my daughter Ann a whore,
       And an ill woman is she.

43 'That was not all he did to me,
       Ere he went frae the town;
   My sons sae true he fiercely slew,
       Amang the bent sae brown.'

44 Then out it spake her daughter Ann,
       She stood by the king's knee:
   'Ye lie, ye lie, my mother dear,
       Sae loud 's I hear you lie.

45 'He has not broke your bigly bowers,
     Nor has he stole your fee,
   Nor made your daughter Ann a whore;
     A good woman I 'll be.

46 'Altho he slew your three bauld sons,
     He weel might be forgien;
   They were well clad in armour bright,
     Whan my love was him lane.'

47 'Well spoke, well spoke,' the king replied,
     'This tauking pleases me;
   For ae kiss o your lovely mouth,
     I 'll set your true-love free.'

48 She 's taen the king in her arms,
     And kissd him cheek and chin;
   He then set her behind her love,
     And they went singing hame.

72

THE CLERK'S TWA SONS O OWSENFORD

A. 'The Clerk's Twa Sons o Owsenford,' Kinloch MSS, V, 403.

B. 'The Clerks o Owsenfoord,' Dr Joseph Robertson's Note-Book, "Adversaria," p. 67.

C. 'The Clerks of Oxenford,' Buchan's Ballads of the North of Scotland, I, 281.

D. 'The Clerks Two Sons of Oxenfoord,' Motherwell's MS., p. 433.

A, AS sung, had a sequel of six stanzas, which is found separately and seems to belong with another ballad, 'The Wife of Usher's Well.' Robert Chambers combined A with Buchan's version, C, and the six concluding stanzas with 'The Wife of Usher's Well,' and divided his ballad into two parts, "on account of the great superiority of what follows over what goes before, and because the latter portion is in a great measure independent of the other:" The Scottish Ballads, pp 345–50. His second reason for a division is better than his first. It is quite according to precedent for a ballad to end with a vow like that in A 17, D 14: see 'Clerk Saunders.'

D has some amusing dashes of prose, evidently of masculine origin: "They thought their father's service mean, their mother's no great affair," 2; "When he was certain of the fact, an angry man was he," 6; "That I may ride to fair Berwick, and see what can be done," 8. We have here a strong contrast with both the blind-beggar and the housemaid style of corruption; something suggesting the attorney's clerk rather than the clerk of Owsenford, but at least not mawkish.

There are ballads both in Northern and in Southern Europe which have a certain amount of likeness with 'The Clerk's Twa Sons,' but if the story of all derives from one original, time has introduced great and even unusual variations.

In the Scottish ballad two youths go to Paris to study, and have an amour with the mayor's daughters, for which they are thrown into prison and condemned to be hanged. The Clerk, their father, comes to the prison, asks them what is their offence, and learns that it is a little dear bought love. He offers the mayor a ransom for their lives, and is sternly refused. The mayor's two daughters beg for their true-love's lives with the same bad success. The students are hanged, and the father goes home to tell his wife that they are put to a higher school. She, A [he, D], vows to pass the rest of her days in penance and grief.

A very well known German ballad, found

also in the Low Countries and in Scandinavia, has the following story.* A youth is lying in a dungeon, condemned to be hanged. His father comes to the town, and they exchange words about the severity of his prison. The father then goes to the lord of the place and offers three hundred florins as a ransom. Ransom is refused: the boy has a gold chain on his neck which will be his death. The father says that the chain was not stolen, but the gift of a young lady, who reared the boy as a page, or what not. There is no dear bought love in the case. The father, standing by the gallows, threatens revenge, but his son deprecates that: he cares not so much for his life as for his mother's grief. Within a bare half year, more than three hundred men pay with their lives for the death of the boy.†

A Spanish and Italian ballad has resemblances with the Scottish and the German, and may possibly be a common link: 'Los tres estudiantes,' Milá, Romancerillo, p. 165, No 208, A-L, previously, in Observaciones, etc., p. 104, No 6, 'Los estudiantes de Tolosa;' 'Los estudians de Tortosa,' Briz y Candi, I, 101; 'Gli scolari di Tolosa,' Nigra, Rivista Contemporanea, XX, 62. Three students

meet three girls, and attempt some little jests with them: ask them for a kiss, Milá, H; throw small pebbles at them, Milá, D; meet one girl on a bridge and kiss her, Nigra. For this the girls have them arrested by an accommodating catchpoll, and they are hanged by a peremptory judge. The youngest student weeps all the time; the eldest tries to console him; their brother serves a king or duke, and if he hears of what has been done will kill judge, constable, and all their scribes. The brother gets word somehow, and comes with all speed, but the three clerks are hanged before he arrives. He gives the town of Tolosa to the flames, the streets run with the blood of the judge, and horses swim in the blood of the girls, Milá, C, Briz; the streets are washed with the blood of women, walls built of the heads of men, Milá, A; etc.

In a pretty passage in Buchan's not altogether trustworthy version, C 35–38, the clerks ask back their faith and troth before they die. For this ceremony see 'Sweet William's Ghost.'

Aytoun's ballad is translated by Knortz Schottische Balladen, p. 72, No 23.

A

Kinloch MSS, V, 403, in the handwriting of James Chambers, as sung to his maternal grandmother, Janet Grieve, seventy years before, by an old woman, a Miss Ann Gray, of Neidpath Castle, Peeblesshire; January 1, 1829.

1 O I will sing to you a sang,
     But oh my heart is sair!
   The clerk's twa sons in Owsenford
     Has to learn some unco lair.

* 'Das Schloss in Oesterreich,' 'Der unschuldige Tod des jungen Knaben.' One stanza in Forsters Frische Liedlein, 1540, II, No 77 (Böhme); broadside of 1606, Erk's Liederhort, p. 15, No 6ᵃ; broadside of 1647, Eschenburg, in Deutsches Museum, 1776, p. 399, and Denkmäler Altdeutscher Dichtkunst, 1799, p. 446, = Uhland, p. 300, No 125; late broadside, Wunderhorn, 1806, I, 220. From oral tradition: Gräter's Bragur, VI, I, 205; Erk, Neue Sammlung, I, 20, No 16; Erk's Liederhort, p. 12, No 6; Hoffmann u. Richter, p. 17, No 8; Fiedler, p. 172, No 12; Jeitteles, in Archiv für Litteraturgeschichte, IX, 362, No 5; Schlossar, Deutsche Volkslieder aus Steiermark, p. 346, No 314; Wittstock, Sagen u. Lieder aus dem Nösner Gelande, p. 44, No 15; Frommann, Deutsche Mundarten, V, 391; Meinert, p. 53. (The last is an independent version; the rest have all one type.) Low-German, Niederdeutsche Volkslieder, he-

rausgegeben vom Vereine für niederdeutsche Sprachforschung, p. 56, No 84. Dutch, Hoffmann, Niederländische Volkslieder, p. 84, No 25. Norse: Afzelius, II, 62, No 40, from a seventeenth century broadside; Atterbom's Poetisk Kalender, 1816, p. 32; Wigström, Folkdiktning, I, 64, No 30; Aminson, Bidrag, etc., IV, 4, No 26, A, B, fragments; Nyerup, Udvalg af Danske Viser, I, 57, No 14; Lindeman, Norske Fjeldmelodier, Tekst Bilag, I, 3 f, No 10. There is a Swedish broadside of 1642, a Danish of 1697.

† Meinert's ballad, which, though it sometimes betrays artifice, has a fresher tone than the others, makes the chain the young lady's love-token: but this love is no count in the indictment. Uhland, IV, 145, cites from a manuscript chronicle a story of a highwayman, a widow's son, thrice imprisoned and twice ransomed; to no purpose, as far as I can see.

2 They hadna been in fair Parish
   A twelvemonth an a day,
 Till the clerk's twa sons o Owsenford
   Wi the mayor's twa daughters lay.

3 O word 's gaen to the mighty mayor,
   As he saild on the sea,
 That the clerk's twa sons o Owsenford
   Wi his twa daughters lay.

4 'If they hae lain wi my twa daughters,
   Meg an Marjorie,
 The morn, or I taste meat or drink,
   They shall be hangit hie.'

5 O word 's gaen to the clerk himself,
   As he sat drinkin wine,
 That his twa sons in fair Parish
   Were bound in prison strong.

6 Then up and spak the clerk's ladye,
   And she spak powrfully :
 'O tak with ye a purse of gold,
   Or take with ye three,
 And if ye canna get William,
   Bring Andrew hame to me.'

       *   *   *   *   *

7 'O lye ye here for owsen, dear sons,
   Or lie ye here for kye?
 Or what is it that ye lie for,
   Sae sair bound as ye lie?'

8 'We lie not here for owsen, dear father,
   Nor yet lie here for kye,
 But it 's for a little o dear bought love
   Sae sair bound as we lie.'

9 O he 's gane to the mighty mayor,
   And he spoke powerfully :
 'Will ye grant me my twa sons' lives,
   Either for gold or fee ?
 Or will ye be sae gude a man
   As grant them baith to me ? '

10 'I 'll no grant ye yere twa sons' lives,
    Neither for gold or fee,
  Nor will I be sae gude a man
    As gie them back to thee ;
  Before the morn at twelve o'clock
    Ye 'll see them hangit hie.'

11 Up an spak his twa daughters,
    An they spak powrfully :
  'Will ye grant us our twa loves' lives,
    Either for gold or fee ?
  Or will ye be sae gude a man
    As grant them baith to me.'

12 'I 'll no grant ye yere twa loves' lives,
    Neither for gold or fee,
  Nor will I be sae gude a man
    As grant their lives to thee ;
  Before the morn at twelve o'clock
    Ye 'll see them hangit hie.'

13 O he 's taen out these proper youths,
    And hangd them on a tree,
  And he 's bidden the clerk o Owsenford
    Gang hame to his ladie.

14 His lady sits on yon castle-wa,
    Beholding dale an doun,
  An there she saw her ain gude lord
    Come walkin to the toun.

15 'Ye 're welcome, welcome, my ain gude lord,
    Ye 're welcome hame to me ;
  But where away are my twa sons ?
    Ye should hae brought them wi ye.'

16 'It 's I 've putten them to a deeper lair,
    An to a higher schule ;
  Yere ain twa sons ill no be here
    Till the hallow days o Yule.'

17 'O sorrow, sorrow come mak my bed,
    An dool come lay me doon !
  For I 'll neither eat nor drink,
    Nor set a fit on ground.'

— • —

                B

Noted down from a female servant by Dr Joseph Robertson, July 15, 1829 ; "Adversaria," p. 67.

       *   *   *   *   *

1 'DE weel, de weel, my twa young sons,
   An learn weel at the squeel ;
 Tak no up wi young women-kin,
   An learn to act the feel.'

2 But they had na been in Blomsbury
　　A twalmon and a day,
　Till the twa pretty clerks o Owsenfoord
　　Wi the mayr's dauchters did lay.

3 Word has gaen till the auld base mayr,
　　As he sat at his wine,
　That the twa pretty clerks o Owsenford
　　Wi his daughters had lien.

4 Then out bespak the auld base mayr,
　　An an angry man was he :
　'Tomorrow, before I eat meat or drink,
　　I 'll see them hanged hie.'

5 But word has gaen to Owsenfoord

　　.　　.　　.　　.　　.

　　Before the letter was read,
　　She let the tears doun fa.

　　*　　　*　　　*　　　*　　　*

6 'Your sons are weel, an verra weel,
　　An learnin at the squeel ;
　But I fear ye winna see your sons
　　At the holy days o Yeel.'

7 Their father he went to Bloomsbury,
　　He turnit him roun about,

An there he saw his twa braw sons,
　　In the prison, leukin out.

8 'O lie ye there for owsen, my sons,
　　Or lie ye there for kye ?
　Or lie ye there for dear fond love,
　　Si closs as ye de lie ? '

9 'We lie na here for owsen, father,
　　We lie na here for kye,
　But we lie here for dear fond love,
　　An we 're condemned to die.'

　　*　　　*　　　*　　　*　　　*

10 Then out bespak the clerks' fader,
　　An a sorry man was he :
　'Gae till your bowers, ye lillie-flowers,
　　For a' this winna dee.'

11 Then out bespak the aul base mayr,
　　An an angry man was he :
　'Gar to your bowers, ye vile base whores,
　　Ye 'll see them hanged hie.'

　　*　　　*　　　*　　　*　　　*

———◆———

C

Buchan's Ballads of the North of Scotland, I, 281.

1 I 'LL tell you a tale, or I 'll sing you a song,
　　Will grieve your heart full sair ;
　How the twa bonny clerks o Oxenford
　　Went aff to learn their lear.

2 Their father lovd them very weel,
　　Their mother muckle mair,
　And sent them on to Billsbury,
　　To learn deeper lear.

3 Then out it spake their mother dear :
　　' Do weel, my sons, do weel,
　And haunt not wi the young women,
　　Wi them to play the fiel.'

4 Their father sware them on their souls,
　　Their mother on their life,

Never to lie wi the auld mayor's daughters,
　　Nor kiss the young mayor's wife.

5 But they hadna been in Billsbury
　　A twallmonth and a day,
　Till the twa bonny clerks o Oxenford
　　With the mayor's twa daughters lay.

6 As these twa clerks they sat and wrote,
　　The ladies sewed and sang ;
　There was mair mirth in that chamber
　　Than all fair Ferrol's land.

7 But word 's gane to the wicked mayor,
　　As he sat at the wine,
　That the twa bonny clerks o Oxenford
　　With his twa daughters had lyne.

8 'O have they lain with my daughters dear,
　　Heirs out ower a' my land,

The morn, ere I eat or drink,
    I 'll hang them with my hand.'

9 Then he has taen the twa bonny clerks,
    Bound them frae tap to tae,
Till the reddest blood in their body
    Out ower their nails did gae.

10 ' Whare will I get a little wee boy,
    Will win gowd to his fee,
That will rin on to Oxenford,
    And that right speedilie ? '

11 Then up it starts a bonny boy,
    Gold yellow was his hair ;
I wish his father and mother joy,
    His true-love muckle mair.

12 Says, Here am I, a little wee boy,
    Will win gowd to my fee,
That will rin on to Oxenford,
    And that right speedilie.

13 ' Where ye find the grass green growing,
    Set down your heel and rin,
And where ye find the brigs broken,
    Ye 'll bend your bow and swim.

14 ' But when ye come to Oxenford,
    Bide neither to chap nor ca,
But set your bent bow to your breast,
    And lightly loup the wa.'

15 Where he found the grass green growing,
    He slackt his shoes and ran,
And where he found the brigs broken,
    He bent his bow and swam.

16 And when he came to Oxenford,
    Did neither chap nor ca,
But set his bent bow to his breast,
    And lightly leapt the wa.

17 ' What news, what news, my little wee boy ?
    What news hae ye to me ?
How are my sons in Billsbury,
    Since they went far frae me ? '

18 ' Your sons are well, and learning well,
    But at a higher school,
And ye 'll never see your sons again,
    On the holy days o Yule.'

19 ' Wi sorrow now gae make my bed,
    Wi care and caution lay me down ;
That man on earth shall neer be born
    Shall see me mair gang on the groun.

20 ' Take twenty pounds in your pocket,
    And ten and ten to tell them wi,
And gin ye getna hynde Henry,
    Bring ye gay Gilbert hame to me.'

21 Out it speaks old Oxenford,
    A sorry, sorry man, was he :
' Your strange wish does me surprise,
    They are baith there alike to me.

22 ' Wi sorrow now I 'll saddle my horse,
    And I will gar my bridle ring,
And I shall be at Billsbury
    Before the small birds sweetly sing.'

23 Then sweetly sang the nightingale,
    As she sat on the wand,
But sair, sair, mournd Oxenford,
    As he gaed in the strand.

24 When he came to Billsbury,
    He rade it round about,
And at a little shott-window
    His sons were looking out.

25 ' O lye ye there, my sons,' he said,
    ' For oxen, or for kye ?
Or is it for a little o deep dear love,
    Sae sair bound as ye lye ? '

26 ' We lye not here, father,' they said,
    ' For oxen, nor for kye ;
It 's all for a little o deep dear love,
    Sae sair bound as we lye.

27 ' O borrow 's, borrow 's, father,' they said,
    ' For the love we bear to thee ! '
' O never fear, my pretty sons,
    Well borrowed ye shall be.'

28 Then he 's gane to the wicked mayor,
    And hailed him courteouslie :
' Good day, good day, O Billsbury,
    God make you safe and free ! '
' Come sit you down, brave Oxenford,
    What are your wills with me ? '

29 'Will ye gie me my sons again,
     For gold or yet for fee?
   Will ye gie me my sons again,
     For 's sake that died on tree?'

30 'I winna gie you your sons again,
     For gold nor yet for fee;
   But if ye 'll stay a little while,
     Ye 'se see them hanged hie.'

31 Ben it came the mayor's daughters,
     Wi kirtle, coat alone;
   Their eyes did sparkle like the gold,
     As they tript on the stone.

32 'Will ye gie us our loves, father,
     For gold or yet for fee?
   Or will ye take our own sweet life,
     And let our true-loves be?'

33 He 's taen a whip into his hand,
     And lashd them wondrous sair:
   Gae to your bowers, ye vile rank whores,
     Ye 'se never see them mair.

34 Then out it speaks old Oxenford,
     A sorry man was he:
   'Gang to your bowers, ye lily-flowers,
     For a' this maunna be.'

35 Out it speaks him hynde Henry:
     'Come here, Janet, to me;

Will ye gie me my faith and troth,
  And love, as I gae thee?'

36 'Ye shall hae your faith and troth,
     Wi God's blessing and mine;'
   And twenty times she kissd his mouth,
     Her father looking on.

37 Then out it speaks him gay Gilbert:
     'Come here, Margaret, to me;
   Will ye gie me my faith and troth,
     And love, as I gae thee?'

38 'Yes, ye shall get your faith and troth,
     Wi God's blessing and mine;'
   And twenty times she kissd his mouth,
     Her father looking on.

39 'Ye 'll take aff your twa black hats,
     Lay them down on a stone,
   That nane may ken that ye are clerks
     Till ye are putten down.'

40 The bonny clerks they died that morn,
     Their loves died lang ere noon;
   Their father and mother for sorrow died,
     They all died very soon.

41 These six souls went up to heaven,
     I wish sae may we a'!
   The mighty mayor went down to hell,
     For wrong justice and law.

———•———

D

Motherwell's MS., p. 433, from James Nicol, Strichen.

1 OH I will tell a tale of woe,
     Which makes my heart richt sair;
   The Clerk's two sons of Oxenfoord
     Are too soon gone to lair.

2 They thought their father's service mean,
     Their mother's no great affair;
   But they would go to fair Berwick,
     To learn [some] unco lair.

3 They had not been in fair Berwick
     A twelve month and a day,
   Till the clerk's two sons of Oxenfoord
     With the mayor's two daughters lay.

4 This word came to the mighty mayor,
     As he hunted the rae,
   That the clerks two sons of Oxenfoord
     With his two daughters lay.

5 'If they have lain with my daughters,
     The heirs of all my land,
   I make a vow, and will keep it true,
     To hang them with my hand.'

6 When he was certain of the fact,
     An angry man was he,
   And he has taken these two brothers,
     And hanged them on the tree.

7 Word it has come to Oxenfoord's clerk,
     Ere it was many day,

That his two sons sometime ago
  With the mayor's two daughters lay.

8 'O saddle a horse to me,' he cried,
  'O do it quick and soon,
That I may ride to fair Berwick,
  And see what can be done.'

9 But when he came to fair Berwick
  A grieved man was he,
When that he saw his two bonnie sons
  Both hanging on the tree.

10 'O woe is me,' the clerk cried out,
  'This dismal sight to see,
All the whole comfort of my life
  Dead hanging on the tree!'

11 He turned his horse's head about,
  Making a piteous moan,
And all the way to Oxenfoord
  Did sad and grievously groan.

12 His wife did hastily cry out,
  'You only do I see;
What have you done with my two sons,
  You should have brought to me?'

13 'I put them to some higher lair,
  And to a deeper scule;
You will not see your bonnie sons
  Till the haly days of Yule.

14 'And I will spend my days in grief,
  Will never laugh nor sing;
There's never a man in Oxenfoord
  Shall hear my bridle ring.'

A. 3¹, 5¹, 6³, 7¹, 9¹. Oh.
  5³. in Owsenford. 14². day an doom.
B. *In the margin as a note (see* A 1) :

  I will sing a sang to you,
    But o my heart is sair !

The twa pretty clerks o Owsenfoord
  As they went to their lair.

7². twinit, MS. ?
8⁴. sic loss.
C. 28³. oh.

73

LORD THOMAS AND FAIR ANNET

A. 'Lord Thomas and Fair Annet,' Percy's Reliques, 1765, II, 293 ; III, 240, ed. 1767.

B. 'The Nut-Brown Bride,' Kinloch MSS, I, 1.

C. 'The Brown Bride and Lord Thomas,' Motherwell's MS., p. 157.

D. 'Lord Thomas and Fair Ellinor.' a. Pepys Ballads, III, 316, No 312. b, c, d, other broadside copies. e, f, g, h, i, recited copies.

E. 'Sweet Willie and Fair Annie,' Jamieson's Popular Ballads, I, 22.

F. 'Sweet Willie and Fair Annie,' Kinloch MSS, III, 127, V, 339.

G. Skene MSS, p. 104.

H. 'Fair Annie and Sweet Willie,' Gibb MS., p. 64.

THE copy of 'Lord Thomas and Fair Annet' in Herd, 1769, p. 246, 1776, I, 24, and in the Musical Museum, p. 553, No 535, is Percy's, A.

The English version of this ballad, 'Lord Thomas and Fair Ellinor,' given, with alterations, in Percy's Reliques, III, 82, 1765,* is a broadside of Charles the Second's time, printed for I. Clarke, W. Thackeray, and T. Passenger, and licensed by L'Estrange, who was censor from 1663 to 1685. This copy has become traditional in Scotland and Ireland. The Scottish traditional copy, 'Lord Thomas and Fair Annet,' given by Percy in the Reliques (unfortunately with some corrections, but these cannot have been many), is far superior, and one of the most beautiful of our ballads, and indeed of all ballads. 'Fair Margaret and Sweet William,' "a more pathetic story of the man who loves one woman and marries another," begins in the same way, with the last long talk before parting. The conclusion is that the forsaken maid dies of grief, not by the hand of her incensed rival, and it is most natural that the two stories should be blended in tradition, as they are here in E-H, E 31 ff, F 27 ff, G 24 ff, H 37 ff belonging to 'Fair Margaret and Sweet William.'

There is a copy of 'Lord Thomas and Fair Ellinor,' written over for the ballad-mongers, and of course much less in the popular style, in Pepys, IV, 48, No 45, and Roxburghe, II, 553, with the title 'The Unfortunate Forrester, or, Fair Eleanor's Tragedy.' In this Fair Ellinor stabs herself and Lord Thomas then kills himself with the same dagger.†

Norse ballads have the story of 'Lord Thomas and Fair Annet,' coming very close in details. Those forms which are nearest to the English resemble more the mixed versions, E-H, than the simple, A-D. But in none of the Norse ballads is love thwarted because it stands upon the choice of friends. A man abandons a woman who is in all but the name his wife, and who regards herself, and is evidently regarded by others, as standing in

no dishonorable relation to him. There is again a bifurcation in the catastrophe. The forsaken mistress submits and hangs herself in the one case, in the other she takes a fierce revenge. The latter conclusion may well, as Grundtvig holds, be the more original, but the ballads which have the other will here be put first, as being nearer to the English.

(1.) A. 'Herr Peder och Liten Kerstin,' Afzelius, I, 49, No 9, Grundtvig, IV, 219, Wigström, Folkdiktning, II, 5, broadsides of the eighteenth century and traditional copies derived therefrom. B. 'Herr Peders Slegfred,' broadside of the seventeenth century, Grundtvig, IV, 216, No 210; Danske Viser, III, 365, No 157; Kristensen, II, 177, No 52. C. A traditional fragment, Grundtvig, IV, 220, Bilag 2, from Cavallius and Stephens's collection. (2.) D. 'Liti Kerstis hevn,' Landstad, p. 559, No 67. E. Manuscript of the seventeenth century, Grundtvig, IV, 215. F. 'Liten Kerstins Hämd,' c. 1700, Arwidsson, I, 305, No 45.

Sir Peter and Liten Kerstin sit at table talking merrily, A, B, E. Peter informs Kerstin that he is to be married. She says she shall not fail to be present; he, that the wedding will be too far away for anybody to come. She shall come, if asked, though it be in Rome, B. If you come, says Peter, you must not wear your gold. She will wear it, for it was got by no dishonor, B, E. Peter rides off, Kerstin wrings her hands: alack for the maid that trusts a loon! He makes the preparations for his bridal, and she orders her clothes, which are of the richest description, all pearls and gold.‡ She has her horse shod, as in English, B 21, C 12, E 22. When she enters the hall, wives and maids stand up, B. She pours wine for the guests. The bride asks who she is, and is told that it is Sir Peter's mistress.§ She has more gold on her

---

* I have been enabled to restore the original readings by the ever ready kindness of Professor Skeat.

† London, printed for W. T[hackeray], T. P[assenger], and W. W. [Whitwood?]. This impression is therefore contemporary with the other.

‡ In D, E she borrows the fine things of her sister. Minute particulars are given in D. We all wonder how Fair Annet, whose face should be her fortune, comes by so much. Her

horse's shoes and bells would have made her a nice little dowry; and then she has, F 20, as much gold above her brow as would buy an earldom, like the oriental Susie Py. This comes of a reckless use of commonplaces, without regard to keeping.

§ Some of the versions have traits of 'Fair Annie.' In F the woman is a king's sister, and is not living with Sir Peter.

kirtle's hem, says the bride, than all that Sir Peter owns. Why, if he had her, did he come seeking me? After the usual long delay the bride is conducted to the bride-house, Kerstin carrying the torch before her. Kerstin even puts the bride to bed. She leaves the room, saying, **A**, I trow I shall come here no more, goes into the orchard, and hangs herself with her hair. Sir Peter is informed of what has happened, rushes to the orchard, takes Kerstin down, has a grave dug deep and broad, sets his sword against a stone, and runs on it. The next day, as so often, there are three dead, Sir Peter, Kerstin, and the bride, **A**, **B**. In **C**, Peter hangs himself on the same tree.

Not so moving, but considerably more powerful and original, is the other termination of the story. In **E**, after Kerstin has lighted the bride to the bride-house, she draws a knife and kills Peter. She tells the bride that this should have been her death too, had she not spoken her so fair. In **D**, **F**, she sets fire to the house and burns the bride on the bridegroom's arm.

Sir Peter awakes, but he wakes not ere
The flame is playing in the young bride's hair.

Sir Peter springs from his bed, oer late ;
He saw Little Kersti go out through the gate.

' Ah, dear Little Kersti, now help thou me !
Another time shall I help thee.'

And it was Little Kersti, her laugh he heard :
' I wot how well you keep your word.' *

A Southern ballad has something of the outline of the English and Norse, and sounds like a thin echo of them. **A**. Poésies populaires de la France, MS., III, fol. 158, Burgundy. **B**. Buchon, Noëls et Chants p. de la Franche-Comté, p. 90, No 31, ' J'ai fait un rêve.' **C**.

Beaurepaire, La Poésie p. en Normandie, p. 50. **D**. Ampère, Instructions, p. 34, Bretagne. **E**. Guillon, Chansons p. de l'Ain, p. 161, ' Chante, rossignolet.' **F**. Arbaud, Chants p. de la Provence, II, 139, ' Lou premier Jour de Mai.' **G**. Ferraro, Canti p. monferrini, p. 8, No 7, ' Il primo amore.'

A youth is obliged by his father to give up his love for a bride who is less beautiful but richer. He has a dream that his love is dead, and carries her a rose, **B**, **D**. He invites her to the wedding : she will not come to the ceremony, but to the dance. She has three gowns made for the occasion, the third embroidered with gold, or of gold stuff. She falls dead while dancing : she falls on the right, he on the left. In **G**, after his love has died, the bridegroom draws his sword and kills himself. **C** and one copy of **D** have the phenomenon of the sympathetic plants, as in English **A**, **B**, **E**, **F**, **G**.

E 3 is a sort of commonplace when unequal matches are in question. So in a fragment in Herd's manuscripts, I, 55, II, 187 :

' I hae nae houses, I hae nae lands,
I hae nae gowd or fee, Sir ;
I am oer low to be your bryde,
Your loon I 'll never be, Sir.'

And again Motherwell's MS., p. 37. It is Lady Grey's answer to King Edward in the Third Part of Henry VI, III, 2 :

' I know I am too mean to be your queen,
And yet too good to be your concubine.'

So Crescentia, the Koloczaer Codex, Mailáth u. Köffinger, p. 260, v. 565 ff.

With regard to **B** 20, ' I 'll na put on the dowie green,' Kinloch remarks that green is considered unfortunate in love matters, the couplet running,

Og deð var liti Kersti, sá högt hon lóg:
'eg veit du helde sá vel dit órð!'
Landstad, 33–36.

Upon which the good pastor, who loved the things nevertheless, remarks, What a culpable style of life, what moral depravation, many of these ballads depict !

---

* Herre Per vaknað inki för dá
at login leikað i Áselitis hár.

Herre Per springe han up af si seng,
dá ság han liti Kersti pá gata geng.

' Aa kære liti Kersti, no hjölper du meg !
en annen sinn skal eg hjölpe deg.'

> Green is love deen,
> Yellow 's forsaken ;

whereas blue is looked upon as a most fortunate color : "blue is love true." "To be married in a green colored dress is ominous of misfortune, for according to the proverb :

> They that marry in green,
> Their sorrow is soon seen.

And no young woman in the North would wear that color on her wedding day. An old lady of my acquaintance, whose marriage had proved unfortunate, used seriously to warn young women to beware of being married in green, for she attributed her own misfortunes solely to her having been married in a green gown, which she had put on contrary to the sage advice of her seniors, in whose minds the belief was more firmly rooted, and who had wished her to wear in its stead a blue dress, as being the more lucky color. To dance in green stockings is a proverbial phrase applied to an elder sister when the younger is first married, intimating that she may mourn her hapless fate, as she has now no chance of being married. To dream of green is believed to be the presage of misfortune." Kinloch MSS, I, 15 f.

A is translated by Bodmer, II, 44, Doenniges, p. 125. **D**, Percy's copy, by Eschenburg, in Ursinus, Balladen und Lieder, 1777, p. 69 ; by Bodmer, I, 106 ; by Talvj, Versuch u. s. w., p. 497 ; Döring, p. 191 ; Doenniges, p. 121 ; Arentsschild, Albion u. Erin, p. 535 ; von Marées, p. 36 ; Knortz, Lieder u. Romanzen Alt-Englands, p. 175, No 47 ; Loève-Veimars, p. 123.

Norse **A** is translated by W. and M. Howitt, Literature and Romance of Northern Europe, I, 258 ; **B** by Prior, III, 363.

A

Percy's Reliques, 1765, II, 293, " given, with some corrections, from a MS. copy transmitted from Scotland."

1 Lord Thomas and Fair Annet
   Sate a' day on a hill ;
   Whan night was cum, and sun was sett,
   They had not talkt their fill.

2 Lord Thomas said a word in jest,
   Fair Annet took it ill :
   ' A, I will nevir wed a wife
   Against my ain friends' will.'

3 ' Gif ye wull nevir wed a wife,
   A wife wull neir wed yee : '
   Sae he is hame to tell his mither,
   And knelt upon his knee.

4 ' O rede, O rede, mither,' he says,
   ' A gude rede gie to mee ;
   O sall I tak the nut-browne bride,
   And let Faire Annet bee ? '

5 ' The nut-browne bride haes gowd and gear,
   Fair Annet she has gat nane ;

And the little beauty Fair Annet haes
   O it wull soon be gane.'

6 And he has till his brother gane :
   ' Now, brother, rede ye mee ;
   A, sall I marrie the nut-browne bride,
   And let Fair Annet bee ? '

7 ' The nut-browne bride has oxen, brother,
   The nut-browne bride has kye ;
   I wad hae ye marrie the nut-browne bride,
   And cast Fair Annet bye.'

8 ' Her oxen may dye i the house, billie,
   And her kye into the byre,
   And I sall hae nothing to mysell
   Bot a fat fadge by the fyre.'

9 And he has till his sister gane :
   ' Now, sister, rede ye mee ;
   O sall I marrie the nut-browne bride,
   And set Fair Annet free ? '

10 ' I 'se rede ye tak Fair Annet, Thomas,
   And let the browne bride alane ;

Lest ye sould sigh, and say, Alace,
    What is this we brought hame ! '

11 'No, I will tak my mither's counsel,
    And marrie me owt o hand ;
And I will tak the nut-browne bride,
    Fair Annet may leive the land.'

12 Up then rose Fair Annet's father,
    Twa hours or it wer day,
And he is gane into the bower
    Wherein Fair Annet lay.

13 'Rise up, rise up, Fair Annet,' he says,
    'Put on your silken sheene ;
Let us gae to St. Marie's kirke,
    And see that rich weddeen.'

14 'My maides, gae to my dressing-roome,
    And dress to me my hair ;
Whaireir yee laid a plait before,
    See yee lay ten times mair.

15 'My maids, gae to my dressing-room,
    And dress to me my smock ;
The one half is o the holland fine,
    The other o needle-work.'

16 The horse Fair Annet rade upon,
    He amblit like the wind ;
Wi siller he was shod before,
    Wi burning gowd behind.

17 Four and twenty siller bells
    Wer a' tyed till his mane,
And yae tift o the norland wind,
    They tinkled ane by ane.

18 Four and twenty gay gude knichts
    Rade by Fair Annet's side,
And four and twenty fair ladies,
    As gin she had bin a bride.

19 And whan she cam to Marie's kirk,
    She sat on Marie's stean :
The cleading that Fair Annet had on
    It skinkled in their een.

20 And whan she cam into the kirk,
    She shimmerd like the sun ;
The belt that was about her waist
    Was a' wi pearles bedone.

21 She sat her by the nut-browne bride,
    And her een they wer sae clear,
Lord Thomas he clean forgat the bride,
    Whan Fair Annet drew near.

22 He had a rose into his hand,
    He gae it kisses three,
And reaching by the nut-browne bride,
    Laid it on Fair Annet's knee.

23 Up than spak the nut-browne bride,
    She spak wi meikle spite :
'And whair gat ye that rose-water,
    That does mak yee sae white ? '

24 'O I did get the rose-water
    Whair ye wull neir get nane,
For I did get that very rose-water
    Into my mither's wame.'

25 The bride she drew a long bodkin
    Frae out her gay head-gear,
And strake Fair Annet unto the heart,
    That word spak nevir mair.

26 Lord Thomas he saw Fair Annet wex pale,
    And marvelit what mote bee ;
But whan he saw her dear heart's blude,
    A' wood-wroth wexed hee.

27 He drew his dagger, that was sae sharp,
    That was sae sharp and meet,
And drave it into the nut-browne bride,
    That fell deid at his feit.

28 'Now stay for me, dear Annet,' he sed,
    'Now stay, my dear,' he cry'd ;
Then strake the dagger untill his heart,
    And fell deid by her side.

29 Lord Thomas was buried without kirk-wa,
    Fair Annet within the quiere,
And o the tane thair grew a birk,
    The other a bonny briere.

30 And ay they grew, and ay they threw,
    As they wad faine be neare ;
And by this ye may ken right weil
    They were twa luvers deare.

B

Kinloch MSS, I, 1, from the recitation of Mary Barr, Lesmahago.

1 SWEET WILLIE and Fair Annie
    Sat a' day on yon hill;
Though they had sat til the leventh o June,
    They wad na got their fill.

2 But Willie spak a word amiss,
    Fair Annie took it ill:
' I 'll neer marry a tocherless lass
    Agen my ain friends' will.'

3 Then on she lap, and awa she gat,
    As fast as she could hie:
' Fare ye weel now, Sweet Willie,
    It 's fare ye weel a wee.'

4 Then he is gane to his father's ha,
    And tirled at the pin;
Then up and rase his father proud.
    And loot Sweet Willie in.

5 ' Come riddle us, riddle us, father dear,
    Yea both of us into ane;
Whether sall I marry Fair Annie,
    Or bring the brown bride hame?'

6 ' The brown bride she has houses and land,
    And Annie she has nane;
Sae on my blessing, my auld son,
    Bring ye Brown Bride hame.'

7 Then he is to his mither's bouer,
    And tirled at the pin;
Then up and rose his mother dear
    To let Sweet Willie in.

8 ' Come riddle us, riddle us, mother dear,
    Yea baith o us into ane;
Whether sall I marry Fair Annie,
    Or bring the brown bride hame?'

9 ' The brown bride she has gowd and gear,
    Fair Annie she has nane;
And for my blessing, my auld son,
    Bring ye Brown Bride hame.'

10 Then he is to his sister's bouer,
    And tirled at the pin;
And wha sae ready as his sister dear
    To let her brither in.

11 ' Come riddle us, riddle us, sister fair,
    Us baith yea into ane;
Whether sall I marry Fair Annie,
    Or bring the brown bride hame?'

12 ' The brown bride she has horse and kye,
    And Annie she has nane;
But for my love, my brither dear,
    Bring hame the fair woman.

13 ' Your horse may dee into the staw,
    The kye into the byre,
And ye 'll hae nocht but a howther o dirt,
    To feed about your fire.'

14 Then he is to Fair Annie's bouer,
    And tirled at the pin;
And wha sae ready as Fair Annie
    To let Sweet Willie in.

15 ' You 're welcome here to me, Willie,
    You 're welcome here to me:'
' I 'm na welcome to thee, Annie,
    I 'm na welcome to thee,
For I 'm come to bid ye to my wedding,
    It 's gey sad news to thee.'

16 ' It 's gey sad news to me, Willie,
    The saddest ye could tell;
It 's gey sad news to me, Willie,
    That shoud been bride mysel.'

17 Then she is to her father gane,
    And bowed low on her knee:
.   .   .   .   .   .
.   .   .   .   .   .

18 ' Come riddle us, riddle us, father dear,
    Us baith yea into ane;
Whether sall I gang to Willie's wedding,
    Or sall I stay at hame?'

19 ' Whare ane will be your frien, Annie,
    Twenty will be your fae;'
' But prove it gude, or prove it bad,
    To Willie's wedding I 'll gae.'

20 ' I 'll na put on the grisly black,
    Nor yet the dowie green,
But I 'll put on a scarlet robe
    To sheen like onie queen.'

21 She 's orderd the smiths to the smithy,
    To shoe her a riding steed;
She has orderd the tailors to her bouer,
    To dress her a riding weed.

22 She has calld her maries to her bour,
    To lay gowd on her hair:
'Whare e'er ye put ae plait before,
    See ye lay ten times mair.'

23 The steed Fair Annie rade upon,
    He bounded like the wind;
Wi silver he was shod before,
    Wi burning gowd behind.

24 And four and twenty siller bells
    War tiëd til his mane;
Wi ae blast o the norland wind
    They tinkled ane by ane.

25 And whan she cam unto the place,
    And lichted on the green,
Ilka ane that did her see
    Thought that she was a queen.

26 'Is this your bride, Sweet Willie?' she said,
    'I think she 's wondrous wan;
Ye micht have had as fair a bride
    As eer the sun sheend on.'

27 'O haud your tongue, Fair Annie,' he said,
    'Wi your talk let me abee;
For better I loe your little finger
    Than the brown bride's haill bodie.'

28 Then out and spak the nut-brown bride,
    And she spak out of spite:
'O whare gat ye the water, Annie,
    That washd your face sae white?'

29 'O I gat een the water,' quo she,
    'Whare ye will neer get nane;
It 's I gat een the water,' quo she,
    'Aneath yon marble stane.'

30 Then out and spake the nut-brown bride,
    And she spak yet again:
'O whare gat ye the claith, Annie,
    That dried your face sae clean?'

31 'O I gat een the claith,' quo she,
    'Whare ye will neer get nane;
It 's I gat een the claith,' quo she,
    'Aneath yon bouer o bane.'

32 The brown bride had a little penknife,
    Which she kept secret there;
She stabbd Fair Annie to the heart,
    A deep wound and a sair.

33 It 's out and spak he Sweet Willie,
    And he spak yet again:
'O what 's the matter wi thee, Annie,
    That ye do look sae wan?'

34 'Oh are ye blind, Willie?' she said,
    'Or do ye no weel see?
I think ye micht see my heart's blude,
    Come rinning by my knee.'

35 Then Willie took a little sword,
    Which he kept secret there,
And strak the brown bride to the heart,
    A word she neer spak mair.

36 And after that a' this was dune,
    He drew it through the strae,
And through his ain fair bodie
    He causd the cauld iron gae.

37 The last words that Sweet Willie spak,
    His heart was almaist gane;
'May never a young man like me
    Have sic a sad wedding.

38 'For gear will come, and gear will gang,
    And gear 's ae but a lend,
And monie a ane for warld's gear
    A silly brown bride brings hame.'

39 Sweet Willie was buried in Mary's kirk,
    And Annie in Mary's quire,
And out o the ane there grew a birk,
    And out o the ither a brier.

40 And ae they grew, and ae they threw,
    Until the twa did meet,
That ilka ane micht plainly see
    They were true lovers sweet.

C

Motherwell's MS., p. 157, from the recitation of Agnes Laird, Kilbarchan, 1825.

1 ' Come read my rede, O mother dear,
　　Come riddle it all in one ;
　O whether will I take Fair Annie,
　　Or bring the brown bride home ? '

2 ' The brown, brown bride has kye and ewes,
　　Fair Annie she has none ;
　She has nothing but a bonny, bonny face,
　　And that 'll soon be gone.'

3 ' Where will I get a pretty little boy,
　　That 'll rin my errands soon,
　That will rin to Fair Annie's bower,
　　And bid her to my wedding ? '

4 ' Here am I, a pretty little boy,
　　That 'll rin your errands soon,
　That will rin to Fair Annie's bower,
　　And bid her to your wedding.'

5 ' Forbid her to put on her silks so black,
　　Or yet her silks so brown ;
　But she must put on her suddled silks,
　　That she wears up and down.

6 ' Forbid her to put on her silks so green,
　　Or yet her silks so gray ;
　But she must put on her suddled silks,
　　That she wears every day.'

7 When he gade to Fair Annie's bower,
　　He tirled at the pin ;
　So ready was Fair Annie hersell
　　To open and let him in.

8 ' What news, what news, my little boy ?
　　What news hast thou to me ? '
　' You must prepare for Lord Thomas' wedding,
　　And that 's bad news for thee.'

9 ' Good news, good news,' Fair Annie says,
　　' Good news is it for me,
　For me to be bride and him bridegroom,
　　And that 's good news for me.'

10 　' He forbids thee to put on thy silks so black,
　　Or yet thy silks so brown ;
　But thou must put on thy suddled silks,
　　That thou wears up and down.

11 ' He forbids you to put on thy silks so green,
　　Or yet thy silks so gray ;
　But thou must on thy suddled silks,
　　That thou wears every day.'

12 ' There are smiths into my smiddy-bour
　　That 'll dress to me a steed,
　There are tailors in my tailor-house
　　That 'll dress to me a weed.

13 ' There are maidens in my maiden-bower
　　That 'll lay gold in my hair,
　And where eer there were ane link before,
　　It shall be nine times mair.'

14 Then Annie got herself attired,
　　In all things very fine,
　With red ribbons, and silks so fair,
　　That owre her shoulders shine.

15 When she came to Lord Thomas' yett,
　　She shined amang them a',
　And the buttons on Lord Thomas' coat
　　Brusted and brak in twa.

16 ' Brown, brown is your steed,' she says,
　　' But browner is your bride ;
　But gallant is that handkerchy
　　That hideth her din hide.'

17 ' O hold thy peace, Fair Annie,' he says,
　　' Speak not of that to me,
　For happy is that bonny, bonny lad
　　That leads his life with thee.'

18 Then out bespoke the brown, brown bride,
　　And she spoke out with spite :
　' O whare gets thou that water-cherry,
　　That washes thee so white ? '

19 ' I got in my father's garden,
　　Below an olive tree,
　And although thou war to seek long seven
　　years
　That water thou 'll never see.

20 ' Tho thou hast got Lord Thomas' hand
　　That water thou 'll neer see ;
　For thou 's sunbrunt from thy mother's womb,
　　And thou 'll never be like me.'

＊　　＊　　＊　　＊　　＊

D

a. Pepys Ballads, III, 316, No 312. b. A Collection of Old Ballads, I, 249, 1723. c. Ritson, Select Collection of English Songs, II, 187, 1783. d. Buchan's Gleanings, p. 86. e, f, g, h, i, recited copies.

1 LORD THOMAS he was a bold forrester,
    And a chaser of the king's deer ;
Faire Ellinor was a fair woman,
    And Lord Thomas he loved her dear.

2 ' Come riddle my riddle, dear mother,' he said,
    ' And riddle us both as one,
Whether I shall marry Fair Ellinor,
    And let the brown girl alone.'

3 ' The brown girl she has got houses and lands,
    And Fair Ellinor she has got none ;
Therefore I charge you on my blessing
    To bring me the brown girl home.'

4 And as it befell on a high holidaye,
    As many did more beside,
Lord Thomas he went to Fair Ellinor,
    That should have been his bride.

5 But when he came to Fair Ellinor's bower,
    He knocked there at the ring ;
But who was so ready as Fair Ellinor
    For to let Lord Thomas in.

6 ' What news, what news, Lord Thomas,' she said,
    ' What news hast thou brought unto me ? '
' I am come to bid thee to my wedding,
    And that is bad news to thee.'

7 ' Oh God forbid, Lord Thomas,' she said,
    ' That such a thing should be done ;
I thought to have been thy bride my own self,
    And you to have been the brid's-groom.

8 ' Come riddle my riddle, dear mother,' she
    sayd,
    ' And riddle it all in one ;
Whether I shall go to Lord Thomas's wedding,
    Or whether I shall tarry at home.'

9 ' There 's many that are your friends, daughter,
    And many that are your fo ;
Therefore I charge you on my blessing,
    To Lord Thomas's wedding don't go.'

10 ' There 's many that are my friends, mother,
    If a thousand more were my foe,
Betide my life, betide my death,
    To Lord Thomas's wedding I 'le go.'

11 She cloathed herself in gallant attyr e,
    And her merry men all in green,
And as they rid thorough everye towne,
    They took her to have been a queene.

12 But when she came to Lord Thomas 's gate,
    She knocked there at the ring ;
But who was so ready as Lord Thomas
    To lett Fair Ellinor in.

13 ' Is this your bride ? ' Fair Ellin she sayd,
    ' Methinks she looks wondrous browne ;
Thou mightest have had as fair a woman
    As ever trod on the ground.'

14 ' Despise her not, Fair Ellin,' he sayd,
    ' Despise her not now unto mee ;
For better I love thy little finger
    Than all her whole body.'

15 This browne bride had a little penknife,
    That was both long and sharp,
And betwixt the short ribs and the long
    Prickd Fair Ellinor to the heart.

16 ' Oh Christ now save thee,' Lord Thomas he
    said,
    ' Methinks thou lookst wondrous wan ;
Thou wast usd for to look with as fresh a
    colour
    As ever the sun shin'd on.'

17 ' Oh art thou blind, Lord Thomas ? ' she sayd,
    ' Or canst thou not very well see ?
Oh dost thou not see my own heart's blood
    Runs trickling down my knee ? '

18 Lord Thomas he had a sword by his side,
    As he walked about the hall ;
He cut off his bride's head from her shoulders,
    And he threw it against the wall.

19 He set the hilte against the ground,
    And the point against his heart ;
There was never three lovers that ever met
    More sooner they did depart.

E

Jamieson's Popular Ballads, I, 22, from the recitation of Mrs W. Arrot, of Aberbrothick, as learned by her when a child from an elderly maid-servant.

1 SWEET WILLIE and Fair Annie
    Sat a' day on a hill,
And though they had sitten seven year,
    They neer wad had their fill.

2 Sweet Willie said a word in haste,
    And Annie took it ill:
' I winna wed a tocherless maid,
    Against my parents' will.'

3 ' Ye 're come o the rich, Willie,
    And I 'm come o the poor;
I 'm oer laigh to be your bride,
    And I winna be your whore.'

4 O Annie she 's gane till her bower,
    And Willie down the den,
And he 's come till his mither's bower,
    By the lei light o the moon.

5 ' O sleep ye, wake ye, mither?' he says,
    ' Or are ye the bower within?'
' I sleep richt aft, I wake richt aft;
    What want ye wi me, son?

6 ' Whare hae ye been a' night, Willie?
    O wow, ye 've tarried lang!'
' I have been courtin Fair Annie,
    And she is frae me gane.

7 ' There is twa maidens in a bower;
    Which o them sall I bring hame?
The nut-brown maid has sheep and cows,
    And Fair Annie has nane.'

8 ' It 's an ye wed the nut-brown maid,
    I 'll heap gold wi my hand;
But an ye wed her Fair Annie,
    I 'll straik it wi a wand.

9 ' The nut-brown maid has sheep and cows,
    And Fair Annie has nane;
And Willie, for my benison,
    The nut-brown maid bring hame.'

10 ' O I sall wed the nut-brown maid,
    And I sall bring her hame;

But peace nor rest between us twa,
    Till death sinder 's again.

11 ' But, alas, alas!' says Sweet Willie,
    ' O fair is Annie's face!'
' But what 's the matter, my son Willie?
    She has nae ither grace.'

12 ' Alas, alas!' says Sweet Willie,
    ' But white is Annie's hand!'
' But what 's the matter, my son Willie?
    She hasna a fur o land.'

13 ' Sheep will die in cots, mither,
    And owsen die in byre;
And what 's this warld's wealth to me,
    An I get na my heart's desire?

14 ' Whare will I get a bonny boy,
    That wad fain win hose and shoon,
That will rin to Fair Annie's bower,
    Wi the lei light o the moon?

15 ' Ye 'll tell her to come to Willie's weddin,
    The morn at twal at noon;
Ye 'll tell her to come to Willie's weddin,
    The heir o Duplin town.

16 ' She manna put on the black, the black,
    Nor yet the dowie brown,
But the scarlet sae red, and the kerches sae
    white,
    And her bonny locks hangin down.'

17 He is on to Annie's bower,
    And tirled at the pin,
And wha was sae ready as Annie hersel
    To open and let him in.

18 ' Ye are bidden come to Willie's weddin,
    The morn at twal at noon;
Ye are bidden come to Willie's weddin,
    The heir of Duplin town.

19 ' Ye manna put on the black, the black,
    Nor yet the dowie brown,
But the scarlet sae red, and the kerches sae
    white,
    And your bonny locks hangin down.'

20 ' It 's I will come to Willie's weddin,
    The morn at twal at noon;

It 's I will come to Willie's weddin,
   But I rather the mass had been mine.

21 'Maidens, to my bower come,
   And lay gold on my hair ;
   And whare ye laid ae plait before,
   Ye 'll now lay ten times mair.

22 'Taylors, to my bower come,
   And mak to me a weed ;
   And smiths, unto my stable come,
   And shoe to me a steed.'

23 At every tate o Annie's horse mane
   There hang a silver bell,
   And there came a wind out frae the south,
   Which made them a' to knell.

24 And whan she came to Mary-kirk,
   And sat down in the deas,
   The light that came frae Fair Annie
   Enlightend a' the place.

25 But up and stands the nut-brown bride,
   Just at her father's knee :
   'O wha is this, my father dear,
   That blinks in Willie's ee ? '
   'O this is Willie's first true-love,
   Before he loved thee.'

26 'If that be Willie's first true-love,
   He might hae latten me be ;
   She has as much gold on ae finger
   As I 'll wear till I die.

27 'O whare got ye that water, Annie,
   That washes you sae white ? '
   'I got it in my mither's wambe,
   Whare ye 'll neer get the like.

28 'For ye 've been washd in Dunny's well,
   And dried on Dunny's dyke,
   And a' the water in the sea
   Will never wash ye white.'

29 Willie 's taen a rose out o his hat,
   Laid it in Annie's lap :
   .   .   .   .   .
   'Hae, wear it for my sake.'

30 'Tak up and wear your rose, Willie,
   And wear 't wi mickle care ;

For the woman sall never bear a son
   That will make my heart sae sair.'

31 Whan night was come, and day was gane,
   And a' man boun to bed,
   Sweet Willie and the nut-brown bride
   In their chamber were laid.

32 They werena weel lyen down,
   And scarcely fa'n asleep,
   Whan up and stands she Fair Annie,
   Just up at Willie's feet.

33 'Weel brook ye o your brown, brown bride,
   Between ye and the wa ;
   And sae will I o my winding sheet,
   That suits me best ava.

34 'Weel brook ye o your brown, brown bride,
   Between ye and the stock ;
   And sae will I o my black, black kist,
   That has neither key nor lock.'

35 Sad Willie raise, put on his claise,
   Drew till him his hose and shoon,
   And he is on to Annie's bower,
   By the lei light o the moon.

36 The firsten bower that he came till,
   There was right dowie wark ;
   Her mither and her three sisters
   Were makin to Annie a sark.

37 The nexten bower that he came till,
   There was right dowie cheir ;
   Her father and her seven brethren
   Were makin to Annie a bier.

38 The lasten bower that he came till,
   .   .   .   .   .
   .   .   .   .   .
   And Fair Annie streekit there.

39 He 's lifted up the coverlet,
   .   .   .   .   .
   .   .   .   .   .
   .   .   .   .   .

40 'It 's I will kiss your bonny cheek,
   And I will kiss your chin,
   And I will kiss your clay-cald lip,
   But I 'll never kiss woman again.

41 'The day ye deal at Annie's burial
    The bread but and the wine;
    Before the morn at twall o'clock,
    They 'll deal the same at mine.'

42 The tane was buried in Mary's kirk,
    The tither in Mary's quire,

And out o the tane there grew a birk,
    And out o the tither a brier.

43 And ay they grew, and ay they drew,
    Untill they twa did meet,
    And every ane that past them by
    Said, Thae 's been lovers sweet!

F

Kinloch MSS, III, 127, stanzas 1–17; the remainder in Dr
John Hill Burton's papers. Another copy in Kinloch MSS,
V, 339. Both in Dr Burton's handwriting.

1 SWEET WILLIE and Fair Annie,
    As they sat on yon hill,
    If they hed sat frae morn till even,
    They hed no talked their fill.

*   *   *   *   *

2 Willie's dune him hame again,
    As fast as gang could he:
    'An askin, an askin, my mother,
    And I pray ye 'll grant it me.

3 'Oh will I merry the nut-brown maid,
    Wi her oxen and her kye?
    Or will I merry my Fair Annie,
    That hes my heart for aye?'

4 'Oh if ye merry your Fair Annie,
    Your mither's malison you 'll wun;
    But if ye merry the nut-brown may,
    Ye will get her blessin.'

5 'Oh voe 's me, mother,' Willie said,
    'For Annie's bonny face!'
    'Little metter o that, my son Willie,
    When Annie hesna grace.'

6 'Oh voe 's me, mither,' Willie said,
    'For Annie's bonny han!'
    'And what 's the metter, son Willie,
    When Annie hesna lan?

7 'But ye will merry the nut-brown may,
    Wi her oxen and her kye;
    But ye will merry the nut-brown may,
    For she hes my hert for aye.'

8 Out and spak his sister Jane,
    Where she sat be the fire:
    'What 's the metter, brother Willie?
    Tack ye your heart's desire.

9 'The oxen may die into the pleuch,
    The cow drown i the myre;
    And what 's the metter, brother Willie?
    Tak ye your heart's desire.'

10 'Whare will I get a bonny boy,
    That will wun hose and shune,
    That will run on to Anny's bower,
    And come right sune again?'

11 'Ye 'll bid her come to Willie's weddin,
    The morn is the day;
    Ye 'll bid her come to Willie's weddin,
    And no make no delay.

12 'Ye 'll forbid her to put on the black, the
        black,
    Or yet the dowie brown;
    But the white silk and the reed skarlet,
    That will shine frae town to town.'

13 He is on to Anie's bower,
    And tirled at the pin,
    And wha was sae ready as Annie hersel
    To let the ladie in.

14 'Ye 'r bidden to come to Willie's weddin,
    The morn is the day;
    Ye 'r bidden come to Willie's weddin,
    And no mack no delay.

15 'Ye 'r forbidden to put on the black, the black,
    Or yet the dowie brown;
    But the white silk and the red scarlet,
    That will shine frae town to town.

16 'Ye 'r forbidden to put on the black, the black,
Or yet the dowie gray;
But the white silk and the red scarlet,
That will shine frae brae to brae.'

17 'It's I will come to Willie's weddin,
Gif the morn be the day;
It's I will come to Willie's weddin,
And no mack no delay.'

18 Annie's steed was silver shod,
And golden graithed behin;
At every teet o her horse mane
A silver bell did ring.

19 When Annie was in her sadle set,
She glanced like the moon;
There was as much gould abov her brow
Would buy an earldom.

20 When Annie was on her sadel set,
She glanced like the fire;
There was as much gould above her brow
Was worth a yearl's hire.

21 Annie gaed in the heigh, heigh hill,
And Willie the dowie glen;
Annie alane shone brighter
Than Willie and a' his men.

22 'Oh wha is that, my ane Willie,
That glances in your ee?'
'Oh it is Annie, my first fore love,
Come till see you and me.'

23 'Oh far got ye that water, Annie,
That washes ye so wan?'
'Oh I got it aneth yon marble stane,
Where ye will nere get nane.

24 'Ye've been brunt sare anent the sun,
And rocket i the reek;
And tho ye wad wash till doom's day,
Ye wad never be so white.'

25 'If this be Annie, your first fore love,
Come our weddin to see,
She has by far owr brent a brow
To lat ye bide by me.'

26 When bells were rung, and mass was sung,
And a' men bun to bed,
Sweet Willie and his nut-brown bride
In ae chamber were laid.

27 The hedna weel layn down, layn down,
But nor hed fallen asleep,
When up and started Fair Annie,
And stud at Willie's feet.

28 'Vo be to you, nut-brown bride,
Wi yer oxen and your sheep!
It is Annie, my first fore love,
And I fear sair she is dead.

29 'Vo be te you, nut-brown bride,
An ill death you betide!
For you've parted me and my first fore love,
And I fear death is her guide.

30 'You'll seddle to me the black, the black,
You'll seddle to me the brown,
Till I ride on to Annie's bower
And see how she is bune.'

31 When he came to Fair Annie's bower,
And lighted and gaed in,

. . . . . .

. . . . . .

32 Her father was at her heed, her heed,
Her mother at her feet,
Her sister she was at her side,
Puttin on her winding sheet.

33 'It's kiss will I yer cheek, Annie,
And kiss will I your chin,
And I will kiss your wan, wan lips,
Tho there be no breath within.

34 'Ye birl, ye birle at my luve's wake
The white bread and the wine,
And or the morn at this same time
Ye'll birlc the same at mine.'

35 They birled, they birled at Annies wake
The white bread and the wine,
And ere the morn at that same time
At his they birled the same.

36 The one was buried at Mary's kirk,
The other at Mary's quire,
And throw the one there sprang a birk,
And throw the other a brier.

37 And ay at every year's ane
They grew them near and near,
And every one that passed them by
Said, They be lovers dear.

G

Skene MS., p. 104; northeast of Scotland, 1802–03.

1 SWEET WILLIE and Fair Annë,
    They sat on yon hill,
And frae the morning till night
    This twa neer talked their fill.

2 Willie spak a word in jest,
    And Annë took it ill :
' We 's court na mare maidens,
    Against our parents' will.'

3 ' It 's na against our parents' will,'
    Fair Annie she did say,

.   .   .   .   .

.   .   .   .   .

4 Willie is hame to his bower,
    To his book all alane,
And Fair Annie is to her bower,
    To her book and her seam.

5 Sweet Willie is to his mother dear,
    Fell low down on his knee :
' An asking, my mother dear,
    And ye grant it to me ;
O will I marry the nut-brown may,
    An lat Fair Annie gae ? '

6 ' The nut-brown may has ousen, Willie,
    The nut-brown may has key ;
' An ye will winn my blessing, Willie,
    And latt Fair Annie be.'

7 He did him to his father dear,
    Fell low down on his knee :
' An asking, my father,
    An ye man grant it me.'

8 ' Ask on, my ae son Willie,
    Ye 'r sur yer askin 's free ;
Except it is to marry her Fair Annie,
    And that manna be.'

9 Out spak his little sister,
    As she [sat] by the fire :
' The ox-leg will brack in the plough,
    And the cow will drown in the mire.

10 ' An Willie will ha nathing
    But the dam to sitt by the fire ;

Fair Annie will sit in her beagly bower,
    An winn a earl's hire.'

11 ' Fair faa ye, my little sister,
    A guid dead mat ye die !
An ever I hae goud,
    Well tochered sall ye be.'

12 He 's awa to Fair Annie,
    As fast as gan could he :
' O will ye come to my marriage ?
    The morn it is to be.'

13 ' O I will come to yer marriage,
    The morn, gin I can win.'

.   .   .   .   .

.   .   .   .   .

14 Annie did her to her father dear,
    Fell low down on her knee :
' An askin, my father,
    And ye man grant it me ;
Lat me to Sweet Willie's marriage,
    The morn it is to be.'

15 ' Yer horse sall be siller shod afore,
    An guid red goud ahin,
An bells in his mane,
    To ring against the win.'

16 She did her to her mother dear,
    Fell low down on her knee :
' Will ye lat me to Willie's marriage ?
    The morn it is to be ; '
' I 'll lat ye to Willie's marriage,
    An we the morn see.'

17 Whan Annie was in her saddle set
    She flam'd against the fire ;
The girdle about her sma middle
    Wad a won an earl's hire.

18 Whan they came to Mary kirk,
    And on to Mary quire,
' O far gat ye that watter, Ann,
    That washes ye sae clear ? '
                .

19 ' I got it in my father's garden,
    Aneth a marbell stane ;

.   .   .   .   .

.   .   .   .   .

.

20 'O whar gat ye that water, Annie,
　　That washes ye sae fite?'
'I gat it in my mother's womb,
　　Whar ye['s] never get the like.

21 'For ye ha been christned wi moss-water,
　　An roked in the reak,
An ser brunt in yer mither's womb,
　　For I think ye'll neer be fite.'

22 The nut-brown bride pat her hand in
　　.　　.　　.　　at Annie['s] left ear,
And gin her　　.　　.　　.
　　A deep wound and a sare.

23 Than . . Annie ged on her horse back,
　　An fast away did ride,
But lang or cock's crowing,
　　Fair Annie was dead.

24 Whan bells were rung, and mess was sung,
　　An a' man boun to bed,
Sweet Willie and the nut-brown bride
　　In a chamber were laid.

25 But up und wakend him Sweet Willie
　　Out of his dreary dream:
'I dreamed a dream this night,
　　God read a' dream to guid!

26 'That Fair Annies bowr was full of gentle-
　　men,
　　An herself was dead;
But I will on to Fair Annie,
　　An si't if it be guid.'

27 Seven lang mile or he came near,
　　He heard a dolefull chear,
Her father and her seven brithern,
　　Walking at her bier;
The half of it guid red goud,
　　The other silver clear.

28 'Ye deal at my love's leak
　　The white bread an the wine;
But on the morn at this time
　　Ye's dee the like at mine.'

29 The ane was buried at Mary kirk,
　　The ither at Mary quire;
Out of the ane grew a birk,
　　Out of the ither a briar.

30 An aye the langer that they grew,
　　They came the ither near,
An by that ye might a well kent
　　They were twa lovers dear.

H

Gibb MS., p. 64.

1 FAIR ANNIE and Sweet Willie,
　　As they talked on yon hill,
Though they had talked a lang summer day,
　　They wad na hae talked their fill.

2 'If you would be a good woman, Annie,
　　An low leave a' your pride,
In spite of a' my friends, Annie,
　　I wad mak you my bride.'

3 'Thick, thick lie your lands, Willie,
　　An thin, thin lie mine;
An little wad a' your friends think
　　O sic a kin as mine.

4 'Thick, thick lie your lands, Willie,
　　Down by the coving-tree;

An little wad a' your friends think
　　O sic a bride as me.

5 'O Fair Annie, O Fair Annie,
　　This nicht ye've said me no;
But lang or ever this day month
　　I'll make your heart as sore.'

6 It's Willie he went home that night,
　　An a sick man lay he down;
An ben came Willie's auld mither,
　　An for nae gude she came.

＊　　＊　　＊　　＊　　＊

7 'It's if ye marry Fair Annie,
　　My malison ye's hae;
But if ye marry the nut-brown may,
　　My blessin an ye's hae.'

8 'Mother, for your malison,
    An mother, for your wis,
It's I will marry the nut-brown may,

.   .   .   .   .

9 .   .   .   .   .
.   .   .   .   .
It's up an spak his sister,

.   .   .   .   .

10 'The owsen may hang in the pleugh,
    The kye drown in the myre,
An he 'll hae naething but a dirty drab
    To sit doun by the fire.'

*   *   *   *   *

11 'Where will I get a bonny boy,
    That will win hose and shoon,
That will rin on to Annie's bower,
    An haste him back again?'

12 'It's I have run your errands, Willie,
    An happy hae I been;
It's I will rin your errands, Willie,
    Wi the saut tears in my een.'

13 'When ye come to Annie's bower,
    She will be at her dine;
And bid her come to Willie's weddin,
    On Monday in good time.

14 'Tell her neither to put on the dowie black,
    Nor yet the mournfu brown,
But the gowd sae reed, and the silver white,
    An her hair weel combed down.

15 'Tell her to get a tailor to her bower,
    To shape for her a weed,
And a smith to her smithy,
    To shoe for her a steed.

16 'To be shod wi silver clear afore,
    An gold graithed behind,
An every foot the foal sets down,
    The gold lie on the ground.'

17 It's when he came to Annie's bower,
    It's she was at her dine:
'Ye 're bidden come to Willie's weddin,
    On Monday in good time.

18 'You 're neither to put on the dowie black,
    Nor get the mournfu brown,

But the gowd sae reid, an the silver white,
    An yere hair well combed doun.

19 'You 're to get a tailor to your bower,
    To shape for you a weed,
And likewise a smith to your smithy,
    To shoe for you a steed.

20 'To be shod with silver clear afore,
    An gold graithed behind,
An every foot the foal sets down,
    The gold lie on the ground.'

21 'It's I will come to Willie's weddin,
    I rather it had been mine;
It's I will come to Willie's weddin,
    On Monday in good time.

22 'It's I 'll send to Willie a toweld silk,
    To hing below his knee.
An ilka time he looks on it,
    He 'll hae gude mind o me.

*   *   *   *   *

23 'An askin, father, an askin,
    An I hope you will grant me;
For it is the last askin
    That ever I 'll ask of thee.'

24 'Ask me, Annie, gold,' he said,
    'An ask me, Annie, fee,
But dinna ask me Sweet Willie,
    Your bedfellow to be.'

25 'It's I will ask you gold, father,
    Sae will I ask you fee,
But I needna ask you Sweet Willie,
    My bedfellow to be.

26 'For I am bidden to Willie's weddin,
    On Monday in good time,

.   .   .   .   .
.   .   .   .   .

*   *   *   *   *

27 On every tait o her horse's mane
    A siller bell did hing,
An on every tait o her horse's tail
    A golden bell did ring.

28 Twal and twal rade her afore,
    An twal an twal ahind,

An twal an twal on every side,
　To hold her frae the wind.

29 Fair Annie shined mair on the top o the hill
　　Than Willie did in the glen ;
　　Fair Annie shined mair on the heid o the hill
　　Than Willie wi a' his men.

30 Whan she came to Mary's kirk,
　　She lighted on the stane ;
　　An when she came to the kirk-door,
　　She bade the bride gae in.

31 'Clear, clear is your day, Willie,
　　But brown, brown is your bride ;
　　Clear, clear is her lawn curches,
　　But weel dunned is her hide.'

32 'Where got ye yon water, Annie,
　　That has made you so white ? '
　　'I got it in my father's garden,
　　Below yon hollan dyke.

33 'But ye hae been washed i the moss water,
　　An rocked in the reek ;
　　Ye hae been brunt in your mither's wame,
　　An ye will neer be white.'

34 'Whatna fool were ye, Willie,
　　To lay your love on me ;
　　She 's mair gowd on her heid this day
　　Than I 'll wear till I die ! '

35 'I 've laid nae love on you, brown may,
　　I 've laid nae love on you ;
　　I 've mair love for Fair Annie this day
　　Than I 'll hae for you till I dee.'

* 　* 　* 　* 　*

36 'If you will neither eat nor drink,
　　You 'll see good game an play ; '
　　But she turned her horse head to the hill,
　　An swift she rode away.

* 　* 　* 　* 　*

37 When they were all at supper set,
　　.　　.　　.　　.
　　Till he went to Fair Annie's bower,
　　By the ley licht o the mune.

38 An when he came to Annie's bower,
　　Annie was lying deid,
　　An seven o Annie's sisters an sisters' bairns
　　Were sewing at Annie's weed.

39 'It 's I will take your hand, Annie,
　　Since ye wald neer take mine ;
　　The woman shall never have the hand
　　That I 'll touch after thine.

40 'An I will kiss your mouth, Annie,
　　Since ye will never kiss mine ;
　　The woman shall never have the lips
　　That I 'll kiss after thine.

* 　* 　* 　* 　*

41 .　　.　　.　　.　　.
　　'As much breid ye deal at Annie's dairgie
　　Tomorrow ye 's deal at mine.'

———◆———

A. "Some traditionary copies of the ballad have
　this stanza, which is the 19th in order :

　And four and twenty milk-white swans,
　　Wi their wings stretchd out wide,
　To blaw the stour aff the highway,
　　To let Fair Annie ride."
　　　　(Motherwell's Minstrelsy, p. lxviii, 19.)

　Compare 'Lord Ingram and Chiel Wyet,' C 22.
C. 6³, 10³. silk. 13¹. The maidens.
D. a. A Tragical Story of Lord Thomas and Fair

Ellinor. Together with the downfall of the
Brown Girl.
3⁴. And bring. 9¹. many of your.
9⁴, 12¹. Thomas his.
10⁴. Thomas's his. 15³. But betwixt.
b. A Tragical Ballad on the unfortunate Love
of Lord Thomas and fair Ellinor, together
with the Downfal of the Brown Girl.
1³. a fine. 2³. marry with. 3¹. land.
3⁴. Bring me. 4¹. As it.
4². many more did. 6⁴. for thee.
7⁴. bridegroom. 9¹. many that are.

9⁴, 10⁴, 12¹. Thomas's. 10². And if.

11³. through. 11⁴. to be some.

13¹. Ellinor said. 13². wonderful.

13³. mightst. 14². now *wanting*.

15³. And. 16³. Thou us'd to look.

18⁴. he *wanting*.

19³. There never were three lovers met.

19⁴. That sooner did.

c. 1³. a fine. 2³. marry with.

3². And *wanting*. 3³. thee on.

3⁴. To bring. 5⁴. For *wanting*.

6⁴. for thee. 7⁴. bridegroom.

9¹. many that are.

8³, 9⁴, 10⁴, 12¹. Thomases. 10³. or betide.

11³. through. 13³. You might.

14². now *wanting*. 15³. And.

15⁴. She prickd. 16². wain.

d. 3². she 's got land, she says.

4². many more do. 5². at the pin.

8⁴. I shall let it alone. 9². foes.

10². If a thousand were our foes.

10³. me life, me death.

10⁴. To Lord Thomas's I 'll go.

12². at the pin.

After 12 :

He took her by the lily-white hand,
   And led her through the hall ;
He set her in the noblest chair,
   Among the ladies all.

15². both keen. 16¹. now save me.

16³. usest to look as good a colour.

After 17 :

' O dig my grave,' Lord Thomas replied,
   ' Dig it both wide and deep,
And lay Fair Eleanor by my side
And the brown girl at my feet.'

18⁴. And flung.

19³, ⁴. There never were three lovers sure
   That sooner did depart.

e. *Motherwell's MS., p.* 293, *from the recitation of Widow McCormick, February* 23, 1825 ; *learned of an old woman in Dumbarton, thirty years before.*

1 ' Come riddle me, riddle me, mother,' he says,
   ' Come riddle me all in one,

Whether I 'll goe to court Fair Helen
   Or fetch you the brown girl home.'

2 ' It 's many 's the ones your friends,' she says,
   ' And many 's the ones your fone;
My blessing be on you, dear son,' she says,
   ' Go fetch me the brown girl home.'

3 He dressed himself all in green,
   Thorough the road he went,
And every village that he came to,
   They took him to be a king.

4 Till that he came to Fair Helen's gate ;
   He tinkled low at the ring ;
Who was so ready as Fair Helen herself
   To let Lord Thomas in.

5 ' You 're welcome, you 're welcome, Lord Thomas,'
      she says,
   ' What news have you brought to me ? '
' I 've come to bid you to my wedding,
   And that is bad news to thee.'

6 ' It 's God forbid, Lord Thomas,' she said,
   ' That sic an a thing should be,
But I for to be the body of the bride,
   And you to be the bridegroom.'

7 ' Come riddle me, riddle me, mother,' she says,
   ' Come riddle me all in one,
Whether I 'll go to Lord Thomas' wedding,
   Or mourn all day at home.'

8 ' Many 's the ones your friend,' she says,
   ' And many 's the ones your fone ;
' My blessing be on you, dear daughter,' she says,
   ' And mourn all day at home.'

9 ' Many 's the ones my friends, mother,' she says,
   ' And many 's the ones my fae,
But I will go to Lord Thomas' wedding
   Should I lose my life by the way.'

10 She dressed herself all in green,
   Thorow the road she went,
And every village that she came to,
   They took her for to be a queen.

11 Till that she came to Lord Thomas' gates ;
   She tinkled low at the ring ;
Who was so ready as Lord Thomas himself
   To let Fair Helen in.

12 ' Where have you got this brown girl ? ' she says,
   ' I think she looks wonderful brown ;
You might have had as pretty a bride
   As ever the sun shined on.'

13 It's up and starts the brown girl's mother,
   And an angry woman was she:
'Where have you got the roseberry-water
   That washes your face so clear?'

14 'It's I have gotten that roseberry-water
   Where that she could get none;
For I have got it in my mother's womb,
   Where in her mother's womb there was
      none.'

15 She took up a little pen-knife,
   That was baith sharp and small,
She stuck Fair Helen fornents the heart,
   And down the blood did fall.

16 'What ailes you, Fair Helen?' he says,
   'I think you look wonderful pale:

.   .   .   .   .   .

.   .   .   .   .   .

17 'What ailes you, Lord Thomas?' she says,
   'Or don't you very well see?
O don't you see my very heart's blood
   Coming trinkling down by my knee?'

18 He took up a little small sword,
   That hung low by his knee,
And he cut off the brown girl's head,
   And dashed it against the wall.

19 He set the sword all in the ground,
   And on it he did fall;
So there was an end of these three lovers,
   Thro spite and malice all.

   8². foe *in the margin.*
   19⁴. All thro spite and malice *is noted as
      if it were what was recited.*
f. *From Miss Clara Mackay, Woodstock, New
   Brunswick, 1881, derived from her great
   grandmother. The title is* 'Lord Thomas.'
   1². The keeper of our king's gear.
   4, 7 *are wanting.*
   11². Her merry maids all in green.
   After 12:

      He took her by the lily-white hand,
         And led her through the hall,
      And sat her in a chair of gold,
         Amidst her merry maids all.

   15². both clean and sharp.
   After 17:

'No, I am not blind,' Lord Thomas he said,
   'But I can plainly see,
And I can see your dear heart's blood
   Runs trickling down your knee.'

18². It was both keen and small.
18⁴. And flung.
After 19, *as in* d:

      'Oh dig me a grave,' Lord Thomas he said,
         'And dig it both wide and deep,
      And lay Fair Ellinor at my side,
         The brown girl at my feet.'

g. *Recited to me by Ellen Healy, 1881, as
   learned by her of a young girl living near
   Killarney, Ireland, about 1867.*
   2². come riddle me oer and oer: *so* 8².
   2⁴, 3⁴. the pretty brown girl bring home.
   After 3:

      He dressed himself up in a suit of green,
         And his merrymen all in white;
      There was not a town that he rode through
         But they took him to be a knight.

9 'Lord Thomas has got company enough,
   Fair Ellinor, you have none;
Therefore I charge you with my blessing,
   Fair Ellinor, stay at home.'

11 She dressed herself up in a suit of white,
   And her merrymen all in green;
There was not a town that she rode through
   But they took her to be a queen.

After 12:

      He took her by the lily-white hand,
         And by the waist so small,
      And set her at the head of the table,

   .   .   .   .   .

After 13:

      Up spoke the pretty brown girl,
         She said   .   .   .   .
      'Where did you get the water
         That washed your skin so white?'

      'There is a well in my father's land,
         A place you'll never see,

.   .   .   .   .   .

.   .   .   .   .   .

14 *wanting.*

19. *Imperfectly remembered.*

Lord Thomas he stabbed the pretty brown
girl, and then he stabbed himself; and
he said, Bury the pretty brown girl at
my feet, and Fair Ellinor in my arms.

A red rose grew out of Fair Ellinor, and
a sweet briar out of Lord Thomas's
grave, and they grew until they met.

h. *An Irish version, recited by Ellen Daily,
Taunton, Massachusetts.*

2². Come riddle me all at once.

2⁴· Or the bonny brown girl.

4. He dressed himself up in a suit of fine
    clothes,
        With merry men all in white;
    And there was not a town that he rode
        through
    But they took him to be a knight.

5². very low at her ring.

10³,⁴. ' Let the wind blow high or low,
        To Lord Thomas's wedding I'll go.'

11. She dressed herself up in a suit of fine
    clothes,
        With merry maids all in green;
    And there was not a town that she rode
        through
    But they took her to be a queen.

12². very low at his ring.

After 12:

He took her by the lily-white hand,
    And led her along the hall;
He handed her to the head of the table,
    Among the ladies all.

After 13:

Then out spoke the bonny brown girl some
words with spirit, saying:

' Where did you get the water so clear,
    That washed your face so white?'

' There is a well in my father's yard
    That is both clear and spring,

And if you were to live till the day you die
    That doon you never shall see.'

14 *is wanting.*

After 19:

' Bury my mother at my head,
    Fair Ellenor by my side,
And bury the bonny brown girl at the end
        of the church,
    Where she will be far from me.'

.   .   .   .   .   .

.   .   .   .   .   .

Out of Fair Ellen there grew a red rose,
    And out of Lord Thomas there grew a
        sweet-briar.

They grew so tall, they sprung so broad,
    They grew to a steeple top;
Twelve o'clock every night
    They grew to a true lover's knot.

i. *Communicated by Mr W. W. Newell, as
    recited by an Irish maid-servant in
    Cambridge, Massachusetts.*

1, 4–7, 10 *are wanting.*

After 12:

He took her by the lily-white hand,
    And led her through the hall,
Until he put her sitting at the head of the
        table,
    Amongst the gentleman all.

13, 14. ' Is this your bride, Lord Thomas?'
        they said,
        Or is *this* your bride?' said they
    ' O 't is better I love her little finger
        Than all *her* whole boday.'

*The stanza which describes Lord Thomas's
dress and the effect he produced occurs in
e, g, h; that in which Lord Thomas
leads Ellinor through the hall and conducts her to her place is found in d, f, g,
h, i; the colloquy about the water which
washes Ellinor so white in e, g, h; Lord
Thomas's directions about the burial in
d, f, h; the plants growing from the
grave in g, h. None of these are in the
English broadside.*

*A fragment in Pitcairn's MSS, III, 35, is
derived from the English broadside.*

F. *The copy in Kinloch MSS, V, 339, b, seems to
be a revision of the other. The two portions
of that which is apparently the earlier, a,
became separated by some accident or oversight. For stanzas 18–37 I have not the
original, but a transcript. After 1, b inserts Jamieson's second stanza, E 2.*

4. ye merry *twice.*

5³. *altered to* What's metter, son Willie, *to
conform to* 6³ : b, And what's the matter.

12¹. Ye'll tell her to come. 12³. Yer bidden
come. 13¹. Yer forbidden. *Anticipating*

14, 15. *Corrected in* b *as here, and partly
in* a.

18². a, gold engraved, b, golden graved : *cf.* H,
16, 20. 22³. Oh is it : *corrected in* b.

25³. She has by far *struck out and* Fair Annie
written above : b, Fair Annie hes oer.

G. *The division of stanzas and of verses has in
some cases required regulation. The handwriting is in places difficult, and I cannot
be sure that the spelling in every case is what
the writer intended.*

7⁴. mann ? 16⁵. Willie. 20². fett ?
21³. ser brunt (?) 21⁴. faett ? 23¹. Whan.
25³. *perhaps* dreams.
28¹. deal *illegible, a conjecture.* 29³. grave ?

74

FAIR MARGARET AND SWEET WILLIAM

A. a. 'Fair Margaret's Misfortune,' etc., Douce Ballads, I, fol. 72. b. 'Fair Margaret and Sweet William,' Ritson, A Select Collection of English Songs,
1783, II, 190. c. 'Fair Margaret and Sweet William,' Percy's Reliques, 1765, III, 121. d. Percy's
Reliques, 1767, III, 119.

B. Percy Papers; communicated by the Dean of Derry,
February, 1776.

C. Percy Papers ; communicated by Rev. P. Parsons,
April 7, 1770.

A, a, b, c are broadside or stall copies, a of
the end of the seventeenth century, b "modern" in Percy's time, and they differ incon-
siderably, except that a has corrupted an important line.* Of d, Percy says, Since the first
edition some improvements have been inserted,
which were communicated by a lady of the
first distinction, as she had heard this song repeated in her infancy. Herd, in The Ancient
and Modern Scots Songs, 1769, p. 295, follows
Percy. As Percy has remarked, the ballad is
twice quoted in Beaumont and Fletcher's
'Knight of the Burning Pestle,' 1611. Stanza
5 runs thus in Act 2, Scene 8, Dyce, II, 170 :

When it was grown to dark midnight,
  And all were fast asleep,
In came Margaret's grimly ghost,
  And stood at William's feet.

The first half of stanza 2 is given, in Act 3,
Scene 5, Dyce, p. 196, with more propriety
than in the broadsides, thus :

You are no love for me, Margaret,
  I am no love for you.

The fifth stanza of the ballad, as cited in
'The Knight of the Burning Pestle,' says the
editor of the Reliques, has "acquired an importance by giving birth to one of the most
beautiful ballads in our own or any language"
[that is, 'Margaret's Ghost'], "the elegant
production of David Mallet, Esq., who, in the
last edition of his poems, 3 vols, 1759, informs
us that the plan was suggested by the four
verses quoted above, which he supposed to be
the beginning of some ballad now lost."† The
ballad supposed to be lost has been lately re-

* "The common title of this ballad, which is a favorite
of the stalls, is 'Fair Margaret's Misfortunes : '" Motherwell,
Minstrelsy, p. lxviii, note 18.

† Reliques, 1765, III, 121, 310.

covered, in a copy of the date 1711, with the title 'William and Margaret, an Old Ballad,' and turns out to be substantially the piece which Mallet published as his own in 1724, Mallet's changes being comparatively slight. 'William and Margaret' is simply 'Fair Margaret and Sweet William' rewritten in what used to be called an elegant style. Nine of the seventeen stanzas are taken up with a rhetorical address of Margaret to false William, who then leaves his bed, raving, stretches himself on Margaret's grave, thrice calls her name, thrice weeps full sore, and dies. See The Roxburghe Ballads, in the Ballad Society's reprint, III, 671, with Mr Chappell's remarks there, and in the Antiquary, January, 1880. The ballad of 1711 seems to have been founded upon some copy of the popular form earlier than any we now possess, or than any known to me, for the last half of stanza 5 runs nearly as it occurs in Beaumont and Fletcher (see also B 7), thus:

In glided Margaret's grimly ghost,
And stood at William's feet.

'Fair Margaret and Sweet William' begins like 'Lord Thomas and Fair Annet,' and from the fifth stanza on is blended with a form of that ballad represented by versions E-H. The *brown* girl, characteristic of 'Lord Thomas and Fair Annet,' has slipped into A 14, 15, B 8, of 'Fair Margaret and Sweet William.' The catastrophe of 'Fair Margaret and Sweet William' is repeated in 'Lord Lovel,' and it will be convenient to notice under the head of the latter, which immediately follows, some ballads out of English which resemble both, especially in the conclusion.

A c is translated by Bodmer, II, 31, Döring, p. 199; A d by Herder, 1778, I, 124, von Marées, p. 40, Knortz, Lieder u. Romanzen Alt-Englands, No 61.

————•————

A

a. Douce Ballads, I, fol. 72. b. Ritson, A Select Collection of English Songs, 1783, II, 190. c. Percy's Reliques, 1765, III, 121. d. Percy's Reliques, 1767, III, 119.

1 As it fell out on a long summer's day,
    Two lovers they sat on a hill;
  They sat together that long summer's day,
    And could not talk their fill.

2 'I see no harm by you, Margaret,
    Nor you see none by me;
  Before tomorrow eight a clock
    A rich wedding shall you see.'

3 Fair Margaret sat in her bower-window,
    A combing of her hair,
  And there she spy'd Sweet William and his
        bride,
    As they were riding near.

4 Down she layd her ivory comb,
    And up she bound her hair;
  She went her way forth of her bower,
    But never more did come there.

5 When day was gone, and night was come,
    And all men fast asleep,
  Then came the spirit of Fair Margaret,
    And stood at William's feet.

6 'God give you joy, you two true lovers,
    In bride-bed fast asleep;
  Loe I am going to my green grass grave,
    And am in my winding-sheet.'

7 When day was come, and night was gone,
    And all men wak'd from sleep,
  Sweet William to his lady said,
    My dear, I have cause to weep.

8 'I dreamd a dream, my dear lady;
    Such dreams are never good;
  I dreamd my bower was full of red swine,
    And my bride-bed full of blood.'

9 'Such dreams, such dreams, my honoured
        lord,
    They never do prove good,
  To dream thy bower was full of swine,
    And [thy] bride-bed full of blood.'

10 He called up his merry men all,
    By one, by two, and by three,
    Saying, I 'll away to Fair Margaret's bower,
    By the leave of my lady.

11 And when he came to Fair Margaret's bower,
    He knocked at the ring ;
    So ready was her seven brethren
    To let Sweet William in.

12 He turned up the covering-sheet :
    ' Pray let me see the dead ;
    Methinks she does look pale and wan,
    She has lost her cherry red.

13 ' I 'll do more for thee, Margaret,
    Than any of thy kin ;
    For I will kiss thy pale wan lips,
    Tho a smile I cannot win.'

14 With that bespeak her seven brethren,
    Making most pitious moan :
    ' You may go kiss your jolly brown bride,
    And let our sister alone.'

15 ' If I do kiss my jolly brown bride,
    I do but what is right ;

For I made no vow to your sister dear,
    By day or yet by night.

16 ' Pray tell me then how much you 'll deal
    Of your white bread and your wine ;
    So much as is dealt at her funeral today
    Tomorrow shall be dealt at mine.'

17 Fair Margaret dy'd today, today,
    Sweet William he dy'd the morrow ;
    Fair Margaret dy'd for pure true love,
    Sweet William he dy'd for sorrow.

18 Margaret was buried in the lower chancel,
    Sweet William in the higher ;
    Out of her breast there sprung a rose,
    And out of his a brier.

19 They grew as high as the church-top,
    Till they could grow no higher,
    And then they grew in a true lover's knot,
    Which made all people admire.

20 There came the clerk of the parish,
    As you this truth shall hear,
    And by misfortune cut them down,
    Or they had now been there.

B

Communicated to Percy by the Dean of Derry, as written down from memory by his mother, Mrs Bernard ; February, 1776.

1 SWEET WILLIAM would a wooing ride,
    His steed was lovely brown ;
    A fairer creature than Lady Margaret
    Sweet William could find none.

2 Sweet William came to Lady Margaret's
    bower,
    And knocked at the ring,
    And who so ready as Lady Margaret
    To rise and to let him in.

3 Down then came her father dear,
    Clothed all in blue :
    ' I pray, Sweet William, tell to me
    What love 's between my daughter and
    you ? '

4 ' I know none by her,' he said,
    ' And she knows none by me ;
    Before tomorrow at this time
    Another bride you shall see.'

5 Lady Margaret at her bower-window,
    Combing of her hair,
    She saw Sweet William and his brown bride
    Unto the church repair.

6 Down she cast her iv'ry comb,
    And up she tossd her hair,
    She went out from her bowr alive,
    But never so more came there.

7 When day was gone, and night was come,
    All people were asleep,
    In glided Margaret's grimly ghost,
    And stood at William's feet.

8 'How d' ye like your bed, Sweet William?
  How d' ye like your sheet?
And how d 'ye like that brown lady,
  That lies in your arms asleep ?'

9 'Well I like my bed, Lady Margaret,
  And well I like my sheet ;
But better I like that fair lady
  That stands at my bed's feet.'

10 When night was gone, and day was come,
  All people were awake,
The lady waket out of her sleep,
  And thus to her lord she spake.

11 'I dreamd a dream, my wedded lord,
  That seldom comes to good ;
I dreamd that our bowr was lin'd with white
    swine,
  And our brid-chamber full of blood.'

12 He called up his merry men all,
  By one, by two, by three,
'We will go to Lady Margaret's bower,
  With the leave of my wedded lady.'

13 When he came to Lady Margaret's bower,
  He knocked at the ring,

And who were so ready as her brethren
  To rise and let him in.

14 'Oh is she in the parlor,' he said,
  'Or is she in the hall ?
Or is she in the long chamber,
  Amongst her merry maids all ?'

15 'She 's not in the parlor,' they said,
  'Nor is she in the hall ;
But she is in the long chamber,
  Laid out against the wall.'

16 'Open the winding sheet,' he cry'd,
  'That I may kiss the dead ;
That I may kiss her pale and wan
  Whose lips used to look so red.'

17 Lady Margaret [died] on the over night,
  Sweet William died on the morrow ;
Lady Margaret died for pure, pure love,
  Sweet William died for sorrow.

18 On Margaret's grave there grew a rose,
  On Sweet William's grew a briar ;
They grew till they joind in a true lover's knot
  And then they died both together.

* * * * *

C

Communicated to Percy by Rev. P. Parsons, of Wye,
April 7, 1770.

1 As Margaret stood at her window so clear,
  A combing back her hair,
She saw Sweet William and his gay bride
  Unto the church draw near.

2 Then down she threw her ivory comb,
  She turned back her hair ;
There was a fair maid at that window,
  She 's gone, she 'll come no more there.

3 In the night, in the middle of the night,
  When all men were asleep,
There walkd a ghost, Fair Margaret's ghost,
  And stood at his bed's feet.

4 Sweet William he dremed a dream, and he
    said,
  'I wish it prove for good ;

My chamber was full of wild men's wine,
  And my bride-bed stood in blood.'

5 Then he calld up his stable-groom,
  To saddle his nag with speed :
'This night will I ride to Fair Margaret'
    bowr,
  With the leave of my lady.

6 'Oh is Fair Margaret in the kitchen ?
  Or is she in the hall?
.   .   .   .   .
  .   .   .   .

7 'No. she is not in the kitchen,' they cryed,
  'Nor is she in the hall ;
But she is in the long chamber,
  Laid up against the wall.'

8 Go with your right side to Newcastle,
  And come with your left side home,
There you will see those two lovers
  Lie printed on one stone.

A. a. Fair Margaret's Misfortune, or, Sweet William's Frightful Dreams on his Wedding Night. With the Sudden Death and Burial of those Noble Lovers. . . . Printed for S. Bates, at the Sun and Bible, in Gilt-Spur Street. *Sarah Bates published about 1685. Chappell.*

    3[1]. set. 4[1]. lay.

    5[4]. Which causd him for to weep : *caught probably from* 7[4]. *See the quotation in Beaumont and Fletcher, and the other broadside copies.*

    13[2]. my kin. 18[1]. channel.

b. 1[1]. out upon a day. 1[3]. a long.

    2[4]. you shall. 3[4]. a riding.

    4[3]. went away first from the.

    4[4]. more came.

    5[4]. And stood at William's bed-feet.

    6[1]. you true. 6[3]. grass green.

    6[4]. I am. 9[4]. thy bride-bed.

    10[1]. called his. 12[1]. Then he.

    12[3]. she looks both. 14[1]. the seven.

    14[3], 15[1]. brown dame.

    16[2]. Of white. 18[2]. And William.

    19[3]. there they. 19[4]. all the. 20[1]. Then.

c. 2[3]. at eight. 2[4]. you shall.

    3[3]. She spyed. 3[4]. a riding.

    4[4]. more came. 5[3]. There came.

    5[4]. And stood at William's feet.

    6[1]. you lovers true. 6[4]. I 'm.

    9[4]. And they. 12[1]. Then he.

    14[1]. the seven. 17. William dyed.

    18[2]. And William. 19[3]. there they.

    19[4]. Made all the folke. 20[1]. Then.

d. *Variations not found in* c : "Communicated by a lady of the first distinction, as she had heard this song repeated in her infancy."

3[2]. Combing her yellow hair.

3[3]. There she spyed.

4. Then down she layd her ivory combe,
    And braided her hair in twain ;
  She went alive out of her bower,
    But neer came alive in 't again.

6. ' Are you awake, Sweet William? ' shee said,
    ' Or, Sweet William, are you asleep ?
  God give you joy of your gay bride-bed,
    And me of my winding-sheet.'

11[3]. And who so ready as her.

15[3]. I neer made a vow to yonder poor corpse.

16. ' Deal on, deal on, my merry men all,
    Deal on your cake and your wine ;
  For whatever is dealt at her funeral today
    Shall be dealt tomorrow at mine.'

19[1]. They grew till they grew unto the.

19[2]. And then they. 19[3]. they tyed.

19[4]. the people.

C. "The ballad of Sweet William," *writes Parsons to Percy*, " was the same as yours in the stanzas I have omitted. . . . The person from whom I took the thirty-fifth line [*thirty-first, here* 4[3]] sang it thus :

    My chamber was full of wild men's wine,

which is absolute nonsense, yet, if altered to ' wild men and swine,' is perfect sense."

75

LORD LOVEL

A. 'Lady Ouncebell,' communicated to Bishop Percy by the Rev. P. Parsons, of Wye, 1770 and 1775.

B. 'Lord Lavel,' Kinloch MSS, I, 45.

C. 'Lord Travell,' communicated by Mr Alexander Laing, of Newburgh-on-Tay.

D. 'Lord Lovel,' Kinloch MSS, VII, 83; Kinloch's Ancient Scottish Ballads, p. 31.

E. Communicated by Mr J. F. Campbell, of Islay, as learned about 1850.

F. 'Lord Lovel,' communicated by Mr Robert White, of Newcastle-on-Tyne.

G. 'Lord Revel,' Harris MS., fol. 28 b.

H. 'Lord Lovel.' a. Broadside in Dixon's Ancient Poems, Ballads and Songs of the Peasantry of England, p. 78, Percy Society, vol. XIX. b. Davidson's Universal Melodist, I, 148.

I. Percy Papers, communicated by Principal Robertson.

I IS made up of portions of several ballads. The first stanza is derived from 'Sweet William's Ghost,' the second and third possibly from some form of 'Death and the Lady,' 4–11 from 'Lady Maisry.' The eighth stanza of **E** should, perhaps, be considered as taken from 'Lord Thomas and Fair Annet,' since in no other copy of 'Lord Lovel' and in none of 'Fair Margaret and Sweet William' does the hero die by his own hand.

In 'Fair Margaret and Sweet William,' as also in 'Lord Thomas and Fair Annet,' a lover sacrifices his inclination to make a marriage of interest. In 'Lord Lovel' the woman dies, not of affection betrayed, but of hope too long deferred, and her laggard but not unfaithful lover sinks under his remorse and

grief. 'Lord Lovel' is peculiarly such a ballad as Orsino likes and praises: it is silly sooth, like the old age. Therefore a gross taste has taken pleasure in parodying it, and the same with 'Young Beichan.' But there are people in this world who are amused even with a burlesque of Othello.[*]

There are several sets of ballads, very common in Germany and in Scandinavia, which, whether they are or are not variations of the same original, at least have a great deal in common with 'Lord Lovel' and 'Fair Margaret and Sweet William.'

Of these, one which more closely resembles the English is 'Der Ritter und die Maid,' of German origin, but found also further north.[†]

A knight and maid have been together till

---

[*] It can scarcely be too often repeated that such ballads as this were meant only to be sung, not at all to be recited. As has been well remarked of a corresponding Norwegian ballad, 'Lord Lovel' is especially one of those which, for their due effect, require the support of a melody, and almost equally the comment of a burden. No burden is preserved in the case of 'Lord Lovel,' but we are not to infer that there never was one. The burden, which is at least as important as the instrumental accompaniment of modern songs, sometimes, in these little tragedies, foreshadows calamity from the outset, sometimes, as in the Norwegian ballad referred to, is a cheerful-sounding formula, which in the upshot enhances by contrast the gloom of the conclusion. "A simple but lifelike story, supported by the burden and the air, these are the means by which such old romances seek to produce an impression:" Landstad, to 'Herr Stragi,' p. 541.

[†] (1), 'Das Lied vom Herren und der Magd,' 1771, Düntzer u. Herder, Briefe Goethe's an Herder, I, 157. (2), 'Eyn klegliche Mordgeschicht, von ey'm Graven vnnde eyner Meyd,' Nicolai, Eyn feyner kleyner Almanach, 1777, I, 39, No 2; with variations, Kretzschmer, I, 89, No 54, Uhland, p. 220, No 97 A. (3), 'Der Ritter und das Mägdlein,' Erk, Liederhort, p. 81, No 26, a traditional variety of (2). (4), Wunderhorn, 1806, I, 50 = Erlach, II, 531, Mittler, No 91. (5), 'Des Prinzen Reue,' Meinert, p. 218, 1817. (6), Alemannia, II, 185, after a manuscript of von Arnim. (7), Erk's edition of the Wunderhorn, IV, 304. (8), Hoffmann u. Richter, Schlesische Volkslieder, p. 9, No 4. (9), Erk u. Irmer, IV, 62, No 56. (10), 'Zu späte Reue,' Fiedler, p. 161. (11), 'Der Erbgraf,' Simrock, p. 33, No 12, compounded, but partly oral. (12), 'Der Ritter und seine Dame,' Pröhle, p. 19, No 13. (13), Meier, p. 316, No 177. (14–16),

morning. She weeps; he tells her that he will pay for her honor, will give her an underling and money. She will have none but him, and will go home to her mother. The mother, on seeing her, asks why her gown is long behind and short before, and offers her meat and drink. The daughter refuses them, goes to bed, and dies. So far there is no dallying with the innocence of love, as in the English ballad; the German knight is simply a brutal man of pleasure. But now the knight has a dream, as in 'Fair Margaret and Sweet William;' it is that his love has died. He bids his squire or groom to saddle, and rides to find out what has happened. On his way he hears an ominous bell; further on he sees a grave digging; then he meets men carrying a bier. Set down the bier, he cries, that I may see my love. He turns back the cloth and looks at the dead. She has suffered for him, he will suffer for her. He draws his sword and runs it through his heart. They are buried in one coffin, or in the same grave. In some of the ballads lilies rise from the grave; in a Swedish version ('Jungfruns död'), a linden, the leaves of which intermingle.

Next to this we may put a Norwegian and a Swedish ballad, which, having perhaps lost something at the beginning, cannot safely be classed: 'Maarstíg aa hass möy,' Bugge, p. 127, No 26, A, B; 'Herr Malmstens dröm,' Afzelius, III, 104, No 85. Maarstíg dreams that his love's gold ring has got upon another finger, that her gold belt is off her lithe waist, her cloak or her hair is cut to bits, her shoes are full of blood; Malmsten that his love's heart breaks. The pages are ordered to saddle, and Maarstíg, or Malmsten, rides to find

what there is in the dream. Maarstíg encounters two maids, who are just from a wake. "Who is dead?" "Maalfrí, thy sweet love." He rides on, meets the bier, bids the bearers set it down, and looks at the dead. Let them dig the grave, he cries, wide and deep, it shall be his bride-house; let them dig the grave deep and long, that is where bride and bridegroom shall go. He sets his sword against a stone, and falls on it. With slight variations, the course of the story is the same for Malmsten. Another Swedish ballad, 'Den sörjande,' Djurklou, p. 106, No 7, lacks even so much introduction as the dream. The lover orders his horse, hears the funeral bell, sees the grave-digging, meets the bier, looks at his dead mistress, and kills himself. A fragment in Dybeck's Runa, 1845, p. 15, begins with the ride and stops short of the death.

These last ballads apparently give us the middle and end of a story which has also some sort of beginning in the following: Danish, 'Den elskedes Død,' Kristensen, II, 39, No 20, A-D, and in many unprinted copies from oral tradition, besides two from MSS of the sixteenth century, communicated to me by Grundtvig; Swedish, 'Hertig Nils,' Arwidsson, II, 21, No 72, 'Peder Palleson,' Arwidsson, No 71, II, 18, 437; Norwegian, 'Herr Stragi,' Landstad, p. 537, No 61.* A lover and his mistress have parted, have been long parted. She is sick, dying, or even dead. In the Danish manuscript copies we are distinctly told that she has grieved herself to death on his account. Word is sent him by carrier-pigeons, a bird, a page; or he is informed by a spae-wife (Landstad). He leaps over the table, spilling mead and wine (Kristensen), and rides faster than the doves fly. The rest

---

Ditfurth, II, 4–8, Nos 6, 7, 8. (17–22), Wagner, in Deutsches Museum, 1862, II, 758–68. (23), 'Der Herr und seine Dame,' Peter, I, 193, No 10. (24), Parisius, p. 33, No 10. (25), Adam Wolf, p. 11, No 6. (26), Alfred Müller, p. 98. (27), 'Die traurige Begegnung,' Paudler, p. 21, No 13.

Scandinavian, from the German: 'Ungersvennens Dröm,' Fagerlund, Anteckningar, p. 196; 'Jungfruns död,' Wigström, Folkdiktning, I, 52; and besides these Swedish copies, a Danish broadside, from the beginning of this century, which is very common. 'Stolten Hellelille,' "Tragica, No 22," 1657, Danske Viser, III, 184, No 130 (translated by Prior, III, 214), a somewhat artificial piece, has the outline of 'Der

Ritter u. die Maid,' and is a hundred years older than any known copy of the German ballad.

A Wendish ballad, founded on the German, is very like (4): Haupt and Schmaler, I, 139, No 136.

A Dutch ballad, in the Antwerpener Liederbuch, No 45, Hoffmann, Niederländische Volkslieder, p. 61, No 15, Willems, p. 154, No 60, Uhland, No 97 B, has some points of the above, but is a very different story.

* There is a Finnish form of this ballad, probably derived from the Swedish; also another Swedish version in Westergötlands Fornminnesförenings Tidskrift, 1869, häfte 1, which I have not yet seen.

of the tale is much as before, with those minor diversities that are to be expected. The lover commonly kills himself, but dies of heart-break in ' Peder Palleson' and one of the sixteenth century Danish copies. In the latter he hears the bells, says he shall never arrive alive, dies without the house and she within; in the former the maid dies in the upper room, the swain on the wild moor. In the Danish manuscript copies the man is laid south in the churchyard, the maid north [west, east], two roses spring from their breasts and span the church-roof, and there they shall stay till doom; in Kristensen it is two lilies, in Arwidsson a linden.

With these last may belong a German ballad of a young Markgraf, who marries a very young wife, goes for her mother upon the approach of a threatening childbirth, and, returning, has encounters similar to those in ' Der Ritter und die Maid.' In some instances it is a Reiter, or Jäger, "wohlgemuth," not married, or in secret relations with his love, who, coming to a wood or heath, hears a bell that alarms him; etc. In the end he generally kills himself, sometimes dies of a broken heart. Lilies in several cases rise from the young woman's grave, or their grave.*

A Romaic ballad has the characteristic features of the English, German, and Scandinavian stories, with a beginning of its own, as these also have : ' Η Εὐγενοῦλα,' ' Ο Χάρος καὶ ἡ Κόρη,' etc. (1) Zambelios, p. 715, 2 = Passow, No 415 ; (2) Passow, No 418 ; (3) Fauriel, p. 112, No 6 = Passow, No 417 ; (4) Marcellus, II, 72 = Passow, No 414 ; (5) Chasiotis, p. 169, No 5 ; (6) Passow, No 416 ; (7) Arabantinos, p. 285, No 472 ; (8) Tommaseo, III, 307 f ; (9) Jeannaraki, p. 239, No 301 ; and

no doubt elsewhere, for the ballad is a favorite. A young girl, who has nine brothers and is betrothed (or perhaps newly married) to a rich pallikar, professes not to fear Death. Death immediately shows his power over her. Her lover, coming with a splendid train to celebrate his nuptials, sees a cross on her mother's gate, a sign that some one has died. In (2) he lifts a gold handkerchief from the face of the dead, and sees that it is his beloved. Or he finds a man digging a grave, and asks for whom the grave is, and is told. " Make the grave deep and broad," he cries ; "make it for two," and stabs himself with his dagger. A clump of reeds springs from one of the lovers, a cypress [lemon-tree] from the other, which bend one towards the other and kiss whenever a strong breeze blows.†

In a Catalan ballad, a young man hears funeral bells, asks for whom they ring, is told that it is for his love, rides to her house, finds the balcony hung with black, kneels at the feet of the dead, and uncovers her face. She speaks and tells him where his gifts to her may be found, then bids him order the carpenter to make a coffin large enough for two. He draws his dagger and stabs himself ; there are two dead in one house ! ' La mort de la Nuvia,' Briz y Candi, I, 135, Milá, Romancerillo, p. 321 f, No 337 A₁₁, B₁₁ ; found also in Majorca.

As will readily be supposed, some of the incidents of this series of ballads are found in traditional song in various connections.

D is translated by Grundtvig, Engelske og skotske Folkeviser, p. 194, No 29 ; by Rose Warrens, Schottische Volkslieder der Vorzeit, p. 115, No 25.

* (1), "Bothe, Frühlings-Almanach," p. 132, 1806 ; ' Hans Markgraf,' Büsching u. von der Hagen, p. 30 ; Erlach, II, 136 ; Mittler, No 133. (2), ' Alle bei Gott die sich lieben,' Wunderhorn, II, 250, 1808, Mittler, No 128. (3), ' Alle bei Gott die sich lieben,' Hoffmann u. Richter, p. 12, No 5, Mittler, No 132. (4), ' Der Graf u. die Bauerntochter,' Ditfurth, II, 8, No 9. (5), ' Vom jungen Markgrafen,' Pogatschnigg u. Hermann, II, 179, No 595. (6), ' Die junge Mutter,' Paudler, p. 22, No 14.

(7), ' Jungfer Dörtchen ist todt,' Parisius, p. 36, No 10. (8), ' Liebchens Tod,' Erk u. Irmer, VI, 4, No 2 ; Mittler, No 130. (9), ' Jägers Trauer,' Pröhle, p. 86, No 57 ; Mittler, No 129. (10), ' Das unverdiente Kränzlein,' Meinert,

p. 32 ; Mittler, No 131. For plants springing from lovers' graves, as here and in Nos 73, 74, see vol. i, 96 ff.

† In (2) the lover is warned of mishap by a bird, and the bird is a nightingale, as in Kristensen, II, No 20 A. A bird of some sort figures in all the Danish ballads referred to, printed and unprinted, and in the Swedish ' Hertig Nils ;' also in the corresponding Finnish ballad. The nightingale warns to the same effect in a French ballad, Beaurepaire, p. 52. The lover goes straight to his mistress's house, and learns that they are burying her ; then makes for the cemetery, hears the bells, the priests chanting, etc., and approaches the bier. The dead gives him some information, followed by some admonition.

A

Percy Papers, communicated by the Rev. P. Parsons, of Wye, from singing; May 22, 1770, and April 19, 1775.

1 'AND I fare you well, Lady Ouncebell,
    For I must needs be gone,
  And this time two year I 'll meet you again,
    To finish the loves we begun.'

2 'That is a long time, Lord Lovill,' said she,
    'To live in fair Scotland;'
  'And so it is, Lady Ouncebell,
    To leave a fair lady alone.'

3 He had not been in fair Scotland
    Not half above half a year,
  But a longin mind came into his head,
    Lady Ouncebell he woud go see her.

4 He called up his stable-groom,
    To sadle his milk-white stead;
  Dey down, dey down, dey down dery down,
    I wish Lord Lovill good speed.

5 He had not been in fair London
    Not half above half a day,
  But he heard the bells of the high chapel ring,
    They rang with a ceserera.

6 He asked of a gentleman,
    That set there all alone,
  What made the bells of the high chapel ring,
    The ladys make all their moan.

7 'One of the king's daughters are dead,' said he,
    'Lady Ouncebell was her name;
  She died for love of a courtous young night,
    Lord Lovill he was the same.'

8 He caused her corps to be set down,
    And her winding sheet undone,
  And he made a vow before them all
    He 'd never kiss wowman again.

9 Lady Ouncebell died on the yesterday,
    Lord Lovill on the morrow;
  Lady Ouncebell died for pure true love,
    Lord Lovill died for sorrow.

10 Lady Ouncebell was buried in the high chancel,
    Lord Lovill in the choir;
  Lady Ouncebell's breast sprung out a sweet rose,
    Lord Lovill's a bunch of sweet brier.

11 They grew till they grew to the top of the church,
    And then they could grow no higher;
  They grew till they grew to a true-lover's not,
    And then they tyed both together.

12 An old wowman coming by that way,
    And a blessing she did crave,
  To cut off a bunch of that true-lover's not,
    And buried them both in one grave.

———✦———

B

Kinloch MSS, I, 45, from the recitation of Mary Barr, of Lesmahago, "aged upwards of 70," May, 1827.

1 LORD LAVEL he stands at his stable-door,
    Kaiming his milk-white steed;
  And by and cam Fair Nancybelle,
    And wished Lord Lavel good speed.

2 'O whare are ye going, Lord Lavel?' she said,
    'I pray ye tell to me:'
  'O I am going to merry England,
    To win your love aff me.'

3 'And when will ye return again?' she said,
    'Lord Lavel, pray tell to me:'

'Whan seven lang years are past and gane,
    Fair Nancybelle, I 'll return to thee.'

4 ''T is too lang, Lord Lavel,' she said,
    ''T is too lang for me;
  'T is too long, Lord Lavel,' she said,
    'A true lover for to see.'

*   *   *   *   *

5 He had na been in merry England
    A month but barely three,
  Till languishing thoughts cam into his mind,
    And Nancybelle fain wad he see.

6 He rade, and he rade, alang the hieway,
   Till he cam to yonder toun;
  He heard the sound o a fine chapel-bell,
   And the ladies were mourning roun.

7 He rade, and he rade, alang the hieway,
   Till he cam to yonder hall;
  He heard the sound o a fine chapel-bell,
   And the ladies were mourning all.

8 He asked wha it was that was dead,
   The ladies did him tell:
  They said, It is the king's daughter,
   Her name is Fair Nancybelle;
  She died for the love of a courteous young
    knicht,
   His name is Lord Lavel.

9 'O hast thou died, Fair Nancybelle,
   O hast thou died for me!

O hast thou died, Fair Nancybelle!
   Then I will die for thee.'

10 Fair Nancybelle died, as it might be, this
    day,
   Lord Lavel he died tomorrow;
  Fair Nancybelle died with pure, pure love,
   Lord Lavel he died with sorrow.

11 Lord Lavel was buried in Mary's kirk,
   Nancybelle in Mary's quire;
  And out o the ane there grew a birk,
   Out the other a bonny brier.

12 And ae they grew, and ae they threw,
   Until they twa did meet,
  That ilka ane might plainly see
   They war twa lovers sweet.

C

Communicated by Mr Alexander Laing, 1873, as taken
down from the recitation of Miss Fanny Walker, of Mount
Pleasant, near Newburgh-on-Tay.

1 LORD TRAVELL stands in his stable-door,
   Dressing his milk-white steed,
  An bye comes Lady Ounceville:
   'I wish you muckle speed.

2 'Oh whar are ye gaun, Lord Travell?' she
    says,
   'Whar are gaun frae me?'
  'I am gaun to London town,
   Some strange things for to see.'

3 'Whan will ye be back, Lord Travell?' she
    says,
   'Whan will ye be back to me?'
  'I will be back in seven lang years,
   To wed my gay ladie.'

4 'Oh that is too lang for me,' she says,
   'Oh that is too lang for me;
  Oh that is too lang for me,' she says,
   'To wed thy gay ladie.'

5 He hadna been in London town
   A week but only three,
  Whan a boding voice thirld in his ear,
   That Scotland he maun see.

6 He rade an he rode alang the highway,
   Till he cam to yon little town:
  'Oh is there ony body dead?
   The bells they mak sic a sound.'

7 He rade an he rode alang the highway,
   Till he cam to yon little town:
  'Oh is there ony body dead?
   The folk gae mournin round.'

8 'Oh yes indeed, there is ane dead,
   Her name is Ounceville;
  An she has died for a courteous knicht,
   His name is Lord Travell.'

9 'Oh hand ye aboot, ye gentlemen,
   The white bread an the wine,
  For the morn's nicht aboot this time
   Ye 'll do the same for mine!'

D

Kinloch MSS, VII, 83, from the recitation of a lady of Roxburghshire; Kinloch's Ancient Scottish Ballads, p. 31.

1 LORD LOVEL stands at his stable-door,
    Mounted upon a grey steed,
And bye cam Ladie Nanciebel,
    And wishd Lord Lovel much speed.

2 'O whare are ye going, Lord Lovel?
    My dearest, tell unto me:'
'I am going a far journey,
    Some strange countrey to see.

3 'But I'll return in seven long years,
    Lady Nanciebel to see:'
'Oh seven, seven, seven long years,
    They are much too long for me.'

*   *   *   *   *

4 He was gane about a year away,
    A year but barely ane,
Whan a strange fancy cam intil his head
    That faire Nanciebel was gane.

5 It's then he rade, and better rade,
    Untill he cam to the toun,
And there he heard a dismal noise,
    For the church bells au did soun.

6 He asked what the bells rang for;
    They said, It's for Nanciebel;
She died for a discourteous squire,
    And his name is Lord Lovel.

7 The lid of the coffin he opened up,
    The linens he faulded doun,
And ae he kissd her pale, pale lips,
    And the tears cam trinkling doun.

8 'Weill may I kiss these pale, pale lips,
    For they will never kiss me;
I'll mak a vow, and I'll keep it true,
    That I'll neer kiss ane but thee.'

9 Lady Nancie died on Tuesday's nicht,
    Lord Lovel upon the niest day;
Lady Nancie died for pure, pure love,
    Lord Lovel for deep sorraye.

E

Communicated by J. F. Campbell, Esq., as learned from the singing of an English gentleman, about 1850.

1 'Now fare ye well, Lady Oonzabel,
    For I must needs be gone,
To visit the king of fair Scotland,
    Oh I must be up and ride.'

2 So he called unto him his little foot-page,
    To saddle his milk-white steed;
Hey down, hey down, hey derry, hey down,
    How I wish my Lord Lovel good speed!

3 He had not been in fair Scotland,
    Not passing half a year,
When a lover-like thought came into his head,
    Lady Oonzabel he would go see her.

4 So he called unto him his little foot-page,
    To saddle his milk-white steed;
Hey down, hey down, hey derry, hey down,
    How I wish my Lord Lovel good speed.

5 He had not been in fair England,
    Not passing half a day,
When the bells of the high chappel did ring,
    And they made a loud sassaray.

6 He asked of an old gentleman
    Who was sitting there all alone,
Why the bells of the high chappel did ring,
    And the ladies were making a moan.

7 'Oh, the king's fair daughter is dead,' said he;
    'Her name's Lady Oonzabel;
And she died for the love of a courteous young knight,
    And his name it is Lord Lovel.'

*   *   *   *   *

8 He caused the bier to be set down,
    The winding sheet undone,
And drawing forth his rapier bright,
    Through his own true heart did it run.

9 Lady Oonzabel lies in the high chappel,
  Lord Lovel he lies in the quier;
And out of the one there grew up a white rose,
  And out of the other a brier.

10 And they grew, and they grew, to the high
    chappel top;
  They could not well grow any higher;
And they twined into a true lover's knot,
  So in death they are joined together.

F

Communicated by Mr Robert White, of Newcastle-on-Tyne.

1 As LORD LOVEL was at the stable-door,
  Mounting his milk-white steed,
Who came by but poor Nancy Bell,
  And she wished Lovel good speed.

2 'O where are ye going, Lord Lovel?' she said,
  'How long to tarry from me?'
'Before six months are past and gone,
  Again I'll return to thee.'

3 He had not been a twelvemonth away,
  A twelvemonth and a day,
Till Nancy Bell grew sick and sad,
  She pined and witherd away.

4 The very first town that he came to,
  He heard the death-bell knell;

The very next town that he came to,
  They said it was Nancy Bell.

5 He orderd the coffin to be broke open,
  The sheet to be turned down,
And then he kissd her cold pale lips,
  Till the tears ran tricklin down.

6 The one was buried in St. John's church,
  The other in the choir;
From Nancy Bell sprang a bonny red rose,
  From Lord Lovel a bonny briar.

7 They grew, and they grew, to the height o the
    church,
  To they met from either side,
And at the top a true lover's knot
  Shows that one for the other had died.

G

Harris MS., fol. 28 b, from the recitation of Mrs Molison, Dunlappie.

1 LORD REVEL he stands in his stable-door,
  He was dressing a milk-white steed;
A lady she stands in her bour-door,
  A dressin with haste an speed.

2 'O where are you goin, Lord Revel,' she said,
  'Where are you going from me?'
'It's I am going to Lonnon toun,
  That fair city for to see.'

3 'When will you be back, Lord Revel?' she
    said,
  'When will you be back to me?'
'I will be back in the space of three years,
  To wed you, my gey ladie.'

4 'That's too long a time for me,' she said,
  'That's too long a time for me;
For I'll be dead long time ere that,
  For want of your sweet companie.'

5 He had not been in Lonnon toun
  A month but barely three,
When word was brought that Isabell
  Was sick, an like to dee.

6 He had not been in Lonnon toun
  A year but barely ane,
When word was brought from Lonnon toun
  That Isabell was gane.

7 He rode an he rode along the high way,
  Till he came to Edenborrow toon:
Is there any fair lady dead,' said he,
  'That the bells gie such a tone?'

8 'Oh yes, there's a ladie, a very fine ladie,
  Her name it is Isabell ;
  She died for the sake of a young Scottish
      knight,
  His name it is Lord Revel.'

9 'Deal well, deal well at Isabell's burial
  The biscuit and the beer,
  An gainst the morrow at this same time
  You 'll aye deal mair and mair.

10 'Deal well, deal well at Isabell's burial
   The white bread and the wine,

An gainst the morn at this same time
  You 'll deal the same at mine.'

11 They dealt well, dealt weel at Isabell's burial
   The biscuit an the beer,
   And gainst the morn at that same time
   They dealt them mair an mair.

12 They dealt weel, dealt weel at Isabell's burial
   The white bread an the wine,
   An gainst the morn at that same time
   They dealt the same again.

H

a. London broadside of 1846, in Dixon's Ancient Poems, Ballads, and Songs of the Peasantry of England, p. 78, Percy Society, vol. XIX. b. Davidson's Universal Melodist, I, 148.

1 LORD LOVEL he stood at his castle-gate,
  Combing his milk-white steed,
  When up came Lady Nancy Belle,
  To wish her lover good speed, speed,
  To wish her lover good speed.

2 'Where are you going, Lord Lovel?' she said,
  'Oh where are you going?' said she ;
  'I'm going, my Lady Nancy Belle,
  Strange countries for to see.'

3 'When will you be back, Lord Lovel?' she
      said,
  'Oh when will you come back?' said she ;
  'In a year or two, or three, at the most,
  I'll return to my fair Nancy.'

4 But he had not been gone a year and a day,
  Strange countries for to see,
  When languishing thoughts came into his
      head,
  Lady Nancy Belle he would go see.

5 So he rode, and he rode, on his milk-white
      steed,
  Till he came to London town,

And there he heard St Pancras bells,
  And the people all mourning round.

6 'Oh what is the matter?' Lord Lovel he said,
  'Oh what is the matter?' said he ;
  'A lord's lady is dead,' a woman replied,
  'And some call her Lady Nancy.'

7 So he ordered the grave to be opened wide,
  And the shroud he turned down,
  And there he kissed her clay-cold lips,
  Till the tears came trickling down.

8 Lady Nancy she died, as it might be, today,
  Lord Lovel he died as tomorrow ;
  Lady Nancy she died out of pure, pure grief,
  Lord Lovel he died out of sorrow.

9 Lady Nancy was laid in St. Pancras church,
  Lord Lovel was laid in the choir ;
  And out of her bosom there grew a red rose,
  And out of her lover's a briar.

10 They grew, and they grew, to the church-stee-
      ple too,
   And then they could grow no higher ;
   So there they entwined in a true-lover's knot,
   For all lovers true to admire.

I

Percy Papers, communicated by Principal Robertson, the historian.

1 THERE came a ghost to Helen's bower,
     Wi monny a sigh and groan:
   'O make yourself ready, at Wednesday at een,
     Fair Helen, you must be gone.'

2 'O gay Death, O gallant Death,
     Will you spare my life sae lang
   Untill I send to merry Primrose,
     Bid my dear lord come hame?'

3 'O gay Helen, O galant Helen,
     I winna spare you sae lang;
   But make yoursell ready, again Wednesday at
       een,
     Fair Helen, you must be gane.'

4 'O where will I get a bonny boy,
     That would win hose and shoon,
   That will rin fast to merry Primrose,
     Bid my dear lord come soon?'

5 O up and speak a little boy,
     That would win hose and shoon:
   'Aft have I gane your errants, lady,
     But by my suth I 'll rin.'

6 When he came to broken briggs
     He bent his bow and swam,
   And when he came to grass growing
     He cast off his shoon and ran.

7 When he came to merry Primrose,
     His lord he was at meat:
   'O my lord, kend ye what I ken,
     Right little wad ye eat.'

8 'Is there onny of my castles broken doun,
     Or onny of my towers won?
   Or is Fair Helen brought to bed
     Of a daughter or a son?'

9 'There 's nane of [your] castles broken doun,
     Nor nane of your towers won,
   Nor is Fair Helen brought to bed
     Of a doghter or a son.'

10 'Gar sadle me the black, black steed,
     Gar sadle me the brown;
   Gar sadle me the swiftest horse
     Eer carried man to town.'

11 First he bursted the bonny black,
     And then he bursted the brown,
   And then he bursted the swiftest steed
     Eer carried man to town.

12 He hadna ridden a mile, a mile,
     A mile but barelins ten,
   When he met four and twenty gallant knights
     Carrying a dead coffin.

13 'Set down, set down Fair Helen's corps,
     Let me look on the dead;'
   And out he took a little pen-knife,
     And he screeded the winding-sheet.

14 O first he kist her rosy cheek,
     And then he kist her chin,
   And then he kist her coral lips,
     But there 's nae life in within.

15 'Gar deal, gar deal the bread,' he says,
     'The bread bat an the wine,
   And at the morn at twelve o'clock
     Ye 's gain as much at mine.'

16 The tane was buried in Mary's kirk,
     The tother in Mary's choir,
   And out of the tane there sprang a birch,
     And out of the tother a briar.

17 The tops of them grew far sundry,
     But the roots of them grew neer,
   And ye may easy ken by that
     They were twa lovers dear.

———◆———

A. *The copy sent Percy in 1770 was slightly re-*
   vised by Parsons; the original was commu-
   nicated in 1775.
     3³. along in.   4⁴. coud speed.
     6³. make.   6⁴. their mourn.

10⁴. *Parsons corrects* bunch *to* branch.
G.   7⁴. bell.
H. a. 10¹. church-steeple too, *perhaps a misprint*
       for top.
     b. *This is an attempt to burlesque the broad-*

side by vulgarizing two or three words, as lovier, buzzum, *and inserting one stanza.*

2⁴, 4². Foreign countries.
3⁸. In a year, or two or three, or four.
4¹. twelve months and a day.
6⁸. dead, the people all said.
7². to be turned. 7⁴. Whilst.
After 7 :

Then he flung his self down by the side
of the corpse,
With a shivering gulp and a guggle;

Gave two hops, three kicks, heavd a
sigh, blew his nose,
Sung a song, and then died in the
struggle.

10¹. church-steeple top.
10⁸. they twin'd themselves into.
I. 3². 'you,' *as if changed or supplied.*
5². *Crossed out. In a different hand,* **Just**
at the lady's chin.
7⁴. would wad ye. 11⁸. swifted.
13⁴. *Perhaps* scriebed.

76

THE LASS OF ROCH ROYAL

A. 'Fair Isabell of Rochroyall,' Elizabeth Cochrane's Song-Book, p. 151, No 114.

B. 'The Bonny Lass of Lochroyan, or Lochroyen,' Herd's MSS, I, 144, II, 60; Herd's Scottish Songs, 1776, I, 149.

C. 'Lord Gregory,' Pitcairn's MSS, III, 1.

D. 'Fair Anny,' Jamieson-Brown MS., fol. 27; 'Fair Annie of Lochroyan,' Jamieson's Popular Ballads, I, 36.

E. a. 'Love Gregor,' Alexander Fraser Tytler's Brown MS., No 2. **b.** 'The Lass of Lochroyan,' Scott's Minstrelsy, II, 49, 1802.

F. Herd's MSS, I, 31, II, 65.

G. 'Love Gregory,' Buchan's MSS, II, 149; Buchan's Ballads of the North of Scotland, II, 198; Dixon, Scottish Traditional Versions of Ancient Ballads, Percy Society, vol. xvii, p. 60.

H. 'The Lass of Aughrim,' an Irish version, communicated by Mr G. C. Mahon, of Ann Arbor, Michigan.

I. 'Oh open the door, Lord Gregory,' Johnson's Museum, I, 5, No 5, four stanzas.

J. Motherwell's Note-Book, p. 12, two stanzas.

K. Stenhouse's Johnson's Museum, IV, *107, one stanza.

A, NEVER as yet published, is from a manuscript of the first half of the last century. B, the earliest printed copy, was given by Herd, from his manuscript, in 1776, with his usual fidelity. Scott followed, in 1802, with a copy obtained from Mrs Brown by Alexander Fraser Tytler in 1800, introducing six stanzas from B and five from F, and a few readings from two recited copies. This compounded copy is the one that is most generally known. Jamieson printed, in 1806, D, a version written down from Mrs Brown's reci-

tation in 1783, giving it not quite *verbatim*, as he says (he changes, for instance, Rochroyal to Lochroyan), but in general adhering to his text. E a, the copy principally used by Scott, is, to a considerable extent, a repetition of D, but is by no means an imperfectly remembered version of its predecessor (which was written down seventeen years earlier), filled out by Mrs Brown's improvised inventions. E a has stanzas not found in D, two of which occur in B, and is to be regarded as a blending of two independent versions known to

Mrs Brown, which no doubt had much in common, though not so much as **D** and **E a**. The whole of the fragment **F** has not been published hitherto, but five of the eight stanzas are interpolated into Scott's copy, including the two last, which are shown by the very style to be spurious. Fairy charms have been exercised on Lord Gregory, according to the final stanza of **F**, and Lord Gregory calls his dame " witch mother " in **C** 10. But there appears to be no call for magic or witchcraft in the case. A man who is asleep is simply not informed by an ill disposed mother that a woman whom he would like to see is at the door; that is all.*

A, the oldest copy, has a preliminary history wanting in the others. Isabel of Rochroyal has a dream about her lover. She orders her horse, to ride till she comes to some hold. She meets a company, who ask her questions about a first and a second young may, which *she* seems to understand, but which are not made intelligible to us. They then ask whether she be Isabel of Rochroyal, and she answers that she is that same lady, banished from kith and kin; why, we are not informed, but we might conjecture that it would be on account of her relations with Love Gregory. She is directed to Gregory's castle, tirls at the pin, and begs admission. Gregory's mother answers as and for her son, and demands proofs of her being the lass of Rochroyal. These are given, and the mother says that Gregory is gone to sea. Hereupon Isabel breaks out into exclamations as to her helpless condition; who will take care of her? who will be the bairn's father till Gregory come home? The mother replies that she will do all that is necessary for her, but there is none to be her bairn's father till Gregory return. This is in itself unnatural, since the mother is hostile to her son's love, and it is counter to what we read in the other versions. In **B** as in **A**, to be sure, the lass is said to be banished from her kin, but her kin nevertheless show a disposition to do all that is

in their power in the way of kind attentions. The other copies say nothing of her family being alienated. The father in **D** even furnishes his daughter with a bonny ship, to go to her true-love. If we seek to reconcile these accounts, we must take the banishment as a separation for which only the fates are responsible, and suppose that verses are lost in **A** after 17 which narrated Annie's return to her own family. The lass says, st. 22, that she will set her foot on ship-board, having been told by the mother, st. 17, that Gregory is on the sea. Gregory, in turn, has his dream, that his love has been knocking at the door, and his mother tells him that she has not been gone half an hour, and gets his curses for not informing him. Gregory orders his swiftest horse, to ride till he comes to some hold, and presently meets a funeral train who are carrying his love to burial. This conclusion, found also in **B**, **C**, is that of ' Lord Lovel ' and ' Fair Margaret and Sweet William,' and must perhaps be set aside as not the original one. In **B** Gregory kills himself, as Lord Lovel does in one copy, **E**.

The whole story as **A** actually stands, notwithstanding that the lass says she will take ship, seems to pass on land. Two different relations may have been confounded. In the other versions Love Gregory is somewhere over sea, and in **B**, **F** his lass is indebted for his direction, not to a company who are raking over the lea, but to a sea-rover, who shows a consideration not to be looked for from his class.†　The maid, repulsed by Gregory's mother, and supposing herself to be cast off by Gregory himself, sails away from his castle, and in **D**, **E** encounters a storm, and is wrecked. In **D** Gregory rushes to the strand near which his castle lies, sees Annie sailing away, witnesses the wreck of her vessel, plunges into the sea and brings her body to land, and dies of heartbreak. So in **E**, with the difference that Annie's body is thrown ashore by the waves, and that the tale does not finish with the death of Gregory, which we know must have followed.

---

* Jamieson tells us, p. 44, that when a boy he had frequently heard the ballad chanted in Morayshire, and no mention was ever made of " fairy charms."

† **C** 3, 4 are evidently misplaced, and belong in that part of the story where **B** 8, 9 occur.

Why the lovers are parted, why Gregory winna come to the lass, and she must go to him, is not accounted for in C-G. We may deduce from A and B, though the story in these versions as we have it is not altogether consistent, that the lass was banished from kith and kin on account of her connection with Gregory (which in B 16 and H 9 is said to have been irregular) and flying to her lover, found no acceptance with his mother.

Cunningham has rewritten this ballad, Scottish Songs, I, 298, and several songs have been composed on the story: by Burns and Dr Wolcott (Peter Pindar), Thomson's Select Melodies of Scotland, I, 37, ed. 1822; Jamieson, Popular Ballads, I, 46; and by an anonymous writer in a London periodical, cited by Dixon, Scottish Traditional Versions of Ancient Ballads, p. 99.

Roch- or Rough-royal, A, D, E, F, Ruchlawhill, C, I have not found, but there is a Rough castle in Stirlingshire. Loch Ryan runs up into the north-west corner of Wigtown, a shire at the south-west extremity of Scotland. Aughrim is in the county of Roscommon, Ireland.

As the mother in this ballad, feigning to be her son, requires the lady at the gate to legitimate herself by mentioning some of the tokens which have been exchanged between her and her lover, so in other ballads a wife demands conclusive proofs that a man claiming to be her long absent husband is what he pretends to be. E. g., some forms of the French ballad of 'Germaine:'

'Ouvre ta port', Germin', c'est moi qu'est ton mari.'
'Donnez-moi des indic's de la première nuit,
Et par là je croirai que vous êt's mon mari.'

'T'en souviens-tu, Germin', de la première nuit,
Où tu étais monté' sur un beau cheval gris,
Placée entre tes frèr's et moi ton favori?'

'Donnez-moi des indic's de la deuxième nuit,
Et par là je croirai que vous êt's mon mari,
Et par là je croirai que vous êt's mon mari.'

'T'en souviens-tu, Germin', de la deuxième nuit?
En te serrant les doigts ton anneau y cassa,
Tu en as la moitié, et l'autre la voilà.'

Champfleury, Chansons populaires des Provinces, p. 196.

Cf. Poésies pop. de la France, MS., IV, fol. 189; Puymaigre, p. 11, 2d ed., I, 50 f; Beaurepaire, p. 76; Fleury, p. 267; Rathery, in Le Moniteur, Aug. 26, 1853, p. 945 f, 'Le Sire de Créqui;' Wolf, Volkslieder aus Venetien, No 81, p. 59; Ferraro, Canti p. monferrini, No 26, p. 33. And again in Romaic: Ἡ Ἀναγνώρισις, etc.; Fauriel, II, 422–25; Tommaseo, III, 141–44, 148–50; Marcellus, Chants du Peuple en Grèce, I, 328; Schmidt, Griechische Märchen, u. s. w., p. 192, No 57; Chasiotis, p. 29, No 28; Zambelios, p. 718, No 5; Jeannaraki, p. 237, No 300; Arabantinos, pp 209, 211, Nos 347, 348; Passow, pp 321–28, Nos 441–446; Manousos, p. 103 = Fauriel, II, 423. Several of the ballads in Passow are of course repetitions.*

D is translated, after Jamieson, by Grundtvig, Engelske og skotske Folkeviser, No 16; E b, Scott's compounded version, by Schubart, p. 93, Doenniges, p. 33, Gerhard, p. 21, Wolff, Halle der Völker, I, 52, and by Rosa Warrens, Schottische Volkslieder der Vorzeit, No 39, with a change or two from Aytoun; Allingham's compounded version by Knortz, Lieder u. Romanzen Alt-Englands, No 63.

A

E. Cochrane's Songbook, p. 151, No 114.

1 FAIR ISABELL of Rochroyall,
    She dreamed where she lay,

She dreamd a dream of her love Gregory,
    A litle before the day.

* Liebrecht has noted many of the above in his 'Volkskunde.' A man requires identification of a woman in a very ill preserved ballad in Motherwell's MS., p. 320.

2 O huly, huly rose she up,
 And huly she put on,
And huly, huly she put on
 The silks of crimsion.

3 ' Gar sadle me the black,' she sayes,
 ' Gar sadle me the broun ;
Gar sadle me the swiftest steed
 That ever rode the toun.

4 ' Gar shoe him with the beat silver,
 And grind him with the gold ;
Gar put two bells on every side,
 Till I come to some hold.'

5 She had not rode a mile, a mile,
 A mile but barely three,
Till that she spyed a companie
 Come rakeing oere the lee.

6 ' O whether is this the first young may,
 That lighted and gaed in ;
Or is this the second young may,
 That neer the sun shined on ?
Or is this Fair Isabell of Roch Royall,
 Banisht from kyth and kin.'

7 ' O I am not the first young may,
 That lighted and gaed in ;
Nor neither am I the second young may,
 That neer the sun shone on ;

8 ' But I 'm Fair Isabell of Roch Royall
 Banisht from kyth and kin ;
I 'm seeking my true-love Gregory,
 And I woud I had him in.'

9 ' O go your way to yon castle,
 And ride it round about,
And there you 'll find Love Gregory ;
 He 's within, without any doubt.'

10 O she 's away to yon castle,
 She 's tirled at the pin :
' O open, open, Love Gregory,
 And let your true-love in.'

11 ' If you be the lass of the Rochroyall,
 As I trow not you be,
You will tell me some of our love-tokens,
 That was betwixt you and me.'

12 ' Have you not mind, Love Gregory,
 Since we sat at the wine ;

When we changed the rings off our fingers,
 And ay the worst fell mine ?

13 ' Mine was of the massy gold,
 And thine was of the tin ;
Mine was true and trusty both,
 And thine was false within.'

14 If you be [the] lass of the Roch Royall,
 As I trow not you be,
You will tell me some other love-token
 That was betwixt you and me.'

15 ' Have you not mind, Love Gregory,
 Since we sat at the wine,
We changed the smocks off our two backs,
 And ay the worst fell mine ?

16 ' Mine was of the holland fine,
 And thine was course and thin ;
So many blocks have we two made,
 And ay the worst was mine.'

17 ' Love Gregory, he is not at home,
 But he is to the sea ;
If you have any word to him,
 I pray you leave 't with me.'

  * * * * *

18 ' O who will shoe my bony foot ?
 Or who will glove my hand ?
Or who will bind my midle jimp
 With the broad lilly band ?

19 ' Or who will comb my bony head
 With the red river comb ?
Or who will be my bairn's father
 Ere Gregory he come home ? '

20 ' O I 's gar shoe thy bony foot,
 And I 's gar glove thy hand,
And I 's gar bind thy midle jimp
 With the broad lilly band.

21 ' And I 's gar comb thy bony head
 With the red river comb ;
But there is none to be thy bairn's father
 Till Love Gregory he come home.

22 ' I 'll set my foot on the ship-board,
 God send me wind and more !
For there 's never a woman shall bear a son
 Shall make my heart so sore.'

23 'I dreamed a dream now since yestreen,
     That I never dreamed before;
  I dreamd that the lass of the Rochroyall
     Was knocking at the door.'

24 'Ly still, ly still, my é dear son,
     Ly still, and take a sleep;
  For it 's neither ane hour, nor yet a half,
     Since she went from the gate.'

25 'O wo be to you, ill woman,
     And ane ill death mott you die!
  For you might have come to my bed-side,
     And then have wakened me.

26 'Gar sadle me the black,' he sayes,
     'Gar sadle me the broun;
  Gar sadle me the swiftest steed
     That ever rode the toun.

27 'Gar shoe him with the beat silver,
     Gar grind him with the gold;
  Cause put two bells on every side,
     Till I come to some hold.'

28 They sadled him the black, the black,
     So did they him the broun;
  So did they him the swiftest steed
     That ever rode to toun.

29 They shoed him with the beat silver,
     They grind him with the gold;
  They put two bells on every side,
     Till he came to some hold.

30 He had not rode a mile, a mile,
     A mile but barely three,
  Till that he spyed her comely corps
     Come raking oere the lee.

31 'Set doun, set doun these comely corps,
     Let me look on the dead:'
  And out he 's ta'en his little pen-knife,
     And slitted her winding sheet.

32 And first he kist her cheek, her cheek,
     And then he kist her chin;
  And then he kist her rosy lips,
     But there was no breath within.

33 'Gar deall, gar deall for my love sake
     The spiced bread and the wine;
  For ere the morn at this time,
     So shall you deall for mine.

34 'Gar deall, gar deall for my love sake
     The pennys that are so small.;
  For ere the morn at this time,
     So shall you deall for all.'

35 The one was buried in Mary kirk,
     The other in Mary quire;
  Out of the one there sprung a birk,
     Out of the other a bryar;
  So thus you may well know by that
     They were two lovers dear.

B

Herd's MS, I, 144; II, 60, the first ten lines; Herd's
Scottish Songs, 1776, I, 149.

1 'O WHA will shoe thy bonny feet?
     Or wha will glove thy hand?
  Or wha will lace thy midle jimp,
     With a lang, lang London whang?

2 'And wha will kame thy bonny head,
     With a tabean brirben kame?
  And wha will be my bairn's father,
     Till Love Gregory come hame?'

3 'Thy father 'll shoe his bonny feet,
     Thy mither 'll glove his hand;

Thy brither will lace his middle jimp,
   With a lang, lang London whang.

4 'Mysel will kame his bonny head,
     With a tabean brirben kame;
  And the Lord will be the bairn's father,
     Till Love Gregory come hame.'

5 Then she 's gart build a bonny ship,
     It 's a' cored oer with pearl,
  And at every needle-tack was in 't
     There hang a siller bell.

6 And she 's awa .   .   .
     To sail upon the sea;

She 's gane to seek Love Gregory,
    In lands whereer he be.

7 She hadna saild a league but twa,
    O scantly had she three,
Till she met with a rude rover,
    Was sailing on the sea.

8 ' O whether is thou the Queen hersel,
    Or ane o her maries three ?
Or is thou the lass of Lochroyan,
    Seeking Love Gregory ? '

9 ' O I am not the Queen hersell,
    Nor ane o her maries three ;
But I am the lass o Lochroyan,
    Seeking Love Gregory.

10 ' O sees na thou yone bonny bower ?
    It 's a' cored oer with tin ;
When thou hast saild it round about,
    Love Gregory is within.'

11 When she had saild it round about,
    She tirled at the pin :
' O open, open, Love Gregory,
    Open, and let me in !
For I am the lass of Lochroyan,
    Banisht frae a' my kin.'

12 ' If thou be the lass of Lochroyan,
    As I know no thou be,
Tell me some of the true tokens
    That past between me and thee.'

13 ' Hast thou na mind, Love Gregory,
    As we sat at the wine,
We changed the rings aff ither's hands,
    And ay the best was mine ?

14 ' For mine was o the gude red gould,
    But thine was o the tin ;
And mine was true and trusty baith,
    But thine was fa'se within.

15 ' If thou be the lass of Lochroyan,
    As I know na thou be,
Tell me some mair o the true tokens
    Past between me and thee.'

16 ' And has na thou na mind, Love Gregory,
    As we sat on yon hill,

Thou twin'd me of my [maidenhead,]
    Right sair against my will ?

17 ' Now open, open, Love Gregory,
    Open, and let me in !
For the rain rains on my gude cleading,
    And the dew stands on my chin.'

18 Then she has turnd her round about :
    ' Well, since that it be sae,
Let never woman that has born a son
    Hae a heart sae full of wae.

19 ' Take down, take down that mast o gould,
    Set up a mast of tree ;
For it dinna become a forsaken lady
    To sail so royallie.'

20 ' I dreamt a dream this night, mother,
    I wish it may prove true,
That the bonny lass of Lochroyan
    Was at the gate just now.'

21 ' Lie still, lie still, my only son,
    And sound sleep mayst thou get,
For it 's but an hour or little mair
    Since she was at the gate.'

22 Awa, awa, ye wicket woman,
    And an ill dead may ye die !
Ye might have ither letten her in,
    Or else have wakened me.

23 ' Gar saddle to me the black,' he said,
    ' Gar saddle to me the brown ;
Gar saddle to me the swiftest steed
    That is in a' the town.'

24 Now the first town that he cam to,
    The bells were ringing there ;
And the neist toun that he cam to,
    Her corps was coming there.

25 ' Set down, set down that comely corp,
    Set down, and let me see
Gin that be the lass of Lochroyan,
    That died for love o me.'

26 And he took out the little penknife
    That hang down by his gare,
And he 's rippd up her winding-sheet,
    A lang claith-yard and mair.

27 And first he kist her cherry cheek,
    And syne he kist her chin,
And neist he kist her rosy lips ;
    There was nae breath within.

28 And he has taen his little penknife,
    With a heart that was fou sair,
He has given himself a deadly wound,
    And word spake never mair.

C

Pitcairn's MSS, III, 1, from the singing of Widow Stevenson.

*   *   *   *   *

1 SHE sailed west, she sailed east,
    She sailed mony a mile,
Until she cam to Lord Gregor's yett,
    And she tirled at the pin.

2 'It 's open, open, Lord Gregory,
    Open, and let me in ;
For the rain drops on my gouden hair,
    And drops upon your son.'

3 ' Are you the Queen of Queensberry ?
    Or one of the marys three ?
Or are you the lass of Ruchlaw hill,
    Seeking Lord Gregory ? '

4 ' I 'm not the Queen of Queensberry,
    Nor one of the marys three ;
But I am the bonny lass of Ruchlawhill,
    Seeking Lord Gregory.'

5 ' Awa, awa, ye fause thief,
    I will not open to thee
Till you tell me the first token
    That was tween you and me.'

6 ' Do not you mind, Lord Gregory,
    When we birled at the wine,
We changed the rings of our fingers,
    And ay the best was mine ?

7 ' For mine was true and trusty goud,
    But yours it was of tin ;
Mine was of the true and trusty goud,
    But yours was fause within.'

8 She turned about her bonny ship,
    Awa then did she sail:
' The sun shall never shine on man
    That made my heart so sare.'

9 Then up the old mother she got,
    And wakened Lord Gregory :
' Awa, awa, ye fause gudeson,
    A limmer was seeking thee.'

10 ' It 's woe be to you, witch-mother,
    An ill death may you die !
For you might hae set the yet open,
    And then hae wakened me.'

11 It 's up he got, and put on his clothes,
    And to the yet he ran ;
The first sight of the ship he saw,
    He whistled and he sang.

12 But whan the bonny ship was out o sight,
    He clapped his hands and ran,

.   .   .   .   .

.   .   .   .   .

13 The first kirktoun he cam to,
    He heard the death-bell ring,
The second kirktoun he cam to,
    He saw her corpse come in.

14 ' Set down, set down this bonny corpse,
    That I may look upon ;
If she died late for me last night,
    I 'll die for her the morn.

15 ' Be merry, merry, gentlemen,
    Be merry at the bread and wine ;
For by the morn at this time o day
    You 'll drink as much at mine.'

16 The one was buried in Mary's isle,
    The other in Mary's quire ;
Out of the one there grew a thorn,
    And out of the other a brier.

17 And aye they grew, and aye they blew,
    Till their twa taps did meet ;
And every one that passed thereby
    Might see they were lovers sweet.

D

Jamieson-Brown MS., fol. 27; Jamieson's Popular Ballads, I, 36.

1 ' O WHA will shoe my fu fair foot ?
    An wha will glove my han ?
  An wha will lace my middle gimp
    Wi the new made London ban ?

2 ' Or wha will kemb my yellow hair,
    Wi the new made silver kemb ?
  Or wha 'll be father to my young bairn,
    Till Love Gregor come hame ? '

3 Her father shoed her fu fair foot,
    Her mother glovd her han ;
  Her sister lac'd her middle gimp
    Wi the new made London ban.

4 Her brother kembd her yellow hair,
    Wi the new made silver kemb,
  But the king o heaven maun father her bairn,
    Till Love Gregor come hame.

5 ' O gin I had a bony ship,
    An men to sail wi me,
  It 's I would gang to my true-love,
    Since he winna come to me.'

6 Her father 's gien her a bonny ship,
    An sent her to the stran ;
  She 's tane her young son in her arms,
    An turnd her back to the lan.

7 She had na been o the sea saillin
    About a month or more,
  Till landed has she her bonny ship
    Near her true-love's door.

8 The night was dark, an the win blew caul,
    An her love was fast asleep,
  An the bairn that was in her twa arms
    Fu sair began to weep.

9 Long stood she at her true-love's door,
    An lang tirld at the pin ;
  At length up gat his fa'se mither,
    Says, Wha 's that woud be in ?

10 ' O it is Anny of Roch-royal,
    Your love, come oer the sea,
  But an your young son in her arms ;
    So open the door to me.'

11 ' Awa, awa, you ill woman,
    You 've na come here for gude ,
  You 're but a witch, or wile warlock,
    Or mermaid o the flude.'

12 ' I 'm na a witch, or wile warlock,
    Nor mermaiden,' said she ;
  ' I 'm but Fair Anny o Roch-royal ;
    O open the door to me.'

13 ' O gin ye be Anny o Roch-royal,
    As [I] trust not ye be,
  What taiken can ye gie that ever
    I kept your company ? '

14 ' O dinna ye mind, Love Gregor,' she says,
    ' Whan we sat at the wine,
  How we changed the napkins frae our necks,
    It 's na sae lang sin syne ?

15 ' An yours was good, an good enough,
    But nae sae good as mine ;
  For yours was o the cumbruk clear,
    But mine was silk sae fine.

16 ' An dinna ye mind, Love Gregor,' she says,
    ' As we twa sat at dine,
  How we changed the rings frae our fingers,
    But ay the best was mine?

17 ' For yours was good, an good enough,
    Yet nae sae good as mine ;
  For yours was of the good red gold,
    But mine o the diamonds fine.

18 ' Sae open the door now, Love Gregor,
    An open it wi speed,
  Or your young son that is in my arms
    For cauld will soon be dead.'

19 ' Awa, awa, you ill woman,
    Gae frae my door for shame ;
  For I hae gotten another fair love,
    Sae ye may hye you hame.'

20 ' O hae you gotten another fair love,
    For a' the oaths you sware ?
  Then fair you well now, fa'se Gregor,
    For me you 's never see mair.'

21 O heely, heely gi'd she back,
    As the day began to peep ;

She set her foot on good ship-board,
    An sair, sair did she weep.

22 Love Gregor started frae his sleep,
    An to his mither did say,
I dreamd a dream this night, mither,
    That maks my heart right wae.

23 'I dreamd that Anny of Roch-royal,
    The flowr o a' her kin,
Was standin mournin at my door,
    But nane would lat her in.'

24 'O there was a woman stood at the door,
    Wi a bairn intill her arms,
But I woud na lat her within the bowr,
    For fear she had done you harm.'

25 O quickly, quickly raise he up,
    An fast ran to the stran,
An there he saw her Fair Anny,
    Was sailin frae the lan.

26 An 'Heigh, Anny!' an 'Hou, Anny!
    O Anny, speak to me!'
But ay the louder that he cried Anny,
    The louder roard the sea.

27 An 'Heigh, Anny!' an 'Hou, Anny!
    O Anny, winna you bide?'

But ay the langer that he cried Anny,
    The higher roard the tide.

28 The win grew loud, an the sea grew rough,
    An the ship was rent in twain,
An soon he saw her Fair Anny
    Come floating oer the main.

29 He saw his young son in her arms,
    Baith tossd aboon the tide;
He wrang his hands, than fast he ran,
    An plung'd i the sea sae wide.

30 He catchd her by the yallow hair,
    An drew her to the strand,
But cauld an stiff was every limb
    Before he reachd the land.

31 O first he kissd her cherry cheek,
    An then he kissd her chin;
An sair he kissd her ruby lips,
    But there was nae breath within.

32 O he has mournd oer Fair Anny
    Till the sun was gaing down,
Then wi a sigh his heart it brast,
    An his soul to heaven has flown.

E

a. Alexander Fraser Tytler's Brown MS., No 2, written down from Mrs Brown's recitation in 1800. b. Scott's Minstrelsy, II, 49, 1802.

1 'O WHA will shoe my fu fair foot?
    And wha will glove my hand?
And wha will lace my middle jimp,
    Wi the new made London band?

2 'And wha will kaim my yellow hair,
    Wi the new made silver kaim?
And wha will father my young son,
    Till Love Gregor come hame?'

3 'Your father will shoe your fu fair foot,
    Your mother will glove your hand;
Your sister will lace your middle jimp
    Wi the new made London band.

4 'Your brother will kaim your yellow hair,
    Wi the new made silver kaim;
And the king of heaven will father your bairn,
    Till Love Gregor come haim.'

5 'But I will get a bonny boat,
    And I will sail the sea,
For I maun gang to Love Gregor,
    Since he canno come hame to me.'

6 O she has gotten a bonny boat,
    And saild the sa't sea fame;
She langd to see her ain true-love,
    Since he could no come hame.

7 'O row your boat, my mariners,
    And bring me to the land,
For yonder I see my love's castle,
    Closs by the sa't sea strand.'

8 She has taen her young son in her arms,
      And to the door she 's gone,
   And lang she 's knocked and sair she ca'd,
      But answer got she none.

9 ' O open the door, Love Gregor,' she says,
      ' O open, and let me in ;
   For the wind blaws thro my yellow hair,
      And the rain draps oer my chin.'

10 ' Awa, awa, ye ill woman,
      You 'r nae come here for good ;
   You 'r but some witch, or wile warlock,
      Or mer-maid of the flood.'

11 ' I am neither a witch nor a wile warlock,
      Nor mer-maid of the sea,
   I am Fair Annie of Rough Royal ;
      O open the door to me.'

12 ' Gin ye be Annie of Rough Royal —
      And I trust ye are not she —
   Now tell me some of the love-tokens
      That past between you and me.'

13 ' O dinna you mind now, Love Gregor,
      When we sat at the wine,
   How we changed the rings frae our fingers ?
      And I can show thee thine.

14 ' O yours was good, and good enneugh,
      But ay the best was mine ;
   For yours was o the good red goud,
      But mine o the dimonds fine.

15 ' But open the door now, Love Gregor,
      O open the door I pray,
   For your young son that is in my arms
      Will be dead ere it be day.'

16 ' Awa, awa, ye ill woman,
      For here ye shanno win in ;
   Gae drown ye in the raging sea,
      Or hang on the gallows-pin.'

17 When the cock had crawn, and day did dawn,
      And the sun began to peep,
   Then it raise him Love Gregor,
      And sair, sair did he weep.

18 ' O I dreamd a dream, my mother dear,
      The thoughts o it gars me greet,

That Fair Annie of Rough Royal
      Lay cauld dead at my feet.'

19 ' Gin it be for Annie of Rough Royal
      That ye make a' this din,
   She stood a' last night at this door,
      But I trow she wan no in.'

20 ' O wae betide ye, ill woman,
      An ill dead may ye die !
   That ye woudno open the door to her,
      Nor yet woud waken me.'

21 O he has gone down to yon shore-side,
      As fast as he could fare ;
   He saw Fair Annie in her boat,
      But the wind it tossd her sair.

22 And ' Hey, Annie ! ' and ' How, Annie !
      O Annie, winna ye bide ? '
   But ay the mair that he cried Annie,
      The braider grew the tide.

23 And ' Hey, Annie ! ' and ' How, Annie !
      Dear Annie, speak to me ! '
   But ay the louder he cried Annie,
      The louder roard the sea.

24 The wind blew loud, the sea grew rough,
      And dashd the boat on shore ;
   Fair Annie floats on the raging sea,
      But her young son raise no more.

25 Love Gregor tare his yellow hair,
      And made a heavy moan ;
   Fair Annie's corpse lay at his feet,
      But his bonny young son was gone.

26 O cherry, cherry was her cheek,
      And gowden was her hair,
   But clay cold were her rosey lips,
      Nae spark of life was there.

27 And first he 's kissd her cherry cheek,
      And neist he 's kissed her chin ;
   And saftly pressd her rosey lips,
      But there was nae breath within.

28 ' O wae betide my cruel mother,
      And an ill dead may she die !
   For she turnd my true-love frae my door,
      When she came sae far to me.'

F

Herd MS., I, 31, II, 65.

1 ' O WHA will lace my steys, mother ?
      O wha will gluve my hand ?
   O wha will be my bairn's father,
      While my luve cums to land ? '

2 ' O sall I lace your steys, dochter,
      O sall I gluve your hand ;
   And God will be your bairn's father,
      While your luve cums to land.'

3 Now she 's gard build a bonie schip,
      Forbidden she wad nae be ;
   She 's gane wi four score mariners,
      Sailand the salt, salt sea.

4 They had nae saild but twenty legues,
      Bot twenty legues and three,
   When they met wi the ranke robers,
      And a' their companie.

5 ' Now whether are ye the Queen hersell ?
      For so ye weel micht bee,
   Or are ye the lass o the Ruch Royal,
      Seekand Lord Gregorie ? '

6 ' O I am neither the Queen,' she sed,
      ' Nor sick I seem to be ;
   But I am the lass o the Ruch Royal,
      Seekand Lord Gregorie.'

*   *   *   *   *

7 And when she saw the stately tower,
      Shynand sae cleere and bricht,
   Whilk proud defies the jawing wave,
      Built on a rock a hicht,

8 Sche sailed it round, and sailed it sound,
      And loud, loud cried she,
   ' Now break, now break, ye fairy charms,
      And let the prisoner free.'

———————

G

Buchan's MSS. II, 149 ; Buchan's Ballads of the North of Scotland, II, 198.

1 IT fell on a Wodensday,
      Love Gregory 's taen the sea,
   And he has left his lady Janet,
      And a weary woman was she.

2 But she had na been in child-bed
      A day but barely three,
   Till word has come to Lady Janet
      Love Gregory she would never see.

3 She 's taen her mantle her middle about,
      Her cane into her hand,
   And she 's awa to the salt-sea side,
      As fast as she could gang.

4 ' Whare will I get a curious carpenter,
      Will make a boat to me ?
   I'm going to seek him Love Gregory,
      In 's lands where eer he be.'

5 ' Here am I, a curious carpenter,
      Will make a boat for thee,
   And ye may seek him Love Gregory,
      But him ye 'll never see.'

6 She sailed up, she sailed down,
      Thro many a pretty stream,
   Till she came to that stately castle,
      Where Love Gregory lay in.

7 ' Open, open, Love Gregory,
      O open, and lat me in ;
   Your young son is in my arms,
      And shivering cheek and chin.'

8 ' Had awa, ye ill woman,
      Had far awa frae me ;
   Ye 're but some witch, or some warlock,
      Or the mermaid, troubling me.

9 ' My lady she 's in Lochranline,
      Down by Lochlearn's green ;
   This day she wadna sail the sea,
      For goud nor warld's gain.

10 ' But if ye be my lady Janet,
       As I trust not well ye be,
    Come tell me oer some love-token
       That past 'tween thee an me.'

11 ' Mind on, mind on now, Love Gregory,
       Since we sat at the wine ;

The rings that were on your fingers,
I gied thee mine for thine.

12 'And mine was o the good red goud,
    Yours o the silly tin,
    And mine 's been true, and very true,
    But yours had a fause lynin.

13 'But open, open, Love Gregory,
    Open, and let me in;
    Your young son is in my arms,
    He 'll be dead ere I win in.'

14 'Had awa, ye ill woman,
    Had far awa frae me;
    Ye 're but some witch, or some warlock,
    Or the mermaid, troubling me.

15 'But if ye be my lady Janet,
    As I trust not well ye be;
    Come tell me o'er some love-token
    That past tween thee and me.'

16 'Mind on, mind on, Love Gregory,
    Since we sat at the wine;
    The shifts that were upon your back,
    I gave thee mine for thine.

17 'And mine was o the good holland,
    And yours o the silly twine,
    And mine 's been true, and very true,
    But yours had fause lynin.'

*   *   *   *   *

H

Communicated by Mr G. C. Mahon, of Ann Arbor, Michigan, as sung by a laborer, at Tyrrelspass, West Meath, Ireland, about 1830.

1 'OH who 'll comb my yellow locks,
    With the brown berry comb?
    And who 'll be the child's father,
    Until Gregory comes home?'

2 'Oh   .   .   .   .
    .   .   .   .   .   .
    And God will be the child's father,
    Until Gregory comes home.'

*   *   *   *   *

3 'The dew wets my yellow locks,
    The rain wets my skin,
    The babe 's cold in my arms,
    Oh Gregory, let me in!'

4 'Oh if you be the lass of Aughrim,
    As I suppose you not to be,
    Come tell me the last token
    Between you and me.'
    The dew wets, etc.

5 'Oh Gregory, don't you remember
    One night on the hill,
    When we swapped rings off each other's hands,
    Sorely against my will?'

Mine was of the beaten gold,
    Yours was but black tin.'
    The dew wets, etc.

6 'Oh if you be the lass of Aughrim,
    As I suppose you not to be,
    Come tell me the last token
    Between you and me.'
    The dew wets, etc.

7 'Oh Gregory don't you remember
    One night on the hill,
    When we swapped smocks off each other's
        backs,
    Sorely against my will?
    Mine was of the holland fine,
    Yours was but Scotch cloth.'
    The dew wets, etc.

8 'Oh if you be the lass of Aughrim,
    As I suppose you not to be,
    Come tell me the last token
    Between you and me.'
    The dew wets, etc.

9 'Oh Gregory, don't you remember,
    In my father's hall,
    When you had your will of me?
    And that was worse than all.'
    .   .   .   .   .
    .   .   .   .   .
    The dew wets, etc.

I

Johnson's Museum, I, 5, No 5, 1787.

1 'OH open the door, Lord Gregory,
    Oh open, and let me in ;
  The rain rains on my scarlet robes,
    The dew drops oer my chin.'

2 'If you are the lass that I lovd once,
    As I true you are not she,
  Come give me some of the tokens
    That past between you and me.'

3 'Ah wae be to you, Gregory,
    An ill death may you die !
  You will not be the death of one,
    But you 'll be the death of three.

4 'Oh don't you mind, Lord Gregory,
    'T was down at yon burn-side
  We changd the ring of our fingers,
    And I put mine on thine ? '

J

Motherwell's Note-Book, p. 12.

1 ' O WHA will shoe my pretty little foot?
    And wha will glove my hand ?
  And who will lace my middle jimp
    Wi this lang London whang ?

2 'And wha will comb my yellow, yellow hair,
    Wi this fine rispen kame ?
  And wha will be my bairn's father,
    Till Lord Gregory come hame ? '

K

Stenhouse's Johnson's Museum, IV, *107, communicated
by Kirkpatrick Sharpe, " as generally sung by the people of
Galloway and Dumfriesshire."

' O OPEN the door, Love Gregory,
    O open, and let me in ;
  The wind blows through my yellow hair,
    And the dew draps oer my chin.'

A. 8². kine.
    11. His mother: *margin of the MS.*
    20. Mother: *margin.* 22. Lady.
    23. Gregory: *margin.* 24. Mother: *margin.*
B. 1³. who. 2², 4². *Herd prints* Tabean birben.
    12. His mother speaks to her from the house
        and she thinks it him: *margin of the
        MS.*
    14¹. has (?). 15 *follows* 17 *in the MS.*
    16³. *Herd prints* maidenhead.
    20. The son speaks : *margin.*
    25¹. corp (?).
C. *After* 2. Then Lord Gregory's mother an-
        swers, counterfeiting her son.
    After 4. The mother, still counterfeiting her
        son, says.
    *The old woman who sang the ballad, says Pit-
        cairn, murmured over these words as a
        sort of recitative, and then resumed the
        song, with a slight variation of voice.*

D. 3⁴. linnen ; *probably a way of pronouncing*
        London.
    Jamieson adopts several readings from E a,
        *besides making some slight alterations of his
        own, and inserts these two stanzas, "* from
        memory," *between* 21 *and* 22 :

    Tak down, tak down the mast o goud,
        Set up the mast o tree ;
    Ill sets it a forsaken lady
        To sail sae gallantlie.

    Tak down, tak down the sails o silk,
        Set up the sails o skin ;
    Ill sets the outside to be gay
        Whan there 's sic grief within.

    For the first of these see B 19.
E. a. quha, ze, *etc., of the MS. are printed* wha,
        ye, *etc.*

b. *Scott's version, described as composed from* **B, E a, F,** *and two recited copies, is rather* **E a,** *excepting* 6[3, 4] *and* 16, *interpolated with six stanzas from* **B,** *five from* **F,** *and two lines from other sources, with a few verbal changes. It is, neglecting these verbal changes (also in part derived from* **B, E a, F),** *made up thus:*
1–5 = **E a** 1–5; 6 = **F** 3[1] + **F** 3[4] + *two lines from other sources;* 7–9 = **F** 4–6; 10 = **B** 10; 11 = **F** 7; 12 = **E a** 7; 13 = **F** 8; 14–20 = **E a** 8–14; 21 = **B** 16; 22 = **E a** 15; 23–25 = **B** 15, 18, 19; 26 = **E a** 17; 27 = **B** 20; 28–38 = **E a** 18–28; 39 = **E a** 28[1-3] + **B** 25[4].

Scott has Lord Gregory *for* Love Gregor, *or* Love Gregory, *throughout, and* Lochroyan *for* Rough (Roch) Royal.

3[4]. Till Lord Gregory come to land.

6[3, 4]. The sails were o the light-green silk,
The tows o taffety.

24[3, 4]. Fair Annie floated through the faem,
But the babie raise no more.

G. 4[4]. Ands lands : *Buchan prints* In 's.
6[2]. For mony : *Buchan prints* Thro mony.
12[4]. fause reason : *Buchan prints* fause lynin.
14[3]. *Buchan prints* or vile warlock.

H. "I find myself quite unable to arrange the fragments of the 'Lass of Aughrim' in anything like decent symmetry. The idea that I have of the arrangement is that the Lass begins with a sort of soliloquy, lamenting her condition; that she sings this at the door of a castle, shut against her; that she hears Gregory's voice within, and then appeals to him for admittance; and then comes the dialogue between them.

"The [third] stanza, as I heard the thing sung, was repeated as a burden after all the succeeding stanzas, even when the Lad and not the Lass speaks; but I do not think it followed the [first two] stanzas; they were a sort of introduction." *Mr Mahon, December,* 1884, *May,* 1885.

77

SWEET WILLIAM'S GHOST

A. 'Sweet William's Ghost,' Ramsay's Tea Table Miscellany, "4th volume, 1740;" here from the London edition of 1763, p. 324.

B. Herd's MSS, I, 177, II, 49, stanzas 27 ff.

C. 'Marjorie and William,' Motherwell's MS., p. 262, 'William and Marjorie,' Motherwell's Minstrelsy, p. 186.

D. Dr Joseph Robertson's Note-Book, 'Adversaria,' p. 86.

E. 'Sweet William and May Margaret,' Kinloch's Ancient Scottish Ballads, p. 241.

F. Jamieson's Popular Ballads, I, 83, stanzas 26 ff.

G. Minstrelsy of the Scottish Border, III, 183, ed. 1833.

RAMSAY'S copy, **A**, was reprinted by Percy, Reliques, 1765, III, 128, and by Herd, 1769, p. 194, 1776, I, 76. Percy remarks that the concluding stanza seems modern. There can be no doubt that both that and the one before it are modern; but, to the extent of Margaret's dying on her lover's grave, they are very likely to represent original verses not remembered in form. B constitutes, in Herd's MSS, and F, in Jamieson's Popular Ballads, the termination of a copy of 'Clerk Saunders.' Scott appended the three stanzas given as **G** to the later edition of his *rifacimento* of the copies of 'Clerk Saunders' in Herd's MSS, and says

of them: " I am informed by the reciter that
it was usual to separate from the rest that
part of the ballad which follows the death of
the lovers, as belonging to another story."
The first part of **F** was evidently derived from
' Proud Lady Margaret,' No. 47.

Motherwell notes, Minstrelsy, p. lxiii, 6,
that in recited copies he had heard this stanza
repeated, " which does not occur in printed
copies " (and can easily be spared), after **A**
14.*

My meikle tae is my gavil-post,
  My nose is my roof-tree,
My ribs are kebars to my house,
  And there is nae room for thee.

The story of this ballad seems to have become disordered in most of the versions. **A**
alone, the first published, has perhaps retained
the original form. The principal idea is, however, preserved in all the full versions, **A-E**;
the dead lover returns to ask back his unful-
filled troth-plight. His mistress, not knowing
that he is dead, demands that he shall first
come within her bower and kiss her, **A, B, C.**
He answers that if he does this her days will
not be long. She persists; he shall take her
to kirk,† and wed her with a ring, **A, E.** He
then tells her distinctly that he is dead, and
she returns to him his faith and troth. She
streaks her troth on a long wand and gives it
to him through a window, **B.** In **A** she
stretches out her white hand, " to do her
best; " in **C** " takes up " her white hand, and
strikes him on the breast; in **E** takes her
white hand and smooths it on his breast; all
of which are possibly corruptions of the ceremony performed in **B.** In **D** she takes a silver key and strikes him three times on the
breast. She follows the dead till he comes to
his grave, **A, B, C, D (?) F,** which is wrongly
said in **A, E** to be far beyond the sea. She
asks if there is room for her in his grave, and
is told there is not, **A, F** [there is room, **B,
D**]. She dies at his grave, **A**; is told that
her days will not be long, **F**; in **G**, goes weeping away.

* Motherwell probably meant 13.
† So **E** 10; **A** 9 has, in Ramsay, kirk-yard, which obviously requires to be corrected.

Margaret will not give William back his
faith and troth, in **B, D, E**, unless he resolves
certain questions about the state of the dead;
what becomes of women that die in travail;
where the women go who hang themselves
for sin; where unbaptized children. Mere
curiosity does not sort well with this very
seriously conceived ballad, and these passages
have probably grown out of a not unnatural
inquiry on the part of Margaret as to her
lover's personal state, extended in **E** 12 to
" tell me the pleasures o heaven, and pains o
hell how they be." The scene at the grave in
C 11–13 may be judged grotesque, but is not
trivial or unimpressive. These verses may be
supposed not to have belonged to the earliest
form of the ballad, and one does not miss them
from **A**, but they cannot be an accretion of
modern date.

Sir Walter Scott informs us, in the Advertisement to The Pirate, that the lady whose
affections had been engaged by Goff, the historical prototype of Cleveland, " went up to
London to see him before his death, and that,
arriving too late, she had the courage to request a sight of his body; and then touching
the hand of the corpse, she formally resumed
the troth-plight which she had bestowed."
" Without going through this ceremony," Scott
goes on to say, " she could not, according to
the superstition of the country, have escaped
a visit from the ghost of her departed lover,
in the event of her bestowing upon any living
suitor the faith which she had plighted to the
dead." ‡

' Sweet William's Ghost ' has much in common with one of the most beautiful and celebrated of the Scandinavian ballads, and may
well be a different development of the same
story:

Danish. ' Fæstemanden i Graven ' (' Aage
og Else '), Grundtvig, No 90, II, 492–97, III,
870–74, **A** from a manuscript of the seventeenth century, **B** from about 1700, **C** from
recent tradition. Swedish. ' Sorgens Magt,'
A, B, Afzelius, No 6, I, 29, II, 204; **C**, Ar-

‡ In a note in the Kinloch MSS, VII, 277, Kinloch says
that Sir Walter Scott told him that he had received this
story from an old woman in Shetland.

widsson, No 91, II, 103; D, Wigström, Skånska Visor, No 8, the same, Folkdiktning, I, 17, No 6, 'Den döde brudgummen:' all from recent tradition.

According to the oldest version, Danish A,* from which the others do not materially vary, a man dies just as he is to be married. His love grieves for him passionately. The dead hears her under the ground, comes to her bower with his coffin on his back, and knocks. She lets him in after he has proved himself to be " a spirit of health " by uttering the name of Jesus, combs his hair, and asks him how it is under the black earth (cf. English, E 12). It is like the bliss of heaven. May she follow him into his grave? It is like blackest hell. Every time she weeps for him his coffin is filled with lappered blood. But when she sings and is happy, his grave is all hung with rose-leaves. The cock crows, the white, the red, the black; he takes up his coffin and goes wearily back to the graveyard. His love follows through the mirk wood (so Swedish A 9, cf. English B 11), to the churchyard, and into the church. Then his yellow hair falls away, his rosy color wans. He bids her go home and never weep for him more. " Look up at the sky, the night is going; " and as she looks he slips into his grave. She goes sadly home, prays God that she may not live out a year and a day, falls sick, and dies within a month.

The Scandinavian ballad agrees in many particulars with the conclusion of the second lay of Helgi Hundingsbani in the older Edda. Helgi, having been slain by Sigrún's brother, is bitterly bewailed by Sigrún. He quits his barrow to come to her. Sigrún will kiss him, but his hair is thick with hoar-frost, he is drenched in blood, and how is this? These are the grim tears that Sigrún has shed, every one of which falls on his breast. Sigrún says she will sleep in his arms as though he were

alive, and goes into the barrow with him. The end of the story is lost; according to a prose tradition which professes to supply the close, Sigrún soon died of grief. The source of the later ballads is perceptible here.

In the English ballad the dead lover returns of his own motion, simply to ask back his troth; in the Scandinavian, his betrothed grieves him out of his grave, " hon sörjer sin fästeman ur graf,' and the object of his visit is to admonish her to restrain her tears, which prevent his happy repose. A fragmentary story with this turn, which perhaps may even have been a variety of 'Sweet William's Ghost,' will be found in the ballad which follows this.

In a somewhat popular German ballad, 'Der todte Freier,' a dead man comes to the window of his betrothed in the night and calls her. She does not recognize him; says he smells of the ground. He has been eight years in the ground, and that may be. He bids her summon father, mother, and friends, for her bridegroom has come. She is decked as for her wedding; at the first sound of the bell makes her will or receives the sacrament, and dies at the second.†

A young man goes to the grave of his betrothed and asks his love-tokens back; she refers him to her mother, and tells him she will join him in a year: Haupt u. Schmaler, I, 88, No 55. This returning of gifts by the dead is not an infrequent phenomenon: Čelakowský, I, 4, No 2 = Wenzig, Slawische Volkslieder, p. 57, and III, 16, No 6; Beaurepaire, p. 53, Le Héricher, Lit. pop. de Normandie, p. 160 f; Briz y Candi, I, 140, Milá, Observaciones, p. 155, No 50, Milá, Romancerillo, pp 320–22, No 337, D, E, A^{11}, B^{11}.

A is translated by Grundtvig, Engelske og skotske Folkeviser, p. 34, No 4; by Herder, Book III, No 8; Bodmer, II, 36; Wacker-

---

* The ballad has been often translated, mostly after the compounded form in the Danske Viser, No 29: Prior, III, 76 (Danish A), 81; "London Magazine, 1820, I, 152;" Borrow, Foreign Quarterly Review, 1830, VI, 62, and p. 47 of his Romantic Ballads; Buchanan, p. 112.

† Hoffmann von Fallersleben in Deutsches Museum, 1852, II, 162 = Erk's Wunderhorn, IV, 73, and Liederhort, p. 75,

No 24ª, Mittler, No 545; Wagner in Deutsches Museum, 1862, II, 802, 803; Liederhort, No 24, p. 74; Ditfurth, II, 1, No 2; Meier, p. 355, No 201; Peter, I, 199, No 14; A. Müller, p. 95; Meinert, p. 3 = Erlach, IV, 196, Erk's Wunderhorn, IV, 74, Liederhort, p. 76, No 24b, Zuccalmaglio, p. 130, No 60, Mittler, No 544; Schleicher, Volkstümliches aus Sonneberg, p. 112, No 22.

nagel, Altdeutsche Blätter, I, 189; Döring, p. 391; Knortz, Lieder u. Romanzen Alt-Englands, p. 86, No 23; von Marées, p. 24. C by Grundtvig, p. 319, No 90; Wolff, Halle der Völker, I, 30, Hausschatz, p. 205; Knortz, as above, p. 179, No 49. A compound of **D**, **C**, **A**, by Rosa Warrens, Schottische Volkslieder, p. 53, No 12.

A

Ramsay's Tea Table Miscellany, "4th volume, 1740;" here from the London edition of 1763, p. 324.

1 THERE came a ghost to Margret's door,
   With many a grievous groan,
And ay he tirled at the pin,
   But answer made she none.

2 'Is that my father Philip,
   Or is 't my brother John?
Or is 't my true-love, Willy,
   From Scotland new come home?'

3 ''T is not thy father Philip,
   Nor yet thy brother John;
But 't is thy true-love, Willy,
   From Scotland new come home.

4 'O sweet Margret, O dear Margret,
   I pray thee speak to me;
Give me my faith and troth, Margret,
   As I gave it to thee.'

5 'Thy faith and troth thou 's never get,
   Nor yet will I thee lend,
Till that thou come within my bower,
   And kiss my cheek and chin.'

6 'If I shoud come within thy bower,
   I am no earthly man;
And shoud I kiss thy rosy lips,
   Thy days will not be lang.

7 'O sweet Margret, O dear Margret,
   I pray thee speak to me;
Give me my faith and troth, Margret,
   As I gave it to thee.'

8 'Thy faith and troth thou 's never get,
   Nor yet will I thee lend,
Till you take me to yon kirk,
   And wed me with a ring.'

9 'My bones are buried in yon kirk-yard,
   Afar beyond the sea,
And it is but my spirit, Margret,
   That 's now speaking to thee.'

10 She stretchd out her lilly-white hand,
   And, for to do her best,
'Hae, there 's your faith and troth, Willy,
   God send your soul good rest.'

11 Now she has kilted her robes of green
   A piece below her knee,
And a' the live-lang winter night
   The dead corp followed she.

12 'Is there any room at your head, Willy?
   Or any room at your feet?
Or any room at your side, Willy,
   Wherein that I may creep?'

13 'There 's no room at my head, Margret,
   There 's no room at my feet;
There 's no room at my side, Margret,
   My coffin 's made so meet.'

14 Then up and crew the red, red cock,
   And up then crew the gray:
'Tis time, tis time, my dear Margret,
   That you were going away.'

15 No more the ghost to Margret said,
   But, with a grievous groan,
Evanishd in a cloud of mist,
   And left her all alone.

16 'O stay, my only true-love, stay,'
   The constant Margret cry'd;
Wan grew her cheeks, she closd her een,
   Stretchd her soft limbs, and dy'd.

B

Herd's MSS, I, 177, II, 49, stanzas 27 ff.

1 WHAN bells war rung, an mass was sung,
    A wat a' man to bed were gone,
  Clark Sanders came to Margret's window,
    With mony a sad sigh and groan.

2 ' Are ye sleeping, Margret,' he says,
    ' Or are ye waking, presentlie ?
  Give me my faith and trouthe again,
    A wat, trew-love, I gied to thee.'

3 ' Your faith and trouth ye 's never get,
    Nor our trew love shall never twain,
  Till ye come with me in my bower,
    And kiss me both cheek and chin.'

4 ' My mouth it is full cold, Margret.
    It has the smell now of the ground ;
  And if I kiss thy comely mouth,
    Thy life-days will not be long.

5 ' Cocks are crowing a merry mid-larf,
    I wat the wild fule boded day ;
  Gie me my faith and trouthe again,
    And let me fare me on my way.'

6 ' Thy faith and trouth thou shall na get,
    Nor our trew love shall never twin,
  Till ye tell me what comes of women
    Awat that dy's in strong traveling.'

7 ' Their beds are made in the heavens high,
    Down at the foot of our good Lord's knee,
  Well set about wi gilly-flowers,
    A wat sweet company for to see.

8 ' O cocks are crowing a merry midd-larf,
    A wat the wilde foule boded day ;
  The salms of Heaven will be sung,
    And ere now I 'le be misst away.'

9 Up she has tain a bright long wand,
    And she has straked her trouth thereon ;
  She has given [it] him out at the shot-window,
    Wi many a sad sigh and heavy groan.

10 ' I thank you, Margret, I thank you, Margret,
    And I thank you hartilie ;
  Gine ever the dead come for the quick,
    Be sure, Margret, I 'll come again for thee.'

11 It 's hose an shoon an gound alane
    She clame the wall and followed him,
  Untill she came to a green forest,
    On this she lost the sight of him.

12 ' Is their any room at your head, Sanders ?
    Is their any room at your feet ?
  Or any room at your twa sides ?
    Whare fain, fain woud I sleep.'

13 ' Their is na room at my head, Margret,
    Their is na room at my feet ;
  There is room at my twa sides,
    For ladys for to sleep.

14 ' Cold meal is my covering owre,
    But an my winding sheet ;
  My bed it is full low, I say,
    Down among the hongerey worms I sleep.

15 ' Cold meal is my covering owre,
    But an my winding sheet ;
  The dew it falls na sooner down
    Then ay it is full weet.'

C

Motherwell's MS., p. 262, Motherwell's Minstrelsy, p.
186, from the recitation of Mrs McCormick, and learned by
her in Dumbarton, from an old woman, thirty years before:
January 19, 1825.

1 LADY MARJORIE, Lady Marjorie,
    Sat sewing her silken seam ;
  By her came a pale, pale ghost,
    With many a sich and mane.

2 ' Are ye my father, the king ? ' she says,
    ' Or are ye my brother John ?
  Or are you my true-love, Sweet William,
    From England newly come ? '

3 ' I'm not your father, the king,' he says,
    ' No, no, nor your brother John ;
  But I'm your true love, Sweet William,
    From England that's newly come.'

4 'Have ye brought me any scarlets so red?
  Or any silks so fine?
Or have ye brought me any precious things,
  That merchants have for sale?'

5 'I have not brought you any scarlets sae red,
  No, no, nor the silks so fine;
But I have brought you my winding-sheet,
  Oer many 's the rock and hill.

6 'O Lady Marjory, Lady Marjory,
  For faith and charitie,
Will you give to me my faith and troth,
  That I gave once to thee?'

7 'O your faith and troth I 'll not give thee,
  No, no, that will not I,
Until I get one kiss of your ruby lips,
  And in my arms you come [lye].'

8 'My lips they are so bitter,' he says,
  'My breath it is so strong,
If you get one kiss of my ruby lips,
  Your days will not be long.

9 'The cocks they are crowing, Marjory,' he says,
  'The cocks they are crawing again;
It 's time the deid should part the quick,
  Marjorie, I must be gane.'

10 She followed him high, she followed him low,
  Till she came to yon church-yard;
O there the grave did open up,
  And young William he lay down.

11 'What three things are these, Sweet William,'
    she says,
  'That stands here at your head?'
'It 's three maidens, Marjorie,' he says,
  'That I promised once to wed.'

12 'What three things are these, Sweet William,'
    she says,
  'That stands here at your side?'
'It is three babes, Marjorie,' he says,
  'That these three maidens had.'

13 'What three things are these, Sweet William,'
    she says,
  'That stands here at your feet?'
It is three hell-hounds, Marjorie,' he says,
  'That 's waiting my soul to keep.'

14 She took up her white, white hand,
  And she struck him in the breast,
Saying, Have there again your faith and
    troth,
  And I wish your soul good rest.

D

From tradition: Dr Joseph Robertson's Note-Book, "Adversaria," p. 86.

1 LADY MARGARET was in her wearie room,
  Sewin her silken seam,
And in cam Willie, her true-love,
  Frae Lundin new come hame.

2 'O are ye my father Philip,
  Or are ye my brither John?
Or are ye my true-love, Willie,
  Frae London new come home?'

3 'I 'm nae your father Philip,
  Nor am I your brother John;
But I am your true-love, Willie,
  An I 'm nae a levin man.

4 'But gie me my faith and troth, Margrat,
  An let me pass on my way;

For the bells o heaven will be rung,
  An I 'll be mist away.'

5 'Yere faith and troth ye 'se never get,
  Till ye tell me this ane;
Till ye tell me where the women go
  That hang themsell for sin.'

6 'O they gang till the low, low hell,
  Just by the devil's knee;
It 's a' clad ower wi burnin pitch,
  A dreadfu sicht to see.'

7 'But your faith and troth ye 'se never get,
  Till you tell me again;
Till you tell me where the children go
  That die without a name.'

8 'O they gang till the high, high heaven,
  Just by our Saviour's knee,

An it's a' clad ower wi roses red,
  A lovelie sicht to see.

9 'But gie me my faith and troth, Margrat,
  And let me pass on my way;
For the psalms o heaven will be sung,
  An I'll be mist away.'

10 'But your faith and troth yese never get
  Till ye tell me again;
Till ye tell me where the women go
  That die in child-beddin.'

11 'O they gang till the hie, hie heaven,
  Just by our Saviour's knee,
And every day at twal o clock
  They're dipped oer the head.

12 'But gie me my faith and troth, Margret,
  And let me pass on my way;
For the gates o heaven will be shut,
  And I'll be mist away.'

13 Then she has taen a silver key,
  Gien him three times on the breast;
Says, There's your faith and troth, Willie,
  I hope your soul will rest.

14 'But is there room at your head, Willie?
  Or is there room at your feet?
Or is there room at any o your sides,
  To let in a lover sweet?'

15 'There is nae room at my head, Margrat,
  There's nae room at my feet,
But there is room at baith my sides,
  To lat in a lover sweet.'

E

Kinloch's Ancient Scottish Ballads, p. 241.

1 As May Margret sat in her bouerie,
  In her bouer all alone,
At the very parting o midnicht
  She heard a mournfu moan.

2 'O is it my father? O is it my mother?
  Or is it my brother John?
Or is it Sweet William, my ain true-love,
  To Scotland new come home?'

3 'It is na your father, it is na your mother,
  It is na your brother John;
But it is Sweet William, your ain true-love,
  To Scotland new come home.'

4 'Hae ye brought me onie fine things,
  Onie new thing for to wear?
Or hae ye brought me a braid o lace,
  To snood up my gowden hair?'

5 'I've brought ye na fine things at all,
  Nor onie new thing to wear,
Nor hae I brought ye a braid of lace,
  To snood up your gowden hair.

6 'But Margaret, dear Margaret,
  I pray ye speak to me;

O gie me back my faith and troth,
  As dear as I gied it thee.'

7 'Your faith and troth ye sanna get,
  Nor will I wi ye twin,
Till ye come within my bouer,
  And kiss me, cheek and chin.'

8 'O should I come within your bouer,
  I am na earthly man;
If I should kiss your red, red lips,
  Your days wad na be lang.

9 'O Margaret, dear Margaret,
  I pray ye speak to me;
O gie me back my faith and troth,
  As dear as I gied it thee.'

10 'Your faith and troth ye sanna get,
  Nor will I wi ye twin,
Till ye tak me to yonder kirk,
  And wed me wi a ring.'

11 'My banes are buried in yon kirk-yard,
  It's far ayont the sea;
And it is my spirit, Margaret,
  That's speaking unto thee.'

12 'Your faith and troth ye sanna get,
  Nor will I twin wi thee,

Till ye tell me the pleasures o heaven,
  And pains of hell how they be.'

13 'The pleasures of heaven I wat not of,
  But the pains of hell I dree;
There some are hie hangd for huring,
  And some for adulterie.'

F

Jamieson's Popular Ballads, I, 83, stanzas 26 ff.

1 WHEN seven years were come and gane,
  Lady Margaret she thought lang;
And she is up to the hichest tower,
  By the lee licht o the moon.

2 She was lookin oer her castle high,
  To see what she might fa,
And there she saw a grieved ghost,
  Comin waukin oer the wa.

3 'O are ye a man of mean,' she says,
  'Seekin ony o my meat?
Or are you a rank robber,
  Come in my bower to break?'

4 'O I'm Clerk Saunders, your true-love,
  Behold, Margaret, and see,
And mind, for a' your meikle pride,
  Sae will become of thee.'

5 'Gin ye be Clerk Saunders, my true-love,
  This meikle marvels me;
O wherein is your bonny arms,
  That wont to embrace me?'

G

Minstrelsy of the Scottish Border, III, 183, ed. 1833, the
last three stanzas.

*   *   *   *   *

1 'BUT plait a wand o bonny birk,
  And lay it on my breast,
And shed a tear upon my grave,
  And wish my saul gude rest.

14 Then Margret took her milk-white hand,
  And smoothd it on his breast:
'Tak your faith and troth, William,
  God send your soul good rest!'

6 'By worms they're eaten, in mools they're
    rotten,
  Behold, Margaret, and see,
And mind, for a' your mickle pride,
  Sae will become o thee.'

*   *   *   *   *

7 O, bonny, bonny sang the bird,
  Sat on the coil o hay;
But dowie, dowie was the maid
  That followd the corpse o clay.

8 'Is there ony room at your head, Saunders?
  Is there ony room at your feet?
Is there ony room at your twa sides,
  For a lady to lie and sleep?'

9 'There is nae room at my head, Margaret,
  As little at my feet;
There is nae room at my twa sides,
  For a lady to lie and sleep.

10 'But gae hame, gae hame now, May Margaret,
  Gae hame and sew your seam;
For if ye were laid in your weel made bed,
  Your days will nae be lang.'

---

2 'And fair Margret, and rare Margret,
  And Margret o veritie,
Gin eer ye love another man,
  Neer love him as ye did me.'

3 Then up and crew the milk-white cock,
  And up and crew the grey;
The lover vanishd in the air,
  And she gaed weeping away.

A. 8³. yon kirk-yard.

B. 1², And every one *is substituted for* **A** wat a' man, *no doubt by a reviser.*

1⁴, 9⁴. grown.

5¹, 8¹. mid larf, midd larf *I retain, though I do not understand* larf.

9². on it *struck out at the end of the line, and* thereon *written over. Qy* it on?

14⁴. *A line is drawn through* Down *and the.*

15¹. is my bed, *written after* weet, *is struck out. The copy in Herd's second volume is a tran-* script *of the other, and its variations have* apparent authority.

C. 7⁴. *MS.* come (lye).

9⁴. away *written over* be gane.

10². *Motherwell prints* churchyard green.

14¹. white *thrice.*

Motherwell makes not a few slight changes printing.

D. 15¹. at my head, Willie.

E. 8 *follows* 10 *in Kinloch.*

78

THE UNQUIET GRAVE

A. 'The Unquiet Grave,' Folk-Lore Record, I, 60, 1868.

B. Notes and Queries, Fifth Series, VII, 436.

C. Notes and Queries, Fifth Series, VII, 387.

D. 'The Ghost and Sailor,' Buchan's MSS, I, 268.

THE vow in the second stanza of all the copies is such as we find in ' Bonny Bee-Ho'm,' and elsewhere (see p. 156 f of this volume), and **A**, **B**, **D** 4, 5, **C** 3, 4 are nearly a repetition of 'Sweet William's Ghost,' **A** 5, 6, **B** 3, 4, **C** 7, 8, **D** 7, 10. This may suggest a suspicion that this brief little piece is an aggregation of scraps. But these repetitions would not strike so much if the ballad were longer, and we must suppose that we have it only in an imperfect form. Even such as it is, however, this fragment has a character of its own. It exhibits the universal popular belief that excessive grieving for the dead interferes with their repose. We have all but had ' The Unquiet Grave' before, as the conclusion of two versions of ' The Twa Brothers : '

She ran distraught, she wept, she sicht,
    She wept the sma brids frae the tree,
She wept the starns adown frae the lift,
    She wept the fish out o the sea.

' O cease your weeping, my ain true-love,
    Ye but disturb my rest ; '
' Is that my ain true lover, John,
    The man that I loe best ? '

' 'T is naething but my ghaist,' he said,
    ' That 's sent to comfort thee ;
O cease your weeping, my true-love,
    And 't will gie peace to me.'

                        (I, 440, C 18–20.)

She put the small pipes to her mouth,
    And she harped both far and near,
Till she harped the small birds off the briers,
    And her true-love out of the grave.

' What 's this ? what 's this, Lady Margaret ? he says,
    ' What 's this you want of me ? '
' One sweet kiss of your ruby lips,
    That 's all I want of thee.'

' My lips they are so bitter,' he says,
    ' My breath it is so strong,
If you get one kiss of my ruby lips,
    Your days will not be long.'

                        (I, 439, B 10–12.)

Sir Walter Scott has remarked that the belief that excessive grieving over lost friends destroyed their peace was general throughout Scotland : Redgauntlet, Note 2 to Letter XI. See also Gregor's Notes on the Folk-Lore of he North-East of Scotland, p. 69. We have ecent testimony that this belief survives in England (1868), Folk Lore Record, I, 60. It as held in Ireland that inordinate tears would ierce a hole in the dead: Killinger, Erin, VI, 5, 449 (quoting a writer that I have not lentified).

The common notion is that tears wet the hroud or grave-clothes. Scott relates a story f a Highlander who was constrained to come ack and say to a kinswoman: My rest is disurbed by your unnecessary lamentation; our tears scald me in my shroud.

Mrs Grant of Laggan tells a similar story. An only sister had lost an only brother. Night fter night she sat up, weeping incessantly and alling upon his name. At length her brother ppeared to her in his shroud, and seemed wet nd shivering. "Why," said he, "am I disurbed with the extravagance of thy sorrow? Till thou art humble and penitent for this ebellion against the decrees of Providence, very tear thou sheddest falls on this dark hroud without drying, and every night thy ears still more chill and encumber me." Esays on the Superstitions of the Highlanders f Scotland, ed. New York, 1813, p. 95 f.

A dead boy appears to his mother, and begs er to cease weeping, for all her tears fall pon his shirt and wet it so that he cannot leep. The mother gives heed, her child comes gain and says, Now my shirt is dry, and I ave peace. Grimms, K. u. H. märchen, No 09.

In another form of this tradition a child as to carry all its mother's tears in a large itcher, and cannot keep up with a happy little band to which it would belong, 'Die Macht ler Thränen,' Erk, Neue Sammlung, III, I, No 35 = Wunderhorn, IV, 95, Liederhort, p. 8, No 3, Mittler, No 557; Hoffmann u. Richter, . 341, No 290; Börner, Volkssagen aus dem Orlagau, pp 142, 152; or lags behind because ts clothes are heavy with these tears, Geiler von Kaisersberg's Trostspiegel, 1510, cited by Rochholz in Wolf's Zeitschrift für deutsche Mythologie, II, 252; Thomas Cantipratensis, Bonum Universale, "l. ii, c. 53, § 17," about 1250; or the child collects its mother's tears n its hands, Müllenhoff, No 196.

A wife's tears wet her dead husband's shirt in the German ballad 'Der Vorwirth:' Meinert, p. 13 = Erk's Wunderhorn, IV, 96, Erk's Liederhort, p. 160, No 46ᵃ, Mittler, No 555; Hoffmann in Deutsches Museum, 1852, II, 161 = Wunderhorn, IV, 98, Liederhort, p. 158, No 46, Mittler, No 556; Peter, I, 200, No 15.

Saint Johannes Eleemosynarius and a couple of his bishops are fain to rise from their graves because their stoles are wet through with a woman's tears, Legenda Aurea, c. 27, § 12, Grässe, p. 132, last half of the thirteenth century (cited by Liebrecht); and Saint Vicelin, because his robes are drenched with the tears of his friend Eppo, Helmold, Chronica Slavorum, l. i, 78, p. 15, ed. Lappenberg, last half of the twelfth century (cited by Müllenhoff).

Sigrún weeps bitter tears for Helgi's death every night ere she sleeps. The hero comes out of his mound to comfort her, but also to tell her how she discommodes him. He is otherwise well off, but every drop pierces, cold and bloody, to his breast: Helgakviða Hundingsbana II, 45. So in some of the ballads which apparently derive from this lay, the tears of Else or Kerstin fill her lover's coffin with blood: Grundtvig, II, 495, 497, No 90, A 17, B 8; Afzelius, I, 31, No 6, st. 14, Wigström, Folkdiktning, I, 18, st. 9.

Almost the very words of the Highland apparition in Scott's tale are used by an Indian sage to a king who is inconsolable for the loss of his wife; "the incessant tears of kinsfolk burn the dead, so it is said:" Kâlidâsas, Raghuvansa, VIII, 85, ed. Stenzler, p. 61 of his translation. Another representation is that the dead have to swallow the rheum and tears of their mourning relations, and therefore weeping must be abstained from: Yâjnavalkya's Gesetzbuch, Sanskrit u. Deutsch, Stenzler, III, 11, p. 89.

The ancient Persians also held that immoderate grief on the part of survivors was detrimental to the happiness of the dead. Weeping for the departed is forbidden, because the water so shed forms an impediment before the bridge Tchînavar (over which souls pass to heaven). Sad-der, Porta XCVII, Hyde, Vete-

rum Persarum et Parthorum Religionis Historia, p. 486, ed. Oxford, 1700.   Again, Ardai
Viraf, seeing a deep and fetid river, which
is carrying away a multitude of souls in all
the agony of drowning, and asking what this
is, is told : The river that you see before you
is composed of the tears of mankind, tears
shed, against the express command of the Almighty, for the departed ; therefore, when you
return again to the earth inculcate this to
mankind, that to grieve immoderately is in the
sight of God a most heinous sin ; and the river
is constantly increased by this folly, every
tear making the poor wretches who float on it
more distant from ease and relief. The Ardai
Viraf Nameh, translated from the Persian, by
J. A. Pope, London, 1816, p. 53 f.*

The Greeks and Romans also reprehend
obstinate condolement as troubling the dead,
and perhaps, if we had the popular views of
the subject, these might be found to have taken
an expression like some of the above.   In Lucian De Luctu, c. 16, the ghost of a son who
had died in the bloom of youth is made to reproach the disconsolate father in these words :
ὦ κακόδαιμον ἄνθρωπε, τί κέκραγας ; τί δέ μοι παρέ
χεις πράγματα ; †

See, also, Maurer, Isländische Volkssagen,
p. 312 f, No 9 ; Luzel, I, 65, ' La jeune fille et
l'âme de sa mère ;' Karadshitch, I, 272, No
368, Talvj, I, 84, ed. 1853 ; Kapper, Gesänge
der Serben, II, 116 ; Nibelungen, 2302, ed
Bartsch ; Blaas, in Germania, XXV, 429, No
34 ; Grimm, Deutsche Mythologie, III, 447,
No 397 ; Müllenhoff, No 195 ; Wunderhorn,
IV, 94, last stanza ; Wolf, Beiträge zur
deutschen Mythologie, I, 215, No 149 .

A

Communicated to the Folk Lore Record, I, 60, by Miss
Charlotte Latham, as written down from the lips of a girl in
Sussex.

1 ' THE wind doth blow today, my love,
    And a few small drops of rain ;
I never had but one true-love,
    In cold grave she was lain.

2 ' I 'll do as much for my true-love
    As any young man may ;
I 'll sit and mourn all at her grave
    For a twelvemonth and a day.'

3 The twelvemonth and a day being up,
    The dead began to speak :
' Oh who sits weeping on my grave,
    And will not let me sleep ? '

4 ' 'T is I, my love, sits on your grave,
    And will not let you sleep ;
For I crave one kiss of your clay-cold lips,
    And that is all I seek.'

5 ' You crave one kiss of my clay-cold lips ;
    But my breath smells earthy strong ;
If you have one kiss of my clay-cold lips,
    Your time will not be long.

6 ' 'T is down in yonder garden green,
    Love, where we used to walk,
The finest flower that ere was seen
    Is withered to a stalk.

7 ' The stalk is withered dry, my love,
    So will our hearts decay ;
So make yourself content, my love,
    Till God calls you away.'

* Rochholz has cited the Raghuvansa in Deutscher Unsterblichkeits Glaube, p. 208 ; the other oriental citations are
made by Kuhn, Wolf's Zeitschrift für deutsche Mythologie,
I, 62 f.

† Schenkl, in Germania, XI, 451 f ; who also cites Tibullus, I, 1, 67, Propertius, IV, 11, 1, and inscriptions, as Gruter, p. 1127, 8.

B

Notes and Queries, Fifth Series, VII, 436, cited by W. R. S. R., from the Ipswich Journal, 1877: from memory, after more than seventy years.

1 ' How cold the wind do blow, dear love,
    And see the drops of rain !
  I never had but one true-love,
    In the green wood he was slain.

2 ' I would do as much for my own true-love
    As in my power doth lay ;
  I would sit and mourn all on his grave
    For a twelvemonth and a day.'

3 A twelvemonth and a day being past,
    His ghost did rise and speak :
  ' What makes you mourn all on my grave ?
    For you will not let me sleep.'

4 ' It is not your gold I want, dear love,
    Nor yet your wealth I crave ;
  But one kiss from your lily-white lips
    Is all I wish to have.

5 ' Your lips are cold as clay, dear love,
    Your breath doth smell so strong ; '
  ' I am afraid, my pretty, pretty maid,
    Your time will not be long.'

C

" From a yeoman in Suffolk, who got it from his nurse ; " B. Montgomerie Ranking, in Notes and Queries, Fifth Series, VII, 387.

1 ' COLD blows the wind oer my true-love,
    Cold blow the drops of rain ;
  I never, never had but one sweetheart,
    In the greenwood he was slain.

2 ' I did as much for my true-love .
    As ever did any maid ;

* * * * *

3 ' One kiss from your lily-cold lips, true-love,
    One kiss is all I pray,
  And I 'll sit and weep all over your grave
    For a twelvemonth and a day.'

4 ' My cheek is as cold as the clay, true-love,
    My breath is earthy and strong ;
  And if I should kiss your lips, true-love,
    Your life would not be long.'

D

Buchan's MSS, I, 268.

1 ' PROUD BOREAS makes a hideous noise,
    Loud roars the fatal fleed ;
  I loved never a love but one,
    In church-yard she lies dead.

2 ' But I will do for my love's sake
    What other young men may ;
  I 'll sit and mourn upon her grave,
    A twelvemonth and a day.'

3 A twelvemonth and a day being past,
    The ghost began to speak :

' Why sit ye here upon my grave,
    And will not let me sleep ? '

4 ' One kiss of your lily-white lips
    Is all that I do crave ;
  And one kiss of your lily-white lips
    Is all that I would have.'

5 ' Your breath is as the roses sweet,
    Mine as the sulphur strong ;
  If you get one kiss of my lips,
    Your days would not be long.

6 ' Mind not ye the day, Willie,
    Sin you and I did walk ?
  The firstand flower that we did pu
    Was witherd on the stalk.'

7 'Flowers will fade and die, my dear,
    Aye as the tears will turn ;
And since I 've lost my own sweet-heart,
    I 'll never cease but mourn.'

8 'Lament nae mair for me, my love,
    The powers we must obey ;
But hoist up one sail to the wind,
    Your ship must sail away.'

79

THE WIFE OF USHER'S WELL

A. 'The Wife of Usher's Well,' Minstrelsy of the Scottish Border, II, 111, ed. 1802.

B. 'The Clerk's Twa Sons o Owsenford,' stanzas 18 23, Kinloch MSS, V, 403.

B FORMS the conclusion, as already said, to a beautiful copy of 'The Clerk's Twa Sons o Owsenford,' recited by the grandmother of Robert Chambers.

A motive for the return of the wife's three sons is not found in the fragments which remain to us. The mother had cursed the sea when she first heard they were lost, and can only go mad when she finds that after all she has not recovered them ; nor will a little wee while, B 5, make any difference. There is no indication that the sons come back to forbid obstinate grief, as the dead often do. But supplying a motive would add nothing to the impressiveness of these verses. Nothing that we have is more profoundly affecting.

A is translated by Grundtvig, Engelske og skotske Folkeviser, No 14; by Freiligrath Zwischen den Garben, II, 227, ed. Stuttgart 1877 ; by Doenniges, p. 61 ; by Rosa Warrens Schottische Volkslieder, No 9, with insertion of B 5, 6 ; and by Knortz, Lieder und Romanzen Alt-Englands, p. 227, after Allingham.

A

Minstrelsy of the Scottish Border, II, 111, 1802, from the recitation of an old woman residing near Kirkhill, in West Lothian.

1 THERE lived a wife at Usher's Well,
    And a wealthy wife was she ;
She had three stout and stalwart sons,
    And sent them oer the sea.

2 They hadna been a week from her,
    A week but barely ane,
Whan word came to the carline wife
    That her three sons were gane.

3 They hadna been a week from her,
    A week but barely three,
Whan word came to the carlin wife
    That her sons she 'd never see.

4 'I wish the wind may never cease,
    Nor fashes in the flood,
Till my three sons come hame to me,
    In earthly flesh and blood.'

5 It fell about the Martinmass,
    When nights are lang and mirk,
The carlin wife's three sons came hame,
    And their hats were o the birk.

6 It neither grew in syke nor ditch,
    Nor yet in ony sheugh ;
But at the gates o Paradise,
    That birk grew fair eneugh.

*   *   *   *   *

7 'Blow up the fire, my maidens,
    Bring water from the well ;

For a' my house shall feast this night,
    Since my three sons are well.'

8 And she has made to them a bed,
    She 's made it large and wide,
    And she 's taen her mantle her about,
    Sat down at the bed-side.

*   *   *   *   *

9 Up then crew the red, red cock,
    And up and crew the gray ;
    The eldest to the youngest said,
    'T is time we were away.

10 The cock he hadna crawd but once,
    And clappd his wings at a',
    When the youngest to the eldest said,
    Brother, we must awa.

11 ' The cock doth craw, the day doth daw,
    The channerin worm doth chide ;
    Gin we be mist out o our place,
    A sair pain we maun bide.

12 ' Fare ye weel, my mother dear !
    Fareweel to barn and byre !
    And fare ye weel, the bonny lass
    That kindles my mother's fire ! '

———◆———

B

Kinloch MSS, V, 403, stanzas 18–23. In the handwriting
f James Chambers, as sung to his maternal grandmother,
anet Grieve, seventy years before, by an old woman, a Miss
nn Gray, of the Neidpath Castle, Peeblesshire : January 1,
829.

1 THE hallow days o Yule are come,
    The nights are lang an dark,
    An in an cam her ain twa sons,
    Wi their hats made o the bark.

2 ' O eat an drink, my merry men a',
    The better shall ye fare,
    For my twa sons the are come hame
    To me for evermair.'

3 She has gaen an made their bed,
    An she 's made it saft an fine,

An she 's happit them wi her gay mantel,
    Because they were her ain.

4 O the young cock crew i the merry Linkem,
    An the wild fowl chirpd for day ;
    The aulder to the younger did say,
    Dear brother, we maun away.

5 ' Lie still, lie still a little wee while,
    Lie still but if we may ;
    For gin my mother miss us away
    She 'll gae mad or it be day.'

6 O it 's they 've taen up their mother's mantel,
    An they 've hangd it on the pin :
    ' O lang may ye hing, my mother's mantel,
    Or ye hap us again ! '

———◆———

A. 4². fishes. *The correction is suggested in ed.* 1833 *of the Border Minstrelsy. Aytoun reads* freshes.

80

OLD ROBIN OF PORTINGALE

Percy MS., p. 90; Hales and Furnivall, I, 235.

THIS fine ballad was printed in the Reliques of Ancient English Poetry, III, 48, ed.
of 1765, "with considerable corrections." The
information given by a page, the reward promised and the alternative punishment threatened
him, the savage vengeance taken on the lady
and the immediate remorse, are repeated in
'Little Musgrave,' No 81. So the "Sleep
you, wake you" of 4², a frequent formula for
such occasions,* which we find in 'Earl Brand,'
No 7, D 1, 'King Arthur and King Cornwall,'
No 30, st. 49³; 'Clerk Saunders,' No 69, F 4;
'Willie and Lady Maisry,' No 70, B 2, 11; 'The
Bent sae Brown,' No 71, st. 5; 'Lord Thomas
and Fair Annet,' No 73, E 5; 'Sweet William's
Ghost,' No 77, B 2; 'Jellon Grame,' A 4;
'The Drowned Lovers,' Buchan, I, 140, st. 11;
'Jock o the Side,' Caw's Museum, st. 16;
'Kinmont Willie,' Scott, st. 35; 'The Baron
of Brackley,' Scarce Ancient Ballads, st. 2;
the song or ballad in 'King Lear,' III, 6, 40;
Ravenscroft's Pammelia, 1609, No 30; the

interlude of 'The Four Elements' (Steevens)
Íslenzk Fornkvæði, II, 115, st. 26, 27; 'Der
todte Freier,' Erk's Liederhort, p. 75, No 24ᵃ
Deutsches Museum, 1852, II, 167 = Mittle:
No 545, Wunderhorn, IV, 73, etc., and
Deutsches Museum, 1862, II, 803, No 10
Ampère, Instructions, p. 36; Coussemaker
No 48, st. 5; Kolberg, Pieśni ludu Polskiego
No 7e, st. 8; etc.

Old Robin, instead of attaching a cross o:
red cloth to the right shoulder of his coat o:
cloak, shapes the cross in his shoulder "o:
white flesh and of red," st. 32; that is, burn
the cross in with a hot iron, as was done some
times by the unusually devout or superstitious
or for a pious fraud: Mabillon, Annales, a
annum 1095, cited by Michaud, Histoire de
Croisades, I, 110, note, ed. 1825.

Translated by Bodmer, I, 153; by Knortz
Lieder und Romanzen Alt-Englands, No 66.

---

1 GOD let neuer soe old a man
    Marry soe yonge a wiffe
As did Old Robin of Portingale;
    He may rue all the dayes of his liffe.

2 Ffor the maiors daughter of Lin, God wott,
    He chose her to his wife,
And thought to haue liued in quiettnesse
    With her all the dayes of his liffe.

3 They had not in their wed-bed laid,
    Scarcly were both on sleepe,
But vpp shee rose, and forth shee goes
    To Sir Gyles, and fast can weepe.

4 Saies, Sleepe you, wake you, faire Sir Gyles?
    Or be not you within?
    .   .   .   .   .   '
    .   .   .   .   .

5 'But I am waking, sweete,' he said,
    'Lady, what is your will?'
'I haue vnbethought me of a wile,
    How my wed lord we shall spill.

6 'Four and twenty knights,' she sayes,
    'That dwells about this towne,
Eene four and twenty of my next cozens,
    Will helpe to dinge him downe.'

7 With that beheard his litle foote-page,
    As he was watering his masters steed;

* As Sir Frederick Madder has observed, who cites some of
the instances given.

Soe s . . . . . .
    His verry heart did bleed.

8 He mourned, sikt, and wept full sore ;
    I sweare by the holy roode,
  The teares he for his master wept
    Were blend water and bloude.

9 With *that* beheard his deare m*a*ster,
    As [he] in his garden sate ;
  Says, Euer alacke, my litle page,
    What causes thee to weepe ?

10 'Hath any one done to thee wronge,
    Any of thy fellowes here ?
  Or is any of thy good friends dead,
    W*hic*h makes thee shed such teares ?

11 ' Or if it be my head-kookes-man,
    Greiued againe he shalbe,
  Nor noe man w*i*thin my howse
    Shall doe wrong vnto thee.'

12 ' But it is not yo*ur* head-kookes-man,
    Nor none of his degree ;
  But [f]or to morrow, ere it be noone,
    You are deemed to die.

13 ' And of that thanke yo*ur* head-steward,
    And after, yo*ur* gay ladie : '
  ' If it be true, my litle foote-page,
    Ile make thee heyre of all my land.'

14 ' If it be not true, my deare m*a*ster,
    God let me neuer thye : '
  ' If it be not true, thou litle foot-page,
    A dead corse shalt thou be.'

15 He called downe his head-kookes-man,
    Cooke in kitchen sup*er* to dresse :
  ' All and anon, my deare m*a*ster,
    Anon att yo*ur* request.'

16 .   .   .   .   .

  .   .   .   .   .
  ' And call you downe my faire lady,
    This night to supp w*i*th mee.'

17 A*n*d downe then came *that* fayre lady,
    Was cladd all in purple and palle ;
  The rings *that* were vpon her fingers
    Cast light thorrow the hall.

18 'What is yo*ur* will, my owne wed lo*rd*,
    What is yo*ur* will w*i*th mee ? '
  ' I am sicke, fayre lady,
    Sore sicke, and like to dye.'

19 ' But and you be sicke, my owne wed lo*rd*,
    Soe sore it greiueth mee ;
  But my fiue maydens and my selfe
    Will goe and make yo*ur* bedd.

20 'A*n*d at the wakening of yo*ur* first sleepe
    You shall haue a hott drinke made,
  And at the wakening of yo*ur* next sleepe
    Yo*ur* sorrowes will haue a slake.'

21 He put a silke cote on his backe,
    Was thirteen inches folde,
  And put a steele cap vpon his head,
    Was gilded w*i*th good red gold.

22 A*n*d he layd a bright browne sword by his
    side,
    And another att his ffeete,
  And full well knew Old Robin then
    Whether he shold wake or sleepe.

23 And about the middle time of the night
    Came twenty four good knights in ;
  Si*r* Gyles he was the formost man,
    Soe well he knew *that* ginne.

24 Old Robin, w*i*th a bright browne sword,
    Si*r* Gyles head he did winne ;
  Soe did he all those twenty four,
    Neu*er* a one went quicke out [agen].

25 None but one litle foot-page,
    Crept forth at a window of stone,
  And he had two armes when he came in,
    And [when he went out he had none].

26 Vpp then came *that* ladie light,
    W*i*th torches burning bright ;
  Shee thought to haue brought Si*r* Gyles a
    drinke,
    But shee found her owne wedd k*n*i*gh*t.

27 And the first thinge *that* this ladye stumbled
    vpon
    Was of Si*r* Gyles his ffoote ;
  Sayes, Euer alacke, and woe is me,
    Here lyes my sweete hart-roote !

28 And the *second* thing *tha*t this ladie stumbled
        on
    Was of S*i*r Gyles his head;
    Sayes, Euer alacke, and woe is me,
    Heere lyes my true-loue deade !

29 Hee cutt the papps beside he[r] brest,
    And bad her wish her will ;
    And he cutt the eares beside her heade,
    And bade her wish on still.

30 ' Mickle is the mans blood I haue spent,
    To doe thee and me some good ; '

Sayes, Euer alacke, my fayre lady,
    I thinke *tha*t I was woode !

31 He calld then vp his little foote-page,
    And made him heyre of all his land,

    .   .   .   .   .

    .   .   .   .   .

32 And he shope the crosse in his right sholder,
    Of the white flesh and the redd,
    And he went him into the holy land,
    Wheras Christ was quicke and dead.

6¹, ⁸, 23², 24³.   24.   8¹. sist.
11¹, 12¹. bookes man : *cf*. 15¹.
14². never dye.
15². Cooke *seems to be wrongly repeated*.
19³. 5.   20³. first sleep.   21². 13.

25³.   2.   25⁴. *So Hales and Furnivall.*
26¹. ladie bright.   *Qy* fayre ?   26². burning light.
28¹.   2ᵈ.   30². thee & and.
32³. sent him.
    And *always for* &.

81

LITTLE MUSGRAVE AND LADY BARNARD

A. ' Little Musgrave and the Lady Barnard.' **a.** Wit Restord, 1658, in the reprint " Facetiæ," London, 1817, I, 293. **b.** Wit and Drollery, 1682, p. 81.

B. Percy MS., p. 53; Hales and Furnivall, I, 119.

C. a. ' Little Mousgrove and the Lady Barnet,' Pepys Ballads, I, 364. **b.** Pepys Ballads, III, 314. **c.** Roxburghe Ballads, III, 146. **d.** Roxburghe Ballads, III, 340. **e.** Bagford Ballads, I, 36.

D. ' Lord Barnard,' Kinloch MSS, I, 287.

E. ' Young Musgrave,' Campbell MSS, II, 43.

F. ' Lord Barnaby,' Jamieson's Popular Ballads, I, 170.

G. ' Wee Messgrove,' Motherwell's MS., p. 643.

H. ' Little Musgrave,' Motherwell's MS., p. 120.

I. ' Little Sir Grove,' Motherwell's MS., p. 305.

J. ' Lord Barnabas' Lady,' Motherwell's MS., p. 371.

K. Dr Joseph Robertson's Journal of Excursions, No 5.

L. ' Lord Barnett and Little Munsgrove,' Buchan's MSS, I, 27 : Scottish Traditional Versions of Ancient Ballads, Percy Society, XVII, 21.

M. ' Little Mushiegrove,' Motherwell's Minstrelsy, Appendix, p. xx, XXI, one stanza.

N. ' Little Massgrove,' communicated by Miss Reburn, as learned in County Meath, Ireland, two stanzas.

A COPY of this ballad in Dryden's Miscellany, III, 312, 1716, agrees with the one in Wit and Drollery. That in Ritson's Select Collection of English Songs, II, 215, 1783, agrees with Dryden's save in two or three words. The broadside C a was printed for

Henry Gosson, who is said by Chappell to have published from 1607 to 1641. If the lower limit be correct, this is the earliest impression known.* The other broadsides, C b-e, are later, but all of the seventeenth century. Percy inserted the ballad in his Reliques, III, 67, 1765, making a broadside in the British Museum his basis, and correcting as usual.

Percy remarks: This ballad is ancient, and has been popular; we find it quoted in many old plays. Cases cited by him are: Beaumont and Fletcher's Knight of the Burning Pestle, v, 3, Dyce II, 223, of about 1611:

And some they whistled, and some they sung,
  Hey down, down
And some did loudly say,
Ever as the lord Barnet's horn blew,
  Away, Musgrave, away!

Again, Sir William Davenant's play ' The Wits,' where Sir Thwack boasts, " I sing Musgrove, and for the Chevy Chase no lark comes near me," Act III, p. 194, of ed. 1672; and ' The Varietie,' a comedy, Act IV, 1649. In Beaumont and Fletcher's ' Bonduca,' v, 2, Dyce, V, 88, dating before March, 1619, we find this stanza, which is perhaps A 26, loosely remembered:

She set the sword unto her breast,
  Great pity it was to see
That three drops of her life-warm blood
  Run trickling down her knee.

And two stanzas in Fletcher's ' Monsieur Thomas,' IV, 11, Dyce VII, 375, earlier than 1639, may well be A 11, 12 parodied:

If this be true, thou little tiny page,
  This tale that thou tellst me,
Then on thy back will I presently hang
  A handsome new livery.

But if this be false, thou little tiny page,
  As false it well may be,
Then with a cudgel of four foot long
  I 'll beat thee from head to toe.

Jamieson says, in a prefatory note to F, that he had heard ' Little Musgrave ' repeated, with very little variation, both in Morayshire and the southern counties of Scotland. All the Scottish versions are late, and to all seeming derived, indirectly or immediately, from print.† As a recompense we have a fine ballad upon the same theme, ' The Bonny Birdy,' which is not represented in England.

In the English broadside and most of the northern versions the lovers try a bribe, a threat, or both, to make the page keep counsel. In some of these Musgrave, when detected, ejaculates a craven imprecation of woe to the fair woman that lies in his arms asleep, G 23, H 16, I 14, J 20, L 37. In I the men are brothers; in E, F Musgrave has a wife of his own; in C, G Lord Barnard kills himself; in E he is hanged! None of these divergences from the story as we have it in A are improvements, but it is an improvement that the lady should die by stroke of steel as in C, E, H, J, K, L, in exchange for the barbarity of A. The penance in L is a natural and common way of ending such a tragedy. The collecting of the lady's heart's blood in a basin of pure silver, G 28–30, is probably borrowed from ' Lammikin,' where this trait is very effective.

The heathen child, B 13¹, is a child unchristened. An unbaptized child seems still to be called so in Norway, and so is a woman between childbirth and churching. In modern Icelandic usage a boy or girl before confirmation is called heathen, from confusion between baptism and confirmation: Ivar Aasen, at the word heiden; Vigfusson, at the word heiðinn.‡

K 12,

O he 's taen out a lang, lang brand,
  And stripped it athwart the straw,

explains a corruption in E 18², where the manuscript reads, He 's struck *her* in the straw, and another in J 9. The sword is

---

* C a was most obligingly copied, and C b collated, for me by Professor Skeat with his own hand.

† L, one of two copies in Buchan's MSS, would certainly have been but the slightest loss if omitted, as another, MSS II, 152, being a broadside made over for the stalls, has been.

‡ Pagani appellati interdum infantes quorum certis ex causis differebatur baptismus; Ducange, s. v. Pagani, who cites, Infans infirmus et paganus commendatus presbytero, etc. Ethnicus was used in the same way.

wiped or whetted on straw in 'Clerk Saunders,' A 15, C 13, D 8, G 17; 'Willie and Lady Maisry,' B 19; 'Lord Thomas and Fair Annet,' B 36; 'Lady Diamond,' Buchan, II, 206, st. 8. Child Maurice dries his sword on the grass, John Steward dries his on his sleeve, A 27, 28; Glasgerion dries his sword on his sleeve, A 22; Horn wipes his sword on his arm, King Horn, ed. Wissmann, 622 f.

A

a. Wit Restord, 1658, in the reprint 'Facetiæ,' London, 1817, I, 293. b. Wit and Drollery, 1682, p. 81.

1 As it fell one holy-day,
    Hay downe
  As many be in the yeare,
When young men and maids together did goe,
  Their mattins and masse to heare,

2 Little Musgrave came to the church-dore;
  The preist was at private masse;
But he had more minde of the faire women
  Then he had of our lady['s] grace.

3 The one of them was clad in green,
  Another was clad in pall,
And then came in my lord Bernard's wife,
  The fairest amonst them all.

4 She cast an eye on Little Musgrave,
  As bright as the summer sun;
And then bethought this Little Musgrave,
  This lady's heart have I woonn.

5 Quoth she, I have loved thee, Little Musgrave,
  Full long and many a day;
'So have I loved you, fair lady,
  Yet never word durst I say.'

6 'I have a bower at Buckelsfordbery,
  Full daintyly it is deight;
If thou wilt wend thither, thou Little Musgrave,
  Thou's lig in mine armes all night.'

7 Quoth he, I thank yee, faire lady,
  This kindnes thou showest to me;
But whether it be to my weal or woe,
  This night I will lig with thee.

8 With that he heard, a little tynë page,
  By his ladye's coach as he ran:

'All though I am my ladye's foot-page,
  Yet I am Lord Barnard's man.

9 'My lord Barnard shall knowe of this,
  Whether I sink or swim;'
And ever where the bridges were broake
  He laid him downe to swimme.

10 'A sleepe or wake, thou Lord Barnard,
  As thou art a man of life,
For Little Musgrave is at Bucklesfordbery,
  A bed with thy own wedded wife.'

11 'If this be true, thou little tinny page,
  This thing thou tellest to me,
Then all the land in Bucklesfordbery
  I freely will give to thee.

12 'But if it be a ly, thou little tinny page,
  This thing thou tellest to me,
On the hyest tree in Bucklesfordbery
  Then hanged shalt thou be.'

13 He called up his merry men all:
  'Come saddle me my steed;
This night must I to Buckellsfordbery,
  For I never had greater need.'

14 And some of them whistld, and some of them sung,
  And some these words did say,
And ever when my lord Barnard's horn blew,
  'Away, Musgrave, away!'

15 'Methinks I hear the thresel-cock,
  Methinks I hear the jaye;
Methinks I hear my lord Barnard,
  And I would I were away.'

16 'Lye still, lye still, thou Little Musgrave,
  And huggell me from the cold;
'T is nothing but a shephard's boy,
  A driving his sheep to the fold.

17 'Is not thy hawke upon a perch?
      Thy steed eats oats and hay;
   And thou a fair lady in thine armes,
      And wouldst thou bee away?'

18 With that my lord Barnard came to the dore,
      And lit a stone upon;
   He plucked out three silver keys,
      And he opend the dores each one.

19 He lifted up the coverlett,
      He lifted up the sheet:
   'How now, how now, thou Littell Musgrave,
      Doest thou find my lady sweet?'

20 'I find her sweet,' quoth Little Musgrave,
      'The more 't is to my paine;
   I would gladly give three hundred pounds
      That I were on yonder plaine.'

21 'Arise, arise, thou Littell Musgrave,
      And put thy clothës on;
   It shall nere be said in my country
      I have killed a naked man.

22 'I have two swords in one scabberd,
      Full deere they cost my purse;
   And thou shalt have the best of them,
      And I will have the worse.'

23 The first stroke that Little Musgrave stroke,
      He hurt Lord Barnard sore;

The next stroke that Lord Barnard stroke,
   Little Musgrave nere struck more.

24 With that bespake this faire lady,
      In bed whereas she lay:
   'Although thou 'rt dead, thou Little Musgrave,
      Yet I for thee will pray.

25 'And wish well to thy soule will I,
      So long as I have life;
   So will I not for thee, Barnard,
      Although I am thy wedded wife.'

26 He cut her paps from off her brest;
      Great pitty it was to see
   That some drops of this ladie's heart's blood
      Ran trickling downe her knee.

27 'Woe worth you, woe worth, my mery men all
      You were nere borne for my good;
   Why did you not offer to stay my hand,
      When you see me wax so wood?

28 'For I have slaine the bravest sir knight
      That ever rode on steed;
   So have I done the fairest lady
      That ever did woman's deed.

29 'A grave, a grave,' Lord Barnard cryd,
      'To put these lovers in;
   But lay my lady on the upper hand,
      For she came of the better kin.'

———◆———

B

Percy MS., p. 53, Hales and Furnivall, I, 119.

*   *   *   *   *

1 .   .   .   .   .
   .   .   .   .   .
   'Ffor this same night att [Bucklesfeildberry]
   Litle Musgreue is in bed with thy wife.'

2 'If it be trew, thou litle foote-page,
      This tale thou hast told to mee,
   Then all my lands in Buckle[s]feildberry
      I 'le freely giue to thee.

3 'But if this be a lye, thou little foot-page,
      This tale thou hast told to mee,

Then on the highest tree in Bucklesfeildberry
   All hanged that thou shalt bee.'

4 Saies, Vpp and rise, my merrymen all,
      And saddle me my good steede,
   For I must ride to Bucklesfeildberry;
      God wott I had neuer more need!

5 But some they whistled, and some thé sunge,
      And some they thus cold say,
   When euer as Lord Barnetts horne blowes,
      'Away, Musgreue, away!'

6 'Mie thinkes I heare the throstlecocke,
      Me thinkes I heare the iay,
   Me thinkes I heare Lord Barnetts horne,
      Away, Musgreue, away!'

7 'But lie still, lie still, Litle Musgreue,
    And huddle me from the cold,
For it is but some sheaperds boy,
    Is whistling sheepe ore the mold.

8 'Is not thy hauke vpon a pearch,
    Thy horsse eating corne and hay?
And thou, a gay lady in thine armes,
    And yett thou wold goe away!'

9 By this time Lord Barnett was come to the dore,
    And light vpon a stone,
And he pulled out three silver kayes,
    And opened the dores euery one.

10 And first he puld the couering downe,
    And then puld downe the sheete;
Saies, How now? How now, Litle Musgreue?
    Dost find my gay lady sweet?

11 'I find her sweete,' saies Litle Musgreue,
    ' The more is my greefe and paine;'

   .   .   .   .   .

   .   .   .   .

  *   *   *   *   *

12 .   .   .   .   .

' Soe haue I done the fairest lady
    That euer wore womans weede.

13 ' Soe haue I done a heathen child,
    Which ffull sore greiueth mee,
For which Ile repent all the dayes of my life,
    And god be with them all three!'

———◆———

C

a. Pepys Ballads, I, 364, No 187. b. Pepys Ballads, III, 314, No 310. c. Roxburghe Ballads, III, 146. d. Roxburge Ballads, III, 340. e. Bagford Ballads, I, 36.

1 As it fell on a light holyday,
    As many more does in the yeere,
Little Mousgrove would to the church and
        pray,
    To see the faire ladyes there.

2 Gallants there were of good degree,
    For beauty exceeding faire,
Most wonderous lovely to the eie,
    That did to that church repaire.

3 Some came downe in red velvet,
    And others came downe in pall,
But next came downe my Lady Barnet,
    The fairest amongst them all.

4 She cast a looke upon Little Mousgrove,
    As bright as the summer's sunne;
Full well perceived then Little Mousgrove
    Lady Barnet's love he had wonne.

5 Then Lady Barnet most meeke and mild
    Saluted this Little Mousgrove,
Who did repay her kinde courtesie
    With favour and gentle love.

6 ' I have a bower in merry Barnet,
    Bestrowed with cowslips sweet;
If that it please you, Little Mousgrove,
    In love me there to meete,

7 ' Within mine armes one night to sleepe,
    For you my heart have wonne,
You need not feare my suspicious lord,
    For he from home is gone.'

8 ' Betide me life, betide me death,
    This night I will sleepe with thee,
And for thy sake I 'le hazzard my breath,
    So deare is thy love to me.'

9 ' What shall wee doe with our little foot-page,
    Our counsell for to keepe,
And watch for feare Lord Barnet comes,
    Whilest wee together doe sleepe?'

10 ' Red gold shall be his hier,' quoth he,
    ' And silver shall be his fee,
If he our counsell safely doe keepe,
    That I may sleepe with thee.'

11 ' I will have none of your gold,' said he,
    ' Nor none of your silver fee;
If I should keepe your counsell, sir,
    'T were great disloyaltie.

12 'I will not be false unto my lord,
    For house nor yet for land;
But if my lady doe prove untrue,
    Lord Barnet shall understand.'

13 Then swiftly runnes the little foot-page,
    Unto his lord with speed,
Who then was feasting with his deare friends,
    Not dreaming of this ill deede.

14 Most speedily the page did haste,
    Most swiftly did he runne,
And when he came to the broken bridge
    He lay on his brest and swumme.

15 The page did make no stay at all,
    But went to his lord with speed,
That he the truth might say to him
    Concerning this wicked deed.

16 He found his lord at supper then,
    Great merriment there they did keepe:
'My lord,' quoth he, 'this night, on my word,
    Mousgrove with your lady does sleepe.'

17 'If this be true, my little foot-page,
    And true as thou tellest to me,
My eldest daughter I 'le give to thee,
    And wedded thou shalt be.

18 'If this be a lye, my little foot-page,
    And a lye as thou tellest to mee,
A new paire of gallowes shall straight be set,
    And hanged shalt thou be.'

19 'If this be a lye, my lord,' said he,
    'A lye that you heare from me,
Then never stay a gallowes to make,
    But hang me up on the next tree.'

20 Lord Barnet then cald up his merry men,
    Away with speed he would goe;
His heart was so perplext with griefe,
    The truth of this he must know.

21 'Saddle your horses with speed,' quoth he,
    'And saddle me my white steed;
If this be true as the page hath said,
    Mousgrove shall repent this deed.'

22 He charg'd his men no noise to make,
    As they rode all along on the way;

'Nor winde no hornes,' quoth he, 'on your life,
    Lest our comming it should betray.'

23 But one of the men, that Mousgrove did love,
    And respected his friendship most deare,
To give him knowledge Lord Barnet was
        neere,
    Did winde his bugle most cleere.

24 And evermore as he did blow,
    'Away, Mousgrove, and away;
For if I take thee with my lady,
    Then slaine thou shalt be this day.'

25 'O harke, fair lady, your lord is neere,
    I heare his little horne blow;
And if he finde me in your armes thus,
    Then slaine I shall be, I know.'

26 'O lye still, lye still, Little Mousgrove,
    And keepe my backe from the cold;
I know it is my father's shepheard,
    Driving sheepe to the pinfold.'

27 Mousgrove did turne him round about,
    Sweete slumber his eyes did greet;
When he did wake, he then espied
    Lord Barnet at his bed's feete.

28 'O rise up, rise up, Little Mousgrove,
    And put thy clothës on;
It shall never be said in faire England
    I slew a naked man.

29 'Here 's two good swords,' Lord Barnet said,
    'Thy choice, Mousgrove, thou shalt make;
The best of them thy selfe shalt have,
    And I the worst will take.'

30 The first good blow that Mousgrove did strike,
    He wounded Lord Barnet sore;
The second blow that Lord Barnet gave,
    Mousgrove could strike no more.

31 He tooke his lady by the white hand,
    All love to rage did convert,
That with his sword, in most furious sort,
    He pierst her tender heart.

32 'A grave, a grave,' Lord Barnet cryde,
    'Prepare to lay us in;
My lady shall lie on the upper side,
    Cause she 's of the better kin.'

33 Then suddenly he slue himselfe,
    Which grieves his friends full sore ;
    The deaths of these thra worthy wights
    With teares they did deplore.

34 This sad mischance by lust was wrought ;
    Then let us call for grace,
    That we may shun this wicked vice,
    And mend our lives apace.

D

Kinloch MSS, I, 287.

1 THERE were four and twenty gentlemen
    A playing at the ba,
    And lusty Lady Livingstone
    Cuist her ee out oure them a'.

2 She cuist her ee on Lord Barnard,
    He was baith black and broun ;
    She cuist her ee on Little Musgrave,
    As bricht as the morning sun.

3 .   .   .   .   .   .
    ' What 'll I gie ye, my Little Musgrave,
    Ae nicht wi me to sleep ? '

4 ' Ae nicht wi you to sleep,' he says,
    ' O that wad breed meikle strife ;
    For the ring on your white finger
    Shows you Lord Barnard's wife.'

5 ' O Lord Barnard he is gane frae hame,
    He 'll na return the day ;
    He has tane wi him a purse o goud,
    For he 's gane hind away.'

6 Up startit then the wylie foot-page,
    .   .   .   .   .
    ' What will ye gie to me,' he said,
    ' Your council for to keep ? '

7 ' O goud sall be my little boy's fee,
    And silver sall be his hire ;
    But an I hear a word mair o this,
    He sall burn in charcoal fire.'

8 But the wylie foot-page to the stable went,
    Took out a milk-white steed,
    And away, away, and away he rade,
    Away wi meikle speed.

9 It 's whan he cam to the water-side,
    He smoothd his breist and swam,
    And whan he cam to gerss growing,
    He set down his feet and ran.

10 ' Whan he cam to Lord Barnard's towr
    Lord Barnard was at meat ;
    He said, ' If ye kend as meikle as me,
    It 's little wad ye eat.'

11 ' Are onie o my castles brunt ? ' he says,
    ' Or onie my towrs won ?
    Or is my gay ladie broucht to bed,
    Of a dochter or a son ? '

12 ' There is nane o your castles brunt,
    Nor nane o your towrs won ;
    Nor is your gay ladie broucht to bed,
    Of a dochter or a son.

13 ' But Little Musgrave, that gay young man,
    Is in bed wi your ladie,
    .   .   .   .   .

14 ' If this be true ye tell to me,
    It 's goud sall be your fee ;
    But if it be fause ye tell to me,
    I 'se hang ye on a tree.'

*   *   *   *   *

15 Whan they cam to yon water-side,
    They smoothd their breists and swam ;
    And whan they cam to gerss growing,
    They set doun their feet and ran.

*   *   *   *   *

16 ' How do ye like my sheets ? ' he said,
    ' How do ye like my bed ?
    And how do ye like my gay ladie,
    Wha 's lying at your side ? '

17 ' O I do like your sheets,' he said,
    ' Sae do I like your bed ;
    But mair do I like your gay ladie,
    Wha 's lying at my side.'

18 ' Get up, get up, young man,' he said,
    ' Get up as swith 's ye can ;
    Let it never be said that Lord Barnard
    Slew in bed a nakit man.'

* * * * *

19 'How do ye like his bluidy cheeks?
　　Or how do ye like me?'
　'It 's weill do I like his bluidy cheeks,
　　Mair than your haill bodie.'

20 Then she has kissd his bluidy cheeks,
　　It 's oure and oure again,'

. . . . . .

———•———

E

Campbell MSS, II, 43.

1 Four and twenty gay ladies
　　Were playing at the ba,
　And [out] came Lord Barnaby's lady,
　　The fairest o them a'.

2 She coost her eyes on Little Musgrave,
　　And he on her again;
　She coost her eyes on Little Musgrave,
　　As they twa lovers had been.

3 'I have a hall in Mulberry,
　　It stands baith strong and tight;
　If you will go to there with me,
　　I 'll lye with you all night.'

4 'To lye with you, madam,' he says,
　　'Will breed both sturt and strife;
　I see by the rings on your fingers
　　You are Lord Barnaby's wife.'

5 'Lord Barnaby 's to the hunting gone,
　　And far out oer the hill,
　And he will not return again
　　Till the evening tide untill.'

6 They were not well lain down,
　　Nor yet well fallen asleep,
　Till up started Lord Barnaby's boy,
　　Just up at their bed-feet.

7 She took out a little penknife,
　　Which hung down low by her gair:
　'If you do not my secret keep,
　　A word ye 's neer speak mair.'

8 The laddie gae a blythe leer look,
　　A blythe leer look gave he,
　And he 's away to Lord Barnaby,
　　As fast as he can hie.

* * * * *

9 'If these tidings binna true,
　　These tidings ye tell to me,
　A gallows-tree I 'll gar be made
　　And hanged ye shall be.

10 'But if these tidings are true,
　　These tidings ye tell me,
　The fairest lady in a' my court
　　I 'll gar her marry thee.'

11 He 's taen out a little horn,
　　He blew baith loud and sma,
　And aye the turning o the tune
　　'Away, Musgrave, awa!'

12 They were not well lain down,
　　Nor yet well fallen asleep,
　Till up started Lord Barnaby,
　　Just up at their bed-feet.

13 'O how like ye my blankets, Musgrave?
　　And how like ye my sheets?
　And how like ye my gay lady,
　　So sound in your arms that sleeps?'

14 'Weel I like your blankets, Sir,
　　And far better yere sheets;
　And better far yere gay lady,
　　So sound in my arms that sleeps.'

15 'Get up, get up, now, Little Musgrave,
　　And draw to hose and sheen;
　It 's neer be said in my country
　　I 'd fight a naked man.

16 'There is two swords into my house,
　　And they cost me right dear;
　Take you the best, and I the worst,
　　I 'll fight the battle here.'

17 The first stroke that Lord Barnaby gave,
　　It was baith deep and sore;
　The next stroke that Lord Barnaby gave,
　　A word he never spoke more.

18 He 's taen out a rapier then,
　　He 's struck it in the straw,
　And thro and thro his lady's sides
　　He gard the cauld steel gae.

19 'I am not sae wae for Little Musgrave,
　　As he lys cauld and dead;
　But I 'm right wae for his lady,
　　For she 'll gae witless wud.

20 'I'm not sae wae for my lady,
　　For she lies cauld and dead;
　But I'm right wae for my young son,
　　Lies sprawling in her blood.'

21 First crew the black cock,
　　And next crew the sparrow;
　And what the better was Lord Barnaby?
　　He was hanged on the morrow.

F

Jamieson's Popular Ballads and Songs, I, 170.

1 'I HAVE a tower in Dalisberry,
　　Which now is dearly dight,
　And I will gie it to Young Musgrave,
　　To lodge wi me a' night.'

2 'To lodge wi thee a' night, fair lady,
　　Wad breed baith sorrow and strife;
　For I see by the rings on your fingers
　　You're good Lord Barnaby's wife.'

3 'Lord Barnaby's wife although I be,
　　Yet what is that to thee?
　For we'll beguile him for this ae night,
　　He's on to fair Dundee.

4 'Come here, come here, my little foot-page,
　　This gold I will give thee,
　If ye will keep thir secrets close
　　'Tween Young Musgrave and me.

5 'But here I hae a little pen-knife,
　　Hings low down by my gare;
　Gin ye winna keep thir secrets close,
　　Ye'll find it wonder sair.'

6 Then she's taen him to her chamber,
　　And down in her arms lay he;
　The boy coost aff his hose and shoon,
　　And ran to fair Dundee.

7 When he cam to the wan water,
　　He slackd his bow and swam,
　And when he cam to growin grass,
　　Set down his feet and ran.

8 And when he cam to fair Dundee,
　　Wad neither chap nor ca,
　But set his braid bow to his breast,
　　And merrily jumpd the wa.

9 'O waken ye, waken ye, my good lord,
　　Waken, and come away!'
　'What ails, what ails my wee foot-page,
　　He cries sae lang ere day?

10 'O is my bowers brent, my boy?
　　Or is my castle won?

Or has the lady that I loe best
　　Brought me a daughter or son?'

11 'Your ha's are safe, your bowers are safe,
　　And free frae all alarms,
　But, oh! the lady that ye loe best
　　Lies sound in Musgrave's arms.'

12 'Gae saddle to me the black,' he cried,
　　'Gae saddle to me the gray;
　Gae saddle to me the swiftest steed,
　　To hie me on my way.'

13 'O lady, I heard a wee horn toot,
　　And it blew wonder clear;
　And ay the turning o the note,
　　Was, Barnaby will be here!

14 'I thought I heard a wee horn blaw,
　　And it blew loud and high;
　And ay at ilka turn it said,
　　Away, Musgrave, away!'

15 'Lie still, my dear, lie still, my dear,
　　Ye keep me frae the cold;
　For it is but my father's shepherds,
　　Driving their flocks to the fold.'

16 Up they lookit, and down they lay,
　　And they're fa'en sound asleep;
　Till up stood good Lord Barnaby,
　　Just close at their bed-feet.

17 'How do you like my bed, Musgrave?
　　And how like ye my sheets?
　And how like ye my fair lady,
　　Lies in your arms and sleeps?'

18 'Weel like I your bed, my lord,
　　And weel like I your sheets,
　But ill like I your fair lady,
　　Lies in my arms and sleeps.

19 'You got your wale o se'en sisters,
　　And I got mine o five;
　Sae tak ye mine, and I's tak thine,
　　And we nae mair sall strive.'

20 'O my woman's the best woman
　　That ever brak world's bread,

And your woman 's the worst woman
  That ever drew coat oer head.

21 ' I hae twa swords in ae scabbert,
  They are baith sharp and clear;
  Tak ye the best, and I the warst,
  And we 'll end the matter here.

22 ' But up, and arm thee, Young Musgrave,
  We 'll try it han to han ;
  It 's neer be said o Lord Barnaby,
  He strack at a naked man.'

23 The first straik that Young Musgrave got,
  It was baith deep and sair,

And down he fell at Barnaby's feet,
  And word spak never mair.

*   *   *   *   *

24 ' A grave, a grave,' Lord Barnaby cried,
  ' A grave to lay them in ;
  My lady shall lie on the sunny side,
  Because of her noble kin.'

25 But oh, how sorry was that good lord,
  For a' his angry mood,
  Whan he beheld his ain young son
  All weltring in his blood !

G

Motherwell's MS., p. 643, from the recitation of Mrs Mc-Conechie, Kilmarnock.

1 LORD BARNARD's awa to the green wood,
  To hunt the fallow deer ;
  His vassals a' are gane wi him,
  His companie to bear.

2 His lady wrate a braid letter,
  And seald it wi her hand,
  And sent it aff to Wee Messgrove,
  To come at her command.

3 When Messgrove lookt the letter on,
  A waefu man was he ;
  Sayin, Gin I'm gript wi Lord Barnard's wife,
  Sure hanged I will be.

4 When he came to Lord Barnard's castel
  He tinklit at the ring,
  And nane was so ready as the lady hersell
  To let Wee Messgrove in.

5 ' Welcome, welcome, Messgrove,' she said,
  ' You 're welcome here to me ;
  Lang hae I loed your bonnie face,
  And lang hae ye loed me.

6 ' Lord Barnard is a hunting gane,
  I hope he 'll neer return,
  And ye sall sleep into his bed,
  And keep his lady warm.'

7 ' It cannot be,' Messgrove he said,
  ' I ween it cannot be ;
  Gin Lord Barnard suld come hame this nicht,
  What wuld he do to me ? '

8 ' Ye naething hae to fear, Messgrove,
  Ye naething hae to fear ;

I 'll set my page without the gate,
  To watch till morning clear.'

9 But wae be to the wee fut-page,
  And an ill death mat he die !
  For he 's awa to the green wood,
  As hard as he can flee.

10 And whan he to the green wood cam,
  'T was dark as dark could bee,
  And he fand his maister and his men
  Asleep aneth a tree.

11 ' Rise up, rise up, maister,' he said,
  ' Rise up, and speak to me ;
  Your wife 's in bed wi Wee Messgrove,
  Rise up richt speedilie.'

12 ' Gin that be true ye tell to me,
  A lord I will mak thee ;
  But gin it chance to be a lie,
  Sure hanged ye sall be.'

13 ' It is as true, my lord,' he said,
  ' As ever ye were born ;
  Messgrove 's asleep in your lady's bed,
  All for to keep her warm.'

14 He mounted on his milk-white steed,
  He was ane angry man ;
  And he reachd his stately castell gate
  Just as the day did dawn.

15 He put his horn unto his mouth,
  And he blew strong blasts three ;
  Sayin, He that 's in bed with anither man's wife,
  He suld be gaun awa.

16 Syne out and spak the Wee Messgrove,
  A frichtit man was he ;

' I hear Lord Barnard's horn,' he said,
   ' It blaws baith loud and hie.'

17 ' Lye still, lye still, my Wee Messgrove,
   And keep me frae the cauld ;
   'T is but my father's shepherd's horn,
   A sounding in the fauld.'

18 He put his horn unto his mouth,
   And he blew loud blasts three ;
   Saying, He that 's in bed wi anither man's wife,
   'T is time he was awa.

19 Syne out and spak the Wee Messgrove,
   A frichtit man was he :
   ' Yon surely is Lord Barnard's horn,
   And I maun een gae flee.'

20 ' Lye still, lye still, Messgrove,' she said,
   ' And keep me frae the cauld ;
   'T is but my father's shepherd's horn,
   A sounding in the fauld.'

21 And ay Lord Barnard blew and blew,
   Till he was quite wearie ;
   Syne he threw down his bugle horn,
   And up the stair ran he.

22 ' How do you like my blankets, Sir ?
   How do you like my sheets ?
   How do ye like my gay ladie,
   That lies in your arms asleep ? '

23 ' Oh weel I like your blankets, Sir,
   And weel I like your sheet ;
   But wae be to your gay ladie,
   That lyes in my arms asleep ! '

24 ' I 'll gie you ae sword, Messgrove,
   And I will take anither ;
   What fairer can I do, Messgrove,
   Altho ye war my brither ? '

25 The firsten wound that Messgrove gat,
   It woundit him richt sair ;
   And the second wound that Messgrove gat,
   A word he neer spak mair.

26 ' Oh how do ye like his cheeks, ladie ?
   Or how do ye like his chin ?
   Or how do ye like his fair bodie,
   That there 's nae life within ? '

27 ' Oh weel I like his cheeks,' she said,
   ' And weel I like his chin ;
   And weel I like his fair bodie,
   That there 's nae life within.'

28 ' Repeat these words, my fair ladie,
   Repeat them ower agane,
   And into a basin of pure silver
   I 'll gar your heart's bluid rin.'

29 ' Oh weel I like his cheeks,' she said,
   ' And weel I like his chin ;
   And better I like his fair bodie
   Than a' your kith and kin.'

30 Syne he took up his gude braid sword,
   That was baith sharp and fine,
   And into a basin of pure silver
   Her heart's bluid he gart rin.

31 ' O wae be to my merrie men,
   And wae be to my page,
   That they didna hald my cursed hands
   When I was in a rage ! '

32 He leand the halbert on the ground,
   The point o 't to his breast,
   Saying, Here are three sauls gaun to heaven,
   I hope they 'll a' get rest.

H

Motherwell's MS., p. 120.

1 LITTLE MUSGRAVE is to the church gone,
   Some ladies for to sply ;
   Doun came one drest in black,
   And one came drest in brown,
   And down and came Lord Barlibas' lady,
   The fairest in a' the town.

*   *   *   *   *

2 ' I know by the ring that 's on your finger
   That you 'r my Lord Barlibas' lady : '
   ' Indeed I am the Lord Barlibas' lady,
   And what altho I bee ? '

*   *   *   *   *

3 ' Money shall be your hire, foot-page,
   And gold shall be your fee ;
   You must not tell the secrets
   That 's between Musgrove and me.'

4 ' Money shall not be hire,' he said,
   ' Nor gold shall be my fee ;

But I 'll awa to my own liege lord,
  With the tidings you 've told to me.'

5 When he cam to the broken brig,
  He coost aff his clothes and he swimd,
And when he cam to Lord Barlibas' yett,
  He tirled at the pin.

6 'What news, what news, my little foot-page ?
  What news have ye brocht to me ?
Is my castle burnt ? ' he said,
  ' Or is my tower tane ?
Or is my lady lighter yet,
  Of a daughter or son ? '

7 ' Your castle is not burnt,' he says,
  ' Nor yet is your tower tane,
Nor yet is your lady brocht to bed,
  Of a daughter or a son ;
But Little Musgrove is lying wi her,
  Till he thinks it is time to be gane.'

8 ' O if the news be a lie,' he says,
  ' That you do tell unto me,
I 'll ca up a gallows to my yard-yett,
  And hangd on it thou shallt be.

9 ' But if the news be true,' he says,
  ' That you do tell unto me,
I have a young fair dochter at hame,
  Weel wedded on her you shall be.'

10 He called upon his merry men,
  By thirties and by three :
' Put aff the warst, put on the best,
  And come along with me.'

11 He put a horn to his mouth,
  And this he gard it say :
' The man that 's in bed wi Lord Barlibas' lady,
  It 's time he were up and away.'

12 ' What does yon trumpet mean ? ' he sayd,
  ' Or what does yon trumpet say ?

I think it says, the man that 's in bed wi Lord
  Barlibas' lady,
It 's time he were up and away.'

13 ' O lie you still, my Little Musgrove,
  And cover me from the cold,
For it is but my father's sheepherd,
  That 's driving his sheep to the fold.'

14 . . . . . .
  In a little while after that,
Up started good Lord Barlibas,
  At Little Musgrove his feet.

15 ' How do you like my blankets ? ' he says,
  ' Or how do you like my sheets ?
Or how do you like mine own fair lady,
  That lies in your arms and sleeps ? '

16 ' I like your blankets very well,
  And far better your sheets;
But woe be to this wicked woman,
  That lies in my arms and sleeps ! '

17 ' Rise up, rise up, my Little Musgrove,
  Rise up, and put your clothes on ;
It 's neer be said on no other day
  That I killed a naked man.

18 ' There is two swords in my chamber,
  I wot they cost me dear ;
Take you the best, give me the warst,
  We 'll red the question here.'

19 The first stroke that Lord Barlibas struck,
  He dang Little Musgrove to the ground ;
The second stroke that Lord Barlibas gave
  Dang his lady in a deadly swound.

20 ' Gar mak, gar mak a coffin,' he says,
  ' Gar mak it wide and long,
And lay my lady at the right hand,
  For she 's come of the noblest kin.'

I

Motherwell's MS., p. 305, from the recitation of Rebecca
Dunse, 4th May, 1825 : one of her mother's songs, an old
woman.

*   *   *   *   *

1 ' It 's gold shall be your hire,' she says,
  ' And silver shall be your fee,
If you will keep the secrets
  Between Little Sir Grove and me.'

2 ' Tho gold should be my hire,' he says,
  ' And silver should be my fee,
It 's I 'll not keep the secret
  Betwixt Little Sir Grove and thee.'

3 Up he rose, and away he goes,
  And along the plain he ran,
And when he came to Lord Bengwill's castle,
  He tinkled at the pin ;
And who was sae ready as Lord Bengwill himsell
  To let this little page in.

4 'Is any of my towers burnt?' he said,
   ' Or any of my castles taen ?
Or is Lady Bengwill brought to bed,
   Of a daughter or a son ?'

5 'It's nane of your towers are burnt,' he said,
   ' Nor nane of your castles taen ;
But Lady Bengwill and Little Sir Grove
   To merry bed they are gane.'

6 'If this be true that you tell me,
   Rewarded you shall be ;
And if it's a lie that you tell me,
   You shall be hanged before your ladie's ee.

7 'Get saddled to me the black,' he says,
   ' Get saddled to me the brown ;
Get saddled to me the swiftest steed
   That ever man rode on.'

8 The firsten town that he came to,
   He blew baith loud and schill,
And aye the owre-word o the tune
   Was, ' Sir Grove, I wish you well.'

9 The nexten town that he came to,
   He blew baith loud and long,
And aye the owre-word of the tune
   Was ' Sir Grove, it is time to be gone.'

10 ' Is yon the sound of the hounds ?' he says,
   ' Or is yon the sound of the deer ?
But I think it's the sound of my brother's horn,
   That sounds sae schill in my ear.'

11 ' Lye still, lye still, Sir Grove,' she says,
   ' And keep a fair lady from cold ;
It's but the sound of my father's herd-boys,
   As they're driving the sheep to the fold.'

12 They lay down in each other's arms,
   And they fell fast asleep,
And neer a one of them did wake
   Till Lord Bengwill stood at their feet.

13 ' How do you love my soft pillow ?
   Or how do you love my sheets ?
Or how do you love my fair lady,
   That lies in your arms and sleeps ? '

14 ' Full well I love your soft pillow,
   Far better I love your sheets ;
But woe be to your fair lady,
   That lies in my arms and sleeps ! '

15 ' Rise up, rise up, Sir Grove,' he says,
   ' Some clothes there put you upon ;
Let it never be said in fair England
   I fought with a naked man.'

16 ' Oh where shall I go, or where shall I fly,
   Or where shall I run for my life ?
For you've got two broadswords into your hand,
   And I have never a knife.'

17 ' You shall take the one sword,' he says,
   ' And I shall take the other,
And that is as fair I'm sure to day
   As that you are my born brother.'

18 ' Hold your hand, hold your hand, my brother dear,
   You've wounded me full sore ;
You may get a mistress in every town,
   But a brother you'll never get more.'

19 The very first stroke that Lord Bengwill gave him,
   He wounded him full sore ;
The very next stroke that Lord Bengwill gave him,
   A word he never spoke more.

20 He's lifted up Lady Bengwill,
   And set her on his knee,
Saying, Whether do you love Little Sir Grove
   Better than you do me ?

21 ' Full well I love your cherry cheeks,
   Full well I love your chin,
But better I love Little Sir Grove, where he lies,
   Than you and all your kin.'

*   *   *   *   *

22 ' A grave, a grave,' Lord Bengwill cried,
   ' To put these lovers in,
And put Lady Bengwill uppermost,
   For she's come of the noblest kin.'

———◆———

J

Motherwell's MS., p. 371, from the recitation of Agnes
Lyle, Kilbarchan.

1 FOUR and twenty ladies fair
   Was playing at the ba,

And out cam the lady, Barnabas' lady,
   The flower amang them a'.

2 She coost an ee on Little Mossgrey,
   As brisk as any sun,
And he coost anither on her again,
   And they thocht the play was won.

3 'What would you think, Little Mossgrey,
   To lye wi me this nicht?
Good beds I hae in Barnabey,
   If they were ordered richt.'

4 'Hold thy tongue, fair lady,' he says,
   'For that would cause much strife;
For I see by the rings on your fingers
   That you 're Lord Barnabas' wife.'

5 'Lord Barnabas' lady indeed I am,
   And that I 'll let you ken,
But he 's awa to the king's court,
   And I hope he 'll neer come hame.'

6 Wi wrapped arms in bed they lay
   Till they fell both asleep,
When up and starts Barnabas' boy,
   And stood at their bed-feet.

7 'How likes thou the bed, Mossgrey?
   Or how likes thou the sheets?
Or how likes thou my master's lady,
   Lyes in thy arms and sleeps?'

8 'Weel I love the bed,' he said,
   'And far better the sheets;
But foul may fa your master's lady,
   Lies in my arms and sleeps!'

9 She pulled out a rusty sword,
   Was sticking by the stroe;
Says, Tell no tidings of me, my boy,
   Or thou 'll neer tell no moe.

10 He 's awa to the king's court,
   As fast as he can dree;
He 's awa to the king's court,
   For to tell Barnaby.

11 'Are there any of my biggins brunt?
   Or any of my young men slain?
Or is my lady brocht to bed,
   Of a dochter or a son?'

12 'There is none of your biggings brunt,
   There 's none of your young men slain;
But Little Mossgrey and your lady
   They are both in a bed within.'

13 'If that be true, my bonnie boy,
   Thou tellest unto me,
I have not a dochter but only one,
   And married ye shall be.

14 'But if it be a lie, my bonnie boy,
   You 're telling unto me,
On the highest tree of Bailsberry,
   Thereon I 'll gar hang thee.'

15 There was a man in the king's court
   Had a love to Little Mossgrey;
He took a horn out of his pocket,
   And blew both loud and hie:
'He that 's in bed wi Barnabas' lady,
   It 's time he were away!'

16 'Oh am I not the maddest man
   Ere lay in a woman's bed!
I think I hear his bridle ring,
   But and his horse feet tread.'

17 'Lye still, lye still, Little Mossgrey,
   And keep me from the cold;
It 's but my father's small sheep-herd,
   Calling his sheep to the fold.'

18 With wrapped arms in bed they lay
   Till they fell both asleep,
Till up and darts Barnabas himsell,
   And stood at their bed-fit.

19 'How likest thou the bed, Mossgrey?
   And how loves thou the sheets?
And how loves thou my lady fair,
   Lyes in your arms and sleeps?'

20 'Well I love your bed,' he says,
   'And far better your sheets;
But foul may fa your lady fair,
   Lyes in my arms and sleeps!'

21 'Rise, O rise, Little Mossgrey,
   Put on your hose and shoon;
I 'll neer hae 't said in a far countrie
   I killed a naked man.'

22 Slowly, slowly rose he up,
   And slowly put he on,
And slowly down the stairs he goes,
   And thinking to be slain.

23 'Here 's two swords,' Barnabas said,
   'I wad they cost me dear;
Tak thou the best, I 'll tak the warst,
   We 'll try the battle here.'

24 The first stroke that Mossgrey got,
   It was baith sharp and sore;
And the next stroke his lady got,
   One word she neer spak more.

25 'Ye 'll mak a coffin large and wide,
   And lay this couple in;
And lay her head on his right hand,
   She 's come o the highest kin.'

K

Dr Joseph Robertson's Journal of Excursions, No 5, taken down from a man in the parish of Leochel, Aberdeenshire, February 12, 1829.

1 It 's four and twenty bonny boys
      Were playin at the ba,
  And out it cums Lord Barnet's ladie,
      And playit out ower them a'.

2 And aye she shot it 's Little Mousgray,
      As clear as any sun :
  ' O what wad ye gie, it 's Little Mousgray,
      It 's in O my arms to won? '

3 ' For no, for no, my gay ladie,
      For no, that maunna be ;
  For well ken I by the rings on your fingers,
      Lord Barnet's ladie are ye.'

4 When supper was over, and mass was sung,
      And a' man boun for bed,
  It 's Little Mousgray and that lady
      In ae chamber was laid.

5 It 's up and starts her little foot-page,
      Just up at her bed-feet :
  ' Hail weel, hail weel, my little foot-page,
      Hail well this deed on me,
  An ever I lee my life to brook,
      I 'se pay you well your fee.'

6 Out it spaks it 's Little Mousgray :
      ' I think I hear a horn blaw ;
  She blaws baith loud and shill at ilka turning of the
          tune,
      Mousgray, gae ye your wa ! '

7 ' Lie still, lie still, it 's Little Mousgray,
      Had the caul win frae my back ;
  It 's bat my father's proud shepherds,
      The 're huntin their hogs to the fauld.'

8 O up it starts the bold Barnet :

  .   .   .   .   .   .

  .   .   .   .   .   .

9 ' Win up, win up, it 's Little Mousgray,
      Draw ti your stockins and sheen ;
  I winna have it for to be said
      I killed a naked man.

10 ' There is two swords in my scabbart,
      They cost me many a pun ;
  Tak ye the best, and I the warst,
      And we sall to the green.'

11 The firsten strok Lord Barnet strak,
      He wound Mousgray very sore ;
  The nexten stroke Lord Barnet strak,
      Mousgray spak never more.

12 O he 's taen out a lang, lang brand,
      And stripped it athwart the straw,
  And throch and throu his ain ladie
      And he 's gart it cum and ga.

13 There was nae main made for that ladie,
      In bower whar she lay dead !
  But a' was for her bonny young son,
      Lay blobberin amang the bluid.

———◆———

L

Buchan's MSS, I, 27 ; Scottish Traditional Versions of Ancient Ballads, Percy Society, XVII, 21.

1 Four an twenty handsome youths
      Were a' playing at the ba,
  When forth it came him Little Munsgrove,
      The flower out ower them a'.

2 At times he lost, at times he wan,
      Till the noon-tide o the day,
  And four an twenty gay ladies
      Went out to view the play.

3 Some came down in white velvet,
      And other some in green ;
  Lord Burnett's lady in red scarlet,
      And shin'd like ony queen.

4 Some came down in white velvet,
      And other some in pale ;
  Lord Burnett's lady in red scarlet,
      Whose beauty did excell.

5 She gae a glance out ower them a',
      As beams dart frae the sun ;
  She fixed her eyes on Little Munsgrove,
      For him her love lay on.

6 ' Gude day, gude day, ye handsome youth,
      God make ye safe and free ;
  What woud ye gie this day, Munsgrove,
      For ae night in bower wi me ? '

7 ' I darena for my lands, lady,
      I darena for my life ;

I ken by the rings on your fingers
Ye are Lord Burnett's wife.'

8 'It woud na touch my heart, Munsgrove,
Nae mair than 't woud my tae,
To see as much o his heart's blood
As twa brands coud let gae.

9 'I hae a bower in fair Strathdon,
And pictures round it sett,
And I hae ordered thee, Munsgrove,
In fair Strathdon to sleep.'

10 Her flattering words and fair speeches,
They were for him too strong,
And she 's prevailed on Little Munsgrove
With her to gang along.

11 When mass was sung, and bells were rung,
And a' man bound for bed,
Little Munsgrove and that lady
In ae chamber were laid.

12 'O what hire will ye gie your page,
If he the watch will keep,
In case that your gude lord come hame
When we 're fair fast asleep ?'

13 'Siller, siller 's be his wage,
And gowd shall be his hire;
But if he speak ae word o this,
He 'll die in a burning fire.'

14 'The promise that I make, Madam,
I will stand to the same;
I winna heal it an hour langer
Than my master comes hame.'

15 She 's taen a sharp brand in her hand,
Being in the tidive hour ;
He ran between her and the door,
She never saw him more.

16 Where he found the grass grow green,
He slacked his shoes an ran,
And where he found the brigs broken,
He bent his bow an swam.

17 Lord Burnett ower a window lay,
Beheld baith dale and down ;
And he beheld his ain foot-page
Come hastening to the town.

8 'What news, what news, my little wee boy,
Ye bring sae hastilie ?'
'Bad news, bad news, my master,' he says,
'As ye will plainly see.'

19 'Are any of my biggins brunt, my boy ?
Or are my woods hewed down ?
Or is my dear lady lighter yet,
O dear daughter or son ?'

20 'There are nane o your biggins brunt, master,
Nor are your woods hewn down;
Nor is your lady lighter yet,
O dear daughter nor son.

21 'But ye've a bower in fair Strathdon,
And pictures round it sett,
Where your lady and Little Munsgrove
In fair Strathdon do sleep.'

22 'O had your tongue ! why talk you so
About my gay ladye ?
She is a gude and chaste woman
As in the North Countrie.'

23 'A word I dinna lie, my lord,
A word I dinna lie ;
And if ye winna believe my word,
Your ain twa een shall see.'

24 'Gin this be a true tale ye tell,
That ye have tauld to me,
I 'll wed you to my eldest daughter,
And married you shall be.

25 'But if it be a fause story
That ye hae tauld to me,
A high gallows I 'll gar be built,
And hanged shall ye be.'

26 He 's called upon his landlady,
The reckoning for to pay,
And pulled out twa hands fou o gowd ;
Says, We 'll reckon anither day.

27 He called upon his stable-groom,
To saddle for him his steed,
And trampled ower yon rocky hills
Till his horse hoofs did bleed.

28 There was a man in Lord Burnett's train
Was ane o Munsgrove's kin,
And aye as fast as the horsemen rade,
Sae nimbly 's he did rin.

29 He set a horn to his mouth,
And he blew loud and sma,
And aye at every sounding's end,
'Awa, Munsgrove, awa!'

30 Then up it raise him Little Munsgrove,
And drew to him his sheen ;
'Lye still, lye still,' the lady she cried,
'Why get ye up sae seen ?'

31 'I think I hear a horn blaw,
　　And it blaws loud and sma;
　　And aye at every sounding's end,
　　Awa, Munsgrove, awa!'

32 'Lye still, lye still, ye Little Munsgrove,
　　Had my back frae the wind ;
　　It 's but my father's proud shepherd,
　　Caing his hogs to town.'

33 'I think I hear a horn blaw,
　　And it blaws loud and shrill,
　　And aye at every sounding's end
　　Bids Munsgrove take the hill.'

34 'Lye still, my boy, lye still, my sweet,
　　Had my back frae the cauld ;
　　It 's but the sugh o the westlin wind,
　　Blawing ower the birks sae bauld.'

35 He turned him right and round about,
　　And he fell fast asleep ;
　　When up it started Lord Burnett,
　　And stood at their bed-feet.

36 'Is 't for love o my blankets, Munsgrove ?
　　Or is 't for love o my sheets ?
　　Or is 't for love o my gay lady ?
　　Sae soun in your arms she sleeps!'

37 'It 's nae for love o your blankets, my lord,
　　Nor yet for love o your sheets ;
　　But wae be to your gay ladye,
　　Sae soun in my arms she sleeps!'

38 'Win up, win up, ye Little Munsgrove,
　　Put all your armour an ;
　　It 's never be said anither day
　　I killed a naked man.

39 'I hae twa brands in ae scabbard,
　　Cost me merks twenty-nine ;
　　Take ye the best, gie me the warst,
　　For ye 're the weakest man.'

40 The first an stroke that Munsgrove drew
　　Wounded Lord Burnett sair ;
　　The next an stroke Lord Burnett drew,
　　Munsgrove he spake nae mair.

41 He turned him to his ladye then,
　　And thus to her said he :
　　'All the time we 've led our life
　　I neer thought this o thee.

42 'How like ye now this well-faird face,
　　That stands straight by your side ?
　　Or will ye hate this ill-faird face,
　　Lyes weltering in his blude ? '

43 'O better love I this well-faird face,
　　Lyes weltering in his blude,
　　Then eer I 'll do this ill-faird face,
　　That stands straight by my side.'

44 Then he 's taen out a sharp dagger,
　　It was baith keen and smart,
　　And he has wounded that gay ladye
　　A deep wound to the heart.

45 'A grave, a grave,' cried Lord Burnett,
　　'To bury these two in,
　　And lay my ladye in the highest flat,
　　She 's chiefest o the kin.

46 'A grave, a grave,' said Lord Burnett,
　　'To bury these two in ;
　　Lay Munsgrove in the lowest flat,
　　He 's deepest in the sin.

47 'Ye 'll darken my windows up secure,
　　Wi staunchions round about,
　　And there is not a living man
　　Shall eer see me walk out.

48 'Nae mair fine clothes my body deck,
　　Nor kame gang in my hair,
　　Nor burning coal nor candle light
　　Shine in my bower mair.'

————◆————

M

Motherwell's Minstrelsy, Appendix, p. xx, XXI

It fell upon a Martinmas time,
　　When the nobles were a' drinking wine,

That Little Mushiegrove to the kirk he did go,
　　For to see the ladies come in.

N

Communicated by Miss Margaret Reburn, as heard in County Meath, Ireland, about 1860.

1 'How do you like my rug?' he said,
  'And how do you like my sheets?

And how do you like my false ladie,
  That lies in your arms asleep?'

2 'Well I like your rug my lord,
  And well I like your sheets;
But better than all your fair ladie,
  That lies in my arms asleep.'

A. a. 3^2. in pale. 6^2. geight. 6^3. wilt wed.
      9^2. or sinn. 17^3. thou fair.
      29^8. on upper.

   b. 1^4. Their masses and mattins.
      2^2. *omits* private. 3^2. pale. 3^4. among.
      4^4. I have. 5^4. Yet word I never durst.
      6^2. daintily bedight. 7^1. lady fair.
      7^2. you shew. 7^4. will I.
      8^1. All this was heard by.
      8^3. Quo he, though I am my ladies page.
      8^4. my lord. 9^2. Although I lose a limb.
      9^8. whereas. 10^4. thy none.
      11^4. *omits* will. 14^3. when as the.
      14^4. Away, thou little Musgrave.
      15^3. Bernards horn. 16^4. to fold.
      17^1. the perch. 17^3. thy fair.
      18^2. lighted upon a stone.
      19^4. Doest find my lady so sweet.
      20^3. hunder'd pound. 21^4. That I killed.
      25^3. not do. 25^4. Though I.
      26^1. *omits* That: heart. 27^2. ne're were.
      28^2. on a.

B. 5^4. Musgerue. 6 *is written in the MS. after* 8, *but a marginal note by the scribe directs this stanza to be put two higher than it is written.* Furnivall.
   8^4. awaw. 9^8. out 3.
   11^2. *Between here and* 12^8 *half a page is gone.*
   13^4. all 3.

C. a. The lamentable Ditty of Little Mousgrove and the Lady Barnet. . . . . London, printed for H. Gosson. *Stanzas of eight lines.*
   b. London: printed for J. Clark, W. Thackeray, and T. Passenger.
   c. A Lamentable Ballad of the Little Musgrove and the Lady Barnet. . . . . London, printed for F. Coles, T. Vere, J. Wright, and J. Clarke.
   e. London: printed by and for W. O., and are to be sold by the Booksellers.
   a. 15^8. might lay. *After* 16 : The second part.

b., c. Musgrove *throughout.*
   1^1. light *wanting.* 1^2. more be.
   2^4. which did to the.
   3^2. some came. c. pale.
   3^8. The next: the lady. 3^4. c. among.
   4^1. upon. 4^3. well thou perceived.
   5^1. The: most *wanting.* 5^8. b. reply.
   6^8. that you please. 7^2. my love.
   8^1. b. my life: my death. 8^2. will lye.
   8^4. c. my love to thee. 9^8. come.
   9^4. While: doe *wanting.*
   10^8. So he: doe *wanting.* 11^1. he said.
   13^1. ran this. 13^8. b. He then.
   13^8. his own. 14^2. c. he did.
   14^4. bent his. 15^2. to the.
   15^8. b. my say. c. may say.
   16^2. there *wanting.* c. did make.
   16^8. upon. 16^4. doth.
   17^2. that thou. b. telst. 17^8. to *wanting.*
   18^2. as *wanting.* b. to *wanting.*
   18^8. shall be set up. 18^4 thou shalt.
   19^2. thou hearest of. c. And a.
   19^8. Never stay a pair of gallows to make.
      b. to *wanting.*
   19^4. me on.
   20^1. Lord Barnet calld his merry men all.
   20^8. was so. 21^1. he said.
   21^4. b. his deed. 22^1. to make no noise.
   22^2. all . . . on *wanting.* 22^8. horn.
   23^1. c. of them that.
   23^8. him notice: was come.
   23^4. wind the. 24^1. did sound.
   24^8. if he. 26^4. into the.
   27^8. awake: did espy. b. then he.
   27^4. the beds. 28^2. cloathing.
   28^8. c. never shall. 28^8. England fair.
   28^4. That I. 29^1. b. Here is two swords.
   29^2. c. The choice: Musgrove shall.
   29^8. shall. 30^1. good *wanting.*
   $30^{1,8}$. that *wanting.* 31^2. did *wanting.*
   31^8. And with: furious wise.
   32^4. she 's the better skin: c. she is.

33². b. grieved. c. grievd.
33³. c. death of these worthy.
34¹. c. mischief. 34³. b. shun the.
34⁴. And fly from sin.
d. 1¹. a high. 9¹. with this.
11³. counsel, Madam. 21². my milk-white.
23⁴. wind his bugle horn clear.
33³. these three lovely.
e. 1¹. a high. 1³. Little *wanting*.
3⁸. Then next. 8¹. my life: my death.
13³. He then. 15³. might tell to.
19². that *wanting*. 26⁴. unto the.

28². an *for* on. 29¹. Here is two.
29². Musgrove thy choice now make.
31³. most *wanting*. 34³. shun the.
E. 10¹. this tidings. 12³. Banburry.
15³. It neer. 18². struck her.
19⁴. wud: (with it) *in margin.*
G. 10¹. (cam) to the green wood cam.
H. 13¹. Oh.
I. 9³. old word.
K. 2¹. *Corrupt:* cf. A4, C4, D2, *etc.*
13². lay slain.
L. 9⁴. On. 48¹. decks.

82

THE BONNY BIRDY

Jamieson-Brown MS., fol. 42; Jamieson's Popular Ballads, I, 162.

JAMIESON, in printing this ballad, gave the husband the name Lord Randal, made many changes, and introduced several stanzas, "to fill up chasms." But the chasms, such as they are, are easily leapt by the imagination, and Jamieson's interpolations are mere bridges of carpenter's work. The admirably effective burden is taken into the story at stanza 11. As Jamieson remoulds the ballad, it is no burden, but a part of the dialogue throughout.

The main part of the action is the same as in 'Little Musgrave.' The superior lyrical quality of the Scottish ballad makes up for its inferiority as a story, so that on the whole it cannot be prized much lower than the noble English ballad.

Cunningham has rewritten the ballad in his own style, pretending, as often, to have known another recited copy: 'Sir Hugh,' Songs of Scotland, II, 130.

1 THERE was a knight, in a summer's night,
  Was riding oer the lee,   diddle
An there he saw a bonny birdy,
  Was singing upon a tree.   diddle
    O wow for day!   diddle
    An dear gin it were day!   diddle
    Gin it were day, an gin I were away!
    For I ha na lang time to stay.   diddle

2 'Make hast, make hast, ye gentle knight,
    What keeps you here so late?
  Gin ye kent what was doing at hame,
    I fear you woud look blate.'

3 'O what needs I toil day an night,
    My fair body to kill,
  Whan I hae knights at my comman,
    An ladys at my will?'

4 'Ye lee, ye lee, ye gentle knight,
    Sa loud 's I hear you lee;
  Your lady 's a knight in her arms twa
    That she lees far better nor the.'

5 'Ye lee, you lee, you bonny birdy,
    How you lee upo my sweet!

I will tak out my bonny bow,
　　An in troth I will you sheet.'

6 'But afore ye hae your bow well bent,
　　An a' your arrows yare,
I will flee till another tree,
　　Whare I can better fare.'

7 'O whare was you gotten, and whare was ye
　　　clecked?
　　My bonny birdy, tell me:'
'O I was clecked in good green wood,
　　Intill a holly tree;
A gentleman my nest herryed,
　　An ga me to his lady.

8 'Wi good white bread an farrow-cow milk
　　He bade her feed me aft,
An ga her a little wee simmer-dale wanny,
　　To ding me sindle and saft.

9 'Wi good white bread an farrow-cow milk
　　I wot she fed me nought,
But wi a little wee simmer-dale wanny
　　She dang me sair an aft:
Gin she had deen as ye her bade,
　　I woudna tell how she has wrought.'

10 The knight he rade, and the birdy flew,
　　The live-lang simmer's night,
Till he came till his lady's bowr-door,
　　Then even down he did light:

The birdy sat on the crap of a tree,
　　An I wot it sang fu dight.

11 'O wow for day!　　　diddle
　　An dear gin it were day!　　　diddle
Gin it were day, an gin I were away!
　　For I ha na lang time to stay.'　　　diddle

12 'What needs ye lang for day,　　　diddle.
　　An wish that you were away?　　　diddle
Is no your hounds i my cellar,
　　Eating white meal an gray?'　　　diddle
　　　O wow, etc.

13 'Is nae your steed in my stable,
　　Eating good corn an hay?
An is nae your hawk i my perch-tree,
　　Just perching for his prey?
An is nae yoursel i my arms twa?
　　Then how can ye lang for day?'

14 'O wow for day!　　　diddle
　　An dear gin it were day!　　　diddle
For he that's in bed wi anither man's wife
　　Has never lang time to stay.'　　　diddle

15 Then out the knight has drawn his sword,
　　An straiked it oer a strae,
An thro and thro the fa'se knight's waste
　　He gard cauld iron gae:
An I hope ilk ane sal sae be servd
　　That treats ane honest man sae.

———————————

*The burden stands thus in the manuscript after
the first stanza :*

　O wow for day,　　diddle
　An dear gin it were day,　　diddle

Gin it were day,　diddle
I were away,
For I ha na lang time to stay.　diddle

13¹. nae you. (?)

CHILD MAURICE

A. 'Childe Maurice,' Percy MS., p. 346; Hales and Furnivall, II, 502.

B. 'Child Noryce,' Motherwell's MS., p. 255; Motherwell's Minstrelsy, p. 282.

C. 'Bob Norice,' Motherwell's MS., p. 510.

D. 'Gill Morice,' Motherwell's MS., p. 480.

E. 'Chield Morice,' Motherwell's MS., p. 165; Motherwell's Minstrelsy, p. 269.

F. a. 'Gil Morrice,' Percy's Reliques, III, 93, 1765. b. Letter of T. Gray, June, 1757 (?).

G. Jamieson's Popular Ballads, I, 18, three stanzas; Jamieson, in The Scots Magazine, 1803, LXV, 698, two stanzas.

———◆———

A was printed from the Percy manuscript by Jamieson, in his Popular Ballads, I, 8. Of B Motherwell says, 1827 : " By testimony of a most unexceptionable description, but which it would be tedious here to detail, the editor can distinctly trace this ballad as existing in its present shape at least a century ago."

In his preface to the copy of the ballad in the Reliques of Ancient Poetry (F), Percy remarks : " The following piece has lately run through two editions in Scotland, the second printed at Glasgow in 1755, 8vo. Prefixed to them both is an advertisement, setting forth that the preservation of this poem was owing ' to a lady, who favored the printers with a copy as it was carefully collected from the mouths of old women and nurses ; ' and ' any reader that can render it more correct or complete ' is desired to oblige the public with such

improvements. In consequence of this advertisement sixteen additional verses have been produced and handed about in manuscript, which are here inserted in their proper places." The copy printed in 1755 * and earlier had already " received very considerable modern improvements," as Percy goes on to say, the most noticeable of which is a conclusion of eight stanzas, in the taste of the middle of the last century. These, as also the four stanzas which had been handed about in manuscript, are omitted from this reprint.

Home's tragedy of Douglas, produced in Edinburgh in 1756, was founded upon the story of Gil Morice, and the popularity of the play seems to have given vogue to the ballad.† The sophisticated copy passed into recitation, and may very likely have more or less infected those which were repeated from ear-

---

* The edition of 1755 is not known now to exist. Mr David Laing showed Motherwell a copy, without place or date, with the title : Gill Morice, An Ancient Scots Poem. The foundation of the tragedy called Douglas, as it is now acted in the Concert-Hall, Canongate. There was no material difference between this edition and that which was reprinted in the Reliques, except that it lacked the four stanzas which Percy introduced. Motherwell's Minstrelsy, p. 259, note.

In Herd's MSS, I, 7, II, 70, there are half a dozen more stanzas, from The Weekly Magazine, August 13, 1772, which continue the story still further. My lady flings herself over a craig, my lord seeks death in battle. But, as Sir Walter Scott notes in the margin, these verses are " formed on the conclusion of Douglas, which tragedy is founded on the

original ballad." These stanzas are printed by Jamieson, I, 21.

Mr Macmath has communicated to me an early copy of ' Gil Morice,' without place or date, in conjunction with a parody, entitled The Seven Champions of the Stage, printed in 1757, which satirizes Parson Home's efforts to get his Agis and his Douglas acted by Garrick. This copy of ' Gil Morice ' might be another edition of that which Mr Laing possessed. Its variations, which are of slight consequence, will be given in the notes to F.

† The name of the heroine in the tragedy of Douglas was originally Lady Barnard, as in the ballad ; it was altered to Lady Randolph when the play was produced in London. Motherwell, p. 257, note.

lier tradition. An old woman (Mrs Thomson, the reciter of E), who was born about the time when the ballad was printed, told Motherwell that she had learned 'Chield Morice' in her infancy from her grandmother, but at a later period of her life committed to memory 'Gil Morice,' " which began, with young lasses like her, to be a greater favorite and more fashionable than the set which her grandmother and old folks used to sing." *

Gray writes to Mason, June, 1757 (?): " I have got the old Scotch ballad on which Douglas was founded ; it is divine, and as long as from hence [Cambridge] to Aston." † He cites the first fifteen lines.

The copy in Smith's Scottish Minstrel, III, 106, is Herd's (Percy's), with omissions and changes. 'Child Nourice,' a fragment, in Buchan's MSS, I, 143, is of recent make.

The name of Barnard, a name, says Aytoun, quite foreign to Scotland, may have been adopted from 'Little Musgrave.' There is a marked similarity in the conclusion of the two ballads.

Aytoun, in his compilation, I, 147, 149, rejects the two stanzas, F 13, 14, beginning, " And when he came to broken brigue," as taken from 'Lady Maisry.' These stanzas are the most favorite of all commonplaces,

and belong as much to one ballad as another. They occur in one version or another of ' Lord Ingram,' ' Little Musgrave,' ' The Clerk's Twa Sons,' etc., and wearisomely often in the ballads in Buchan's collection.

The popularity of 'Gil Morice' since the middle of the last century has caused the story to be localized. The green wood, says Motherwell, was believed to be " the ancient forest of Dundaff, in Stirlingshire, and Lord Barnard's castle to have occupied a precipitous cliff overhanging the Water of Carron, on the lands of Halbertshire." Gil Morice, " according to the unvarying traditions of the country, was remarkable for the extreme length and loveliness of his yellow hair." Motherwell considers that the embellishments of the ballad may have been suggested by these traditions. But why should not these traditions have been derived from the embellished ballad ? There had already been nearly fourscore years for them to grow up at the date of the publication of his Minstrelsy.

B is translated by Wolff, Halle der Völker, I, 11, Hausschatz, p. 222 ; F by Loève-Veimars, p. 316, with some retrenchment ; Allingham's copy by Knortz, Lieder u. Romanzen Alt-Englands, No 31.

A

Percy MS., p. 346 ; Hales and Furnivall, II, 502.

1 CHILDE MAURICE hunted ithe siluer wood,
   He hunted itt round about,
   And noebodye *that* he ffound therin,
   Nor none there was with-out.

2 .   .   .   .   .   .
   .   .   .   .   .
   And he tooke his siluer combe in his hand,
   To kembe his yellow lockes.

3 He sayes, Come hither, thou litle ffoot-page,
   That runneth lowlye by my knee,
   Ffor thou shalt goe to Iohn Stewards wiffe
   And pray her speake with mee.

4 '.   .   .   .   .
   .   .   .   .   .
   I, and greete thou doe *that* ladye well,
   Euer soe well ffroe mee.

5 ' And, as itt ffalls, as many times
   As knotts beene knitt on a kell,

* Minstrelsy, p. 269, note. Mr Aytoun considers that E is only the copy printed in the middle of the last century purged, in the process of oral transmission, of what was not to the popular taste, "and altered more." There is no doubt that a copy learned from print may be transformed in this way, but it is certain that old tradition does not come to a stop when a ballad gets into print. Mrs Thomson's account

of the matter Aytoun does not heed. It is difficult to understand why Aytoun printed the stanzas from Percy's Reliques, at I, 149 f, 2d ed., except as a simple courtesy to his correspondent.

† Already cited in The Ballad Minstrelsy of Scotland, Glasgow, 1871, p. 316.

Or marchant men gone to leeue London,
  Either to buy ware or sell.

6 ' And, as itt ffalles, as many times
    As any hart can thinke,
  Or schoole-masters are in any schoole-house,
    Writting with pen and inke :
  Ffor if I might, as well as shee may,
    This night I wold with her speake.

7 ' And heere I send her a mantle of greene,
    As greene as any grasse,
  And bidd her come to the siluer wood,
    To hunt with Child Maurice.

8 ' And there I send her a ring of gold,
    A ring of precyous stone,
  And bidd her come to the siluer wood,
    Let ffor no kind of man.'

9 One while this litle boy he yode,
    Anobther while he ran,
  Vntill he came to Iohn Stewards hall,
    I-wis he neuer blan.

10 And of nurture the child had good,
    Hee ran vp hall and bower ffree,
  And when he came to this lady ffaire,
    Sayes, God you saue and see !

11 ' I am come ffrom Ch[i]ld Maurice,
    A message vnto thee ;
  And Child Maurice, he greetes you well,
    And euer soe well ffrom mee.

12 ' And, as itt ffalls, as oftentimes
    As knotts beene knitt on a kell,
  Or marchant-men gone to leeue London,
    Either ffor to buy ware or sell.

13 ' And as oftentimes he greetes you well
    As any hart can thinke,
  Or schoolemasters [are] in any schoole,
    Wryting with pen and inke.

14 ' And heere he sends a mantle of greene,
    As greene as any grasse,
  And he bidds you come to the siluer wood,
    To hunt with Child Maurice.

15 ' And heere he sends you a ring of gold,
    A ring of the precyous stone ;

He prayes you to come to the siluer wood,
  Let ffor no kind of man.'

16 ' Now peace, now peace, thou litle ffoot-page,
    Ffor Christes sake, I pray thee !
  Ffor if my lord heare one of these words,
    Thou must be hanged hye !'

17 Iohn Steward stood vnder the castle-wall,
    And he wrote the words euerye one,

 .   .   .   .   .   .

 .   .   .   .   .   .

18 And he called vnto his hors-keeper,
    ' Make readye you my steede !'
  I, and soe hee did to his chamberlaine,
    ' Make readye thou my weede !'

19 And he cast a lease vpon his backe,
    And he rode to the siluer wood,
  And there he sought all about,
    About the siluer wood.

20 And there he ffound him Child Maurice
    Sitting vpon a blocke,
  With a siluer combe in his hand,
    Kembing his yellow locke[s.]

  *   *   *   *   *

21 But then stood vp him Child Maurice,
    And sayd these words trulye :
  ' I doe not know your ladye,' he said,
    ' If that I doe her see.'

22 He sayes, How now, how now, Child Mau-
      rice ?
    Alacke, how may this bee ?
  Ffor thou hast sent her loue-tokens,
    More now then two or three.

23 ' Ffor thou hast sent her a mantle of greene,
    As greene as any grasse,
  And bade her come to the siluer woode,
    To hunt with Child Maurice.

24 ' And thou [hast] sent her a ring of gold,
    A ring of precyous stone,
  And bade her come to the siluer wood,
    Let ffor noe kind of man.

25 ' And by my ffaith, now, Child Maurice,
    The tone of vs shall dye !'

'Now be my troth,' sayd Child Maurice,
  'And *that* shall not be **I**.'

26 But hee pulled forth a bright browne sword,
     And dryed itt on the grasse,
   And soe ffast he smote att Iohn Steward,
     I-wisse he neuer [did] rest.

27 Then hee pulled fforth his bright browne
     sword,
   And dryed itt on his sleeue,
   And the ffirst good stroke Iohn Stewart
     stroke,
   Child Maurice head he did cleeue.

28 And he pricked itt on his swords poynt,
     Went singing there beside,
   And he rode till he came to *that* ladye
     ffaire,
   Wheras this ladye lyed.

29 And sayes, Dost thou know Child Maurice
     head,
   If *that* thou dost itt see?
   And lapp itt soft, and kisse itt offt,
     Ffor thou louedst him better than mee.'

30 But when shee looked on Child Maurice head,
     Shee neuer spake words but three :
   'I neuer beare no child but one,
     And you haue slaine him trulye.'

31 Says, Wicked be my merrymen all,
     I gaue meate, drinke, and clothe !
   But cold they not haue holden me
     When I was in all *that* wrath !

32 'Ffor I haue slaine one of the curteousest
     *knigh*ts
   *Tha*t euer bestrode a steed,
   Soe haue I done one [of] the fairest ladyes
     *Tha*t euer ware womans weede ! '

———◆———

B

Motherwell's MS., p. 255 ; Motherwell's Minstrelsy, p.
282. From the singing of Widow McCormick, Paisley, January 19, 1825. Learned by her of an old woman in Dumbarton : Motherwell's Note Book, fol. 4.

1 CHILD NORYCE is a clever young man,
     He wavers wi the wind ;
   His horse was silver-shod before,
     With the beaten gold behind.

2 He called to his little man John,
     Saying, You don't see what I see ;
   For O yonder I see the very first woman
     That ever loved me.

3 'Here is a glove, a glove,' he said,
     'Lined with the silver grey ;
   You may tell her to come to the merry green-
     wood,
   To speak to Child Nory.

4 'Here is a ring, a ring,' he says,
     'It 's all gold but the stane ;
   You may tell her to come to the merry green-
     wood,
   And ask the leave o nane.'

5 'So well do I love your errand, my master,
     But far better do I love my life ;
   O would ye have me go to Lord Barnard's cas-
     tle,
   To betray away his wife ?'

6 'O don't I give you meat,' he says,
     'And don't I pay you fee ?
   How dare you stop my errand ?' he says ;
     'My orders you must obey.'

7 O when he came to Lord Bernard's castle,
     He tinkled at the ring ;
   Who was as ready as Lord Barnard himself
     To let this little boy in ?

8 'Here is a glove, a glove,' he says,
     'Lined with the silver grey ;
   You are bidden to come to the merry green-
     wood,
   To speak to Child Nory.

9 'Here is a ring, a ring,' he says,
     'It 's all gold but the stane ;
   You are bidden to come to the merry green-
     wood,
   And ask the leave o nane.'

10 Lord Barnard he was standing by,
    And an angry man was he :
'O little did I think there was a lord in the
      world
    My lady loved but me ! '

11 O he dressed himself in the holland smock,
    And garments that was gay,
And he is away to the merry green-wood,
    To speak to Child Nory.

12 Child Noryce sits on yonder tree,
    He whistles and he sings :
'O wae be to me,' says Child Noryce,
    'Yonder my mother comes ! '

13 Child Noryce he came off the tree,
    His mother to take off the horse :
'Och alace, alace,' says Child Noryce,
    'My mother was neer so gross ! '

14 Lord Barnard he had a little small sword,
    That hung low down by his knee ;

He cut the head off Child Noryce,
    And put the body on a tree.

15 And when he came home to his castell,
    And to his ladie's hall,
He threw the head into her lap,
    Saying, Lady, there 's a ball !

16 She turned up the bloody head,
    She kissed it frae cheek to chin :
'Far better do I love this bloody head
    Than all my royal kin.

17 'When I was in my father's castel,
    In my virginity,
There came a lord into the North,
    Gat Child Noryce with me.'

18 'O wae be to thee, Lady Margaret,' he sayd,
    'And an ill death may you die ;
For if you had told me he was your son,
    He had neer been slain by me.'

C

Motherwell's MS., p. 510, from the singing of Mrs Storie, wife of William Storie, laborer, Lochwinnoch. A song of Mrs Storie's grandmother.

1 BOB NORICE is to the grein-wud gane,
    He is awa wi the wind ;
His horse is siller-shod afore,
    In the shynand gowd ahind.

2 He said unto his wee boy John,
    I sie what ye dinna sie ;
I see the ⌊first⌋ woman that I eer luvit,
    Or ever luvit me.

3 'Gae tak to hir this pair o gluvis,
    They 're o the siller-gray,
And tell her to cum to the merrie grein-wud
    An speik to Bob Norice.

4 'Gae tak to her this gay gowd ring,
    And it 's aw gowd but the stane,
And tell her to cum to the merrie grein-wud,
    And ask the leive o nane.

5 'Gae tak to her this braw manteil,
    It 's a' silk but the sleive,

And tell her to cum to the merrie green-wud,
    And ax nae bauld Barnet's leive.'

6 'I daurna gang to Lord Barnet's castel,
    I daurna gang for my lyfe ;
I daurna gang to Lord Barnet's castell,
    To twyne him o his wife.'

7 'Do I nae pay you gowd ?' he said,
    'Do I nae pay you fee ?
How daur you stand my bidding, Sir,
    Whan I bid you to flee ? '

8 'Gif I maun gang to Lord Barnet's castel,
    Sae sair agane my will,
I vow a vow, and I do protest,
    It sall be dune for ill.'

9 But whan he came to Lord Barnet's castel
    He tinklet at the ring ;
Tha war nane sae ready as Lord Barnet himsell
    To let the wee calland in.

10 'What news, what news, my bonnie wee boy ?
    What news hae ye to me ? '
'Nae news, nae news, Lord Barnet,' he said,
    'But your ladie I fain would see.

11 'Here is a pair o gluves to her,
       Thay'r o the silver gray ;
   And tell her to cum to the merrie green-wud,
       And speik to Bob Norice.

12 'Here is a gay gowd ring to her,
       It 's aw gowd but the stane ;
   And she maun cum to the merrie green-wud,
       And speir the leive o nane.

13 'Here is a gay manteil to her,
       It 's aw silk but the sleive ;
   And she maun cum to the merrie grein-wud,
       And ask not bauld Barnet's leive.'

14 Then out bespack the yellow nurse,
       Wi the babie on her knee,
   Sayand, Gif thay be cum frae Bob Norice,
       They are welcum to me.

15 'O haud your tung, ye yellow nurse,
       Aloud an I heir ye lie ;
   For they 're to Lord Barnet's lady,
       I trew that this be she.'

16 Lord Barnet 's to a dressing-room,
       And buskt him in woman's array,
   And he 's awa to the merrie green-wud,
       To speik to Bob Norrice.

17 Bob Norrice he sits on a tree,
       He is whissland and singand ;

Says, Merrie, merrie may my hert be,
       I see my mither cumand.

18 Bob Norice he cam doun frae the trie,
       To help his mother to licht fra her horss ;
   'Och alace, ·alace,' says Bob Norice,
       'My mither was neer sae gross !'

19 Lord Barnet had a not-brown sword,
       That huug down by his knee,
   And he has cut Bob Norice heid
       Aff frae his fair bodie.

20 He tuke the bluidy head in his hand,
       And he brocht it to the ha,
   And flang it into his lady's lap,
       Sayand, Lady, there is a ba !

21 She took the bluidy heid in her hand,
       And kisst it frae cheik to chin,
   Sayand, Better I lyke that weil faurit face
       Nor aw my royal kin.

22 'Whan I was in my father's bour,
       A' in my dignity,
   An Englis lord a visit came,
       Gat Bob Norice wi me.'

23 Then out bespak Lord Barnet syne,
       And a wae, wae man was he,
   Sayand, Gif I had kent he was your son,
       He wuld neer been killit be me.

D

Motherwell's MS., p. 480, from the recitation of Widow
Michael, a very old woman, as learned by her in Banffshire
seventy years before.   August, 1826.

1 GILL MORICE stood in stable-door,
       With red gold shined his weed ;
   A bonnie boy him behind,
       Dressing a milk-white steed.

2 'Woe 's me for you, maister,
       Your name it waxes wide ;
   It is not for your rich, rich robes,
       Nor for your meikle pride,
   But all is for yon lord's ladie,
       She lives on Ithan side.'

3 'Here 's to thee, my bonnie wee boy,
       That I pay meat and fee ;
   You will run on to Ithan side
       An errand unto me.'

4 'If ye gar me that errand run,
       Sae sair against my will,
   I 'll make a vow, and keep it true,
       I 'll do your errand ill.'

5 'I fear nae ill of thee, boy,
       I fear nae ill of thee ;
   I fearna ill of my bonnie boy,
       My sister's son are ye.

6 'Ye 'll tak here this green manteel,
       It 's lined with the frieze ;

Ye 'll bid her come to gude green-wood,
  To talk with Gill Morice.

7 ' Ye 'll tak here this sark o silk,
  Her ain hand sewed the sleeve ;
Ye 'll bid her come to gude green-wood,
  And ask not Burnard's leave.'

8 When he gade to Ithan side
  They were hailing at the ba,
And four and twenty gay ladyes
  They lookd ower castle wa.

9 ' God mak you safe, you ladies all,
  God mak you safe and sure ;
But Burnard's lady amang you all,
  My errand is to her.

10 ' Ye 'll tak here this green manteel,
  It 's a' lined wi the frieze ;
Ye 're bidden come to gude green-wood
  And speak to Gill Morice.

11 ' Ye 'll tak here this sark of silk,
  Your ain hand sewed the sleeve ;
Ye 're bidden come to gude green-wood,
  And ask not Burnard's leave.'

12 Up it stood the little nurice,
  She winked with her ee :
' Welcome, welcome, bonnie boy,
  With luve-tidings to me.

13 ' Ye lie, ye lie, ye false nurice,
  Sae loud 's I hear ye lie ;
It 's to the lady of the house,
  I 'm sure ye are not shee.'

14 Then out and spoke him bold Burnard,
  Behind the door stood he :
' I 'll go unto gude green-wood,
  And see what he may be.

15 ' Come, bring to me the gowns of silk,
  Your petticoats so small,
And I 'll go on to gude green-wood,
  I 'll try with him a fall.'

16 Gill Morice stood in gude green-wood,
  He whistled and he sang :
' I think I see the woman come
  That I have loved lang.'

17 ' What now, what now, ye Gill Morice,
  What now, and how do ye ?
How lang hae ye my lady luved ?
  This day come tell to me.'

18 ' First when I your lady loved,
  In green-wood amang the thyme,
I wot she was my first fair love
  Or ever she was thine.

19 ' First when I your lady loved,
  In green-wood amang the flouirs,
I wot she was my first fair love
  Or ever she was yours.'

20 He 's taen out a lang, lang brand
  That he was used to wear,
And he 's taen aff Gill Morice head,
  And put it on a spear :
The soberest boy in a' the court
  Gill Morice head did bear.

21 He 's put it in a braid basin,
  And brocht it in the ha,
And laid it in his lady's lap ;
  Said, Lady, tak a ba !

22 ' Play ye, play ye, my lady,' he said,
  ' Play ye frae ha to bower ;
Play ye wi Gill Morice head,
  He was your paramour.'

23 ' He was not my paramour,
  He was my son indeed ;
I got him in my mother's bower,
  And in my maiden-weed.

24 ' I got him in my mother's bower,
  Wi meikle sin and shame ;
I brocht him up in good green-wood,
  Got mony a shower o rain.

25 ' But I will kiss his bluidy head,
  And I will clap his chin ;
I 'll make a vow, and keep it true,
  I 'll never kiss man again.

26 ' Oftimes I by his cradle sat,
  And fond to see him sleep ;
But I may walk about his grave,
  The saut tears for to weep.'

27 ' Bring cods, bring cods to my ladye,
    Her heart is full of wae ; '
' None of your cods, Burnet,' she says,
    ' But lay me on the strae.'

28 ' Pox on you, my lady fair,
    That wudna telled it me ;
If I had known he was your son,
    He had not been slain by me ;
And for ae penny ye wud hae gien
    I wud hae gien him three.'

29 ' Keep weel your land, Burnet,' she said,
    ' Your land and white monie ;
There 's land eneuch in Norroway
    Lies heirless I wot the day.'

30 The one was killed in the mornin air,
    His mother died at een,
And or the mornin bells was rung
    The threesome were a' gane.

E

Motherwell's MS., p. 165 ; Motherwell's Minstrelsy, p. 269.
From the recitation of Mrs Thomson, Kilbarchan, seventy
years of age, as learned from her mother at the Water of
Leven, Dumbarton, when she was ten years old. March, 1825.

1 Chield Morrice was an earl's son,
    His name it waxed wide ;
It was nae for his parentage,
    Nor yet his meikle pride,
But it was for a lady gay,
    That lived on Carron side.

2 ' O Willie, my man, my errand gang,
    And you maun rin wi speed ;
When other boys run on their feet,
    On horseback ye shall ride.

3 ' O master dear, I love you weel,
    And I love you as my life,
But I will not go to Lord Barnard's ha,
    For to tryst forth his wife.

4 ' For the baron he 's a man of might,
    He neer could bide a taunt,
And ye shall see or it be late
    How meikle ye 'll hae to vaunt.'

5 ' O you must rin my errand, Willie,
    And you must rin wi speed,
And if you don't obey my high command
    I 'll gar your body bleed.

6 ' And here it is a gay manteel,
    It 's a' gowd but the hem ;
Bid her come speak to Chield Morice,
    Bring naebody but her lane.

7 ' And here it is a holland smock,
    Her own hand sewed the sleeve ;

Bid her come speak to Chield Morice,
    Ask not the baron's leave.'

8 ' Since I must run this errand for you,
    So sore against my will,
I 've made a vow, and I 'll keep it true,
    It shall be done for ill.'

9 For he did not ask the porter's leave,
    Tho he stood at the gate,
But straight he ran to the big hall,
    Where great folk sat at meat.

10 ' Good hallow, gentle sir and dame,
    My errand canna wait ;
Dame, ye must go speak to Chield Morice,
    Before it be too late.

11 ' And here it is a gay manteel,
    It' s a' goud but the hem ;
Ye must come speak to Child Morice,
    Bring nae body but your lane.

12 ' And here it is a holland smock,
    Your ain hand sewed the sleeve ;
You must come speak to Chield Morice,
    Ask not the baron's leave.'

13 O aye she stamped wi her foot,
    And winked wi her ee,
But a' that she could say or do,
    Forbidden he wad na be.

14 ' It 's surely to my bouir-woman,
    It canna be to me : '
' I brocht it to Lord Barnard's lady,
    And I trow that thou art she.'

15 Out then spak the wylie nurse,
    Wi the bairn just on her knee :

'If this be come fra Chield Morice,
    It's dear welcome to me.'

16 'Thou lies, thou lies, thou wylie nurse,
    Sae loud's I hear thee lie;
  I brought it to Lord Barnard's lady,
    And I trow thou binna she.'

17 Then up and rose him the bold baron,
    And an angry man was he;
  He took the table wi his foot,
    And keppd it wi his knee,
  Till silver cup and ezar dish
    In flinders they did flee.

18 'Go bring me one of thy cleeding,
    That hings upon the pin,
  And I'll awa to the good green-wood,
    And crack wi your leman.'

19 'I would have you stay at home, Lord Bar-
    nard,
    I would have you stay at home;
  Never wyte a man for violence douce
    That never thought you wrong.'

20 And when he to the green-wood went,
    No body saw he there
  But Chield Morice, on a milk-white steed,
    Combing down his yellow hair.

21 Chield Morice sat in the gay green-wood,
    He whistled and he sang:
  'O what means a' thir folks coming?
    My mother tarries lang.'

22 'No wonder, no wonder, Chield Morice,' he
    said,
  'My lady loved thee weel;
  For the whitest bit of my body
    Is blacker than thy heel.

23 'But nevertheless now, Chield Morice,
    For a' thy gay beautie,
  O nevertheless, Chield Morice,
    Thy head shall go with me.'

24 He had a rapier by his side,
    Hung low down by his knee;
  He struck Chield Morrice on the neck,
    Till aff his head did flee.

25 Then he's taen up that bloody head,
    And stuck it on a spear,
  And the meanest man in a' his train
    Gat Chield Morice head to bear.

26 The lady looked owre the castle-wa,
    Wi meikle dool and down,
  And there she saw Chield Morice head,
    Coming trailing to the town.

27 But he's taen up this bluidy head,
    And dashed it gainst the wa:
  'Come down, come down, you ladies fair,
    And play at this foot-ba.'

28 Then she's taen up this bluidy head,
    And she kissed it both cheek and chin:
  'I would rather hae a kiss o that bluidy
    head
  Than a' thy earldom.

29 'I got him in my father's bouir,
    Wi meikle sin and shame,
  And I brought him up in gay green-wood,
    Beneath the heavy rain.

30 'Many a day have I rockd thy cradle,
    And fondly seen thee sleep,
  But now I'll go about thy grave,
    And sore, sore will I weep.'

31 'O woe be to thee, thou wild woman,
    And an ill deid may thou die!
  For if ye had tauld me he was your son,
    He should hae ridden and gane wi me.'

32 'O hold your tongue, you bold baron,
    And an ill death may ye die!
  He had lands and rents enew of his ain,
    He needed nane fra thee.'

33 'Then I'll curse the hand that did the
    deed,
    The heart that thought him ill,
  The feet that carried me speedilie
    This comely youth to kill.'

34 This lady she died gin ten o'clock,
    Lord Barnard died gin twall,
  And bonnie boy now, Sweet Willie,
    What's come o him I canna tell.

F

a. Percy's Reliques, III, 93, 1765.   b. Letter of T. Gray to Mason, June, 1757 (?): Gray's Works, ed. Gosse, II, 316.

1 GIL MORRICE was an erles son,
    His name it waxed wide ;
It was nae for his great riches,
    Nor yet his mickle pride,
Bot it was for a lady gay,
    That livd on Carron side.

2 ' Whair sall I get a bonny boy,
    That will win hose and shoen,
That will gae to Lord Barnard's ha,
    And bid his lady cum ?

3 ' And ye maun rin errand, Willie,
    And ye may rin wi pride ;
When other boys gae on their foot,
    On horseback ye sall ride.'

4 ' O no ! Oh no ! my master dear,
    I dare nae for my life ;
I 'll no gae to the bauld baron's,
    For to triest furth his wife.'

5 ' My bird Willie, my boy Willie,
    My dear Willie,' he sayd,
' How can ye strive against the stream ?
    For I sall be obeyd.'

6 ' Bot, O my master dear,' he cry'd,
    ' In grene-wod ye 're your lain ;
Gi owre sic thochts, I walde ye rede,
    For fear ye should be tain.'

7 ' Haste, haste, I say, gae to the ha,
    Bid hir cum here wi speid ;
If ye refuse my heigh command,
    I 'll gar your body bleid.

8 ' Gae bid hir take this gay mantel,
    'T is a' gowd but the hem ;
Bid hir cum to the gude grene-wode,
    And bring nane bot hir lain.

9 ' And there it is, a silken sarke,
    Hir ain hand sewd the sleive ;
And bid hir cum to Gill Morice,
    Speir nae bauld baron's leave.'

10 ' Yes, I will gae your black errand,
    Though it be to your cost ;

Sen ye by me will nae be warnd,
    In it ye sall find frost.

11 ' The baron he 's a man of might,
    He neir could bide to taunt ;
As ye will see, before it 's nicht,
    How sma ye hae to vaunt.

12 ' And sen I maun your errand rin,
    Sae sair against my will,
I 'se mak a vow, and keip it trow,
    It sall be done for ill.'

13 And when he came to broken brigue,
    He bent his bow and swam ;
And when [he] came to grass growing,
    Set down his feet and ran.

14 And when he came to Barnard's ha,
    Would neither chap nor ca,
Bot set his bent bow to his breist,
    And lichtly lap the wa.

15 He wauld nae tell the man his errand,
    Though he stude at the gait ;
Bot straiht into the ha he cam,
    Whair they were set at meit.

16 ' Hail ! hail ! my gentle sire and dame,
    My message winna waite ;
Dame, ye maun to the gude grene-wod,
    Before that it be late.

17 ' Ye 're bidden tak this gay mantel,
    'T is a' gowd bot the hem ;
You maun gae to the gude grene-wode,
    Evn by your sel alane.

18 ' And there it is, a silken sarke,
    Your ain hand sewd the sleive ;
Ye maun gae speik to Gill Morice,
    Speir nae bauld baron's leave.'

19 The lady stamped wi hir foot,
    And winked wi hir ee ;
But a' that she coud say or do,
    Forbidden he wad nae bee.

20 ' It 's surely to my bowr-woman ;
    It neir could be to me :'
' I brocht it to Lord Barnard's lady ;
    I trow that ye be she.'

21 Then up and spack the wylie nurse,
The bairn upon hir knee :
'If it be cum frae Gill Morice,
It 's deir welcum to mee.'

22 'Ye leid, ye leid, ye filthy nurse,
Sae loud 's I heire ye lee ;
I brocht it to Lord Barnard's lady ;
I trow ye be nae shee.'

23 Then up and spack the bauld baron,
An angry man was hee ;
He 's tain the table wi his foot,
Sae has he wi his knee,
Till siller cup and ezar dish
In flinders he gard flee.

24 'Gae bring a robe of your cliding,
That hings upon the pin,
And I 'll gae to the gude grene-wode,
And speik wi your lemman.'

25 'O bide at hame, now, Lord Barnard,
I warde ye bide at hame ;
Neir wyte a man for violence
That neir wate ye wi nane.'

26 Gil Morice sate in gude grene-wode,
He whistled and he sang :
'O what mean a' the folk coming ?
My mother tarries lang.'

27 The baron came to the grene-wode,
Wi mickle dule and care,
And there he first spied Gill Morice,
Kameing his yellow hair.

28 'Nae wonder, nae wonder, Gill Morice,
My lady loed thee weel ;
The fairest part of my body
Is blacker than thy heel.

29 'Yet neir the less now, Gill Morice,
For a' thy great bewty,
Ye 's rew the day ye eir was born ;
That head sall gae wi me.'

30 Now he has drawn his trusty brand,
And slaited on the strae,

And thro Gill Morice fair body
He 's gard cauld iron gae.

31 And he has tain Gill Morice head,
And set it on a speir ;
The meanest man in a' his train
Has gotten that head to bear.

32 And he has tain Gill Morice up,
Laid him across his steid,
And brocht him to his painted bowr,
And laid him on a bed.

33 The lady sat on castil-wa,
Beheld baith dale and doun,
And there she saw Gill Morice head
Cum trailing to the toun.

34 'Far better I loe that bluidy head,
Bot and that yellow hair,
Than Lord Barnard, and a' his lands,
As they lig here and thair.'

35 And she has tain hir Gill Morice,
And kissd baith mouth and chin :
'I was once as fow of Gill Morice
As the hip is o the stean.

36 'I got ye in my father's house,
Wi mickle sin and shame ;
I brocht thee up in gude green-wode,
Under the heavy rain.

37 'Oft have I by thy cradle sitten,
And fondly seen thee sleip ;
Bot now I gae about thy grave,
The saut tears for to weip.'

38 And syne she kissd his bluidy cheik,
And syne his bluidy chin :
'O better I loe my Gill Morice
Than a' my kith and kin !'

39 'Away, away, ye ill woman,
And an il deith mait ye dee !
Gin I had kend he 'd bin your son,
He 'd neir bin slain for mee.'

G

Jamieson's Popular Ballads, I, 18 ; Jamieson, in The Scots Magazine, 1803, LXV, 698, stanzas 1, 3.

1 GIL MORRICE sat in silver wood,
   He whistled and he sang :
 ' Whar sall I get a bonny boy
   My errand for to gang ? '

2 He ca'd his foster-brither Willie :
 ' Come, win ye hose and shoon,

   And gae unto Lord Barnard's ha,
   And bid his lady come.'

*   *   *   *   *

3 And she has taen the bloody head,
   And cast it i the brim,
   Syne gathered up her robes o green,
   And fast she followed him.

A.   1[1]. siluen : *compare* 7[3], 8[3], 14[3], 15[3], *etc.*
   2[3, 4]. *In the MS., these go with* 3 : *compare* 20.
   3[2]. rumeth.
   4[3, 4]. *These precede what is printed as* 6.
   5[1], 6[1], 12[1]. out many.
   6[3]. as schoole masters : *compare* 13[3].
   6[5, 6]. *These lines may be the last half of a stanza. There is nothing corresponding in the page's repetition of his master's message.*
   17[1, 2]. *Joined in the MS. with* 18.
   18[4]. then my.
   21. *At least one stanza must be lost after* 20.
   22[1, 2] *precede* 21, *and* 22[3, 4] *make a stanza with* 21[3, 4] : *the order being* 22[1, 2], 21, 22[3, 4].
   22[4]. 2 or 3.
   26[1]. *Only half the* n *in the MS.   Furnivall.*
   30[2]. but 3.   32[1]. curteouset.
   And *for* & *throughout.*

B.   2[3]. For *is a later insertion.*   2[3], 6[1]. Oh.
   6[1, 2]. *Originally,* O do I not, And do I not.
   9[3]. to go to : come *written over* go.
   13[2], 14[3]. of.   14[2]. That *is a later insertion.*
   18[2]. And *is a later insertion.*
   18[4]. *Originally,* He should neer have been.

C.   " This ballad was forwarded to me by my good friend Andrew Crawfurd, of John's Hill, Lochwinnoch.   He wrote it from the recitation of Mrs Storie, wife of William Storie, laborer, in Lochwinnoch.   It was a song of Mrs Storie's grandmother.   It is queried if this should not be Babe Norice. . . . The interlineary corrections were made in consequence of Mrs Storie singing the ballad over to myself."   *Motherwell.   The interlineary corrections have been adopted.   The earlier readings follow.*
   Barnard *for* Barnet.
   5[4]. speir nae bauld baron's.   6[1]. Barnard's ha.

   8[3]. and I doubly vow.   10[1]. wee lad.
   12[1]. gay *wanting.*   13[1]. braw manteil.
   13[4]. nae bauld baron's.   16[1]. to a busking gane.
   16[2]. drest him.   19[1]. Barnard liftit his.
   19[3]. has sneddit.   19[4]. And aff frae his bodie.
   20[4]. lady *wanting.*
   The affected spelling I suppose to be Crawfurd's.
   7[4], 9[1]. quhan.
       In the Appendix to his Minstrelsy, p. xvii, Motherwell adopts the reading Babe Norice *in* 1[1], *and prints* burning gowd *in* 1[4].

D.   " This copy is from the recitation of Margaret Paterson, *alias* widow Michael, a very old woman residing at Dovecote Ha, Barhead. She is a native of Banffshire, and learned the ballad there in her infancy. She mentions that she has heard it sung with many variations, but this copy was considered to be the right way. It is seventy years since she committed it to her memory. 4th August, 1826."   *Motherwell.*

E.   *In his Minstrelsy, p. 269, Motherwell says that the reciter learned the ballad from her grandmother.   He goes on to say :* She mentions that at a later period of her life she also committed to memory ' Gill Morice,' which began with young lasses like her to be a greater favorite and more fashionable than the set which her grandmother and other old folks used to sing, under the title of ' Chield Morice.'
   17[5]. *Written* and dezar dish, *the* d *of* and *being carried on to the word following.*
   19[3]. douce *makes no apparent sense.   Motherwell prints* done.
   20[1]. *Stood originally* And when he came to the green wood.
   26[2]. *No doubt a corruption of the familiar* Beheld baith dale and down.

29⁴. heaviy, *perhaps representing the actual sound. Motherwell prints* heavy.

F. a. *In eight-line stanzas. Wh and y are substituted for the initial* quh *and* z *cherished by ballad imitators.*

  5⁴. shall.   30⁴. He 's gar.

  b. 1². fame it wexed.   1⁴. Nae for.
  1⁶. Carron's.   3¹. Ye maun rin this.
  3². maun rin.   3⁸. feet.
  4¹. Ah na, ah na.

The four stanzas which follow, " produced and handed about in manuscript," in consequence of an advertisement, were introduced into his copy by Percy.
After 26:

His hair was like the threeds of gold,
  Drawne frae Minerva's loome;
His lipps like roses drapping dew,
  His breath was a' perfume.

His brow was like the mountain snae,
  Gilt by the morning beam;
His cheeks like living roses glow,
  His een like azure stream.

The boy was clad in robes of grene,
  Sweete as the infant spring,
And like the mavis on the bush
  He gart the vallies ring.

After 27 :

That sweetly wavd around his face,
  That face beyond compare;
He sang sae sweet, it might dispel
  A' rage but fell dispair.

The following stanzas were appended to the ballad in the edition reprinted by Percy :

' Obraid me not, my Lord Barnard,
  Obraid me not for shame !
With that saim speir O pierce my heart,
  And put me out o pain.

' Since nothing bot Gill Morice head
  Thy jelous rage could quell,

Let that saim hand now tak hir life
  That neir to thee did ill.

' To me nae after days nor nichts
  Will eir be saft or kind ;
I 'll fill the air with heavy sighs,
  And greet till I am blind.'

' Enouch of blood by me 's bin spilt,
  Seek not your death frae mee ;
I rather lourd it had been my sel
  Than eather him or thee.

' With waefo wae I hear your plaint ;
  Sair, sair I rew the deid,
That eir this cursed hand of mine
  Had gard his body bleid.

' Dry up your tears, my winsom dame,
  Ye neir can heal the wound ;
Ye see his head upon the speir,
  His heart's blude on the ground.

' I curse the hand that did the deid,
  The heart that thocht the ill,
The feet that bore me wi sik speid
  The comely youth to kill.

' I 'll ay lament for Gill Morice,
  As gin he were my ain ;
I 'll neir forget the dreiry day
  On which the youth was slain.'

The copy lent me by Mr Macmath lacks the four stanzas inserted by Percy, but has the eight given immediately above. The following are the variations from F.
  2¹. will I.   7⁴. thy body.
  10². thy cost.
  18⁸. maun cum.   26¹. sits.
  26⁸. means a' these folks.
  26⁴. she tarrys.
  27¹. And whan he cam to guid.
  27⁸. first saw.   27⁴. Kemeing down.
  28². Than my, *misprint.*   30⁴. gard.
  34⁴. they lay.   35⁴. hip was.
The eight stanzas follow which are printed immediately above.

84

BONNY BARBARA ALLAN

A. a. 'Bonny Barbara Allan,' Tea-Table Miscellany, IV, 46, ed. 1740; here from the edition of London, 1763, p. 343. **b.** 'Sir John Grehme and Barbara Allan,' Percy's Reliques, 1765, III, 131.

B. a. 'Barbara Allen's Cruelty,' etc., Roxburghe Ballads, II, 25; reprint of the Ballad Society, III, 433.

b. Roxburghe Ballads, III, 522. **c.** Broadside formerly belonging to Percy. **d.** Percy's Reliques, 1765, III, 125.

C. 'Barbara Allan,' Motherwell's MS., p. 288, from recitation.

A a is wrongly said by Stenhouse, The Scots Musical Museum, IV, 213, to have appeared in Ramsay's Miscellany in 1724. It is not even in the edition of 1733, but, according to Mr Chappell, was first inserted in that of 1740. Ramsay's copy is repeated in Herd, 1769, p. 29, 1776, I, 19, Johnson's Museum, p. 230, No 221, and Ritson's Scotish Song, II, 196. **C** was perhaps derived from Ramsay, but possibly may have come down by purely oral tradition. Some later copies of **B** have Reading Town for Scarlet Town (Chappell).

The Scottish ballad is extended in Buchan's MSS, I, 90, Motherwell's MS., p. 671, to forty-one stanzas. In this amplified copy, which has no claim to be admitted here, the dying lover leaves his watch and gold ring, his Bible and penknife, a mill and thirty ploughs, nine meal-mills and the freights of nine ships, all

to tocher Barbara Allan. This is the ballad referred to by Charles Kirkpatrick Sharpe in Stenhouse's edition of the Museum, IV, 300*, as sung by the peasantry of Allandale. Doubtless it was learned by them from some stall-print.

Pepys makes this entry in his Diary, January 2, 1666 : " In perfect pleasure I was to hear her [Mrs Knipp, an actress] sing, and especially her little Scotch song of Barbary Allen." Goldsmith, in his third essay, 1765, p. 14, writes : The music of the finest singer is dissonance to what I felt when an old dairy-maid sung me into tears with ' Johnny Armstrong's Last Good-night,' or ' The Cruelty of Barbara Allen.' *

A b is translated by Loève-Veimars, p. 379, von Marées, p. 34; **B d** by Bodmer, I, 85.

A

a. The Tea-Table Miscellany, IV, 46, ed. 1740; here from the London edition of 1763, p. 343. b. Percy's Reliques, III, 131, ed. 1765, " with a few conjectural emendations from a written copy."

1 IT was in and about the Martinmas time,
   When the green leaves were a falling,
   That Sir John Græme, in the West Country,
   Fell in love with Barbara Allan.

2 He sent his men down through the town,
   To the place where she was dwelling :
   ' O haste and come to my master dear,
   Gin ye be Barbara Allan.'

3 O hooly, hooly rose she up,
   To the place where he was lying,

---

* Pepys is cited by James Farquhar Graham, The Scottish Songs, II, 157, and Goldsmith by Chappell, The Roxburghe Ballads, III, 433.

And when she drew the curtain by,
    'Young man, I think you 're dying.'

4 'O it 's I 'm sick, and very, very sick,
    And 't is a' for Barbara Allan :'
'O the better for me ye 's never be,
    Tho your heart's blood were a spilling.

5 'O dinna ye mind, young man,' said she,
    'When ye was in the tavern a drinking,
That ye made the healths gae round and
    round,
    And slighted Barbara Allan ? '

6 He turnd his face unto the wall,
    And death was with him dealing :

'Adieu, adieu, my dear friends all,
    And be kind to Barbara Allan.'

7 And slowly, slowly raise she up,
    And slowly, slowly left him,
And sighing said, she coud not stay,
    Since death of life had reft him.

8 She had not gane a mile but twa,
    When she heard the dead-bell ringing,
And every jow that the dead-bell geid,
    It cry'd, Woe to Barbara Allan !

9 'O mother, mother, make my bed !
    O make it saft and narrow !
Since my love died for me to-day,
    I 'll die for him to-morrow.'

B

a. Roxburghe Ballads, II, 25 ; reprint of the Ballad Society, III, 433. b. Roxburghe Ballads, III, 522. c. A broadside formerly belonging to Bishop Percy. d. Percy's Reliques, 1765, III, 125.

1 In Scarlet Town, where I was bound,
    There was a fair maid dwelling,
Whom I had chosen to be my own,
    And her name it was Barbara Allen.

2 All in the merry month of May,
    When green leaves they was springing,
This young man on his death-bed lay,
    For the love of Barbara Allen.

3 He sent his man unto her then,
    To the town where she was dwelling :
'You must come to my master dear,
    If your name be Barbara Allen.

4 'For death is printed in his face,
    And sorrow 's in him dwelling,
And you must come to my master dear,
    If your name be Barbara Allen.'

5 'If death be printed in his face,
    And sorrow 's in him dwelling,
Then little better shall he be
    For bonny Barbara Allen.'

6 So slowly, slowly she got up,
    And so slowly she came to him,

And all she said when she came there,
    Young man, I think you are a dying.

7 He turnd his face unto her then :
    'If you be Barbara Allen,
My dear,' said he, ' come pitty me,
    As on my death-bed I am lying.'

8 'If on your death-bed you be lying,
    What is that to Barbara Allen ?
I cannot keep you from [your] death ;
    So farewell,' said Barbara Allen.

9 He turnd his face unto the wall,
    And death came creeping to him :
'Then adieu, adieu, and adieu to all,
    And adieu to Barbara Allen ! '

10 And as she was walking on a day,
    She heard the bell a ringing,
And it did seem to ring to her
    'Unworthy Barbara Allen.'

11 She turnd herself round about,
    And she spy'd the corps a coming :
'Lay down, lay down the corps of clay,
    That I may look upon him.'

12 And all the while she looked on,
    So loudly she lay laughing,
While all her friends cry'd [out] amain,
    'Unworthy Barbara Allen ! '

13 When he was dead, and laid in grave,
   Then death came creeping to she :
' O mother, mother, make my bed,
   For his death hath quite undone me.

14 ' A hard-hearted creature that I was,
   To slight one that lovd me so dearly ;

I wish I had been more kinder to him,
   The time of his life when he was near me.'

15 So this maid she then did dye,
   And desired to be buried by him,
And repented her self before she dy'd,
   That ever she did deny him.

C

Motherwell's MS., p. 288 ; from Mrs Duff, Kilbirnie, February 9, 1825.

1 It fell about the Lammas time,
   When the woods grow green and yellow,
There came a wooer out of the West
   A wooing to Barbara Allan.

2 ' It is not for your bonny face,
   Nor for your beauty bonny,
But it is all for your tocher good
   I come so far about ye.'

3 ' If it be not for my comely face,
   Nor for my beauty bonnie,
My tocher good ye 'll never get paid
   Down on the board before ye.'

4 ' O will ye go to the Highland hills,
   To see my white corn growing?
Or will ye go to the river-side,
   To see my boats a rowing ? '

5 O he 's awa, and awa he 's gone,
   And death 's within him dealing,
And it is all for the sake of her,
   His bonnie Barbara Allan.

6 O he sent his man unto the house,
   Where that she was a dwelling :
' O you must come my master to see,
   If you be Barbara Allan.'

7 So slowly aye as she put on,
   And so stoutly as she gaed till him,
And so slowly as she could say,
   ' I think, young man, you 're lying.'

8 ' O I am lying in my bed,
   And death within me dwelling;
And it is all for the love of thee,
   My bonny Barbara Allan.'

9 She was not ae mile frae the town,
   Till she heard the dead-bell ringing :
' Och hone, oh hone, he 's dead and gone,
   For the love of Barbara Allan ! '

A. b. 1³. o the.   4⁴. a *wanting*.
     5¹. Remember ye nat in the tavern, sir.
     5². Whan ye the cups wer fillan.
     5³. How ye.   6⁴. And *wanting*.   7¹. Then
     hooly, hooly.   7². And hooly, hooly.
     8². deid-bell knellan.   8³. that *wanting*.
     8⁴. It *wanting*.   9⁴. I 'se.

B. a. Barbara Allen's Cruelty, or, The Young-
        man's Tragedy.   With Barbara Allen's
        Lamentation for her Unkindness to her
        Lover and her Self. . . . Printed for P.
        Brooksby, J. Deacon, J. Blare, J. Back.
        Black Letter.
     13⁴. undone we.
   b. Barbara Allen's Cruelty, or, The Young
        Man's Tragedy.   *No name of printer.*
     1³. for my own.   2². they were.
     2⁴. the sake of.

3⁴. name is.   4⁴. thy name is.
5³. Then *wanting*.   6¹. she came to him.
6³. came to him.   6⁴. a *wanting*.
7². you are.
7⁴. As I am on my death-bed lying.
8¹. If you are on your death-bed lying.
8³. from your.
8⁴. Then farewell : said *wanting*.
9². on him.
9³. and *wanting* : to you all.
10¹. And *wanting* : out one day.
10². bells.   10³. And they.
11². And saw.   11³. corps said she.
12³. cry'd out.   13¹. in his.
13⁴. will quite undo me.
14¹. A *wanting*.   14³. more kind.
14⁴. In time of life.   15³. eer.

16. As she was lying down to die,
    A sad feud she fell in ;
    She said, I pray take warning by
    Hard-hearted Barbara Allen.

c. *Title the same as in* a. Printed and sold at
the Printing-office in Bow-Church-Yard,
London.

1^3. for my own. 2^2. they wore.
3^4. name is. 4^3. And thou.
4^4. thy name is. 5^3. O little.
6^1. she came to him. 6^3. came to him.
6^4. a *wanting*. 7^2. you are.
7^4. As I am on my death-bed lying.
8^3. from your.
8^4. Then farewell : said *wanting*.
9^2. on him. 9^3. to you all.
10^1. And *wanting : out one day*.
10^2. bells. 10^3. And they.
11^2. And espy'd. 11^3. corps said she.
12^3. cry'd out.
13^4. will quite undo me.
14^1. A *wanting*. 14^3. more kind.

14^4. In time of life.
15^4. eer. 16 *as in* b.
d *was " given, with some corrections, from
an old printed copy in the editor's possession." That these corrections were considerable, we know from the $*_*^*$ at the
end. The old printed copy is very likely
to have been* c, *and, if so, the ballad was
simply written over. It does not seem
necessary to give the variations under
the circumstances. In* 2^3 *Percy has*
Yong Jemmye Grove.
C. 2^1. bonny *should perhaps be* comely, *as in* 3^1.
4^2. *Originally written* To see my white . . .
courting.
5^2. *Originally* dwelling. 5^3. *Originally* it 's.
5^4. The *is written over* His, *probably as a conjecture.*
7^2. *After* stoutly, slowly ? *as a conjectural emendation.*
7^4. lying. ' *An ingenious friend ' of Percy's
suggested the transposition of* lying *and* dying *in* A $3^{2, 4}$.

85

LADY ALICE

A. ' Lady Alice.' a. Bell's Ancient Poems, Ballads,
and Songs of the Peasantry of England, p. 127. b.
Notes and Queries, Second Series, I, 418. c. Notes
and Queries, Second Series, I, 354.

B. ' Giles Collins and Proud Lady Anna,' Gammer
Gurton's Garland, p. 38, ed. 1810.

THIS little ballad, which is said to be still
of the regular stock of the stalls, is a sort of
counterpart to ' Lord Lovel.' A writer in

Notes and Queries, Second Series, I, 418, says :
This old song was refined and modernized by
the late Richard Westall, R. A.

A

a. Bell's Ancient Poems, Ballads, and Songs of the Peasantry of England, p. 127, a stall copy. b. Edward Hawkins,
in Notes and Queries, Second Series, I, 418. c. Notes and
Queries, Second Series, I, 354, as heard sung forty years
before 1856, " Uneda," Philadelphia.

1 LADY ALICE was sitting in her bower-window,
    Mending her midnight quoif,

And there she saw as fine a corpse
    As ever she saw in her life.

2 ' What bear ye, what bear ye, ye six men tall ?
    What bear ye on your shoulders ?'
' We bear the corpse of Giles Collins,
    An old and true lover of yours.'

3 ' O lay him down gently, ye six men tall,
    All on the grass so green,
And tomorrow, when the sun goes down,
    Lady Alice a corpse shall be seen.

4 ' And bury me in Saint Mary's church,
    All for my love so true,
And make me a garland of marjoram,
    And of lemon-thyme, and rue.'

5 Giles Collins was buried all in the east,
    Lady Alice all in the west,
And the roses that grew on Giles Collins's
        grave,
    They reached Lady Alice's breast.

6 The priest of the parish he chanced to pass,
    And he severed those roses in twain;
Sure never were seen such true lovers before,
    Nor eer will there be again.

B

Gammer Gurton's Garland, p. 38, ed. 1810.

1 GILES COLLINS he said to his old mother,
    Mother, come bind up my head,
And send to the parson of our parish,
    For tomorrow I shall be dead.   dead,
    For tomorrow I shall be dead.

2 His mother she made him some water-gruel,
    And stirrd it round with a spoon;
Giles Collins he ate up his water-gruel,
    And died before 't was noon.

3 Lady Anna was sitting at her window,
    Mending her night-robe and coif;
She saw the very prettiest corpse
    She 'd seen in all her life.

4 ' What bear ye there, ye six strong men,
    Upon your shoulders so high?'
' We bear the body of Giles Collins,
    Who for love of you did die.'

5 ' Set him down, set him down,' Lady Anna
        she cry'd,
    ' On the grass that grows so green;
Tomorrow, before the clock strikes ten,
    My body shall lye by hisn.'

6 Lady Anna was buried in the east,
    Giles Collins was buried in the west;
There grew a lilly from Giles Collins
    That touchd Lady Anna's breast.

7 There blew a cold north-easterly wind,
    And cut this lilly in twain,
Which never there was seen before,
    And it never will again.

A. a. 1^2. At midnight mending her quoif.
    b. 1^2. Mending her midnight coif.
        3^3. before the sun.
        4. *wanting*. 5^3. grow, *misprinted*.
        6^1. pass by. 6^2. And severd these.
        6^4. ever there will.
    c. 1^1. at her. 1^2. A mending her midnight coif.

1^3. the finest corpse. 1^4. That ever.
2^2. Upon your shoulders strong.
2^3. Sir Giles.
3, 4. *wanting*.
5^1. Lady Alice was. 5^2. Giles Collins all.
5^3. A lily grew out of. 5^4. And touched.
6. *wanting*.

86

YOUNG BENJIE

A. 'Young Benjie,' Minstrelsy of the Scottish Border, III, 251, ed. 1803; III, 10, ed. 1833.

B. 'Bondsey and Maisry,' Buchan's Ballads of the North of Scotland, II, 265.

'VERKEL VEJEMANDSØN,' Grundtvig, IV, 151, No 198, invites a comparison with 'Young Benjie,' although the ballads, in the form in which they are now extant, are widely divergent. Verkel Vejemandsøn, seeing maid Gundelild shining in her virgin crown, makes a fiendish vow to rob her of it. He rides up to her house and asks where her father and mother are. They are away from home. He carries her off on his horse into the thickest of a wood, and bids her hold the beast while he makes a bed of leaves. He loses her in the thicket, and cannot find her, though he looks for her a day and two days. She goes to the strand and throws herself into the sea, saying, It was a very different bride-bed that my mother meant me to have. She is drawn out in a fisherman's net. Verkel swears that he has not seen her for eight years, but he is convicted of his crime, on evidence not given, and "clothes three stakes;" that is, he is hanged, and parts of his body are exposed on the wheels which crown the three posts of a gallows.

Sir Walter Scott's observations on the passage in which the drowned maid reveals the author of her death are too interesting to be spared :

"In this ballad the reader will find traces of a singular superstition, not yet altogether discredited in the wilder parts of Scotland. The lykewake, or watching a dead body, in itself a melancholy office, is rendered, in the idea of the assistants, more dismally awful by the mysterious horrors of superstition. In the interval betwixt death and interment, the disembodied spirit is supposed to hover round its mortal habitation, and, if invoked by certain rites, retains the power of communicating, through its organs, the cause of its dissolution. Such inquiries, however, are always dangerous, and never to be resorted to unless the deceased is suspected to have suffered *foul play*, as it is called. It is the more unsafe to tamper with this charm in an unauthorized manner, because the inhabitants of the infernal regions are, at such periods, peculiarly active. One of the most potent ceremonies in the charm, for causing the dead body to speak, is setting the door ajar, or half open. On this account the peasants of Scotland sedulously avoid leaving the door ajar while a corpse lies in the house. The door must either be left wide open or quite 'shut; but the first is always preferred, on account of the exercise of hospitality usual on such occasions. The attendants must be likewise careful never to leave the corpse for a moment alone, or, if it is left alone, to avoid, with a degree of superstitious horror, the first sight of it.

"The following story, which is frequently related by the peasants of Scotland, will illustrate the imaginary danger of leaving the door ajar. In former times a man and his wife lived in a solitary cottage on one of the extensive Border fells. One day the husband died suddenly, and his wife, who was equally afraid of staying alone by the corpse, or leaving the dead body by itself, repeatedly went to the door, and looked anxiously over the lonely moor for the sight of some person approaching. In her confusion and alarm she accidentally left the door ajar, when the corpse suddenly started up and sat in the bed, frowning and grinning at her frightfully. She sat alone, crying bitterly, unable to avoid the fascination of the dead man's eye, and too much terrified to break the sullen silence, till a Catholic priest, passing over the wild, entered the cottage. He first set the door quite open, then put his little finger in his mouth, and said the paternoster backwards; when the horrid look of the corpse relaxed, it fell back on the bed, and behaved itself as a dead man ought to do.

"The ballad is given from tradition. I have been informed by a lady of the highest literary eminence [Miss Joanna Baillie], that she has heard a ballad on the same subject, in which the scene was laid upon the banks of the Clyde. The chorus was,

> O Bothwell banks bloom bonny,

and the watching of the dead corpse was said to have taken place in Bothwell church."

A is translated by Schubart, p. 164; by Gerhard, p. 88; by Knortz, Schottische Balladen, No 31.

———◆———

A

Minstrelsy of the Scottish Border, III, 251, ed. 1803; III, 10, ed. 1833. From tradition.

1 Of a' the maids o fair Scotland
    The fairest was Marjorie,
And Young Benjie was her ae true-love,
    And a dear true-love was he.

2 And wow! but they were lovers dear,
    And loved fu constantlie;
But ay the mair, when they fell out,
    The sairer was their plea.

3 And they hae quarrelled on a day,
    Till Marjorie's heart grew wae,
And she said she 'd chuse another luve,
    And let Young Benjie gae.

4 And he was stout, and proud-hearted,
    And thought o 't bitterlie,
And he 's gaen by the wan moon-light
    To meet his Marjorie.

5 'O open, open, my true-love,
    O open, and let me in!'
'I dare na open, Young Benjie,
    My three brothers are within.'

6 'Ye lied, ye lied, ye bonny burd,
    Sae loud 's I hear ye lie;
As I came by the Lowden banks,
    They bade gude een to me.

7 'But fare ye weel, my ae fause love,
    That I hae loved sae lang!
It sets ye chuse another love,
    And let Young Benjie gang.'

8 Then Marjorie turned her round about,
    The tear blinding her ee:
'I darena, darena let thee in,
    But I 'll come down to thee.'

9 Then saft she smiled, and said to him,
    O what ill hae I done?
He took her in his armis twa,
    And threw her oer the linn.

10 The stream was strang, the maid was stout,
    And laith, laith to be dang,
But ere she wan the Lowden banks
    Her fair colour was wan.

11 Then up bespak her eldest brother,
    'O see na ye what I see?'
And out then spak her second brother,
    'It 's our sister Marjorie!'

12 Out then spak her eldest brother,
    'O how shall we her ken?'
And out then spak her youngest brother,
    'There 's a honey-mark on her chin.'

13 Then they 've taen up the comely corpse,
    And laid it on the grund:
'O wha has killed our ae sister,
    And how can he be found?

14 'The night it is her low lykewake,
    The morn her burial day,
And we maun watch at mirk midnight,
    And hear what she will say.'

15 Wi doors ajar, and candle-light,
    And torches burning clear,

The streikit corpse, till still midnight,
　They waked, but naething hear.

16 About the middle o the night
　　The cocks began to craw,
　And at the dead hour o the night
　　The corpse began to thraw.

17 'O wha has done the wrang, sister,
　　Or dared the deadly sin?
　Wha was sae stout, and feared nae dout,
　　As thraw ye oer the linn?'

18 'Young Benjie was the first ae man
　　I laid my love upon;
　He was sae stout and proud-hearted,
　　He threw me oer the linn.'

19 'Sall we Young Benjie head, sister?
　　Sall we Young Benjie hang?

Or sall we pike out his twa gray een,
　And punish him ere he gang?'

20 'Ye mauna Benjie head, brothers,
　　Ye mauna Benjie hang,
　But ye maun pike out his twa gray een,
　　And punish him ere he gang.

21 'Tie a green gravat round his neck,
　　And lead him out and in,
　And the best ae servant about your house
　　To wait Young Benjie on.

22 'And ay, at every seven year's end,
　　Ye 'll tak him to the linn;
　For that 's the penance he maun drie,
　　To scug his deadly sin.'

B

Buchan's Ballads of the North of Scotland, II, 265.

1 'O come along wi me, brother,
　　Now come along wi me;
　And we 'll gae seek our sister Maisry,
　　Into the water o Dee.'

2 The eldest brother he stepped in,
　　He stepped to the knee;
　Then out he jumpd upo the bank,
　　Says, This water 's nae for me.

3 The second brother he stepped in,
　　He stepped to the quit;
　Then out he jumpd upo the bank,
　　Says, This water 's wondrous deep.

4 When the third brother stepped in,
　　He stepped to the chin;
　Out he got, and forward wade,
　　For fear o drowning him.

5 The youngest brother he stepped in,
　　Took 's sister by the hand;
　Said, Here she is, my sister Maisry,
　　Wi the hinny-draps on her chin.

6 'O if I were in some bonny ship,
　　And in some strange countrie,
　For to find out some conjurer,
　　To gar Maisry speak to me!'

7 Then out it speaks an auld woman,
　　As she was passing by:
　'Ask of your sister what you want,
　　And she will speak to thee.'

8 'O sister, tell me who is the man
　　That did your body win?
　And who is the wretch, tell me, likewise,
　　That threw you in the lin?'

9 'O Bondsey was the only man
　　That did my body win;
　And likewise Bondsey was the man
　　That threw me in the lin.'

10 'O will we Bondsey head, sister?
　　Or will we Bondsey hang?
　Or will we set him at our bow-end,
　　Lat arrows at him gang?'

11 'Ye winna Bondsey head, brothers,
　　Nor will ye Bondsey hang;
　But ye 'll take out his twa grey een,
　　Make Bondsey blind to gang.

12 'Ye 'll put to the gate a chain o gold,
　　A rose garland gar make,
　And ye 'll put that in Bondsey's head,
　　A' for your sister's sake.'

87

PRINCE ROBERT

A. 'Prince Robert,' Scott's Minstrelsy, II, 124, ed. 1802; III, 269, ed. 1833.

B. 'Earl Robert,' Motherwell's MS., p. 149; Motherwell's Minstrelsy, p. 200.

C. 'Lord Robert and Mary Florence,' Motherwell's MS., p. 321.

D. 'Prince Robert,' Harris MS., fol. 29.

PRINCE ROBERT'S mother poisons him because he has married against her will. He sends for his bride to come, but she is in time only for the funeral. The mother will give her nothing of her son's, not even the ring on his finger, all that she asks for. The bride's heart breaks before the mother's face.

There are other ballad-stories of a mother's

poisoning because of displeasure at a son's match, but I know of none which demands comparison with this very slender tale.

A is translated by Schubart, p. 122; by Doenniges, p. 57; **A** and **B** combined by Rosa Warrens, Schottische Volkslieder, No 36.

A

Scott's Minstrelsy, II, 124, ed. 1802; III, 269, ed. 1833: from the recitation of Miss Christian Rutherford.

1 PRINCE ROBERT has wedded a gay ladye,
    He has wedded her with a ring;
   Prince Robert has wedded a gay ladye,
    But he daur na bring her hame.

2 'Your blessing, your blessing, my mother dear,
    Your blessing now grant to me!'
   'Instead of a blessing ye sall have my curse,
    And you 'll get nae blessing frae me.'

3 She has called upon her waiting-maid,
    To fill a glass of wine;
   She has called upon her fause steward,
    To put rank poison in.

4 She has put it to her roudes lip,
    And to her roudes chin;
   She has put it to her fause, fause mouth,
    But the never a drop gaed in.

5 He has put it to his bonny mouth,
    And to his bonny chin,
   He 's put it to his cherry lip,
    And sae fast the rank poison ran in.

6 'O ye hae poisoned your ae son, mother,
    Your ae son and your heir;
   O ye hae poisoned your ae son, mother,
    And sons you 'll never hae mair.

7 'O where will I get a little boy,
    That will win hose and shoon,
   To rin sae fast to Darlinton,
    And bid Fair Eleanor come?

8 Then up and spake a little boy,
    That wad win hose and shoon,
   'O I 'll away to Darlinton,
    And bid Fair Eleanor come.'

9 O he has run to Darlinton,
    And tirled at the pin;
   And wha was sae ready as Eleanor's sell
    To let the bonny boy in?

10 'Your gude-mother has made ye a rare dinour,
    She 's made it baith gude and fine;
   Your gude-mother has made ye a gay dinour,
    And ye maun cum till her and dine.'

11 It 's twenty lang miles to Sillertoun town,
    The langest that ever were gane;

But the steed it was wight, and the ladye was
 light,
  And she cam linkin in.

12 But when she came to Sillertoun town,
   And into Sillertoun ha,
 The torches were burning, the ladies were
   mourning,
   And they were weeping a'.

13 'O where is now my wedded lord,
   And where now can he be?
 O where is now my wedded lord?
   For him I canna see.'

14 'Your wedded lord is dead,' she says,
   'And just gane to be laid in the clay;
 Your wedded lord is dead,' she says,
   'And just gane to be buried the day.

15 'Ye 'se get nane o his gowd, ye 'se get nane o
   his gear,
 Ye 'se get nae thing frae me;
 Ye 'se na get an inch o his gude broad land,
   Tho your heart suld burst in three.'

16 'I want nane o his gowd, I want nane o his
   gear,
   I want nae land frae thee;
 But I 'll hae the ring that 's on his finger,
   For them he did promise to me.'

17 'Ye 'se na get the ring that 's on his finger,
   Ye 'se na get them frae me;
 Ye 'se na get the ring that 's on his finger,
   An your heart suld burst in three.'

18 She 's turn'd her back unto the wa,
   And her face unto a rock,
 And there, before the mother's face,
   Her very heart it broke.

19 The tane was buried in Marie's kirk,
   The tother in Marie's quair,
 And out o the tane there sprang a birk,
   And out o the tother a brier.

20 And thae twa met, and thae twa plat,
   The birk but and the brier,
 And by that ye may very weel ken
   They were twa lovers dear.

B

Motherwell's MS. p. 149, ; Motherwell's Minstrelsy, p. 200:
from the recitation of Mrs Thomson, Kilbarchan, a native of
Bonhill, Dumbartonshire, aged betwixt sixty and seventy.

1 It 's fifty miles to Sittingen's Rocks,
   As eer was ridden or gane;
 And Earl Robert has wedded a wife,
   But he dare na bring her hame.
 And Earl Robert has wedded a wife,
   But he dare na bring her hame.

2 His mother, she called to her waiting-maid,
   To bring her a pint o wine:
 'For I dinna weel ken what hour of the day
   That my son Earl Robert shall dine.'

3 She 's put it to her fause, fause cheek,
   But an her fause, fause chin;
 She 's put it to her fause, fause lips,
   But never a drap went in.

4 But he 's put it to his bonny cheek,
   Aye and his bonny chin;
 He 's put it to his red rosy lips,
   And the poison went merrily doun.

5 'O where will I get a bonny boy,
   That will win hose and shoon,
 That will gang quickly to Sittingen's Rocks,
   And bid my lady come?'

6 It 's out then speaks a bonny boy,
   To Earl Robert was something akin:
 'Many a time have I ran thy errand,
   But this day wi the tears I 'll rin.'

7 Bat when he came to Sittingin's Rocks,
   To the middle of a' the ha,
 There were bells a ringing, and music playing,
   And ladies dancing a'.

8 'What news, what news, my bonny boy?
   What news have ye to me?
 Is Earl Robert in very good health,
   And the ladies of your countrie?'

9 'O Earl Robert 's in very good health,
   And as weel as a man can be;
 But his mother this night has a drink to be
   druken,
   And at it you must be.'

10 She called to her waiting-maid,
    To bring her a riding-weed,
  And she called to her stable-groom,
    To saddle her milk-white steed.

11 But when she came to Earl Robert's bouir,
    To the middle of a' the ha,
  There were bells a ringing, and sheets doun
      hinging,
    And ladies mourning a'.

12 'I 've come for none of his gold,' she said,
    ' Nor none of his white monie,
  Excepting a ring of his smallest finger,
    If that you will grant me.'

13 'Thou 'll not get none of his gold,' she said,
    ' Nor none of his white monie ;

Thou 'll not get a ring of his smallest finger,
    Tho thy heart should break in three.'

14 She set her foot unto a stane,
    Her back unto a tree ;
  She set her foot unto a stane,
    And her heart did break in three.

15 The one was buried in Mary's kirk,
    The other in Mary's quire ;
  Out of the one there grew a birk,
    From the other a bonnie brier.

16 And these twa grew, and these twa threw,
    Till their twa craps drew near ;
  So all the warld may plainly see
    That they loved each other dear.

C

Motherwell's MS., p. 321, from Agnes Laird, Kilbarchan,
June 21, 1825.

1 LORD ROBERT and Mary Florence,
    They were twa children young ;
  They were scarse seven years of age
    Till love began to spring.

2 Lord Robert loved Mary Florence,
    And she lovd him above power ;
  But he durst not for his cruel mother
    Bring her unto his bower.

3 It was nineteen miles to Strawberry Castle,
    As good as ever was rode or gane,
  But the lord being light, and the steed being
      swift,
    Lord Robert was hame gin noon.

4 'A blessing, a blessing, dear mother,' he cries,
    ' A blessing I do crave ! '
  'A blessing, a blessing, my son Lord Robert,
    And a blessing thou shalt have.'

5 She called on her chamber-maid
    To fill up a glass of wine,
  And so clever was her cursed fingers
    To put the rank poison in.

6 'O wae be to you, mother dear,' he cries,
    ' For working such a wae ;

For poisoning of your son Lord Robert,
    And children you have nae mae.

7 'O where will I get a pretty little boy
    That 'll rin him my errands sune ?
  That will rin unto Strawberry Castle,
    And tell Mary Florence to cum ? '

8 'Here am I, a pretty little boy,
    Your eldest sister's son,
  That will rin unto Strawberry Castle,
    And tell Mary Florence to come.'

9 When he came unto Strawberry Castle
    He tirled at the pin,
  And so ready was Mary Florence hersell
    To open and let him in.

10 'What news, what news, my pretty little boy ?
    What news hast thou brocht here ? '
  With sichin and sabbin and wringing his
      hands,
    No message he could refer.

11 'The news that I have gotten,' he says,
    ' I cannot weel declair ;
  But my grandmother has prepard a feast,
    And fain she would hae thee thair.'

12 She called on her stable-groom
    To dress her swiftest steed ;

For she knew very weel by this pretty little
    boy
  That Lord Robert was dead.

13 And when she came to Knotingale Castle
    She tirled at the pin,
  And so ready was Lord Robert's mother
    To open and let her in.

14 'What news, what news, Mary Florence?' she
    says,
  'What news has thou to me?'
  'I came to see your son Lord Robert,
    And fain would I him see.

15 'I came not for his gude red gold,
    Nor for his white monie,
  But for the ring on his wee finger,
    And fain would I it see.'

16 'That ring thou cannot see, Mary Florence,
    That ring thou 'll never see;
  For death was so strong in Lord Robert's
    breast
  That the gold ring burst in three.'

17 She has set her foot unto a stone,
    Her back unto a tree;
  Before she left Knotingale Castle
    Her heart it brak in three.

D

Harris MS., fol. 29, from the recitation of Mrs Molison.

1 PRINCE ROBERT he has wedded a wife,
    An he daurna bring her hame;
  The queen   .   .   .
    His mither was much to blame.

*   *   *   *   *

2 'It is the fashion in oor countrie, mither,
    I dinna ken what it is here,
  To like your wife better than your mither,
    That . . . bought you sae dear.'

3 She called upon her best marie,
    An tippet her wi a ring,
  To bring to her the rank poison,
    To gie Prince Robert a dram.

4 She put it to her cheek, her cheek,
    She put it to her chin;
  She put it to her fause, fause lips,
    But neer a drap gaed in.

5 She put it to his cheek, his cheek,
    She put it to his chin;
  She put it to his rosy lips,
    An the rank poison gaed in.

6 'Whare will I get a bonnie boy,
    Wha will win meat an fee,
  Wha will rin on to . . . bower,
    Bring my gude ladie to me?'

7 'Here am I, a bonnie boy,
    Willin to win meat an fee,
  Wha will rin on to . . . bower,
    An bring your gude ladie.'

8 'Whan you come to broken brig,
    Tak aff your coat an swim;
  An whan you come to grass growin,
    Tak aff your shoon an rin.'

9 An whan he cam to broken brig,
    He coost his coat an swam,
  An whan he cam to grass growin,
    Set doon his feet an ran.

10 An whan he cam to the ladie's bower,
    He fand her a' her lane,

*   *   *   *   *

11 An syne she kissed his wan, wan lips,

A. 13^1, 13^3. Oh.
    16^3, 17^1, 17^3. ring, *ed.* 1802; rings, *ed.* 1833.
B. 2^2. *Changed in the MS. to* O bring me.
    7^2, 11^2. a' *added later.*

9^2. a *added later.*
15^3. grew an; *the next word looks like* buk, *but is erased, and* birk *substituted. Motherwell printed* bush.

88

YOUNG JOHNSTONE

A. 'The Cruel Knight,' Herd, The Ancient and Modern Scots Songs, 1769, p. 305 ; I, 165, ed. 1776.

B. a. 'Young Johnstone,' Motherwell's Minstrelsy, p. 193. **b.** 'The Young Johnstone,' Finlay's Scottish Historical and Romantic Ballads, II, 71.

C. 'Sweet William and the Young Colonel,' Motherwell's MS., p.,310.

D. 'Johnston Hey and Young Caldwell,' Motherwell's MS., p. 639.

E. 'Lord John's Murder,' Buchan's Ballads of the North of Scotland, II, 20.

F. 'Young Johnston,' Motherwell's Minstrelsy, Appendix, p. xx, XVIII, one stanza.

PINKERTON inserted Herd's 'Cruel Knight,' A, in his Select Scotish Ballads, I, 69, with alterations and omissions. Motherwell enters in his Note-Book, p. 6, that he had received from Mrs Gentles, Paisley, 'The Young Johnstone,' "different in some measure from the copy in Finlay's Ballads." Of the version printed in his Minstrelsy (B a), undoubtedly that which was derived from Mrs Gentles, he says, "for a few verbal emendations recourse has been had to Mr Finlay's copy (B b)." These versions should therefore not have differed considerably, Finlay suppressed "Young Johnstone's reason for being sae late a coming in," "as well as a concluding stanza of inferior merit;" in this rejection he was not followed by Motherwell. Christie, I, 156, gives E "with some alterations from the way it was sung" by an old woman; petty variations, such as one must think could not have impressed themselves upon a memory unapt to retain things of more importance. 'Young Johnstone' in Chambers's Twelve Romantic Scottish Ballads, p. 19, is made up mostly from B a, B b, E, like the copy in the same editor's Scottish Ballads, p. 293, but handles tradition very freely.

E seems to be A altered, or imperfectly remembered, with the addition of a few stanzas. Motherwell remarks of his version, what is true of all the others but E, that the ballad throws no light on Young Johnstone's motive for stabbing his lady. An explanation was afforded by the reciter: "The barbarous act was committed unwittingly, through Young Johnstone's suddenly waking from sleep, and, in that moment of confusion and alarm, unhappily mistaking his mistress for one of his pursuers." And this is the turn which is given to the act in E 13 :

'Ohon, alas, my lady gay,
  To come sae hastilie !
I thought it was my deadly foe,
  Ye had trysted into me.'

The apology may go for what it is worth. Awake or waking, Young Johnstone's first instinct is as duly to stab as a bull-dog's is to bite.

C 5, 9, 13 are taken from 'The Lass of Roch Royal:' cf. No 76, B 17, C 2, E 9, H 3. D 6 recalls 'Fair Margaret and Sweet William,' No 74, A 8, B 11 ; A 13, B 25, C 26, D 30, E 15, 'Lord Thomas and Fair Annet,' No 73, B 34, D 17 ; D 31, 32, 'The Twa Brothers,' No 49, B 4, C 4, 5, D 5, 7, E 6, 7, F 5, 6, G 4, 5.

A, with the last two stanzas of B a, is translated by Rosa Warrens, Schottische Volkslieder, No 27 ; E by Gerhard, p. 157 ; Aytoun, II, 110 by Knortz, Schottische Balladen, No 30, p. 94, with abridgment ; Pinkerton's copy by Grundtvig, No 20, p. 136.

A

Herd's Ancient and Modern Scots Songs, 1769, p. 305.

1 THE knight stands in the stable-door,
   As he was for to ryde,
When out then came his fair lady,
   Desiring him to byde.

2 'How can I byde? how dare I byde?
   How can I byde with thee?
Have I not killd thy ae brother?
   Thou hadst nae mair but he.'

3 'If you have killd my ae brother,
   Alas, and woe is me!
But if I save your fair body,
   The better you'll like me.'

4 She's tane him to her secret bower,
   Pinnd with a siller pin,
And she's up to her highest tower,
   To watch that none come in.

5 She had na well gane up the stair,
   And entered in her tower,
When four and twenty armed knights
   Came riding to the door.

6 'Now God you save, my fair lady,
   I pray you tell to me,
Saw you not a wounded knight
   Come riding by this way?'

7 'Yes, bloody, bloody was his sword,
   And bloody were his hands;

But if the steed he rides be good,
   He's past fair Scotland's strands.

8 'Light down, light down then, gentlemen,
   And take some bread and wine;
The better you will him pursue
   When you shall lightly dine.'

9 'We thank you for your bread, lady,
   We thank you for your wine;
I would gie thrice three thousand pounds
   Your fair body was mine.'

10 Then she's gane to her secret bower,
   Her husband dear to meet;
But he drew out his bloody sword,
   And wounded her sae deep.

11 'What aileth thee now, good my lord?
   What aileth thee at me?
Have you not got my father's gold,
   But and my mother's fee?'

12 'Now live, now live, my fair lady,
   O live but half an hour,
There's neer a leech in fair Scotland
   But shall be at thy bower.'

13 'How can I live? how shall I live?
   How can I live for thee?
See you not where my red heart's blood
   Runs trickling down my knee?'

*   *   *   *   *

B

a. Motherwell's Minstrelsy, p. 193, from the recitation of Mrs Gentles, Paisley. **b.** Finlay's Scottish Ballads, II, 71, from two recited copies.

1 YOUNG Johnstone and the young Colnel
   Sat drinking at the wine:
'O gin ye wad marry my sister,
   It's I wad marry thine.'

2 'I wadna marry your sister
   For a' your houses and land;
But I'll keep her for my leman,
   When I come oer the strand.

3 'I wadna marry your sister
   For a' your gowd so gay;
But I'll keep her for my leman,
   When I come by the way.'

4 Young Johnstone had a little small sword,
   Hung low down by his gair,
And he stabbed it through the young Colnel,
   That word he neer spak mair.

5 But he's awa to his sister's bower,
   He's tirled at the pin:
'Whare hae ye been, my dear brither,
   Sae late a coming in?'

'I hae been at the school, sister,
　　Learning young clerks to sing.'

6 'I 've dreamed a dreary dream this night,
　　I wish it may be for good ;
　They were seeking you with hawks and hounds,
　　And the young Colnel was dead.'

7 'Hawks and hounds they may seek me,
　　As I trow well they be ;
　For I have killed the young Colnel,
　　And thy own true-love was he.'

8 'If ye hae killed the young Colnel,
　　O dule and wae is me !
　But I wish ye may be hanged on a hie gallows,
　　And hae nae power to flee.'

9 And he 's awa to his true-love's bower,
　　He 's tirled at the pin :
　'Whar hae ye been, my dear Johnstone,
　　Sae late a coming in ?'
　'It 's I hae been at the school,' he says,
　　'Learning young clerks to sing.'

10 'I have dreamed a dreary dream,' she says,
　　'I wish it may be for good ;
　They were seeking you with hawks and hounds,
　　And the young Colnel was dead.'

11 'Hawks and hounds they may seek me,
　　As I trow well they be ;
　For I hae killed the young Colnel,
　　And thy ae brother was he.'

12 'If ye hae killed the young Colnel,
　　O dule and wae is me !
　But I care the less for the young Colnel,
　　If thy ain body be free.

13 'Come in, come in, my dear Johnstone,
　　Come in and take a sleep ;
　And I will go to my casement,
　　And carefully I will thee keep.'

14 He had not weel been in her bower-door,
　　No not for half an hour,
　When four and twenty belted knights
　　Came riding to the bower.

15 'Well may you sit and see, lady,
　　Well may you sit and say ;

Did you not see a bloody squire
　　Come riding by this way ?'

16 'What colour were his hawks ?' she says,
　　'What colour were his hounds ?
　What colour was the gallant steed,
　　That bore him from the bounds ?'

17 'Bloody, bloody were his hawks,
　　And bloody were his hounds ;
　But milk-white was the gallant steed,
　　That bore him from the bounds.'

18 'Yes, bloody, bloody were his hawks,
　　And bloody were his hounds ;
　And milk-white was the gallant steed,
　　That bore him from the bounds.

19 'Light down, light down now, gentlemen,
　　And take some bread and wine ;
　And the steed be swift that he rides on,
　　He 's past the brig o Lyne.'

20 'We thank you for your bread, fair lady,
　　We thank you for your wine ;
　But I wad gie thrice three thousand pound
　　That bloody knight was taen.'

21 'Lie still, lie still, my dear Johnstone,
　　Lie still and take a sleep ;
　For thy enemies are past and gone,
　　And carefully I will thee keep.'

22 But Young Johnstone had a little wee sword,
　　Hung low down by his gair,
　And he stabbed it in fair Annet's breast,
　　A deep wound and a sair.

23 'What aileth thee now, dear Johnstone ?
　　What aileth thee at me ?
　Hast thou not got my father's gold,
　　Bot and my mither's fee ?'

24 'Now live, now live, my dear ladye,
　　Now live but half an hour,
　And there 's no a leech in a' Scotland
　　But shall be in thy bower.'

25 'How can I live ? how shall I live ?
　　Young Johnstone, do not you see
　The red, red drops o my bonny heart's blood
　　Rin trinkling down my knee ?

26 ' But take thy harp into thy hand,
    And harp out owre yon plain,
    And neer think mair on thy true-love
    Than if she had never been.'

27 He hadna weel been out o the stable,
    And on his saddle set,
    Till four and twenty broad arrows
    Were thrilling in his heart.

C

Motherwell's MS., p. 310, from the recitation of Jeanie Nicol, May 4, 1825.

1 SWEET WILLIAM and the young Colnel
    One day was drinking wine :
    ' It's I will marry your sister,
    If ye will marry mine.'

2 ' I will not marry your sister,
    Altho her hair be brown ;
    But I 'll keep her for my liberty-wife,
    As I ride thro the town. '

3 William, having his two-edged sword,
    He leaned quite low to the ground,
    And he has given the young Colnel
    A deep and a deadly wound.

4 He rade, he rade, and awa he rade,
    Till he came to his mother's bower ;
    ' O open, open, mother,' he says,
    ' And let your auld son in.

5 ' For the rain rains owre my yellow hair,
    And the dew draps on my chin,
    And trembling stands the gallant steed
    That carries me from the ground.'

6 ' What aileth thee, Sweet William ? ' she says,
    ' What harm now hast thou done ? '
    ' Oh I hae killed the young Colnel,
    And his heart's blood sair does run.'

7 ' If ye hae killed the young Colnel,
    Nae shelter ye 'll get frae me ;
    May the two-edged sword be upon your heart,
    That never hath power to flee ! '

8 He rade, he rade, and awa he rade,
    Till he came to his sister's bower ;
    ' Oh open, open, sister,' he says,
    ' And let your brother in.

9 ' For the rain rains on my yellow hair,
    And the dew draps on my chin,
    And trembling stands the gallant steed
    That carries me from the ground.'

10 ' What aileth thee, Sweet William ? ' she says,
    ' What harm now hast thou done ? '
    ' Oh I have killed the young Colnel,
    And his heart's blood sair doth run.'

11 ' If ye hae killed the young Colnel,
    Nae shelter ye 'll get frae me ;
    May the two-edged sword be upon your heart,
    That never hath power to flee ! '

12 He rade, he rade, and awa he rade,
    Till he came to his true-love's bower ;
    ' Oh open, oh open, my true-love,' he says,
    ' And let your sweetheart in.

13 ' For the rain rains on my yellow hair,
    And the dew draps on my chin,
    And trembling stands the gallant steed
    That carries me from the ground.'

14 ' What aileth thee, Sweet William ? ' she says,
    ' What harm now hast thou done ? '
    ' Oh I hae killed thy brother dear,
    And his heart's blood sair doth run.'

15 ' If ye hae killed my brother dear,
    It 's oh and alace for me !
    But between the blankets and the sheets
    It 's there I will hide thee ! '

16 She 's taen him by the milk-white hand,
    She 's led him thro chambers three,
    Until she came to her own chamber :
    ' It 's there I will hide thee.

17 ' Lye down, lye down, Sweet William,' she says,
    ' Lye down and take a sleep ;
    It 's owre the chamber I will watch,
    Thy fair bodie to keep.'

18 She had not watched at the chamber-door
    An hour but only three,
    Till four and twenty belted knichts
    Did seek his fair bodie.

19 ' O did you see the hunt ? ' she says,
    ' Or did you see the hounds ?
    Or did you see that gallant steed,
    That last rade thro the town ? '

20 ' What colour was the fox ? ' they said,
    ' What colour was the hounds ?
    What colour was the gallant steed,
    That 's far yont London toun ? '

21 ' O dark grey was the fox,' she said,
    ' And light grey was the hounds,
    But milk-white was the gallant steed
    That 's far yont London town.'

22 ' Rise up, rise up, Sweet William,' she says,
    ' Rise up, and go away ;
    For four and twenty belted knights
    Were seeking thy bodye.'

23 Sweet William, having his two-edged sword,
    He leaned it quite low to the ground,
    And he has given his own true-love
    A deep and a deadly wound.

24 ' What aileth thee, Sweet William ? ' she says,
    ' What harm now have I done ?
    I never harmed a hair of your head
    Since ever this love began.'

25 ' Oh live, oh live, my own true-love,
    Oh live but half an hour,
    And the best doctor in London town
    Shall come within thy bower.'

26 ' How can I live ? how shall I live ?
    How can I live half an hour ?
    For don't you see my very heart's blood
    All sprinkled on the floor ? '

27 William, having his two-edged sword,
    He leaned it quite low to the ground,
    And he has given his own bodie
    A deep and a deadly wound.

D

Motherwell's MS., p. 639, from the recitation of an Irish-woman, wife of John French, a porter at the quay of Ayr.

1 JOHNSTON HEY and Young Caldwell
    Were drinking o the wine :
    ' O will ye marry my sister ?
    And I will marry thine.'

2 ' I winna marry your sister,
    Altho her locks are broun ;
    But I 'll make her my concubine,
    As I ride through the toun.'

3 Syne Johnston drew a gude braid sword,
    That hang down by his knee,
    And he has run the Young Caldwell
    Out through the fair bodie.

4 Up he gat, and awa he rade,
    By the clear light o the moon,
    Until he came to his mother's door,
    And there he lichtit doun.

5 ' Whare hae ye been, son Willie,' she said,
    ' Sae late and far in the night ? '
    ' O I hae been at yon new slate house,
    Hearing the clergy speak.'

6 ' I dreamd a dream. son Willie,' she said,
    ' I doubt it bodes nae gude ;
    That your ain room was fu o red swine,
    And your bride's bed daubd wi blude.'

7 ' To dream o blude, mither,' he said,
    ' It bodeth meikle ill ;
    And I hae slain a Young Caldwell,
    And they 're seeking me to kill.'

8 ' Gin ye hae slain a Young Caldwell,
    Alace and wae is me !
    But gin your fair body 's free frae skaith,
    The easier I will be.'

9 Up he gat, and awa he rade,
    By the clear licht o the mune,
    Until he cam to his sister's bower,
    And there he lichtit doun.

10 'Whare hae ye been, brither,' she said,
  'Sae late and far in the night?'
  'O I hae been in yon new slate house,
  Hearing the clergy speak.'

11 'I dreamd a dream, brither,' she said,
  'I doubt it bodes nae gude;
  I dreamd the ravens eat your flesh,
  And the lions drank your blude.'

12 'To dream o blude, sister,' he said,
  'It bodeth meikle ill;
  And I hae slain a Young Caldwell,
  And they're seeking me to kill.'

13 'Gin ye hae slain a Young Caldwell,
  Alace and wae is me!
  To be torn at the tail o wild horses
  Is the death I weet ye'll die.'

14 Up he gat, and awa he rade,
  By the clear light o the mune,
  Untill he cam to his true-love's bower,
  And there he lichtit doun.

15 'Whare hae ye been, Love Willie,' she said,
  'Sae late and far in the night?'
  'O I hae been in yon new sklate house,
  Hearing the clergy speak.'

16 'I dreamd a dream, Willie,' she said,
  'I doubt it bodes nae gude;
  I dreamd the ravens ate your flesh,
  And the lions drank your blude.'

17 'To dream o ravens, love,' he said,
  'Is the loss o a near friend;
  And I hae killd your brither dear,
  And for it I'll be slain.'

18 'Gin ye hae slain my ae brither,
  Alace and wae is me!
  But gin your fair body's free frae skaith,
  The easier I will be.'

19 'Lye doun, lye doun, Love Willie,' she said,
  'Lye doun and tak a sleep;
  And I will walk the castel wa,
  Your fair bodie to keep.'

20 He laid him doun within her bowr,
  She happit him wi her plaid,

And she's awa to the castle-wa,
  To see what would betide.

21 She hadna gane the castle round
  A time but only three,
  Till four and twenty beltit knichts
  Cam riding ower the lea.

22 And whan they came unto the gate,
  They stude and thus did say:
  'O did ye see yon bludie knicht,
  As he rade out this way?'

23 'What colour was his hawk?' she said,
  'What colour was his hound?
  What colour was the gudely steed
  The bludie knicht rade on?'

24 'Nut-brown was his hawk,' they said,
  'And yellow-fit was his hound,
  And milk-white was the goodly steed
  The bluidie knicht rade on.'

25 'Gin nut-brown was his hawk,' she said,
  'And yellow-fit was his hound,
  And milk-white was the gudely steed,
  He's up to London gone.'

26 They spurrd their steeds out ower the lea,
  They being void o fear;
  Syne up she gat, and awa she gade,
  Wi tidings to her dear.

27 'Lye still, lye still, Love Willie,' she said,
  'Lye still and tak your sleep;'
  Syne he took up his good braid sword,
  And wounded her fu deep.

28 'O wae be to you, Love Willie,' she said,
  'And an ill death may ye die!
  For first ye slew my ae brither,
  And now ye hae killd me.'

29 'Oh live, oh live, true-love,' he said,
  'Oh live but ae half hour,
  And there's not a docter in a' London
  But sall be in your bower.'

30 'How can I live, Love Willie,' she said,
  'For the space of half an hour?
  Dinnae ye see my clear heart's blood
  A rinnin down the floor?'

31 'Tak aff, tak aff my holland sark,
　　And rive 't frae gare to gair,
　　And stap it in my bleeding wounds ;
　　They 'll may be bleed nae mair.'

32 Syne he took aff her holland sark,
　　And rave 't frae gare to gair,
　　And stappit it in her bleeding wounds,
　　But aye they bled the mair.

33 'Gae dress yoursell in black,' she said,
　　' And gae whistling out the way,
　　And mourn nae mair for your true-love
　　When she 's laid in the clay.'

34 He leaned his halbert on the ground,
　　The point o 't to his breast,
　　Saying, Here three sauls ['s] gaun to heaven ;
　　I hope they 'll a' get rest.

E

Buchan's Ballads of the North of Scotland, II, 20.

1 LORD JOHN stands in his stable door,
　　Says he, I will gae ride,
　　His lady, in her bigly bower?
　　Desired him to bide.

2 'How can I bide ? how can I bide ?
　　How shall I bide wi thee ?
　　When I hae killd your ae brother ;
　　You hae nae mair but he.'

3 ' If ye hae killd my ae brother,
　　Alas, and wae is me !
　　If ye be well yoursell, my love,
　　The less matter will be.

4 ' Ye 'll do you to yon bigly bower,
　　And take a silent sleep,
　　And I 'll watch in my highest tower,
　　Your fair body to keep.'

5 She has shut her bigly bower,
　　All wi a silver pin,
　　And done her to the highest tower,
　　To watch that nane come in.

6 But as she looked round about,
　　To see what she could see,
　　There she saw nine armed knights
　　Come riding oer the lea.

7 ' God make you safe and free, lady,
　　God make you safe and free !
　　Did you see a bludy knight
　　Come riding oer the lea ? '

8 ' O what like was his hawk, his hawk ?
　　And what like was his hound ?
　　If his steed has ridden well,
　　He 's passd fair Scotland's strand.

9 ' Come in, come in, gude gentlemen,
　　And take white bread and wine ;
　　And aye the better ye 'll pursue,
　　The lighter that ye dine.'

10 ' We thank you for your bread, lady,
　　We thank you for the wine,
　　And I woud gie my lands sae broad
　　Your fair body were mine.'

11 She has gane to her bigly bower,
　　Her ain gude lord to meet ;
　　A trusty brand he quickly drew,
　　Gae her a wound sae deep.

12 ' What harm, my lord, provokes thine ire
　　To wreak itself on me,
　　When thus I strove to save thy life,
　　Yet served for sic a fee ? '

13 ' Ohon, alas, my lady gay,
　　To come sae hastilie !
　　I thought it was my deadly foe,
　　Ye had trysted into me.

14 ' O live, O live, my gay lady,
　　The space o ae half hour,
　　And nae a leech in a' the land
　　But I 'se bring to your bower.'

15 ' How can I live ? how shall I live ?
　　How can I live for thee ?
　　Ye see my blude rin on the ground,
　　My heart's blude by your knee.

16 ' O take to flight, and flee, my love,
　　O take to flight, and flee !
　　I woudna wish your fair body
　　For to get harm for me.'

17 ' Ae foot I winna flee, lady,
　　Ae foot I winna flee ;

I 've dune the crime worthy o death,
  It 's right that I shoud die.

8 ' O deal ye well at my love's lyke
  The beer but an the wine ;

For ere the morn, at this same time,
  Ye 'll deal the same at mine.'

F

Motherwell's Minstrelsy, Appendix, p. xx, XVIII.

As Willie and the young Colnel
  Were drinking at the wine,

' O will ye marry my sister ? ' says Will,
  ' And I will marry thine.'

A. 10⁴. very deep, *in the edition of* 1776.
B. a. 4¹. *Motherwell informs us*, p. 200, *that the
      original reading was* little small sword ;
      also he stabbed in 4³.
   b. *Finlay's version is compounded from two,
      and Motherwell's, since it adopts read-
      ings from Finlay's, is compounded from
      three ; but Motherwell's has nevertheless
      been preferred, on account of its retain-
      ing stanzas which Finlay omitted. Be-
      sides, Motherwell gives us to understand
      that his changes are few.*
      3². gowd and fee.   3⁴. come oer the sea.
      4¹. nut-brown sword.   4³. he ritted.
      5². And he 's.   5³. dear Johnstone.
      5⁵, ⁶. *wanting.*
      6¹, 10¹. dreamed a dream this night, she says.
      6², 10². be good.
      7¹, 11¹. They are seeking me with hawks and
          hounds.
      8², 12². A dule.   9¹. his lover's.   9⁵, ⁶. *wanting.*
      12³. But I gie na sae much for.
      12⁴. is free.   13⁴. I 'll thee.
      14¹, ². She hadna weel gane up the stair,
          And entered in her tower.
      14³. Till.   4⁴. the door.
      15¹, ². O did you see a bloody squire,
          A bloody squire was he.
      15³. O did you see.   15⁴. riding oer the lea.
      16¹. she cried.   17⁸. And.
      19¹. But light ye down now.
      19³. be good he rides upon.   19⁴. of Tyne.

20¹. bread, ladie.   20³. But *wanting* : pounds.
20⁴. Your fair bodie was mine.
21³, ⁴. For there 's four an l twenty belted
      knights
  Just gone out at the gate.
22¹. had a wee penknife.
22³, ⁴. And he ritted it through his dear ladie,
    And wounded her sae sair.

25. How can I live, my dear Johnstone ?
    How can I live for thee ?
  O do ye na see my red heart's blood
    Run trickling down my knee ?

26. But go thy way, my dear Johnstone,
    And ride along the plain,
  And think no more of thy true love
    Than she had never been.

27. *wanting.*
C. 19¹. Oh.   25¹. O : *the first.*
D. 1³, 5³, 15³. Oh.   15¹. he been.
    18¹. ae *corrected from* ain.
    19³. wa *corrected from* round.
    24¹. she said.   29¹. O : *the first.*
    Caldwell *is an obvious corruption of* Colonel.
E. *The alterations according to the singing of
    Christie's old woman are, as usual with him
    in such cases, utterly insignificant.*
    2¹. How can I bide, how shall.   2². How can.
    3⁴. will it.   6³. she did see.   10². for your.
    15³. rins.

89

FAUSE FOODRAGE'

A. ' Fa'se Footrage,' Alexander Fraser Tytler's Brown MS., No 3.

B. 'The Eastmure King and the Westmure King, Motherwell's MS., p. 341.

C. ' Eastmuir King,' Harris MS., No 18, fol. 22.

A WAS printed in the Minstrelsy of the Scottish Border, II, 73, 1802, " chiefly " from Mrs Brown's MS. ; in fact, with not quite forty petty alterations. Scott remarks that the ballad has been popular in many parts of Scotland.   Christie, I, 172, had heard it sung by an old Banffshire woman, who died in 1866, at the age of nearly eighty, with very little difference from Scott's copy.*

The resemblance of the verse in A 31, ' The boy stared wild like a gray gose-hawke,' to one in ' Hardyknute,' ' Ncrse een like gray gosshawk stared wild,' struck Sir Walter Scott as suspicious, and led him " to make the strictest inquiry into the authenticity of the song. But every doubt was removed by the evidence of a lady of high rank [Lady Douglas of Douglas, sister to Henry, Duke of Buccleuch, as we are informed in the edition of 1833], who not only recollected the ballad as having amused her infancy, but could repeat many of the verses." It is quite possible that Mrs Brown may unconsciously have adopted this verse from the tiresome and affected Hardyknute, so much esteemed in her day. One would be only too glad were this the only corruption which the ballad had undergone. On the contrary, while not calling in question the substantial genuineness of the ballad, we must admit that the form in which we have received it is an enfeebled one, without much flavor or

color ; and some such feeling no doubt affected Sir Walter's mind, more than the reminiscence of ' Hardyknute,' which, of itself, is of slight account.

A tale ' How the king of Estmure Land married the king's daughter of Westmure Land ' is mentioned in " The Complaint of Scotland," and there has been considerable speculation as to what this tale might be, and also as to what localities Estmure Land and Westmure Land might signify. Seeing no clue to a settlement of these questions, I pass them by, with the simple comment that no king of Estmure Land marries the king of Westmure Land's daughter in this ballad or any other.

Three kings (King Easter and King Wester, A, the Eastmure king and the Westmure king, B, C, and King Honor, A, the king of Onorie, B, King Luve, C), court a lady, and the third, who woos for womanhood and beauty, B, wins her. The Eastmure king, B, the Westmure, C, kills his successful rival on his wedding-day. According to the prosaic, not at all ballad-like, and evidently corrupted account in A, there is a rebellion of nobles four months after the marriage, and a certain False Foodrage takes it upon himself to kill the king. The murderer spares the queen, and if she gives birth to a girl will spare her child also, but if she bears a boy the boy is to die.

---

* " As far as he can remember, the old woman gave the story in fewer verses."   Christie gives the ballad from Scott (omitting stanzas 10–18), " with slight alterations from the way she sung it."   These alterations are : 1¹, has *omitted*. 4¹, Then some *for* O some.   26³, fair castle *for* bonny castle (bonny in Scott, 1833 ; fair in Scott, 1802).   29², is right *for*

was right.   29⁴, Ere ever you *for* Or ever ye.   Dean Christie's memory, it seems, retains the most inconsiderable variations, while it is not so good for larger things.   See the note at Christie, I, 128, ' Willie and Earl Richard's Daughter,' in this volume, and other ballads.

In A the queen escapes from custody before her time comes, and gives birth to a boy in the swines' sty. Lots are cast to see who shall go find the queen (the narrative is very vague here), and the lot falls on Wise William, who sends his wife in his stead. The queen induces this woman to exchange children with her, Wise William's wife having a girl. After some years Wise William reveals to the boy that he is rightful lord of the castle (and we may suppose royal dignity) which False Foodrage has usurped. The boy kills False Foodrage and marries Wise William's daughter. Some of these incidents are wanting in B. For Wise William's wife we have simply a poor woman in the town.

'Fause Foodrage' is closely related to a Scandinavian ballad, especially popular in Denmark, where it is found in not less than twenty-three manuscripts:

Danish. A, ' Ung Villum,' Danske Viser, No 126, III, 135, 66 stanzas; B, ' Vold og Mord,' Levninger, II, 64, No 12, 64 stanzas; C, ' Lille Villum,' Kristensen, I, 305, No 111, 15 stanzas ; also, Tragica, No 18, not seen. **Icelandic.** ' Kvæði af Loga í Vallarhlíð,' Íslenzk fornkvæði, I, 235, No 28, 55 stanzas. **Swedish.** ' Helleman Unge,' Arwidsson, I, 132, No 15, 13 stanzas (imperfect). **Färöe,** in unprinted copies. There are more incidents in the Danish ballad, and too many, but something, without doubt, has been lost from the English, which, however, preserves these essential points: A man that has wedded a woman who had another lover is killed by his competitor shortly after his marriage; a boy is born, who is passed off as a girl; this boy, before he has attained manhood, slays his father's murderer.

In the Danish ' Young William,' A, Svend of Voldesløv, rich in gold, woos Lisbet, who prefers William for his good qualities. Svend shuts himself up in his room, sick with grief. His mother and sister come and go. The mother will get him a fairer maid, and gives him the good rede not to distress himself about a girl that is plighted to another man. The sister gives a bad rede, to kill William, and so get the bride. The mother remarks that a son is coming into being who would revenge his father's death. The business can be done, says Svend, before that son is born, and immediately after takes occasion to meet William as he is passing through a wood, and kills him. Forty weeks gone, Lisbet gives birth to a son, but Svend is told that she has borne a daughter. Young William attains to the age of eighteen, and is a stalwart youth, given to games of strength. One day when he is putting the stone with a peasant, the two fall out, and the peasant, being roughly treated, calls out, You had better avenge your father's death. Young William hastens to his mother, and asks whether his father's death had been by violence, and, if so, who killed him. The mother thinks him too young to wield a sword: he must summon Svend to a court. This is done. Svend informs his uncle that he is summoned to court by William, and asks what he is to do. The uncle had always been told that Lisbet's child was a girl. I shall never live to see the day, says Svend, when I shall beat a woman at tricks. Svend goes to the court, attended by many of his uncle's men. William charges him with the murder of his father, for which no compensation has been offered. Svend says not a penny will be paid, and William draws his sword and cuts him down. For killing Svend William is summoned to court by Svend's brother, Nilus. Nilus demands amends. William says they are quit, with brother against father, and he will marry Nilus's sister (whom he has already carried off). Never, says Nilus, for which William finds it necessary to kill *him*. He then rides to his mother, who asks what amends have been offered for his father's death, and, on hearing that William has killed both the murderer and his brother, clasps him to her heart, for all her grief is now over.

No other Scandinavian copy besides Danish A has the killing of Nilus, which may be regarded as an aftergrowth. In the Icelandic version, the sister, so far from putting her brother up to the murder, bursts into tears when her brother tells what he has done, because she knows that revenge will follow. The murderer offers himself to his former love in place of her husband, at the very moment when she is bowed in anguish over the dead body. She replies significantly, He is not far from me that shall revenge him. All the Scandinavian copies have the three chief points of the story except the Swedish, which lacks the first half.

Another Scandinavian ballad has many of the features of 'Young William:' Danish, 'Liden Engel,' A, Danske Viser, No 127, III, 147; B, Levninger, II, 82, No 13; C, Kristensen, I, 254, No 97, a fragment. Norwegian, 'Unge Ingelbrett,' Bugge, p. 110, No 23, derived from the Danish. According to Danish A, and for the most part B, Liden Engel (who, by the way, is of Westerris) carries off a bride by force. Her brother burns him and all his people in a church in which they have taken refuge, the lady being saved by lifting her on shields up to a window, whence she is taken by her natural friends. It is the mother that suggests the setting of the church on fire, and the first act of the daughter, after getting out of the church with singed hair, is to fall on her bare knees and pray that she may have a son who will take vengeance on her brother. A son is born, and called after his father, but his existence is as far as possible kept secret. As he grows up his mother is always saying to him, Thine uncle was the death of thy father. The boy wishes to serve the king; the mother says, Go, but remember thy father's death. The

king observes that the youth has always a weight on his mind, and on his asking the cause Little Engel answers that his uncle had slain his father and paid no boot. The king says, If you wish to revenge his death, as it is quite proper you should, I will lend you three hundred men. When the uncle is informed that Little Engel is coming against him he declares that he had never heard of such a person before: so the secret has been well kept. Little Engel burns his uncle and all his people in a stone chamber in which they had shut themselves up.

In the Norwegian-Danish ballad Engel, or Ingelbrett, the second simply kills his uncle with a sword. The offence given in this case is not the carrying off a bride by force, but the omitting to ask the brother's consent to the marriage, though that of all the rest of the family had been obtained: another instance of the danger of such neglect in addition to those already mentioned in the preface to 'The Cruel Brother,' I, 142.

'Fause Foodrage' has some affinity with 'Jellon Grame.'

Scott's copy is translated by Schubart, p. 102; Wolff, Halle der Völker, I, 33, and Hausschatz, p. 211; Doenniges, p. 51; Knortz, Schottische Balladen, No 28.

'Ung Villum' is translated by Prior, III, 422, No 170; 'Liden Engel' by the same, III, 379, No 164.

A

Alexander Fraser Tytler's Brown MS., No 3.

1 KING EASTER has courted her for her gowd,
    King Wester for her fee,
King Honor for her lands sae braid,
    And for her fair body.

2 They had not been four months married,
    As I have heard them tell,
Until the nobles of the land
    Against them did rebel.

3 And they cast kaivles them amang,
    And kaivles them between,
And they cast kaivles them amang
    Wha shoud gae kill the king.

4 O some said yea, and some said nay,
    Their words did not agree;
Till up it gat him Fa'se Footrage,
    And sware it shoud be he.

5 When bells were rung, and mass was sung,
    And a' man boon to bed,

King Honor and his gay ladie
In a hie chamer were laid.

6 Then up it raise him Fa'se Footrage,
While a' were fast asleep,
And slew the porter in his lodge,
That watch and ward did keep.

7 O four and twenty silver keys
Hang hie upon a pin,
And ay as a door he did unlock,
He has fastend it him behind.

8 Then up it raise him King Honor,
Says, What means a' this din!
Now what 's the matter, Fa'se Footrage?
O wha was 't loot you in?

9 'O ye my errand well shall learn
Before that I depart;'
Then drew a knife baith lang and sharp
And pierced him thro the heart.

10 Then up it got the Queen hersell,
And fell low down on her knee:
'O spare my life now, Fa'se Footrage!
For I never injured thee.

11 'O spare my life now, Fa'se Footrage!
Until I lighter be,
And see gin it be lad or lass
King Honor has left me wi.'

12 'O gin it be a lass,' he says,
'Well nursed she shall be;
But gin it be a lad-bairn,
He shall be hanged hie.

13 'I winna spare his tender age,
Nor yet his hie, hie kin;
But as soon as eer he born is,
He shall mount the gallows-pin.'

14 O four and twenty valiant knights
Were set the Queen to guard,
And four stood ay at her bower-door,
To keep baith watch and ward.

15 But when the time drew till an end
That she should lighter be,
She cast about to find a wile
To set her body free.

16 O she has birled these merry young men
Wi strong beer and wi wine,
Until she made them a' as drunk
As any wallwood swine.

17 'O narrow, narrow is this window,
And big, big am I grown!'
Yet thro the might of Our Ladie
Out at it she has won.

18 She wanderd up, she wanderd down,
She wanderd out and in,
And at last, into the very swines' stye,
The Queen brought forth a son.

19 Then they cast kaivles them amang
Wha should gae seek the Queen,
And the kaivle fell upon Wise William,
And he 's sent his wife for him.

20 O when she saw Wise William's wife,
The Queen fell on her knee;
'Win up, win up, madame,' she says,
'What means this courtesie?'

21 'O out of this I winna rise
Till a boon ye grant to me,
To change your lass for this lad-bairn
King Honor left me wi.

22 'And ye maun learn my gay gose-hawke
Well how to breast a steed,
And I shall learn your turtle-dow
As well to write and read.

23 'And ye maun learn my gay gose-hawke
To wield baith bow and brand,
And I shall learn your turtle-dow
To lay gowd wi her hand.

24 'At kirk or market where we meet,
We dare nae mair avow
But, Dame how does my gay gose-hawk?
Madame, how does my dow?'

25 When days were gane, and years came on,
Wise William he thought long;
Out has he taen King Honor's son,
A hunting for to gang.

26 It sae fell out at their hunting,
Upon a summer's day,

That they cam by a fair castle,
    Stood on a sunny brae.

27 'O dinna ye see that bonny castle,
    Wi wa's and towers sae fair?
Gin ilka man had back his ain,
    Of it you shoud be heir.'

28 'How I shoud be heir of that castle
    In sooth I canna see,
When it belongs to Fa'se Footrage,
    And he's nae kin to me.'

29 'O gin ye shoud kill him Fa'se Footrage,
    You woud do what is right;
For I wot he killd your father dear,
    Ere ever you saw the light.

30 'Gin ye should kill him Fa'se Footrage,
    There is nae man durst you blame;
For he keeps your mother a prisoner,
    And she dares no take you hame.'

31 The boy stared wild like a gray gose-hawke,
    Says, What may a' this mean!

'My boy, you are King Honor's son,
    And your mother's our lawful queen.'

32 'O gin I be King Honor's son,
    By Our Ladie I swear,
This day I will that traytour slay,
    And relieve my mother dear.'

33 He has set his bent bow till his breast,
    And lap the castle-wa,
And soon he's siesed on Fa'se Footrage,
    Wha loud for help gan ca.

34 'O hold your tongue now, Fa'se Footrage,
    Frae me you shanno flee;'
Syne pierced him through the foul fa'se heart,
    And set his mother free.

35 And he has rewarded Wise William
    Wi the best half of his land,
And sae has he the turtle-dow
    Wi the truth of his right hand.

B

Motherwell's MS., p. 341.

1 THE Eastmure king, and the Westmure king,
    And the king of Onorie,
They have all courted a pretty maid,
    And guess wha she micht be.

2 The Eastmure king courted her for gold,
    And the Westmure king for fee,
The king of Onore for womanheid,
    And for her fair beautie.

3 The Eastmure king swore a solemn oath,
    He would keep it till May,
That he would murder the king of Onore,
    Upon his wedding day.

4 When bells was rung, and psalms was sung,
    And all men boune for sleep,
Up and started the Eastmure king
    At the king of Onore's head.

5 He has drawn the curtains by —
    Their sheets was made of dorn —

And he has murdered the king of Onore,
    As innocent as he was born.

6 This maid she awak'd in the middle of the night,
    Was in a drowsy dream;
She found her bride's-bed swim with blood,
    Bot and her good lord slain.

7 'What will the court and council say?
    What will they say to me?
What will the court and council say
    But this night I've murderd thee?'

8 Out and speaks the Eastmure king:
    'Hold your tongue, my pretty may,
And come along with me, my dear,
    And that court ye'll never see.'

9 He mounted her on a milk-white steed,
    Himself upon a gray;
She turnd her back against the court,
    And weeping rode away.

10 'Now if you be with child,' he says,
    'As I trew well you be,

If it be of a lassie-bairn,
　　I 'll give her nurses three.

11 'If it be a lassie-bairn,
　　If you please she 'll get five;
　　But if it be a bonnie boy,
　　I will not let him live.'

12 Word is to the city gone,
　　And word is to the town,
　　And word is to the city gone,
　　She 's delivered of a son.

13 But a poor woman in the town
　　In the same case does lye,
　　Wha gived to her her woman-child,
　　Took awa her bonnie boy.

14 At kirk or market, whereer they met,
　　They never durst avow,
　　But 'Thou be kind to my boy,' she says,
　　'I 'll be kind to your bonnie dow.'

15 This boy was sixteen years of age,
　　But he was nae seventeen,
　　When he is to the garden gone,
　　To slay that Eastmure king.

16 'Be aware, be aware, thou Eastmure king,
　　Be aware this day of me;
　　For I do swear and do declare
　　Thy botcher I will be.'

17 'What aileth thee, my bonnie boy?
　　What aileth thee at me?
　　I 'm sure I never did thee wrang;
　　Thy face I neer did see.'

18 'Thou murdered my father dear,
　　When scarce conceived was I;
　　Thou murdered my father dear,
　　When scarce conceived was me:'
　　So then he slew that Eastmure king,
　　Beneath that garden tree.

C

Harris MS., No 18, fol. 22: derived from Jannie Scott, an old Perthshire nurse, about 1790.

1 EASTMUIR king, and Wastmuir king,
　　And king o Luve, a' three,
　　It 's they coost kevils them amang,
　　Aboot a gay ladie.

2 Eastmuir king he wan the gowd,
　　An Wastmuir king the fee,

But king o Luve, wi his lands sae broad,
　　He 's won the fair ladie.

3 Thae twa kings, they made an aith,
　　That, be it as it may,
　　They wad slay him king o Luve,
　　Upon his waddin day.

4 Eastmuir king he brak his aith,
　　An sair penance did he;
　　But Wastmuir king he made it oot,
　　An an ill deid mat he dee!

B. 4⁴. Onore's feet *originally*.　　5³. Onores.

90

JELLON GRAME.

A. a. 'Jellon Grame and Lillie Flower,' A. Fraser Tytler's Brown MS., No 4. b. 'Jellon Grame,' Scott's Minstrelsy, II, 20, 1802.

B. 'Hind Henry,' Motherwell's MS., p. 443.

C. 'May-a-Row,' Buchan's Ballads of the North of Scotland, II, 231.

D. 'Lady Margerie,' Cromek's Remains of Nithsdale and Galloway Song, p. 222.

'JELLON GRAME' was first given to the world in Scott's Minstrelsy, in 1802. The editor says of this copy, A b, " This ballad is published from tradition, with some conjectural emendations. It is corrected by a copy in Mrs Brown's MS. [A a], from which it differs in the concluding stanzas. Some verses are apparently modernized." The only very important difference between Scott's version and Mrs Brown's is its having four stanzas of its own, the four before the last two, which are evidently not simply modernized, but modern.

There is a material difference between the story furnished by A and what we learn from the three other copies. Jellon Grame sends for his love Lillie Flower to come to the wood. She is very eager to go, though warned by the messenger that she may never come back. Jellon Grame, who has already dug her grave, kills her because her father will hang him when it is discovered that she has had a child by him. He brings up the child as his sister's son. One day, when the boy asks why his mother does not take him home, Jellon Grame (very unnaturally) answers, I slew her, and there she lies: upon which the boy sends an arrow through him.

In B, C, D, the man is Henry, Hind Henry, B, C; the maid is May Margerie, B, May-a-Roe, C, Margerie, D. Margerie, in B, receives a message to come to the wood to make her love a shirt, which surprises her, for no month had passed in the year that she had not made him three. Nevertheless, she goes, though warned by her mother that there is a plot against her life. She is stopped in the wood

by Hind Henry, who kills her because she loves Brown Robin. Word is carried that Margerie has been slain; her sister hastens to the wood, takes under her care the child which Margerie was going with, and calls him Brown Robin, after his father. The lad goes to the wood one day after school to pull a hollin wand, and meets Hind Henry at the place where the mother had been killed. No grass is growing just there, and the boy asks Hind Henry why this is so. Hind Henry, not less frank than Jellon Grame, says, That is the very spot where I killed your mother. The boy catches at Henry's sword and runs him through.

C has nearly the same incidents as B, diluted and vulgarized in almost twice as many verses. Brown Robin is made to be Hind Henry's brother. The sister does not appear in the action, and the child is brought up by the murderer, as in A, but is named Robin Hood, after that bold robber. On hearing from Hind Henry how his mother had come to her death, young Robin sends an arrow to his heart.

A story is supplied from the " traditions of Galloway " for the fragmentary, and perhaps heterogeneous, verses called D; I suppose by Allan Cunningham. Margerie was beloved by two brothers, and preferred the elder. Henry, the younger, forged a billet to her by which he obtained a meeting in a wood, when he reproached her for not returning his feelings: sts 1, 2. " She expostulated with him on the impropriety of bringing her into an unfrequented place for the purpose of winning affections which, she observed, were not hers to bestow ; " but expostulations as to improprieties producing but slight effect in " those rude times," told him plainly that she was with child by his brother. Henry drew his sword and killed Margerie. The elder brother, who was hunting, was apprised of mischief by the omens in stanza 4. " Astonished at this singular phenomenon, he immediately flew to the bower of his mistress, where a page informed him she was gone to the 'silver wood,' agreeably to his desire. Thither he spurred his horse, and, meeting Henry with his bloody sword still in his hand, inquired what he had been killing." The other replied as in stanza 5. " A mutual explanation took place, and Henry fell by the sword of his unhappy brother."

The resemblance of this ballad at the beginning to ' Child Maurice' will not escape notice. Silver Wood, or the silver wood, is found in ' Child Maurice,' **A** 1, **G** 1. **A** 14, **B** 10, **C** 15, is a commonplace : see No 66, **A** 28, 29, **B** 20, 21, **D** 9, **E** 40 ; No 70, **B** 25 ; No 81, **K** 13. **B** 13 is found in ' Willie and Earl Richard's Daughter,' **B** 24 : cf. **A** 15. The phenomenon in **D** 4 we have had in No 65, **D** 17.

' Jellon Grame,' and particularly versions **B, C, D,** may be regarded as a counterpart to ' Fause Foodrage,' and especially to versions **B, C,** of that ballad. In ' Fause Foodrage,' **B, C,** and ' Jellon Grame,' **B, C, D,** a woman has two lovers. The one who is preferred is killed by the other in ' Fause Foodrage ;' in ' Jellon Grame' the woman herself is killed by the lover she has rejected. This kind of interchange is familiar in ballads. In both ' Fause Foodrage ' and ' Jellon Grame ' the son of the woman, before he comes to manhood, takes vengeance on the murderer.

' Jellon Grame,' as well as ' Fause Foodrage,' has certainly suffered very much in transmission. It is interesting to find an ancient and original trait preserved even in so extremely corrupted a version as **C** of the present ballad, a circumstance very far from unexampled. In stanza 18 we read that the child who is to avenge his mother " grew as big in ae year auld as some boys woud in three," and we have a faint trace of the same extraordinary thriving in **B** 15 : " Of all the youths was at that school none could with him compare." So in one of the Scandinavian ballads akin to ' Fause Foodrage,' and more remotely to ' Jellon Grame,' the corresponding child grows more in two months than other boys in eight years :

> Mei voks unge Ingelbrett
> í dei maanar tvaa
> hell híne smaabonni
> vokse paa aatte aar.

Bugge, Norske Folkeviser, No 23, st. 17, p. 113.

This is a commonplace : so again Bugge, No 5, sts 7, 8, p. 23. Compare Robert le Diable, and Sir Gowther.

In **B** 14 we are told that the boy was called by his father's name (**C** 17 is corrupted). This is a point in the corresponding Scandinavian ballads : Danske Viser, No 126, st. 21, No 127, st. 34 ; Levninger, No 12, st. 26, No 13, st. 18 ; Íslenzk fornkvæði, No 28, st. 33 b ; Bugge, No 23, st. 16 ; Kristensen, I, No 97, sts 7, 11, No 111, st. 9.

A b is translated by Schubart, p. 69 ; by Arndt, Blütenlese, p. 234.

A

a. A. Fraser Tytler's Brown MS., No 4. b. Scott's Minstrelsy, II, 20, 1802.

1 O JELLON GRAME sat in Silver Wood,
   He whistled and he sang,

   And he has calld his little foot-page,
     His errand for to gang.

2 ' Win up, my bonny boy,' he says,
     ' As quick as eer you may ;
   For ye maun gang for Lillie Flower,
     Before the break of day.'

3 The boy he 's buckled his belt about,
  And thro the green-wood ran,
  And he came to the ladie's bower-door,
  Before the day did dawn.

4 'O sleep ye, or wake ye, Lillie Flower?
  The red run 's i the rain : '
  'I sleep not aft, I wake right aft ;
  Wha 's that that kens my name ? '

5 'Ye are bidden come to Silver Wood,
  But I fear you 'll never win hame ;
  Ye are bidden come to Silver Wood,
  And speak wi Jellon Grame.'

6 'O I will gang to Silver Wood,
  Though I shoud never win hame ;
  For the thing I most desire on earth
  Is to speak wi Jellon Grame.'

7 She had no ridden a mile, a mile,
  A mile but barely three,
  Ere she came to a new made grave,
  Beneath a green oak tree.

8 O then up started Jellon Grame,
  Out of a bush hard bye :
  'Light down, light down now, Lillie Flower,
  For it 's here that ye maun ly.'

9 She lighted aff her milk-white steed,
  And knelt upon her knee :
  'O mercy, mercy, Jellon Grame !
  For I 'm nae prepar'd to die.

10 'Your bairn, that stirs between my sides,
  Maun shortly see the light ;
  But to see it weltring in my blude
  Woud be a piteous sight.'

11 'O shoud I spare your life,' he says,
  'Until that bairn be born,
  I ken fu well your stern father
  Woud hang me on the morn.'

12 'O spare my life now, Jellon Grame !
  My father ye neer need dread ;
  I 'll keep my bairn i the good green wood,
  Or wi it I 'll beg my bread.'

13 He took nae pity on that ladie,
  Tho she for life did pray ;
  But pierced her thro the fair body,
  As at his feet she lay.

14 He felt nae pity for that ladie,
  Tho she was lying dead ;
  But he felt some for the bonny boy,
  Lay weltring in her blude.

15 Up has he taen that bonny boy,
  Gien him to nurices nine,
  Three to wake, and three to sleep,
  And three to go between.

16 And he 's brought up that bonny boy,
  Calld him his sister's son ;
  He thought nae man would eer find out
  The deed that he had done.

17 But it sae fell out upon a time,
  As a hunting they did gay,
  That they rested them in Silver Wood,
  Upon a summer-day.

18 Then out it spake that bonny boy,
  While the tear stood in his eye,
  'O tell me this now. Jellon Grame,
  And I pray you dinna lie.

19 'The reason that my mother dear
  Does never take me hame?
  To keep me still in banishment
  Is baith a sin and shame.'

20 'You wonder that your mother dear
  Does never send for thee ;
  Lo, there 's the place I slew thy mother,
  Beneath that green oak tree.'

21 Wi that the boy has bent his bow,
  It was baith stout and lang,
  And through and thro him Jellon Grame
  He 's gard an arrow gang.

22 Says, Lye you thare now, Jellon Grame,
  My mellison you wi ;
  The place my mother lies buried in
  Is far too good for thee.

B

Motherwell's MS., p. 443.

1 WORD has come to May Margerie,
   In her bower where she sat :
'You are bid come to good green-wood,
   To make your love a shirt.'

2 'I wonder much,' said May Margerie,
   'At this message to me ;
There is not a month gone of this year
   But I have made him three.'

3 Then out did speak her mother dear,
   A wise woman was she ;
Said, Stay at home, my daughter May,
   They seek to murder thee.

4 'O I'll cast off my gloves, mother,
   And hang them up, I say ;
If I come never back again,
   They will mind you on May.

5 'Go saddle my horseback,' she said,
   'It's quick as ever you may,
And we will ride to good green-wood ;
   It is a pleasant day.'

6 And when she came to good green-wood,
   It's through it they did ride ;
Then up did start him Hind Henry,
   Just at the lady's side.

7 Says, Stop, O stop, you May Margerie,
   Just stop I say to thee ;
The boy that leads your bridle reins
   Shall see you red and blue.

8 It's out he drew a long, long brand,
   And stroked it ower a strae,
And through and through that lady's sides
   He made the cauld weapon gae.

9 Says, Take you that now, May Margerie,
   Just take you that from me,
Because you love Brown Robin,
   And never would love me.

10 There was less pity for that lady,
   When she was lying dead,
As was for her bony infant boy,
   Lay swathed amang her bleed.

11 The boy fled home with all his might,
   The tear into his ee :
'They have slain my lady in the wood,
   With fear I'm like to die.'

12 Her sister's ran into the wood,
   With greater grief and care,
Sighing and sobbing all the way,
   Tearing her cloaths and hair.

13 Says, I'll take up that fair infant,
   And lull him on my sleeve ;
Altho his father should wish me woe,
   His mother to me was leeve.

14 Now she has taken the infant up,
   And she has brought him hame,
And she has called him Brown Robin,
   That was his father's name.

15 And when he did grow up a bit,
   She put him to the lair,
And of all the youths was at that school
   None could with him compare.

16 And it fell once upon a day
   A playtime it was come,
And when the rest went from the school,
   Each one to their own home,

17 He hied him unto good green-wood,
   And leapt from tree to tree ;
It was to pull a hollin wand,
   To play his ownself wi.

18 And when he thus had passed his time,
   To go home he was fain,
He chanced to meet him Hind Henry,
   Where his mother was slain.

19 'O how is this,' the youth cried out,
   'If it to you is known,
How all this wood is growing grass,
   And on that small spot grows none ?'

20 'Since you do wonder, bonnie boy,
   I shall tell you anon ;
That is indeed the very spot
   I killed your mother in.'

21 He catched hold of Henry's brand,
   And stroked it ower a strae,

And thro and thro Hind Henry's sides
 He made the cauld metal gae.

22 Says, Take you that, O Hind Henry,
 O take you that from me,

For killing of my mother dear,
 And her not hurting thee.

C

Buchan's Ballads of the North of Scotland, II, 231.

1 WHEN spring appeard in all its bloom,
 And flowers grew fresh and green,
As May-a-Roe she set her down,
 To lay gowd on her seam.

2 But word has come to that lady,
 At evening when 't was dark,
To meet her love in gude greenwood,
 And bring to him a sark.

3 ' That 's strange to me,' said May-a-Roe,
 ' For how can a' this be ?
A month or twa is scarcely past
 Sin I sent my lovie three.'

4 Then May-a-Roe lap on her steed,
 And quickly rade away ;
She hadna ridden but hauf a mile,
 Till she heard a voice to say :

5 ' Turn back, turn back, ye ventrous maid,
 Nae farther must ye go ;
For the boy that leads your bridle rein
 Leads you to your overthrow.'

6 But a' these words she neer did mind,
 But fast awa did ride ;
And up it starts him Hynde Henry,
 Just fair by her right side.

7 ' Ye 'll tarry here, perfidious maid,
 For by my hand ye 'se dee ;
Ye married my brother, Brown Robin,
 Whan ye shoud hae married me.'

8 ' O mercy, mercy, Hynde Henry,
 O mercy have on me !
For I am eight months gane wi child,
 Therefore ye 'll lat me be.'

9 ' Nae mercy is for thee, fair maid,
 Nae mercy is for thee ;
You married my brother, Brown Robin,
 Whan ye shoud hae married me.'

10 ' Ye will bring here the bread, Henry,
 And I will bring the wine,
And ye will drink to your ain love,
 And I will drink to mine.'

11 ' I winna bring here the bread, fair maid,
 Nor yet shall ye the wine,
Nor will I drink to my ain love,
 Nor yet shall ye to thine.'

12 ' O mercy, mercy, Hynde Henry,
 Until I lighter be !
Hae mercy on your brother's bairn,
 Tho ye hae nane for me.'

13 ' Nae mercy is for thee, fair maid,
 Nae mercy is for thee ;
Such mercy unto you I 'll gie
 As what ye gae to me.'

14 Then he 's taen out a trusty brand,
 And stroakd it ower a strae,
And thro and thro her fair body
 He 's gart cauld iron gae.

15 Nae meen was made for that lady,
 For she was lying dead ;
But a' was for her bonny bairn,
 Lay spartling by her side.

16 Then he 's taen up the bonny bairn,
 Handled him tenderlie,
And said, Ye are o my ain kin,
 Tho your mother ill used me.

17 He 's washen him at the crystal stream,
 And rowd him in a weed,
And namd him after a bold robber
 Who was calld Robin Hood.

18 Then brought to the next borough's town,
 And gae him nurses three ;
He grew as big in ae year auld
 As some boys woud in three.

19 Then he was sent to guid squeel-house,
 To learn how to thrive ;
He learnd as muckle in ae year's time
 As some boys would in five.

20 ' But I wonder, I wonder,' said little Robin,
   ' Gin eer a woman bare me;
For mony a lady spiers for the rest,
   But nae ane spiers for me.

21 ' I wonder, I wonder,' said little Robin,
   ' Were I of woman born;
Whan ladies my comrades do caress,
   They look at me wi scorn.'

22 It fell upon an evening-tide,
   Was ae night by it lane,
Whan a' the boys frae guid squeel-house
   Were merrily coming hame,

23 Robin parted frae the rest,
   He wishd to be alane;
And when his comrades he dismist,
   To guid greenwood he 's gane.

24 When he came to guid greenwood,
   He clamb frae tree to tree,
To pou some o the finest leaves,
   For to divert him wi.

25 He hadna pu'd a leaf, a leaf,
   Nor brake a branch but ane,
Till by it came him Hynde Henry,
   And bade him lat alane.

26 ' You are too bauld a boy,' he said,
   ' Sae impudent you be,
As pu the leaves that 's nae your ain,
   Or yet to touch the tree.'

27 ' O mercy, mercy, gentleman,
   O mercy hae on me!
For if that I offence hae done,
   It was unknown to me.'

28 ' Nae boy comes here to guid greenwood
   But pays a fine to me;
Your velvet coat, or shooting-bow,
   Which o them will ye gie?'

29 ' My shooting-bow arches sae well,
   Wi it I canno part;
Lest wer 't to send a sharp arrow
   To pierce you to the heart.'

30 He turnd him right and round about,
   His countenance did change:

   ' Ye seem to be a boy right bauld;
   Why can ye talk sae strange?

31 ' I 'm sure ye are the bauldest boy
   That ever I talkd wi;
As for your mother, May-a-Roe,
   She was neer sae bauld to me.'

32 ' O, if ye knew my mother,' he said,
   ' That 's very strange to me;
And if that ye my mother knew,
   It 's mair than I coud dee.'

33 ' Sae well as I your mother knew,
   Ance my sweet-heart was she;
Because to me she broke her vow,
   This maid was slain by me.'

34 ' O, if ye slew my mother dear,
   As I trust ye make nae lie,
I wyte ye never did the deed
   That better paid shall be.'

35 ' O mercy, mercy, little Robin,
   O mercy hae on me!'
   ' Sic mercy as ye pae my mother,
   Sic mercy I 'll gie thee.

36 ' Prepare yourself, perfidious man,
   For by my hand ye 'se dee;
Now come 's that bluidy butcher's end
   Took my mother frae me.'

37 Then he hae chosen a sharp arrow,
   That was baith keen and smart,
And let it fly at Hynde Henry,
   And piercd him to the heart.

38 These news hae gaen thro Stirling town,
   Likewise thro Hunting-ha;
At last it reachd the king's own court,
   Amang the nobles a'.

39 When the king got word o that,
   A light laugh then gae he,
And he 's sent for him little Robin,
   To come right speedilie.

40 He 's putten on little Robin's head
   A ribbon and gowden crown,
And made him ane o 's finest knights,
   For the valour he had done.

D

Cromek's Remains of Nithsdale and Galloway Song, p. 222.

*   *   *   *   *

1 'D' YE mind, d' ye mind, Lady Margerie,
    When we handed round the beer?
Seven times I fainted for your sake,
    And you never dropt a tear.

2 'D' ye mind, d' ye mind, Lady Margerie,
    When we handed round the wine?
Seven times I fainted for your sake,
    And you never fainted once for mine.'

*   *   *   *   *

3 And he's taen the baby out of her womb
    And thrown it upon a thorn:

'Let the wind blow east, let the wind blow west,
    The cradle will rock its lone.'

*   *   *   *   *

4 But when brother Henry's cruel brand
    Had done the bloody deed,
The silver-buttons flew off his coat,
    And his nose began to bleed.

*   *   *   *   *

5 'O I have been killing in the silver wood
    What will breed mickle woe;
I have been killing in the silver wood
    A dawdy and a doe.'

*   *   *   *   *

A. a. 10^4. piteouus.
    b. 1^2. he sharpd his broad-sword lang.
        1^4. An errand.
        2^2. quickly as ye.
        3^1. boy has. 3^3. ladye's bower.
        4^1. or *omitted*. 4^2. red sun's on.
        $4^{3,\,4}$. *wanting*.
        $5^{1,\,2}$. *as* $4^{3,\,4}$: I doubt ye'll.
        $5^{3,\,4}$. *wanting*.
        6. *wanting*. 7^1. had na.
        8^2. there bye.
        9^4. no. 11^2. were born.
        11^3. Full weel I ken your auld.
        12^2. ye need na. 12^3. babe in gude.
        13^1. on Lillie Flower.
        14^1. for Lillie Flower.
        14^2. Where she. 14^3. bonny bairn.
        14^4. That lay.
        15^3. Three to sleep and three to wake.
        16^1. he bred.
        16^3. And he thought no eye could ever see.
        17^1. O so it fell upon a day.
        17^2. When hunting they might be.
        17^3. That *omitted*.
        17^4. Beneath that green aik tree.

18–20.

And mony were the green wood flowers
    Upon the grave that grew,
And marvelld much that bonny boy
    To see their lovely hue.

'What's paler than the prymrose wan?
    What's redder than the rose?
What's fairer than the lilye flower
    On this wee know that grows?'

O out and answered Jellon Grame,
    And he spake hastilie;
'Your mother was a fairer flower,
    And lies beneath this tree.

'More pale she was, when she sought my grace,
    Than prymrose pale and wan,
And redder than rose her ruddy heart's blood,
    That down my broad-sword ran.'

22^1. Lie ye. 22^2. gang you wi.

B. 12^1. sisters ran: into *altered to* unto.

91

FAIR MARY OF WALLINGTON

A. 'Fair Mary of Wallington,' Lovely Jenny's Garland, three copies, as early as 1775.

B. 'Lady Mazery,' Herd's MSS: a, I, 186; b, II, 89.

C. 'The Bonny Earl of Livingston,' Alexander Fraser Tytler's Brown MS., No 5.

D. 'The Laird o Livingstone,' Dr John Hill Burton's MS., No 2.

E. 'Mild Mary,' Motherwell's MS., p. 123.

F. 'Lord Darlington.' a. Buchan's Ballads of the North of Scotland, I, 183. b. The Borderer's Table Book, VII, 178.

'FAIR MARY OF WALLINGTON' was communicated to Bishop Percy, with other "old Scots Songs," in 1775, by Roger Halt, and presumably in a copy of the garland from which it is here printed. A was given by Ritson, from an inferior edition, with corrections, and the title changed to 'Fair Mabel of Wallington,' in The Northumberland Garland, 1793, p. 38 of the reprint of Northern Garlands, 1809. Ritson's copy is repeated in Bell's Rhymes of Northern Bards, 1812, p. 147, and in Richardson's Borderer's Table Book, VI, 141.

The story is very well preserved and very well told in A. All the seven sisters of a family are destined to die of their first child. Five having so died already, one of the remaining two expresses a resolution never to marry, since she is sure that she will go the way of the others. She is told that a knight has been there, asking for her hand. Then in three quarters of a year they may come to her burial. When her husband's mother welcomes her to her castle and bowers, the bride responds, under the operation of her melancholy conviction, I think they'll soon be yours. At the end of three quarters of a year she sends messages to her family: to her mother to come to her sickening or her wake; * to her

sister to remain in maidenhood, and escape the doom of the family. When the mother arrives the young wife is in extremities.† She gives rings to her mother, who is all to blame, gives rings to her husband, and with a razor opens her side, and takes out an heir for the house. In D we are told that five boys had been cut from their mothers, Mary's sisters, before. In B the remaining sister declares that no man shall ever lie by her side; but her mother says she shall marry though she live but three quarters of a year: so, nearly, in C.

A Breton ballad, 'Pontplancoat,' A, Luzel, I, 382, B, p. 386, exhibits such correspondences with the English and Scottish that we cannot hesitate to assume that it has the same source.

In the first version Pontplancoat marries Marguerite for his third wife. He is obliged by affairs to leave her, and has a dream which disturbs him so much that he returns home the same night. This dream is that his wife has been three days in travail, and it proves true. A spoon is put in the lady's mouth, an incision made in her right side, and a son taken out. This is Pontplancoat's third son, and each of them has been extracted from his mother's side. He has had three wives of the

---

* The stanza which should convey this part of the message is wanting, but may be confidently supplied from the errand-boy's repetition.

† The three steeds in **B** 23–25, the tiring out of the black and of the brown, and the endurance of the white, are found

in 'Lady Maisry,' No 65, **B, C, E, F,** and this passage perhaps belongs to that ballad. It may, however, have been a commonplace. There is something similar in Bugge, p. 130, No 26 **B,** 6–8, and Landstad, p. 512, No 57, 24–27. For the milk-white geese, **E** 7, see No 66, **C** 22, No 73, **A,** note.

name of Marguerite, and they have all died in this way.

Marguerite, in the other version, is told by her mother that she is to marry Pontplancoat. Marguerite signifies her obedience, but Pontplancoat has already had four wives of her name, all of whom " had been opened," and she shall be the fifth. As before, Pontplancoat is obliged to go away, and during his absence he receives letters which inform him that his wife is in labor and that the chances are against a normal delivery. He returns instantly. The lady has been three days in labor. A silver ball is put into her mouth, her right side opened with a knife, and a son extracted. Pontplancoat has four sons besides, all of whom have been brought into the world in this way.

English A is localized in Northumberland, and Mary made the wife of a Sir William Fenwick of Wallington. According to notes of Percy, he had not been able to find a Sir William Fenwick, lord of Wallington, with a wife of the name of Mary. Were a Sir William and Lady Mary Fenwick authenticable, a nice historical question would arise between them and some baron and baroness of the family Pontplancoat in Finistère, Brittany.

An extensively disseminated Scandinavian ballad has been assumed to be of kin with ' Mary of Wallington,' and in one version or another has resemblances which may possibly come from unity of origin, but the general likeness is certainly not striking. The published texts are: Norwegian, ' Maalfrí,' Bugge, Gamle norske Folkeviser, p. 122, No 25, A, B. Icelandic, ' Málfríðar kvæði,' Íslenzk fornkvæði, I, 208, No 24, A-D. Swedish, ' Herr Peder och Malfred,' Afzelius, I, 70, No 14. Danish, A, ' Esben og Malfred,' " Tragica, No 26," Danske Viser, III, 208, No 133; B, C, Kristensen, I, 232, No 87, A, B; D, E, ' Malfreds Død,' Kristensen, II, 232, No 69, A, B; F, ' Liden Malfreds Vise,' Feilberg, Fra Heden, p. 119; G, ' Herr Peder og Liden Malfred,' Berggreen's Danske Folkesange, 3d ed., p. 172, No 88. The Danish ballad is preserved in ten manuscripts, and Grundtvig possessed not less than twenty-two traditionary Danish versions and two Swedish, which he did not live to print.

The Norwegian ballad is most like, or least unlike, the English. Maalfrí, a king's only daughter, is married to Karl, king of England. It was spaed to her when she was yet a maid that she should die of her twelfth lying in ; she has already born eleven children. The king purposing to leave her for a time, she reminds him of the prophecy. He defies spaewives and goes, but after three days dreams that Maalfrí's cloak is cut in two, that her hair is cut to bits, etc. ; and this sends him home, when he learns that two sons have been cut from her side. He throws himself on his sword. Maalfrí, Malfred, is, in the other Norse ballads, also an only daughter, and dies in her twelfth child-birth, in all but Icelandic B, C, D, where the first is fatal to her. There are no other important diversities, and the resemblances in the details of the Norse and the English ballads are these two: the wife being fated to die of her first child in Icelandic B, C, D, and the Cæsarean operation in the Norwegian versions.

It is barely worth mentioning that there is also a German ballad, in which a maid (only eleven years old in most of the versions) begs her mother not to give her to a husband, because she will not live more than a year if married, and dies accordingly in child-birth: ' Hans Markgraf,' " Bothe, Frühlings-Almanach, 1806, p. 132," reprinted in Büsching und von der Hagen's Volkslieder, p. 30, Erlach, II, 136, Mittler, No 133; " Alle bei Gott die sich lieben," Wunderhorn, 1808, II, 250, Erlach, IV, 127, Mittler, No 128; Hoffmann und Richter, Schlesische Volkslieder, p. 12, No 5, Mittler, No 132. To these may be added ' Der Graf und die Bauerntochter,' Ditfurth, II, 8, No 9 ; ' Der Mutter Fluch,' Meinert, p. 246. In these last it is the mother who objects to the marriage, on account of her daughter's extreme youth.*

---

* Uhland, Schriften zur Geschichte der Dichtung und Sage, IV, 107, cites the chair of stone in English A 12, 18, as bringing to mind Bothe, st. 14, Wunderhorn, st. 12, where he mother sits down auf einen breiten Stein, an ein harten Stein, and breaks her heart. The chair of stone in the English ballad, like the chair of oak, is a customary seat of the mother's, and she is very far from breaking her heart. Nothing can be built on such accidents.

A

Lovely Jenny's Garland, three copies, as early as 1775, but without place or date.

1 WHEN we were silly sisters seven,
    sisters were so fair,
Five of us were brave knights' wives,
    and died in childbed lair.

2 Up then spake Fair Mary,
    marry woud she nane;
If ever she came in man's bed,
    the same gate wad she gang.

3 'Make no vows, Fair Mary,
    for fear they broken be;
Here 's been the Knight of Wallington,
    asking good will of thee.'

4 'If here 's been the knight, mother,
    asking good will of me,
Within three quarters of a year
    you may come bury me.'

5 When she came to Wallington,
    and into Wallington hall,
There she spy'd her mother dear,
    walking about the wall.

6 'You 're welcome, daughter dear,
    to thy castle and thy bowers;'
'I thank you kindly, mother,
    I hope they 'll soon be yours.'

7 She had not been in Wallington
    three quarters and a day,
Till upon the ground she could not walk,
    she was a weary prey.

8 She had not been in Wallington
    three quarters and a night,
Till on the ground she coud not walk,
    she was a weary wight.

9 'Is there neer a boy in this town,
    who 'll win hose and shun,
That will run to fair Pudlington,
    and bid my mother come?'

10 Up then spake a little boy,
    near unto a-kin;
'Full oft I have your errands gone,
    but now I will it run.'

11 Then she calld her waiting-maid
    to bring up bread and wine:
'Eat and drink, my bonny boy,
    thou 'll neer eat more of mine.

12 'Give my respects to my mother,
    [as] she sits in her chair of stone,
And ask her how she likes the news,
    of seven to have but one.

13 ['Give my respects to my mother,
    as she sits in her chair of oak,
And bid her come to my sickening,
    or my merry lake-wake.]

14 'Give my love to my brother
    William, Ralph, and John,
And to my sister Betty fair,
    and to her white as bone.

15 'And bid her keep her maidenhead,
    be sure make much on 't,
For if eer she come in man's bed,
    the same gate will she gang.'

16 Away this little boy is gone,
    as fast as he could run;
When he came where brigs were broke,
    he lay down and swum.

17 When he saw the lady, he said,
    Lord may your keeper be!
'What news, my pretty boy,
    hast thou to tell to me?'

18 'Your daughter Mary orders me,
    as you sit in a chair of stone,
To ask you how you like the news,
    of seven to have but one.

19 'Your daughter gives commands,
    as you sit in a chair of oak,
And bids you come to her sickening,
    or her merry lake-wake.

20 'She gives command to her brother
    William, Ralph, and John,
[And] to her sister Betty fair,
    and to her white as bone.

21 'She bids her keep her maidenhead,
    be sure make much on 't,

For if eer she came in man's bed,
    the same gate woud she gang.'

22 She kickt the table with her foot,
    she kickt it with her knee,
The silver plate into the fire,
    so far she made it flee.

23 Then she calld her waiting-maid
    to bring her riding-hood,
So did she on her stable-groom
    to bring her riding-steed.

24 ' Go saddle to me the black [the black,]
    go saddle to me the brown,
Go saddle to me the swiftest steed
    that eer rid [to] Wallington.'

25 When they came to Wallington,
    and into Wallington hall,
There she spy'd her son Fenwick,
    walking about the wall.

26 ' God save you, dear son,
    Lord may your keeper be !
Where is my daughter fair,
    that used to walk with thee ? '

27 He turnd his head round about,
    the tears did fill his ee :
' 'T is a month,' he said, ' since she
    took her chambers from me.'

28 She went on   .   .   .
    and there were in the hall
Four and twenty ladies,
    letting the tears down fall.

29 Her daughter had a scope
    into her cheek and into her chin,
All to keep her life
    till her dear mother came.

30 ' Come take the rings off my fingers,
    the skin it is so white,
And give them to my mother dear,
    for she was all the wite.

31 ' Come take the rings off my fingers,
    the veins they are so red,
Give them to Sir William Fenwick,
    I 'm sure his heart will bleed.'

32 She took out a razor
    that was both sharp and fine,
And out of her left side has taken
    the heir of Wallington.

33 There is a race in Wallington,
    and that I rue full sare ;
Tho the cradle it be full spread up,
    the bride-bed is left bare.

B

Herd's MSS : a, I, 186 ; b, II, 89.

1 ' WHEN we were sisters seven,
    An five of us deyd wi child,
And there is nane but you and I, Mazery,
    And we 'll go madens mild.'

2 But there came knights, and there came
    squiers,
An knights of high degree ;
She pleasd hersel in Levieston,
    Thay wear a comly twa.

3 He has bought her rings for her fingers,
    And garlands for her hair,
The broochis till her bosome braid ;
    What wad my love ha mair ?

And he has brought her on to Livingston,
    And made her lady thear.

4 She had na been in Liveingston
    A twelvemonth and a day,
Till she was as big wi bairn
    As ony lady could gae.

5 The knight he knocked his white fingers,
    The goude rings flew in twa :
' Halls and bowers they shall go wast
    Ere my bonny love gie awa ! '

6 The knight he knocked his white fingers,
    The goude rings flew in foure :
' Halls and bowers they shall go waste
    Eren my bonny lady gie it ore ! '

7 The knight he knocked his white fingers,
    The lady[s] sewed and sung;
  It was to comfort Lady Mazery,
    But her life-days wear na long.

8 'O whare will I get a bonny boy,
    That will win both hoos and shoon,
  That will win his way to Little Snoddown,
    To my mother, the Queen?'

9 Up and stands a bonny boy,
    Goude yellow was his hair;
  I wish his mother mickle grace at him,
    And his trew-love mickle mare.

10 'Here am I a bonny boy,
    That will win baith hoos an shoon,
  That will win my way to Little Snoddown,
    To thy mother, the Queen.'

11 'Here is the rings frae my fingers,
    The garlonds frae my hair,
  The broches fray my bosom braid;
    Fray me she 'll nere get mare.

12 'Here it is my weeding-goun,
    It is a' goude but the hem;
  Gi it to my sister Allen,
    For she is left now bird her lane.

13 'When you come whare brigs is broken,
    Ye 'l bent your bow and swim;
  An when ye come whare green grass grows,
    Ye 'l slack your shoon and run.

14 'But when you come to yon castle,
    Bide neither to chap nor ca,
  But you 'l set your bent bow to your breast,
    And lightly loup the wa,
  And gin the porter be half-gate,
    Ye 'll be ben throw the ha.'

15 O when he came whare brigs was broken,
    He bent his bow and swam;
  An when he came where green grass grows,
    He slackd his shoon an ran.

16 And when he came to yon castel,
    He stayed neither to chap no ca'l,
  But bent his bow unto his breast,
    And lightly lap the wa'l;
  And gin the porter was hafe-gate,
    He was ben throw the ha'l.

17 'O peace be to you, ladys a'l!
    As ye sit at your dine
  Ye ha little word of Lady Mazerë,
    For she drees mickel pine.

18 'Here is the rings frae her fingers,
    The garlands frae her hair,
  The broches frae her bosome brade;
    Fray her ye 'l nere get mare.

19 'Here it is her weeding-goun,
    It is a' goude but the hem;
  Ye 'll ge it to her sister Allen,
    For she is left bird her lane.'

20 She ca'd the table wi her foot,
    And coped it wi her tae,
  Till siller cups an siller cans
    Unto the floor did gae.

21 'Ye wash, ye wash, ye bonny boy,
    Ye wash, and come to dine;
  It does not fit a bonny boy
    His errant for to tine.

22 'Ge saddle to me the black, the black,
    Ge saddle to me the brown,
  Ge saddle to me the swiftest steed
    That ever rid frae a town.'

23 The first steed they saddled to her,
    He was the bonny black;
  He was a good steed, an a very good steed,
    But he tiyrd eer he wan the slack.

24 The next steed they saddled to her,
    He was the bonny brown;
  He was a good steed, an a very good steed,
    But he tiyird ere he wan the town.

25 The next steed they saddled to her,
    He was the bonny white;
  Fair fa the mair that fo'd the fole
    That carried her to Mazeree['s] lear!

26 As she gaed in at Leivingston,
    Thair was na mickel pride;
  The scobs was in her lovely mouth,
    And the razer in her side.

27 'O them that marrys your daughter, lady,
    I think them but a foole;
  A married man at Martimass,
    An a widdow the next Yule!'

28 'O hold your toung now, Livingston,
　　Let all your folly abee ;
　I bear the burden in my breast,
　　Mun suffer them to dee.'

29 Out an speaks her Bird Allen,
　　For she spake ay through pride ;

C

Alexander Fraser Tytler's Brown MS., No 5.

1 'O WE were sisters seven, Maisry,
　　And five are dead wi child ;
　There is nane but you and I, Maisry,
　　And we 'll go maidens mild.'

2 She hardly had the word spoken,
　　And turnd her round about,
　When the bonny Earl of Livingston
　　Was calling Maisry out.

3 Upon a bonny milk-white steed,
　　That drank out of the Tyne,
　And a' was for her Ladie Maisry,
　　To take her hyne and hyne.

4 Upon a bonny milk-white steed,
　　That drank out o the Tay,
　And a' was for her Lady Maisry,
　　To carry her away.

5 She had not been at Livingston
　　A twelve month and a day,
　Until she was as big wi bairn
　　As any ladie coud gae.

6 She calld upon her little foot-page,
　　Says, Ye maun run wi speed,
　And bid my mother come to me,
　　For of her I 'll soon have need.

'That man shall near be born,' she says,
　'That shall ly down by my side.'

30 'O hold your toung now, Bird Allen,
　　Let all your folly abee ;
　For you shall marry a man,' she says,
　'Tho ye shoud live but rathes three.'

7 'See, there is the brootch frae my hause-bane
　It is of gowd sae ried ;
　Gin she winna come when I 'm alive,
　　Bid her come when I am dead.'

8 But ere she wan to Livingston,
　　As fast as she coud ride,
　The gaggs they were in Maisry's mouth,
　　And the sharp sheers in her side.

9 Her good lord wrang his milk-white hands,
　　Till the gowd rings flaw in three :
　'Let ha's and bowers and a' gae waste,
　　My bonny love 's taen frae me !'

10 'O hold your tongue, Lord Livingston,
　　Let a' your mourning be ;
　For I bare the bird between my sides,
　　Yet I maun thole her to die.'

11 Then out it spake her sister dear,
　　As she sat at her head :
　'That man is not in Christendoom
　　Shall gar me die sicken dead.'

12 'O hold your tongue, my ae daughter,
　　Let a' your folly be,
　For ye shall be married ere this day week
　　Tho the same death you should die.'

D

Dr John Hill Burton's MS., No 2.

1 'HERE it is was sisters seven,
　　And five is died with child ;
　Was non but you and I, Hellen,
　　And we'se be maidens mild.'

2 They hadna been maidens o bonny Snawdon
　　A twalvemonth and a day,
　When lairds and lords a courting came,
　　Seeking Mary away.

3 The bonny laird of Livingstone,
　　He liket Mary best ;
　He gae her a ring, a royal ring,
　　And he wedded her at last.

4 She hed na been lady o Livingstone
     A twalvemonth and a day,
  When she did go as big wi bairn
     As iver a woman could be.

*   *   *   *   *

7 The knights were wringin their white fingers,
     And the ladys wer tearin their hair;
  It was a' for the lady o Livingstone,
     For a word she never spake mare.

8 Out and spake her sister Hellen,
     Where she sat by her side;
  'The man shall never be born,' she said,
     'Shall ever make me his bride.

9 'The man,' she said, 'that would merry me,
     I 'de count him but a feel,

To merry me at Whitsunday,
     And bury me at Yele.'

10 Out and spak her mother dear,
     Whare she sat by the fire:
   'I bare this babe now from my side,
     Maun suffer her to die.

11 'And I have six boys now to my oyes,
     And none of them were born,
   But a hole cut in their mother's side,
     And they from it were shorne.'

12 .   .   .   .   .
    .   .   .   .   .   .
    .   .   .   .   .

E

Motherwell's MS., p. 123, from the recitation of Mrs Mac-
queen, Lochwinnoch.

1 'ARISE, arise, dochter,' she said,
     'My bidding to obey;
  The bravest lord in all Scotland
     This night asked you of me.'

2 'O haud your tongue, mother,' she said,
     'These words they do me wrang;
  For gin I lye in a man's bed,
     My days will no be lang.

3 'There were seven sisters o us a',
     We were a' clad in white;
  And five of them were married,
     And in child-bed they died.'

4 'Ye shall not be drest in black,
     Nor sall ye be in broun;
  But ye'se be drest in shining gowd,
     To gae glittering thro the town.

5 'Your father sall ride before you,' she said,
     'And your brother sall ride ahin;
  Your horses fore-feet siller shod,
     And his hind anes wi gowd shall shine.

6 'Wi four and twenty buirdlie men
     Atween ye and the wun,
  And four and twenty bonnie mays
     Atween ye and the sun.

7 'Four and twenty milk-white geese,
     Stretching their wings sae wide,
  Blawing the dust aff the high-way,
     That Mild Mary may ride.'

8 They took to them their milk-white steeds,
     Set her upon a grey,
  And wi a napkin in her hand
     Weeping she rade away.

9 O they rade on that lee-lang nicht,
     And part o the neist day also,
  And syne she saw her auld good mother
     Stand in the gates below.

10 'You 'r welcome, welcome, dochter,' she said,
     'To your biggins and your bowers;'
   'I thank ye kindly, mither,' she said,
     'But I doubt they 'll sune be yours.'

*   *   *   *   *

F

a. Buchan's Ballads of the North of Scotland, I, 183.
b. The Borderer's Table Book, VII, 178, communicated by
J. H. Dixon; "transcribed from a MS. copy in possession of
an antiquarian friend," collated with a.

1 ' O we were seven brave sisters,
    Five of us died wi child,
And nane but you and I, Maisry,
    So we'll gae maidens mild.'

2 'O had your tongue, now Lady Margaret,
    Let a' your folly be;
I'll gar you keep your true promise
    To the lad ayont the sea.'

3 'O there is neither lord nor knight
    My love shall ever won,
Except it be Lord Darlington,
    And here he winna come.'

4 But when the hour o twall was past,
    And near the hour o one,
Lord Darlington came to the yetts,
    Wi thirty knights and ten.

5 Then he has wedded Lady Margaret,
    And brought her oer the sea,
And there was nane that lived on earth
    Sae happy as was she.

6 But when nine months were come and gane
    Strong travailling took she,
And nae physician in the land
    Could ease her maladie.

7 'Where will I get a little wee boy,
    Will won baith meat and fee,

That will gae on to Seaton's yetts,
    Bring my mother to me?'

8 'O here am I, a little wee boy,
    That will won meat and fee,
That will gae on to Seaton's yetts,
    And bring your mother to thee.'

9 Then he is on to Seaton's yetts,
    As fast as gang could he;
Says, Ye must come to Darlington,
    Your daughter for to see.

10 But when she came to Darlington,
    Where there was little pride,
The scobbs were in the lady's mouth,
    The sharp sheer in her side.

11 Darlington stood on the stair,
    And gart the gowd rings flee:
'My ha's and bowers and a' shall gae waste,
    If my bonny love die for me.'

12 'O had your tongue, Lord Darlington,
    Let a' your folly be;
I boor the bird within my sides,
    I'll suffer her to die.

13 'But he that marries my daughter,
    I think he is a fool;
If he marries her at Candlemas,
    She'll be frae him ere Yule.

14 'I had seven ance in companie,
    This night I go my lane;
And when I come to Clyde's water,
    I wish that I may drown.'

———◆———

A. *The copy of the garland here used is much
more correct than the other two, but still not
carefully printed.   The garland gives the
ballad in eight stanzas of eight verses.*
  1¹. so were sisters.
  6². bower: *perhaps we should read* towers.
  8². weight, *which makes sense, but, taking
     rhyme into account, the change seems
     requisite: cf.* 30².
  15². came: come *in the other copies.*
  16². swim.   19¹. of aik?
  19². weary lake-wake? *if so, also* 13².

27¹. his eyes.   28². downfal.
30¹. finger.   30². weight.
31¹. of: veine.

B. a. *Stanzas 5–7 should come after 26, but the
changes which have been traditionally
made in 7, to adapt the passage to its actual position, render the restoration of the
right order impracticable.   7¹ is not com-
forting.*
   2². An lords?   3³. brooch is.
  12⁴. now to bird: *cf.* 19⁴.
  13². bent: *so the other copy.*

13⁴. Ye.   14². clap nor cae' : *cf.* 16².
15¹. come.   16². war (?).   17¹. a¹.
19⁸. to my.   20². coped : caped ?
21. *After this these lines are struck out :*

     Nor yet do (to ?) a well-ford made
       Her errant for to set (let ?).

22¹. Ga.   23⁴. stack (?).
29². throught.   30⁴. luve, *in my copy.*
The spelling is in several places doubtful.
b *appears to be a transcript of* a : *the spelling*
   is somewhat regulated.
3⁸. broatch is.   6². in twa.
8². wun.   8⁸. will rin.
8³, 10⁸. Little Snod Down.
9⁸. of him.   12⁴. bird her lane.
16⁸. into.   18⁸. broch is.
20². caped it.   21¹, ². Gae wash.
22¹, ², ⁸. Go, Go, Gae.   23⁴. slack.
25⁴. lear *wanting.*   26⁸. scobs *wanting.*
30⁴. live : rather.

C.   10⁴. here : e *added in different ink.*

D.   1⁴. maiden.   7¹. ringin.
    9¹. that wᵈ.   10⁸. I hear.
E.   6². the win' *originally :* i *seems to have*
     been changed to u.
F. a.   13¹. But her.
  b.   2⁴. the lord.
    3². my true love eer shall be.
    3⁴. And he winna come here to me.
    5¹. It 's he.   6⁸. And neer a leech in a'.
    7². That will win meat.
    7⁴. And bring your.

    8. O out then spake the little foot-page,
       And knelt on bended knee :
     O here, *etc.*

    8². will win both.
    11¹. Lord Darlington.   12⁸. side.
    13¹ He that marries a daughter o mine.
    13². I wot.   13⁸. Candemas tide.
    13⁴. at Yule.
    14⁸. When I come to the salt water.

92

BONNY BEE HOM

A. 'Bonny Bee Ho'm,' Alexander Fraser Tytler's Brown MS., No 6 ; Jamieson's Popular Ballads, I, 185.

B. 'The Enchanted Ring,' Buchan's Ballads of the North of Scotland, I, 169.

——◆——

A WAS given from the manuscript by Jamieson " verbatim," that is, with a few slight variations ; the first stanza earlier, in the Scots Magazine, October, 1803, p. 700.

For the ring (chain, A 7) that makes a man invulnerable, and that which indicates by the discoloration of the stone that his love is dead

or untrue, see 'Hind Horn,' I, 200 f ; for the vows in A 3, 4, B 3, 'Clerk Saunders,' at p. 156 f of this volume.* The like vows are adopted into a song called 'The Lowlands of Holland,' found in Herd's MSS, I, 97, and inserted in his Scottish Songs, 1776, II, 2 ; a fragment, but all that concerns us.†

* Also 'Bonny Molly Stewart,' Maidment's Scotish Ballads and Songs, 1859, p. 128, and the Reply to 'Cromlet's Lilt,' Maidment's Scotish Ballads and Songs, Historical and Traditionary, 1868, II, 59.

† There are six double stanzas in Johnson's Museum, p. 118, to which Stenhouse, IV, 115, adds a concluding one, the fourth of Herd's. "This ballad," Stenhouse was informed, "was composed about the beginning of the last century by a young widow in Galloway, whose husband was drowned on a voyage to Holland." His authority was probably traditional, and all the information except the date, and, to be accurate, the widowhood, is found in the song itself. Motherwell, Minstrelsy, Introduction, p. lxxii, note 37, ob-

serves that neither Herd's nor Johnson's copy is so full " as one which may occasionally be met with in stall editions published about sixty years ago :" 1827. Logan, who prints two vulgar versions, or rather perversions, in which a bridegroom is pressed into the king's sea-service on the night of his marriage, Pedlar's Pack, p. 22, says : " A more lengthened version of the same ballad in the Scotch dialect will be found in Book First of A Selection of Scots Songs, Harmonised. . . . By Peter Urbani, Professor of Music, Edinburgh, circa 1794." Christie, I, 236, says that 'The Lowlands of Holland ' was sung in his father's family, in Aberdeenshire, as far back as the middle of the last century. Herd's copy is translated by Talvj, Charakteristik, p. 594.

1 'My love has built a bony ship, and set her
      on the sea,
  With seven score good mariners to bear her
      company ;
  There 's three score is sunk, and three score
      dead at sea,
  And the Lowlands of Holland has twin'd my
      love and me.

2 'My love he built another ship, and set her on
      the main,
  And nane but twenty mariners for to bring her
      hame ;
  But the weary wind began to rise, and the sea
      began to rout,
  My love then and his bonny ship turnd wither-
      shins about.

3 'There shall neither coif come on my hea
      nor comb come in my hair ;
  There shall neither coal nor candle-light shin
      in my bower mair ;
  Nor will I love another one until the day
      die,
  For I never lovd a love but one, and he
      drowned in the sea.'

4 'O had your tongue, my daughter dear, be sti
      and be content ;
  There are mair lads in Galloway, ye neen na
      sair lament : '
  'O there is none in Gallow, there 's none at a
      for me,
  For I never lovd a love but one, and he
      drowned in the sea.'

A

Alexander Fraser Tytler's Brown MS., No 6.

1 By Arthur's Dale as late I went
      I heard a heavy moan ;
  I heard a ladie lammenting sair,
      And ay she cried Ohone !

2 'Ohon, alas ! what shall I do,
      Tormented night and day !
  I never loved a love but ane,
      And now he 's gone away.

3 'But I will do for my true-love
      What ladies woud think sair ;
  For seven year shall come and go
      Ere a kaim gang in my hair.

4 'There shall neither a shoe gang on my foot,
      Nor a kaim gang in my hair,
  Nor eer a coal nor candle-light
      Shine in my bower nae mair.'

5 She thought her love had been on the sea,
      Fast sailling to Bee Hom ;
  But he was in a quiet chamer,
      Hearing his ladie's moan.

6 'Be husht, be husht, my ladie dear,
      I pray thee mourn not so ;
  For I am deep sworn on a book
      To Bee Hom for to go.'

7 She has gien him a chain of the beaten gowd,
      And a ring with a ruby stone :
  'As lang as this chain your body binds,
      Your blude can never be drawn.

8 'But gin this ring shoud fade or fail,
      Or the stone shoud change its hue,
  Be sure your love is dead and gone,
      Or she has proved untrue.'

9 He had no been at Bonny Bee Hom
      A twelve month and a day,
  Till, looking on his gay gowd ring,
      The stone grew dark and gray.

10 'O ye take my riches to Bee Hom,
      And deal them presentlie,
  To the young that canna, the auld that maunna.
      And the blind that does not see.'

11 Now death has come into his bower,
      And split his heart in twain ;
  So their twa souls flew up to heaven,
      And there shall ever remain.

B

Buchan's Ballads of the North of Scotland, I, 169.

1 IN Lauderdale I chanc'd to walk,
   And heard a lady's moan,
Lamenting for her dearest dear,
   And aye she cried, Ohon!

2 'Sure never a maid that eer drew breath
   Had harder fate than me;
I'd never a lad but one on earth,
   They forc'd him to the sea.

3 'The ale shall neer be brewin o malt,
   Neither by sea nor land,
That ever mair shall cross my hause,
   Till my love comes to hand.

4 'A handsome lad, wi shoulders broad,
   Gold yellow was his hair;
None of our Scottish youths on earth
   That with him could compare.'

5 She thought her love was gone to sea,
   And landed in Bahome;
But he was in a quiet chamber,
   Hearing his lady's moan.

6 'Why make ye all this moan, lady?
   Why make ye all this moan?
For I'm deep sworn on a book,
   I must go to Bahome.

7 'Traitors false for to subdue
   Oer seas I'll make me boun,
That have trepand our kind Scotchmen,
   Like dogs to ding them down.'

8 'Weell, take this ring, this royal thing,
   Whose virtue is unknown;
As lang's this ring's your body on,
   Your blood shall neer be drawn.

9 'But if this ring shall fade or stain,
   Or change to other hue,

Come never mair to fair Scotland,
   If ye're a lover true.'

10 Then this couple they did part,
   With a sad heavy moan;
The wind was fair, the ship was rare,
   They landed in Bahome.

11 But in that place they had not been
   A month but barely one,
Till he lookd on his gay gold ring,
   And riven was the stone.

12 Time after this was not expir'd
   A month but scarcely three,
Till black and ugly was the ring,
   And the stone was burst in three.

13 'Fight on, fight on, you merry men all,
   With you I'll fight no more;
I will gang to some holy place,
   Pray to the King of Glore.'

14 Then to the chapel he is gone,
   And knelt most piteouslie,
For seven days and seven nights,
   Till blood ran frae his knee.

15 'Ye'll take my jewels that's in Bahome,
   And deal them liberallie,
To young that cannot, and old that mannot,
   The blind that does not see.

16 'Give maist to women in child-bed laid,
   Can neither fecht nor flee;
I hope she's in the heavens high,
   That died for love of me.'

17 The knights they wrang their white fingers,
   The ladies tore their hair;
The women that neer had children born,
   In swoon they down fell there.

18 But in what way the knight expir'd,
   No tongue will eer declare;
So this doth end my mournful song,
   From me ye'll get nae mair.

———◆———

A. 10^3. To the young that canna
   The auld that that maunna.

B. 11^3. Till they. 12^4. And stone.

93
LAMKIN

A. 'Lamkin,' Jamieson's Popular Ballads, I, 176.

B. 'Lambert Linkin,' Motherwell's MS., p. 15 ; Motherwell's Minstrelsy, p. 290.

C. 'Lamerlinkin,' Motherwell's MS., p. 9.

D. 'Bold Rankin,' Maidment's New Book of Old Ballads, p. 73 ; Whitelaw's Book of Scottish Ballads, p. 246, V.

E. 'Lambkin,' Kinloch MSS, V, 246 ; retouched by Kinloch, II, 27.

F. 'Long Lankyn.' **a.** Notes and Queries, Second Series, II, 324. **b.** Notes and Queries, Fourth Series, II, 281.

G. 'Long Lonkin,' Richardson's Borderer's Table Book, 1846, VIII, 410 ; Fisher's Drawing Room Scrap Book, 1835, p. 11.

H. 'Bauld Rankin,' Kinloch MSS, I, 306.

I. Skene MSS, p. 75.

J. 'Lammikin,' Kinloch MSS, V, 371.

K. 'Long Longkin,' Percy Papers, communicated by Rev. P. Parsons, 1775.

L. 'Lamkin,' Motherwell's MS., p. 14.

M. 'Cruel Lammikin.' **a.** Dr Joseph Robertson's Note-Book, Adversaria, p. 60. **b.** Kinloch MSS, VI, 31.

N. 'Lamkin,' Dr Joseph Robertson's Note-Book, Journal of Excursions, No 2.

O. 'Lammikin,' Kinloch MSS, V, 375.

P. 'Lammikin,' Herd's MSS, I, 25; Herd's Scottish Songs, 1776, I, 145.

Q. 'Lammikin,' Finlay's Scottish Ballads, II, 45.

R. 'Lammikin,' Finlay's Scottish Ballads, II, 55.

S. 'Lambkin,' Motherwell's Note-Book, fol. 13.

T. Recited by Ellen Healy, as sung by a woman living near Killarney.

U. 'Lamkin.' **a.** Allingham's Ballad Book, p. xxxiii. **b.** The same, p. 297, No 56.

V. Harris MS., No 28, fol. 27 b.

'LAMMIKIN : an Old Scotch Ballad,' Aberdeen, Lewis and James Smith, 1862, said to be edited by the Rev. Dr John Burnett Pratt, Episcopal minister at Cruden, Aberdeenshire, is made up of A, B, P, Q, R, with such alterations as seemed good to the editor, and a few interpolated stanzas.

'Long Lonkin,' edited by A. O. Bell, C. E., York, 1846 (Notes and Queries, Fourth Series, III, 93), I have not seen, but presume it to be a compounded copy.

The story is told without material variation in all the numerous versions. A mason has built a castle for a nobleman, cannot get his pay, and therefore seeks revenge. The name given the builder is Lamkin, A, C, E, L, M, N, S, U ; Lammikin, J, O, P, Q ; Lankin, Lonkin, F b, G, I ; Lantin, T ; Long Lankyn, or Long Longkin, F a, G, K ; Rankin, D, H ; Balankin, or Lambert Linkin, B ; Balcanqual, R. That of the nobleman is Lord Wearie, Weire, A, M, P, Q, U b ; Lord Earie, N ; Erley, Earley, J ; Murray, I ; Arran, C ; Montgomery, E ; Cassilis, S ; he is lord of Prime Castle, B. The lord, having occasion to leave his family, fears mischief from the man whom he has wronged, and enjoins his wife to keep the castle well fastened. Precautions are taken, but nevertheless his enemy effects an entrance through some aperture that has not been secured, B, C,

F, G, H, P, R, U b, or by connivance with a nurse, A, D, E, I. Most of the servants are away. To get at the lady, Lamkin, as we may call him, by advice of the nurse inflicts some hurt on the babe in the cradle, stabbing it, or "nipping" it, and its cries bring the mother down. The lady proffers large sums of gold to save her life, but Lamkin does not care for gold now. He gloats over his opportunity, and bids the nurse, or a maid-servant, or even one of the daughters of the house, to scour a silver bason to hold the lady's noble blood. The lord has a presentiment of calamity at home, and, returning, finds his house red with the blood of his wife and child. Lamkin is hanged, B, F, I, or burned, C, H, or boiled in a pot full of lead, D. The nurse is burned, A, B, D, F, H, or hanged, C, Q, or boiled in a caldron, I.*

In K, the oldest version, except perhaps P, which is greatly inferior, Lady Betty is called down by Longkin to see her mother's blood running, then Lady Nelly to see her sister's blood running, Lady Jenny to see Lady Nelly's, etc. In F, T, the mother, very unnaturally, offers Lamkin her daughter as wife, in ransom of her own life. In C, D, a servant offers her life for her lady; in D, G, K, a daughter for her mother.

Motherwell remarks, p. lxx of his Minstrelsy, note 27: "There is a 'Lambirkyns wod' near Dupplin, in Perthshire. Can this have got its name from the cruel mason who the ballad assures us 'lived in the wode'? If so,

it must be very ancient. It is localized, too, I believe, at Balwearie, in Fifeshire; but there are few places where the ballad is remembered but which have also some ancient edifice in the neighborhood reared by the hands of Lammikin.† Indeed, it seems questionable how some Scottish lairds could well afford to get themselves seated in the large castles they once occupied unless they occasionally treated the mason after the fashion adopted in this ballad." And again, at p. 291: "There can be little doubt that the epithet Linkin Mr Lambert acquired from the secrecy and address with which he insinuated him into that notable strength [Prime Castle]. Indeed, all the names of Lammerlinkin, Lammikin, Lamkin, Lankin, Linkin, Belinkin, can easily be traced out as abbreviations of Lambert Linkin." It might be inferred, however, from the mason's seemingly resentful inquiry in A 8-11, J 3-6, Where's the men, women, bairns, lady, that call me Lamkin? that the view in these particular versions was that Lamkin was a sobriquet applied in derision of the meekness with which the builder had submitted to his injury. Linkin, it will be observed, occurs only in B, and it is far more likely that Lamkin, or Lammikin, which is found in a full dozen copies, is a simply ironical designation for the bloody mason, the terror of countless nurseries.‡

A is translated by Talvj, Versuch, etc., p. 571; Allingham's ballad by Knortz, Lieder und Romanzen Alt-Englands, p. 162.

* Of boiling to death see Ducange, Caldariis decoquere, and other places cited by Robertson, Materials for the History of Thomas Becket, I, xxxii, note, and 128. This was especially a punishment for coiners, and was sanctioned as the penalty for poisoners by a statute of 22 Henry VIII, c. 29, repealed 1 Edward VI.

† More about the locality in Notes and Queries, First Series, II, 270.

‡ "Balcanquel is an ancient Scottish surname, and is sometimes corrupted, for the more agreeable sound, into Beluncan. All reciters agree that Lammikin, or Lambkin, is not the name of the hero, but merely an epithet." Finlay, Scottish Ballads, II. 56.

A

Jamieson's Popular Ballads, I, 176, communicated by Mrs Brown.

1 It 's Lamkin was a mason good
  as ever built wi stane;
He built Lord Wearie's castle,
  but payment got he nane.

2 'O pay me, Lord Wearie,
    come, pay me my fee:'
  'I canna pay you, Lamkin,
    for I maun gang oer the sea.'

3 'O pay me now, Lord Wearie,
    come, pay me out o hand:'

'I canna pay you, Lamkin,
    unless I sell my land.'

4 'O gin ye winna pay me,
    I here sall mak a vow,
Before that ye come hame again,
    ye sall hae cause to rue.'

5 Lord Wearie got a bonny ship,
    to sail the saut sea faem ;
Bade his lady weel the castle keep,
    ay till he should come hame.

6 But the nourice was a fause limmer
    as eer hung on a tree ;
She laid a plot wi Lamkin,
    whan her lord was oer the sea.

7 She laid a plot wi Lamkin,
    when the servants were awa,
Loot him in at a little shot-window,
    and brought him to the ha.

8 'O whare 's a' the men o this house,
    that ca me Lamkin ? '
'They 're at the barn-well thrashing ;
    't will be lang ere they come in.'

9 'And whare 's the women o this house,
    that ca me Lamkin ? '
'They 're at the far well washing ;
    't will be lang ere they come in.'

10 'And whare 's the bairns o this house,
    that ca me Lamkin ? '
'They 're at the school reading ;
    't will be night or they come hame.'

11 'O whare 's the lady o this house,
    that ca's me Lamkin ? '
'She 's up in her bower sewing,
    but we soon can bring her down.'

12 Then Lamkin 's tane a sharp knife,
    that hang down by his gaire,
And he has gien the bonny babe
    a deep wound and a sair.

13 Then Lamkin he rocked,
    and the fause nourice sang,
Till frae ilkae bore o the cradle
    the red blood out sprang.

14 Then out it spak the lady,
    as she stood on the stair :
'What ails my bairn, nourice,
    that he 's greeting sae sair ?

15 'O still my bairn, nourice,
    O still him wi the pap ! '
'He winna still, lady,
    for this nor for that.'

16 'O still my bairn, nourice,
    O still him wi the wand ! '
'He winna still, lady,
    for a' his father's land.'

17 'O still my bairn, nourice,
    O still him wi the bell ! '
'He winna still, lady,
    till ye come down yoursel.'

18 O the firsten step she steppit,
    she steppit on a stane ;
But the neisten step she steppit,
    she met him Lamkin.

19 'O mercy, mercy, Lamkin,
    hae mercy upon me !
Though you 've taen my young son's life,
    ye may let mysel be.'

20 'O sall I kill her, nourice,
    or sall I lat her be ? '
'O kill her, kill her, Lamkin,
    for she neer was good to me.'

21 'O scour the bason, nourice,
    and mak it fair and clean,
For to keep this lady's heart's blood,
    for she 's come o noble kin.'

22 'There need nae bason, Lamkin,
    lat it run through the floor ;
What better is the heart's blood
    o the rich than o the poor ? '

23 But ere three months were at an end,
    Lord Wearie came again ;
But dowie, dowie was his heart
    when first he came hame.

24 'O wha's blood is this,' he says,
    'that lies in the chamer ? '

'It is your lady's heart's blood;
  't is as clear as the lamer.'

25 'And wha's blood is this,' he says,
    'that lies in my ha?'
   'It is your young son's heart's blood;
    't is the clearest ava.'

26 O sweetly sang the black-bird
     that sat upon the tree;
   But sairer grat Lamkin,
     when he was condemnd to die.

27 And bonny sang the mavis,
     out o the thorny brake;
   But sairer grat the nourice,
     when she was tied to the stake.

B

Motherwell's MS., p. 15; from the recitation of Mrs Thomson, Kilbarchan, February 25, 1825.

1 BALANKIN was as gude a mason
    as eer picked a stane;
  He built up Prime Castle,
    but payment gat nane.

2 The lord said to his lady,
    when he was going abroad,
  O beware of Balankin,
    for he lyes in the wood.

3 The gates they were bolted,
    baith outside and in;
  At the sma peep of a window
    Balankin crap in.

4 'Good morrow, good morrow,'
    said Lambert Linkin:
  'Good morrow to yoursell, sir,'
    said the false nurse to him.

5 'O where is your good lord?'
    said Lambert Linkin:
  'He's awa to New England,
    to meet with his king.'

6 'O where is his auld son?'
    said Lambert Linkin:
  'He's awa to buy pearlings,
    gin our lady lye in.'

7 'Then she'll never wear them,'
    said Lambert Linkin:
  'And that is nae pity,'
    said the false nurse to him.

8 'O where is your lady?'
    said Lambert Linkin:

'She's in her bower sleeping,'
    said the false nurse to him.

9 'How can we get at her?'
    said Lambert Linkin:
  'Stab the babe to the heart,
    wi a silver bokin.'

10 'That would be a pity,'
     said Lambert Linkin:
   'No pity, no pity,'
     said the false nurse to him.

11 Balankin he rocked,
     and the false nurse she sang,
   Till all the tores of the cradle
     wi the red blood down ran.

12 'O still my babe, nurice,
     O still him wi the knife!'
   'He'll no be still, lady,
     tho I lay doun my life.'

13 'O still my babe, nurice,
     O still him wi the kame!'
   'He'll no be still, lady,
     till his daddy come hame.'

14 'O still my babe, nurice,
     O still him wi the bell!'
   'He'll no be still, lady,
     till ye come doun yoursell.'

15 'It's how can I come down,
     this cauld winter nicht,
   Without eer a coal,
     or a clear candle-licht?'

16 'There's two smocks in your coffer,
     as white as a swan;
   Put one of them about you,
     it will shew you licht down.'

17 She took ane o them about her,
    and came tripping doun ;
But as soon as she viewed,
    Balankin was in.

18 ' Good morrow, good morrow,'
    said Lambert Linkin :
' Good morrow to yoursell, sir,'
    said the lady to him.

19 ' O save my life, Balankin,
    till my husband come back,
And I 'll gie you as much red gold
    as you 'll hold in your hat.'

20 ' I 'll not save your life, lady,
    till your husband come back,
Tho you would give me as much red gold
    as I could hold in a sack.

21 ' Will I kill her ? ' quo Balankin,
    ' will I kill her, or let her be ? '
' You may kill her,' said the false nurse,
    ' she was neer good to me ;
And ye 'll be laird of the castle,
    and I 'll be ladie.'

22 Then he cut aff her head
    fram her lily breast-bane,

And he hung 't up in the kitchen,
    it made a' the ha shine.

23 The lord sat in England,
    a drinking the wine :
' I wish a' may be weel
    with my lady at hame ;
For the rings of my fingers
    the 're now burst in twain ! '

24 He saddled his horse,
    and he came riding doun,
But as soon as he viewed,
    Balankin was in.

25 He had na weel stepped
    twa steps up the stair,
Till he saw his pretty young son
    lying dead on the floor.

26 He had not weel stepped
    other twa up the stair,
Till he saw his pretty lady
    lying dead in despair.

27 He hanged Balankin
    out over the gate,
And he burnt the fause nurice,
    being under the grate.

C

Motherwell's MS., p. 9 : from Edward King, weaver, Kilbarchan, taken from the recitation of his mother, an old woman.

1 LAMERLINKIN, as gude a mason
    as eer laid a stane,
Built a house to Lord Arran,
    but entrance had nane.

2 Says the lord to his lady,
    when going abroad,
Take care of Lamerlinkin,
    wha bides in the wood.

3 ' I care not for Lamkin,
    nor none of his kin ;
My house is plastered outside,
    and bolted within.'

4 The gates they were locked,
    baith outside and in,
But there was a wee hole
    that let Lamkin creep in.

5 ' Good woman, good woman,'
    said Lamerlinkin :
' Good woman, good woman,'
    said the fause nurse to him.

6 ' Where 's the lord o this house ?
    is he not within ? '
' He 's up in Old England,
    he 's dining wi the king.'

7 ' Where 's the lady of this house ?
    or is she not within ? '
' She 's up in her high room,
    and cannot come down.'

8 'Where is the maids o this house?
    or are they not within?'
  'They are at the well washing,
    and cannot get in.'

9 'Where is the men o this house?
    or are they not within?'
  'They are at the barn threshing,
    and cannot win hame.'

10 'O what will I do,
    to mak her come doun?'
  'We 'll kill her auld son,
    to mak her come doun.'

11 He took out a pen-knife,
    baith pointed and sharp,
  And he stabbed the babie
    three times in the heart.

12 Lamerlinkin did rock,
    and the fause nurse did sing;
  Ower the four-cornered cradle
    the red blood did spring.

13 'O please my babie, nurse,
    O please him wi wands!'
  'He 'll no be pleased, madam,
    for a' his father's lands.'

14 'O please my babie, nurse,
    O please him wi keys!'
  'He 'll no be pleased, madam,
    let me do what I please.'

15 'O please my babie, nurse,
    O please him with bells!'
  'He 'll no be pleased, madam,
    till you come down yoursell.

16 'How can I come doun
    this cold frosty night,

Without coal or candle
    for to shew me light?'

17 'The gold rings on your finger
    are bright as the sun;
  You may see to cum doun the stair
    with the light o them.'

18 O then she came doun the stair,
    stepping step by step;
  So ready was Lamkin
    to grip her in his lap.

19 'Save my life, Lamkin,
    till five minutes break,
  And I 'll give thee gold,
    the fu o a peck.'

20 'I 'll no save your life,
    till five minutes break,
  Tho thou should give me gold,
    the fu of a sack.'

21 'O Jeany, O Jeany,
    O scour the bason clean,
  That your lady's noble blood
    may be kepped clean.'

22 'O no, no, no, Lambkin,
    my heart will be sare;
  O take my life, Lambkin,
    let my lady go.'

*   *   *   *   *

23 He sent for the false nurse,
    to give her her fee;
  All the fee that he gave her
    was to hang her on a tree.

24 He sent for Lamerlinkin,
    to give him his hire;
  All the hire that he gave him
    was to burn him in the fire.

D

Maidment's New Book of Old Ballads, p. 73, No XX; Whitelaw's Book of Scottish Ballads, p. 246, No V: from a manuscript copy, in the possession of W. H. Logan, Edinburgh, derived from oral tradition.

1 SAID the lord to his lady,
    Beware of Rankin ;
For I am going to England,
    to wait on the king.

2 ' No fears, no fears,'
    said the lady, said she,
' For the doors shall be bolted,
    and the windows pindee.

3 ' Go bar all the windows,
    both outside and in ;
Don't leave a window open,
    to let Bold Rankin in.'

4 She has barred all the windows,
    both outside and in ;
But she left one of them open,
    to let Bold Rankin in.

5 ' O where is the master of this house ? '
    said Bold Rankin ;
' He 's up in Old England,'
    said the false nurse to him.

6 ' O where is the mistress of this house ? '
    said Bold Rankin ;
' She 's up in the chamber sleeping,'
    said the false nurse to him.

7 ' O how shall we get her down ? '
    said Bold Rankin ;
' By piercing the baby,'
    said the false nurse to him.

8 ' Go please the baby, nursy,
    go please it with a bell ; '
' It will not be pleased, madam,
    till you come down yoursel.'

9 ' How can I come down stairs,
    so late into the night,
Without coal or candle,
    to shew me the light ?

10 ' There is a silver bolt
    lies on the chest-head ;

Give it to the baby,
    give it sweet milk and bread.'

11 She rammed the silver bolt
    up the baby's nose,
Till the blood it came trinkling
    down the baby's fine clothes.

12 ' Go please the baby, nursie,
    go please it with the bell : '
' It will not please, madam,
    till you come down yoursel.

13 ' It will neither please with breast-milk,
    nor yet with pap ;
But I pray, loving lady,
    Come and roll it in your lap.'

14 The first step she stepit,
    she steppit on a stone ;
And the next step she stepit,
    she met Bold Rankin.

15 ' O Rankin, O Rankin,
    spare me till twelve o'clock,
And I will give you as many guineas
    as you can carry on your back.'

16 ' What care I for as many guineas
    as seeds into a sack,
When I cannot keep my hands off
    your lily-white neck ? '

17 ' O will I kill her, nursie,
    or let her abee ? '
' O kill her,' said the false nurse,
    ' she was never good to me.'

18 ' Go scour the bason, lady,
    both outside and in,
To hold your mother's heart's blood,
    sprung from a noble kin.'

19 ' To hold my mother's heart's blood
    would make my heart full woe ;
O rather kill me, Rankin,
    and let my mother go.'

20 ' Go scour the bason, servants,
    both outside and in,
To hold your lady's heart's blood,
    sprung from a noble kin.'

1 'To hold my lady's heart's blood
   would make my heart full woe ;
O rather kill me, Rankin,
   and let my lady go.'

2 'Go scour the bason, nursy,
   both outside and in,
To hold your lady's heart's blood,
   sprung from a noble kin.'

3 'To hold my lady's heart's blood
   would make my heart full glad ;
Ram in the knife, Bold Rankin,
   and gar the blood to shed.

4 ' She 's none of my comrades,
   she 's none of my kin ;
Ram in the knife, Bold Rankin,
   and gar the blood rin.'

5 'O will I kill her, nursy,
   or let her abee ? '
'O kill her,' said the false nurse,
   ' she was never good to me.'

*   *   *   *

26 'I wish my wife and family
   may be all well at home ;
For the silver buttons of my coat
   they will not stay on.'

27 As Betsy was looking
   oer her window so high,
She saw her dear father
   come riding by.

28 'O father, dear father,
   don't put the blame on me
It was false nurse and Rankin
   that killed your lady.'

29 O was n't that an awful sight,
   when he came to the stair,
To see his fairest lady
   lie bleeding there !

30 The false nurse was burnt
   on the mountain hill-head,
And Rankin was boiled
   in a pot full of lead.

E

Kinloch MSS, V, 246, from Mary Barr.

LAMBKIN was as good a mason
   as ever laid stone ;
He builded Lord Montgomery's castle,
   but payment got none.

He builded the castle
   without and within ;
But he left an open wake
   for himself to get in.

Lord Montgomery said to his lady,
   when he went abroad,
Take care of Bold Lambkin,
   for he is in the wood.

'Gar bolt the gate, nourice,
   without and within,
Leave not the wake open,
   to let Bold Lambkin in.'

5 She bolted the gates,
   without and within,
But she left the wake open,
   to let Bold Lambkin in.

6 'Gude morrow, gude morrow,'
   says Bold Lambkin then ;
'Gude morrow, gude morrow,'
   says the false nurse to him.

7 'Where is Lord Montgomery ?
   or where is he gone ? '
'He is gone up to England,
   to wait on the king.'

8 'Where are the servants ?
   and where are they gone ? '
'They are all up to England,
   to wait upon him.'

9 'Where is your lady ?
   or where is she gone ? '
'She is in her bower sitting,
   and sewing her seam.'

10 'O what shall we do
     for to make her come down?'
   'We 'll kill the pretty baby,
     that 's sleeping so sound.'

11 Lambkin he rocked,
     and the false nurse she sung,
   And she stabbed the babe to the heart
     with a silver bodkin.

12 'O still my babe, nourice,
     O still him with the pap:'
   'He 'll no be stilled, madam,
     for this nor for that.'

13 'O still my babe, nourice,
     go still him with the keys:'
   'He 'll no be stilled, madam,
     let me do what I please.'

14 'O still my babe, nourice,
     go still him with the bell:'
   'He 'll no be stilled, madam,
     till you come down yoursel.'

15 'How can I come down,
     this cold winter night,
   When there 's neither coal burning,
     nor yet candle-light?'

16 'The sark on your back
     is whiter than the swan;
   Come down the stair, lady,
     by the light of your hand.'

17 The lady she cam down
     the stair trip for trap;

Who so ready as Bold Lambkin
  to meet her in the dark?

18 'Gude morrow, gude morrów,'
     said Bold Lambkin then;
   'Gude morrow, gude morrow,'
     said the lady to him.

19 'O where is Lord Montgomery?
     or where is he gone?'
   'O he is up to England,
     to wait on the king.'

20 'O where are your servants?
     or where are they gone?'
   'They are all up to England,
     to wait upon him.

21 'I 'll give you as much gold, Lambkin,
     as you 'll put in a peck,
   If you 'll spare my life
     till my lord comes back.'

22 'Tho you would [give] me as much
     as I could put in a sack,
   I would not spare thy life
     till thy lord comes back.'

23 Lord Montgomery sate in England,
     drinking with the king;
   The buttons flew off his coat,
     all in a ring.

24 'God prosper, God prosper
     my lady and son!
   For before I get home
     they will all be undone.'

F

a. Notes and Queries, Second Series, II, 324, as sung by a nurse nearly a century ago [1856] in Northumberland. b. Notes and Queries, Fourth Series, II, p. 281, from Northamptonshire, communicated by Mr B. H. Cowper.

1 SAID my lord to his ladye,
     as he mounted his horse, (bis)
   Take care of Long Lankyn,
     who lies in the moss.   (bis)

2 Said my lord to his ladye,
     as he rode away,

Take care of Long Lankyn,
  who lies in the clay.

3 Let the doors be all bolted,
     and the windows all pinned,
   And leave not a hole
     for a mouse to creep in.

4 Then he kissed his fair ladye,
     and he rode away;
   He must be in London
     before break of day.

5 The doors were all bolted,
    and the windows were pinned,
All but one little window,
    where Long Lankyn crept in.

6 'Where is the lord of this house?'
    said Long Lankyn:
'He is gone to fair London,'
    said the false nurse to him.

7 'Where is the ladye of this house?'
    said Long Lankyn:
'She's asleep in her chamber,'
    said the false nurse to him.

8 'Where is the heir of this house?'
    said Long Lankyn:
'He's asleep in his cradle,'
    said the false nurse to him.

*   *   *   *

9 'We'll prick him, and prick him,
    all over with a pin,
And that will make your ladye
    to come down to him.'

10 So he pricked him and pricked,
    all over with a pin,
And the nurse held a basin
    for the blood to run in.

11 'Oh nurse, how you sleep!
    Oh nurse, how you snore!'
And you leave my little son Johnstone
    to cry and to roar.'

12 'I've tried him with suck,
    and I've tried him with pap;
So come down, my fair ladye,
    and nurse him in your lap.'

13 'Oh nurse, how you sleep!
    Oh nurse, how you snore!
And you leave my little son Johnstone
    to cry and to roar.'

14 'I've tried him with apples,
    I've tried him with pears;
So come down, my fair ladye,
    and rock him in your chair.'

15 'How can I come down,
    't is so late in the night,
When there's no candle burning,
    nor fire to give light?'

16 'You have three silver mantles
    as bright as the sun;
So come down, my fair ladye,
    by the light of one.'

*   *   *   *

17 'Oh spare me, Long Lankyn,
    oh spare me till twelve o'clock,
You shall have as much gold
    as you can carry on your back.'

18 'If I had as much gold
    as would build me a tower,'
.   .   .   .   .   .

19 'Oh spare me, Long Lankyn,
    oh spare me one hour,
You shall have my daughter Betsy,
    she is a sweet flower.'

20 'Where is your daughter Betsy?
    she may do some good;
She can hold the silver basin,
    to catch your heart's blood.'

*   *   *   *

21 Lady Betsy was sitting
    in her window so high,
And she saw her father,
    as he was riding by.

22 'Oh father, oh father,
    don't lay the blame on me;
'T was the false nurse and Long Lankyn
    that killed your ladye.'

*   *   *   *   *

23 Then Long Lankyn was hanged
    on a gallows so high,
And the false nurse was burnt
    in a fire just by.

G

Richardson's Borderer's Table Book, VIII, 410, 1846, communicated by Mrs Blackett, Newcastle, as taken down from the recitation of an old woman of Ovington, Northumberland, "several years ago;" previously in Fisher's Drawing Room Scrap Book, 1835, p. 11.

1 THE lord said to his ladie,
        as he mounted his horse,
Beware of Long Lonkin,
        that lies in the moss.

2 The lord said to his ladie,
        as he rode away,
Beware of Long Lonkin,
        that lies in the clay.

3 'What care I for Lonkin,
        or any of his gang?
My doors are all shut,
        and my windows penned in.'

4 There were six little windows,
        and they were all shut,
But one little window,
        and that was forgot.

5 .   .   .   .   .

And at that little window
        long Lonkin crept in.

6 'Where's the lord of the hall?'
        says the Lonkin:
'He's gone up to London,'
        says Orange to him.

7 'Where's the men of the hall?'
        says the Lonkin:
'They're at the field ploughing,'
        says Orange to him.

8 'Where's the maids of the hall?'
        says the Lonkin:
'They're at the well washing,'
        says Orange to him.

9 'Where's the ladies of the hall?'
        says the Lonkin:
'They're up in their chambers,'
        says Orange to him.

10 'How shall we get them down?'
        says the Lonkin:
'Prick the babe in the cradle,'
        says Orange to him.

11 'Rock well my cradle,
        and bee-ba my son;
You shall have a new gown
        when the lord he comes home.'

12 Still she did prick it,
        and bee-ba she cried:
'Come down, dearest mistress,
        and still your own child.'

13 'Oh still my child, Orange,
        still him with a bell:'
'I can't still him, ladie,
        till you come down yoursell.'

*   *   *   *

14 'Hold the gold basin,
        for your heart's blood to run in,'
.   .   .   .   .

15 'To hold the gold basin,
        it grieves me full sore;
Oh kill me, dear Lonkin,
        and let my mother go.'

----♦----

H

Kinloch MSS, I, 306.

1 BAULD RANKIN was as gude a mason
        as eer biggit wi stane;
He has biggit a bonny castle,
        but siller he gat nane.

*   *   *   *   *

2 'Gae bar the gates,' the lady said,
        'gae bar them out and in;
Leave not a door open,
        lest Rankin should come in.'

3 They've bard them on the outer side,
        sae hae they on the in;
But left the cellar-door open,
        and Bauld Rankin crap in.

4 'Where's a' the women o the house?'
    says Bauld Rankin:
'They 're at the well washing,'
    says the fause nurse to him.

5 'Where's a' the men of this house?'
    says the Bauld Rankin:
'They are at the barn thrashing,'
    says the fause nurse to him.

6 'Where's the lady of this house?'
    says the Bauld Rankin:
'She's in the chamber, sleeping,'
    says the fause nurse to him.

7 'How will we get her wakent?
    how will we get her down?'
'We'll pierce the baby's heart's blood,'
    says the fause nurse to him.

* * * * *

8 'Come, please the babe, nurse,
    come please it wi the keys:'
'It'll no be pleased, madam,
    tho I'll down on my knees.'

9 'Come, please the babe, nurse,
    come, please it wi the knife:'
'It'll no be pleased, madam,
    should I lay down my life.'

10 'Come, please the babe, nurse,
    come, please it wi the bell:'
'It'll no be pleased, madam,
    till ye come down yoursel.'

11 'How can I come down, how can I come,
    sae late in the night,
And neither coal nor candle,
    for to shew me light?'

12 The first step she steppit,
    she steppit on a stane;
The next step she steppit,
    she met the Bauld Rankin.

13 'O spare my life, Rankin,
    O spare it most dear!
I'll gie you as monie guineas
    as birds in the air.

14 'O spare my life, Rankin,
    O save it most sweet!
I'll gie you as monie guineas
    as there's stanes in the street.'

* * * *

15 'I wish my wife and bairns
    may be all well at hame;
For the buttons on my waistcoat
    they winna bide on.

16 'I wish my wife and family
    may be all well at home;
For the rings upon my fingers
    they winna bide on.'

* * * *

17 He has kindled a big bane-fire,
    in the middle o the closs,
And he has burned Bauld Rankin,
    likewise the fause nurse.

———◆———

I

* * * *

Skene MSS, p. 75, North of Scotland, 1802–03.

1 LANCKIN was as guid a mason
    as ever did use stane;
He biggit Lord Murray's house,
    an payment neer got nane.

2 It fell ance on a day
    Lord Murray went frae hame,
An Lankin came to the fause nourice,

.   .   .   .   .

3 'O still my bairn, nourice,
    still him wi the knife:'
'He winna still, lady,
    Tho I should lay down my life.'

4 'O still my bairn, nurice,
    still him wi the bell:'
'He winna still, lady,
    till ye come down yersel.'

5 The first [step she steppit],
    she came on the marble stane ;
  The next step [she steppit],
    she met him Lankin.

6 'O spare my life, Lankin,
    an I 'll gie ye a peck o goud ;
  An that dinna please ye,
    I 'll heap it wi my hand.'

7 'O will I kill the lady, nurice,
    or will I lat her be?'
  'O kill her, Lankin,
    she was never guid to me.'

8 'O wanted ye yer meat, nurice?
    or wanted ye yer fee?
  Or wanted ye the othir bounties
    ladys are wont to gie?'

9 .   .   .   .   .
  'O kill her, Lankin,
    she was never guid to me.'

10 'Gae wash a bason, nurice,
    an ye wash it clean,
  To cape this ladie's blood ;
    she is come o high kine.'

11 'I winna wash a bason,
    nor will I wash it clean,
  To cape this ladie's blood,
    tho she 's come o high kine.'

    *   *   *   *

12 Bonny sang yon bird,
    as he sat upon the tree,
  But sare grat Lankin,
    for he was hangit hie.

13 Bonny sang the bird,
    that sat upon the hill,
  But sare grat the nurice,
    whan the caudron gan to boil.

14 .   .   .   .   .
    Lankin was hangit hie,
  And the fause nourice burnt
    in the caudron was she.

———•———

J

Kinloch MSS, V, 371, in the handwriting of Dr John Hill
Burton.

1 O LAMMIKIN was as good a mason
    as ever bigget stane ;
  He 's bigget Lord Erley's castle,
    but money he got nane.

2 It fell out upon a time
    Lord Earley went from home ;
  He left his lady in his castle,
    but and his young son.

    *   *   *   *

3 'Where is the lord o this house,
    that calls me Lammikin?'
  'He 's on the sea sailing,
    he will not come home.'

4 'Where are the men o this house,
    that call me Lammikin?'
  'They are at the barn threshing,
    they will not come in.'

5 'Where are the maids of this house,
    that call me Lammikin?'
  'They are at the well washing,
    they will not come in.'

6 'Where is the lady o this house,
    that calls me Lammikin?'
  'She 's in her room shewing,
    she will not come down.'

7 'How shall we contrive
    for to make her come down?'
  'We 'll stick her dear infant,
    and make her come down.'

8 O Lammikin he rocket,
    and the fause nurice sung,
  While out o the cradle
    the infant's blude sprung.

9 'O still my bairn, nurice,'
    the lady did cry :
  'He will not still, lady,
    for you nor for I.'

10 ' O still my bairn, nurice,
  still him wi the wan : '
' He will not still, lady,
  for a' his father's lan.'

11 ' Oh still my bairn, nurice,
  still him wi the keys : '
' Oh he winna still, lady,
  for a' his father's leys.'

12 ' Oh still my bairn, nurice,
  still him wi the bell : '
' Oh he winna still, lady,
  till ye come down yersell.'

13 The firsten step that lady stepped,
  it was upon a stone ;
The nexten step that lady stepped,
  she saw him Lammikin.

14 The nexten step that lady stepped
  was in her own child's blood,

   .   .   .   .

   *   *   *   *

15 ' Oh will I kill her, nurice,
  or will I let her be ? '
' Kill her, dear Lammikin,
  she was never gude to me.'

16 ' Oh wanted you meat, nurice ?
  or wanted you fee ?
Or wanted you anything
  that a lady can gie ? '

17 ' I wanted no meat, lady,
  nor wanted I fee,
But I wanted mony a thing
  that a lady could gie.'

   *   *   *   *

K

Communicated to Percy by Rev. P. Parsons, of Wye, near
Ashford, Kent, April 19, 1775.

1 My lord said to my lady,
  when he went from home,
Take care of Long Longkin,
  he lies in the lone.

2 My lady said to my lord,
  when he went abroad,

   .   .   .   .

3 ' I care not for Longkin,
  nor none of his kin,
For my gate 's fast barrd,
  and my windows shut in.'

4 My lord was not gone
  many miles from the place,
Untill the false Longkin
  came straight to the place.

   *   *   *   *

5 ' Pinch the bairn, nourry,
  pinch it very sore,
Untill the mother
  shall come down below.'

6 ' Still the bairn, nury,
  still it with the pap : '
' It wont be stilld, madam,
  with neither this nor that.'

7 ' Still the bairn, nury,
  still it with a bell : '
' It wont be stilld, madam,
  till you cum down yoursell.'

   *   *   *   *

8 ' Come down, Lady Betty,
  the flower of all your kin,
And see your mother's heart's blood,
  so freely running.

9 Down came Lady Betty,
  her heart full of woe :
' Oh take my life, Longkin,
  and let my mother go.'

10 'Come down, Lady Nelly,
       the flower of all your kin,
   And see your sister's heart's blood,
       so freely running.'

11 Down came Lady Nelly,
       her heart full of woe :
   'Oh take my life, Longkin,
       and let my sister go.'

12 'Come down, Lady Jenny, etc.

L

Motherwell's MS., p. 14, from Mr W. Steele, Greenock.

*   *   *   *   *

1 'O WHERE 's the men of this house?'
       quo the Lamkin :
   'They 're in the barn threshing,'
       quo the false nurse within.

2 'O where 's the women of the house ?'
       quo the Lamkin :
   'They 're at the well washing,'
       quo the false nurse within.

3 'O where 's the lord of this house ?'
       quo the Lamkin :
   'He 's in the wood hunting,'
       quo the false nurse within.

4 'O where 's the lady of the house ?'
       quo the Lamkin :

'She 's in her bower dressing,'
       quo the false nurse within.

*   *   *   *

5 'O please my babie, nourrice,
       O please him with the keys : '
   'He 'll no be pleased, madam,
       let me do what I please.'

6 'O please my babie, nourrice,
       O please him with the bell : '
   'He 'll no be pleased, madam,
       till ye come down yoursell.'

*   *   *   *

7 There was blood in the chaumer,
       and blood in the ha,
   And blood in his ladie's room,
       which he liked warst of a'.

*   *   *   *

M

a. Dr Joseph Robertson's Note-Book, Adversaria, p. 60, from tradition. b. Kinloch MSS, VI, 31, in Dr Robertson's handwriting.

*   *   *   *   *

1 BUT it fell out upon a day
       Lord Wearie was to gae frae hame,
   And he has left his lady gay
       In his castell to stay her lane.

*   *   *   *   *

2 Lamkin rocked,
       and fausse nourice sang,
   And a' the four tors o the cradle
       red blood sprang.

3 'O still my bairn, nourice,
       O still him wi the wan :
   'He winna still, lady,
       for a' his father's lan.'

4 'O still my bairn, nourice,
       O still him wi the keys :
   'He winna still, lady,
       for a' his father's leys.'

5 'O still my bairn, nourice,
       O still him wi the pap : '
   'He winna still, lady,
       for this nor for that.'

6 'O still my bairn, nourice,
       O still him wi the bell : '

'He winna still, lady,
    untill ye cum down yersell.'

7 The firsten step she steppet,
    she stepped on a stane,
And the nexten step she stepped,
    she keppit him fause Lamkin.

8 The thirden step she steppit,
    she saw her young son's red blood run on,

  •   •   •   •   •

9 'Ye 've killed my bairn, Lamkin,
    but lat mysell be ;
Ye 'se be as weel payit a mason
    as was ever payd a fee.'

N

Dr Joseph Robertson's Journal of Excursions, 1828–29, No 2.

1 LAMKIN was as gude a mason
    as ever biggit stone ;
He biggit Laird Earie's house,
    and payment he got none.

2 O it fell ance upon a day
    Laird Earie went from home,
And Lamkin came cravin
    his lady alone.

3 'O far 's the laird o this place ?
    O neerice, tell me : '
'He 's on the sea sailin,
    O Lamkin,' said she.

4 'O far 's the lady o this place ?
    neerice, tell me : '
'She 's up the stair dressin,
    O Lamkin,' said she.

5 'O far 's the bairns o this place ?
    neerice, tell me : '
'The 're at the scheel •   •
    O Lamkin,' said she.
'O will I get a word o her,
    neerice ? ' said he.

    *   *   *   *

6 The first step that lady steppet
    she steppd on a stone ;
The next step that lady stept
    she met wi Lamkin.

    *   *   *   *

7 Ere the basin was washen,
    or haf made clean,
The ladie's heart-bleed
    was rinnin in the reem.

O

Kinloch MSS, V, 375, from Mrs Forbes, Milne's Court, Edinburgh, in the handwriting of Robert Chambers.

    *   *   *   *   *

1 'You have two bright diamonds,
    as bright as the stars,
Put one on each finger,
    they 'll show you doun stairs.'

2 The first step this lady took,
    she dreaded no harm ;
But the second step this lady took,
    she was in Lammikin's arms.

3 'Will I kill her, nursie,
    or will I let her be ? '
'Oh yes, kill her, Lammikin,
    she was never gude to me.'

4 'How can [ye] say so, nursie ?
    how can ye say so ?
For your head neer did ache
    but my heart it was sore.

5 'Oh spare my life, nursie,
    oh spare my life, spare ;
Ye 'll have as mony gowd guineas
    as there 's birds in the air.

6 'Oh spare my life, nursie,
    till my lord comes back ;
Ye 'll have as mony gowd guineas
    as the fou of a sack.'

7 'Oh yes kill her and .   .
    .   .   .   .   .
.   .   .   .   .
    .   .   .   .   .

P

Herd's MSS, I, 25.

1 A BETTER mason than Lammikin
    nevir builded wi the stane,
Wha builded Lord Weire's castill,
    but wages nevir gat nane.

*   *   *   *   *

2 They stecked doors, they stecked yates,
    close to the cheik and the chin ;
They stecked them a' but a little wickit,
    and Lammikin crap in.

3 'Now where 's the lady of this castle ?
    nurse, tell to Lammikin :'
'She 's sewing up intill her bowir,'
    the fals nourrice she sung.

4 'What sall we do, what sall we say,
    to gar her cum there down ? '

Q

Finlay's Scottish Ballads, II, 45.

1 LAMMIKIN was as gude a mason
    as ever hewed a stane ;
He biggit Lord Weire's castle,
    but payment gat he nane.

*   *   *   *   *

2 'Where are the lads o this castle ?'
    says the Lammikin :
'They are a' wi Lord Weire, hunting,'
    the false nourice did sing.

8 'Go scour the silver basin,
    go scour it fine,
For our lady's heart's blude
    is gentle to tine.

9 'Go scour the silver skewer,
    oh scour it richt fine,
For our lady's heart's blude
    is gentle to tine.'

'We 'll nip the baby in the cradle,
    the fals nourrice she sung.

5 Lammikin nipped the bonie babe,
    while loud fals nourice sings ;
Lammikin nipped the bony babe,
    while hich the red blude springs.

6 'O gentil nourice, please my babe,
    O please him wi the keys :'
'He 'll no be pleased, gay lady,
    gin I 'd sit on my knees.'

7 'Gude gentil nourice, please my babe,
    O please him wi a knife :'
'He winna be pleased, mistress myne,
    gin I wad lay down my lyfe.'

8 'Sweet nourice, loud, loud cries my babe,
    O please him wi the bell :'
'He winna be pleased, gay lady,
    till ye cum down yoursell.'

3 'Where are the lasses o this castle ?'
    says the Lammikin :
'They are a' out at the washing,'
    the false nourice did sing.

4 'But where 's the lady o this house ?'
    says the Lammikin :
'She is in her bower sewing,'
    the false nourice did sing.

5 'Is this the bairn o this house ?'
    says the Lammikin :
'The only bairn Lord Weire aughts,'
    the false nourice did sing.

*   *   *   *   *

'Still my bairn, nourice,
  O still him if ye can :'
'He will not still, madam,
  for a' his father's lan.'

7 'O gentle nourice, still my bairn,
  O still him wi the keys :'
'He will not still, fair lady,
  let me do what I please.'

8 'O still my bairn, kind nourice,
  O still him wi the ring :'
'He will not still, my lady,
  let me do any thing.'

    *   *   *   *

9 The first step she stepped,
  she stepped on a stane ;
The next step she stepped,
  she met the Lammikin.

    *   *   *   *

10 'O nourice, wanted ye your meat ?
  or wanted ye your fee ?

Or wanted ye for any thing
  a fair lady could gie ? '

11 'I wanted for nae meat, ladie,
  I wanted for nae fee ;
But I wanted for a hantle
  a fair lady could gie.'

    *   *   *   *

12 'I wish a' may be weel,' he says,
  ' wi my ladie at hame ;
For the rings upon my fingers
  are bursting in twain.'

    *   *   *   *

13 'There 's bluid in my nursery,
  there 's bluid in my ha,
There 's bluid in my fair lady's bower,
  an that 's warst of a'.'

14 O sweet, sweet sang the birdie,
  upon the bough sae hie,
But little cared false nourice for that,
  for it was her gallows-tree.

    *   *   *   *

———◆———

R

Finlay's Scottish Ballads, II, 55, "from a manuscript formerly written by an old lady."

1 WHEN Sir Guy and his train
  gaed to hunt the wild boar,
He gard bar up his castle,
  behind and before.

2 And he bade his fair lady
  guard weel her young son,
For wicked Balcanqual
  great mischief had done.

3 So she closed a' the windows,
  without and within,
But forgot the wee wicket,
  and Balcanqual crap in.

    *   *   *   *

4 Syne Balcanqual he rocked,
  and fause nourice sang,

Till through a' the cradle
  the baby's blood sprang.

5 'O please the bairn, nourice,
  and please him wi the keys :'
'He 'll no be pleased, madam,
  for a' that he sees.'

6 And Balcanqual ay rocked,
  while fause nourice sang,
And through a' the cradle
  the baby's blood ran.

7 'Please the bairn, nourice,
  and please him wi the knife :'
'He 'll no be pleased, madam,
  tho I 'd gie my life.'

8 And Balcanqual still rocked,
  and fause nourice sang,
While through a' the cradle
  the baby's blood ran.

9 'Now please the bairn, nourice,
        and please him wi the bell :'
  'He 'll no be pleased, madam,
        till ye come yoursell.'

10 Down came this fair lady,
        tripping down the stair,
   To see her sick bairn,
        but returned never mair.

S

Motherwell's Note-Book, fol. 13.

1 LAMBKIN was as brave a builder
        as eer built a stane,
  And he built Lord Cassillis house,
        an for payment he gat nane.

T

Recited to me by Ellen Healy, January 14, 1881, as sung
by Moll Lochnie, a woman of about seventy, at a place near
Killarney, before 1867.

1 'WHERE is the lord ?
        or is he within ?'
  'He 's gone to New England,
        to dine with the king.'

2 'Where is his horses ?
        or where is his men ?'
  'They 're gone to New England,
        to wait upon him.'

3 'Where is his lady ?
        or is she within ?'
  'She 's in her bedchamber,
        all in her lying in.'

4 'Can I get at her,
        with thousands of lands?
  Can I get at her,
        to make her understand ?'

5 'You cannot get at her,
        with thousands of lands ;
  You cannot get at her,
        to make her understand.'

6 'Lady, come down,
        and please your child,'

11 'Now scour the bason, Jenny,
        and scour 't very clean,
   To haad this lady's blood,
        for she 's of noble kin.'

    *   *   *   *

2 My lord said to my lady,
        when he went abroad,
  Tak care o fause Lamkin,
        for he sleeps in the wood.

    .   .   .   .   .

7 'Can't you please my child
        with white bread and breast-wine ? '
  'O lady, come down,
        and please him awhile.'

8 'How can I go down,
        this cold winter's night,
  Without a fire in the kitchen,
        or candle to light ?'

9 'You 've got nine bright lamps,
        just as bright as the king ;
  Lady, come down,
        and light one of them.'

10 .   .   .   .   .
        .   .   .   .
   False Lantin he took her
        so brave in his arms.

11 Saying, Where is your friend,
        or where is your foe,
   That will hold the gold basin,
        your heart's blood to flow ?

12 'My nurse is not my friend,
        my nurse is my foe ;
   She 'll hold the gold basin,
        my heart's blood to flow.

3 'O spare my life
    for one summer's day,
And I'll give you as much money
    as there's sand in the sea.'

4 'I'll not spare your life
    for one summer's day,
And I wont have as much money
    as there's sand in the sea.'

5 'O spare me my life
    until one o'clock,
And I'll give you Queen Betsie,
    the flower of the flock.'

6 'O mama, dear mama,
    then please him awhile;

U

a. The Ballad Book, by William Allingham, p. xxxiii,
t of a version sung by a nurse in the family of a relative
Ireland.   b. The same, p. 297, No 56, a compounded ver-
n.

1 As my lord and my lady
    were out walking one day,
Says my lord to my lady,
    Beware of Lamkin.

2 'O why should I fear him,
    or any such man,

V

Harris MS., No 28, fol. 27 b, Miss Seymour, Lethnot.

I WALD be very sorry
    to wash a basin clean,

My dada is coming,
    he's dressed in great style.'

17 False Lantin he heard
    the words from the high,
Saying, Your mama is dead,
    and away I will fly.

18 'O dada, dear dada,
    do not blame me,
'T is nurse and false Lantin
    betrayed your ladie.'

19 'I'll bury my mama
    against the wall,
And I'll bury my baba,
    white all, white all.'

When my doors are well barrd,
    and my windows well pinnd?'

*   *   *   *

3 'O keep your gold and silver,
    it will do you some good ;
It will buy you a coffin,
    when you are dead.'

4 There's blood in the kitchen,
    and blood in the hall,
And the young Mayor of England
    lies dead by the wall.

To haud my mither's heart's blude,
    that's comin, an I ken.

2¹², 22². *Motherwell suggests* mother *for* lady.
After 22, "a stanza, forgotten by the reciter,
   which purported that on the night his lady
   was murdered, the ring on Lord Arran's
   finger broke."
b. 1¹. he got on. 1², 2². who lives.
    3¹. The doors are . . . windows are.
    3². There is not . . . where a mouse can.

4². For he. 5¹. the windows all pinned.
5². But one : Lankin.
7². she's in her high chamber.
8¹. young heir. 9¹. we'll prick him, we'll.
10¹. They pricked him, they.
10². false nurse . . . drop in.
11². my son Johnson.
12², 14², 16². Come down.

13. *wanting.*   14². and nurse.

15². And there 's no fire burning, nor lamp.

16². all by.

17². much money.   18. *wanting.*

19, 20, 21. Nancy.   20². golden basin.

22², 23¹. Long *wanting.*   23². close by.

G.   "A friend of the lady who contributed our copy of this ballad gave a transcript to Miss Landon, who published it in the Drawing Room Scrap Book for 1835, in which, without any authority, she lays the scene of the murder in Cumberland."

Variations in the Drawing Room Scrap Book:

7¹, 8¹, 9¹. Where are.

11, 13 *are given in* Halliwell's Nursery Rhymes of England, *ed.* 1874, *p.* 212, *No* 403, *with only this variation :* 11², when ye lord.

I.   5¹. marble stane, *indistinct in the MS.*

7¹. O . . . her gang.

K.   *After* 4.   He was in league with the nurse, who let him in to one of the low rooms.

After 12.   Whilst he and the nurse are plundering the house, the lord comes home, and avenges himself upon these wicked villains.

L.   2¹. woman.

M.   a. *After* 1.   And a' the servants were frae hame ; Lamkin made up wi the fauss norice.

2 *follows* 8.

b. *Begins with a stanza very near to* N 1 :

> Lamkin was as gude a mason
> As ever laid a stane,
> And he has built Lord Wearie a castle,
> But payment he got nane.

1¹. once upon : Wearie went frae.

2 *follows* 6.

2¹. Lamkin he rockit and the.

2². Till to the four tors o the cradle the.

3¹. a wand.   8 *is omitted.*

9². as eer was paid.

N.   6¹. first steppd.

P.   *Eleven of the nineteen stanzas of Herd's version are spurious, and many of the others have been tampered with.   The metre is disturbed or changed.*

Stanza 4 *is omitted in Herd's printed copy.*

After 1 *follow :*

> 'Sen ye winnae gie me my guerdon, lord,
>   Sen ye winnae gie me my hyre,

> Yon proud castle, sae stately built,
>   I sall gar reek wi the fyre.

> 'Sen ye winna gie me my wages, lord,
>   Ye sall hae caus to rue :'
> And syne he brewed a black revenge,
>   And syne he vowed a vow.

> 'Now byde at hame, my luve, my lyfe,
>   I warde ye byde at hame ;
> Oh gang nae to this day's hunting,
>   To leave me a' my lane.

> 'Yestrene, yestrene, I dreamt my bower
>   Of red, red blude was fu ;
> Gin ye gang to this black hunting,
>   I sall hae caus to rue.'

> 'Wha looks to dreams, my winsome dame ?
>   Ye hae nae caus to feare :'
> And syne he 's kist her comely cheik,
>   And syne the starting teare.

> And syne he 's gane to the good greene wode,
>   And she to her painted bowir,
> And she 's gard steck doors, windows, yates,
>   Of castle, ha and tower.

After 8 *follow these five stanzas, found also i̇* *Herd's MSS, II,* 97 :

> And when she saw the red, red blude,
>   A loud scrich scriched she :
> 'O monster, monster, spare the child
>   Wha never skaithed thee.

> 'O spare, gif in your bluidy briest
>   Albergs not heart of stane ;
> O spare, and ye sall hae of gould
>   What ye can carry hame.'

> 'Dame, I want not your gowd,' he sayd,
>   'Dame, I want not your fee ;
> I hae been wronged by your lord,
>   Ye sall black vengence drie.

> 'Here are nae serfs to guard your halls,
>   Nae trusty spearsmen here ;
> They sound the horn in good greene wode,
>   And chase the doe and deer.

> 'Tho merry sounds the gude greene wode,
>   Wi huntsmen hounds and horn,
> Your lord sall rue eer sets yon sun
>   He hes done me skaith and scorn.'

*   *   *   *   *

For quha, ze, *etc.,* wha, ye *are printed.*

Q. *Of the thirty-five stanzas printed by Finlay,
seventeen, or* 2, 3, 5–9, 12 (?), 14, 16 (?), 18,
19, 21–25, *are derived from Herd's version,*
P, *all his spurious verses being retained.
There are some variations, due to imperfect
recollection. Of the remaining eighteen,* 4,
28, 29, 31, 34 *are clearly by a modern pen.
There are some twelve genuine stanzas,* 1,
10, 11, 13, 15, 17, 20, 26, 27, 30, 32, 33,
*which are independent of Herd. Two more,
Finlay's* 12, 16, *have been left with these
because they vary considerably from Herd,
and may possibly be traditional. So may
the following be, Finlay's* 35 *and last; but
I think it is not.*

> They carried him a' airts o wind,
> And mickle pain had he;
> At last before Lord Weire's gate
> They hanged him on the tree.

R. *This second version of Finlay's has been written over. His fourth stanza and his last six
owe nothing to tradition. Finlay himself
"restored" the name of Balwearie from a
recited copy "in preference to that of* Sr.
Guy, *or* Gray, *which the* MS. *bears, as it
makes the ballad* appear *more decidedly
local."*

After 3:

> Then up spak fause nourice:
> 'haste up to the tower,
> Somebody knocks at the gate,
> bauldly and dowr.'

After 11:

> She's lifted her baby,
> and kissed cheek and chin,
> And his ance rosy lips,
> but nae breath was within.

> 'Fare weel, my sweet baby,
> ye've left me alane;
> But I see my death coming,
> I needna make mane.'

> They've taen this fair lady,
> and tied her wi bands,
> And in her sweet heart's blood
> they've dipped their hands.

> For Balcanqual and nourice
> had vowd her to slae,
> Because their ill deeds
> made Balwearie their fae.

> Balwearie and his train
> cam hame weary at een,
> Nae voice gied them welcome,
> nae light could be seen.

> 'Open, dear lady,
> my castle to me:'
> Nae voice gied an answer,
> nae voice was to gie.

S. "Lambkin. . . . 27 stanzas."

T. *After* 5: "The nurse said this, and the false
Lantin stabbed the baby. He bribed the
nurse to make the lady come down and
please the child. It told how he stabbed
the baby, what kind of knife he had, and
how he put it through the baby."

U. b. *Allingham's copy is principally composed of
14 stanzas of* A, 9 *of* G, 5 *of* Q, 1 *of* B.
*So much of the following stanzas as is in
larger type may be regarded as derived,
partially or wholly, from the "copy taken
down from the mouth of an Irish nurse in
the family of a relative of the editor."*

> 6 What care I for Lamkin,
> or any of his gang?
> I'll keep my doors weel guarded,
> my windows all pennd in.'

> 7 When all the doors were guarded,
> and all the windows shut,
> There was still one little window,
> and that one was forgot.

> 13 'And how are we to bring her down?'
> says the Lamkin:
> 'Pinch the babe in the cradle here,'
> says the fause nourice to him.

> 18 The first step the lady stepped,
> she stepped on a stane;
> The last step the lady stepped,
> there she met Lamkin.

> 19 'O mercy, mercy, Lamkin,
> have mercy upon me!
> O harm ye not my little son,
> I pray you let him be.'

23 Lord Weare he sat in England,
     a drinking o the wine ;
     He felt his heart fu heavy
       at this very same time.

25 He sailed in his bonny ship
     upon the saut sea-faem ;

     He leapd up on his horse
     and swiftly he rade hame.

27 'O whas blude is this,' he says,
     'that lies in the bower ? '
     'It is your lady's heart's blude,
      where Lamkin he slew her.'

94

YOUNG WATERS

Percy's Reliques, 1765, II, 172.

PERCY took this ballad "from a copy printed not long since at Glasgow, in one sheet 8vo," and he informs us that the world was indebted for its publication to the Lady Jean Hume, sister to the Earl of Hume. Maidment, Scotish Ballads and Songs, Historical and Traditionary, II, 62, gives the title of the first edition as follows: Young Waters, an Ancient Scotish Poem, never before printed. Glasgow: printed and sold by Robert and Andrew Foulis. MDCCLV. Small 4to, pp. 8. He does not say whether he prints from the original edition. The ballad was repeated in Herd's Ancient and Modern Scots Songs, 1769, p. 238; in Ritson's Scotish Song, 1794, II, 181, with the variation of a word or two; and in Pinkerton's Select Scotish Ballads, 1783, I, 72, with arbitrary changes.

Motherwell, Minstrelsy, Introduction, p. lxviii, note 16, says he had never met with any traditionary version of this ballad. There is a copy in the Skene MSS, p. 23, which in all likelihood was learned by the writer from print. Buchan, who may generally be relied upon to produce a longer ballad than anybody else, has 'Young Waters' in thirty-nine stanzas, "the only complete version which he had ever met." Of this copy I will only say that everything which is not in the edition of 1755 (itself a little the worse for editing) is a counterfeit of the lowest description. Nevertheless it is given in an appendix; for much the same reason that thieves are photographed.

It is possible, and Aytoun, I, 93, thinks highly probable, that this ballad may have been founded on some real event in Scottish history; but Aytoun shows a commendable discretion in his conclusion that, "though various conjectures have been hazarded as to its origin, none appear sufficiently plausible to warrant their adoption," an opinion in which Maidment fully concurs. Chambers, who unhesitatingly accepted Buchan's ballad, did not, in 1829, entertain the least doubt that Young Waters was one of the Scottish nobles executed by James I after his return from his captivity in England, and very probably Walter Stuart, second son of the Duke of Albany : The Scottish Ballads, p. 34. Thirty years later he had no more doubt that the ballad was composed by Lady Wardlaw.

A Scandinavian ballad, historical to the extent that one version has historical names, exhibits the principal incidents of the short story of 'Young Waters.' Danish. 'Folke Lovmandsøn og Dronning Helvig,' texts of the 16th century, Grundtvig, III, 691, No 178, A–D.* Swedish. A, 'Falkvard Lagermanson,' tradition of this century, Arwidsson, II,

* D, which is made up from the three others, is translated by Prior, II, 160, No 65.

62, No 80. **B**, manuscript of the last century, Grundtvig, III, 697. The king and queen, Danish **B**, are Magnus I of Sweden and his wife Helvig (died 1290, 1325). Folke Lovmandsøn is in high favor with dames and maids, but especially with the queen, to whose service he is devoted. A little wee page plays the part of the wily lord of 'Young Waters' in exciting the king's jealousy. The innocent young knight is rolled down hill in a tun set with knives.

Translated by Grundtvig, No 7, p. 48 ; Herder, II, 68 ; Döring, p. 383 ; Allingham's copy by Knortz, Lieder und Romanzen Alt-Englands, No 8, p. 33 ; Buchan's by Gerhard, p. 8.

---

1 ABOUT Yule, when the wind blew cule,
　　And the round tables began,
　　A there is cum to our king's court
　　Mony a well-favoured man.

2 The queen luikt owre the castle-wa,
　　Beheld baith dale and down,
　　And then she saw Young Waters
　　Cum riding to the town.

3 His footmen they did rin before,
　　His horsemen rade behind ;
　　Ane mantel of the burning gowd
　　Did keip him frae the wind.

4 Gowden-graithd his horse before,
　　And siller-shod behind ;
　　The horse Young Waters rade upon
　　Was fleeter than the wind.

5 Out then spake a wylie lord,
　　Unto the queen said he,
　　' O tell me wha 's the fairest face
　　Rides in the company ? '

6 ' I 've sene lord, and I 've sene laird,
　　And knights of high degree,
　　But a fairer face than Young Waters
　　Mine eyne did never see.'

7 Out then spack the jealous king,
　　And an angry man was he :
　　' O if he had been twice as fair,
　　You micht have excepted me.'

8 ' You 're neither laird nor lord,' she says,
　　' Bot the king that wears the crown ;
　　There is not a knight in fair Scotland
　　But to thee maun bow down.'

9 For a' that she could do or say,
　　Appeasd he wad nae bee,
　　Bot for the words which she had said,
　　Young Waters he maun dee.

10 They hae taen Young Waters,
　　And put fetters to his feet ;
　　They hae taen Young Waters,
　　And thrown him in dungeon deep.

11 ' Aft I have ridden thro Stirling town
　　In the wind bot and the weit ;
　　Bot I neir rade thro Stirling town
　　Wi fetters at my feet.

12 ' Aft have I ridden thro Stirling town
　　In the wind bot and the rain ;
　　Bot I neir rade thro Stirling town
　　Neir to return again.'

13 They hae taen to the heiding-hill
　　His young son in his craddle,
　　And they hae taen to the heiding-hill
　　His horse bot and his saddle.

14 They hae taen to the heiding-hill
　　His lady fair to see,
　　And for the words the queen had spoke
　　Young Waters he did dee.

Quhen, zoung, *etc., are printed* when, young.
3³. And *corrected to* Ane *in the second edition of the Reliques.*

5¹. But. *Ritson, Maidment*, Out.
10¹, ³. Waters and : and *is carried on to the following line.*

APPENDIX.

Buchan's Ballads of the North of Scotland, I, 15.

1 It fell about the gude Yule time,
   When caps and stoups gaed roun,
Down it came him Young Waters,
   To welcome James, our king.

2 The great, the great, rade a' together,
   The sma came a' behin,
But wi Young Waters, that brave knight,
   There came a gay gatherin.

3 The horse Young Waters rade upon,
   It cost him hunders nine ;
For he was siller-shod before,
   And gowd-graith had behin.

4 At ilka tippit o his horse mane
   There hang a siller bell ;
The wind was loud, the steed was proud,
   And they gae a sindry knell.

5 The king he lay ower 's castle-wa,
   Beheld baith dale and down,
And he beheld him Young Waters,
   Come riding to the town.

6 He turnd him right and round about,
   And to the queen said he,
Who is the bravest man, my dame,
   That ever your een did see ?

7 'I 've seen lairds, and I 've seen lords,
   And knights o high degree,
But a braver man than Young Waters
   My een did never see.'

8 He turnd him right and roun about,
   And ane angry man was he :
'O wae to you, my dame, the queen,
   Ye might hae excepted me !'

9 'Ye are nae laird, ye are nae lord,
   Ye are the king that wears the crown ;
There 's nae a lord in fair Scotland
   But unto you maun a' bow down.'

10 'O lady, for your love-choicing,
    Ye shall win to your will ;
The morn, or I eat or drink,
    Young Waters I 'll gar kill.'

11 'And nevertheless,' the king coud say,
    'Ye might hae excepted me ;
Yea for yea,' the king coud say,
    'Young Waters he shall die.

12 'Likewise for your ill-wyled words,
    Ye sall hae cause to mourn ;
Gin ye hadna been sae big wi child,
    Ye on a hill sud burn.'

13 Young Waters came before the king,
    Fell low down on his knee :
'Win up, win up, Young Waters,
    What 's this I hear o thee ?'

14 'What ails the king at me,' he said,
    'What ails the king at me?'
'It is tauld me the day, sir knight,
    Ye 've done me treasonie.'

15 'Liars will lie on fell gude men,
    Sae will they do on me ;
I wudna wish to be the man
    That liars on wudna lie.'

16 'Nevertheless,' the king coud say,
    'In prison strang gang ye ;
O yea for yea,' the king coud say,
    'Young Waters, ye shall die.'

17 Syne they hae taen him Young Waters,
    Laid him in prison strang,
And left him there wi fetters boun,
    Making a heavy mane.

18 'Aft hae I ridden thro Striveling town
    Thro heavy wind and weet ;
But neer rade I thro Striveling town
    Wi fetters on my feet.

19 'Aft hae I ridden thro Striveling town
    Thro heavy wind and rain ;
But neer rade I thro Striveling town
    But thought to ridden 't again.'

20 They brought him to the heading-hill,
    His horse bot and his saddle ;
And they brought to the heading-hill
    His young son in his cradle.

21 And they brought to the heading-hill
    His hounds intill a leish ;
And they brought till the heading-hill
    His gos-hawk in a jess.

22 King James he then rade up the hill,
    And mony a man him wi,
And called on his trusty page
    To come right speedilie.

23 'Ye 'll do ye to the Earl o Mar,
    For he sits on yon hill ;
Bid him to loose the brand frae his bodie,
    Young Waters for to kill.'

24 'O gude forbid,' the Earl he said,
     'The like sud eer fa me,
My bodie eer sud wear the brand
     That gars Young Waters die.'

25 Then he has loosd his trusty brand
     And casten 't in the sea ;
Says, Never lat them get a brand
     Till it come back to me.

26 The scaffold it prepared was,
     And he did mount it hie,
And a' spectators that were there,
     The saut tears blint their ee.

27 'O had your tongues, my brethren dear,
     And mourn nae mair for me ;
Ye 're seeking grace frae a graceless face,
     For there is nane to gie.

28 'Ye 'll tak a bit o canvas claith
     And pit it ower my ee ;
And Jack, my man, ye 'll be at hand
     The hour that I sud die.

29 'Syne aff ye 'll tak my bluidy sark,
     Gie it fair Margaret Grahame ;
For she may curse the dowie dell
     That brought King James him hame.

30 'Ye 'll bid her mak her bed narrow,
     And mak it naeways wide ;
For a brawer man than Young Waters
     Will neer streek by her side.

31 'Bid her do weel to my young son,
     And gie him nurses three ;
For gin he live to be a man,
     King James will gar him die.'

32 He calld upon the headsman, then,
     A purse o gowd him gae ;
Says, Do your office, headsman, boy,
     And mak nae mair delay.

33 O head me soon, O head me clean,
     And pit me out o pine ;
For it is by the king's command ;
     Gang head me till his min.

34 Tho by him I 'm condemnd to die,
     I 'm lieve to his ain kin ;
And for the truth, I 'll plainly tell,
     I am his sister's son.

35 'Gin ye 're my sister's son,' he said,
     'It is unkent to me ;'
'O mindna ye on your sister Bess,
     That lives in the French countrie ? '

36 'Gin Bess then be your mither dear,
     As I trust well she be,
Gae hame, gae hame, Young Waters,
     Ye 'se neer be slain by me.'

37 But he lay by his napkin fine,
     Was saft as ony silk,
And on the block he laid his neck,
     Was whiter than the milk.

38 Says, Strike the blow, ye headsman, boy,
     And that right speedilie ;
It 's never be said, Here gaes a knight
     Was ance condemnd to die.

39 The head was taen frae Young Waters,
     And mony tears for him shed ;
But mair did mourn for fair Margaret,
     As raving she lyes mad.

95

THE MAID FREED FROM THE GALLOWS

A. Communicated to Bishop Percy, 1770.

B. 'The Broom o the Cathery Knowes,' Motherwell's MS., p. 290.

C. Notes and Queries, Sixth eries, VII, 275, 1883.

D. Skene MSS, p. 61, stanzas 19–24 : 1802–03.

E. 'Lady Maisry,' Buchan's MSS, II, 186; 'Warenston and the Duke of York's Daughter,' Buchan's

Ballads of the North of Scotland, II, 190, stanzas 16–22.

F. Notes and Queries, Sixth Series, VI, 476, 1882.

G. a. 'The Golden Key,' Notes and Queries, Sixth Series, VI, 415. **b.** The same, p. 269.

H. 'The Golden Ball.' **a.** Baring-Gould's Appendix to Henderson's Notes on the Folk Lore of the Northern Counties of England and the Borders, 1866, p. 333. **b.** Notes and Queries, Sixth Series, X, 354, 1884.

D, E form the conclusion of a ballad which belongs to the series of 'Mary Hamilton,' or 'The Queen's Mary,' and give an entirely wrong turn to that distressful tragedy.

F had become a children's game, the last stage of many old ballads : see the notes. In G and H the verses are set in a popular tale, and a characteristic explanation is furnished of the danger which the heroine has incurred : she has lost a golden key, or a golden ball, which had been entrusted to her. See, again, the notes.

All the English versions are defective and distorted, as comparison will show. In many others, both from northern and southern Europe, a young woman has fallen into the hands of corsairs; father, mother, brother, sister, refuse to pay ransom, but her lover, in one case husband, stickles at no price which may be necessary to retrieve her.

We will begin with the best ballad of the cycle, the **Sicilian** 'Scibilia Nobili,' communicated to Nuove Effemeridi Siciliane, Nuova Serie, I, 528, 1874, by Salvatore Struppa, as sung by a peasant woman in the neighborhood of Marsala, 151 verses.[*] Tunisian cor-

sairs, learning of the marriage of the king's daughter, fit out a strong force, and when they are near port change caps, to pass for Christians. They knock at Scibilia's door, and, on her refusing to open, her husband being a-hunting, burst the door in, and carry her on board ship. Her husband goes to the shore weeping, and offers her captors her weight in gold; they will not give her up for a shipful. He begs to be allowed a word with her : why has she let herself be carried off, and who will nurse her boy? She refuses to eat, drink, or sleep. The sailors fall asleep, and Scibilia drops into the sea. They take silk ladders to recover her; she weeps always. (It would be superfluous to do more than point to the fact that the story is not well compacted, or altogether rational, as we have it.) The lady, turning to a sailor, says, Can you tell me how the wind is? If north or south, I will go to my father. No opposition is made by the pirates, who had but just now refused a shipful of gold for her. "My dear father, will you ransom me?" "For how much, my dear daughter?" "Three lions, three falcons, and four pillars of gold." "I cannot lose so

[*] Liebrecht was the first to call attention to this ballad-cycle, Zur Volkskunde, p. 222, repeating, with enlargement, an article in Zeitschrift für deutsche Philologie, IX, 53. He gives the Sicilian text, and a Balearic and a Färöe, presently to be noticed, with translations, and points out other parallels. Reifferscheid made additions in his Westfälische Volkslieder, p. 10, p. 138 ff. I have not at hand the Effemeridi for 1874.

much money : how much better lose you !''
She is urged by her captors to eat and drink,
but will not eat, drink, or sleep, for her boy
is starving. She again makes for the coast,
weeping ever, and the foregoing scene, from
the inquiry as to the wind, is repeated with
mother, brother, sister. All say it is better
to lose her than so much money. She finally
tries her husband, who answers, Better lose
all this gold ; it is enough if you are not lost.
And after three days the father died. " And
let him die ; I will dress all in red.'' And
after three days the mother died. " And let
her die ; I will dress all in yellow.'' And
after three days the brother died. " And let
him die ; I will dress all in green.'' And
after three days the sister died. " And let
her die ; I will dress all in white. And if
my dear husband dies, I will dress in black.''

Spanish. A. a, 'La Donzella,' Die Ba-
learen in Wort und Bild geschildert, II, 263
(privately printed by the Archduke Ludwig
Salvator, Leipzig, 1871, a book which I have
not been able to obtain), Liebrecht, Zur
Volkskunde, p. 231 ; b, Briz, Cansons de la
Terra, IV, 15, from a Majorcan *revista*. **B.**
'Lo Rescat,' Briz, IV, 13. **C.** 'La Cautiva,'
Milá, Romancerillo, p. 257, No 261. In **A** a
maid, who is embroidering a handkerchief by
the seashore, lacking silk, hails a vessel, and
asks if they have any. She is invited to come
aboard and see if they have what she requires.
She falls asleep, and the sailors put off. This
beginning is like that of another very common
ballad. The maid is wakened by the singing
of the sailors, and asks them to put into the
port where her father is. What follows corresponds to the English ballad. " Father, will
you ransom me ? The Moors offer me for
sale.'' " Dear daughter, how much do they
ask ? '' " I am yours for a hundred crowns.''
" Daughter, I will not pay a penny for you.''
The scene is repeated with mother, brother,
and sister, all of whom make the same answer
as the father, and then with the lover ; but his
reply is, I would not give you up for all the
world.

The first five stanzas of **A** are wanting in **B**,
which begins, accordingly, at the point where
the maid asks to have the ship put about. The
sister is omitted in **B**, as also in **A** b. **C** is
shortened still further, beginning with the appeal to the father, and omitting both sister
and brother.

Färöe. ' Frísa Vísa,' communicated by
Hammershaimb, with other ballads, to the
Antiquarisk Tidsskrift, 1849–51, p. 95. Frisian pirates are carrying away a maid. She
weeps and beats her hands, and cries, Wait,
my father will ransom me ; he will ransom me
with his castles ; he will not let me perish in
Friesland. The father answers, I have only
two castles ; neither of them can I give up for
thee ; indeed thou mayst perish in Friesland.
The Frisians are starting off again. The maid
begs them to stop ; her mother will redeem
her with her kirtles. But the mother says, I
have but two kirtles, and neither of them can
I give up for thee ; indeed thou mayst perish
in Friesland. Once more the Frisians are
about to put off. The maid says her lover
will redeem her with his ships. The lover
loyally responds, I have only two ships ; both
will I gladly part with for thee ; thou shalt
not perish in Friesland. It appears from a
note of Hammershaimb that the ballad might
be extended indefinitely by the maid's calling
upon brother, sister, and friends to redeem her
with their respective valuables.*

Icelandic. A ballad briefly mentioned at
p. 20 f of the volume of the Antiquarisk Tidsskrift, before cited. The Frisians call out,
Bear the Danish maid to the ships ! ' Bide,
Frisians, bide ; my kinsfolk will redeem me.'
Upon the sixth appeal, to her lover, the maid
is ransomed.

Swedish. ' Den Bortsålda,' the same ballad as the Färöe and the Icelandic, with an
absurd introductory stanza, in which the maid
is said to have been sold into the heathen
land by her parents for a bit of bread ; whence
the title. **A. a,** Afzelius, No 15, I, 73 ; †
b, Hofberg, Nerikes Gamla Minnen, p. 256,
No 5. **B.** Afzelius, I, 134. **C.** Rancken, Nå-

---

* " *Legen* kan nu fortsættes videre '' might imply that the
ballad was used as a game ; but it is presumable that the
author would have been explicit, had he meant this.

† Translated by George Stephens in the Foreign Quarterly Review, XXVI, 31.

gra prof af folksång, p. 6, No 2, with collation of three other copies. **D.** Eva Wigström, Folkdiktning, I, 62, No 29. **E.** Öberg, in Aminson, Bidrag, I, 23. **F.** Axelson, Vester-dalarne, p. 174, No 2, three stanzas, the rest said to be "entirely like" the Afzelius copies, which differ considerably. A maid is in the hands of sea-rovers, and they are on the point of rowing off with her. She wrings her hands, and calls to them to wait a while. She sees her father coming, who will redeem her with his oxen, and so she shall escape going to the heathen land to pine away. The father says he has but oxen two: the one he shall be using, the other he shall keep — låta stå ; and she will not scape going to the heathen land. The sailors lower their oars. The maid wrings her hands, and calls to them again to wait; she sees her mother coming, who will redeem her with her gold caskets. The mother says she has of gold caskets but two: the one she shall be using, the other shall let stay. The maid sees her sister, who will redeem her with her gold crowns. The sister has but two gold crowns, one of which she shall be using, the other will let be. The maid sees her brother, who will redeem her with his foals. The brother has but two foals: the one he shall be using, the other he will let be, and she will not scape from going to the heathen land to pine away. Then the maid sees her true-love coming, and calls to him to redeem her with his gold rings. "Of gold rings," he says, "I have no more than twelve : with six I shall redeem thee, six thou shalt have thyself ; so thou scapest going to the heathen land to pine away."

This is the story in **A**, and the chief variations of the other copies are in the things which the maid proposes to her kindred and her lover to redeem her with, and the number of these which they profess to have. The spuriousness of the introductory stanza, in which the girl is said to have been sold into the heathen land for dire need, is evident. The family have two oxen, two gold caskets, two gold crowns, two foals ; or even houses, gold caskets, gold chains, mills, more than five, **B**, and no doubt everything handsome about

them. In **D** the father is even a king. **E, F** lack this beginning. **C** concludes with a permissible imprecation on the part of the lover :

'Cursed be thy father, cursed be thy mother,
Cursed be thy sister, and even so thy brother!'

In **Danish** the ballad occurs in manuscripts, and has been printed as a broadside : Bergström's Afzelius, II, 63.

German. A. Gräter's Idunna und Hermode, 1814, p. 76, communicated by Abrahamson, one of the editors of the Danske Viser, as learned by him from a maid-servant of his mother, in Sleswig, not long after 1750. **B.** 'Liebesprobe,' Kretzschmer-Zuccalmaglio, II, 54, No 22, "from North Germany," apparently a little retouched. **C.** 'Des Liebsten Liebe die grösste Liebe,' Hoffmann und Richter, p. 43, No 23, Silesia. **D.** 'Loskauf,' Erk's Liederhort, p. 136, No 40, Saxony. **E.** 'Das losgekaufte Mädchen,' Erk und Irmer, II, 52, No 53, Saxony. **F.** 'Loskauf,' Erk's Liederhort, p. 138, No 40ᵃ, Brandenburg. **G.** 'O Schipmann,' Reiffenberg, p. 138, Westphalia. **H.** 'O Schipmann,' Reiffenberg, p. 10, No 5, Westphalia. **I.** 'Loskauf,' Uhland, p. 267, No 117, Westphalia. **J.** Köhler, in Anzeiger für deutsches Alterthum, VI, 268, from Friedrich Kind in " Abend-Zeitung, 1819, No 164, Kind's Erzählungen, 1822, p. 77," Auserwählte Unterhaltungen, Wien, 1827, I, 20. 'Die Losgekaufte,' in Kretzschmer, I, 181, is rewritten ; 'Loskauf,' in Simrock, No 39, p. 90, is made up from a variety of copies. Several of the versions come very near to one another, especially C-F, nor is there any noteworthy difference in the story of the whole series, save a single point in the last three. A maid whom seamen are carrying off begs them to stop or put back to land; she has a father who will not abandon her. She begs her father to part with coat, house, hat, watch, or bull, to save her from drowning ; the father refuses. Then, as before, she successively and vainly entreats her mother to redeem her with gold chain, ring, apron, gown, or silver trinkets ; her brother with silver buckles, hat, horse, sword, or coat; her sister with apron, dress, shoes, green wreath, or pearl wreath. Two of the four relatives are wanting in H, I, J. All of her blood refusing to ransom the maid, she calls upon her lover to sacrifice sword, horse, ring, golden hill, to save her, or, in H, I, J, to sell himself to the oar, and the lover is ready in every case. The redemption is not from slavery in a foreign land, but from drowning.

Esthonian. The ballad is known all over Esthonia, and a copy composed of two closely resembling versions is given by Neus, Ehstnische Volkslieder, p. 109, 'Die Ausgelöste.' A girl, taken captive in war, asks that the boats may put in, in order that she may find some one to buy her off. She appeals first to her mother, who might redeem her with the best of three aprons which she possesses, one of which is of gold web, another of silver, another of brass. A daughter, answers the mother, is a thing of to-day and to-morrow; my aprons are for life. Her father is next asked to ransom her with the best of three bulls which he owns, which have a horn of gold, silver, and brass respectively. His daughter is his for two days, his bulls for life. The brother is entreated to save her by the sacrifice of the best of his three horses, which have severally manes of gold, silver, and brass. His sister is his for two days, his horse for life. The sister is asked to part with the best of her three wreaths, which are of gold, silver, brass, for an only sister's sake. A sister is hers for a month or two, her wreath for life. Finally the maid turns to her truelove, who has three hats, one of brass, one of silver, one of gold, and entreats him to devote the best to her redemption. How long lasts a hat? he exclaims. A couple of days; but my betrothed for life! Another copy of the same ballad is given by Neus in Dorpater Jahrbücher, V, 228.

The ballad is equally popular in Finland: 'Lunastettava neiti,' Kanteletar, 1864, p. 283,

No 26, p. 285, No 27, ed. 1840, III, 131, 137, 273 f; Rancken, Några prof, p. 9.

In various Slavic ballads the man and maid change parts, and the man is ransomed by the generosity of his mistress when his kinsfolk have failed him.

Two Wendish ballads, Haupt and Schmaler, A, No 74, B, No 75, I, 107 ff, begin, like the popular German ballad 'Der Schäfer und der Edelmann,' with a shepherd's being thrown into prison by a nobleman for wearing a costume beyond his rank, and proud words besides. He sees his father coming, A, and asks him to pawn half a hundred sheep and get him out. The father prefers his half hundred sheep. He sees his mother coming, and asks her to pawn two cows and release him. She prefers her cows. He sees his brother coming, and asks him to pawn his horse. His brother prefers his horse. He sees his sister coming, and asks her to pawn a fine gown, but the gown again is much dearer in his sister's eyes. He sees his love coming, and asks her to pawn her coral necklace for his ransom, which she does, and he is released. In B he writes to father, mother, and sister to ransom him; they all tell him that if he were good for anything he would not be in prison. His love flies to him and ransoms him.[*]

Russian. Čelakowský, II, 106,[†] Sakharof, IV, 171, No 13. A young man in prison writes to father and mother for ransom; the whole family will have nothing to do with malefactors and robbers. His love, when written to, calls to her women to get her gold together, all that shall be needed to free him.

Little-Russian. Golovatsky, I, 48, No 8. An imprisoned youth writes to his father, Wilt thou ransom me, or shall I perish? How much must he give? Forty saddled horses. Better he should perish. He writes to his mother; she must give forty oxen with their yokes. She declines. He writes to his love;

---

[*] In the same collection, No 297, I, 297, there is no refusal on the part of the kindred, but what they offer is insufficient, and the maid succeeds by outbidding them. So in some of the corresponding German ballads, as Hoffmann und Richter, Nos 9, 10; Erk's Liederhort, Nos 51, 51ᵃ, 51ᵇ; Elwert, Ungedruckte Reste alten Gesangs, p. 43, = Liederhort, 51ᶜ; Longard, p. 22, No 11; Fiedler, p. 141. In Ulmann's Let-

tische Volkslieder, 1874, p. 168 (cited by Reiffenberg), 'Der losgekaufte Soldat,' a conscript writes to father, mother, brother, sister, to buy him off, and they devote horses, cows, lands, dowry, to this object, but do not succeed. His mistress sells her wreath and frees him.

[†] Goetze, Stimmen des russischen Volks, p. 150; Wenzig, Slawische Volkslieder, p. 151.

she must furnish forty geese with their goslings. I will spin, she says, spin lustily, buy geese, and ransom thee. No 7, I, 46, is to the same effect, but lacks the close.

Slovenian. 'Rodbina,' 'Kinship,' Vraz, Narodne Pĕsni ilirske, p. 141.* A hero in prison asks his father to release him; the three horses he must give are too much. He asks his mother; the three castles she must give are too much. He asks his brother; the

* Translated by Anastasius Grün, Volkslieder aus Krain, p. 30.

three rifles he must give are too much. He asks his sister; the three fair tresses she must sacrifice are too much. He asks his love; she must give her white hand. Not too much is my white hand, she says; easy to give for thee hand and life besides.

A Little-Russian ballad in Waclaw z Oleska, p. 226, and a Polish in Waldbrühl's Balalaika, p. 504, have the same theme, Love stronger than Blood (woman's love here), but do not belong with the pieces already cited as to form.

————————◆————————

A

Communicated to Percy, April 7, 1770, by the Rev. P. Parsons, of Wey, from oral tradition.

* * * * *

1 'O good Lord Judge, and sweet Lord Judge,
 Peace for a little while!
Methinks I see my own father,
 Come riding by the stile.

2 'Oh father, oh father, a little of your gold,
 And likewise of your fee!
To keep my body from yonder grave,
 And my neck from the gallows-tree.'

3 'None of my gold now you shall have,
 Nor likewise of my fee;
For I am come to see you hangd,
 And hanged you shall be.'

4 'Oh good Lord Judge, and sweet Lord Judge,
 Peace for a little while!
Methinks I see my own mother,
 Come riding by the stile.

5 'Oh mother, oh mother, a little of your gold,
 And likewise of your fee,
To keep my body from yonder grave,
 And my neck from the gallows-tree!'

6 'None of my gold now shall you have,
 Nor likewise of my fee;
For I am come to see you hangd,
 And hanged you shall be.'

7 'Oh good Lord Judge, and sweet Lord Judge,
 Peace for a little while!

Methinks I see my own brother,
 Come riding by the stile.

8 'Oh brother, oh brother, a little of your gold,
 And likewise of your fee,
To keep my body from yonder grave,
 And my neck from the gallows-tree!'

9 'None of my gold now shall you have,
 Nor likewise of my fee;
For I am come to see you hangd,
 And hanged you shall be.'

10 'Oh good Lord Judge, and sweet Lord Judge,
 Peace for a little while!
Methinks I see my own sister,
 Come riding by the stile.

11 'Oh sister, oh sister, a little of your gold,
 And likewise of your fee,
To keep my body from yonder grave,
 And my neck from the gallows-tree!'

12 'None of my gold now shall you have,
 Nor likewise of my fee;
For I am come to see you hangd,
 And hanged you shall be.'

13 'Oh good Lord Judge, and sweet Lord Judge,
 Peace for a little while!
Methinks I see my own true-love,
 Come riding by the stile.

14 'Oh true-love, oh true-love, a little of your gold,
 And likewise of your fee,

To save my body from yonder grave,
  And my neck from the gallows-tree.'

15 ' Some of my gold now you shall have,
  And likewise of my fee,

For I am come to see you saved,
  And saved you shall be.'

———•———

B

Motherwell MS., p. 290, from the recitation of Widow
McCormick; learned in Dumbarton.

*   *   *   *   *

1 ' It 's hold your hand, dear judge,' she says,
  ' O hold your hand for a while !
For yonder I see my father a coming,
  Riding many 's the mile.

2 ' Have you any gold, father ? ' she says,
  ' Or have you any fee ?
Or did you come to see your own daughter
    a hanging,
  Like a dog, upon a tree ? '

3 ' I have no gold, daughter,' he says,
  ' Neither have I any fee ;
But I am come to see my ain daughter hanged,
  And hanged she shall be.'

4 ' Hey the broom, and the bonny, bonny broom,
  The broom o the Cauthery Knowes !
I wish I were at hame again,
  Milking my ain daddie's ewes.

5 ' Hold your hand, dear judge,' she says,
  ' O hold your hand for a while !
For yonder I see my own mother coming,
  Riding full many a mile.

6 ' Have you any gold, mother ? ' she says,
  ' Or have you any fee ?
Or did you come to see your own daughter
    hanged,
  Like a dog, upon a tree ? '

7 ' I have no gold, daughter,' she says,
  ' Neither have I any fee ;
But I am come to see my own daughter
    hanged,
  And hanged she shall be.'

8 ' Hey the broom, the bonnie, bonnie broom,
  The broom o the Cauthery Knowes !
I wish I were at hame again,
  Milking my ain daddie's ewes.

9 ' Hold your hand, dear judge,' she says,
  ' O hold your hand for a while !
For yonder I see my ae brother a coming,
  Riding many 's the mile.

10 ' Have you any gold, brother ? ' she says,
  ' Or have you any fee ?
Or did you come to see your ain sister a hang-
    ing,
  Like a dog, upon a tree ? '

11 ' I have no gold, sister,' he says,
  ' Nor have I any fee ;
But I am come to see my ain sister hanged,
  And hanged she shall be.'

12 ' Hey the broom, the bonnie, bonnie broom,
  The broom o the Cathery Knowes !
I wish I were at hame again,
  Milking my ain daddie's ewes.

13 ' Hold your hand, dear judge,' she says,
  ' O hold your hand for a while !
For yonder I see my own true-love coming,
  Riding full many a mile.

14 ' Have you any gold, my true-love ? ' she says,
  ' Or have you any fee ?
Or have you come to see your own love
    hanged,
  Like a dog, upon a tree ? '

*   *   *   *   *

C

Notes and Queries, Sixth Series, VII, 275, 1883 : communicated by the Rev. E. Venables, Precentor of Lincoln, as sung by a nurse-maid from Woburn, near High Wycombe, Buckinghamshire, " between fifty and sixty years ago."

1 ' HOLD up thy hand, most righteous judge,
　　Hold up thy hand a while !
　For here I see my own dear father,
　　Come tumbling over the stile.

2 ' Oh hast thou brought me silver or gold,
　　Or jewels, to set me free ?
　Or hast thou come to see me hung ?
　　For hanged I shall be.

3 ' If I could get out of this prickly bush,
　　That prickles my heart so sore,

If I could get out of this prickly bush,
　I 'd never get in it no more.'

4 ' Oh I have brought nor silver nor gold,
　　Nor jewels, to set thee free ;
　But I have come to see thee hung,
　　For hanged thou shall be.

*　　*　　*　　*　　*

5 ' It 's I have brought thee silver and gold,
　　And jewels, to set thee free ;
　I have not come to see thee hung,
　　For hanged thou shall not be.'

6 ' Now I have got out of this prickly bush,
　　That prickled my heart so sore,
　And I have got out of this prickly bush,
　　I 'll never get in it no more.'

D

Skene MSS, p. 61, stanzas 19–24 : taken down in the north or northeast of Scotland, 1802–03.

1 .　.　　.　　.　.
　　' O had your hand a while !
　For yonder comes my father,
　　I 'm sure he 'l borrow me.

2 ' O some of your goud, father,
　　An of your well won fee !
　To save me [frae the high hill],
　　[And] frae the gallow-tree.'

3 ' Ye 's get nane of my goud,
　　Nor of my well won fee,

For I would gie five hundred poun
　To see ye hangit lie.'

4 .　.　　.　.　.　　.
　　' O had yer hand a while !
　Yonder is my love Willie,
　　Sure he will borrow me.

5 ' O some o your goud, my love Willie,
　　An some o yer well won fee !
　To save me frae the high hill,
　　And frae the gallow-tree.'

6 ' Ye 's get a' my goud,
　　And a' my well won fee,
　To save ye fra the headin-hill,
　　And frae the gallow-tree.'

E

Buchan's MSS, II, 186, stanzas 16–22.

1 ' HOLD your hands, ye justice o peace,
　　Hold them a little while !
　For yonder comes my father and mother,
　　That 's travelld mony a mile.

2 ' Gie me some o your gowd, parents,
　　Some o your white monie,
　To save me frae the head o yon hill,
　　Yon greenwood gallows-tree.'

3 ' Ye 'll get nane o our gowd, daughter,
　　Nor nane o our white monie,
　For we have travelld mony a mile,
　　This day to see you die.'

4 ' Hold your hands, ye justice o peace,
　　Hold them a little while !
　For yonder comes him Warenston,
　　The father of my chile.

5 ' Give me some o your gowd, Warenston,
　　Some o your white monie,

To save me frae the head o yon hill,
    Yon greenwood gallows-tree.'

6 'I bade you nurse my bairn well,
    And nurse it carefullie,
And gowd shoud been your hire, Maisry,
    And my body your fee.'

7 He 's taen out a purse o gowd,
    Another o white monie,
And he 's tauld down ten thousand crowns,
    Says, True-love, gang wi me.

F

Notes and Queries, Sixth Series, VI, 476, 1882 : "sung in Forfarshire, forty years ago."

1 'STOP, stop, . . .
  . . . .
I think I see my father coming,
  . . . .

2 'O hae ye brocht my silken cloak,
    Or my golden key?
Or hae ye come to see me hanged,
    On this green gallows-tree?'

3 'I've neither brocht your silken cloak,
    Nor your golden key,
But I have come to see you hanged,
    On this green gallows-tree.'

*   *   *   *   *

4 'I've neither brocht your silken cloak,
    Nor your golden key,
But I am come to set you free
    From this green gallows-tree.'

G

a. Notes and Queries, Sixth Series, VI, 415, 1882. b. The same, p. 269.

1 'HANGMAN, hangman, stop a minute,
  . . . .
I think I see my father coming,
  . . . .

2 'Father, father, have you found the key,
    And have you come to set me free?

Or have you come to see me hanged,
    Upon this gallows-tree?'

*   *   *   *   *

3 'I have not come to see you hanged,
    Upon the gallows-tree,
For I have found the golden key,'
  . . . .

H

a. Baring-Gould's Appendix to Henderson's Notes on the Folk Lore of the Northern Counties of England and the Borders, 1866, p. 333, Yorkshire. b. Notes and Queries, Sixth Series, X, 354, 1884.

1 'STOP, stop! . . .
  . . . .
I think I see my mother coming,
  . . . .

2 'Oh mother, hast brought my golden ball,
    And come to set me free?
  . . . .

3 'I've neither brought thy golden ball,
    Nor come to set thee free,
But I have come to see thee hung,
    Upon this gallows-tree.'

4 'Stop, stop! . . .
  . . . .
I think I see my father coming,
  . . . .

5 'O father, hast brought my golden ball,
    And come to set me free?
  . . . .

6 ' I 've neither brought thy golden ball,
    Nor come to set thee free,
But I have come to see thee hung,
    Upon this gallows-tree.'

7 ' Stop, stop !   .   .   .

    I see my sweet-heart coming,

8 ' Sweet-heart, hast brought my golden ball,
    And come to set me free ?

9 ' Aye, I have brought thy golden ball,
    And come to set thee free;
I have not come to see thee hung,
    Upon this gallows-tree.'

———◆———

B. *The title,* 'The Broom o the Cathery Knowes,'
    *is not prefixed to the ballad, but is given in
    the Index.*
    5⁴. *Changed by Motherwell to* many 's the mile,
    as in 1.
    12. Hey the broom, &c.
C. *This version, which the Rev. E. Venables has
    also communicated to me in manuscript, was
    tagged on to a fragment of* 'Hugh of Lin-
    coln.'
    After 4: " Mother, brother, sister, uncle, aunt,
    etc., succeed. At last comes the own true
    love, who replies."
D. 2³, ⁴. *Restored from stanza* 5.
F. " It was sung in Forfarshire forty years ago by
    girls during the progress of some game,
    which I do not now distinctly recollect. **A**
    lady, at the point of being executed, cries
    Stop, stop ! I think I see my father coming.
    Then, addressing her father, she asks," *as in
    stanza* 2 ; " to which the father replies," *as
    in stanza* 3. " Mother, brother, sister, are
    each addressed in turn, and give the same
    answer. Last of all the fair sinner sees her
    lover coming, and on putting the question to
    him is answered thus," *as in stanza* 4 ;
    " whereupon the game ends." *W. F.* (2),
    Saline Manse, Fife.
G. a. *Before stanza* 1: " I think the title of this
    ballad is ' The Golden Key.' The sub-
    stance of it is that a woman has lost a
    gold key, and is about to be hung, when
    she exclaims, *as in stanza* 1. Then fol-
    lows" *stanza* 2. *After* 2: " Father,
    mother, brother, sister, all in turn come
    up, and have not found the lost key. At
    last the sweet-heart appears, who ex-
    claims triumphantly," *as in stanza* 3. " I
    write this from memory. I never saw it
    in print." *H. Fishwick.*

b. " A lady writes to me, My mother used to
    hear, in Lancashire and Cheshire, a ballad
    of which she only recollects three lines :

> And I 'm not come to set you free,
> But I am come to see you hanged,
> All under the gallows-tree.

The last line was repeated, I believe, in
every verse." *William Andrews.*
H. a. *The verses form part of a Yorkshire story
    called* The Golden Ball. *A man gives
    a golden ball to each of two lasses, and if
    either loses the ball she is to be hanged.
    The younger, while playing with her ball,
    tosses it over a park-paling ; the ball runs
    away over the grass into a house, and is
    seen no more.*
    " Now t' lass was taken to York to be
    hanged. She was brought out on t' scaf-
    fold, and t' hangman said, Now, lass, tha
    must hang by t' neck till tha be'st dead.
    But she cried out, Stop, stop," *etc., stanzas*
    1–3.
    " Then the hangman said, Now, lass, say
    thy prayers, for tha must dee." *Stanzas*
    4–6 *follow. The maid thinks she sees her
    brother coming, her sister, uncle, aunt,
    cousin. The hangman then says,* " I
    wee-nt stop no longer, tha 's making gam
    of me. Tha must be hung at once. But
    now she saw her sweetheart coming through
    the crowd, and he had over head i t' air
    her own golden ball. So she said," *as in
    stanzas* 7–9.
b. *Miss Kate Thompson, of Newcastle-or-
    Tyne, had when a child frequently been
    told the story of* The Golden Ball *by a
    woman who was a native of the Border-
    land. A rich lady possessed a golden*

*ball, which she held in high esteem. A
poor girl, her servant, had to clean this
ball every day, and it was death to lose
it. One day when she was cleaning the
ball near a stream it disappeared. The
girl was condemned to die, and had
mounted the scaffold. The story was all
in prose up to the execution, when the
narrator broke into rhyme:*

'Stop the rope! stop the rope!
For here I see my mother coming.

'Oh mother, have you brought the
    golden ball,
    And come to set me free?
Or are you only here to see me die,
    Upon the high, high gallows-tree?'

*The mother answers that she has only
come to see her die. Other relatives follow, and last of all comes the lover, who
produces the ball, and the execution is
stopped. Miss Thompson adds that two
Northumbrian servants in her house remember the story so.*

96

THE GAY GOSHAWK

A. 'The Gay Goss Hawk,' Jamieson-Brown MS., fol. 15, No 6.

B. Motherwell's MS., p. 230.

C. 'The Jolly Goshawk,' Motherwell's MS., p. 435; Motherwell's Minstrelsy, p. 353.

D. 'The Gay Goss-hawk,' Motherwell's Note-Book, 27; Motherwell's MS., p. 415.

E. 'The Gay Goss-hawk,' Minstrelsy of the Scottish Border, II, 7, 1802.

F. Communicated by Miss Reburn, as sung in County Meath, Ireland.

G. 'The Scottish Squire,' Buchan's Ballads of the North of Scotland, II, 245.

THE 'Gay Goshawk' first appeared in print in the second volume of Scott's Minstrelsy, in 1802. Scott's copy was formed partly from Mrs Brown's version, **A**, "and partly from a MS. of some antiquity *penes Edit.*" This compounded copy is now given, **E**, with those portions which are contained in the Brown MS. printed in smaller type, in order that what is peculiar to the other manuscript may be distinguished. A second copy of **A** was made for William Tytler under the direction of the reciter in 1783, but has not been recovered. There were 28 stanzas, as in **A**, and the first stanza has been given by Anderson in Nichols's Illustrations, VII, 176. **C** was furnished Motherwell by Buchan from a manuscript sent

him, and Buchan says that he himself took down from recitation the vilely dilated and debased **G**: Ballads of the North of Scotland, II, 340.

A ballad widely known in France has the central idea of the Gay Goshawk, a maid's feigning death to escape from a father to a lover whom she is not permitted to marry, but in the development of the story there is no likeness. A version of this ballad, 'Belle Isambourg,' was printed as early as 1607 in a collection with the title Airs de Cour, p. 40, and was republished by Rathery in the Moniteur of August 26, 1853, p. 946, afterwards in Haupt's Französische Volkslieder, p. 92. The king wishes to give Fair Isambourg a husband, but her heart is fixed on a handsome knight, whom she loves more than all her kin together, though he is poor. The king shuts her up in a dark tower, thinking that this treatment will bring about a change, but it does not. Isambourg sees her lover riding towards or by the tower at full speed. She calls to him to stop, and says:

> Malade et morte m'y feray,
> Porter en terre m'y lairray,
> Pourtant morte je ne seray.

> Puis apres je vous prie amy,
> Qu'à ma chapelle à Sainct-Denis
> Ne m'y laissez pas enfouir.

Isambourg is now proclaimed to be dead, and is carried to burial by three princes and a knight. Her lover, hearing the knelling and chanting, puts himself in the way and bids the bearers stop. Since she has died for loving him too well, he wishes to say a De profundis. He rips open a little of the shroud, and she darts a loving smile at him. Everybody is astonished.

Other versions, derived from oral tradition, have a more popular stamp: (1.) Poésies populaires de la France, MS., III, 54, 'La fille du roi et le Prince de Guise,' learned at Maubeuge, about 1760. (2.) III, 47, 'Le beau Déon,' Auvergne. (3.) III, 49, 'La princesse de la Grand' Tour,' Berry. (4.) III, 50 (the hero being Léon), Berry. (5.) III, 53, Caudebec. (6.) III, 56, Pamiers, Languedoc. (7.) III, 57, and II, 52, Orléans. (8.) 'La fille d'un prince,' Buchon, Noëls et chants p. de la Franche-Comté, p. 82, No 16. (9.) 'La fille d'un prince,' Rondes et Chansons p. illustrées, Paris, 1876, p. 286. (10.) 'La princesse,' Guillon, Chansons p. de l'Ain, p. 87. (11.) 'La maîtresse captive,' Puymaigre, Chants p. messins, I, 87. (12.) Le Héricher, Littérature p. de Normandie, p. 153 f. (13.) 'De Dion et de la fille du roi,' Ampère, Instructions, p. 38, the first fourteen stanzas; Auvergne. (14.) G. de Nerval, La Bohème Galante, ed. 1866, p. 70, and Les Faux Saulniers, ed. 1868, p. 346, the story completed in Les Filles du Feu, ed. 1868, p. 132; or, in the collection lately made from his works,

Chansons et Ballades p. du Valois, p. 16, VIII. The last two have a false termination, as already remarked under No 4, I, 42.

In these traditional versions, the father pays a visit to the princess after she has been confined seven years, and asks how she is. One side is eaten away by worms, her feet are rotting in the irons. She begs a few sous to give the jailer to loosen her fetters. Millions are at her disposal if she will give up her lover. Rather rot, is her reply. Rot, then, says her father. The lover comes by and throws a few words of writing into the tower, directing her to counterfeit death. The rest is much the same. In several versions the king yields.

There are many other ballads in which a girl, for one reason or another, feigns death. In 'Les trois capitaines,' or 'La jolie fille de la Garde,' etc., Arbaud, I, 143, Decombe, Ch. p. d'Ille-et-Vilaine, p. 150, No 51, Champfleury, Ch. p. des Provinces, p. 95, Bujeaud, II, 174, 'La Bohème Galante,' ed. 1866, p. 71 f, Chansons du Valois, p. 19, IX, Puymaigre, Vieux Auteurs, II, 478, E. Legrand, Romania, X, 369, No 6, the object is to save her honor;* so in Marcoaldi, p. 162, No 10, Ferraro, C. p. monferrini, p. 41, No 31. The well-disposed hostess of an inn administers a sleeping-draught, in Arbaud's ballad and in Decombe's. The object is to avoid becoming a king's mistress, in 'Kvindelist,' Grundtvig, IV, 394, No 235, 'Hertig Hillebrand och hans Syster,' Arwidsson, I, 380 No 61; in a Bohemian ballad, to avoid marrying a Turk, 'Oklamaný Turek,' 'The Turk duped,' Celakovský, III, 11 (translated in Bowring's Cheskian Anthology, p. 129) Erben, p. 485, etc., etc.; to move a lover who is on the point of deserting, Hoffmann, Niederländische Volkslieder, p. 61, No 15, Willems, No 60, Uhland, No 97 B.

In 'Willie's Lyke-Wake,' No 25, I, 247, a man feigns death in order to capture a coy maid, or a maid refused him by her parents.

Birds are not seldom employed as posts in ballads: see 'Sweet William,' Motherwell's Minstrelsy, p. 307, Milá, Romancerillo, No 258; Hartung, Romanceiro, I, 193 (dove).

---

* Or her soul, in a copy which terminates with a miracle, Victor Smith, Chansons du Velay, etc., Romania, IV, 114: where see note 2.

A falcon carries a letter, in Afzelius, III, 116, No 87, and Milá, No 258 K, and Marko Kraljevitch sends a letter by a falcon from his prison, Karadshitch, II, 383. For a love-message of a general sort, not involving business, the nightingale is usually and rightly selected. On the other hand, a nightingale first orders a ring of a goldsmith, and afterwards delivers it to a lady, in Uhland, No 15.* In this ballad the goshawk is endowed with the nightingale's voice. The substitution of a parrot in G, a bird that we all know can talk, testifies to the advances made by reason among the humblest in the later generations.† A parrot, says Buchan, " is by far a more likely messenger to carry a love-letter or deliver a verbal message," II, 341. The parrot goes well with the heroine swooning on a sofa (stanza 33) and the step-dame sitting on the sofa's end (stanza 36).

Thieves drop three drops of *wax* on the breast of a servant-girl who is feigning sleep, and she shows no sign of feeling, in a Catalan ballad, Milá, Romancerillo, p. 104, No 114, vv 13–16, Observaciones, p. 147, No 43, Briz, I, 147. ‡

Translated by Grundtvig, Engelske og skotske Folkeviser, No 32, after E, C, G. After D by Talvj, Versuch, u. s. w., p. 560; Schubart, p. 57; Doenniges, p. 19; Gerhard, p. 37; Loève-Veimars, p. 264. By Knortz, Lieder Alt-Englands, No 2, after C; by Rosa Warrens, Schottische Volkslieder, No 38, after C and E, sometimes following Aytoun, I, 178.

A

Jamieson-Brown MS., No 6, pt 15.

1 'O WELL 's me o my gay goss-hawk,
　That he can speak and flee ;
　He 'll carry a letter to my love,
　Bring back another to me.'

2 ' O how can I your true-love ken,
　Or how can I her know ?
　Whan frae her mouth I never heard couth,
　Nor wi my eyes her saw.'

3 'O well sal ye my true-love ken,
　As soon as you her see ;
　For, of a' the flowrs in fair Englan,
　The fairest flowr is she.

4 ' At even at my love's bowr-door
　There grows a bowing birk,
　An sit ye down and sing thereon,
　As she gangs to the kirk.

5 ' An four-and-twenty ladies fair
　Will wash and go to kirk,
　But well shall ye my true-love ken,
　For she wears goud on her skirt.

6 ' An four and twenty gay ladies
　Will to the mass repair,
　But well sal ye my true-love ken,
　For she wears goud on her hair.'

7 O even at that lady's bowr-door
　There grows a bowin birk,
　An she set down and sang thereon,
　As she ged to the kirk.

8 'O eet and drink, my marys a',
　The wine flows you among,
　Till I gang to my shot-window,
　An hear yon bonny bird's song.

9 'Sing on, sing on, my bonny bird,
　The song ye sang the streen,
　For I ken by your sweet singin
　You 're frae my true-love sen.'

---

* See Uhland, III, 109 f, 171.

† The contrast presented by darker ages, when cheap literature was unknown, may be seen from these verses :

> Ma mie reçoit de mes lettres
> 　Pàr l'alouette des champs ;
> Elle m'envoie les siennes
> 　Par le rossignol chantant.

> Sans savoir lire ni écrire
> 　Nous lisons ce qui est dedans ;

> Il y a dedans ces lettres,
> 　'Aime moi, je t'aime tant.'
> 　　　　　(Le Moniteur, May 27, 1853.)

‡ The " red, red lead " of D 7, 8 I had at first supposed to show a carelessness about epithets, like the " roses blue " of a Danish ballad. But considering that the red lead is to be *rubbed on*, one may ask whether some occult property of minium may have been known to the mother.

10 O first he sang a merry song,
   An then he sang a grave,
   An then he peckd his feathers gray,
   To her the letter gave.

11 'Ha, there's a letter frae your love,
   He says he sent you three;
   He canna wait your love langer,
   But for your sake he'll die.

12 'He bids you write a letter to him;
 • He says he's sent you five;
   He canno wait your love langer,
   Tho you're the fairest woman alive.'

13 'Ye bid him bake his bridal-bread,
   And brew his bridal-ale,
   An I'll meet him in fair Scotlan
   Lang, lang or it be stale.'

14 She's doen her to her father dear,
   Fa'n low down on her knee:
   'A boon, a boon, my father dear,
   I pray you, grant it me.'

15 'Ask on, ask on, my daughter,
   An granted it sal be;
   Except ae squire in fair Scotlan,
   An him you sall never see.'

16 'The only boon, my father dear,
   That I do crave of the,
   Is, gin I die in southin lands,
   In Scotland to bury me.

17 'An the firstin kirk that ye come till,
   Ye gar the bells be rung,
   An the nextin kirk that ye come till,
   Ye gar the mess be sung.

18 'An the thirdin kirk that ye come till,
   You deal gold for my sake,
   An the fourthin kirk that ye come till,
   You tarry there till night.'

19 She is doen her to her bigly bowr,
   As fast as she coud fare,

An she has tane a sleepy draught,
That she had mixed wi care.

20 She's laid her down upon her bed,
   An soon she's fa'n asleep,
   And soon oer every tender limb
   Cauld death began to creep.

21 Whan night was flown, an day was come,
   Nae ane that did her see
   But thought she was as surely dead
   As ony lady coud be.

22 Her father an her brothers dear
   Gard make to her a bier;
   The tae half was o guide red gold,
   The tither o silver clear.

23 Her mither an her sisters fair
   Gard work for her a sark;
   The tae half was o cambrick fine,
   The tither o needle wark.

24 The firstin kirk that they came till,
   They gard the bells be rung,
   An the nextin kirk that they came till,
   They gard the mess be sung.

25 The thirdin kirk that they came till,
   They dealt gold for her sake,
   An the fourthin kirk that they came till,
   Lo, there they met her make!

26 'Lay down, lay down the bigly bier,
   Lat me the dead look on;'
   Wi cherry cheeks and ruby lips
   She lay an smil'd on him.

27 'O ae sheave o your bread, true-love,
   An ae glass o your wine,
   For I hae fasted for your sake
   These fully days is nine.

28 'Gang hame, gang hame, my seven bold
      brothers,
   Gang hame and sound your horn;
   An ye may boast in southin lans
   Your sister's playd you scorn.'

B

Motherwell's MS., p. 230 : from the recitation of Mrs Bell, f Paisley, and of Miss Montgomerie, of Edinburgh, her sister.

1 Out then spoke the king of Scotland,
    And he spak wondrous clear :
Where will I get a boy, and a pretty little boy,
    That will my tidings bear ?

2 Out then spak a pretty little bird,
    As it sat on a brier :
What will ye gie me, king of Scotland, he
      said,
    If I your tidings will bear ?

3 'One wing of the beaten gowd,
    And another of the silver clear ;
It's all unto thee, my pretty little bird,
    If thou my tidings will bear.'

4 The bird flew high, the bird flew low,
    This bird flew to and fro,
Until that he came to the king of England's
      dochter,
    Who was sitting in her bower-window.

5 'Here is a gift, a very rare gift,
    And the king has sent you three ;
He says if your father and mother winna let,
    You may come privately.

6 'Here is a gift, and a very rare gift,
    The king has sent you five ;
He says he will not wait any longer on you,
    If there be another woman alive.'

7 She's away to her mother dear,
    Made a low beck on her knee :
'What is your asking of me, daughter ?
    Queen of Scotland you never shall be.'

8 'That's not my asking of thee, mother,
    That's not my asking of thee ;
But that if I die in merry England,
    In Scotland you will bury me.'

9 She's awa to her father dear,
    Made a low beck on her knee :
'What is your asking of me, daughter ?
    Queen of Scotland you never shall be.'

10 'That's not my asking of thee, father,
    That's not my asking of thee ;

But that if I die in merry England,
    In Scotland you will bury me.'

11 She walked to and fro,
    She walked up and down,
But ye wud na spoken three words to an
      end
    Till she was in a deep swoon.

12 Out then spoke an auld witch-wife,
    And she spoke random indeed :
Honoured madam, I would have you to try
    Three drops of the burning lead.

13 Her mother went weeping round and round,
    She dropped one on her chin ;
'Och and alace,' her mother did say,
    'There is no breath within ! '

14 Her mother went weeping round and round,
    She dropt one on her briest ;
'Och and alace,' her mother did cry,
    'For she's died without a priest ! '

15 Her mother went weeping round and round,
    She dropped one on her toe ;
'Och and alace,' her mother did cry,
    'To Scotland she must goe !

16 'Call down, call down her sisters five,
    To make to her a smock ;
The one side of the bonny beaten gold,
    And the other of the needle-work.

17 'Call down, call down her brothers seven,
    To make for her a bier ;
The one side of the bonny beaten gold,
    And the other of the silver clear.'

18 Many a mile by land they went,
    And many a league by sea,
Until that they came to the king of Scotland,
    Who was walking in his own valley.

19 'Here is a gift, and a very rare gift,
    And you to have made her your own ;
But now she is dead, and she's new come from
      her steed,
    And she's ready to lay in the ground.'

20 O he has opened the lid of the coffin,
    And likewise the winding sheet,

And thrice he has kissed her cherry, cherry
  cheek,
  And she smiled on him full sweet.

21 'One bit of your bread,' she says,
  'And one glass of your wine;
  It's all for you and your sake
  I've fasted long days nine.

22 'One glass of your wine,' she says,
  'And one bit of your bread;

For it's all for you and for your sake
  I suffered the burning lead.

23 'Go home, go home, my brothers seven,
  You may go blow your horn;
  And you may tell it in merry England
  That your sister has given you the scorn.

24 'Go home, go home, my brothers seven,
  Tell my sisters to sew their seam;
  And you may tell it in merry England
  That your sister she is queen.'

———◆———

C

Motherwell's MS., p. 435; communicated by Peter Buchan, from a MS. which had been sent him.

1 'O WELL is me, my jolly goshawk,
  That ye can speak and flee,
  For ye can carry a love-letter
  To my true-love from me.'

2 'O how can I carry a letter to her,
  When her I do not knaw?
  I bear the lips to her never spake,
  And the eyes that her never saw.'

3 'The thing of my love's face is white
  It's that of dove or maw;
  The thing of my love's face that's red
  Is like blood shed on snaw.

4 'And when you come to the castle,
  Light on the bush of ash,
  And sit you there and sing our loves,
  As she comes from the mass.

5 'And when she goes into the house,
  Sit ye upon the whin;
  And sit you there and sing our loves,
  As she goes out and in.'

6 And when he flew to that castel,
  He lighted on the ash;
  And there he sat and sang their loves,
  As she came from the mass.

7 And when she went into the house,
  He flew unto the whin;
  And there he sat and sang their loves,
  As she went out and in.

8 'Come hither, come hither, my maidens all,
  And sip red wine anon,
  Till I go to my west window,
  And hear a birdie's moan.'

9 She's gone unto her west window,
  And fainly aye it drew,
  And soon into her white silk lap
  The bird the letter threw.

10 'Ye're bidden send your love a send,
  For he has sent you twa;
  And tell him where he can see you,
  Or he cannot live ava.'

11 'I send him the rings from my white fingers,
  The garlands off my hair;
  I send him the heart that's in my breast:
  What would my love have mair?
  And at the fourth kirk in fair Scotland,
  Ye'll bid him meet me there.'

12 She hied her to her father dear,
  As fast as gang could she:
  'An asking, an asking, my father dear,
  An asking ye grant me;
  That, if I die in fair England,
  In Scotland bury me.

13 'At the first kirk of fair Scotland,
  You cause the bells be rung;
  At the second kirk of fair Scotland,
  You cause the mass be sung.

14 'At the third kirk of fair Scotland,
  You deal gold for my sake;
  And the fourth kirk of fair Scotland,
  O there you'll bury me at.

15 'And now, my tender father dear,
    This asking grant you me;'
'Your asking is but small,' he said,
    'Weel granted it shall be.'

16 She hied her to her mother dear,
    As fast as gang could she :
'An asking, an asking, my mother dear,
    An asking ye grant me ;
That if I die in fair England
    In Scotland bury me.

17 'And now, my tender mother dear,
    This asking grant you me;'
'Your asking is but small,' she said,
    'Weel granted it shall be.'

18 She hied her to her sister dear,
    As fast as gang could she:
'An asking, an asking, my sister dear,
    An asking ye grant me ;
That if I die in fair England,
    In Scotland bury me.

19 'And now, my tender sister dear,
    This asking grant you me :'
'Your asking is but small,' she said,
    'Weel granted it shall be.'

20 She hied her to her seven brothers,
    As fast as gang could she :
'An asking, an asking, my brothers seven,
    An asking ye grant me ;
That if I die in fair England,
    In Scotland ye bury me.

21 'And now, my tender brothers dear,
    This asking grant you me :'
'Your asking is but small,' they said,
    'Weel granted it shall be.'

22 Then down as dead that lady drapd,
    Beside her mother's knee;
Then out it spoke an auld witch-wife,
    By the fire-side sat she.

23 Says, Drap the hot lead on her cheek,
    And drop it on her chin,
And drop it on her rose-red lips,
    And she will speak again :
For much a lady young will do,
    To her true-love to win.

24 They drapd the het lead on her cheek,
    So did they on her chin ;
They drapt it on her red-rose lips,
    But they breathed none again.

25 Her brothers they went to a room,
    To make to her a bier ;
The boards of it was cedar wood,
    And the plates ow it gold so clear.

26 Her sisters they went to a room,
    To make to her a sark ;
The cloth of it was satin fine,
    And the steeking silken wark.

27 'But well is me, my jolly goshawk,
    That ye can speak and flee ;
Come shew to me any love-tokens
    That you have brought to me.'

28 'She sends you the rings from her fingers,
    The garlands from her hair;
She sends you the heart within her breast;
    And what would you have mair?
And at the fourth kirk of fair Scotland,
    She bids you meet her there.'

29 'Come hither, all my merry young men,
    And drink the good red wine ;
For we must on to fair Scotland,
    To free my love frae pine.'

30 At the first kirk of fair Scotland,
    They gart the bells be rung ;
At the second kirk of fair Scotland,
    They gart the mass be sung.

31 At the third kirk of fair Scotland,
    They dealt gold for her sake ;
And the fourth kirk of fair Scotland
    Her true-love met them at.

32 'Set down, set down the corpse,' he said,
    'Till I look on the dead ;
The last time that I saw her face,
    She ruddy was and red ;
But now, alas, and woe is me !
    She 's wallowit like a weed.'

33 He rent the sheet upon her face,
    A little above her chin ;
With lily-white cheeks, and lemin een,
    She lookt and laughd to him.

34 'Give me a chive of your bread, my love,
　　A bottle of your wine ;
　For I have fasted for your love
　　These long days nine ;
　There 's not a steed in your stable
　　But would have been dead ere syne.

35 'Go home, go home, my seven brothers,
　　Go home and blow the horn ;
　For you can say in the south of England
　　Your sister gave you a scorn.

36 'I came not here to fair Scotland
　　To lye amang the meal ;
　But I came here to fair Scotland
　　To wear the silks so weel.

37 'I came not here to fair Scotland
　　To ly amang the dead ;
　But I came here to fair Scotland
　　To wear the gold so red.'

———————

D

Motherwell's Note-Book, pp 27–30, Motherwell's MS., pp
415–17 ; from Agnes Laird, Kilbarchan, August 24, 1825.

1 'O WHERE 'LL I get a pretty little bird
　　That 'll go my errand soon,
　That will fly to the Queen of England's doch-
　　ter,
　　And bid my trew-luve come ? '

2 'Here am I, a pretty little bird,
　　That 'll go your errands soon,
　That will fly to the Queen of England's daugh-
　　ter,
　　And bid your trew-luve come.'

3 This wee birdie 's taken its flight,
　　And it 's flown owre the sea,
　Until it cam to the Queen of England's daugh-
　　ter ;
　　She 's sitting in her bower-windie.

4 Then out bespoke these nine ladies,
　　As they sat in a ring :
　'O we 'll awa to the west window,
　　To hear this birdie sing.'

5 This wee birdie 's taken its flight,
　　And it 's flown owre them a',
　And at the lady's left shoulder
　　It loot a letter fa.

6 She has taken the letter up,
　　And read it speedilie :
　' O mother, the queen, O mother, the queen,
　　Grant this request to me ;
　Whenever I do chance for to die,
　　In Scotland gar bury me.'

*　　*　　*　　*　　*

7 'Bring to me the red, red lead,
　　And rub it on her chin ;
　It 's Oh and alace for my dochter Janet !
　　But there is not a breath within.

8 'Bring to me the red, red lead,
　　And rub it on her toe ;
　It 's Oh and alace for my daughter Janet !
　　To Scotland she must go.'

9 'Rise up, rise up, ye seven sisters,
　　And make her winding sheet,
　With the one side of the beaten gold,
　　And the other o the needle-wark.

10 'Rise up, rise up, ye seven brethren,
　　And make her carriage-bier,
　With the one side of the beaten gold,
　　And the other o the silver clear.'

11 They 've carried east, they 've carried west,
　　They 've carried her high and low,
　Until that they came to the king of Scotland,
　　Was sitting in his bower-window.

12 'Here is a token of your trew-love,
　　And here is a token come down,
　For she is dead, and she 's ready to be buried,
　　And she wants to be laid in your ground.'

13 He 's taen out his mickle knife,
　　And tore her winding sheet,
　And there she lay like the crimson red,
　　And she smiled in his face so sweet.

14 'Go home, go home, you seven brethren,
　　Go home and saw your corn,
　For she is fit for the queen of Scotland now,
　　And she 's gien you the scorn.

15 'Go home, go home, you seven sisters,
　　Go home and sew your seam,
　For she is fit for the queen of Scotland now,
　　And she 's ready to be my queen.'

———·———

E

Minstrelsy of the Scottish Border, II, 7, 1802; III, 151,
1833.

1 'O WALY, waly, my gay goss-hawk,
　　Gin your feathering be sheen!'
　'And waly, waly, my master dear,
　　Gin ye look pale and lean!

2 'O have ye tint at tournament
　　Your sword, or yet your spear?
　Or mourn ye for the southern lass,
　　Whom you may not win near?'

3 'I have not tint at tournament
　　My sword, nor yet my spear,
　But sair I mourn for my true-love,
　　Wi mony a bitter tear.

4 'But weel 's me on ye, my gay goss-hawk,
　　Ye can baith speak and flee;
　Ye sall carry a letter to my love,
　　Bring an answer back to me.'

5 'But how sall I your true-love find,
　　Or how suld I her know?
　I bear a tongue neer wi her spake,
　　An eye that neer her saw.'

6 'O weel sall ye my true-love ken,
　　Sae sune as ye her see,
　For of a' the flowers of fair England,
　　The fairest flower is she.

7 'The red that 's on my true-love's cheik
　　Is like blood-drops on the snaw;
　The white that is on her breast bare
　　Like the down o the white sea-maw.

8 'And even at my love's bouer-door
　　There grows a flowering birk,
　And ye maun sit and sing thereon,
　　As she gangs to the kirk.

9 'And four-and-twenty fair ladyes
　　Will to the mass repair,

　　But weel may ye my ladye ken,
　　　The fairest ladye there.'

10 Lord William has written a love-letter,
　　Put it under his pinion gray,
　And he is awa to southern land,
　　As fast as wings can gae.

11 And even at that ladye's bour
　　There grew a flowering birk,
　And he sat down and sang thereon,
　　As she gaed to the kirk.

12 And weel he kent that ladye feir
　　Amang her maidens free,
　For the flower that springs in May morning
　　Was not sae sweet as she.

13 [He lighted at the ladye's yate,
　　And sat him on a pin,
　And sang fu sweet the notes o love,
　　Till a' was cosh within.]

14 And first he sang a low, low note,
　　And syne he sang a clear,
　And aye the oerword of the sang
　　Was, Your love can no win here.

15 'Feast on, feast on, my maidens a',
　　The wine flows you amang,
　While I gang to my shot-window,
　　And hear yon bonny bird's sang.

16 'Sing on, sing on, my bonny bird,
　　The sang ye sung yestreen;
　For weel I ken by your sweet singing
　　Ye are frae my true-love sen.'

17 O first he sang a merry sang,
　　And syne he sang a grave,
　And syne he peckd his feathers gray,
　　To her the letter gave.

18 'Have there a letter from Lord William;
　　He says he 's sent ye three;

He canna wait your love langer,
　　But for your sake he 'll die.'

19 ' Gae bid him bake his bridal bread,
　　And brew his bridal ale,
　And I sall meet him at Mary's kirk,
　　Lang, lang·ere it be stale.'

20 The lady 's gane to her chamber,
　　And a moanfu woman was she,
　As gin she had taen a sudden brash,
　　And were about to die.

21 ' A boon, a boon, my father deir,
　　A boon I beg of thee ! '
　' Ask not that paughty Scotish lord,
　　For him you neer shall see.

22 ' But, for your honest asking else,
　　Weel granted it shall be : '
　' Then, gin I die in southern land,
　　In Scotland gar bury me.

23 ' And the first kirk that ye come to,
　　Ye 's gar the mass be sung,
　And the next kirk that ye come to,
　　Ye 's gar the bells be rung.

24 ' And when ye come to St Mary's kirk,
　　Ye 's tarry there till night : '
　And so her father pledged his word,
　　And so his promise plight.

25 She has taen her to her bigly bour,
　　As fast as she could fare,
　And she has drank a sleepy draught,
　　That she had mixed wi care.

26 And pale, pale grew her rosy cheek,
　　That was sae bright of blee,
　And she seemed to be as surely dead
　　As any one could be.

27 They drapt a drap o the burning red gowd,
　　They drapt it on her chin ;
　' And ever alas,' her mother cried,
　　' There is nae life within ! '

28 They drapt a drap o the burning red gowd,
　　They drapt it on her breast-bane ;

' Alas,' her seven bauld brothers said,
　　' Our sister 's dead and gane ! '

29 Then up arose her seven brethren,
　　And hewd to her a bier ;
　They hewd it frae the solid aik,
　　Laid it oer wi silver clear.

30 Then up and gat her seven sisters,
　　And sewed to her a kell,
　And every steek that they pat in
　　Sewd to a siller bell.

31 The first Scots kirk that they cam to,
　　They gard the bells be rung ;
　The next Scots kirk that they cam to,
　　They gard the mass be sung.

32 But when they cam to St Mary's kirk,
　　There stude spearmen all on raw,
　And up and started Lord William,
　　The chieftane amang them a'.

33 ' Set down, set down the bier,' he said,
　　' Let me looke her upon : '
　But as soon as Lord William touched her hand,
　　Her colour began to come.

34 She brightened like the lily-flower,
　　Till her pale colour was gone ;
　With rosy cheek, and ruby lip,
　　She smiled her love upon.

35 ' A morsel of your bread, my lord,
　　And one glass of your wine,
　For I hae fasted these three lang days,
　　All for your sake and mine.

36 ' Gae hame, gae hame, my seven bauld brothers,
　　Gae hame and blaw your horn ;
　I trow you wad hae gien me the skaith,
　　But I 've gien you the scorn.

37 ' Ah woe to you, you light woman,
　　An ill death may you die !
　For we left father and mother at hame
　　Breaking their hearts for thee.'

F

From Miss Margaret Reburn, as sung in County Meath, Ireland, about 1860.

* * * * *

1 SHE got three drops of boiling lead,
   And dropped them on her hand :
   ' Oh and alas, my daughter dear,
   I 'd rather all my land ! '

2 She got three drops of boiling lead,
   And dropped them on her chin :

' Oh and alas, my daughter dear,
   There is no life within ! '

3 She got three drops of boiling lead,
   And dropped them on her toe :
   ' Oh and alas, my daughter dear,
   To fair Scotland you must go ! '

* * * * *

4 ' Give me a cake of the new made bread,
   And a cup of the new made wine,
   For for your sake, Lord Thomas,' she said,
   ' I fasted those days nine.'

G

Buchan's Ballads of the North of Scotland, II, 245, "from recitation."

1 WHEN grass grew green on Lanark plains,
   And fruit and flowers did spring,
   A Scottish squire in cheerfu strains,
   Sae merrily thus did sing :

2 ' O well fails me o my parrot
   That he can speak and flee ;
   For he will carry love-letters
   Between my love and me.

3 ' And well fails me o my parrot
   He can baith speak and gang ;
   And he will carry love-letters
   To the maid in South England.'

4 ' O how shall I your love find out ?
   Or how shall I her know ?
   When my tongue with her never spake,
   Nor my eyes her ever saw.'

5 ' O what is red of her is red
   As blude drappd on the snaw ;
   And what is white o her is white
   As milk, or the sea-maw.

6 ' Even before that lady's yetts
   You'll find a bowing birk ;
   And there ye 'll sit, and sing thereon,
   Till she gaes to the kirk.

7 ' Then even before that lady's yetts
   You 'll find a bowing ash ;
   And ye may sit and sing thereon,
   Till she comes frae the mass.

8 ' And even before that lady's window
   You 'll find a bed o tyme ;
   And ye may sit and sing thereon,
   Till she sits down to dine.

9 ' Even abeen that lady's window
   There 's fixd a siller pin ;
   And a' these words that I tell you,
   Ye 'll sit and sing therein.

10 ' Ye 'll bid her send her love a letter,
   For he has sent her five ;
   And he 'll never send anither ane,
   To nae woman alive.

11 ' Ye 'll bid her send her love a letter,
   For he has sent her seven ;
   And he 'll never send anither send,
   To nae maid under heaven.'

12 This little bird then took his flight,
   Beyond the raging sea,
   And lighted at that lady's yetts,
   On tower o gowd sae hie.

13 Even before that lady's yetts
   He found a bowing birk ;
   And there he sat, and sang thereon,
   Till she went to the kirk.

14 Even before that lady's yetts
   He found a bowing ash ;
   And then he sat and sang thereon,
   Till she came frae the mass.

15 Even before that lady's window
   He found a bed o tyme ;
   And then he sat and sang thereon,
   Till she sat down to dine.

16 Even abeen that lady's window
    Was fixd a siller pin ;
  And a' the words that were tauld him,
    He sat and sang them in.

17 ' You 're bidden send your love a letter,
    For he has sent you five ;
  Or he 'll never send anither send,
    To nae woman alive.

18 ' You 're bidden send your love a letter,
    For he has sent you seven ;
  And he 'll never send anither send,
    To nae maid under heaven.'

19 ' Sit in the hall, good ladies all,
    And drink the wine sae red,
  And I will to yon small window,
    And hear yon birdie's leed.

20 ' Sing on, sing on, my bonny bird,
    The sang ye sung just now ; '
  ' I 'll sing nae mair, ye lady fair,
    My errand is to you.'

21 ' If ye be my true-lovie's bird,
    Sae well 's I will you ken ;
  You will gae in at my gown-sleeve,
    Come out at my gown-hem.'

22 ' That I am come frae your true-love,
    You soon shall see right plain ;
  And read these lines below my wing,
    That I hae brought frae him.'

23 When she looked these lines upon,
    She read them, and she leuch :
  ' O well fails me, my true-love, now,
    O this I hae eneuch.

24 ' Here is the broach on my breast-bane,
    The garlings frae my hair,
  Likewise the heart that is within ;
    What woud my love hae mair ?

25 ' The nearest kirk in fair Scotland,
    Ye 'll bid him meet me there : '
  She has gane to her dear father,
    Wi heart perplexd and sair.

26 When she came to her auld father,
    Fell low down on her knee :
  ' An asking, asking, father dear,
    I pray you grant it me.'

27 ' Ask what you will, my dear daughter,
    And I will grant it thee ;
  Unless to marry yon Scottish squire ;
    That 's what shall never be.'

28 ' O that 's the asking, father,' she said,
    ' That I 'll neer ask of thee ;
  But if I die in South England,
    In Scotland ye 'll bury me.'

29 ' The asking 's nae sae great, daughter,
    But granted it shall be ;
  And tho ye die in South England,
    In Scotland we 'll bury thee.'

30 She has gane to her step-mother,
    Fell low down on her knee :
  ' An asking, asking, mother dear,
    I pray you grant it me.'

31 ' Ask what ye please, my lily-white dove,
    And granted it shall be : '
  ' If I do die in South England,
    In Scotland bury me.'

32 ' Had these words spoke been in again,
    I woud not granted thee ;
  You hae a love in fair Scotland,
    Sae fain 's you woud be tee.'

33 She scarce was to her chamber gane
    Nor yet was well set down,
  Till on the sofa where she sat
    Fell in a deadly swoon.

34 Her father and her seven brithers,
    They made for her a bier ;
  The one half o 't was gude red gowd,
    The other siller clear.

35 Her seven sisters were employed
    In making her a sark ;
  The one half o 't was cambric fine,
    The other needle-wark.

36 Then out it speaks her auld step-dame,
    Sat on the sofa's end :
  Ye 'll drap the het lead on her cheek,
    Sae do you on her chin ;
  For women will use mony a wile
    Their true-loves for to win.

37 Then up it raise her eldest brither,
    Into her bower he 's gane ;
  Then in it came her youngest brither,
    The het leed to drap on.

38 He drapt it by her cheek, her cheek,
    Sae did he by her chin ;
  Sae did he by her comely hause ;
    He knew life was therein.

39 The bier was made wi red gowd laid,
    Sae curious round about ;

A private entrance there contriv'd,
    That her breath might win out.

40 The first an kirk in fair Scotland,
    They gard the bells be rung;
The niest an kirk in fair Scotland,
    They causd the mass be sung.

41 The third an kirk in fair Scotland,
    They passd it quietly by;
The fourth an kirk in fair Scotland,
    Clerk Sandy did them spy.

42 'O down ye 'll set this corpse o clay,
    Lat me look on the dead;
For I may sigh, and say, alas!
    For death has nae remeid.'

43 Then he has cut her winding sheet
    A little below her chin,
And wi her sweet and ruby lips
    She sweetly smil'd on him.

44 'Gie me a sheave o your white bread,
    A bottle o your wine;
For I hae fasted for your sake
    Fully these lang days nine.

45 'Gae hame, gae hame, my seven brithers,
    Gae hame and blaw your trumpet;
And ye may tell to your step-dame
    This day she is affronted.

46 'I camna here to fair Scotland
    To lye amo the dead;
But came to be Clerk Sandy's wife,
    And lay gowd on my head.

47 'Gae hame, gae hame, my seven brithers,
    Gae hame and blaw your horn;
And ye may tell in fair England
    In Scotland ye got the scorn.

48 'I came not here to fair Scotland
    To mix amang the clay;
But came to be Clerk Sandy's wife,
    And wear gowd to my tae.'

49 'Sin ye hae gien us this ae scorn,
    We shall gie you anither;
Ye shall hae naething to live upon
    But the bier that brought you hither.'

———•———

A. *Written in stanzas of two long lines.*
    1. *In the Tytler-Brown MS.*

    O well 's me o my gay goss hawke
        That he can speake and flee,
    Will carry a letter to my love,
        Bring another back to me.

B. 20¹. Oh.   24¹. by brothers.
C. 2¹. Oh.   12². shee.
    After 16: etc., repeated as above.
    After 18²: etc., as above.
    After 20: etc., as to father, mother, etc. *The verses not written out (and not printed in the Minstrelsy) have been supplied accordingly.*
    30². bells *altered in the MS. from* mass.
    26³. clothe.
    29³. *In the Minstrelsy Motherwell has substituted* England *for* Scotland.
    34⁶. *Motherwell prints* dead ere syne.
D. *In his Note-Book, p.* 27, *Motherwell says that he got this copy of the ballad from* Agnes Laird; *in the MS., p.* 415, *from* Agnes Lyle. *Page* 26 *of the Note-Book shows that* Laird *is right.*
E. *The edition of* 1833 *inserts stanza* 13, *and substitutes for* 27, 28 *the following*:

Then spake her cruel step-minnie:
    'Tak ye the burning lead,
And drap a drap on her bosome,
    To try if she be dead.'

They took a drap o boiling lead,
    They drappd it on her breast;
'Alas, alas,' her father cried,
    'She 's dead without the priest!'

She neither chatterd with her teeth,
    Nor shiverd with her chin;
'Alas, alas,' her father cried,
    'There is nae breath within!'

After 36 *is inserted*:

'Commend me to my grey father,
    That wished my saul gude rest,
But wae be to my cruel step-dame,
    Garrd burn me on the breast.'

And mother, 37³, *is changed to* sisters. *The step-mother clearly does not belong to this ballad.*

97

BROWN ROBIN

A. 'Brown Robin.' **a.** Jamieson-Brown MS., fol. 37. **b.** Abbotsford MS., "Scottish Songs."

B. 'Love Robbie,' Christie's Traditional Ballad Airs, I, 136.

C. 'Brown Robyn and Mally,' Buchan's Ballads of the North of Scotland, II, 299.

'BROWN ROBIN' was No 7 in William Tytler's Brown MS. The first stanza is cited by Anderson, Nichols's Literary Illustrations, VII, 177, and there were twenty-one stanzas, as in **A a**. **A b** may have been a copy of the Tytler-Brown version. It does not seem to have been tampered with so much as other ballads in the same manuscript. The story undoubtedly stops at the right point in **A**, with the escape of the two lovers to the wood. The sequel in **C** is not at all beyond the inventive ability of Buchan's blind beggar, and some other blind beggar may have contrived the cane and the whale, the shooting and the hanging, in **B**.

Brown Robin is lover or husband of May Margerie, or May a Roe = Lillie Flower, in 'Jellon Grame,' No 90, **B** 14, **C** 7, and again of White Lilly in 'Rose the Red and White Lilly,' No 103, **A** 7 ff.

We have money given over the wall by an eloping lady, as in **B** 4, 5, **C** 5, also in 'Willie o Douglas Dale,' No 101, **C** 4, 5.

A 1, nearly, is stanza 5 in Jamieson's 'Glenkindie;' see p. 141 of this volume, note to **B**. **C** is translated by Gerhard, p. 175.

A

a. Jamieson-Brown MS., fol. 37. b. Abbotsford MS., "Scottish Songs."

1 THE king but an his nobles a' } *bis*
   Sat birling at the wine; }
He would ha nane but his ae daughter
   To wait on them at dine.

2 She's servd them butt, she's servd them ben,
   Intill a gown of green,
But her ee was ay on Brown Robin,
   That stood low under the rain.

3 She's doen her to her bigly bowr,
   As fast as she coud gang,
An there she's drawn her shot-window,
   An she's harped an she sang.

4 'There sits a bird i my father's garden,
   An O but she sings sweet!

I hope to live an see the day
   Whan wi my love I'll meet.'

5 'O gin that ye like me as well
   As your tongue tells to me,
What hour o the night, my lady bright,
   At your bowr sal I be?'

6 'Whan my father an gay Gilbert
   Are baith set at the wine,
O ready, ready I will be
   To lat my true-love in.'

7 O she has birld her father's porter
   Wi strong beer an wi wine,
Untill he was as beastly drunk
   As ony wild-wood swine:
She's stown the keys o her father's yates
   An latten her true-love in.

8 Whan night was gane, an day was come,
    An the sun shone on their feet,
  Then out it spake him Brown Robin,
    I 'll be discoverd yet.

9 Then out it spake that gay lady :
    My love, ye need na doubt ;
  For wi ae wile I 've got you in,
    Wi anither I 'll bring you out.

10 She 's taen her to her father's cellar,
    As fast as she can fare ;
  She 's drawn a cup o the gude red wine,
    Hung 't low down by her gare ;
  An she met wi her father dear
    Just coming down the stair.

11 ' I woud na gi that cup, daughter,
    That ye hold i your han
  For a' the wines in my cellar,
    An gantrees whare the stan.'

12 ' O wae be to your wine, father,
    That ever 't came oer the sea ;
  'T 'is pitten my head in sick a steer
    I my bowr I canna be.'

13 ' Gang out, gang out, my daughter dear,
    Gang out an tack the air ;
  Gang out an walk i the good green wood,
    An a' your marys fair.'

14 Then out it spake the proud porter —
    Our lady wishd him shame —
  ' We 'll send the marys to the wood,
    But we 'll keep our lady at hame.'

15 ' There 's thirty marys i my bowr,
    There 's thirty o them an three ;
  But there 's nae ane amo them a'
    Kens what flowr gains for me.'

16 She 's doen her to her bigly bowr,
    As fast as she could gang,
  An she has dresst him Brown Robin
    Like ony bowr-woman.

17 The gown she pat upon her love
    Was o the dainty green,
  His hose was o the saft, saft silk,
    His shoon o the cordwain fine.

18 She 's pitten his bow in her bosom,
    His arrow in her sleeve,
  His sturdy bran her body next,
    Because he was her love.

19 Then she is unto her bowr-door,
    As fast as she coud gang ;
  But out it spake the proud porter —
    Our lady wishd him shame —
  ' We 'll count our marys to the wood,
    An we 'll count them back again.'

20 The firsten mary she sent out
    Was Brown Robin by name ;
  Then out it spake the king himsel,
    ' This is a sturdy dame.'

21 O she went out in a May morning,
    In a May morning so gay,
  But she came never back again,
    Her auld father to see.

—◆—

B

Christie's Traditional Ballad Airs, I, 136, from the recitation of an old woman in Buckie, Enzie, Banffshire.

1 ' A FEATHERD fowl 's in your orchard, father,
    O dear, but it sings sweet !
  What would I give, my father dear,
    That bonnie bird to meet !
  What would I give, etc.

2 ' O hold your tongue, my daughter Mary,
    Let a' your folly be ;
  There 's six Scots lords tomorrow, child,
    That will a' dine wi me,

And ye maun serve them a', Mary,
    As 't were for meat and fee.'

3 She served them up, sae has she down,
    The footmen a' the same,
  But her mind was aye on Love Robbie,
    Stood out below the rain.

4 A hundred pun o pennies roun,
    Tied in a towel so sma,
  She has gien to him Love Robbie,
    Out oer the castle-wa ;
  Says, Tak ye that, my love Robbie.
    And mysel ye may hae.

5 A hundred pun o pennies roun,
   Tied in a napkin white,
She has gien to him Love Robbie,
   Out oer the garden-dyke;
Says, Tak ye that, my Love Robbie,
   And mysel gin ye like.

6 'If this be true ye tell to me,
   As your tongue woudna lee,
I shall be in your bigly bower
   Before the clock strike three;
I shall be in your bigly bower,
   Dressd like a gay ladye.'

7 When bells were rung, and mass was sung,
   And all men bound for bed,
Love Robbie came to Mary's bower,
   Dressd like a comely maid.

8 They had not kissd nor love clappëd,
   As lovers when they meet,
Till sighing said he Love Robbie,
   My life, my life I doubt.

9 'Your life, your life, you Love Robbie,
   Your life you needna doubt;
For it was wiles brought in Robbie,
   And wiles will lat him out.'

10 Then in it came her father dear,
   And stood upon the floor,
And she filld the cup of good red wine,
   Said, Father, will ye drink more?

11 'O better I love the cup, Mary,
   The cup that's in your hand,
Than all my barrels full of wine,
   On the gantrees where they stand.'

12 'O woe be to your wine, father,
   It eer came oer the sea!
If I getna the air o good greenwood
   O I will surely dee.'

13 'There's seven maries in your bower,
   There's seven o them and three,
And I'll send them to good greenwood,
   For flowers to shortsome thee.'

14 'There's seven maries in my bower,
   There's seven o them and three,
But there's nae a mary mang them a'
   Can pu flowers to shortsome me:'

'Then by my sooth,' said her father dear,
   'Let yoursel gang them wi.'

15 She dressd hersel in the royal red,
   Love Robbie was in dainty green;
Love Robbie's brand was about his middle,
   And he shone like ony queen.

16 The firsten ane that took the floor,
   Love Robbie was that ane:
'Now by my sooth,' said the proud porter,
   'She is a sonsie dame;
I would not care now very much
   To turn her in again.'

17 'I'd fain see any woman or man,
   Of high or low degree,
Would turn a mary in again
   That once came out with me.'

18 They had not been in good greenwood,
   Pu'd a flower but only three,
Till the porter stood behind a bush,
   And shot him Love Robbie.

19 Now word has come to her father dear,
   In the chamber where he lay,
Lady Mary's sick in good greenwood,
   And cannot come away.

20 He's taen his mantle him about,
   His cane into his han,
And he is on to good greenwood,
   As fast as he could gang.

21 'O want you fish out o the fleed,
   Or whale out o the sea?
Or is there any one alive
   This day has angerd thee?'

22 'I want not fish out o the fleed,
   Nor whale out o the sea;
But woe be to your proud porter,
   Sae sair's he's angerd me!
He's shot the fairest flower this day,
   That would hae comfort me.'

23 'O hold your tongue, my daughter Mary,
   Let a' your folly be;
Tomorrow ere I eat or drink
   High hangëd shall he be.'

C

Buchan's Ballads of the North of Scotland, II, 299.

1 'THERE is a bird in my father's orchard,
  And dear, but it sings sweet!
I hope to live to see the day]
  This bird and I will meet.'

2 'O hold your tongue, my daughter Mally,
  Let a' your folly be;
What bird is that in my orchard
  Sae shortsome is to thee?

3 'There are four-an-twenty noble lords
  The morn shoud dine wi me;
And ye maun serve them a', Mally,
  Like one for meat and fee.'

4 She servd the nobles all as one,
  The horsemen much the same;
But her mind was aye to Brown Robyn,
  Beneath the heavy rain.

5 Then she's rowd up a thousand pounds
  Intil a servit white,
And she gae that to Brown Robyn,
  Out ower the garden-dyke:
Says, Take ye that, my love Robyn,
  And mysell gin ye like.

6 'If this be true, my dame,' he said,
  'That ye hae tauld to me,
About the hour o twall at night,
  At your bower-door I'll be.'

7 But ere the hour o twall did chap,
  And lang ere it was ten,
She had hersell there right and ready
  To lat Brown Robyn in.

8 They hadna kissd nor love clapped
  Till the birds sang on the ha;
'O,' sighing says him Brown Robyn,
  'I wish I were awa!'

9 They hadna sitten muckle langer
  Till the guards shot ower the way;
Then sighing says him Brown Robyn,
  'I fear my life this day.'

10 'O had your tongue, my love Robyn,
  Of this take ye nae doubt;
It was by wiles I brought you in,
  By wiles I'll bring you out.'

11 Then she's taen up a cup o wine,
  To her father went she;
'O drink the wine, father,' she said,
  'O drink the wine wi me.'

12 'O well love I the cup, daughter,
  But better love I the wine;
And better love I your fair body
  Than a' the gowd in Spain.'

13 'Wae be to the wine, father,
  That last came ower the sea;
Without the air o gude greenwood,
  There's nae remeid for me.'

14 'Ye've thirty maries in your bower,
  Ye've thirty and hae three;
Send ane o them to pu a flower,
  Stay ye at hame wi me.'

15 'I've thirty maries in my bower,
  I've thirty o them and nine;
But there's nae a marie amo them a'
  That kens my grief and mind.

16 'For they may pu the nut, the nut,
  And sae may they the slae,
But there's nane amo them a' that kens
  The herb that I woud hae.'

17 'Well, gin ye gang to gude greenwood,
  Come shortly back again;
Ye are sae fair and are sae rare,
  Your body may get harm.'

18 She dressd hersell into the red,
  Brown Robyn all in green,
And put his brand across his middle,
  He was a stately dame.

19 The first ane stepped ower the yett,
  It was him Brown Robyn;
'By my sooth,' said the proud porter,
  'This is a stately dame.

20 'O wi your leave, lady,' he said,
  'And leave o a' your kin,
I woudna think it a great sin
  To turn that marie in.'

21 'O had your tongue, ye proud porter,
  Let a' your folly be;
Ye darena turn a marie in
  That ance came forth wi me.'

22 ' Well shall I call your maries out,
    And as well shall I in ;
For I am safe to gie my oath
    That marie is a man.'

23 Soon she went to gude greenwood,
    And soon came back again ;
' Gude sooth,' replied the proud porter,
    ' We 've lost our stately dame.'

24 ' My maid 's faen sick in gude greenwood,
    And sick and liken to die ;
The morn before the cocks do craw,
    That marie I maun see.'

25 Out it spake her father then,
    Says, Porter, let me know
If I will cause her stay at hame,
    Or shall I let her go ?

26 ' She says her maid 's sick in the wood,
    And sick and like to die ;
I really think she is too gude
    Nor ever woud make a lie.'

27 Then he whispered in her ear,
    As she was passing by,
' What will ye say if I reveal
    What I saw wi my eye ? '

28 ' If ought ye ken about the same,
    O heal that well on me,
And if I live or brook my life,
    Rewarded ye shall be.'

29 Then she got leave o her father
    To gude greenwood again,
And she is gane wi Brown Robyn,
    But 't was lang ere she came hame.

30 O then her father began to mourn,
    And thus lamented he :
' O I woud gie ten thousand pounds
    My daughter for to see.'

31 ' If ye will promise,' the porter said,
    ' To do nae injury,
I will find out your daughter dear,
    And them that 's gane her wi.'

32 Then he did swear a solemn oath,
    By a' his gowd and land,
Nae injury to them 's be dune,
    Whether it be maid or man.

33 The porter then a letter wrote,
    And seald it wi his hand,
And sent it to that lady fair,
    For to return hame.

34 When she came to her father's ha,
    He received her joyfullie,
And married her to Brown Robyn ;
    Now a happy man was he.

35 She hadna been in her father's ha
    A day but barely three,
Till she settled the porter well for life,
    Wi gowd and white monie.

A. a. *Written in stanzas of two long lines.*
    The first stanza, as given by Anderson, is :

The king Val(?) and his nobles a'
    Sat drinking at the wine ;
He woud ha nane but his ae daughter
    To wait on them at dine.

    18¹. boson : *the king's daughter must have
        been* " a sturdy dame " *too.*
    21². so gray.   *The sun was up : see stanza
        8.*
    b. 1². Were drinking.
    2¹. She served them butt.
    2². Baith knights and gallants sheen.

2³. was still.   3². might gang.
3³. And she has.
4¹. in yonder tree.   4². vow but he.
4⁴. my love and I shall.
5¹. Gin ye luve me as weel, fair maid.
6¹. my auld father.   6². Sit drinking.
6³. will I.
7¹. has hired the proud porter.
7². Wi the ale but and the.
7⁵,⁶. She 's slipped aff hir silken sheen,
    And saftly trippd she down ;
She 's stown the key o hir father's
    yate,
    And let hir true love in.
8². shined.   8³. out and spake.

9¹. O out and spake.

9⁸. As wi ae wile I hae brought.

10¹, ². *wanting.*

10⁵. she has met her auld.

10⁶. Came creeping up.   11. *wanting.*

12². ever it crossd.   12⁸. It has put.

12⁴. canna stay.   13⁴. Wi a'

14¹. and spake.   14². send him.

14⁴. But keep the princess.

15⁴. flowr 's gude.

16¹. hied her.   16². Sae fast as she might.

16³, ⁴. She 's putten a goun upon hir love
      Was of the dainty green.

17¹, ². The girdle round his stately waist
      Wi gowd and silver shone.

17⁸. His stockings o.

17⁴. And his shune o the cordovan.

18¹. She put.   18². up her.

18⁸. her fair side next.   19. *wanting.*

20⁸. By the faith o my body, then said the
      king.

20⁴. a lusty.   21¹. gaed out.   21². sae gay.

98

BROWN ADAM

A. 'Brown Adam,' Jamieson-Brown MS., fol. 17.

B. 'Broun Edom,' Harris MS., fol. 27 b, No 26.

C. 'Brown Adam the Smith,' Buchan MSS, I, 46.

'BROWN ADAM' was No 14 of the fifteen ballads furnished William Tytler by Mrs Brown in 1783: Anderson, in Nichols's Illustrations, VII, 178. The ballad was first printed in the Minstrelsy of the Scottish Border, II, 16, 1802, with the omission of Mrs Brown's second stanza, and some changes. Scott remarks that he had seen a copy printed on a single sheet.

C 1, 3, 6, 7 are very close to A 1, 2, 3, 4. A 2 was not printed by Scott, and if these stanzas were borrowed, A 2 must have been taken from the Jamieson MS., to which other cases of correspondence warrant a suspicion that one of Buchan's contributors had access. C has the usual marks of Buchan's copies, great length, vulgarity, and such extravagance and absurdity as are found in stanzas 23, 26, 29.

A Danish ballad, from manuscripts of the sixteenth century and later, has a remote likeness to 'Brown Adam:' 'Den afhugne Haand,' Grundtvig, No 199, IV, 153. Lawi Pedersøn, who has shown bad faith to women, makes love to Lutzelil, who knows his ways, and re-jects him summarily. Lawi rides off in wrath, saying that she shall be sorry for it. The maid is afraid to go to church for nine months, but ventures at Easter. Lawi stops her in a wood. She begs him to do her no harm, feigns to be amenable, and gives him an assignation at an off-lying apartment in which she sleeps with her maids; then rides away, laughing over her successful evasion. She tells her father how she has met Lawi, and begs him to be on the watch. Lawi comes at night, knocks, and is answered, according to the formula of Danish ballads, that she has made no appointment and he cannot come in. Lawi threatens to take off the door, and does so. Lutzelil's father is standing ready with his sword, and cuts off Lawi's hand.

The copy in Scott's Minstrelsy is translated by Grundtvig, Engelske og skotske Folkeviser, No 45, p. 291; by Schubart, p. 65; Arndt, Blütenlese, p. 231; Rosa Warrens, Schottische Volkslieder, No 29, p. 130; Knortz, Schottische Balladen, No 2, p. 5.

A

Jamieson-Brown MS., fol. 17.

1 O WHA woud wish the win to blaw,
   Or the green leaves fa therewith?
   Or wha wad wish a leeler love
     Than Brown Adam the Smith?

2 His hammer's o the beaten gold,
   His study's o the steel,
   His fingers white are my delite,
   He blows his bellows well.

3 But they ha banishd him Brown Adam
   Frae father and frae mither,
   An they ha banishd him Brown Adam
   Frae sister and frae brither.

4 And they ha banishd Brown Adam
   Frae the flowr o a' his kin;
   An he's biggit a bowr i the good green wood
   Betwen his lady an him.

5 O it fell once upon a day
   Brown Adam he thought lang,
   An he woud to the green wood gang,
   To hunt some venison.

6 He's ta'en his bow his arm oer,
   His bran intill his han,
   And he is to the good green wood,
   As fast as he coud gang.

7 O he's shot up, an he's shot down,
   The bird upo the briar,
   An he's sent it hame to his lady,
   Bade her be of good cheer.

8 O he's shot up, an he's shot down,
   The bird upo the thorn,
   And sent it hame to his lady,
   And hee'd be hame the morn.

9 Whan he came till his lady's bowr-door
   He stood a little foreby,
   And there he heard a fu fa'se knight
   Temptin his gay lady.

10 O he's taen out a gay gold ring,
   Had cost him mony a poun:
   'O grant me love for love, lady,
   An this sal be your own.'

11 'I loo Brown Adam well,' she says,
   'I wot sae does he me;
   An I would na gi Brown Adam's love
   For nae fa'se knight I see.'

12 Out has he ta'en a purse of gold,
   Was a' fu to the string:
   'Grant me but love for love, lady,
   An a' this sal be thine.'

13 'I loo Brown Adam well,' she says,
   'An I ken sae does he me;
   An I woudna be your light leman
   For mair nor ye coud gie.'

14 Then out has he drawn his lang, lang bran,
   And he's flashd it in her een:
   'Now grant me love for love, lady,
   Or thro you this sal gang!'

15 'O,' sighing said that gay lady,
   'Brown Adam tarrys lang!'
   Then up it starts Brown Adam,
   Says, I'm just at your han.

16 He's gard him leave his bow, his bow,
   He's gard him leave his bran;
   He's gard him leave a better pledge,
   Four fingers o his right han.

B

Harris MS., fol. 27 b, No 26.

1 .   .   .   .   .
  .   .   .   .
   For wha ere had a lealer luve
   Than Broun Edom the smith?

2 His studie was o the beaten gowd,
   His hammer o the pith;
   His cords waur o the gude green silk,
   That blew his bellows with.

3 It fell out ance upon a time
   Broun Edom he thoucht lang,
   That he wald gae to see his luve,
   By the le licht o the mune.

C

Buchan MSS, I, 46.

1 O WHA woud wish the win to blaw,
  The green leaves fa therewith?
O wha would wish a leeler luve
  Than Brown Adam the Smith?

2 O he forsook the royal court,
  And knights and lords sae gude,
And he is to the black smithy,
  To learn to shoe a steed.

3 His hammer-shaft o gude red gowd,
  His studdy o the steel,
His fingers whyte, and maids' delight,
  And blaws his bellows weel.

4 He being a favourite with the king
  Caused him get mony a fae,
And sae their plots they did contrive
  To work him grief and wae.

5 Of treason then he was accused
  By his fause enemie,
Which caused the king to make a vow
  That banishd he shoud be.

6 Then banishd hae they Brown Adam
  Frae father and frae mither,
And banishd hae they him Brown Adam
  Frae sister and frae brither.

7 And they hae banishd him Brown Adam,
  The flower o a' his kin;
He built a bower in gude green wood,
  For his true love and him.

8 But it fell ance upon a day
  The king's young son thought lang,
And minded him on Brown Adam,
  Oft rade on his right han.

9 Then he sent for him Brown Adam,
  To shoe his milk-white steed,
That he might see him ance in court,
  Mang knights o noble bleed.

10 When Brown Adam he read these lines,
  A light laugh then gae hee:
' What's this that's made their hearts to fa,
  They lang sae sair for mee?'

11 Then out it speaks his gay ladye:
  Brown Adam, bide wi mee;
For if ye gang to court, I fear
  Your face I'll never see.

12 ' Cheer up your heart, my ain true-love,
  Let naething cause your grief;
Though I be absent for some days,
  Ye seen will get relief.'

13 Then he has kissd his gay ladye,
  And rade alang the lay,
And hunted a' the wild birds there,
  As he rade on the way.

14 He shot the bunting o the bush,
  The linnet o the brier,
And sent them on to gude green wood,
  His ladye's heart to cheer.

15 He shot the bunting o the bush,
  The linnet o the wand,
And sent them on to his ladye,
  Forbade her to think lang.

16 He shot the bunting o the bush,
  The linnet o the thorn,
And sent them on to his ladye,
  Said he'd be hame the morn.

17 A thought then came into his mind,
  As he rade on the way,
Some evil in his absence might
  Befa his ladye gay.

18 Now when he had the prince' steed shod,
  And bound again to ryde,
He turned his horse to Ringlewood;
  Some days he meant to byde.

19 But when he turned to Ringlewood,
  Ae foot's horse woudna ryde;
Whan he turned to his luver's bower,
  He flew like ony glyde.

20 When he drew near to his luve's bower,
  There he alighted down,
For the hearing o his great horse tramp
  Ere he wan to the town.

21 Whan he came to his luver's bower,
  He heard a dolefu din;
He wasna aware o a fu fause knight,
  His true-love's bower within.

22 He bound his steed to his ain stall,
  And gae him corn and hay,
And listened at a shott-window,
  To hear what he would say.

23 The first and thing the knight drew out,
  It was a coffer fine;
It was as fu o gude black silk,
  Make ladyes for to shine.

24 'Ye are too lack o luve, ladye,
　　And that 's a hatefu thing ;
　Luve me, and lat Brown Adam be,
　　And a' this shall be thine.'

25 'O well I like Brown Adam,' she said,
　　'I wyte hee hates nae mee ;
　I winna forsake him Brown Adam
　　For a' your gifts an thee.'

26 The next and thing the knight drew out,
　　It was a coffer small ;
　It was as fou o shambo gluves,
　　Woud had her hands frae caul.

27 'Ye are too lack o luve, ladye,
　　An that 's a hatefu thing ;
　Luve me, an lat Brown Adam be,
　　An a' this shall be thine.'

28 'O well like I Brown Adam,' she said,
　　'I 'm sure he hates nae me ;
　I winna forsake him Brown Adam
　　For a' your gifts an thee.'

29 The next and thing the knight drew out
　　It was a coffer fine ;
　It was as fu of gude red gowd
　　As a guinea coud get in.

30 'You are too lack o luve, ladye,
　　And that 's a hatefu thing ;
　Luve me, and lat Brown Adam be,
　　And a' this shall be thine.'

31 'O well I like Brown Adam,' she said,
　　'I 'm sure hee hates nae mee ;
　I winna forsake him Brown Adam
　　For a' the gowd ye 'll gie.'

32 Then his mild mood did quickly change,
　　And grew mair fierce and cruel,
　And then drew out a trusty brand,
　　Which made her heart to pruel.

33 'Since I by you am slighted sae,
　　Since I frae you maun part,

I swear a vow before I gae,
　That this shall pierce your heart.'

34 'But still I like Brown Adam,' she said,
　　'I wat hee hates nae mee ;
　And if he knew my troubles now
　　At my call woud hee be.

35 'Although he were sax miles awa,
　　He 'd seen be at my han ;
　But wae is me, sae may I say,
　　Brown Adam tarries lang !'

36 He hit the door then wi his foot,
　　Made a' the bands to flee :
　'Cheer up your heart, my luve Janet,
　　Your love 's nae far frae thee.'

37 Then he drew out a trusty brand,
　　And chassd him thro the ha ;
　The knight jumpd to a shott-window,
　　And woud hae been awa.

38 'Stay still, stay still,' Brown Adam said,
　　'Make nae sic haste frae mee ;
　You or I maun rue the race
　　That I came ower the lee.'

39 Then frae the knight he 's taen a wad,
　　His mantle and his brand ;
　Likewise he 's taen anither wad,
　　His sword and his sword-hand.

40 He threw him ower the shott-window,
　　Bade him lie there wi care,
　And never come back to gude green wood
　　To marr fair ladies mair.

41 'O I am brown,' said Brown Adam,
　　'And I was never whyte ;
　But my love has robes o different hues,
　　To wear at her delyght.

42 'Her kirchies be o cambricks fine,
　　Wi gowd pinnd to the chin ;
　Her robes shall be o the scarlet hue
　　She shall gang daily in.'

————

A. *Anderson cites the first stanza, in exact agree-
　　ment with the Jamieson MS., except that
　　the third line begins with O.*

3². mother (?).
7⁴. Beede (?).
15². long.

99

JOHNIE SCOT

A. ' Jack, the Little Scot,' Jamieson-Brown MS., fol. 5.

B. ' McNaughtan,' Glenriddell MSS, XI, 78.

C. ' Johnie Scot,' Motherwell's MS., p. 213.

D. ' Johnnie Scot,' Motherwell's MS., p. 205.

E. ' McNachton,' Motherwell's MS., p. 113.

F. ' Bonnie Johnie Scot,' Motherwell's MS., p. 211.

G. ' Johnie Scott,' Motherwell's Note-Book, p. 35 ; Motherwell's MS., p. 394.

H. ' Love Johny,' Kinloch MSS, VI, 53.

I. ' Johnie Buneftan,' Kinloch MSS, VII, 39, 41, 43, 45, 47, 49.

J. Kinloch MSS, VII, 40, 42, 46, 49.

K. ' Johnie, the Little Scot,' Kinloch MSS, I, 311.

L. ' Johnie Scott,' Campbell MSS, I, 57.

M. ' Lord Johnnie Scott,' Campbell MSS, II, 335.

N. ' Lord John,' Buchan's Gleanings, p. 122.

O. ' Johnie Scot,' communicated by Mr Macmath.

P. Motherwell's Note-Book, p. 11.

A WAS No 2 of the fifteen ballads in William Tytler's lost Brown MS. : Nichols's Illustrations, VII, 176. There is a copy of A in the Abbotsford MS., " Scottish Songs," fol. 24, with many wilful alterations and a few readings from tradition. The ballad printed in Motherwell's Minstrelsy, p. 204, is a compound of C, D, E, and the one in Kinloch's Ancient Scottish Ballads, p. 77, is made up from I, J, " recited versions obtained in the north and west " of Scotland, with some slight changes.

The story of ' Willie o Winsbury,' No 100, has considerable resemblance to that of ' Johnie Scot,' but Willie's extreme beauty moves the king, the lady's father, to offer his daughter to him in marriage, without a combat. Mrs Brown's version of ' Willie o Douglas Dale,' No 101, A, begins with the first stanza of her version of ' Johnie Scot,' A. So does ' Young Betrice,' another ballad of hers, No 5 of William Tytler's MS. :

> Young Betrice was as brave a knight
>   As ever saild the sea,
> And he 's taen him to the court of France,
>   To serve for meat and fee.

Anderson, who cites this stanza, Nichols's Illustrations, as above, remarks : " The conduct of the story is different from that of No 2 [' Jack, the Little Scot '], which it resembles. Some of the lines are in ' Gil Morrice.' " ' Young Betrice ' may possibly be a variety of ' Hugh Spencer : ' see ' Hugh Spencer,' C.

There is resemblance to ' Child Maurice,' No 83, besides the commonplace of the messenger-boy, in the sending of a token to the lady, A 12, 13, D 6, E 2, H 4, 5, J 4, M 8, N 11, 12; ' Child Maurice,' A 7, 8, B 3, 4, C 3, 4, 5, D, E 6, 7, F 17, 18. In the present ballad the token is a sark of silk (M 8, simply shirt) ; so in ' Child Maurice,' D 7, F 18. The blessing on the errand-boy, A 8, is found in ' Fair Mary of Wallington,' No 91, B 9.

While John, the Scot, is in service at the English court, the king's daughter becomes with child to him. She is thrown into prison. Johnie, who has fled to Scotland, sends a messenger to her with a token which she will recognize, urging her to come to him. An answer is returned that she is in chains. Johnie resolves to go to the rescue. He is warned of the danger, but a body of Scots attends him, five hundred men, **A-D, O**, twenty-four, **E, G, I**; all unmarried, **B, D, E, G, H, I, O**. When he arrives at the English court, the king asks his name. His name is Pitnachton, **A** 26; McNaughtan, **B** 17, **E** 14, cf. **C** 16; Auchney, **H** 21; Buneftan, **I** 14; Johnie Scot, Love John, **C** 17, **K** 12, **L** 13, **N** 26; Earl Hector, **D** 18. The king will hang the Scot on his daughter's account. Resistance is threatened by Johnie's friends. The king has a champion who will fight them three by three, **A** 29, **B** 20, **E** 18, **F** 17, **N** 30. This champion is an Italian, **A** 29, **I** 17, **L** 16, **N** 31, **O** 8; an Itilian, **H** 27; Talliant, Tailliant, **C** 22, **D** 23, **F** 17, **G** 16. The Scot kills the Italian in a duel. In **C** 24, **D** 25, **F** 19, **G** 18, the Italian jumps over Johnie's head, skims over it like a swallow, and is apparently run through while so doing. Johnie calls for a priest to marry his love and him, the king for a clerk to write the tocher. But tocher is refused by the Scot, who wants only his dearly won lady.

The champion is described in **A** 31 as a gurious (grugous, gruous?) ghost; in **H** 27 as a greecy (frightful) ghost; in **L** 18 he is a fearsome sight, with three women's-spans between his brows and three yards between his shoulders; in the Abbotsford copy of **A**, 29, 30, a grisly sight, with a span between his eyes, between his shoulders three and three, and Johnie scarcely reaching his knee. These points are probably taken from another and a later ballad, which is perhaps an imitation, and might almost be called a parody, of Johnie Scot, 'Lang Johnny Moir:' see Buchan's Ballads of the North of Scotland, I, 248.

The process of striping a sword oer a stane or to the stran, **N** 28, **H** 28, striking it across the plain, **A** 32, **K** 14, is that of whetting or wiping, already noted under No 81, II, 243 f. To the places cited there may be added 'Child Maurice,' **F** 30, 'Jellon Grame,' No 90, **B** 8, 21, **C** 14, 'The Baffled Knight,' No 112, **A** 10. **G** 20^2 is a manifest corruption, a repetition of 17^2; **K** 14 has been corrected, in conformity with **A** 32.

The Rev. Andrew Hall, in his Interesting Roman Antiquities recently discovered in Fife, 1823, p. 216, relates the following story, on traditional authority.* James Macgill, of Lindores, had killed Sir Robert Balfour, of Denmiln, in a duel which he had wished to avoid, about the year 1679. Macgill "immediately went up to London in order to procure his pardon, which it seems the king, Charles the Second, offered to grant him upon condition of his fighting an Italian gladiator or bravo, or, as he was then called, a bully; which, it is said, none could be found to do. . . . Accordingly a large stage was erected for the exhibition before the king and court. . . . Sir James, it is said, stood on the defensive till the bully had spent himself a little, being a taller man than Sir James. In his mighty gasconading and bravadoing he actually leaped over the knight as if he would swallow him alive, but in attempting to do this a second time Sir James run his sword up through him, and then called out, 'I have spitted him; let them roast him who will.' This not only procured his pardon, but he was also knighted on the spot."

The exploit of Johnie Scot, and, if you please, of Sir James Macgill, has been achieved as well on the south side of the English Channel. The Breton seigneur Les Aubrays, or Lizandré, of St Brieux, is ordered by the French king to undertake a combat with his wild Moor. Les Aubrays asks a page, who brings the king's command, about the Moor's fashion of fighting. The Moor is master of devilish magic, and has herbs about him by virtue of which any wounds he may get are soon healed. The Breton is told, among other things, that he must throw holy water at the Moor the moment the savage draws, and when the Moor makes a leap in the air he must receive him on the point of his sword. These instructions are followed with perfect success. When the Moor is "swimming" in the air, Lizandré so disposes his sword as to take him on it. Luzel, 'Lezobre,' etc., 'Les Aubrays et le More du Roi,' second and third versions, I, 300–03, 294, 295; 'Le Géant

---

* Pointed out to Motherwell by Charles Kirkpatrick Sharpe.

Lizandré,' II, 568–71, 'Le Géant Les Aubrays,' 576–79; Poésies populaires de la France, MS., vol. i, near the beginning. Though the brave Breton is called giant in the title of Luzel's last two versions, nothing is said in the ballads of his being of unusual proportions. He is victorious in nineteen fights, but it is because of his profuse liberality to St Anne; it borders on the irreligious, therefore, to call him a giant.*

The copy in Motherwell's Minstrelsy, p. 204, is translated by Wolff, Halle der Völker, I, 15, Hausschatz, p. 210.

——◆——

A

Jamieson-Brown MS., fol. 5.

1 O JOHNEY was as brave a knight
　　As ever saild the sea,
　An he's done him to the English court,
　　To serve for meat and fee.

2 He had nae been in fair England
　　But yet a little while,
　Untill the kingis ae daughter
　　To Johney proves wi chil.

3 O word's come to the king himsel,
　　In his chair where he sat,
　That his ae daughter was wi bairn
　　To Jack, the Little Scott.

4 'Gin this be true that I do hear,
　　As I trust well it be,
　Ye pit her into prison strong,
　　An starve her till she die.'

5 O Johney's on to fair Scotland,
　　A wot he went wi speed,
　An he has left the kingis court,
　　A wot good was his need.

6 O it fell once upon a day
　　That Johney he thought lang,
　An he's gane to the good green wood,
　　As fast as he coud gang.

7 'O whare will I get a bonny boy,
　　To rin my errand soon,
　That will rin into fair England,
　　An haste him back again?'

8 O up it starts a bonny boy,
　　Gold yallow was his hair,
　I wish his mither meickle joy,
　　His bonny love mieckle mair.

9 'O here am I, a bonny boy,
　　Will rin your errand soon;
　I will gang into fair England,
　　An come right soon again.'

10 O whan he came to broken briggs,
　　He bent his bow and swam;
　An whan he came to the green grass growan,
　　He slaikid his shoone an ran.

11 Whan he came to yon high castèl,
　　He ran it roun about,
　An there he saw the king's daughter,
　　At the window looking out.

12 'O here's a sark o silk, lady,
　　Your ain han sewd the sleeve;
　You'r bidden come to fair Scotlan,
　　Speer nane o your parents leave.

13 'Ha, take this sark o silk, lady,
　　Your ain han sewd the gare;
　You're bidden come to good green wood,
　　Love Johney waits you there.'

14 She's turnd her right and roun about,
　　The tear was in her ee:
　'How can I come to my true-love,
　　Except I had wings to flee?

15 'Here am I kept wi bars and bolts,
　　Most grievous to behold;

---

* "Les Aubrays est le nom d'une seigneurie du pays de Retz, apportée en mariage, en 1455, à Rolland de Lannion, par Guyonne de Grezy, dame des Aubrays. La ballade ne peut pas, par conséquent, être antérieure à cette époque, et nous la croyons bien plus moderne." M. Pol de Courcy, Luzel, I, 306. The ballad can be no older, unless the Seigneur Les Aubrays has displaced an earlier hero; but what means have we of deciding that question?

My breast-plate 's o the sturdy steel,
    Instead of the beaten gold.

16 ' But tak this purse, my bonny boy,
    Ye well deserve a fee,
  An bear this letter to my love,
    An tell him what you see.'

17 Then quickly ran the bonny boy
    Again to Scotlan fair,
  An soon he reachd Pitnachton's towrs,
    An soon found Johney there.

18 He pat the letter in his han
    An taul him what he sa,
  But eer he half the letter read,
    He loote the tears doun fa.

19 ' O I will gae back to fair Englan,
    Tho death shoud me betide,
  An I will relieve the damesel
    That lay last by my side.'

20 Then out it spake his father dear,
    My son, you are to blame;
  An gin you 'r catchd on English groun,
    I fear you 'll neer win hame.

21 Then out it spake a valiant knight,
    Johny's best friend was he;
  I can commaun five hunder men,
    An I 'll his surety be.

22 The firstin town that they came till,
    They gard the bells be rung;
  An the nextin town that they came
    till,
    They gard the mess be sung.

23 The thirdin town that they came till,
    They gard the drums beat roun;
  The king but an his nobles a'
    Was startld at the soun.

24 Whan they came to the king's palace
    They rade it roun about,
  An there they saw the king himsel,
    At the window looking out.

25 ' Is this the Duke o Albany,
    Or James, the Scottish king?
  Or are ye some great foreign lord,
    That 's come a visiting?'

26 ' I 'm nae the Duke of Albany,
    Nor James, the Scottish king;
  But I 'm a valiant Scottish knight,
    Pitnachton is my name.'

27 ' O if Pitnachton be your name,
    As I trust well it be,
  The morn, or I tast meat or drink,
    You shall be hanged hi.'

28 Then out it spake the valiant knight
    That came brave Johney wi;
  Behold five hunder bowmen bold,
    Will die to set him free.

29 Then out it spake the king again,
    An a scornfu laugh laugh he;
  I have an Italian i my house
    Will fight you three by three.

30 ' O grant me a boon,' brave Johney cried;
    ' Bring your Italian here;
  Then if he fall beneath my sword,
    I 've won your daughter dear.'

31 Then out it came that Italian,
    An a gurious ghost was he;
  Upo the point o Johney's sword
    This Italian did die.

32 Out has he drawn his lang, lang bran,
    Struck it across the plain:
  ' Is there any more o your English dogs
    That you want to be slain?'

33 ' A clark, a clark,' the king then cried,
    ' To write her tocher free;'
  ' A priest, a priest,' says Love Johney,
    ' To marry my love and me.

34 ' I 'm seeking nane o your gold,' he says,
    ' Nor of your silver clear;
  I only seek your daughter fair,
    Whose love has cost her dear.'

B

Glenriddell MSS, XI, 78 : 1791.

1 JOHNNY 's into England gane,
  Three quarters of a year ;
  Johnny 's into England gane,
  The king's banner to bear.

2 He had na been in England lang,
  But and a little while,
  Untill the king's daughter
  To Johnny gaes wi child.

3 Word is to the kitchin gane,
  And word is to the ha,
  And word is to the king's palace,
  Amang the nobles a'.

4 Word 's gane to the king's palace,
  The palace where she sat,
  That his ae daughter gaes wi child
  To Jock, the Little Scot.

5 'If she be wi child,' he says,
  'As I trow well she be,
  I 'll put her into strang prison,
  And hang her till she die.'

6 But up and spak young Johnny,
  And O he spake in time :
  Is there never a bony boy here
  Will rin my errand soon ?

7 That will gae to yon castle,
  And look it round about ?
  And there he 'll see a fair lady,
  The window looking out.

8 Up then spak a bony boy,
  And a bony boy was he :
  I 'll run thy errand, Johnny, he said,
  Untill the day I die.

9 'Put on your gown o silk, madam,
  And on your hand a glove,
  And gang into the good green-wood,
  To Johnny, your true-love.'

10 'The fetters they are on my feet,
   And O but they are cauld !
   My bracelets they are sturdy steel,
   Instead of beaten gold.

11 'But I will write a lang letter,
   And seal it tenderlie,
   And I will send to my true-love,
   Before that I do die.'

12 The first look that Johnny lookd,
   A loud laughter gae he ;
   But the next look that Johnny gae,
   The tear blinded his ee.

13 He says, I 'll into England gae,
   Whatever may betide,
   And a' to seek a fair woman
   That sud hae been my bride.

14 But up and speaks his father,
   And O he spak in time :
   If that ye into England gae,
   I 'm feerd ye neer come hame.

15 But up then speaks our gude Scotch king,
   And a brisk young man was he :
   He 's hae five hunder o my life-guard,
   To bear him companie.

16 When Johnny was on saddle set,
   And seemly for to see,
   There was not a married man
   Into his companie.

17 When Johnny sat on saddle-seat,
   And seemly to behold,
   The hair that hang on Johnny's head
   Was like the threads o gold.

18 When he cam to .   .   .
   He gard the bells a' ring,
   Untill the king and a' his court
   Did marvel at the thing.

19 'Is this the brave Argyle,' he said,
   'That 's landed and come hame ?
   Is this the brave Argyle,' he said,
   'Or James, our Scottish king ? '

20 'It 's no the brave Argyle,' they said,
   'That 's landed and come hame ;
   But it is a brave young Scottish knight,
   McNaughtan is his name.'

21 'If McNaughtan be his name,' he says,
   'As I trow weel it be,

The fairest lady in a' my court
　　Gangs wi child to thee.'

22 'If that she be wi child,' he says,
　　'As I wat weel she be,
　　I 'll mak it lord o a' my land,
　　And her my gay lady.'

23 'I have a champion in my court
　　Will fight you a' by three ; '
　　But up then speaks a brisk young man,
　　And a brisk young man was he :
　　I will fight to my life's end,
　　Before poor Johnny die.

24 The king but and his nobles a'
　　Went out into the plain,
　　The queen but and her maidens a',
　　To see young Johnny slain.

25 The first wound that Johnny gae the cham-
　　pion
　　Was a deep wound and sair ;
　　The next wound that he gae the champion,
　　He never spak mair.

26 'A priest, a priest,' young Johnny cries,
　　'To wed me and my love ; '
　　'A clerk, a clerk,' the king he cries,
　　'To sign her tocher gude.'

27 'I 'll hae nane o your goud,' he says,
　　'I 'll hae nane o your gear,
　　But a' I want is my true-love,
　　For I hae bought her dear.'

28 He took out a little goat-horn,
　　And blew baith loud and shill ;
　　The victry 's into Scotland gane,
　　Tho sair against their will.

───────◆───────

C

Motherwell's MS., p. 213 : from the recitation of Mrs
Thomson, Kilbarchan.

1 O JOHNIE 's to the hunting gone,
　　Unto the woods sae wild,
　　And Earl Percy's old daughter
　　To Johnie goes with child.

2 O word is to the kitchen gone,
　　And word is to the ha,
　　And word is to the highest towers,
　　Amang the nobles a'.

3 'If she be with child,' her father said,
　　'As woe forbid it be,
　　I 'll put her into a prison strong,
　　And try the veritie.'

4 'But if she be with child,' her mother said,
　　'As woe forbid it be,
　　I 'll put her intil a dungeon dark,
　　And hunger her till she die.'

5 Then she has wrote a braid letter,
　　And sealed it wi her hand,
　　And sent it to the merry green wood,
　　Wi her own boy at command.

6 The first line of the letter he read,
　　His heart was full of joy ;
　　But he had not read a line past two
　　Till the salt tears blind his eye.

7 'O I must up to England go,
　　What ever me betide,
　　For to relieve that fair ladie
　　That lay last by my side.'

8 Out and spak his father then,
　　And he spak all in time :
　　Johnie, if ye to England go,
　　I fear ye 'll neer return.

9 But out and spak his uncle then,
　　And he spak bitterlie :
　　Five hundred of my good life-guards
　　Shall go along with thee.

10 When they were mounted on their steeds,
　　They were comely to behold ;
　　The hair that hung owre Johnie's shoulders
　　Was like the yellow gold.

11 The first town that they came to,
　　They made the bells to ring ;
　　And when they rode the town all owre,
　　They made the trumpets sound.

12 When they came to Earl Percy's gates,
  They rode them round about,
  And who saw he but his own true-love,
  At a window looking out!

13 'The doors they are bolted with iron and
      steel,
  The windows round about;
  My feet they are in fetters strong;
  And how can I get out?

14 'My garters they are of the lead,
  And oh but they be cold!
  My breast-plate's of the beaten steel,
  Instead of beaten gold.'

15 But when they came to Earl Percy's yett,
  They tirled at the pin;
  None was so ready as Earl Percy
  To open and let them in.

16 'Art thou the King of Aulsberry,
  Or art thou the King of Spain?
  Or art thou one of our gay Scots lords,
  M⸰Nachtan by thy name?'

17 'I'm not the King of Aulsberry,
  Nor yet the King of Spain;
  But I am one of our gay Scots lords,
  Johnie Scot I am called by name.'

18 'If Johnie Scot be thy name,' he said,
  'As I trow weel it be,
  The fairest lady in a' our court
  Gaes big with child to thee.'

19 'If she be with child,' fair Johnie said,
  'As I trow weel she be,
  I'll make it heir owre a' my land,
  And her my gay ladie.'

20 'But if she be with child,' her father said,
  'As I trow weel she be,
  Tomorrow morn again eight o clock
  High hanged thou shalt be.'

21 But out and spak his uncle then,
  And he spak bitterlie:
  Before that we see Johnie Scot slain,
  We 'll a' fight till we die.

22 'But is there ever a Tailliant about your court,
  That will fight duels three?
  Before that I be hanged or slain,
  On the Tailliant's sword I'll die.'

23 But some is to the good green wood,
  And some is to the plain,
  Either to see fair Johnie hanged,
  Or else to see him slain.

24 And they began at eight o clock of the morning,
  And they fought on till three,
  Till the Tailliant, like a swallow swift,
  Owre Johnie's head did flee.

25 But Johnie being a clever young boy,
  He wheeled him round about,
  And on the point of Johnie's broad sword
  The Tailliant he slew out.

26 'A priest, a priest,' fair Johnie cried,
  'To wed my love and me;'
  'A clerk, a clerk,' her father cried,
  'To sum the tocher free.'

27 'I'll have none of your gold,' fair Johnie said,
  'Nor none of your white monie;
  But I will have my own fair bride,
  For I vow that I've bought her dear.'

28 He's taen his true-love by the hand,
  He led her up the plain:
  'Have you any more of your English dogs
  You want for to have slain?'

29 He took a little horn out of his pocket,
  He blew it baith loud and shill,
  And honour 's into Scotland gone,
  In spite of England's skill.

D

Motherwell MS., p. 205 : **a**, "words and tune from Mrs McNiccol," of Paisley, native of the parish of Houston ; **b**, variations from "John Lindsay, cowfeeder, Wallace Street, Paisley."

1 O JOHNNIE Scot walks up and down
　　Among the woods sae wild ;
　Who but the Earl of Percy's ae daughter
　　To him goes big with child !

2 O word is to the kitchen gone,
　　And word 's gone to the hall,
　And word is to King Henry gane,
　　And amongst his nobles all.

3 O Johnnie 's called his waiting-man,
　　His name was Germanie :
　' O thou must to fair England go,
　　Bring me that fair ladie.'

4 He rode till he came to Earl Percy's gate,
　　He tirled at the pin ;
　' O who is there ? ' said the proud porter,
　　' But I daurna let thee in.'

5 So he rade up, and he rode down,
　　Till he rode it round about ;
　Then he saw her at a wee window,
　　Where she was looking out.

6 ' O thou must go to Johnnie Scot,
　　Unto the woods so green,
　In token of thy silken shirt,
　　Thine own hand sewed the seam.'

7 ' How can I go to Johnnie Scot ?
　　Or how can I get out ?
　My breast plate 's o the hard, hard iron,
　　With fetters round about.

8 ' But I will write a lang letter,
　　And give it unto thee,
　And thou must take that to Johnnie Scot,
　　See what answer he sends to me.'

9 When Johnnie looked the letter upon
　　A sorry man was he ;
　He had not read one line but two
　　Till the saut tear did blind his ee.

10 ' O I must to fair England go,
　　Whatever me betide,
　All for to fight for that gay ladie
　　That last lay by my side.'

11 O out and spoke his father then,
　　And he spoke well in time :
　O if you to fair England go,
　　I doubt your coming home.

12 ' O no, O no,' said good King James,
　　' Before such a thing shall be,
　I 'll send five hundred of my life-guards,
　　To bear Johnnie company.'

13 When they were all on saddle set,
　　Most pleasant to behold,
　The hair that hung over Johnnie's neck
　　Was like the links of gold.

14 When they were all marching away,
　　Most beautiful to see,
　There was not so much as a married man
　　In Johnnie's company.

15 O Johnnie was the foremost man
　　In the company that did ride ;
　King James he was the second man,
　　Wi his rapier by his side.

16 They rode till they came to Earl Percy's yate,
　　They tirled at the pin :
　' O who is there ? ' said the proud porter ;
　　' But I daurnot let thee in.

17 ' Is it the Duke of York,' he said,
　　' Or James, our Scotish king ?
　Or is it one of the Scotish lords,
　　From hunting new come home ? '

18 ' It 's not the Duke of York,' he said,
　　' Nor James, our Scotish king ;
　But it is one of the Scotish lords,
　　Earl Hector is my name.'

19 When Johnnie came before the king,
　　He fell low down on his knee :
　' O the brawest lady in a' my court
　　With child goes big to thee.'

20 ' O if she be with child,' Johnnie said,
　　' As I trew well she be,
　I will make it heir of all my land,
　　And her my gay ladie.'

21 ' But if she be with child,' said the king,
　　' As I trew well she be,
　Before the morn at ten o clock
　　High hanged thou shalt be.'

22 'O no, O no,' said good King James,
   'Before such a thing shall be,
Before that Johnnie Scot be hanged,
   We 'll a' fight till we die.'

23 'But there is a Talliant in my court,
   Of men he will fight five ;
Go bring them out to the green wood,
   See wha will gain the prize.'

24 Lords and ladies flocked all,
   They flocked all amain,
They flocked all to the green wood,
   To see poor Johnnie slain.

25 This Talliant he could find no way
   To be poor Johnnie's dead,

But, like unto a swallow swift,
   He jumped oer Johnnie's head.

26 But Johnnie was a clever man,
   Cunning and crafty withal,
And up on the top of his braid sword
   He made this Talliant fall.

27 'A priest, a priest,' then Johnnie cried,
   'To marry my love and me ;'
'A clerk, a clerk,' her father cried,
   'To sum the tocher free.'

28 'I 'll take none of your gold,' Johnnie said,
   'Nor none of your other gear,
But I 'll just have my own true-love,
   This day I 've won her dear.'

E

Motherwell's MS., p. 113 ; from the recitation of T. Risk.

1 McNAUGHTON's unto England gane,
   The king's banner to bear :
'O do you see yon castle, boy ?
   It 's walled round about;
There you will spy a fair ladye,
   In the window looking out.'

2 'Here is a silken sark, fair lady,
   Thine own hand sewed the sleeve,
And thou must go to yon green wood,
   To Johnnie thy true-love.'

3 'The castle it is high, my boy,
   And walled round about ;
My feet are in the fetters strong,
   And how can I get out ?

4 'My garters o the gude black iron,
   And they are very cold ;
My breast plate 's of the sturdy steel,
   Instead of beaten gold.

5 'But had I paper, pen and ink,
   And candle at my command,
It 's I would write a lang letter
   To John in fair Scotland.'

6 The first line that Johnnie looked on,
   A loud, loud lauch leuch he ;

The second line that Johnnie looked on,
   The tear did blind his ee.

7 Says, I must unto England go,
   Whatever me betide,
For to relieve my own fair lady,
   That lay last by my side.

8 Then up and spoke Johnnie's auld mither,
   A well spoke woman was she :
If you do go to England, Johnnie,
   I may take farewell o thee.

9 Then up and spoke Johnnie's old father,
   A well spoke man was he :
It 's twenty-four of my gay troop
   Shall go along with thee.

10 When Johnie was on saddle set,
   Right comely to be seen,
There was not so much as a married man
   In Johnie's companie ;
There was not so much as a married man,
   Not a one only but ane.

11 The first gude toun that Johnie came to,
   He made the bells be rung ;
The next gude toun that Johnie came to,
   He made the psalms be sung.

12 The next gude toun that Johnie came to,
   He made the drums beat round,

Till the king and all his merry men
  A-marvelled at the sound.

13 'Are you the Duke of Mulberry,
    Or James, our Scotish king?
  Are you the Duke of Mulberry,
    From Scotland new come home?'

14 'I'm not the Duke of Mulberry,
    Nor James, our Scotish king;
  But I am a true Scotishman,
    McNaughtoun is my name.'

15 'If McNaughtoun be your name,' he said,
    'As I trew well it be,
  The fairest lady in a' my court
    She goes with child to thee.

16 'If McNauchton be your name,' he said,
    'As I trew well it be,
  Tomorrow morn by eight o clock
    O hanged you shall be.'

17 O Johnie had a bonnie little boy,
    His name was Germany:
  'Before that we be all hanged, my sovereign,
    We'll fight you till we die.'

18 'Say on, say on, my bonnie little boy,
    It is well spoken of thee,
  For there is a campioun in my court
    Shall fight you three by three.'

19 Next morning about eight o'clock
    The king and his merry men,

The queen and all her maidens fair,
  Came whistling down the green,
To see the cruel fight begin,
  And see poor Johnnie slain.

20 They fought on, and Johnie fought on,
    Wi swords of tempered steel,
  Until the drops of red, red blood
    Ran prinkling down the field.

21 They fought on, and Johnie fought on,
    They fought so manfullie
  They left not a man alive in all the king's
      court,
    Not a man only but three.

22 'A priest, a priest,' poor Johnie cries,
    'To wed my love and me;'
  'A clerk, a clerk,' the king did cry,
    'To write her portion free.'

23 'I'll have none of your gold,' he says,
    'Nor none of your white money,
  But I will have mine own fair lady,
    Who has been dear to me.'

24 Johnie put a horn unto his mouth,
    He blew it wondrous schill;
  The sound is unto Scotland gane,
    Sair against all their will.

25 He put his horn to his mouth,
    He blew it ower again,
  And aye the sound the horn cried,
    'McNaughtoun's cure to them!'

———◆———

F

Motherwell's MS., p. 211; from the recitation of Agnes
Laird, Kilbarchan, 21 June, 1825.

1 WORD has to the kitchen gane,
    And word has to the ha,
  And word has to the king himsell,
    In the chamber where he sat,
  That his ae daughter gaes wi bairn
    To bonnie Johnie Scot.

2 Word has to the kitchen gane,
    And word has to the ha,
  And word has to the queen hersell,
    In the chamber where she sat,

That her ae dochter gaes wi bairn
  To bonnie Johnie Scot.

3 'O if she be wi bairn,' he says,
    'As I trew well she be,
  We'll put her in a prison strang,
    And try her verity.'

4 'O if she be wi bairn,' she says,
    'As I trew weel she be,
  We'll put her in a dungeon dark,
    And hunger her till she die.'

5 Now she has written a letter,
    And sealed it with her hand,

And sent it unto Johnie Scot,
  To come at her command.

6 The first lang line that he looked to,
  He laughed at the same ;
  The neist lang line that he did read,
  The tears did blin his een.

7 'Once more to England I must go,
  May God be my sure guide !
  And all to see that lady fair
  That last lay by my side.'

8 Then out bespoke our Scotish king,
  And he spoke manfullie :
  I and three thousand of my guards
  Will bear you companye.

9 They all were mounted on horseback,
  So gallantly they rode ;
  The hair that hung owre Johnie's shoulders
  Was like the links of goud.

10 When they came to the king of England's
    gate,
  They knocked at the pin ;
  So ready was the king himsell
  To open and let them in.

11 'Are you the Duke [of York],' he says,
  ' Or are ye the King of Spain ?
  Or are ye some of the gay Scots boys,
  From hunting now come hame ?'

12 'I am not the Duke of York,' he says,
  ' Nor yet the King of Spain ;
  But I am one of the gay Scots boys,
  From hunting just come hame.'

13 'If you are one of the Scots boys,
  As I trew weel you be,
  The fairest lady in my hall
  Gaes big wi child to thee.'

14 'Then if she be wi bairn,' he says,
  ' As I trew weel she be,
  I 'll make him heir of a' my gear,
  And her my fair ladye.'

15 'If she be wi bairn,' her father says,
  ' As I trew weel she be,
  Before the morn at ten o'clock
  High hanged thou shall be.'

16 Then out bespake our Scotish king,
  And he spoke manfullie :
  Before that Johnie Scott be slain,
  We 'll all fight till we die.

17 'I have a Talliant in my house
  We 'll fight your men by three ;'
  ' Bring out your trooper,' Johnie says,
  ' For fain I would him see.'

18 Some gade unto the high mountain,
  Some gade unto the plain,
  Some at high windows looked out,
  To see poor Johnie slain.

19 The Talliant he fought on a while,
  Thinking Johnie would retire,
  And then he, like a swallow swifte,
  Owre Johnie's head did flee.

20 But Johnie was a clever man,
  And turned about with speed,
  And on the edge of his broadsword
  He slew the Talliant dead.

21 Then he has brought the lady out,
  And sat her on a dapple-gray,
  And being mounted on before,
  They briskly rode away.

22 Now the honour unto Scotland came,
  In spite of England's skill ;
  The honour unto Scotland came
  In spite of England's will.

———◆———

G

Motherwell's Note-Book, p. 35, Motherwell MS., p. 394 ;
from the singing of Agnes Lyle, of Kilbarchan, 24 August,
1825.

1 JOHNIE SCOTT 's a hunting gone,
  To England woods so wild,

Until the king's old dochter dear
  She goes to him with child.

2 'If she be with bairn,' her mother says,
  ' As I trew weel she be,
  We 'll put her in a dark dungeon,
  And hunger her till she die.'

3 'If she be with bairn,' her father says,
   'As oh forbid she be!
We 'll put her in a prison strong,
   And try the veritie.'

4 The king did write a long letter,
   Sealed it with his own hand,
And he sent it to Johnie Scot,
   To speak at his command.

5 When Johnie read this letter long,
   The tear blindit his ee:
'I must away to Old England;
   King Edward writes for me.'

6 Out and spak his mother dear,
   She spoke aye in time:
Son, if thou go to Old England,
   I fear thou 'll neer come hame.

7 Out and spoke a Scotish prince,
   And a weel spoke man was he:
Here 's four and twenty o my braw troops,
   To bear thee companie.

8 Away they gade, awa they rade,
   Away they rade so slie;
There was not a maried man that day
   In Johnie's companie.

9 The first good town that they passed thro,
   They made their bells to ring;
The next good town that they passed thro,
   They made their music sing.

10 The next gude town that they passed thro,
   They made their drums beat round,
The king and a' his gay armies
   Admiring at the sound.

11 When they came to the king's court,
   They travelled round about,
And there he spied his own true-love,
   At a window looking out.

12 'O fain wald I come down,' she says,
   'Of that ye needna dout;
But my garters they 're of cauld, cauld iron,
   And I can no win out.

13 'My garters they 're of cauld, cauld iron,
   And it is very cold;

My breast-plate is of sturdy steel,
   Instead o beaten gold.'

14 Out and spoke the king himsell,
   And an angry man was he:
The fairest lady in a' my court,
   She goes with child to thee.

15 'If your old doughter be with child,
   As I trew weel she be,
I 'le make it heir of a' my land,
   And her my gay lady.'

16 'There is a Talliant in my court,
   This day he 's killed three;
And gin the morn by ten o'clock
   He 'll kill thy men and thee.'

17 Johnie took sword into his hand,
   And walked cross the plain;
There was many a weeping lady there,
   To see young Johnie slain.

18 The Talliant never knowing this,
   Now he 'll be Johnie's dead,
But, like unto a swallow swift,
   He flew out owre his head.

19 Johnie was a valliant man,
   Weel taught in war was he,
And on the point of his broad sword
   The Talliant stickit he.

20 Johnie took sword into his hand,
   And walked cross the plain:
'Are there here any moe of your English
   dogs
   That 's wanting to be slain?

21 'A priest, a priest,' young Johnie cries,
   'To wed my bride and me;'
'A clerk, a clerk,' her father cries,
   'To tell her tocher wi.'

22 'I 'm wanting none of your gold,' he says,
   'As little of your gear;
But give me just mine own true-love,
   I think I 've won her dear.'

23 Johnie sets horn into his mouth,
   And he blew loud and schrill;
The honour it 's to Scotland come,
   Sore against England's will.

H

Kinloch MSS, VI, 53, in an unknown hand.

1 ' WHERE will I gett a bony boy,
      That would fain win hose and shoon,
   That will go on to yon palace,
      And haste him back again ? '

2 ' Here am I, a bony boy,
      That would fain win hose and shoon,
   That will go on to yon palace,
      And haste me back again.'

3 ' When you come to yon palace,
      You 'l run it round about ;
   There you 'l see a gay lady,
      At the window looking out.

4 ' Give hir this shirt of silk,
      Hir own hand sewed the slive,
   And bid her come to good green woods,
      Spear no hir parents' leave.

5 ' Give hir this shirt of silk, boy,
      Hir own hand sewed the gare ;
   You 'l bid her come to good green woods,
      Love Johny, I 'll meet hir there.'

6 When he came to yon palace,
      He ran it round about,
   And there he saw a gay lady,
      At the window looking out.

7 ' Take here this shirt of silk, lady,
      Your own hand sewed the slive ;
   You 're biden come to good green woods,
      Spire no your parents' leave.

8 ' Take here this shirt of silk, lady,
      Your own hand sewed the gare ;
   You 're biden come to good green woods,
      Love Johny 'll meet you there.'

9 ' The staunchens they are strong, boy,
      Dear, vow but they are stout !
   My feet they are in strong fetters,
      And how shall I win out ?

10 ' My garters is of the cold iron,
       Dear, vow but they are cold !
    And three splits of the sturdy steel,
       Instead of beaten goold.

11 ' But I will write a braud leter,
       And sign it with my hand,
    And I will send it to Love Johny,
       Weel may he understand.'

12 And she has wrote [a] braud leter,
       And signd it with hir hand,
    And sent it on to Love Jony,
       Weel did he understand.

13 When he got this letter,
       A light laugh did he gie ;
    But or he read it half down through,
       The salt tears blinded 's ee.

14 Says, I 'll awa to fair England,
       What ever may betide,
    And all is for the fair lady
       That lay close by my side.

15 Out it spoke Jony's mother,
       And she spoke ay through pride ;
    Says, If ye go to fair England,
       Sir, better to you bide.

16 When Jony was on his sadle set,
       And seemly to behold,
    Every tet o Love Jony's hair
       Was like the threads of goold.

17 When Jony was on his sadle set,
       And seemly for to see,
    There was not a maried man
       In a' Jony's company.

18 The first town that they came till,
       They gard the bells be rung ;
    The next town that they came till,
       They gard the mess bee sung.

19 When they came to the king's palace,
       The drums they did beat round,
    And the quien and her marys all
       Amased at the sound.

20 ' Is this the Duke of Mulberry,
       Or James, our Scottish king ?
    Or is it any noble lord
       That 's going a visiting ? '

21 ' It 's not the Duke of Mulberry,
       Nor James, our Scottish king ;

But it is Jack, the Little Scot,
  And Auchney is his name.'

22 'If Auchney bee your name,' he said,
  'As I trust weel it be,
  The fairest lady in all my court
  She goes with bairn to the.'

23 'If she be with bairn,' he said,
  'As I doubt not nor she be,
  I will make it heir oer all my land,
  And hir my gay lady.'

24 The king he swore a solemn oath,
  And a solemn oath swore he,
  'The morn, before I eat or drink,
  High hanged he shall be!'

  *   *   *   *

25 The king and his nobles all
  Went out into the plain,
  And the quen and hir marys all,
  To see Love Johny slain.

26 They fought up, and they fought down,
  With swords of temperd steel,
  But not a drop of Johny's blood
  In that day he did spill.

27 Out they brought the Itilian,
  And a greecy ghost was he,
  But by the edge o Love Johny's sword
  That Itilian did die.

28 Johny's taen his neat drawn sword,
  And stript it to the stran:
  'Is there any more of your English dogs
  That wants for to be slain?'

29 'A clerck, a clerck,' now says the king,
  'To sign her tocher free;'
  'A priest, a priest,' said Love Johny,
  'To mary my dear and me.

30 'I fought not for your goold, your goold,
  I fought not for your gear,
  But I fought for my rose Mary,
  And vow! I 've bought hir dear.'

  ————◆————

I

Kinloch MSS, VII, 39, 41, 43, 45, 47, 49.

1 JOHNIE is up to London gane,
  Three quarters o the year,
  And he is up to London gane,
  The king's banner for to bear.

2 He had na been in fair London
  A twalmonth and a day,
  Till the king's ae daughter
  To Johnie gangs wi child.

3 O word is to the kitchen gane,
  And word is to the ha,
  And word is to the king himsel
  Amang his nobles a'.

  *   *   *   *

4 She has wrote a braid letter,
  She has wrote it tenderly,
  And she 's wrote a braid letter,
  To lat her Johnie see

5 That her bower is very high,
  It 's aw weel walled about;
  Her feet are in the fetters strang,
  Her body looking out.

6 Her garters are of cauld iron,
  And they are very cold;
  Her breist-plate is o the sturdy steel,
  Instead o the beaten gold.

7 Whan he lookit the letter on,
  A licht lauch gaed he;
  But eer he read it til an end,
  The tear blindit his ee.

8 'I maun up to London gang,
  Whatever me betide,
  And louse that lady out o prison strang;
  She lay last by my side.'

9 Up spak Johnie's ae best man,
  That stood by Johnie's knie:
  Ye 'll get twenty four o my best men,
  To bear ye companie.

10 When Johnie was in his saddle set,
   A pleasant sicht to see,
There was na ae married man
   In Johnie's companie.

11 The first toun that he cam till,
   He made the mass be sung;
The niest toun that he cam till,
   He made the bells be rung.

12 When he cam to fair London,
   He made the drums gae round;
The king and his nobles aw
   They marvelld at the sound.

13 'Is this the Duke of Winesberry,
   Or James, the Scotish king?
Or is it a young gentleman,
   That wants for to be in?'

14 'It's na the Duke of Winesberry,
   Nor James, the Scotish king;
But it is a young gentleman,
   Buneftan is his name.'

15 Up spak the king himsel,
   An angry man was he:
The morn eer I eat or drink
   Hie hangit sall he be.

16 Up spak Johnie's ae best man,
   That stood by Johnie's knie:
Afore our master he be slain
   We'll aw fecht till we die.

17 Up spak the king himsel,
   And up spak he:

I have an Italian in my court
   That will fecht ye manifullie.

18 'If ye hae an Italian in your court,
   Fu fain wad I him see;
If ye hae an Italian in your court,
   Ye may bring him here to me.'

19 The king and his nobles aw
   Went tripping doun the plain,
Wi the queen and her maries aw,
   To see fair Johnie slain.

20 Even anent the prison-door
   The battle did begin;

   .   .   .   .

   .   .   .   .

21 They foucht up, and they foucht doun,
   Wi swerds o tempered steel,
Til Johnie wi his gude braidswerd
   Made the Italian for to yield.

22 He has kickd him with his foot,
   And he has kickd him oure the plain:
'Onie mair Italians in your court
   Ye want for to be slain?'

23 'A clerk, a clerk,' the king cried,
   'To sign her tocher-fee;'
'A priest, a priest,' young Johnie said,
   'To marry her and me.

24 'For I want nane o your gowd,
   Nor nane o your weel won fee;
I only want your fair dochter,
   I have won her mannfullie.'

————◆————

J

Kinloch MSS, VII, 40, 42, 46, 49.

1 O word is to the queen hersel,
   In parlour whare she sat,
That the king's dochter goes wi child
   To Jock, that little Scot.

2 O word is to the king himsel,
   And an angry man was he;
Says, I will put her in cold prison,
   And hunger her till she dee.

3 The ladie was laid in cold prison,
   By the king, a grievous man;
And up and starts a little boy,
   Upon her window-stane.

4 Says, Here's a silken shift, ladye,
   Your ane hand sewed the sleeve,
And ye maun gang to yon greenwud,
   And of your freends speir na leave.

5 'My bouer is very hie,' said the lady,
   'And it's wondrous hie round about;

My feet are lockit in the iron fetters,
　　And how can I get out?

6 ' But I will write a braid letter,
　　And seal it tenderlie,
　And send it to yon greenwud,
　　And let young Johnie see.'

7 O Johnie's to his father gane,
　　And til him did say,
　O I maun up to London, father,
　　And fecht for that lady gay.

8 His father spak but ae word,
　　Says, I speak it in time;
　For an ye gang to London, Johnie,
　　I fear your coming hame.

K

Kinloch MSS, I, 311.

1 JOHNIE's up to England gane,
　　Three quarters o a year;
　Johnie's up to England gane,
　　The king's banner to bear.

2 He had not in fair England been
　　A month 't was barely ane,
　When the fairest lady o the court
　　To Johnie wi child is gane.

3 Word is to the kitchen gane,
　　And word 's gane to the ha;
　Word 's gane to the high, high rooms,
　　Among the nobles a'.

4 And word o 't to the king is gane,
　　In the chamber where he sat,
　His only daughter goes wi child
　　To Johnie, the Little Scot.

5 ' O if she be wi child,' he says,
　　' As I trow weel she be,
　I 'll lock her up in strong prison,
　　And punish her till she dee.'

6 Then she has wrote a long letter,
　　And seald it without a blot,
　And she has sent it to fair Scotland,
　　To Johnie, the Little Scot.

9 And out and spak anither youth,
　　And a pretty youth was he:
　Afore I see young Johnie dung
　　I 'll fecht for him till I dee.

*　　*　　*　　*

10 He has wallowd it, he has wallowd it,
　　He 's wallowd it again;
　Cries, Onie mae o your English dogs
　　That wants for to be slain?

11 He set the horn until his mouth,
　　And he has blawn baith loud and shill;
　The victor 's doun to Scotland gane,
　　Richt sair against their will.

7 The first line that he did read,
　　In laughter loud was he;
　But or he gat the hindmost read
　　The tear blindit his ee.

8 ' Get ready for me the black, black steed,
　　Get ready for me the brown,
　And saddle to me the swiftest horse
　　Eer carried man to town.'

9 Whan he cam to Edinburgh town,
　　He made the bells to ring,
　And when he cam to merry Carlisle,
　　He made the monks to sing.

10 When he cam to the king's gates,
　　He made his drums beat round;
　The king bot and his nobles a'
　　They wonderd at the sound.

11 ' Is this [the] King of France,' he **cried,**
　　' Or is 't the King of Spain?
　Or is it Johnie, the Little Scot,
　　That 's wanting to be slain?'

12 ' It 's neither the King of France,' he said,
　　' Nor is 't the King of Spain;
　But it is Johnie, the Little Scot,
　　That 's come to claim his ain.'

*　　*　　*　　*　　*

13 They foucht it ance, they foucht it twice,
　　They foucht it oure again,
　Till draps o blood, like draps o rain,
　　War rinning to the plain.

14 Then Johnie drew a nut-brown brand,
　　And strook it oure the plain,
　Saying, Are there onie mae o your English-
　　　men
　　That 's wanting to be slain ?

15 ' A clerk, a clerk,' the king he cried,
　　' To sign her tocher-fee ; '
　' A priest, a priest,' then Johnie cried,
　　' To marry my love and me.

16 ' I 'll hae nane o your gowd,' he says,
　　' As little o your gear ;
　But I 'll hae her, my ain true-love,
　　For I 'm sure I 've coft her dear.'

L

Campbell MSS, I, 57.

1 JOHNNIE SCOTT 's a hunting gane,
　　To England's woods sae wild ;
　The fairest flower of all England
　　To Johnie provd big with child.

2 It 's word 's going up, and word 's going down,
　　Going to the king's bower,
　That his dear daughter was with child,
　　That was his daily flower.

3 ' If she be with child,
　　As I suppose she be,
　I 'll put her into prison strong,
　　And hunger her till she die.'

4 The king he wrote a letter broad,
　　And sealed it with his hands,
　And sent it down to Johnie Scott,
　　In Scotland where he stands.

5 The first line that Johnie lookd on,
　　A merry man was he ;
　The next line that he lookd on,
　　The salt tears blinded his eye.

6 Out then spoke his old father,
　　Who neer spoke out of time :
　And if you go to England, son,
　　I doubt your coming home.

7 Out then spoke our Scottish James,
　　Sitting low by Johnie's knee :
　Fifteen score of my life-guards
　　Shall ride in your company.

8 When Johnie came to the king's court
　　He rode it round about,

And there he spied his own true-love,
　　From the jail-window looking out.

9 ' Come down, true-love,' said Johnie Scott,
　　' And now you 'll ride behind me ;
　Before I leave fair England
　　Some life shall die for thee.'

10 ' My feet are in the fetters strong,
　　I 'm belted round about ;
　My breastplate is of the stubborn steel,
　　Instead of beaten gold.'

11 When Johnie came to the king's bower
　　He tinkled at the ring ;
　Who was so ready as the king himself
　　To let proud Johnie in !

12 ' Are ye the Duke of Marlborough,' he said,
　　' Or James, our Scottish king ?
　Or are you my bastard son,
　　From Scotland new come home ? '

13 ' I 'm not the Duke of Marlborough,' he said,
　　' Nor James, our Scottish king ;
　But I am just a good Scotch lad,
　　And Johnie Scott 's my name.'

14 ' If you be Johnie Scott,' says he,
　　' As I suppose you be,
　The fairest flower in all England
　　Is big with child by thee.'

15 ' If she be big with child,' said he,
　　' As I hope her to be,
　I 'll make it heir of all my lands,
　　And she my gay lady.'

16 ' O no,' then the king he crys,
　　' There 's no such thing will be ;

There is an Italian in my court,
  And by his hands ye 'll die.'

17 'I 'll stand my ground,' says Johnnie
      Scott,
  ' I 'll stand it till I die ;
  I 'll stand my ground,' says Johnnie Scott,
  ' One foot I 'd scorn to fly.'

18 When the Italian was brought out,
    A fearsome sight was he ;
  Between his brows three women's spang,
    His shoulders was yards three.

19 As Johnnie, being a crafty lad,
    Well tried at the sword was he,
  Upon the point of his broad sword
    He made the Italian die.

———————

M

Campbell MSS, II, 335.

1 LORD JOHNNIE 's up to England gane,
    Three quarters of an year ;
  Lord Johnnie 's up to England gone,
    The king's banner to bear.

2 He had not been in fair England,
    Three quarters he was not,
  Till the king's eldest daughter
    Goes with child to Lord Johnnie Scott.

3 Word has to the kitchen gone,
    And word 's gone to the hall,
  And word 's gone to the high, high room,
    Among the nobles all.

4 And word has gaen to the king himsel,
    In his chamber where he sat,
  That his eldest daughter goes wi child
    To good Lord Johnnie Scott.

5 ' Gin that be true,' the king replied,
    ' As I suppose it be,
  I 'll put her in a prison strong,
    And starve her till she die.'

      *   *   *   *   *

6 ' O where will I get a little page,
    That will win baith hose and shoon,
  And run into fair Scotland,
    And tell my love to come ? '

      *   *   *   *   *

7 ' What news, what news, my little page ?
    What news hae ye brought to me ? '
  ' Bad news, bad news, my master dear,
    The king's daughter maun die.

8 ' Here is a shirt, O master dear,
    Her ain hand sewd the sleeve ;
  She bad me run and tell ye this,
    And ask nae person's leave.

9 ' They have her in a prison strong,
    And in a dungeon deep ;
  Her feet are in the fetters strong,
    And they 've left her to weep.

10 ' Her feet are in the cold, cold iron,
    Instead of beaten gold ;
  Her garters are of the cauld, cauld iron,
    And O but they are cold ! '

      *   *   *   *   *

11 ' A clerk, a clerk,' the king did cry,
    ' To cry the toucher-fee ; '
  ' A priest, a priest,' Lord Johnnie cry'd,
    ' To join my love and me.

12 ' I want none of your gold,' he said,
    ' Nor as little want I a fee ;
  But I do want your daughter dear,
    My wedded wife to be.'

N

Buchan's Gleanings, p. 122.

1 LORD JOHN he 's on to England gone,
    To England gone is he ;
  Love John he 's on to England gone,
    The king's banneret to be.

2 He hadna been in fair England
    O but a little while,
  Till faen in love wi the king's daughter,
    And to him she 's with chile.

3 Now word is to the kitchen gane,
    And word is to the ha,
  And word is to the king's high court,
    And that was warst of a'.

4 Out then spake the king himsell,
    An angry man was he :
  I 'll put her into prison strong,
    And starve her till she die.

5 Love John he 's on to Scotland gone,
    I wat he 's on wi speed ;
  Love John he 's on to Scotland gone,
    And as good was his need.

6 He hadna been in fair Scotland
    But a very short tide,
  Till he minded on the damsel
    That lay last by his side.

7 'Whare will I get a bonny boy,
    Will win baith meat and fee,
  That will run on to fair England,
    And haste him back to me ?'

8 'O here am I, a bonny boy,
    Will win baith meat and fee,
  That will run on to fair England,
    And haste him back to thee.'

9 'Where ye find the grass grow green,
    Ye 'll slack your shoes and rin ;
  And when ye find the brigs broken,
    Ye 'll bend your bow and swim.

10 'And when ye come to the king's high court,
    Ye 'll rin it round about,
  And there ye 'll see a lady gay,
    At a window looking out.

11 'Bid her take this shirt of silk,
    Her ain hand sewed the sleeve ;
  Bid her come to good green-wood,
    At her parents spier nae leave.

12 'Bid her take this shirt of silk,
    Her ain hand sewed the gair ;
  Bid her come to good green-wood,
    Love John he waits her there.'

13 Where he found the grass grow green,
    He slackd his shoes and ran ;
  Where he fan the brigs broken,
    He bent his bow and swam.

14 When he came to the king's high court,
    He ran it round about ;
  And there he saw the lady gay,
    At the window looking out.

15 'Ye 're bidden take this shirt of silk,
    Yere ain hand sewed the sleeve ;
  Ye 're bidden come to good green-wood,
    At your parents spier nae leave.

16 'Ye 're bidden take this shirt of silk,
    Yere ain hand sewed the gair ;
  Ye 're bidden come to good green-wood,
    Love John he waits you there.'

17 'My feet are in the fetters strong,
    Instead of silken sheen ;
  My breast-plate 's of the cold iron,
    Instead of gold so fine.

18 'But I will write a broad letter,
    And seal it with my hand,
  And send it off to my Love Johnny,
    And let him understand.'

19 The first line that he looked on,
    A loud laughter laught he ;
  But ere he read it to the end,
    The tear blinded his ee.

20 'O I will on to fair England,
    Whatever me betide,
  For to relieve the damsel
    That lay last by my side.'

21 Out it spake his father dear,
    A noble lord was he :

If ye gang to England, Johnny,
Ye 'll neer come back to me.

22 Out it spake a noble lord,
A noble lord, I wat, was he :
Fifteen of our Scottish lords
Will bear his honour companie.

23 The first town that they eer came till,
They gart the bells be rung ;
The next town that they came till,
They gart the mass be sung.

24 And when they came to the king's court,
They gart the trumpet soun,
Till the king and all his merry young
men
Did marvel at the tune.

25 ' Is this the Duke of Marlborough,
Or James, the Scottish king ?
Or is it else some Scottish lord,
Come here a visiting ? '

26 ' It 's not the Duke of Marlborough,
Nor James, the Scottish king :
It is Love John of fair Scotland,
Come here a visiting.'

27 ' If this be John of fair Scotland,
He 's dearly welcome to me ;

The morn ere he eat or drink,
High hanged he shall be.'

28 He 's taen his broadsword in his hand,
And stripd it oer a stane ;
Then thro and thro the king's high court
With broadsword now is gane.

29 They fought it up, they fought it down,
Till they were weary men,
When the blood, like drops of rain,
Came trickling down the plain.

30 Out it spake the king himsel,
Ane angry man was he :
I have ane Italian within my court
Will fight ye three and three.

31 Out it came that ae Italian,
As pale as death was he,
And on the point of Johnny's sword
That ae Italian did die.

32 ' A clerk, a clerk,' the king he cried,
' And seal her tocher wi ; '
' A priest, a priest,' Lord John he cried,
' That we may married be.

33 ' For I want neither gold,' he said,
' Nor do I want your gear ;
But I do want my ain true-love,
For I have bought her dear.'

O

Communicated by Mr William Macmath, of Edinburgh,
from his aunt, Miss Jane Webster, formerly of Airds of
Kells, now (December, 1882) of Dalry, Kirkcudbrightshire,
who learned it from the late Miss Jane Hannay, Newton
Stewart.

* * * * *

1 Out then spak his auld faither,
And a blythe auld man was he,
Saying, I 'll send five hunner o my brisk young
men,
To bear Johnie companie.

2 And when they were on saddle set,
They were a pleasant sight for to see,
For there was na ae married man
In a' Johnie's companie.

3 And when they were on saddle set,
They were a pleasant sight to behold,
For the hair that hung down Johnie's back
Was like the links of gold.

4 And when they came to Newcastle,
They reined their horses about ;
Wha did he see but his ain Jeanie,
At a window looking out !

5 ' Come doun, come doun, Jeanie,' he says,
' Come doun, come doun to me ; '
' I canna come doun, Johnie,' she says,
' For King Edward has bolted me.

6 ' My stockings are o the heavy iron,
I feel them very cold ;
And my breast-plate 's o the sturdy steel,
Instead of beaten gold.'

*   *   *   *   *

7 .   .   .   .   .

     ' I 'll make it heir o a' my lands,
       And her my gay lady.'

P

Motherwell's Note-Book, p. 11.

1 JOHNIE 's up to England gone,
     Three quarters of a year;
     Johnie 's up to England gone,
     The king's banner to bear.

2 He hadna been in fair England
     A month but only three,

8 'There is an Italian in this court;
     This day he has slain knights three;
     And before tomorrow at eight o'clock
     The Italian will slay thee.'

           The king he had but one dochter,
     And she fell in love with he.

3 And word is up, and word is down,
     And word is to the ha,
     And word is to the king's court gane,
     Amang the nobles a'.

4 Now word is to the king himsell,
     On throne where he did sit,
     That his ae dochter goes wi child
     To John that little Scot.

A. *Written in stanzas of two long lines in the*
     Jamieson MS.
4², 27². *MS.* will?   8³. I wist.   15³. plates.
The first stanza is given thus by Anderson in
     Nichols's Illustrations :

       Johnie was as brave a knight
         As ever sailed the sea,
       And he is to the English court,
         To serve for meat and fee.

The Abbotsford copy omits stanzas 4, 9, 34.
     Most of the many changes are, beyond doubt,
     arbitrary, but the following are more or
     less countenanced by other versions.
1³· ⁴. And he is up to fair England,
     The king's braid banner to bear.
     Cf. B, E, I, K, M, N, P.
19⁴. That should have been my bride.
     Cf. B 10.

30. Out then cam that Italian knight,
     A grisly sight to see;
     Between his een there was a span,
     Between his shoulders three and three.

     And forth then came brave John the Scot,
     He scarcely reachd his knee;

     Yet on the point of Johny's brand
     The Italian knight did die.

       Cf. L 18.

B. *Written in stanzas of two lines.* 16³. And there.
C. 3². forgid.   14³. plates.   16⁴. be thy.
     23³. Johnie slain.   24⁴. Johnie's dread.
     26⁴. free *changed in MS. to* fee. *Cf.* A 33²,
     D 27⁴, E 22⁴, H 29²; fee, I 23², K 15², M
     11².
D. a. *The last two lines of each stanza are repeated*
     in singing.
     8⁴. *Originally* to thee.
     25². dead *changed to* deid.
   b. *Title,* Lord Johnnie Scot.
     The variations are generally written above the
     readings of a, *or otherwise distinctly indi-*
     cated.
     1¹. It 's Johnie.   1³. And who.
     3³. It 's thou.   3⁴. gay ladie.
     4¹. rode till her father's gate.   5¹. It 's he.
     6¹. to the green woods.
     6². To Johnnie Scot thy luve.   6⁴. the sleeve.
     7¹. to the green woods.   10³. ladie gay.
     11¹. out then . . . father dear.
     11². spoke out.   11³. If thou unto.
     11⁴. doubt thy.   12¹. Out then spoke our.
     12². And he spoke manfullie.

13, 14. *These stanzas are often transposed.*
13⁴. the yellow gold.
14². Most pleasant for to.
18¹. I 'm not.   18². James your.
18³. But I 'm.   20¹. he said.   21¹. he said.
22¹. Out then spoke our.   23⁴. the day.
24¹. all did flock.   24². In coaches all amain.
24⁸. all did flock.   25⁴. oer his head.
26³. on the point.
The reciter had heard another ballad which detailed the same events, and but little differing in any respect, which went under the name of 'McNaughton's Valour,' or, 'Naughton's Valour.'

E. 13⁴. *Originally* now come, *altered to* new come.
17². *Var.* And a well spoke boy was he.
18³. *Var.* champion.
19³. *Originally written* Likewise the queen and her maidens fair.
20⁴. trinkling down?   *Motherwell.*

25⁴. *Var.* McNaughton and his men !
"McNaughtoun's cure to ye !" is Devil relieve ye !   *Motherwell.*
F. 3¹, 4¹. Oh.
G. 8². the rade.   8³. Theyre.
The second copy has these few differences, attributable to Motherwell :
1³. England's.   2¹, 3¹. said.   7⁴. bear him.
23¹. set unto.   23². schill.   23³. Scotland gone.
H. 8⁴. Johny I 'll.   19². They drums.
20¹. muberry.   26³. Johny.   27³. But but.
26, 27 *should, perhaps, be transposed ; but compare* N 29–31.
I. 2². *Kinloch corrects* day *to* while.
After 3.   A verse a-wanting.   It is about the king putting his daughter in prison.
K. 14². shook: *cf.* A 32².
L. 3⁴. dies (?).   17³. say.
P. 2⁴. *Var.* goes with child to : *perhaps a change of Motherwell's.*

100

WILLIE O WINSBURY

A. ' Willie o Winsbury,' Campbell MSS, II, 38.

B. Herd's MSS, I, 29 ; II, 98.

C. ' Lord Thomas of Winsbury,' Kinloch MSS, I, 315.

D. Percy Papers, communicated by the Rev. P. Parsons, about 1775.

E. ' Johnnie Barbour,' Notes and Queries, Fifth Series, VII, 387.

F. ' Willie of Winsberye,' Motherwell's MS., p. 404.

G. ' Lord Thomas o Winsbury,' Buchan's MSS, II, 174 ; ' Lord Thomas of Winesberry and the King's Daughter,' Buchan's Ballads of the North of Scotland, II, 212.

H. ' Lord Thomas of Winesberrie,' Kinloch's Ancient Scottish Ballads, p. 92.

I. ' Lord Thomas of Winsberry,' a, b, stall copies ; c, Buchan's Gleanings, p. 127.

THE main points of the story of this ballad are the same in all the copies. The king of Scotland, C, F, of France, H, I, has been away from home a considerable time, in Spain, A, C, F, G, a prisoner, A, F, a-hunting, C, H, I, and during his absence his daughter has become with child by William or Thomas of Winsbury. The father threatens to hang the young man, but on seeing him is so struck with his beauty that he exonerates his daughter, and offers her in marriage to her lover, with a large dowry. Winsbury accepts the lady, but declines gold and land, having enough of his own. In H he says he shall be king when he goes back to Scotland ; in the other copies he appears to be only a man of very good estate.

From the hero turning out to be a royal person from Scotland, in H, Kinloch, Ancient Scot-

ish Ballads, p. 89, is led to imagine that the
ballad may relate to James V of Scotland, who
married a daughter of Francis I. His reasons
are, first, that James *disguised himself* when
he went to inspect the Duke of Vendôme's
daughter (to whom he was in a way betrothed),
so as not to be known to her or to her parents.
Secondly, that when James, not fancying this
lady, passed on, it was at a *hunting*-party
that he met the French princess, who became
so enamored of him that she would have no
other husband. That the poor princess had
long been sick, and "was not able to travel
out of the realm to no other countrie" (on
a milk-white steed, C 13), and that she died
about six months after her marriage, does
not come into the ballad.* Buchan thinks
Winsbury's rank to be fixed by his version,

G, as that of a chamberlain, and therefore
cannot admit the plausibility of a disguised
James V.

The two English copies, D, E, both imperfect, change the hero's name to Johnnie Barbary ('lately come from Spain,' cf. B 5) or
Johnnie Barbour. Motherwell, in a manuscript annotation to Kinloch's Ancient Scottish
Ballads, mentions that he had obtained from
recitation a copy in which the name was
Sweet Willie of Salisbury. The change from
a king to a lady neat and trim in D 1 is a corruption that one would have hardly looked for
" from the spinning-wheel."

The stanza which notes the reluctance of
the young man to come at call, C 9, D 6, F 12,
occurs in all copies of 'The Knight and
Shepherd's Daughter.'

A

Campbell MSS, II, 38.

1 THE king he hath been a prisoner,
    A prisoner lang in Spain, O
And Willie o the Winsbury
    Has lain lang wi his daughter at hame. O

2 'What aileth thee, my daughter Janet,
    Ye look so pale and wan?
Have ye had any sore sickness,
    Or have ye been lying wi a man?
Or is it for me, your father dear,
    And biding sae lang in Spain?'

3 'I have not had any sore sickness,
    Nor yet been lying wi a man;
But it is for you, my father dear,
    In biding sae lang in Spain.'

4 'Cast ye off your berry-brown gown,
    Stand straight upon the stone,
That I may ken ye by yere shape,
    Whether ye be a maiden or none.'

5 She's coosten off her berry-brown gown,
    Stooden straight upo yon stone;
Her apron was short, and her haunches were
    round,
    Her face it was pale and wan.

6 'Is it to a man o might, Janet?
    Or is it to a man of fame?
Or is it to any of the rank robbers
    That's lately come out o Spain?'

7 'It is not to a man of might,' she said,
    'Nor is it to a man of fame;
But it is to William of Winsbury;
    I could lye nae langer my lane.'

8 The king's called on his merry men all,
    By thirty and by three:
'Go fetch me William of Winsbury,
    For hanged he shall be.'

9 But when he cam the king before,
    He was clad o the red silk;
His hair was like to threeds o gold.
    And his skin was as white as milk.

---

* " A William Wynnesbury, who was yeoman of the Guard
at the time of Henry VIII, used generally to act as Lord of
Misrule in the years 1508–19, and he was Friar Tuck at
Greenwich in May, 1515 (see Collier's Annals of the Stage,
and J. S. Brewer's Letters and Papers of Henry VIII), and
this, no doubt, made the name popular with the ballad-mak-

ers." Ward, Catalogue of Romances, etc., I, 532. Undeni-
ably the Lord Winsbury of our ballad might be said to have
acted as a lord of misrule, but it was hardly an English (or
Scots) ballad-maker of the sixteenth century that made this
ballad; and Mr. Ward, probably, did not intend so to be
understood.

10 'It is nae wonder,' said the king,
      'That my daughter's love ye did win ;
   Had I been a woman, as I am a man,
      My bedfellow ye should hae been.

11 'Will ye marry my daughter Janet,
      By the truth of thy right hand ?
   I 'll gie ye gold, I 'll gie ye money,
      And I 'll gie ye an earldom o land.'

12 'Yes, I 'll marry yere daughter Janet,
      By the truth of my right hand ;
   But I 'll hae nane o yer gold, I 'll hae nane
      yer money,
      Nor I winna hae an earldom o land.

13 'For I hae eighteen corn-mills,
      Runs all in water clear,
   And there 's as much corn in each o them
      As they can grind in a year.'

B

Herd's MSS, I, 29 ; II, 98.

*   *   *   *   *

1 'WHAT aileth ye, my dochter Dysmill,
      Ye look sae pale and wan ?
   Hae ye had ony sair sickness,
      Or ill luve wi a man ?

2 'Cast aff, cast aff your bony brown goun,
      And lay 't down on the stane,
   And I sall tell ye ay or no
      Ye hae layn wi a man.'

3 She has taen aff her bony brown gown,
      She has laid it on the stane ;
   Her waist was big, her side was round,
      Her fair colour was gane.

4 'Now is it to a man of micht,
      Or to a man of mean ?
   Or is it to the ranke robber
      That robs upon the main ? '

5 'O it 's nor to a man of micht,
      Nor to a man of mean ;

   But it 's to Willie Winchberrie,
      That came frae France and Spain.'

6 The king he 's turnd him round about,
      An angry man was he :
   'Gar bring to me your fals leman,
      Wha sall high hanged be.'

7 Then Dysmill turnd her round about,
      The tear blinded her ee :
   'Gin ye begin to hang, father,
      Ye maun begin wi mee.'

8 When Willie he cam to the king,
      His coat was o the silk ;
   His hair was like the thread o gowd,
      His skin white as the milk.

9 'Ne wonder, ne wonder,' quoth the king,
      'My dochter shoud like ye ;
   Gin ye were a woman, as ye 're a man,
      My bedfellow ye sould be.

10 'Now will ye marry my dochter Dysmill,
      By the truth o your right hand ?
   Now will ye marry my dochter Dysmill,
      And be a lord o the land ? '

C

Kinloch MSS, I, 315.

1 THE king has been long seven years away,
      Long seven years away frae hame ;
   Our king has been long seven years away,
      A hunting oer in Spain.

*   *   *   *   *

2 'What aileth thee, my ae daughter,
      Thou lookst so pale and wan ?
   Hast thou had any sore sickness,
      Or hast thou loved man ? '

3 'I have not had any sore sickness,
      To make me look sae wan ;
   But it is for your own majestie,
      You staid sae lang in Spain.'

4 'Cast aff, cast aff thy silken gown,
    And lay it on yon stane,
And I 'll tell to thee if with child you be,
    Or if ye be with nane.'

5 She 's casten aff her costly gown,
    That 's made o the silk sae fine ;
Her stays were sae strait she could na
      loot,
    And her fair colour was wan.

6 'Oh is it to any mighty man ?
    Or any lord of fame ?
Or is it to the rank robbers
    That I sent out o Spain ? '

7 'It is no to the rank robbers
    That you sent out o Spain ;
But it is to Thomas of Winsbury,
    For I dought na lie my lane.'

8 'If it be to Lord Thomas,' he says,
    ' It 's hanged shall he be : '
'If you hang Thomas of Winsbury,
    You 'll get na mair gude o me.'

9 The king 's called up his merry men all,
    By one, by two, and three ;
Lord Thomas should hae been the foremost
      man,
    But the hindmost man was he.

10 'No wonder, no wonder,' the king he said,
    ' My daughter loved thee ;
For wert thou a woman, as thou art a man,
    My bedfellow thou shouldst be.

11 'O will you marry my daughter dear,
    By the faith of thy right hand ?
And thou shalt reign, when I am dead,
    The king over my whole land.'

12 'I will marry your daughter dear,
    With my heart, yea and my hand ;
But it never shall be that Lord Winsbury
    Shall rule oer fair Scotland.'

13 He 's mounted her on a milk-white steed,
    Himself on a dapple-grey,
And made her a lady of as much land
    She could ride in a whole summer day.

—◆—

D

Communicated to Percy by the Rev. P. Parsons, of Wey, apparently in 1775. "This I had from the spinning-wheel."

1 THERE was a lady fine and gay,
    She was so neat and trim ;
She went unto her own garden-wall,
    To see her own ships come in.

2 And there she spied her daughter Jane,
    Who lookd so pale and wan :
' What, have you had some long sickness,
    Or lain with some young man ? '

3 'No, I have had no long sickness,
    Nor lain with no young man : '
Her petticoats they were so short,
    She was full nine months gone.

4 'Oh is it by some nobleman ?
    Or by some man of fame ?
Or is it by Johnny Barbary,
    That 's lately come from Spain ? '

5 'No, it is by no nobleman,
    Nor by no man of fame ;
But it is by Johnny Barbary,
    That 's lately come from Spain.'

6 Then she calld down her merry men,
    By one, by two, by three ;
Johnny Barbary used to be the first,
    But now the last came he.

7 'Oh will you take my daughter Jane,
    And wed her out of hand ?
And you shall dine and sup with me,
    And be heir of my land.'

8 'Yes, I will take your daughter Jane,
    And wed her out of hand ;
And I will dine and sup with you,
    But I do not want your land.'

9 Then she calld down her merry men,
    With a shrill and a pleasant voice :
' Come, let us all now mery be,
    Since she has made such a happy choice.'

E

Notes and Queries, Fifth Series, VII, 387, 1877: communicated by B. Montgomerie Ranking, as "heard sung years ago by a West Country fisherman."

*   *   *   *   *   *

1 'OH daughter, oh daughter,' her father he said,
   'What makes you look so pale?
.   .   .   .   .
   Or are you in love with any man?'

2 .   .   .   .   .
   'But if it be one of my own sailor lads,
   High hanged he shall be.'

3 Johnnie Barbour he cam doun the stair,
   His shirt was of the silk;
His two bonnie black een were rolling in his
   head,
   And his skin was as white as milk.

4 'Oh are you ready to marry my daughter,
   And take her by the hand,
And to eat and drink with me at the table,
   And be heir of all my land?'

5 'Oh it 's I am ready to marry your daughter,
   And take her by the hand,
And to eat and drink with her at the table,
   And to fight for all your land.'

———————

F

Motherwell's MS., p. 404; from the recitation of Agnes Laird, of Kilbarchan, August 24, 1825.

1 OUR king hath been a poor prisoner,
   And a poor prisoner in Spain; O
When seven long years was past and gone,
   Our Scotish king came hame.   O

2 As he was riding along the way,
   He met with his dear dochter:
'What ails thee, what ails thee, my dochter dear,
   Thou looks so pale and wan?

3 'Have ye had any sore sickness,
   Or have ye lovd a man?
Or is it for me, my dochter dear,
   I have been so long in Spain?'

4 'I have had no sore sickness,
   Nor yet have I loved a man;
But it is for you, my father dear,
   Thou 've been so long in Spain.'

5 'Cast aff, cast aff thy brown silk gown,
   And spread it on yonder stone,
And I will tell you by and by
   Whether thou art a maid or none.'

6 She 's coosten off her brown silk gown,
   And spread it on yonder stone,

And her belly was big, and her face pale and
   wan,
   And she was about half gone.

7 'Is it to a man o micht?
   Or to a man of fame?
Or is it to one of the rank rebels
   That I sent out of Spain?'

8 'It is not to a man of micht,
   Nor to a man of fame,
Nor yet to one of the rank rebels
   That ye sent out o Spain;
But it is to Willie o Winsberry,
   Thy very own serving-man.'

9 'If it be to Willie o Winsberry,
   As I trew well it be,
Gin the morn at ten o the clock
   It 's hanged shall he be.'

10 As the king was riding up the gate
   He met Willie clothed in scarlet red,
And his hair was as yellow as the beam,
   beam gold,
   And his breast as white as milk.

11 'No wonder, no wonder,' quo the king,
   'My dochter luvit thee;
For if thou was a woman, as thou 'rt a
   man,
   My bedfellow thou should be.'

12 The king called down his merry men all,
 By one, by two, and by three;
 Sweet Willie should ha been the foremost
 man,
 But the hindmost man drew he.

13 'Will you take my dochter Jean,
 By the faith of her richt hand?

And you shall sup and dine with me,
 And heir the third part of my land.'

14 'I will take your dochter Jean,
 By the faith of her richt hand,
 And I will sup and dine with you,
 But a fig for all your land;
 For I've as much land in Winsberry
 As we'll ride in a long summer's day.'

———

G

Buchan's MSS, II, 174; Buchan's Ballads of the North
of Scotland, II, 212.

1 SEVEN years the king he staid
 Into the land of Spain,
 And seven years True Thomas was
 His daughter's chamberlain.

2 But it fell ance upon a day
 The king he did come home;
 She baked and she benjed ben,
 And did him there welcome.

3 'What aileth you, my daughter Janet,
 You look sae pale and wan?
 There is a dreder in your heart,
 Or else you love a man.'

4 'There is no dreder in my heart,
 Nor do I love a man;
 But it is for your lang byding
 Into the land of Spain.'

5 'Ye'll cast aff your bonny brown gown,
 And lay it on a stone,
 And I'll tell you, my jelly Janet,
 If ever ye lovd a man.'

6 She's cast aff her bonny brown gown,
 And laid it on a stone;
 Her belly was big, her twa sides high,
 Her colour it was quite gane.

7 'Is it to a man o the might, Janet,
 Or is it till a man o the main?
 Or is it to one o my poor soldiers,
 That I brought hame frae Spain?'

8 'It's not till a man o the might,' she says,
 'Nor yet to a man o the main;

But it's to Thomas o Winsbury,
 That cannot longer len.'

9 'O where are all my wall-wight men,
 That I pay meat and fee,
 That will go for him True Thomas,
 And bring him in to me?
 For the morn, ere I eat or drink,
 High hanged shall he be.'

10 She's turnd her right and round about,
 The tear blinded her ee:
 'If ye do any ill to True Thomas,
 Ye's never get gude o me.'

11 When Thomas came before the king
 He glanced like the fire;
 His hair was like the threads o gold,
 His eyes like crystal clear.

12 'It was nae wonder, my daughter Janet,
 Altho ye loved this man;
 If he were a woman, as he is a man,
 My bed-fellow he would been.

13 'O will ye marry my daughter Janet?
 The truth's in your right hand;
 Ye's hae some o my gold, and some o my
 gear,
 And the twalt part o my land.'

14 'It's I will marry your daughter Janet;
 The truth's in my right hand;
 I'll hae nane o your gold, nor nane o your
 gear,
 I've enough in my own land.

15 'But I will marry your daughter Janet
 With thirty ploughs and three,
 And four and twenty bonny breast-mills,
 And a' on the water o Dee.'

H

Kinloch's Scottish Ballads, p. 92.

1 It fell upon a time, when the proud king of
    France
  Went a hunting for five months and more,
That his dochter fell in love with Thomas of
    Winesberrie,
  From Scotland newly come oer.

2 Whan her father cam hame frae hunting the
    deer,
  And his dochter before him cam,
Her belly it was big, and her twa sides round,
  And her fair colour was wan.

3 'What ails thee, what ails thee, my dochter
    Janet?
  What maks thee to look sae wan?
Ye 've either been sick, and very, very sick,
  Or else ye hae lain wi a man.'

4 'Ye 're welcome, ye 're welcome, dear father,'
    she says,
  'Ye 're welcome hame to your ain,
For I hae been sick, and very, very sick,
  Thinking lang for your coming hame.

5 'O pardon, O pardon, dear father,' she says,
  'A pardon ye 'll grant me:'
'Na pardon, na pardon, my dochter,' he says,
  'Na pardon I 'll grant thee.

6 'O is it to a man of micht,
  Or to a man of mean?
Or is it to onie of thae rank robbers
  That I sent hame frae Spain?'

7 'It is not to a man of micht,
  Nor to a man of mean;
But it is to Thomas o Winesberrie,
  And for him I suffer pain.'

8 'If it be to Thomas o' Winesberrie,
  As I trust well it be,
Before I either eat or drink,
  Hie hangit sall he be.'

9 When this bonnie boy was brought afore the
    king,
  His claithing was o the silk,
His fine yellow hair hang dangling doun,
  And his skin was like the milk.

10 'Na wonder, na wonder, Lord Thomas,' he
    says,
  'My dochter fell in love wi thee,
For if I war a woman, as I am a man,
  My bed-fellow ye shoud be.

11 'Then will ye marry my dochter Janet,
  To be heir to a' my land?
O will ye marry my dochter Janet,
  Wi the truth o your richt hand?'

12 'I will marry your dochter Janet,
  Wi the truth o my richt hand;
I 'll hae nane o your gowd, nor yet o your
    gear,
  I 've eneuch in fair Scotland.

13 'But I will marry your dochter Janet,
  I care na for your land,
For she 's be a queen, and I a king,
  Whan we come to fair Scotland.'

———◆———

I

a. A stall copy printed by M. Randall, Stirling. b. A
stall copy by C. Randall, Stirling. c. Buchan's Gleanings,
p. 127.

1 It fell upon a time that the proud king of
    France
  Went a hunting for five months and more;
His daughter fell in love with Lord Wins-
    berry,
  Who from Scotland was newly come oer.

2 'You 're welcome, welcome, dear father,' she
    said,
  'You 're welcome again to your own;
For I have been sick, and very, very sick,
  Thinking long for your coming home.'

3 'Put off, put off your gown of green,' he says,
  'And spread it on yonder green,
And tell them from me that in mourning you
    are,
  Or that ye have lain with a man.'

4 She's put off her gown of green,
   And spread it on the strand;
   Her haunches were round, and her belly was
       big,
   From her face the colour is gone.

5 'O is it to a man of might,' he says,
   'Or is it to a man that's mean?
   Or is it to one of those rank rebels,
   That lately from Scotland came?'

6 'O it is to a man of might,' she says,
   'It is not to one that is mean;
   It is to Lord Thomas of Winsberry,
   And for him I must suffer pain.'

7 The king called up his merry men all,
   By one, by two, and by three:
   'Go fetch me Lord Thomas of Winsberry,
   For tomorrow he shall die.'

8 They sought him up, they sought him down,
   As fast as fast could be;
   There they found Lord Thomas of Winsberry,
   Sitting under an orange tree.

9 'Get up, get up, Lord Thomas,' they said,
   'Get up, and bound your way;
   For the king has sworn by his honoured crown
   That tomorrow is thy dying-day.'

10 'O what have I robbd, or what have I stolen,
   Or what have I killed or slain,

That I should be afraid to speak to your king?
For I have done him no wrong.'

11 Lord Thomas came tripping up the stair,
   His cloathing was of the silk;
   His fine yellow hair hung dangling down,
   His skin was white as the milk.

12 And when he came before the king
   He kneeled down on his knee;
   Says, What is your will with me, my liege,
   What is your will with me?

13 'I think no wonder, Lord Thomas,' he says,
   'That my daughter fell in love with thee;
   If thou wert a woman, as thou art a man,
   My bed-fellow thou wouldst be.

14 'Will ye marry my daughter Jean,
   By the faith of thy right hand?
   Thou'se have part of my gold, part of my
       gear,
   And a third part of my land.'

15 'Yes, I will marry thy daughter Jean,
   By the faith of my right hand;
   I'll have none of your gold, none of your gear;
   I have enough in fair Scotland.'

16 He has mounted her on a milk-white steed,
   Himself on a dapple-grey;
   He's got as much land in fair Scotland
   As they can ride in a summer's day.

A. O *is added, in singing, to every second and*
     fourth verse. 1². oh.
   9³. the reeds of, *in my copy.*
   11². of my.

B. Quhat, ze, etc., are *printed* what, ye.

C. 9. *Given thus in Kinloch's annotated copy of*
     his Ancient Scottish Ballads; derived from
     Motherwell:

   The king called doun his merry men,
     By thirties and by three;
   Lord Thomas, that used to be the first,
     The hindmost man was he.

D. 3². altered, *wrongly, to* But lain with a.
   9². shrrill.

F. O *is added, in singing, to every second and*
     fourth verse.
   1³, ⁴. *Thus in Motherwell's Note-Book, p.*
     27:

   Seven long years was past and gone
     When our Scotish king came home. O

   16. *Given thus in Kinloch's annotated copy of*
     his Ancient Scottish Ballads, as the con-
     cluding verse of Mr Motherwell's copies and
     that of Buchan:

   He mounted her on a milk-white steed,
     Himself on a dapple-grey,
   And they've as muckle land in braid Scot-
       land
     As can be rode in a lang simmer's day.

G. *Some trifling changes are made by Buchan in printing.*

　8[4]. ben, *printed by Buchan* len.

I. a. 14[2]. of my : *so* b. 16[1]. her *wanting.*

　b. 2[3]. and very sick. 4[1, 2]. *wanting.*

5[2]. that is. 5[3]. these. 8[2]. As fast as they.
9[3]. his *wanting.* 11[3]. hang. 13[4]. should be.
c. 2[2]. You are. 3[1]. Put off your. 5[2]. that is.
　5[3]. these. 7[4]. Sitting under an orange tree.
8. *wanting.* 14[2]. of my. 14[3]. Thou 'llt.

101

WILLIE O DOUGLAS DALE

A. 'Willy o Douglass-dale,' Jamieson-Brown MS., fol. 8.

B. a. 'Dame Oliphant, or, Willie o Douglass Dale,' Buchan MSS, II, 117. b. 'The Earl of Douglas and

Dame Oliphant,' Buchan's Ballads of the North of Scotland, II, 181 ; 'Lord Willie Douglas,' Motherwell's MS., p. 619.

C. 'Douglass Dale,' Kinloch MSS, V, 327.

A WAS among the fifteen ballads furnished by Mrs Brown to William Tytler in 1783, No 8. The first stanza is cited by Dr Anderson in Nichols's Illustrations, VII, 177. There is a copy in the Abbotsford MS. "Scottish Songs," fol. 16, in which the text is considerably altered ; stanzas 7, 12, 19, 22–24 are omitted, and 25 is inserted between 30 and 31. B b inserts two stanzas after B a 15, and adds one at the end. The copy in Christie's Traditional Ballad Airs, II, 32, is an abridgment of B b as made over in The Ballad Minstrelsy of Scotland, Glasgow, 1871, p. 63. C has an appendage of two stanzas which belong to another ballad, and are transferred accordingly.

The first part of the story of this ballad, or down to the birth of the boy, is repeated in 'Willie and Earl Richard's Daughter' (hitherto called 'The Birth of Robin Hood'), which immediately follows. This portion of the ballad has resemblances to 'Leesome Brand,' No 15.*

A 9, B 15, is a popular passage the like of which is found in many ballads : as 'Child Waters,' A 2, 3 ; 'Lady Maisry,' H 7, 8 ;

'Willie o Winsbury,' A 5, C 5, D 3 ; 'Willie and Earl Richard's Daughter,' A 4 ; 'Der Ritter und die Magd,' Düntzer u. Herder, Briefe Goethe's, I, 157, st. 6 ; Nicolai, I, 40, No 2, st. 6 ; Wunderhorn, 1806, I, 50, st. 11, Erk, IV, 304, st. 5 ; Erk's Liederhort, p. 81, st. 10 ; Hoffmann u. Richter, No. 4, st. 4 ; Meier, Schwäbische Volkslieder, No 177, st. 9 ; Ditfurth, II, Nos 6, 7, 8, st. 5 ; Uhland, No 97 A, st. 5 ; Mittler, No 91, st. 6 ; 'Schön Elselein,' 'Das Schwabentöchterlein,' Böhme, No 51[a], st. 11, No 51[b], st. 8 (= Mittler, No 218 ; Uhland, No 257) ; 'Þiðriks kvæði konúngs,' Islenzk fornkvæði, II, 218, No 57, st. 6 ; Haupt u. Schmaler, V. l. der Wenden, I, 160, No 136, st. 7 ; Sakellarios, Τὰ Κυπριακά, III, 52, No 20, vv 5–9 ; Guillon, Ch. p. de l'Ain, 'La Fille d'un Boulanger,' p. 201, sts 1, 2 ; Milá, Romancerillo, 'La infanta seducida,' p. 249, No 258, l. 4 ; 'De la infanta y el hijo del rey de Francia,' Wolf y Hofmann, Primavera, II, 91, No 158, verses 5, 6 ; Aigner, Ungarische Volksdichtungen, p. 86, st. 1, p. 215, st. 2.

The very ill-timed question in B 20 occurs in 'Young Hunting,' No 68, K 8, 'Clerk Saunders,' No 69, F 5, Buchan, Ballads of the North of Scotland, 'Auld Matrons,' II, 238, st. 4, and 'Willie's Fatal Visit,' II, 260, st. 7.

---

* For the five hundred pounds in A 12, C 4, 5, cf. 'Leesome Brand,' A 12, 18, and the corresponding Scandinavian ballads.

For others in this passage see 'Rose the Red and White Lily.' The bribe of gowns in B 29 is found in 'Young Hunting,' B 9, C 7, K 13.

The historical foundation for this ballad suggested in The Ballad Minstrelsy of Scotland, Glasgow, 1871, p. 63, cannot be seriously entertained.

A

Jamieson-Brown MS., fol. 8.

1 O WILLY was as brave a lord
    As ever saild the sea,
And he has gane to the English court,
    To serve for meat and fee.

2 He had nae been at the kingis court
    A twelvemonth and a day,
Till he longd for a sight o the king's daughter,
    But ane he coud never see.

3 O it fell ance upon a day
    To the green wood she has gane,
An Willy he has followd her,
    With the clear light o the moon.

4 He looted him low, by her did go,
    Wi his hat intill his hand :
' O what 's your will wi me, Sir Knight?
    I pray keep your hat on.'

5 ' O I am not a knight, Madam,
    Nor never thinks to be ;
For I am Willy o Douglassdale,
    An I serve for meat and fee.'

6 ' O I 'll gang to my bowr,' she says,
    ' An sigh baith even an morn
That ever I saw your face, Willy,
    Or that ever ye was born.

7 ' O I 'll gang to my bowr,' she says,
    ' An I 'll pray baith night an day,
To keep me frae your tempting looks,
    An frae your great beauty.'

8 O in a little after that
    He keepit Dame Oliphant's bowr,
An the love that passd between this twa,
    It was like paramour.

9 ' O narrow, narrow 's my gown, Willy,
    That wont to be sae wide ;

An short, short is my coats, Willy,
    That wont to be sae side ;
An gane is a' my fair colour,
    An low laid is my pride.

10 ' But an my father get word of this,
    He 'll never drink again ;
An gin my mother get word of this,
    In her ain bowr she 'll go brain ;
An gin my bold brothers get word this,
    I fear, Willy, you 'll be slain.'

11 ' O will you leave your father's court,
    An go along wi me ?
I 'll carry you unto fair Scotland,
    And mak you a lady free.'

12 She pat her han in her pocket
    An gae him five hunder poun :
' An take you that now, Squire Willy,
    Till awa that we do won.'

13 Whan day was gane, and night was come,
    She lap the castle-wa ;
But Willy kepit his gay lady,
    He was laith to let her fa.

14 Whan night was gane, an day come in,
    An lions gaed to their dens,
An ay the lady followd him,
    An the tears came hailing down.

15 ' O want ye ribbons to your hair ?
    Or roses to your shoone ?
Or want ye as meickle dear bought love
    As your ain heart can contain ? '

16 ' I want nae ribbons to my hair,
    Nor roses till my shoone ;
An Ohone, alas, for dear bought love !
    I have mair nor I can contain.'

17 O he 's pu'd the oak in good green wood,
    An he 's made to her a fire ;

He coverd it oer wi withred leaves,
      An gard it burn thro ire.

18 He made a bed i the good green wood,
      An he 's laid his lady down,
   An he 's coverd her oer wi fig-tree leaves,
      But aι his ain night-gown.

19 'O had I a bunch o yon red roddins,
      That grows in yonder wood,
   But an a drink υ water clear,
      I think it woud do me good.'

20 He 's pu'd her a bunch o yon red roddins,
      That grew beside yon thorn,
   But an a drink o water clear,
      Intill his hunting-horn.

21 He 's bent his bow, and shot the deer,
      An thro the green wood gane,
   An ere that he came back again
      His lady took travailing.

22 'O up ye tak that horn,' she says,
      'An ye blaw a blast for me;
   Gin my father be in good green wood,
      Sae seen 's he 'll come me ti.'

23 'O gin there be a man on earth
      That ye loo better nor me,
   Ye blaw the horn yoursel,' he says,
      'For it 's never be blawn by me.'

24 O he 's bent his bow, an shot the deer,
      An thro the green wood has he gane,
   An lang or he came back again
      His lady bare him a son.

25 O up has he tane his bonny young son,
      An washn him wi the milk,
   An up has he tane his gay lady,
      An rowd her i the silk.

26 He 's bent his bow, and shot the deer,
      An thro the green wood has he gane,
   Till he met wi a well-fard may,
      Her father's flock feeding.

27 'Ye leave your father's flock feeding,
      An go along wi me;
   I 'll carry you to a lady fair,
      Will gi you both meat and fee.'

28 O whan she came the lady before,
      She 's fa'n down on her knee:
   'O what 's your will wi me, my dame?
      An a dame you seem to be.'

29 'O I 'm Dame Oliphant, the king's daughter,
      Nae doubt but ye 've heard o me;
   Will you leave your father's flock feeding,
      An go to Scotlan wi me?

30 'An ye sal get a nouriship
      Intill an earldome,
   An I will gar provide for the
      To marry some brave Scotsman.'

31 The may she keepit the bonny boy,
      An Willy led his lady,
   Untill they took their fair shippin,
      Then quikly hame came they.

32 The win was fair, an the sea was clear,
      An they a' wan safe to lan;
   He 's haild her lady of Douglassdale,
      Himsel the lord within.

————•————

B

a. Buchan MSS, II, 117. b. Buchan's Ballads of the
North of Scotland, II, 181; Motherwell's MS., p. 619.

1 WILLIE was an earl's ae son,
      And an earl's ae son was he,
   But he thought his father lack to sair,
      And his mother of low degree.

2 But he is on to fair England,
      To sair for meat an fee,

And all was for Dame Oliphant,
      A woman of great beauty.

3 He hadna been in fair England
      A month but barely ane,
   Ere he dreamd that fair Dame Oliphant
      Gied him a gay gold ring.

4 He hadna been in fair England
      A month but barely four,

Ere he dreamd that fair Dame Oliphant
  Gied him a red rose flower,
Well set about with white lilies,
  Like to the paramour.

5 It fell ance upon a day
  Dame Oliphant thought lang,
And she gaed on to good green wood,
  As fast as she could gang.

6 As Willie stood in his chamber-door,
  And as he thought it good,
There he beheld Dame Oliphant,
  As she came thro the wood.

7 He's taen his bow his arm oer,
  His sword into his hand,
And he is on to good green wood,
  As fast as he could gang.

8 And there he found Dame Oliphant,
  Was lying sound asleep,
And aye the sounder she did sleep
  The nearer he did creep.

9 But when she wakend from her sleep
  An angry maid was she,
Crying, Had far away frae me, young man,
  Had far away frae me!
For I fear ye are the Scottish knight
  That beguiles young ladies free.

10 'I am not the Scottish knight,
  Nor ever thinks to be;
I am but Willie o Douglass Dale,
  That serves for meat an fee.'

11 'If ye be Willie o Douglass Dale,
  Ye 're dearly welcome to me;
For oft in my sleep have I thought on
  You and your merry winking ee.'

12 But the cocks they crew, and the horns blew,
  And the lions took the hill,
And Willie he gaed hame again,
  To his hard task and till;
And likewise did Dame Oliphant,
  To her book and her seam.

13 Till it fell ance upon a day
  Dame Oliphant thought lang,
And she went on to Willie's bower-yates,
  As fast as she could gang.

14 'O are ye asleep now, Squire Willie?
  O are you asleep?' said she;
O waken, waken, Squire Willie,
  O waken, and speak to me.

15 'For the gowns that were oer wide, Willie,
  They winna meet on me,
And the coats that were oer side, Willie,
  They winna come to my knee;
And if the knights of my father's court get word,
  I 'm sure they 'll gar you die.'

* * * * *

16 But she 's taen a web of the scarlet,
  And she tare it fine an sma,
And even into Willie's arms
  She leapt the castle-wa;
And Willie was wight and well able,
  And he keept her frae a fa.

17 But the cocks they crew, and the horns blew,
  And the lions took the hill,
And Willie's ladie followed him,
  And the tears did twinkle still.

18 'O want ye ribbons to your hair?
  Or roses to your sheen?
Or want ye chains about your neck?
  Ye 'se get mair ere that be deen.'

19 'I want not ribbons to my hair,
  Nor roses to my sheen,
And there 's mair chains about my neck
  Nor ever I 'll see deen;
But I have as much dear bought love
  As my heart can contain.'

20 'Will ye go to the cards or dice?
  Or to the table ee?
Or to a bed, so well down spread,
  And sleep till it be day?'

21 'I 've mair need of the roddins, Willie,
  That grow on yonder thorn;
Likewise a drink o Marywell water,
  Out of your grass-green horn.

22 'I 've mair need of a fire, Willie,
  To had me frae the cauld;
Likewise a glass of your red wine,
  Ere I bring my son to the fauld.'

23 He 's got a bush o roddins till her,
    That grows on yonder thorn;
  Likewise a drink o Marywell water,
    Out of his grass-green horn.

24 He carried the match in his pocket
    That kindled to her the fire,
  Well set about wi oaken spells,
    That leamd oer Lincolnshire.

25 And he has bought to his lady
    The white bread and the wine;
  And the milk he milked from the goats,
    He fed his young son on.

26 Till it fell ance upon a day
    Dame Oliphant thought lang:
  ' O gin ye hae a being, Willie,
    I pray ye hae me hame.'

27 He 's taen his young son in his arms,
    His lady by the hand,

And they 're down thro good green wood,
    As fast as they could gang.

28 Till they came to a shepherd-may,
    Was feeding her flocks alone;
  Said, Will ye gae alang wi me,
    And carry my bonny young son?

29 The gowns that were shapen for my
        back,
    They shall be sewd for thine;
  And likewise I 'll gar Squire Willie
    Gie you a braw Scotsman.

30 When they came on to Willie's bower-
        yates,
    And far beyont the sea,
  She was haild the lady o Douglass Dale,
    And Willie an earl to be:
  Likewise the maid they brought awa,
    She got a braw Scotsman.

C

Kinloch MSS, V, 327, in the handwriting of Dr John Hill
Burton.

1 Sweet Sir William of Douglas Dale,
    A knight's ae son was he;
  He dreamed of dear Dame Oliphant,
    Lang ere he did her see.

2 He dreamed a woman of great beauty
    Gave him a red rose flower,
  Well busket abou̶ ̶ wi the lillies white,
    Just like the paramour.

3 O sweet Sir William of Douglas Dale,
    A knight's ae son was he,
  And he is on to the king's high court,
    To serve for meat and fee.

    *   *   *   *   *

4 Five hundred pounds of Spanish gold,
    Tied in a towal so white,
  And that she has given her Lord William,
    Out oer the castle-dyke.

5 Five hundred pounds of Spanish gold,
    Tied in a towel sae sma,

And that she has given her own true-love,
    Out ore the castle-wa.

6 She rowed hersell in a robe o silk,
    To loup the castle-wa;
  He ceppet her in his armes twa,
    And he let not her get a fa.

    *   *   *   *   *

7 The cocks do craw, and the day does daw,
    And the wild fowl bodes on hill;
  The lassie she followed her Sweet William,
    And let the tears down fall.

    *   *   *   *   *

8 ' O want you ribbons to your hair?
    Or roses to your sheen?
  Or want ye as much of feel daft love
    As your heart can contain?'

9 ' I want nor ribbons to my hair,
    Nor roses to my sheen;
  I 've got as much o dear bought love
    As my heart can contain.'

    *   *   *   *   *

10 He carried a flint in his pocket,
   And he strack to her a fire,
   And he buskit it roun wi the leaves o oak,
   And gart it burn wi ire.

11 He 's taen his big coat him about,
   And his gun into his hand,
   And he has gone to good green wood,
   To kill some venison.

12 He 's taen his big coat him about,
   And his gun into his han,
   But lang ere he came back again
   She bare his dear young son.

13 He rowed her in his muckle coat.
   But in his good night-gown,
   And he fed her wi the good goat-milk,
   Till she was well able to gang.

14 He 's taen his young son in his arm,
   His lady in his hand,
   And they are down thro good green wood,
   As fast as they can gang.

15 And they came to a shepherd's daughter,
   Was feeding at her sheep ;
   Says, Will ye go to Douglass Dale,
   Wi my yong son to keep ?

16 O I will gee you gold, maiden,
   And I will gee you fee,
   Gin ye will go to Douglas Dale,
   Wi my yong son and me.

17 She 's taen his young son in her arm,
   And kissed baith cheek and chin ;
   Says, I will go to Douglas Dale,
   As fast as I can win.

18 He 's taen his big coat him about,
   And his lady in his hand,
   And they are off to Douglas Dale,
   As fast as they can gang.

19 And when they came to Douglas Dale
   A happy man was he,
   For his lady, and his young son,
   And his nurse, a' three.

———————

A. *The stanzas are written in the MS. in two long lines. The first stanza, as given by Anderson, is :*

   Willie was as brave a lord
     As ever saild the sea,
   And he 's gone to the English court,
     To serve for meat and fee.

   1³. Enlish. 6², 7², 14¹, 24¹. & *for* an.
   22⁴. tie (?). 24¹. the bow.
B. a. 27³. And there.
   b. 15¹. *Omits* For.
   After 15, *inserts :*

   ' Dame Oliphant, Dame Oliphant,
       A king's daughter are ye ;
   But woud ye leave your father and mother,
       And gang awa wi me ? '

   ' O I woud leave my father and mother,
       And the nearest that eer betide,
   And I woud nae be feard to gang,
       Gin ye war by my side.'

17⁴. trinkle.   19³. there are.   19⁴. Then ever.
20². table play.   23². grow.   26⁴. pray you.
After 30, *inserts :*

   And lang and happy did they live,
     But now their days are deen,
   And in the kirk o sweet Saint Bride
     Their graves are growing green.

Motherwell makes some alterations in his copy : as 1³, laigh to sair ; 12⁴, *and* toil ; *whateer, in the second line of the second inserted stanza, above ; besides others which are purely arbitrary. He has* table eye *in* 20², *where Buchan prints* table play, *and* living, *with being written over, in* 26³.
C. 3¹, 8¹, 16¹. Oh. 6³. ceppit ? 16¹·². gie ?
There are appended to this version two stanzas of which Burton says: The reciter of this ballad is obstinate in persisting that the last two stanzas belong to it. They are evidently taken from ' The Birth of Robin Hood,' and have no connection with this ballad. See the following ballad.

102

WILLIE AND EARL RICHARD'S DAUGHTER

A. 'The Birth of Robin Hood,' Jamieson's Popular Ballads, II, 44.

B. 'The Birth of Robin Hood,' Buchan's Ballads of the North of Scotland, II, 1.

C. Kinloch's MSS, V, 330 f, two stanzas.

A WAS taken down from Mrs Brown's recitation by Jamieson in 1800, and published in his collection in 1806, "without the alteration of a single word." C wrongly forms the conclusion of 'Willie o Douglas Dale,' the preceding ballad. The copy in Christie's Traditional Ballad Airs, I, 128, is an abridgment of B, with a very few trivial changes.

The first half of the story in A, 1–9, is that of 'Willie of Douglas Dale,' A, 1–24, and there is a partial verbal correspondence.* In the latter a shepherd's daughter is engaged as nurse to the boy born in the wood, and Dame Oliphant is taken home by her lover and made lady of Douglas Dale. In the present ballad the lady's father tracks his daughter to the wood, finds the new-born child, adopts him as his grandson, and gives him the name Robin Hood, Willie [Archibald] disappearing from the scene.

The first part of B 4–18 is a variety of the wide-spread tragic ballad of 'Leesome Brand,'

No 15. So, also, is the larger part of 'Willie o Douglas Dale,' with the tragic features dropped.

This ballad certainly does not belong to the cycle of Robin Hood, and for this reason the title hitherto borne by it could not be retained. The connection with Robin Hood was in all probability mediated by the name Brown Robin. Brown Robin plays the part of Willie [Archibald] in 'Rose the Red and White Lily,' A 25–29. Brown Robin's son, in 'Jellon Grame,' is called Robin after Robin Hood, B 14, C 7, 17. Brown Robin carries off his love to the wood in the ballad of the same name. The Earl of Huntingdon, B 3, 21, has no place in the ancient traditional ballads of Robin Hood, but is of later literary invention. A 17, B 1, C 1, may, however, very well have belonged to some Robin Hood ballad.

A is translated by Grundtvig, Engelske og skotske Folkeviser, p. 22, No 3.

A

Jamieson's Popular Ballads, II, 44, from Mrs Brown's recitation.

1 O WILLIE 's large o limb and lith,
    And come o high degree,
  And he is gane to Earl Richard,
    To serve for meat and fee.

2 Earl Richard had but ae daughter,
    Fair as a lily-flower,
  And they made up their love-contract
    Like proper paramour.

3 It fell upon a simmer's nicht,
    Whan the leaves were fair and green,

---

* Compare No 102, **A** 1³, ⁴, and No 101, **A** 1³, ⁴; 2³, ⁴ and 8³, ⁴; 3 and 3; 4 and 9¹, ², ⁵, ⁶; 5 and 10¹, ², ⁵, ⁶; 7¹, 8²⁴ and 13; 9⁸ and 24⁴. Also No 102, **A** 3, and No 101, **B** 13; 4¹, ², 5¹, ⁴ and 15¹, ², ⁵, ⁶; 8 and 16. Also, No 102, **A** 1, and No 101, **C** 3; 8 and 6.

That Willie met his gay ladie
Intil the wood alane.

4 'O narrow is my gown, Willie,
That wont to be sae wide;
And gane is a' my fair colour,
That wont to be my pride.

5 'But gin my father should get word
What 's past between us twa,
Before that he should eat or drink,
He 'd hang you oer that wa.

6 'But ye 'll come to my bower, Willie,
Just as the sun gaes down,
And kep me in your arms twa,
And latna me fa down.'

7 O whan the sun was now gane down,
He 's doen him till her bower,
And there, by the lee licht o the moon,
Her window she lookit oer.

8 Intill a robe o red scarlet
She lap, fearless o harm;
And Willie was large o lith and limb,
And keppit her in his arm.

9 And they 've gane to the gude green wood,
And, ere the night was deen,
She 's born to him a bonny young son,
Amang the leaves sae green.

10 Whan night was gane, and day was come,
And the sun began to peep,
Up and raise the Earl Richard
Out o his drowsy sleep.

11 He 's ca'd upon his merry young men,
By ane, by twa, and by three:
'O what 's come o my daughter dear,
That she 's nae come to me?

12 'I dreamt a dreary dream last night,
God grant it come to gude!
I dreamt I saw my daughter dear
Drown in the saut sea flood.

13 'But gin my daughter be dead or sick,
Or yet be stown awa,
I mak a vow, and I 'll keep it true,
I 'll hang ye ane and a'!'

14 They sought her back, they sought her fore,
They sought her up and down;
They got her in the gude green wood,
Nursing her bonny young son.

15 He took the bonny boy in his arms,
And kist him tenderlie;
Says, Though I would your father hang,
Your mother 's dear to me.

16 He kist him oer and oer again:
'My grandson I thee claim,
And Robin Hood in gude green wood,
And that shall be your name.'

17 And mony ane sings o grass, o grass,
And mony ane sings o corn,
And mony ane sings o Robin Hood
Kens little whare he was born.

18 It wasna in the ha, the ha,
Nor in the painted bower,
But it was in the gude green wood,
Amang the lily-flower.

B

Buchan's Ballads of the North of Scotland, II, 1.

1 Mony ane talks o the grass, the grass,
And mony ane o the corn,
And mony ane talks o gude Robin Hood
Kens little whar he was born.

2 He was gotten in a earl's ha,
And in a lady's bower,

And born into gude greenwood,
Thro mony cauld winter's shower.

3 His father was the earl's own steward,
Sprung frae sma pedigree;
His mother, Earl Huntingdon's ae daughter,
For he had nane else but she.

4 When nine months were near an end,
And eight months they were gone,

The lady's cheeks wi tears were wet,
    And thus she made her moan :

5 ' What shall I say, my love Archibald,
    This day for you and me ?
I will be laid in cauld irons,
    And ye 'll be hanged on tree.'

6 ' What aileth my love Clementina ?
    What gars you mourn sae sair ? '
' You know,' said she, ' I 'm with child to thee,
    These eight lang months and mair.'

7 ' Will ye gae to my mother's bower,
    Stands on yon stately green ?
Or will ye gae to the gude greenwood,
    Where ye will not be seen ? '

8 ' I winna gang to your mother's bower,
    Stands on yon stately green ;
But I will on to gude greenwood,
    For I will not be seen.'

9 He 's girt his sword down by his side,
    Took his lady by the hand,
And they are on thro gude greenwood,
    As fast as they could gang.

10 With slowly steps these couple walkd,
    About miles scarcely three.
When this lady, being sair wearied out,
    Lay down beneath a tree.

11 ' O for a few of yon junipers,
    To cheer my heart again,
And likewise for a gude midwife,
    To ease me of my pain ! '

12 ' I 'll bring to you yon junipers,
    To cheer your heart again,
And I 'll be to you a gude midwife,
    To ease you of your pain.'

13 ' Had far awa frae me, Archibald,
    For this will never dee ;
That 's nae the fashion o our land,
    And it 's nae be used by me.

14 ' Ye 'll take your small-sword by your side,
    Your buckler and your bow,
And ye 'll gae down thro gude greenwood,
    And hunt the deer and roe.

15 ' You will stay in gude greenwood,
    And with the chase go on,
Until yon white hind pass you by,
    Then straight to me ye 'll come.'

16 He 's girt his sword then by his side,
    His buckler and his bow,
And he is on thro gude greenwood,
    To hunt the deer and roe.

17 And in the greenwood he did stay,
    And with the chase gaed on,
Until the white hind passd him by,
    Then to his love he came.

18 He girt his sword then by his side,
    Fast thro greenwood went he,
And there he found his love lie dead,
    Beneath the green oak tree.

19 The sweet young babe that she had born
    Right lively seemed to be ;
' Ohon, alas ! ' said young Archibald,
    ' A mournful scene to me !

20 ' Altho my sweet babe is alive,
    This does increase my woe ;
How to nourish a motherless babe
    Is mair than I do know.'

21 He looked east, he looked west,
    To see what he could see,
Then spied the Earl o Huntingdon,
    And mony a man him wi.

22 Then Archibald fled from the earl's face,
    Among the leaves sae green,
That he might hear what might be said,
    And see, and nae be seen.

23 The earl straight thro the greenwood came,
    Unto the green oak tree,
And there he saw his daughter dead,
    Her living child her wi.

24 Then he 's taen up the little boy,
    Rowed him in his gown-sleeve ;
Said, Tho your father 's to my loss,
    Your mother 's to me leave.

25 And if ye live until I die,
    My bowers and lands ye 'se heir ;

You are my only daughter's child;
  But her I never had mair.

26 Ye 'se hae all kinds of nourishment,
  And likewise nurses three;
  If I knew where the fause knave were,
  High hanged should he be.

27 His daughter he buried in gude church-yard,
  All in a mournful mood,
  And brought the boy to church that day,
  And christend him Robin Hood.

28 This boy was bred in the earl's ha
  Till he became a man,
  But loved to hunt in gude greenwood,
  To raise his noble fame.

C

Kinloch MSS, V, 330 f, the last two stanzas of 'Douglass Dale.'

1 MONY ane speaks o grass, o grass,
  And mony mare o corn,
  And mony ane sings o Robin Heed
  Kens little whare he was born.

2 He was born in good green wood,
  At the fut o yon olive tree;
  His father was a knight's ae son,
  And his mother a lady free.

B. *Christie says of his copy that the words sung by his maternal grandfather "were somewhat, as far as the Editor can remember, like those given by Buchan, and that some slight alterations were made by him from the way the Editor heard the ballad sung."*

The alterations in Christie's eighteen stanzas are:
1^3. mony talk. 1^4. That kenna.
8^4. Whare I will. 15^1. in the.
15^3. a white. 18^2. gaed he.
25^4. I neer. 28^1. The.

103

ROSE THE RED AND WHITE LILY

A. 'Rose the Red and White Lilly,' Jamieson-Brown MS., fol. 1.
B. 'Rose the Red and White Lillie,' Buchan's Ballads of the North of Scotland, I, 67.

C. 'The Wedding of Robin Hood and Little John,' Kinloch's Ancient Scottish Ballads, p. 69.

A WAS No 6 of the fifteen ballads written down by Mrs Brown for William Tytler in 1783: Anderson, in Nichols's Illustrations, VII, 176. This copy was printed by Scott in his Minstrelsy, II, 60, 1802, "chiefly from Mrs Brown's MS.," but with numerous alterations. Kinloch's annotated copy of his Ancient Scottish Ballads supplies an additional stanza of C; the 17th.

The story in A is that Rose the Red and

White Lily have a bad step-mother, who, however, has two good sons that love these maids: Brown Robin, Lily, and Arthur, Rose. The maids build a bower, in which the young people make very merry, and the step-mother, to spoil sport, tells her sons that they must sail the sea. Brown Robin goes to the wood, and Arthur to the king's court. The maids disguise themselves as men, and take service with their lovers: White Lily under the name of Roge the Round, and Rose the Red under that of Sweet Willy. Before they part they make a mutual vow that at three blasts of a horn the one shall come to the other's help. Once upon a time, when Robin and his men are putting the stone, Roge sets it seven foot beyond all the rest, but, having exerted herself too much in so doing, is fain to lean her back against an oak and utters a moan, by which Brown Robin perceives that Roge is a woman. Forty weeks after this Roge has occasion for the aid of a bower-wife. Brown Robin proffers his help, but it is declined; nevertheless, with an apparent but not a real inconsistency, the lady asks him to blow her horn, for she has a brother at the court who will come to her upon the sound. Robin replies that if she has a brother whom she loves better than him she may blow the horn herself. This she does, and Sweet Willy comes at once. Brown Robin will let no man enter the bower without a fight. Rose the Red is wounded, and avows herself to be a woman. Brown Robin is distressed: he wished never to see a woman's blood, for the sake of a maid named White Lily. Roge the Round reveals herself as that same. Word comes to the king's court that Brown Robin's man has borne a son, and the king declares that he will go to the wood to inquire into this marvel. Arthur will go with him, to find a foot-page who had left him. Arrived at the wood, Arthur blows his horn, and Sweet Willy comes running to him. Arthur asks the page why he had run away, and is told that it was to see a brother that lives in the wood. The king enters the bower, and finds White Lily nursing her son. This leads to an explanation on the part of Rose the Red. Brown

Robin, coming in from hunting, starts to see the king. The king bids him have no fear, but quit the wood and come to court. Brown Robin and White Lily, Arthur and Rose the Red, go to church and are married.

In B the two maids, ill-treated by their step-mother, betake themselves to the wood, where they meet, not Brown Robin, but Robin Hood, and take service with him. Rose and Lily change parts; Rose, under the name of Nicholas, consorting with Robin Hood, and Lily, *alias* Roger Brown, with Little John. It is not, however, Robin Hood and Little John who turn out to be their lovers, but "a lad in the company," and "another youth among the company," stanzas 30, 51. Nothing is said of the king.

In the fragmentary C the maids are daughters of a king. Their proper names are not given, and we do not learn that the step-mother has a pair of sons. In consequence of the harshness of their step-mother, these king's daughters go to the wood as Nicholas and Rogee Roun, to seek Robin Hood, and they are discovered to be maids by a song which Rogee sings. Rogee is wedded to Robin Hood, and Nicholas to Little John.

It is easy to see that the Robin Hood of B, C, was suggested by the Brown Robin of A. The name Barnsdale in A 12, 51 has certainly been adopted from the Robin Hood cycle, but in the present ballad is the residence of the father of Rose and Lily, not that of Robin Hood.

The only part of the ballad which has the stamp of indubitably ancient tradition is the child-birth in the wood, and this scene is the rightful, and perhaps exclusive, property of 'Leesome Brand,' No 15: see I, 182. A 24–29, B 40–47, are found again in 'Willie o Douglas Dale,' A 15–17, 22, 23, B 18, 19, 22, 24, C 8–10, and the first part of 'Willie o Douglas Dale,' as well as of the ballad which immediately precedes the present, commonly called 'The Birth of Robin Hood,' is a variation of 'Leesome Brand.'

Robin Hood has no love-story in any ancient ballad, though his name has been foisted into modern love-ballads, as in 'Robin Hood and the Tanner's Daughter,' No 8 C. Maid Marian is a late accretion. There is a piteously vulgar broadside, in which Maid Marian, being parted from Robin Hood, dresses herself "like a page" (but armed fully), meets Robin Hood, also under disguise, and has an hour's fight with him. There is so far a resemblance in this to A 30 ff, B 49, that a woman disguised as a page fights with Robin Hood. I suppose

the resemblance to be accidental, but whether it be or not, the question of 'Rose the Red and White Lily' being originally a Robin Hood ballad is not affected.

A 3, B 5, is like C 6 of 'The Clerk's Twa Sons o Owsenford,' No 72.

Scott's copy is translated by Doenniges, p. 40.

A

Jamieson-Brown MS., fol. 1.

1 O ROSE the Red and White Lilly,
    Their mother dear was dead,
    And their father married an ill woman,
    Wishd them twa little guede.

2 Yet she had twa as fu fair sons
    As eer brake manis bread,
    And the tane of them loed her White Lilly,
    An the tither lood Rose the Red.

3 O biggit ha they a bigly bowr,
    And strawn it oer wi san,
    And there was mair mirth i the ladies'
        bowr
    Than in a' their father's lan.

4 But out it spake their step-mother,
    Wha stood a little foreby:
    I hope to live and play the prank
    Sal gar your loud sang ly.

5 She 's calld upon her eldest son:
    Come here, my son, to me;
    It fears me sair, my eldest son,
    That ye maun sail the sea.

6 'Gin it fear you sair, my mither dear,
    Your bidding I maun dee;
    But be never war to Rose the Red
    Than ye ha been to me.'

7 'O had your tongue, my eldest son,
    For sma sal be her part;
    You 'll nae get a kiss o her comely mouth
    Gin your very fair heart should break.'

8 She 's calld upon her youngest son:
    Come here, my son, to me;
    It fears me sair, my youngest son,
    That ye maun sail the sea.

9 'Gin it fear you sair, my mither dear,
    Your bidding I maun dee;
    But be never war to White Lilly
    Than ye ha been to me.'

10 'O haud your tongue, my youngest son,
    For sma sall be her part;
    You 'll neer get a kiss o her comely mouth
    Tho your very fair heart should break.'

11 When Rose the Red and White Lilly
    Saw their twa loves were gane,
    Then stopped ha they their loud, loud sang,
    And tane up the still mournin;
    And their step-mother stood listnin by,
    To hear the ladies' mean.

12 Then out it spake her White Lilly:
    My sister, we 'll be gane;
    Why should we stay in Barnsdale,
    To waste our youth in pain?

13 Then cutted ha they their green cloathing
    A little below their knee,
    An sae ha they there yallow hair,
    A little aboon there bree;
    An they 've doen them to haely chapel,
    Was christened by Our Lady.

14 There ha they chang'd their ain twa names,
    Sae far frae ony town,
    An the tane o them hight Sweet Willy,
    An the tither o them Roge the Roun.

15 Between this twa a vow was made,
  An they sware it to fulfil ;
That at three blasts o a bugle-horn,
  She 'd come her sister till.

16 Now Sweet Willy 's gane to the kingis court,
  Her true-love for to see,
An Roge the Roun to good green wood,
  Brown Robin's man to be.

17 As it fell out upon a day
  They a' did put the stane,
Full seven foot ayont them a'
  She gard the puttin-stane gang.

18 She leand her back against an oak,
  And gae a loud Ohone !
Then out it spake him Brown Robin,
  But that 's a woman's moan !

19 'O ken ye by my red rose lip ?
  Or by my yallow hair ?
Or ken ye by my milk-white breast ?
  For ye never saw it bare ? '

20 'I ken no by your red rose lip,
  Nor by your yallow hair ;
Nor ken I by your milk-white breast,
  For I never saw it bare ;
But come to your bowr whaever sae likes,
  Will find a lady there.'

21 'O gin ye come to my bowr within,
  Thro fraud, deceit, or guile,
Wi this same bran that 's in my han,
  I swear I will the kill.'

22 'But I will come thy bowr within,
  An spear nae leave,' quoth he ;
'An this same bran that 's i my han
  I sall ware back on the.'

23 About the tenth hour of the night
  The ladie's bower-door was broken,
An eer the first hour of the day
  The bonny knave-bairn was gotten.

24 When days were gane, and months were run,
  The lady took travailing,
And sair she cry'd for a bowr-woman,
  For to wait her upon.

25 Then out it spake him Brown Robin :
  Now what needs a' this din ?

For what coud any woman do
  But I coud do the same ?

26 ' 'T was never my mither's fashion,' she says,
  ' Nor sall it ever be mine,
That belted knights shoud eer remain
  Where ladies dreed their pine.

27 ' But ye take up that bugle-horn,
  An blaw a blast for me ;
I ha a brother i the kingis court
  Will come me quickly ti.'

28 ' O gin ye ha a brither on earth
  That ye love better nor me,
Ye blaw the horn yoursel,' he says,
  ' For ae blast I winna gie.'

29 She 's set the horn till her mouth,
  And she 's blawn three blasts sae shrill ;
Sweet Willy heard i the kingis court,
  And came her quickly till.

30 Then up it started Brown Robin,
  An an angry man was he :
' There comes nae man this bowr within
  But first must fight wi me.'

31 O they hae fought that bowr within
  Till the sun was gaing down,
Till drops o blude frae Rose the Red
  Came hailing to the groun.

32 She leand her back against the wa,
  Says, Robin, let a' be ;
For it is a lady born and bred
  That 's foughten sae well wi thee.

33 O seven foot he lap a back ;
  Says, Alas, and wae is me !
I never wisht in a' my life,
  A woman's blude to see ;
An a' for the sake of ae fair maid
  Whose name was White Lilly.

34 Then out it spake her White Lilly,
  An a hearty laugh laugh she :
She 's lived wi you this year an mair,
  Tho ye kentna it was she.

35 Now word has gane thro a' the lan,
  Before a month was done,
That Brown Robin's man, in good green wood,
  Had born a bonny young son.

36 The word has gane to the kingis court,
　An to the king himsel;
　'Now, by my fay,' the king could say,
　'The like was never heard tell!'

37 Then out it spake him Bold Arthur,
　An a hearty laugh laugh he:
　I trow some may has playd the loun,
　And fled her ain country.

38 'Bring me my steed,' then cry'd the king,
　'My bow and arrows keen;
　I'l ride mysel to good green wood,
　An see what's to be seen.'

39 'An't please your grace,' said Bold Arthur,
　'My liege, I'll gang you wi,
　An try to fin a little foot-page,
　That's strayd awa frae me.'

40 O they've hunted i the good green wood
　The buck but an the rae,
　An they drew near Brown Robin's bowr,
　About the close of day.

41 Then out it spake the king in hast,
　Says, Arthur, look an see
　Gin that be no your little foot-page
　That leans against yon tree.

42 Then Arthur took his bugle-horn,
　An blew a blast sae shrill;
　Sweet Willy started at the sound,
　An ran him quickly till.

43 'O wanted ye your meat, Willy?
　Or wanted ye your fee?
　Or gat ye ever an angry word,
　That ye ran awa frae me?'

44 'I wanted nought, my master dear;
　To me ye ay was good;
　I came but to see my ae brother,
　That wons in this green wood.'

45 Then out it spake the king again,
　Says, Bonny boy, tell to me
　Wha lives into yon bigly bowr,
　Stands by yon green oak tree?

46 'O pardon me,' says Sweet Willy,
　'My liege, I dare no tell;
　An I pray you go no near that bowr,
　For fear they do you fell.'

47 'O haud your tongue, my bonny boy,
　For I winna be said nay;
　But I will gang that bowr within,
　Betide me weel or wae.'

48 They've lighted off their milk-white steeds,
　An saftly enterd in,
　An there they saw her White Lilly,
　Nursing her bonny yong son.

49 'Now, by the rood,' the king coud say,
　'This is a comely sight;
　I trow, instead of a forrester's man,
　This is a lady bright!'

50 Then out it spake her Rose the Red,
　An fell low down on her knee:
　O pardon us, my gracious liege,
　An our story I'll tell thee.

51 Our father was a wealthy lord,
　That wond in Barnsdale;
　But we had a wicked step-mother,
　That wrought us meickle bale.

52 Yet she had twa as fu fair sons
　As ever the sun did see,
　An the tane o them lood my sister dear,
　An the tither sayd he lood me.

53 Then out it spake him Bold Arthur,
　As by the king he stood:
　Now, by the faith o my body,
　This shoud be Rose the Red!

54 Then in it came him Brown Robin,
　Frae hunting o the deer,
　But whan he saw the king was there,
　He started back for fear.

55 The king has taen him by the hand,
　An bade him naithing dread;
　Says, Ye maun leave the good green wood,
　Come to the court wi speed.

56 Then up he took White Lilly's son,
　An set him on his knee;
　Says, Gin ye live to wiald a bran,
　My bowman ye sall bee.

57 The king he sent for robes of green,
　An girdles o shinning gold;
　He gart the ladies be arrayd
　Most comely to behold.

58 They 've done them unto Mary Kirk,
   An there gat fair wedding,
   An fan the news spread oer the lan,
   For joy the bells did ring.

59 Then out it spake her Rose the Red,
   An a hearty laugh laugh she :
   I wonder what would our step-dame say,
   Gin she this sight did see !

B

Buchan's Ballads of the North of Scotland, I, 67.

1 Now word is gane thro a' the land,
  Gude seal that it sae spread !
  To Rose the Red and White Lillie,
  Their mither dear was dead.

2 Their father 's married a bauld woman,
  And brought her ower the sea,
  Twa sprightly youths, her ain young sons,
  Intill her companie.

3 They fixd their eyes on those ladies,
  On shipboard as they stood,
  And sware, if ever they wan to land,
  These ladies they woud wed.

4 But there was nae a quarter past,
  A quarter past but three,
  Till these young luvers a' were fond
  O other's companie.

5 The knights they harped i their bower,
  The ladies sewd and sang ;
  There was mair mirth in that chamer
  Than a' their father's lan.

6 Then out it spak their step-mither,
  At the stair-foot stood she :
  I 'm plagued wi your troublesome noise !
  What makes your melodie ?

7 O Rose the Red, ye sing too loud,
  White Lillie, your voice is strang ;
  But gin I live and brook my life,
  I 'se gar you change your sang.

8 'We maunna change our loud, loud song
  For nae duke's son ye 'll bear ;
  We winna change our loud, loud song,
  But aye we 'll sing the mair.

9 'We never sung the sang, mither,
  But we 'll sing ower again ;

We 'll take our harps into our hands,
  And we 'll harp, and we 'll sing.'

10 She 's calld upon her twa young sons,
   Says, Boun ye for the sea ;
   Let Rose the Red and White Lillie
   Stay in their bower wi me.

11 'O God forbid,' said her eldest son,
   'Nor lat it ever be,
   Unless ye were as kind to our luves
   As gin we were them wi.'

12 'Yet never the less, my pretty sons,
   Ye 'll boun you for the faem ;
   Let Rose the Red and White Lillie
   Stay in their bowers at hame.'

13 'O when wi you we came alang,
   We felt the stormy sea,
   And where we go, ye neer shall know,
   Nor shall be known by thee.'

14 Then wi her harsh and boisterous word
   She forc'd these lads away,
   While Rose the Red and White Lillie
   Still in their bowers did stay.

15 But there was not a quarter past,
   A quarter past but ane,
   Till Rose the Red in rags she gaed,
   White Lillie's claithing grew thin.

16 Wi bitter usage every day,
   The ladies they thought lang ;
   'Ohon, alas !' said Rose the Red,
   'She 's gard us change our sang.

17 'But we will change our own fu names,
   And we 'll gang frae the town,
   Frae Rose the Red and White Lillie
   To Nicholas and Roger Brown.

18 'And we will cut our green claithing
   A little aboon our knee,

And we will on to gude greenwood,
    Twa bauld bowmen to be.'

19 ' Ohon, alas ! ' said White Lillie,
    ' My fingers are but sma,
And tho my hands woud wield the bow,
    They winna yield at a'.'

20 ' O had your tongue now, White Lillie,
    And lat these fears a' be ;
There 's naething that ye 're awkward in
    But I will learn thee.'

21 Then they are on to gude greenwood,
    As fast as gang coud they ;
O then they spied him Robin Hood,
    Below a green aik tree.

22 ' Gude day, gude day, kind sir,' they said,
    ' God make you safe and free : '
' Gude day, gude day,' said Robin Hood,
    ' What is your wills wi me ? '

23 ' Lo here we are, twa banishd knights,
    Come frae our native hame ;
We 're come to crave o thee service,
    Our king will gie us nane.'

24 ' If ye be twa young banishd knights,
    Tell me frae what countrie : '
' Frae Anster town into Fifeshire ;
    Ye know it as well as we.'

25 ' If a' be true that ye hae said,
    And tauld just now to me,
Ye 're welcome, welcome, every one ;
    Your master I will be.

26 ' Now ye shall eat as I do eat,
    And lye as I do lye ;
Ye salna wear nae waur claithing
    Nor my young men and I.'

27 Then they went to a ruinous house,
    And there they enterd in,
And Nicholas fed wi Robin Hood,
    And Roger wi Little John.

28 But it fell ance upon a day
    They were at the putting-stane,
Whan Rose the Red she viewd them a',
    As they stood on the green.

29 She hit the stane then wi her foot,
    And kepd it wi her knee,
And spaces three aboon them a'
    I wyte she gard it flee.

30 She sat her back then to a tree,
    And gae a loud Ohon !
A lad spak in the companie,
    I hear a woman's moan.

31 ' How know you that, young man ? ' she said,
    ' How know you that o me ?
Did eer ye see me in that place
    Ae foot my ground to flee ?

32 ' Or know ye by my cherry cheeks ?
    Or by my yellow hair ?
Or by the paps on my breast-bane ?
    Ye never saw them bare.'

33 ' I know not by your cherry cheeks,
    Nor by your yellow hair ;
But I know by your milk-white chin,
    On it there grows nae hair.

34 ' I never saw you in that cause
    Ae foot your ground to flee ;
I 've seen you stan wi sword in han
    Mang men's blood to the knee.

35 ' But if I come your bower within,
    By night, or yet by day,
I shall know before I go
    If ye be man or may.'

36 ' O if you come my bower within,
    By night, or yet by day,
As soon 's I draw my trusty brand,
    Nae lang ye 'll wi me stay.'

37 But he is haunted to her bower,
    Her bigly bower o stane,
Till he has got her big wi bairn,
    And near sax months she 's gane.

38 Whan three mair months were come and gane,
    They gaed to hunt the hynde ;
She wont to be the foremost ane,
    But now stayd far behynd.

39 Her luver looks her in the face,
    And thus to her said he ;

I think your cheeks are pale and wan;
    Pray, what gaes warst wi thee?

40 O want ye roses to your breast?
    Or ribbons to your sheen?
  Or want ye as muckle o dear bought luve
    As your heart can conteen?

41 'I want nae roses to my breast,
    Nae ribbons to my sheen;
  Nor want I as muckle dear bought luve
    As my heart can conteen.

42 'I'd rather hae a fire behynd,
    Anither me before,
  A gude midwife at my right side,
    Till my young babe be bore.'

43 'I'll kindle a fire wi a flint-stane,
    Bring wine in a green horn;
  I'll be midwife at your right side,
    Till your young babe be born.'

44 'That was neer my mither's custom,
    Forbid that it be mine!
  A knight stan by a lady bright
    Whan she drees a' her pine.

45 'There is a knight in gude greenwood,
    If that he kent o me,
  Thro stock and stane and the hawthorn
    Sae soon 's he woud come me tee.'

46 'If there be a knight in gude greenwood
    Ye like better than me,
  If ance he come your bower within,
    Ane o us twa shall dee.'

47 She set a horn to her mouth,
    And she blew loud and shrill;
  Thro stock and stane and the hawthorn
    Brave Roger came her till.

48 'Wha's here sae bauld,' the youth replied,
    'Thus to encroach on me?'
  'O here I am,' the knight replied,
    'Hae as much right as thee.'

49 Then they fought up the gude greenwood,
    Sae did they down the plain;
  They niddart ither wi lang braid-swords,
    Till they were bleedy men.

50 Then out it spak the sick woman,
    Sat under the greenwood tree;
  O had your han, young man, she said,
    She's a woman as well as me.

51 Then out it speaks anither youth,
    Amang the companie;
  Gin I had kent what I ken now,
    'T is for her I woud dee.

52 'O wae mat worth you, Rose the Red,
    An ill death mat ye dee!
  Altho ye tauld upo yoursell,
    Ye might hae heald on me.'

53 'O for her sake I was content
    For to gae ower the sea;
  For her I left my mither's ha,
    Tho she proves fause to me.'

54 But whan these luvers were made known,
    They sung right joyfullie,
  Nae blyther was the nightingale,
    Nor bird that sat on tree.

55 Now they hae married these ladies,
    Brought them to bower and ha;
  And now a happy life they lead;
    I wish sae may we a'.

C

Kinloch's Ancient Scottish Ballads, annotated by the editor, p. 69.

1 THE king has wedded an ill woman,
    Into some foreign land;
  His daughters twa, that stood in awe,
    They bravely sat and sang.

2 Then in became their step-mother,
    Sae stately steppin ben:
  'O gin I live and bruik my life,
    I'll gar ye change your tune.'

3 'O we sang neer that sang, ladie,
    But we will sing again;

And ye neer boor that son, ladie,
We wad lay our love on.

4 'But we will cow our yellow locks
   A little abune our bree,
   And we will on to gude greenwud,
   And serve for meat and fee.

5 'And we will kilt our gay claithing
   A little below the knee,
   And we will on to gude greenwud,
   Gif Robin Hood we see.

6 'And we will change our ain twa names,
   When we gae frae the toun;
   The tane we will call Nicholas,
   The tither Rogee Roun.'

7 Then they hae cowd their yellow locks
   A little abune their bree,
   And they are on to gude greenwud,
   To serve for meat and fee.

8 And they hae kilt their gay claithing
   A little below their knee,
   And they are on to gud greenwud,
   Gif Robin Hood they see.

9 And they hae chang'd thair ain twa names,
   Whan they gaed frae the toun;
   The tane they 've called Nicholas,
   The tither Rogee Roun.

10 And they hae staid in gude greenwud,
   And never a day thoucht lang,
   Till it fell ance upon a day
   That Rogee sang a sang.

11 'Whan we were in our father's bouer,
   We sewd the silken seam;
   But now we walk the gude greenwud,
   And bear anither name.

12 'When we were in our father's ha,
   We wore the beaten gold;
   But now we wear the shield sae sharp;
   Alas, we 'll die with cold!'

13 Then up bespak him Robin Hood,
   As he to them drew near:
   'Instead of boys to carry the bow,
   Two ladies we 've got here.'

14 So they had not been in gud greenwud
   A twalmonth and a day,
   Till Rogee Roun was as big wi bairn
   As onie lady could gae.

15 'O wae be to my stepmother,
   That garrd me leave my hame!
   For I 'm wi bairn to Robin Hood,
   And near nine month is gane.

16 'O wha will be my bouer-woman?
   Na bouer-woman is here;
   O wha will be my bouer-woman,
   Whan that sad time draws near?'

17 Then up bespak him Robin Hood,
   At the foot o yon greenwud tree:
   O hold your tongue, fair Rogee Roun,
   For married ye sall be.

18 The tane was wedded to Robin Hood,
   And the tither to Little John;
   And it was a' owing to their stepmother,
   That garrd them leave their hame.

———◆———

A. *Written, like all the ballads in the MS., in
   stanzas of two long lines.*
   1. *Anderson cites this stanza, giving the last
   line,* Wist them twa little quee'd.
   8^1. younges. 8^3. youngst.
   13^1. greed. 21^4. sear. 26^3. beltest kights.
   47^4. well? 49^1. the the king.
   *Scott's variations, the contrary not being al-
   leged, must be supposed to be his own.
   Scott inserts after* 10:

Sae Bauld Arthur 's gane to our king's court,
   His hie chamberlain to be;
But Brown Robin he has slain a knight,
   And to grene wood he did flee.

$11^{5, 6}$ *are* $12^{1, 2}$ *in the MS., making a stanza
with* $12^{1, 2}$; $12^{3, 4}$ *make an eight-line stanza
with* 13. $11^{5, 6}$ *are omitted by Scott.*
$13^{5, 6}$ *make the last half of a stanza in Scott,
which begins:*

And left hae they that bonny bour,
  To cross the raging sea.
20³, ⁴ *are omitted by Scott.*
33⁵, ⁶ *make the last half of a stanza in Scott,*
  which runs :

And that all for the knightly vow
  I swore to Our Ladye,
But mair, *etc.*
57 *follows* 53 *in Scott, and* 59 *is omitted.*
B. 7². While Lillie.   43². horn green.

104

PRINCE HEATHEN

A. 'The Disconsolate Lady,' The Jovial Rake's Garland, n. d., p. 6, No 4.

B. 'Prince Heathen,' Buchan's MSS, I, 97 ; Motherwell's MS., p. 665.

THE fragment **A** (pointed out to me by Svend Grundtvig) is partly explained by **B**, which is no doubt some stall-copy, reshaped from tradition. Motherwell's copy was derived from Buchan.

The story, which reads like an old one extremely corrupted, is none too intelligible even in the longer form. Lady Margery is sitting in her bower-door. Prince Heathen comes by and gives her a ring. She refuses him her love. He swears that he will make her greet ; she swears that he shall not. He takes her maidenhead : still she will not greet. He tells her that he has killed her father, mother, and seven brothers : still she will not greet. He puts her in a vault of stone, fastened with five and thirty locks : she will not greet [go, **A**], but rues. He comes back from the mountains, and asks her how she is faring. Dying, she

says. He takes her out upon the green, allowing her no female service, and she brings forth a son. How is it with her now? Dying. She asks for a drink of water : he will not give her a drop until she wraps up her young son. She has nothing to wrap the babe in ; he gives her his horse-sheet ; her tears fall fast. "Bonny may, now you greet!" he exclaims [" will you go now?" **A**]. But she greets not for him ; it is for her young son, wrapped so roughly. Prince Heathen, satisfied, as far as we can see, now that he has subdued her proud will, orders his son to be rolled in silk and washed in milk, according to the usage of Scottish nursery : see No 5, B 61, C 82, 83, E 32, F 57, G 33 ; No 20, C 8 ; No 63, B 35, C 35, F 22, J 47 ; No 101, A 25. Having broken her spirit, he loves her well.

A

The Jovial Rake's Garland, n. d., p. 6, No 4, Bodleian Library, Douce PP, 164.

1 LADY MARGERY MAY sits in her bower,
  Sewing at her seem ;
By there comes a heathen knight,
  From her her maidenhead has tane.

2 He has put her in a tower strong,
  With double locks on fifty doors :

' Lady Margery May, will you ga now? '
' O ye heathen knight, not yet for you.

3 ' I am asking, you heathen knight ;
  What I am asking will you grant to
    me ?
Will ye let one of your waitmen
  A drink of your well bring to me ? '

4 ' Meat nor drink you shall never get,
  Nor out of that shall you never come,

Meat nor drink shall you never get,
   Until you bear to me daughter or son.'

5 Thus time drew on, and further on,
   For travail came this young lady to ;
   She travailed up, so did she down,
   But lighter could she never be.

6 ' An asking, an asking, you heathen knight ;
   An asking will you grant to me ?

B

Buchan's MSS, I, 97 ; Motherwell's MS., p. 665.

1 LADY MARGARET sat in her bower-door,
   Sewing at her silken seem,
   When by it came Prince Heathen then,
   An gae to her a gay gold ring.

2 He turnd about, an gied a bow ;
   She said, Begone, I love na you ;
   When he sware by his yellow hair
   That he woud gar her greet fu sair.

3 But she sware by her milk-white skin
   Prince Heathen shoud gar her greet nane :
   ' O bonny may, winna ye greet now ? '
   ' Ye heathenish dog, nae yet for you.'

4 He 's taen her in his arms twa,
   Laid her between him an the wa,
   An ere he let her free again,
   Her maidenhead frae her he 's taen.
   ' O bonny may, winna ye greet now ? '
   ' Ye heathenish dog, nae yet for you.'

5 ' I killd your father in his bed,
   And your gay mother by his side,
   And your seven brothers, ane by ane,
   And they were seven pretty men.
   O bonny may, winna ye greet now ? '
   ' Ye heathenish dog, nae yet for you.'

6 ' I 'll put you in a vault o stone,
   Where five an thirty locks hing on ;
   Naebody there then shall you see,
   For I will keep the keys wi me.
   O bonny may, winna ye greet now ? '
   ' Ye heathenish dog, nae yet for you.'

Will you give me a scread of silk,
   For to row your young son wi ? '

7 He took the horse-sheet in his hand,
   The tears came twinkling down :
   ' Lady Margaret May, will ye ga now ? '
   ' O ye heathen knight, not yet for you.'

8 ' I 'll wash my young son with the milk,
   I will dry my young son with the silk ;
   For hearts will break, and bands will bow ;
   So dear will I love my lady now ! '

7 He 's put her in a vault o stone,
   Where five an thirty locks hing on ;
   Naebody there coud eer her see,
   Prince Heathen kept the keys him wi.
   But ae she cried, What shall I do !
   The heathenish dog has gart me rue.

8 Prince Heathen from the mountains came,
   Attended by his armed men,
   And he 's gane to the bonny may,
   And to the prison where she lay :
   ' O bonny may, what do you now ? '
   ' Ye heathenish dog, dying for you.'

9 ' I 'll take you out upon the green,
   Where women ye shall neer see ane,
   But only me and my young men,
   Till ye bring daughter hame or son.
   O bonny may, what do you now ? '
   ' Ye heathenish dog, dying for you.'

10 He 's taen her out upon the green,
   Where she saw women never ane,
   But only him and 's merry young men,
   Till she brought hame a bonny young son.
   ' O bonny may, what do you now ? '
   ' Ye heathenish dog, dying for you.

11 ' A drink, a drink, frae Prince Heathen's hand,
   Though it were frae yon cauld well strong ! '
   ' O neer a drap, Prince Heathen,' said one,
   ' Till ye row up your bonny young son.'
   ' How can I row up my bonny young son,
   When I hae naething to row him in ? '

12 ' I will lend you my horse's sheet,
   That will row him baith head and feet.'
   As soon 's she took it in her han,

Tears oer her cheeks down rapping ran.
'O bonny may, ye do greet now :'
'Ye heathenish dog, but nae for you.

13 'But a' is for my bonny young son ;
Your sheets are rough to row him in ;
Ohon, alas, sair may I rue
That eer I saw such rogues as you ! '

14 'Ye 'll row my young son in the silk,
An ye will wash him wi the milk,
An lay my lady very saft,
That I may see her very aft.'
When hearts are broken, bands will bow ;
Sae well 's he loved his lady now !

A. 3³. writmen.   5². too.
B. 11². wells.   *Motherwell MS.* well.

There are some trifling deviations in Motherwell's copy.

105

THE BAILIFF'S DAUGHTER OF ISLINGTON

a. Printed for P. Brooksby, Roxburghe Ballads, II, 457.
b. Printed for J. Walter, Douce Ballads, II, fol. 229.
c. Printed for P. Brooksby, Pepys Ballads, III, 258,
No 256. d. Printed for P. Brooksby, Roxburghe Ballads, IV, 56. e. Printed for P. Brooksby, Douce Ballads, II, fol. 230. f. An Aldermary Churchyard copy.

REPRINTED in Percy's Reliques, III, 133, 1765, from the Pepys copy, c, but " with some improvements, communicated by a lady as she heard the same repeated in her youth ; " that is, in fact, a few casual verbal variations, attributable to imperfect recollection of a broadside.   There are much better in a copy which I have received from an Irish lady, partly made over by secondary tradition.   Reprinted also by Ritson, A Select Collection of English Songs, II, 234, 1783, apparently from a, with an arbitrary change in st. 8², and one or two other variations.   Mr F. H. Stoddard informs me that 'The Bailiff's Daughter' is still very much sung, and may be heard any day at a country cricket-match.

A fond youth and a coy maid, a bailiff's daughter, having been parted seven years, the maid disguises herself to go in quest of her lover, and meets him on her way.   He asks her whether she knows the bailiff's daughter. The bailiff's daughter is dead long ago, she replies.   Then he will go into a far country.

The maid, assured of his faith, reveals herself, and is ready to be his bride.

This is the counterpart of a ballad found in other languages (and represented in English by Percy's cento 'The Friar of Orders Gray,' Reliques, I, 225, 1765), in which a man tells a woman that the object of her affection, lover, or more commonly husband, is dead. So runs the story in the following :

Italian.   Marcoaldi, Canti popolari umbri, etc., p. 151, 'La prova d' amore,' Piedmontese ; Gianandrea, C. p. marchigiani, p. 270, No 7, 'La prova d' amore ;' Ferraro, C. p. monferrini, p. 60, No 41, 'Il ritorno,' and C. p. di Ferrara, Cento e Pontelagoscuro, p. 16, No 4, p. 105, No 18 ; Bernoni, C. p. veneziani, Punt. IX, No 1, 'Il ritorno dalla guerra ;' Wolf, Volkslieder aus Venetien, No 91, 'La ragazza ed i soldati ;' Bolza, Canzoni p. comasche, No 53, ' Il riconoscimento ;' Finamore, Storie p. abruzzesi, Archivio, I, 91, No 6, ' Rusine e Ddiamóre ;' Kestner, in Reifferscheid, Westfälische V. l., p. 156, Roman.

Spanish. 'Caballero de lejas tierras,' Juan de Ribera, Nueve Romances, 1605, in Duran, I, 175, No 318, Wolf y Hofmann, Primavera, II, 88, No 156, and a traditional version in a note of Duran, as above, repeated in Primavera. **Catalan.** 'La vuelta del peregrino,' Milá, Observaciones, p. 111, No 12, 'El peregrino,' Romancerillo, p. 154, No 203; 'La tornada del pelegrí,' Briz, V, 65.

Portuguese. 'Bella Infanta,' Almeida-Garrett, II, 7; Bellermann, p. 100, No 12; Braga, C. p. do Archipelago açoriano, p. 298, No 41, Romanceiro Geral, p. 1, 'Dona Infanta,' p. 4, 'Dona Catherina;' Coelho, in Zeitschrift für romanische Philologie, III, 63, 1879 (imperfect).

Romaic. 'Ἡ ἀναγνώρισις,' Zambelios, p. 718, No 5, Kind, Anthologie, 1861, p. 126, No 5, Passow, No 442 : ''Ἡ πιστὴ σύζυγος,' Evlambios, p. 58, Marcellus, I, 332, Passow, No 444 ; Tommaseo, III, 148, Passow, No 445, and III, 150, Passow, No 446 ; Schmidt, Griechische M., S., u. V. l., p. 192, No 57 (see note, p. 272) ; Marcellus, I, 328, Passow, No 441 ; ''Αναγνωρισμός,' Chasiotis, p. 89, No 28; Aravandinos, Nos 347–349, pp. 209–211 ; 'Τὸ γύρισμα,' Oikonomides, p. 132 ; Jeannaraki, p. 237, No 300, with perverted conclusion ; Fauriel, II, 396, Passow, No 447 (fragment). Aravandinos, No 348, is translated by Miss Garnett, Greek Folk Songs, p. 163.

Translated by Bodmer, I, 82 ; Döring, p. 85 ; Arndt, p. 193 ; Von Marées, p. 45 ; Knortz, Lieder u. Romanzen Alt-Englands, No 64.

———•———

1 THERE was a youth, and a well belovd youth,
    And he was a esquire's son,
He loved the bayliff's daughter dear,
    That lived in Islington.

2 She was coy, and she would not believe
    That he did love her so,
No, nor at any time she would
    Any countenance to him show.

3 But when his friends did understand
    His fond and foolish mind,
They sent him up to fair London,
    An apprentice for to bind.

4 And when he had been seven long years,
    And his love he had not seen,
'Many a tear have I shed for her sake
    When she little thought of me.'

5 All the maids of Islington
    Went forth to sport and play ;
All but the bayliff's daughter dear ;
    She secretly stole away.

6 She put off her gown of gray,
    And put on her puggish attire ;
She's up to fair London gone,
    Her true-love to require.

7 As she went along the road,
    The weather being hot and dry,
There was she aware of her true-love,
    At length came riding by.

8 She stept to him, as red as any rose,
    And took him by the bridle-ring :
'I pray you, kind sir, give me one penny,
    To ease my weary limb.'

9 'I prithee, sweetheart, canst thou tell me
    Where that thou wast born ? '
'At Islington, kind sir,' said she,
    · Where I have had many a scorn.'

10 'I prithee, sweetheart, canst thou tell me
    Whether thou dost know
The bailiff's daughter of Islington ? '
    'She's dead, sir, long ago.'

11 'Then will I sell my goodly steed,
    My saddle and my bow ;
I will into some far countrey,
    Where no man doth me know.'

12 'O stay, O stay, thou goodly youth !
    She's alive, she is not dead ;
Here she standeth by thy side,
    And is ready to be thy bride.'

13 'O farewel grief, and welcome joy,
    Ten thousand times and more !

For now I have seen my own true-love,
    That I thought I should have seen no more.'

---

a–f. True Love Requited, or, The Bayliff's Daughter of Islington.

The young man's friends the maid did scorn,
Cause she was poor, and left forlorn ;
They sent the esquire to London fair,
To be an apprentice seven year.
And when he out on 's time was come,
He met his love, a going home,
And then, to end all further strife,
He took the maid to be his wife.

To a North Countrey Tune, or, I have a good old mother at home.
e, f *have* of 's, of his, *in verse* 5.
a. 8². bridal ring, *and so all but* f.
At the end : Printed for P. Brooksby, at the Golden Ball in Pye-Corner. *Brooksby printed* 1672–95 : *Chappell.*
b. 1². a squire's.
Printed for J. Walter, at the Golden Bal[l] in Pye-Corner. *J. Walter's time is* 1690–1720 : *Chappell.*

c. 1². a *wanting.* 6². her *wanting.*
Printed for P. Brooksby, at the Golden Ball in Py-Corner.
d. 3⁴. a apprentice. 6². her *wanting.*
9². was. 12¹. thou well belovd.
Printed for P. Brooksby, at the Golden Ball in West Smithfield.
e. 3¹. a apprentice. 6². her *wanting.*
6⁴. inquire. 8³. a penny.
9². was. 11¹. I sell *wanting.*
12¹. thou well belovd.
Printed for P. Brooksby, at the Golde[n] Ball, near the Bear Tavern, in Pye Corner.
f. 1¹. was was youth. 1². a squire's. 2¹. He was.
2³. would she. 5¹. When all . . . of fair.
6². her ragged. 6³. And she is.
6⁴. After her . . . enquire. 7¹. And as.
8¹. a rose. 8². bridle. 8⁴. For to.
9². Whereat. 10². Whether that. 11¹. I will.
11³. And travel into. 13³. I see.
13⁴. should neer see more.
Printed and sold in Aldermary Churchyard, Bow Lane, London. "1700, *or a little later.*"

106
THE FAMOUS FLOWER OF SERVING-MEN

a. Wood, E. 25, fol. 75, Bodleian Library. b. Pepys, III, 142, No 140, Magdalen College Library, Cambridge. c. A Collection of Old Ballads, I, 216, 1723.

THIS ballad was given in Percy's Reliques, III, 87, 1765, "from a written copy, containing some improvements (perhaps modern ones)." These improvements are execrable in style and in matter, so far as there is new matter, but not in so glaring contrast with the groundwork as literary emendations of traditional ballads. Ritson reprinted in A Select Collection of English Songs, II, 244, 1783, some broadside like that which was followed by c.*

'Sweet Willie' in Kinloch MSS, V, 407 and VII, 197 (the latter printed in Kinloch's

---

* Heber had a copy printed by J. Andrews, who flourished 1655–60.

Ancient Scottish Ballads, p. 96), and also a fragment with the same title in the Harris MS., fol. 20 f, No 15, are derived from the broadside through recitation. A copy in Buchan's MSS, I, 150, is taken directly from print.

In other cases portions of the broadside appear to have entered into combination with traditional verses belonging to some other story, or possibly to some older form of this.

The Dean of Derry communicated to Percy in 1776 the following stanzas, which he wrote down from the recitation of his mother, Mrs Barnard, wife of the Bishop of Derry.*

1 My mother showd me a deadly spight;
   She sent three thieves at darksome night;
   They put my servants all to flight,
   They robd my bower, and they slew my knight.

2 They could not do me much more harm,
   But they slew my baby on my arm;
   They left me nothing to wrap it in
   But the bloody, bloody sheet that it lay in.

3 They left me nothing to make a grave
   But the bloody sword that slew my babe;
   All alone the grave I made,
   And all alone salt tears I shed.

4 All alone the bell I rung,
   And all alone sweet psalms I sung;
   I leant my head against a block,
   And there I cut my lovely locks.

5 I cut my locks, and chang'd my name
   From Fair Eleanore to Sweet William.

Scott inserted in his Border Minstrelsy, III, 83, 1803, seven stanzas under the title of 'The Lament of the Border Widow,' which show broader traces of the sheet-ballad (1–3), and also, as Aytoun has remarked, agreements with

'The Three Ravens' and with 'Fair Helen of Kirconnell' (5–7). 'The Lament of the Border Widow,' " obtained from recitation in the Forest of Ettrick," has been thought to relate to the execution of Cokburne, a border-freebooter, by James V. Those who are interested in such random inventions (as, under pardon, they must be called) will find particulars in Scott's introduction, and a repetition of the same in Maidment's Scotish Ballads and Songs, Historical and Traditionary, II, 170.†

1 My love he built me a bonny bower,
   And clad it a' wi lilye-flour;
   A brawer bower ye neer did see
   Than my true-love he built for me.

2 There came a man, by middle day,
   He spied his sport and went away,
   And brought the king that very night,
   Who brake my bower, and slew my knight.

3 He slew my knight, to me sae dear;
   He slew my knight, and poind his gear;
   My servants all for life did flee,
   And left me in extremitie.

4 I sewd his sheet, making my mane;
   I watched the corpse, myself alane;
   I watched his body, night and day;
   No living creature came that way.

5 I took his body on my back,
   And whiles I gaed, and whiles I sate;
   I diggd a grave, and laid him in,
   And happd him with the sod sae green.

6 But think na ye my heart was sair,
   When I laid the moul on his yellow hair?
   O think na ye my heart was wae,
   When I turnd about, away to gae?

7 Nae living man I 'll love again,
   Since that my lovely knight is slain;

---

* Mrs Barnard makes this note: I remember to have seen a printed ballad, at least seventy years since, in which this was containd, as sung by a youth, overheard by a king he servd, and exalted to become his queen. I fancy these scenes were in Germany, by the names. — Percy regards the verses as a " fragment of an older copy than that printed of 'The Lady turnd Serving-Man.' "

† The Border Widow's Lament has received extraordinary favor. It has been translated by Schubart, p. 209; Talvj, Charakteristik, p. 570; Fiedler, Geschichte der schottischen

Liederdichtung, p. 29; Freiligrath, Zwischen den Garben, II, 229, Stuttgart, 1877; Doenniges, p. 77; Knortz, L. u. R. Alt-Englands, p. 195, No 58. Cunningham furbished up the verses a little in The Songs of Scotland, II, 97. The copy in Chambers's Scottish Songs, I, 174, is Cunningham's, all but the sixth stanza, which is from Scott. — A great deal of nonsense passes in ballads, but I am impelled to ask just here how a lover would go about to clothe a bower with lily-flower. Is the ballad lily a climbing plant?

Wi ae lock of his yellow hair
I'll chain my heart for evermair.

Again, there are six couplets in Johnson's Museum, p. 90, No 89, called, from the burden, 'Oh ono chrio,' which have a little of The Border Widow, and incidentally of The Flower of Serving-Men, winding up with sentiments of transcendent elegance.

Oh was I not a weary wight,
Maid, wife and widow in one night!

When in my soft and yielding arms,
When most I thought him free from harms,

Even at the dead time of the night,
They broke my bower, and slew my knight.

With ae lock of his jet-black hair
I'll tye my heart for ever mair.

Nae sly-tongued youth, or flattering swain,
Shall eer untye this knott again.

Thine still, dear youth, that heart shall be,
Nor pant for aught save heaven and thee.

"Dr Blacklock informed Burns that this song . . . was composed on the horrid massacre at Glencoe": Stenhouse's note, IV, 92.

The English broadside, which may reasonably be believed to be formed upon a predecessor in the popular style, has been held to have a common origin with the Scandinavian ballad 'Maid and Stable Boy,' already spoken of under 'Child Waters' at p. 84 f of this volume. The points of resemblance are that a maid cuts her hair, dons man's clothes, and seeks service with a king. In the end she is married to the king's son, or to a nobleman of his court. The differences, in other respects, are considerable.

Percy's ballad is translated by Bodmer, I, 160; by Merk, Ursinus, p. 79, and Bothe, p. 307; by Döring, p. 329.

———•———

1 You beautious ladies, great and small,
I write unto you one and all,
Whereby that you may understand
What I have suffered in this land.

2 I was by birth a lady fair,
My father's chief and onely heir,
But when my good old father dy'd,
Then was I made a young knight's bride.

3 And then my love built me a bower,
Bedeckt with many a fragrant flower;
A braver bower you never did see
Then my true-love did build for me.

4 But there came thieves late in the night,
They rob'd my bower, and slew my knight,
And after that my knight was slain,
I could no longer there remain.

5 My servants all from me did flye,
In the midst of my extremity,
And left me by my self alone,
With a heart more cold then any stone.

6 Yet, though my heart was full of care,
Heaven would not suffer me to despair;
Wherefore in hast I chang'd my name
From Fair Elise to Sweet William.

7 And therewithal I cut my hair,
And drest my self in man's attire,
My doublet, hose, and bever-hat,
And a golden band about my neck.

8 With a silver rapier by my side,
So like a gallant I did ride;
The thing that I delighted on,
Was for to be a serving-man.

9 Thus in my sumptuous man's array,
I bravely rode along the way;
And at the last it chanced so
That I unto the king's court did go.

10 Then to the king I bowed full low,
My love and duty for to show,
And so much favour I did crave
That I a serving-man's place might have.

11 'Stand up, brave youth, the king replyd,
  'Thy service shall not be denyd ;
  But tell me first what thou canst do ;
  Thou shalt be fitted thereunto.

12 'Wilt thou be usher of my hall,
  To wait upon my nobles all ?
  Or wilt thou be taster of my wine,
  To wait on me when I shall dine ?

13 'Or wilt thou be my chamberlain,
  To make my bed both soft and fine ?
  Or wilt thou be one of my guard ?
  And I will give thee thy reward.'

14 Sweet William, with a smiling face,
  Said to the king, If 't please your grace
  To show such favour unto me,
  Your chamberlain I fain would be.

15 The king then did the nobles call,
  To ask the counsel of them all,
  Who gave consent Sweet William he
  The king's own chamberlain should be.

16 Now mark what strange things came to pass :
  As the king one day a hunting was,
  With all his lords and noble train,
  Sweet William did at home remain.

17 Sweet William had no company then
  With him at home but an old man ;
  And when he saw the coast was clear,
  He took a lute which he had there.

18 Upon the lute Sweet William plaid,
  And to the same he sung and said,
  With a pleasant and most noble voice,
  Which made the old man to rejoyce :

19 'My father was as brave a lord
  As ever Europe did afford ;
  My mother was a lady bright,
  My husband was a valiant knight.

20 'And I my self a lady gay,
  Bedeckt with gorgeous rich array ;
  The bravest lady in the land
  Had not more pleasures to command.

21 'I had my musick every day,
  Harmonious lessons for to play ;
  I had my virgins fair and free,
  Continually to wait on me.

22 'But now, alas ! my husband 's dead,
  And all my friends are from me fled ;
  My former joys are past and gone,
  For now I am a serving-man.'

23 At last the king from hunting came,
  And presently upon the same
  He called for the good old man,
  And thus to speak the king began.

24 'What news, what news, old man ?' quod he ;
  'What news hast thou to tell to me ? '
  'Brave news,' the old man he did say ;
  'Sweet William is a lady gay.'

25 'If this be true thou tellest me
  I 'le make thee a lord of high degree ;
  But if thy words do prove a lye,
  Thou shalt be hanged up presently.'

26 But when the king the truth had found,
  His joys did more and more abound ;
  According as the old man did say,
  Sweet William was a lady gay.

27 Therefore the king without delay
  Put on her glorious rich array,
  And upon her head a crown of gold,
  Which was most famous to behold.

28 And then, for fear of further strife,
  He took Sweet William for his wife ;
  The like before was never seen,
  A serving-man to be a queen.

---

a. Printed for J. Hose, next door but one to the
  Rose Inn, near Holbourn-bridge. John Hose,
  over against Staples-Inn, near Gray's Inn Lane,
  printed, according to Chappell, 1660–1675.

b. Printed for W. Thackeray and T. Passinger. W.

Thackeray's *date, Chappell, is* 1660–1689 ; T.
Passinger's, 1670–1682.

a, b *have for title and preface* :
  The Famous Flower of Serving-men, or,
  The Lady turnd Serving-man.

Her lover being slain, her father dead,
Her bower robd, her servants fled,
She drest her self in mans attire,
She trim'd her locks, she cut her hair,
And therupon she changde her name
From Fair Elise to Sweet William.

To a dainty tune, or Flora Farewel, Summer-
Time, or Love's Tide.

Before 19 : Sweet William's Song.
After 22 : The end of Sweet William's Song.
a. *After* 8 : The Second Part, to the same tune.
b. 8⁴. It was to. 12⁴. I do. 20⁴. pleasure.
c. 2⁴. I was. 8⁴. It was to. 9⁴. I to.
 12⁴. I do. 16¹. thing. 17³. the house.
 18³. a sweet and noble voice.
 20⁴. pleasure. 23³. this good.
 25¹. tellst to.

107

WILL STEWART AND JOHN

A. 'Will Stewart and Iohn,' Percy Manuscript, p.
428; Hales and Furnivall, III, 216.

B. 'Tring Dilly,' Campbell's MSS, II, 30.

THE fragment **B** is disordered as well as
mutilated. B 1 corresponds to A 18, 13 ; 2 to
14 ; 3 to 19, 40 ; 4 to 41, 42 ; 5 to 43 ; 6 to 35,
36 ; 7 to 17. It is simply a confused recollection of some parts of the ballad.

The first stanza furnishes a sort of general
lyrical introduction, and does not belong to
the story, to which, as I conceive, the circumstance that Adlatts Park is wide and broad is
of no more special pertinence than the other
which follows, that grass grows green in our
countrye. See I, 7, note.

Will Stewart, of Argyle Castle, languishes
with love for the Earl of Mar's daughter, and
lies in care-bed. His younger brother, John, a
wiser man, offers to go a-wooing for his brother,
and to forward his object takes service with
the Earl of Mar as chamberlain to his daughter. One Sunday, as John is conveying the
lady home from church, he makes known to
her that he is a messenger. The lady at
first, like Shakspere's Olivia, would rather
he should speak for himself, but upon hearing
what John has to say for his brother is ready
to love Will heartily. She bids her lover
come with a hundred men to a foot-ball match
on Sunday after St Andrew's day. He must

play sixteen games, and if he win the greater
part she shall love him the more. This tidings makes Will Stewart leap from care-bed.
He chooses a hundred men from eleven score
and three, dresses them in green, himself in
scarlet (about which the lady had been particular), meets his mistress at the rendezvous,
gives her a kiss of courtesy, and wins twelve
of the sixteen games. The Earl of Mar invites Will to his house, where the Stewart
avows his love for his daughter; he knows
not whether the lady loves him. "God forbid!" exclaims the earl. "I would rather
thou wert hanged or burned. To thy chamber, lady, or I will beat thee before the
Stewart's eye." Will, with John, who re-
nounces Mar's service, returns to Argyle Castle, and Will leaps into care-bed again. A
parliament is held at Edinburgh, to which
both brothers are summoned. Mar discovers
that Will is an earl's son, and even the king's
cousin, but this discovery has no effect to
change the mind of the peremptory nobleman. Will and John go back to Argyle Castle
when the parliament is done, and Will once
more leaps into care-bed. John, in great con-
cern for his brother, offers to go a-wooing for

him again. He disguises himself as a beggar, comes to Mar's house on a dole-day, makes his way to the lady and sticks by her till all the beggars are gone, and then tells her that he is no beggar, but a messenger. The lady, reproached for her cruelty, says the blame is not hers, and appoints Will to meet her within three days at Martinsdale with a hundred men, they and he dressed as before. Will leaps out of care-bed, chooses a hundred of the best out of eleven score men and three, rides to Martinsdale, and finds the true lady waiting for him. They send for priest and clerk and are married, and she goes home with Will. A twelvemonth after, John is despatched to bid the Earl of Mar to a christening. John frightens the earl with an intimation that his daughter will now be returned on his hands. This brings the wilful father round. The marriage ceremony is performed over again, and Will made Earl of Mar.

As Mr Hales has remarked, Bishop Percy's Folio Manuscript, III, 215, the allusions to manners and customs are highly interesting: as, to foot-ball matches, 27; to the kiss of courtesy, 35^3; to the beating of daughters, 42^4, 43^3; to the dole-day, 66^2; to the beggar's dress and equipment, 61, 78^3.

The superfluous *that* in 3^4, 16^3, 18^4, 38^1, 68^1, 89^2, is common in the ballads of the Percy manuscript.

A

Percy MS., p. 428; Hales and Furnivall, III, 216.

1 ADLATTS parke is wyde and broad,
  And grasse growes greene in our coun-
    trye;
  Eche man can gett the loue of his ladye,
  But alas, I can gett none of mine!

2 Itt's by two men I sing my song,
  Their names is William Stewart and Iohn;
  William he is the elder brother,
  But Iohn hee is the wiser man.

3 But William he is in care-bed layd,
  And for the loue of a ffaire ladye;
  If he haue not the loue of the Erle of Mar's
    daughter,
  In ffaith ffor loue *that* he must dye.

4 Then Iohn was sorry ffor his brother,
  To see him lye and languish soe:
  'What doe you mourne for, brother?' he
    saies,
  'I pray you tell to me your woe.'

5 'Doe [you] mourne for gold, brother?' he
    saies,
  'Or doe you mourne ffor ffee?
  Or doe you mourne for a likesome ladye,
  You neuer saw her with your eye?'

6 'I doe not mourne for gold,' he saies,
  'Nor I doe not mourne for any ffee;
  But I doe mourne for a likesome ladye,
  I neere blinke on her with mine eye.'

7 'But when haruest is gotten, my deere broth-
    er —
  All this is true *that* I tell thee —
  Gentlemen, they loue hunting well,
  And giue wight-men their cloth and ffee.

8 'Then I'le goe a wooing ffor thy sake,
  In all the speed *that* I can gone,
  And for to see this likesome ladye,
  And hope to send thee good tydings home.'

9 Iohn Stewart is gone a wooing for his brother,
  Soe ffarr into ffaire Scottland,
  And left his brother in mikle ffeare,
  Vntill he heard the good tydand.

10 And when he came to the Erle of Mar's his
    house,
  Soe well he could his curtesye,
  And when he came before the erle,
  He kneeled low downe vpon his knee.

11 'O rise vp, rise vp, Iohn Steward,
  Rise vp, now, I doe bidd thee;
  How doth thy ffather, Iohn Steward,
  And all the lords in his countrye?'

12 'And itt please you, my lord, my ffather is
        dead ;
    My brother and I cannott agree ;
    My brother and I am ffallen att discord,
    And I am come to craue a service of thee.'

13 ' O welcome, welcome, Iohn Stewart,
    A welcome man thou art to me ;
    I 'le make thee chamberlaine to my daughter,
    And ffor to tend of that ladye soe ffree.

14 ' And if thou wilt haue a better office,
    Aske, and thou shall haue itt of mee ;
    And where I giue other men a penny of wage,
    Inffaith, Iohn, thou shalt haue three.'

15 And then bespake him Iohn Stewart,
    And these were the words said hee :
    There is no office in your court
    This day that better pleaseth mee.

16 The Ffryday is gone, the Sunday is come —
    All this is true that I doe say —
    And to the church that they be gone,
    Iohn Stewart and the lady gay.

17 And as they did come home againe —
    I-wis itt was a meeten mile —
    Iohn Stewart and the lady gay,
    They thought itt but a [little] while.

18 ' I am a messenger, ladye,' he saies,
    ' I am a messenger to thee : '
    ' O speake ffor thy selfe, Iohn Stewart,' shee
        saies,
    ' A welcome man that thou shalt bee.'

19 ' Nay, by my ffaith,' saies Iohn Stewart,
    ' Which euer, alas, that may not bee !
    He hath a higher degree in honour,
    Allas, ladye, then euer I !

20 ' He is a lord now borne by birth,
    And an erle affter his ffather doth dye ;
    His haire is yellow, his eyes beene gray ;
    All this is true that I tell yee.

21 ' He is ffine in the middle, and small in the
        wast,
    And pleasant in a woman's eye ;
    And more nor this, he dyes for your loue,
    Therefore, lady, show some pittye.'

22 ' If this be soe,' then saies the lady,
    ' If this be true that thou tells mee,
    By my ffaith then, Iohn Stewart,
    I can loue him hartilye.

23 ' Bidd him meete me att St Patr[i]cke's
        Church
    On Sunday after St Andrew's day ;
    The fflower of Scottland will be there,
    And then begins our summer's play.

24 ' And bidd him bring with him a hundred gun-
        ners,
    And rawnke ryders lett them bee,
    And lett them bee of the rankest ryders
    That be to be ffound in that countrye.

25 ' They best and worst, and all in like,
    Bidd him cloth them in one liuerye ;
    And ffor his men, greene is the best,
    And greene now lett their liueryes bee.

26 ' And clothe himselfe in scarlett redd,
    That is soe seemlye ffor to see ;
    Ffor scarlett is a ffaire coulour,
    And pleasant allwayes in a woman's eye.

27 ' He must play sixteene games att ball,
    Against the men of this countrye,
    And if he winn the greater part,
    Then I shall love him more tenderlye.'

28 What the lady said, Iohn Stewart writt,
    And to Argyle Castle sent it hee ;
    And [when] Willie Steward saw the letter,
    Fforth of care-bed then lope hee.

29 Hee mustered together his merry men all,
    Hee mustered them soe louelilye ;
    Hee thought hee had had scarson halfe a hun-
        dred,
    Then had hee eleuen score and three.

30 He chose fforth a hundred of the best
    That were to be ffound in that countrye,
    He cladd them all in one coulour,
    And greene i-wis their liueryes bee.

31 He cladd himselfe in scarlett redd,
    That is soe seemlye ffor to see ;
    Ffor scarlett is a ffaire coulor,
    And seemlye in a woman's eye.

32 And then towards Patricke Church he went,
   With all his men in braue array,
   To gett a sight, if he might,
   And speake with his lady gay.

33 When they came to Patricke's churche,
   Shee kneeled downe by her mother trulye :
   'O mother, if itt please you to giue me leaue,
   The Stewart's horsse ffaine wold I see.'

34 'I 'le giue you leaue, my deere daughter,
   And I and my maide will goe with yee : '
   The lady had rather haue gone her selfe
   Then haue had her mother's companye.

35 When they came before Willie Steward,
   Soe well hee cold his curtesye :
   'I wold kisse your daughter, ladye,' he said,
   'And if your will that soe itt bee.'

36 The ladye's mother was content
   To doe a straunger that curtesye ;
   And when Willie had gotten a kisse,
   I-wis shee might haue teemed him three.

37 Sixteen games were plaid that day there —
   This is the truth as I doe say —
   Willie Stewart and his merry men,
   Thé carryed twelue of them away.

38 And when they games that they were done,
   And all they ffolkes away were gone
   But the Erle of Marr and William Stewart,
   The erle wold needs haue William home.

39 And when they came vnto the erle's howse,
   They walked to a garden greene ;
   Ffor to confferr of their bussines,
   Into the garden they be gone.

40 'I loue your daughter,' saies William Stewart,
   'But I cannott tell whether she loueth mee : '
   'Marry, God defend,' saies the Erle of Mar,
   'That euer soe that itt shold bee !

41 'I had rather a gallowes there was made,
   And hange thee ffor my daughter's sake ;
   I had rather a ffyer were made att a stake,
   And burne thee ffor my daughter's sake !

42 'To chamber, to chamber, gay ladye,' he saies,
   'In the deuill's name now I bidd thee !

And thou gett thee not to the chamber soone,
   I 'le beate thee before the Stewart's eye.'

43 And then bespake William Stewart,
   These were the words said hee :
   'If thou beate thy daughter for my sake,
   Thou 'st beate a hundred men and mee.'

44 Then bespake Iohn Stewart —
   Lord ! an angry man was hee —
   'O churle, if thou wouldest not haue macht
   with my brother,
   Thou might haue answerd him curteouslye.'

45 'O hold thy peace, Iohn Stewart,
   And chamber thy words now, I bidd thee ;
   If thou chamber not thy words soone,
   Thou 'st loose a good service ; soe shalt thou
   doe me.'

46 'Marry ! hang them that cares,' saies Iohn
   Stewart,
   'Either ffor thy service or ffor thee ;
   Services can I haue enoughe,
   But brethren wee must euer bee.'

47 William Stewart and his brother Iohn,
   To Argyle Castle gon they bee ;
   And when Willye came to Argyle Castle,
   Into care-bedd then lope hee.

48 A parliament att Edenborrow was made,
   The king and his nobles all mett there ;
   Thé sent ffor William Stewart and Iohn,
   To come amongst the other peeres.

49 Their clothing was of scarlett redd,
   That was soe seemelye ffor to see ;
   Blacke hatts, white ffeathers plewed with
   gold,
   And sett all on their heads trulye.

50 Their stockings were of twisted silke,
   With garters ffringed about with gold ;
   Their shoes were of the cordevine,
   And all was comelye to behold.

51 And when they came to Edenborrowe,
   They called ffor Iohn Stewart and Willie :
   'I answer in a lord's roome,' saies Will Stew-
   art,
   'But an erle I hope to bee.'

52 'Come downe, come downe,' saies the Lord of
    Marr,
    'I knew not what was thy degree:'
  'O churle, if I might not haue macht with thy
    daughter,
    Itt had not beene long of my degree.

53 'My ffather, hee is the king his brother,
    And then the king is vnckle to me;
  O churle, if I might not haue macht with thy
    daughter,
    Itt·had not beene long of my degree.'

54 'O hold your peace,' then sayd the king,
    'Cozen William, I doe bidd thee;
  Infaith, cozen William, he loues you the
    worsse
    Because you are a-kinn to mee.

55 'I 'le make thee an erle with a siluer wande,
    And adde more honors still to thee;
  Thy brother Ihon shall be a lord,
    Of the best att home in his countrye.

56 'Thy brother Kester shalbe a knight,
    Lands and liuings I will him giue,
  And still hee shall liue in court with mee,
    And I 'le maintaine him whilest he doth
    liue.'

57 And when the parlaiment was done,
    And all the ffolkes away were gone,
  Willye Stewart and Iohn his brother,
    To Argyle Castle they be gone.

58 But when they came to Argyle Castle,
    That was soe ffarr in that countrye,
  He thought soe much then of his loue
    That into care-bedd then lope hee.

59 Iohn Stewart did see his brother soe ill,
    Lord, in his heart that hee was woe!
  'I will goe wooing for thy sake
    Againe yonder gay ladye to.

60 'I 'le cloth my selfe in strange array,
    In a beggar's habbitt I will goe,
  That when I come before the Erle of Marr
    My clothing strange he shall not knowe.'

61 Iohn hee gott on a clouted cloake,
    Soe meete and low then by his knee,
    With four garters vpon one legg,
    Two aboue, and towe below trulye.

62 'But if thou be a beggar, brother,
    Thou art a beggar that is vnknowne;
  Ffor thou art one of the stoutest beggars
    That euer I saw since I was borne.

63 'Heere, geeue the lady this gay gold ringe,
    A token to her that well is knowne;
  And if shee but aduise itt well,
    Shee 'le know some time itt was her owne.'

64 'Stay, by my ffaith, I goe not yett,'
    Iohn Stewart he can replye;
  'I 'le haue my bottle ffull of beere,
    The best that is in thy butterye.

65 'I 'le haue my sachell ffilld full of meate,
    I am sure, brother, [it] will doe noe harme;
  Ffor, before I come to the Erle of Marr's his
    house,
    My lipps, I am sure, they wilbe warme.'

66 And when he came to the Erle of Marr's house,
    By chance itt was of the dole-day;
  But Iohn cold ffind no place to stand,
    Vntill he came to the ladye gaye.

67 But many a beggar he threw downe,
    And made them all with weeping say,
  He is the devill, hee is no beggar,
    That is come fforth of some strange coun-
    trye.

68 And now the dole that itt is delte,
    And all the beggars be gon away,
  Sauing Iohn Stewart, that seemed a beggar,
    And the ladye that was soe gay.

69 'Lady,' sais Iohn, 'I am no beggar,
    As by my clothes you may thinke that I bee;
  I am your servant, Iohn Stewart,
    And I am sent a messenger to thee.'

70 'But if thou be Iohn Stewart,
    As I doe thinke that thou bee,
  Avayle thy capp, avayle thy hoode,
    And I will stand and speake to thee.

71 'How doth thy brother, Iohn Stewart,
    And all the lords in his countrye?'

'O ffye vpon thee, wicked woman!
　My brother he doth the worsse ffor thee.'

72 With *that* the teares stood in her eyes;
　　O lord, shee wept soe tenderlye!
　Sais, Ligg the blame vnto my ffather;
　　I pray you, Iohn Stew*art*, lay itt not to mee.

73 Comend me to my owne true-loue,
　　That liues soe farr in the North countrye,
　And bidd him meete me att Martingsdale,
　　Ffullye w[i]thin these dayes three.

74 Hang them, sais the lady gay,
　　That letts their ffather witting bee!
　I 'le proue a ladye ffull of loue,
　　And be there by the sunn be a quarter highe.

75 And bidd him bring with him a hundred gun-
　　ners,
　　And ranke riders lett them bee;
　Lett them be of the rankest ryders
　　That be to be ffound in *that* countrye.

76 The best and worse, and all in like,
　　Bidd him clothe them in one liuerye;
　And for his men, greene is the best,
　　And greene now lett their lyueryes bee.

77 And cloth himselfe in scarlett redd,
　　That is soe seemelye for to see;
　For scarlett is a ffaire coulor,
　　And pleasant in a woman's eye.

78 What they lady sayd, Iohn Stewart writt,
　　To Argyle Castle sent'itt hee;
　His bagg and his dish and showing horne,
　　Unto three beggars he gaue them all three.

79 And when Willie Stewart saw the letter,
　　Fforth of care-bed then lope hee;
　He thought himselfe as lustye and sound
　　As any man in *that* countrye.

80 He mustered together his merrymen all,
　　He mustered them soe louinglye;
　He thought he had had scarce halfe a hundred,
　　Then had hee eleuen score and three.

81 He chose fforth a hundred of the best
　　That were to be found in *that* companye,

And *p*resentlye they tooke their horsse,
　And to Martingsdale posted hee.

82 And when he came to Martingsdale,
　　He found his loue staying there trulye,
　For shee was a lady true of loue,
　　And was there by [the] sunn was a qwarter
　　highe.

83 Shee kisst Will*iam* Stewart and his brother
　　Iohn,
　　Soe did shee *p*art of his merry men:
　'If the churle, thy ffather, hee were here,
　　He shold not haue thee backe againe.'

84 They sent ffor preist, they sent ffor clarke,
　　And they were marryed there with speede.;
　Will*iam* tooke the lady home with him,
　　And they liued together long time indeed.

85 And in twelue monthe soe they wrought,
　　The lady shee was great with childe;
　The sent Iohn Stewart to the Erle off Marre,
　　To come and christen the barne soe milde.

86 'And if this be soe,' sayes the Erle of Marre,
　　'Iohn Stewart, as thou tells mee,
　I hope in God you haue marryed my daugh-
　　ter,
　　And put her bodye to honestye.'

87 'Nay, by my ffaith,' then saies Iohn Stewart,
　　'Ffor euer alas *that* shall not bee;
　Ffor now wee haue put her body to shame,
　　Thou 'st haue her againe hame to thee.'

88 'I had rather make thee Erle of Marre,
　　And marry my daughter vnto thee;
　For by my ffaith,' sais the Erle of Marr,
　　'Her marryage is marrd in our countrye.'

89 'If this be soe,' then sais Iohn Stewart,
　　'A marryage soone *that* thou shalt see;
　Ffor my brother William, my ffather's heyre,
　　Shall marry thy daughter before thine eye.'

90 They sent ffor preist, thé sent ffor clarke,
　　And marryed there they were with speed;
　And William Stewart is Erle of Marr,
　　And his ffather-in-law dwells with him in-
　　deed.

B

Campbell MSS, II, 30.

1 'SPEAK for yoursell, John Stewart,' he did say,
  'Speak for yoursell, John Stewart,' he did say,
  'Speak for yoursell, John Stewart,' he did say,
    'And soon an answer I will gie to thee;
  The highest service I can give thee
  Is to wait on my daughter Ailly.

2 '.   .   .   .   .
    .   .   .   .   .
  If ever I gie a man a penny wage,
  I 'm sure, John Stewart, ye shall hae three.'

3 'I speak not for mysell,' John Stewart he did
    say,
  'I speak for a lord of a higher degree;
  The message is from my brother William,
  Your loving daughter's husband to be.'

4 '.   .   .   .   .   .
    .   .   .   .   .   .

I 'll rather beat fair Ailly in my leather bang,
As lang as she can either stand or gang.'

5 .   .   .   .   .   .
    .   .   .   .   .   .
  'Ye hadna beat her before my face
  Or ye 'll beat three hundred men and me.'

6 When William came to Mulbery Hall,
  He kissd the ladies one and all;
  But when he cam to fair Ailly,
  She thought he might hae gaen her twa or
    three.

7 Between the kitchen and the garden
    It is calld a measured mile;
  That lady and that lord fell into discourse,
    And they thought they rode it in a short
    while.

  Chorus: Tring dilly, tring dilly, tring ding
             dido,
           Tring dilly, tring dilly, dolo dee.

A. 2¹. by 2.   14⁴. haue 3.   24¹. a 100.
    27⁴. love *is written in the MS. by a later
      hand between* then *and* I.   *Furnivall.*
    29³. a 100ᵈ.   29⁴. 11 score.
    30¹. a 100.   36⁴. him 3.
    37¹. 16 games.   37⁴. 12 of.
    38³. Marrs.   38⁴. & the Erle.   40³. March.
    43⁴. a 100ᵈ: men and nee.
    44⁴. might *has two strokes for the* i *in the MS.*
      Furnivall.
    48⁴. amongst *has four strokes for the* m *in the
      MS.*   *Furnivall.*

51³. in L, *MS.*   *Furnivall.*
52¹. Mars.   60³. March.
61³. 4 garters.   61⁴. 2 aboue.
73⁴. dayes 3.   75¹. a 100ᵈ.   Gunners *has* m *in
  place of* nn.   *Furnivall.*
75³. *Two or three letters appear one over the
  other for the* s *in* ryders.   *Furnivall.*
78⁴. vnto 3, all 3.   80³. a 100 d.
80⁴. 11 score.   81¹. a 100ᵈ.
84³. n *instead of* m *in* home.   *Furnivall.*
85¹. in 12.   85⁴. chrsten.
And *throughout for* &.

108

CHRISTOPHER WHITE

'Christopher White,' Percy MS., p. 513; Hales and Furnivall, III, 494.

——————◆——————

A RICH merchant, burgess of Edinburgh, overhears a lady making moan for Christopher White, who is banished from England. He makes her great offers to abandon Christopher and lay her love on him. She resists these offers at first, and tells him that if she is false to Christopher she cannot be true to him. But silver and gold makes her heart turn and makes her leave good company. After she has been married two or three months tidings come to Edinburgh that all the merchants must to sea; it is for service against Spain, 17[4]. The lady takes advantage of her husband's absence to write to Christopher; she sends him a hundred pound and bids him come to Edinburgh. Christopher first goes to London and obtains pardon of the king of England, then makes for Edinburgh. The lady tells him that she is a merchant's wife, and he shall have enough of the merchant's gold. Christopher, who seems not till then to have known of her marriage, begins an indignant answer, but the lady cuts him short with an offer to go to England with him. They pack up silver and gold and make off to Little England, whatever that may be (perhaps a Percy MS. phrase: see 'Hugh Spencer,' st. 34). The merchant comes back, and is told that his wife has fled with Christopher. He does not care for the loss of silver and gold, but mourns for the lady, who, he frankly owns, had given him due warning of what he might look for.

——————◆——————

1 As I walked fforth one morninge,
  By one place *that* pleased mee,
Wherin I heard a wandering wight,
  Sais, Christopher White is good companye.

2 I drew me neere, and very neere,
  Till I was as neere as neere cold bee;
Loth I was her councell to discreene,
  Because I wanted companye.

3 'Say on, say on, thou well faire mayd,
  Why makest thou moane soe heauilye?'
Sais, All is ffor one wandering wight,
  Is banished fforth of his owne countrye.

4 'I am the burgesse of Edenburrow,
  Soe am I more of townes three;
I haue money and gold great store,
  Come, sweet wench, and ligg thy loue on
    mee.'

5 The merchant pulled forth a bagg of gold
  W*h*ich had hundreds two or three;
Sais, Euery day throughout the weeke
  I 'le comt as much downe on thy knee.

6 'O merchant, take thy gold againe,
  A good liuing 't will purchase thee;
If I be ffalse to Chr*istopher* White,
  Merchant, I cannott be true to thee.'

7 Sais, I haue halls, soe haue I bowers,
  Sais, I haue shipps sayling on the sea;
I ame the burgess of Edenburrowe;
  Come, sweete wench, ligge thy loue on mee.

8 Come on, come, thou well faire mayde,
  Of our matters lett vs goe throughe,
For to-morrowe I 'le marry thee,
  And thy dwelling shalbe in Edenburrough.

9 The lady shee tooke this gold in her hand,
    The teares thé ffell ffast ffrom her eye ;
  Sais, Siluer and gold makes my hart to turne,
    And makes me leaue good companye.

10 They had not beene marryed
    Not ouer monthes two or three,
  But tydings came to Edenburrowe
    That all the merchants must to the sea.

11 Then as this lady sate in a deske,
    Shee made a loue-letter ffull round ;
  She mad a *lettre* to Chr*istopher* White,
    And in itt shee put a hundred pound.

12 She lin'd the letter *with* gold soe red,
    And mony good store in itt was found ;
  Shee sent itt to Chr*istopher* White,
    That was soe ffar in the Scotts ground.

13 Shee bade him then ffrankely spend,
    And looke *that* hee shold merry bee,
  And bid him come to Edenburrowe,
    Now all the merchants be to the sea.

14 But Chr*istopher* came to leeue London,
    And there he kneeled lowly downe,
  And there hee begd his p*ar*don then,
    Of our noble k*ing that* ware the crowne.

15 But when he came to his true-loue's house,
    W*hich* was made both of lime and stone,
  Shee tooke him by the lily-white hand,
    Sais, True-loue, you are welcome home !

16 Welcome, my honey, welcome, my ioy,
    Welcome, my true-loue ; home to mee !
  Ffor thou art hee *that* will lengthen my
      dayes,
    And I know thou art good companye.

17 Chr*istopher*, I am a merchant's wiffe ;
    Chr*istopher*, the more shall be y*our* gaine ;

Siluer and gold you shall haue enough,
    Of the merchant's gold *that* is in Spaine.

18 ' But if you be a merchant's wiffe,
    Something tó much you are to blame ;
  I will thee reade a loue-let*ter*
    Shall sture thy stumpes, thou noble dame.'

19 ' Althoug I be a marchant's wiffe,
    .   .   .   shall   .   .   mine
  .   and g .   .   .   .   .
    Into England I 'le goe w*ith* the.'

20 They packet vp both siluer and plate,
    Siluer and gold soe great plentye,
  And they be gon into Litle England,
    And the marchant must them neu*er* see.

21 And when the merchants they came home,
    Their wiues to eche other can say,
  Heere hath beene good Chr*istopher* White,
    And he hath tane thy wiffe away.

22 They haue packett vp spoone and plate,
    Siluer and gold great plenty,
  And they be gon into Litle England,
    And them againe thow must neu*er* see.

23 ' I care nott ffor my siluer and gold,
    Nor for my plate soe great plentye,
  But I mourne for *that* like-some ladye
    That Chr*istopher* White hath tane ffrom
      mee.

24 ' But one thing I must needs confesse,
    This lady shee did say to me,
  If shee were ffalse to Chr*istopher* White,
    Shee cold neu*er* be true to mee.

25 ' All young men a warning take,
    A warning, looke, you take by mee ;
  Looke *that* you loue y*our* old loues best,
    For infaith they are best companye.'

———◆———

1¹. mornige.   2³. discreeme.   3². thom.
4². townes 3.   5². 2 or.   9². eyes.
10². 2 or 3.   11⁴. 100ᴴ.   15⁴. yoͬ are.
16³. lenghen.   18³. ler*ter*.   18⁴. stue thy.
19². ³. *The MS. is pared away at the bottom*

of p. 513, *and the writing has perished and
part of the paper is broken away at the top
of p.* 514.   *Furnivall.*
20¹. siluer & p : *see* 22¹.
And *for* &, *throughout.*

109

TOM POTTS

A. 'Thomas of Potte,' Percy MS., p. 409; Hales and Furnivall, III, 135.

B. 'The Lovers Quarrel, or, Cupid's Triumph,' etc.
a. London, printed for F. Coles, and others, 1677.

b. Pepys Merriments, I, 189; Ritson, Pieces of Ancient Popular Poetry, p. 115, 1791.

C. 'The Two Constant Lovers in Scotland,' etc., broadside of 1657; Ritson's Ancient Songs, 1790, p. 248.

ALL the copies here printed are of the seventeenth century, and the ballad need not be put much beyond that date. Modernized editions, differing much, were issued in the century following, perhaps earlier, some of which have a Second Part, narrating the happy married life of Tom Potts, Lord Arundel, and Fair Rosamund. See Halliwell's Descriptive Notices of Popular English Histories, p. 17, No 15, Percy Society, vol. xxiii, and the notes to B.

Unequal matches are common enough in ballads and romances, and very naturally, since they are an easy expedient for exciting interest, at least with those who belong to the humbler party. We have other ballad-examples of disparagement on the female side in 'The Bonny Foot-Boy' and 'Ritchie Storie.' No offence seems to be given when King Cophetua weds the Beggar-Maid, but when the Lady of the Strachy marries the Yeoman of the Wardrobe good taste is shocked. Such events would be celebrated only by fellows of the yeoman or of the foot-boy, and surely in the present case the minstrel was not much above the estate of the serving-man. Lord Jockey's reckless liberality throughout, and Lord Phenix's in the end, is a mark of the serving-man's ideal nobleman.

Tom Potts stanches his blood with a charm in A 75[4], B 82[4], just as the sons of Autolycus do that of Ulysses in Odyssey XIX, 457 f. His rejecting of his master's thirty fine horses in favor of the old white cut-tail is a ludicrous repetition of Hugh Spencer's preference of the hack he had brought over sea, and Walter of Aquitaine's predilection for his worn-out charger. See, further on, 'Hugh Spencer's Feats in France.'

There is a Lord Phenix in a sufficiently absurd ballad in Motherwell's MS., 'Jamie o Lee,' p. 654; an English nobleman who steals the Queen of Scotland's jewels and lays the blame on Jamie o Lee, a page of fifteen years, being himself, for rhyme's sake, thretty three. The page worsts his accuser in a duel and makes him confess.

Mr Macmath notes for me that Swift, in The Tale of a Tub (written about 1696), having associated Dryden's Hind and Panther with Tom Thumb, Whittington and his Cat, aud other "prime productions of our society," adduces Tommy Potts as "another piece, supposed by the same hand, by way of supplement to the former:" Scott's edition, XI, 72.

The message to Strawberry Castle occurs also in No 65, D, E, F, and No 87 C.

B is translated by Bothe, p. 315.

A

Percy MS., p. 409; Hales and Furnivall, III, 135.

1 ALL you lords of Scottland ffaire,
    And ladyes alsoe, bright of blee,
    There is a ladye amongst them all,
    Of her report you shall heare of me.

2 Of her bewtye shee is soe bright,
    And of her colour soe bright of blee;
    Shee is daughter to the Lord Arrndell,
    His heyre apparrant ffor to bee.

3 'I 'le see *that* bryde,' Lord Phenix sayes,
    '*That* is a ladye of hye degree,
    And iff I like her countenance well,
    The heyre of all my land shee'st bee.'

4 To *that* ladye ffayre Lord Phenix came,
    And to *that* like-some dame said hee,
    Now God thee saue, my ladye ffaire,
    The heyre of all my land tho'st bee.

5 'Leaue of your suite,' the ladye sayd;
    'You are a lord of honor ffree;
    You may gett ladyes enowe att home,
    And I haue a loue in mine owne countrye.

6 'I haue a louer true of mine owne,
    A servinge-man of a small degree;
    Thomas a Pott, itt is his name,
    He is the ffirst loue *that* euer I had, and the
        last *that* hee shalbee.'

7 'Giue Thomas a Pott then be his name,
    I wott I ken him soe readilye;
    I can spend forty pounds by weeke,
    And hee cannott spend pounds three.'

8 'God giue you good of your gold,' said the
        ladye,
    'And alsoe, sir, of your ffee!
    Hee was the ffirst loue *that* euer I had,
    And the last, sir, shall hee bee.'

9 With *that* Lord Phenix was sore amoued;
    Vnto her ffather then went hee;
    Hee told her ffather how itt was proued,
    How *that* his daughter's mind was sett.

10 'Thou art my daughter,' the Erle of Arrndell
        said,
    'The heyre of all my land to bee;

Thou 'st be bryde to the Lord Phenix,
    Daughter, giue thou 'le be heyre to mee.'

11 For lacke of her loue this ladye must lose,
    Her foolish wooing lay all aside;
    The day is appoynted, and ffreinds are agreede;
    Shee is fforcte to be the Lord Phenix bryde.

12 With *that* the lady began to muse —
    A greeued woman, God wott, was shee —
    How shee might Lord Phenix beguile,
    And scape vnmarryed ffrom him *that* day.

13 Shee called to her her litle ffoote-page,
    To Iacke her boy, soe tenderlye;
    Sayes, Come thou hither, thou litle ffoote-page,
    For indeed I dare trust none but thee.

14 To Strawberry Castle, boy, thou must goe,
    To Thomas Pott there as hee can bee,
    And giue him here this letter ffaire,
    And on Guilford Greene bidd him meete me.

15 Looke thou marke his contenance well,
    And his colour tell to mee;
    And hye thee ffast, and come againe,
    And forty shillings I will giue thee.

16 For if he blush in his fface,
    Then in his hart hee 'se sorry bee;
    Then lett my ffather say what hee will,
    For false to Potts I 'le neuer bee.

17 And giue hee smile then with his mouth,
    Then in his heart hee 'le merry be;
    Then may hee gett him a loue where-euer he
        can,
    For small of his companye my part shalbe.

18 Then one while *that* the boy hee went,
    Another while, God wott, rann hee,
    And when hee came to Strawberry Castle,
    There Thomas Potts hee see.

19 Then he gaue him this letter ffaire,
    And when he began then for to reade,
    They boy had told him by word of mouth
    His loue must be the Lord Phenix bryde.

20 With *that*, Thomas a Pott began to blushe,
    The teares trickeled in his eye:
    'Indeed this letter I cannot reede,
    Nor neuer a word to see or spye.

21 'I pray thee, boy, to me thou 'le be trew,
    And heer 's fiue marke I will giue thee ;
  And all these words thou must peruse,
    And tell thy lady this ffrom mee.

22 'Tell her by ffaith and troth shee is mine
      owne,
    By some part of promise, and soe itt 's be
      found ;
  Lord Phenix shall neuer marry her, by night
      nor day,
    Without he can winn her with his hand.

23 'On Gilford Greene I will her meete,
    And bidd that ladye ffor mee pray ;
  For there I 'le loose my liffe soe sweete,
    Or else the wedding I will stay.'

24 Then backe againe the boy he went,
    As ffast againe as he cold hye ;
  The ladye mett him fiue mile on the way :
    'Why hast thou stayd soe long?' saies shee.

25 'Boy,' said the ladye, 'thou art but younge ;
    To please my mind thou 'le mocke and
      scorne ;
  I will not beleeue thee on word of mouth,
    Vnlesse on this booke thou wilt be sworne.'

26 'Marry, by this booke,' the boy can say,
    'As Christ himselfe be true to mee,
  Thomas Pott cold not his letter reade
    For teares trickling in his eye.'

27 'If this be true,' the ladye sayd,
    'Thou bonny boy, thou tells to mee,
  Forty shillings I did thee promise,
    But heere 's ten pounds I 'le giue itt thee.

28 'All my maids,' the lady sayd,
    'That this day doe waite on mee,
  Wee will ffall downe vpon our knees,
    For Thomas Pott now pray will wee.

29 'If his ffortune be now ffor to winn —
    Wee will pray to Christ in Trinytye —
  I 'le make him the fflower of all his kinn,
    Ffor they Lord of Arrundale he shalbe.'

30 Now lett vs leaue talking of this ladye faire,
    In her prayer good where shee can bee ;
  And I 'le tell you hou Thomas Pott
    For ayd to his lord and master came hee.

31 And when hee came Lord Iockye before,
    He kneeled him low downe on his knee ;
  Saies, Thou art welcome, Thomas Pott,
    Thou art allwayes full of thy curtesye.

32 Has thou slaine any of thy ffellowes,
    Or hast thou wrought me some villanye ?
  'Sir, none of my ffellowes I haue slaine,
    Nor I haue wrought you noe villanye.

33 'But I haue a loue in Scotland ffaire,
    I doubt I must lose her through pouertye ;
  If you will not beleeue me by word of mouth,
    Behold the letter shee writt vnto mee.'

34 When Lord Iockye looked the letter vpon,
    The tender words in itt cold bee,
  'Thomas Pott, take thou no care,
    Thou 'st neuer loose her throughe pouer-
      tye.

35 'Thou shalt have forty pounds a weeke,
    In gold and siluer thou shalt rowe,
  And Harbye towne I will thee allowe
    As longe as thou dost meane to wooe.

36 'Thou shalt haue fortye of thy ffellowes ffaire,
    And forty horsse to goe with thee,
  And forty speares of the best I haue,
    And I my-selfe in thy companye.'

37 'I thanke you, master,' sayd Thomas Pott,
    'Neither man nor boy shall goe with mee ;
  I wold not ffor a thousand pounds
    Take one man in my companye.'

38 'Why then, God be with thee, Thomas Pott !
    Thou art well knowen and proued for a
      man ;
  Looke thou shedd no guiltlesse bloode,
    Nor neuer confound no gentlman.

39 'But looke thou take with him some truce,
    Apoint a place of lybertye ;
  Lett him provide as well as hee cann,
    And as well provided thou shalt bee.'

40 And when Thomas Pott came to Gilford
      Greene,
    And walked there a litle beside,
  Then was hee ware of the Lord Phenix,
    And with him Ladye Rozamund his bryde.

41 Away by the bryde rode Thomas of Pott,
　　But noe word to her *that* he did say;
　　But when he came Lord Phenix before,
　　　He gaue him the right time of the day.

42 'O thou art welcome, Thomas a Potts,
　　Thou serving-man, welcome to mee!
　　How ffares they lo*rd* and m*aster* att home,
　　　And all the ladyes in thy cuntrye?'

43 'Sir, my lo*rd* and my m*aster* is in verry good
　　　health,
　　I wott I ken itt soe readylye;
　　I pray you, will you ryde to one outsyde,
　　　A word or towe to talke w*ith* mee.

44 'You are a nobleman,' sayd Thomas a Potts,
　　'Yee are a borne lo*rd* in Scottland ffree;
　　You may gett ladyes enowe att home;
　　　You shall neuer take my loue ffrom
　　　　mee.'

45 'Away, away, thou Thomas a Potts!
　　Thou seruing-man, stand thou a-side!
　　I wott there's not a serving-man this day,
　　　I know, can hinder mee of my bryde.'

46 'If I be but a seruing-man,' sayd Thomas,
　　'And you are a lord of honor ffree,
　　A speare or two I'le w*ith* you runn,
　　　Before I'le loose her thus cowardlye.'

47 'On Gilford Greene,' Lord Ph*e*nix saies, 'I'le
　　　thee meete;
　　Neither man nor boy shall come hither w*ith*
　　　mee;'
　　'And as I am a man,' said Thomas a Pott,
　　　'I'le haue as ffew in my companye.'

48 With *that* the wedding-day was stayd,
　　The bryde went vnmarryed home againe;
　　Then to her maydens ffast shee loughe,
　　　And in her hart shee was ffull ffaine.

49 'But all my mayds,' they ladye sayd,
　　'*That* this day doe waite on mee,
　　Wee will ffall downe againe vpon our knees,
　　　For Thomas a Potts now pray will wee.

50 'If his ffortune be ffor to winn —
　　Wee'le pray to Christ in Trynitye —
　　I'le make him the fflower of all his kinn,
　　　For the Lord of Arrundale he shalbe.'

51 Now let vs leaue talking of this lady fayre,
　　In her prayers good where shee can bee;
　　I'le tell you the troth how Thomas a Potts
　　　For aide to his lord againe came hee.

52 And when he came to Strawberry Castle,
　　To try ffor his ladye he had but one weeke;
　　Alacke, ffor sorrow hee cannott fforbeare,
　　　For four dayes then he ffell sicke.

53 With *that* his lord and m*aster* to him came,
　　Sayes, I pray thee, Thomas, tell mee w*ith*-
　　　out all doubt,
　　Whether hast thou gotten the bonny ladye,
　　　Or thou man gange the ladye w*ith*oute.

54 'Marry, m*aster*, yett *that* matter is vntryde;
　　Within two dayes tryed itt must bee;
　　He is a lo*rd*, and I am but a seruing-man,
　　　I doubt I must loose her through pouertye.'
　　'Why, Thomas a Pott, take thou no care;
　　　Thou'st neuer loose her through pouertye.

55 'Thou shalt haue halfe my land a yeere,
　　And *that* will raise thee many a pound;
　　Before thou shalt loose thy bonny ladye,
　　　Thou shalt drop angells w*ith* him to the
　　　　ground.

56 'And thou shalt haue forty of thy ffellowes
　　　ffaire,
　　And forty horsses to goe w*ith* thee,
　　And forty speres of the best I haue,
　　　And I my-selfe in thy companye.'

57 'I thanke you, m*aster*,' sayd Thomas a Potts,
　　'But of one thinge, s*ir*, I wold be ffaine;
　　If I shold loose my bonny ladye,
　　　How shall I increase yo*ur* goods againe?'

58 'Why, if thou winn thy lady ffaire,
　　Thou maye well fforth for to pay mee;
　　If thou loose thy lady, thou hast losse enoughe;
　　　Not one penny I will aske thee.'

59 'M*aster*, you haue thirty horsses in one hold,
　　You keepe them ranke and royallye;
　　There's an old horsse, — for him you doe not
　　　care —
　　　This day wold sett my lady ffree.

60 '*That* is a white, with a cutt tayle,
　　Ffull sixteen yeeres of age is hee;

Giffe you wold lend me *that* old horsse,
    Then I shold gett her easilye.'

61 ' Thou takes a ffoolish p*a*rt,' the L*or*d Iockye
    sayd,
  ' And a ffoolish p*a*rt thou takes on thee ;
Thou shalt haue a better then euer he was,
    That forty pounds cost more nor hee.'

62 ' O m*a*ster, those horsses beene wild and
    wicked,
  And litle they can skill of the old traine ;
Giffe I be out of my saddle cast,
    They beene soe wild they 'le neuer be tane
    againe.

63 ' Lett me haue age, sober and wise ;
    Itt is a p*a*rt of wisdome, you know itt
    plaine ;
If I be out of my sadle cast,
    Hee 'le either stand still or turne againe.'

64 ' Thou shalt haue *that* horsse with all my hart,
    And my cote-plate of siluer ffree,
And a hundred men att thy backe,
    For to fight if neede shalbee.'

65 ' I thanke you, m*a*ster,' said Thomas a Potts,
  ' Neither man nor boy shall goe with mee ;
As you are a lord off honor borne,
    Let none of my ffellowes know this of mee.

66 ' Ffor if they wott of my goinge,
    I wott behind me they will not bee ;
Without you keepe them vnder a locke,
    Vppon *that* greene I shall them see.'

67 And when Tho*mas* c*a*me to Gilford Greene,
    And walked there some houres three,
Then was he ware of the L*or*d Phenix,
    And four men in his companye.

68 ' You haue broken yo*ur* vow,' sayd Tho*mas* a
    Pott,
  ' Yo*ur* vowe *that* you made vnto mee ;
You said you wold come yo*ur* selfe alone,
    And you haue brought more then two or
    three.'

69 ' These are my waiting-men,' L*or*d Phenix
    sayd,
  ' *That* euery day doe waite on mee ;
Giffe any of these shold att vs stirr,
    My speare shold runn throwe his bodye.'

70 ' I 'le runn noe race,' said Tho*mas* Potts,
  ' Till *that* this othe heere made may bee :
If the one of vs be slaine,
    The other fforgiuen *that* hee may bee.'

71 ' I 'le make a vow,' L*or*d Phenix sayes,
  ' My men shall beare wittnesse with thee,
Giffe thou slay mee att this time,
    Neuer the worsse beloued in Scottland thou
    shalt bee.'

72 Then they turned their horsses round about,
    To run the race more egarlye ;
L*or*d Phenix he was stiffe and stout,
    He has runn Tho*mas* quite thorrow the
    thye.

73 And beere Tho*mas* out of his saddle ffaire ;
    Vpon the ground there did hee lye ;
He saies, For my liffe I doe not care,
    But ffor the loue of my ladye.

74 But shall I lose my ladye ffaire ?
    I thought shee shold haue beene my wiffe ;
I pray thee, L*or*d Phenix, ryde not away,
    For with thee I will loose my liffe.

75 Tho Tho*mas* a Potts was a seruing-man,
    He was alsoe a phisityan good ;
He clapt his hand vpon his wound,
    With some kind of words he stauncht the
    blood.

76 Then into his sadle againe hee leepe ;
    The blood in his body began to warme ;
He mist L*or*d Phenix bodye there,
    But he run him quite throw the brawne of
    the arme.

77 And he bore him quite out of his saddle ffaire ;
    Vpon the ground there did he lye ;
He said, I pray thee, L*or*d Phenix, rise and
    ffight,
    Or else yeeld this ladye sweete to mee.

78 ' To ffight with thee,' qu*o*th Phenix, ' I cannott
    stand,
    Nor ffor to ffight, I cannott, sure ;
Thou hast run me through the brawne of the
    arme ;
    Noe longer of thy spere I cannott endure.

79 ' Thou 'st haue *that* ladye with all my hart,
    Sith itt was like neuer better to proue.

Nor neuer a noble-man this day,
   That will seeke to take a pore man's loue.'

80 'Why then, be of good cheere,' saies Tho*mas*
   Pott,
   'Indeed your bucher I 'le neuer bee,
For I 'le come and stanche y*our* bloode,
   Giff any thankes you 'le giue to mee.'

81 As he was stanching the Phenix blood,
   These words Tho*mas* a Pott cann to him
   proue :
   'I 'le neuer take a ladye of you thus,
   But here I 'le giue you another choice.

82 'Heere is a lane of two miles longe ;
   Att either end sett wee will bee ;
The ladye shall sitt vs betweene,
   And soe will wee sett this ladye ffree.'

83 'If thou 'le doe soe,' Lo*rd* Phenix sayes,
   'Tho*mas* a Pott, as thou dost tell mee,
Whether I gett her or goe wi*thout* her,
   Heere 's forty pounds I 'le giue itt thee.'

84 And when the ladye there can stand,
   A woman's mind that day to proue,
'Now, by my ffaith,' said this ladye ffaire,
   'This day Tho*mas* a Pott shall haue his
   owne loue.'

85 Toward Tho*mas* a Pott the lady shee went,
   To leape behind him hastilye ;
'Nay, abyde a while,' sayd Lo*rd* Phenix,
   'Ffor better yett proued thou shalt bee.

86 'Thou shalt stay heere wi*th* all thy maids —
   In number wi*th* thee thou hast but three —
Tho*mas* a Pott and I 'le goe beyond yonder wall,
   There the one of vs shall dye.'

87 And when they came beyon*d* the wall,
   The one wold not the other nye ;
Lo*rd* Phenix he had giuen his word
   With Tho*mas* a Pott neuer to ffight.

88 'Giue me a choice,' Lo*rd* Phenix sayes,
   'Tho*mas* a Pott, I doe pray thee ;
Lett mee goe to yonder ladye ffaire,
   To see whether shee be true to thee.'

89 And when hee came *that* ladye too,
   Vnto that likesome dame sayd hee,
Now God thee saue, thou ladye ffaire,
   The heyre of all my land thou 'st bee.

90 Ffor this Tho*mas* a Potts I haue slaine ;
   He hath more then deadlye wounds two or
   three ;
Thou art mine owne ladye, he sayd,
   And marryed together wee will bee.

91 The ladye said, If Tho*mas* a Potts this day
   thou haue slaine,
   Thou hast slaine a better man than eu*er* was
   thee ;
And I 'le sell all the state of my lande
   But thou 'st be hanged on a gallow-tree.

92 With *that* they lady shee ffell in a soone ;
   A greeued woman, I wott, was shee ;
Lo*rd* Phenix hee was readye there,
   Tooke her in his armes most hastilye.

93 'O Lo*rd*, sweete, and stand on thy ffeete,
   This day Tho*mas* a Pott aliue can bee ;
I 'le send ffor thy father, the Lo*rd* of Arrun-
   dale,
   And marryed together I will you see :
Giffe hee will not maintaine you well,
   Both gold and land you shall haue from
   me.'

94 'I 'le see *that* wedding,' my Lo*rd* of Arrundale
   said,
   'Of my daughter's loue *that* is soe ffaire ;
And sith itt will no better be,
   Of all my land Tho*mas* a Pott shall be my
   heyre.'

95 'Now all my maids,' the ladye said,
   'And ladyes of England, faire and ffree,
Looke you neuer change y*our* old loue for no
   new,
   Nor neuer change fo*r* no pouertye.

96 'Ffor I had a louer true of mine owne,
   A seruing-man of a small degree ;
Ffrom Tho*mas* a Pott I 'le turne his name,
   And the Lo*rd* of Arrundale hee shall bee.'

B

a. London, printed for F. Coles, and others, 1677, Bodleian Library, Wood, 259. **b.** Pepys Penny Merriments, I, 189, Magdalen College Library, Cambridge.

1 OF all the lords in Scotland fair,
    And ladies that been so bright of blee,
  There is a noble lady among them all,
    And report of her you shall hear by me.

2 For of her beauty she is bright,
    And of her colour very fair ;
  She 's daughter to Lord Arundel,
    Approvd his parand and his heir.

3 ' I 'le see this bride,' Lord Phenix said,
    ' That lady of so bright a blee,
  And if I like her countenance well,
    The heir of all my lands she 'st be.'

4 But when he came the lady before,
    Before this comely maid came he,
  ' O God thee save, thou lady sweet,
    My heir and parand thou shalt be.'

5 ' Leave off your suit,' the lady said,
    ' As you are a lord of high degree ;
  You may have ladies enough at home,
    And I have a lord in mine own country.

6 ' For I have a lover true of mine own,
    A serving-man of low degree,
  One Tommy Pots it is his name,
    My first love and last that ever shall be.'

7 ' If that Tom Pots is his name,
    I do ken him right verily ;
  I am able to spend fourty pounds a week,
    Where he is not able to spend pounds three.'

8 ' God give you good of your gold,' she said,
    ' And ever God give you good of your fee ;
  Tom Pots was the first love that ever I had,
    And I do mean him the last to be.'

9 With that Lord Phenix soon was movd ;
    Towards the lady did he threat ;
  He told her father, and so it was provd,
    How his daughter's mind was set.

10 ' O daughter dear, thou art my own,
    The heir of all my lands to be ;
  Thou shalt be bride to the Lord Phenix,
    If that thou mean to be heir to me.'

11 ' O father dear, I am your own,
    And at your command I needs must be ;
  But bind my body to whom you please,
    My heart, Tom Pots, shall go with thee.'

12 Alas ! the lady her fondness must leave,
    And all her foolish wooing lay aside ;
  The time is come, her friends have appointed,
    That she must be Lord Phenix bride.

13 With that the lady began to weep ;
    She knew not well then what to say,
  How she might Lord Phenix deny,
    And escape from marriage quite away.

14 See calld unto her little foot-page,
    Saying, I can trust none but thee ;
  Go carry Tom Pots this letter fair,
    And bid him on Guilford Green meet me.

15 For I must marry against my mind,
    Or in faith well proved it shall be ;
  And tell to him I am loving and kind,
    And wishes him this wedding to see.

16 But see that thou note his countenance well,
    And his colour, and shew it to me ;
  And go thy way and hie thee again,
    And forty shillings I will give thee.

17 For if he smile now with his lips,
    His stomach will give him to laugh at the
      heart ;
  Then may I seek another true-love,
    For of Tom Pots small is my part.

18 But if he blush now in his face,
    Then in his heart he will sorry be ;
  Then to his vow he hath some grace,
    And false to him I will never be.

19 Away this lacky-boy he ran,
    And a full speed forsooth went he,
  Till he came to Strawberry Castle,
    And there Tom Pots came he to see.

20 He gave him the letter in his hand ;
    Before that he began to read,
  He told him plainly by word of mouth,
    His love was forc'd to be Lord Phenix
      bride.

21 When he lookd on the letter fair,
    The salt tears blemished his eye ;

Says, I cannot read this letter fair,
    Nor never a word to see or spy.

22 My little boy, be to me true,
    Here is five marks I will give thee ;
  And all these words I must peruse,
    And tell my lady this from me.

23 By faith and troth she is my own,
    By some part of promise, so it 's to be
      found ;
  Lord Phoenix shall not have her night nor
      day,
    Except he can win her with his own hand.

24 On Guilford Green I will her meet ;
    Say that I wish her for me to pray ;
  For there I 'le lose my life so sweet,
    Or else the wedding I mean to stay.

25 Away this lackey-boy he ran,
    Even as fast as he could hie ;
  The lady she met him two miles of the way ;
    Says, Why hast thou staid so long, my boy ?

26 My little boy, thou art but young,
    It gives me at heart thou 'l mock and scorn ;
  I 'le not believe thee by word of mouth,
    Unless on this book thou wilt be sworn.

27 ' Now by this book,' the boy did say,
    ' And Jesus Christ be as true to me,
  Tom Pots could not read the letter fair,
    Nor never a word to spy or see.

28 ' He says, by faith and troth you are his own,
    By some part of promise, so it 's to be
      found ;
  Lord Phenix shall not have you night nor day,
    Except he win you with his own hand.

29 ' On Guilford Green he will you meet ;
    He wishes you for him to pray ;
  For there he 'l lose his life so sweet,
    Or else the wedding he means to stay.'

30 ' If this be true, my little boy,
    These tidings which thou tellest to me,
  Forty shillings I did thee promise,
    Here is ten pounds I will give thee.

31 ' My maidens all,' the lady said,
    ' That ever wish me well to prove,

Now let us all kneel down and pray
    That Tommy Pots may win his love.

32 ' If it be his fortune the better to win,
    As I pray to Christ in Trinity,
  I 'le make him the flower of all his kin,
    For the young Lord Arundel he shall be.'

33 Let 's leave talking of this lady fair,
    In prayers full good where she may be ;
  Now let us talk of Tommy Pots ;
    To his lord and master for aid went he.

34 But when he came Lord Jockey before,
    He kneeled lowly on his knee :
  ' What news, what news, thou Tommy Pots,
    Thou art so full of courtesie ?

35 ' What tydings, what tydings, thou Tommy
    Pots,
  Thou art so full of courtesie ?
  Thou hast slain some of thy fellows fair,
    Or wrought to me some villany.'

36 ' I have slain none of my fellows fair,
    Nor wrought to you no villany,
  But I have a love in Scotland fair,
    And I fear I shall lose her with poverty.

37 ' If you 'l not believe me by word of mouth,
    But read this letter, and you shall see,
  Here by all these suspitious words
    That she her own self hath sent to me.'

38 But when he had read the letter fair,
    Of all the suspitious words in it might be,
  ' O Tommy Pots, take thou no care,
    Thou 'st never lose her with poverty.

39 ' For thou 'st have forty pounds a week,
    In gold and silver thou shalt row,
  And Harvy Town I will give thee
    As long as thou intendst to wooe.

40 ' Thou 'st have forty of thy fellows fair,
    And forty horses to go with thee,
  Forty of the best spears I have,
    And I my self in thy company.'

41 ' I thank you, master,' said Tommy Pots,
    ' That proffer is too good for me ;
  But, if Jesus Christ stand on my side,
    My own hands shall set her free.

42 'God be with you, master,' said Tommy Pots,
     'Now Jesus Christ you save and see;
   If ever I come alive again,
     Staid the wedding it shall be.'

43 'O God be your speed, thou Tommy Pots,
     Thou art well proved for a man;
   See never a drop of blood thou spil,
     Nor yonder gentleman confound.

44 'See that some truce with him you take,
     And appoint a place of liberty;
   Let him provide him as well as he can,
     As well provided thou shalt be.'

45 But when he came to Guilford Green,
     And there had walkt a little aside,
   There was he ware of Lord Phenix come,
     And Lady Rosamond his bride.

46 Away by the bride then Tommy Pots went,
     But never a word to her did say,
   Till he the Lord Phenix came before;
     He gave him the right time of the day.

47 'O welcome, welcome, thou Tommy Pots,
     Thou serving-man of low degree;
   How doth thy lord and master at home,
     And all the ladies in that countrey?'

48 'My lord and master is in good health,
     I trust since that I did him see;
   Will you walk with me to an out-side,
     Two or three words to talk with me?

49 'You are a noble man,' said Tom,
     'And born a lord in Scotland free;
   You may have ladies enough at home,
     And never take my love from me.'

50 'Away, away, thou Tommy Pots;
     Thou serving-man, stand thou aside;
   It is not a serving-man this day
     That can hinder me of my bride.'

51 'If I be a serving-man,' said Tom,
     'And you a lord of high degree,
   A spear or two with you I 'le run,
     Before I 'le lose her cowardly.

52 'Appoint a place, I will thee meet,
     Appoint a place of liberty;
   For there I 'le lose my life so sweet,
     Or else my lady I 'le set free.'

53 'On Guilford Green I will thee meet;
     No man nor boy shall come with me:'
   'As I am a man,' said Tommy Pots,
     'I 'le have as few in my company.'

54 And thus staid the marriage was,
     The bride unmarried went home again;
   Then to her maids fast did she laugh,
     And in her heart she was full fain.

55 'My maidens all,' the lady said,
     'That ever wait on me this day,
   Now let us all kneel down,
     And for Tommy Pots let us all pray.

56 'If it be his fortune the better to win,
     As I trust to God in Trinity,
   I 'le make him the flower of all his kin,
     For the young Lord Arundel he shall be.'

57 When Tom Pots came home again,
     To try for his love he had but a week;
   For sorrow, God wot, he need not care,
     For four days that he fel sick.

58 With that his master to him came,
     Says, Pray thee, Tom Pots, tell me if tho
          doubt
   Whether thou hast gotten thy gay lady,
     Or thou must go thy love without.

59 'O master, yet it is unknown;
     Within these two days well try'd it must be;
   He is a lord, I am but a serving-man,
     I fear I shall lose her with poverty.'

60 'I prethee, Tom Pots, get thee on thy feet;
     My former promises kept shall be;
   As I am a lord in Scotland fair,
     Thou 'st never lose her with poverty.

61 'For thou 'st have the half of my lands a year,
     And that will raise thee many a pound;
   Before thou shalt out-braved be,
     Thou shalt drop angels with him on the
          ground.'

62 'I thank you, master,' said Tommy Pots,
     'Yet there is one thing of you I would fain;
   If that I lose my lady sweet,
     How I 'st restore your goods again?'

63 'If that thou win the lady sweet,
     Thou mayst well forth, thou shalt pay me;

If thou loosest thy lady, thou losest enough;
  Thou shalt not pay me one penny.'

64 'You have thirty horses in one close,
    You keep them all both frank and free;
  Amongst them all there's an old white horse
    This day would set my lady free.

65 'That is an old horse with a cut tail,
    Full sixteen years of age is he;
  If thou wilt lend me that old horse,
    Then could I win her easily.'

66 'That's a foolish opinion,' his master said,
    'And a foolish opinion thou tak'st to thee;
  Thou'st have a better then ever he was,
    Though forty pounds more it cost me.'

67 'O your choice horses are. wild and tough,
    And little they can skill of their train;
  If I be out of my saddle cast,
    They are so wild they'l ner be tain.'

68 'Thou'st have that horse,' his master said,
    'If that one thing thou wilt tell me;
  Why that horse is better than any other,
    I pray thee, Tom Pots, shew thou to me.'

69 'That horse is old, of stomach bold,
    And well can he skill of his train;
  If I be out of my saddle cast,
    He'l either stand still or turn again.'

70 'Thou'st have the horse with all my heart,
    And my plate-coat of silver free;
  An hundred men to stand at thy back,
    To fight if he thy master be.'

71 'I thank you master,' said Tommy Pots,
    'That proffer is too good for me;
  I would not, for ten thousand pounds,
    Have man or boy in my company.

72 'God be with you, master,' said Tommy Pots;
    'Now, as you are a man of law,
  One thing let me crave at your hand;
    Let never a one of my fellows know.

73 'For if that my fellows they did wot,
    Or ken of my extremity,
  Except you keep them under a lock,
    Behind me I am sure they would not be.'

74 But when he came to Guilford Green,
    He waited hours two or three;
  There he was ware of Lord Phenix come,
    And four men in his company.

75 'You have broken your vow,' said Tommy
      Pots,
    'The vow which you did make to me;
  You said you would bring neither man nor
      boy,
    And now has brought more than two or
      three.'

76 'These are my men,' Lord Phenix said,
    'Which every day do wait on me;
  [If] any of these dare proffer to strike,
    I'le run my spear through his body.'

77 'I'le run no race now,' said Tommy Pots,
    'Except now this may be;
  If either of us be slain this day,
    The other shall forgiven be.'

78 'I'le make that vow with all my heart,
    My men shall bear witness with me;
  And if thou slay me here this day,
    In Scotland worse belovd thou never shalt
      be.'

79 They turnd their horses thrice about,
    To run the race so eagerly;
  Lord Phenix he was fierce and stout,
    And ran Tom Pots through the thick o th'
      thigh.

80 He bord him out of the saddle fair,
    Down to the ground so sorrowfully:
  'For the loss of my life I do not care,
    But for the loss of my fair lady.

81 'Now for the loss of my lady sweet,
    Which once I thought to have been my
      wife,
  I pray thee, Lord Phenix, ride not away,
    For with thee I would end my life.'

82 Tom Pots was but a serving-man,
    But yet he was a doctor good;
  He bound his handkerchief on his wound,
    And with some kind of words he stancht his
      blood.

83 He leapt into his saddle again,
    The blood in his body began to warm;
He mist Lord Phenix body fair,
    And ran him through the brawn of the arm.

84 He bord him out of his saddle fair,
    Down to the ground most sorrowfully;
Says, Prethee, Lord Phenix, rise up and fight,
    Or yield my lady unto me.

85 ' Now for to fight I cannot tell,
    And for to fight I am not sure;
Thou hast run me throw the brawn o th' arm,
    That with a spear I may not endure.

86 ' Thou 'st have the lady with all my heart;
    It was never likely better to prove
With me, or any nobleman else,
    That would hinder a poor man of his love.'

87 ' Seeing you say so much,' said Tommy Pots,
    ' I will not seem your butcher to be;
But I will come and stanch your blood,
    If any thing you will give me.'

88 As he did stanch Lord Phenix blood,
    Lord, in his heart he did rejoyce!
' I 'le not take the lady from you thus,
    But of her you 'st have another choice.

89 ' Here is a lane of two miles long;
    At either end we set will be;
The lady shall stand us among,
    Her own choice shall set her free.'

90 ' If thou 'l do so,' Lord Phenix said,
    ' To lose her by her own choice it 's honesty;
Chuse whether I get her or go her without,
    Forty pounds I will give thee.'

91 But when they in that lane was set,
    The wit of a woman for to prove,
' By the faith of my body,' the lady said,
    ' Then Tom Pots must needs have his love.'

92 Towards Tom Pots the lady did hie,
    To get on behind him hastily;
' Nay stay, nay stay,' Lord Phenix said,
    ' Better proved it shall be.

93 ' Stay you with your maidens here —
    In number fair they are but three —

Tom Pots and I will go behind yonder wall,
    That one of us two be proved to dye.'

94 But when they came behind the wall,
    The one came not the other nigh;
For the Lord Phenix had made a vow,
    That with Tom Pots he would never fight.

95 ' O give me this choice,' Lord Phenix said,
    ' To prove whether true or false she be,
And I will go to the lady fair,
    And tell her Tom Pots slain is he.'

96 When he came from behind the wall,
    With his face all bloody as it might be,
' O lady sweet, thou art my own,
    For Tom Pots slain have I.

97 ' Now have I slain him, Tommy Pots,
    And given him death's wounds two or three;
O lady sweet, thou art my own;
    Of all loves, wilt thou live with me?'

98 ' If thou hast slain him, Tommy Pots,
    And given him death's wounds two or three,
I 'le sell the state of my father's lands
    But hanged shall Lord Phenix be.'

99 With that the lady fell in a swound,
    For a grieved woman, God wot, was she;
Lord Phenix he was ready then
    To take her up so hastily.

100 ' O lady sweet, stand thou on thy feet,
    Tom Pots alive this day may be;
I 'le send for thy father, Lord Arundel,
    And he and I the wedding will see.

101 ' I 'le send for thy father, Lord Arundel,
    And he and I the wedding will see;
If he will not maintain you well,
    Both lands and livings you 'st have of me.'

102 ' I 'le see this wedding,' Lord Arundel said,
    ' Of my daughter's luck that is so fair;
Seeing the matter will be no better,
    Of all my lands Tom Pots shall be the heir.'

103 With that the lady began for to smile,
    For a glad woman, God wot, was she;
' Now all my maids,' the lady said,
    ' Example you may take by me.'

104 'But all the ladies of Scotland fair,
    And lasses of England that well would
      prove,
  Neither marry for gold nor goods,
    Nor marry for nothing but only love.

105 'For I had a lover true of my own,
    A serving-man of low degree;
  Now from Tom Pots I 'le change his name,
    For the young Lord Arundel he shall be.'

------·------

C

A white letter sheet in five columns, "published May 29,
1657," The King's Pamphlets, British Museum, 669, f. 20, 55.

1 IN Scotland there are ladies fair,
    There 's ladies of honor and high degree,
      Hey down, down a down derry
  But one excels above all the rest,
    And the Earl of Arundel's daughter is she.
      With hey down, derry down,
      Lang derry down derry

2 Both knights and lords of great account
    Comes thither a wooing for this ladie's sake :
  It fell on a day that Earl Arundell said,
    Daughter, which of these lords will you
      take ?

3 Or which of them now likes thee best ?
    Speak truth to me, but do not lie ;
  Speak truth to me, and do not jest,
    Who must heir my livings when as I die ?

4 Lord Fenix is a lord of high degree,
    And hath both lands and livings free ;
  I tell thee, daughter, thou shalt him have,
    If thou wilt take any counsell at me.

5 With that the young lady fell down of her
      knee,
    And trickling tears ran down her eye :
  'As you are my father, and loves me dear,
    My heart is set where it must be.

6 'On a serving-man which is so poor,
    For all he hath is but pounds three ;
  He was the first lover that ere I had,
    And the last I mean him for to be.'

7 With that her father was sore offended,
    And fast he rode at that same tide,
  Untill he to the Lord Fenix came,
    And said, Take thee my daughter for thy
      bride.

8 The yong ladie cald up Jack, her foot-boy :
    'I dare trust no man alive but thee ;
  Thou must go my earand to Strawbery Castle,
    To the place where Tomy o'th Potts doth
      lye.

9 'And carry this letter, in parchment fair,
    That I have sealed with mine own hand ;
  And when Tomey looks this letter upon,
    Be sure his countenance thou understand.

10 'And if he either laugh or smile,
    He is not sorry at his heart ;
  I must seek a new love where I will,
    For small of Tomey must be my part.

11 'But if he wax red in the face,
    And tricling tears fall from his eyes,
  Then let my father say what he will,
    For true to Tomey I 'le be always.

12 'And thou must tell him by word of mouth,
    If this letter cannot be read at that tyde,
  That this day sennight, and no longer hence,
    I must be Lord William Fenix bride.'

13 The boy took leave of his lady gay,
    And to Strawbery Castle he did him fast
      hie ;
  A serving-man did guide him the way
    To the place where Tomey o'th Pots did lie.

14 'O Christ thee save, good Tomey o'th Pots,
    And Christ thee save as I thee see ;
  Come read this letter, Tomey o'th Potts,
    As thy true-love hath sent to thee.'

15 Then Tomey he waxed red in the face,
    And trickling tears ran down his eyes ;
  But never a letter could he read,
    If he should be hanged on th' gallow-tree.

16 'Shee bid me tell you by word of mouth,
    If this letter could not be read at this tide,

That this day sennight, and no longer hence,
  She must be Lord William Fenix bride.'

17 'Now in faith,' said Tomey, 'she is mine own,
    As all hereafter shall understand ;
Lord Fenix shall not marry her, by night or
    day,
Unless he win her by his own hand.

18 'For on Gilforth Green I will her meet,
    And if she love me, bid her for me pray ;
And there I will lose my life so sweet,
    Or else her wedding I will stay.'

19 He cald this boy unto accounts ;
    Think whether he loved this lady gay !
He gave him forty shilling for his message,
    And all he had was but pounds three.

20 The boy took his leave of Tomey o'th Potts,
    Fearing that he had staid too late ;
The young lady did wait of his comming,
    And met him five miles out of the gate.

21 'O boney boy, thou art not of age,
    Therefore thou canst both mock and scorn ;
I will not beleeve what my love hath said,
    Unlesse thou on this book be sworn.'

22 'Now, in faith, gay lady, I will not lye,'
    And kist the book full soon did he :
'One letter he could not read at that time,
    If he should have been hangd at gallo-tree.

23 'He said in faith you are his own,
    As all hereafter shall understand ;
Lord Fenix shall not marry you by night or
    day,
Unlesse he winn you with his own hand.

24 'For on Gilforth Green he will you meet,
    And if you love him, you must for him
      pray ;
And there he will lose his life so sweet,
    Or else your wedding he will stay.'

25 Let us leave talking of the boy,
    That with his gay lady is turned home ;
Now let us go talk of Tomey o'th Potts,
    And how to his master he is gone.

26 When Tomey came his master before,
    He kneeled down upon his knee :

'What tidings hast thou brought, my man,
    As that thou makes such courtesie ? '

27 'O Christ you save, dear master,' he said,
    'And Christ you save as I you see ;
For God's love, master, come read me this let-
    ter,
Which my true love hath sent to me.'

28 His master took this letter in hand,
    And looked ore it with his eye ;
'In faith, I am fain, my man,' he said,
    'As thou hast a lady so true to thee.'

29 'I have a lady true to me,
    And false to her I 'le never be ;
But ere this day sennight, and no longer hence,
    I must lose my love through rovertie.

30 'Lord Fenix he will her have,
    Because he hath more wealth then I : '
'Now hold thy tongue, my man,' he said,
    'For before that day many a one shall die.

31 'O Tomey,' said he, 'I love thee well,
    And something for thee I will doo ;
For Strawbery Castle shall be thine own
    So long as thou dost mean to woo.

32 'One half of my lands I 'le give thee a year,
    The which will raise thee many a pound ;
Before that thou lose thy bonny sweet-hart,
    Thou shalt drop angels with him to the
      ground.

33 'I have thirty steeds in my stable strong,
    Which any of them is good indeed,
And a bunch of spears hangs them among,
    And a nag to carry thee swift with speed.

34 'My sute of armour thou shalt put on —
    So well it becomes thy fair body —
And when thou comst on Gilford Green
    Thou 'll look more like a lord then he.

35 'My men shall all rise and with thee go,
    And I my self with thee will ride ;
And many a bloody wound will we make
    Before that thou shalt lose thy bride.'

36 'Now Christ reward you, dear master,' he
    said,
    'For the good will you bear to me ;

But I trust to God, in a little space,
    With my own hands to set her free.

37 'I 'le none of your horses, master,' he said,
    'For they cannot well skill of their trade;
  None but your gray nag that hath a cut tail,
    For hee 'll either stand or turn again.

38 'One spear, master, and no more,
    No more with me that I will take,
  And if that spear it will not serve my turn,
    I 'le suffer death for my true-love's sake.'

39 Early in the morning, when day did spring,
    On Gilforth Green betime was he;
  There did he espie Lord Fenix comming,
    And with him a royall company.

40 Gold chains about their necks threescore,
    Full well might seem fine lords to ride;
  The young lady followed far behind,
    Sore against her will that she was a bride.

41 There Tomey passed this lady by,
    But never a word to her did say;
  Then straight to Lord Fenix he is gone,
    And gives him the right time of the day.

42 'O Christ you save, Lord Fenix,' he said,
    'And Christ you save as I you see;'
  'Thou art welcome, Tomey o'th Potts,' he said,
    'A serving-man into our company.

43 'O how doth thy master, Tomy o'th Potts?
    Tell me the truth and do not lye;'
  'My master is well,' then Tomey replide,
    'I thank my lord, and I thank not thee.

44 'O Christ you save Lord Fenix,' he said,
    'And Christ you save as I you see;
  You may have choyce of ladies enough,
    And not take my true-love from me.'

45 With that Lord Fenix was sore offended,
    And fast away he rode at that tide;
  'God forbid,' Lord Fenix he said,
    'A serving-man should hold me from my
      bride!'

46 But afterward Tomey did him meet,
    As one that came not thither to flye,
  And said, Lord Fenix, take thou my love,
    For I will not lose her cowardly.

47 'O meet me here tomorrow,' he said;
    'As thou art a man, come but thy sell;
  And if that I come [with] any more,
    The divell fetch my soul to hell.'

48 And so this wedding-day was staid,
    The lady and lords they turned home;
  The lady made merry her maidens among,
    And said, Tomey I wish thou may win thy
      own.

49 Early in the morning, when day did spring,
    On Gilforth Green betime was he;
  He waited long for Lord Fenix comming,
    But Lord William Fenix he could not see.

50 He waited long and very long,
    Untill the sun waxed very high;
  There was he ware of Lord Fenix coming,
    And with him other men three.

51 'Thou art a false thief, Lord Fenix,' he said,
    'Because thou breakst thy promise with me;
  Thou promisedst me to come by thy self,
    And thou hast brought other men three.

52 'But in regard I call thee thief,
    Because thou hast broken promise with me,
  I vow, and you were as many more,
    Forsaken sure you should not be.'

53 'These are my men,' Lord Fenix said,
    'That every day do wait on me;
  If any of them do strike a stroke,
    In faith then hanged he shall be.'

54 They fetcht a race and rode about,
    And then they met full eagerly;
  Lord Fenix away by Tomey's body glowd,
    And he ran him quite thorow the thigh.

55 Out of his saddle bore him he did,
    And laid his body on the ground;
  His spear he ran thorow Tomey's thigh,
    In which he made a grievous wound.

56 But Tomey quickly start up again;
    For as he was a physitian good,
  He laid his hand upon the wound,
    And quickly he did stanch the blood.

57 Full lightly he leaped to his saddle again,
    Forth of it long he did not stay;

For he weighed more of the ladie's love
   Then of any life he had that day.

58 They fetched a race and rode about,
   The blood in Tomey's body began to warm ;
He away by Lord Fenix body glowde,
   And he ran him quite through the arm.

59 Out of his saddle bore him he hath,
   Of from his steed that mounted so high ;
'Now rise and fight, Lord Fenix,' he said,
   'Or else yeeld the lady unto me.'

60 'I 'll yeeld the lady unto thee ;
   My arm no more my spear will guide ;
It was never better likely to prove,
   To hold a poor serving-man from his bride.'

61 'But if thou wilt thus deal then with me,
   Lest of this matter should rise any voice,
That I have gotten the victory,
   Then thou shalt have another choice.

62 'Yonder is a lane of two miles long ;
   At either end then stand will we ;

Wee 'l set the lady in the midst,
   And whether she come to, take her, for me.'

63 'If thou wilt thus deal,' said Fenix then,
   'Thou 'll save my credit and honor high ;
And whether I win her, or go without her,
   I 'le be willing to give ten pounds to thee.'

64 There was a lane of two miles long ;
   The lady was set in the middle that tide ;
She laught and made merry her maids among,
   And said, Tomey o'th Pots, now I 'le be thy
     bride.

65 Now all you ladies of high degree,
   And maides that married yet would be,
Marry no man for goods or lands,
   Unlesse you love him faithfully.

66 For I had a love of my own, she said,
   At Strawberrie Castle there lived he ;
I 'le change his name from Tomey o'th Pots,
   And the yong *Earl* of *A*rundell now he shall
     be.

A. 6^1. of nine.   6^3. *at the end of the stanza.*
   7^3. spend 40$^{li}_{..}$.
   7^4. pounds 3.
   11^3. *There is a mark like an undotted* i, *in the*
     MS., before the y *of* appoynted. *Furnivall.*
   15^4. 40.
   20^3. camot.
   21^2, 24^3. 5.
   21^3. must pursue.
   27^3. 40^s.
   27^4. 10^{li}.
   29^1. wim.
   33^2, 33^3. *Stanza* 35 *is written between these*
     lines, "but marked by a bracket, and by
     Percy, to go in its proper place." Furni-
     vall.
   35^1. 40^{li}.
   36^1. 40^{tye}.
   36^2, ^{3}. 40.
   36^4. *Only half the* n *of* companye *in the MS.*
     Furnivall.
   37^3. 1000 $^{li}_{..}$.
   46^3. or 2.
   51, 52 *are bracketed as beginning the* 2$^d_{..}$ parte.

51^4. cane.
52^4. for 4.
54^2. 2.
56$^{1,\,2,\,3}$. 40.
57^3. bomy.
59^1. 30.
60^2. 16.
61^3. the euer.
61^4. 40^{li}.
64^3. 100^d.
67^2. 3.
67^4. 4.
68^4. 2 or 3.
72^2. rum.
75^1. Then.
81^1. stamching.
81^2. him praie, *perhaps.*
82^1. 2.
83^4. 40^{li}.
86^2. 3.
90^2. 2 or 3.
93^5. you maintaine.
96^1. owme.
And *for* & *throughout.*

B. The Lovers Quarrel, or, Cupids Triumph, being
   the Pleasant History of Fair Rosamond of
   Scotland : being daughter to the Lord Arundel, whose love was obtained by the valour
   of Tommy Pots, who conquered the Lord
   Phenix, and wounded him, and after obtained
   her to be his wife.

a. London, printed for F. Coles, T. Vere, J.
   Wright and J. Clarke. 1677.

   16⁸. high thee.
   30⁴. then pounds.
   48². since *is torn*.
   68². me tell.
   75⁴. or 3.
   And *for & throughout*.
   After 32 : The Second Part.
   After 56 : The Third Part.

b. 7¹. it is.   13⁴. quite *wanting*.
   15¹. my will.   15⁸. to *wanting*.
   16¹. see you.   16⁸. hye thee.
   17². give me.   18². merry be.
   18⁴. I will.   19¹. run.
   24². So that.   25⁸. three miles.
   26². thoult.   27⁸. this letter.
   27⁴. see or spy.   29². to stay.
   33¹. leaving.
   38⁴, 60⁴, 78⁴. ne'r.
   42². Christ Jesus.
   44¹. him you make.
   46². A serving-man of low degree.
   48⁴. to speak.
   53¹. will you.
   55⁴. Tom.
   58². prithee.
   58⁸. lady gay.
   59⁸. am *wanting*.
   60¹. stand thou on.
   61¹. the *wanting*.
   63². mayst forthwith.
   64⁸. there is.   66². takest.
   66⁸. than.   66⁴. pound.
   69¹. of courage.   69². he can.
   70¹. that horse.
   73¹. that *wanting*.

   73⁸. kept.   74⁴. in their.
   75⁴. then.   77². now that this.
   81⁴. would I.
   82⁴. kind of *wanting*.
   85⁴. I cannot.   87¹. thou say'st.
   89⁴. And her.   90¹. thoult.
   90². loose : 't is.
   91⁴. needs must.
   92². get behind him so.
   93⁸. I 'le.   93⁴. the one.
   94⁴. never try : *right ?*
   96⁴. *Ritson prints* slain is he.
   98⁸. estate.   101⁴. thou 'st have.
   103¹. for *wanting*.
   104¹. ladies in.
   104². ladies of.

   A copy in " Northern Penny Histories," Bodleian Library, Douce, p. p. 172, London, William Dicey, *which may date about* 1725, *is
   somewhat modernized and has not a few
   petty variations. Only the following readings seem worth the noting.*

   9². fast he did.
   15¹. my will.
   19⁸. Salisbury Castle.
   44¹. you make.
   60¹. stand on.   85¹. How for.
   94⁴. never try.   96⁴. have I.
   This copy has an additional stanza :

   106. The lady she did loyal prove,
            As many do in Scotland know,
        And how they spent their days in love
            The Second Book shall plainly show.

C. The two constant Lovers in Scotland, or, A
   pattern of true Love, expressed in this en-
   suing Dialogue between an Earls daughter
   in Scotland and a poor Serving-man ; she refusing to marry the Lord Fenix, which her
   father would force her to take, but clave to
   her first Love, Tomey o'th Pots.
   And *for &.*   29⁸. senninght.   47². self.
   After 38 : The Second Part.

110

THE KNIGHT AND SHEPHERD'S DAUGHTER

A. ' The Beautifull Shepherdesse of Arcadia.' **a.** Roxburghe Ballads, III, 160, 161. **b.** Roxburghe Ballads, II, 30, 31. 27 stanzas.

B. ' Shepherd's Dochter,' Kinloch MSS, V, 255. 33 stanzas.

C. ' Earl Richard,' Kinloch MSS, VII, 69. 30 stanzas.

D. Kinloch MSS, VII, 68, fragments. 16 stanzas.

E. ' Earl Richard, the Queen's Brother.' **a.** Buchan's Ballads of the North of Scotland, II, 81. **b.** Motherwell's MS., p. 459 ; Motherwell's Minstrelsy, p. 377. 60 stanzas.

F. ' Earl Lithgow.' **a.** Buchan's Ballads of the North

of Scotland, II, 91. 63 stanzas. **b.** Christie's Traditional Ballad Airs, I, 184. 22 stanzas.

G. ' Jo Janet,' Gibb MS., No 1. 34 stanzas.

H. ' The Shepherd's Daughter,' Kinloch MSS, V, 20 ; also, Kinloch MSS, VII, 61, and Kinloch's Scottish Ballads, p. 25. 19 stanzas.

I. Communicated by Dr Thomas Davidson, from his own recollection. 11 stanzas.

J. ' Earl Richard,' Dr J. Robertson's Journal of Excursions, No 7. 17 (?) stanzas.

K. ' The Knight and the Shepherd's Daughter,' Motherwell's MS., p. 226. 18 stanzas.

L. Motherwell's Note-Book, p. 1. 3 stanzas.

THE only English version of this ballad is a broadside, found in the Roxburghe Collection.* It was given from a black-letter copy, with changes and the omission of stanza 4, in the Reliques of Ancient English Poetry, 1765, III, 75. Hearne, in his preface to Guilielmi Neubrigensis Historia, I, lxx (cited by Percy), remarks that some impressions were adorned with the picture of a queen, meant, as he maintains, to be Elizabeth, and quotes the first stanza.† From this Percy infers that the ballad was popular in Elizabeth's time, a supposition probable enough in itself, and con-

firmed by the fifteenth stanza occurring (as Percy notes) in Fletcher's comedy of ' The Pilgrim,' 1621.‡

Motherwell, Minstrelsy, Introduction, p. lxvi, says that the ballad was current in Scotland in many shapes (1827).

The copy in Kinloch's Ancient Scottish Ballads, p. 13, is C, with the stanzas given here as D incorporated into it from another version.

Kinloch is fully justified in claiming for the Scottish ballad a decided superiority. The humorous artifices which the lady practises to maintain the character of a beggar's brat are,

---

* And Douce, says Mr Chappell. A Tewkesbury copy, not dated, is mentioned by Halliwell, Notes on Fugitive Tracts, etc., Percy Society, vol. xxix, p. 16, No 9.

 † There was a shepherd's daughter
  Came triping on the way,
  And there she met a courteous knight,
  Which caused her to stay.
  Sing trang dil do lee

 ‡ He called down his merry men all,
  By one, by two, by three ;

  William would fain have been the first,
   But now the last is he.
     Act IV, Sc. 2, Dyce, VIII, 66.

In Beaumont and Fletcher's ' Knight of the Burning Pestle,' we have the following stanza, which resembles **A** 23, but may equally well belong to ' The Douglas Tragedy :' see No 7, **B** 10, **C** 9, **D** 9 :

  He set her on a milk-white steed,
   And himself upon a grey ;
  He never turned his face again,
   But he bore her quite away.
     Act II, Sc. 8, Dyce, II, 172.

as he says, kept up with great spirit and fancy, and, as far as we know, are entirely of Scottish invention. It might perhaps be objected that in the course of tradition they have been exaggerated in later copies to a point threatening weariness.

The passage in which the knight rides off and is followed so closely by the maid, through river and all, A 6–8, B 5–10, etc., is found also in 'Child Waters,' A 11–16, B 4–11, etc., and suits both ballads perhaps equally well.

Parts of this ballad inevitably suggest a parallel with the tales belonging to the class of the 'Marriage of Sir Gawain.' * In the Wife of Bath's Tale, a lusty bachelor who has been out hawking meets a maid walking, and forces her to yield to his will. The offence is brought before King Arthur,† and the knight, as he is also called, is condemned to death. The alternative of marrying is so distasteful to him that he tries every means to avoid it. 'Take all my good,' he says to the woman, 'but let my body go.' But all for naught. Dame Ragnell makes a point of being wedded in high style ; so does our shepherd's daughter in E 37, 38, F 38, 39. In Gower, the knight takes the woman on his horse and rides away sighing ; and they also have a cauld and eerie ride in E 39. The bride becomes, if possible, more and more repulsive in the Gawain tales, and endeavors to make herself so in the ballad. As in the tales, so in the ballad, the bridegroom will not turn about and make much of her, C 29, E 56, G 30. The ugly woman turns out to be a king's daughter in Gower's tale, a most desirable wife in all the others ; and the shepherdess is a king's daughter in B, E, F, K, and at least an excellent match in other copies. The knight is nephew to a king or emperor in three of the tales, and the queen's brother or the king's in nearly all the ballads.‡ Even the Billy Blin in F 60–63,

G 31, 32, cf. D 15, 16, looks like a remnant of the fairy machinery of the Gawain tales.

The tragic ballad of 'Ebbe Galt,' Danske Viser, II, 47, No 63, has several features in common with ' The Knight and Shepherd's Daughter.' Ebbe Galt has been drinking heavily with the king's men. Riding home through a wood, he meets in an evil hour a farmer's pretty wife, and offers her presents to show him the way to the town. She undertakes to do so, though much afraid. They come to the farmer's house. Ebbe Galt begins to ban and beat, and in the end ravishes the woman, using extreme cruelty. She says, Now you have had your will of me, with little good to either of us, for God's sake tell me your name. § He declares himself to be Ebbe Galt. The farmer comes home and is told all. He comforts his wife and goes to make his plaint to the king. If any man in the court has done this, says the king, it shall cost him his life. When he learns that the man is his nephew, he would rather than half Denmark not have pronounced so harsh a doom. Ebbe Galt is summoned to answer for himself. He is not much better sober than drunk, though the ballad lays the fault on ale. He tells the farmer to produce his wife ; she will make no complaint. The woman gives her evidence. She had treated Ebbe Galt with all hospitality as her husband's guest. He had broken in the doors of the room where she was with her children, beaten five maids and killed three swains. Ebbe's father offers his horse and a thousand mark as ransom. The king says that he himself, if it lay in him, would have redeemed the youth with three thousand ; Ebbe Galt shall die. While they are taking him off, Ebbe is flippant : he would not mind losing his life had the woman been prettier.

There is a very favorite Scandinavian ballad, see 'Tærningspillet,' Grundtvig, IV, 402, No

---

* Already remarked by Motherwell, Minstrelsy, p. 378.

† A queen is arbiter in Gower and Chaucer ; so here in versions E, F, G, J.

‡ In K, a vulgar copy, the man is absurdly made a blacksmith's son, though a courtier. Similarly in an old stall copy of which the last stanza is cited by Buchan, II, 318 :

O when she came to her father's yetts,
    Where she did reckon kin,
She was the queen of fair Scotland,
    And he but a goldsmith's son.

§ This is a commonplace, as observed already, I, 446. It occurs also in ' Malfred og Sadelmand,' st. 8, Kristensen, I, 259, No. 99. Ebbe Galt is translated by Prior, II, 87.

238, in which a fair lady challenges a young horse-boy, or boatswain, to play tables with her, and after having won from him all he has, stakes herself against his shoes or the like. The youth now wins ; she makes him handsome offers, rising constantly in value, to let her off, but he will not. God pity me ! she says ; but he reveals to her that her case is not a bad one, for he is the best king's son in the world.‡

An imitation of the English ballad by Laplace, 'Lise et Mainfroi,' 1740, terminates more sentimentally. The shepherdess persists that she will have the hand which the king has awarded her, until she stands before the altar. She then declares that her sense of honor has been satisfied, and resigns a very advantageous match (for she is not a princess in disguise), with " Puisses-tu du moins quelquefois te souvenir de ta bergère ! " Mainfroi exclaims in a transport, Stay, deign to be my wife ! the king and all the court unite in the entreaty, and Lise yields. She certainly is entitled to a statuette in porcelain. See Charles Malo, Les Chansons d'Autrefois, pp. 124–128.

The copy in Percy's Reliques is translated by Bodmer, I, 88.

———•———

A

a. Roxburghe Ballads, III, 160, 161. **b.** The same, II, 30, 31.

1 THERE was a shepherd's daughter
    Came triping on the way,
And there she met a courteous knight,
    Which caused her to stay.
Sing trang dil do lee

2 ' Good morow to you, beautious maid,'
    These words pronounced he ;
'O I shall dye this day,' he said,
    ' If I have not my will of thee.'

3 ' The Lord forbid,' the maid reply'd,
    ' That such a thing should be,
That ever such a courteous yong knight
    Should dye for love of me.'

4 He took her by the middle so small,
    And laid her down on the plain,
And after he had had his will,
    He took her up again.

5 ' Now you have had your wil, good sir,
    And put my body thus to shame,
Even as you are a courteous knight,
    Tel me what is your name.'

6 ' Some men do call me Jack, sweet heart,
    And some do call me John,
But when I come to the king's [fair] court,
    They call me Sweet William.'

7 He set his foot in the stirrop,
    And away then did he ride ;
She tuckt her kirtle about her middle,
    And run close by his side.

8 But when she came to the broad water,
    She set her brest and swom,
And when she was got out again,
    She took her heels and run.

9 He never was the courteous knight
    To say, Fair maid, will you ride?
Nor she never was so loving a maid
    To say, Sir Knight, abide.

10 But when she came to the king's fair court,
    She knocked at the ring ;
So ready was the king himself
    To let this fair maid in.

11 'O Christ you save, my gracious leige,
    Your body Christ save and see !
You have got a knight within your court
    This day hath robbed me.

12 ' What hath he robbed thee of, fair maid ?
    Of purple or of pall ?

‡ Danske Viser, No 186, Grundtvig's **A**, is translated by Dr Prior, who notes the resemblance and the contrast to our ballad, III, 144.

Or hath he took thy gay gold ring,
  From off thy finger small?'

13 'He hath not robbed me, my liege,
  Of purple nor of pall;
  But he hath got my maidenhead,
  Which grieves me worst of all.'

14 'Now if he be a batchelor,
  His body I'le give to thee;
  But if he be a married man,
  High hanged shall he be.'

15 He called down his merry men all,
  By one, by two, and by three;
  Sweet William was us'd to be the first,
  But now the last comes hee.

16 He brought her down full forty pound,
  Ty'd up with[in] a glove:
  'Fair maid, I give the same to the,
  And seek another love.'

17 'O I'le have none of your gold,' she said,
  'Nor I'le have none of your fee;
  But I must have your fair body
  The king hath given me.'

18 Sweet William ran and fetcht her then
  Five hundred pound in gold,
  Saying, Fair maid, take this unto thee;
  Thy fault will never be told.

19 ''T is not your gold that shall me tempt,'
  These words then answered she,
  'But I must have your own body;
  So the king hath granted me.'

20 'Would I had drank the fair water
  When I did drink the wine,

That ever any shepherd's daughter
  Should be a fair lady of mine!

21 'Would I had drunk the puddle-water
  When I did drink the ale,
  That ever any shepherd's daughter
  Should have told me such a tale!'

22 'A shepheard's daughter as I was,
  You might have let me be;
  I'd never come to the king's fair court
  To have craved any love of thee.'

23 He set her on a milk-white steed,
  And himselfe upon a gray;
  He hung a bugle about his neck,
  And so they rode away.

24 But when they came unto the place
  Where marriage rites were done,
  She provd her self a duke's daughter,
  And he but a squire's son.

25 'Now you have married me, sir knight,
  Your pleasures may be free;
  If you make me lady of one good
    town,
  I'le make you lord of three.'

26 'Accursed be the gold,' he said,
  'If thou hadst not bin true,
  That should have parted thee from
    me,
  To have chang'd thee for a new.'

27 Their hearts being then so linked fast,
  And joyning hand in hand,
  He had both purse and person too,
  And all at his command.

———◆———

B

Kinloch MSS, V, 255, in the handwriting of Mr Kinloch.

1 THERE was a shepherd's dochter
  Kept sheep upon yon hill,
  And by cam a gay braw gentleman,
  And wad hae had his will.

2 He took her by the milk-white hand,
  And laid her on the ground,

And whan he got his will o her
  He lift her up again.

3 'O syne ye've got your will o me,
  Your will o me ye've taen,
  'T is all I ask o you, kind sir,
  Is to tell to me your name.'

4 'Sometimes they call me Jack,' he said,
  'Sometimes they call me John,

But whan I am in the king's court,
  My name is Wilfu Will.'

5 Then he loup on his milk-white steed,
  And straught away he rade,
  And she did kilt her petticoats,
  And after him she gaed.

6 He never was sae kind as say,
  O lassie, will ye ride?
  Nor ever had she the courage to say,
  O laddie, will ye bide!

7 Until they cam to a wan water,
  Which was called Clyde,
  And then he turned about his horse,
  Said, Lassie, will ye ride?

8 'I learned it in my father's hall,
  I learned it for my weel,
  That whan I come to deep water,
  I can swim as it were an eel.

9 'I learned it in my mother's bower,
  I learned it for my better,
  That whan I come to broad water,
  I can swim like ony otter.'

10 He plunged his steed into the ford,
  And straught way thro he rade,
  And she set in her lilly feet,
  And thro the water wade.

11 And whan she cam to the king's court,
  She tirled on the pin,
  And wha sae ready 's the king himsel
  To let the fair maid in?

12 'What is your will wi me, fair maid?
  What is your will wi me?'
  'There is a man into your court
  This day has robbed me.'

13 'O has he taen your gold,' he said,
  'Or has he taen your fee?
  Or has he stown your maidenhead,
  The flower of your bodye?'

14 'He has na taen my gold, kind sir,
  Nor as little has he taen my fee,
  But he has taen my maidenhead,
  The flower of my bodye.'

15 'O gif he be a married man,
  High hangit shall he be,
  But gif he be a bachelor,
  His body I 'll grant thee.'

16 'Sometimes they call him Jack,' she said,
  'Sometimes they call him John,
  But whan he 's in the king's court,
  His name is Sweet William.'

17 'There 's not a William in a' my court,
  Never a one but three,
  And one of them is the Queen's brother;
  I wad laugh gif it war he.'

18 The king called on his merry men,
  By thirty and by three;
  Sweet Willie, wha used to be foremost man,
  Was the hindmost a' but three.

19 O he cam cripple, and he cam blind,
  Cam twa-fald oer a tree:
  'O be he cripple, or be he blind,
  This very same man is he.'

20 'O whether will ye marry the bonny may,
  Or hang on the gallows-tree?'
  'O I will rather marry the bonny may,
  Afore that I do die.'

21 But he took out a purse of gold,
  Weel locked in a glove:
  'O tak ye that, my bonny may,
  And seek anither love.'

22 'O I will hae none o your gold,' she says,
  'Nor as little ony of your fee,
  But I will hae your ain body,
  The king has granted me.'

23 O he took out a purse of gold,
  A purse of gold and store;
  'O tak ye that, fair may,' he said,
  'Frae me ye 'll neer get mair.'

24 'O haud your tongue, young man,' she says,
  'And I pray you let me be;
  For I will hae your ain body,
  The king has granted me.'

25 He mounted her on a bonny bay horse,
  Himsel on the silver grey;

He drew his bonnet out oer his een,
    He whipt and rade away.

26 O whan they cam to yon nettle bush,
    The nettles they war spread :
'O an my mither war but here,' she says,
    'These nettles she wad sued.'

27 'O an I had drank the wan water
    Whan I did drink the wine,
That eer a shepherd's dochter
    Should hae been a love o mine !'

28 'O may be I 'm a shepherd's dochter,
    And may be I am nane ;
But you might hae ridden on your ways,
    And hae let me alane.'

29 O whan they cam unto yon mill,
    She heard the mill clap :

.   .   .   .   .
    .   .   .   .

30 'Clap on, clap on, thou bonny mill,
    Weel may thou, I say,
For mony a time thou 's filled my pock
    Wi baith oat-meal and grey.'

31 'O an I had drank the wan water
    Whan I did drink the wine,
That eer a shepherd's dochter
    Should hae been a love o mine !'

32 'O may be I 'm a shepherd's dochter,
    And may be I am nane ;
But you might hae ridden on your ways,
    And hae let me alane.

33 'But yet I think a fitter match
    Could scarcely gang thegither
Than the King of France's auld dochter
    And the Queen of Scotland's brither.'

C

Kinloch's MSS, VII, 69 ; apparently from the recitation of Mrs Charles of Torry, Aberdeen, born in Mearnshire.

1 THERE was a shepherd's dochter
    Kept sheep on yonder hill ;
Bye cam a knicht frae the High College,
    And he wad hae his will.

2 Whan he had got his wills o her,
    His will as he has taen :
'Wad ye be sae gude and kind
    As tell to me your name ?'

3 'Some ca's me Jock, some ca's me John,
    Some disna ken my name,
But whan I 'm into the king's court,
    Mitchcock is my name.'

4 'Mitchcock ! hey !' the lady did say,
    And spelt it oure again ;
'If that 's your name in the Latin tongue,
    Earl Richard is your name !'

5 O jumpt he upon his horse,
    And said he wad go ride ;
Kilted she her green claithing,
    And said she wad na bide.

6 The knicht rade on, the lady ran,
    A live-lang simmer's day,
Till they cam to a wan water
    Was calld the river Tay.

7 'Jump on behind, ye weill-faurd may,
    Or do ye chuse to ride ?'
'No, thank ye, sir,' the lady said,
    'I rather chuse to wade ;'
And afore that he was mid-water,
    She was at the ither side.

8 'Turn back, turn back, ye weill-faurd may,
    My heart will brak in three :'
'And sae did mine in yon bonny hill-side,
    Whan ye wad [na] lat me be.'

9 'Whare gat ye that gay claithing
    This day I see on thee ?'
'My mither was a gude milk-nurse,
    And a gude nourice was she ;
She nursd the Earl of Stockford's daughter,
    And gat aw this to me.'

10 Whan she cam to the king's court,
    She rappit wi a ring ;
Sae ready as the king himsel
    Was to let the lady in !

11 'There is a knicht into your court
    This day has robbed me : '
  'O has he taen your gowd,' he says,
    'Or has he taen your fee ? '

12 'He has na taen my gowd,' she says,
    'Nor yet has he my fee ;
  But he has taen my maiden-head,
    The flowr o my fair bodie.'

13 Then out bespak the queen hersel,
    Wha sat by the king's knee :
  There 's na a knicht in aw our court
    Wad hae dune that to thee,
  Unless it war my brither, Earl Richard,
    And forbid it it war he !

14 Wad ye ken your love,
    Amang a hunder men ?
  'I wad,' said the bonnie ladie,
    'Amang five hunder and ten.'

15 The king made aw his merry men pass,
    By ane, by twa, and three ;
  Earl Richard us'd to be the first man,
    But he was hinmost man that day.

16 He cam hauping on ane foot,
    And winking with ae ee ;
  But 'Ha ! ha ! ' said the bonnie ladie,
    'That same young man are ye.'

17 He 's taen her up to a hie towr-head
    And offerd her hunder punds in a glove :
  'Gin ye be a courteous maid,
    Ye 'll choice anither love.'

18 'What care I for your hunder pund ?
    Na mair than ye wad for mine ;
  What 's a hunder pund to me,
    To a marriage wi a king ! '

19 Whan the marriage it was oure,
    And ilk ane took them horse,
  'It never set a beggar's brat
    At nae knicht's back to be.'

20 The ladie met wi a beggar-wife,
    And gied her half o crown :
  'Tell aw your neebours, whan ye gang hame,
    That Earl Richard's your gude-son.'

21 'O hold your tongue, ye beggar's brat,
    My heart will brak in three ; '

'And sae did mine on yon bonny hill-side,
    Whan ye wad na let me be.'

22 Whan she cam to yon nettle-dyke,
    .   .   .   .   .
  'An my auld mither she was here,
    Sae weill as she wad ye pu.

23 'She wad boil ye weill, and butter ye weill,
    And sup till she war fu,
  And lay her head upon her dish-doup,
    And sleep like onie sow.'

24 Whan she cam to Earl Richard's house,
    The sheets war holland fine :
  'O haud awa thae linen sheets,
    And bring to me the linsey clouts
    I hae been best used in.'

25 ['Awa, awa wi your siller spoons,
    Haud them awa frae me ;
  It would set me better to feed my flocks
    Wi the brose-cap on my knee :
  Sae bring to me the gude ram's horn,
    The spoons I 've been used wi.']

26 'Hold your tongue, ye beggar's brat,
    My heart will brak in three ; '
  'And sae did mine on yon bonnie hill-
    side,
    Whan ye wadna lat me be.'

27 'I wish I had drank the well-water
    Whan first I drank the wine !
  Never a shepherd's dochter
    Wad hae been a love o mine.

28 'O I wish I 'd drank the well-water
    Whan first I drank the beer,
  That ever a shepherd's dochter
    Shoud hae been my only dear ! '

  *   *   *   *   *

29 'Ye 'll turn about, Earl Richard,
    And mak some mair o me ;
  An ye mak me lady o ae puir plow,
    I can mak ye laird o three.'

30 'If ye be the Earl of Stockford's dochter,
    As I 've taen some thouchts ye be,
  Aft hae I waited at your father's yett,
    But your face I coud never see.'

D

Kinloch's MSS, VII, 68; apparently from the recitation of Jenny Watson of Lanark, aged seventy-three. Only such portions of this version were preserved as differed considerably from **C**.

*   *   *   *

1 AND he was never sae discreet
    As bid her loup on and ride,
  And she was neer sae meanly bred
    As for to bid him bide.

2 And whan she cam to yon water,
    It was running like a flude:
  'I 've learned it in my mither's bouer,
    I 've learned it for my gude,
  That I can soum this wan water
    Like a fish in a flude.

3 'I 've learned it in my father's bouer,
    I 've learned it for my better,
  And I will soum this wan water
    As tho I was ane otter.'

*   *   *   *

4 ' Gude day, gude day, my liege the king,
    Gude day, gude day, to thee;'
  'Gude day,' quo he, 'my lady fair,
    What want ye wi me?'

*   *   *   *

5 'Gin he be a single man,
    His bodie I 'll gie thee;
  But gin he be a married man,
    I 'll hang him on a tree.'

*   *   *   *

6 He 's powd out a hundred punds,
    Weel lockit in a glove;

.   .   .   .

7 'I 'll hae nane o your gowd,' she said,
    ' Nor either o your fee;
  But I will hae your ain bodie
    The king has granted me.'

8 'O was ye gentle gotten, maid?
    Or was ye gentle born?
  Or hae ye onie gerss growing?
    Or hae ye onie corn?

9 'Or hae ye onie lands or rents,
    Lying at libertie?
  Or hae ye onie education,
    To dance alang wi me?'

10 'I was na gentle gotten, madam,
    Nor was I gentle born;
  Neither hae I gerss growing,
    Nor hae I onie corn.

11 'I have na onie lands or rents,
    Lying at libertie;
  Nor hae I onie education,
    To dance alang wi thee.'

12 He lap on ae milk-white steed,
    And she lap on anither,
  And then the twa rade out the way
    Like sister and like brither.

13 And whan she cam to Tyne's water,
    She willie did say,
  Fareweil, ye mills o Tyne's water,
    With thee I bid gude-day.

14 Fareweil, ye mills o Tyne's water,
    To you I bid gud-een,
  Whare monie a day I hae filld my pock,
    Baith at midnicht and at een.

*   *   *   *

15 Whan they cam to her father's yett,
    She tirled on the pin;
  And an auld belly-blind man was sitting
        there,
    As they war entering in.

16 ' The meetest marriage,' the belly-blind did
        cry,
    ' Atween the ane and the ither,
  Atween the Earl of Stockford's dochter
    And the Queen o England's brither.'

E

a. Buchan's Ballads of the North of Scotland, II, 81, from Mr Nicol of Strichen, as learned in his youth from old people. b. Motherwell's MS., p. 459, derived, no doubt, from Buchan.

1 EARL RICHARD, once upon a day,
  And all his valiant men so wight,
He did him down to Barnisdale,
  Where all the land is fair and light.

2 He was aware of a damosel —
  I wot fast on she did her bound —
With towers of gold upon her head,
  As fair a woman as could be found.

3 He said, Busk on you, fair ladye,
  The white flowers and the red;
For I would give my bonnie ship
  To get your maidenhead.

4 'I wish your bonnie ship rent and rive,
  And drown you in the sea;
For all this would not mend the miss
  That ye would do to me.'
'The miss is not so great, ladye;
  Soon mended it might be.

5 'I have four an twenty mills in Scotland,
  Stands on the water of Tay;
You 'll have them, and as much flour
  As they 'll grind in a day.'

6 'I wish your bonnie ship rent and rive,
  And drown you in the sea;
For all that would not mend the miss
  That ye would do to me.'
'The miss is not so great, ladye;
  Soon mended it will be.

7 'I have four an twenty milk-white cows,
  All calved in a day;
You 'll have them, and as much haind grass
  As they all on can gae.'

8 'I wish your bonnie ship rent and rive,
  And drown you in the sea;
For all that would not mend the miss
  That ye would do to me.'
'The miss is not so great, ladye;
  Soon mended it might be.

9 'I have four an twenty milk-white steeds,
  All foaled in one year;

You 'll have them, and as much red gold
  As all their backs can bear.'

10 She turned her right and round about,
   And she swore by the mold;
'I would not be your love,' said she,
   'For that church full of gold.'

11 He turned him right and round about,
   And he swore by the mess;
Says, Ladye, ye my love shall be,
   And gold ye shall have less.

12 She turned her right and round about,
   And she swore by the moon;
'I would not be your love,' says she,
   'For all the gold in Rome.'

13 He turned him right and round about,
   And he swore by the moon;
Says, Ladye, ye my love shall be,
   And gold ye shall have none.

14 He caught her by the milk-white hand,
   And by the grass-green sleeve,
And there has taken his will of her,
   Wholly without her leave.

15 The ladye frownd, and sadly blushd,
   And oh, but she thought shame!
Says, If you are a knight at all,
   You surely will tell me your name.

16 'In some places they call me Jack,
   In other some they call me John;
But when into the queen's court,
   O then Lithcock it is my name!'

17 'Lithcock! Lithcock!' the ladye said,
   And oft she spelt it ower again;
'Lithcock! it 's Latin,' the ladye said,
   'Richard 's the English of that name.'

18 The knight he rode, the ladye ran,
   A live-long summer's day,
Till they came to the wan water
   That all men do call Tay.

19 He set his horse head to the water,
   Just thro it for to ride,
And the ladye was as ready as him
   The waters for to wade.

20 For he had never been as kind-hearted
    As to bid the ladye ride,
And she had never been so low-hearted
    As for to bid him bide.

21 But deep into the wan water
    There stands a great big stone ;
He turned his wight horse head about,
    Said, Ladye fair, will ye loup on ?

22 She 's taken the wand was in her hand
    And struck it on the faem,
And before he got the middle-stream
    The ladye was on dry land :
' By help of God and our Lady,
    My help lyes not in your hand !

23 ' I learned it from my mother dear,
    Few are there that have learned better,
When I come to deep water,
    I can swim thro like ony otter.

24 ' I learned it from my mother dear,
    I find I learnd it for my weel,
When I come to a deep water,
    I can swim thro like ony eel.'

25 ' Turn back, turn back, you ladye fair,
    You know not what I see ;
There is a ladye in that castle
    That will burn you and me.'
' Betide me weel, betide me wae,
    That ladye I will see.'

26 She took a ring from her finger,
    And gave it the porter for his fee ;
Says, Take you that, my good porter,
    And bid the queen speak to me.

27 And when she came before the queen,
    There she fell low down on her knee ;
Says, There is a knight into your court
    This day has robbed me.

28 ' O has he robbed you of your gold,
    Or has he robbed you of your fee ? '
' He has not robbed me of my gold,
    He has not robbed me of my fee ;
He has robbed me of my maidenhead,
    The fairest flower of my bodie.'

29 ' There is no knight in all my court,
    That thus has robbed thee,

But you 'll have the truth of his right hand,
    Or else for your sake he 'll die :

30 ' Tho it were Earl Richard, my own brother,
    And, Oh, forbid that it be ! '
Then sighing said the ladye fair,
    I wot the same man is he.

31 The queen called on her merry men,
    Even fifty men and three ;
Earl Richard used to be the first man,
    But now the hindmost man was he.

32 He 's taken out one hundred pounds.
    And told it in his glove ;
Says, Take you that, my ladye fair,
    And seek another love.

33 ' Oh, no ! oh, no ! ' the ladye cried,
    ' That 's what shall never be ;
I 'll have the truth of your right hand,
    The queen it gave to me.'

34 [' I wish I 'd drunken your water, sister,
    When I did drink thus of your ale,
That for a carl's fair daughter
    It does me gar dree all this bale !]

35 ' I wish I had drunk of your water, sister,
    When I did drink your wine,
That for a carle's fair daughter
    It does gar me dree all this pine ! '

36 ' May be I am a carle's daughter,
    And may be never nane ;
When ye met me in the greenwood,
    Why did you not let me alane ? '

37 ' Will you wear the short clothes,
    Or will you wear the side ?
Or will you walk to your wedding,
    Or will you till it ride ? '

38 ' I will not wear the short clothes,
    But I will wear the side ;
I will not walk to my wedding,
    But I to it will ride.'

39 When he was set upon the horse,
    The lady him behin,
Then cauld and eerie were the words
    The twa had them between.

40 She said, Good e'en, ye nettles tall,
    Just there where ye grow at the dyke;
  If the auld carline my mother were here,
    Sae weel 's she would your pates pyke!

41 How she would stap you in her poke —
    I wot at that she wadna fail —
  And boil ye in her auld brass pan,
    And of ye make right good kail!

42 And she would meal you with millering,
    That she gathers at the mill,
  And make you thick as ony daigh:
    And when the pan was brimful,

43 Would mess you up in scuttle-dishes,
    Syne bid us sup till we were fou,
  Lay down her head upon a poke,
    Then sleep and snore like ony sow.

44 'Away, away, you bad woman!
    For all your vile words grieveth me;
  When you hide so little for yourself,
    I 'm sure ye 'll hide far less for me.

45 'I wish I had drunk your water, sister,
    When that I did drink of your wine,
  Since for a carle's fair daughter,
    It aye gars me dree all this pine.'

46 'May be I am a carle's daughter,
    And may be never nane;
  When ye met me in the good greenwood,
    Why did you not let me alane?

47 'Gude een, gude een, ye heather-berries,
    As ye 're growing on yon hill;
  If the auld carline and her bags were here,
    I wot she would get meat her fill.

48 'Late, late at night, I knit our pokes,
    With even four an twenty knots;
  And in the morn at breakfast time
    I 'll carry the keys of an earl's locks.

49 'Late, late at night, I knit our pokes,
    With even four an twenty strings;
  And if you look to my white fingers,
    They have as many gay gold rings.'

50 'Away, away, ye ill woman!
    So sore your vile words grieveth me;
  When you hide so little for yourself,
    I 'm sure ye 'll hide far less for me.

51 'But if you are a carle's daughter,
    As I take you to be,
  How did you get the gay cloathing
    In greenwood ye had on thee?'

52 'My mother, she 's a poor woman,
    She nursed earl's children three,
  And I got them from a foster-sister,
    For to beguile such sparks as thee.'

53 'But if you be a carle's daughter,
    As I believe you be,
  How did you learn the good Latin
    In greenwood ye spoke to me?'

54 'My mother, she 's a mean woman,
    She nursd earl's children three;
  I learnt it from their chaplain,
    To beguile such sparks as ye.'

55 When mass was sung, and bells were rung,
    And all men bound for bed,
  Then Earl Richard and this ladye
    In ae bed they were laid.

56 He turned his face unto the stock,
    And she her's to the stane,
  And cauld and dreary was the love
    That was these twa between.

57 Great mirth was in the kitchen,
    Likewise intill the ha,
  But in his bed lay Earl Richard,
    Wiping the tears awa.

58 He wept till he fell fast asleep,
    Then slept till light was come;
  Then he did hear the gentlemen
    That talked in the room:

59 Said, Saw ye ever a fitter match,
    Betwixt the ane and ither,
  The king of Scotland's fair dochter
    And the queen of England's brither?

60 'And is she the king o Scotland's fair dochter?
    This day, O weel is me!
  For seven times has my steed been saddled,
    To come to court with thee;
  And with this witty lady fair,
    How happy must I be!'

F

a. Buchan's Ballads of the North of Scotland, II, 91; from the recitation of an old person. b. Christie's Traditional Ballad Airs, I, 184.

1 EARL LITHGOW he 's a hunting gane,
　　Upon a summer's day,
　And he 's fa'en in with a weel-far'd maid,
　　Was gathering at the slaes.

2 He 's taen her by the milk-white hand,
　　And by the grass-green sleeve;
　He led her to the foot of a tree,
　　At her he spierd nae leave.

3 The lassie being well learned,
　　She turned her right around;
　Says, Will ye be as good, kind sir,
　　As tell to me your name?

4 'Whiles they call me Jack,' he says,
　　'And whiles they call me John;
　But when I 'm in the queen's high court,
　　Earl Litchcock is my name.'

5 The lassie being well learned,
　　She spelld it ower again;
　Says, Litchcock is a Latin word,
　　But Lithgow is your name.

6 The lassie being well learned,
　　She spelld it ower again;
　Says, Lithgow is a gentle word,
　　But Richard is your name.

7 She has kilted her green claithing
　　A little abeen her knee;
　The gentleman rode, and the lassie ran,
　　Till at the water o Dee.

8 When they were at the water o Dee,
　　And at the narrow side,
　He turned about his high horse head,
　　Says, Lassie, will ye ride?

9 'I learned it in my mother's bower,
　　I wish I had learned it better,
　When I came to. this wan water,
　　To swim like ony otter.

10 'I learned it in my mother's bower,
　　I wish I had learned it weel,
　That when I came to a wan water,
　　To swim like ony eel.'

11 She has kilted her green claithing
　　A little abeen her knee;
　The gentleman rode, the lassie swam,
　　Thro the water o Dee:
　Before he was at the middle o the water,
　　At the other side was she.

12 She sat there and drest hersell,
　　And sat upon a stone;
　There she sat to rest hersell,
　　And see how he 'd come on.

13 'How mony miles hae ye to ride?
　　How mony hae I to gang?'
　'I 've thirty miles to ride,' he says,
　　'And ye 've as mony to gang.'

14 'If ye 've thirty miles to ride,' she says,
　　'And I 've as mony to gae,
　Ye 'll get leave to gang yoursell;
　　It will never be gane by me.'

15 She 's gane to the queen's high court,
　　And knocked at the pin;
　Who was sae ready as the proud porter,
　　To let this lady in!

16 She 's put her hand in her pocket,
　　And gien him guineas three:
　'Ye will gang to the queen hersell,
　　And tell her this frae me.

17 'There is a lady at your yetts
　　Can neither card nor spin;
　But she can sit in a lady's bower,
　　And lay gold on a seam.'

18 He 's gane ben thro ae lang room,
　　And he 's gane ben thro twa,
　Till he came to a lang, lang trance,
　　And then came to the ha.

19 When he came before the queen,
　　Sat low down on his knee:
　'Win up, win up, my proud porter,
　　What makes this courtesie?'

20 'There is a lady at your yetts
　　Can neither card nor spin;
　But she can sit in a lady's bower,
　　And lay gold on a seam.'

21 'If there is a lady at my yetts
　　That cannot card nor spin,

Ye 'll open my yetts baith wide and braid,
And let this lady in.'

22 Now she has gane ben thro ae room,
And she 's gane ben thro twa,
And she gaed ben a lang, lang trance,
Till she came to the ha.

23 When she came before the queen,
Sat low down on her knee :
' Win up, win up, my fair woman,
What makes such courtesie ? '

24 ' My errand it 's to thee, O queen,
My errand it 's to thee ;
There is a man within your courts
This day has robbed me.'

25 ' O has he taen your purse, your purse,
Or taen your penny-fee ?
Or has he taen your maidenhead,
The flower of your bodie ? '

26 ' He hasna taen my purse, my purse,
Nor yet my penny-fee,
But he has taen my maidenhead,
The flower of my bodi '

27 ' It is if he be a batchelor,
Your husband he shall be ;
But if he be a married man,
High hanged he shall be.

28 ' Except it be my brother, Litchcock,
I hinna will it be he ; '
Sighd and said that gay lady,
That very man is he.

29 She 's calld on her merry men a',
By ane, by twa, by three ;
Earl Litchcock used to be the first,
But the hindmost man was he.

30 He came cripple on the back,
Stane blind upon an ee ;
And sighd and said Earl Richard,
I doubt this calls for me.

31 He 's laid down a brand, a brand,
And next laid down a ring ;
It 's thrice she minted to the brand,
But she 's taen up the ring :
There 's not a knight in a' the court,
But calld her a wise woman.

32 He 's taen out a purse of gold,
And tauld it on a stane ;
Says, Take ye that, my fair woman,
And ye 'll frae me be gane.

33 ' I will hae nane o your purse[s] o gold,
That ye tell on a stane ;
But I will hae yoursell,' she says,
' Another I 'll hae nane.'

34 He has taen out another purse,
And tauld it in a glove ;
Says, Take ye that, my fair woman,
And choice another love.

35 ' I 'll hae nane o your purses o gold,
That ye tell in a glove ;
But I will hae yoursell,' she says,
' I 'll hae nae ither love.'

36 But he 's taen out another purse,
And tauld it on his knee ;
Said, Take ye that, ye fair woman,
Ye 'll get nae mair frae me.

37 ' I 'll hae nane o your purses o gold,
That ye tell on your knee ;
But I will hae yoursell,' she says,
' The queen has granted it me.'

38 ' O will ye hae the short claithing,
Or will ye hae the side ?
Or will ye gang to your wedding,
Or will ye to it ride ? '

39 ' I winna hae the short claithing,
But I will hae the side ;
I winna gang to my wedding,
But to it I will ride.'

40 The first town that they came till
They made the mass be sung,
And the next town that they came till
They made the bells be rung.

41 And the next town that they came till
He bought her gay claithing,
And the next town that they came till
They held a fair wedding.

42 When they came to Mary-kirk,
The nettles grew on the dyke :
' If my auld mither, the carlin, were here,
Sae well 's she would you pyke.

43 'Sae well 's she would you pyke,' she says,
    ' She woud you pyke and pou,
    And wi the dust lyes in the mill
    Sae woud she mingle you.

44 ' She 'd take a speen intill her hand,
    And sup ere she be fou,
    Syne lay her head upon a sod,
    And snore like ony sow.'

45 When she came to yon mill-dams,
    Says, Weel may ye clap ;
    I wyte my minnie neer gaed by you
    Wanting mony a lick.

46 He 's drawn his hat out ower his face,
    Muckle shame thought he ;
    She 's driven her cap out ower her locks,
    And a light laugh gae she.

47 When they were wedded, and well bedded,
    And hame at dinner set,
    Then out it spake our bride hersell,
    And she spake never blate.

48 Put far awa your china plates,
    Put them far awa frae me,
    And bring to me my humble gockies,
    That I was best used wi.

49 Put far awa your siller speens,
    Had them far awa frae me,
    And bring to me my horn cutties,
    That I was best used wi.

50 When they were dined and well served,
    And to their dancing set,
    Out it spake our bride again,
    For she spake never blate.

51 If the auld carlin, my mither, were here,
    As I trust she will be,
    She 'll fear the dancing frae us a',
    And gar her meal-bags flee.

52 When bells were rung, and mass was sung,
    And a' men bound for rest,
    Earl Richard and the beggar's daughter
    In ae chamber were placed.

53 ' Had far awa your fine claithing,
    Had them far awa frae me,
    And bring to me my fleachy clouts,
    That I was best used wi.

54 ' Had far awa your holland sheets,
    Had them far awa frae me,
    And bring to me my canvas clouts,
    That I was best used wi.

55 ' Lay a pock o meal beneath my head,
    Another aneath my feet,
    A pock o seeds beneath my knees,
    And soundly will I sleep.'

56 ' Had far awa, ye carlin's get,
    Had far awa frae me ;
    It disna set a carlin's get
    My bed-fellow to be.'

57 ' It 's may be I 'm a carlin's get,
    And may be I am nane ;
    But when ye got me in good greenwood,
    How letna you me alane ? '

58 ' It is if you be a carlin's get,
    As I trust well ye be,
    Where got ye all the gay claithing
    You brought to greenwood with thee ? '

59 ' My mother was an auld nourice,
    She nursed bairns three ;
    And whiles she got, and whiles she
        staw,
    And she kept them a' for me ;
    And I put them on in good greenwood,
    To beguile fause squires like thee.'

60 It 's out then spake the Billy-Blin,
    Says, I speak nane out of time ;
    If ye make her lady o nine cities,
    She 'll make you lord o ten.

61 Out it spake the Billy-Blin,
    Says, The one may serve the other ;
    The King of Gosford's ae daughter,
    And the Queen of Scotland's brother.

62 ' Wae but worth you, Billy-Blin,
    An ill death may ye die !
    My bed-fellow he 'd been for seven years
    Or he 'd kend sae muckle frae me.'

63 ' Fair fa ye, ye Billy-Blin,
    And well may ye aye be !
    In my stable is the ninth horse I 've killd,
    Seeking this fair ladie :
    Now we 're married, and now we 're bedded,
    And in each other's arms shall lie.'

G

Gibb MS., No 1. From recitation; traced to Mrs E. Lindsay, about 1800.

1 Jo JANET has to the greenwood gane,
   Wi a' her maidens free,

.   .   .   .   .

.   .   .   .   .

*   *   *   *   *

2 'Some ca me Jack, some ca me John,
   Some ca me Jing-ga-lee,
But when I am in the queen's court
   Earl Hitchcock they ca me.'

3 'Hitchcock, Hitchcock,' Jo Janet she said,
   An spelled it ower agane,
'Hitchcock it's a Latin word;
   Earl Richard is your name.'

4 But when he saw she was book-learned,
   Fast to his horse hied he;
But she kilted up her gay claithing,
   An fast, fast followed she.

5 Aye he rade, an aye she ran,
   The live-lang simmer's day,
Till they came to the wan water,
   An a' men call it Tay.

6 She has tane the narrow fuird,
   An he has tane the wide,
An ere he was in the middle-water,
   Jo Janet was at the ither side.

7 .   .   .   .   .

.   .   .   .   -

   As swift as eel or otter.

8 An when she cam to the queen's court
   She tirled at the pin,
An wha sae ready as the queen hersel
   To let Jo Janet in!

9 .   .   .   .   .

.   .   .   .   .

'There is a knicht into your court
   This day has robbed me.'

10 'Has he robbed you o your gold, fair may,
   Or robbed you o your fee?

Or robbed you o your maidenhead,
   The flower o your bodie?'

11 'He has nae robbed me o my gold,' she said,
   'Nor o my weel won fee,
But he has robbed me o my maidenhead,
   The flower o my bodie.'

12 'It's if he be a married knight,
   It's hanged he shall be;
But if he be a single knight,
   It's married ye sall be.

13 'There's but three knichts into my court
   This day hae been frae me,
An ane is Earl Richard, my brither,
   An I hope it is na he:'
Then sichin said Jo Janet,
   The very same man is he.

14 The queen has called on her merry men
   By thirty and by three;
He wont to be the foremost man,
   But hinmost in cam he.

15 'Is this your tricks abroad, Richard,
   Is this your tricks abroad,
Wheneer ye meet a bonny may
   To lay her on the road?'

*   *   *   *

16 But he took out a purse o gold,

.   .   .   .   .

Says, Tak you that, my bonny may,
   An seek nae mair o me.

17 'I winna hae your gold,' she said,
   'I winna hae your fee;
I'll hae the troth o your right hand
   The queen has promised me.'

*   *   *   *   *

18 As they rade bye yon bonny mill-town
   Sae fair's the nettles grew;
Quoth she, If my auld mither were here,
   Sae finely's she wad you pu.

19 She wad you nip, she wad you clip,
   Sae finely's she wad you pu,
An pit you on in a wee, wee pat,
   An sup till she were fu,

Syne rowe her heid in her gown-tail,
   An sleep like ony soo.

20 He drew his hat down ower his broos,
   An a doon look gae he,
But she threw her locks out ower her cocks,
   An nae ways dung was she.

21 'It 's if ye be a beggar's brat,
   As I dout na but ye be,
It 's where gat ye the gay claithing
   That hings down to your knee?'

22 'My mither was nurse to Earl Marshall's
     dother,
   An a fine lady is she,
An aye when she gets new claithing
   She casts the auld to me :'
An sichin said Earl Richard,
   My ain true-love is she !

23 But if you be a beggar's brat,
   As I doutna but ye be,
Where got ye the Latin words
   Ye said in greenwood to me ?

24 'My mither was a bad woman,
   She served sic men as thee,
An a' the gear at ever she got
   She waired it a' on me,
An learned me weel the Latin tongue,
   To beguile sic sparks as thee.'

25 'Awa, awa, ye ill woman,
   An ill death mat ye dee!
  .   .   .   .
     .   .   .

26 When they were a' at supper set,
   An siller spoons gaen roun,
It 's, 'Haud awa yer siller spoons,
   Haud them far awa frae me,

An bring to me a guid ramshorn,
   The thing I 'm best used wi.'

27 An when they were at supper set,
   An the ale-caup gaen about,
She took it in her arms twa,
   An sae clean 's she lickit it oot.

28 He drew his hat doun ower his broos,
   An a doun look gae he,
But she threw her locks out ower her cocks,
   An nae ways dung was she.

29 When mass was sung, and bells were rung,
   An a' men boun to bed,
Earl Richard an Jo Janet
   In ae bed they were laid.

30 He turned his face unto the stock,
   An sair, sair did he weep ;
She turned her face unto the wa,
   An sound she fell asleep.

31 .   .   .   .   .
  .   .   .   .
The Billie Blin stood up at their bed-feet.

32 Said, Saw ye ever a fitter match
   Atween the tane and the tither,
The Earl Marshall['s] ae dother
   An the Queen o Scotland's brither ?

33 'Wae be to you for an ill woman,
   An ill death mat ye dee !
For mony 's the mare and mare's foal
   I 've bursten seekin thee.'

34 .   .   .   a cup o wine,
   Quoth, Here 's to thee and me !
If ye mak me lady o ae puir pleugh,
   I 'll mak ye lord o three.

H

Kinloch's MSS, V, 20, in the handwriting of Mr James
Beattie, 1820, and from the recitation of one of the Miss
Beatties, his aunts, native in The Mearns : also Kinloch MS.,
VII, 61, and Kinloch's Scottish Ballads, p. 25.

1 THERE was a shepherd's daughter,
   Kept sheep on yonder hill ;

There came a knight o courage bright,
   And he wad have his will.   Diddle, &c.

2 He 's taen her by the milk-white hand,
   Gien her a gown o green ;
'O take you that, fair may,' he says,
   'There 's nae mair o me to be seen.'

3 'Since ye have taen your wills o me,
    Your wills o me you 've taen,
Since ye have taen your wills o me,
    Pray tell to me your name.'

4 'O some they call me Jack, lady,
    And others call me John ;
But when I 'm in the king's court,
    Sweet William is my name.'

5 She 's kilted up her green clothing
    A little below her knee,
And she is to the king's court,
    As fast as she could gae.

6 And when she came unto the king,
    She knelt low on her knee :
' There is a man into your court
    This day has robbed me.'

7 ' Has he robbd you of your gold,' he says,
    'Or of your white monie ?
Or robbd you of the flowery branch,
    The flower of your bodie ?'

8 'He has not robbd me of my gold,' she
        says,
    ' Nor of my white monie,
But he 's robbd me of the flowery branch,
    The flower of my bodie.'

9 'O if he be a bond-man,
    High hanged shall he be ;
But if he be a free man,
    He'se well provide for thee.'

10 The king 's called on his nobles all,
    By thirty and by three ;
Sweet William should have been the foremost
        man,
    But the hindmost man was he.

11 ' Do you not mind yon shepherd's daughter,
    You met on yonder hill ?

When a' her flocks were feeding round,
    Of her you took your will.'

12 And he 's taen out a purse o gold,
    And tied up in a glove ;
' Take you that, fair may,' he says,
    ' And choice for you a love.'

13 O he 's taen out three hundred pounds,
    Tied up in a purse ;
' See, take you that, fair may,' he says,
    ' And that will pay the nurse.'

14 ' I 'll neither have your gold,' she says,
    ' Nor yet your white monie,
But I will have the king's grant,
    That he has granted me.'

15 Then he 's taen her on a milk-white steed,
    Himsell upon another,
And to his castle they have rode,
    Like sister and like brother.

16 O ilka nettle that they came to,
    ' O well mote you grow !
For mony a day 's my minny and me
    Pilkit at your pow.'

17 O ilka mill that they came to,
    ' O well mote you clack !
For monie a day 's my minnie and me
    Buckled up our lap.'

*   *   *   *   *

18 ' You 're the king of England's ae brother,
    I trust well that you be ;
I 'm the Earl of Stampford's ae daughter,
    And he has nae mair but me.'

19 O saw you eer such a near marriage,
    Between the one and the other,
The Earl of Stampford's ae daughter,
    And the King of England's brother !

I

Communicated by Dr Thomas Davidson, from his own recollection; Aberdeenshire.

1 THERE was a shepherd's daughter,
    Kept flocks on yonder hill,
    And by there cam a courteous knight,
    Wud fain and hae his will.

*   *   *   *

2 'Some do ca me Jock,' he said,
    'And some do ca me John,
    But when I do ride i the king's high court,
    Gulelmus is my name.'

*   *   *   *

3 And when she came to the kinges court
    She tirled at the pin,
    And wha was there but the king himsel,
    To lat this fair maid in!

4 'Now Christ you save, my lord,' she said,
    'Now Christ you save and see;
    There is a knicht into your court
    This day has robbed me.

5 'He's na robbed me o my silken purse,
    Nor o my white money,
    But he's robbed me o my maidenheid,
    The flower o my bodie.'

6 'O gin he be a single man,
    Weel married sall ye be,
    But an he be a married man,
    He's hang upon a tree.'

7 Then he called up his merry men a',
    By one, by two, and by three,
    And William should a been the first,
    But the hindmost man was he.

8 And he cam hirplin on a stick,
    And blin upon an ee,
    But sighand said that gay ladie,
    That same man robbed me.

*   *   *

9 'Gin I had drunk the wan water,
    When I did drink the wine,
    A cairdman's daughter
      Should never be a true-love o mine.'

10 'Maybe I'm a cairdman's daughter,
    And maybe I am nane;
    But when ye did come to good green wood,
    Ye sud hae latten me alane.'

11 She set upon a milk-white steed,
    An himsel on a dapple grey,
    An she had as much lan in fair Scotlan
    'S ye cud ride in a lang simmer's day.

———•———

J

Dr Joseph Robertson's Journal of Excursions, No 7. Taken down from a man in the parish of Leochel, Aberdeenshire, February 12, 1829.

*   *   *   *   *

1 'SOME ca'ss me James, some ca'as me John,
    I carena what they ca me,
    But when I [am] at hame in my ain country,
    It's Lispcock that they ca me.'

2 The lassie being well beuk-learned,
    She spelled it ower again;
    Says, Lispcock in a Latin beuk
    Spells Erl Richard in plain.

3 .   .   .   .   .
    The lassie kilted up her green claithing,
    And fast, fast followed on.

4 Till they cam till a wide water,
      .   .   .   .
    He's turned his hie horse head about,
    Says, Lassie will ye ride?

5 'I learned it in my mother's bower,
    I wish I'd learned it better,
    Whenever I cam to any wide water,
    To soum like ony otter.'

6 The laird he chused the ford to ride,
    The ladie the pot to swim,

And or the laird was half water,
    The ladie was on dry lan.

7 O he rade on to yon hie castell,
    He rade it richt and roun about;
  The laird gaed in at ae back-door,
    But the ladie beet to knock.

8 O out it cam the proud porter,
    Wi his hat into his han,

.   .   .   .   .

.   .   .   .   .

9 She 's pitten her hand in her pocket,
    Pulld out guineas three,
  And that she 's given to the proud porter,
    To cause her to get entrance there.

10 The proud porter ran up the stair,
    O fifteen steps he made but three:
  ' The prettiest lady stands at yer yetts
    That ever my een did see.'

11 .   .   .   .   .

.   .   .   .   .

  ' Goe doun, goe doun, you proud porter,
    Cause her to cum up to me.'

12 When she gaed in before the queen,
    She fell low down on her knee:

' There is a man into your courts
    This day has robbed me.'

13 ' Has he robbed you o your fine clothing,
    Or o your white monie?
  Or taen frae you your maidenhead,
    The flower o your bodie?'

14 ' He hasna robbed me o my fine clothing,
    Nor o my white monie,
  But he 's taen frae me my maidenhead,
    The flower o my bodie.'

15 ' O gin he be a married man,
    High hanged sall he be;
  And gin he be a batchelere,
    Well wedded shall ye be.'

16 O she has called in her merry young men,
    By thirties and by threes;
  Earl Richard should hae been the foremost
    man,
    But the hindmost man was he.

17 He cam limpin on a staff,
    And blinkin on an ee,
  And sichand says that gay ladie,
    That samen man is he.

*   *   *   *

K

Motherwell's MS., p. 226. From the recitation of Widow McCormick, Westbrae, Paisley, 1825; learned of an old woman in Dumbarton, thirty or forty years before.

1 THERE was a shepherd's daughter,
    Kept sheep on yonder hill;
  O by comes a courtier,
    And fain wud hae his will.
      We 'll go no more a roving,
        A roving in the night,
      We 'll go no more a roving,
        Let the moon shine neer so bright.
      O we 'll go [no] more a roving.

2 He took her by the middle so small,
    And by the grass-green sleeve;
  He bended her body unto the ground,
    And of her parents he askd no leave.

3 ' Now since you 've got your will o me,
    And brought my fair bodie to shame,
  All the request I ask of you is,
    Pray tell me what 's your name.'

4 ' O some do call me Jack,' he says,
    ' And some do call me John,
  But when I am in the king's court,
    My name is Sweet William.'

5 She took her petticoats by the band,
    Her mantle oer her arm,
  And she 's awa to the king's court,
    As fast as she could run.

6 When she came to the king's court,
    She tinkled at the ring;
  Who was so ready as the king himsel
    To let this fair maid in!

7   And when she came before the king,
        She kneeled low by his knee ;
    'What 's this ? what 's this, fair maid,' he
        says,
        'What 's this you ask of me ? '

8   .   .   .   .   .

    'There is a knight into your court
        This day has robbed me.'

9   'If he robbed you of your gold,' he said,
        'It 's hanged he must be ;
    If he 's robbed you of your maidenhead,
        His body I grant to thee.'

10 'He 's not robbed me of my gold,' she said,
        'Nor of my white money,
    But he 's robbed me of my maidenhead,
        The flower of my bodie.'

11 He 's called down his merry men all,
        By one, by two, by three ;
    John used to be the foremost man,
        But the hindmost man was he.

12 He took a long purse of gold
        And wrapped it in a glove :
    'Here 's to thee, my dearest dear,
        Go seek some other love.'

13 'I 'll have none of your gold,' she says,
        'Nor any of your white money,
    But I 'll just have your own bodie
        The king has granted to me.'

14 'I wish I was drinking the well-water
        When I drank of the ale,
    Before a shepherd's daughter
        Would tell me such a tale.'

15 He got her on a milk-white steed,
        Himself upon a grey,
    Then on a day   .   .   .
        This couple rode away.

16 It 's when they were coming by the nettle-
        bush,
    She said, So well may you grow !
    For many a day my mammy and me
        Hae pickled at your pow.

17 When they cam by the mill-door, she said,
        So well may you clatter !
    For many a day my mammy and me
        Pickled at your happer.

18 When they came to the king's court,
        They reckoned up their kin ;
    She was a king's one dochter,
        And he but a blacksmith's son.

L

Motherwell's Note-Book, p. 1, recited by Miss Brown, of
Glasgow, after a blind aunt.

*   *   *   *   *

1   'I LEARNED it in my father's bower,
        And I learned it for the better,
    That every water I coudna wade,
        I swam it like an otter.
        With my low silver ee.

2   'I learned it in my father's bower,
        And I learned it for my weel,
    That every water I coudna wade,
        I swam it like an eel.'

*   *   *   *

3   And he cam hirpling on a stick,
        And leaning on a tree :
    'Be he cripple, or be he blind,
        The same man is he.'

A. a. The beautifull Shepherdesse of Arcadia.
       A new pastorell Song of a courteous young
       Knight and a supposed Shepheard's Daugh-
       ter. To a gallant tune, called the Shep-
       heards Delight. . . . London, Printed for

William Gilbertson. *Gilbertson published*
1640–63: *Chappell. Dated* 1655 *in the
Museum Catalogue.*
4, 6. *Burden* Trang dang.   7³. abeut.
10¹. cour.   12⁴. fingets.

18⁴. faults. 24². rights. 27¹. *Perhaps* to linked. *Some trivial errors of the press have been corrected.*

b. The Beautiful Shepherdess of Arcadia : A new Pastoral Song of a courteous young Knight and a supposed Shepherd's Daughter of Arcadia, in Peloponnesus. To the Tune of The Shepherd's Daughter, &c. London : Printed for A. M., W. O., and T. Thackeray, at the sign of the Angel in Duck [Lane]. *Dated* 1680 ? *in the Catalogue.*

3⁸. yong *wanting.* 4¹. about the middle:

4². down *wanting.* 4⁸. had got.

5¹. kind sir. 5². thus *wanting.*

6¹. men *wanting.* 6⁸. fair court.

7¹. into the. 7². he did. 7⁸. her girdle.

9⁸. was never. 10¹. But *wanting.*

11¹. save you. 11⁸. got *wanting.*

12¹. of, sweet-heart.

12⁴. finger. 13². or of.

13⁴. most of. 15⁸. was *wanting.* 16². within.

18⁸. to thee. 18⁴. fault. 19. not thy.

22. *wanting, in my transcript.*

24². rites was. 25². will be. 25⁴. make thee.

26⁸. should a. 27¹. being linked so.

27². joyned.

B. 23⁸. tak he.

C. *C and D were derived from the recitation of Jenny Watson of Lanark and Mrs Charles of Torry, but which from which we are not distinctly told. An incidental expression of Kinloch's, MSS, VII, 59, may warrant the assigning of C to Mrs Charles. C is written on the right hand of the MS. and D on the left, except that the last two stanzas of D are written on the right, and a few readings of D are written above those of C. (The ink of D is blacker.)*

6. *omitted by* Kinloch *in printing.*

7⁴. wade *altered to* wyde, *according to the pronunciation.*

8⁴, 21⁴. na *is wanting.*

14¹. Kinloch *prints* your fause love : *in MS.* [fause].

25. *inserted at p. 23 of* Kinloch's *interleaved copy of his* Ancient Scottish Ballads.

D 1⁸. frae the king's court.

3⁴. Earl Richard is my name. 11¹. anie.

14⁴. *Altered to* At midday and.

16⁸. cried the.

17¹. He powd out a hundred punds.

17². Weel lockit in a glove.

27¹. Hoch ! had I drank the wan water.

27⁸. That . . . a mill-capon.

E. a. 6⁴. for me : *see* 4⁴, 8⁴. 16⁴. Oh.

34. *wanting, supplied from the MS.*

44⁸,⁴, 50⁸,⁴. *unless* hide *is for* heed, *read* heed, *as in* b.

b. 1¹. on a. 13⁸. ye shall be. 18⁴. does.

22¹. wand she had in. 22⁴. on the.

22⁶. help does not lye. 23¹. *omits* it.

23². is there that has. 23⁸. to a.

24⁸. came. 25⁶. will I. 26². *omits* it.

30⁴. samen. 31¹. men all. 31⁴. *omits* man.

34. *omitted in* a. 43². we be.

44⁸,⁴. When you heed so little of yourself,
I 'm sure ye 'll heed far less nor me.

47⁸,⁴. If the auld carle and his bags were here,
I wot he would get meat his fill.

48¹, 49¹. last night.

50. Away, away, you evil woman,
How sore your vile words grieve me !
When you heed so little on yourself,
I know you will heed less on me.

52⁴. as ye. 53¹. you are.

55¹. was rung. 55⁸. the ladye.

55⁴. In one. 56¹. face to. 56⁴. thir twa.

57¹. Great was the mirth. 57². into.

57⁴. And wiping. 60⁴. at thee.

The variations in b *are probably* Motherwell's *improvements. He does not adopt all of them in printing, but makes still other slight changes.*

F. b. "An epitome (*eleven eight-line stanzas*) of Buchan's version, with some slight alterations from the way the editor has heard the ballad sung."

15¹. The lady to the queen's court gaed.

15⁸. And ready was.

16². And gae him gowd sae free.

19². He lout doun. 23². She lout doun.

30². And blind.

33¹, 37¹. I will not hae your purse o gowd.

33⁴. And other. 39². Nor will I hae.

41⁸. And when they came to St. Mary's kirk.

62⁸. My husband.

I. 1². *Var.* Kept hogs. 8⁸. sigh and.

J. 3⁸. in, *perhaps, for* on.

3, 4 ; 8, 9 ; 11, 12. *Written without division in the MS.*

17⁸. sich &.

K. 4¹. Oh.

17⁴. Hae *added later ;* pickled *altered from* pircled.

111

CROW AND PIE

MS. Rawlinson, C. 813, fol. 27 b, beginning of the sixteenth century.   Halliwell's Nugæ Poeticæ, p. 42.

———•———

THIS is not a purely popular ballad, but rather of that kind which, for convenience, may be called the minstrel-ballad. It has, however, popular features, and markedly in stanzas 13, 14; for which see pp. 444, 446 of the first volume, and the ballad preceding this, A 5, 6, B 3, 4, etc. ; also Buchan's Ballads of the North of Scotland, II 144, ' The Baron o Leys.'

———•———

1 THROUGHE a forest as I can ryde,
    To take my sporte yn an mornyng,
  I cast my eye on euery syde,
    I was ware of a bryde syngynge.

2 I sawe a faire mayde come rydyng ;
    I speke to hur of loue, I trowe ;
  She answered me all yn scornyng,
    And sayd, The crowe shall byte yow.

3 ' I pray yow, damesell, scorne me nott ;
    To wyn your loue ytt ys my wyll ;
  For your loue I haue dere bought,
    And I wyll take good hede thertyll.'

4 ' Nay, for God, ser, that I nyll ;
    I tell the, Jenken, as I trowe,
  Thow shalt nott fynde me suche a gyll ;
    Therfore the crowe shall byte yow.'

5 He toke then owt a good golde ryng,
    A purse of velweytt, that was soo fyne :
  ' Haue ye thys, my dere swetyng,
    With that ye wylbe lemman myn.'

6 ' Be Cryst, I dare nott, for my dame,
    To dele with hym þat I doo nott knowe ;
  For soo I myght dyspyse my name ;
    Therfore the crow shall byte yow.'

7 He toke hur abowte the mydell small,
    That was soo faire of hyde and hewe ;

He kyssed hur cheke as whyte as whall,
    And prayed hur þat she wolde vpon hym
      rewe.

8 She scornyd hym, and callyd hym Hew ;
    His loue was as a paynted blowe :
  ' To-day me, to-morowe a newe ;
    Therfore the crow shall byte yow.'

9 He toke hur abowte the mydell small,
    And layd hur downe vpon the grene ;
  Twys or thrys he served hur soo withall,
    He wolde nott stynt yet, as I wene.

10 ' But sythe ye haue i-lyen me bye,
    Ye wyll wedde me now, as I trowe :'
  ' I wyll be aduysed, Gyll,' sayd he,
    ' For now the pye hathe peckyd yow.'

11 ' But sythe ye haue i-leyn me by,
    And brought my body vnto shame,
  Some of your good ye wyll part with me,
    Or elles, be Cryst, ye be to blame.'

12 ' I wylbe aduysed,' he sayde ;
    ' þe wynde ys wast þat thow doyst
      blowe ;
  I haue a-noder þat most be payde ;
    Therfore the pye hathe pecked yow.'

13 ' Now sythe ye haue i-leyn me bye,
    A lyttle thyng ye wyll tell ;

In case that I with chylde be,
>   What ys your name? Wher doo ye
>   dwell?'

14 'At Yorke, at London, at Clerkenwell,
>   At Leycester, Cambryge, at myrye Brys-
>   towe;
>   Some call me Rychard, Robart, Jacke, and
>   Wyll;
>   For now the pye hathe peckyd yow.

15 'But, all medons, be ware be rewe,
>   And lett no man downe yow throwe;

For and yow doo, ye wyll ytt rewe,
>   For then þe pye wyll pecke yow.'

16 'Farewell, corteor, ouer the medoo,
>   Pluke vp your helys, I yow beshrew!
>   Your trace, wher so euer ye ryde or goo,
>   Crystes curse goo wythe yow!

17 'Thoughe a knave hathe by me layne,
>   Yet am I noder dede nor slowe;
>   I trust to recouer my harte agayne,
>   And Crystes curse goo wythe yow!'

1⁴. bryde: qy, bryd? 8². blewe.
16². be shrew yow. 17². nor sleyne.

And *for* &. *Final double* l, *though crossed, has been printed without adding* e.

112

THE BAFFLED KNIGHT

A. a. Ravenscroft's Deuteromelia, or, The Second Part of Musicks Melodie, or Melodious Musicke, London, 1609. 'The Over Courteous Knight,' Ritson's Ancient Songs, 1790, p. 159. **b.** Pills to Purge Melancholy, III, 37, 1719.

B. Pills to Purge Melancholy, V, 112, 1719.

C. a. 'The Baffled Knight, or, The Lady's Policy.' A Collection of Old Ballads, III, 178, 1725. **b.** 'The Lady's Policy, or, The Baffled Knight,' Three Parts (the first fifty stanzas), Pepys Ballads, V, Nos 162–164. **c.** Douce Ballads, III, fol. 52 b. **d.** 'The Baffled Knight, or, The Lady's Policy,' Roxburghe Ballads, III, 674.

D. a. 'The Shepherd's Son,' Herd's Ancient and Modern Scots Songs, p. 328, 1769. **b.** 'Blow the Winds, Heigh ho!' Dixon, Ancient Poems, Ballads and Songs of the Peasantry of England, p. 123, Percy Society, vol. xvii; Bell, p. 80.

E. 'The Knight and Lady,' Motherwell's MS., p. 410.

A b is in the first volume of the editions of 1698, 1707: Chappell, Popular Music, p. 62. B is in the third volume of the edition of 1707, and is also printed in A Complete Collection of Old and New English and Scotch Songs, 8vo, 1735, which I have not seen: Chappell, p. 520.

> * Pepys, V, 169, No 162. An Excellent New Song, calld The Lady's Policy, or, The Baffled Knight. London, printed and sold by T. Moore, 1693. T. Moore printed 1689–93: Chappell.
> Pepys, V, 170, No 163. An Answer to The Baffld Knight,

The original story, represented by A, B, and C 1–17, appears to have been revived at the end of the seventeenth century, and to have been so much relished as to encourage the addition of a Second, Third, and Fourth Part, all of which were afterwards combined, as in C a, c, d.*

> or, The beautiful Lady's Second piece of policy, by which she preserved her Virginity and left the brisk Knight in Pickle. Printed for C. Bate, next the Crown Tavern in West Smithfield. C. Bates printed 1690–1702: Chappell.
> Pepys, V, 171, No 164. The Third Part of the Baffld

Percy inserted a version of C, abridged to forty-five stanzas, in his Reliques, 1765, III, 238, 1767, II, 339, which was "given, with some corrections,* from a MS. copy, and collated with two printed ones in Roman character in the Pepys collection." Although "MS. copy" in Percy's case may mean nothing, while "some corrections" may signify much, it has been thought best to reprint Percy's ballad in an Appendix.

D is repeated in Johnson's Museum, p. 490, No 477, with a slight change in the first line. It probably belongs to the first half of the eighteenth century.

E is, in all probability, a broadside copy modified by tradition. In E, as in two stanzas appended to B (see notes), and in a rifacimento immediately to be mentioned, the all but too politic maid would certainly seem to be encouraging the knight at first.†

'The Politick Maid,' Roxburghe Ballads, I, 306 f, Ballad Society reprint, II, 281, is an edition, after Percy's fashion, of some old form of the ballad, by Richard Climsell (Chappell). It was printed for Thomas Lambert, whose date, according to Mr. Chappell, is 1636–41, and is, therefore, considerably earlier than any known copy of the First Part of C. For the sake of such portions of the original as it preserves, it is given in an Appendix.

There is a Scottish ballad in which the tables are turned upon the maid in the conclusion. This, as being of comparatively recent, and not of popular, but of low literary origin, cannot be admitted here. It can be found in Kinloch's Ballad Book, 'Jock Sheep,' p. 16, and the Kinloch MSS, I, 229, communicated by James Beattie as taken down from the recitation of Miss E. Beattie, Mearnsshire. Other versions are, in the Campbell MSS, 'Dernie Hughie,' II, 233; 'Jock Sheep, or, The Maiden Outwitted,' Buchan MSS, I, 155. Another ballad, brief and silly, in which a

maid ties a gentleman's hands with her apron strings, 'The Abashed Knight,' Buchan's Ballads of the North of Scotland, II, 131, is rejected on similar grounds.

The important points in A, B, and the first part of C are that a knight, coming upon a damsel at a distance from her home, desires to have his will of her. She asks him to take her to her father's hall, where he shall be gratified. Reaching the house, she slips in and leaves the knight without. She jeers at him for not using his opportunity.

A similar story occurs in many European ballads.

Spanish. A. 'De Francia partió la niña,' "Cancionero de Romances, s. a., fol. 259, Can. de Rom. 1550, fol. 274, Silva de 1550, I, fol. 184;" 'La Infantina,' Duran, I, 152, No 284, Wolf y Hofmann, Primavera, II, 82, No 154. A damsel on the way to Paris has lost the road, and is waiting under a tree for an escort. A knight rides by, and she asks him to take her along. He puts her on the crupper, and, when midway, asks for *amores*. The damsel tells him that she is a leper (hija de un malato y de una malatía), which frightens the knight to silence. As they are entering Paris the damsel laughs, and the knight asks why; she laughs at the knight's want of spirit. He proposes to go back for something which he has forgotten. She will not turn back; she is daughter to the king of France, and any man who should touch her would pay dearly for it. **B.** Another copy, from a broadside of the sixteenth century, Duran, I, 152, No 285, Primavera, II, 83, No 154 a, blends the story with that of a princess who has been made to pass seven years in a wood by a fairy's spell, 'A cazar va el caballero,' 'La Infanta encantada,' Duran, I, 159, No 295, Primavera, II, 74, No 151. **C.** 'El Caballero burlado,' from Asturian tradition, Amador de los Rios, Historia de la Litteratura española, VII, 442.

Knight, or, The Witty Lady's new Intreague, by which she left him fetterd in his Boots. Where he lay all Night in her Father's Park, Cursing his woful Misfortune. Printed for I. Deacon, at the Angel in Guilt Spur Street, without Newgate. Jonah Deacon printed 1684–95 : Chappell.

I do not know that the Fourth Part was ever separately printed.

The Pepys copy is not at my disposal except for collation.

* "Bishop Percy found the subject worthy of his best improvements," says Ritson, for once with French neatness: Ancient Songs, p. 159.

† See, further on, the second Danish and the German ballad.

Portuguese. A. 'A Infeitiçada,' Almeida-Garrett, II, 31. B, C, D. Romances da filha do rei de França, 'O caçador e á donzilla,' 'Donzella encantada,' Braga, Cantos p. do Archipelago açoriano, Nos 1, 2, 3, pp. 183–191. E, F. Romances da Infanta de França, 'A Encantada,' Braga, Romanceiro Geral, Nos 10, 11, pp. 26–29. G. 'Infantina' (defective), Coelho, Zeitschrift für romanische Philologie, III, 62.* In all the Portuguese versions the proper story is mixed with that of the Hunter and the Enchanted Princess ('O Caçador,' Almeida-Garrett, II, 17), and in all but F the lady is discovered to be the sister of the knight, a frequent catastrophe in ballads,† certainly a false one in the present instance. In A the damsel represents herself as having been bewitched before baptism, and any man who should come near her would become *malato*.‡ In B, C, D she says she is daughter of a *malato*, and any man approaching her would become *malato*.§ This feature is wanting in E, F, G.

French. A. Gasté, Chansons normandes du XVᵉ siècle, p. 72, No 43, 'Et qui vous passera le bois?' Vaux-de-vire d'Olivier Basselin, etc., Du Bois, p. 190, No 30, Le Bibliophile Jacob, p. 225; Wolff, Altfranzösische Volkslieder, p. 81. B. a. 'La Filho doou Ladre,' Arbaud, II, 90. b. 'La Fille du Lepreux,' Poésies pop. de la France, MS., III, fol. 261. C. 'En allant au bois,' Bujeaud, I, 244. D. 'En revenant de Saint-François,' Guillon, p. 103. E. 'Margueridette,' Bladé, Poésies pop. de l'Armagnac, etc., p. 76. A damsel who is afraid to pass a wood is taken through by a knight, B. Midway he makes love to her; she advises him to keep off; she is the daughter of a leper. When out of the wood she laughs, and, the man asking why, says, because she has come out a maid. He proposes to return, which she will not hear of; he should have plucked his bird while he had it in hand. She declares herself daughter of the king, D; of the seigneur, E; of the chief burgher of the city, A. The knight of B is an officer in E, who takes the maid up on his horse, and in E she feigns to be the hangman's daughter, not a leper's. Inferior copies of the same type are given by Legrand, Romania, X, 392, No 43, Lovell, Chansons Canadiennes, p. 30, Gagnon, p. 92 (much corrupted).

In a variation of this story an orange-girl delivers herself from her predicament by feigning an ague-fit: 'La Marchande d'Oranges,' Rolland, p. 258, No 127, *d*; Poésies pop. de la France, IV, fol. 166, fol. 213 (a fragment at fol. 286 is the latter half of the same copy); Bujeaud, I, 249, and 251 (marchande de pommes). Other copies give the story a different turn.

In another version the man yields to the girl's tears, and is laughed at in the conclusion: 'Le galant maladroit,' Poésies pop. de la France, MS., III, fol. 139, fol. 141; 'La fille bien avisée,' fol. 524; IV, fol. 350, 'Il était un chasseur;' VI, 119 = Rolland, I, 23, No 4, c; Gerard de Nerval, La Bohème Galante, p. 96, ed. 1866 = Les Faux Saulniers, Œuvres complètes, 1868, IV, 398; Buchon, p. 76, No 2; Beaurepaire, p. 33 f; Guillon, p. 101; Tarbé, 'L'honnête Garçon,' II, 137; Rolland, 'L'Occasion manquée,' I, 23, No 4 b; Puymaigre, 'La Rencontre,' p. 113, 2d ed. I, 154. The "moral" is wanting in very few of these.

Still other varieties, with omissions, additions, or changes which need not be particularized, are: 'L'Amant discret,' Puymaigre, p. 112, I, 153; Guillon, pp. 29, 273; 'L'autre jour,' Bladé, P. p. de l'Armagnac, p. 114; 'Praube Moussu,' Bladé, Poésies pop. de la Gascogne, II, 66, Moncaut, p. 356; Rolland, I, 23, No 4, a; 'Lou Pastre,' Bladé, II, 114;

---

* A, E, F in Hardung's Romanceiro, I, 49–55, B, C, D, the same, pp. 59–67.

† As in 'Don Bueso,' Duran, I, lxv, A. de los Rios, in Jahrbuch für romanische u. englische Literatur, III, 282, two copies.

‡ "Curse women, and still more him that trusts them," says the knight at the end of Portuguese A, and so in English A.

§ It has been contended that *malato* signifies a peasant of low condition: see Braga, C. p. do Arch. açor., p. 399; but, on the other hand, Amador de los Rios, as above, VII, 433. Sense requires, if not the specific meaning *leprous*, at least something contagious, and sufficiently serious to make the knight tremble in his saddle, as he does in Portuguese A. Hardung aptly cites from Spanish B: "Fija soy de un malato *que tiene la malatia*." Compare the French ballads.

Bujeaud, I, 254; 'Lou Pastour et la Pastouro,' Daymard, Collection de vieilles chansons recueillies à Serignac, p. 16, which last I have not seen.

Italian. 'La figlia del re,' Ferraro, Canti p. monferrini, p. 76, No 55. A damsel lost in a wood asks a cavalier to show her the way. He takes her on his horse. She, for a reason not given, but to be gathered from the other southern ballads, tells him that she is daughter of a poor man who has had seven years of sickness. Get down from the horse, he says, and I will show you the way. At the end of the wood she tells him she is daughter of a rich merchant, proprietor of many farms. He solicits her to mount again. No; he has had the quail and let it fly; yonder is the castle of her father the king.

Danish. 'I Rosenslund,' Grundtvig, IV, 357, No 230, four copies: A, previously in Levninger, II, 51, No 9, C, "Tragica, No 14," 1657, Danske Viser, III, 94, No 122. D has a false conclusion. In A, the best copy, from MSS of the seventeenth century, a knight who is hawking and hunting finds a damsel in a wood. She has been there all night, she says, listening to the birds. He says, Not so, it is a tryst with a knight; and she owns that this is the case. He proposes that she shall throw over this lover and accept him. She will not give her faith to two, and asks him for his honor's sake to convey her to her bower. She rides, he walks; and when they come to the bower she locks him out, wishing him ill night and laughing as he rides away.

'Den dyre Kaabe,' Grundtvig, IV, 362, No 231, two copies, from MSS of the seventeenth century. A maid and a young man meet in a wood or mead. She invites him to spread both of their cloaks on the ground for a bed. His new scarlet cloak cost him fifteen mark in Stockholm, and he will not spoil it by laying it in the dew. If he will wait, she will go home to her mother's, not far, and bring a bolster. She goes off laughing and leaves him expecting her all that day and the next, but she does not come back. Eight weeks after he meets her at the church door and asks an explanation. He may thank his cloak of scar-

let new for his disappointment; had she been a young man and met a maid, she would not have spared her cloak though it were cloth of gold. The reference to Stockholm points to a Swedish origin for this ballad, but it is not, says Grundtvig, extant in Swedish.

German. 'Das Mäntelein,' "Frankfurter Liederbuch 1584, No 150," Uhland, p. 245, No 106, Mittler, No 32. A young man and maid go out into the green three hours before day. After rebuffing him, she strangely asks him, as if she knew that he would not consent, to spread his cloak on the grass. His cloak cost him fifty pound, and would be spoiled. In the evening, as she stands in her tower, the young man passes and greets her. She answers, The angels above will requite your cloak for my coming off a maid.

The artifice by which the lady disembarrasses herself in the Third Part of the broadside ballad, by pulling off the knight's boots half-way, is a very familiar story, found also in a modern German ballad, Walter, p. 94, No 64. See Les cent nouvelles Nouvelles, 1432 and earlier, No 24, ed. Wright, Paris, 1858, I, 128; Hondorff, Promptuarium Exemplorum, "1572, fol. 310," 1586, 362 b; Kirchhof, Wendunmuth, 1562, ed. Oesterley, III, 228, and other places, besides these, cited by Oesterley, IV, 101.

A modern French ballad, attributed to Favart, which may very probably have had a basis in popular tradition, celebrates the *fille d'honneur* who escapes from the importunity of her seigneur by distracting his attention (as the lady does in the second adventure in English C), and leaping on to the horse from which he had dismounted to make love to her, in some versions taking his valise with her: 'La villageoise avisée,' from Recueil de romances historiques, tendres et burlesques, tant anciennes et modernes, par M. D. L**, 1767, I, 299, in Hoffmann und Richter, Schlesische Volkslieder, p. 354; 'La Bergère rusée,' Puymaigre, pp. 119, 121, or I, 160, 162; Poésies pop. de la France, MS., III, fol. 37, 284, 294, 522, VI, 472; Wolff, Altfranzösische Volkslieder, p. 142; Tarbé, 'La Fille d'Honneur,' II, 147; 'Le Cavalier,' Guillon, p. 175. On this French ballad is founded 'Junkernlust und Mädchenlist,' Hoffmann u. Richter, p. 156, No 132, 'Der Junker und das Mädchen,' Erk u. Irmer, IV, 66, No 60, 'Die Verschmitzte,' Zuccalmaglio, p. 195, No 93. Somewhat similar are 'List der Bedrukte,' Willems, Oude vlaemsche Liederen, p. 215, No 88; 'The Scotchman Outwitted,' Old Ballads, 1723, I, 211, and Ritson's Select Collection of English Songs, 1783, II, 286; 'The Courtier and Country Maid,' Pills to Purge Melancholy, I, 128, ed. 1719.

In a Romaic ballad a maid makes a youngster who solicits her carry her over a river, then holds him off by promises while they cross field and meadow, and when they reach a hamlet sets the dogs at him: Ἡ Ἀπάτη,

"Xanthopoulos, Trapezountia, in Φιλολογικὸς Συνέκδημος, 1849, p. 436;" Kind, Anthologie, 1861, p. 86, Passow, No 481. (Without the dogs, in Ioannidis, p. 276, No 4.)

There is a French ballad in which a maid who is rowing a man over a piece of water receives amorous proposals from him, exacts a large sum of money, lands the gallant, and pushes off: 'La Batelière,' 'La jolie Batelière,' 'La Batelière rusée,' Puymaigre, p. 145, or I, 186, p. 147; Fleury, Littérature orale de la Basse-Normandie, p. 308; Poésies pop. de la France, MS., III, 137; Bujeaud, II, 307; Decombe, p. 323.

Percy's copy is translated by Bodmer, I, 94; by Bothe, 425.

A

a. Ravenscroft's Deuteromelia, or, The Second Part of Musick's Melodie, or Melodious Musicke, etc., E 4, London, 1609. Ritson's Ancient Songs, 1790, p. 159. b. Pills to Purge Melancholy, III, 37, 1719.

1 YONDER comes a courteous knight,
   Lustely raking ouer the lay;
He was well ware of a bonny lasse,
   As she came wandring ouer the way.
Then she sang downe a downe, hey downe
     derry (bis)

2 'Ioue you speed, fayre lady,' he said,
   'Among the leaues that be so greene;
If I were a king, and wore a crowne,
   Full soone, fair lady, shouldst thou be a
     queen.

3 'Also Ioue saue you, faire lady,
   Among the roses that be so red;
If I haue not my will of you,
   Full soone, faire lady, shall I be dead.'

4 Then he lookt east, then hee lookt west,
   Hee lookt north, so did he south;
He could not finde a priuy place,
   For all lay in the diuel's mouth.

5 'If you will carry me, gentle sir,
   A mayde vnto my father's hall,

Then you shall haue your will of me,
   Vnder purple and vnder paule.'

6 He set her vp vpon a steed,
   And him selfe vpon another,
And all the day he rode her by,
   As though they had been sister and brother.

7 When she came to her father's hall,
   It was well walled round about;
She yode in at the wicket-gate,
   And shut the foure-eard foole without.

8 'You had me,' quoth she, 'abroad in the field,
   Among the corne, amidst the hay,
Where you might had your will of mee,
   For, in good faith, sir, I neuer said nay.

9 'Ye had me also amid the field,
   Among the rushes that were so browne,
Where you might had your will of me,
   But you had not the face to lay me downe.'

10 He pulled out his nut-browne sword,
   And wipt the rust off with his sleeue,
And said, Ioue's curse come to his heart
   That any woman would beleeue!

11 When you haue your owne true-loue
   A mile or twaine out of the towne,
Spare not for her gay clothing,
   But lay her body flat on the ground.

B

Pills to Purge Melancholy, V, 112, 1719.

1 THERE was a knight, and he was young,
    A riding along the way, sir,
And there he met a lady fair,
    Among the cocks of hay, sir.

2 Quoth he, Shall you and I, lady,
    Among the grass lye down a ?
And I will have a special care
    Of rumpling of your gown a.

3 'If you will go along with me
    Unto my father's hall, sir,
You shall enjoy my maidenhead,
    And my estate and all, sir.'

4 So he mounted her on a milk-white steed,
    Himself upon another,
And then they rid upon the road,
    Like sister and like brother.

5 And when she came to her father's
        house,
    Which was moated round about, sir,
She stepped streight within the gate,
    And shut this young knight out, sir.

6 'Here is a purse of gold,' she said,
    'Take it for your pains, sir ;
And I will send my father's man
    To go home with you again, sir.

7 'And if you meet a lady fair,
    As you go thro the next town, sir,
You must not fear the dew of the
        grass,
    Nor the rumpling of her gown, sir.

8 'And if you meet a lady gay,
    As you go by the hill, sir,
If you will not when you may,
    You shall not when you will, sir.'

———◆———

C

a. A Collection of Old Ballads, III, 178, 1725. b. Pepys
Ballads, V, 169 ff, Nos 162–164, end of the 17th century, the
first fifty stanzas. c. Douce Ballads, III, fol. 52 b, Dur-
ham : Printed and sold by I. Lane. d. Roxburghe Ballads,
III, 674, 1750 (?).

1 THERE was a knight was drunk with wine
    A riding along the way, sir,
And there he did meet with a lady fine,
    And among the cocks of hay, sir.

2 One favour he did crave of her,
    And askd her to lay her down, sir,
But he had neither cloth nor sheet,
    To keep her from the ground, sir.

3 'There is a great dew upon the grass,
    And if you shoud lay me down, sir,
You would spoil my gay clothing,
    That has cost me many a pound, sir.'

4 'I have a cloak of scarlet red,
    I'll lay it under you, love,
So you will grant me my request
    That I shall ask of you, love.'

5 'And if you'll go to my father's hall,
    That is moated all round about, sir,

There you shall have your will of me,
    Within, sir, and without, sir.

6 'Oh yonder stands my milk-white steed,
    And among the cocks of hay, sir ;
If the king's pinner should chance to
        come,
    He'll take my steed away, sir.'

7 'I have a ring upon my finger,
    It's made of the finest gold, love,
And it shall serve to fetch your steed
    Out of the pinner's fold, love.'

8 'And if you'll go to my father's house,
    Round which there's many a tree, sir,
There you shall have your chamber free,
    And your chamberlain I'll be, sir.'

9 He sate her on a milk-white steed,
    Himself upon another,
And then they rid along the way,
    Like sister and like brother.

10 But when she came to her father's house,
    Which was moated all round about, sir,
She slipd herself within the gate,
    And she lockd the knight without, sir.

11 'I thank you, kind knight, for seeing me here,
    And bringing me home a maiden, sir,
But you shall have two of my father's men
    For to set you as far back again, sir.'

12 He drew his sword out of his scabbard,
    And whet it upon his sleeve, sir,
Saying, Cursed be to evry man
    That will a maid believe, sir!

13 She drew her handkerchief out of her pocket,
    And threw it upon the ground, sir,
Saying, Thrice cursed be to evry maid
    That will believe a man, sir!

14 We have a tree in our garden,
    Some call it of rosemary, sir;
There 's crowing-cocks in our town,
    That will make a capon of you, sir.

15 We have a flower in our garden,
    Some call it a marygold, sir,
And he that would not when he might,
    He shall not when he would, sir.

16 But if you chance for to meet a maid,
    A little below the town, sir,
You must not fear her gay cloathing,
    Nor the wrinkling of her gown, sir.

17 And if you chance for to meet a maid,
    A little below the hill, sir,
You need not fear her screeking out,
    For she quickly will lye still, sir.

18 The baffld knight was by the lass
    Ingeniously outwitted,
And since that time it came to pass
    He was again well fitted.

19 As he was riding cross a plain,
    In boots, spurs, hat and feather,
He met that lady fair again;
    They talkd a while together.

20 He said, Tho you did serve me so,
    And cunningly decoy me,
Yet now, before you further go,
    I must and will enjoy thee.

21 'T was near a spacious river's side,
    Where rushes green were growing,

And Neptune's silver streams did glide,
    Four fathom waters flowing.

22 The lady blushd like scarlet red,
    And trembled at this stranger:
'How shall I guard my maidenhead
    From this approaching danger!'

23 With a lamenting sigh, said she,
    To dye I now am ready;
Must this dishonour fall on me?
    A most unhappy lady!

24 He from his saddle did alight,
    In gaudy rich attire,
And cried, I am a noble knight,
    Who do your charms admire.

25 He took the lady by the hand,
    Who seemingly consented,
And woud no more disputing stand:
    She had a plot invented

26 How she might baffle him again,
    With much delight and pleasure,
And eke unspotted still remain,
    With her pure virgin treasure.

27 'Look yonder, good sir knight, I pray:
    Methinks I do discover,
Well mounted on a dapple-grey,
    My true, entire lover.'

28 The knight, he standing on the brink
    Of the deep floating river,
Thought she, Thou now shalt swim or sink;
    Choose which you fancy rather.

29 Against his back the lady run;
    The waters strait he sounded;
He cry'd out, Love, what have you done!
    Help! help! or I am drowned.

30 Said she, Sir knight, farewel, adieu;
    You see what comes of fooling;
That is the fittest place for you,
    Whose courage wanted cooling.

31 'Love, help me out, and I 'll forgive
    This fault which you 've committed;
'No, no,' says she, 'sir, as I live,
    I think you 're finely fitted.'

32 She rid home to her father's house,
    For speedy expedition,
While the gay knight was soakd like souce,
    In a sad wet condition.

33 When he came mounted to the plain
    He was in rich attire,
Yet when he back returnd again
    He was all muck and mire.

34 A solemn vow he there did make,
    Just as he came from swiming,
He 'd love no lady, for her sake,
    Nor any other women.

35 The baffld knight was foold once more,
    You 'll find by this pleasant ditty,
For she whose charms he did adore
    Was wonderful sharp and witty.

36 Returning from her father's park,
    Just close by a summer bower,
She chanc'd to meet her angry spark,
    Who gave her a frowning lower.

37 The thoughts of what she twice had done
    Did cause him to draw his rapier,
And at the lady then he run,
    And thus he began to vapour:

38 'You chousd me at your father's gate,
    Then tumbld me into the river;
I seek for satisfaction straight;
    Shall I be a fool forever?'

39 He came with resolution bent
    That evening to enjoy her,
And if she did not give consent,
    That minute he would destroy her.

40 'I pray, sir knight, and why so hot
    Against a young silly woman?
Such crimes as these might be forgot;
    For merry intrigues are common.'

41 'What! do you count it mirth,' he cry'd,
    'To tumble me in and leave me?
What if I drowned there had dy'd?
    A dangerous jest, believe me.

42 'Well, if I pardon you this day
    Those injuries out of measure,
It is because without delay
    I mean to enjoy the pleasure.'

43 'Your suit,' she said, 'is not deny'd,
    But think of your boots of leather,
And let me pull them off,' she cry'd,
    'Before we lye down together.'

44 He set him down upon the grass,
    And violets so sweet and tender;
Now by this means it came to pass
    That she did his purpose hinder.

45 For having pulld his boots half-way,
    She cry'd, I am now your betters;
You shall not make of me your prey;
    Sit there, like a thief in fetters.

46 Now finding she had servd him so,
    He rose and began to grumble;
Yet he could neither stand nor go,
    But did like a cripple tumble.

47 The boots stuck fast, and would not stir;
    His folly she soon did mention,
And laughing said, I pray, kind sir,
    How like you my new invention?

48 My laughing fit you must excuse;
    You are but a stingless nettle;
You 'd neer a stood for boots or shooes,
    Had you been a man of mettle.

49 Farewel, sir knight, 't is almost ten;
    I fear neither wind nor weather;
I 'll send my father's serving-men
    To pull off your boots of leather.

50 She laughd outright, as well she might,
    With merry conceits of scorning,
And left him there to sit all night,
    Untill the approaching morning.

51 The fourth part of the baffld knight
    The lady hath fairly acted;
She did his love and kindness slight,
    Which made him almost distracted.

52 She left him in her father's park,
    Where nothing but deer could hear him;
While he lay rouling in the dark,
    There 's never a soul came near him.

53 Until the morning break of day,
    And being warm summer weather,
A shepherd chanc'd to come that way,
    Who pulld on his boots of leather.

54 Then mounting on his milk-white steed,
   He, shaking his ears, was ready,
   And whip and spur he rid with speed
   To find out this crafty lady.

55 'If once this lady I come nigh
   She shall be releasd by no man:
   Why shoud so brave a knight as I
   Be foold by a silly woman!

56 'Three times she has affronted me,
   In crimes which I cannot pardon;
   But if I an't revengd,' said he,
   'Let me not be worth a farthing.

57 'I value not her beauty fair,
   Tho once I did dote upon her;
   This trusty sword shall now repair
   My baffled, blasted honour.'

58 Unto her father's house he came,
   Which every side was moated;
   The fair sweet youthful charming dame,
   His angry brows she noted.

59 Thought she, I'll have the other bout,
   And tumble him in the river;
   And let the Devil help him out,
   Or there he shall soak for ever.

60 He will not let me live at rest,
   Although I have often foild him;
   Therefore once more, I do protest,
   With flattering I'll beguile him.

61 The bridge was drawn, the gates lockd fast,
   So that he could no ways enter;
   She smil'd to him, and cry'd at last,
   Sir knight, if you please to venture,

62 A plank lies over the moat hard by,
   Full seventeen foot in measure;
   There's no body now at home but I;
   Therefore we'll take our pleasure.

63 This word she had no sooner spoke,
   But straight he was tripping over;
   The plank was sawd, and snapping broke;
   He provd an unhappy lover.

D

a. Herd's Ancient and Modern Scots, p. 328, 1769. b. Dixon, Ancient Poems, Ballads and Songs of the Peasantry of England, p. 123, Percy Society, vol. xvii; Bell, p. 80.

1 THERE was a shepherd's son
   Kept sheep upon a hill;
   He laid his pipe and crook aside,
   And there he slept his fill.
      Sing, Fal deral, etc.

2 He looked east, he looked west,
   Then gave an under-look,
   And there he spyed a lady fair,
   Swimming in a brook.

3 He raisd his head frae his green bed,
   And then approachd the maid;
   'Put on your claiths, my dear,' he says,
   'And be ye not afraid.

4 ''Tis fitter for a lady fair
   To sew her silken seam
   Than to get up in a May morning
   And strive against the stream.'

5 'If you'll not touch my mantle,
   And let my claiths alane,
   Then I'll give you as much money
   As you can carry hame.'

6 'O I'll not touch your mantle,
   And I'll let your claiths alane;
   But I'll tak you out of the clear water,
   My dear, to be my ain.'

7 And when she out of the water came,
   He took her in his arms:
   'Put on your claiths, my dear,' he says,
   'And hide those lovely charms.'

8 He mounted her on a milk-white steed,
   Himself upon anither,
   And all along the way they rode,
   Like sister and like brither.

9 When she came to her father's yate
   She tirled at the pin,
   And ready stood the porter there,
   To let this fair maid in.

10 And when the gate was opened,
    So nimbly 's she whipt in ;
    ' Pough ! you 're a fool without,' she says,
      ' And I 'm a maid within.

11 ' Then fare ye well, my modest boy,
    I thank you for your care ;
    But had you done what you should do,
    I neer had left you there.'

12 ' Oh I 'll cast aff my hose and shoon,
    And let my feet gae bare,

And gin I meet a bonny lass,
    Hang me if her I spare.'

13 ' In that do as you please,' she says,
    ' But you shall never more
    Have the same opportunity ; '
    With that she shut the door.

14 There is a gude auld proverb,
    I 've often heard it told,
    He that would not when he might,
    He should not when he would.

E

Motherwell's MS., p. 410 : from the singing of Agnes
Lyle, Kilbarchan, September, 1825.

1 THERE was a knight, was drunk with wine,
    Came riding along the way, sir ;
    He would have had a lady gay
    Amang the quiles of hay, sir.

2 ' What if I should lay thee down,
    Amang the quiles of hay, maid ?
    Sheets nor blankets have I none,
    To keep thy cloathing clean, maid.'

3 ' The wind blaws east, the wind blaws west,
    The wind blaws owre yon thorn, sir ;
    Weel may I wash my cloathing clear,
    And dry them on the morn, sir.'

4 ' What if I should lay thee down,
    Amang the rigs of corn, maid ?
    Then the king's life-guard will come,
    And steal our steeds away, maid.'

5 ' I have ten gold rings on my hand,
    They 're all gold but the stone, sir ;
    I 'll give them to the king's life-guard,
    If he 'll let our steeds alone, sir.

6 ' But see you not yon sunny bank,
    Over yon lily lea, sir,
    Where you and I may crack a while,
    And never one may see, sir ? '

7 He was on a milk-white steed,
    And she was on another,
    And all the live-long winter night
    They rode like sister and brother.

8 When they came to that sunny bank,
    He began to lay her down, sir ;

' O no, O no, kind sir,' she says,
    ' Ye 'll ruffle all my gown, sir.

9 ' My gown it cost my father dear,
    'T was many a mark and pound, sir ;
    And if that ye do lay me down,
    Ye 'll ruffle all my gown, sir.

10 ' But see ye na yon fair castel,
    Over yon lily lea, sir,
    Where you and I may crack a while,
    And never one may see, sir ? '

11 He was on a milk-white steed,
    And she was on another,
    And all the live-long winter night
    They rode like sister and brother.

12 When they came to that fair castel,
    She was at her father's yet ;
    She jumped in at her father's door,
    And left this knight without, sir.

13 She says, I am a maid within,
    You 're but a knave without, sir ;
    There were neer a butcher's son
    Put me in so much doubt, sir.

14 ' Oh if I had thee out,' he said,
    ' But two miles from the town, maid,
    I would lay thee down,' he said,
    ' And never mind thy gown, maid.'

15 ' There is a flower in my father's garden,
    The name o't marigold, sir,
    And he that would not when he might,
    He shall not when he wold, sir.

16 ' But when eer ye meet a pretty maid,
    And two miles from a town, sir,
    Ye may lay her down,' she says,
    And never mind her gown, sir.

17 ' Ye 're like unto my father's steed;
 He 's standing in the lone, sir;
He hings his head above the sheaf,
 But daur not venture on, sir.

18 ' When eer ye meet a pretty maid,
 And two miles from the town, sir,
Ye may lay her down,' she says,
 ' And never mind her gown, sir.

19 ' There is a cock in my father's flock,
 He wears a double comb, sir,
He claps his wings, but craweth not ;
 I fear you be like him, sir.

20 ' But when eer you meet a pretty maid,
 And two miles from a town, sir,
You may lay her down,' she said,
 ' And never mind her gown, sir.'

A. b. 1². the hay. 2⁴. should.
 6¹. up *wanting*. 7³. rode in.
B. *In eight-line stanzas.*
 After 8 follow these two stanzas, which belong
 to a different version of the ballad, and near
 the beginning, not at the end.

 ' There is a dew upon the grass
  Will spoil your damask gown a,
 Which has cost your father dear
  Many shilling and crown a.'

 ' There is a wind blows from the west
  Soon will dry the ground a,
 And I will have a special care
  Of the rumpling of my gown a.'

C. a. 4². under thee : *cf.* b. 22². trembling : cf. b.
 28⁴. thou fancy : *cf.* b.
 b. 1³. did he. 1⁴. amongst.
 2¹. One question. 4². under you.
 6⁴. sir *wanting*. 7³. it will.
 8². That 's moated all round about, sir.
 10². all *wanting*.
 11². me a maiden-head, sir. 11⁴. For *wanting*.
 13³. to *wanting*. 17¹. for *wanting*.
 17³. screeping.
 18. An Answer, *etc.*, *begins here.*
 19¹. cross the. 19³. met with.
 22². trembled. 24⁴. Who doth.
 28³. shall. 28⁴. you fancy.
 31³. said. 31⁴. you are well.
 32³. the old. 34⁴. woman.
 35. The Third Part *begins here.*
 35⁴. Is. 38⁴. Or I 'll be. 40². Again.
 40³. must be. 44¹. sat.
 44². so *wanting*. 44⁴. That *wanting*.
 46¹. that she. 46². rise.
 46³. For he. 48¹. laughing, sir.
 49¹. it 's. 50. *End of* Part III.

c. 1¹. got drunk. 1³. he met.
 1⁴. And *wanting :* amongst.
 2¹. One question. 2³. nor shoes.
 3⁴. has *wanting*. 4³, ⁴. *wanting*.
 6⁴. sir *wanting*.
 8². That is moated all round about, **sir**.
 9¹. set. 9³. And so.
 10¹. he came. 10⁴. she *wanting*.
 11². my maiden-head home, sir.
 11⁴. For *wanting*. 12². wet. 12³. a curse be.
 13. *wanting*. 14². it a.
 14⁴. We ll make. 16¹. for *wanting*.
 16³. not mind. 17¹. for *wanting*.
 17³. squeaking. 18. Part II.
 19¹. a cross the. 19³. met with.
 20². did decoy. 20⁴. enjoy you.
 21⁴. water. 22². trembling. 22³. I guide.
 23². I vow I. 24⁴. Who does.
 25⁴. While she a. 27¹. sir, good knight.
 28¹. than standing. 28². a deep flowing.
 28³. shall.
 28⁴. thou fancest. 29³. out *wanting*.
 30¹. farewel, sir knight.
 31². the fault that. 31³. said.
 31⁴. you are well. 32³. Whilst the knight.
 34⁴. woman. 35. Part III.
 35¹. baffld *wanting*. 36². close *wanting*.
 37³. than be. 38⁴. Or I 'll be.
 39⁴. he 'd. 40³. must be.
 42². These. 43². on your.
 43⁴. down *wanting*. 44¹. sat.
 44². so *wanting*. 44⁴. That *wanting*.
 46¹. that she. 46³. For he.
 48¹. laughing, sir. 48³. never have : boots **nor**.
 49¹. it 's almost dark. 49³. servant **man**.
 51. Part IV.
 51². has. 51³. and service.
 51⁴. him quite. 53². summer's.
 56⁴. worth one. 58¹. he went.
 58². on every. 59². into.

59⁴. Or he shall lye.
60¹. not leave me at.   60⁴. flattery.
61². no way.   61³. on him and said.
62⁴. So that you may use your.
63⁴. sawn.

d. 1⁴. cooks.   3³. gay *wanting*.
    4⁴. of thee.   8⁴. I will.   9¹. sat.
    10⁴. she *wanting*.
    11⁴. as far *wanting*.   12³. curses.
    13³. to *wanting*.   14². of *wanting*.
    14⁴. of thee.   15². calls: a *wanting*.
    16¹. for *wanting*.   16⁴. wrinking.
    17¹. for *wanting*.   17³. shrieking.
    21³. slide.   22². trembled.
    25³. discoursing.   28¹. knight was.
    28². Or.   28⁴. which you.
    29². water.   30⁴. wanting.
    31³. sir *wanting*.   32¹. father.
    37³. did run.   37⁴. he *wanting*.   38². in the.
    39⁴. he 'd.   40². young foolish.
    42². These.   45². now I 'm.
    48³. have stood : nor.   49⁴. To help off thy.
    50³. stay all.   52². none but.
    53⁴. off his.   54³. rode.
    56¹. has she.   56³. ar'n't.   58². on every.
    58³. charming youthful.   62². feet.

D. b. *Burden :*

        And blow the winds, heigh ho !
          Sing blow the winds, heigh ho !
        Clear away the morning dew,
          And blow the winds, heigho !

1². He kept sheep on yonder hill.
1³. and his.   2¹. and he.
2². He took an other look.
2³. lady gay.   2⁴. Was dipping.
3, 4 *are wanting*.
5¹. She said, sir, don't touch my mantle.
5². Come, let.   5³. I will give you.
6¹. I will not.   6². And *wanting*.
6³. I 'll . . . water clear.

7. He did not touch her mantle,
     He let her clothes alone,

But he took her from the clear water,
  And all to be his own.

8¹. He set her.
8³. And there they rode along the road.
After 8 :

    And as he rode along the road
      They spied some cocks of hay ;
    ' Yonder,' he says, ' is a lovely place
      For men and maids to play.'

9¹. And when they came.
9². She pulled at a ring.
9³. ready was the proud porter.
9⁴. For to let the lady.
10¹. gates were open.
10². This lady jumped in.
10³. She says, You are a fool without.
11¹. Good morrow to you, modest.
11³. If you had been what you should have been.
11⁴. I would not have.
For 12–14 :

    ' There is a horse in my father's stable,
      He stands beyond the thorn ;
    He shakes his head above the trough,
      But dares not prey the corn.

    ' There is a bird in my father's flock,
      A double comb he wears ;
    He flaps his wings, and crows full loud,
      But a capon's crest he bears.

    ' There is a flower in my father's garden,
      They call it marygold ;
    The fool that will not when he may,
      He shall not when he wold.'

Said the shepherd's son, as he doft his shoon,
  My feet they shall run bare,
And if ever I meet another maid,
  I rede that maid beware.

APPENDIX.

—◆—

Roxburghe Ballads, I, 306 f; Ballad Society's reprint, II, 281.

THE POLITICK MAID,

or,

A dainty new ditty,
Both pleasant and witty,
Wherein you may see
The maide's policie.

1 THERE was a knight was wine-drunke,
   As he rode on the way,
And there he spide a bonny lasse,
   Among the cocks of hay.
      Sing loud, whistle in the winde,
      Blow merry, merry,
      Up and down in yonder dale,
      With hey tro, nonney, nonney.

2 This gallant knight unto the lasse
   Did present take his way,
But it seemd he had a shame-face,
   He did not court and play.

3 When he came to this bonny lasse,
   He found she was not coy ;
His courtesie she did imbrace,
   And did not say him nay.

4 ' If we should sit us downe here,
   Upon the grasse so greene,
Here's neither sheet nor covering,
   To keep our cloathing cleane.

5 ' And if we should sit downe,' quoth he,
   ' Among the cockes of hay,
Then would come forth the king's pinder,
   And take our steedes away.'

6 ' I have rings on my fingers,
   Made of the purest gold,
That will release our steedes againe
   Out of the king's pinfold.

7 ' Sir knight, if you will goe with me
   Into my father's bowers,
There you may sit and talke with me
   This three or foure houres.'

8 When she came to her father's bowers,
   They were moted round about ;
Then she slipt in at a wicket,
   And left sir knight without.

9 ' Now I am here, a maide, within,
   And you, sir knight, without;
You may lay straw under your feete,
   To keepe you from the gout.

10 ' Henceforth when you doe meet a maide,
    A mile out of the towne,
Sir knight, you must not be affraid
    Of soyling of her gowne.

11 ' And if you chance to meet a maid
    Amongst the cockes of hay,
Sir knight, you must not be affraid
    With her to court, and say
       Sing loud, etc.

12 ' It is a proverb, many say,
    And truth it is in tryall,
He that will not when as he may
    Shall after have denyall.

13 ' And thus, sir knight, now fare you well,
    To you I bid adieu;
And you hereafterwards may tell
    How I have servëd you.'

                                        R. C.

Printed at London for Thomas Lambert, at the signe of the Hors-shoo in Smithfield.

Percy's Reliques, III, 238, 1765.

1 THERE was a knight was drunk with wine
   A riding along the way, sir,
And there he met with a lady fine,
   Among the cocks of hay, sir.

2 ' Shall you and I, O lady faire,
   Among the grass lye downe-a?
And I will have a special care
   Of rumpling of your gowne-a.'

3 ' Upon the grass there is a dewe,
   Will spoil my damaske gowne, sir ;
My gown and kirtle they are newe,
   And cost me many a crowne, sir.'

4 ' I have a cloak of scarlet red,
   Upon the ground I'll throwe it;
Then, lady faire, come lay thy head ;
   We'll play, and none shall knowe it.'

5 ' O yonder stands my steed so free,
   Among the cocks of hay, sir,
And if the pinner should chance to see,
   He'll take my steed away, sir.'

6 ' Upon my finger I have a ring,
　　It 's made of finest gold-a,
　And, lady, it thy steed shall bring
　　Out of the pinner's fold-a.'

7 ' O go with me to my father's hall;
　　Fair chambers there are three, sir;
　And you shall have the best of all,
　　And I 'll your chamberlain bee, sir.'

8 He mounted himself on his steed so tall,
　　And her on her dapple-grey, sir,
　And then they rode to her father's hall,
　　Fast pricking along the way, sir.

9 To her father's hall they arrived strait;
　　'T was moated round about-a;
　She slipped herself within the gate,
　　And lockt the knight without-a.

10 ' Here is a silver penny to spend,
　　And take it for your pain, sir;
　And two of my father's men I 'll send,
　　To wait on you back again, sir.'

11 He from his scabbard drew his brand,
　　And whet it upon his sleeve-a,
　And ' Cursed,' he said, ' be every man
　　That will a maid believe-a!'

12 She drew a bodkin from her haire,
　　And whipd it upon her gown-a:
　' And curst be every maiden faire
　　That will with men lye down-a!

13 ' A tree there is, that lowly grows,
　　And some do call it rue, sir;
　The smallest dunghill cock that crows
　　Would make a capon of you, sir.

14 ' A flower there is, that shineth bright,
　　Some call it marygold-a;
　He that wold not when he might,
　　He shall not when he wold-a.'

15 The knight was riding another day,
　　With cloak and hat and feather;
　He met again with that lady gay,
　　Who was angling in the river.

16 ' Now, lady faire, I 've met with you,
　　You shall no more escape me;
　Remember how not long agoe
　　You falsely did intrap me.'

17 The lady blushed scarlet red,
　　And trembled at the stranger:
　' How shall I guard my maidenhead
　　From this approaching danger!'

18 He from his saddle down did light,
　　In all his riche attyer,
　And cryed, As I am a noble knight,
　　I do thy charms admyer.

19 He took the lady by the hand,
　　Who seemingly consented,
　And would no more disputing stand;
　　She had a plot invented.

20 ' Looke yonder, good sir knight, I praye,
　　Methinks I now discover,
　A riding upon his dapple-grey,
　　My former constant lover.'

21 On tip-toe peering stood the knight,
　　Fast by the river brink-a;
　The lady pusht with all her might:
　　' Sir knight, now swim or sink-a!'

22 Oer head and ears he plunged in;
　　The bottom faire he sounded;
　Then rising up he cried amain,
　　Help, helpe, or else I 'm drowned!

23 ' Now fare you well, sir knight, adieu!
　　You see what comes of fooling;
　That is the fittest place for you;
　　Your courage wanted cooling.'

24 Ere many days, in her father's park,
　　Just at the close of eve-a,
　Again she met with her angry sparke,
　　Which made this lady grieve-a.

25 ' False lady, here thou 'rt in my powre,
　　And no one now can hear thee;
　And thou shalt sorely rue the hour
　　That eer thou dar'dst to jeer me.'

26 ' I pray, sir knight, be not so warm
　　With a young silly maid-a;
　I vow and swear I thought no harm;
　　'T was a gentle jest I playd-a.'

27 ' A gentle jest in soothe,' he cry'd,
　　' To tumble me in and leave me!
　What if I had in the river dy'd?
　　That fetch will not deceive me.

28 ' Once more I 'll pardon thee this day,
　　Tho injurd out of measure;
　But then prepare without delay
　　To yield thee to my pleasure.'

29 ' Well then, if I must grant your suit,
　　Yet think of your boots and spurs, sir;
　Let me pull off both spur and boot,
　　Or else you cannot stir, sir.'

30 He set him down upon the grass,
    And begd her kind assistance;
'Now,' smiling thought this lovely lass,
    'I'll make you keep your distance.'

31 Then pulling off his boots half-way,
    'Sir knight, now I'm your betters;
You shall not make of me your prey;
    Sit there like a knave in fetters.'

32 The knight when she had served soe,
    He fretted, fum'd and grumbled;
For he could neither stand nor goe,
    But like a cripple tumbled.

33 'Farewell, sir knight, the clock strikes ten,
    Yet do not move nor stir, sir;
I'll send you my father's serving-men,
    To pull off your boots and spurs, sir.

34 'This merry jest you must excuse;
    You are but a stingless nettle;
You'd never have stood for boots or shoes
    Had you been a man of mettle.'

35 All night in grievous rage he lay,
    Rolling upon the plain-a;
Next morning a shepherd past that way,
    Who set him right again-a.

36 Then mounting upon his steed so tall,
    By hill and dale he swore-a,
'I'll ride at once to her father's hall;
    She shall escape no more-a.

37 'I'll take her father by the beard,
    I'll challenge all her kindred;
Each dastard soul shall stand affeard;
    My wrath shall no more be hindred.'

38 He rode unto her father's house,
    Which every side was moated;
The lady heard his furious vows,
    And all his vengeance noted.

39 Thought shee, sir knight, to quench your rage
    Once more I will endeavor;
This water shall your fury swage,
    Or else it shall burn forever.

40 Then, faining penitence and feare,
    She did invite a parley:
'Sir knight, if you'll forgive me heare,
    Henceforth I'll love you dearly.

41 'My father he is now from home,
    And I am all alone, sir;
Therefore across the water come,
    And I am all your own, sir.'

42 'False maid, thou canst no more deceive;
    I scorn the treacherous bait-a;
If thou wouldst have me thee believe,
    Now open me the gate-a.'

43 'The bridge is drawn, the gate is barrd,
    My father has the keys, sir;
But I have for my love prepar'd
    A shorter way and easier.

44 'Over the moate I've laid a plank,
    Full seventeen feet in measure;
Then step across to the other bank,
    And there we'll take our pleasure.'

45 These words she had no sooner spoke,
    But strait he came tripping over;
The plank was sawd, it snapping broke,
    And sousd the unhappy lover.

113

THE GREAT SILKIE OF SULE SKERRY

Proceedings of The Society of Antiquaries of Scotland, I, 86, 1852. Communicated by the late Captain F. W. L. Thomas, R. N. ; written down by him from the dictation of a venerable lady of Snarra Voe, Shetland.

THIS Shetland ballad* was reprinted in Colburn's New Monthly Magazine, April, 1864, with spelling Scotticized, and two or three other uncalled-for changes.

"Finns," as they are for the most part called, denizens of a region below the depths of the ocean, are able to ascend to the land above by donning a seal-skin, which then they are wont to lay off, and, having divested themselves of it, they "act just like men and women." If this integument be taken away from them, they cannot pass through the sea again and return to their proper abode, and they become subject to the power of man, like the swan-maidens and mer-wives of Scandinavian and German tradition: Grimm's Mythologie, I, 354 f. Female Finns, under these circumstances, have been fain to accept of human partners. The Great Selchie, or Big Seal, of Shul Skerry, had had commerce with a woman during an excursion to the upper world. See Hibbert's Description of the Shetland Islands, pp. 566–571, and Karl Blind in the Contemporary Review, XL, 404, 1881. A correspondent of Blind gives stanza 3 with a slight variation, thus :

> I am a man, upo da land,
>   I am a selkie i da sea ;
> An whin I 'm far fa every strand
>   My dwelling is in Shöol Skerry.

* The ballad was pointed out to me by Mr Macmath, and ould have followed No 40 had I known of it earlier.

1 AN eartly nourris sits and sings,
    And aye she sings, Ba, lily wean !
  Little ken I my bairnis father,
    Far less the land that he staps in.

2 Then ane arose at her bed-fit,
    An a grumly guest I 'm sure was he :
  'Here am I, thy bairnis father,
    Although that I be not comelie.

3 'I am a man, upo the lan,
    An I am a silkie in the sea :
  And when I 'm far and far frae lan,
    My dwelling is in Sule Skerrie.'

4 'It was na weel,' quo the maiden fair,
    'It was na weel, indeed,' quo she,
  'That the Great Silkie of Sule Skerrie
    Suld hae come and aught a bairn to me.'

5 Now he has taen a purse of goud,
    And he has pat it upo her knee,
  Sayin, Gie to me my little young son,
    An tak thee up thy nourris-fee.

6 An it sall come to pass on a simmer's day,
    When the sin shines het on evera stane,
  That I will tak my little young son,
    An teach him for to swim the faem.

7 An thu sall marry a proud gunner,
    An a proud gunner I 'm sure he 'll be,
  An the very first schot that ere he schoots,
    He 'll schoot baith my young son and me.

6². Quhen.

ADDITIONS AND CORRECTIONS

VOL. I.

1. Riddles Wisely Expounded.

I, 2 b. Russian riddle-songs: Trudy, III, 314, No 44; V, 1073, No 208, 1190, No 6.

The Russian riddle-ballad of the merchant's son. Add : Shein, Russkiya Narodnuiya Pyesni, Plyasovuiya, Dance Songs, Nos 88, 87, 89, p. 233 f.

2. The Elfin Knight.

P. 8 a, second paragraph. Russian ballad of Impossibilities propounded reciprocally by youth and maid (including a shirt): Shein, Russkiya N. P., Plyasovuiya, Nos 85, 86, p. 231 f.

13. Another Clever Wench, in Hurwitz's Hebrew Tales, New York, 1847, p. 154, Nos 61, 62; or Sagen der Hebräer aus dem Englischen, u. s. w., Leipzig, 1828, p. 129, Nos 56, 57.

14 a, line 16. The Rusalka ballad, also in Trudy, III, 190, No 7.

14 a, the first paragraph. In the third or " Forest " book of the Mahā-bhārata, chapters 311–313, is a story that bears marks of being an ancient part of the compilation. Yudhishthira and his four younger brothers are distressed with thirst. The eldest sends these one after another in quest of water. Each reaches a lake and hears a voice of a sprite in the air, " I have the first claim on this lake. Do not drink till you have answered my questions," drinks notwithstanding, and falls as if dead. At last Yudhishthira goes himself, answers the questions, and is offered boons by the sprite. He is very modest, and asks the life of one of his two half-brothers only, not that of either of his full brothers. Whereupon the sprite rewards his virtue by bringing all four to life.

The riddles and questions are spun out at great length, and many are palpable interpolations. A few examples may be given. What is weightier (more reverend) than the earth? One's mother. What is loftier than the heavens? One's father. What is fleeter than the wind? The mind. What are more numerous than the blades of grass? Thoughts. What does not close its eyes while asleep? A fish. What is that which does not move after birth? An egg. What is that which is without heart? A stone. And so on. A paraphrase of parts of these chapters is given by Ed. Arnold, Indian Idylls, Boston, 1883, pp. 212–235.

Similarly, in the Kathā-sarit-sāgara, chapter v, a man escapes death by resolving an ogre's riddle. See Tawney's translation, I, 26, and especially the note, where Benfey is cited as comparing Mahā-bhārata, XIII, 5883 ff.

14 b. Legend of St Andrew : Horstmann, Altenglische Legenden, Neue Folge, 1881, p. 8.

18. A variety of **F**, **G**, Bruce and Stokoe, Northumbrian Minstrelsy, p. 79. ' Whittingham Fair,' popular in the north and west of the county of Northumberland; usually sung as a nursery-ballad.

1 ' Are you going to Whittingham fair ?
    Parsley, sage, rosemary, and thyme
Remember me to one who lives there ;
    For once she was a true-love of mine.

2 ' Tell her to make me a cambric shirt,
Without any seam or needlework.

3 ' Tell her to wash it in yonder well,
Where never spring-water nor rain ever fell.

4 ' Tell her to dry it on yonder thorn,
Which never bore blossom since Adam was born.'

5 ' Now he has asked me questions three,
    Parsley, sage, rosemary, and thyme
I hope he will answer as many for me ;
    For once he was a true-love of mine.

6 ' Tell him to find me an acre of land
Betwixt the salt water and the sea-sand.

7 ' Tell him to plough it with a ram's horn,
And sow it all over with one pepper-corn.

8 ' Tell him to reap it with a sickle of leather,
And bind it up with a peacock's feather.

9 ' When he has done, and finished his work,
O tell him to come, and he 'll have his shirt.'

Another variety of **F**, **G**, communicated by Mr Frank Kidson, Leeds, 1884 ; from tradition.

1 'Oh where are you going?' 'To Scarbro
    fair.'
  Savoury, sage, rosemary and thyme
'Remember me to a lass who lives there;
  For once she was a true lover of mine.

2 'And tell her to make me a cambric shirt,
  Without a needle or thread or ought else;
  And then she shall be a true lover of mine.

3 'And tell her to wash it in yonder well,
  Where water neer sprung nor a drop of rain
    fell;
  And then, etc.

4 'And tell her to hang it on yonder stone,
  Where moss never grew since Adam was born.

5 'And when she has finished and done, her I'll
    repay,
  She can come unto me and married we'll be.'

6 'Oh where are you going?' 'To Scarbro fair.'
'Remember me to a lad who lives there;
  For once he was a true lover of mine.

7 'And tell him to buy me an acre of land
  Between the wide ocean and the sea-sand;
  And then he, etc.

8 'And tell him to plough it with a ram's horn,
  And sow it all over with one pepper-corn.

9 'And tell him to reap 't with a sickle of
    leather,
  And bind it up with a peacock's feather.

10 'And when he has finished, and done his work,
  He can come unto me for his cambric shirt.'

Variations in a fragment of the same, remembered by
another person: F. Kidson.

1¹ Oh are you going to . . .

7 Tell her   .   .   .
  Sow it all over with sand.

9 Reap it with   .   .
    And tie it   .   .   .
      And then she shall be   .   .

3 (after 9):

And tell her to wash it in yonder dry well,
Where no water sprung nor a drop of rain fell,
And tell her to wash it in yonder dry well,
Or never be a true lover of mine.

3. The Fause Knight upon the Road.

P. 21, note, and p. 485. "Die Windsbraut soll man
brav schelten, sich selber aber bekreuzigen, dann weicht
sie. Sie ist des Teufels Braut. Wo eine Windsbraut
auffährt, ist eine Hexe aufgesprungen." Birlinger u.
Buck, Volksthümliches aus Schwaben, I, 192, No 304.
G. L. K.

21. Finnur is a trold in a corresponding Icelandic
story, Árnason, Íslenzkar þjóðsögur, I, 58. G. L. K.

See, for Finn and Finns, Karl Blind in The Contemporary Review, XL, 402 ff., 1881; also, 'The Great
Silkie of Sule Skerry,' No 113, II, 494.

4. Lady Isabel and the Elf-Knight.

P. 24. May Colvin in Ireland. According to a Con-
nemara story given briefly in Once a Week, II, 53 f,
July 2, 1864, one Captain Webb was wont to ill-use
young women, and then strip them and throw them into
the Murthering Hole, not far from Maarn. At last a
girl induced him to turn his back, and then thrust him
into the Hole. P. Z. Round.

24 b. The Flemish ballad is given by Fétis, Histoire
Générale de la Musique, V, 59, "d'après un texte ancien
qui a deux strophes de plus que celui de Willems."
G. L. K.

28 b. 'Ásu kvaeði' in Íslenzk fornkvæði, II, 226, No
60, A-M: this copy D (E-M). Published in 1885.

41, and p. 487 f. Russian form, corrupted.

On the oaken bridge stood Galya, there Galya stood
and drew water, she drew water and spoke with Marko.
"O Marko mine, what dost thou say to me? Come
wander with me, youth; let us wander on foot through
the dark night." One field traversed, a second they
crossed, and in the third lay down on the grass to sleep.
The rain began to sprinkle, the fierce rain to fall, and
Marko began to slumber. "O Marko mine, sleep not
while with me; bare your sword and fight with me."
Young Galya vanquished Marko; she conquered Marko,
and rode, she mounted and rode over the level field.
Galya arrives at the new gate; there stands Marko's
mother, more beautiful than gold. "Young Galya,
what can I say? Have you seen Marko near my
house?" "Oh, hush, mother; weep not, mourn not.
Thy Marko has married in the field; he has taken to
himself a fine young lady, a grave in the meadow."
Trudy, V, 425, No 816.

A man beguiles a girl with tales of a land where the
rivers are of honey, where pears grow on willows, and
maidens are clothed in gold. Trudy, V, 335, No 660.

In one version of this ballad a cuckoo flies up and

bids the maid not listen to the Cossack's tales : " I have flown all over the world, and I have never seen golden mountains, nor eaten pears from willow-trees, nor beheld maidens clad in gold."

41 a, and 487 a. A maid going to the ford for water meets Marko, and suggests that he should propose for her; if her mother will not consent, they will *roam*. They cross one field and two, and lie down on the grass in a third. He is falling asleep, when she wakes him with a cry that they are pursued. Marko is overtaken and his head cut off. Trudy, V, 226, No 454. No 548, p. 278, is nearly the same. No 690, p. 352, resembles in part No 454, and partly Golovatsky, I, 116.

42 a and 488 a, **A**. A lover takes his love by her white hands, leads her to the Danube, seizes her by the white sides, and flings her in. She asks whether she is ugly, or whether it is her ill fate. Trudy, **V**, 166, No 339.

In Poésies pop. de la France, MS., VI, 278, Poésies pop. de la Corrèze, a ballad called 'Chanson du brave Altizar' is mentioned as a variant of 'Dion et la Fille du Roi,' and, fol. 321 of the same volume, a version from Mortain, Basse Normandie, is said to have been communicated, which, however, I have not found. These may both belong with the French ballads at II, 356.

43 a. **E**. Another copy in Guillon, Chansons pop. de l'Ain, p. 85.

Add **I** : 'Monsieur de Savigna,' Decombe, Chansons pop. d'Ille-et-Vilaine, p. 264, No 92. The ballad begins like **A, B**, but the conclusion is inverted. The fair one is thrown into a pond; M. Savigna cuts away with his sword the plant she seizes when she comes up from the bottom the fourth time; *she* asks, If you ever go back, where will you say you left me? and he answers, In the big wood full of robbers.

59. **F**. In the catalogue of the British Museum, " London ? 1710 ? "

60.

G

British Museum, MS. Addit. 20094. 'The Knight and the Chief's Daughter,' communicated to Mr T. Crofton Croker in 1829, as remembered by Mr W. Pigott Rogers, and believed by Mr Rogers to have been learned by him from an Irish nursery-maid.

1 'Now steal me some of your father's gold,
　And some of your mother's fee,
And steal the best steed in your father's stable,
　Where there lie thirty three.'

2 She stole him some of her father's gold,
　And some of her mother's fee,
And she stole the best steed from her father's
　stable,
　Where there lay thirty three.

3 And she rode on the milk-white steed,
　And he on the barb so grey,

Until they came to the green, green wood,
　Three hours before it was day.

4 'Alight, alight, my pretty colleen,
　Alight immediately,
For six knight's daughters I drowned here,
　And thou the seventh shall be.'

5 'Oh hold your tongue, you false knight villain,
　Oh hold your tongue,' said she ;
''T was you that promised to marry me,
　For some of my father's fee.'

6 'Strip off, strip off your jewels so rare,
　And give them all to me ;
I think them too rich and too costly by far
　To rot in the sand with thee.'

7 'Oh turn away, thou false knight villain,
　Oh turn away from me ;
Oh turn away, with your back to the cliff,
　And your face to the willow-tree.'

8 He turned about, with his back to the cliff,
　And his face to the willow-tree ;
So sudden she took him up in her arms,
　And threw him into the sea.

9 'Lie there, lie there, thou false knight villain,
　Lie there instead of me ;
'T was you that promised to marry me,
　For some of my father's fee.'

10 'Oh take me by the arm, my dear,
　And hold me by the hand,
And you shall be my gay lady,
　And the queen of all Scotland.'

11 'I 'll not take you by the arm, my dear,
　Nor hold you by the hand ;
And I won't be your gay lady,
　And the queen of all Scotland.'

12 And she rode on the milk-white steed,
　And led the barb so grey,
Until she came back to her father's castle,
　One hour before it was day.

13 And out then spoke her parrot so green,
　From the cage wherein she lay :
Where have you now been, my pretty colleen,
　This long, long summer's day ?

14 ' Oh hold your tongue, my favourite bird,
    And tell no tales on me ;
    Your cage I will make of the beaten gold,
    And hang in the willow-tree.'

15 Out then spoke her father dear,
    From the chamber where he lay :
    Oh what hath befallen my favourite bird,
    That she calls so loud for day ?

16 ' 'T is nothing at all, good lord,' she said,
    ' 'T is nothing at all indeed ;
    It was only the cat came to my cage-door,
    And I called my pretty colleen.'

5. Gil Brenton.

P. 67 a, line 14.   Add the Icelandic versions of ' Tor-
kild Trundesøn ' recently printed : Íslenzk fornkvæði,
II, 281, No 62, **A** 42 f, **B** 42, **C** 29.

6. Willie's Lady.

P. 85 b, the third paragraph.   " Bei der Entbindung
. . . muss man alle Schlösser im Hause an Thüren und
Kisten aufmachen: so gebiert die Frau leichter." Wuttke,
Der deutsche Volksaberglaube, p. 355, No 574, ed.
1869.   G. L. K.

7. Earl Brand.

P. 96 b, line 1.   In England the north side of the
burial-ground is appropriated to unbaptized children,
suicides, etc.   Brand's Antiquities, ed. Hazlitt, II, 214–
218.
97 b.   Add : **Portuguese.** Roméro, Cantos pop. do
Brazil, No 4, ' D. Duarte e Donzilha,' I, 9 : sicupira
and collar.
Romaic.   Chasiotis, p. 169, No 5, lemon and cypress;
Aravandinos, p. 284 f, Nos 471, 472, cypress and reed.
97 b, and 489 b.   **Russian.** Bezsonof, Kalyeki Perekhozhie, I, 697–700, Nos 167, 168 (Ruibnikof) : Vasily is
laid on the right, Sophia on the left; golden willow and
cypress.   The hostile mother pulls up, breaks down,
the willow ; cuts down, pulls up, the cypress.
Trudy, V, 711, No 309, **A**, man buried under church,
wife under belfry; green maple and white birch. **B–J**,
other copies with variations.   V, 1208, No 50, a Cossack blossoms into a thorn, a maid into an elder; his
mother goes to pull up the thorn, hers to pluck up the
elder.   " Lo, this is no thorn ! it is my son !"   " Lo,
this is no elder ! it is my daughter !"
489 b, eighth line from below, read, for laburnum,
silver willow, and golden willow in the next line but
one ; and also for No 285.
98 a.   **Magyar.** In Ungarische Revue, 1883, pp.
756–59, these three and one more.

Chinese.   Hanpang has a young and pretty wife
named Ho, whom he tenderly loves.   The king, becoming enamored of her, puts her husband in prison, where
he kills himself.   Ho throws herself from a high place,
leaving a letter to the king, in which she begs that she
may be buried in the same tomb as her husband ; but
the king orders them to be put in separate graves.   In
the night cedars spring up from their tombs, which thrive
so extraordinarily that in ten days their branches and
their roots are interlocked.   A. de Gubernatis, La Mythologie des Plantes, II, 53, from Schlegel, Urano-
graphie chinoise, p. 679.   (Already cited by Braga.)

9. The Fair Flower of Northumberland.

P. 116 a, **C** 5[1].   Bed-head should certainly be bed-
stock : cf. **B** 3[1].

10. The Twa Sisters.

P. 119 b.   Färöe versions.   Seven are now known,
and one is printed, from the manuscript collection of
Färöe ballads made by Svend Grundtvig and Jørgen
Bloch, in Hammershaimb, Færøsk Anthologi, No 7, p.
23, ' Harpu rima.'
124 b.   Waldau, Böhmische Granaten, II, 97.   R.
Köhler.   (I have never been able to get the second
volume.)
125 a.

' Siffle, berger, de mon haleine !
    Mon frère m'a tué sous les bois d'Altumène,
    Pour la rose de ma mère, que j'avais trouvée,' etc.

Poésies pop. de la France, MS., VI, 193 bis ; popular
in Champagne : Mélusine, I, col. 424.
125 b, second paragraph.   (7), also in Rochholz,
Schweizersagen aus dem Aargau, II, 126, No 353.   Add
to stories of this group, ' La Flute,' Bladé, Contes pop.
de la Gascogne, II, 100–102.   G. L. K.
The last paragraph.   De Gubernatis, Zoölogical
Mythology, I, 195, cites other similar stories : Afanasief,
Skazki, v, 71, No 17, and two varieties, VI, 133, No
25; the twentieth story of Santo Stefano di Calcinaia,
II, 325.   G. L. K.

11. The Cruel Brother.

P. 143 b, line 27.   Add **D** 3, and the Swedish ballad
at p. 203, stanzas 14–17.

12. Lord Randal.

P. 151 a.   Lt.-Col. W. F. Prideaux, of Calcutta, has
kindly informed me that **E** was printed in The Universal Magazine, 1804.   It is there said to have been
sung, to a very simple and very ancient Scotch tune,

by a peasant-girl at the village of Randcallas, Perthshire. See, also, Notes and Queries, Sixth Series, XII, 134.

152 b. Italian **A** is translated in the Countess Evelyn Martinengo-Cesaresco's Essays in the Study of Folk-Songs, p. 219.

156 b, at the end of the second paragraph. The Čelakovský and the Sakharof ballad are the same. Add: Trudy, V, 432, No 822; p. 915, No 481.

13. Edward.

P. 168 b. **B** is translated also in Seckendorf's Musenalmanach für das Jahr 1808, p. 7, and by Du Méril, Histoire de la Poésie scandinave, p. 467.

14. Babylon, or, The Bonnie Banks o Fordie.

P. 172 b. **Färöe.** Four versions are known; Lyngbye's is repeated in Hammershaimb's Færøsk Anthologi, No 13, p. 45, 'Torkils døtur.'

173. ' La Fille d'un Cabaretier,' Guillon, Chansons pop. de l'Ain, p. 165, has some of the circumstances of No 14. A girl is stopped by three "libertins" in a wood. She gives them her ring and her chain, to ransom her person. They say they will have that too, and kill her when she resists. They then go for breakfast to her father's tavern, and while they are paying their scot the ring falls and is recognized by her mother. The youngest confesses, and they are taken to the forest and burned.

In a Russian ballad the only sister of nine [seven] brothers is given in marriage to a rich merchant, who lives at a distance from her home. After three years the married pair undertake a journey to her native place. On their way they are attacked by nine robbers, who kill her husband, throw her child into the sea, and act their pleasure with her. One of the nine, entering into talk with the woman, discovers that she is his sister. Sakharof, translated in Ralston's Songs of the Russian People, p. 49 f; Ruibnikof, Part III, p. 340, No 62, Part IV, p. 99, No 19; Hilferding, col. 149, No 28, col. 844, No 167, col. 1154, No 248, col. 1265, No 294; Trudy, V, 910, No 479, **A-H.**

15. Leesome Brand.

P. 181 b, line 12. Montanus is Vincenz von Zuccalmaglio; the ballad-editor is Wilhelm.

French. Add **C**, Decombe, No 96, p. 275, ' Le fils du roi d'Espagne.'

182 a, second paragraph, line 6 ff. Say: No 102, ' Willie and Earl Richard's Daughter;' No 103, ' Rose the Red and White Lily;' No 64, ' Fair Janet,' **C** 7, **D** 1; No 63, ' Child Waters,' **J** 39; No 24, ' Bonnie Annie,' **A** 10, **B** 6, 7.

A man's help refused in travail. Add: Sir Beues of Hamtoun, p. 132, v. 3449 ff (Maitland Club).

> Beues is seruise gan hire bede,
> To helpe hire at that nede.
> ' For Godes loue,' she seide, ' nai!
> Leue sire, thow go the wai;
> For forbede, for is pite,
> That no wimmanis priuite
> To no man thourgh me be kouthe.'

16. Sheath and Knife.

P. 185. As an arrow-shot is to fix the place for a grave here and in ' Robin Hood's Death,' so, in many popular tales, arrows are shot to determine where a wife is to be sought: see a Hindoo tale, Asiatic Journal, 1833, XI, 207, Benfey, Pantschatantra, I, 261; Hahn, Griechische Märchen, No 67, II, 31, 285; Afanasief, I, 346, No 23, cited by Ralston, The Nineteenth Century, IV, 1004, 1878; Jagić, in Archiv für slavische Philologie, II, 619, and R. Köhler's notes at p. 620.

17. Hind Horn.

P. 194. The warning by a dream, the preternaturally rapid transportation, and the arrival in time to prevent a second marriage taking effect are found in the story of Aboulfaouaris, Cabinet des Fées, XV, 336 ff, Les Mille et un Jours, Paris, 1840, 228 ff. Rohde, Der griechische Roman, p. 182: F. Liebrecht.

196. Recognition by a ring dropped into a drinking-vessel. See Nigra, Romania, XIV, 255 f, note 2: but Willems and Coussemaker are cited in this book, I, 195 a (3).

197 b, second paragraph. Wernhart von Strätlingen: see the note to I, 350, of Birlinger and Buck, Volksthümliches aus Schwaben.

198 a. The story of the return, by marvellous means, of the seven years abroad husband, in Leskien u. Brugman, Litauische Volkslieder u. Märchen, No 22, p. 437 f: Wollner's notes, p. 571. G. L. K.

198 b, third paragraph. Add: Victor Smith, ' Le Retour du Mari,' Chants pop. du Velay et du Forez, in Romania, IX, 289; Tarbé, Romancero de Champagne, II, 122; " E. Muller, Chansons de mon village, journal Le Mémorial de la Loire du 19 septembre, 1867; Daymard, Collection de vieilles chansons, p. 220 du Bulletin de la Société des études du Lot, 1879 " (V. Smith). Imperfect copies of this ballad in Guillon, Chansons pop. de l'Ain, p. 95, ' Les deux Maris,' p. 39, ' Ma pauvre Elise.'

As a tale in Bladé, Contes pop. de la Gascogne, I, 43. The seigneur is conveyed from the Holy Land by the devil, appears as a beggar, and produces one half of his marriage contract, which fits the half left with his wife. G. L. K.

200 a, second paragraph. Say, in the fourth line, three, six, or twelve. Dobrynya and Nastasya in Hil-

ferding, Nos 23, 26, 33, 38, 43, columns 131, 144, 160,
176, 211, and twenty other places ; Ruibnikof, I, 169,
No 27, III, 90, No 18 ; Miss Hapgood's Epic Songs of
Russia, Dobrynya and Alyosha, p. 253.

18. Sir Lionel.

P. 209 a.　A king's daughter is to be given to the
man that rids the country of a boar : Diarmaid and the
Magic Boar, Campbell, Tales of the West Highlands,
III, 81.

19. King Orfeo.

P. 216 a, first paragraph.　The Bodleian copy, **B**,
also refers to the lay of Orpheus at the end.　G. L. K.
So the Lai de l'Espine, Roquefort, Poésies de Marie de
France, I, 556, v. 185, and Floire et Blanceflor, ed. Du
Méril, p. 231, v. 71 : Zielke, Sir Orfeo, p. 131.

For correspondences between Sir Orfeo and the Irish
epic tale of the Wooing of Etain, see Kittredge, in The
American Journal of Philology, VII, 191 ff.

20. The Cruel Mother.

P. 219 b.　Add to the German versions : **M**, O.
Knoop, Volkssagen, Erzählungen, u. s. w., aus dem öst-
lichen Hinterpommern, Posen, 1885, pp. x, xi : ' Es
trieb ein Schäfer mit Lämmlein raus.'　Fr. Schönwerth,
Aus der Oberpfalz, I, 234, gives a prose tale which is
evidently founded on the ballad of ' The Cruel Mother '
(three children, one in the water, one in dung, one in the
wood).　R. Köhler.
225.

N

Percy Papers, with no account of the derivation.

1　There was a duke's daughter lived at York,
　　All alone and alone a
　　And she fell in love with her father's clarke.
　　Down by the greenwood side a, side a,
　　Down, etc.

2　She loved him seven long years and a day,
　　Till at last she came big-bellied away.

3　She set her back against a thorn,
　　And there she had two pretty babes born.

4　She took out a penknife long and short,
　　And she pierc'd these pretty babes to the ten-
　　der heart.

5　So as she was walking in her father's hall,
　　She saw three pretty babes playing at ball.

6　The one was clothed in purple, the other in
　　pall,
　　And the other was cloathed in no cloths at all.

7　' O pretty babes, pretty babes, will you be
　　mine ?
　　You shall be clothed in scarlet so fine,
　　And ye shall drink ale, beer and wine.'

8　' We are three angels, as other angels be,
　　And the hotest place in hell is reserved for
　　thee.'

O

Pepys Ballads, V, 4, No 2, from a transcript in the Percy
Papers.

1　There was a duke's daughter lived in York,
　　Come bend and bear away the bows of yew
　　So secretly she loved her father's clark.
　　Gentle hearts, be to me true.

2　She loved him long and many a day,
　　Till big with child she went away.

3　She went into the wide wilderness ;
　　Poor she was to be pitied for heaviness.

4　She leant her back against a tree,
　　And there she endurd much misery.

5　She leant her back against an oak,
　　With bitter sighs these words she spoke.

6　She set her foot against a thorne,
　　And there she had two pretty babes born.

7　She took her filliting off her head,
　　And there she ty'd them hand and leg.

8　She had a penknife long [and] sharp,
　　And there she stuck them to the heart.

9　She dug a grave, it was long and deep,
　　And there she laid them in to sleep.

10　The coldest earth it was their bed,
　　The green grass was their coverlid.

11　As she was a going by her father's hall,
　　She see three children a playing at ball.

12　One was drest in scarlet fine,
　　And the other[s was naked] as ere they was
　　born.

13 'O mother, O mother, if these children was
    mine,
    I wold dress them [in] scarlet fine.'

14 'O mother, O mother, when we was thine,
    You did not dress [us] in scarlet fine.

15 'You set your back against a tree,
    And there you endured great misery.

16 'You set your foot against a thorne,
    And there you had us pritty babes born.

17 'You took your filliting off your head,
    And there you bound us, hand to leg.

18 'You had a penknife long and sharp,
    And there you stuck us to the heart.

19 'You dug a grave, it was long and deep,
    And there you laid us in to sleep.

20 'The coldest earth it was our bed,
    The green grass was our coverlid.

21 'O mother, mother, for your sin
    Heaven-gate you shall not enter in.

22 'O mother, mother, for your sin
    Hell-gates stands open to let you in.'

23 The lady's cheeks lookd pale and wan,
    'Alass I,' said she, 'what have I done!'

24 She tore her silken locks of hair,
    And dy'd away in sad despair.

25 Young ladies all, of beauty bright,
    Take warning by her last good-night.

The Duke's Daughter's Cruelty, or, The Wonderful Apparition of two Infants who she murtherd
and buried in a Forrest for to hide her Shame.
Printed for J. Deacon at the Sign of the Angel
in Guil[t]-spur Street.
Either the printer or the transcriber was careless.
5^2. sights. 11^1. gowing.
12^2. was naked *inserted by Percy.*
16^1. you foot ; throne, *and perhaps also in* 6^1.
20^1. coldeth. 23^1. wand. 25^2. waring.
After 10 *is introduced, absurdly, this stanza, derived from* 'The Famous Flower of Serving-
Men :'

She cut her hair, changed her name
From Fair Elinor to Sweet William.

21. The Maid and the Palmer.

P. 228 a.   The Färöe version, 'Mariu vísa,' is No 9
of Hammershaimb's Færøsk Anthologi, p. 35.

22. St Stephen and Herod.

P. 234.   The Färöe 'Rudisar vísa' is No 11 of Hammershaimb's Færøsk Anthologi, p. 39.   Three copies
are now known.
238 b.   A description of San Domingo de la Calzada,
with a narration of the miracle of St James, is cited by
Birlinger from a manuscript of travels by a young German, 1587–93, in Alemannia, XIII, 42–44.   The trav-
eller had heard "the fable" in Italy, too, and had seen
a painting of it at Savona.   R. Köhler.
De Gubernatis, Zoölogical Mythology, II, 283 f, note
2, after citing the legend of San Domingo de la Calzada, adds : A similar wonder is said, by Sigonio, to
have taken place in the eleventh century in the Bo-
lognese ; but instead of St James, Christ and St Peter
appear to perform miracles.   G. L. K.
239.   In The Ely Volume, or, The Contributions of
our Foreign Missions to Science, etc., 2d ed., Boston,
1885, the editor, Dr Laurie, discoursing of the Yezidees,
says they speak of Satan as Melek Taoos, King Peacock, and the cawals (a sort of circuit-riders), "carry
round with them brazen images of a bird on a sort of
Oriental candlestick, as vouchers for their mission, and a
means of blessing to their followers.   One of them gave
Dr Lobdell the following account of the origin of this
name [Melek Taoos].   In the absence of his disciples,
Satan, in the form of a dervish, took Christ down from
the cross and carried him to heaven.   Soon after the
Marys came and asked the dervish where Christ was.
They would not believe his reply, but promised to do so
if he would restore the chicken he was eating to life.
He did so, and when he told them who he was they
adored him.   When he left them he promised always
to appear to them as a beautiful bird, and so the peacock became his symbol."   P. 315.   G. L. K.
241 a and 505.

> Em dezembro, vintecinco,
> Meio da noite chegado,
> Um anjo ia no ar
> A dizer : Elle é já nado.
> Pergunta lo boi : Aonde ?
> La mula pergunta : Quem ?
> Canta lo gallo : Jesus.
> Diz la ovelha : Bethlem.

Azevedo, Romanceiro do Archipelago da Madeira, p. 3.
R. Köhler.
The Taking of Stamboul, in Bezsonof, Kalyeki Pe-
rekhozhie, I, 617, No 138.

25. Willie's Lyke-Wake.

P. 249 f. The story of **A, B, C** in a tale, ' La Fur-narella,' A. de Nino, Usi e Costumi abruzzesi, III, 198, No 37. R. Köhler.

C. Russian, in Trudy, V, 113, No 249.

29. The Boy and the Mantle.

P. 269 b. Stones. Add the Magnet, Orpheus de Lapidibus, Leipsic, 1764, Hamberger, p. 318, translated by Erox, De Gemmis, cap. 25 ; and the Agate, " Albertus Magnus, De Mineralibus, l. II, sect. ii, c. 7: " cited by Du Méril, Floire et Blanceflor, p. clxvi. G. L. K.

269 b, third paragraph. See the English Flor and Blancheflor, ed. Hausknecht, 1885, p. 189, vv. 715–20.

270 b, the first paragraph. Add : Grimm, Deutsche Mythologie, p. 931, ed. 1876. " Ebenso trägt die in-dische Mariatale, so lang ihre Gedanken rein sind, ohne Gefäss das zu Kugeln geballte Wasser : " Kinder-und Hausmärchen, III, 264, 9, ed. 1856. See Benfey, Orient und Occident, I, 719 ff, II, 97. F. Liebrecht. For the Mariatale story (from P. Sonnerat, Voyage aux Indes Orientales, etc.), see ' Paria,' in Goethes lyrische Gedichte, erläutert von H. Düntzer, II, 449 ff, ed. 1875.

The dragon kept by the priests of Lanuvian Juno ate honey-cakes from the hands of pure maids who went down into its cave, but twined round the unchaste and bit them : Aelian, Hist. An., XI, 6, Propertius IV (v), 8. See Die Jungfernprobe in der Drachenhöhle zu Lanuvium, C. A. Böttiger's Kleine Schriften, I, 178 ff. G. L. K.

Note †. In the English ' Virgilius ' it is a brass ser-pent with the same property : Thoms, A Collection of Early Prose Romances, II, p. 34 of Virgilius, ed. 1827: cited by Sir Walter Scott, ' Sir Tristrem,' p. 432, ed. 1833, apropos of the trick of the shameless Ysonde. G. L. K.

271 a. Aqua potationis domini: see, also, Konrad von Fussesbrunnen, Die Kindheit Jesu, ed. Kochen-dörffer, Quellen u. Forschungen, XLIII, p. 81 f, vv. 573–88, 617–21, 673 ff. G. L. K.

A stunned white elephant will be resuscitated if touched by the hand of a chaste woman. A king's eighty thousand wives, and subsequently all the women in his capital, touch the elephant without effect. A serving-woman, devoted to her husband, touches the elephant, and it rises in sound health and begins to eat. Kathā-sarit-sāgara, Book VII, ch. 36, Tawney's trans-lation, p. 329 f : H. H. Wilson's Essays, II, 129 f. (" In the 115th Tale of the Gesta Romanorum, we read that two chaste virgins were able to lull to sleep and kill an elephant that no one else could approach." Tawney's note.) C. R. Lanman.

30. King Arthur and King Cornwall.

P. 277 a, second paragraph. Brags : see Miss Hap-

good's Epic Songs of Russia, p. 300 ; also pp. 48, 50, 61, 65, 161, etc.

280 b, the last paragraph. Färöe **A** is printed by Hammershaimb in Færøsk Anthologi, p. 139, No 20.

31. The Marriage of Sir Gawain.

P. 289. Miss Martha Carey Thomas, in her Disser-tation on Sir Gawain and the Green Knight, etc., Zürich, 1883, pp. 62–64, has shown that the ugly woman in the English romances is probably derived from ' La damoisele hydeuse,' in the Perceval of Chrestien de Troyes, vv. 5996–6015.

32. King Henry.

P. 298, note. So of a frog, Colshorns, p. 139, No 42.

298 b, second paragraph. " In an unpublished story of the Monferrato, communicated to me by Dr Ferraro, a beautiful girl, when plucking up a cabbage, sees under its roots a large room, goes down into it, and finds a serpent there, who promises to make her fortune if she will kiss him and sleep with him. The girl con-sents. After three months the serpent begins to as-sume the legs of a man, then a man's body, and finally the face of a handsome youth, the son of a king, and marries his young deliverer." De Gubernatis, Zoölogi-cal Mythology, II, 418. G. L. K.

34. Kemp Owyne.

P. 307 f. Caspar Decurtius, Märchen aus dem Bündner Oberlande, nach dem Räto-Romanischen er-zählt, Jecklin, Volksthümliches aus Graubünden, Zü-rich, 1874, p. 126, has a tale of a Schlangenjungfrau who is a maid by day and a serpent by night, and is disenchanted by three kisses. G. L. K.

311. The Rev. Robert Lambe sent Percy, under date of January 29, 1768, " the best copy of ' The Laidley Worm ' that he could procure from many incorrect, im-perfect, and nonsensical ones." There are differences between this and the copy printed in Hutchinson,* but one is about as good as the other. In this earlier copy 2 follows 3 and 37 is wanting. 6 and 7 read :

O up then spake the queen herself :
  Who 's this that welcoms me ?
A lord replied, The king's daughter,
  The flower of the North Country.

' Wo be to thee, thou gray-haird man,
  Thou mightst have excepted me ;
Before the morn at this same time
  I 'll bring her to low degree.'

* Not for the first time. A stall-copy among the Percy papers is of the date 1772, and an edition of 1771, from Lambe's manuscript, is transcribed for Percy by Bulman.

And 17, 22 :

> He straightway built a bonny ship,
>   And set her on the sea ;
> Her sails were made of silk so fine,
>   Her masts of rowan-tree.

> The hags came back, finding their charms
>   Most powerfully withstood ;
> For warlocks, witches, cannot work
>   Where there is rowan-tree wood.

Duncan Frasier does not appear in the last stanza :

> Now this fact, as it happened, is
>   For their good sung in rhime,
> Lest they should some important part
>   Forget of it in time.

Along with this earlier copy of Lambe's is found another, undescribed, which shows both agreements and variations : 2 follows 3, and 6, 7 and the final stanza are the same. 17 and 22 are wanting, and there are, therefore, no witches and no rowan-tree. Instead of 21–23, we have this very bad stanza :

> ' Run, run, my men, my sailors send
>   Aboard yon ship so tall,
> And bid them drown the Child of Wind ;
>   But he soon slew them all.'

In the same parcel there is a copy of ' The Laidley Worm' which is somewhat more in the popular tone than the one already printed. It was sent in an undated letter [1775 ?] to J. Bulman, Esq., of Sheepwash, Morpeth, by E. G., that is, Captain E. Grow. "The above," says E. G., " is the Haggworm as I collected it from an old woman. I wrote to the Revrd Mr Lamb for his ballad, and directed him to send to you. . . . I think the inclosed more original then his, for Mr Lamb, tho a good antiquarian, is but a bad poet, and above the one half is his own composing." Mr J. Bulman appears to have transmitted this version to Percy, to whom, upon another occasion, May 25, 1775, he sends " a bold imitation of the song, now lost, of the Laidler Worm (written by Duncan Frazier, the monk on Cheviot, in 1270), by a lady, Miss Graham of Gloriorum, in Northumberland : " of which nothing need be said.

' The Hagg Worm,' obtained from an old woman by Captain E. Grow.

1 Bambrough Castle 's a bonny place,
    Built on a marble stone,
  But long, long did the lady look
    Eer her father came home.

2 She knotted the keys upon a string,
    And with her she has them taen ;
  She cast them oer her left shoulder,
    And to the gates she is gaen.

3 It fell out on a day the king
    Brought his new lady home,
  And all the lordling[s] in his realm
    To welcome them did come.

4 ' You 'r welcome, father,' the lady cries,
    ' To your halls and your towers,
  And so are you, good queen,' said she,
    ' For all that 's here is yours.'

5 ' O who is this,' said the queen,
    ' That welcomes me so high ? '
  Up then spake a greyhaird man,
    An ill dead may he dee !
  'T is the kinges aie daughter,
    The flower of the North Country.

6 ' O woe betyde the[e], greyhaired man,
    An ill dead may thou dee !
  Had she been fairer then she is,
    You might have excepted me.

7 ' I 'll liken her to a laidley worm,
    That warps about the stone,
  And not till Child of Wynd comes back
    Shall she again be wonne.'

8 The lady stood at her bower-door,
    A loud laughter took she :
  ' I hope your prayers will have no pith ;
    You took not God with ye.'

9 She calld on her waiting-maid —
    They calld her Dorothy —
  ' The coffer that my gold lies in,
    I leave to thee the key.

10 ' Her hellish spells seize on my heart,
    And quick will alter me ;
  For eer the seting sun is down
    A laidler worm I 'll be.'

11 Word 's gone east, and word 's gone west,
    And word 's gone oer the sea,
  There 's a laidler worm in Spindlestone Heughs
    Will destroy the North Countree.

12 For seven miles east and seven miles west,
    And seven miles north and south,
  Nea blade of grass or corn will grow,
    For the venom of her mouth.

13 To this day may be seen the cave
    This monsterous worm embowered,
  And the stone trough where seven cows' milk
    She every day devoured.

14 Word 's gone east and word 's gone west,
    Word oer the sea did go ;

The Child of Wynd got wit of it,
   Which filld his heart with woe.

15 'I have no sister but barely one,
    I fear fair Margery !
   I wish I was at Spindlestone Heughs,
    This laidler worm to see.'

16 Up then spoke his eldest brother,
    An angry man was he :
   O thou art young, far over young,
    To sail the stormy sea.

17 'Peace, brother,' said the Child of Wynd,
    'Dear brother, let me be ;
   For when we come to danger dire,
    I must fight when you will flee.

18 'O let us build a bonny ship,
    And set her in the sea ;
   The sails shall be of silken twine,
    The masts of rowon-tree.'

19 They built a ship, the wind and tyde
    Drave them along the deep ;
   At last they saw a stately tower,
    On the rock high and steep.

20 The sea was smooth, the sky was clear ;
    As they approached nigher,
   King Ida's castle well they knew,
    And the banks of Balmburghshire.

21 The queen lookd thro her bower-window,
    To see what she coud see,
   And she espied a gallant ship
    Come sailing along the sea.

22 She calld on her witch-women
    To sink them in the main;
   They hoisted up their silken sails,
    And to Warren bridge they gane.

23 The worm lept up, the worm lept down,
    She plaited round the stane,
   And as the ship came to the land
    She banged them off again.

24 The Child leapd in the shallow water
    That flows oer Budle sand,
   And when he drew his berry-brown sword
    She suffered them to land.

25 When they came to Bamburg castle
    They tirled at the ring ;
   'Who 's that,' said the proud porter,
    'That woud so fain be in ? '

26 ''T is the king's son and Child of Wynd,
    Who have long been oer the sea;

We come to see our sister dear,
   The peirless Margery.'

27 'Heigh a ween, and Oh a ween !
    A ween, a woe-ses me !
   She 's a laidler worm at Spindlestone Heughs,
    These seven years and three.'

28 They highed them stright to Spindleston
    Heughs —
   Grief added to their speed —
   Where out she came a laidler worm,
    And strack their hearts with dread.

29 The Child drew out his berry-brown sword,
    And waved it oer her head,
   And cried, If thou   .   .
   .   .   .   .

30 'O quit thy sword, and bend thy bow,
    And give me kisses three ;
   For if I am not wonne eer the sun goes down,
    Wonne will I never be.'

31 He quit his sword, he bent his bow,
    He gave her kisses three;
   She threw out her fireballs,
    And fiercely made them flee.

32 In she went, and out she came,
    A laidley ask was she :
   'Oh, tho I am a laidley ask,
    No harm I 'll do to thee.

33 'Oh quit thy sword, and bend thy bow,
    And give me kisses three ;
   For if I am not wonne eer the sun goes
    down,
    Wonne will I never be.'

34 He quit his sword, he bent his bow,
    And gave her kisses three;
   But she threw out her fireballs,
    And fiercely made them flee.

35 In she went, and out she came,
    A laidley adder was she ;
   ['Oh, tho I am a laidley adder,
    No harm I 'll do to thee.]

36 'Oh quit thy sword, and bend thy bow,
    And give me kisses three;
   [For if I am not wonne eer the sun goes
    down,
    Wonne will I never be.']

37 He quit his sword, he bent his bow,
    He gave her kisses three;
   She crept into the cave a snake,
    But stept out a lady.

38 ' O quit thy sword, unbend thy bow,
    And give me kisses three;
For tho I am a lady fair,
    I am   .   .   to modesty.'

39 He took his mantle from his back,
    And wrapd his sister in,
And thei 'r away to Bamburg Castle,
    As fast as they coud winne.

40 His absence and her reptile form
    The king had long deplored,
But now rejoiced to see them both
    Again to him restored.

41 The queen he sought, who when he found
    All quailed and sore affraid,
Because she knew her power must yield
    To Child of Wynd, who said:

42 ' O woe be to the[e], wicked woman,
    An ill deed may thou dee !
As thou my sister likened,
    So likened thou shalt be.

43 ' I change thy body to a toad,
    That on the earth doth wend,
And wonne, wonne shalt thou never be
    Untill the world doth end ! '

44 Now on the ground, near Ida's tower,
    She crawls a loathsome toad,
And venom spits on every maid
    She meets upon the road.

8³. with have.

27². *The correction to* woe *is* is obvious, but, not knowing *that there may not have been some such popular interjection as* woe-ses, *I leave it.*

32⁴. to three.

35. In she went, and out she came,
    A laidley adder was she :
' Oh quit thy sword, and bend thy bow,
    And give me kisses three.'

She t[h]rew out her fire-balls, etc., *is written between the second and third lines. There seems to be no occasion for a third discharge of fireballs ; but indeed the fireballs should come before the kisses, anyway.*

42². deed did thou.

37. Thomas Rymer.

P. 322, second paragraph and note. Examples are too numerous to require mention, but it may be noticed that in The Turke and Gowin, Percy MS., ed. Hales and Furnivall, I, 93 f, vv 83–101, the Turk will not let Gawain touch any of the viands set forth in the underground castle, but brings in safe victual for him. G. L. K.

39. Tam Lin.

P. 335. F was learned by Widow McCormick from an old woman in Dumbarton : Motherwell's Note-Book, p. 4.

I. " The variations in the tale of Tamlane " were derived " from the recitation of an old woman residing near Kirkhill, in West Lothian : " Scott's Minstrelsy, II, 102, 1802.

336 b, third paragraph. Add: Aminson, IV, 6, No 27.

338. King Bean, in the form of a flying thing, turns into a handsome youth after bathing in three vessels successively, one of milk and water, one of milk, one of rose-water: Bernoni, Fiabe pop. veneziane, p. 87, No 17, translated by Crane, Italian Popular Tales, p. 12. A green bird bathes in a pan of milk, and becomes a handsome youth, and, bathing in gold basins full of water, this youth turns into a bird again: Pitré, Fiabe, Novelle e Racconti, I, 163, No 18, translated by Crane, p. 2, and note, p. 321. A prince and his two servants, transformed into pigeons, resume their proper shape on plunging into basins of gold, silver, and bronze respectively: a Tuscan story in De Gubernatis, Zoölogical Mythology, II, 299 f, note. G. L. K.

339 b, line 9 ff, Fairy Salve. This feature, in one form or another, occurs in nearly all the stories of mortal women who have helped elf-women in travail that are reported by Árnason, Íslenzkar þjóðsögur, I, 15 ff. G. L. K.

For fairy salve and indiscreet users of it, see, also, J. O'Hanlon, Irish Folk-Lore, Gentleman's Magazine, 1865, Pt II, in the Gentleman's Magazine Library, ed. Gomme, English Traditional Lore, p. 12. G. L. K.

340 a, third line of the second paragraph. Add to Zielke, v. 68: vv. 399–405.

340 a, second paragraph, Ympe-tree. In the lay de Tydorel, published by Gaston Paris in Romania, VIII, 67, a queen goes to sleep, v. 30, soz une ente, with strange results. G. L. K.

40. The Queen of Elfin's Nourice.

P. 358 f. Add : Hunt, Popular Romances of the West of England, ed. 1881, p. 83 ; P. I. Begbie, Supernatural Illusions, London, 1851, I, 44–47 ; Bartsch, Sagen, u. s. w., aus Meklenburg, I, 85, No 95 ; Kuhn, Märkische Sagen, p. 82, No 81, and Sagen, u. s. w., aus Westfalen, I, 285 f, No 331, and note ; Grässe, Sagen des Königreichs Sachsen, 2d ed., I, 73, No 69, I, 395, No 455 ; Peter, Volksthümliches aus Österreichisch-Schlesien, II, 16 ; Lütolf, Sagen, u. s. w., aus Lucern, u. s. w., p. 476, No 478 ; Rochholz, Naturmythen, p. 113 f, No 9, and note, and especially the same author's Schweizersagen aus dem Aargau, I, 339: Wolf, Niederländische Sagen, p. 501, No 417; Árnason, Íslenzkar þjóðsögur, I, 13–22 (eight). G. L. K.

41. Hind Etin.

P. 365. Add to the German ballad: I, Birlinger u. Crecelius, Deutsche Lieder, Festgruss an L. Erk, No 1, 3 stanzas. R. Köhler.

42. Clerk Colvill.

P. 374 b. **Swedish.** ' Prins Olof,' Wigström, Folk-diktning, II, 16, is rationalized; the elf is simply a frilla, mistress.

379 a. Add: Breton **G**, ' Le Sône de la Fiancée,' Revue des Provinces, III, 3e livraison ; Bladé, not seen by me.

380 a. French **C**. Say ' Le Fils Arnaud,' Noëlas, Essai d'un Romancero forézien, 68 verses.

380 b. Add: **HH**, **II**, ' Jean Renaud,' Decombe, Chansons pop. d'Ille-et-Vilaine, Nos 89, 90, pp. 253, 256; **JJ**, Le Limousin. **KK**, Le Loiret, **LL**, La Ven-dée, in Mélusine, II, cols 302–305: the last from " Revue de la Province de l'Ouest, 1856–57, IV, 50."

The first stanza, and four of the concluding, in Poé-sies pop. de la France, MS., VI, 491 and 491 bis.

382 a. Italian **B** also in Rivista di letteratura popo-lare, p. 56, 1877.

43. The Broomfield Hill.

P. 391. Josyan, in Sir Bevis of Hamptoun, preserves her chastity by the use of a rune.

> ' I shall go make me a writ,
> Thorough a clerk wise of wit,
> That there shall no man have grace,
> While that letter is in place,
> Against my will to lie me by,
> Nor do me shame nor villany.'
> She did that letter soon be wrought
> On the manner as she had thought ;
> About her neck she hanged it.

Ellis's English Metrical Romances, London, 1848, p. 256.

391 b, note †. The text of Harleian MS., 2270, com-pared with another copy in Harleian MS., No 5259, is given in Wright's Latin Stories, p. 114, No 126, Percy Society, vol. viii. R. Köhler.

In the Lai de Doon, ed. G. Paris, Romania, VIII, 61 ff, those who sleep in the bed are found dead in the morning, and Doon simply sits up all night. R. Köh-ler.

393 b, last line but one. Uhland, No 104, in Nieder-deutsche Volkslieder, herausgegeben vom Verein für niederdeutsche Sprachforschung, p. 40, No 63.

44. The Twa Magicians.

P. 400 a. Add to the French ballads: **P**, ' Mi-gnonne,' Guillon, p. 248, Ain ; **Q**, Mélusine, I, 338 f, Carcasonne.

401. **Persian.** Chodzko, Specimens of the Popular Poetry of Persia, p. 487, No 61, Songs of the Ghilanis. This and French **Q** are noted by Hasdek in the Rou-manian periodical Columna lui Traian, 1876, p. 44, 1877, p. 301, apropos of ' Cucul și Turturica.' **Dal-matian.** Francesco Carrara, Canti del popolo dalmata, Zara, 1849, p. ix. Revue des Traditions populaires, I, 98. R. Köhler.

402 a, last paragraph. The Welsh text, with an English translation, is given by Stephens, Literature of the Kymry, p. 170: cf. pp. 174, 175. G. L. K.

401. In the Kalevala, Ilmarinen, after the death of his first wife, steals her younger sister, who is very un-willing to accompany him. She threatens to break his sledge to pieces, but it is made of iron. She will turn into a salmon (Schnäpel) in the sea; he will give chase in the form of a pike. She will become an er-mine; he an otter, and pursue her. She will fly off as a lark; he will follow as an eagle. Here the talk of transformation ends: Rune 37, vv. 148–178. The next morning Ilmarinen in his wrath turns the maid into a gull. Kalewala, übertragen von Schiefner, pp. 226–228. G. L. K.

45. King John and the Bishop.

P. 404 a. The Two Noble Kinsmen, V, ii, 67, 68,

Daughter. How far is 't now to the end o the world, my masters ?
Doctor. Why, a day's journey, wench.

G. L. K.

404 b. Death the penalty for not guessing riddles. There is no occasion to accumulate examples, but this Oriental one is worth mentioning. In the tale of Gôsht-i Fryânô, Akht, the sorcerer, will give three and thirty riddles to Gôsht, and if Gôsht shall give no answer, or say, I know not, he will slay him. After answering all the riddles, Gôsht says he will give Akht three on the same terms, and the sorcerer, failing to solve them, is slain. Ardâ-Vîrâf, Pahlavî text, etc., Haug and West, Bombay and London, 1872, pp. 250, 263 f. This tale Köhler has shown to be one with that of the fine Kir-ghish lay ' Die Lerche,' in Radloff, Proben der Volks-litteratur der türkischen Stämme Süd-Sibiriens, III, 780 : see Zeitschrift der deutschen morgenländischen Gesellschaft, XIX, 633 ff.

Additions to the literature, by Dr R. Köhler.

405 b. The tale cited by Vincent of Beauvais is told by Étienne de Bourbon, A. Lecoy de la Marche, Anec-dotes historiques, légendes et apologues, tirés du recueil inédit d'Étienne de Bourbon, No 86.

In an as yet unprinted fifteenth-century Low German poem on the Seven Deadly Sins (Josefs Gedicht von den sieben Todsünden . . . nach der Handschrift bekannt gemacht von Dr Babucke, Oster-Programm des Progymnasiums zu Norden, 1874, p. 18), a king puts an abbot four questions :

De erste vraghe was, wor dat ertrike wende
Unn were hoghest, eft he dat kende ;
De ander, wor dat unghelucke queme
Unn bleve, wan dat eyn ende neme ;
Dat drudde, wo gud de konig were na rade
Wan he stunde in synem besten wade ;
De verde, we syner eldermoder beneme
De maghedom unn dar wedder in greme.

The abbot's swineherd, named Reyneke, answers:

Die erste vraghe, wor de erde hoghest were,
Reyneke sede : In deme hemmel kommet, here,
By dem vadere Cristus syn vordere hant,
Dar is de hoghe unn keret de erde bekant.
De andere, wor dat lucke ghinghe an,
Dar moste dat ungelucke wenden unn stan,
Unn kende nerghen vorder komen.
Dat hebbe ik by my sulven vornomen :
Ghisterne was ik eyn sweyn, nu bin ik beschoren,
Unde byn to eyneme heren koren.

The replies to the third and fourth questions are wanting through the loss of some leaves of the MS. As to the first question, compare the legend of St Andrew, Legenda Aurea, ed. Grässe, p. 21, ubi terra sit altior omni coelo; to which the answer is made, in coelo empyreo, ubi residet corpus Christi. See, also, Gering, Íslendzk Æventýri, No 24, I, 95, II, 77, and note. For the fourth question see Kemble's Salomon and Saturn, p. 295, and Köhler in Germania, VII, 476.

408 b. Other repetitions of the popular tale, many of them with the monk or miller sans souci. Bartsch, Sagen, Märchen u. Gebräuche aus Meklenburg, I, 496 (Pater ohne Sorgen) ; Asbjørnsen, Norske Folke-Eventyr, Ny Samling, 1876, p. 128, No 26 ; Bondeson, Halländske Sagor, p. 103, No 27; the same, Svenska Folksagor, p. 24, No 7 (utan all sorg), cf. p. 22, No 6; Wigström, Sagor och Äfventyr upptecknade i Skåne, p. 109, in Nyare bidrag till kännedom om de svenska landsmålen och svenskt folklif, V, 1 ; Lespy, Proverbes du Pays de Béarn, p. 102 ; Bladé, Contes pop. de la Gascogne, III, 297; Moisant de Brieux, Origines de quelques coutumes anciennes, etc., Caen, 1874, I, 147, II, 100; Armana prouvençau, 1874, p. 33 (parson, bishop, gardener, middle of the earth, weight of the moon, what is my valuation? what am I thinking?) ; Pitré, Fiabe, Novelle, etc., II, 323, No 97 (senza pinseri) ; Imbriani, La novellaja fiorentina, etc., p. 621, V (Milanese, senza pensà); Braga, Contos tradicionaes do povo portuguez, I, 157, No 71, previously in Era Nova, 1881, p. 244 (sem cuidados), and No 160; Krauss,

Sagen u. Märchen der Südslaven, II, 252, No 112 (ohne Sorgen); Erman, Archiv für die wissenschaftliche Kunde von Russland, XXIV, 146 (Czar Peter, kummerloses Kloster); Vinson, Le Folk-Lore du Pays basque, p. 106; Cerquand, Légendes et recits pop. du Pays basque, No 108.

Unterhaltende Räthsel-Spiele in Fragen u. Antworten, gesammelt von C. H. W., Merseburg, 1824, has the story of king, abbot, and shepherd, with the three riddles, How far is it to heaven? How deep is the sea? What is better than a gold coach? The shepherd prompts the abbot, and the abbot answers the king in person. The answer to the third is, the rain that falls between Whitsuntide and St John's. For this reply compare Archiv für slavische Philologie, V, 56, lines 25–36.

408 note *. Add the Æsopian tale, P. Syrku, Zur mittelalterlichen Erzählungsliteratur aus dem Bulgarischen, Archiv für slavische Philologie, VII, 94–97.

410 a. The Jewish-German story is given in Grünbaum's Jüdischdeutsche Chrestomathie, 1882, pp. 440–43. The third question is, What am I thinking? with the usual answer.

410 b. Some additions to the literature in Keller, Fastnachtspiele, Nachlese, p. 338, note to 199.

46. Captain Wedderburn's Courtship.

P. 415 a. Ein taub hat kein lungen: R. Köhler, in Weimarisches Jahrbuch, V, 344, 22.

416 a, second paragraph. Liebrecht's Abstract of Sakellarios's ballad is repeated in Liebrecht, Zur Volkskunde, p. 162 ff.

416, note †. See R. Köhler, Die Pehlevi-Erzählung von Gôsht-i Fryânô, etc., in Zeitschrift der deutschen morgenländischen Gesellschaft, XXIX, 634–36.

417, note †. The one stake with no head on it occurs in the Kalevala. Lemminkäinen, going to the Northland, is warned by his mother that he will find a courtyard planted with stakes, with a head on every stake but one, on which his head will be stuck. Schiefner, Rune 26, vv. 315–22, p. 163. G. L. K.

417 b. Similar are ' Las tres adivinanzas,' Marin, Cantos pop. españoles, I, 395 ; ' Soldatino,' Archivio per Tradizioni popolari, I, 57.

418 a. Drolleries. See R. Köhler's article on Hagen, No 63, in Germania, XIV, 269, written in 1868, to which, Dr K. informs me, he could now make numerous additions.

49. The Twa Brothers.

P. 437 b. Add, though perhaps superfluous: Passow, p. 316, No 437, vv. 37, 38; Legrand, Recueil de Chansons pop. grecques, p. 220, v. 24 ff, p. 330, v. 17 ff; Aravandinos, No 435, v. 7 ff.

53. Young Beichan.

P. 463 a, first paragraph. The French ballad in
Poésies pop. de la France, MS., IV, fol. 404; printed in
Mélusine, II, col. 44. Another copy in Mélusine, I, col.
123.

476. Substitute for **L** this broadside: 'Lord Bateman.'

1 Lord Bateman was a noble lord,
    A noble lord of high degree;
He shipped himself on board a ship,
    Some foreign country he would go see.

2 He sailed East, and he sailed West,
    Until he came to proud Turkey,
When he was taken and put to prison,
    Until his life was almost gone.

3 And in this prison there grew a tree,
    It grew so stout and strong,
Where he was chained by the middle,
    Until his life was almost gone.

4 This Turk he had one only daughter,
    The fairest creature my eyes did see;
She stole the keys of her father's prison,
    And swore Lord Bateman she would set
      free.

5 'Have you got houses? Have you got lands?
    Or does Northumberland belong to thee?
What would you give to the fair young lady
    That out of prison would set you free?'

6 'I have got houses, I have got lands,
    And half Northumberland belongs to me;
I'll give it all to the fair young lady
    That out of prison would set me free.'

7 O then she took me to her father's hall,
    And gave to me the best of wine,
And every health she drank unto him,
    'I wish, Lord Bateman, that you were mine!

8 'Now in seven years I'll make a vow,
    And seven years I'll keep it strong,
If you'll wed with no other woman,
    I will wed with no other man.'

9 O then she took him to her father's harbour,
    And gave to him a ship of fame:
'Farewell, farewell to you, Lord Bateman,
    I'm afraid I neer shall see you again.'

10 Now seven long years are gone and past,
    And fourteen days, well known to thee;
She packed up all her gay clothing,
    And swore Lord Bateman she would go
      see.

11 But when she came to Lord Bateman's cas-
    tle,
    So boldly she did ring the bell;
'Who's there, who's there?' cried the proud
    porter,
    'Who's there? come unto me tell.'

12 'O is this Lord Bateman's castle?
    Or is his Lordship here within?'
'O yes, O yes,' cried the young porter,
    'He's just now taken his new bride in.'

13 'O tell him to send me a slice of bread,
    And a bottle of the best wine,
And not forgetting the fair young lady
    Who did release him when close confined.'

14 Away, away, went this proud young porter,
    Away, away, and away went he,
Until he came to Lord Bateman's chamber;
    Down on his bended knees fell he.

15 'What news, what news, my proud young por-
    ter?
    What news hast thou brought unto me?'
'There is the fairest of all young creatures
    That eer my two eyes did see.

16 'She has got rings on every finger,
    And round one of them she has got three,
And as much gay clothing round her
    As would buy all Northumberland free.

17 'She bids you send her a slice of bread,
    And a bottle of the best wine,
And not forgetting the fair young lady
    Who did release you when close confined.'

18 Lord Bateman he then in a passion flew,
    And broke his sword in splinters three,
Saying, I will give all my father's riches,
    That if Sophia has crossed the sea.

19 Then up spoke the young bride'[s] mother,
    Who never was heard to speak so free:
You'll not forget my only daughter,
    That if Sophia has crossed the sea.

20 'I own I made a bride of your daughter;
   She 's neither the better or worse for me;
   She came to me with her horse and saddle,
   She may go back in her coach and three.'

21 Lord Bateman prepared another marriage,
   With both their hearts so full of glee:
   ' I 'll range no more in foreign countries,
   Now since Sophia has crossed the sea.'

   Pitts, Seven Dials.

P. 485 a, and p. 21, note. See, further, on reproach-
ing or insulting elves and the like, Liebrecht, Zur
Volkskunde, pp. 54–56: Cassel, Der Schwan, 1863,
p. 14. F. Liebrecht.
   Bladé, Contes populaires de la Gascogne, II, 8, 9.
G. L. K.
   485 b. **C.** The second stanza was accidentally
omitted. It is:

   'What 's that ye hae on your back ?'
   ' It 's my dinner and my book.'

487, note. The scene between St George and the
maiden is woven into a Greek tale, ' Der Goldäpfelbaum
und die Höllenfahrt,' Hahn, No 70, II, 55. See, also,
George's legend in Bezsonof, Kalyeki Perekhozhie, I,
506, 509, 520, Nos 117, 118, 120.
   496 a. This copy of ' The Twa Sisters,' **Z,** a variety
of **R,** was derived from ladies in New York, and by
them from a cousin.

1 There was a man lived in the West,
   Sing bow down, bow down
   There was a man lived in the West,
   The bow was bent to me
   There was a man lived in the West,
   He loved his youngest daughter best;
   So you be true to your own true-love
   And I 'll be true to thee.

2 He gave the youngest a beaver hat;
   The eldest she was mad at that.

3 He gave the youngest a gay gold ring;
   The eldest she had nothing.

4 As they stood by the river's brim,
   The eldest pushed the youngest in.

5 ' Oh dear sister, hand me your hand,
   And I 'll give you my house and land.'

6 ' Oh dear sister, hand me your glove,
   And you shall have my own true-love.'

7 First she sank and then she swam,
   She swam into the miller's dam.

8 The miller, with his line and hook,
   He caught her by the petticoat.

9 He robbed her of her gay gold ring,
   And then he threw her back again.

10 The miller, he was burnt in flame,
   The eldest sister fared the same.

503 a, fourth paragraph. Add: Bellermann, p. 100,
No 12.

VOL. II.

54. The Cherry-Tree Carol.

P. 1. Printed in Bullen's Carols and Poems, 1886,
p. 29, with the stanzas in this order: **A** 1–8, **B** 8, **A** 9,
B 9–15, **B** 17. Bullen remarks, As regards the text of
this carol, no two copies are found to agree, and one is
obliged to adopt an eclectic method: p. 252.
   A Dutch carol, keeping the palms, J. A. and L. J. Alberdingk-Thijm, Oude en nieuwere Kerstliederen, p.
174, No 87.

55. The Carnal and the Crane.

P. 7. Printed in Bullen's Carols and Poems, 1886,
p. 49, with Sandys's text, **a.**
   Legend of the Sower. I omitted to mention ' La
Fuito en Egypto,' in Arbaud, I, 33 ff. The legend of
the sower is the subject of a carol in the Bible des
Noëls, printed at Caen: Beaurepaire in Le Héricher,
Littérature pop. de Normandie, p. 81 f. Also, of a
Dutch carol, J. A. and L. J. Alberdingk-Thijm, Oude
en nieuwere Kerstliederen, p. 138, No 70.
   Victor Smith gives two copies in Noëls du Velay
et du Forez, Romania, VIII, 420 f. R. Köhler. In the
second the quail plays the part of the partridge, the
swallow befriends the Virgin. V. Smith refers also to
Eugène Muller, Chansons de mon Village, journal Le
Mémorial de la Loire du 23 septembre, 1867.

Dr R. Köhler has furnished me with these additional
references.
   A French Life of the Virgin, cited from a MS. of the
thirteenth century, by Reinsch, Pseudo-Evangelien, pp.
60–64.
   Ferdinand Wolf, Jahrbuch für romanische und englische Literatur, III, 73, cites from Didron, Annales
Archéologiques, XVI, 315, 1856, a mystery of The
Flight into Egypt, which has the legend of the Sower,
in Noëls dramatiques des Flamands de France, publiés

par l'abbé Carnel. This mystery was apparently written in the eighteenth century, for representation by a charity-school.

The legend is popularly preserved in Ireland, and a species of beetle is the Virgin's enemy, in place of the partridge or quail (p. 8, note †) : E. Adams in Transactions of the London Philological Society, cited by Rolland, Faune populaire de la France, III, 326. The same story in Notes and Queries, Fourth Series, X, 183.

The miraculous harvest is the subject of a Catalan popular tale, ' La Menta y 'l Gaitx,' Maspons y Labrós, Lo Rondallayre, II, 28. A hawk seconds the mint in calling out, Under the sheaf ! Again, simply, without the trait of the malicious plant or bird, in Leite de Vasconcellos, Tradições pop. de Portugal, p. 106. (Juniper, according to Italian tradition, saves the Virgin during her flight, when broom and chick-pea are on the point of revealing her whereabouts by their noise : De Gubernatis, Mythologie des Plantes, II, 153.)

The legend has been transferred by tradition to St Radegund, Acta Sanctorum Augusti, III, 66 ; to St Macrina, pursued by Gargantua, Sébillot, Gargantua dans les Traditions populaires, p. 173; and even to Luther, von Schulenburg, Wendische Volkssagen, p. 47. It is cited from the 145th book of the works of Bernard de Bluet d'Arberes, by P. L. Jacob, Dissertations Bibliographiques, p. 195.

56. Dives and Lazarus.

P. 10. Printed in A. H. Bullen's Carols and Poems, 1886, p. xviii, from a Birmingham broadside of the last century, differing only in a few words from A.

57. Brown Robyn's Confession.

P. 13. I neglected to refer to the throwing over of Bonnie Annie in No 24, I, 244. Add: ' Les Pèlerins de Saint-Jacques,' Decombe, Chansons pop. d'Ille-et-Vilaine, p. 284, No 98.

As to detention of ships by submarine people, see R. Köhler, in Zeitschrift für deutsches Alterthum, XXIX, 456–458.

15. For other cases of guilty men who endanger ships being ascertained by lot and thrown into the sea, see R. Köhler's Vergleichende Anmerkungen, prefixed to Karl Warnke's edition of the Lais of Marie de France, p. C, Eliduc, I. Köhler cites ' Tristan le Léonois,' in which Sadoc, a nephew of Joseph of Arimathea, is the offender who is thus disposed of. Wesselofsky, Archiv für slavische Philologie, IX, 288 ff (as pointed out to me by Dr Köhler), makes the admirable suggestion that Sadok (in Hebrew, The Just) is the original of the Russian Sadko.

The story of Sadko, in Miss Hapgood's Epic Songs of Russia, p. 313.

19 b. Mermaids boding storms : Hunt, Popular Romances of the West of England, ed. 1881, p. 15. G. L. K.

58. Sir Patrick Spens.

P. 20 b. A a is translated in Seckendorf's Musenalmanach für das Jahr 1808, p. 9.

59. Sir Aldingar.

P. 33, note. Octavian, ed. Sarrazin, p. 8, 195 ff, p. 72, 157 ff.

40 a, the second paragraph. There are five copies of the Färöe ballad. The copy in the Antiquarisk Tidsskrift was made up from four. A fifth, printed by Hammershaimb in Færøsk Anthologi, p. 188, No 25, has a widely divergent and very inferior story. There is no ordeal by battle. Óluva asks to be subjected to three probations, sea, fire, and a snake-house, and comes off triumphantly. Mýlint, her slanderer, is so absurd as to propose to try the snake-house, and is torn to pieces ere he is half in. Óluva goes into a cloister.

60. King Estmere.

P. 49, note †. " Was *lough a loud laughter* the reading of the folio ? " " A loud laughter the ladie lought," Percy Folio, I, 190, ' The Lord of Learne,' v. 215. G. L. K.

51, and 54, stanza 49. Riding into Hall. Sir Percival rides so close to King Arthur that his mare kisses Arthur's forehead, v. 494 ff; knocks off the king's hat, Chrestien de Troyes, 2125 ff (the kissing is a mistranslation); he binds his mare in the hall, v. 599, Thornton Romances. Lancelot rides into hall in Morte Arthur, v. 1555, p. 60, ed. Furnivall. Dame Tryamour rides into hall in the English Launfal, v. 973 ff, Ritson, Met. Rom., I, 212; Lanval, v. 617 ff, Warnke, Lais der Marie de France, p. 111.

Floris ende Blancefloer, ed. Moltzer, p. 29, v. 1055 : F. Liebrecht.

Floire et Blanceflor, ed. Du Méril, v. 665 f, p. 28. Torrent of Portugal, ed. Halliwell, v. 1143 ff, p. 49 : Torrent and others ride into the king's hall during meat, Torrent even ' up to the lady.' Le Bel Inconnu, ed. Hippeau, vv. 71–89, p. 4. Ipomydon, ed. Weber, vv. 1651 ff, III, 341: Ipomydon, disguised as a fool, goes to the king's court on a rouncy, and when told to go to meat ties his horse ' fast him by ; ' into the hall came riding a may. G. L. K.

51 b, the third paragraph. " En ces temps-là, dit la Chronique Générale d'Espagne, les rois, comtes, nobles, et tous les chevaliers, afin d'être prêts à toute heure, tenaient leurs chevaux dans la salle où ils couchaient avec leurs femmes: Taine, Les Origines de la France contemporaine, I, 10 f." F. Liebrecht. " E

assy los reyes e condes e los altos omes e todos los otros caualleros que se presçiauan de armas, todos parauan los cauallos dentro en las camaras donde tenien sus lechos donde dormian con sus mugeres, porque, luego que oyan dar el apellido, touiessen prestos sus cauallos e sus armas, e que caualgassen luego sin otra tardança ninguna." Crónica de España, ed. 1541, Third Part, fol. cclxxv.

61. Sir Cawline.

P. 56. I have omitted to refer to the close resemblance to Sir Eglamour, Thornton Romances, p. 121, Percy MS., Hales and Furnivall, II, 341. See 'Sir Lionel,' I, 209.

56 b, line 19 f. Compare the sword given by Cristabelle to Sir Eglamour, v. 265 f:

Saint Poule fonde hyt in the Grekes sea.

57 a. In the Lai de l'Espine, erroneously ascribed by Roquefort to Marie de France, the hero, holding watch for the sake of adventure at the Gué de l'Espine, en la nuit de la Saint Jéhan, tilts with eldritch knights and wins a horse from one of them. The horse disappears, much as in the story in Gervase of Tilbury. G. L. K.

62. Fair Annie.

P. 67, note ‡. More cases in Dr R. Köhler's annotation to 'Le Fraisne,' Warnke, Lais der Marie de France, p. LXIV ff. See, also, Liebrecht, Germania, XXVIII, 114 f. [The passage concerning Guinea negroes, Köhler, p. LXXIV, occurs also, perhaps originally, in Astley's Voyages, III, 83, whence it is cited by Sir John Lubbock, Mental and Social Condition of Savages, p. 36, ed. 1882. G. L. K.]

63. Child Waters.

P. 85 b. Percy's ballad is translated in Seckendorf's Musenalmanach für das Jahr 1808, p. 120.

66. Lord Ingram and Chiel Wyet.

P. 127 a. Sword in bed.
Add the following references, communicated by Dr R. Köhler. Gonzenbach, Sicilianische Märchen, Nos 39, 40, I, 272, 279 ; Bladé, Contes p. de la Gascogne, I, 284 ; Leskien u. Brugman, Litauische Volkslieder u. Märchen, p. 394, Märchen 11, and Wollner's note, p. 548 ; Pio, Νεοελληνικὰ Παραμύθια, No 10, p. 174 ; a Latin tale in Jahrbuch für romanische u. englische Literatur, XI, 231 ; Prym u. Socin, Syrische Sagen u. Märchen, No 7, p. 25 ; Gaster, Beiträge zur vergleichenden Sagen- u. Märchenkunde, p. 28 ; Generides, ed. Furnivall, p. 202, v. 6511 ff, ed. Wright, 3921 ff ; the French

Bevis of Hampton, and (through Amis and Amiloun) one version of the Seven Sages, epitomized in Loiseleur des Longchamps, Essai sur les Fables indiennes, Rajna, Ricerchi intorno ai Reali di Francia, p. 121, and Origini dell' Epopea francese, p. 406 ; Lane, Thousand and One Nights, III, 346, Story of Seyf El-Mulook (A. Weber) ; Weber, Ueber eine Episode im Jaimini-Bhârata, Monatsberichte der Berliner Akademie, 1869, p. 40 ; Reinisch, Die Nuba-Sprache, I, 190 ; Consiglieri Pedroso, Portuguese Folk-Tales, Folk-Lore Society, No 25, p. 100 (lance for sword).

The King of the Crows (a man by night) puts a naked sword between himself and his wife. Bladé, Contes pop. de la Gascogne, I, 21. G. L. K.

127 b. Jumping over tables. See, also, I, 502 a, note to p. 194, and 502 b, note to 198 b. Add to the Polish ballads in the last, Roger, p. 13, Nos 25, 26: in 25 the bride jumps three, in 26 she jumps four and knocks over a fifth with her foot. R. Köhler notes a Slavic ballad of the same set, translated by Max Waldau, Deutsches Museum, 1851, I, 134. Nastasya (see I, 200) jumps over a table to get to Dobrynya, Hilferding, col. 810, No 157 ; Miss I. F. Hapgood's Epic Songs of Russia, p. 267.

Herr Lave, in the favorite and excellent Scandinavian ballad, 'Herr Lave og Herr Jon,' jumps over the table when he is told "nu sover Hr. Jon hos unge Bruddin," Kristensen, II, 304, No 86, C 13 : so Kristensen, I, 172, No 62, A 5 ; Wigström, Folkdiktning, I, 71, No 34, stanza 15 ; Öberg, Filikromen, III, 32, 35, stanza 15 ; Grundtvig, No 275, ' Hr. Find og Vendel rod,' stanza 12. Liebrecht, Englische Studien, IX, 447, adds E. Wigström, Folkdiktning, I, 14, ' Agneta och bergamannen,' stanza 18.

Alexander, in disguise, jumps over Darius's table, Kyng Alisaunder, 4236–39, Weber, I, 174 ; Garadue jumps the table in the Lai du Corn, Wolf, Ueber die Lais, vv. 551–54, p. 340. The Soudan of Dammas, Kyng of Tars, vv. 97 ff, Ritson, II, 160, and King Richard, Richard Coer de Lion, vv. 1795–98, Weber, II, 71, smite the table down. G. L. K.

67. Glasgerion.

P. 137 a, second paragraph. Landau notes various unpleasant stories resembling Boccaccio's, Quellen des Dekameron, pp. 70 f, 74 ff, ed. 1884.

137 a, note *. The comparison between Chaucer's Glascurion and the Welsh Geraint had already been made by Price, Essay on the Remains of Ancient Lit. in the Welsh, etc., 1845, Literary Remains of the Rev. Thomas Price, 1854, I, 152. G. L. K.

137 b, line 18. Insert : Briz, V, 73.

Line 20. Add : the harping of Wäinämöinen, Kalevala, Rune 41, v. 31 ff, Schiefner, p. 240. Daghda, the Druid, performs in the hall of his enemies the three feats which give distinction to a harper : makes the women cry tears, the women and youth burst into laughter, and the entire host fall asleep. O'Curry, Manners and Customs of the Ancient Irish, III, 214 : cf. D'Arbois de Jubainville, Cours de la Litt. Celtique, II, 190 f.   G. L. K.

68. Young Hunting.

P. 143, note ‡.   Danske Samlinger, Norske Magasin, are cited by Grundtvig, IV, 151.

143.   Discovery of drowned bodies.   See, further, Dennys, The Folk-Lore of China, p. 64; Liebrecht, Volkskunde, p. 332, No 169, and Englische Studien, IX, 447 ; Mélusine, II, cols 252, 253.

69. Clerk Saunders.

P. 158 b, at the end of the first paragraph.   Supply the Portuguese versions, accidentally omitted: 'Dona Branca,' Braga, Cantos pop. do Archipelago açoriano, p. 233; 'Dom Alberto,' p. 236, 'Flor de Marilia,' p. 237.

72. The Clerk's Twa Sons o Owsenford.

P. 174.   Add to the Spanish and Italian ballad : 'Les trois Clercs,' Decombe, as above, p. 267, No 93; 'Les trois Écoliers,' Mélusine, I, col. 243 f ; 'La Légende de Pontoise' (corrupted), Poésies p. de la France, MS., I, fol. 82, Mélusine, II, 18 f.

73. Lord Thomas and Fair Annet.

P. 179 b.   F.   After Kinloch MSS, III, 127, insert: and Dr John Hill Burton's papers.

182.   Green and blue.

> " Oh green 's forsaken,
> And yellow 's forsworn,
> And blue 's the sweetest
> Color that 's worn."

This is given (apropos of an emerald engagement-ring) as a popular rhyme in William Black's Three Feathers, chap. ix.   The scene is in Cornwall.

> " Then shall ye were a shelde of blewe,
> In token ye shall be trewe,"

says the king's daughter of Hungary in the Squyr of Lowe Degre, vv. 205, 206, Ritson, III, 153.   See Rochholz, Altdeutsches Bürgerleben, pp. 277, 278.   G. L. K.

75. Lord Lovel.

204 and 212.

J

Communicated by Mr Macmath, as derived from his aunt, Miss Jane Webster, who learned it from her mother, Janet Spark, Kirkcudbrightshire.

1 Lord Lovel was standing at his stable-door,
    Kaiming down his milk-white steed,
When by came Lady Anzibel,
    Was wishing Lord Lovel good speed, good
      speed,
    Was wishing Lord Lovel good speed.

2 'O where are you going, Lord Lovel?' she
      said,
    'O where are you going?' said she :
'I'm going unto England,
    And there a fair lady to see.'

3 'How long will you stay, Lord Lovel?' she
      said,
    'How long will you stay?' says she :
'O three short years will soon go by,
    And then I'll come back to thee.'

P. 205 a, note.   Add: (28) a copy in B. Seuffert, Maler Müller, Berlin, 1877, p. 455 f : R. Köhler. (Dropped in the second edition, 1881.)

205 b, note *.   The Finnish version is 'Morsiamen kuolo,' Kanteletar, 1864, p. viii.

P. 206.   Add: Decombe, 'Derrièr' la Trinité,' p. 210, No 75, 'En chevauchant mon cheval rouge,' p. 212, No 76; Ampère, Instructions, p. 36, Bulletin du Comité, etc., I, 252, 'Les chevaux rouges.'

77. Sweet William's Ghost.

P. 227, note ‡.   Sir Walter Scott, in his Introduction to The Pirate, ed. 1846, p. viii, and note, p. 136, informs us that the old woman was Bessie Millie, living at Stromness, Pomona, Orkney (not Shetland).   W. Macmath.

227 b.   Asking back troth.   The Child of Bristow's father, who has been charged by his son to come back from purgatory at intervals of a fortnight, asks back his troth three times, and gets it after he is ransomed by his son: Hazlitt, Early Popular Poetry, I, 120, 124, 128.

78. The Unquiet Grave.

P. 235 a.   Add these versions of the tale of the child that is obliged to carry its mother's tears in a pitcher, or whose clothes are wet with its mother's tears : 'Das Thränenkrüglein,' Bechstein, Märchenbuch, 1845, p. 109, 1879, p. 110; Wucke, Sagen der mittleren Werra, 1864, I, 133; also, II, 31; Krainz, Mythen u. Sagen aus dem steirischen Hochlande, p. 405, No 309 [and Sagen aus Steirmark, p. 50, No 44]; Jäcklin, Volksthümliches aus Graubünden, Cur, 1878, p. 18, versified by the editor; Friedrich Müller, Siebenbürgische Sagen, 1857, p. 47, No 64, and Wien, 1885, No 87; von Shulenburg, Wendische Volkssagen, p. 238; Krauss, Sagen u. Märchen der Südslaven, II, 307, No 132. J. W. Wolf, Deutsche Märchen u. Sagen, p. 162, No 42, gives the story from Thomas Cantipratensis, and in a note, at p. 595, says, dieselbe Sage ist auch muhammedanisch, doch muss ich leider die nähere Nachweise darüber für ein anderes Mal ersparen. R. Köhler.

Schambach u. Müller, Niedersächsische Sagen, No 233, p. 220, and note at p. 364; Lütolf, Sagen aus Lucern, p. 515. G. L. K.

236 a. Better in the Pahlavî text, Arḍâ-Vîrâf, Haug and West, Bombay and London, 1872, ch. 16, p. 165. Srôsh, the pious, and Åtarô, the angel, said thus. This river is the many tears which men shed from the eyes as they make lamentation and weeping for the departed. They shed those tears unlawfully, and they swell to this river. Those who are not able to cross over are those for whom, after their departure, much lamentation and weeping were made, and those who cross more easily are those for whom less was made. Speak forth to the world thus: When you are in the world, make no lamentation and weeping unlawfully; for so, much harm and difficulty may happen to the souls of your departed.

236 b. Add: the legend Santo Antonio e a Princeza, Estacio da Veiga, Romanceiro do Algarve, p. 178, Hardung, Romanceiro Portuguez, II, 151 f; and to note ‡, Jacobs, Anthologia Græca, II, 799, Appendix Epigrammatum, 125, ed. 1814. F. Liebrecht.

80. Old Robin of Portingale.

P. 240 a. Add: ‘Willie's Fatal Visit,’ Buchan, II, 259 f, stanza 5; ‘Wallace and his Leman,’ p. 226, stanza 2.

240 b, second paragraph, fourth line. Say: burns or cuts.

> And with a knyfe son gerte he schare
> A crose appone his schuldir bare.

Sir Isumbras, Thornton Romances, ed. Halliwell, p. 94, v. 135 f.

King Richard, in Richard Coer de Lion, v. 1726, Weber, II, 68, says: "Upon my flesch I bare the croys." Certain young men who had refused to take the cross, having got worsted in a fight with robbers, condignly, three days afterwards, crucem quem antea spreverant in carne sibi invicem ultronei affixerunt. Giraldus Cambrensis, Itinerarium Cambriæ, ii, 7, Opera, ed. Dimock, VI, 126. G. L. K.

81. Little Musgrave and Lady Barnard.

P. 243 b, third paragraph. Heathen child: so Sir Beues of Hamtoun, v. 3558, p. 136 (Maitland Club).

244. For wiping or whetting the sword, see turther under No 99, p. 378.

89. Fause Foodrage.

P. 297 a, third paragraph. A Färöe version, ‘Sveinur í Vallalið,’ one of five known, is printed by Hammershaimb, Færøsk Anthologi, No 19, p. 124.

90. Jellon Grame.

P. 303 b, the first paragraph. Add to Bugge, No 5, Landstad's version, No 18, stanzas 6, 7, p. 224. The trait of the extraordinary growth of the boy who is to avenge his father is preserved also in the Färöe ‘Sveinur í Vallalið’ (a variety of ‘Ung Villum,’ II, 297 a), Hammershaimb, Færøsk Anthologi, p. 131, stanzas 44, 45. Again in ‘Ivar Erlingen og Riddarsonen,’ Landstad, No 13, stanzas 22, 23, p. 161. Sigurd grows more in one month than other bairns in six in some Färöe versions of ‘Regin Smith,’ as Lyngbye, p. 58, stanzas 33, 34; the verses having, perhaps, been adopted from other ballads: see Hammershaimb, Sjúrðar kvæði, p. 6, note 2. This marvellous growth occurs in some popular tales, as ‘Der Grindkopf’ (Italian), Köhler, in Jahrbuch für rom. u. eng. Literatur, VIII, 253, Gonzenbach, Sicilianische Volksmärchen, I, 158, No 26.

91. Fair Mary of Wallington.

P. 310 b, last paragraph, eleventh line. After Wunderhorn, etc., insert: ‘Von der jungen Markgräfin,’ Seckendorf's Musenalmanach für das Jahr 1808, p. 23.

93. Lamkin.

P. 320 and 339.

W

‘Bloody Lambkin,’ communicated by Mr Macmath as derived from his aunt, Miss Jane Webster, who learned it from her aunt, Minnie Spark, Kirkcudbrightshire.

* * * *

1 And it was weel built,
    without and within,
Except a little hole,
    to let Bloody Lambkin come in.

* * *

2 He stabbed her young son,
    wi the silver bodkin,
Till oot o the cradle
    the reed blude did rin.

3 'Oh still my babe, nourrice,
  still him wi the keys:'
'He 'll no be still, madam,
  let me do what I please.'

4 'Oh still my babe, nourrice,
  still him wi the knife:'
'He 'll no be still, madam,
  na, no for my life.'

5 'Oh still my babe, still my babe,
  still him wi the bell:'
'He 'll no be still, madam,
  till ye come down yoursel.'

6 'How can I come down,
  this cold frosty night?
I have neither coal nor candle,
  for to show me light!'

*   *   *   *

7 'O haud your tongue, nourrice,
  sae loud as ye lee;
Ye 'd neer a cut finger
  but I pitied thee.'

95. Maid Freed from the Gallows.

P. 349 b. Add: Antonovitch and Dragomanof, Historical Songs of the Little-Russian People, Kief, 1874, I, 102, No 34; Chodzko, Les Chants historiques de l'Ukraine, p. 72. A Cossack writes to his father from prison, begging to be ransomed. 'How much?' asks the father. 'Eight oxen to every house, with their plows.' If he must give so much, the son will have to die. The son writes to his mother. 'How much do they ask?' 'Eight milch-cows, with their calves.' At that rate he will have to die. He writes to his love. 'How much must be paid?' 'Seven hundred ducks from each house.' She would rather part with all she has than let him die.

100. Willie o Winsbury.

P. 398. This copy, **J**, which resembles **D**, was communicated by Mr Macmath as derived, September 13, 1886, from his aunt, Miss Jane Webster, who learned it above fifty years ago at Airds of Kells, Kirkcudbrightshire, from the singing of Samuel Galloway. "Barborough may be spelt Barburgh, Barbara, or even, perhaps, Barbary."

1 There was a lass in the North Countrie,
  And her clothing it was the green,

And she 's looked ower her father's castle-wa,
  For to see her father's ships sail in, in,
  For to see her father's ships on sea.

2 'What aileth thee, dear daughter?' he said,
  'What makes thee so pale and wan?
I 'm afraid you 've got some sore sickness,
  Or have lain wi some young man, man,
  Or have lain wi some young man.'

3 'O I have got no sore sickness,
  Nor I 've lain with no young man;
But the thing that grieves me to the heart
  Is my true-love is staying too long.'
  That my true-love, etc.

4 'O is he a lord, or a duke, or a knight,
  Or a man of birth or fame?
Or is he one of my own servant-men,
  That is lately come from Spain?'

5 'He 's neither a lord, nor a duke, nor a knight,
  Nor a man of birth or fame;
But he is one of your own servant-men,
  That is lately come from Spain.'

6 'O call him down, the Spanish dog,
  O call him down to me,
For before eight o'clock next morning
  Hanged he shall be, be,
  Aye, hanged on a tree.'

7 'It 's oh forbid, dear father,' she said,
  'That anything there should be,
For if that you hang John Barborough,
  You 'll get nae mair good o me.'

8 He 's called down his merry men all,
  By one and by two and by three;
John Barborough was to be the first,
  But the last man down came he.

*   *   *   *   *

9 .   .   .   .
.   .   .   .
For every pound that he laid down,
  John Barborough laid down three.

Dr Davidson has given me a stanza, derived from Aberdeenshire, which is close to **G** 10.

She turned her right an round about,
  Wi the saut tear in her ee:

' O gin ye hang my True Tammas,
Ye 'se never see guid o me.'

To be Corrected in the Print.

I, 67 a, line 15. *Read* Trundesøn.

279 b, note §, first citation. *Read* 31² *for* 29².

319, note *, second line. *Read* later *for* Latin.

322, note *, last line but one. *Read* baciata.

392 b, third line. O *has dropt out of* Oesterley.

392 b, third paragraph, second line. *Read* husband's sons are.

400 b, first line. *Read* și.

400 b, sixth line from the bottom. *Read* Čelakovský.

407 b, second paragraph, last line but one. *Read* abbot be cook.

486 a, **CC**, first line, and 504 a, 219 b, fifth line. *Read* Schlossar.

II, 10 b, second paragraph, last line. *Read* 97 *for* 47.

78 b, stanza 26². *Read* frae *for* from.

82 a, third stanza from the bottom, second verse. *Read* Orris.

85 a, first paragraph, last line. *Read* **J** 30 *for* **F** 30.

99 a, **A** 31¹, third line. *Read* 32³ for 31¹.

133, **D** 4¹. *Read* Lord Ingram.

136 b, second paragraph, second line. *Read* III, 113–118.

137 b, third paragraph, second line. *Read* Barnard.

143, note ‡. *Read* Samlinger . . . Norske Magasin.

185 a, stanza 21³. *Drop* the.

206 a, third paragraph (7), and 215 b, second paragraph, last line but four. *Read* Aravandinos.

215 b, second paragraph, last line but five. *Read* 89 *for* 29.

256, **K** 2⁴. *Read* in o my arms.

326, stanza 8¹. *Read* O go please it.

352, stanza 20². *Read* No tho (No *having been arbitrarily struck out*).

It is intended to follow the spelling of sources or to note departures from it. The following undesigned variations from the spelling of the texts have been observed. Undoubtedly there are others. All that shall be detected will be registered, and literal conformity restored if the opportunity shall offer.

I, 145 b, 21². *Read* silver-shode.

II, 48 a, **C** 1³. *Read* rottens.

78, 4³. *Read* welcome.

78, 22². *Read* angring.

78, 24². *Read* bot.

91, **D** 24³. *Read* ha an.

91, **D** 27¹, ². *Read* ye 'el.

91, **D** 29³. *Read* mether an.

107, **D** 15². *Read* spak.

108, **E** 2⁴. *Read* die.

111, notes, **E** 1³. *Read* labour.

190, **F** 13⁴. *Read* Te.

207, **B** 3¹. *Read* whan. 4³. *Read* lang.

209, **D** 4⁴. *Read* fair. 5⁴. *Read* aw.

248, **D** 1³. *Read* Levingstone.

248, **D** 5³, 7¹, 14². *Read* gowd.

326, 12¹, 17¹. *Read* nursy.

CATALOGUE OF DOVER BOOKS

Literature, History of Literature

ARISTOTLE'S THEORY OF POETRY AND THE FINE ARTS, edited by S. H. Butcher. The celebrated Butcher translation of this great classic faced, page by page, with the complete Greek text. A 300 page introduction discussing Aristotle's ideas and their influence in the history of thought and literature, and covering art and nature, imitation as an aesthetic form, poetic truth, art and morality, tragedy, comedy, and similar topics. Modern Aristotelian criticism discussed by John Gassner. lxxvi + 421pp. 5⅜ x 8.　　　　　　　　T42 Paperbound **$2.00**

INTRODUCTIONS TO ENGLISH LITERATURE, edited by B. Dobrée. Goes far beyond ordinary histories, ranging from the 7th century up to 1914 (to the 1940's in some cases.) The first half of each volume is a specific detailed study of historical and economic background of the period and a general survey of poetry and prose, including trends of thought, influences, etc. The second and larger half is devoted to a detailed study of more than 5000 poets, novelists, dramatists; also economists, historians, biographers, religious writers, philosophers, travellers, and scientists of literary stature, with dates, lists of major works and their dates, keypoint critical bibliography, and evaluating comments. The most compendious bibliographic and literary aid within its price range.

Vol. I. THE BEGINNINGS OF ENGLISH LITERATURE TO SKELTON, (1509), W. L. Renwick, H. Orton. 450pp. 5⅛ x 7⅞.　　　　　　　　　　　　　　T75 Clothbound **$4.50**

Vol. II. THE ENGLISH RENAISSANCE, 1510-1688, V. de Sola Pinto. 381pp. 5⅛ x 7⅞.
T76 Clothbound **$4.50**

Vol. III. AUGUSTANS AND ROMANTICS, 1689-1830, H. Dyson, J. Butt. 320pp. 5⅛ x 7⅞.
T77 Clothbound **$4.50**

Vol. IV. THE VICTORIANS AND AFTER, 1830-1940's, E. Batho, B. Dobrée. 360pp. 5⅛ x 7⅞.
T78 Clothbound **$4.50**

EPIC AND ROMANCE, W. P. Ker. Written by one of the foremost authorities on medieval literature, this is the standard survey of medieval epic and romance. It covers Teutonic epics, Icelandic sagas, Beowulf, French chansons de geste, the Roman de Troie, and many other important works of literature. It is an excellent account for a body of literature whose beauty and value has only recently come to be recognized. Index. xxiv + 398pp. 5⅜ x 8.
T355 Paperbound **$2.00**

THE POPULAR BALLAD, F. B. Gummere. Most useful factual introduction; fund of descriptive material; quotes, cites over 260 ballads. Examines, from folkloristic view, structure; choral, ritual elements; meter, diction, fusion; effects of tradition, editors; almost every other aspect of border, riddle, kinship, sea, ribald, supernatural, etc., ballads. Bibliography. 2 indexes. 374pp. 5⅜ x 8.　　　　　　　　　　　　　T548 Paperbound **$1.85**

MASTERS OF THE DRAMA, John Gassner. The most comprehensive history of the drama in print, covering drama in every important tradition from the Greeks to the Near East, China, Japan, Medieval Europe, England, Russia, Italy, Spain, Germany, and dozens of other drama producing nations. This unsurpassed reading and reference work encompasses more than 800 dramatists and over 2000 plays, with biographical material, plot summaries, theatre history, etc. "Has no competitors in its field," THEATRE ARTS. "Best of its kind in English," NEW REPUBLIC. Exhaustive 35 page bibliography. 77 photographs and drawings. Deluxe edition with reinforced cloth binding, headbands, stained top. xxii + 890pp. 5⅜ x 8.　　　　T100 Clothbound **$6.95**

THE DEVELOPMENT OF DRAMATIC ART, D. C. Stuart. The basic work on the growth of Western drama from primitive beginnings to Eugene O'Neill, covering over 2500 years. Not a mere listing or survey, but a thorough analysis of changes, origins of style, and influences in each period; dramatic conventions, social pressures, choice of material, plot devices, stock situations, etc.; secular and religious works of all nations and epochs. "Generous and thoroughly documented researches," Outlook. "Solid studies of influences and playwrights and periods," London Times. Index. Bibliography. xi + 679pp. 5⅜ x 8.
T693 Paperbound **$2.75**

A SOURCE BOOK IN THEATRICAL HISTORY (SOURCES OF THEATRICAL HISTORY), A. M. Nagler. Over 2000 years of actors, directors, designers, critics, and spectators speak for themselves in this potpourri of writings selected from the great and formative periods of western drama. On-the-spot descriptions of masks, costumes, makeup, rehearsals, special effects, acting methods, backstage squabbles, theatres, etc. Contemporary glimpses of Molière rehearsing his company, an exhortation to a Roman audience to buy refreshments and keep quiet, Goethe's rules for actors, Belasco telling of $6500 he spent building a river, Restoration actors being told to avoid "lewd, obscene, or indecent postures," and much more. Each selection has an introduction by Prof. Nagler. This extraordinary, lively collection is ideal as a source of otherwise difficult to obtain material, as well as a fine book for browsing. Over 80 illustrations. 10 diagrams. xxiii + 611pp. 5⅜ x 8.　　　T515 Paperbound **$3.00**

CATALOGUE OF DOVER BOOKS

WORLD DRAMA, B. H. Clark. The dramatic creativity of a score of ages and eras — all in two handy compact volumes. Over ⅓ of this material is unavailable in any other current edition! 46 plays from Ancient Greece, Rome, Medieval Europe, France, Germany, Italy, England, Russia, Scandinavia, India, China, Japan, etc. — including classic authors like Aeschylus, Sophocles, Euripides, Aristophanes, Plautus, Marlowe, Jonson, Farquhar, Goldsmith, Cervantes, Molière, Dumas, Goethe, Schiller, Ibsen, and many others. This creative collection avoids hackneyed material and includes only completely first-rate works which are relatively little known or difficult to obtain. "The most comprehensive collection of important plays from all literature available in English," SAT. REV. OF LITERATURE. Introduction. Reading lists. 2 volumes. 1364pp. 5⅜ x 8.　　　　　　　　　　　　　　　　 Vol. 1, T57 Paperbound **$2.25**
Vol. 2, T59 Paperbound **$2.50**

MASTERPIECES OF THE RUSSIAN DRAMA, edited with introduction by G. R. Noyes. This only comprehensive anthology of Russian drama ever published in English offers complete texts, in 1st-rate modern translations, of 12 plays covering 200 years. Vol. 1: "The Young Hopeful," Fonvisin; "Wit Works Woe," Griboyedov; "The Inspector General," Gogol; "A Month in the Country," Turgenev; "The Poor Bride," Ostrovsky; "A Bitter Fate," Pisemsky. Vol. 2: "The Death of Ivan the Terrible," Alexey Tolstoy "The Power of Darkness," Lev Tolstoy; "The Lower Depths," Gorky; "The Cherry Orchard," Chekhov; "Professor Storitsyn," Andreyev; "Mystery Bouffe," Mayakovsky. Bibliography. Total of 902pp. 5⅜ x 8.
Vol. 1 T647 Paperbound **$2.00**
Vol. 2 T648 Paperbound **$2.00**

EUGENE O'NEILL: THE MAN AND HIS PLAYS, B. H. Clark. Introduction to O'Neill's life and work. Clark analyzes each play from the early THE WEB to the recently produced MOON FOR THE MISBEGOTTEN and THE ICEMAN COMETH revealing the environmental and dramatic influences necessary for a complete understanding of these important works. Bibliography. Appendices. Index. ix + 182pp. 5⅜ x 8.　　　　　　　　　　　　 T379 Paperbound **$1.35**

THE HEART OF THOREAU'S JOURNALS, edited by O. Shepard. The best general selection from Thoreau's voluminous (and rare) journals. This intimate record of thoughts and observations reveals the full Thoreau and his intellectual development more accurately than any of his published works: self-conflict between the scientific observer and the poet, reflections on transcendental philosophy, involvement in the tragedies of neighbors and national causes, etc. New preface, notes, introductions. xii + 228pp. 5⅜ x 8.　　　　　 T741 Paperbound **$1.50**

H. D. THOREAU: A WRITER'S JOURNAL, edited by L. Stapleton. A unique new selection from the Journals concentrating on Thoreau's growth as a conscious literary artist, the ideals and purposes of his art. Most of the material has never before appeared outside of the complete 14-volume edition. Contains vital insights on Thoreau's projected book on Concord, thoughts on the nature of men and government, indignation with slavery, sources of inspiration, goals in life. Index. xxxiii + 234pp. 5⅜ x 8.　　　　　　　　　　　 T678 Paperbound **$1.65**

THE HEART OF EMERSON'S JOURNALS, edited by Bliss Perry. Best of these revealing Journals, originally 10 volumes, presented in a one volume edition. Talks with Channing, Hawthorne, Thoreau, and Bronson Alcott; impressions of Webster, Everett, John Brown, and Lincoln; records of moments of sudden understanding, vision, and solitary ecstasy. "The essays do not reveal the power of Emerson's mind . . . as do these hasty and informal writings," N.Y. Times. Preface by Bliss Perry. Index. xiii + 357pp. 5⅜ x 8.　　 T477 Paperbound **$1.85**

FOUNDERS OF THE MIDDLE AGES, E. K. Rand. This is the best non-technical discussion of the transformation of Latin pagan culture into medieval civilization. Covering such figures as Tertullian, Gregory, Jerome, Boethius, Augustine, the Neoplatonists, and many other literary men, educators, classicists, and humanists, this book is a storehouse of information presented clearly and simply for the intelligent non-specialist. "Thoughtful, beautifully written," AMERICAN HISTORICAL REVIEW. "Extraordinarily accurate," Richard McKeon, THE NATION. ix + 365pp. 5⅜ x 8.　　　　　　　　　　　　　　　　　　　　 T369 Paperbound **$2.00**

PLAY-MAKING: A MANUAL OF CRAFTSMANSHIP, William Archer. With an extensive, new introduction by John Gassner, Yale Univ. The permanently essential requirements of solid play construction are set down in clear, practical language: theme, exposition, foreshadowing, tension, obligatory scene, peripety, dialogue, character, psychology, other topics. This book has been one of the most influential elements in the modern theatre, and almost everything said on the subject since is contained explicitly or implicitly within its covers. Bibliography. Index. xlii + 277pp. 5⅜ x 8.　　　　　　　　　　　　　　　　　　　　 T651 Paperbound **$1.75**

HAMBURG DRAMATURGY, G. E. Lessing. One of the most brilliant of German playwrights of the eighteenth-century age of criticism analyzes the complex of theory and tradition that constitutes the world of theater. These 104 essays on aesthetic theory helped demolish the regime of French classicism, opening the door to psychological and social realism, romanticism. Subjects include the original functions of tragedy; drama as the rational world; the meaning of pity and fear, pity and fear as means for purgation and other Aristotelian concepts; genius and creative force; interdependence of poet's language and actor's interpretation; truth and authenticity; etc. A basic and enlightening study for anyone interested in aesthetics and ideas, from the philosopher to the theatergoer. Introduction by Prof. Victor Lange. xxii + 265pp. 4½ x 6⅜.　　　　　　　　　　　　　 T32 Paperbound **$1.45**

Philosophy, Religion

GUIDE TO PHILOSOPHY, C. E. M. Joad. A modern classic which examines many crucial problems which man has pondered through the ages: Does free will exist? Is there plan in the universe? How do we know and validate our knowledge? Such opposed solutions as subjective idealism and realism, chance and teleology, vitalism and logical positivism, are evaluated and the contributions of the great philosophers from the Greeks to moderns like Russell, Whitehead, and others, are considered in the context of each problem. "The finest introduction," BOSTON TRANSCRIPT. Index. Classified bibliography. 592pp. 5⅜ x 8.
T297 Paperbound **$2.00**

HISTORY OF ANCIENT PHILOSOPHY, W. Windelband. One of the clearest, most accurate comprehensive surveys of Greek and Roman philosophy. Discusses ancient philosophy in general, intellectual life in Greece in the 7th and 6th centuries B.C., Thales, Anaximander, Anaximenes, Heraclitus, the Eleatics, Empedocles, Anaxagoras, Leucippus, the Pythagoreans, the Sophists, Socrates, Democritus (20 pages), Plato (50 pages), Aristotle (70 pages), the Peripatetics, Stoics, Epicureans, Sceptics, Neo-platonists, Christian Apologists, etc. 2nd German edition translated by H. E. Cushman. xv + 393pp. 5⅜ x 8.
T357 Paperbound **$1.85**

ILLUSTRATIONS OF THE HISTORY OF MEDIEVAL THOUGHT AND LEARNING, R. L. Poole. Basic analysis of the thought and lives of the leading philosophers and ecclesiastics from the 8th to the 14th century—Abailard, Ockham, Wycliffe, Marsiglio of Padua, and many other great thinkers who carried the torch of Western culture and learning through the "Dark Ages": political, religious, and metaphysical views. Long a standard work for scholars and one of the best introductions to medieval thought for beginners. Index. 10 Appendices. xiii + 327pp. 5⅜ x 8.
T674 Paperbound **$1.85**

PHILOSOPHY AND CIVILIZATION IN THE MIDDLE AGES, M. de Wulf. This semi-popular survey covers aspects of medieval intellectual life such as religion, philosophy, science, the arts, etc. It also covers feudalism vs. Catholicism, rise of the universities, mendicant orders, monastic centers, and similar topics. Unabridged. Bibliography. Index. viii + 320pp. 5⅜ x 8.
T284 Paperbound **$1.85**

AN INTRODUCTION TO SCHOLASTIC PHILOSOPHY, Prof. M. de Wulf. Formerly entitled SCHOLASTICISM OLD AND NEW, this volume examines the central scholastic tradition from St. Anselm, Albertus Magnus, Thomas Aquinas, up to Suarez in the 17th century. The relation of scholasticism to ancient and medieval philosophy and science in general is clear and easily followed. The second part of the book considers the modern revival of scholasticism, the Louvain position, relations with Kantianism and Positivism. Unabridged. xvi + 271pp. 5⅜ x 8.
T296 Clothbound **$3.50**
T283 Paperbound **$1.75**

A HISTORY OF MODERN PHILOSOPHY, H. Höffding. An exceptionally clear and detailed coverage of western philosophy from the Renaissance to the end of the 19th century. Major and minor men such as Pomponazzi, Bodin, Boehme, Telesius, Bruno, Copernicus, da Vinci, Kepler, Galileo, Bacon, Descartes, Hobbes, Spinoza, Leibniz, Wolff, Locke, Newton, Berkeley, Hume, Erasmus, Montesquieu, Voltaire, Diderot, Rousseau, Lessing, Kant, Herder, Fichte, Schelling, Hegel, Schopenhauer, Comte, Mill, Darwin, Spencer, Hartmann, Lange, and many others, are discussed in terms of theory of knowledge, logic, cosmology, and psychology. Index. 2 volumes, total of 1159pp. 5⅜ x 8.
T117 Vol. 1, Paperbound **$2.25**
T118 Vol. 2, Paperbound **$2.25**

ARISTOTLE, A. E. Taylor. A brilliant, searching non-technical account of Aristotle and his thought written by a foremost Platonist. It covers the life and works of Aristotle; classification of the sciences; logic; first philosophy; matter and form; causes; motion and eternity; God; physics; metaphysics; and similar topics. Bibliography. New Index compiled for this edition. 128pp. 5⅜ x 8.
T280 Paperbound **$1.00**

THE SYSTEM OF THOMAS AQUINAS, M. de Wulf. Leading Neo-Thomist, one of founders of University of Louvain, gives concise exposition to central doctrines of Aquinas, as a means toward determining his value to modern philosophy, religion. Formerly "Medieval Philosophy Illustrated from the System of Thomas Aquinas." Trans. by E. Messenger. Introduction. 151pp. 5⅜ x 8.
T568 Paperbound **$1.25**

LEIBNIZ, H. W. Carr. Most stimulating middle-level coverage of basic philosophical thought of Leibniz. Easily understood discussion, analysis of major works: "Theodicy," "Principles of Nature and Grace," "Monadology"; Leibniz's influence; intellectual growth; correspondence; disputes with Bayle, Malebranche, Newton; importance of his thought today, with reinterpretation in modern terminology. "Power and mastery," London Times. Bibliography. Index. 226pp. 5⅜ x 8.
T624 Paperbound **$1.35**

CATALOGUE OF DOVER BOOKS

AN ESSAY CONCERNING HUMAN UNDERSTANDING, John Locke. Edited by A. C. Fraser. Unabridged reprinting of definitive edition; only complete edition of "Essay" in print. Marginal analyses of almost every paragraph; hundreds of footnotes; authoritative 140-page biographical, critical, historical prolegomena. Indexes. 1170pp. 5⅜ x 8.

T530 Vol. 1 (Books 1, 2) Paperbound **$2.25**
T531 Vol. 2 (Books 3, 4) Paperbound **$2.25**
2 volume set **$4.50**

THE PHILOSOPHY OF HISTORY, G. W. F. Hegel. One of the great classics of western thought which reveals Hegel's basic principle: that history is not chance but a rational process, the realization of the Spirit of Freedom. Ranges from the oriental cultures of subjective thought to the classical subjective cultures, to the modern absolute synthesis where spiritual and secular may be reconciled. Translation and introduction by J. Sibree. Introduction by C. Hegel. Special introduction for this edition by Prof. Carl Friedrich. xxxix + 447pp. 5⅜ x 8.

T112 Paperbound **$2.00**

THE PHILOSOPHY OF HEGEL, W. T. Stace. The first detailed analysis of Hegel's thought in English, this is especially valuable since so many of Hegel's works are out of print. Dr. Stace examines Hegel's debt to Greek idealists and the 18th century and then proceeds to a careful description and analysis of Hegel's first principles, categories, reason, dialectic method, his logic, philosophy of nature and spirit, etc. Index. Special 14 x 20 chart of Hegelian system. x + 526pp. 5⅜ x 8.

T254 Paperbound **$2.25**

THE WILL TO BELIEVE and HUMAN IMMORTALITY, W. James. Two complete books bound as one. THE WILL TO BELIEVE discusses the interrelations of belief, will, and intellect in man; chance vs. determinism, free will vs. determinism, free will vs. fate, pluralism vs. monism; the philosophies of Hegel and Spencer, and more. HUMAN IMMORTALITY examines the question of survival after death and develops an unusual and powerful argument for immortality. Two prefaces. Index. Total of 429pp. 5⅜ x 8.

T291 Paperbound **$2.45**

THE WORLD AND THE INDIVIDUAL, Josiah Royce. Only major effort by an American philosopher to interpret nature of things in systematic, comprehensive manner. Royce's formulation of an absolute voluntarism remains one of the original and profound solutions to the problems involved. Part One, Four Historical Conceptions of Being, inquires into first principles, true meaning and place of individuality. Part Two, Nature, Man, and the Moral Order, is application of first principles to problems concerning religion, evil, moral order. Introduction by J. E. Smith, Yale Univ. Index. 1070pp. 5⅜ x 8.

T561 Vol. 1 Paperbound **$2.75**
T562 Vol. 2 Paperbound **$2.75**
Two volume set **$5.50**

THE PHILOSOPHICAL WRITINGS OF PEIRCE, edited by J. Buchler. This book (formerly THE PHILOSOPHY OF PEIRCE) is a carefully integrated exposition of Peirce's complete system composed of selections from his own work. Symbolic logic, scientific method, theory of signs, pragmatism, epistemology, chance, cosmology, ethics, and many other topics are treated by one of the greatest philosophers of modern times. This is the only inexpensive compilation of his key ideas. xvi + 386pp. 5⅜ x 8.

T217 Paperbound **$2.00**

EXPERIENCE AND NATURE, John Dewey. An enlarged, revised edition of the Paul Carus lectures which Dewey delivered in 1925. It covers Dewey's basic formulation of the problem of knowledge, with a full discussion of other systems, and a detailing of his own concepts of the relationship of external world, mind, and knowledge. Starts with a thorough examination of the philosophical method; examines the interrelationship of experience and nature; analyzes experience on basis of empirical naturalism, the formulation of law, role of language and social factors in knowledge; etc. Dewey's treatment of central problems in philosophy is profound but extremely easy to follow. ix + 448pp. 5⅜ x 8.

T471 Paperbound **$2.00**

THE PHILOSOPHICAL WORKS OF DESCARTES. The definitive English edition of all the major philosophical works and letters of René Descartes. All of his revolutionary insights, from his famous "Cogito ergo sum" to his detailed account of contemporary science and his astonishingly fruitful concept that all phenomena of the universe (except mind) could be reduced to clear laws by the use of mathematics. An excellent source for the thought of men like Hobbes, Arnauld, Gassendi, etc., who were Descarte's contemporaries. Translated by E. S. Haldane and G. Ross. Introductory notes. Index. Total of 842pp. 5⅜ x 8.

T71 Vol. 1, Paperbound **$2.00**
T72 Vol. 2, Paperbound **$2.00**

THE CHIEF WORKS OF SPINOZA. An unabridged reprint of the famous Bohn edition containing all of Spinoza's most important works: Vol. I: The Theologico-Political Treatise and the Political Treatise. Vol. II: On The Improvement Of Understanding, The Ethics, Selected Letters. Profound and enduring ideas on God, the universe, pantheism, society, religion, the state, democracy, the mind, emotions, freedom and the nature of man, which influenced Goethe, Hegel, Schelling, Coleridge, Whitehead, and many others. Introduction. 2 volumes. 826pp. 5⅜ x 8.

T249 Vol. I, Paperbound **$1.50**
T250 Vol. II, Paperbound **$1.50**

CATALOGUE OF DOVER BOOKS

THE SENSE OF BEAUTY, G. Santayana. A revelation of the beauty of language as well as an important philosophic treatise, this work studies the "why, when, and how beauty appears, what conditions an object must fulfill to be beautiful, what elements of our nature make us sensible of beauty, and what the relation is between the constitution of the object and the excitement of our susceptibility." "It is doubtful if a better treatment of the subject has since been published," PEABODY JOURNAL. Index. ix + 275pp. 5⅜ x 8.
T238 Paperbound **$1.00**

PROBLEMS OF ETHICS, Moritz Schlick. The renowned leader of the "Vienna Circle" applies the logical positivist approach to a wide variety of ethical problems: the source and means of attaining knowledge, the formal and material characteristics of the good, moral norms and principles, absolute vs. relative values, free will and responsibility, comparative importance of pleasure and suffering as ethical values, etc. Disarmingly simple and straightforward despite complexity of subject. First English translation, authorized by author before his death, of a thirty-year old classic. Translated and with an introduction by David Rynin. Index. Foreword by Prof. George P. Adams. xxi + 209pp. 5⅜ x 8.
T946 Paperbound **$1.45**

AN INTRODUCTION TO EXISTENTIALISM, Robert G. Olson. A new and indispensable guide to one of the major thought systems of our century, the movement that is central to the thinking of some of the most creative figures of the past hundred years. Stresses Heidegger and Sartre, with careful and objective examination of the existentialist position, values—freedom of choice, individual dignity, personal love, creative effort—and answers to the eternal questions of the human condition. Scholarly, unbiased, analytic, unlike most studies of this difficult subject, Prof. Olson's book is aimed at the student of philosophy as well as at the reader with no formal training who is looking for an absorbing, accessible, and thorough introduction to the basic texts. Index. xv + 221pp. 5⅜ x 8½.
T55 Paperbound **$1.45**

SYMBOLIC LOGIC, C. I. Lewis and C. H. Langford. Since first publication in 1932, this has been among most frequently cited works on symbolic logic. Still one of the best introductions both for beginners and for mathematicians, philosophers. First part covers basic topics which easily lend themselves to beginning study. Second part is rigorous, thorough development of logistic method, examination of some of most difficult and abstract aspects of symbolic logic, including modal logic, logical paradoxes, many-valued logic, with Prof. Lewis' own contributions. 2nd revised (corrected) edition. 3 appendixes, one new to this edition. 524pp. 5⅜ x 8.
S170 Paperbound **$2.00**

WHITEHEAD'S PHILOSOPHY OF CIVILIZATION, A. H. Johnson. A leading authority on Alfred North Whitehead synthesizes the great philosopher's thought on civilization, scattered throughout various writings, into unified whole. Analysis of Whitehead's general definition of civilization, his reflections on history and influences on its development, his religion, including his analysis of Christianity, concept of solitariness as first requirement of personal religion, and so on. Other chapters cover views on minority groups, society, civil liberties, education. Also critical comments on Whitehead's philosophy. Written with general reader in mind. A perceptive introduction to important area of the thought of a leading philosopher of our century. Revised index and bibliography. xii + 211pp. 5⅜ x 8½.
T996 Paperbound **$1.50**

WHITEHEAD'S THEORY OF REALITY, A. H. Johnson. Introductory outline of Whitehead's theory of actual entities, the heart of his philosophy of reality, followed by his views on nature of God, philosophy of mind, theory of value (truth, beauty, goodness and their opposites), analyses of other philosophers, attitude toward science. A perspicacious lucid introduction by author of dissertation on Whitehead, written under the subject's supervision at Harvard. Good basic view for beginning students of philosophy and for those who are simply interested in important contemporary ideas. Revised index and bibliography. xiii + 267pp. 5⅜ x 8½.
T989 Paperbound **$1.50**

MIND AND THE WORLD-ORDER, C. I. Lewis. Building upon the work of Peirce, James, and Dewey, Professor Lewis outlines a theory of knowledge in terms of "conceptual pragmatism." Dividing truth into abstract mathematical certainty and empirical truth, the author demonstrates that the traditional understanding of the a priori must be abandoned. Detailed analyses of philosophy, metaphysics, method, the "given" in experience, knowledge of objects, nature of the a priori, experience and order, and many others. Appendices. xiv + 446pp. 5⅜ x 8.
T359 Paperbound **$2.25**

SCEPTICISM AND ANIMAL FAITH, G. Santayana. To eliminate difficulties in the traditional theory of knowledge, Santayana distinguishes between the independent existence of objects and the essence our mind attributes to them. Scepticism is thereby established as a form of belief, and animal faith is shown to be a necessary condition of knowledge. Belief, classical idealism, intuition, memory, symbols, literary psychology, and much more, discussed with unusual clarity and depth. Index. xii + 314pp. 5⅜ x 8.
T235 Clothbound **$3.50**
T236 Paperbound **$1.50**

LANGUAGE AND MYTH, E. Cassirer. Analyzing the non-rational thought processes which go to make up culture, Cassirer demonstrates that beneath both language and myth there lies a dominant unconscious "grammar" of experience whose categories and canons are not those of logical thought. His analyses of seemingly diverse phenomena such as Indian metaphysics, the Melanesian "mana," the Naturphilosophie of Schelling, modern poetry, etc., are profound without being pedantic. Introduction and translation by Susanne Langer. Index. x + 103pp. 5⅜ x 8.
T51 Paperbound **$1.25**

Music

A GENERAL HISTORY OF MUSIC, Charles Burney. A detailed coverage of music from the Greeks up to 1789, with full information on all types of music: sacred and secular, vocal and instrumental, operatic and symphonic. Theory, notation, forms, instruments, innovators, composers, performers, typical and important works, and much more in an easy, entertaining style. Burney covered much of Europe and spoke with hundreds of authorities and composers so that this work is more than a compilation of records . . . it is a living work of careful and first-hand scholarship. Its account of thoroughbass (18th century) Italian music is probably still the best introduction on the subject. A recent NEW YORK TIMES review said, "Surprisingly few of Burney's statements have been invalidated by modern research . . . still of great value." Edited and corrected by Frank Mercer. 35 figures. Indices. 1915pp. 5⅜ x 8. 2 volumes. **T36 The Set, Clothbound $12.50**

A DICTIONARY OF HYMNOLOGY, John Julian. This exhaustive and scholarly work has become known as an invaluable source of hundreds of thousands of important and often difficult to obtain facts on the history and use of hymns in the western world. Everyone interested in hymns will be fascinated by the accounts of famous hymns and hymn writers and amazed by the amount of practical information he will find. More than 30,000 entries on individual hymns, giving authorship, date and circumstances of composition, publication, textual variations, translations, denominational and ritual usage, etc. Biographies of more than 9,000 hymn writers, and essays on important topics such as Christmas carols and children's hymns, and much other unusual and valuable information. A 200 page double-columned index of first lines — the largest in print. Total of 1786 pages in two reinforced clothbound volumes. 6¼ x 9¼. **The set, T333 Clothbound $17.50**

MUSIC IN MEDIEVAL BRITAIN, F. Ll. Harrison. The most thorough, up-to-date, and accurate treatment of the subject ever published, beautifully illustrated. Complete account of institutions and choirs; carols, masses, and motets; liturgy and plainsong; and polyphonic music from the Norman Conquest to the Reformation. Discusses the various schools of music and their reciprocal influences; the origin and development of new ritual forms; development and use of instruments; and new evidence on many problems of the period. Reproductions of scores, over 200 excerpts from medieval melodies. Rules of harmony and dissonance; influence of Continental styles; great composers (Dunstable, Cornysh, Fairfax, etc.); and much more. Register and index of more than 400 musicians. Index of titles. General Index. 225-item bibliography. 6 Appendices. xix + 491pp. 5⅝ x 8¾. **T705 Clothbound $10.00**

THE MUSIC OF SPAIN, Gilbert Chase. Only book in English to give concise, comprehensive account of Iberian music; new Chapter covers music since 1941. Victoria, Albéniz, Cabezón, Pedrell, Turina, hundreds of other composers; popular and folk music; the Gypsies; the guitar; dance, theatre, opera, with only extensive discussion in English of the Zarzuela; virtuosi such as Casals; much more. "Distinguished . . . readable," Saturday Review. 400-item bibliography. Index. 27 photos. 383pp. 5⅜ x 8. **T549 Paperbound $2.00**

ON STUDYING SINGING, Sergius Kagen. An intelligent method of voice-training, which leads you around pitfalls that waste your time, money, and effort. Exposes rigid, mechanical systems, baseless theories, deleterious exercises. "Logical, clear, convincing . . . dead right," Virgil Thomson, N.Y. Herald Tribune. "I recommend this volume highly," Maggie Teyte, Saturday Review. 119pp. 5⅜ x 8. **T622 Paperbound $1.25**

WILLIAM LAWES, M. Lefkowitz. This is the definitive work on Lawes, the versatile, prolific, and highly original "King's musician" of 17th century England. His life is reconstructed from original documents, and nearly every piece he ever wrote is examined and evaluated: his fantasias, pavans, violin "sonatas," lyra viol and bass viol suites, and music for harp and theorbo; and his songs, masques, and theater music to words by Herrick ("Gather Ye Rosebuds"), Jonson, Suckling, Shirley, and others. The author shows the innovations of dissonance, augmented triad, and other Italian influences Lawes helped introduce to England. List of Lawes' complete works and several complete scores by this major precursor of Purcell and the 18th century developments. Index. 5 Appendices. 52 musical excerpts, many never before in print. Bibliography. x + 320pp. 5⅜ x 8. **T706 Clothbound $10.00**

THE FUGUE IN BEETHOVEN'S PIANO MUSIC, J. V. Cockshoot. The first study of a neglected aspect of Beethoven's genius: his ability as a writer of fugues. Analyses of early studies and published works demonstrate his original and powerful contributions to composition. 34 works are examined, with 143 musical excerpts. For all pianists, teachers, students, and music-minded readers with a serious interest in Beethoven. Index. 93-item bibliography. Illustration of original score for "Fugue in C." xv + 212pp. 5⅝ x 8⅜. **T704 Clothbound $6.00**

CATALOGUE OF DOVER BOOKS

JOHANN SEBASTIAN BACH, Philipp Spitta. The complete and unabridged text of the definitive study of Bach. Written some 70 years ago, it is still unsurpassed for its coverage of nearly all aspects of Bach's life and work. There could hardly be a finer non-technical introduction to Bach's music than the detailed, lucid analyses which Spitta provides for hundreds of individual pieces. 26 solid pages are devoted to the B minor mass, for example, and 30 pages to the glorious St. Matthew Passion. This monumental set also includes a major analysis of the music of the 18th century: Buxtehude, Pachelbel, etc. "Unchallenged as the last word on one of the supreme geniuses of music," John Barkham, SATURDAY REVIEW SYNDICATE. Total of 1819pp. 2 volumes. Heavy cloth binding. 5⅜ x 8. T252 The set, Clothbound **$12.50**

THE LIFE OF MOZART, O. Jahn. Probably the largest amount of material on Mozart's life and works ever gathered together in one book! Its 1350 authoritative and readable pages cover every event in his life, and contain a full critique of almost every piece he ever wrote, including sketches and intimate works. There is a full historical-cultural background, and vast research into musical and literary history, sources of librettos, prior treatments of Don Juan legend, etc. This is the complete and unaltered text of the definitive Townsend translation, with foreword by Grove. 5 engraved portraits from Salzburg archives. 4 facsimiles in Mozart's hand. 226 musical examples. 4 Appendixes, including complete list of Mozart's compositions, with Köchel numbers (fragmentary works included). Total of xxviii + 1352pp. Three volume set. 5⅜ x 8.

T85 Vol. I Clothbound **$5.00**
T86 Vol. II Clothbound **$5.00**
The set **$10.00**

BEETHOVEN'S QUARTETS, J. de Marliave. The most complete and authoritative study ever written, enjoyable for scholar and layman alike. The 16 quartets and Grand Fugue are all analyzed bar by bar and theme by theme, not over-technically, but concentrating on mood and effects. Complete background material for each composition: influences, first reviews, etc. Preface by Gabriel Fauré. Introduction and notes by J. Escarra. Translated by Hilda Andrews. 321 musical examples. xxiii + 379pp. 5⅜ x 8. T694 Paperbound **$1.85**

STRUCTURAL HEARING: TONAL COHERENCE IN MUSIC, Felix Salzer. Written by a pupil of the late Heinrich Schenker, this is not only the most thorough exposition in English of the Schenker method but also extends the Schenker approach to include modern music, the middle ages, and renaissance music. It explores the phenomenon of tonal organization by means of a detailed analysis and discussion of more than 500 musical pieces. It casts new light for the reader acquainted with harmony upon the understanding of musical compositions, problems of musical coherence, and connection between theory and composition. "Has been the foundation on which all teaching in music theory has been based at this college," Leopold Mannes, President of The Mannes College of Music. 2 volumes. Total of 658pp. 6½ x 9¼. The set, T418 Clothbound **$8.00**

ANTONIO STRADIVARI: HIS LIFE AND WORK (1644-1737), W. Henry Hill, Arthur F. Hill, and Alfred E. Hill. Still the only book that really delves into life and art of the incomparable Italian craftsman, maker of the finest musical instruments in the world today. The authors, expert violin-makers themselves, discuss Stradivari's ancestry, his construction and finishing techniques, distinguished characteristics of many of his instruments and their locations. Included, too, is story of introduction of his instruments into France, England, first revelation of their supreme merit, and information on his labels, number of instruments made, prices, mystery of ingredients of his varnish, tone of pre-1684 Stradivari violin and changes between 1684 and 1690. An extremely interesting, informative account for all music lovers, from craftsman to concert-goer. Republication of original (1902) edition. New introduction by Sydney Beck, Head of Rare Book and Manuscript Collections, Music Division, New York Public Library. Analytical index by Rembert Wurlitzer. Appendixes. 68 illustrations. 30 full-page plates. 4 in color. xxvi + 315pp. 5⅜ x 8½. T425 Paperbound **$2.25**

THREE CLASSICS IN THE AESTHETIC OF MUSIC, Claude Debussy, Ferrucio Busoni, and Charles Ives. Three very different points of view by three top-ranking modern composers. "M. Croche, the Dilettante-Hater" consists of twenty-five brief articles written by Debussy between the years 1901 and 1905, a sparkling collection of personal commentary on a wide range of topics. Busoni's "Toward a New Aesthetic of Music" considers the nature of absolute music in an attempt to suggest answers to the question, What are the aims of music?, and discusses modern systems of tonality and harmony, the concept of unity of keys, etc. Ives's "Essays Before a Sonata," a literary complement to the movements of the author's "Concord, 1845" piano sonata, contains his most mature analysis of his art. Stimulating reading for musicians, music lovers, and philosophers of the arts. iv + 188pp. 5⅜ x 8½. T320 Paperbound **$1.45**

Dover Classical Records

Now available directly to the public exclusively from Dover: top-quality recordings of fine classical music for only $2 per record! Almost all were released by major record companies to sell for $5 and $6. These recordings were issued under our imprint only after they had passed a severe critical test. We insisted upon:

First-rate music that is enjoyable, musically important and culturally significant.

First-rate performances, where the artists have carried out the composer's intentions, in which the music is alive, vigorous, played with understanding and sensitivity.

First-rate sound—clear, sonorous, fully balanced, crackle-free, whir-free.

Have in your home music by major composers, performed by such gifted musicians as Elsner, Gitlis, Wührer, Beveridge Webster, the Barchet Quartet, Gimpel, etc. Enthusiastically received when first released, many of these performances are definitive. The records are not seconds or remainders, but brand new pressings made on pure vinyl from carefully chosen master tapes. "All purpose" 12" monaural 33⅓ rpm records, they play equally well on hi-fi and stereo equipment. Fine music for discriminating music lovers, superlatively played, flawlessly recorded: there is no better way to build your library of recorded classical music at remarkable savings. There are no strings; this is not a come-on, not a club, forcing you to buy records you may not want in order to get a few at a lower price. Buy whatever records you want in any quantity, and never pay more than $2 each. Your obligation ends with your first purchase. And that's when ours begins. Dover's money-back guarantee allows you to return any record for any reason, even if you don't like the music, for a full, immediate refund—no questions asked.

MOZART: STRING QUARTETS: IN A (K. 464) AND C ("DISSONANT") (K. 465), Barchet Quartet. The final two of the famous Haydn Quartets, high-points in the history of music. The A Major was accepted with delight by Mozart's contemporaries, but the C Major, with its dissonant opening, aroused strong protest. Today, of course, the remarkable resolutions of the dissonances are recognized as major musical achievements. "Beautiful warm playing," MUSICAL AMERICA. "Two of Mozart's loveliest quartets in a distinguished performance," REV. OF RECORDED MUSIC. (Playing time 58 mins.)   HCR 5200 **$2.00**

MOZART: STRING QUARTETS: IN G (K. 80), D (K. 156), and C (K. 157), Barchet Quartet. The early chamber music of Mozart receives unfortunately little attention. First-rate music of the Italian school, it contains all the lightness and charm that belongs only to the youthful Mozart. This is currently the only separate source for the composer's work of this period. "Excellent," HIGH FIDELITY. "Filled with sunshine and youthful joy; played with verve, recorded sound live and brilliant," CHRISTIAN SCI. MONITOR. (playing time 51 mins.)   HCR 5201 **$2.00**

MOZART: SERENADES: #9 IN D ("POSTHORN") (K. 320), #6 IN D ("SERENATA NOTTURNA") (K. 239), Pro Musica Orch. of Stuttgart, under Edouard van Remoortel. For Mozart, the serenade was a highly effective form, since he could bring to it the immediacy and intimacy of chamber music as well as the free fantasy of larger group music. Both these serenades are distinguished by a playful, mischievous quality, a spirit perfectly captured in this fine performance. "A triumph, polished playing from the orchestra," HI FI MUSIC AT HOME. "Sound is rich and resonant, fidelity is wonderful," REV. OF RECORDED MUSIC. (Playing time 51 mins.)   HCR 5202 **$2.00**

MOZART: DIVERTIMENTO FOR VIOLIN, VIOLA AND CELLO IN E FLAT (K. 563); ADAGIO AND FUGUE IN F MINOR (K. 404a), Kehr Trio. The divertimento is one of Mozart's most beloved pieces, called by Einstein "the finest and most perfect trio ever heard." It is difficult to imagine a music lover who will not be delighted by it. This is the only recording of the lesser known Adagio and Fugue, written in 1782 and influenced by Bach's Well-Tempered Clavichord. "Extremely beautiful recording, strongly recommended," THE OBSERVER. "Superior to rival editions," HIGH FIDELITY. (Playing time 51 mins.)   HCR 5203 **$2.00**

SCHUMANN: KREISLERIANA (OPUS 16) AND FANTASIA IN C (OPUS 17), Vlado Perlemuter, Piano. The vigorous Romantic imagination and the remarkable emotional qualities of Schumann's piano music raise it to a special eminence in 19th-century creativity. Both these pieces are rooted to the composer's tortuous romance with his future wife, Clara, and both receive brilliant treatment at the hands of Vlado Perlemuter, Paris Conservatory, proclaimed by Alfred Cortot "not only a great virtuoso but also a great musician." "The best Kreisleriana to date," BILLBOARD. (Playing time 55 mins.)   HCR 5204 **$2.00**

CATALOGUE OF DOVER BOOKS

SCHUMANN: TRIOS #1 IN D MINOR (OPUS 63) AND #3 IN G MINOR (OPUS 110), Trio di Bolzano. The fiery, romantic, melodic Trio #1 and the dramatic, seldom heard Trio #3 are both movingly played by a fine chamber ensemble. No one personified Romanticism to the general public of the 1840's more than did Robert Schumann, and among his most romantic works are these trios for cello, violin and piano. "Ensemble and overall interpretation leave little to be desired," HIGH FIDELITY. "An especially understanding performance," REV. OF RECORDED MUSIC. (Playing time 54 mins.) HCR 5205 **$2.00**

SCHUBERT: QUINTET IN A ("TROUT") (OPUS 114), AND NOCTURNE IN E FLAT (OPUS 148), Friedrich Wührer, Piano and Barchet Quartet. If there is a single piece of chamber music that is a universal favorite, it is probably Schubert's "Trout" Quintet. Delightful melody, harmonic resources, musical exuberance are its characteristics. The Nocturne (played by Wührer, Barchet, and Reimann) is an exquisite piece with a deceptively simple theme and harmony. "The best Trout on the market—Wührer is a fine Viennese-style Schubertian, and his spirit infects the Barchets," ATLANTIC MONTHLY. "Exquisitely recorded," ETUDE. (Playing time 44 mins.) HCR 5206 **$2.00**

SCHUBERT: PIANO SONATAS IN C MINOR AND B (OPUS 147), Friedrich Wührer. Schubert's sonatas retain the structure of the classical form, but delight listeners with romantic freedom and a special melodic richness. The C Minor, one of the Three Grand Sonatas, is a product of the composer's maturity. The B Major was not published until 15 years after his death. "Remarkable interpretation, reproduction of the first rank," DISQUES. "A superb pianist for music like this, musicianship, sweep, power, and an ability to integrate Schubert's measures such as few pianists have had since Schnabel," Harold Schonberg. (Playing time 49 mins.) HCR 5207 **$2.00**

STRAVINSKY: VIOLIN CONCERTO IN D, Ivry Gitlis, Cologne Orchestra; DUO CONCERTANTE, Ivry Gitlis, Violin, Charlotte Zelka, Piano, Cologne Orchestra; JEU DE CARTES, Bamberg Symphony, under Hollreiser. Igor Stravinsky is probably the most important composer of this century, and these three works are among the most significant of his neoclassical period of the 30's. The Violin Concerto is one of the few modern classics. Jeu de Cartes, a ballet score, bubbles with gaiety, color and melodiousness. "Imaginatively played and beautifully recorded," E. T. Canby, HARPERS MAGAZINE. "Gitlis is excellent, Hollreiser beautifully worked out," HIGH FIDELITY. (Playing time 55 mins.) HCR 5208 **$2.00**

GEMINIANI: SIX CONCERTI GROSSI, OPUS 3, Helma Elsner, Harpsichord, Barchet Quartet, Pro Musica Orch. of Stuttgart, under Reinhardt. Francesco Geminiani (1687-1762) has been rediscovered in the same musical exploration that revealed Scarlatti, Vivaldi, and Corelli. In form he is more sophisticated than the earlier Italians, but his music delights modern listeners with its combination of contrapuntal techniques and the full harmonies and rich melodies charcteristic of Italian music. This is the only recording of the six 1733 concerti: D Major, B Flat Minor, E Minor, G Minor, E Minor (bis), and D Minor. "I warmly recommend it, spacious, magnificent, I enjoyed every bar," C. Cudworth, RECORD NEWS. "Works of real charm, recorded with understanding and style," ETUDE. (Playing time 52 mins.) HCR 5209 **$2.00**

MODERN PIANO SONATAS: BARTOK: SONATA FOR PIANO; BLOCH: SONATA FOR PIANO (1935); PROKOFIEV, PIANO SONATA #7 IN B FLAT ("STALINGRAD"); STRAVINSKY: PIANO SONATA (1924), István Nádas, Piano. Shows some of the major forces and directions in modern piano music: Stravinsky's crisp austerity; Bartok's fusion of Hungarian folk motives; incisive diverse rhythms, and driving power; Bloch's distinctive emotional vigor; Prokofiev's brilliance and melodic beauty couched in pre-Romantic forms. "A most interesting documentation of the contemporary piano sonata. Nadas is a very good pianist." HIGH FIDELITY. (Playing time 59 mins.) HCR 5215 **$2.00**

VIVALDI: CONCERTI FOR FLUTE, VIOLIN, BASSOON, AND HARPSICHORD: #8 IN G MINOR, #21 IN F, #27 IN D, #7 IN D; SONATA #1 IN A MINOR, Gastone Tassinari, Renato Giangrandi, Giorgio Semprini, Arlette Eggmann. More than any other Baroque composer, Vivaldi moved the concerto grosso closer to the solo concert we deem standard today. In these concerti he wrote virtuosi music for the solo instruments, allowing each to introduce new material or expand on musical ideas, creating tone colors unusual even for Vivaldi. As a result, this record displays a new area of his genius, offering some of his most brilliant music. Performed by a top-rank European group. (Playing time 45 mins.) HCR 5216 **$2.00**

LÜBECK: CANTATAS: HILF DEINEM VOLK; GOTT, WIE DEIN NAME, Stuttgart Choral Society, Swabian Symphony Orch.; PRELUDES AND FUGUES IN C MINOR AND IN E, Eva Hölderlin, Organ. Vincent Lübeck (1654-1740), contemporary of Bach and Buxtehude, was one of the great figures of the 18th-century North German school. These examples of Lübeck's few surviving works indicate his power and brilliance. Voice and instrument lines in the cantatas are strongly reminiscent of the organ: the preludes and fugues show the influence of Bach and Buxtehude. This is the only recording of the superb cantatas. Text and translation included. "Outstanding record," E. T. Canby, SAT. REVIEW. "Hölderlin's playing is exceptional," AM. RECORD REVIEW. "Will make [Lübeck] many new friends," Philip Miller. (Playing time 37 mins.) HCR 5217 **$2.00**

CATALOGUE OF DOVER BOOKS

DONIZETTI, BETLY (LA CAPANNA SVIZZERA), Soloists of Compagnia del Teatro dell'Opera Comica di Roma, Societa del Quartetto, Rome, Chorus and Orch. Betly, a delightful one-act opera written in 1836, is similar in style and story to one of Donizetti's better-known operas, L'Elisir. Betly is lighthearted and farcical, with bright melodies and a freshness character- istic of the best of Donizetti. Libretto (English and Italian) included. "The chief honors go to Angela Tuccari who sings the title role, and the record is worth having for her alone," M. Rayment, GRAMOPHONE REC. REVIEW. "The interpretation . . . is excellent . . . This is a charming record which we recommend to lovers of little-known works," DISQUES.
HCR 5218 **$2.00**

ROSSINI: L'OCCASIONE FA IL LADRO (IL CAMBIO DELLA VALIGIA), Soloists of Compagnia del Teatro dell'Opera Comica di Roma, Societa del Quartetto, Rome, Chorus and Orch. A charm- ing one-act opera buffa, this is one of the first works of Rossini's maturity, and it is filled with the wit, gaiety and sparkle that make his comic operas second only to Mozart's. Like other Rossini works, L'Occasione makes use of the theme of impersonation and attendant amusing confusions. This is the only recording of this important buffa. Full libretto (English and Italian) included. "A major rebirth, a stylish performance . . . the Roman recording engineers have outdone themselves," H. Weinstock, SAT. REVIEW. (Playing time 53 mins.)
HCR 5219 **$2.00**

DOWLAND: "FIRST BOOKE OF AYRES," Pro Musica Antiqua of Brussels, Safford Cape, Director. This is the first recording to include all 22 of the songs of this great collection, written by John Dowland, one of the most important writers of songs of 16th and 17th century Eng- land. The participation of the Brussels Pro Musica under Safford Cape insures scholarly ac- curacy and musical artistry. "Powerfully expressive and very beautiful," B. Haggin. "The musicianly singers . . . never fall below an impressive standard," Philip Miller. Text included. (Playing time 51 mins.)
HCR 5220 **$2.00**

FRENCH CHANSONS AND DANCES OF THE 16TH CENTURY, Pro Musica Antiqua of Brussels, Safford Cape, Director. A remarkable selection of 26 three- or four-part chansons and de- lightful dances from the French Golden Age—by such composers as Orlando Lasso, Crecquil- lon, Claude Gervaise, etc. Text and translation included. "Delightful, well-varied with respect to mood and to vocal and instrumental color," HIGH FIDELITY. "Performed with . . . dis- crimination and musical taste, full of melodic distinction and harmonic resource," Irving Kolodin. (Playing time 39 mins.)
HCR 5221 **$2.00**

GALUPPI: CONCERTI A QUATRO: #1 IN G MINOR, #2 IN G, #3 IN D, #4 IN C MINOR, #5 IN E FLAT, AND #6 IN B FLAT, Biffoli Quartet. During Baldassare Galuppi's lifetime, his instru- mental music was widely renowned, and his contemporaries Mozart and Haydn thought highly of his work. These 6 concerti reflect his great ability; and they are among the most interesting compositions of the period. They are remarkable for their unusual combinations of timbres and for emotional elements that were only then beginning to be introduced into music. Performed by the well-known Biffoli Quartet, this is the only record devoted exclu- sively to Galuppi. (Playing time 47 mins.)
HCR 5222 **$2.00**

HAYDN: DIVERTIMENTI FOR WIND BAND, IN C; IN F; DIVERTIMENTO A NOVE STROMENTI IN C FOR STRINGS AND WIND INSTRUMENTS, reconstructed by H. C. Robbins Landon, performed by members of Vienna State Opera Orch.; MOZART DIVERTIMENTI IN C, III (K. 187) AND IV (K. 188), Salzburg Wind Ensemble. Robbins Landon discovered Haydn manuscripts in a Bene- dictine monastery in Lower Austria, edited them and restored their original instrumentation The result is this magnificent record. Two little-known divertimenti by Mozart—of great charm and appeal—are also included. None of this music is available elsewhere (Playing time 58 mins.)
HCR 5223 **$2.00**

PURCELL: TRIO SONATAS FROM "SONATAS OF FOUR PARTS" (1697): #9 IN F ("GOLDEN"), #7 IN C, #1 IN B MINOR, #10 IN D, #4 IN D MINOR, #2 IN E FLAT, AND #8 IN G MINOR, Giorgio Ciompi, and Werner Torkanowsky, Violins, Geo. Koutzen, Cello, and Herman Chessid, Harpsichord. These posthumously-published sonatas show Purcell at his most advanced and mature. They are certainly among the finest musical examples of pre-modern chamber music. Those not familiar with his instrumental music are well-advised to hear these outstanding pieces. "Performance sounds excellent," Harold Schonberg. "Some of the most noble and touching music known to anyone," AMERICAN RECORD GUIDE. (Playing time 58 mins.)
HCR 5224 **$2.00**

BARTOK: VIOLIN CONCERTO; SONATA FOR UNACCOMPANIED VIOLIN, Ivry Gitlis, Pro Musica of Vienna, under Hornstein. Both these works are outstanding examples of Bartok's final period, and they show his powers at their fullest. The Violin Concerto is, in the opinion of many authorities, Bartok's finest work, and the Sonata, his last work, is "a masterpiece" (F. Sackville West). "Wonderful, finest performance of both Bartok works I have ever heard," GRAMOPHONE. "Gitlis makes such potent and musical sense out of these works that I suspect many general music lovers (not otherwise in sympathy with modern music) will discover to their amazement that they like it. Exceptionally good sound," AUDITOR. (Playing time 54 mins.)
HCR 5211 **$2.00**

Social Sciences

SOCIAL THOUGHT FROM LORE TO SCIENCE, H. E. Barnes and H. Becker. An immense survey of sociological thought and ways of viewing, studying, planning, and reforming society from earliest times to the present. Includes thought on society of preliterate peoples, ancient non-Western cultures, and every great movement in Europe, America, and modern Japan. Analyzes hundreds of great thinkers: Plato, Augustine, Bodin, Vico, Montesquieu, Herder, Comte, Marx, etc. Weighs the contributions of utopians, sophists, fascists and communists; economists, jurists, philosophers, ecclesiastics, and every 19th and 20th century school of scientific sociology, anthropology, and social psychology throughout the world. Combines topical, chronological, and regional approaches, treating the evolution of social thought as a process rather than as a series of mere topics. "Impressive accuracy, competence, and discrimination . . . easily the best single survey," Nation. Thoroughly revised, with new material up to 1960. 2 indexes. Over 2200 bibliographical notes. Three volume set. Total of 1586pp. 5⅜ x 8.

T901 Vol I   Paperbound **$2.50**
T902 Vol II   Paperbound **$2.50**
T903 Vol III   Paperbound **$2.35**
The set **$7.35**

FOLKWAYS, William Graham Sumner. A classic of sociology, a searching and thorough examination of patterns of behaviour from primitive, ancient Greek and Judaic, Medieval Christian, African, Oriental, Melanesian, Australian, Islamic, to modern Western societies. Thousands of illustrations of social, sexual, and religious customs, mores, laws, and institutions. Hundreds of categories: Labor, Wealth, Abortion, Primitive Justice, Life Policy, Slavery, Cannibalism, Uncleanness and the Evil Eye, etc. Will extend the horizon of every reader by showing the relativism of his own culture. Prefatory note by A. G. Keller. Introduction by William Lyon Phelps. Bibliography. Index. xiii + 692pp. 5⅜ x 8.   T508 Paperbound **$2.49**

PRIMITIVE RELIGION, P. Radin. A thorough treatment by a noted anthropologist of the nature and origin of man's belief in the supernatural and the influences that have shaped religious expression in primitive societies. Ranging from the Arunta, Ashanti, Aztec, Bushman, Crow, Fijian, etc., of Africa, Australia, Pacific Islands, the Arctic, North and South America, Prof. Radin integrates modern psychology, comparative religion, and economic thought with first-hand accounts gathered by himself and other scholars of primitive initiations, training of the shaman, and other fascinating topics. "Excellent," NATURE (London). Unabridged reissue of 1st edition. New author's preface. Bibliographic notes. Index. x + 322pp. 5⅜ x 8.

T393 Paperbound **$1.85**

PRIMITIVE MAN AS PHILOSOPHER, P. Radin. A standard anthropological work covering primitive thought on such topics as the purpose of life, marital relations, freedom of thought, symbolism, death, resignation, the nature of reality, personality, gods, and many others. Drawn from factual material gathered from the Winnebago, Oglala Sioux, Maori, Baganda, Batak, Zuni, among others, it does not distort ideas by removing them from context but interprets strictly within the original framework. Extensive selections of original primitive documents. Bibliography. Index. xviii + 402pp. 5⅜ x 8.   T392 Paperbound **$2.25**

A TREATISE ON SOCIOLOGY, THE MIND AND SOCIETY, Vilfredo Pareto. This treatise on human society is one of the great classics of modern sociology. First published in 1916, its careful catalogue of the innumerable manifestations of non-logical human conduct (Book One); the theory of "residues," leading to the premise that sentiment not logic determines human behavior (Book Two), and of "derivations," beliefs derived from desires (Book Three); and the general description of society made up of non-elite and elite, consisting of "foxes" who live by cunning and "lions" who live by force, stirred great controversy. But Pareto's passion for isolation and classification of elements and factors, and his allegiance to scientific method as the key tool for scrutinizing the human situation made his a truly twentieth-century mind and his work a catalytic influence on certain later social commentators. These four volumes (bound as two) require no special training to be appreciated and any reader who wishes to gain a complete understanding of modern sociological theory, regardless of special field of interest, will find them a must. Reprint of revised (corrected) printing of original edition. Translated by Andrew Bongiorno and Arthur Livingston. Index. Bibliography. Appendix containing index-summary of theorems. 48 diagrams. Four volumes bound as two. Total of 2063pp. 5⅜ x 8½.   The set Clothbound **$15.00**

THE POLISH PEASANT IN EUROPE AND AMERICA, William I. Thomas, Florian Znaniecki. A seminal sociological study of peasant primary groups (family and community) and the disruptions produced by a new industrial system and immigration to America. The peasant's family, class system, religious and aesthetic attitudes, and economic life are minutely examined and analyzed in hundreds of pages of primary documentation, particularly letters between family members. The disorientation caused by new environments is scrutinized in detail (a 312-page autobiography of an immigrant is especially valuable and revealing) in an attempt to find common experiences and reactions. The famous "Methodological Note" sets forth the principles which guided the authors. When out of print this set has sold for as much as $50. 2nd revised edition. 2 vols. Vol. 1: xv + 1115pp. Vol. 2: 1135pp. Index. 6 x 9.

T478 Clothbound 2 vol. set **$12.50**

Language Books and Records

GERMAN: HOW TO SPEAK AND WRITE IT. AN INFORMAL CONVERSATIONAL METHOD FOR SELF STUDY, Joseph Rosenberg. Eminently useful for self study because of concentration on elementary stages of learning. Also provides teachers with remarkable variety of aids: 28 full- and double-page sketches with pertinent items numbered and identified in German and English; German proverbs, jokes; grammar, idiom studies; extensive practice exercises. The most interesting introduction to German available, full of amusing illustrations, photographs of cities and landmarks in German-speaking cities, cultural information subtly woven into conversational material. Includes summary of grammar, guide to letter writing, study guide to German literature by Dr. Richard Friedenthal. Index. 400 illustrations. 384pp. 5⅜ x 8½.
T271 Paperbound **$2.00**

FRENCH: HOW TO SPEAK AND WRITE IT. AN INFORMAL CONVERSATIONAL METHOD FOR SELF STUDY, Joseph Lemaitre. Even the absolute beginner can acquire a solid foundation for further study from this delightful elementary course. Photographs, sketches and drawings, sparkling colloquial conversations on a wide variety of topics (including French culture and custom), French sayings and quips, are some of aids used to demonstrate rather than merely describe the language. Thorough yet surprisingly entertaining approach, excellent for teaching and for self study. Comprehensive analysis of pronunciation, practice exercises and appendices of verb tables, additional vocabulary, other useful material. Index. Appendix. 400 illustrations. 416pp. 5⅜ x 8½.
T268 Paperbound **$2.00**

DICTIONARY OF SPOKEN SPANISH, Spanish-English, English-Spanish. Compiled from spoken Spanish, emphasizing idiom and colloquial usage in both Castilian and Latin-American. More than 16,000 entries containing over 25,000 idioms—the largest list of idiomatic constructions ever published. Complete sentences given, indexed under single words—language in immediately useable form, for travellers, businessmen, students, etc. 25 page introduction provides rapid survey of sounds, grammar, syntax, with full consideration of irregular verbs. Especially apt in modern treatment of phrases and structure. 17 page glossary gives translations of geographical names, money values, numbers, national holidays, important street signs, useful expressions of high frequency, plus unique 7 page glossary of Spanish and Spanish-American foods and dishes. Originally published as War Department Technical Manual TM 30-900. iv + 513pp. 5⅜ x 8.
T495 Paperbound **$1.75**

SPEAK MY LANGUAGE: SPANISH FOR YOUNG BEGINNERS, M. Ahlman, Z. Gilbert. Records provide one of the best, and most entertaining, methods of introducing a foreign language to children. Within the framework of a train trip from Portugal to Spain, an English-speaking child is introduced to Spanish by a native companion. (Adapted from a successful radio program of the N. Y. State Educational Department.) Though a continuous story, there are a dozen specific categories of expressions, including greetings, numbers, time, weather, food, clothes, family members, etc. Drill is combined with poetry and contextual use. Authentic background music is heard. An accompanying book enables a reader to follow the records, and includes a vocabulary of over 350 recorded expressions. Two 10″ 33⅓ records, total of 40 minutes. Book. 40 illustrations. 69pp. 5¼ x 10½.
T890 The set **$4.95**

AN ENGLISH-FRENCH-GERMAN-SPANISH WORD FREQUENCY DICTIONARY, H. S. Eaton. An indispensable language study aid, this is a semantic frequency list of the 6000 most frequently used words in 4 languages—24,000 words in all. The lists, based on concepts rather than words alone, and containing all modern, exact, and idiomatic vocabulary, are arranged side by side to form a unique 4-language dictionary. A simple key indicates the importance of the individual words within each language. Over 200 pages of separate indexes for each language enable you to locate individual words at a glance. Will help language teachers and students, authors of textbooks, grammars, and language tests to compare concepts in the various languages and to concentrate on basic vocabulary, avoiding uncommon and obsolete words. 2 Appendixes. xxi + 441pp. 6½ x 9¼.
T738 Paperbound **$2.45**

NEW RUSSIAN-ENGLISH AND ENGLISH-RUSSIAN DICTIONARY, M. A. O'Brien. Over 70,000 entries in the new orthography! Many idiomatic uses and colloquialisms which form the basis of actual speech. Irregular verbs, perfective and imperfective aspects, regular and irregular sound changes, and other features. One of the few dictionaries where accent changes within the conjugation of verbs and the declension of nouns are fully indicated. "One of the best," Prof. E. J. Simmons, Cornell. First names, geographical terms, bibliography, etc. 738pp. 4½ x 6¼.
T208 Paperbound **$2.00**

96 MOST USEFUL PHRASES FOR TOURISTS AND STUDENTS in English, French, Spanish, German, Italian. A handy folder you'll want to carry with you. How to say "Excuse me," "How much is it?", "Write it down, please," etc., in four foreign languages. Copies limited, no more than 1 to a customer.
FREE

Trubner Colloquial Manuals

These unusual books are members of the famous Trubner series of colloquial manuals. They have been written to provide adults with a sound colloquial knowledge of a foreign language, and are suited for either class use or self-study. Each book is a complete course in itself, with progressive, easy to follow lessons. Phonetics, grammar, and syntax are covered, while hundreds of phrases and idioms, reading texts, exercises, and vocabulary are included. These books are unusual in being neither skimpy nor overdetailed in grammatical matters, and in presenting up-to-date, colloquial, and practical phrase material. Bilingual presentation is stressed, to make thorough self-study easier for the reader.

COLLOQUIAL HINDUSTANI, A. H. Harley, formerly Nizam's Reader in Urdu, U. of London. 30 pages on phonetics and scripts (devanagari & Arabic-Persian) are followed by 29 lessons, including material on English and Arabic-Persian influences. Key to all exercises. Vocabulary. 5 x 7½. 147pp.　　　　　　　　　　　　　　　　　　　　　　　　　Clothbound **$1.75**

COLLOQUIAL PERSIAN, L. P. Elwell-Sutton. Best introduction to modern Persian, with 90 page grammatical section followed by conversations, 35-page vocabulary. 139pp.
　　　　　　　　　　　　　　　　　　　　　　　　　　　　　　Clothbound **$1.75**

COLLOQUIAL ARABIC, DeLacy O'Leary. Foremost Islamic scholar covers language of Egypt, Syria, Palestine, & Northern Arabia. Extremely clear coverage of complex Arabic verbs & noun plurals; also cultural aspects of language. Vocabulary. xviii + 192pp. 5 x 7½.
　　　　　　　　　　　　　　　　　　　　　　　　　　　　　　Clothbound **$2.50**

COLLOQUIAL GERMAN, P. F. Doring. Intensive thorough coverage of grammar in easily-followed form. Excellent for brush-up, with hundreds of colloquial phrases. 34 pages of bilingual texts. 224pp. 5 x 7½.　　　　　　　　　　　　　　　　　　　　　　　　Clothbound **$1.75**

COLLOQUIAL SPANISH, W. R. Patterson. Castilian grammar and colloquial language, loaded with bilingual phrases and colloquialisms. Excellent for review or self-study. 164pp. 5 x 7½.
　　　　　　　　　　　　　　　　　　　　　　　　　　　　　　Clothbound **$1.75**

COLLOQUIAL FRENCH, W. R. Patterson. 16th revision of this extremely popular manual. Grammar explained with model clarity, and hundreds of useful expressions and phrases; exercises, reading texts, etc. Appendixes of new and useful words and phrases. 223pp. 5 x 7½.
　　　　　　　　　　　　　　　　　　　　　　　　　　　　　　Clothbound **$1.75**

COLLOQUIAL CZECH, J. Schwarz, former headmaster of Lingua Institute, Prague. Full easily followed coverage of grammar, hundreds of immediately useable phrases, texts. Perhaps the best Czech grammar in print. "An absolutely successful textbook," JOURNAL OF CZECHO-SLOVAK FORCES IN GREAT BRITAIN. 252pp. 5 x 7½.　　　　　　　Clothbound **$3.00**

COLLOQUIAL RUMANIAN, G. Nandris, Professor of University of London. Extremely thorough coverage of phonetics, grammar, syntax; also included 70-page reader, and 70-page vocabulary. Probably the best grammar for this increasingly important language. 340pp. 5 x 7½.
　　　　　　　　　　　　　　　　　　　　　　　　　　　　　　Clothbound **$2.50**

COLLOQUIAL ITALIAN, A. L. Hayward. Excellent self-study course in grammar, vocabulary, idioms, and reading. Easy progressive lessons will give a good working knowledge of Italian in the shortest possible time. 5 x 7½.　　　　　　　　　　　　Clothbound **$1.75**

COLLOQUIAL TURKISH, Yusuf Mardin. Very clear, thorough introduction to leading cultural and economic language of Near East. Begins with pronunciation and statement of vowel harmony, then 36 lessons present grammar, graded vocabulary, useful phrases, dialogues, reading, exercises. Key to exercises at rear. Turkish-English vocabulary. All in Roman alphabet. x + 288pp. 4¾ x 7¼.　　　　　　　　　　　　　　　　　　Clothbound **$4.00**

DUTCH-ENGLISH AND ENGLISH-DUTCH DICTIONARY, F. G. Renier. For travel, literary, scientific or business Dutch, you will find this the most convenient, practical and comprehensive dictionary on the market. More than 60,000 entries, shades of meaning, colloquialisms, idioms, compounds and technical terms. Dutch and English strong and irregular verbs. This is the only dictionary in its size and price range that indicates the gender of nouns. New orthography. xvii + 571pp. 5½ x 6¼.　　　　　　　　　　　　　　T224 Clothbound **$2.75**

LEARN DUTCH, F. G. Renier. This book is the most satisfactory and most easily used grammar of modern Dutch. The student is gradually led from simple lessons in pronunciation, through translation from and into Dutch, and finally to a mastery of spoken and written Dutch. Grammatical principles are clearly explained while a useful, practical vocabulary is introduced in easy exercises and readings. It is used and recommended by the Fulbright Committee in the Netherlands. Phonetic appendices. Over 1200 exercises; Dutch-English, English-Dutch vocabularies. 181pp. 4¼ x 7¼.　　　　　　　　　　　　T441 Clothbound **$2.25**

CATALOGUE OF DOVER BOOKS

INVITATION TO GERMAN POETRY record. Spoken by Lotte Lenya. Edited by Gustave Mathieu, Guy Stern. 42 poems of Walther von der Vogelweide, Goethe, Hölderlin, Heine, Hofmannsthal, George, Werfel, Brecht, other great poets from 13th to middle of 20th century, spoken with superb artistry. Use this set to improve your diction, build vocabulary, improve aural comprehension, learn German literary history, as well as for sheer delight in listening. 165-page book contains full German text of each poem; English translations; biographical, critical information on each poet; textual information; portraits of each poet, many never before available in this country. 1 12″ 33⅓ record; 165-page book; album. **The set $4.95**

ESSENTIALS OF RUSSIAN record, A von Gronicka, H. Bates-Yakobson. 50 minutes of spoken Russian based on leading grammar will improve comprehension, pronunciation, increase vocabulary painlessly. Complete aural review of phonetics, phonemics—words contrasted to highlight sound differences. Wide range of material: talk between family members, friends; sightseeing; adaptation of Tolstoy's "The Shark;" history of Academy of Sciences; proverbs, epigrams; Pushkin, Lermontov, Fet, Blok, Maikov poems. Conversation passages spoken twice, fast and slow, let you anticipate answers, hear all sounds but understand normal speed. 12″ 33⅓ record, album sleeve. 44-page manual with entire record text. Translation on facing pages, phonetic instructions. **The set $4.95**

Note: For students wishing to use a grammar as well, set is available with grammar-text on which record is based, Gronicka and Bates-Yakobson's "Essentials of Russian" (400pp., 6 x 9, clothbound; Prentice Hall), an excellent, standard text used in scores of colleges, institutions. Augmented set: book, record, manual, sleeve **$10.70**

DICTIONARY OF SPOKEN RUSSIAN, English-Russian, Russian-English. Based on phrases and complete sentences, rather than isolated words; recognized as one of the best methods of learning the idiomatic speech of a country. Over 11,500 entries, indexed by single words, with more than 32,000 English and Russian sentences and phrases, in immediately useable form. Probably the largest list ever published. Shows accent changes in conjugation and declension; irregular forms listed in both alphabetical place and under main form of word. 15,000 word introduction covering Russian sounds, writing, grammar, syntax. 15-page appendix of geographical names, money, important signs, given names, foods, special Soviet terms, etc. Travellers, businessmen, students, government employees have found this their best source for Russian expressions. Originally published as War Department Technical Manual TM 30-944. iv + 573pp. 5⅝ x 8⅜. T496 Paperbound **$2.75**

THE GIFT OF LANGUAGE, M. Schlauch. Formerly titled THE GIFT OF TONGUES, this is a middle-level survey that avoids both superficiality and pedantry. It covers such topics as linguistic families, word histories, grammatical processes in such foreign languages as Aztec, Ewe, and Bantu, semantics, language taboos, and dozens of other fascinating and important topics. Especially interesting is an analysis of the word-coinings of Joyce, Cummings, Stein and others in terms of linguistics. 232 bibliographic notes. Index. viii + 342pp. 5⅜ x 8. T243 Paperbound **$1.85**

Prices subject to change without notice.

Dover publishes books on art, music, philosophy, literature, languages, history, social sciences, psychology, handcrafts, orientalia, puzzles and entertainments, chess, pets and gardens, books explaining science, intermediate and higher mathematics, mathematical physics, engineering, biological sciences, earth sciences, classics of science, etc. Write to:

Dept. catrr.
Dover Publications, Inc.
180 Varick Street, N.Y. 14, N.Y.